AUSTRALIAN
PRIMARY
THE FUTURE OF AUSTRALIAN ENGLISH
OXFORD
THESAURUS

SECOND EDITION

Compiled by
Anne Knigh

GW01066249

OXFORD

UNIVERSITY PRESS

AUSTRALIA & NEW ZEALAND

OXFORD
UNIVERSITY PRESS

Oxford University Press is a department of the University of Oxford. It furthers the University's objective of excellence in research, scholarship, and education by publishing worldwide. Oxford is a registered trademark of Oxford University Press in the UK and in certain other countries.

Published in Australia by
Oxford University Press
253 Normanby Road, South Melbourne, Victoria 3205, Australia

© Oxford University Press 1994, 2001

The moral rights of the author have been asserted.

First published 1994
Second edition 2001
Reprinted 2001, 2002, 2003, 2004, 2005,
2006, 2007, 2008, 2009, 2010, 2011, 2012, 2013, 2014, 2015

National Library of Australia Cataloguing-in-Publication data

The Australian primary Oxford thesaurus.
2nd ed.

ISBN 978 0 19 551056 0.

1. English language—Synonyms and antonyms—Dictionaries, Juvenile.
2. English language—Australia—Synonyms and antonyms—Dictionaries, Juvenile.

423

Reproduction and communication for educational purposes
The Australian *Copyright Act 1968* (the Act) allows a maximum of one chapter or 10% of the pages of this work, whichever is the greater, to be reproduced and/or communicated by any educational institution for its educational purposes provided that the educational institution (or the body that administers it) has given a remuneration notice to Copyright Agency Limited (CAL) under the Act.

For details of the CAL licence for educational institutions contact:

Copyright Agency Limited
Level 15, 233 Castlereagh Street
Sydney NSW 2000
Telephone: (02) 9394 7600
Facsimile: (02) 9394 7601
Email: info@copyright.com.au

Typeset by Desktop Concepts Pty Ltd, Melbourne
Printed in Hong Kong by Sheck Wah Tong Printing Press Ltd

Links to third party websites are provided by Oxford in good faith and for information only. Oxford disclaims any responsibility for the materials contained in any third party website referenced in this work.

OWLS
OXFORD
DICTIONARY
WORD AND
LANGUAGE
SERVICE

Do you have a query about words, their origin, meaning, use, spelling, pronunciation, or any other aspect of international English? Then write to OWLS at the Australian National Dictionary Centre, Australian National University, Canberra ACT 0200 (email ANDC@anu.edu.au). All queries will be answered using the full resources of *The Australian National Dictionary* and *The Oxford English Dictionary*. The Australian National Dictionary Centre and Oxford University Press also produce *Ozwords*, a biannual newsletter which contains interesting items about Australian words and language. Subscription is free – please contact the *Ozwords* subscription manager at Oxford University Press, GPO Box 2784, Melbourne, VIC 3001, or ozwords. au@oup.com

Preface

The *Australian Primary Oxford Thesaurus* is an alphabetical listing of words with their synonyms (words of similar meaning) and antonyms (words of opposite meaning). Each entry provides a set of words of similar or related meaning to the word you look up, so that you can choose the word which best expresses what you want to say.

You can use the thesaurus to find:

- an alternative word for an overused one, such as **nice** or **get**

- a more formal word for an everyday word, such as **attire** for **clothes**, or **laud** for **praise**

- a slang alternative to a standard word, such as **humungous** for **big**, or **porky** for **lie**

- a more specific word for a general one, such as **canoe** for **boat**, or **mackintosh** for **coat**

- the names for the male, female, or young of some animals

- the opposites of many words.

Or you can use it to find a word which you know exists but cannot recall, by looking up a word with a similar meaning.

The *Australian Primary Oxford Thesaurus* is designed to be straightforward to use. If clarification is needed, a guide to the layout of entries is provided in the following pages.

The help given by Brian Knight and George Turner on the first edition of the *Thesaurus* is once again gratefully acknowledged. I should also like to thank Bronwyn Knight for her invaluable assistance in the preparation of this edition.

Anne Knight
2001

How the thesaurus is set out

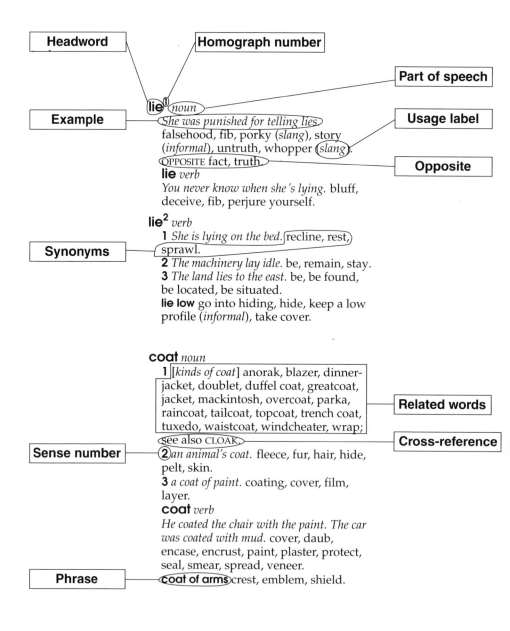

Headword

Homograph number

Part of speech

Example

Usage label

Opposite

lie¹ *noun*
She was punished for telling lies.
falsehood, fib, porky (*slang*), story
(*informal*), untruth, whopper (*slang*).
OPPOSITE fact, truth.
lie *verb*
You never know when she's lying. bluff,
deceive, fib, perjure yourself.

Synonyms

lie² *verb*
1 *She is lying on the bed.* recline, rest,
sprawl.
2 *The machinery lay idle.* be, remain, stay.
3 *The land lies to the east.* be, be found,
be located, be situated.
lie low go into hiding, hide, keep a low
profile (*informal*), take cover.

Related words

Cross-reference

Sense number

coat *noun*
1 [*kinds of coat*] anorak, blazer, dinner-
jacket, doublet, duffel coat, greatcoat,
jacket, mackintosh, overcoat, parka,
raincoat, tailcoat, topcoat, trench coat,
tuxedo, waistcoat, windcheater, wrap;
see also CLOAK.
2 *an animal's coat.* fleece, fur, hair, hide,
pelt, skin.
3 *a coat of paint.* coating, cover, film,
layer.
coat *verb*
*He coated the chair with the paint. The car
was coated with mud.* cover, daub,
encase, encrust, paint, plaster, protect,
seal, smear, spread, veneer.

Phrase

coat of arms crest, emblem, shield.

Headwords
The headword is the first word of each entry and is printed in bold type. Entries are arranged in alphabetical order of headwords.

Homograph numbers
Words which have the same spelling but different meaning or origin are called homographs. They have separate entries in the thesaurus and their headwords are distinguished by raised numbers.

Parts of speech
The headword is followed by a part-of-speech label printed in italics indicating how the word is used in a sentence, for example as a *noun, verb, adverb, adjective, preposition, pronoun, interjection*, or *conjunction*. Where a word may be used as more than one part of speech, the headword is repeated on a new line with the new part-of-speech label, followed by its set of synonyms.

Sense numbers
Different senses of the headword are numbered, and each sense starts on a new line.

Examples
Example phrases or sentences printed in italics help to identify the different senses of the headword or show how the word is used in context.

Synonyms
Synonyms are words which are the same or nearly the same in meaning. They are listed alphabetically for each sense of the headword or phrase. It is important to remember that no two words have exactly the same meaning or tone, so care must be taken to ensure that the synonym selected is the most appropriate word for a particular context.

Opposites
Opposites and contrasting words are given for many headwords and are introduced by the labels OPPOSITE or CONTRASTS WITH.

Phrases
Where a word is often used as part of a phrase, the phrase is printed in bold and found at the entry for the main word in the phrase. Synonyms and opposites are given for the phrase.

Usage labels
If a synonym is restricted in use, it is followed by a label printed in italics in brackets. A label following either the part of speech or a sense number applies to the headword or to the phrase printed in bold type. Words may be restricted to a particular region or subject area, or may be classed as formal, informal, slang, old use, or derogatory. *Informal* indicates that the word is normally used in informal or spoken English rather than formal writing, while *slang* warns that it is used very informally, or restricted to a particular group. A *derogatory* use is one that is intentionally insulting.

Cross-references
Cross-references printed in small capitals and introduced by 'see' or 'see also' are provided for some entries instead of, or as well as, a list of synonyms.

Related words
Some entries contain lists of words which are not synonyms of the headword, but specific varieties, breeds, etc. These lists are preceded by an explanatory note in italics in square brackets.

Proprietary terms

This book includes some words which are, or are asserted to be, proprietary names or trade marks. Their inclusion does not imply that they have acquired for legal purposes a non-proprietary or general significance, nor is any other judgement implied concerning their legal status. In cases where the editor has some evidence that a word is used as a proprietary name or trade mark this is indicated by the label *trade mark*, but no judgement concerning the legal status of such words is made or implied thereby.

Aa

abandon *verb*
1 *Do not abandon a person in need.* desert, ditch (*informal*), forsake, jilt, leave, leave in the lurch, run out on (*informal*), walk out on (*informal*).
2 *They had to abandon ship.* desert, evacuate, leave, quit, vacate.
3 *The space launch was abandoned because of the storm.* cancel, discontinue, drop, give up, postpone, scrap.
OPPOSITE continue.
4 *He just abandoned his job.* abdicate, chuck in (*informal*), give up, quit, resign, throw in (*informal*).
OPPOSITE keep.

abbey *noun*
convent, friary, monastery, nunnery, priory, religious house.

abbreviate *verb*
'Christine' is abbreviated to 'Chris'. abridge, contract, reduce, shorten.
OPPOSITE lengthen.

abbreviation *noun*
Use the full name rather than the abbreviation. acronym, contraction, shortening.

abdomen *noun*
belly, gut (*informal*), paunch, stomach, tummy (*informal*).

abduct *verb*
The man abducted the girl. carry off, kidnap, seize, snatch (*informal*).

abide *verb*
1 (*old use*) *They had to abide in the same house.* dwell, live, remain, reside, stay.
2 *She can't abide the smell of garlic.* bear, endure, put up with, stand, stomach, suffer, take, tolerate.
abide by *We must abide by the rules.* accept, comply with, follow, keep to, obey, observe, stick to.
OPPOSITE disobey.

ability *noun*
mathematical ability. aptitude, capability, capacity, cleverness, competence, expertise, genius, gift, knack, know-how, potential, proficiency, prowess, skill, talent.
OPPOSITE inability, incompetence.

able *adjective*
1 *He is able to attend the class.* allowed, authorised, available, eligible, fit, free, permitted.
OPPOSITE unable.
2 *an able student.* accomplished, adept, capable, clever, competent, gifted, intelligent, proficient, qualified, skilful, talented.
OPPOSITE incompetent.

abnormal *adjective*
an abnormal reaction. atypical, bizarre, curious, deviant, eccentric, exceptional, extraordinary, freakish, irregular, odd, peculiar, queer, rare, singular, strange, uncommon, unconventional, unnatural, unusual, weird.
OPPOSITE normal.

abode *noun*
see HOME.

abolish *verb*
They succeeded in abolishing slavery. cancel, do away with, eliminate, end, eradicate, get rid of, put an end to, remove, stamp out, wipe out.
OPPOSITE retain.

abolition *noun*
the abolition of capital punishment. cancellation, elimination, ending, eradication, removal.
OPPOSITE retention.

abominable *adjective*
1 *an abominable crime.* abhorrent, appalling, atrocious, contemptible, despicable, detestable, disgusting, foul, hateful, heinous, horrible, loathsome, odious, repugnant, vile.

2 (*informal*) *abominable weather.* atrocious (*informal*), awful (*informal*), bad, crook (*Australian informal*), dreadful (*informal*), foul, frightful (*informal*), lousy (*informal*), shocking (*informal*), terrible (*informal*), unpleasant.

aboriginal *adjective*
the aboriginal inhabitants. earliest, first, indigenous, native, original.
OPPOSITE immigrant.

abound *verb*
The river abounds with fish. be full, overflow, swarm, teem.

about *preposition*
1 *Look about you.* around, close to, near.
2 *an article about drug abuse.* concerning, connected with, dealing with, involving, on, regarding, relating to.
about *adverb*
1 *about 150 centimetres tall.* almost, approximately, around, more or less, nearly, roughly.
2 *They're somewhere about.* around, near, nearby.
be about to *He was about to leave.* be going to, be on the point of, be on the verge of, be ready to.

above *adverb*
1 *noises from above.* overhead, upstairs.
2 *discussed above.* before, earlier, previously.
OPPOSITE below.
above *preposition*
1 *above the clouds. above the bridge.* higher than, on top of, over, upstream from.
2 *above 50,000.* beyond, greater than, higher than, more than, over.
OPPOSITE below.
3 *the officer above corporal.* higher than, superior to.
above board *All his business dealings were above board.* clean, fair, honest, honourable, legal, legitimate, open, straight.
OPPOSITE underhand.

abrasion *noun*
The victim suffered abrasions. graze, lesion, scrape, scratch.

abroad *adverb*
He travelled abroad. overseas.

abrupt *adjective*
1 *an abrupt halt.* hasty, quick, rapid, sharp, sudden, swift, unexpected.
OPPOSITE gradual.
2 *an abrupt manner.* blunt, brisk, brusque, curt, gruff, impolite, rude, short.
OPPOSITE polite.

absence *noun*
an absence of three weeks. absenteeism, non-attendance, truancy.
OPPOSITE attendance, presence.

absent *adjective*
Five children were absent. away, elsewhere, missing, off.
OPPOSITE present.
absent *verb*
absent yourself from *He absented himself from school.* bludge (*Australian informal*), play hookey from (*informal*), play truant from, skive off (*informal*), stay away from, wag (*informal*).
OPPOSITE attend.

absent-minded *adjective*
daydreaming, distracted, dreamy, far-away, forgetful, inattentive, oblivious, preoccupied, scatterbrained, scatty (*informal*).
OPPOSITE alert.

absolute *adjective*
1 *an absolute delight. an absolute disaster.* complete, downright, out-and-out, outright, perfect, positive, pure, sheer, thorough, total, utter.
2 *They needed absolute proof.* categorical, certain, conclusive, definite, firm, positive, reliable, sure.
OPPOSITE dubious.
3 *The monarch has absolute power.* complete, omnipotent, sovereign, supreme, total, unconditional, unlimited, unqualified, unrestricted.
OPPOSITE limited.

absorb *verb*
1 *The sponge absorbs water.* draw up, mop up, soak up, suck up, take up.
2 *The student absorbed the information.* assimilate, digest, take in.
absorbed in *absorbed in thought.* engrossed in, immersed in, interested in, lost in, preoccupied with.

absorbing *adjective*
an absorbing book. captivating, engrossing, fascinating, gripping, interesting.
OPPOSITE boring.

abstract *adjective*
abstract ideas. academic, intangible, intellectual, theoretical.
OPPOSITE concrete, practical.
abstract *noun*
an abstract of the book. outline, précis, summary, synopsis.

absurd *adjective*
We laughed at his absurd suggestion. comic, crazy, farcical, foolish, funny, illogical, laughable, ludicrous, mad, nonsensical, outrageous, preposterous, ridiculous, senseless, silly, strange, stupid, unreasonable, zany.
OPPOSITE reasonable.

abundance *noun*
an abundance of food. heaps (*informal*), lashings (*informal*), loads (*informal*), lots (*informal*), oodles (*informal*), plenty, stacks (*informal*), tons (*informal*), wealth.
OPPOSITE lack, shortage.

abundant *adjective*
an abundant supply of fruit. ample, bountiful, copious, generous, large, lavish, liberal, plentiful, profuse.
OPPOSITE inadequate, insufficient.
abundant in The river is abundant in fish. abounding in, full of, overflowing with, teeming with.
OPPOSITE deficient in, lacking in.

abuse *noun*
1 physical abuse. child abuse. assault, ill-treatment, maltreatment, mistreatment.
2 verbal abuse. curses, insults, invective, obscenities, slander, swearing.
OPPOSITE compliments.
abuse *verb*
1 She abused her position. exploit, misuse.
2 The man had abused the child physically. assault, harm, hurt, ill-treat, maltreat, mistreat, molest.
3 She abused the person on the telephone. attack, be rude to, curse, insult, revile, slander, swear at.

abusive *adjective*
abusive language. derogatory, disparaging, impolite, insulting, obscene, offensive, pejorative, rude, scornful, slanderous.
OPPOSITE complimentary, polite.

abysmal *adjective* (*informal*)
The food was abysmal. abominable (*informal*), appalling (*informal*), atrocious (*informal*), dreadful (*informal*), shocking (*informal*), terrible (*informal*); see also BAD.

abyss *noun*
It sank into the abyss. bottomless pit, chasm, hole.

academic *adjective*
1 academic books. educational, pedagogic, scholastic.
2 an academic person. bookish, highbrow, intellectual, learned, scholarly, studious.
OPPOSITE practical.
3 The question is purely academic. abstract, hypothetical, speculative, theoretical.
OPPOSITE practical.

accelerate *verb*
The driver accelerated to overtake. go faster, quicken, speed up, step on it (*informal*).
OPPOSITE decelerate, slow down.

accent *noun*
1 The accent is on the first syllable in the word 'tangent'. emphasis, prominence, stress.
2 She speaks with an Irish accent. brogue, dialect, intonation, pronunciation.
accent *verb*
Accent the first syllable. accentuate, emphasise, stress.

accentuate *verb*
The report accentuates the problems in the company. accent, draw attention to, emphasise, highlight, stress.

accept *verb*
1 She accepted the prize. get, receive, take.
OPPOSITE refuse, reject.
2 He accepted responsibility. admit, assume, bear, shoulder, take, undertake.
OPPOSITE evade.

a
b
c
d
e
f
g
h
i
j
k
l
m
n
o
p
q
r
s
t
u
v
w
x
y
z

3 *She finds it hard to accept change.* agree to, consent to, go along with, put up with, reconcile yourself to, resign yourself to, take, tolerate, welcome. OPPOSITE reject.
4 *Do you accept that I am right?* acknowledge, admit, agree, believe, think. OPPOSITE dispute.

acceptable *adjective*
acceptable behaviour. adequate, appropriate, passable, pleasing, proper, satisfactory, seemly, suitable, tolerable. OPPOSITE unacceptable, unsatisfactory.

access *noun*
Access to the house was restricted. admission, admittance, approach, entrance, entry, way in.
access *verb*
She was unable to access the information. retrieve.

accessible *adjective*
The computer is down and the information is not accessible. attainable, available, handy, obtainable, retrievable. OPPOSITE inaccessible, irretrievable.

accessory *noun*
1 *accessories for the vacuum cleaner.* attachment, extension, extra, fitting.
2 *an accessory to murder.* abetter, accomplice, assistant, associate.

accident *noun*
1 *a tragic accident.* calamity, catastrophe, disaster, misadventure, misfortune, mishap.
2 *a car accident.* collision, crash, pile-up (*informal*), prang (*slang*), smash.
3 *It happened by accident.* chance, coincidence, fluke, fortune, luck.

accidental *adjective*
an accidental discovery. chance, coincidental, fluky, fortuitous, serendipitous, unexpected, unintentional, unplanned. OPPOSITE deliberate, planned.

accident-prone *adjective*
disaster-prone, jinxed (*informal*), unlucky.

acclaim *verb*
The spectators acclaimed the winning team. applaud, cheer, clap, hail, praise, salute, welcome.

acclimatise *verb*
He has acclimatised to the cold. adapt, adjust, become accustomed, get used.

accommodate *verb*
1 *The family can accommodate two visitors.* billet, board, house, put up, take in.
2 *The cottage accommodates eight.* fit, house, sleep.

accommodation *noun*
rented accommodation. billet, digs (*informal*), home, house, housing, lodgings, premises, quarters, residence.

accompany *verb*
1 *A bodyguard accompanies the princess everywhere.* attend, be with, chaperone, escort, go with, partner, tag along with, travel with.
2 *The teacher accompanied the cellist on the piano.* back up, play with, support.

accomplish *verb*
She accomplished what was required. achieve, attain, bring off, carry out, complete, do, finish, fulfil, succeed in. OPPOSITE fail.

accomplished *adjective*
an accomplished writer. able, brilliant, experienced, expert, gifted, proficient, skilful, skilled, talented. OPPOSITE amateurish, inexpert.

accomplishment *noun*
1 *social accomplishments.* ability, attainment, gift, skill, talent.
2 *Climbing Mount Everest was her latest accomplishment.* achievement, attainment, deed, exploit, feat.

accord *noun*
All parties signed the accord. agreement, compact, pact, treaty.
of your own accord *She wrote the letter of her own accord.* off your own bat, of your own free will, of your own volition, spontaneously, unasked, voluntarily, willingly.

accordingly *adverb*
She stopped at the shops, and accordingly was late. consequently, hence, so, therefore, thus.

account *noun*
1 *He paid the account.* bill, invoice, receipt, statement.

2 *We read an account of these events.* description, explanation, history, log, narrative, record, report, story, tale.

account *verb*
account for *Not even a headache could account for his rudeness.* excuse, explain, give grounds for, justify.
take into account *His age will be taken into account.* allow for, consider, take into consideration.
OPPOSITE disregard.

accumulate *verb*
1 *They accumulated books over the years.* acquire, amass, collect, gather, hoard, stockpile, store up.
2 *The miser's funds accumulated.* build up, grow, increase, multiply, pile up.
OPPOSITE diminish.

accuracy *noun*
correctness, exactness, faithfulness, fidelity, meticulousness, precision, truth.
OPPOSITE inaccuracy.

accurate *adjective*
an accurate representation. careful, correct, exact, factual, faithful, meticulous, perfect, precise, right, true.
OPPOSITE inaccurate.

accusation *noun*
a false accusation. allegation, charge, imputation, indictment.

accuse *verb*
He was accused of spying. blame, charge, impeach, incriminate, indict, point the finger at (*informal*).
OPPOSITE acquit, exonerate.

accustomed *adjective*
1 *at the accustomed time.* customary, established, expected, familiar, fixed, habitual, normal, regular, set, usual.
2 *accustomed to the conditions.* acclimatised, adjusted, used.
OPPOSITE unused.

ace *noun*
He's an ace at golf. champion, expert, master, star, winner.

ache *verb*
Her head ached. be painful, be sore, hurt, pound, throb.

ache *noun*
1 *Rest relieved the ache in her body.* discomfort, hurt, pain, pang, soreness.
2 *the ache of a broken heart.* agony, anguish, distress, grief, misery, pain, sorrow, suffering.

achieve *verb*
1 *She achieved her goal.* accomplish, attain, carry out, fulfil, reach, realise, succeed in.
2 *He achieved fame.* acquire, attain, earn, gain, get, obtain, win.

achievement *noun*
proud of his achievements. accomplishment, attainment, deed, feat; see also SUCCESS.
OPPOSITE failure.

acid *adjective*
an acid taste. acidic, sharp, sour, tangy, tart, vinegary.
OPPOSITE sweet.

acknowledge *verb*
1 *He acknowledged that they were right.* accept, admit, agree, concede, confess, grant, recognise.
OPPOSITE deny.
2 *She acknowledged all her sympathy cards.* answer, reply to, respond to.

acknowledgement *noun*
1 *an acknowledgement of guilt.* acceptance, admission, confession.
OPPOSITE denial.
2 *All applications received a written acknowledgement.* answer, reply, response.
3 *an acknowledgement for bravery.* notice, recognition, reward, thanks.

acne *noun*
see PIMPLE.

acquaintance *noun*
I wouldn't call her a friend, simply an acquaintance. associate, colleague, contact.

acquire *verb*
He acquired many possessions. buy, collect, come by, gain, get, obtain, pick up, procure, purchase, secure.
OPPOSITE dispose of.

a
b
c
d
e
f
g
h
i
j
k
l
m
n
o
p
q
r
s
t
u
v
w
x
y
z

acquisition *noun*
the library's acquisitions. accession,
possession, purchase.

acquit *verb*
The judge acquitted him after new evidence.
absolve, clear, exonerate, let off, release,
vindicate.
OPPOSITE convict.

acrobat *noun*
gymnast, tightrope walker, trapeze
artist.

act *noun*
1 his brave acts. accomplishment,
achievement, action, deed, exploit, feat,
undertaking.
2 an act of parliament. decree, edict, law,
statute.
3 the comedian's act. performance,
routine, show, sketch, skit.
4 (informal) Her tears were just an act.
deception, front, hoax, pretence, sham,
show.

act *verb*
1 Act sensibly! behave, conduct yourself.
2 The brakes did not act. function,
operate, work.
3 The children acted as fairies in the play.
appear, impersonate, perform, play,
portray.
4 She's not really upset: she's just acting.
fake, feign, make believe, pretend,
sham.

acting *adjective*
the acting principal. deputy, interim,
provisional, substitute, temporary.
OPPOSITE permanent.

action *noun*
1 They put the plan into action. activity,
motion, operation, performance,
practice, work.
2 a brave action. act, deed, exploit, feat,
move, step, undertaking.
3 a holiday packed with action. activity,
adventure, drama, excitement,
happenings, incidents.
4 legal action. lawsuit, proceedings,
prosecution.
5 He was killed in action. battle, combat,
conflict, fighting, warfare.

activate *verb*
Pressing the button activates the brakes. set
off, start, switch on, trigger, turn on.

active *adjective*
1 an active toddler. an active eighty-year-
old. dynamic, energetic, full of beans
(informal), hyperactive, lively, sprightly,
spry.
OPPOSITE inactive.
2 active games such as tennis. energetic,
lively, physical, strenuous, vigorous.
OPPOSITE passive.
3 an active member. busy, diligent, hard-
working, industrious, involved,
occupied, participating.
OPPOSITE inactive, nominal.
4 an active volcano. functioning,
operative, working.
OPPOSITE dormant, extinct.

activist *noun*
a political activist. agitator, campaigner,
crusader, lobbyist, protester, stirrer.

activity *noun*
1 The hall was a hive of activity. action,
bustle, excitement, hurly-burly, hustle,
industry, liveliness, movement.
OPPOSITE inactivity.
2 physical activity. exercise, exertion.
OPPOSITE inactivity.
3 leisure activities. hobby, occupation,
pastime, project, pursuit, undertaking.

actor *noun*
actress, performer, player, star, trouper;
[group of actors] cast, company, troupe.

actual *adjective*
an actual incident. authentic, confirmed,
factual, genuine, real, true.
OPPOSITE fictitious.

actually *adverb*
He was actually surprised. genuinely,
indeed, in fact, really, truly.

acute *adjective*
acute pain. excruciating, extreme,
intense, keen, piercing, severe, sharp,
shooting, stabbing.
OPPOSITE mild.

adamant *adjective*
He was adamant that they would not have a
dog. determined, firm, inflexible,
resolute, resolved, stubborn,

unyielding.
OPPOSITE flexible.

adapt *verb*
1 *The play was adapted for television.* adjust, alter, change, convert, edit, modify, remake, rewrite, transform.
2 *The koalas adapted to their new habitat.* acclimatise, adjust, become accustomed to, become used to.

adaptable *adjective*
an adaptable person. accommodating, amenable, easygoing, flexible, malleable, versatile.
OPPOSITE inflexible.

add *verb*
1 *He added the figures.* add up, combine, sum, total, tot up (*informal*).
OPPOSITE subtract.
2 *He added his name to the list.* affix, append, attach, join, tack on.
OPPOSITE remove.
add to *This added to the weight of the parcel.* augment, enlarge, increase, swell.
OPPOSITE reduce.
add up *She added up the bill.* calculate, compute, count, reckon, total, tot up (*informal*), work out.
add up to *It added up to $5.* amount to, come to, make, total.

addict *noun*
1 *drug addict.* druggie (*informal*), junkie (*slang*), user (*informal*).
2 *a television addict.* enthusiast, fan, fanatic, freak (*informal*), lover, nut (*informal*).

addicted *adjective*
She is addicted to heroin. dependent on, hooked on (*slang*).

addiction *noun*
drug addiction. dependence, habit, obsession.

addition *noun*
1 *He did the addition in his head.* calculation, computation, totalling, totting up (*informal*).
OPPOSITE subtraction.
2 *an addition to a building.* annexe, extension, wing.

3 *an addition to a document.* appendix, attachment, codicil, postscript, rider, supplement.

additional *adjective*
additional help. added, backup, extra, further, more, new, other, supplementary.

address *noun*
1 *He lives at a new address.* abode (*old use*), domicile, location, residence.
2 *The minister's address was brief.* lecture, sermon, speech, talk.
address *verb*
1 *She addressed her students.* lecture, speak to, talk to.
2 *He eventually addressed the problem.* apply yourself to, attend to, focus on, tackle, turn to.

adequate *adjective*
1 *adequate supplies.* ample, enough, sufficient.
OPPOSITE insufficient.
2 *an adequate standard.* acceptable, all right, fair, OK (*informal*), passable, satisfactory, tolerable.
OPPOSITE inadequate, unsatisfactory.

adhere *verb*
The chewing gum adhered to the shoe. attach, cling, hold fast, stick.
adhere to *We must adhere to the rules.* abide by, comply with, follow, keep to, stick to.

adhesive *adjective*
adhesive tape. gummed, sticky.
adhesive *noun*
cement, fixative, glue, gum, paste.

adjacent *adjective*
adjacent blocks of land. adjoining, bordering, neighbouring, next-door.

adjourn *verb*
They adjourned the meeting until next week. break off, defer, discontinue, interrupt, postpone, put off, suspend.

adjudicate *verb*
The teacher adjudicated the debate. arbitrate, judge, referee, umpire.

adjudicator *noun*
arbitrator, judge, referee, umpire.

a
b
c
d
e
f
g
h
i
j
k
l
m
n
o
p
q
r
s
t
u
v
w
x
y
z

adjust *verb*
1 *She adjusted the volume.* alter, regulate, set.
2 *The dress needed adjusting.* adapt, alter, change, fit, modify, reshape.
3 *She had to adjust to being at home again.* acclimatise, adapt, become accustomed, get used, reconcile yourself.

ad lib *adverb*
She spoke ad lib. impromptu, off the cuff, off the top of your head (*informal*).
ad lib *adjective*
ad lib remarks. extempore, impromptu, off the cuff, unrehearsed.
OPPOSITE prepared.
ad lib *verb* (*informal*)
She had not learned the music, but she ad libbed very well. extemporise, improvise, play it by ear (*informal*).

administer *verb*
1 *He administers a trust fund.* control, direct, govern, look after, manage, oversee, run, supervise.
2 *The teacher administered the punishment.* carry out, deal out, dispense, give, hand out, mete out, provide.

administrator *noun*
the territory's administrator. chief, controller, director, executive, governor, head, manager, superintendent.

admirable *adjective*
admirable conduct. commendable, excellent, exemplary, honourable, laudable, praiseworthy, worthy.
OPPOSITE deplorable.

admiration *noun*
He was full of admiration for their achievements. approval, commendation, praise, respect, veneration.

admire *verb*
The people admire their leader. appreciate, approve of, esteem, idolise, look up to, praise, regard highly, respect, revere, think highly of, venerate.
OPPOSITE despise.

admirer *noun*
The actor has many admirers. devotee, fan, follower, supporter.

admission *noun*
1 *free admission.* admittance, entrance, entry.
2 *an admission of guilt.* acceptance, acknowledgement, confession, declaration, disclosure, statement.
OPPOSITE denial.

admit *verb*
1 *Only people over eighteen are admitted.* allow in, let in, permit entry, take in.
OPPOSITE exclude.
2 *I admit that I don't know the answer.* accept, acknowledge, concede, confess, grant, own up.
OPPOSITE deny.

admittance *noun*
Strictly no admittance! access, admission, entrance, entry.

ado *noun*
without further ado. bother, commotion, fuss, kerfuffle (*informal*), to-do, trouble.

adolescence *noun*
puberty, teens, youth.

adolescent *adjective*
teenage, youthful.
adolescent *noun*
teenager, youngster, youth.

adopt *verb*
He adopted a false name. assume, choose, take up, use.

adorable *adjective*
an adorable baby. appealing, cute (*informal*), darling, dear, delightful, irresistible, likeable, lovable, lovely, sweet (*informal*).

adore *verb*
1 *The man adored his wife.* cherish, dote on, idolise, love.
OPPOSITE hate.
2 *They adore God.* exalt, glorify, hallow, honour, laud (*formal*), praise, revere, venerate, worship.
3 (*informal*) *She adores jazz.* be fond of, enjoy, like, love.
OPPOSITE hate.

adorn *verb*
They adorned the hall with flowers. array, deck out, decorate, festoon, ornament.

adult *adjective*
an adult penguin. developed, full-sized, grown-up, mature.
OPPOSITE immature.
adult *noun*
grown-up.
OPPOSITE child, minor.

adultery *noun*
divorced on the grounds of adultery. infidelity, unfaithfulness.
OPPOSITE fidelity.

advance *verb*
1 *They advanced towards the city.* approach, go ahead, go forward, go on, make headway, move forward, proceed, progress.
OPPOSITE retreat.
2 *They advanced the date of their wedding.* bring forward, hasten.
OPPOSITE defer, postpone.
3 *She advanced a month's pocket money.* lend, prepay.
advance *noun*
1 *a scientific advance.* breakthrough, development, headway, improvement, progress.
2 *an advance on next week's pocket money.* loan, prepayment.
in advance *She paid her fees in advance.* ahead, beforehand, up front.
OPPOSITE later.

advanced *adjective*
1 *an advanced age.* elderly, mature, old, ripe.
OPPOSITE tender, young.
2 *advanced studies.* complicated, difficult, hard, higher.
OPPOSITE elementary.
3 *advanced technology.* innovative, modern, new, revolutionary, sophisticated, up-to-date.
OPPOSITE obsolete.

advantage *noun*
1 *Language skills are an advantage.* asset, benefit, blessing, bonus, boon, help, plus.
OPPOSITE disadvantage, handicap.
2 *It will be to your advantage.* benefit, gain, profit.
take advantage of capitalise on, cash in on, exploit, make the most of, make use of, use.

advantageous *adjective*
an advantageous position. beneficial, favourable, good, helpful, profitable, useful, valuable.
OPPOSITE unhelpful.

adventure *noun*
1 *an unforgettable adventure.* escapade, experience, exploit, incident.
2 *a life filled with adventure.* danger, excitement, risk, uncertainty.

adventurous *adjective*
an adventurous explorer. bold, brave, daring, enterprising, intrepid, venturesome.

adversary *noun*
She defeated her adversary. enemy, foe, opponent, rival.

adverse *adjective*
She suffered no adverse effects. bad, detrimental, harmful, ill, unfavourable, untoward.
OPPOSITE favourable, good.

adversity *noun*
in sickness and adversity. affliction, calamity, catastrophe, disaster, distress, hardship, misfortune, trouble.
OPPOSITE prosperity.

advertise *verb*
The company advertises their products. make known, plug (*informal*), promote, publicise, push (*informal*).

advertisement *noun*
ad (*informal*), advert (*informal*), blurb, commercial, notice, plug (*informal*), promotion, publicity, trailer.

advice *noun*
1 *She asked for my advice as to what to do.* counsel, guidance, opinion, recommendation, suggestion, tip.
2 *We received advice that the goods had been sent.* information, news, notification, word.

advisable *adjective*
It is advisable to remain silent. prudent, recommended, sensible, wise.
OPPOSITE foolish, inadvisable.

a
b
c
d
e
f
g
h
i
j
k
l
m
n
o
p
q
r
s
t
u
v
w
x
y
z

advise *verb*
1 *He advised them to sell the house.*
counsel, recommend, suggest, urge,
warn.
2 *She advised them of their rights.* inform,
notify, tell.

adviser *noun*
a financial adviser. consultant,
counsellor, guide, mentor.

aerial *adjective*
an aerial view. bird's-eye, overhead.
aerial *noun*
a TV aerial. antenna.

aeroplane *noun*
plane; see also AIRCRAFT.

affair *noun*
1 *That's not your affair.* business,
concern, responsibility, thing.
2 *business affairs.* activity, business,
concern, dealing, interest, matter,
operation.
3 *a sad and sorry affair.* business, case,
episode, event, happening, incident,
occurrence.
4 *an affair with a married woman.* fling,
liaison, love affair, relationship,
romance.

affect *verb*
1 *The changes did not affect them.* concern,
have an effect on, have an impact on,
impinge on, touch.
2 *Tuberculosis affected his lungs.* attack,
damage, infect, strike.

affection *noun*
caring, fondness, liking, love,
tenderness, warmth.

affectionate *adjective*
an affectionate husband. caring, devoted,
doting, fond, kind, loving, tender-
hearted, warm-hearted.
OPPOSITE cold-hearted, indifferent.

affirm *verb*
He affirmed that he had written the letter.
assert, confirm, declare, state, swear.

afflict *verb*
The disease afflicted her in childhood.
distress, oppress, plague, torment,
trouble.

affliction *noun*
1 *She bore affliction bravely.* adversity,
distress, hardship, misery, misfortune,
pain, suffering, trouble.
2 *Doctors tried to treat her affliction.*
ailment, condition, disease, disorder,
illness, malady, sickness, trouble.

affluent *adjective*
the affluent society. prosperous, rich,
wealthy, well-heeled (*informal*), well off,
well-to-do.
OPPOSITE poor.

afford *verb*
*They can't afford a new car. She can afford
$100 for the tickets.* bear the expense of,
manage, pay for, spare.

afraid *adjective*
1 *She is afraid of the dark.* alarmed,
anxious, apprehensive, fearful,
frightened, nervous, panic-stricken,
scared, terrified, timid, worried.
OPPOSITE brave, unafraid.
2 *I'm afraid there isn't any more.*
apologetic, regretful, sorry.

after *preposition*
1 *Close the door after you.* behind.
2 *after my bedtime.* following, later than,
past.
OPPOSITE before.
3 *He asked after you.* about, concerning,
regarding.

afterwards *adverb*
after, later, next, subsequently.

again *adverb*
Try again. afresh, anew, another time,
once more.

against *preposition*
1 *We're against capital punishment.* anti,
averse to, opposed to.
OPPOSITE for, in favour of.
2 *the A team against the B team.* in
opposition to, opposing, versus.

age *noun*
1 *the age in which we live.* days, epoch,
era, period, time.
2 (*informal*) *I haven't seen him for ages.*
donkey's years (*informal*), eternity
(*informal*), yonks (*slang*).

age *verb*
The wine has aged well. develop, grow older, mature, mellow, ripen.

aged *adjective*
1 *aged people.* elderly, old, retired.
OPPOSITE young.
2 *an aged cheddar.* mature, ripe, vintage.

agency *noun*
a travel agency. bureau, business, company, firm, office, organisation.

agenda *noun*
the agenda for the meeting. list, plan, programme, schedule.

agent *noun*
1 *an agent for a company.* broker, delegate, middleman, negotiator, proxy, representative, spokesperson.
2 *a secret agent.* intelligence officer, mole (*informal*), spy.

aggravate *verb*
1 *Washing with soap aggravated the rash.* compound, exacerbate, inflame, intensify, worsen.
OPPOSITE improve.
2 (*informal*) *Rock music aggravates some people.* annoy, bother, exasperate, get on someone's nerves, irritate, provoke.
OPPOSITE please.

aggressive *adjective*
1 *aggressive behaviour.* attacking, belligerent, combative, hostile, militant, pugnacious, warlike.
OPPOSITE friendly.
2 *an aggressive salesperson.* assertive, forceful, insistent, persistent, pushy, self-assertive, zealous.
OPPOSITE retiring.

agile *adjective*
an agile dancer. flexible, lithe, nimble, quick-moving, sprightly, spry, supple.
OPPOSITE clumsy, stiff.

agitate *verb*
1 *agitate the mixture.* beat, churn, shake, stir, toss, whisk.
2 *The patient became agitated.* disturb, excite, fluster, perturb, ruffle, stir up, trouble, unsettle, upset, work up, worry.
OPPOSITE pacify.

3 *The students were agitating against logging.* campaign, lobby, protest, stir.

agitator *noun*
political agitators. activist, campaigner, lobbyist, protester, rabble-rouser, stirrer.

agonising *adjective*
agonising pain. acute, excruciating, intolerable, painful, severe, unbearable.
OPPOSITE mild.

agony *noun*
anguish, distress, pain, suffering, torment, torture.

agree *verb*
1 *Father and son never agree.* be unanimous, concur, see eye to eye.
OPPOSITE differ.
2 *They agreed that we had grounds for complaint.* accept, admit, allow, concede, grant.
3 *He agreed to speak at the ceremony.* consent, undertake.
4 *Their answers agree.* accord, be consistent, be in harmony, coincide, correspond, fit, match, tally.
OPPOSITE disagree.
agree to *She agreed to our plan.* accept, approve, back, consent to, endorse, OK (*informal*), support.
OPPOSITE reject.
agree with *Curry does not agree with me.* be good for, suit.

agreeable *adjective*
1 *an agreeable person.* amiable, congenial, friendly, likeable, nice, pleasant; see also PLEASANT.
2 *We'll go ahead if you're agreeable.* amenable, in accord, in agreement, in favour, willing.
OPPOSITE against, unwilling.

agreement *noun*
1 *No agreement could be reached on what to do.* accord, concord, consensus, harmony, unanimity.
OPPOSITE disagreement.
2 *An agreement was signed by both parties.* accord, arrangement, bargain, contract, covenant, deal, pact, settlement, treaty.

aground *adverb & adjective*
beached, grounded, marooned, shipwrecked, stranded.

a
b
c
d
e
f
g
h
i
j
k
l
m
n
o
p
q
r
s
t
u
v
w
x
y
z

ahead *adverb*
1 *moving ahead.* forwards, on, onwards.
OPPOSITE backwards.
2 *Their team is ahead.* in advance, in front, in the lead.
OPPOSITE behind.

aid *verb*
1 *He aided the robber.* abet, assist, collaborate with, cooperate with, help.
OPPOSITE hinder.
2 *The computer aids their essay writing.* advance, facilitate, further, promote.
3 *The government aids their organisation.* back, contribute to, give to, subscribe to, subsidise.
4 *He aided the injured man.* assist, help, lend a hand to, minister to, relieve, succour.

aid *noun*
1 *She could not have managed without their aid.* assistance, backing, collaboration, cooperation, help, succour, support.
OPPOSITE hindrance, opposition.
2 *financial aid.* charity, contribution, donation, funding, grant, relief, sponsorship, subsidy, support.

ailment *noun*
The doctor treated his ailment. affliction, complaint, condition, disease, disorder, illness, infection, infirmity, malady, sickness, trouble.

aim *verb*
1 *He aimed the gun at the bird.* direct, focus, level, point, train.
2 *She aims to be famous.* aspire, endeavour, intend, plan, purpose, seek, strive, try.

aim *noun*
What is his aim? ambition, goal, intention, object, objective, plan, point, purpose, target.

aimless *adjective*
an aimless existence. drifting, goalless, pointless, purposeless.
OPPOSITE purposeful.

air *noun*
1 *flying through the air.* atmosphere, sky.
2 *Open the window and let in some air.* breeze, draught, wind.

3 *an air of mystery.* appearance, atmosphere, aura, feeling, impression, look, mood.
4 *He whistled a happy air.* melody, strain, tune.

air *verb*
1 *She aired the room.* freshen, open up, ventilate.
2 *You can air your grievances.* express, get off your chest, make known, reveal, say, tell, voice.

air hostess flight attendant, hostess, hostie (*Australian informal*), steward, stewardess.

in the air
1 *Rumours are in the air.* abroad, around, circulating, current.
2 *Plans are still in the air.* uncertain, undecided, unresolved.

aircraft *noun*
[*kinds of aircraft*] aeroplane, airliner, airship, biplane, bomber, fighter, glider, helicopter, jet, jumbo jet, jump jet, microlight, monoplane, plane, seaplane, turbojet.

airport *noun*
aerodrome, airfield, airstrip, landing strip.

airy *adjective*
an airy room. breezy, draughty, fresh, ventilated, well-ventilated.
OPPOSITE stuffy.

aisle *noun*
The theatre has two aisles for ease of access. corridor, gangway, gap, passage, passageway, path.

alarm *noun*
1 *The burglar set off the alarm.* alert, bell, signal, siren, warning.
2 *He jumped up in alarm.* anxiety, apprehension, consternation, dismay, dread, fear, fright, panic, terror, trepidation, worry.

alarm *verb*
The loud knock alarmed them. agitate, dismay, disturb, frighten, panic, perturb, petrify, put the wind up (*informal*), scare, startle, terrify, unnerve.
OPPOSITE reassure.

album *noun*
1 *a photo album.* book, display book.
2 *the group's latest album.* collection, compilation, disc, record, recording.

alcohol *noun*
booze (*informal*), drink, grog (*Australian informal*), liquor, spirits, wine.

alcoholic *adjective*
alcoholic drinks. intoxicating, spirituous.
alcoholic *noun*
a reformed alcoholic. dipsomaniac, drunk, drunkard, wino (*informal*).
OPPOSITE teetotaller.

alcove *noun*
an alcove in a room. bay, niche, nook, recess.

alert *adjective*
A nurse must be alert. attentive, awake, aware, careful, observant, on the ball (*informal*), on the lookout, on your toes, ready, vigilant, wary, watchful.
OPPOSITE careless, inattentive.
alert *verb*
He alerted them to the dangers. caution, forewarn, prepare, warn.

alias *noun*
assumed name, false name, nickname, pen-name, pseudonym, stage name.

alien *noun*
1 *enemy aliens.* foreigner, outsider, stranger.
OPPOSITE native.
2 *an alien from another planet.* extraterrestrial.
alien *adjective*
1 *an alien practice.* exotic, foreign, outlandish, strange, unfamiliar.
OPPOSITE familiar.
2 *Cruelty is alien to her character.* contrary, foreign, inconsistent, uncharacteristic.
OPPOSITE consistent.

alienate *verb*
She alienated people with her rudeness. estrange, turn away, turn off.

alight[1] *verb*
1 *The passengers alighted from the bus.* descend, disembark, get down, get off.
OPPOSITE board.

2 *The bird alighted on a branch.* land, perch, settle.

alight[2] *adjective*
The house was alight. ablaze, blazing, burning, on fire.

alike *adjective*
akin, comparable, equivalent, identical, indistinguishable, similar, synonymous.
OPPOSITE different, unlike.

alive *adjective*
The animal was still alive. animate, breathing, existing, live, living, quick (*old use*), surviving.
OPPOSITE dead.
alive to *He is alive to the possible dangers.* alert to, aware of, conscious of, mindful of.
OPPOSITE unaware of.
alive with *The river was alive with boats.* crawling with (*informal*), full of, packed with, swarming with, teeming with.

allege *verb*
He alleged that he was innocent. affirm, assert, claim, declare, state.

allegiance *noun*
swear allegiance to the king. devotion, duty, faithfulness, fidelity, loyalty.
OPPOSITE disloyalty, treason.

allegory *noun*
fable, parable.

allergy *noun*
an allergy to dust. reaction, sensitivity.

alley *noun*
back street, lane, passage, passageway, path.

alliance *noun*
The two parties formed an alliance. association, coalition, confederation, league, partnership, union.

allot *verb*
allot time, places, things, etc. allocate, apportion, assign, dispense, distribute, dole out, give out, ration, share out.

allotment *noun*
1 *an annual allotment of $10,000.* allocation, allowance, quota, ration, share.

a
b
c
d
e
f
g
h
i
j
k
l
m
n
o
p
q
r
s
t
u
v
w
x
y
z

2 *a building allotment.* block, lot, plot, section (*Australian historical*).

allow *verb*
1 *They allowed her to come.* approve, authorise, enable, let, permit.
OPPOSITE forbid.
2 *He was allowed $200 a year for expenses.* allocate, allot, assign, give, grant, permit, provide.

allowance *noun*
1 *They used up their water allowance.* allocation, allotment, portion, quota, ration.
2 *He was paid an allowance.* annuity, benefit, dole, endowment, grant, payment, pension, pocket money, stipend, subsidy.
make allowances for *make allowances for her failing eyesight.* allow for, bear in mind, make concessions for, take into account, take into consideration; see also EXCUSE.

all right *adjective*
1 *The car was badly damaged but the driver was all right.* fine, OK (*informal*), safe, safe and sound, unharmed, uninjured, unscathed.
2 *The food at camp was all right.* acceptable, fine, OK (*informal*), passable, satisfactory.

ally *noun*
They are friends and allies. associate, colleague, confederate, friend, partner.
OPPOSITE enemy.
ally *verb*
They allied themselves against the common enemy. band together, combine, join forces, side, team up, unite.

almighty *adjective*
Almighty God. all-powerful, omnipotent, sovereign, supreme.

almost *adverb*
They ate almost half of the cake. all but, approximately, close to, nearly, not quite, practically.

alone *adjective*
She likes to be alone. apart, by yourself, isolated, on your own, separate, single, solitary, solo, unaccompanied, unaided, unassisted; see also LONELY.

alone *adverb*
You alone can help. exclusively, just, only, solely.

alongside *preposition*
His car was parked alongside ours. adjacent to, beside, close to, next to.

aloud *adverb*
The children read aloud. audibly, out loud.
OPPOSITE silently.

also *adverb*
additionally, as well, besides, furthermore, in addition, moreover, too.

alter *verb*
She had her dress altered to fit better. He altered his story for the police. adapt, adjust, amend, change, convert, modify, remodel, reshape, revise, transform, vary.

alternate *adjective*
She comes on alternate Tuesdays. every other, every second.
alternate *verb*
Her mood alternates between happiness and despair. change, interchange, rotate, swing, switch, take turns, vary.

alternative *noun*
The two alternatives are Sydney or Melbourne. choice, option, possibility.
alternative *adjective*
1 *an alternative proposal.* different, other, second.
2 *alternative medicine.* non-conventional, unconventional.

altitude *noun*
elevation, height.

altogether *adverb*
1 *He was not altogether satisfied.* absolutely, completely, entirely, on the whole, quite, thoroughly, totally, utterly, wholly.
OPPOSITE partially.
2 *There were ten altogether.* all told, in all, in total, in toto.

always *adverb*
1 *He always arrives late.* consistently, every time, invariably, regularly.

2 *They are always arguing.* constantly, continually, continuously, eternally, forever, perpetually, repeatedly.
3 *You can always cancel your appointment.* in any case, in any event, whatever happens.

amalgamate *verb*
Their club amalgamated with ours. combine, incorporate, integrate, join, merge, mix, unite.
OPPOSITE separate.

amateur *noun*
layman, layperson, laywoman, non-professional.
OPPOSITE professional.

amaze *verb*
astonish, astound, bewilder, dumbfound, flabbergast, nonplus, overwhelm, shock, stagger, startle, stun, stupefy, surprise, take aback.

amazement *noun*
astonishment, bewilderment, shock, surprise, wonder.

ambassador *noun*
attaché, consul, diplomat, envoy, representative.

ambiguous *adjective*
an ambiguous answer. equivocal, imprecise, indefinite, uncertain, unclear, vague.
OPPOSITE clear, unambiguous.

ambition *noun*
1 *His ambition is to be a doctor.* aim, aspiration, desire, dream, goal, intention, objective, purpose.
2 *He lacks ambition.* drive, enterprise, enthusiasm, get-up-and-go (*informal*), motivation, push, zeal.

ambitious *adjective*
an ambitious person. aspiring, enterprising, go-ahead, keen, pushy, zealous.
OPPOSITE apathetic.

amble *verb & noun*
dawdle, ramble, saunter, stroll, walk, wander.

ambush *noun*
set up an ambush. snare, trap.

ambush *verb*
The bushrangers ambushed the gold escort. attack, ensnare, lie in wait for, pounce on, swoop on, trap, waylay.

amend *verb*
He amended the text. adapt, adjust, alter, change, correct, edit, improve, modify, rectify, revise.

amends *plural noun*
make amends for *The penitent man wanted to make amends for his crime.* atone for, compensate for, make reparation for, make restitution for.

amenity *noun*
a resort with many amenities. convenience, facility, feature.

amiable *adjective*
an amiable person. affable, agreeable, amicable, friendly, genial, good-natured, kind, kindly, pleasant.
OPPOSITE unfriendly.

amicable *adjective*
on amicable terms. cordial, friendly, harmonious, peaceful.
OPPOSITE hostile.

ammunition *noun*
bullets, cartridges, grenades, missiles, projectiles, rounds, shells, shot, shrapnel.

amnesty *noun*
an amnesty for all political prisoners. pardon, reprieve.

among *adverb*
a rose among thorns. amid, amidst, amongst, in the middle of, in the midst of, surrounded by.

amount *noun*
a large amount. extent, lot (*informal*), mass, measure, quantity, sum, total, volume.
amount *verb*
amount to *It amounted to $99.20.* add up to, come to, equal, make, total.

amphibian *noun*
[*various amphibians*] axolotl, frog, newt, salamander, toad.

a
b
c
d
e
f
g
h
i
j
k
l
m
n
o
p
q
r
s
t
u
v
w
x
y
z

ample *adjective*
1 *They have ample supplies of food.* abundant, copious, enough, generous, lavish, plentiful, profuse, sufficient. OPPOSITE insufficient.
2 *a person of ample build.* big, large, stout. OPPOSITE slight.

amplify *verb*
1 *amplify sound.* boost, enhance, increase, intensify, magnify, strengthen. OPPOSITE reduce.
2 *Please amplify your story.* add to, develop, elaborate on, enlarge upon, expand, fill out, supplement. OPPOSITE condense.

amuse *verb*
She tried to amuse the patients. cheer up, delight, divert, entertain.

amusement *noun*
1 *a source of amusement.* delight, enjoyment, entertainment, fun, merriment, mirth, pleasure, recreation.
2 *different amusements.* distraction, diversion, entertainment, game, hobby, interest, pastime, sport.

amusing *adjective*
see FUNNY.

analyse *verb*
1 *The specimen was analysed in the laboratory.* break down, dissect, divide, separate, take apart.
2 *He analysed the data.* examine, interpret, investigate, study.

analysis *noun*
an analysis of the causes. breakdown, examination, interpretation, investigation, study.

anarchy *noun*
chaos, confusion, disorder, lawlessness. OPPOSITE law, order.

ancestor *noun*
forebear, forefather, predecessor. OPPOSITE descendant.

ancestry *noun*
He was proud of his French ancestry. ancestors, blood, descent, extraction, forebears, genealogy, lineage, origin, roots, stock. OPPOSITE progeny.

anchor *verb*
The fisherman anchored the boat. berth, moor, secure, tie up.

ancient *adjective*
1 *in ancient times.* bygone, early, former, old, olden, prehistoric, primitive. OPPOSITE modern.
2 *an ancient encyclopedia.* antiquated, antique, archaic, obsolete, old, old-fashioned, out-of-date. OPPOSITE modern, new.

anecdote *noun*
narrative, story, tale, yarn (*informal*).

angel *noun*
a host of angels. archangel, cherub, messenger of God, seraph.

angelic *adjective*
1 *the angelic choir.* celestial, cherubic, heavenly, seraphic.
2 *an angelic child.* good, innocent, kind, pure. OPPOSITE devilish.

anger *noun*
He could not hide his anger. annoyance, displeasure, exasperation, fury, indignation, ire, irritation, outrage, rage, temper, vexation, wrath.
anger *verb*
His arrogance angered them. annoy, bug (*informal*), displease, enrage, exasperate, incense, infuriate, irritate, madden, outrage, provoke, rile (*informal*), vex. OPPOSITE pacify, please.

angle *noun*
1 *an angle of 45 degrees.* bend, corner.
2 *written from a woman's angle.* outlook, perspective, point of view, position, slant, standpoint, viewpoint.
angle *verb*
He angled the screen towards them. slant, slope, tilt, turn, twist.

angling *noun*
fishing.

angry *adjective*
an angry person. annoyed, bad-tempered, cross, displeased, enraged, exasperated, furious, hot under the collar (*informal*), incensed, indignant, infuriated, irate, irritated, livid (*informal*), mad (*informal*), outraged,

riled (*informal*), ropeable (*Australian informal*), shirty (*informal*), snaky (*Australian informal*), up in arms, wild. OPPOSITE calm, pleased.

be *or* **become angry** blow your stack (*informal*), blow your top (*informal*), do your block (*Australian informal*), do your lolly (*informal*), explode, flare up, flip your lid (*informal*), fly off the handle (*informal*), freak (out) (*informal*), fume, get steamed up (*informal*), go crook (*Australian informal*), go off the deep end (*informal*), hit the roof (*informal*), lose your temper, rage, seethe.

anguish *noun*
suffer mental anguish. agony, distress, grief, misery, pain, sorrow, suffering, torment, torture, woe.

animal *noun*
beast, brute, creature; [*animals*] fauna, livestock, wildlife; [*various animals*] aardvark, alligator, antelope, ape, armadillo, ass, axolotl, baboon, badger, bandicoot, bat, bear, beaver, bettong, bilby, bison, bobcat, buffalo, bull, bullock, camel, caribou, cat, cattle, cheetah, chimpanzee, chipmunk, cougar, cow, coyote, crocodile, cuscus, deer, dog, dolphin, donkey, dromedary, echidna, elephant, elk, fox, frog, gazelle, gibbon, giraffe, glider, gnu, goat, gopher, gorilla, guinea pig, hamster, hare, hedgehog, hippopotamus, horse, hyena, impala, jackal, jaguar, jellyfish, kangaroo, koala, leopard, lion, lizard, llama, lynx, mole, monkey, moose, mouse, newt, numbat, ocelot, octopus, orang-utan, otter, ox, pademelon, panda, panther, pig, platypus, polar bear, porcupine, porpoise, possum, potoroo, puma, quokka, quoll, rabbit, raccoon, rat, reindeer, rhinoceros, salamander, seal, sea lion, sheep, skunk, snake, spider, squid, squirrel, tiger, toad, tortoise, turtle, wallaby, walrus, weasel, whale, wildebeest, wolf, wombat, worm, yak, zebra; see also BIRD, FISH, INSECT, SHELLFISH.

animate *adjective*
an animate being. alive, breathing, live, living, sentient.
OPPOSITE inanimate.

animate *verb*
A new leader was needed to animate the group. buck up (*informal*), energise, enliven, excite, fire up, inspire, liven up, motivate, perk up (*informal*), rouse, stimulate.

animated *adjective*
an animated conversation. active, bright, energetic, enthusiastic, excited, exuberant, lively, passionate, spirited, vigorous, vivacious.
OPPOSITE lifeless.

animosity *noun*
He showed no animosity towards his replacement. antagonism, bitterness, enmity, hatred, hostility, ill will, malevolence, malice, resentment.
OPPOSITE friendliness.

annexe *noun*
the hotel annexe. addition, extension, wing.

annihilate *verb*
The bomb annihilated the entire population. destroy, eliminate, eradicate, exterminate, extinguish, get rid of, kill, murder, obliterate, slaughter, wipe out.

anniversary *noun*
birthday, jubilee; [*some specific anniversaries*] centenary (= 100 years), sesquicentenary (= 150 years), bicentenary (= 200 years).

announce *verb*
The couple announced their engagement. advertise, broadcast, declare, disclose, make known, proclaim, publicise, publish, report, tell.

announcement *noun*
advertisement, bulletin, communiqué, declaration, disclosure, notice, notification, proclamation, publication, report, statement.

announcer *noun*
broadcaster, compère, disc jockey, DJ, herald, master of ceremonies, MC, newsreader, presenter.

annoy *verb*
aggravate (*informal*), anger, badger, bother, bug (*informal*), distress, drive someone mad (*informal*), drive someone

a
b
c
d
e
f
g
h
i
j
k
l
m
n
o
p
q
r
s
t
u
v
w
x
y
z

up the wall (*informal*), exasperate, get on someone's nerves, harass, hassle, infuriate, irk, irritate, madden, nark (*informal*), needle (*informal*), pester, plague, provoke, rile (*informal*), rub someone up the wrong way (*informal*), trouble, try, upset, vex, worry.
OPPOSITE please.

annoyed *adjective*
angry, cranky, crook (*Australian informal*), cross, displeased, exasperated, fed up (*informal*), irritated, mad, miffed (*informal*), narked (*informal*), needled (*informal*), peeved (*informal*), put out, riled (*informal*), shirty (*informal*), upset, vexed.
OPPOSITE pleased.

annual *adjective*
yearly.

anonymous *adjective*
an anonymous caller. nameless, unidentified, unknown, unnamed.
OPPOSITE familiar.

another *adjective*
1 *They each had another helping.* additional, extra, further, second.
2 *There is another kind you can buy.* alternative, different.
OPPOSITE same.

answer *noun*
1 *the answer to my question.* rejoinder, reply, response, retort.
OPPOSITE question.
2 *the answer to all her problems.* explanation, solution.
answer *verb*
1 *He answered aggressively.* rejoin, reply, respond, retort.
2 *She answered the problem.* resolve, solve, work out.
answer back argue, be cheeky, contradict, disagree, talk back.

antagonism *noun*
antagonism between the two families. animosity, conflict, discord, friction, hatred, hostility, opposition, rivalry.
OPPOSITE harmony.

antenna *noun*
1 *an insect's antenna.* feeler.
2 *a TV antenna.* aerial.

anthem *noun*
The choir sang the anthem. canticle, chorale, hymn, psalm.

anthology *noun*
an anthology of poetry. collection, miscellany, selection, treasury.

anticipate *verb*
1 *The man anticipated the journalist's question.* forestall, pre-empt.
2 (*informal*) *They anticipated trouble.* expect, forecast, foresee, predict.

anticlimax *noun*
The party was an anticlimax. comedown, disappointment, flop (*slang*), let-down.

antics *plural noun*
She was not amused by their silly antics. capers, fooling around, mischief, pranks, shenanigans (*informal*), tomfoolery, tricks.

antidote *noun*
1 *an antidote to a poison.* antitoxin, antivenene.
2 *an antidote to depression.* corrective, countermeasure, cure, remedy.

antiquated *adjective*
His ideas are antiquated. archaic, behind the times, obsolete, old-fashioned, out of date, primitive, quaint, unfashionable.
OPPOSITE modern.

antique *adjective*
an antique bicycle. antique furniture. ancient, antiquated, archaic, old, old-fashioned, veteran, vintage.
antique *noun*
collectable, collector's item, heirloom, relic.

antiseptic *noun*
The surfaces were wiped with antiseptic. bactericide, disinfectant, germicide.

antonym *noun*
'Good' and 'bad' are antonyms. opposite.
OPPOSITE synonym.

anxiety *noun*
The thought of the interview filled him with anxiety. apprehension, concern, dismay, dread, fear, misgiving, nervousness, stress, tension, trepidation, uneasiness, worry.
OPPOSITE calmness.

anxious *adjective*
1 *anxious about the outcome.* afraid, apprehensive, concerned, fearful,

nervous, tense, troubled, uneasy, uptight (*informal*), worried.
OPPOSITE carefree.
2 *anxious to please.* desperate, eager, keen, longing, wanting.
OPPOSITE loath.

apart *adverb*
1 *Husband and wife live apart now.* independently, separately.
OPPOSITE together.
2 *tear apart.* asunder, into pieces.
apart from aside from, except, excluding, not counting, not including, other than, save.
OPPOSITE including.

apartment *noun*
bedsit (*British*), condominium (*American*), flat, home unit (*Australian*), penthouse, rooms, unit (*Australian*).

apathetic *adjective*
an apathetic audience. indifferent, passive, unconcerned, unemotional, uninterested, unmoved, unresponsive.
OPPOSITE enthusiastic.

ape *noun*
[*various apes*] chimpanzee, gibbon, gorilla, orang-utan.
ape *verb*
The child aped the teacher. copy, imitate, mimic.

apex *noun*
a good view from the apex. acme, crest, height, peak, pinnacle, summit, tip, top, vertex, zenith.

apologetic *adjective*
She was apologetic for being late. contrite, penitent, regretful, remorseful, repentant, sorry.
OPPOSITE unrepentant.

apologise *verb*
beg pardon, express regret, repent, say sorry.

apology *noun*
He offered an apology for his behaviour. defence, excuse, explanation.

apostle *noun*
Paul was an apostle of Christ. evangelist, messenger, missionary.

appal *verb*
They were appalled by the destruction. disgust, dismay, horrify, outrage, shock, sicken, terrify.

appalling *adjective*
an appalling crime. abominable, atrocious, awful, dire, dreadful, frightful, ghastly, hideous, horrendous, outrageous, repulsive, shocking, sickening, terrible.

apparatus *noun*
He set up the apparatus for the job. appliance, contraption, device, equipment, gear, instrument, machine, machinery, tool.

apparent *adjective*
1 *His unhappiness is apparent.* clear, conspicuous, evident, manifest, obvious, patent, plain, unmistakable, visible.
2 *Do not be deceived by her apparent reluctance.* ostensible, outward, seeming, superficial.

appeal *verb*
1 *She appealed for help.* apply, ask, beg, entreat, implore, petition, plead, request, solicit.
2 *Cruises do not appeal to me.* attract, entice, fascinate, interest, lure, tempt.
appeal *noun*
1 *an appeal for help.* call, entreaty, petition, plea, request.
2 *It does not hold much appeal.* attraction, charm, fascination, interest, temptation.

appear *verb*
1 *The cat always appears at mealtimes.* arrive, attend, be present, come, emerge, front up (*informal*), materialise, show up, turn up.
2 *Janet appears as Eliza in the school play.* act, perform, play, star, take the part of.
3 *The story appeared in the newspapers.* be published, be reported, come out.
4 *She appeared unwell.* give an impression of being, look, seem.

appearance *noun*
1 *Music heralded the appearance of the official party.* advent, arrival, coming.
OPPOSITE disappearance.
2 *He always has a sad appearance.* air, aspect, demeanour, expression, look, manner.

a b c d e f g h i j k l m n o p q r s t u v w x y z

3 *an appearance of normality.* front, impression, pretence, semblance, show.

appease *verb*
The manager appeased the angry customer. calm, pacify, quiet, quieten, soothe, tranquillise.

appendix *noun*
an appendix to a report. addendum, addition, attachment, supplement.

appetising *adjective*
appetising food. appealing, delicious, mouth-watering, tasty, tempting.

appetite *noun*
an appetite for rich food. an appetite for power. craving, desire, fondness, hunger, keenness, liking, longing, passion, stomach, taste, thirst.

applaud *verb*
1 *The audience applauded enthusiastically.* clap, give an ovation, give someone a big hand (*informal*).
2 *We applaud your action.* acclaim, approve, commend, compliment, congratulate, praise.
OPPOSITE condemn.

applause *noun*
thunderous applause. clapping, hand (*informal*), ovation; see also APPROVAL.

appliance *noun*
kitchen appliances. apparatus, contraption, device, equipment, gadget, implement, instrument, machine, utensil.

applicable *adjective*
The rules were not applicable to his case. appropriate, fitting, pertinent, relevant, suitable.
OPPOSITE inapplicable.

applicant *noun*
an applicant for a job, scholarship, etc. candidate, competitor, entrant, interviewee, job-seeker.

application *noun*
1 *His application for assistance was refused.* appeal, claim, petition, request, submission.
2 *The student shows great application.* commitment, dedication, diligence, effort, industry, perseverance.

apply *verb*
1 *Apply the ointment twice daily.* put on, smear, spread.
2 *They had to apply force to open the door.* employ, exercise, use, utilise.
3 *You must apply the rules fairly.* administer, enforce, put into effect.
4 *It does not apply to me.* be relevant, concern, pertain, refer, relate.
apply for *He applied for work.* ask for, audition for, put in for, register for, request, seek.

appoint *verb*
They appointed him secretary. choose, elect, name, nominate, select.

appointment *noun*
1 *an appointment to see someone.* arrangement, date, engagement, interview, meeting, rendezvous.
2 *The appointment of Mary Jones as new state secretary was welcomed.* choice, election, selection.
3 *He took up his appointment.* job, office, position, post, situation.

appreciate *verb*
1 *He appreciated what he was given.* be grateful for, be thankful for, cherish, prize, think highly of, treasure, value.
2 *I appreciate your desire for privacy.* realise, recognise, understand.
3 *House values are appreciating all the time.* go up, improve, increase, rise.
OPPOSITE depreciate.

appreciative *adjective*
an appreciative customer. grateful, thankful.

apprehend *verb*
The police apprehended the culprit. arrest, capture, catch, detain, nab (*informal*), nail, nick (*slang*), seize, take into custody.

apprehension *noun*
She faced the exam with apprehension. anxiety, concern, dread, fear, foreboding, nervousness, trepidation, uneasiness, worry.

apprehensive *adjective*
afraid, anxious, edgy (*informal*), fearful, frightened, nervous, troubled, uneasy, worried.

apprentice *noun*
beginner, cadet, learner, novice, probationer, pupil, trainee.

approach *verb*
1 *A storm is approaching. The holidays are approaching.* advance, come near, draw near, loom, near.
2 *They approached the problem from a different angle.* go about, handle, set about, tackle.
3 *They approached the bank for a loan.* appeal to, apply to, ask.

approach *noun*
1 *The dog barked at the approach of strangers.* advance, arrival, coming, nearing.
2 *The approach to the city is congested.* access, entry, way, way in.
OPPOSITE exit.
3 *a different approach to the problem.* attitude, manner, method, procedure, style, technique, way.

approachable *adjective*
an approachable boss. accessible, affable, easygoing, friendly.
OPPOSITE aloof.

appropriate *adjective*
an appropriate comment. an appropriate time. applicable, apt, fitting, pertinent, proper, relevant, right, seemly, suitable, timely.
OPPOSITE inappropriate, unsuitable.

approval *noun*
1 *Their performance won the audience's approval.* acclaim, admiration, applause, appreciation, commendation, favour, praise.
OPPOSITE condemnation.
2 *The plans received council approval.* acceptance, agreement, assent, authorisation, blessing, consent, endorsement, go-ahead, OK (*informal*), permission, sanction, support.

approve *verb*
The committee approved the expenditure. agree to, allow, assent to, authorise, consent to, endorse, pass, permit, sanction, support.
OPPOSITE reject.

approve of *He approves of what they are doing.* admire, applaud, be pleased with, commend, like, praise.
OPPOSITE disapprove.

approximate *adjective*
an approximate figure. ballpark (*informal*), close, estimated, inexact, rough.

approximately *adverb*
approximately 200 years old. about, almost, approaching, around, close to, nearly, roughly.

apron *noun*
pinafore.

apt *adjective*
1 *an apt remark.* applicable, appropriate, fitting, relevant, suitable.
OPPOSITE inappropriate.
2 *He is apt to be careless.* inclined, liable, likely, tending.
OPPOSITE unlikely.
3 *an apt student.* bright, clever, intelligent, quick, sharp, smart.
OPPOSITE slow.

aptitude *noun*
an aptitude for mathematics. ability, capability, capacity, flair, gift, knack, skill, talent.

arbitrary *adjective*
an arbitrary choice. capricious, chance, indiscriminate, random, subjective, unreasoned, whimsical.
OPPOSITE reasoned.

arbitrator *noun*
adjudicator, arbiter, judge, referee, umpire.

arc *noun*
arch, bend, bow, crescent, curve.

arcade *noun*
cloister, gallery, mall, passage, walk.

arch *noun*
1 *a single-arch bridge.* archway, span, vault.
2 *He bent over to form an arch.* arc, bow, curve, semicircle.

arch *verb*
The cat arched her back. bend, bow, curve, hump.

a
b
c
d
e
f
g
h
i
j
k
l
m
n
o
p
q
r
s
t
u
v
w
x
y
z

archaic *adjective*
ancient, antiquated, antique, obsolete, old, olden, old-fashioned, out of date. OPPOSITE modern.

ardent *adjective*
an ardent football fan. avid, eager, earnest, enthusiastic, fervent, keen, passionate, zealous.

arduous *adjective*
an arduous task. difficult, exhausting, gruelling, hard, laborious, onerous, strenuous, taxing, tough.
OPPOSITE easy.

area *noun*
1 *the area of a playing field.* extent, measurement, size.
2 *They live in the same area.* district, locality, neighbourhood, precinct, quarter, region, territory, vicinity, zone.
3 *a picnic area.* place, space, spot.
4 *in the area of information technology.* domain, field, realm, sphere.

arena *noun*
The athletes entered the arena. amphitheatre, field, ground, pitch, ring, stadium.

argue *verb*
1 *They argued over everything.* barney (*informal*), bicker, debate, differ, disagree, dispute, feud, fight, haggle, have words, quarrel, quibble, row (*informal*), spar, squabble, wrangle.
2 *He argued that all people are born equal.* assert, contend, declare, maintain, reason, show.

argument *noun*
1 *two people having an argument over trivia.* altercation, barney (*informal*), blue (*Australian informal*), clash, controversy, debate, disagreement, dispute, feud, fight, quarrel, row (*informal*), squabble, tiff, wrangle.
2 *the argument for free education.* case, defence, grounds, justification, reason, reasoning.

argumentative *adjective*
belligerent, contentious, contrary, quarrelsome.

arid *adjective*
arid regions. desert, dry, parched, waterless; see also BARREN.
OPPOSITE well-watered.

arise *verb*
1 *A problem has arisen.* appear, come up, crop up, emerge, occur, originate, present itself.
2 (*old use*) *He arose and walked away.* get up, rise, stand up.

aristocrat *noun*
lady, lord, noble, nobleman, noblewoman, peer, peeress.

aristocratic *adjective*
an aristocratic gentleman. blue-blooded, noble, titled, upper-class.
OPPOSITE plebeian.

arm^1 *noun*
1 *an animal's arms.* forelimb, limb, tentacle (*of an octopus*).
2 *an arm of a tree.* bough, branch, limb.

arm^2 *verb*
The men armed themselves with batons. equip, furnish, provide, supply.
armed services air force, armed forces, army, defence forces, forces, military, navy, services.
arms *plural noun*
policemen carrying arms. firearms, weapons.

armada *noun*
an armada of ships. convoy, fleet, navy.

armistice *noun*
The countries signed an armistice. ceasefire, peace, peace treaty, truce.

armour *noun*
chain mail, mail, protective covering.

arms *plural noun*
see ARM^2.

army *noun*
1 *The army kept the peace in the town.* armed forces, armed services, military, soldiers, troops.
2 *an army of helpers.* crowd, horde, host, mob, multitude, throng.

aroma *noun*
bouquet, fragrance, odour, perfume, savour, scent, smell.

aromatic *adjective*
an aromatic curry. fragrant, pungent, spicy, strong-smelling.

around *adverb*
1 He's never around when you want him. about, close by, in the vicinity, near, nearby.
2 He travels around. about, here and there, hither and thither.
3 an audience of around 500 people. about, approximately, close to, nearly, roughly.
around *preposition*
The nurse put screens around the bed. encircling, on all sides of, round, surrounding.

arouse *verb*
1 The noise aroused the neighbours. awake, awaken, rouse, stir, waken, wake up.
2 Try not to arouse suspicion. cause, excite, inspire, provoke, rouse, stimulate, stir up.

arrange *verb*
1 The books are arranged according to subject. array, classify, display, group, lay out, line up, order, organise, position, put in order, rank, set out, sort.
2 He arranged a meeting. contrive, fix, organise, plan, prepare, schedule, set up, wangle (*slang*).
3 The music has been arranged for two recorders. adapt, orchestrate, score, set.

arrangement *noun*
1 the arrangement of books on the shelves. array, classification, display, grouping, layout, line-up, order, organisation, set-up, system.
2 a financial arrangement. agreement, bargain, contract, deal, plan, provision, settlement, understanding.
3 a musical arrangement. adaptation, orchestration, setting, version.

array *noun*
an array of ornaments. arrangement, collection, display, exhibit, line-up, series, show.

arrears *plural noun*
1 The boss paid the arrears. back pay, debt, outstanding amount.

2 They caught up on the arrears of work. backlog, build-up, pile-up.
in arrears in arrears with the rent. behind, late, overdue.
OPPOSITE in advance, up to date.

arrest *verb*
1 The progress of the cancer was arrested. check, curb, halt, prevent, stop.
2 The police arrested the thief. apprehend, capture, catch, detain, nab (*informal*), nail, nick (*slang*), seize, take into custody.

arrival *noun*
the arrival of the official party. advent, appearance, approach, coming, entrance, entry.
OPPOSITE departure.

arrive *verb*
They finally arrived in Sydney at eight o'clock. appear, come, disembark, enter, get in, land, roll up (*informal*), show up, touch down, turn up; see also REACH.
OPPOSITE depart.

arrogant *adjective*
cocky, conceited, condescending, contemptuous, disdainful, egotistic, haughty, high and mighty, lofty, overbearing, presumptuous, proud, scornful, self-important, snobbish, snooty (*informal*), stuck-up (*informal*), supercilious, vain.
OPPOSITE modest.

arsenal *noun*
an arsenal of weapons. ammunition dump, armoury, arms depot, magazine, store.

arsonist *noun*
firebug (*informal*), pyromaniac.

art *noun*
the art of saying a lot in a few words. craft, flair, gift, knack, skill, talent, technique, trick.

artful *adjective*
as artful as a fox. clever, crafty, cunning, deceitful, ingenious, scheming, shifty, shrewd, sly, tricky, wily.
OPPOSITE artless.

a
b
c
d
e
f
g
h
i
j
k
l
m
n
o
p
q
r
s
t
u
v
w
x
y
z

article *noun*
1 *an article of jewellery.* item, object, piece, thing.
2 *a newspaper article.* essay, feature, item, piece, report, story, write-up.

articulate *adjective*
an articulate speaker. an articulate speech. clear, coherent, eloquent, fluent, intelligible, lucid, understandable.
OPPOSITE inarticulate.
articulate *verb*
She articulated each word with care. enunciate, pronounce, say, speak, utter.

artificial *adjective*
1 *artificial grass.* bogus, counterfeit, fake, false, imitation, man-made, manufactured, phoney (*informal*), pseudo, sham, synthetic.
OPPOSITE natural, real.
2 *His sympathy is artificial.* affected, false, feigned, forced, hollow, insincere, phoney (*informal*), pretended, skin-deep, superficial.
OPPOSITE genuine, sincere.

artist *noun*
1 [*kinds of artist*] cartoonist, engraver, graphic designer, illustrator, painter, photographer, portraitist, sculptor.
2 *The concert artists appeared on stage.* artiste, entertainer, musician, performer.

artistic *adjective*
an artistic design. aesthetic, attractive, beautiful, creative, decorative, imaginative, tasteful.

ascend *verb*
They ascended the mountain. The plane ascended. climb, go up, mount, rise, scale, soar.
OPPOSITE descend.

ascent *noun*
a steep ascent. climb, gradient, hill, incline, rise, slope.
OPPOSITE descent.

ascertain *verb*
Try to ascertain what is wrong. determine, discover, establish, find out, identify, learn, uncover, work out.

ashamed *adjective*
abashed, embarrassed, humiliated, mortified, red-faced, shamefaced, sheepish.

ashes *plural noun*
cinders, embers, remains.

aside *adverb*
Step aside. away, out of the way, to one side, to the side.
aside from apart from, besides, in addition to, other than.

ask *verb*
1 *Ask the teacher.* enquire of, inquire of, interrogate, query, question, quiz.
OPPOSITE answer.
2 *He asked for help.* appeal, apply, beg, demand, entreat, implore, petition, plead, pray, request, seek, solicit.
3 *She asked me to dinner.* invite, summon.

asleep *adverb & adjective*
asleep in the hammock. dormant, dozing, hibernating, napping, resting, sleeping, slumbering, snoozing.
OPPOSITE awake.
fall asleep doze off, drop off, flake out (*informal*), go to sleep, nod off.

aspect *noun*
1 *All aspects of the problem had been considered.* angle, detail, facet, feature, side.
2 *The room has a northerly aspect.* outlook, prospect, view.

ass *noun*
1 *He rode an ass.* donkey, jackass (*male*), jenny (*female*).
2 (*informal*) *Don't be an ass.* see FOOL.

assail *verb*
The rioters assailed the police with stones. assault, attack, bombard, lay into, set upon.

assailant *noun*
assaulter, attacker, mugger.

assassin *noun*
executioner, hit man (*slang*), killer, murderer.

assassinate *verb*
The President was assassinated. execute, kill, murder, slay.

assault *noun*
They launched an assault on the enemy's military buildings. attack, charge, offensive, onslaught, raid, strike.
assault *verb*
1 He assaulted the police officer. assail, attack, beat up, hit, mug, set upon, strike.
2 The woman had been sexually assaulted. molest, rape.

assemble *verb*
1 A crowd assembled to welcome the princess. collect, come together, congregate, flock, gather, group, meet, muster, rally, swarm, throng.
OPPOSITE scatter.
2 The machines are assembled in Adelaide. build, construct, fit together, make up, manufacture, put together.
OPPOSITE dismantle.

assembly *noun*
The mayor spoke to the assembly. conference, congregation, congress, convention, council, crowd, gathering, group, meeting, mob, multitude, rally, throng.

assert *verb*
He asserted that he was innocent. allege, argue, claim, contend, declare, insist, maintain, state, swear.

assertive *adjective*
She became more confident and assertive. aggressive, authoritative, bold, dogmatic, forceful, pushy, self-assertive, strong-willed.
OPPOSITE submissive.

assess *verb*
1 The teacher assessed the student's work. appraise, evaluate, grade, judge, mark, rate.
2 The damage was assessed at $10,000. appraise, calculate, estimate, gauge, reckon, value, work out.

asset *noun*
Brains are definitely an asset. advantage, benefit, blessing, boon, help.
OPPOSITE disadvantage, liability.
assets *plural noun*
The company was forced to sell some of its assets. capital, holdings, means, possessions, property, resources, wealth.
OPPOSITE liabilities.

assign *verb*
1 Books were assigned to each pupil. allocate, allot, deal out, distribute, give out.
2 The teacher assigned the new boy to the job of library monitor. appoint, delegate, designate, nominate, select.

assignment *noun*
He always completes his assignments just before the deadline. homework, job, project, task, work.

assimilate *verb*
1 The students assimilated the information. absorb, digest, take in; see also LEARN.
2 The immigrants assimilated quickly. become absorbed, blend in, integrate.

assist *verb*
He likes to assist people. abet, aid, back, collaborate with, cooperate with, help, lend a hand, relieve, serve, support.
OPPOSITE hinder.

assistance *noun*
aid, backing, backup, collaboration, cooperation, help, reinforcement, relief, service, support.
OPPOSITE hindrance.

assistant *noun*
abetter, accessory, accomplice, aide, deputy, helper, offsider (*Australian*), sidekick (*informal*), subordinate.

associate *verb*
1 She associates with many different people. fraternise, hang around (*informal*), hang out (*informal*), keep company, mix, socialise.
2 They associated summer with swimming. connect, identify, link, relate.
associate *noun*
a business associate. colleague, fellow-worker, partner, workmate; see also COMPANION.

association *noun*
1 an association between the two ideas. connection, link, relation, relationship, tie-up.
2 She belongs to a sporting association. alliance, body, club, federation, group, league, organisation, society, union.

a
b
c
d
e
f
g
h
i
j
k
l
m
n
o
p
q
r
s
t
u
v
w
x
y
z

assorted *adjective*
assorted chocolates. different, diverse, miscellaneous, mixed, varied.

assortment *noun*
array, collection, hotchpotch, mixture, range, selection, variety.

assume *verb*
1 *We assumed that you knew the way.* believe, expect, guess, imagine, presume, suppose, think.
2 *He has assumed that responsibility.* accept, adopt, take on, undertake.
3 *He assumed a grave expression.* acquire, adopt, affect, put on.

assumed *adjective*
an assumed name. false, fictitious, made-up.

assumption *noun*
His assumption proved to be wrong. guess, hypothesis, presumption, supposition, surmise, theory.

assurance *noun*
1 *They gave an assurance that the parcel would be delivered.* commitment, guarantee, oath, pledge, promise, undertaking.
2 *life assurance.* see INSURANCE.
3 *She conducts herself with assurance.* confidence, poise, self-assurance, self-confidence.

assure *verb*
1 *He assured her that he would come.* declare, give your word, guarantee, pledge, promise, swear, vow.
2 *He tried the door to assure himself that it was locked.* convince, persuade, prove to, reassure.
3 *Preparation assures success.* ensure, guarantee, make sure of, secure.

astonish *verb*
The news astonished her. amaze, astound, dumbfound, flabbergast, nonplus, shock, stagger, startle, stun, stupefy, surprise, take aback.

astonishment *noun*
gaze in astonishment. amazement, surprise, wonder.

astound *verb*
see ASTONISH.

astray *adverb*
go astray *Her purse has gone astray.* be lost, be mislaid, be misplaced, go missing, go walkabout (*informal*).

astronaut *noun*
cosmonaut, spaceman, spacewoman.

astronomical *adjective*
an astronomical amount of money. colossal, enormous, exorbitant, huge, incredible (*informal*), massive, unbelievable, vast.
OPPOSITE tiny.

athletic *adjective*
an athletic person. active, brawny, muscular, robust, sporty (*informal*), strapping, strong.

athletics *plural noun*
school athletics. games, races, sport, sports, track and field events.

atmosphere *noun*
1 *the earth's atmosphere.* aerospace, air, sky.
2 *a happy atmosphere.* air, ambience, climate, environment, feeling, mood, tone.

atom *noun*
He does not have an atom of sense. bit, iota, jot, molecule, ounce, particle, scrap, skerrick (*Australian informal*), speck, trace.

atone *verb*
atone for *He has atoned for his misconduct.* compensate for, make amends for, make up for, pay for, pay the penalty for.

atrocious *adjective*
1 *an atrocious crime.* abominable, appalling, barbaric, brutal, cruel, despicable, evil, heinous, horrific, monstrous, savage, vicious, wicked.
2 (*informal*) *atrocious weather.* abominable (*informal*), bad, dreadful (*informal*), foul, shocking (*informal*), terrible (*informal*), unpleasant.

attach *verb*
She attached the documents to the letter. affix, bind, connect, couple, fasten, fix, glue, join, link, pin, secure, staple, stick,

tack, tie.
OPPOSITE detach.

attached *adjective*
They are very attached to one another.
close, devoted, fond (of).

attachment *noun*
The vacuum cleaner came with various attachments. accessory, extra, fitting.

attack *verb*
1 *The thieves attacked the travellers.* ambush, assail, assault, beat up, molest, mug, pounce on, set upon.
OPPOSITE defend.
2 *The city was attacked at night.* besiege, bombard, invade, raid, storm, strike.
3 *The critics attacked the artist and his work.* condemn, criticise, knock (*informal*), pan (*informal*), revile, slam (*informal*), slate (*informal*).
OPPOSITE praise.
4 *The disease attacked his liver.* affect, damage, harm, infect, injure.
5 *Let's attack the washing-up.* begin, get stuck into (*informal*), make inroads on, set about, start, tackle.

attack *noun*
1 *an attack on the city.* ambush, assault, blitz, bombardment, charge, offensive, onslaught, raid, strike.
OPPOSITE defence.
2 *an attack of sneezing.* bout, fit, outbreak, seizure.

attain *verb*
He attained the required standard. accomplish, achieve, arrive at, gain, obtain, reach.

attempt *verb*
He attempted to climb the mountain. endeavour, strive, try, venture.
attempt *noun*
Their first attempt met with failure. effort, endeavour, go, try.

attend *verb*
1 *She attends their meetings.* appear at, be present at, go to, show up at (*informal*), turn up at, visit.
2 *The doctor is attending the patient.* care for, look after, take care of.
attend to *He is attending to the problem.* deal with, handle, see to, take care of.

attendance *noun*
Her attendance at the function was requested. appearance, presence.
OPPOSITE absence.

attendant *noun*
aide, assistant, chaperone, companion, escort, helper, servant, steward, usher.

attention *noun*
1 *attention to detail.* care, concentration, concern, heed, notice, regard.
2 *attract attention.* notice, publicity, recognition.
pay attention concentrate, listen, pay heed, watch.

attentive *adjective*
1 *an attentive pupil.* alert, careful, diligent, observant, vigilant, watchful.
OPPOSITE inattentive.
2 *She is attentive to their needs.* aware, considerate, mindful, thoughtful.

attic *noun*
garret, loft.

attitude *noun*
1 *Her attitude is always cheerful.* disposition, frame of mind, manner, mood, outlook.
2 *the company's attitude towards conservation.* feeling, opinion, position, stance, stand, standpoint, thoughts, view, viewpoint.

attract *verb*
1 *A magnet attracts iron.* draw, pull.
OPPOSITE repel.
2 *The bright lights of the big city attracted him.* appeal to, draw, entice, fascinate, interest, lure.

attraction *noun*
1 *the attraction of visiting new places.* appeal, attractiveness, charm, fascination, lure, pull.
2 *tourist attractions.* drawcard, feature, interest.

attractive *adjective*
1 *an attractive offer.* appealing, enticing, interesting, inviting, pleasing, tempting.
OPPOSITE unattractive.
2 *an attractive person.* beautiful, bonny (*Scottish*), captivating, charming, enchanting, fascinating, good-looking,

a
b
c
d
e
f
g
h
i
j
k
l
m
n
o
p
q
r
s
t
u
v
w
x
y
z

handsome, irresistible, lovely, nice, pleasant, pretty, striking, stunning, sweet (*informal*).
OPPOSITE plain, ugly.
3 *an attractive outfit.* becoming, flattering.

audible *adjective*
audible sounds. clear, discernible, distinct, perceptible.
OPPOSITE inaudible.

audience *noun*
She spoke to the audience. congregation, crowd, listeners, spectators, viewers.

audition *noun*
an audition for a film. screen test, test, trial, try-out.

auditorium *noun*
hall, theatre.

austere *adjective*
an austere way of life. frugal, hard, harsh, plain, puritanical, restrained, self-denying, self-disciplined, severe, simple, spartan, strict.
OPPOSITE indulgent.

authentic *adjective*
an authentic passport. actual, genuine, real, true, trustworthy.
OPPOSITE fake.

author *noun*
the author of a literary work. biographer, composer, creator, dramatist, essayist, novelist, playwright, poet, writer.

authorise *verb*
1 *He authorised the sale.* agree to, allow, approve, give permission for, OK (*informal*), permit, sanction.
OPPOSITE forbid.
2 *She is authorised to collect the rent.* entitle, license, permit.

authority *noun*
1 *a position of authority.* command, control, dominion, influence, power, right, sovereignty.
2 *He had authority to search the house.* approval, consent, permission, sanction, warrant.
3 *She is an authority on wines.* connoisseur, expert, judge, specialist.

autograph *noun*
signature.

automatic *adjective*
1 *an automatic device.* automated, computerised, electronic, mechanised, programmed, pushbutton, self-operating.
OPPOSITE manual.
2 *an automatic reaction.* instinctive, involuntary, mechanical, reflex, spontaneous, unconscious, unthinking.
OPPOSITE conscious.
3 *an automatic suspension of licence.* inevitable, mandatory, necessary, obligatory.

autumn *noun*
Autumn follows summer. fall (*American*).

auxiliary *adjective*
auxiliary services. ancillary, assisting, backup, helping, reserve, support, supporting.

available *adjective*
Is the car available? accessible, at your disposal, free, handy, obtainable, ready, usable.

avenge *verb*
He wanted to avenge the crime. get even for, get your own back for (*informal*), repay, take revenge for; see also RETALIATE.
OPPOSITE forgive.

avenue *noun*
see ROAD.

average *adjective*
1 *The average mark for the class was 65.* mean.
2 *a man of average intelligence.* intermediate, mediocre, medium, middling, normal, ordinary, regular, standard, usual.
OPPOSITE exceptional.

avert *verb*
1 *People averted their eyes.* turn away.
2 *They managed to avert disaster.* fend off, prevent, stave off, ward off.

aviator *noun*
airman, airwoman, aviatrix (*female, old use*), flyer, pilot.

avid *adjective*
an avid reader. eager, enthusiastic, keen, passionate.
OPPOSITE reluctant.

avoid *verb*
1 *He avoided the tidying.* dodge, escape, evade, get out of, shirk, sidestep, skirt.
OPPOSITE face.
2 *He avoided the new boy.* cold-shoulder, elude, give a wide berth to, ignore, keep away from, shun, steer clear of.
OPPOSITE confront.

awake *verb*
1 *I awoke to the sound of thunder.* awaken, stir, wake, wake up.
2 *The noise awoke us.* arouse, awaken, rouse, wake, wake up.
awake *adjective*
He lay awake for hours. sleepless, wakeful, wide awake.
OPPOSITE asleep.

awaken *verb*
see AWAKE.

award *verb*
The prize is awarded to the top student. bestow, confer, give, grant, present.
award *noun*
the presentation of awards. badge, colours, cup, decoration, honour, medal, prize, scholarship, trophy.

aware *adjective*
aware of *I am aware of the risks.* alert to, conscious of, familiar with, informed about, mindful of.
OPPOSITE ignorant.
be aware of see KNOW.

awe *noun*
filled with awe. admiration, amazement, fear, respect, reverence, veneration, wonder.
OPPOSITE contempt.

awe-inspiring *adjective*
an awe-inspiring sight. amazing, astonishing, awesome, breathtaking, impressive, magnificent, marvellous, stupendous, wonderful.

awesome *adjective*
an awesome responsibility. daunting, fearsome, formidable, terrible.

awful *adjective*
1 *an awful accident. awful weather.* abominable, appalling, atrocious, bad, disgusting, dreadful, foul, frightful, ghastly, horrible, nasty, shocking, terrible, unpleasant.
2 (*informal*) *an awful lot of money.* big, huge, impressive, large, tremendous.

awfully *adverb*
1 *He behaved awfully.* abominably, appallingly, atrociously, badly, deplorably, dreadfully, frightfully, horribly, nastily, poorly, shockingly, terribly, unpleasantly.
2 (*informal*) *awfully pretty.* exceedingly, extremely, terribly (*informal*), very.

awkward *adjective*
1 *an awkward tool.* cumbersome, inconvenient, unmanageable, unwieldy.
OPPOSITE user-friendly.
2 *an awkward spot to get to.* difficult, hard, inconvenient, tricky, troublesome.
OPPOSITE convenient.
3 *an awkward person, always having accidents.* bumbling, bungling, clumsy, gauche, gawky, uncoordinated, ungainly.
OPPOSITE coordinated.
4 *He felt awkward about it.* embarrassed, ill at ease, self-conscious, uncomfortable, uneasy.
OPPOSITE comfortable.

axe *noun*
adze, battleaxe, chopper, cleaver, hatchet, mogo, tomahawk.
axe *verb*
The programme was axed. abolish, cancel, discontinue, do away with, eliminate, get rid of, give the chop (*informal*), scrap, terminate, wind up.

axle *noun*
The wheel turned on the axle. arbor, rod, shaft, spindle.

a
b
c
d
e
f
g
h
i
j
k
l
m
n
o
p
q
r
s
t
u
v
w
x
y
z

Bb

babble *verb*
1 *I can't understand what she's babbling about.* chatter, gabble, gibber, jabber, mumble, yabber (*Australian informal*).
2 *the soothing sound of a creek babbling along.* burble, gurgle, murmur.

baby *noun*
1 *The mother fed her baby.* babe, child, infant, toddler, tot.
OPPOSITE adult.
2 *an animal's baby.* offspring, young.
baby *verb*
They baby the child too much. indulge, mollycoddle, pamper, spoil.

babyish *adjective*
childish, immature, infantile, juvenile, sooky (*Australian informal*).
OPPOSITE mature.

babysit *verb*
see MIND.

babysitter *noun*
childminder, minder, nanny, sitter.

back *noun*
1 *His back was injured.* backbone, spinal column, spine, vertebral column.
2 *They stood at the back of the line.* end, rear, tail.
OPPOSITE front.
3 *the back of a ship.* poop, stern.
OPPOSITE bow.
4 *the back of the painting.* reverse, underside.
OPPOSITE front.
back *adjective*
1 *back legs.* hind, rear.
OPPOSITE front.
2 *a back issue.* earlier, former, past, previous.
OPPOSITE current, future.
back *verb*
1 *She backed the car into the space.* move backwards, reverse.
2 *The government is backing their new venture.* aid, assist, encourage, endorse, help, promote, sponsor, subsidise,

support.
OPPOSITE oppose.
3 *Which horse did he back in the race?* bet on, gamble on.
back away *He backed away from the others.* move backwards, pull back, retire, retreat, withdraw.
back down *It was an unpopular decision, but he refused to back down.* back-pedal, backtrack, concede, give in, submit, surrender, yield.
back out of *He found a way to back out of the agreement.* escape from, get out of, go back on, renege on, withdraw from, wriggle out of.
back up *She backed up everything he said.* affirm, confirm, corroborate, document, reinforce, second, substantiate, support, verify.
OPPOSITE contradict.
go back see RETURN.

backbone *noun*
1 *an animal's backbone.* back, spinal column, spine, vertebral column.
2 *The country needs a leader with backbone.* courage, determination, grit, guts (*informal*), pluck, resolve.

backfire *verb*
Their plan backfired. boomerang, fail, rebound, recoil.

background *noun*
1 *a pale blue background.* backcloth, backdrop, setting.
OPPOSITE foreground.
2 *the historical background of the play.* circumstances, context, environment, setting.
3 *The applicant's background suited him to the job.* education, experience, history, training, upbringing.

backing *noun*
1 *The club receives the school's backing.* aid, approval, assistance, endorsement, funding, help, sponsorship, subsidy, support.
OPPOSITE opposition.

2 *musical backing.* accompaniment.

backlog *noun*
a backlog of letters to answer. arrears, build-up, stockpile.

backpack *noun*
haversack, knapsack, pack, rucksack.

backpacker *noun*
see HIKER, TRAVELLER.

backside *noun*
see BOTTOM.

backup *noun*
The team provides the driver with backup. aid, assistance, help, support.
backup *adjective*
backup supplies. emergency, reserve, spare, stand-by.

backward *adjective*
1 *a backward glance.* rearward.
OPPOSITE forward.
2 *a backward place.* primitive, underdeveloped, undeveloped.
OPPOSITE advanced.
3 *a backward child.* handicapped, retarded, slow.
OPPOSITE gifted, precocious.

backwards *adverb*
in reverse, rearwards.
OPPOSITE forwards.
backwards and forwards back and forth, hither and thither, to and fro.
go backwards see DETERIORATE, REVERSE.

bacteria *plural noun*
see MICROBE.

bad *adjective*
1 *a bad person. a bad deed.* abhorrent, abominable, atrocious, awful, base, beastly, corrupt, criminal, cruel, deplorable, depraved, despicable, detestable, disgraceful, dishonest, dishonourable, evil, hateful, immoral, infamous, loathsome, malevolent, malicious, mean, nasty, naughty, notorious, sinful, ungodly, unrighteous, unworthy, vile, villainous, wicked.
OPPOSITE good, virtuous.
2 *bad weather.* appalling (*informal*), atrocious (*informal*), dreadful (*informal*), foul, grim, inclement, lousy (*informal*),

rotten (*informal*), shocking (*informal*), terrible (*informal*), unpleasant.
OPPOSITE fair, fine.
3 *a bad accident.* appalling, awful, dire, disastrous, dreadful, frightful, ghastly, grave, hideous, horrendous, horrible, horrific, nasty, serious, severe, shocking, terrible.
4 *The food had gone bad.* decayed, foul, mildewed, mouldy, off, putrid, rancid, rotten, spoiled, tainted.
OPPOSITE fresh.
5 *a bad smell.* foul, nauseating, obnoxious, offensive, revolting, stinking, vile.
OPPOSITE fragrant.
6 *The workman did a bad job.* defective, deficient, faulty, incompetent, inferior, poor, shoddy, substandard, unsatisfactory, unsound.
OPPOSITE good.
7 *She went to the doctor because she felt bad.* crook (*Australian informal*), ill, off colour, poorly, sick, unhealthy, unwell.
OPPOSITE well.
8 *He felt bad about what happened.* ashamed, conscience-stricken, guilty, regretful, remorseful, sad, sorry, unhappy, upset.
9 *Lollies are bad for your teeth.* damaging, dangerous, destructive, detrimental, harmful, hurtful, injurious, ruinous, unhealthy.
OPPOSITE beneficial.
bad language abuse, curses, expletives, obscenities, profanities, swear words.

baddy *noun* (*informal*)
the goodies and the baddies. criminal, crook (*informal*), miscreant, villain.

badge *noun*
crest, emblem, insignia, logo, medal, shield, sign, symbol.

badger *verb*
He badgered them into going. bully, harass, hassle (*informal*), hound, nag, pester.

bad-tempered *adjective*
angry, cantankerous, crabby, cranky, cross, crotchety, grouchy, gruff, grumpy, hot-tempered, ill-tempered, irascible, irritable, moody, peevish, petulant, quarrelsome, shirty (*informal*),

a
b
c
d
e
f
g
h
i
j
k
l
m
n
o
p
q
r
s
t
u
v
w
x
y
z

short-tempered, snaky (*Australian informal*), stroppy (*informal*), testy.
OPPOSITE easygoing, good-humoured.

baffle *verb*
The problem had me baffled. bamboozle (*informal*), bewilder, confound, confuse, mystify, perplex, puzzle, stump.

bag *noun*
[*kinds of bag*] backpack, carry bag, case, dilly bag (*Australian*), duffel bag, handbag, haversack, kitbag, knapsack, pack, port (*Australian*), pouch, purse (*American*), rucksack, sack, satchel, schoolbag, shopping bag, shoulder bag, suitcase, swag (*Australian*), travelling bag, tucker bag (*Australian informal*).

baggage *noun*
bags, cases, luggage, suitcases, trunks.

baggy *adjective*
baggy trousers. floppy, loose, roomy.
OPPOSITE tight.

bags *verb* (*informal*)
I bags that seat at the front. claim, lay claim to, reserve.

bail[1] *noun*
He was released on bail. bond, guarantee, security, surety.
bail *verb*
bail out *They wanted us to bail the firm out.* assist, help, relieve, rescue.

bail[2] *verb*
bail up (*Australian*)
1 *She always gets bailed up by her friends at the shops.* buttonhole, corner, detain, waylay.
2 *The bushrangers bailed them up on a lonely track.* hold up, rob, stick up (*informal*).

bait *noun*
Cheese was used as a bait to catch the mouse. attraction, enticement, lure, temptation.
bait *verb*
Baiting bears is a cruel sport. badger, goad, provoke, tease, torment.

bake *verb*
1 *The chicken was baked in the oven.* cook, roast.
2 *The bricks were baked in the sun.* dry, fire, harden.

balance *noun*
1 *weigh on the balance.* scales, weighing machine.
2 *lose your balance.* equilibrium, poise, stability, steadiness.
3 *We took what we needed and gave away the balance.* difference, excess, leftovers, remainder, residue, rest, surplus.
balance *verb*
The two sides balanced each other. cancel out, counteract, counterbalance, equalise, even out, level, neutralise, offset.

balanced *adjective*
balanced reporting. even-handed, fair, impartial, unbiased.

balcony *noun*
1 *The house has a balcony outside the bedroom.* deck, terrace, veranda.
2 *a balcony in the theatre.* gallery, the gods (*informal*), upper dress circle.

bald *adjective*
1 *a bald head.* hairless, shaved.
OPPOSITE hairy, hirsute.
2 *a bald tyre.* smooth, worn.

bale[1] *noun*
a bale of wool. bundle, pack, package, parcel.

bale[2] *verb*
bale out *The airman baled out before the plane crashed.* eject, jump out, parachute.

ball[1] *noun*
bead, drop, globe, pellet, sphere.

ball[2] *noun*
dance, formal, social.

ballerina *noun*
ballet-dancer, dancer.

ballot *noun*
They held a secret ballot. election, plebiscite, poll, referendum, vote.

ban *verb*
The government banned cigarette advertising. forbid, outlaw, prohibit, proscribe.
OPPOSITE permit.

ban *noun*
a ban on the sale of fireworks. boycott, embargo, moratorium, prohibition, veto.

band *noun*
1 a band of red on each sleeve. annulus, circle, hoop, line, loop, ring, strip, stripe.
2 bands holding a thing together. belt, brace, cord, elastic, loop, ribbon, strap, string, tie.
3 a band of gangsters. body, bunch, clique, company, gang, group, mob, pack, party.
4 She plays flute in the band. ensemble, group, orchestra.
band *verb*
The newcomers banded together for moral support. ally, associate, gather, group, join, team up, unite.

bandage *noun*
dressing, gauze, plaster, tourniquet.

bandit *noun*
brigand, buccaneer, bushranger, criminal, crook (*informal*), gangster, highwayman, outlaw, pirate, robber, thief.

bandstand *noun*
platform, rotunda, stage.

bandy-legged *adjective*
bow-legged.
OPPOSITE knock-kneed.

bang *verb*
1 Some fireworks bang; others fizz. blast, boom, crash, detonate, explode, pop.
2 Don't bang the door down. bash, hammer, hit, knock, pound, slam, strike, thump.
bang *noun*
1 We were startled by a loud bang. blast, boom, clap, clatter, crash, explosion, pop, thud.
2 The bang on the head gave him a nasty lump. blow, bump, hit, knock, punch, whack.

bangle *noun*
anklet, armlet, bracelet.

banish *verb*
He was banished from the country. cast out, deport, drive out, exile, expel, oust, remove, send away, transport.
OPPOSITE admit.

banisters *plural noun*
It's fun to slide down the banisters. handrail, stair-rail.

bank¹ *noun*
1 a river bank. brink, edge, embankment, shore, side, slope, verge.
2 a sand bank. mass, mound, pile.
bank *verb*
1 The leaves banked up in the gutters. accumulate, collect, heap, pile.
2 The plane banked as it prepared to land. incline, lean, list, pitch, tilt.

bank² *noun*
money in the bank. kitty, pool, reserve, store.
bank *verb*
He banks $100 each week. deposit, invest, put aside, save.
bank on We are banking on your success. bargain on, count on, depend on, pin your hopes on, rely on.

bankrupt *adjective*
The company is bankrupt. broke (*informal*), bust (*informal*), in liquidation, insolvent, ruined.
OPPOSITE solvent.

banner *noun*
1 Supporters waved the team's banner. flag, pennant, standard.
2 The protesters carried banners. placard, sign.

banquet *noun*
dinner, feast, meal, repast (*formal*).

baptise *verb*
He was baptised 'John'. christen, name.

bar *noun*
1 a wooden bar. bail, batten, beam, block, girder, pole, rail, rod, stake, stick.
2 The chart shows bars of different colours. band, column, oblong, rectangle, strip, stripe.
3 a bar of soap. block, cake, hunk, lump, piece, slab.
4 a bar to progress. barrier, block, impediment, obstacle, restriction.
5 They drank at the bar. counter, saloon.
6 a snack bar. kiosk, shop, stall.

a
b
c
d
e
f
g
h
i
j
k
l
m
n
o
p
q
r
s
t
u
v
w
x
y
z

bar *verb*
1 *He was barred from entering the meeting.* ban, exclude, forbid, keep out, outlaw, prevent, prohibit.
2 *The policeman barred our way.* block, impede, obstruct.
behind bars imprisoned, in jail, in prison.
OPPOSITE free.

barbarian *adjective*
a barbarian tribe. barbarous, primitive, savage, uncivilised, uncultivated, uncultured.
OPPOSITE civilised.

barbaric *adjective*
barbaric customs. barbarous, brutal, cruel, inhuman, rough, savage, vicious, wild.

barber *noun*
haircutter, hairdresser.

bare *adjective*
1 *bare bodies.* exposed, naked, nude, unclothed, uncovered, undressed.
OPPOSITE clad, dressed.
2 *bare trees.* denuded, leafless, stripped.
3 *the bare facts.* bald, plain, unadorned, unembellished.
OPPOSITE embellished.
4 *The house was bare.* empty, unfurnished, vacant.
5 *the bare necessities of life.* basic, meagre, mere, scant.
bare *verb*
The dog bared its teeth. expose, reveal, show.

barely *adverb*
He barely had time to eat. hardly, only just, scarcely.

bargain *noun*
1 *The two sides struck a bargain.* accord, agreement, contract, covenant, deal, pact.
2 *There were some bargains at the sales.* give-away (*informal*), good buy, snip (*informal*), special, steal (*informal*).
bargain *verb*
The customer bargained with the salesman. barter, discuss terms, haggle, negotiate.
bargain for see EXPECT.
bargain on *He can't bargain on their*

support. bank on, count on, depend on, expect, rely on.

barge *verb*
They barged into another boat. bump, collide, crash, knock, lurch, slam.
barge in *He barged in on our conversation.* burst in, butt in, interrupt, intrude.

bark *noun*
a dog's bark. bay, bow-wow, growl, woof, yap, yelp.
bark *verb*
The dog barked. bay, growl, woof, yap, yelp.

barn *noun*
outbuilding, outhouse, shed.

baron *noun*
see NOBLEMAN.

barrack *verb*
barrack for (*Australian*)
They barracked for the local team. cheer on, egg on, support.

barracks *noun*
army barracks. billet, camp, garrison, quarters.

barrage *noun*
1 *a barrage across a river.* barrier, dam, wall.
2 *a barrage of bullets. a barrage of questions.* bombardment, firing, hail, onslaught, volley.

barrel *noun*
a wine barrel. butt, cask, drum, hogshead, keg, tun; see also CONTAINER.

barren *adjective*
1 *barren land.* arid, bare, desert, infertile, lifeless, unproductive, waste.
OPPOSITE fertile.
2 *a barren couple.* childless, infertile, sterile.
OPPOSITE fertile.

barricade *noun*
The area was sealed off with barricades. barrier, blockade, fence.
barricade *verb*
The police barricaded the building. block off, fence off, obstruct, shut off.

barrier *noun*
1 *We were not allowed past the barrier.*
bar, barricade, boom, fence, gate,
obstruction, partition, rail, screen, wall.
2 *a barrier to communication.* bar, block,
hindrance, impediment, obstacle,
restriction, stumbling block.

barrister *noun*
advocate, attorney (*American*), counsel;
see also LAWYER.

barrow *noun*
cart, handcart, wheelbarrow.

barter *verb*
They bartered cigarettes for food.
exchange, swap, trade.

base *noun*
1 *The ornament has a flat base.* bottom,
foundation, pedestal, stand, support.
OPPOSITE apex.
2 *a military base.* camp, depot,
headquarters, installation, post, station.
base *verb*
1 *It was based on fact.* build, establish,
found, ground, root.
2 *The manager is based in Canberra.*
locate, post, station.
base *adjective*
base motives. bad, contemptible,
cowardly, despicable, dishonourable,
evil, ignoble, immoral, low, mean,
selfish, underhand, wicked.
OPPOSITE honourable.

basement *noun*
cellar, crypt, vault.

bash *verb*
The intruder bashed the householder.
assault, attack, batter, beat, clout, hit,
mug, punch, strike, thump.
bash *noun*
1 *a bash on the head.* blow, hit, knock,
punch, thump.
2 (*informal*) *Have a bash at it.* see TRY.

bashful *adjective*
coy, demure, diffident, reserved,
reticent, self-conscious, sheepish, shy.
OPPOSITE bold.

basic *adjective*
1 *the basic problem.* fundamental,
primary, root, underlying;

see also CENTRAL.
OPPOSITE secondary.
2 *basic mathematics.* elementary,
fundamental, rudimentary, simple.
OPPOSITE advanced.
3 *The house is very basic.* no-frills
(*informal*), plain, primitive, simple,
spartan.
4 *a basic income for survival.* essential,
minimum, necessary.

basically *adverb*
at bottom, at heart, essentially, for the
most part, fundamentally.

basin *noun*
a basin of water. bowl, container, dish,
font, sink, washbasin, washbowl.

basis *noun*
the basis of a good story. base, beginning,
foundation, starting point.

bask *verb*
The dog basked in the sun. sunbake,
sunbathe, sun yourself, warm yourself.

basket *noun*
carrier, hamper, pannier, punnet.

bass *adjective*
a bass sound. deep, low.

bat *noun*
a bat used in games. club, racquet, stick.
bat *verb*
The cricketers practised batting the ball. see
HIT.

batch *noun*
a batch of scones. bunch, collection,
group, lot, number, set.

bathe *noun*
1 *The nurse bathed the wound.* clean,
cleanse, rinse, wash.
2 *They bathed in the river.* bogey
(*Australian*), paddle, swim, take a dip.

bathers *plural noun* (*informal*)
bathing costume, bathing suit, bikini,
cossie (*Australian informal*), one-piece,
swimmers (*Australian informal*),
swimming costume, swimsuit, togs
(*Australian informal*), trunks, two-piece.

baton *noun*
cane, rod, staff, stick, truncheon, wand.

a
b
c
d
e
f
g
h
i
j
k
l
m
n
o
p
q
r
s
t
u
v
w
x
y
z

batter *verb*
He battered his wife when he was drunk. assault, bash, beat, belt (*slang*), clobber (*slang*), hit, pound, strike, thump, wallop (*slang*), whack.

battle *noun*
He died in the battle. action, campaign, clash, combat, conflict, confrontation, encounter, engagement, fighting, hostilities, offensive, strife, war, warfare; see also FIGHT.
battle *verb*
see FIGHT.

battler *noun* (*Australian*)
the little Aussie battler. fighter, struggler, toiler, worker.

battleship *noun*
see WARSHIP.

baulk *verb*
The horse baulked at the fence. hesitate, jib, prop, pull up, shy, stop.

bawl *verb*
1 The sergeant bawled his orders. bellow, cry out, roar, shout, yell.
2 The child bawled her eyes out. cry, howl, sob, wail, weep.

bay[1] *noun*
ships in the bay. bight, cove, estuary, gulf, inlet.

bay[2] *noun*
1 a parking bay. compartment, division, space.
2 The piano sits in a bay of the lounge room. alcove, niche, nook, recess.

bay[3] *verb*
The dogs bayed. bark, cry, howl, yelp.
keep at bay see WARD OFF (at WARD).

bazaar *noun*
The school bazaar raised $3000. charity sale, fair, fête, flea market (*informal*), garage sale, jumble sale, trash and treasure market.

be *verb*
1 He is still in Sydney. be alive, dwell, exist, live, remain, reside.
2 The box is on the shelf. be found, be located, be situated, sit.
3 Easter will be in March this year. fall, happen, occur, take place.
4 She won't be at school today. attend, be present.
5 He wants to be a doctor. become.

beach *noun*
coast, sands, seashore, seaside, shore.

beacon *noun*
The beacon alerted us to the danger. flare, lighthouse, signal fire, signal light, signal station.

bead *noun*
beads of perspiration. bubble, drop, droplet.
beads *plural noun*
necklace, rosary.

beady *adjective*
beady eyes. bright, shiny, small.

beaker *noun*
cup, glass, tumbler.

beam *noun*
1 roof beams. board, girder, joist, plank, rafter, support, timber.
2 a beam of light. gleam, ray, shaft, streak, stream.
beam *verb*
1 beam a radio programme. beam light. broadcast, emit, radiate, send out, transmit.
2 She beamed with pleasure. grin, smile.

bear *verb*
1 The tree-house cannot bear a heavy weight. carry, hold up, support, take.
2 They came bearing gifts. bring, carry, convey, deliver, transport.
3 He bore the scars. have, possess, show, wear.
4 He can't bear the noise. abide, cope with, endure, put up with, stand, suffer, tolerate.
5 She bore a set of twins. bring forth, give birth to, have, produce.

bearable *adjective*
acceptable, endurable, sustainable, tolerable.
OPPOSITE intolerable.

beard *noun*
facial hair, goatee, whiskers, ziff (*Australian slang*).

bearing *noun*
1 *soldierly bearing.* air, behaviour, carriage, demeanour, deportment, manner, posture, stance.
2 *It has no bearing on the matter.* connection, relation, relationship, relevance.

bearings *plural noun*
find your bearings. location, position, whereabouts.

beast *noun*
1 *A country vet looks after big beasts.* animal, brute, creature, quadruped.
2 *The person who did this was a beast.* brute, fiend, monster, savage.

beastly *adjective*
1 *his beastly instinct.* animal, bestial.
2 (*informal*) *That was a beastly thing to do.* abominable, awful, disgusting, hateful, horrible, mean, nasty, rotten, unpleasant.

beat *verb*
1 *He beat the boy until he cried.* bash, baste, batter, belt (*slang*), cane, clobber (*slang*), clout (*informal*), club, flog, hit, knock, lash, lay into (*informal*), pound, quilt (*Australian slang*), slap, smack, smite, spank, stoush (*Australian slang*), strike, thrash, thump, thwack, trounce, wallop (*slang*), whack, whip.
2 *The sun beat down.* burn, shine.
3 *Beat the eggs.* agitate, mix, stir, whip, whisk.
4 *Her heart beat unevenly.* flutter, palpitate, pound, throb, thump.
5 *He beat all his opponents.* clobber (*slang*), conquer, defeat, euchre, get the better of, lick (*informal*), outdo, outstrip, outwit, overcome, overwhelm, pulverise, rout, slaughter, stonker (*Australian slang*), surpass, thrash, triumph over, trounce, vanquish; see also WIN.
6 *It beats me.* baffle, bamboozle (*informal*), bewilder, perplex, puzzle, stump.

beat *noun*
1 *the beat in music.* accent, pulse, rhythm, stress.
2 *a police officer's beat.* circuit, course, path, round, route.

beat up *He beat up the driver and robbed him.* assault, attack, bash up, batter, mug, thrash.

beautiful *adjective*
1 *She was beautiful to look at.* appealing, attractive, bonny (*Scottish*), captivating, charming, delightful, exquisite, fair (*old use*), glorious, good-looking, gorgeous, handsome, irresistible, lovely, pleasing, pretty, radiant, stunning.
OPPOSITE ugly.
2 *The student does beautiful work.* brilliant, excellent, fine, good; see also EXCELLENT.
3 *beautiful landscapes.* picturesque, pretty, scenic.

beautify *verb*
They beautified the house before selling it. adorn, decorate, enhance, improve, prettify, smarten up, tizzy up (*Australian*).

beauty *noun*
1 *a thing of beauty. a woman's beauty.* attractiveness, elegance, glamour, good looks, handsomeness, loveliness, magnificence, prettiness, radiance, splendour.
OPPOSITE ugliness.
2 *One of the beauties of this method is that it is simple.* advantage, attraction, benefit, blessing, good point.
OPPOSITE disadvantage.

because *conjunction*
He was sad because his cat had died. as, for, since.
because of *She was absent because of illness.* as a result of, by reason of, on account of, owing to, thanks to.

beckon *verb*
He beckoned to the child to come to him. gesture, motion, signal.

become *verb*
1 *She became a doctor.* change into, develop into, grow into, turn into.
2 *Yellow becomes her.* befit, be right for, flatter, look good on, suit.
become of *What became of Henry?* befall (*formal*), happen to.

becoming *adjective*
see ATTRACTIVE, SUITABLE.

a
b
c
d
e
f
g
h
i
j
k
l
m
n
o
p
q
r
s
t
u
v
w
x
y
z

bed *noun*
1 [*kinds of bed*] berth, bunk, camp bed, cot, cradle, crib, divan, folding bed, four-poster, hammock, sofa bed, stretcher, trundle bed, waterbed.
2 *The curry was served on a bed of rice.* base, bottom, foundation.
3 *a dry river bed.* bottom, channel, course.
4 *a garden bed.* border, patch, plot, strip.

bedclothes *plural noun*
bedding, bed linen, covers, linen; [*various bedclothes*] bedspread, blanket, bolster, continental quilt, counterpane, coverlet, Doona (*trade mark*), duvet, eiderdown, pillow, pillowcase, pillowslip, quilt, sheet.

bedlam *noun*
With so many performers it was bedlam backstage. chaos, confusion, madhouse (*informal*), mayhem, pandemonium, rumpus, uproar.

bedraggled *adjective*
He came in bedraggled after his walk in the rain. dishevelled, messy, ruffled, scruffy, unkempt, untidy, wet.
OPPOSITE well-groomed.

bedroom *noun*
chamber (*old use*), dormitory.

bee *noun*
a hive of bees. bumble-bee, drone, honey bee, queen, worker.

bee-keeper *noun*
apiarist.

beer *noun*
ale, bitter, lager, stout.

before *adverb*
They had been there before. beforehand, earlier, formerly, in the past, previously.
before *preposition*
Thunder comes before lightning. ahead of, earlier than, in front of, prior to.
OPPOSITE after.

beforehand *adverb*
The meal was prepared beforehand. earlier, in advance, in anticipation, in readiness.

beg *verb*
1 *He's always begging for money.* cadge, scrounge, sponge.
2 *She begged them to stay.* ask, beseech, entreat, implore, plead, request.

beggar *noun*
1 *She gave money to the beggar in the street.* cadger, down-and-out, mendicant, scrounger, sponger, tramp.
2 (*informal*) *You cheeky beggar!* fellow, person, rascal, wretch (*informal*).

begin *verb*
1 *The game begins at twelve o'clock.* commence, get going, get under way, kick off (*informal*), open, start.
OPPOSITE end, finish.
2 *He began a pizza delivery service.* commence, create, embark on, establish, found, initiate, introduce, launch, open, set up, start.
3 *The problems begin when people cannot agree.* appear, arise, commence, crop up, emerge, originate, spring up, start.

beginner *noun*
apprentice, learner, new chum (*Australian informal*), novice, recruit, starter, trainee.
OPPOSITE old hand.

beginning *noun*
1 *the beginning of the race.* commencement, opening, outset, start.
2 *the beginning of a new movement.* birth, creation, dawn, founding, genesis, inception, introduction, onset, origin, rise, root, source, starting point.
3 *the beginning of a novel.* introduction, opening, preamble, preface, prelude, prologue.
OPPOSITE end.

begrudge *verb*
She begrudges him his promotion. envy, grudge, mind, object to, resent.

behalf *noun*
on behalf of as a representative of, for, representing.

behave *verb*
1 *She can predict how you will behave.* act, conduct yourself, react.
2 *The car behaved well in the snow.* function, operate, perform, run, work.

3 *We hope you all behave yourselves.* be polite, be well-mannered, mind your manners.
OPPOSITE misbehave.

behaviour *noun*
actions, conduct, demeanour, deportment, manners.

behead *verb*
decapitate, guillotine; see also EXECUTE.

behind *adverb*
1 *They sat behind.* at the back, at the rear, in the back, in the rear.
2 *He is behind with his payment.* in arrears, late, overdue.

behind *preposition*
1 *He ran behind the main group.* after, at the back of, at the rear of, following.
2 *Our car is parked behind that one.* beyond, on the far side of, on the other side of.
3 *Some countries are behind others in development.* less advanced than, trailing.

behind *noun*
He fell on his behind. see BOTTOM.
behind someone's back deceitfully, in secret, secretly, slyly, sneakily.
behind the scenes backstage, in the background, in the wings, unobtrusively.
behind the times antiquated, obsolete, old-fashioned, out of date.

beige *adjective*
a beige colour. biscuit, buff, coffee, fawn, neutral.

being *noun*
1 *come into being.* existence, life.
2 *living beings.* animal, creature, entity, individual, living thing, mortal, person.

belch *verb*
1 *He belched after drinking the lemonade.* bring up wind, burp (*informal*).
2 *The funnel belched black smoke.* discharge, emit, give off, send out, spew.

belief *noun*
1 *Her belief in God will always remain firm.* confidence, faith, reliance, trust.
OPPOSITE disbelief.

2 *It was her belief that the man was innocent.* conviction, judgement, opinion, thought, view.
3 *people of many different beliefs.* conviction, creed, doctrine, faith, ideology, persuasion, philosophy, religion.

believable *adjective*
acceptable, convincing, credible, plausible.
OPPOSITE incredible, unlikely.

believe *verb*
1 *I would not believe all that he says.* accept, credit, rely on, trust.
OPPOSITE disbelieve, mistrust.
2 *I believe that you can do it.* be certain, be convinced, be sure, have faith.
OPPOSITE doubt.
3 *I believe it's going to rain.* guess (*informal*), reckon, suppose, think.

believer *noun*
religious believers. convert, disciple, follower, supporter.
OPPOSITE unbeliever.

bell *noun*
an alarm bell. the church bells. alarm, carillon, chime, peal, ring, signal.

bellow *verb*
The leader bellowed his instructions. bawl, roar, shout, yell.

belly *noun*
abdomen, guts (*informal*), paunch, stomach, tummy (*informal*).

belong *verb*
The clothes belong in the drawers. go, have a place.
belong to
1 *The house belongs to me.* be owned by, be the property of.
2 *We belong to the club.* be a member of, be associated with.

belongings *plural noun*
effects, gear (*informal*), goods, possessions, property, stuff (*informal*), things (*informal*).

beloved *adjective*
a beloved child. adored, cherished, darling, dear, loved, precious, treasured.

a b c d e f g h i j k l m n o p q r s t u v w x y z

beloved *noun*
a letter to your beloved. boyfriend, darling, fiancé, fiancée, girlfriend, love, lover, sweetheart.

below *adverb*
1 *go below.* beneath, downstairs, downstream, underneath.
2 *see chapter 2 below.* further on.
OPPOSITE above.
below *preposition*
1 *located below the bridge.* beneath, downstream from, under, underneath.
2 *temperatures below zero.* less than, lower than.
OPPOSITE above.

belt *noun*
1 *a leather belt.* band, girdle, sash, strap.
2 *They live in the wheat belt.* area, district, region, strip, zone.
belt *verb*
He belted the child. beat, flog, hit, lash, strap, thrash, whip; see also HIT.

bench *noun*
1 *The children sat on a bench.* form, pew, seat.
2 *She chopped the meat on the kitchen bench.* counter, table, work surface, worktop.
the bench judges, magistrates.

bend *verb*
1 *The force bent the metal.* angle, arch, bow, buckle, contort, curl, curve, distort, flex, kink, loop, twist, warp.
OPPOSITE straighten.
2 *The plant bent towards the light.* incline, lean.
3 *The road bends sharply.* curve, turn, twist, wind.
4 *She bent down to tie her laces.* bow, crouch, duck, kneel, stoop.
bend *noun*
a bend in the road. angle, corner, curve, kink, loop, turn, twist.

beneath *preposition*
1 *beneath the surface.* below, under, underneath.
OPPOSITE above.
2 *He considered the work beneath him.* unfit for, unworthy of.

benefactor *noun*
The costs were paid by an anonymous benefactor. donor, patron, philanthropist, sponsor, supporter.

beneficial *adjective*
advantageous, constructive, favourable, good, helpful, positive, profitable, rewarding, useful, valuable.
OPPOSITE harmful.

benefit *noun*
1 *It was a benefit to know some French.* advantage, asset, blessing, boon, help, profit, use.
OPPOSITE handicap.
2 *He was paid a government benefit.* allowance, assistance, dole (*informal*), handout (*informal*), income support, payment.
benefit *verb*
1 *The discovery will benefit mankind.* aid, assist, help, serve.
2 *Who benefited from the sale?* gain, profit.

benign *adjective*
a benign tumour. harmless.
OPPOSITE malignant.

bent *noun*
She has a bent for photography. aptitude, flair, gift, leaning, liking, skill, talent.
bent *adjective*
a bent back. a bent ruler. arched, bowed, contorted, crooked, curved, distorted, hunched, twisted, warped.
bent on He was bent on winning. determined on, intent on, set on.

bequeath *verb*
She bequeathed her jewellery to her daughter. hand down, leave, pass on, will.

bequest *noun*
endowment, gift, inheritance, legacy, settlement.

beret *noun*
see CAP.

berserk *adjective*
beside yourself, crazy, demented, deranged, frantic, frenzied, insane, mad, wild.
OPPOSITE calm.

berth *noun*
1 *a six-berth cabin.* bed, bunk.
2 *a berth for a ship.* anchorage, dock, landing stage, moorings, pier, quay, wharf.
berth *verb*
The ship berthed. anchor, dock, land, moor, tie up.

beside *preposition*
The car drew up beside ours. alongside, close to, near to, next to.
beside the point immaterial, irrelevant, unconnected.
OPPOSITE to the point.

besides *preposition*
There were five applicants besides her. apart from, aside from, as well as, excluding, in addition to, not counting.
besides *adverb*
We don't want to go; and besides, we weren't invited. also, anyway, furthermore, in addition, in any case, moreover, too.

besiege *verb*
1 *The enemy besieged the town.* blockade, encircle, encompass, lay siege to, surround.
2 *He was besieged with requests for autographs.* assail, badger, beset, harass, hound, pester.

best *adjective*
best practice. the best doctor in the field. finest, first-rate, foremost, greatest, leading, superlative, supreme, top, top-notch (*informal*), unequalled, unrivalled, unsurpassed.
OPPOSITE worst.

bet *noun*
He had a bet on a horse. flutter (*informal*), gamble, punt, risk, stake, wager.
bet *verb*
1 *She bet $2 on the winning horse.* gamble, punt, risk, stake, wager.
2 (*informal*) *I bet he'll be late.* be certain, be convinced, be sure, predict.

betray *verb*
1 *betray a friend.* be disloyal to, dob in (*Australian informal*), double-cross, grass (on) (*slang*), inform on, rat on (*informal*), tell on (*informal*).

2 *betray a secret.* blab, disclose, expose, give away, let slip, reveal, tell.
OPPOSITE keep.

better[1] *adjective*
1 *better quality.* finer, greater, superior.
OPPOSITE worse.
2 *She feels better now.* cured, fitter, healed, healthier, improved, on the mend (*informal*), recovered, stronger, well.
better *verb*
He bettered the world record by two seconds. beat, do better than, exceed, improve on, surpass, top.
get better *The patient is getting better.* convalesce, improve, rally, recover, recuperate.
OPPOSITE deteriorate.
get the better of beat, conquer, defeat, outdo, outwit, overcome.

better[2] *noun*
gambler, punter.

beverage *noun*
drink, liquid, refreshment.

beware *verb*
Buyer beware! Beware of the dog! be careful, be cautious, be on your guard, be wary, look out, mind, take heed, watch out.

bewilder *verb*
We were bewildered by his behaviour. baffle, bamboozle (*informal*), confuse, nonplus, perplex, puzzle, stump.

bewitch *verb*
1 *The sorcerer bewitched the cat.* cast a spell on, jinx (*informal*), point the bone at (*Australian*).
2 *He was bewitched by her beauty.* captivate, charm, delight, enchant, enthral, entrance, fascinate, spellbind.

beyond *preposition*
1 *They walked beyond the town.* farther than, further than, past.
2 *beyond the age of 25.* after, later than, over, past.

bias *noun*
1 *The newspaper shows a bias towards one political party.* favouritism, inclination, leaning, prejudice, slant.
OPPOSITE impartiality.

a
b
c
d
e
f
g
h
i
j
k
l
m
n
o
p
q
r
s
t
u
v
w
x
y
z

2 *The skirt is cut on the bias.* cross, diagonal.

biased *adjective*
biased reporting. distorted, one-sided, prejudiced, slanted, unbalanced, unfair. OPPOSITE impartial.

Bible *noun*
a verse from the Bible. Holy Writ, Scripture, the Scriptures, the Word of God.

bicycle *noun*
bike (*informal*), cycle, push-bike (*informal*), two-wheeler (*informal*); [*kinds of bicycle*] BMX, moped, mountain bike, penny farthing, racing bike, tandem.

bid *noun*
1 *She put in a bid of $10 for the vase.* offer, proposal, tender.
2 *He made a bid for the presidency.* attempt, effort, try.
bid *verb*
He bid $200 for the stamp collection. offer, propose, tender.

big *adjective*
1 *a big building. a big man.* ample, broad, bulky, colossal, enormous, fat, giant, gigantic, ginormous (*slang*), great, hefty, huge, hulking, humungous (*slang*), immense, jumbo (*informal*), king-sized, large, lofty, mammoth, massive, mighty, monstrous, monumental, outsize, spacious, stupendous, tall, tremendous, vast. OPPOSITE little, small.
2 *a big amount.* astronomical, colossal, considerable, enormous, excessive, exorbitant, extravagant, handsome, hefty, immeasurable, incalculable, large, sizeable, staggering, substantial, tidy (*informal*). OPPOSITE small.
3 *my big brother.* elder, grown-up, older. OPPOSITE little.
4 *It was the big match.* critical, grand, great, important, major, momentous, significant, vital. OPPOSITE minor.
5 (*informal*) *That's big of you.* big-hearted, generous, kind, unselfish. OPPOSITE mean.
big dipper roller coaster, switchback.

bike *noun*
see BICYCLE, MOTORCYCLE.

bikini *noun*
two-piece; see also BATHERS.

bill¹ *noun*
1 *She can't pay the bill.* account, invoice, statement, tab (*informal*).
2 *The billposters had stuck new bills over old ones.* advertisement, flyer, notice, placard, poster.
3 *a parliamentary bill.* draft legislation, proposed legislation.
4 *a $20 bill.* banknote, note.

bill² *noun*
a bird's bill. beak.

billet *verb*
The students were billeted with families. accommodate, house, lodge, put up.

billow *noun*
see WAVE.
billow *verb*
1 *Smoke billowed forth.* rise, roll, swell.
2 *The wind caused skirts to billow.* balloon, puff out, swell.

billycart *noun* (*Australian*)
go-cart, hill trolley.

bin *noun*
1 *a storage bin.* can, container, crate, receptacle, skip, tin.
2 *a household bin for rubbish.* dustbin, garbage bin, garbage can, garbage tin, rubbish bin, Sulo (*trade mark*), trash can, wheelie bin.

bind *verb*
1 *He bound the parcel with string.* attach, fasten, hold together, secure, strap, tie, truss.
2 *They were bound by ties of friendship.* connect, join, link, unite.
3 *Bind his wounds.* bandage, cover, dress, swathe, wrap.
4 *The blanket was bound with satin.* edge, finish, hem, trim.
5 *The contract bound him to stay in the job for three years.* compel, constrain, force, oblige, require.
bind *noun* (*informal*)
I'm in a bit of a bind. difficulty, dilemma, fix, jam (*informal*), predicament, quandary, spot (*informal*).

binder *noun*
He put all his papers into a binder. cover, file, folder.

binoculars *plural noun*
field glasses, opera glasses.

biography *noun*
life story, memoirs, reminiscences.

bird *noun*
a feathered bird. birdie (*informal*), chick, cock, fledgeling, fowl, hen, nestling; [*various birds*] albatross, bellbird, blackbird, boobook, bowerbird, brolga, budgerigar, butcherbird, canary, cassowary, cockatoo, corella, cormorant, crane, crow, cuckoo, curlew, currawong, dove, eagle, emu, falcon, finch, flamingo, flycatcher, frogmouth, galah, hawk, heron, honeyeater, ibis, jabiru, jay, kestrel, kingfisher, kiwi, kookaburra, lark, lorikeet, lyrebird, macaw, magpie, miner, mopoke, muttonbird, nightingale, ostrich, owl, parakeet, parrot, partridge, peacock, pelican, penguin, petrel, pheasant, pigeon, puffin, quail, raven, robin, rook, rosella, seagull, shearwater, shrike, sparrow, spoonbill, starling, stork, swallow, swan, swift, thrush, vulture, whipbird, willy wagtail, woodpecker, wren; see also POULTRY.
bird's-eye view aerial view, overhead view.

Biro *noun* (*trade mark*)
ballpoint, pen.

birth *noun*
1 *The hospital has a special birth unit.* childbirth, confinement, delivery, labour, nativity.
2 *the birth of a new industry.* beginning, creation, founding, genesis, origin, start.
birth control contraception, family planning.
give birth to bear, bring forth, deliver, produce, reproduce.

birthday *noun*
anniversary.

biscuit *noun*
bickie (*informal*), cookie, cracker, wafer.

bisect *verb*
cut in half, halve.

bistro *noun*
They ate a meal at the bistro. bar, brasserie, café, restaurant.

bit *noun*
1 *It doesn't make a bit of difference.* iota, jot, ounce, scrap, skerrick (*Australian informal*), speck.
2 *a bit of cheese.* chip, chunk, crumb, fragment, hunk, lump, morsel, particle, piece, portion, segment, slice.
3 *Wait a bit.* jiffy (*informal*), minute, moment, second, tick (*informal*).
bit by bit by degrees, gradually, little by little, progressively.

bitchy *adjective*
catty (*informal*), malicious, mean, nasty, spiteful, vindictive.

bite *verb*
1 *He bit into his apple.* champ, crunch, gnaw, munch, nibble; see also EAT.
2 *The insect bit him.* nip, sting, wound.
bite *noun*
1 *an insect bite.* nip, sting, wound.
2 *a bite of apple.* morsel, mouthful, piece.

biting *adjective*
1 *a biting wind.* bitter, cold, harsh, penetrating, piercing, sharp.
OPPOSITE mild.
2 *He made some biting remarks.* caustic, critical, cutting, sarcastic, sharp, stinging.

bitter *adjective*
1 *a bitter taste.* acrid, harsh, sharp.
OPPOSITE sweet.
2 *bitter memories.* distressing, painful, sad, sorrowful, unpleasant.
OPPOSITE happy.
3 *bitter comments.* hostile, rancorous, resentful, spiteful, vicious.
4 *a bitter wind.* biting, cold, freezing, harsh, piercing, sharp.

bizarre *adjective*
People stared at her bizarre costume. curious, eccentric, fantastic, grotesque, odd, outlandish, peculiar, strange, unusual, weird.
OPPOSITE ordinary.

a
b
c
d
e
f
g
h
i
j
k
l
m
n
o
p
q
r
s
t
u
v
w
x
y
z

black *adjective*
1 *a black colour.* ebony, inky, jet-black, pitch-black, raven, sable, sooty, swarthy. OPPOSITE white.
2 *The sky was black.* dark, moonless, overcast, starless.
3 *The chimney sweep's hands were black.* blackened, dirty, filthy, grimy, grubby, sooty. OPPOSITE clean.
4 *She gave me a black look.* angry, furious, hostile, menacing, sullen, threatening.
5 *a black mood.* depressed, dismal, gloomy, glum, melancholy, sad, sombre. OPPOSITE bright.
6 *He committed a black deed.* deadly, evil, hateful, malicious, sinister, wicked.
black out see FAINT.

blacken *verb*
1 *The wall was blackened by the fire.* darken, dirty, soil, stain.
2 *The newspapers blackened his character.* defame, denigrate, malign, smear, speak ill of, sully, tarnish.

blackmail *verb*
hold to ransom, threaten.
blackmail *noun*
extortion.

blackout *noun*
1 *When there is a blackout we use candles.* power cut, power failure.
2 *He suffers occasional blackouts.* faint, loss of consciousness, swoon.

blade *noun*
1 *The knife has a sharp blade.* cutting edge, edge.
2 *a blade of grass.* frond, leaf, shoot.

blame *verb*
They blamed him for the accident. accuse, charge, condemn, criticise, find guilty, hold responsible, make accountable, reproach, reprove.
blame *noun*
She took the blame for what happened. censure, criticism, fault, guilt, rap (*informal*), reprimand, reproach, responsibility.

blameless *adjective*
blameless conduct. guiltless, innocent, irreproachable, unimpeachable.

bland *adjective*
The food tastes bland. flavourless, insipid, mild, plain, tasteless, uninteresting, wishy-washy. OPPOSITE tasty.

blank *adjective*
1 *a blank sheet of paper.* clean, empty, plain, unfilled, unmarked, unused.
2 *a blank face.* deadpan, emotionless, expressionless, impassive, poker-faced.
blank *noun*
fill the blanks. gap, space.

blanket *noun*
1 *We need extra blankets on the bed.* cover, covering, rug.
2 *a thick blanket of fog.* cloak, covering, layer, mantle, sheet.

blare *verb*
The trumpets blared. blast, boom, resound, roar, sound, trumpet.

blasphemous *adjective*
His remarks were considered blasphemous. disrespectful, impious, irreligious, irreverent, profane, sacrilegious, ungodly. OPPOSITE reverent.

blasphemy *noun*
disrespect, impiety, irreverence, profanity, sacrilege. OPPOSITE reverence.

blast *noun*
1 *a blast of wind.* draught, gust, rush.
2 *hear a blast of horns.* blare, boom, honk, toot.
3 *a bomb blast.* detonation, discharge, explosion.
blast *verb*
1 *The miners blasted the rock.* blow up, detonate, explode; see also DESTROY.
2 *We were blasted for being late.* see TELL OFF (at TELL).

blast-off *noun*
the blast-off of the spacecraft. launch, lift-off, take-off.

blatant *adjective*
blatant dishonesty. flagrant, obvious, open, overt, unashamed, unconcealed. OPPOSITE concealed.

blaze *noun*
1 *The firemen extinguished the blaze.* conflagration, fire, flames, inferno.
2 *a blaze of anger.* burst, fit, outburst, rage.
blaze *verb*
Lights were blazing. burn, flame, flare, glow, shine.

blazer *noun*
jacket; see also COAT.

bleach *verb*
blanch, fade, lighten, peroxide, whiten.

bleak *adjective*
1 *bleak weather.* bitter, chilly, cold, dreary, wintry.
OPPOSITE sunny.
2 *a bleak setting.* bare, barren, desolate, dismal, windswept.
3 *The future looks bleak.* black, depressing, dismal, gloomy, grim, hopeless, unpromising.
OPPOSITE bright.

bleary *adjective*
bleary eyes. blurred, cloudy, filmy, fuzzy, misty, watery.
OPPOSITE clear.

bleed *verb*
The patient bled. haemorrhage, lose blood.

bleep *noun & verb*
beep, signal.

blemish *noun*
skin without blemishes. blotch, defect, discoloration, fault, flaw, imperfection, mark, scar, spot, stain.

blend *verb*
1 *The ingredients are blended in the machine.* combine, fuse, incorporate, integrate, mingle, mix.
OPPOSITE separate.
2 *The colours blend well.* fit, go together, harmonise.
OPPOSITE clash.
blend *noun*
a blend of apple and pear juice. combination, fusion, mix, mixture.

bless *verb*
1 *The priest blessed the house.* consecrate, dedicate, hallow, sanctify.
OPPOSITE curse.

2 *They bless God.* adore, glorify, hallow, laud (*formal*), praise.
OPPOSITE curse.

blessed *adjective*
1 *the Blessed Virgin Mary.* beatified, consecrated, hallowed, holy, revered, sacred, sanctified.
2 (*old use*) *Blessed are the pure in heart.* fortunate, happy.

blessing *noun*
1 *The project had his blessing.* approval, consent, favour, OK (*informal*), support.
OPPOSITE disapproval.
2 *The minister pronounced the blessing.* benediction, grace, prayer, thanksgiving.
3 *The rain was a blessing to farmers.* asset, boon, gift, godsend, help.
OPPOSITE misfortune.

blight *noun*
1 *Blight had affected the plants.* disease, fungus, mildew, pestilence, rust.
2 *a blight on society.* affliction, bane, curse, plague, scourge.
blight *verb*
His plans were blighted by a family tragedy. damage, dash, frustrate, mar, ruin, spoil, wreck.
OPPOSITE enhance.

blind *adjective*
1 *a blind person.* sightless, unsighted, visually impaired.
OPPOSITE sighted.
2 *blind obedience.* mindless, uncritical, unreasoning, unthinking.
blind *verb*
He blinded them with science. bamboozle (*informal*), confuse, dazzle, overawe, overwhelm; see also DECEIVE.
blind *noun*
The blinds are sold with the house. screen, shade, shutter, venetian blind.
blind alley *He drove the car into a blind alley.* cul-de-sac, dead end, no through road.

blink *verb*
The lights blinked. flash, flicker, glimmer, shimmer, sparkle, twinkle, wink.

bliss *noun*
Six weeks of holidays will be bliss. delight, ecstasy, happiness, heaven, joy,

a
b
c
d
e
f
g
h
i
j
k
l
m
n
o
p
q
r
s
t
u
v
w
x
y
z

paradise, pleasure, rapture.
OPPOSITE hell, misery.

blissful *adjective*
delightful, happy, heavenly, joyous,
wonderful.

blister *noun*
bubble, swelling.

blitz *noun*
The police had a blitz on speeding drivers.
attack, campaign, crackdown (*informal*),
offensive, onslaught.

blizzard *noun*
snowstorm; see also STORM.

bloated *adjective*
a bloated stomach. distended, enlarged,
inflated, puffed up, swollen.

blob *noun*
a blob of mayonnaise. bead, dollop, drop,
splash, splotch, spot.

block *noun*
1 *a block of wood, metal, soap, etc.* bar,
brick, cake, chunk, cube, hunk, ingot,
slab, wedge.
2 (*Australian*) *Their house is on a large
suburban block.* acreage, allotment, plot,
section (*Australian historical*).
3 *Their house is built on blocks.* pile, stilt,
support.
4 *The police set up a road block.* barrier,
blockade, obstacle, obstruction.
block *verb*
1 *Parked trucks blocked the traffic.* bar,
blockade, hamper, hinder, hold back,
impede, obstruct, stop.
2 *The leaves blocked the drain.* bung up,
choke, clog, fill up, jam, stop up.
OPPOSITE clear.

blockade *noun*
The soldiers set up a blockade. barricade,
barrier, block, siege.

blockage *noun*
barrier, block, blockade, bottleneck,
jam, obstacle, obstruction, stoppage.

bloke *noun* (*informal*)
He's a nice bloke. boy, chap (*informal*),
character, fellow (*informal*), guy
(*informal*), man.

blond, blonde *adjective*
blond hair. fair, flaxen, golden, light.
OPPOSITE dark.

blood *noun*
1 *of royal blood.* ancestry, descent,
family, line, lineage, parentage, race,
stock.
2 *my own flesh and blood.* family,
kinsfolk, kith and kin, relations,
relatives.

bloodbath *noun*
see MASSACRE.

blood-curdling *adjective*
chilling, frightening, hair-raising,
horrific, horrifying, spine-chilling,
terrifying.

bloodshed *noun*
carnage, killing, massacre, murder,
slaughter, slaying, wounding.

bloodthirsty *adjective*
bloodthirsty soldiers. brutal, ferocious,
fierce, homicidal, murderous, savage,
vicious.

bloody *adjective*
1 *bloody hands.* bleeding, bloodstained.
2 *a bloody battle.* cruel, gory, violent; see
also BLOODTHIRSTY.
OPPOSITE bloodless.

bloom *noun*
a bouquet of red blooms. blossom, bud,
flower.
bloom *verb*
Her plants are blooming. blossom, flower.

blossom *noun*
The peach tree is in blossom. bloom,
flower.
blossom *verb*
1 *The tree blossomed.* bloom, flower.
2 *Her talent has blossomed.* bloom,
develop, flourish, grow, thrive.

blot *noun*
1 *blots of ink.* blotch, mark, smudge,
splotch, spot, stain.
2 *a blot on the landscape.* blight, eyesore.
3 *a blot on his character.* blemish, defect,
fault, stain.
blot *verb*
1 *He blotted his page with his leaky pen.*
smudge, spot, stain.

2 *Blot the spill with paper towel.* absorb, dry, soak up.

blot out *He tried to blot out the bad memories.* cover, mask, obliterate, obscure, wipe out.

blotch *noun*
blemish, blot, mark, patch, spot.

blouse *noun*
shirt.

blow¹ *verb*
1 *The wind blew very fiercely.* blast, bluster, gust, roar, whistle.
2 *The breeze blew the smell of the bakery our way.* carry, convey, drive, move, send, waft.
3 *He blew his trumpet.* blare, blast, play, sound, toot.
4 *The policeman asked him to blow in the bag.* breathe out, exhale, puff.
5 *(slang) I blew it.* botch, bungle, muff, ruin, spoil, wreck.

blow out *He blew out the candle.* extinguish, put out, snuff.

blow up
1 *blow up the air mattress.* fill, inflate, pump up.
OPPOSITE deflate.
2 *(informal) blow up a photograph.* enlarge.
OPPOSITE reduce.
3 *The story was blown up by the newspapers.* exaggerate, magnify, overstate.
OPPOSITE play down.
4 *The bomb blew up.* detonate, explode, go off.
5 *The building was blown up.* blast, bomb, burst apart, destroy, shatter.

blow² *noun*
1 *knocked down by a heavy blow.* bang, bash, belt *(slang)*, clout *(informal)*, hit, king-hit *(Australian informal)*, knock, punch, rap, slap, smack, stroke, thump, thwack, wallop *(slang)*, whack.
2 *Losing his house was a terrible blow.* bombshell, calamity, disaster, misfortune, setback, shock, upset.

blubber *noun*
fat, flab *(informal)*.
blubber *verb*
cry, snivel, sob, weep.

bludge *verb (Australian informal)*
1 *Some work hard while others bludge.* idle, loaf, skive *(informal)*, slack, take it easy.
2 *He's been bludging school.* see WAG.
3 *He hasn't any money and is forced to bludge off others.* see SCROUNGE.
bludge *noun (Australian informal)*
The job was a bludge. breeze *(informal)*, child's play, cinch *(informal)*, piece of cake *(informal)*, pushover *(informal)*, snack *(Australian informal)*.

bludger *noun (Australian informal)*
He worked hard and had no time for bludgers. freeloader *(informal)*, idler, layabout, loafer, parasite, shirker, slacker, sponger.

blue *adjective*
1 *a blue colour.* aqua, aquamarine, azure, cobalt (blue), indigo, navy (blue), powder blue, Prussian blue, royal blue, sapphire, sky blue, turquoise, ultramarine.
2 *blue skies.* clear, cloudless.
3 *feeling blue.* depressed, downcast, down in the dumps *(informal)*, gloomy, low, melancholy, sad, unhappy.
blue *noun*
1 *(Australian informal) They had a blue over the handling of the money.* altercation, argument, barney *(informal)*, disagreement, quarrel, row.
2 *(Australian informal) He made a terrible blue.* see BLUNDER.
blues *plural noun*
see DEPRESSION.

blueprint *noun*
a blueprint for change. design, outline, pattern, plan, scheme.

bluff *verb*
1 *The card player bluffed his opponent.* deceive, dupe, fool, hoodwink, mislead, take in, trick.
2 *I knew he was only bluffing.* fake, pretend, sham.
bluff *noun*
We weren't sure whether what he said was just a bluff. deception, pretence, sham, trick.

blunder *verb*
She blundered into the room. lumber, lurch, stagger, stumble.

a
b
c
d
e
f
g
h
i
j
k
l
m
n
o
p
q
r
s
t
u
v
w
x
y
z

blunder *noun*
He committed a blunder. blue (*Australian informal*), booboo (*slang*), bungle, clanger (*informal*), howler (*informal*), mistake, slip-up (*informal*).

blunt *adjective*
1 *a blunt knife.* dull, unsharpened.
OPPOSITE sharp.
2 *a blunt refusal.* abrupt, candid, curt, direct, frank, open, outspoken, upfront (*informal*).
OPPOSITE subtle.
blunt *verb*
She blunted the knife. dull.
OPPOSITE sharpen, whet.

blurred *adjective*
The picture is blurred. blurry, confused, dim, distorted, foggy, fuzzy, hazy, indistinct, misty, out of focus, unclear.
OPPOSITE clear.

blush *verb*
colour, flush, glow, go red, redden.
OPPOSITE pale.

blustery *adjective*
blustery conditions. blowy, gusty, rough, squally, stormy, wild, windy.

board *noun*
1 *wooden boards.* beam, plank, sheet, slat, timber.
2 *on the company's board.* committee, council, panel.
board *verb*
1 *They boarded the ship, bus, etc.* catch, embark, get on, go on board.
OPPOSITE alight, disembark.
2 *Some country students board with city families.* live, lodge, reside.

boast *verb*
He boasted about his successes. be conceited, blow your own trumpet, brag, congratulate yourself, crow, have tickets on yourself (*Australian informal*), show off, skite (*Australian informal*), swank (*informal*), talk big (*informal*).
OPPOSITE hide your light under a bushel.

boaster *noun*
braggart, show-off, skite (*Australian informal*).

boastful *adjective*
cocky (*informal*), conceited, proud, swaggering, swanky (*informal*), vain.
OPPOSITE modest.

boat *noun*
craft, vessel; [*various boats*] barge, canoe, catamaran, cutter, dinghy, ferry, gondola, houseboat, hydrofoil, junk, kayak, ketch, launch, lifeboat, motor boat, pontoon, punt, raft, rowing boat, sailing boat, sampan, skiff, sloop, speedboat, trawler, tug, yacht; see also SHIP.

bob *verb*
1 *bob up and down.* bounce, curtsy, jerk, jig, jump, leap.
2 *bob your head.* duck, nod.
bob up appear, come up, show up, turn up.

bodily *adjective*
having a bodily form. corporal, physical.

body *noun*
1 *The artist studied the human body.* anatomy, figure, form, physique, shape.
2 *The body was taken to the morgue.* carcass, corpse, remains.
3 *The spots are on his body and not on his limbs or face.* torso, trunk.
4 *an aeroplane body.* fuselage, hull, shell.
5 *He belongs to a student body.* see GROUP.
6 *a foreign body in your eye.* object, thing.
7 *This fabric lacks body.* solidity, strength, substance.

bodyguard *noun*
escort, guard, minder, protector.

bog *noun*
fen, marsh, mire, mudflat, quagmire, quicksand, swamp, wetlands.
bog *verb*
The car was bogged in the mud. immobilise, stick, trap.

boggy *adjective*
boggy ground. marshy, miry, muddy, spongy, swampy, wet.

bogyman *noun*
She is frightened of the bogyman. bogy, devil, evil spirit, goblin.

boil[1] *verb*
The casserole is boiling. Boil the kettle.
bubble, cook, heat, seethe, simmer, stew.

boil[2] *noun*
abscess, carbuncle, gumboil, inflammation.

boiling *adjective*
see HOT.

boisterous *adjective*
boisterous children. active, energetic, exuberant, high-spirited, lively, noisy, rough, rowdy, unruly, vivacious, wild.
OPPOSITE quiet.

bold *adjective*
1 *a bold leader.* brave, confident, courageous, daring, fearless, game, heroic, intrepid, unafraid.
OPPOSITE timid.
2 *bold behaviour.* assertive, audacious, brazen, cheeky, forward, immodest, impudent, presumptuous, shameless.
OPPOSITE coy, shy.
3 *bold colours.* bright, conspicuous, showy, striking, strong, vibrant, vivid.
OPPOSITE pale.

bolster *noun*
cushion, pillow, support.
bolster *verb*
bolster confidence. bolster the economy.
boost, encourage, prop up, reinforce, shore up, strengthen, support.

bolt *noun*
1 *the bolt on a door.* bar, catch, latch, lock.
2 *a bolt of lightning.* flash, shaft.
bolt *verb*
1 *Have you bolted the door?* fasten, latch, lock, secure.
2 *The animal bolted.* dart off, dash off, escape, run away, run off, take off, tear off.
3 *She bolts her food.* gobble, gulp, guzzle, shovel in, wolf.
a bolt from the blue bombshell, shock, surprise, thunderbolt.
bolt upright erect, straight.

bomb *noun*
1 *The building was destroyed by a bomb.* device (*euphemism*), explosive, grenade, incendiary, missile.
2 (*Australian informal*) *They drive an old bomb.* heap (*informal*), jalopy (*informal*), rust bucket (*informal*), wreck.
bomb *verb*
The city was bombed at night. attack, blitz, blow up, bombard, shell.

bombard *verb*
1 *The soldiers bombarded the building.* attack, besiege, blitz, bomb, fire at, pelt, shell.
2 *They bombarded her with questions.* assail, attack, besiege, hound.

bond *noun*
1 *a bond of friendship.* attachment, connection, link, relationship, tie.
2 *The trainee enters into a bond with the employer.* agreement, bargain, contract, deal.
3 *a bond on a flat.* bond money, deposit, guarantee, security.
bond *verb*
The glue bonds the two surfaces together. adhere, bind, cement, connect, fasten, fuse, join, link, stick, tie.
bonds *plural noun*
The prisoner burst his bonds. chains, fetters, handcuffs, manacles, ropes, shackles.

bondage *noun*
captivity, enslavement, slavery.
OPPOSITE freedom.

bone *verb*
The butcher boned the meat. fillet.

bonfire *noun*
see FIRE.

bonnet *noun*
1 *She knitted the baby a bonnet.* cap, hat.
2 *the car bonnet.* hood (*American*).

bonus *noun*
They received a bonus. addition, extra, reward, supplement, tip.
OPPOSITE penalty.

bony *adjective*
After dieting she had a bony look. angular, gaunt, lean, scrawny, skinny, thin.
OPPOSITE plump.

boo *verb*
The audience booed. heckle, hoot, jeer, scoff.
OPPOSITE cheer.

a
b
c
d
e
f
g
h
i
j
k
l
m
n
o
p
q
r
s
t
u
v
w
x
y
z

book *noun*
1 *We read his latest book.* publication, release, volume, work; [*kinds of book*] almanac, annual, anthology, atlas, dictionary, directory, encyclopedia, guidebook, handbook, manual, novel, omnibus, textbook, thesaurus, yearbook.
2 *She records everything in her book.* account book, album, daybook, diary, exercise book, journal, ledger, logbook, memo book, notebook, passbook, pocketbook, scrapbook, sketchbook.
3 *The Old Testament is made up of thirty-nine books.* division, part, section.
book *verb*
1 *The police booked him for speeding.* charge, fine.
2 *We booked seats for the concert.* order, reserve.

booklet *noun*
a booklet explaining immunisation. brochure, handbook, handout, leaflet, pamphlet.

boom *verb*
1 *Her voice boomed in the empty cave.* echo, resonate, resound, reverberate.
2 *Business is booming.* expand, flourish, grow, prosper, thrive.
OPPOSITE slacken.
boom *noun*
1 *the boom of the drums.* bang, blast, reverberation, roar, rumble, thunder.
2 *a boom in the film industry.* expansion, growth, improvement, upturn.
OPPOSITE decline.

boomerang *verb*
The plan boomeranged on the instigators. backfire, rebound, recoil.

boost *verb*
1 *He boosted the boy up to see over the wall.* hoist, lift, push, raise.
2 *The visit boosted morale.* assist, bolster, encourage, heighten, improve, increase, lift, raise, strengthen.
OPPOSITE lower.
boost *noun*
a financial boost from the government. assistance, encouragement, help, impetus, shot in the arm, stimulus.

booster *noun*
A tetanus booster is required once every ten years. immunisation, injection, inoculation, jab (*informal*), shot, vaccination.

boot *noun*
1 *He wore boots in the rain.* gumboot, wellington; see also SHOE.
2 *the boot of the car.* trunk (*American*).
boot *verb*
He booted the ball. kick, punt.
boot out (*slang*)
He was booted out of his job. chuck out (*informal*), dismiss, eject, expel, kick out (*informal*), remove, sack (*informal*), throw out.

booth *noun*
1 *a booth selling magazines.* kiosk, stall, stand.
2 *a telephone booth.* box, compartment, cubicle, enclosure.

booty *noun*
The thieves shared the booty. gains, loot, pickings, plunder, spoils, swag (*informal*), takings.

booze *noun* (*informal*)
There was no booze at the party. alcohol, drink, grog (*Australian*), liquor.

border *noun*
1 *They crossed the border of the country.* boundary, frontier, limit.
2 *the border of a lake.* brink, circumference, edge, margin, perimeter, rim, verge.
3 *a decorative border.* binding, edge, edging, frame, frieze, fringe, hem, margin, strip.

borderline *adjective*
a borderline case. doubtful, line-ball (*Australian*), touch-and-go, uncertain.

bore[1] *verb*
He bored through the surface. drill, gouge, penetrate, perforate, pierce.
bore *noun*
1 *the bore of a gun.* calibre, diameter, gauge.
2 (*Australian*) *Their water comes from a bore.* artesian bore, artesian well.

bore[2] *verb*
He bores me stiff. send to sleep, tire, weary.
OPPOSITE interest.

bored *adjective*
fed up, jack (*Australian slang*), jaded, tired.

boredom *noun*
apathy, dreariness, dullness, monotony, tedium.

boring *adjective*
a boring job. dreary, dull, monotonous, repetitious, routine, tedious, tiresome, unexciting, uninteresting.
OPPOSITE exciting.

borrow *verb*
1 He had to borrow the tools. be lent, have the loan of.
OPPOSITE lend.
2 He borrowed their methods. adopt, copy, take over, use.

bosom *noun*
breasts, bust, chest.

boss *noun* (*informal*)
The boss gave him the time off.
administrator, chief, director, employer, foreman, governor (*slang*), head, leader, manager, master, overseer, proprietor, superintendent, supervisor.
boss *verb* (*informal*)
She bosses her friends around. give orders to, order about, push around, tell what to do.

bossy *adjective*
autocratic, dictatorial, domineering, imperious, masterful, officious, overbearing, tyrannical.

botch *verb*
They botched the job. bungle, make a hash of (*informal*), make a mess of, mess up, muck up (*informal*), muff (*informal*), spoil, wreck.

bother *verb*
1 Everyone must stop bothering her. annoy, disturb, harass, hassle (*informal*), irritate, pester, plague, trouble, upset, worry.

2 She didn't even bother to phone. care, concern yourself, take the time, take the trouble, trouble yourself.
3 He didn't seem bothered that they hadn't arrived. concern, distress, disturb, perturb, put out (*informal*), trouble, upset, worry.
bother *noun*
1 The bus strike was a bit of a bother. inconvenience, irritation, nuisance, pest, problem.
2 He found the house without any bother. difficulty, fuss, hassle (*informal*), to-do, trouble, worry.

bottle *noun*
container; [*kinds of bottle*] carafe, decanter, flagon, flask, magnum, phial, vial.
bottle up She bottled up her grief. conceal, hide, keep back, suppress.
OPPOSITE give vent to.

bottleneck *noun*
blockage, hold-up, jam, obstruction.

bottom *noun*
1 the bottom of a statue. base, foot, foundation, pedestal, support.
OPPOSITE top.
2 the bottom of the ocean. bed, depths, floor.
3 the bottom of a vase. underneath, underside.
4 He fell and bruised his bottom. backside (*informal*), behind (*informal*), bum (*slang*), buttocks, posterior, rear (*informal*), rump, seat.
bottom *adjective*
the bottom level. base, ground, lowest.
OPPOSITE top.

bottomless *adjective*
deep, inexhaustible, infinite.

bough *noun*
the tree's boughs. branch, limb.

boulder *noun*
gibber (*Australian*), rock, stone.

bounce *verb*
1 The ball bounced quite unexpectedly. rebound, recoil, ricochet.
2 She bounced out of bed. bob, bound, hop, jump, leap, spring.

a
b
c
d
e
f
g
h
i
j
k
l
m
n
o
p
q
r
s
t
u
v
w
x
y
z

bouncing *adjective*
a bouncing baby. bonny, healthy, thriving.

bouncy *adjective*
a bouncy surface. elastic, resilient, springy.

bound¹ *verb*
The school is bounded by four streets. border, enclose, limit, surround.
bounds *plural noun*
His generosity knew no bounds. boundaries, limitations, limits.
out of bounds off limits.

bound² *verb*
The dog bounded over the gate. bob, bounce, gallop, hurdle, jump, leap, lope, spring, vault.
bound *noun*
bob, bounce, gallop, hurdle, jump, leap, lope, spring, vault.

bound³ *adjective*
bound for bound for Australia. destined for, en route for, heading for, off to, travelling to.

bound⁴ *adjective*
house-bound. confined, restricted, tied.
bound to He is bound to win. certain to, destined to, sure to.

boundary *noun*
border, bounds, circumference, edge, frontier, limit, margin, perimeter, threshold.

boundless *adjective*
boundless energy. endless, infinite, limitless, unbounded, unlimited, vast.
OPPOSITE finite, limited.

bountiful *adjective*
a bountiful supply of fresh vegetables. abundant, ample, copious, generous, lavish, liberal, plentiful, prolific.
OPPOSITE meagre.

bouquet *noun*
The bride carried a bouquet of flowers. bunch, corsage, posy, spray.

bout *noun*
1 bouts of work. period, session, spell, stint, stretch, turn.

2 a bout of hayfever. attack, fit, outbreak.
3 a boxing bout. competition, contest, fight, match, round.

boutique *noun*
see SHOP.

bow¹ *verb*
He bowed as a sign of respect. bend, bob, curtsy, genuflect, kneel, nod, stoop.

bow² *noun*
a ship's bow. fore, front, prow.
OPPOSITE stern.

bowels *plural noun*
an animal's bowels. entrails, guts, innards (informal), insides (informal), intestines.

bowl¹ *noun*
a bowl of soup. basin, dish, tureen.

bowl² *verb*
bowl a ball. deliver, fling, hurl, lob, pitch, roll, throw, toss.
bowl over I was bowled over by the news. flabbergast, floor, overwhelm, stun, surprise.

box¹ *noun*
1 carton, case, chest, container, crate, pack, package, receptacle, trunk.
2 a witness box. compartment, stall, stand.
3 a sentry-box. a telephone box. booth, cabin, cubicle, hut, shelter.
box in She feels boxed in living in an apartment block in the inner city. box up, confine, coop up, enclose, hem in, shut in, surround.

box² *verb*
1 He boxes as a sport. fight, spar.
2 He threatened to box the boy's ears. clout (informal), cuff, punch, slap, thump; see also HIT.

boxer *noun*
fighter, pugilist, sparring partner.

boxing *noun*
fighting, fisticuffs, pugilism.

boy *noun*
child, fellow, guy (informal), kid (informal), lad, male, schoolboy, youngster, youth.

boycott *verb*
People boycotted the shop in protest. avoid, ban, blacklist, shun, stay away from.
boycott *noun*
a boycott on the company's products. ban, blacklist, embargo, prohibition.

boyfriend *noun*
date (*informal*), escort, fellow, male companion, suitor.

boyish *adjective*
1 *a man with a boyish face.* childish, immature, juvenile, young, youthful.
OPPOSITE mature.
2 *a girl with a boyish appearance.* masculine.
OPPOSITE feminine, girlish.

brace *noun*
1 *a leg brace.* calliper, support.
2 *a brace of partridge.* couple, pair.
brace *verb*
The wobbly chair needs to be braced. reinforce, strengthen, support, tighten.
braces *plural noun*
trousers kept up with braces. straps, suspenders (*American*).
brace yourself He braced himself for the bad news. prepare yourself, steady yourself, steel yourself.

bracelet *noun*
armlet, bangle, wristlet.

bracket *noun*
1 *a bracket on the wall.* shelf, support.
2 *He read the words in the brackets.* brace, parenthesis.
3 *an income bracket.* category, class, division, group, range, set.

brag *verb*
He likes to brag about his successes. blow your own trumpet (*informal*), boast, crow, show off, skite (*Australian informal*), swank (*informal*).

braid *noun*
1 *The dress is trimmed with braid.* ribbon, trimming.
2 *hair in braids.* plait.

brain *noun*
1 *He wanted a job which used his brain.* intellect, intelligence, mind, reason, sense, wit.

2 *He was labelled a brain.* egghead (*informal*), genius, intellectual, whiz-kid (*informal*).

brainwash *verb*
The cult members had been brainwashed. condition, indoctrinate.

brainwave *noun*
brainstorm, idea, inspiration, thought; see also IDEA.

brainy *adjective*
bright, brilliant, clever, gifted, intellectual, intelligent, smart, studious.
OPPOSITE stupid.

brake *verb*
You must brake at a stop sign. halt, pull up, slow down, stop.

branch *noun*
1 *a tree branch.* bough, limb, offshoot.
2 *a branch of an organisation.* arm, department, division, office, part, section, subdivision.
branch *verb*
The river branches here. divide, fork, split, subdivide.
branch out The business branched out into new areas. diversify, expand, extend, open out, spread.

brand *noun*
a brand of car. make, marque, trade mark.
brand *verb*
He brands his cattle. identify, label, mark, stamp.

brandish *verb*
The robber was brandishing a knife. flourish, swing, wave.

brave *adjective*
a brave soldier. bold, courageous, daring, fearless, gallant, game, heroic, intrepid, lion-hearted, plucky, undaunted, valiant.
OPPOSITE cowardly.
brave *verb*
He braved the cold. defy, endure, face, weather, withstand.

bravery *noun*
boldness, courage, daring, fearlessness, gallantry, grit (*informal*), guts (*informal*),

a
b
c
d
e
f
g
h
i
j
k
l
m
n
o
p
q
r
s
t
u
v
w
x
y
z

heroism, nerve, pluck, prowess, valour.
OPPOSITE cowardice.

brawl *noun*
The argument turned into a brawl. clash, confrontation, fight, fisticuffs, free-for-all, punch-up (*informal*), quarrel, row, scrap (*informal*), scuffle, set-to (*informal*), skirmish, stoush (*Australian slang*), struggle, tussle.

brawny *adjective*
a brawny rower. beefy, burly, hefty, muscular, nuggety (*Australian*), stocky, strong, sturdy, thickset.
OPPOSITE scrawny.

bray *noun*
a donkey's bray. hee-haw, neigh, whinny.

brazen *adjective*
a brazen hussy. audacious, bold, cheeky, forward, impertinent, impudent, insolent, shameless.
OPPOSITE modest.

breach *noun*
1 *a breach of the rules.* breaking, infringement, transgression, violation.
2 *a breach in the fence.* break, crack, gap, hole, opening, space, split.
breach *verb*
He breached the agreement. break, infringe, transgress, violate.

breadth *noun*
broadness, extent, magnitude, range, span, spread, thickness, width.
CONTRASTS WITH depth, length.

break *verb*
1 *break into pieces.* burst, bust (*informal*), collapse, come apart, crack, crash, crumble, demolish, disintegrate, fall apart, fracture, fragment, shatter, smash, snap, splinter, split; see also DIVIDE.
OPPOSITE join.
2 *break a machine.* bust (*informal*), damage, destroy, ruin, wreck.
OPPOSITE mend.
3 *break a promise.* dishonour, go back on, renege on.
OPPOSITE honour, keep.
4 *break a law.* breach, disobey, infringe, transgress, violate.
OPPOSITE abide by, obey.

5 *break for coffee.* adjourn, discontinue, interrupt, pause, stop.
6 *break a record.* beat, exceed, outdo, outstrip, surpass.
break *noun*
1 *a break in a hose, rock, etc.* breach, breakage, burst, chink, crack, fracture, gash, leak, rift, rupture, slit, smash, split, tear.
2 *a break in the line of cars.* gap, hole, interruption, opening, space.
3 *a break from work.* breather, interlude, intermission, interruption, interval, lull, pause, playtime, recess, respite, rest, spell (*Australian*); see also HOLIDAY.
4 *Give him a break.* chance, opening, opportunity.
break down
1 *Break down the barriers of prejudice.* destroy, do away with, eliminate, get rid of.
OPPOSITE build up.
2 *The engine broke down.* conk out (*informal*), fail, go bung (*Australian informal*), go on the blink (*informal*), malfunction, pack up (*informal*), seize up, stop working.
3 *When he heard the news he broke down.* collapse, crack up (*informal*), cry, go to pieces (*informal*), weep.
4 *Vegetable matter breaks down.* decay, decompose, rot.
break in
1 *break in on a private discussion.* barge in, burst in, butt in, interrupt, intrude.
2 *break in a horse.* discipline, tame, train.
break of day see DAWN.
break off
1 *break off a piece.* detach, pull off, sever, snap off.
2 *break off an engagement.* cease, discontinue, end, finish, stop, terminate.
break out
1 *Fighting broke out.* begin, commence, erupt, start.
2 *break out of jail.* see ESCAPE.
break up
1 *The couple broke up.* divorce, part, separate, split up.
OPPOSITE reunite.
2 *School breaks up in December.* adjourn, discontinue, end, finish, stop.
OPPOSITE resume.

breakable *adjective*
brittle, delicate, flimsy, fragile, weak.
OPPOSITE indestructible, unbreakable.

breakdown *noun*
1 *mechanical breakdown.* collapse, crash
(*Computing*), failure, hitch, malfunction,
stoppage.
2 *a breakdown of the figures.* analysis,
run-down.

break-in *noun*
The police investigated the break-in.
burglary, forced entry, robbery.

breakneck *adjective*
at breakneck speed. dangerous, fast,
headlong, reckless.

breakthrough *noun*
a breakthrough in the treatment of cancer.
advance, development, discovery,
progress.

break-up *noun*
1 *a marriage break-up.* breakdown,
collapse, failure, separation, split-up.
2 *school break-up.* end of term.

breakwater *noun*
The beach is protected by a breakwater.
jetty, mole, pier.

breast *noun*
bosom, bust, chest.

breath *noun*
a deep breath. exhalation, gasp,
inhalation, pant, puff, respiration.

breathe *verb*
1 *The walkers breathed deeply.* exhale,
inhale, pant, puff, respire.
2 *You mustn't breathe a word of it.* let out,
utter, whisper.

breathless *adjective*
Walking uphill makes her breathless.
gasping, out of breath, panting, puffed,
short of breath, winded.

breathtaking *adjective*
a breathtaking performance. amazing,
astounding, awe-inspiring, exciting,
overwhelming, spectacular,
stupendous.

breed *verb*
1 *These animals breed well.* bear young,
multiply, produce young, reproduce.

2 *He breeds dogs.* raise, rear.
3 *Lies only breed more lies.* create,
generate, give rise to, lead to, result in,
yield.

breed *noun*
a breed of dog. kind, sort, type, variety.

breeze *noun*
1 *a cool breeze.* draught, wind.
2 (*informal*) *She found the task a breeze.*
bludge (*Australian informal*), cinch
(*informal*), piece of cake (*informal*),
pushover (*informal*), snack (*Australian
informal*), walkover.

breeze *verb* (*informal*)
They breezed in late again. drift, flit, sail,
waltz (*informal*), wander.

breezy *adjective*
1 *a breezy place.* draughty, exposed,
windswept.
OPPOSITE sheltered.
2 *a breezy day.* blowy, fresh, windy.

brevity *noun*
the brevity of a speech. briefness,
conciseness, curtness, shortness,
succinctness, terseness.
OPPOSITE long-windedness.

brew *verb*
1 *I'll brew the tea.* infuse, make, prepare.
2 *He brews his own beer.* ferment, make.
3 *Trouble is brewing.* develop, fester,
gather force, hatch.

bribe *noun*
backhander (*informal*), carrot, graft
(*informal*), hush money, incentive,
inducement, pay-off (*informal*), sling
(*Australian informal*), sweetener
(*informal*).

bribe *verb*
He tried to bribe the policeman. buy, buy
off, corrupt, grease someone's palm
(*slang*), influence, pervert, sling
(*Australian informal*), tempt.

bridal *adjective*
the bridal party. marriage, matrimonial,
nuptial, wedding.

bridge *noun*
a bridge over the river. crossing, span;
[*kinds of bridge*] aqueduct, drawbridge,
flyover, footbridge, overpass, pontoon
bridge, suspension bridge, swing
bridge, viaduct.

a
b
c
d
e
f
g
h
i
j
k
l
m
n
o
p
q
r
s
t
u
v
w
x
y
z

bridge *verb*
The road bridges the chasm. cross, extend across, span, straddle, traverse.

brief[1] *adjective*
1 *brief happiness.* ephemeral, fleeting, momentary, passing, short-lived, temporary, transient.
OPPOSITE lasting.
2 *a brief report.* abridged, concise, short, succinct, terse.
OPPOSITE long, wordy.
in brief briefly, concisely, in a nutshell, in short, in summary, succinctly.

brief[2] *noun*
1 *a barrister's brief.* case.
2 *an architect's brief to design a fireproof house.* directions, guidelines, instructions.
brief *verb*
They briefed the premier before he addressed the meeting. fill in (*informal*), inform, instruct, prepare.

brigade *noun*
the fire brigade. band, crew, force, group, squad, team.

brigand *noun*
bandit, buccaneer, bushranger, desperado, gangster, highwayman, outlaw, pirate, robber, thief.

bright *adjective*
1 *Summer is full of bright days.* clear, cloudless, fair, fine, sunny.
OPPOSITE dull, overcast.
2 *a bright colour.* bold, brilliant, flashy, gaudy, intense, showy, strong, vivid.
OPPOSITE dull.
3 *bright lights.* beaming, blazing, dazzling, glaring, gleaming, glistening, glittering, glowing, radiant, shining, sparkling.
OPPOSITE dull.
4 *a bright personality.* animated, cheerful, gay, happy, jolly, lively, merry, sparkling, vivacious.
OPPOSITE dreary, dull.
5 *a bright student.* able, brainy, brilliant, clever, gifted, ingenious, intelligent, quick-witted, sharp, smart, talented.
OPPOSITE dull, slow.

brighten *verb*
1 *The room needs brightening.* illuminate, lighten, light up.
2 *Visitors brighten the patients.* animate, buck up (*informal*), cheer up, enliven, liven up, perk up.

brilliant *adjective*
1 *brilliant lights.* blazing, bright, dazzling, glaring, gleaming, radiant, shining, sparkling.
2 *a brilliant scholar.* brainy, bright, clever, gifted, ingenious, intelligent, smart, talented.
OPPOSITE dim-witted.
3 (*informal*) *a brilliant party.* see EXCELLENT.

brim *noun*
The jar was full to the brim. brink, edge, lip, rim, top.

brine *noun*
salt water, sea water.

bring *verb*
1 *The postman brings the mail.* carry, convey, deliver.
2 *She brought her friend home.* accompany, conduct, escort, fetch, lead, take, transport, usher.
3 *War brings sadness and loss.* cause, create, generate, give rise to, lead to, produce, result in, yield.
bring about *The new government brought about change.* accomplish, achieve, cause, produce.
bring in
1 *They brought in a new rule.* initiate, institute, introduce, start.
2 *The scheme brought in a lot of money.* earn, net, produce, yield.
bring off *Can he bring off his plan?* accomplish, achieve, carry off, pull off.
bring out
1 *The article brought out the consequences of passive smoking.* draw attention to, emphasise, highlight, point out, show.
2 *The students bring out a weekly newsletter.* issue, produce, publish, release.
bring up
1 *Parents bring up their children.* care for, look after, nurture, raise, rear, train.

2 *He brought up the subject.* broach, introduce, mention, raise.
OPPOSITE drop.
3 *She brought up her dinner.* see VOMIT.

brink *noun*
the brink of a lake. bank, border, brim, edge, margin, perimeter, verge.

brisk *adjective*
at a brisk pace. energetic, fast, keen, lively, quick, rapid, snappy, vigorous.
OPPOSITE slow.

bristle *noun*
hair, stubble, whisker.

brittle *adjective*
The plastic had become brittle in the sun. breakable, crisp, fragile, hard.

broad *adjective*
1 *a broad area.* big, extensive, great, large, sweeping, vast, wide.
OPPOSITE narrow.
2 *a broad Australian accent.* clear, explicit, marked, obvious, strong, unmistakable.
3 *the broad outline.* basic, general, overall, vague.
OPPOSITE detailed.

broadcast *verb*
The programme is broadcast on Tuesdays. air, relay, screen, send out, telecast, televise, transmit.
broadcast *noun*
radio and television broadcasts. programme, show, telecast, transmission.

broaden *verb*
The river broadened out. enlarge, expand, extend, open out, spread out, widen.
OPPOSITE narrow.

broad-minded *adjective*
flexible, liberal, open-minded, permissive, tolerant, understanding, unprejudiced.
OPPOSITE narrow-minded.

brochure *noun*
booklet, catalogue, flyer, handout, leaflet, pamphlet, prospectus.

broke *adjective* (*informal*)
She is broke until next pay-day. bankrupt, destitute, penniless, skint (*informal*), stony-broke (*slang*); see also POOR.

broken-hearted *adjective*
desolate, devastated, forlorn, grief-stricken, heartbroken, wretched.

broker *noun*
They bought the shares through a broker. agent, dealer, intermediary, middleman.

bronze *adjective*
see BROWN.

brooch *noun*
badge, clasp, pin.

brood *noun*
The mother bird looks after her brood. clutch, family, litter, offspring, young.
brood *verb*
He's brooding over his loss. dwell (on), fret, meditate, mull, ponder, reflect, stew (*informal*), sulk, think.

brook *noun*
a fast-flowing brook. creek (*Australian*), rivulet, stream, watercourse.

broth *noun*
bouillon, consommé, soup, stock.

brother *noun*
1 *He has a brother and a sister.* male sibling.
2 see MONK.

brotherly *adjective*
fraternal; see also FRIENDLY.

brow *noun*
1 *She plucks her brows.* eyebrow.
2 *He wrinkled his brow.* forehead.

brown *adjective*
1 *a brown colour.* auburn, bay, beige, biscuit, bronze, buff, camel, chestnut, chocolate, coffee, copper, fawn, hazel, khaki, mocha, ochre, rust, sepia, tan, tawny, walnut.
2 *brown bodies on the beach.* bronzed, dark-skinned, suntanned, tanned.
3 *brown bread.* rye, wholemeal.
brown *verb*
1 *His skin browns in summer.* bronze, suntan, tan.

a
b
c
d
e
f
g
h
i
j
k
l
m
n
o
p
q
r
s
t
u
v
w
x
y
z

2 *Brown the cheese.* cook, grill, toast.

brown-haired *adjective*
brunette, dark-haired.

browse *verb*
1 *The cattle are browsing.* feed, graze.
2 *He browsed through his notes.* flick through, flip through, glance through, leaf through, look through, scan, skim (through), thumb through.

bruise *verb*
He bruised his leg. blacken, damage, discolour, injure, mark.

brumby *noun (Australian)*
bronco, warrigal (*Australian*), wild horse.

brush *noun*
a brush with the law. clash, confrontation, dealings, encounter, skirmish.
brush *verb*
1 *She brushed the table.* clean, dust, polish, scrub, smooth, sweep, tidy.
2 *The bullet brushed her arm.* graze, touch.
brush aside *He brushed the problem aside.* dismiss, disregard, ignore, reject, sweep aside.
brush up on *She's brushing up on her French before going overseas.* go over, revise, study.

brutal *adjective*
a brutal attack. atrocious, barbarous, beastly, bloodthirsty, callous, cruel, ferocious, inhuman, inhumane, merciless, ruthless, savage, vicious.
OPPOSITE humane.

brute *noun*
1 animal, beast, creature.
2 *The man was a brute.* beast, bully, monster, ogre.

bubble *verb*
The liquid bubbled. boil, effervesce, fizz, foam, froth, seethe, simmer.

bubbly *adjective*
1 *Lemonade is bubbly.* aerated, carbonated, effervescent, fizzy, foamy, frothy, sparkling.
OPPOSITE flat, still.

2 *a bubbly personality.* animated, exuberant, sparkling, vivacious.

buccaneer *noun*
adventurer, brigand, corsair (*old use*), marauder, pirate, privateer.

buck *verb*
1 *The horse bucked.* jump, leap, start.
2 *(informal) Don't buck the system.* fight, oppose, resist.
buck up *(informal)*
1 *You'd better buck up, or we'll be late.* get a move on (*informal*), hasten, hurry up, make haste, rush.
2 *The patient bucked up when her visitors arrived.* brighten, cheer up, liven up, perk up.

bucket *noun*
pail, scuttle.

buckle *noun*
catch, clasp, clip, fastening.
buckle *verb*
1 *She buckled her shoes.* do up, fasten.
OPPOSITE unbuckle.
2 *The car's bonnet had buckled in the smash.* bend, collapse, crumple, distort, give way, twist, warp.

bud *noun*
shoot, sprout.
bud *verb*
The tree is starting to bud. burgeon, develop, grow, sprout.

budding *adjective*
a budding poet. developing, promising, up-and-coming.
OPPOSITE established.

buddy *noun (informal)*
chum (*informal*), cobber (*Australian informal*), companion, comrade, confidant, confidante, crony, friend, mate, pal (*informal*).

budge *verb*
1 *He refused to budge from his spot.* move, shift, stir.
2 *Once she had made up her mind she would not budge.* back down, change your mind, yield.

budget *noun*
1 *The Treasurer prepared the Budget.* estimate, plan.

2 *She has a budget of $100 for clothes.* allocation, allowance.
budget *verb*
The committee budgeted $5000 for painting. allocate, allow, estimate, plan, set aside.

buffer *noun*
The bumper bar is fitted with rubber buffers. cushion, damper, guard, pad, shield.

buffet *noun*
1 *We ate in the buffet.* café, cafeteria, snack bar; see also RESTAURANT.
2 *The glasses are in the buffet.* china cupboard, sideboard.

bug *noun* (*informal*)
1 *bed bugs.* insect, mite.
2 *She was sick with a tummy bug.* bacterium, germ, infection, microbe, micro-organism, virus, wog (*Australian informal*).
3 *a bug in the software.* defect, error, fault, flaw, problem.
bug *verb* (*informal*)
1 *Our phone calls were bugged.* eavesdrop on, listen in on, tap.
2 *What's bugging you?* annoy, bother, irritate, trouble.

build *verb*
1 *build a house, boat, etc.* assemble, construct, erect, form, make, put together, put up, raise.
OPPOSITE destroy, dismantle.
2 *a relationship built on trust.* base, establish, found, ground.
build *noun*
a person of slender build. figure, frame, physique, shape.
build up
1 *Their funds are building up.* accrue, accumulate, amass, grow.
OPPOSITE dwindle.
2 *The pressure built up.* escalate, grow, increase, intensify, rise, strengthen.
3 *They have steadily built up their business.* develop, enlarge, establish, expand, increase.
OPPOSITE wind down.

building *noun*
construction, edifice, premises, structure.

bulb *noun*
a light bulb. globe.

bulge *noun*
bump, curve, hump, lump, swelling.
bulge *verb*
His stomach bulged. bloat, distend, enlarge, expand, protrude, stick out, swell.

bulk *noun*
1 magnitude, mass, size, volume, weight.
2 *He had finished the bulk of the work.* best part, lion's share, majority, most.
in bulk *He buys dog food in bulk.* in quantity, in volume, wholesale.

bulky *adjective*
a bulky parcel. big, cumbersome, heavy, huge, large, unwieldy, voluminous.
OPPOSITE small.

bulldoze *verb*
They bulldozed the burnt-out building. clear, demolish, flatten, level, raze.

bulletin *noun*
1 *a news bulletin.* announcement, broadcast, communiqué, dispatch, message, notice, report, statement.
2 *He edits the school bulletin.* magazine, newsletter.

bullfighter *noun*
matador, picador, toreador.

bull's-eye *noun*
Her dart hit the bull's-eye. bull, centre, middle.

bully *noun*
Stay away from that bully. intimidator, ruffian, tormentor, tough, tyrant.
bully *verb*
He bullies the other boys. frighten, harass, intimidate, oppress, persecute, pick on, push around (*informal*), stand over, terrorise, threaten, torment, tyrannise.

bum *noun*
see BOTTOM.

bump *verb*
1 *She's always bumping herself on things.* hit, hurt, injure, knock.
2 *We bumped along on the gravel road.* bounce, bucket, jerk, jolt, shake.

a
b
c
d
e
f
g
h
i
j
k
l
m
n
o
p
q
r
s
t
u
v
w
x
y
z

bump *noun*
1 *I heard a bump.* bang, collision, crash, knock, thud, thump.
2 *bumps and bruises.* bulge, hump, lump, swelling.
bump into (*informal*)
I bumped into an old friend today. come across, meet, run into, see.
bump off see KILL.
bump up see RAISE.

bumpy *adjective*
1 *a bumpy road.* corrugated, potholed, rough, uneven.
OPPOSITE smooth.
2 *a bumpy trip.* bouncy, jarring, jolting, rough.
OPPOSITE smooth.

bunch *noun*
1 *a bunch of flowers.* bouquet, corsage, posy, spray.
2 *a bunch of bananas.* cluster, hand.
3 *a bunch of papers.* batch, bundle, collection, lot, pack, quantity, set, sheaf, wad.
4 *hair tied in bunches.* pigtail.
5 (*informal*) *a noisy bunch of people.* crowd, gang, group, lot, mob, team.
bunch *verb*
The people bunched together to keep warm. cluster, crowd, gather, herd, huddle, squash up.

bundle *noun*
a bundle of papers, clothes, etc. bale, bunch, collection, package, parcel, set, sheaf, swag (*Australian*).
bundle *verb*
1 *They bundled the books together.* pack, package, tie, wrap.
2 *They bundled him into a taxi.* pack off, push, shove, thrust.

bung[1] *noun*
a bung for a cask. cork, plug, stopper.
bung *verb* (*informal*)
Bung it in the bin. put, shove, stick (*informal*), throw, toss.
bunged up *My nose is bunged up.* blocked (up), clogged up, congested, stuffed up.

bung[2] *adjective* (*Australian informal*)
go bung *The fridge has gone bung.* be on the blink (*informal*), be out of order,

break down, conk out (*informal*), fail, go kaput (*informal*), pack up (*informal*).

bungle *verb*
They bungled the job. botch, foul up (*informal*), goof (*slang*), mess up, mismanage, muff (*informal*), ruin, spoil, wreck.

bunk *noun*
bed, berth.

buoy *noun*
The ship's course was marked out with buoys. float, marker.
buoy *verb*
buoy up *They were buoyed up with new hope.* boost, cheer, encourage, sustain, uplift.
OPPOSITE weigh down.

burden *noun*
1 *The horse carried a heavy burden.* load, weight.
2 *They share each other's burdens.* care, concern, problem, trouble, worry.
burden *verb*
He was burdened with problems. encumber, lumber, oppress, saddle, weigh down, worry.

bureau *noun*
1 desk, writing-desk.
2 *a travel bureau.* agency, branch, department, division, office.

bureaucrat *noun*
administrator, functionary, official, public servant.

burglar *noun*
The owner disturbed the burglar. housebreaker, intruder, robber, thief.

burglary *noun*
break-in, breaking and entering, larceny, robbery, stealing, theft.

burial *noun*
entombment, interment; see also FUNERAL.
burial ground see CEMETERY.

burly *adjective*
a burly footballer. beefy, brawny, hefty, muscular, nuggety (*Australian*), stocky, stout, strapping, strong, sturdy, thickset, tough.
OPPOSITE skinny, weak.

burn *verb*
1 *She burnt the toast, a cloth, etc.* blacken, brown, char, ignite, kindle, scald, scorch, sear, set alight, set fire to, set on fire, singe, toast.
2 *They burnt the corpse.* cremate.
3 *Their house was burnt in the bushfire.* consume, destroy, gut, incinerate.
4 *The bush was burning.* be ablaze, be alight, be on fire, blaze, catch fire, flame, flare, smoulder.
5 *This fabric burns.* be flammable, be inflammable.
6 *Her cheeks were burning.* feel hot, flush, redden.

burning *adjective*
1 *a burning ambition.* ardent, deep, intense, passionate, strong.
2 *a burning question.* crucial, important, pressing, urgent, vital.

burp *verb* (*informal*)
belch, bring up wind.

burrow *noun*
an animal's burrow. den, hole, lair, tunnel, warren.
burrow *verb*
1 *The wombat burrowed under the fence.* dig, excavate, tunnel.
2 *He burrowed into the box to find the letter.* delve, fossick (*Australian informal*), rummage, search.

bursar *noun*
the school bursar. accountant, financial controller, treasurer.

bursary *noun*
allowance, endowment, grant, scholarship.

burst *verb*
1 *The tyre burst.* blow out, break, bust (*informal*), disintegrate, explode, puncture, rip, rupture, split, tear.
2 *He burst the bag.* break open, bust (*informal*), force open, pop open.
3 *He burst into the room.* barge, fly, run, rush.
4 *She burst into tears.* break, collapse, dissolve, erupt.
burst *noun*
1 *a burst of gunfire.* blaze, explosion, outburst, round, volley.
2 *a burst of activity.* effort, rush, spurt.

bursting *adjective*
see FULL.

bury *verb*
1 *bury a body.* entomb, inter, lay to rest.
OPPOSITE exhume.
2 *bury the evidence.* conceal, cover up, hide, submerge.
OPPOSITE unearth.

bus *noun*
coach, minibus, omnibus.

bush *noun*
1 *She has several small bushes in her garden.* plant, shrub.
2 *Large areas of the country are bush.* brush, forest, scrub, woodland, woods.
3 (*Australian*) *They sold their house in the city to live in the bush.* backblocks (*Australian*), country, donga (*Australian*), inland, interior, mallee (*Australian*), mulga (*Australian*), outback (*Australian*), sticks (*Australian informal*).

bushed *adjective*
1 (*Australian*) *The walkers were bushed.* lost.
2 (*informal*) *It's been a long day, and I'm bushed.* done in (*informal*), exhausted, tired out, whacked (*informal*), worn out.

bushfire *noun*
blaze, conflagration, fire; see also FIRE.

bushie *noun* (*Australian informal*)
bush-dweller, bushwhacker, countryman, countrywoman, farmer.
OPPOSITE city-dweller.

bushranger *noun*
The carriage was held up by bushrangers. bandit, brigand, escapee, highwayman, outlaw, robber.

bushwalker *noun*
hiker, rambler, trekker, walker.

bushy *adjective*
1 *bushy land.* scrubby, shrubby.
2 *a bushy tail.* bristly, fluffy, fuzzy, hairy, shaggy, thick, woolly.

business *noun*
1 *It's not his business to mend fuses.* duty, function, job, responsibility, task, work.
2 *He's in the plumbing business.* career, employment, field, industry, job, line,

a
b
c
d
e
f
g
h
i
j
k
l
m
n
o
p
q
r
s
t
u
v
w
x
y
z

occupation, profession, trade, vocation, work.
3 *Business was brisk before Christmas.* buying and selling, commerce, trade, trading.
4 *They run their own printing business.* company, concern, corporation, enterprise, establishment, firm, outfit (*informal*), practice, venture.
5 *This business has nothing to do with you.* affair, concern, issue, matter, situation, subject, topic.

businesslike *adjective*
a businesslike approach. efficient, methodical, organised, practical, professional, systematic.
OPPOSITE unprofessional.

businessman, businesswoman *noun*
entrepreneur, executive, industrialist, merchant, trader, tycoon.

busker *noun*
She threw a dollar into the busker's hat. street entertainer, street performer.

bust[1] *noun*
1 *a marble bust of the King.* sculpture.
2 *a woman's bust.* bosom, breast, chest.

bust[2] *verb* (*informal*)
1 *With his weight he'll bust the chair.* break, burst, collapse, crack.
2 *The police busted the dealer.* arrest, capture, catch, nab (*informal*), nick (*slang*), raid.
go bust *The business went bust.* fail, go bankrupt, go broke (*informal*).

bustle *verb*
She bustled round the house tidying up. dash, hasten, hurry, hustle, rush, tear.
bustle *noun*
He likes the bustle of the big city. activity, busyness, commotion, excitement, hurly-burly, hurry, hustle.

busy *adjective*
1 *He is kept busy.* active, employed, engaged, industrious, involved, occupied, on the go (*informal*), snowed under (*informal*), working.
OPPOSITE idle.
2 *a busy life.* active, bustling, frenetic, frenzied, full, hectic, lively.
OPPOSITE quiet.

busybody *noun*
interferer, meddler, mischief-maker, Nosy Parker (*informal*), snooper (*informal*), stickybeak (*Australian informal*).

but *adverb*
We can but try. only.
but *conjunction*
He studied hard but he failed the test. however, nevertheless, still, yet.
but *preposition*
There is no one here but me. apart from, aside from, except, other than.
but *noun*
ifs and buts. objection.

butcher *verb*
The soldiers butchered the enemy. kill, massacre, murder, slaughter, slay.

butt[1] *noun*
1 *a rifle butt.* handle, shaft, stock.
2 *cigarette butts.* end, remnant, stub.
OPPOSITE tip.
3 *cheque butts.* counterfoil, stub.

butt[2] *noun*
He is often the butt of their jokes. object, subject, target, victim.
butt *verb*
The goat is butting her. bump, knock, poke, prod, push, ram.
butt in interfere, interrupt, intervene, meddle, poke your nose in (*informal*).

buttocks *plural noun*
backside (*informal*), behind (*informal*), bottom, bum (*slang*), haunches, posterior, rear (*informal*), rump, seat.

button *noun*
All at the press of a button. control, knob, switch.
button *verb*
Button your cardigan! do up, fasten.

buttonhole *verb*
The teacher buttonholed the boy in the corridor. accost, bail up (*Australian*), corner, detain, waylay.

buttress *noun*
a church wall with flying buttresses. prop, reinforcement, stay, support.

buttress *verb*
The walls of the church were buttressed.
brace, prop up, reinforce, shore up,
support.

buy *verb*
1 *She is buying a car.* acquire, come by,
gain, get, obtain, pay for, procure,
purchase.
OPPOSITE sell.
2 (*slang*) *No one would buy that excuse.*
accept, believe, swallow.
OPPOSITE reject.

buy *noun*
a good buy. acquisition, deal, purchase;
see also BARGAIN.

buyer *noun*
client, consumer, customer, patron,
purchaser, shopper.
OPPOSITE seller, vendor.

buzz *noun*
1 *the buzz of traffic.* burr, drone, hum,
vibration, whirr.
2 (*informal*) *Give me a buzz.* bell
(*informal*), call, ring (*informal*), telephone
call.

buzz *verb*
Bees buzz. burr, drone, hum, throb,
whirr.
buzz off see LEAVE.

by *preposition*
1 *They live by the river.* alongside,
beside, near, next to.
2 *They drove to Melbourne by the coast
road.* along, via.
3 *They came by night.* at, during.
4 *by artificial means.* through, using.
5 *Cinderella had to be home by midnight.*
before, no later than.
6 *They do things by the book.* according
to, following.

by *adverb*
1 *Put a little by for the future.* aside,
away, in reserve.
2 *They walk by every day.* past.
by and by before long, presently, soon.
by and large all things considered,
generally speaking, on the whole.
by yourself alone, single-handed,
unaccompanied, unaided, unassisted.

bye-bye *interjection* (*informal*)
adieu, bye (*informal*), cheerio, farewell,
goodbye, hooray (*Australian informal*),
see you (*informal*), see you later
(*informal*), ta-ta (*informal*).

bygone *adjective*
in bygone days. ancient, former, olden,
past.
OPPOSITE future.

bypass *noun*
The bypass avoids the city traffic. detour,
deviation, ring road, ring route.

by-product *noun*
consequence, offshoot, side benefit, side
effect, spin-off.

bystander *noun*
an innocent bystander. eyewitness,
observer, onlooker, passer-by,
spectator, witness.
OPPOSITE participant.

a b c d e f g h i j k l m n o p q r s t u v w x y z

cabin *noun*
1 *a log cabin.* chalet, hut, lodge, shack, shanty.
2 *a cabin on a ship.* berth, compartment, room.

cabinet *noun*
a china cabinet. buffet, case, chest, closet, cupboard, locker, sideboard, wall unit.

cable *noun*
1 *electrical cables.* cord, flex, lead, wire.
2 *a mooring cable.* chain, cord, guy, hawser, line, rope.
3 *He sent a cable from England to Australia.* telegram, wire (*informal*).

cackle *verb*
1 *The hen cackled.* cluck, squawk.
2 *The woman cackled.* see LAUGH.

cadet *noun*
a police cadet. learner, novice, recruit, trainee.

café *noun*
bistro, brasserie, buffet, cafeteria, coffee shop, eatery (*informal*), milk bar, restaurant, snack bar, tea room.

cage *noun*
The animals are in cages. aviary, coop, enclosure, hutch, pen.
cage *verb*
He caged the animals. confine, coop up, lock up, pen, shut in.

cake *noun*
1 [*kinds of cake*] baba, bun, cheesecake, cupcake, doughnut, eclair, flan, gateau, lamington, muffin, pastry, scone, sponge, tart, torte.
2 *fish cakes.* croquette, patty.
3 *a cake of soap.* bar, block, hunk, lump, piece, slab.
cake *verb*
The car was caked with mud. coat, cover, encrust.

calamity *noun*
The town has not recovered from the calamity. accident, catastrophe, disaster, misadventure, misfortune, mishap, tragedy.

calculate *verb*
1 *He calculated the cost.* add up, assess, compute, count, figure out, reckon, total, tot up (*informal*), work out.
2 *The statement was calculated to annoy people.* aim, design, intend, mean, plan.

calculating *adjective*
a calculating person. crafty, cunning, devious, plotting, scheming, shrewd, sly, wily.
OPPOSITE guileless.

calculation *noun*
His calculation was out by 10%. answer, computation, estimate, forecast, result, sum.

calendar *noun*
a pocket calendar. daybook, diary, programme, schedule, timetable.

calf *noun*
heifer, mickey (*Australian*), poddy (*Australian*).

call *noun*
1 *He heard a call for help.* bellow, cooee (*informal*), cry, exclamation, roar, scream, shout, shriek, yell.
2 *They paid a call on her.* visit.
3 *He responded to the call for volunteers.* appeal, invitation, plea, request, summons.
4 *There's no call for concern.* cause, grounds, justification, need, reason.
5 *He gave me a call.* bell (*informal*), buzz (*informal*), phone call, ring, telephone call.
call *verb*
1 *He called to the people below.* bellow, cooee (*informal*), cry, cry out, exclaim, roar, scream, shout, shriek, yell.
2 *They called their cat 'Puss'.* address as, baptise, christen, dub, label, name, nickname.
3 *What is that thing called?* describe as, name, term.

4 *She slept until she was called for breakfast.* arouse, awaken, rouse, waken.
5 *Call the doctor.* contact, fetch, page, phone, ring, send for, summon, telephone.
6 *We were called to board the aircraft.* ask, bid, command, invite, order, summon.

call for
1 *Such behaviour calls for strong discipline.* demand, deserve, justify, necessitate, occasion, require, warrant.
2 *Her friend called for her at 8.* collect, fetch, get, pick up.

call off see CANCEL.

call on
1 *The nurse will call on you tomorrow.* drop in on, look in on, pay a visit to, see, visit.
2 *They called on people to give generously.* appeal to, ask, entreat, implore, invite, request.

call up *He was called up to serve in Vietnam.* conscript, draft (*American*), recruit, summon.

calling *noun*
He had found his calling in life. career, employment, job, mission, niche, occupation, profession, trade, vocation.

callous *adjective*
a callous person. cold-hearted, cruel, hard-hearted, harsh, heartless, insensitive, merciless, pitiless, ruthless, thick-skinned, uncaring, unfeeling, unsympathetic.
OPPOSITE sensitive.

calm *adjective*
1 *a calm day.* balmy, mild, quiet, still.
OPPOSITE windy.
2 *calm seas.* even, flat, motionless, quiet, smooth, steady, still.
OPPOSITE choppy, wild.
3 *He stays calm in a crisis.* collected, composed, cool, level-headed, nonchalant, peaceful, placid, relaxed, sedate, serene, stoical, tranquil, unexcited, unfazed (*informal*), unflappable (*informal*), unruffled.
OPPOSITE agitated, excited.

calm *noun*
the calm after the storm. calmness, lull, peace, quietness, serenity, stillness, tranquillity; see also CALMNESS.

calm *verb*
He tried to calm their fears. allay, alleviate, appease, lull, pacify, quell, quieten, relieve, soothe, still, subdue.
OPPOSITE arouse.

calm down collect yourself, compose yourself, cool off, relax, settle, simmer down.

calmness *noun*
His calmness in a crisis is appreciated. calm, composure, coolness, nonchalance, poise, presence of mind, serenity.
OPPOSITE panic.

camel *noun*
[*kinds of camel*] Bactrian camel, dromedary.

camouflage *verb*
His green clothes camouflaged him in the bush. conceal, cover up, disguise, hide, mask, screen.

camp *noun*
They set up camp by the creek. base, bivouac, encampment, tent.
camp *verb*
They camped by the river. encamp, pitch your tent.

campaign *noun*
a military campaign. an advertising campaign. action, battle, blitz, crusade, drive, fight, manoeuvre, offensive, operation, strategy, war.
campaign *verb*
They campaigned for the release of political prisoners. agitate, battle, canvass, crusade, fight, lobby, press, push, strive, work.

campus *noun*
The school has two campuses. grounds, property, site.

can *noun*
caddy, canister, tin; see also CONTAINER.
can *verb*
She cans the fruit. preserve, tin.

canal *noun*
1 *boating on a canal.* channel, watercourse, waterway.
2 *the alimentary canal.* duct, passage, tube.

a
b
c
d
e
f
g
h
i
j
k
l
m
n
o
p
q
r
s
t
u
v
w
x
y
z

cancel *verb*
1 *The game was cancelled.* abandon, call off, scrap, scrub (*informal*), stop, wash out (*informal*).
2 *She cancelled her subscription.* discontinue, give up, stop, withdraw. OPPOSITE continue, renew.
3 *He cancelled the amount on the docket.* cross out, delete, erase, obliterate, scratch out, wipe out.
cancel out *The two actions cancel out one another.* balance out, counteract, counterbalance, negate, neutralise, offset, undo.

cancer *noun*
carcinoma, growth, malignancy, melanoma, tumour.

candid *adjective*
a candid reply. blunt, direct, forthright, frank, honest, open, outspoken, plain, sincere, straight, straightforward, upfront (*informal*).
OPPOSITE evasive.

candidate *noun*
applicant, competitor, contender, contestant, entrant, examinee, interviewee, nominee, runner.

candy *noun*
see LOLLY.

cane *noun*
He walked with a cane. rod, staff, stick, walking stick.
cane *verb*
The teacher caned the boy. beat, hit, flog, lash, strike, thrash, whack.

canister *noun*
a tea canister. caddy, can, tin.

canoe *noun*
dugout, kayak.

canopy *noun*
a bed with a canopy. awning, cover, covering.

canteen *noun*
1 *the office canteen.* cafeteria, dining room, restaurant, snack bar.
2 *the school canteen.* tuck shop.

canvass *verb*
Politicians canvassed up to the eve of the election. campaign, electioneer, solicit votes.

canyon *noun*
chasm, defile, gorge, gully, pass, ravine, valley.

cap *noun*
1 *He wears a cap.* hat, head-covering, headgear; [*kinds of cap*] beanie, beret, bonnet, deerstalker, fez, mob cap, mortarboard, nightcap, skullcap, yarmulke.
2 *the cap for the bottle.* cover, lid, top.

capability *noun*
a student of great capability. ability, aptitude, calibre, capacity, competence, potential, proficiency, prowess, skill, talent.

capable *adjective*
a capable secretary. able, accomplished, adept, clever, competent, effective, efficient, expert, gifted, proficient, skilful, skilled, smart, talented.
OPPOSITE inept.

capacity *noun*
1 *the capacity of the trunk.* dimensions, size, volume.
2 *the capacity to think critically.* ability, aptitude, capability, competence, gift, potential, power, skill, talent.
3 *in his capacity as chairman.* duty, function, position, post, role.

cape[1] *noun*
She wore a cape. cloak, mantle, poncho, shawl, stole, wrap.

cape[2] *noun*
They sailed round the cape. head, headland, point, promontory.

caper *verb*
The baby animals capered about in the paddock. bound, cavort, dance, frisk, frolic, gambol, hop, jump, leap, play, prance, romp, scamper, skip.

capital *adjective*
1 *the capital city.* chief, important, leading, main, major, principal.
2 *capital letters.* big, block, upper case.

capital *noun*
The business needs more capital. assets, finance, funds, means, money, principal, resources, wealth.

capitalism *noun*
free enterprise, private enterprise.

capsize *verb*
The boat capsized. flip over, keel over, overturn, tip over, turn over, turn turtle.

capsule *noun*
The doctor prescribed capsules. pill, tablet; see also MEDICINE.

captain *noun*
the ship's captain. commander, master, skipper; see also CHIEF.

caption *noun*
She read the caption accompanying the picture. heading, headline, subtitle, surtitle, title.

captivate *verb*
She captivated him with her smile. attract, capture, charm, delight, enchant, enthral, entrance, fascinate, mesmerise, seduce.
OPPOSITE repel.

captive *noun*
The chief released the captives after ten days. convict, detainee, hostage, prisoner.

captivity *noun*
held in captivity. bondage, confinement, custody, detention, imprisonment, internment, slavery.
OPPOSITE freedom.

capture *verb*
1 *The police captured the burglar.* apprehend, arrest, catch, nab (*informal*), nail, nick (*slang*), seize.
2 *The film captured their interest.* catch, hold, take, win.
capture *noun*
the capture of the criminal. apprehension, arrest, seizure.

car *noun*
auto (*informal*), automobile (*American*), motor, motor car, motor vehicle, vehicle, wheels (*slang*); [*an old or dilapidated car*] banger, bomb (*Australian*), heap, jalopy, rust bucket; [*kinds of car*] convertible, coupé, fastback, four-wheel drive, hatchback, hearse, hot rod, limousine, panel van (*Australian*), saloon, sedan, soft-top, sports car, station wagon (*Australian*), ute (*Australian informal*), utility (*Australian*), van, wagon (*informal*).

caravan *noun*
1 *a holiday caravan.* camper, campervan, mobile home, trailer (*American*).
2 *a gypsy caravan.* carriage, cart, van, wagon.

carcass *noun*
a sheep's carcass. body, corpse, remains.

care *noun*
1 *She always works with care.* attention, carefulness, caution, concentration, diligence, meticulousness, precision, thoroughness, thought.
OPPOSITE carelessness.
2 *She left the children in her sister's care.* charge, control, custody, hands, keeping, protection, supervision.
3 *not a care in the world.* anxiety, bother, burden, concern, problem, trouble, worry.
care *verb*
She cares about what happens. be concerned, be interested, bother, concern yourself, mind, worry.
care for
1 *She cares for sick children.* attend to, look after, mind, mother, nurse, take care of, tend, watch over.
2 *He cares for her.* be fond of, be keen on, cherish, like, love.
take care *Take care not to be deceived.* be careful, be cautious, beware, be wary, look out, take heed, take pains, watch out.
take care of
1 *He took good care of the children.* keep an eye on, look after, mind, supervise, take charge of, watch over.
OPPOSITE neglect.
2 *He took care of the banking.* attend to, deal with, take charge of.

career *noun*
a career in engineering. calling, employment, job, occupation, profession, trade, vocation, work.

a
b
c
d
e
f
g
h
i
j
k
l
m
n
o
p
q
r
s
t
u
v
w
x
y
z

career *verb*
The car careered into the wall. hurtle, run, rush, shoot, speed.

carefree *adjective*
blithe, breezy, casual, cheerful, contented, easygoing, footloose, happy-go-lucky, laid-back (*informal*), light-hearted, nonchalant, relaxed, untroubled.
OPPOSITE troubled.

careful *adjective*
1 *a careful worker.* accurate, conscientious, diligent, fastidious, methodical, meticulous, neat, organised, painstaking, pernickety (*informal*), precise, rigorous, scrupulous, systematic, thorough.
OPPOSITE slapdash.
2 *a careful driver.* alert, attentive, cautious, mindful, on guard, prudent, vigilant, wary, watchful.
OPPOSITE negligent, reckless.

careless *adjective*
1 *careless work.* disorganised, hit-or-miss, imprecise, inaccurate, inexact, lax, messy, shoddy, slapdash, slipshod, sloppy, slovenly, untidy.
OPPOSITE meticulous.
2 *a careless driver.* absent-minded, inattentive, irresponsible, lax, negligent, rash, reckless, slack.
OPPOSITE cautious.
3 *a careless comment.* inconsiderate, indiscreet, insensitive, tactless, thoughtless, uncaring, unthinking.

caress *verb*
He caressed her tenderly. cuddle, embrace, fondle, hug, kiss, pat, pet, stroke, touch.

caretaker *noun*
curator, custodian, janitor, keeper, sexton, steward, verger, warden.

cargo *noun*
a ship carrying a cargo of cars. consignment, freight, goods, load.

caricature *noun*
a clever caricature of a famous person. cartoon, parody, satire, send-up (*informal*), spoof (*informal*), take-off (*informal*).

carnival *noun*
celebration, fair, festival, fête, fiesta, gala, jamboree, Mardi Gras, pageant, show.

carol *noun*
Christmas carols. hymn, song.

carpentry *noun*
cabinetmaking, joinery, woodwork.

carpet *noun*
1 *the hall carpet.* floor covering, mat, rug, runner.
2 *a carpet of leaves.* blanket, covering, layer.

carriage *noun*
1 *a horse-drawn carriage.* buggy, chariot, coach, curricle, gig, phaeton, post-chaise, sulky, trap, wagon.
2 *a railway carriage.* car, coach.
3 *The entrants were marked on beauty and carriage.* bearing, deportment, posture, stance.

carry *verb*
1 *She carried the TV from the sitting room.* bring, cart (*informal*), fetch, lift, lug, move, remove, take, transfer.
2 *Ships and trucks carry live sheep.* cart, convey, ferry, freight, haul, ship, transport.
3 *She always carries a bag.* bring, have, take.
4 *The floor could not carry the weight of the piano.* bear, hold up, support, take.
carry on
1 *He carried on working till he was eighty.* continue, go on, keep on, persevere, persist, remain.
2 *They are carrying on a business.* conduct, manage, run.
3 (*informal*) *What's he carrying on about now?* complain, go on, rant, rave, spout.
carry out *He carried out his duties.* accomplish, complete, conduct, discharge, do, execute, finish, fulfil, perform, undertake.

cart *noun*
barrow, billycart, dray, float, go-cart, handcart, trolley, wagon.
cart *verb*
see CARRY.

carton *noun*
box, case, container, pack, package, packet.

cartoon *noun*
1 *a political cartoon.* caricature, comic, comic strip, drawing.
2 *TV cartoons.* animated film, animation.

carve *verb*
1 *He carved the ornament out of wood.* chip, chisel, fashion, hew, sculpt (*informal*), sculpture, shape.
2 *She carved her name on the base.* engrave, etch, inscribe.
3 *He carved the roast.* cut, slice.

cascade *noun*
cataract, falls, rapids, waterfall.

case[1] *noun*
1 *He cited many cases of injustice.* example, illustration, instance, occurrence, situation.
2 *a court case.* action, dispute, hearing, lawsuit, proceedings, suit, trial.
3 *the case against smoking.* arguments, facts.

case[2] *noun*
1 *The case protects its contents.* box, cabinet, canteen (*of cutlery*), capsule, carton, cartridge, casing, casket, chest, coffer, container, covering, crate, envelope, holder, holster, housing, jacket, pack, packaging, receptacle, sheath, shell, skin, sleeve, wrapper.
2 *The travellers were laden with cases.* attaché case, bag, briefcase, holdall, port (*Australian*), portmanteau, suitcase, trunk; [*cases*] baggage, luggage.

cash *noun*
1 *He does not carry any cash.* banknotes, change, coins, currency, money, notes, paper money.
2 (*informal*) *They are short of cash.* capital, dosh (*slang*), dough (*slang*), finance, funds, means, money, resources, riches, wealth.
cash *verb*
They cashed their investment. redeem, turn into cash.
cash in on *He cashed in on the situation.* capitalise on, exploit, make the most of, profit from, take advantage of.

cask *noun*
a cask of wine. barrel, butt, hogshead, keg, tub, tun, vat.

casket *noun*
a jewellery casket. box, case, chest, coffer, container.

casserole *noun*
Dinner was a hearty casserole. cassoulet, fricassee, goulash, hotpot, ragout, stew.

cast *verb*
1 *He cast the box into the sea.* chuck (*informal*), drop, eject, fling, heave, hurl, launch, pitch, shy, sling, throw, toss.
2 *The snake cast its skin.* discard, shed, slough, throw off.
3 *He was able to cast light on the situation.* shed, throw.
4 *He cast his eyes on the box.* direct, turn.
5 *She cast a statue in bronze.* fashion, model, mould, sculpt, shape.
cast *noun*
1 *a bronze cast of the animal's foot.* form, mould, shape.
2 *The play has a famous cast.* actors, company, performers, players, troupe.
cast off *She cast off her old clothes.* discard, get rid of, give away, pass on, reject, throw away.

castle *noun*
château, citadel, fort, fortress, mansion, palace, stronghold.

casual *adjective*
1 *a casual encounter.* accidental, chance, fortuitous, unexpected, unforeseen, unplanned.
OPPOSITE arranged.
2 *a casual comment.* offhand, passing, random, spontaneous, unthinking.
3 *a casual manner.* apathetic, blasé, carefree, careless, easygoing, happy-go-lucky, lackadaisical, laid-back (*informal*), lax, light-hearted, nonchalant, offhand, relaxed, slap-happy (*informal*), unconcerned.
OPPOSITE serious.
4 *casual clothes.* informal, leisure, sports.
OPPOSITE dressy, formal.
5 *casual work.* erratic, irregular, occasional, temporary.
OPPOSITE permanent.

casualty *noun*
the casualties of war. fatality, victim.

a
b
c
d
e
f
g
h
i
j
k
l
m
n
o
p
q
r
s
t
u
v
w
x
y
z

cat *noun*
feline, kitten, moggie (*informal*), puss, pussy (*informal*), tom, tomcat; [*various breeds of cat*] Abyssinian, Angora, Burmese, Manx, Persian, Russian blue, Siamese.

catalogue *noun*
The books are listed in the catalogue. directory, file, index, list, register.
catalogue *verb*
He catalogued all their compact discs. index, list, record, register.

catapult *noun*
He killed a bird with his catapult. ging (*Australian informal*), shanghai (*Australian*), sling, slingshot.

cataract *noun*
cascade, falls, waterfall.

catastrophe *noun*
flood, fire, and other catastrophes. accident, blow, calamity, disaster, misadventure, misfortune, mishap, tragedy.

catastrophic *adjective*
a catastrophic nuclear accident. calamitous, devastating, dire, disastrous.

catch *verb*
1 *He caught a big fish.* capture, ensnare, hook, net, snare, trap.
OPPOSITE release.
2 *They caught the thief.* apprehend, arrest, capture, cop (*informal*), corner, grab, intercept, nab (*informal*), nail, nick (*slang*), pick up, seize.
3 *She caught him as he fell.* clutch, grab, grasp, grip, hang on to, hold on to, seize, snatch.
OPPOSITE drop.
4 *They caught him raiding the fridge.* detect, discover, find, spot, surprise.
5 *Her jumper caught on a wire.* entangle, jam, snag, stick.
6 *He caught hepatitis.* become infected with, come down with, contract, get.
catch *noun*
1 *The fisherman had a good catch.* bag, booty, haul, prize, take.
2 *The proposal looks good, but there must be a catch.* difficulty, disadvantage, drawback, hitch, problem, snag, trap.
3 *He fastened the catch.* bolt, clasp, fastener, hook, latch, lock.

catch on (*informal*)
1 *Short skirts have caught on.* become fashionable, become popular, take off.
2 *The pupil caught on quickly.* comprehend, cotton on (*informal*), latch on (*informal*), learn, understand.

catching *adjective*
a catching disease. communicable, contagious, infectious.

catchy *adjective*
a catchy tune. attractive, haunting, memorable, popular, tuneful.

category *noun*
The questions fell into different categories. class, classification, division, group, grouping, kind, rank, set, sort, type.

cater *verb*
They cater for weddings. cook, provide food, supply food.
cater to *The staff cater to their every whim.* indulge, pander to, satisfy.

cattle *plural noun*
bullocks, bulls, calves, cows, heifers, livestock, oxen, steers, stock.

catty *adjective*
a catty person. bitchy (*informal*), malicious, mean, nasty, sly, spiteful, vicious.

cause *noun*
1 *the cause of the problem.* basis, bottom, origin, root, source.
OPPOSITE effect.
2 *no cause for concern.* basis, call, grounds, justification, need, reason.
3 *a worthy cause.* aim, goal, object, principle, purpose.
cause *verb*
Her attitude causes problems. bring about, create, generate, give rise to, induce, lead to, occasion, produce, provoke, result in, spark off.

caution *noun*
1 *Caution is needed when handling guns.* alertness, attention, attentiveness, care, carefulness, prudence, vigilance, wariness.
OPPOSITE carelessness.
2 *The policeman gave him a caution.* admonition, reprimand, warning.

caution *verb*
1 *She cautioned him about the dangers.*
advise, alert, counsel, forewarn, warn.
2 *The policeman cautioned the driver.*
admonish, reprimand, warn.

cautious *adjective*
a cautious driver. He was cautious when questioned. alert, attentive, careful, circumspect, guarded, mindful, prudent, vigilant, wary, watchful.
OPPOSITE heedless, rash.

cave *noun*
cavern, cavity, den, dugout, grotto, hole, hollow, pothole.
cave *verb*
cave in *The roof caved in.* collapse, fall in, subside.

cavity *noun*
1 *a cavity in the rock.* cave, crater, gap, hole, hollow, pit, pocket.
2 *The dentist found no cavities.* caries, decay, hole.

cease *verb*
1 *The noise ceased.* cut out, die away, peter out, stop.
2 *He ceased work.* break off, conclude, desist, discontinue, end, finish, halt, knock off (*informal*), leave off, quit, stop, suspend, terminate.
OPPOSITE begin, continue.

ceasefire *noun*
armistice, truce.

ceaseless *adjective*
her ceaseless complaining. constant, continual, continuous, endless, eternal, everlasting, incessant, interminable, non-stop, permanent, perpetual, persistent, relentless.

cede *verb*
He ceded his rights to his brother. give up, hand over, relinquish, surrender, yield.
OPPOSITE keep.

ceiling *noun*
a wage ceiling. cap, limit, upper limit.

celebrate *verb*
1 *She celebrated her birthday with a party.* commemorate, keep, mark, observe, remember.
2 *It's your birthday, so let's celebrate.* make merry, party, rejoice, revel.

celebrated *adjective*
a celebrated musician. acclaimed, distinguished, eminent, famous, illustrious, notable, noted, popular, prominent, renowned, respected, well-known.
OPPOSITE unknown.

celebration *noun*
1 *They attended an anniversary celebration.* carnival, festival, gala, jamboree, jubilee, observance, party.
2 *a night of celebration.* festivity, jollification, merrymaking, partying, revelry.

celebrity *noun*
1 *a television celebrity.* big name, identity (*Australian informal*), luminary, personality, star.
OPPOSITE nonentity.
2 *The show brought him celebrity.* eminence, fame, popularity, prestige, prominence, renown, stardom.
OPPOSITE obscurity.

celibate *adjective*
The priest vowed to remain celibate. chaste, single, unmarried, unwed, virginal.
OPPOSITE married.

cell *noun*
1 *The prisoners are confined in cells.* compartment, cubicle, den, dungeon, room.
2 *cells in honeycomb.* cavity, compartment, hole.

cellar *noun*
basement, crypt, dugout, vault.

cement *verb*
He cemented the pieces together. bond, braze, fuse, glue, join, paste, solder, stick, unite, weld.

cemetery *noun*
burial ground, churchyard, graveyard.

censor *verb*
Some parts of the book have been censored. ban, cut out, delete, expurgate, remove.

censure *noun*
Such behaviour warrants her parents' censure. condemnation, criticism, disapproval, rebuke, reproach, reproof.
OPPOSITE approval.

a
b
c
d
e
f
g
h
i
j
k
l
m
n
o
p
q
r
s
t
u
v
w
x
y
z

censure *verb*
He was censured for his disobedience.
castigate, chide (*old use*), rap over the knuckles, rebuke, reprimand, reprove, scold, upbraid.
OPPOSITE commend.

central *adjective*
1 *a central position.* innermost, medial, median, middle.
OPPOSITE outer.
2 *the central issue.* chief, core, essential, foremost, fundamental, key, main, major, paramount, primary, principal.
OPPOSITE marginal, minor.

centre *noun*
the centre of a target, city, etc. bull's-eye, core, focus, headquarters, heart, hub, middle, midpoint, nucleus.
OPPOSITE edge, perimeter.
centre *verb*
Attention was centred on the main arena. concentrate, focus, home in.

ceremonial *adjective*
a ceremonial occasion. formal, ritual, ritualistic, solemn, stately.

ceremony *noun*
1 *They attended the wedding ceremony.* celebration, event, function, occasion, rite, ritual, sacrament, service.
2 *He served us without ceremony.* decorum, formality, pageantry, pomp, protocol, ritual.
OPPOSITE informality.

certain *adjective*
1 *He is certain that he is right.* assured, confident, convinced, definite, positive, sure.
OPPOSITE uncertain, unsure.
2 *Victory was certain.* assured, destined, fated, guaranteed, inescapable, inevitable, sure, unavoidable.
3 *It is certain that he is lying.* definite, indisputable, indubitable, irrefutable, plain, undeniable, undoubted, unquestionable.
OPPOSITE doubtful.
4 *a certain cure.* dependable, fail-safe, guaranteed, infallible, reliable, sure, sure-fire (*informal*), trustworthy, unfailing.
OPPOSITE doubtful.

5 *a certain person who will remain nameless.* particular, specific.

certainly *adverb*
1 *There is certainly some truth in that.* assuredly, clearly, definitely, indubitably, surely, undoubtedly, without doubt.
2 *'Will you come to his concert?'* *'Certainly.'* absolutely, by all means, of course, yes.

certainty *noun*
1 *He couldn't say with certainty.* assurance, certitude, confidence, conviction.
OPPOSITE doubt.
2 *He's a certainty to win.* cert (*slang*), cinch (*informal*), foregone conclusion, moral certainty, sure thing (*informal*).

certificate *noun*
Successful candidates receive a certificate. award, credentials, degree, diploma, document, licence, paper, qualification.

certified *adjective*
a certified practitioner. accredited, authorised, chartered, licensed, official, qualified.

certify *verb*
He certified that this was a true copy. affirm, attest, confirm, declare, endorse, guarantee, testify, verify, vouch.

chain *noun*
1 *The rescuers formed a human chain.* column, cordon, line, row.
2 *a chain of mountains.* line, range, row, series, tier.
3 *a chain of events.* combination, progression, sequence, series, set, string, succession, train.
chain *verb*
The prisoners were chained together. bind, fasten, fetter, handcuff, join, link, secure, tie.
chains *plural noun*
The prisoner was in chains. bonds, fetters, handcuffs, irons, manacles, shackles.

chair *noun*
He sat in his chair. place, seat; [*kinds of chair*] armchair, banana chair, chaise longue, deckchair, dining chair, easy chair, high chair, recliner chair, rocking chair, throne, wheelchair.

chair *verb*
The principal chaired the meeting.
conduct, direct, lead, preside over, run.

chairperson *noun*
the chairperson of a meeting. chair,
chairman, chairwoman, moderator,
president, speaker (*in a legislative
assembly*).

challenge *noun*
He issued a challenge. dare, invitation,
provocation, summons, trial.
challenge *verb*
1 He challenged the man to a fight. dare,
defy, invite, summon.
2 The problem challenged the students.
stimulate, stretch, tax, test, try.
3 He challenged the judge's decision.
contest, dispute, object to, protest
against, query, question.
OPPOSITE accept.

challenging *adjective*
challenging work. demanding, inspiring,
stimulating, testing, thought-
provoking.
OPPOSITE easy.

chamber *noun*
1 a council chamber. hall, meeting room.
2 The parliament has two chambers.
assembly, council, house, legislative
body.
3 a lawyer's chambers. office, room.
4 (*old use*) a lady's chamber. bedroom,
boudoir, room.

champion *noun*
1 a racing champion. ace, conqueror,
hero, title-holder, victor, winner.
2 a champion of citizens' rights. advocate,
defender, patron, protector, supporter,
upholder.

championship *noun*
see COMPETITION.

chance *noun*
1 They met by chance. accident,
coincidence, destiny, fate, fluke,
fortune, luck.
OPPOSITE design.
2 There is a chance that he could lose.
danger, likelihood, possibility,
probability, prospect, risk.
OPPOSITE certainty.

3 She wasn't given a chance to speak. look-
in (*informal*), opening, opportunity,
turn.
chance *adjective*
a chance meeting. accidental, casual,
coincidental, fortuitous, lucky,
unexpected, unintentional, unplanned.
OPPOSITE planned.

change *verb*
1 They changed their plans. adapt, adjust,
alter, amend, chop and change, modify,
rearrange, reform, reorganise, revise,
transform, vary.
OPPOSITE keep, maintain.
2 These events changed her attitude to life.
affect, alter, have an effect on, have an
impact on, influence, revolutionise.
3 Their relationship changed. alter,
develop, evolve; see also DETERIORATE,
IMPROVE.
4 His mood changes. fluctuate, shift,
swing.
5 The frog changed into a handsome prince.
become, be transformed, convert,
mutate, transform, turn.
6 They changed places. exchange,
interchange, replace, substitute, swap,
switch, trade.
change *noun*
1 a change of policy. a noticeable change.
about-turn, adjustment, alteration,
amendment, conversion, deviation,
difference, fluctuation, innovation,
metamorphosis, modification,
mutation, rearrangement, reform,
reorganisation, reversal, revision,
revolution, shift, substitution, swap,
switch, transfiguration, transformation,
transition, U-turn, variation, variety.
2 He pocketed the change. coins, coppers,
silver.

changeable *adjective*
a changeable person. capricious, erratic,
fickle, inconsistent, inconstant, moody,
temperamental, unpredictable,
unreliable, unsteady, variable, volatile.
OPPOSITE constant, steady.

channel *noun*
1 He sailed the boat through the channel.
narrows, passage, strait, watercourse,
waterway.
2 The water runs away in a channel. canal,
ditch, drain, duct, dyke, furrow,

a
b
c
d
e
f
g
h
i
j
k
l
m
n
o
p
q
r
s
t
u
v
w
x
y
z

groove, gully, gutter, outlet, sluice, trench, trough.
3 *a television channel.* band, frequency, station, wavelength.

chant *noun*
religious chants. canticle, psalm, song.
chant *verb*
The crowd chanted their slogan. recite, sing.

chaos *noun*
The earthquake left the city in chaos. bedlam, confusion, disarray, disorder, havoc, mess, muddle, pandemonium, turmoil, upheaval.
OPPOSITE order.

chaotic *adjective*
confused, disorderly, disorganised, jumbled, messy, muddled, out of control, topsy-turvy, uncontrolled, unruly.
OPPOSITE orderly.

chap *noun* (*informal*)
bloke (*informal*), boy, fellow, guy (*informal*), lad (*informal*), man, person.

chapel *noun*
see CHURCH.

chaplain *noun*
a prison chaplain. clergyman, clergywoman, minister, padre, pastor, priest.

chapter *noun*
a chapter of a book. division, part, section, subdivision.

char *verb*
The meat was charred. blacken, brown, scorch, sear, singe, toast.

character *noun*
1 *the distinctive character of something.* attributes, characteristics, features, flavour, make-up, nature, peculiarities, qualities, traits.
2 *She has a cheerful character.* attitude, disposition, manner, nature, personality, spirit, temperament.
3 *He was an unpleasant character.* chap (*informal*), fellow, human being, individual, person, specimen, type (*informal*).

4 *The old man was a real character.* card (*informal*), eccentric, individual, oddball (*informal*), oddity, weirdo (*informal*).
5 *She played several characters in the show.* part, persona, role.
6 *printed characters.* figure, letter, sign, symbol.

characteristic *adjective*
her characteristic walk. distinctive, individual, particular, peculiar, recognisable, special, typical, unique.
characteristic *noun*
He described the butterfly's characteristics. aspect, attribute, feature, hallmark, mark, peculiarity, property, quality, trait.

charge *noun*
1 *high charges for services.* cost, expense, fare, fee, levy, payment, price, rate, tariff, terms, toll.
2 *The children were left in her charge.* care, command, control, custody, keeping, protection, responsibility, supervision.
3 *The charge was assault.* accusation, allegation, complaint, indictment.
charge *verb*
1 *They charged $100 as a deposit.* ask, debit, demand, levy, require.
2 *The police charged her with the crime.* accuse, blame, book, impeach, indict.
OPPOSITE absolve, acquit.
3 *The troops charged the building.* assault, attack, rush, storm.

charitable *adjective*
see GENEROUS.

charity *noun*
1 *She refused to accept charity.* alms (*old use*), contributions, donations, financial assistance, handouts.
2 *He does not give to any charity.* fund, good cause, institution.

charm *noun*
1 *a person with great charm.* appeal, attractiveness, charisma, magnetism.
2 *The fairy's charm had worn off.* incantation, magic, sorcery, spell, witchcraft, witchery, wizardry.
3 *She carried a lucky charm.* amulet, mascot, talisman, trinket.
charm *verb*
She charmed them with her dance. attract, bewitch, captivate, delight, enchant,

enthral, entrance, fascinate, hold spellbound, hypnotise, mesmerise.

charming *adjective*
a charming young lady. appealing, attractive, beguiling, captivating, delightful, enchanting, enthralling, fascinating, likeable, pleasant, sweet (*informal*).
OPPOSITE repulsive.

chart *noun*
1 *a chart of the seas.* map, plan.
2 *The figures are set out in the chart.* diagram, graph, histogram, table.

charter *verb*
They chartered a bus. hire, lease, rent.

chase *verb*
They chased the thief. follow, hound, hunt, pursue, run after, track, trail.

chasm *noun*
a chasm in the rock. abyss, breach, canyon, cavity, cleft, crack, fissure, gap, gorge, hole, opening, ravine, rift.

chassis *noun*
a car chassis. frame, framework, substructure.

chat *noun*
Her friend popped in for a chat. chinwag (*informal*), conversation, gossip, natter (*informal*), talk, yak (*informal*).
chat *verb*
They chatted for hours. chatter, converse, gossip, have a word, natter (*informal*), talk, yak (*informal*).

chatter *verb*
The audience chattered until the lights went out. babble, chat, gabble, gossip, jabber, natter (*informal*), prattle, talk, yak (*informal*).

chatty *adjective*
see TALKATIVE.

cheap *adjective*
1 *cheap prices.* bargain, budget, competitive, cut-price, discount, economical, inexpensive, low, reasonable, reduced.
OPPOSITE dear.
2 *He bought a cheap and nasty camera which did not work well.* inferior, poor,

rubbishy, second-rate, shoddy, tacky (*informal*), tinny, trashy, worthless.
OPPOSITE first-rate.

cheat *verb*
1 *He cheated in the test.* break the rules, copy, crib (*informal*).
2 *The salesman cheated his customers.* bamboozle (*informal*), bluff, con (*informal*), deceive, defraud, diddle (*informal*), double-cross, dupe, fleece, have on (*informal*), hoax, hoodwink, outwit, rip off (*informal*), rob, rook, rort (*Australian slang*), short-change, swindle, take for a ride (*informal*), trick, welsh on.
cheat *noun*
They caught the cheats. charlatan, con man (*informal*), crook (*informal*), embezzler, extortioner, fraud, rogue, rorter (*Australian slang*), shark, sharp (*informal*), sharper, shicer (*Australian slang*), shyster (*informal*), swindler, trickster.

check *verb*
1 *The supervisor checks their work.* audit, correct, double-check, examine, inspect, look over, mark, monitor, screen, test, verify, vet.
2 *She checked how he was going.* ascertain, check on, check out, check up, find out, inquire, investigate, suss out (*informal*).
3 *His progress was checked by his health problems.* curb, frustrate, hamper, hinder, hold back, impede, inhibit, limit, restrict, retard, slow down, stop, stunt, thwart.
OPPOSITE accelerate.
check *noun*
He gave the car a thorough check. check-up, examination, going-over (*informal*), inspection, investigation, once-over (*informal*), probe, scrutiny, search, test.
check in arrive, book in, register.
check out depart, go, leave.

cheek *noun*
1 *He had food on his cheek.* chap, jowl.
2 *She had the cheek to say that!* audacity, boldness, effrontery, gall (*slang*), hide (*informal*), impertinence, impudence, insolence, nerve, presumption, temerity.

a b c d e f g h i j k l m n o p q r s t u v w x y z

cheeky *adjective*
cheeky behaviour. a cheeky person.
arrogant, audacious, bold, brazen, discourteous, disrespectful, forward, fresh (*informal*), impertinent, impolite, impudent, insolent, pert, presumptuous, rude, saucy, shameless.
OPPOSITE polite.

cheer *noun*
happy and full of good cheer. cheerfulness, gaiety, gladness, glee, good spirits, happiness, jollity, joy, merriment, mirth, pleasure.
OPPOSITE gloom.
cheer *verb*
1 *They cheered their team.* applaud, barrack for (*Australian*), clap, encourage, shout for, support.
OPPOSITE hiss at, jeer.
2 *The cards cheered the sick man.* brighten, buck up (*informal*), comfort, console, divert, encourage, gladden, hearten, perk up.
OPPOSITE sadden.

cheerful *adjective*
a cheerful person. a cheerful manner.
blithe, bright, carefree, cheery, chirpy, contented, elated, exhilarated, exuberant, gay, glad, gleeful, good-humoured, happy, happy-go-lucky, jolly, jovial, joyful, joyous, jubilant, light-hearted, lively, merry, optimistic, perky, positive, radiant, upbeat (*informal*).
OPPOSITE dismal, sad.

chemist *noun*
1 *The chemist dispenses the medicine.* apothecary (*old use*), dispenser, druggist, pharmacist.
2 *She picked up her medicine at the chemist.* dispensary, drugstore (*American*), pharmacy.

cherish *verb*
1 *He cherished his wife and children.* adore, be fond of, care for, dote on, hold dear, love, nurture, prize, protect, treasure, value.
OPPOSITE despise.
2 *He cherished the hope that they would return.* cling to, harbour, nourish, nurse, nurture, sustain.
OPPOSITE abandon.

chest *noun*
1 *a toy chest. a treasure chest.* ark, box, case, casket, coffer, crate, ottoman, strongbox, trunk.
2 *The jumper fits over her chest.* bosom, breast, bust, ribcage, thorax.
chest of drawers bureau, chest, dresser, lowboy, tallboy.

chew *verb*
The dog chewed the slipper. champ, chomp, crunch, gnaw, grind, masticate, munch, nibble; see also EAT.

chick *noun*
The birds look after their chicks. chicken, fledgeling, nestling.

chicken *noun*
1 *Chickens are kept for their flesh.* chook (*Australian informal*), fowl, hen, rooster.
2 *Don't be a chicken.* see COWARD.
chicken *verb*
chicken out back out, opt out, pike out (*Australian informal*), pull out, withdraw.

chief *noun*
The people respect their chief. boss, captain, chieftain, commander, director, employer, governor, head, leader, manager, master, overseer, president, principal, ruler, superintendent, supervisor.
chief *adjective*
1 *the chief engineer.* head, leading, senior.
2 *of chief importance.* basic, cardinal, central, dominant, essential, first, foremost, fundamental, greatest, highest, key, leading, main, major, overriding, paramount, predominant, primary, prime, principal, supreme.
OPPOSITE least, secondary.

chiefly *adverb*
especially, for the most part, generally, in the main, mainly, mostly, particularly, primarily, principally.

child *noun*
1 *A child must be accompanied by an adult.* babe, baby, boy, girl, infant, juvenile, kid (*informal*), lad, lass, minor, piccaninny, toddler, tot, youngster, youth.
OPPOSITE adult.

2 *the child of famous parents.* daughter, offspring, son.

childhood *noun*
boyhood, girlhood, infancy, youth.
OPPOSITE adulthood.

childish *adjective*
Her behaviour was childish. babyish, immature, infantile, juvenile, naive, puerile, silly.
OPPOSITE mature.

childlike *adjective*
childlike pleasure. innocent, naive, simple, trusting, youthful.

chill *noun*
a chill in the air. chilliness, coldness, crispness, iciness, nip.
chill *verb*
They chilled the drinks. cool, refrigerate.
OPPOSITE warm.

chilly *adjective*
chilly weather. cold, crisp, freezing, frosty, icy, nippy (*informal*), wintry.
OPPOSITE warm.

china *noun*
They ate off her best china. crockery, dinner service, porcelain, pottery, tableware.

chink *noun*
a chink in the wall. aperture, breach, cleft, crack, cranny, fissure, gap, hole, opening, slit, split.

chip *noun*
1 *chips of wood, glass, etc.* bit, flake, fragment, piece, shaving, sliver, splinter.
2 *a potato chip.* crisp, French fry.
chip *verb*
She chipped the plate. break, damage, nick, splinter.

chirp *verb*
The sparrows chirped. cheep, chirrup, peep, tweet, twitter.

chirpy *adjective*
He was feeling quite chirpy. bright, cheerful, happy, light-hearted, lively, perky, vivacious.
OPPOSITE depressed.

chivalrous *adjective*
chivalrous behaviour. considerate, courteous, gallant, gentlemanly, heroic, honourable, noble, polite.
OPPOSITE unchivalrous.

chock-a-block *adjective*
The room was chock-a-block with reporters. chockers (*informal*), chock-full, crammed, crowded, full, jam-packed (*informal*), packed.

choice *noun*
1 *I have no choice.* alternative, option.
2 *a wide choice of holidays.* array, assortment, collection, range, selection, variety.
3 *He found it hard to make a choice.* decision, election, pick, preference, selection.

choir *noun*
choral group, choristers, chorus, ensemble, singers.

choke *verb*
1 *He choked the man.* asphyxiate, smother, stifle, strangle, suffocate, throttle.
2 *She choked in the thick smoke.* gag, gasp.
3 *The roads were choked with cars.* block, clog, congest, crowd, jam, obstruct, pack.

choose *verb*
They chose him as their spokesperson. appoint, decide on, draw lots for, elect, name, nominate, opt for, pick, prefer, select, settle on, single out, vote for.

choosy *adjective* (*informal*)
a choosy customer. fastidious, finicky, fussy, particular, pernickety (*informal*), picky (*informal*), selective.
OPPOSITE indifferent.

chop *verb*
1 *He chopped the wood.* cleave, cut, fell, hack, hew, split.
2 *He chopped the vegetables.* chip, cube, cut, dice, mince.

chopper *noun*
1 *cut with a chopper.* axe, cleaver, hatchet, tomahawk.
2 (*informal*) *fly a chopper.* helicopter.

a
b
c
d
e
f
g
h
i
j
k
l
m
n
o
p
q
r
s
t
u
v
w
x
y
z

choppy *adjective*
choppy seas. rough, stormy, turbulent.
OPPOSITE smooth.

chore *noun*
a domestic chore. duty, errand, job, task, work.

chorus *noun*
They joined in the chorus. jingle, refrain.

christen *verb*
He was christened 'Peter'. baptise, name; see also CALL.

christening *noun*
a baby's christening. baptism.

Christmas *noun*
Xmas, yuletide (*old use*).

chronic *adjective*
a chronic problem. ceaseless, constant, continuing, continuous, lifelong, lingering, long-standing, perennial, permanent, persistent, unending.
OPPOSITE intermittent, temporary.

chubby *adjective*
a chubby child. dumpy, fat, obese, overweight, plump, podgy, rotund, round, stout, tubby.
OPPOSITE skinny.

chuck *verb* (*informal*)
1 *She chucked the rubbish in the bin.* cast, fling, heave, hurl, pitch, sling, throw, toss.
2 *He chucked his job.* chuck in (*informal*), give up, leave, quit, resign, throw in, toss in (*informal*).
chuck out (*informal*)
1 *She chucked out her old clothes.* discard, ditch (*informal*), get rid of, throw away, throw out.
2 *He was chucked out of school.* boot out (*slang*), cast out, expel, kick out (*informal*), throw out (*informal*).

chuckle *noun* & *verb*
chortle, giggle, laugh, snigger, titter.

chunk *noun*
a chunk of cheese. hunk, lump, mass, piece, slab, wedge, wodge.

church *noun*
1 *They visited several churches.* abbey, basilica, cathedral, chapel, minster, sanctuary, shrine, tabernacle, temple.
2 *Church is at 11 o'clock.* devotions, divine service, service, worship.
3 *leaders of all the Christian churches.* denomination.
church *adjective*
church music. ecclesiastical, religious, sacred.
OPPOSITE secular.

churn *verb*
1 *He churned the cream.* beat, stir, whip, whisk.
2 *The waiting had churned her up inside.* agitate, disturb, stir up, upset.

cinch *noun* (*informal*)
Getting into the finals will be a cinch. breeze (*informal*), child's play, doddle (*informal*), piece of cake (*informal*), pushover (*informal*), snack (*Australian informal*), walkover.

cinders *plural noun*
The cinders were still hot. ashes, embers.

cinema *noun*
She works in cinema. films, flicks (*informal*, *old use*), movies (*informal*), pictures (*informal*).

circle *noun*
1 band, disc, halo, hoop, loop, ring, round.
2 *The craft completed its circle of the earth.* circuit, circumnavigation, lap, loop, orbit, revolution.
3 *a circle of friends.* clique, company, group, set, sphere, world.
circle *verb*
1 *The explorer circled the globe.* circumnavigate, go round, orbit, tour.
2 *She circled the mistakes.* encircle, ring.

circuit *noun*
1 *a racing circuit.* course, ring, track.
2 *The car broke down on the fiftieth circuit.* circle, lap, loop, orbit, revolution.

circular *adjective*
a circular shape. round.
circular *noun*
Office circulars consume a lot of paper. bulletin, flyer, leaflet, memorandum, newsletter, notice.

circulate *verb*
1 *Blood circulates through the body.* flow, go round, move round.

2 *They circulated the letter.* distribute, issue, pass round, release, send round.

circumference *noun*
the circumference of a circle. boundary, edge, limit, margin, perimeter.

circumstance *noun*
the circumstances of the case. background, condition, context, detail, event, fact, particular, position, situation.

citizen *noun*
1 *She became an Australian citizen.* national.
2 *the citizens of Sydney.* dweller, inhabitant, native, resident.

city *noun*
big smoke (*slang*), metropolis, town.
OPPOSITE country.

civic *adjective*
a civic centre. civic pride. citizen's, communal, community, local, municipal, public.

civil *adjective*
1 *civil rights.* citizen's, civic.
2 *civil war.* domestic, home, internal.
3 *They are always civil to visitors.* cordial, courteous, obliging, polite, respectful, well-mannered.
OPPOSITE rude.

civilised *adjective*
a civilised society. cultivated, cultured, developed, educated, enlightened, refined, sophisticated.
OPPOSITE barbaric.

claim *verb*
1 *She claimed her share.* ask for, bags (*informal*), demand, lay claim to, request, require.
OPPOSITE renounce.
2 *He claimed that he was innocent.* allege, assert, declare, insist, maintain, make out, pretend, state.
OPPOSITE deny.
claim *noun*
1 *They pursued a claim for higher wages.* application, call, demand, request.
2 *He has no claim on the land.* entitlement, right, title.

clamber *verb*
They clambered over the fence. climb, crawl, scramble.

clammy *adjective*
His body felt clammy. damp, dank, humid, moist, sticky, sweaty, wet.

clamour *noun*
The clamour in the streets woke the neighbourhood. commotion, din, hubbub, hullabaloo, noise, outcry, racket, row, rumpus, shouting, uproar.

clamp *noun*
The pieces were held together with a clamp. brace, clasp, clip, fastener, grip, support, vice.
clamp *verb*
The pieces were clamped together in a vice. clasp, clip, fasten, grip, secure.

clan *noun*
a Scottish clan. family, group, line, tribe.

clang *noun*
the clang of bells or saucepan lids. chime, clank, clash, clink, jangle, peal, ringing.

clap *noun*
1 *a thunder clap.* bang, burst, crack, explosion, peal.
2 *Give them a big clap.* applause, hand (*informal*).
clap *verb*
The audience clapped the performers. applaud, cheer.
OPPOSITE boo.

clarify *verb*
She clarified what she meant. clear up, elucidate, explain, make clear, shed light on, spell out.
OPPOSITE confuse, obscure.

clarity *noun*
the clarity of the water. clearness, purity, transparency.
OPPOSITE murkiness.

clash *verb*
1 *The cymbals clashed.* clang, clank, clatter, crash, jangle, rattle.
2 *The two parties clashed over use of the reserve.* battle, disagree, dispute, feud, fight, quarrel, squabble, wrangle.
3 *Their views clashed.* be opposed, conflict, differ, diverge.
OPPOSITE harmonise.
clash *noun*
1 *a clash between rivals.* battle, combat, conflict, confrontation, contest, disagreement, fight, skirmish.

a
b
c
d
e
f
g
h
i
j
k
l
m
n
o
p
q
r
s
t
u
v
w
x
y
z

2 *a clash of colours. a personality clash.* conflict, discord, disharmony, incompatibility, mismatch.
OPPOSITE harmony, match.

clasp *noun*
The clasp on the necklace is broken. brooch, buckle, catch, clip, fastener, hook, lock.
clasp *verb*
1 *She clasped the two edges together with a pin.* catch, clip, fasten, join, secure.
2 *They clasped one another tightly.* clutch, embrace, grasp, grip, hold, hug, squeeze.

class *noun*
1 *a class of things, people, etc.* category, classification, division, family, genre, genus, group, kind, league, order, set, sort, species, subset, type, variety.
2 *a social class.* caste, level, order, rank, station.
3 *The girls are in the same class at school.* form, grade, group, set, year.
4 *He missed the class and had to catch up.* lesson, session.
class *verb*
She classed the specimens according to colour. arrange, categorise, classify, grade, group, label, rank, sort.

classic *adjective*
1 *a classic performance.* excellent, exemplary, first-class, first-rate, model, outstanding.
2 *a classic case of malnutrition.* archetypal, standard, typical.
classic *noun*
Some books are considered classics. masterpiece.

classical *adjective*
classical works. ageless, enduring, standard, traditional.

classification *noun*
the classification of birds. arrangement, categorisation, grouping; see also CLASS.

classify *verb*
He classified the books according to subject. arrange, categorise, class, grade, group, label, order, organise, rank, sort.

clatter *noun*
the clatter of plates in the sink. banging, clack, clang, clank, jangle, rattle.

clause *noun*
a clause of a contract. article, condition, paragraph, provision, proviso, section, stipulation.

claw *noun*
nail, nipper, pincer, talon.
claw *verb*
The lion clawed its victim. maul, scratch, slash, tear.

clean *adjective*
1 *a clean bathroom. clean clothes.* cleansed, disinfected, fresh, hygienic, immaculate, laundered, sanitary, scoured, scrubbed, spick and span, spotless, sterilised, unsoiled, washed.
OPPOSITE dirty.
2 *a clean sheet of paper.* blank, fresh, new, unmarked, unused.
OPPOSITE used.
3 *clean air.* clear, fresh, pure, uncontaminated, unpolluted.
OPPOSITE polluted.
4 *a clean joke.* decent, innocent, inoffensive, respectable.
OPPOSITE dirty, rude.
clean *verb*
They cleaned the house, clothes, themselves, etc. bath, bathe, brush, cleanse, disinfect, dry-clean, dust, groom, launder, mop, purge, purify, rinse, sanitise, scour, scrub, shampoo, shower, sponge, sterilise, swab, sweep, swill, tidy (up), vacuum, wash, wipe.
OPPOSITE dirty, soil.

cleanser *noun*
antiseptic, detergent, disinfectant, sanitiser, soap.

clear *adjective*
1 *a clear liquid.* clean, crystal-clear, limpid, pure, see-through, transparent.
OPPOSITE opaque.
2 *clear skies.* blue, bright, cloudless, fair, starry, sunny, unclouded.
OPPOSITE cloudy, overcast.
3 *clear skin.* perfect, spotless, unblemished.
OPPOSITE spotty.
4 *a clear conscience.* easy, guilt-free, untroubled.
OPPOSITE guilty.
5 *a clear call.* audible, distinct.
OPPOSITE indistinct.

6 *clear handwriting.* bold, legible, neat, plain, precise, readable.
OPPOSITE illegible.

7 *a clear picture.* focused, precise, sharp, well-defined.
OPPOSITE blurred.

8 *a clear contrast.* definite, distinct, marked, noticeable, obvious, pronounced, sharp, stark, strong, visible, vivid.
OPPOSITE fuzzy.

9 *a clear case of cheating.* apparent, blatant, clear-cut, definite, evident, obvious, patent, plain, straightforward, unmistakable.
OPPOSITE doubtful.

10 *The message was clear.* coherent, comprehensible, crystal-clear, intelligible, lucid, plain, unambiguous, unconcealed, understandable, unmistakable.
OPPOSITE vague.

11 *a clear path.* empty, free, open, passable, unobstructed.
OPPOSITE blocked.

12 *His clear pay is $300.* net.
OPPOSITE gross.

clear *verb*
1 *The fog cleared.* disappear, evaporate, fade, lift, melt, vanish.
2 *He cleared the pipe.* clean, free, unblock.
3 *The building must be cleared.* empty, evacuate, vacate.
4 *The athletes cleared the hurdles.* bound over, jump over, leap over, spring over, vault.
5 *The plans were cleared by the council.* approve, authorise, OK (*informal*), pass.
OPPOSITE reject.
6 *He was cleared of any wrongdoing.* absolve, acquit, exonerate, vindicate.
OPPOSITE accuse.
7 *They cleared $100.* make, make a profit of, net.

clear off see LEAVE.

clear up
1 *She cleared up her desk.* clean up, sort out, straighten up, tidy up.
2 *They cleared up the matter.* clarify, explain, resolve, settle, sort out.

clearing *noun*
a clearing in the forest. gap, glade, opening, space.

clench *verb*
He clenched his teeth. clamp together, close, grit, set.

clergy *noun*
a member of the clergy. ministry, priesthood; [*various members of the clergy*] archbishop, archdeacon, bishop, canon, cardinal, chaplain, clergyman, clergywoman, cleric, curate, deacon, deaconess, dean, minister, padre, parson, pastor, preacher, priest, primate, rector, vicar.
OPPOSITE laity.

clerk *noun*
bookkeeper, office worker, record-keeper, secretary.

clever *adjective*
1 *a clever person.* able, accomplished, adept, artful, astute, brainy, bright, brilliant, canny, crafty, cunning, deft, dexterous, expert, gifted, intelligent, perceptive, quick-witted, resourceful, sharp-witted, shrewd, skilful, slick, sly, smart, talented, wily, wise, witty.
OPPOSITE slow, stupid.
2 *a clever plan.* ingenious, inventive, neat, nifty (*informal*), smart, strategic.
OPPOSITE stupid.

cliché *noun*
His speech was full of clichés. banality, hackneyed phrase, platitude.

click *verb*
The two parts click together. catch, fasten, snap.

client *noun*
The company looks after its clients. consumer, customer, patron, shopper, user; [*clients*] clientele.

cliff *noun*
a house perched on the cliffs. bluff, crag, escarpment, precipice, scarp.

climate *noun*
The place has a mild climate. weather.

climax *noun*
The film reached its climax. crisis, culmination, highlight, peak, pinnacle, summit.

a
b
c
d
e
f
g
h
i
j
k
l
m
n
o
p
q
r
s
t
u
v
w
x
y
z

climb *verb*
1 *He climbed the fence.* clamber over, go over, mount, scale.
2 *The plane was climbing steadily.* ascend, go up, rise, soar.
OPPOSITE descend.

cling *verb*
The plastic clings to the bowl. adhere, attach, stick.
cling to *The child clung to her mother.* clasp, clutch, embrace, grasp, grip, hang on to, hold on to, hug.
OPPOSITE let go of.

clinic *noun*
He saw a doctor at the clinic. health centre, hospital, infirmary, medical centre, surgery.

clink *verb*
The coins clinked in the bowl. jangle, jingle, ring, tinkle.

clip[1] *noun*
The bag does up with a clip. clasp, fastener, grip, hook.
clip *verb*
He clipped the papers together. attach, fasten, fix, join, pin, staple.

clip[2] *verb*
She clipped her hair. Clip the hedge. bob, crop, cut, prune, shear, shorten, snip, trim.
clip *noun*
a film clip. excerpt, extract, segment, snippet, trailer.

clippers *plural noun*
cutters, scissors, secateurs, shears, snips.

cloak *noun*
1 *She wore a cloak.* burnous, cape, coat, mantle, poncho, shroud, wrap.
2 *a cloak of secrecy.* cloud, cover, mantle, pall, screen, shroud, veil.

clock *noun*
The clocks show different times. chronometer, timepiece; [*kinds of clock*] alarm clock, digital clock, grandfather clock, sundial.

clog *verb*
Leaves clogged the gutters. block, bung up, choke, jam, obstruct, stop up.

close[1] *adjective*
1 *Christmas is close.* at hand, imminent, impending, near, nigh.
2 *The shops are close.* accessible, adjacent, near, neighbouring.
OPPOSITE distant.
3 *at close range.* point-blank, short.
OPPOSITE long.
4 *close friends.* affectionate, attached, dear, devoted, familiar, fond, inseparable, intimate.
5 *a close contest.* even, level-pegging, narrow, neck and neck, tight.
6 *a close fit.* cramped, narrow, tight.
OPPOSITE loose.
7 *a close inspection.* careful, concentrated, detailed, minute, searching, thorough.
OPPOSITE cursory, superficial.
8 *Keep a close eye on the bags.* alert, attentive, careful, keen, sharp, vigilant, watchful.
9 *a close atmosphere.* airless, humid, muggy, oppressive, stale, stifling, stuffy, sultry.
OPPOSITE airy.
close *adverb*
Don't stand too close. close by, near, within cooee (*Australian informal*).
close to *There were close to fifty people present.* almost, approximately, nearly.

close[2] *verb*
1 *She closed the door.* bar, bolt, fasten, latch, lock, seal, secure, shut, slam.
OPPOSITE open.
2 *He closed up all the holes.* block, bung, clog, cork, fill, plug, seal, stop.
3 *The police closed off the area.* barricade, cordon off, rope off, seal off.
4 *The speaker closed the meeting.* conclude, end, finish, stop, terminate, wind up.
OPPOSITE open.
close *noun*
The concert came to a close. completion, conclusion, end, finale, finish, halt, stop, termination.
OPPOSITE beginning, opening.

closeness *noun*
1 *the closeness of a copy to the original.* likeness, resemblance, similarity.
2 *closeness to the shops.* nearness, proximity.

closet *noun*
cupboard, wardrobe.

clot *verb*
The cream clotted. coagulate, solidify, thicken.

cloth *noun*
She bought cloth to make a dress. fabric, material, stuff, textile.

clothe *verb*
They were clothed in their Sunday best. array, attire, deck, dress.

clothes *plural noun*
She enjoys wearing new clothes. apparel (*formal*), attire (*formal*), clobber (*slang*), clothing, costume, dress, garb, garments, gear (*informal*), get-up (*informal*), kit, outfit, raiment (*old use*), rig (*informal*), togs (*informal*), uniform, vestments, wardrobe, wear.

cloud *noun*
1 *flying through the clouds.* fog, haze, mist, vapour; [*kinds of cloud*] altocumulus, altostratus, cirrocumulus, cirrostratus, cirrus, cumulonimbus, cumulostratus, cumulus, nimbostratus, nimbus, stratocumulus, stratus.
2 *a cloud of secrecy.* cloak, mantle, pall, shroud, veil.
cloud *verb*
1 *The sky clouded over.* darken, dim, grow overcast.
OPPOSITE clear.
2 *Tears clouded his vision.* blur, distort, fog, impair, muddy, obscure.

cloudless *adjective*
a cloudless sky. blue, bright, clear, fair, starlit, starry, sunny, unclouded.
OPPOSITE cloudy.

cloudy *adjective*
1 *a cloudy sky.* dull, gloomy, grey, heavy, leaden, overcast.
OPPOSITE cloudless.
2 *a cloudy liquid.* hazy, milky, muddy, murky, opaque.
OPPOSITE clear, transparent.

clout *noun* (*informal*)
an organisation with political clout. influence, muscle, power, strength, sway, weight.

clout *verb*
He was clouted on the head. see HIT.

clown *noun*
We were amused by the clown. buffoon, comedian, comic, fool, jester, joker, wag, zany.

club *noun*
1 *He hit the snake with his club.* bat, baton, bludgeon, cudgel, nulla-nulla, stick, truncheon, waddy.
2 *a student club.* alliance, association, fellowship, group, guild, league, organisation, society, union.
club *verb*
He clubbed the animal to death. batter, beat, bludgeon, clobber, cudgel, hit, strike, wallop.

clue *noun*
no clues to the mystery. cue, guide, hint, idea, indication, inkling, key, lead, pointer, sign, suggestion, tip.

clump *noun*
a clump of hair, weeds, etc. bunch, cluster, group, mass, tuft.

clumsy *adjective*
a clumsy worker. awkward, blundering, bungling, fumbling, gawky, heavy-handed, inept, unco (*informal*), uncoordinated, ungainly, unskilful.
OPPOSITE deft.

cluster *noun*
a cluster of people, animals, etc. assembly, batch, bunch, collection, congregation, crowd, gathering, group, herd, hive, huddle, swarm, throng.
cluster *verb*
They clustered together to keep warm. assemble, bunch, collect, congregate, crowd, flock, gather, group, herd, huddle, throng.
OPPOSITE scatter.

clutch *verb*
He clutched his case. clasp, cling to, grasp, grip, hang on to, hold, hug.
OPPOSITE let go.

clutter *noun*
They tidied up the clutter. jumble, litter, mess, muddle.

a
b
c
d
e
f
g
h
i
j
k
l
m
n
o
p
q
r
s
t
u
v
w
x
y
z

clutter *verb*
She cluttered her desk with papers. crowd, litter, mess up, scatter, strew.
OPPOSITE tidy up.

coach *noun*
1 a horse-drawn coach. carriage, stagecoach.
2 She saw Europe by coach. bus.
3 a maths coach. instructor, teacher, trainer, tutor.
coach *verb*
He coached the chess team. instruct, teach, train, tutor.

coalition *noun*
a coalition of two parties. alliance, amalgamation, association, bloc, partnership, union.

coarse *adjective*
1 a coarse material. harsh, loose-weave, prickly, rough, scratchy.
OPPOSITE fine, smooth.
2 coarse manners. coarse language. boorish, common, crude, foul, impolite, improper, indecent, low, offensive, rough, rude, uncouth, vulgar.
OPPOSITE polite, refined.

coast *noun*
The road follows the coast. beach, coastline, foreshore, seashore, seaside, shore.
coast *verb*
He turned off the engine and coasted down the hill. cruise, drift, freewheel, glide.

coat *noun*
1 [kinds of coat] anorak, blazer, dinner-jacket, doublet, duffel coat, greatcoat, jacket, mackintosh, overcoat, parka, raincoat, tailcoat, topcoat, trench coat, tuxedo, waistcoat, windcheater, wrap; see also CLOAK.
2 an animal's coat. fleece, fur, hair, hide, pelt, skin.
3 a coat of paint. coating, cover, film, layer.
coat *verb*
He coated the chair with the paint. The car was coated with mud. cover, daub, encase, encrust, paint, plaster, protect, seal, smear, spread, veneer.
coat of arms crest, emblem, shield.

coating *noun*
a protective coating. coat, cover, covering, film, glaze, layer, outside, overlay, sealant, skin, surface, veneer.

coax *verb*
They coaxed her into giving a speech. cajole, entice, induce, persuade, sweet-talk (*informal*), talk into, tempt.

cock *noun*
the cock and the hens. cockerel, rooster.
cock *verb*
The dog cocked his ears. prick up, raise, tilt, tip.

cock-eyed *adjective* (*informal*)
1 a cock-eyed painting. askew, awry, crooked, lopsided.
OPPOSITE straight.
2 a cock-eyed scheme. absurd, crazy, foolish, hare-brained, mad, stupid, wild.
OPPOSITE sensible.

cocky *adjective*
The new fellow is too cocky. arrogant, brash, bumptious, cocksure, conceited, impudent, opinionated, overconfident, self-assured, self-confident, vain.
OPPOSITE modest.

code *noun*
1 a code of ethics. laws, principles, regulations, rules, system.
2 a message in code. cipher, signs.
code *verb*
He coded the message. encode, encrypt.
OPPOSITE decipher.

coffin *noun*
box, casket, sarcophagus.

coherent *adjective*
a coherent speech. articulate, clear, connected, consistent, intelligible, logical, rational, structured, understandable.
OPPOSITE incoherent, rambling.

coil *verb*
He coiled the wire round the spool. bend, curl, entwine, kink, loop, roll, turn, twine, twirl, twist, wind, wrap.
coil *noun*
a coil of wire. circle, curl, helix, kink, loop, ring, spiral, twist, whorl.

coin *noun*
1 *a 20-cent coin.* bit, piece.
2 *a purse bursting with coins.* cash, change, copper, money, silver.
coin *verb*
1 *A new $5 piece has been coined.* mint, strike.
2 *She coined the word.* create, devise, invent, make up, originate.

coincide *verb*
1 *The two events coincided.* be concurrent, clash, happen simultaneously, happen together.
2 *Their accounts coincide.* accord, agree, be the same, correspond, match.
OPPOSITE disagree.

coincidence *noun*
They were on the same bus by coincidence. accident, chance, fluke, luck.

cold *adjective*
1 *cold weather.* biting, bitter, bleak, chilly, cool, crisp, freezing, frigid, frosty, glacial, icy, nippy (*informal*), perishing (*informal*), subzero, wintry.
OPPOSITE hot.
2 *She feels cold.* chilly, cool, freezing, frozen, numb, shivery.
OPPOSITE hot.
3 (*informal*) *knocked out cold.* insensible, unconscious.
4 *a cold person.* aloof, callous, clinical, cold-hearted, cool, distant, frigid, hard-hearted, heartless, hostile, indifferent, insensitive, severe, stand-offish, stony, uncaring, undemonstrative, unemotional, unfeeling, unfriendly, unsympathetic.
OPPOSITE ardent, warm.

cold-blooded *adjective*
a cold-blooded killer. brutal, callous, cold-hearted, cruel, heartless, inhuman, inhumane, merciless, pitiless, ruthless, savage, unemotional, unfeeling.
OPPOSITE humane.

collaborate *verb*
The two teams collaborated on the work. cooperate, join forces, work together.

collaborator *noun*
1 *collaborators on the project.* ally, assistant, associate, colleague, co-worker, fellow worker, helper, partner.
2 *a wartime collaborator.* fraterniser, quisling, traitor.

collapse *verb*
1 *The runner collapsed after the race.* faint, fall down, flake out (*informal*), keel over, pass out, swoon.
2 *She collapsed into the chair.* crumple, drop, fall, flop, sink, slump.
3 *The building collapsed with an explosion.* buckle, cave in, crumble, crumple, disintegrate, fall down, give way, tumble down.
4 *The financial system has collapsed.* break down, crash, fail, fold, go bung (*Australian informal*), go bust (*informal*).
collapse *noun*
1 *the collapse of the building.* cave-in, destruction, fall, ruin.
2 *the collapse of a political system.* breakdown, disintegration, downfall, failure.

colleague *noun*
a business colleague. associate, co-worker, fellow worker, partner, workmate; see also COLLABORATOR.

collect *verb*
1 *He collected antiques.* accumulate, acquire, heap up, hoard, pile up, save, stockpile, store.
2 *A crowd of shoppers collected at the door.* assemble, cluster, come together, congregate, flock, gather, group, herd, rally, swarm, throng.
OPPOSITE disperse.
3 *She collected the dry-cleaning.* bring, fetch, get, obtain, pick up.
4 *She collects money for charities.* ask for, obtain, raise, receive, solicit.
OPPOSITE distribute.

collection *noun*
1 *the rubbish collection.* pick-up.
2 *the church collection.* donations, gifts, offering, offertory.
3 *a collection of things.* accumulation, anthology, arrangement, array, assortment, batch, bundle, compendium, compilation, corpus, group, heap, hoard, jumble, mass, medley, miscellany, mixture, pile, selection, series, set, stack, stockpile, store, storehouse, swag (*Australian*), treasury, variety.

a
b
c
d
e
f
g
h
i
j
k
l
m
n
o
p
q
r
s
t
u
v
w
x
y
z

4 *a collection of people.* assembly, band, bevy, body, bunch, cluster, company, congregation, crowd, flock, gathering, group, herd, horde, host, mass, mob, multitude, pack, swarm, throng.

college *noun*
academy, conservatorium, institute, school, seminary, university.

collide *verb*
collide with *The car collided with a bus.* bump into, crash into, hit, knock into, ram into, run into, slam into, smash into, strike.

collision *noun*
People were hurt in the collision. crash, impact, pile-up (*informal*), prang (*informal*), smash.

colloquial *adjective*
a colloquial expression. casual, chatty, conversational, familiar, informal.
OPPOSITE formal.

colonist *noun*
immigrant, pioneer, settler.

colony *noun*
1 *the colony of South Australia.* dependency, dominion, province, settlement, territory.
2 *a colony of bees.* community, group, hive.

colossal *adjective*
a colossal amount. a colossal building. big, enormous, extensive, gigantic, great, huge, humungous (*slang*), immense, large, mammoth, massive, mighty, monstrous, monumental, stupendous, towering, tremendous, vast, whopping (*slang*).
OPPOSITE small.

colour *noun*
1 *bright colours.* dye, hue, paint, pigment, shade, tinge, tint, tone.
2 *Her cheeks have a natural colour.* bloom, glow, redness, ruddiness.
OPPOSITE pallor.
colour *verb*
1 *They coloured the eggs for Easter.* dye, paint, stain, tinge, tint.
2 *Her cheeks coloured with embarrassment.* blush, flush, glow, redden.

3 *The information coloured his judgement.* affect, bias, distort, influence, prejudice, taint.

colourful *adjective*
1 *a colourful drawing.* bright, brilliant, flashy, gaudy, gay, loud, multicoloured, showy, vibrant, vivid.
OPPOSITE colourless.
2 *a colourful story.* descriptive, graphic, interesting, lively, vivid.
OPPOSITE dull.

colourless *adjective*
1 *a colourless liquid.* clear, transparent.
2 *The invalid was colourless.* anaemic, ashen, pale, pasty, sickly, wan, washed out, waxen, white.
OPPOSITE ruddy.
3 *a colourless performance.* boring, drab, dreary, dull, insipid, lacklustre, lifeless, monotonous, nondescript, ordinary, tame, unexciting, unimaginative, wishy-washy.
OPPOSITE colourful.

column *noun*
1 *Columns support the roof.* pile, pillar, pole, post, shaft, support, upright.
2 *a newspaper column.* article, feature, piece.
3 *a column of armoured vehicles.* file, line, parade, procession, queue, row, string, train.

comb *verb*
1 *She combed her hair.* groom, tidy.
2 *He combed the ruins for evidence.* fossick through (*Australian informal*), ransack, rummage through, scour, search.

combat *noun*
killed in combat. action, battle, clash, conflict, confrontation, contest, duel, fight, hostility, skirmish, struggle, war.
combat *verb*
Doctors are trying to combat the disease. battle, counter, fight, oppose, resist, tackle.

combination *noun*
a combination of colours. alliance, amalgam, amalgamation, blend, composite, fusion, merger, mix, mixture, partnership, union.

combine *verb*
  1 *She combined the ingredients.* bind, blend, incorporate, lump together, mix, put together.
  2 *The two schools combined to form a new one.* amalgamate, band together, consolidate, federate, integrate, join forces, merge, team up, unite.
  OPPOSITE separate.

come *verb*
  1 *Come here.* advance, approach, draw near.
  2 *The guests came on time.* appear, arrive, drop in, lob in (*Australian slang*), roll up (*informal*), show up, turn up.
  3 *The bus eventually came to my stop.* arrive at, get to, reach.
  4 *What came next?* happen, occur, take place.
  come about *He told us how the meeting came about.* arise, come to pass, happen, occur, take place.
  come across (*informal*) *He came across the evidence by accident.* chance upon, come upon, discover, find, happen on, stumble on.
  come after see FOLLOW.
  come back *The rash came back.* reappear, recur, resurface, return.
  come before see PRECEDE.
  come down
  1 *The plane came down quickly.* descend, land.
  2 *Prices came down.* drop, fall, nosedive, plunge.
  come out
  1 *The sun came out.* appear, become visible, emerge.
  2 *The truth came out.* become known, be published, be revealed, emerge, leak out.
  3 *The stain came out.* be removed, disappear, wash out.
  come round *The patient is coming round.* come to, rally, recover, regain consciousness, revive.
  come to
  1 *The bill came to $50.* add up to, amount to, equal, tot up to.
  2 *The boxer came to.* see COME ROUND.
  come up
  1 *The diver came up for air.* ascend, pop up, rise, surface.

  2 *A problem has come up.* arise, crop up, occur.
  come up with *She came up with a new idea.* contribute, produce, propose, put forward, submit, suggest.

comedian, comedienne *noun*
  The comedian entertained us with his jokes. comic, humorist, jester, joker, wag, wit.

comedy *noun*
  farce, fun, hilarity, humour, joking, satire, slapstick.
  OPPOSITE tragedy.

comfort *noun*
  1 *They live in comfort.* contentment, ease, luxury, opulence.
  OPPOSITE discomfort, hardship.
  2 *He provided comfort to the grieving family.* consolation, relief, solace, support, sympathy.
  OPPOSITE aggravation.
comfort *verb*
  She comforted them with kind words. cheer, console, encourage, reassure, relieve, soothe, sympathise with.
  OPPOSITE distress.

comfortable *adjective*
  1 *a comfortable bed.* comfy (*informal*), cosy, luxurious, relaxing, restful, snug, soft.
  OPPOSITE uncomfortable.
  2 *a comfortable job.* cushy (*informal*), easy, pleasant, soft (*informal*).
  OPPOSITE demanding, hard.
  3 *He makes his guests feel comfortable.* at ease, at home, contented, relaxed.
  OPPOSITE uneasy.

comic *noun*
  see COMEDIAN.

comical *adjective*
  a comical situation. absurd, amusing, comic, farcical, funny, hilarious, humorous, laughable, ludicrous, nonsensical, ridiculous, silly, zany.
  OPPOSITE serious, tragic.

coming *noun*
  the coming of the king. advent, approach, arrival.

command *noun*
  1 *They follow his commands.* commandment, decree, direction,

a
b
c
d
e
f
g
h
i
j
k
l
m
n
o
p
q
r
s
t
u
v
w
x
y
z

directive, edict, instruction, order,
precept, summons.
2 *Who is in command?* authority, charge,
control, leadership, power, rule.
3 *She has a good command of English.*
control, grasp, mastery, understanding.
command *verb*
1 *She commanded them to be silent.* bid,
call upon, charge, direct, instruct, order,
prescribe, require, summon, tell.
2 *The officer commanded the expedition.* be
in charge of, control, direct, govern,
head, lead, manage, rule, supervise.
3 *He commands their respect.* deserve,
earn.

commandment *noun*
the Ten Commandments. command, law,
order, precept, principle, rule.

commemorate *verb*
They like to commemorate Anzac Day.
celebrate, mark, observe, remember.
OPPOSITE forget, ignore.

commence *verb*
1 *The show commenced at 8 o'clock.* begin,
get going, get under way, kick off
(*informal*), open, start.
OPPOSITE finish.
2 *He commenced the negotiations.* begin,
embark on, enter upon, initiate, launch,
open, start.
OPPOSITE conclude.

commencement *noun*
beginning, birth, dawn, founding,
genesis, inception, onset, opening,
origin, outset, start.
OPPOSITE end.

commend *verb*
The judges commended the book. acclaim,
applaud, approve, laud (*formal*), praise,
recommend.
OPPOSITE condemn.

commendable *adjective*
commendable behaviour. admirable,
laudable, meritorious, praiseworthy,
worthy.

comment *noun*
He wrote his comments in the margin.
annotation, note, observation, opinion,
reference, reflection, remark, statement.
comment *verb*
He merely commented that they were late.
mention, observe, remark, say.

commentary *noun*
*The broadcaster provided a commentary on
the game.* account, description,
narration, report.

commentator *noun*
a sports commentator. broadcaster,
commenter, journalist, narrator,
presenter, reporter.

commerce *noun*
business, trade.

commercial *adjective*
a commercial venture. business,
economic, money-making.
commercial *noun*
a show without commercials. ad (*informal*),
advert (*informal*), advertisement, plug
(*informal*).

commission *noun*
1 *a commission to paint a portrait.*
assignment, duty, job, mission, order,
task.
2 *a commission of inquiry.* board,
committee, council, panel.
3 *An insurance salesman earns a
commission.* brokerage, cut (*informal*),
fee, percentage, share.

commit *verb*
1 *He committed the crime.* carry out, do,
perform, perpetrate.
2 *He committed himself to big repayments.*
bind, pledge, promise.

commitment *noun*
1 *He is trying to reduce his commitments.*
duty, obligation, responsibility, tie.
2 *She honoured her commitment to make a
donation.* pledge, promise, undertaking,
vow.
3 *The party expects members' total
commitment.* allegiance, dedication,
devotion, loyalty.

committee *noun*
The club appointed a committee. board,
council, panel, working party.

common *adjective*
1 *It was common knowledge.* general,
popular, public, universal, well-known.
OPPOSITE private.
2 *a common interest.* joint, mutual
(*informal*), shared.
3 *a common problem. a common
occurrence.* commonplace, customary,

everyday, familiar, frequent, general, habitual, prevalent, regular, routine, standard, universal, usual, widespread.
OPPOSITE rare, unusual.
4 *the common house spider.* common or garden (*informal*), normal, ordinary, plain, simple, standard, typical.
OPPOSITE special.
5 (*derogatory*) *common behaviour.* boorish, coarse, crude, rude, uncouth, unrefined, vulgar.
OPPOSITE refined.
common sense gumption (*informal*), intelligence, judgement, nous (*informal*), sense.

commonplace *adjective*
a commonplace event. common, customary, everyday, familiar, mundane, normal, ordinary, regular, routine, usual.
OPPOSITE rare.

commotion *noun*
She was woken by the commotion outside. ado, ballyhoo, clamour, din, disturbance, fracas, furore, fuss, hubbub, hullabaloo, kerfuffle (*informal*), noise, pandemonium, racket, riot, rumpus, shindy (*informal*), stir, to-do, tumult, turmoil, unrest, uproar.

communal *adjective*
a communal kitchen. common, joint, public, shared.
OPPOSITE private.

communicate *verb*
1 *She communicated her views.* announce, broadcast, convey, declare, disclose, express, impart, indicate, make known, pass on, relate, report, reveal, say, show, signal, speak, state, voice.
OPPOSITE withhold.
2 *He does not communicate with people.* converse, correspond, get in touch, make contact, speak, talk, write.

communication *noun*
1 *a lack of communication.* conversation, correspondence, dialogue, speaking, writing.
2 *a handwritten communication from the Premier.* advice, announcement, bulletin, communiqué, dispatch, information, letter, memorandum, message, news, note, notice, notification, report, statement.

communicative *adjective*
He was not very communicative. chatty, forthcoming, informative, open, talkative.
OPPOSITE reserved.

community *noun*
1 *The police appealed to the community for information.* citizens, nation, people, populace, public, residents, society.
2 *They live in a quiet community.* area, district, environment, locality, municipality, neighbourhood, suburb.
3 *the business community.* group, people, sector, set.

community *adjective*
1 *widespread community support.* popular, public.
2 *a community centre.* civic, local, municipal, neighbourhood.

compact *adjective*
1 *The house is compact.* poky, small, tiny.
OPPOSITE spacious.
2 *a compact calculator.* little, neat, portable, small.
OPPOSITE bulky.

companion *noun*
assistant, associate, attendant, buddy (*informal*), chaperone, chum (*informal*), cobber (*Australian informal*), comrade, crony, escort, friend, mate, pal (*informal*), partner, playmate, sidekick (*informal*).

company *noun*
1 *They enjoy his company.* companionship, fellowship, friendship, society.
2 *They're expecting company.* callers, guests, visitors.
3 *a theatrical company.* crew, ensemble, group, society, troupe.
4 *He spoke to the assembled company.* assembly, audience, congregation, crowd, gathering, group, mob, throng, troop.
5 *an insurance company.* business, concern, corporation, establishment, firm, institution, organisation.

compare *verb*
1 *He compared the two plans.* contrast, juxtapose, weigh up.
2 *He compared the human body to a machine.* liken.

a
b
c
d
e
f
g
h
i
j
k
l
m
n
o
p
q
r
s
t
u
v
w
x
y
z

compare with *His latest book does not compare with his earlier ones.* compete with, match, rival.

comparison *noun*
1 *He made a comparison of the two schemes.* contrast, juxtaposition.
2 *There is no comparison between the two things.* analogy, likeness, parallel, resemblance, similarity.

compartment *noun*
divided into compartments. area, bay, booth, box, carrel, cubby hole, cubicle, division, niche, pigeon-hole, pocket, recess, section, slot, space, stall.

compassion *noun*
He had compassion for the injured man. concern, feeling, mercy, pity, sympathy, tenderness.
OPPOSITE indifference.

compassionate *adjective*
a compassionate judge. humane, kind-hearted, lenient, merciful, soft-hearted, sympathetic, tender-hearted, warm-hearted.
OPPOSITE hard-hearted, pitiless.

compatible *adjective*
1 *a compatible couple.* like-minded, well-matched, well-suited.
OPPOSITE incompatible.
2 *Their explanations are not compatible.* consistent, in accord, in agreement.
OPPOSITE contradictory, inconsistent.

compel *verb*
They compelled him to leave. coerce, constrain, drive, force, make, oblige, press, pressure, push, require.

compensate *verb*
The company compensated her for the loss. indemnify, make amends, make up, recompense, reimburse, repay.

compensation *noun*
She received $10,000 in compensation for the injury. compo (*Australian slang*), damages, indemnity, recompense, redress, reparation, restitution.

compère *noun*
the compère of a programme. announcer, host, master of ceremonies, MC, presenter.

compete *verb*
1 *Four teams are competing.* enter, participate, take part.
2 *The cars competed for the best position.* battle, contend, contest, fight, rival, strive, struggle, vie.

competent *adjective*
a competent worker. able, adept, capable, effective, efficient, handy, practical, proficient, qualified, skilful, skilled, trained.
OPPOSITE inept.

competition *noun*
1 *The school won the mathematics competition.* challenge, championship, contest, game, match, meet, quiz, rally, tournament.
2 *competition for export markets.* opposition, rivalry.

competitor *noun*
competitors in a race, contest, etc. candidate, challenger, contender, contestant, entrant, opponent, participant, player, rival.

compile *verb*
He is compiling the material for the book. accumulate, assemble, collate, collect, gather, organise, put together.

complacent *adjective*
You must keep striving and not allow yourself to be complacent. content, pleased with yourself, self-satisfied, smug.

complain *verb*
He complained that it was unfair. beef (*slang*), bitch (*informal*), gripe (*informal*), grizzle (*informal*), grumble, moan, object, protest, whine, whinge (*informal*).

complaint *noun*
1 *no complaints about the food.* beef (*slang*), criticism, grievance, gripe (*informal*), grizzle (*informal*), grumble, objection, protest.
2 *He suffers from a chest complaint.* affliction, ailment, disease, disorder, illness, malady, sickness.

complete *adjective*
1 *a complete jigsaw set.* entire, full, intact, total, unbroken, whole.
OPPOSITE incomplete.
2 *the complete story.* comprehensive, full, unabridged, uncut, whole.
OPPOSITE incomplete, partial.
3 *The work is now complete.* accomplished, concluded, done, ended, finished.
OPPOSITE unfinished.
4 *complete stupidity.* absolute, downright, out-and-out, outright, perfect, positive, proper, pure, sheer, thorough, total, utter.

complete *verb*
1 *He completed the work in time.* accomplish, achieve, carry out, conclude, end, finalise, finish, fulfil, round off, wind up, wrap up (*informal*).
OPPOSITE begin.
2 *Complete the form in black ink.* fill in, fill out.

completely *adverb*
completely satisfied. absolutely, altogether, entirely, fully, perfectly, quite, thoroughly, totally, utterly, wholly.

complex *adjective*
a complex structure. complicated, elaborate, intricate, involved, sophisticated.
OPPOSITE simple.

complex *noun*
She has a complex about her ears. fixation, hang-up (*informal*), obsession, preoccupation, thing (*informal*).

complexion *noun*
a healthy complexion. colour, skin, tone.

complicated *adjective*
1 *a complicated machine.* complex, elaborate, intricate, sophisticated.
OPPOSITE simple.
2 *a complicated issue.* complex, difficult, intricate, involved, knotty, messy, problematical, tricky.
OPPOSITE straightforward.

complication *noun*
Things proceeded without any complications. difficulty, hitch, obstacle, problem, setback, snag, stumbling block.

compliment *noun*
She received many compliments for her work. bouquet, commendation, congratulations, flattery, honour, praise, tribute.
OPPOSITE insult.

compliment *verb*
He complimented the students on their fine results. applaud, commend, congratulate, flatter, pay tribute to, praise.
OPPOSITE criticise, reproach.

complimentary *adjective*
1 *a complimentary review.* admiring, approving, favourable, flattering, positive.
OPPOSITE critical.
2 *a complimentary drink.* free, free of charge, on the house (*informal*).

component *noun*
Spare components are expensive. bit, constituent, element, ingredient, module, part, piece, unit.

compose *verb*
1 *The group was composed of interesting people.* constitute, form, make up.
2 *She composed a story, music, etc.* compile, concoct, construct, create, formulate, invent, make up, produce, put together, write.

composition *noun*
1 *The children wrote a composition.* article, essay, paper, story.
2 *a musical composition.* creation, opus, piece, work.
3 *the composition of the group.* constitution, make-up, structure.

compound[1] *noun*
a chemical compound. a compound of two words. alloy, amalgam, blend, combination, composite, mixture.

compound *verb*
Worry compounded her problems. add to, aggravate, complicate, exacerbate, increase, worsen.

compound[2] *noun*
The animals are kept in the compound. enclosure, pen, pound, yard.

a
b
c
d
e
f
g
h
i
j
k
l
m
n
o
p
q
r
s
t
u
v
w
x
y
z

comprehend *verb*
She did not comprehend the seriousness of the situation. appreciate, conceive, fathom, follow, grasp, perceive, realise, see, take in, understand.

comprehension *noun*
He has some comprehension of the problem. awareness, conception, grasp, insight, perception, understanding.

compress *verb*
She compressed the foam to fill the cushion. compact, condense, cram, crush, pack down, press, squash, squeeze.

comprise *verb*
The house comprises eight rooms. be made up of, consist of, contain, include.

compromise *noun*
The negotiator helped them to reach a compromise. bargain, deal, happy medium, middle course, trade-off.
compromise *verb*
They agreed to compromise. make a deal, make concessions, meet halfway, strike a bargain.

compulsory *adjective*
a compulsory suspension. mandatory, necessary, obligatory, prescribed, required, unavoidable.
OPPOSITE optional.

compute *verb*
He computed the petrol consumption for the trip. add up, calculate, reckon, total, tot up, work out.

comrade *noun*
They remained comrades throughout their lives. ally, associate, buddy (*informal*), chum (*informal*), cobber (*Australian informal*), colleague, companion, crony, fellow, friend, mate, pal (*informal*), partner.

con *verb* (*informal*)
She felt she'd been conned. cheat, deceive, have (*slang*), hoax, hoodwink, mislead, rip off (*informal*), swindle, trick.
con *noun* (*informal*)
It turned out to be a con. confidence trick, hoax, swindle, swizz (*informal*), trick.
con man (*informal*)
Don't be deceived by that con man. charlatan, cheat, confidence man, fraud, humbug, impostor, phoney (*informal*), quack, swindler, trickster.

conceal *verb*
1 He concealed the microphone. bury, camouflage, cover up, hide, obscure, plant, screen, secrete.
OPPOSITE expose.
2 She concealed her feelings. bottle up, cover up, disguise, hide, keep secret, mask, repress, suppress, withhold.
OPPOSITE reveal.

conceited *adjective*
a conceited champion. arrogant, boastful, bumptious, cocky, egotistical, haughty, immodest, proud, self-important, self-satisfied, smug, stuck-up (*informal*), swollen-headed (*informal*), vain.
OPPOSITE humble, modest.

conceive *verb*
1 The woman conceived. become pregnant.
2 He conceived a way to save the building. contrive, create, devise, dream up, envisage, hatch, imagine, plan, think up.

concentrate *verb*
concentrate on They all concentrated on the lesson. apply yourself to, be absorbed in, focus on, pay attention to, put your mind to.

concentrated *adjective*
concentrated chicken stock. condensed, intense, reduced, strong.
OPPOSITE dilute.

concept *noun*
She grasped the concept. belief, idea, notion, principle, thought.

conception *noun*
1 She was involved in the scheme from its conception. beginning, birth, creation, formulation, inception, origin, outset.
OPPOSITE termination.
2 His conception of the future was different from theirs. concept, idea, image, impression, notion, picture, understanding, vision.

concern *verb*
1 The story concerns a group of rabbits. be about, deal with, have to do with, involve, surround.

2 *The news concerns everybody.* affect, apply to, be important to, interest, matter to, relate to, touch.
3 *His disappearance concerned them.* bother, disturb, perturb, trouble, worry.

concern *noun*
1 *Their safety is his concern.* affair, business, responsibility.
2 *She showed no concern for their feelings.* attention, care, consideration, heed, interest, regard.
OPPOSITE indifference.
3 *He hasn't a concern in the world.* anxiety, burden, care, problem, trouble, worry.
4 *a going concern.* business, company, corporation, enterprise, establishment, firm, organisation.

concerned *adjective*
concerned parents. anxious, caring, distressed, interested, involved, troubled, uneasy, worried.
OPPOSITE unconcerned.

concerning *preposition*
a discussion concerning school uniform. about, regarding, relating to.

concert *noun*
The group gave a free concert. gig (*informal*), performance, recital, show.

concession *noun*
travel concessions. discount, privilege, reduction, right.

concise *adjective*
a concise description. brief, compact, condensed, pithy, short, succinct, summary, terse.
OPPOSITE wordy.

conclude *verb*
1 *The service concluded with the blessing.* cease, close, come to an end, end, finish, stop, terminate.
OPPOSITE begin, start.
2 *He concluded the interview.* bring to an end, close, complete, end, finish, round off, stop, terminate, wind up.
OPPOSITE begin, start.
3 *She concluded that something had gone wrong.* decide, deduce, gather, infer, judge, reason.

conclusion *noun*
1 *the conclusion of the show.* close, completion, end, ending, finish, termination.
OPPOSITE start.
2 *The researcher announced his conclusions.* decision, deduction, finding, judgement, verdict.

condemn *verb*
1 *She condemned them for their destructive behaviour.* blame, censure, criticise, denounce, disapprove of, rebuke.
OPPOSITE praise.
2 *The judge condemned him.* convict, declare guilty, sentence.
OPPOSITE acquit.

condense *verb*
1 *He condensed the pan juices to make a sauce.* boil down, concentrate, reduce, thicken.
2 *He condensed his speech.* abbreviate, abridge, compress, cut, reduce, shorten.
OPPOSITE lengthen.

condition *noun*
1 *He sold the car in good condition.* order, repair, shape, state.
2 *The runner was in fine condition.* fettle, fitness, form, health, shape.
3 *She has a heart condition.* affliction, ailment, complaint, disease, disorder, illness, malady, problem.
4 *The contract specified certain conditions.* prerequisite, provision, proviso, qualification, requirement, stipulation, term.

condition *verb*
He was conditioned to respond to the bell. accustom, teach, train.

conditions *plural noun*
Working conditions are good. circumstances, environment, situation, surroundings.

condone *verb*
They cannot condone stealing. disregard, forgive, ignore, overlook, tolerate, turn a blind eye to.

conduct *verb*
1 *She conducted them to their seats.* direct, escort, guide, lead, pilot, show, steer, take, usher.
2 *She conducted the meeting.* be in charge of, chair, direct, lead, preside over.

a
b
c
d
e
f
g
h
i
j
k
l
m
n
o
p
q
r
s
t
u
v
w
x
y
z

3 *He conducts the business from home.* administer, carry on, control, direct, manage, operate, run.

conduct *noun*
an award for good conduct. actions, behaviour, deportment, manners.

conduct yourself *He knew how to conduct himself in public.* act, behave.

conductor *noun*
orchestral conductor. director, maestro.

conference *noun*
the annual dental conference. assembly, congress, convention, forum, gathering, meeting, symposium.

confess *verb*
He confessed that he had smashed the window. acknowledge, admit, declare, disclose, own up.
OPPOSITE conceal, deny.

confide *verb*
She confided her secret to her friend. confess, disclose, divulge, tell, trust.

confidence *noun*
1 *He has confidence in his staff.* belief, faith, reliance, trust.
OPPOSITE mistrust.
2 *She went into the exam with confidence.* boldness, coolness, courage, self-assurance, self-confidence, self-reliance.
3 *She said it with such confidence.* assurance, authority, certainty, conviction.
OPPOSITE uncertainty.
confidence trick see CON.

confident *adjective*
1 *They were confident about the outcome.* certain, positive, sure.
OPPOSITE unsure.
2 *a confident player.* bold, daring, fearless, self-assured, self-confident.
OPPOSITE diffident.

confidential *adjective*
The information is confidential. classified, hush-hush (*informal*), intimate, personal, private, secret.
OPPOSITE public.

confine *verb*
1 *The problem was confined to a small area.* keep, limit, restrict.
2 *The animals are confined in cages.* box in, coop up, enclose, imprison, intern, jail, keep, pen, shut in, shut up.
OPPOSITE let loose.

confirm *verb*
Others confirmed what the boy said. attest to, back up, bear out, corroborate, establish, prove, reinforce, substantiate, support, validate, verify, witness to.
OPPOSITE contradict, disprove.

confiscate *verb*
She confiscated the comics. impound, seize, take away.

conflict *noun*
1 *Lives were lost in the conflict.* action, battle, clash, combat, encounter, fight, fray, strife, struggle, war.
2 *a conflict of interests.* clash, difference, divergence.
OPPOSITE harmony.
3 *Their different beliefs caused conflict.* antagonism, confrontation, disagreement, discord, friction, hostility, opposition, strife.
conflict *verb*
His story conflicts with theirs. be at odds, be incompatible, clash, contradict, disagree, diverge.
OPPOSITE agree.

conform *verb*
She refuses to conform. comply, toe the line (*informal*).
OPPOSITE rebel.
conform to
1 *He won't conform to the rules.* abide by, comply with, follow, keep to, obey, submit to.
OPPOSITE disobey.
2 *It does not conform to the standard measurements.* coincide with, comply with, correspond to, fit, match.
OPPOSITE differ from.

confront *verb*
1 *They confronted many problems.* encounter, face, meet.
2 *He confronted his rival.* brave, challenge, defy, face up to, oppose, stand up to.
OPPOSITE avoid.

confuse *verb*
1 *He confused the socks in the drawer.* jumble, mix up, muddle, scramble.
OPPOSITE sort out.
2 *The changes confused her.* baffle, bewilder, confound, disconcert,

disorientate, fluster, mislead, mix up, mystify, nonplus, perplex, puzzle, rattle (*informal*).
3 *She confused her with someone else.* mistake, mix up, muddle.
OPPOSITE distinguish.

confused *adjective*
1 *The man was confused.* baffled, bewildered, bushed (*Australian informal*), disoriented, flustered, hazy, mixed-up, muddled, perplexed.
2 *a confused account.* chaotic, disorganised, garbled, higgledy-piggledy, incoherent, jumbled, messy, muddled, topsy-turvy, unclear.
OPPOSITE clear.

confusion *noun*
1 *a scene of confusion.* anarchy, bedlam, chaos, commotion, disorder, disorganisation, havoc, jumble, mayhem, mess, muddle, pandemonium, riot, shambles, tumult, turmoil, upheaval, uproar.
OPPOSITE order.
2 *Labels will eliminate confusion.* misunderstanding, mix-up, muddle.

congeal *adjective*
The sauce congealed on the plate. coagulate, set, solidify, thicken.

congested *adjective*
1 *The roads were congested.* blocked, chock-a-block, choked, crowded, jammed, overcrowded, packed.
OPPOSITE empty.
2 *Her nose was congested.* blocked, clogged up, stuffed up.
OPPOSITE clear.

congratulate *verb*
He congratulated the winner. applaud, commend, compliment, praise.

congratulations *plural noun*
Congratulations on your birthday. compliments, felicitations, good wishes, greetings.

congregate *verb*
The people congregated at the entrance. assemble, cluster, collect, converge, crowd, flock, gather, group, herd, huddle, mass, meet, muster, rally, swarm, throng.
OPPOSITE disperse.

congregation *noun*
The minister spoke to his congregation. flock, parishioners.

congress *noun*
attend a congress. assembly, conference, convention, council, gathering, meeting, symposium.

conjuring *noun*
a performer skilled at conjuring. legerdemain, magic, sleight of hand, tricks.

conjuror *noun*
illusionist, magician.

connect *verb*
1 *She connected the ends.* attach, couple, fasten, hitch, join, link, secure, tie, unite.
OPPOSITE disconnect.
2 *He connected the two ideas.* associate, correlate, link, relate.
OPPOSITE separate.

connection *noun*
1 *a faulty connection.* bond, hook-up, join, joint, junction, link.
2 *a connection between the two events.* association, correlation, correspondence, interconnection, link, relationship, tie-up.

conquer *verb*
1 *They conquered the enemy.* beat, crush, defeat, get the better of, lick (*informal*), overcome, overpower, overthrow, rout, stonker (*Australian slang*), subdue, thrash, triumph over, trounce, vanquish.
OPPOSITE surrender to.
2 *She conquered her disability.* overcome, rise above, surmount.
OPPOSITE give in to.

conqueror *noun*
champion, vanquisher, victor, winner.
OPPOSITE loser.

conquest *noun*
the conquest of a country. annexation, capture, defeat, invasion, occupation, takeover.
OPPOSITE surrender.

conscience *noun*
You must vote according to your conscience. ethics, morals, principles, scruples.

a
b
c
d
e
f
g
h
i
j
k
l
m
n
o
p
q
r
s
t
u
v
w
x
y
z

conscientious *adjective*
a conscientious worker. careful, dedicated, diligent, dutiful, hard-working, honest, meticulous, painstaking, particular, responsible, rigorous, scrupulous, thorough.
OPPOSITE careless.

conscious *adjective*
1 *The patient was conscious.* alert, awake, aware.
OPPOSITE unconscious.
2 *a conscious insult.* calculated, deliberate, intended, intentional, premeditated.
OPPOSITE unintentional.

conscript *verb*
He was conscripted to serve in Vietnam. call up, draft (*American*).
OPPOSITE volunteer.

consecutive *adjective*
five consecutive wins. in a row, straight, successive, uninterrupted.

consensus *noun*
a consensus of opinion. agreement, harmony, unanimity.
OPPOSITE divergence.

consent *verb*
consent to *They consented to his marrying their daughter.* agree to, allow, approve, authorise, permit.
OPPOSITE refuse.
consent *noun*
He signed the form to give his consent. acceptance, agreement, approval, assent, authorisation, endorsement, go-ahead, leave, OK (*informal*), permission, sanction.
OPPOSITE refusal.

consequence *noun*
1 *The consequences of his mistake were felt for a long time.* aftermath, effect, outcome, ramification, repercussion, result, sequel, upshot.
OPPOSITE cause.
2 *The matter is of no consequence.* account, gravity, importance, moment, seriousness, significance.
OPPOSITE unimportance.

consequently *adverb*
accordingly, as a result, hence, so, therefore, thus.

conservation *noun*
conservation of the environment. maintenance, preservation, protection, safe keeping, saving.
OPPOSITE destruction.

conservationist *noun*
environmentalist, green (*informal*), greenie (*Australian informal*).

conservative *adjective*
1 *a conservative attitude.* conventional, old-fashioned, orthodox, reactionary, traditional.
OPPOSITE progressive.
2 *a conservative estimate.* cautious, low, moderate.
OPPOSITE excessive.

conservatory *noun*
a tropical conservatory. glasshouse, greenhouse, hothouse.

conserve *verb*
They tried to conserve their supplies. hold on to, keep, maintain, preserve, save.
OPPOSITE waste.
conserve *noun*
apricot conserve. jam, jelly, preserve.

consider *verb*
1 *They considered the merits of the case.* contemplate, deliberate over, examine, look at, meditate on, mull over, ponder, reflect on, study, think about, weigh.
2 *You must consider people's feelings.* allow for, bear in mind, pay heed to, respect, take into account.
OPPOSITE disregard.
3 *She considered herself lucky.* believe, deem, judge, reckon, regard, think.

considerable *adjective*
a considerable amount. appreciable, big, extensive, fair, goodly, large, noticeable, significant, sizeable, substantial, tidy (*informal*).
OPPOSITE slight.

considerate *adjective*
A considerate guest helps the host. attentive, helpful, kind, neighbourly, obliging, polite, sensitive, thoughtful,

unselfish.
OPPOSITE inconsiderate, thoughtless.

consist *verb*
consist of *The flat consists of three rooms.*
be composed of, comprise, contain,
include.

consistency *noun*
the consistency of whipped cream. density,
firmness, solidity, stiffness, texture,
thickness.

consistent *adjective*
1 *The quality is consistent.* constant,
dependable, invariable, reliable, stable,
steady, unchanging, uniform.
OPPOSITE variable.
2 *Her version was consistent with his.*
compatible, corresponding, in
accordance, in agreement, in keeping.
OPPOSITE inconsistent.

console *verb*
He consoled the losers with a small gift.
cheer, comfort, encourage, relieve,
soothe.
OPPOSITE upset.

conspicuous *adjective*
1 *a conspicuous building.* impressive,
noticeable, obtrusive, obvious,
ostentatious, prominent, showy,
striking, visible.
OPPOSITE inconspicuous.
2 *conspicuous bravery.* distinguished,
notable, outstanding, remarkable.

conspiracy *noun*
a conspiracy to blow up the building.
intrigue, plot, scheme.

conspire *verb*
*They conspired to overthrow the
government.* collaborate, collude,
connive, intrigue, plot, scheme.

constable *noun*
see POLICE OFFICER (at POLICE).

constant *adjective*
1 *constant problems.* ceaseless, chronic,
continual, continuous, endless,
everlasting, incessant, never-ending,
perennial, permanent, perpetual,
persistent, regular, repeated, unending.
OPPOSITE occasional.

2 *a constant friend.* dependable, devoted,
faithful, firm, loyal, reliable, steadfast,
true, trustworthy.
OPPOSITE fickle.
3 *a constant speed.* even, fixed,
invariable, level, stable, steady,
unchanging, uniform, unvarying.
OPPOSITE variable.

constituent *noun*
*He analysed the substance into its
constituents.* component, element,
ingredient, material, part, unit.

constitute *verb*
Twelve months constitute a year.
compose, form, make up.

constitution *noun*
1 *a society's constitution.* charter, laws,
principles, rules.
2 *She has a strong constitution.* health,
physique.

constrict *verb*
Her shoes constrict her feet painfully.
compress, cramp, pinch, squeeze.

construct *verb*
The builders constructed the house.
assemble, build, erect, fabricate, form,
make, manufacture, produce, put
together.
OPPOSITE demolish, destroy.

construction *noun*
a concrete construction. building, edifice,
structure.

constructive *adjective*
constructive criticism. beneficial, helpful,
positive, practical, productive, useful,
valuable.
OPPOSITE destructive.

consult *verb*
He consulted his lawyer. confer with,
discuss with, refer to, speak to, talk
with.

consultant *noun*
a financial consultant. adviser, expert,
specialist.

consultation *noun*
*The members held a consultation over the
matter.* conference, discussion, hearing,
interview, meeting, talk.

a
b
c
d
e
f
g
h
i
j
k
l
m
n
o
p
q
r
s
t
u
v
w
x
y
z

consume *verb*
1 *He consumed all their supper.* devour, eat up, gobble up, guzzle, knock back, swallow.
2 *Fire consumed the building.* burn, demolish, destroy, devastate, gut.
3 *Their supplies were consumed in no time.* drain, exhaust, use up, utilise.

consumer *noun*
buyer, client, customer, patron, purchaser, user.

consumption *noun*
petrol consumption. use, utilisation.

contact *noun*
1 *The two surfaces must be in contact.* connection, touch.
2 *There is no contact between the two groups.* communication, liaison.
contact *verb*
He tried to contact his friend. communicate with, correspond with, get in touch with, reach, speak to, talk to.

contagious *adjective*
a contagious disease. catching, communicable, infectious.

contain *verb*
1 *The box contains jewels.* enclose, hold, house.
2 *The cake contains butter and eggs.* be composed of, consist of, include, incorporate.

container *noun*
holder, receptacle, vessel; [*various containers*] bag, barrel, basket, bin, bottle, box, bucket, caddy, can, canister, carton, cartridge, case, cask, casket, chest, crate, cup, dish, drum, jar, keg, packet, pot, pouch, punnet, sachet, sack, skip, tank, tin, trunk, tub, vat.

contaminate *verb*
The water was contaminated by the chemicals. adulterate, foul, infect, poison, pollute, spoil, taint.
OPPOSITE purify.

contemplate *verb*
1 *He contemplated the scene.* eye, gaze at, look at, observe, regard, stare at, study, survey, view, watch.

2 *She contemplated her next step.* consider, deliberate over, meditate on, ponder, reflect on, think over.
3 *He did not contemplate marriage.* have in mind, intend, plan.

contemporary *adjective*
contemporary designs. current, latest, modern, new, present-day, recent, trendy (*informal*), up-to-date, up-to-the-minute.
OPPOSITE old-fashioned.

contempt *noun*
He treated the visitor with contempt. disdain, disgust, dislike, disrespect, hatred, loathing, scorn.
OPPOSITE respect.

contemptible *adjective*
a contemptible scoundrel. abominable, base, dastardly, despicable, detestable, hateful, loathsome, low, mean, miserable, odious, pitiful, shameful, vile, worthless.
OPPOSITE honourable.

contemptuous *adjective*
She gave the others a contemptuous look. disdainful, haughty, insolent, scornful, sneering, snooty (*informal*), supercilious.
OPPOSITE respectful.

contend *verb*
1 *Two teams contended for the trophy.* battle, clash, compete, contest, fight, strive, struggle, vie.
2 *He contends that he is innocent.* allege, argue, assert, claim, declare, insist, maintain.
contend with *He has to contend with many problems.* cope with, deal with, face, grapple with, tackle.

content¹ *adjective*
She is content with very little. contented, fulfilled, gratified, happy, pleased, satisfied.
OPPOSITE discontented.
content *verb*
Nothing seems to content him. gratify, please, satisfy.

content² *noun*
The essay is marked on form and content. gist, material, matter, substance.

contents *plural noun*
components, constituents, content, elements, ingredients, parts.

contest *noun*
a close contest. battle, bout, championship, combat, competition, conflict, duel, fight, game, match, race, rally, struggle, tournament.
contest *verb*
1 *Five people contested the seat.* battle for, compete for, contend for, fight for, struggle for, vie for.
2 *He will contest the point.* argue, challenge, debate, dispute, question.
OPPOSITE accept.

contestant *noun*
candidate, challenger, competitor, contender, entrant, opponent, participant, player, rival.

context *noun*
seen in its social context. background, circumstances, environment, setting, situation, surroundings.

continual *adjective*
their continual arguments. constant, endless, everlasting, frequent, habitual, incessant, perpetual, recurrent, regular, repeated.
OPPOSITE occasional.

continuation *noun*
the continuation of the story. extension, resumption, sequel, supplement.

continue *verb*
1 *They continued with the treatment.* carry on, keep going, keep on, persevere, persist, proceed.
OPPOSITE discontinue, stop.
2 *He continued as captain.* keep on, remain, stay, survive.
3 *The dry weather continued.* endure, go on, hold, last, persist.
OPPOSITE cease.
4 *They continued the story after the break.* pick up, recommence, resume, take up.
OPPOSITE break off.
5 *They continued the contract.* extend, maintain, prolong, protract, renew.
OPPOSITE terminate.

continuous *adjective*
1 *a continuous line.* connected, unbroken.
OPPOSITE broken.

2 *continuous rain.* ceaseless, constant, endless, everlasting, incessant, interminable, never-ending, non-stop, permanent, perpetual, persistent, relentless, solid, steady, unceasing, uninterrupted, unrelieved.
OPPOSITE intermittent.

contour *noun*
the contours of her body. form, lines, outline, profile, shape.

contract *noun*
They signed the contract. agreement, bargain, bond, charter, covenant, deal, deed, pact, policy, treaty, undertaking.
contract *verb*
1 *The metal contracted as it cooled.* become smaller, shrink.
OPPOSITE expand.
2 *The muscle contracted.* tense, tighten.
OPPOSITE relax.
3 *She contracted to do the work at home.* agree, arrange, negotiate, undertake.
4 *He contracted bronchitis.* acquire, catch, come down with, develop, get, pick up.

contradict *verb*
She contradicted what he said. counter, deny, oppose.
OPPOSITE agree with, back up.

contradictory *adjective*
contradictory explanations. conflicting, incompatible, inconsistent, opposing.
OPPOSITE consistent.

contraption *noun* (*informal*)
He invented a new kitchen contraption. apparatus, appliance, device, gadget, gizmo (*informal*), implement, machine, tool.

contrary *adjective*
1 *the contrary view.* conflicting, contradictory, converse, opposite.
OPPOSITE same.
2 *a contrary child.* defiant, disobedient, headstrong, intractable, obstinate, perverse, pigheaded, rebellious, recalcitrant, stroppy (*informal*), stubborn, unreasonable, wayward, wilful.
OPPOSITE biddable.
contrary *noun*
The contrary is true. antithesis, converse, opposite, reverse.

a
b
c
d
e
f
g
h
i
j
k
l
m
n
o
p
q
r
s
t
u
v
w
x
y
z

contrast *noun*
1 *a contrast of the two poems.* comparison.
2 *a marked contrast in their attitudes.*
difference, dissimilarity, distinction.
OPPOSITE similarity.

contrast *verb*
1 *He contrasted their styles.* compare,
differentiate, distinguish, set against
each other.
2 *Her ideas contrasted with theirs.* differ
(from), disagree.
OPPOSITE resemble.

contribute *verb*
*Everyone contributed money for the
present.* chip in (*informal*), donate, give,
pitch in (*informal*), provide, put in,
subscribe, supply.
contribute to *Good teaching contributed to
his success.* have a hand in, play a part
in.

contribution *noun*
a financial contribution. donation, gift,
grant, handout, help, offering,
offertory, subscription.

contrive *verb*
He contrived a meeting between them.
arrange, engineer, manage, plan, plot,
scheme, wangle (*slang*).

control *noun*
1 *He has control of his class. The company
is under overseas control.* authority,
charge, command, direction,
domination, influence, jurisdiction,
leadership, management, mastery,
power, rule, supervision, sway.
2 *the machine's controls.* button, dial,
instrument, joystick, knob, lever,
switch.

control *verb*
1 *She controls the organisation.*
administer, command, direct,
dominate, govern, head, lead, manage,
oversee, preside over, rule, supervise.
2 *He controls the machine.* handle,
manage, manipulate, operate, regulate.
3 *He could not control his temper.* bridle,
check, contain, curb, hold back, master,
repress, restrain, subdue.
OPPOSITE unleash.

controversial *adjective*
a controversial subject. contentious,
debatable, disputable, moot.

controversy *noun*
His actions sparked off a controversy.
argument, debate, dispute, quarrel, row
(*informal*), wrangle.

convenient *adjective*
1 *a convenient arrangement.* handy,
helpful, practical, suitable, timely,
useful, well-timed.
OPPOSITE inconvenient.
2 *a convenient set of shops.* accessible,
handy.
OPPOSITE inaccessible.

convent *noun*
The nuns live in a convent. abbey,
cloister, nunnery, priory, religious
community.

convention *noun*
1 *She attended the annual convention.*
assembly, conference, congress,
gathering, jamboree, meeting, rally.
2 *He did not follow conventions.* custom,
etiquette, formality, rule, tradition.

conventional *adjective*
conventional methods. accepted,
accustomed, customary, established,
mainstream, normal, ordinary,
orthodox, regular, standard, traditional,
usual.
OPPOSITE unconventional.

converge *verb*
Five roads converge at the roundabout.
come together, intersect, join, meet,
merge.
OPPOSITE diverge, radiate.

conversation *noun*
chat, chatter, chinwag (*informal*),
dialogue, discussion, gossip, natter
(*informal*), talk, yak (*informal*).

convert *verb*
He converted the sofa into a bed. adapt,
change, modify, transform, turn.

convey *verb*
1 *The truck conveys supplies.* bear, bring,
carry, deliver, haul, take, transfer,
transport.
2 *The wires convey electricity.* carry,
conduct, transmit.
3 *The writer conveyed his message clearly.*
communicate, impart, make known,
put across, tell.

convict *verb*
She was convicted of the crime. condemn,
declare guilty.
OPPOSITE acquit.
convict *noun*
The convicts were transported to Australia.
criminal, felon, lag (*slang*), prisoner.

conviction *noun*
1 She spoke with conviction. assurance,
certainty, confidence, earnestness,
fervour.
OPPOSITE doubt.
2 They do not share the same convictions.
belief, creed, faith, opinion, view.

convince *verb*
She convinced the others that she was right.
assure, persuade, prove to, satisfy, win
over.

convoy *noun*
a convoy of ships. armada, company,
fleet, flotilla, group.

convulsion *noun*
The child had a fever with convulsions. fit,
paroxysm, seizure, spasm.

cook *verb*
cook the dinner. make, prepare, put
together; [*various ways to cook*] bake,
barbecue, boil, braise, broil, casserole,
fry, grill, parboil, poach, roast, sauté,
simmer, steam, stew, toast.
cook *noun*
He works as a cook. chef.

cookery *noun*
cooking, cuisine.

cool *adjective*
1 cool weather. chilly, cold, nippy
(*informal*).
OPPOSITE warm.
2 She remains cool in a crisis. calm,
collected, composed, laid-back
(*informal*), level-headed, nonchalant,
relaxed, sedate, self-possessed, serene,
unemotional, unexcited, unflappable
(*informal*), unflustered.
OPPOSITE excited.
3 She received a cool reception. cold,
frosty, half-hearted, hostile, icy,
lukewarm, unenthusiastic, unfriendly,
unwelcoming.
OPPOSITE friendly, warm.

4 (*informal*) The party was cool. She tries to
look cool. see EXCELLENT, TRENDY.
cool *noun* (*informal*)
He lost his cool. calmness, composure,
self-control.
cool *verb*
He cooled the drinks. chill, freeze,
refrigerate.
OPPOSITE heat, warm.

coop *noun*
a chicken coop. cage, enclosure, pen.
coop *verb*
coop up He was cooped up in his room.
box in, cage in, confine, imprison, keep,
pen in, shut up.

cooperate *verb*
The people cooperated with the police.
collaborate, join forces, pull together,
work together; see also HELP.

cooperation *noun*
The biography was written with his
cooperation. assistance, collaboration,
contribution, help, involvement,
participation, support, teamwork.

cooperative *adjective*
a cooperative person. accommodating,
helpful, obliging, willing.
OPPOSITE uncooperative.

coordinate *verb*
The leader coordinates the work of the
various groups. integrate, orchestrate,
organise, synchronise.

coordinator *noun*
a project coordinator. controller, director,
manager, organiser.

cope *verb*
cope with He copes with all sorts of
problems. contend with, deal with,
endure, face, handle, manage,
withstand.

copy *noun*
He could not distinguish the copy from the
original. carbon copy, counterfeit,
double, duplicate, facsimile, fake,
forgery, imitation, likeness, photocopy,
print, replica, reproduction, twin.
OPPOSITE original.
copy *verb*
1 He copied the document. duplicate,
forge, photocopy, print, reproduce.

a
b
c
d
e
f
g
h
i
j
k
l
m
n
o
p
q
r
s
t
u
v
w
x
y
z

2 *The student copied his friend's essay.*
crib, plagiarise.
3 *The actor copies people's mannerisms.*
ape, imitate, mimic, parody, take off
(*informal*).

cord *noun*
tied with cord. cable, lace, line, rope,
string, twine.

core *noun*
1 *the core of an object.* centre, heart,
inside, middle.
2 *the core of the problem.* centre, crux,
essence, gist, heart, nitty-gritty
(*informal*), nucleus.

cork *noun*
He closed the cask with a cork. bung, plug,
stopper.

corkscrew *noun*
The road into the valley was a corkscrew.
helix, spiral.

corner *noun*
1 *the corners of a room.* angle.
2 *The car approached the corner.* bend,
crossroads, curve, intersection, junction,
turn.

corner *verb*
They cornered him in the shop. bail up
(*Australian*), buttonhole, capture, catch,
trap.

corny *adjective*
a corny joke. feeble, hackneyed,
outworn, trite, weak.

coronation *noun*
crowning, enthronement.

corporation *noun*
1 *a business corporation.* company, firm,
organisation.
2 *a municipal corporation.* council.

corpse *noun*
The corpse was buried. body, carcass,
remains.

correct *adjective*
1 *His answer was correct.* accurate, exact,
faultless, flawless, perfect, precise,
proper, right, spot on (*informal*), true.
OPPOSITE incorrect, wrong.
2 *correct behaviour.* acceptable,
appropriate, conventional, decent,
decorous, fitting, impeccable, proper,

right, seemly, suitable.
OPPOSITE improper.

correct *verb*
1 *The fault can be corrected.* cure, fix,
mend, put right, rectify, remedy, repair.
2 *He corrected the draft.* adjust, alter,
amend, improve, revise.
3 *The teacher corrected their work.* assess,
check, mark.
4 *She was always correcting her child.*
admonish, censure, chasten, chastise,
discipline, rebuke, reprimand, reprove,
scold.

correspond *verb*
1 *This information corresponds with what
I'd previously heard.* accord, agree, be
consistent, coincide, conform, fit,
match, square, tally.
OPPOSITE disagree.
2 *They corresponded regularly.*
communicate, exchange letters, keep in
touch, send letters, write.

correspondence *noun*
She answers her correspondence promptly.
communications, letters, mail,
messages.

correspondent *noun*
the newspaper's European correspondent.
journalist, reporter, writer.

corresponding *adjective*
corresponding positions. analogous,
equivalent, like, matching, parallel,
similar.

corridor *noun*
hall, hallway, lobby, passage,
passageway.

corrode *verb*
The car was corroded by rust. consume,
destroy, eat away, erode, oxidise, rot,
rust, wear away.

corrugated *adjective*
corrugated cardboard. furrowed, grooved,
ribbed, ridged, wrinkled.
OPPOSITE flat.

corrupt *adjective*
1 *a corrupt official.* bent (*slang*), crooked,
dishonest, shady, shonky (*Australian
informal*), unscrupulous.
OPPOSITE honest.

2 *leading a corrupt life.* degenerate, depraved, evil, immoral, iniquitous, perverted, sinful, wicked.
OPPOSITE moral.
corrupt *verb*
He tried to corrupt the official. bribe, buy off, influence, lead astray, pervert, tempt.

corruption *noun*
police corruption. moral corruption. bribery, degeneracy, depravity, dishonesty, fraud, graft, immorality, perversion, sinfulness, unscrupulousness, vice, wickedness.
OPPOSITE honesty, morality.

cosmetics *plural noun*
beauty products, make-up.

cost *noun*
He cannot meet the cost. charge, expense, fare, fee, outlay, overheads, payment, price, rate, tariff, toll.
cost *verb*
The book costs $30. be priced at, be worth, sell for.

costly *adjective*
costly presents. dear, exorbitant, expensive, precious, pricey (*informal*), valuable.
OPPOSITE cheap.

costume *noun*
1 *ceremonial costume.* apparel (*formal*), attire (*formal*), clothes, clothing, dress, garb, garments, gear (*informal*), outfit, raiment, regalia, uniform, vestments.
2 *a swimming costume.* suit.

cosy *adjective*
a cosy house. comfortable, comfy (*informal*), friendly, homely, relaxing, secure, snug, warm.
OPPOSITE uncomfortable.

cot *noun*
cradle, crib.

cottage *noun*
cabin, chalet, hut, lodge, shack, weekender (*Australian*); see also HOUSE.

cotton *noun*
thread, yarn.

couch *noun*
He reclined on the couch. chaise longue, chesterfield, divan, settee, sofa.

council *noun*
1 *school council. council of elders.* assembly, board, committee, conference, congress, synod.
2 *a municipal council.* corporation.

counsellor *noun*
a careers counsellor. adviser, guide, mentor.

count[1] *verb*
1 *She counted her blessings.* add up, calculate, enumerate, number, sum up, tally, total, tot up (*informal*).
2 *He did not count the visitors in his calculations.* consider, include, reckon with, take into account.
OPPOSITE exclude.
3 *Looks don't count.* be important, carry weight, matter, rate highly, signify.
count *noun*
1 *an official count.* census, poll, stocktaking.
2 *The final count was 500.* amount, figure, number, reckoning, tally, total.
3 *He was found guilty on four counts.* charge, point.
count on *She counted on their support.* assume, bank on, depend on, expect, reckon on, rely on.

count[2] *noun*
see NOBLEMAN.

counter[1] *noun*
1 *a shop counter.* bar, checkout, stand.
2 *The game uses counters.* disc, piece, token.

counter[2] *verb*
She countered his statement with the facts. contradict, negate, oppose, rebut.

counterfeit *adjective*
a counterfeit note. bogus, dud (*informal*), fake, forged, imitation, phoney (*informal*), sham.
OPPOSITE genuine.
counterfeit *verb*
They counterfeited $50 notes. copy, fake, forge, imitate, reproduce.

countess *noun*
see NOBLEWOMAN.

a
b
c
d
e
f
g
h
i
j
k
l
m
n
o
p
q
r
s
t
u
v
w
x
y
z

countless *adjective*
It happened on countless occasions.
endless, frequent, innumerable, many,
numerous.
OPPOSITE few.

country *noun*
1 *He rules the country.* commonwealth,
democracy, duchy, emirate, kingdom,
land, monarchy, nation, principality,
realm, republic, state, territory.
2 *Forty per cent of the country voted for
him.* citizens, community, inhabitants,
nation, people, populace, population,
public.
3 *They left the city to live in the country.*
backblocks (*Australian*), backwoods,
bush (*Australian*), inland, interior,
outback (*Australian*), rural district,
sticks (*informal*).
OPPOSITE city, town.
4 *rugged country.* countryside, land,
landscape, region, scenery, terrain,
territory.
country *adjective*
country life. agricultural, farming,
pastoral, provincial, rural, rustic.
OPPOSITE urban.

countryman, countrywoman *noun*
1 *The countryman rarely visits the city.*
bushie (*Australian informal*), farmer.
OPPOSITE city-dweller.
2 *a fellow countryman.* compatriot.

couple *noun*
1 *a couple of birds.* brace, pair.
2 *They toasted the happy couple.* duo, pair,
twosome.
couple *verb*
He coupled the cars together. connect,
hitch, join, link, tie, yoke.

coupon *noun*
*She sent in the coupons to collect the
refund.* entry form, form, ticket, token,
voucher.

courage *noun*
The policeman showed great courage.
boldness, bravery, daring,
determination, fearlessness, fortitude,
gallantry, grit, guts (*informal*), heroism,
mettle, nerve, pluck, prowess, spirit,
spunk (*informal*), valour.
OPPOSITE cowardice.

courageous *adjective*
bold, brave, daring, dauntless,
determined, fearless, gallant, game,
heroic, intrepid, lion-hearted, plucky,
resolute, spirited, stoical, stout-hearted,
unafraid, valiant.
OPPOSITE cowardly.

course *noun*
1 *The spacecraft was on course.* direction,
line, orbit, path, route, track.
2 *a language course.* classes, curriculum,
lessons, programme.
3 *a course of blood transfusions.* sequence,
series.
4 *The cars tested out the course.* circuit,
racecourse, track.
of course certainly, naturally,
obviously.

court *noun*
1 *the royal court.* attendants, courtiers
(*old use*), entourage, household, retinue,
train.
2 *He was summoned to appear before the
court.* bar, bench, lawcourt, tribunal.
court *verb*
*He courted the lady for two years before
proposing.* date (*informal*), go out with,
woo (*old use*).

courteous *adjective*
chivalrous, civil, considerate,
diplomatic, gallant, gracious, polite,
proper, respectful, tactful, thoughtful,
well-behaved, well-bred, well-
mannered.
OPPOSITE discourteous, rude.

courtesy *noun*
She treats people with courtesy. chivalry,
civility, consideration, deference,
diplomacy, good manners, politeness,
respect, tact, thoughtfulness.
OPPOSITE discourtesy, rudeness.

courtyard *noun*
court, forecourt, patio, quad (*informal*),
quadrangle, yard.

cove *noun*
The ship sheltered in the cove. bay, inlet.

cover *verb*
1 *He covered the books in plastic.* encase,
enclose, protect, shield, wrap.

2 *The body was covered with clothes.*
clothe, drape, dress, swaddle, swathe, wrap.
3 *She covered the wound with gauze.*
bandage, bind, dress.
OPPOSITE expose.
4 *The hills are covered in mist.* blot out, camouflage, cloak, conceal, envelop, hide, mask, obscure, screen, shroud, surround, veil.
5 *His shoes are covered with mud.* cake, coat, encrust, plaster, smear, spread.
6 *The forest covers a large area.* extend over, occupy, span, stretch over, take up.
7 *They covered five kilometres in an hour.* travel, traverse.
8 *The report covers the main issues.* deal with, include, survey, take in.
OPPOSITE exclude.

cover *noun*
1 *a protective cover.* armour, canopy, cap, case, casing, coating, cocoon, covering, hood, housing, lid, mantle, mask, outside, overlay, roof, screen, sheath, shell, shield, shroud, skin, sleeve, slip, surface, top, veneer, wrapping.
2 *a cover for a book.* binding, jacket, wrapper.
3 *a cover for papers.* binder, envelope, file, folder, portfolio.
4 *He ran for cover.* hiding place, protection, refuge, sanctuary, shelter.
cover up *He tried to cover up the truth.* bury, conceal, hide, hush up, suppress, whitewash.
OPPOSITE expose.

covet *verb*
She coveted his car. crave, desire, fancy, hanker after, long for, want.

coward *noun*
He was a coward in the face of danger. chicken (*informal*), cry-baby, scaredy-cat (*informal*), sissy, sook (*Australian informal*), wimp (*informal*).
OPPOSITE hero.

cowardly *adjective*
It was cowardly to run away. chicken-hearted, dastardly, faint-hearted, fearful, gutless (*informal*), pusillanimous, spineless, timid, timorous, yellow (*informal*).
OPPOSITE brave, heroic.

coy *adjective*
She was coy with strangers. bashful, demure, diffident, modest, self-conscious, sheepish, shy, timid, underconfident.
OPPOSITE forward.

crabby *adjective*
a crabby person. bad-tempered, cantankerous, cross, crotchety, grouchy (*informal*), grumpy, irritable, peevish, snaky (*Australian informal*), sour, sullen, surly.
OPPOSITE cheerful.

crack *noun*
1 *a crack of a whip.* crackle, pop, snap.
2 *cracks in the walls, ice, etc.* break, chink, cranny, crevasse, crevice, fissure, fracture, gap, hole, hollow, opening, rift, slit, split.
3 (*informal*) *She had a crack at it.* attempt, bash (*informal*), go, stab (*informal*), try, whack (*informal*).
crack *verb*
1 *The thunder cracked.* clap, crackle, strike.
2 *The glass cracked.* break, chip, fracture, shatter, splinter, split.
3 *She cracked the code.* break, decipher, solve, work out.
4 *He finally cracked under the strain.* break down, collapse, crack up, fall apart, give way, go to pieces.

crackle *noun*
The radio show was marred by crackle. atmospherics, interference, static.

cradle *noun*
a baby's cradle. basket, bassinet, cot, crib.

craft *noun*
1 *the craft of lacemaking.* art, handicraft, skill, technique, trade.
2 *travel in a craft.* aircraft, boat, raft, ship, spacecraft, vessel.

craftsmanship *noun*
She admired the craftsmanship. artistry, handiwork, skill, workmanship.

crafty *adjective*
as crafty as a fox. artful, astute, calculating, canny, clever, cunning, deceitful, devious, knowing, shifty (*informal*), shrewd, sly, sneaky, subtle,

a
b
c
d
e
f
g
h
i
j
k
l
m
n
o
p
q
r
s
t
u
v
w
x
y
z

tricky, underhand, wily.
OPPOSITE guileless.

crag *noun*
The animal was perched on a crag. cliff,
precipice, rock, scarp.

cram *verb*
1 He crammed his clothes in the case. force,
jam, pack, push, ram, squash, squeeze,
stuff.
2 The lift was crammed with people.
crowd, fill, overfill, pack.
3 She crammed for two weeks before the
exams. revise, study, swot (*informal*).

cramp *verb*
Lack of money cramped his style. hamper,
limit, restrict, stunt, thwart.

cramped *adjective*
1 cramped living conditions. confined,
narrow, poky, tight.
OPPOSITE spacious.
2 cramped writing. crabbed, illegible,
small.

crane *noun*
A crane is used for moving heavy objects.
cherry picker, davit, derrick, hoist.
crane *verb*
She craned her neck to see. stretch.

crank *noun*
a health-food crank. eccentric, fanatic,
freak (*informal*), maniac, nut (*informal*),
weirdo (*informal*).

cranky *adjective*
1 She became cranky and impatient. bad-
tempered, crabby, cross, crotchety,
grouchy (*informal*), irritable, peevish,
snaky (*Australian informal*), surly.
OPPOSITE agreeable.
2 He has cranky ideas. bizarre, eccentric,
odd, peculiar, quirky, strange, weird.
OPPOSITE conventional.

crash *noun*
1 They heard a loud crash. bang, boom,
clang, clank, clatter, smash, wham.
2 a car crash. accident, collision, pile-up
(*informal*), prang (*slang*), smash.
3 a financial crash. collapse, failure.
crash *verb*
1 The plates crashed to the floor during the
earthquake. clatter, fall, shatter, smash,
topple, tumble.

2 The thunder crashed. bang, boom, clap,
clatter, crack, peal.
3 The car crashed into a bus. bang, bump,
knock, ram, run, slam, smash; see also
COLLIDE.
4 The plane crashed into a field. crash-
land, nosedive, plummet, plunge.

crate *noun*
a crate of bottles. box, carton, case, tea
chest.

crater *noun*
moon craters. the crater of a volcano.
cavity, hole, hollow, pit.

craving *noun*
a craving for chocolates. desire, fancy,
hankering, hunger, longing, thirst,
wish, yearning, yen.

crawl *verb*
1 She crawled under the bed. creep, move
on all fours, slither, squirm, worm your
way, wriggle, writhe.
2 The cars crawled along. edge forward,
go at a snail's pace, inch forward, move
slowly.
3 (*informal*) He was unpopular because he
crawled to the teacher. grovel, kowtow,
lick someone's boots, suck up (*informal*),
toady.

craze *noun*
Yo-yos were the latest craze. enthusiasm,
fad, fashion, mania, passion, rage, thing
(*informal*), vogue.

crazy *adjective*
1 crazy people. barmy (*slang*), batty
(*slang*), berserk, bonkers (*slang*),
crackers (*slang*), cuckoo (*informal*), daft
(*informal*), demented, deranged, flaky
(*slang*), insane, loony (*informal*), loopy
(*informal*), mad, mental (*informal*), nuts
(*informal*), nutty (*informal*), off your
head, out of your mind, potty (*informal*),
round the bend (*informal*), screwy
(*informal*), troppo (*Australian slang*),
unbalanced, unhinged, wacky (*slang*).
OPPOSITE sane.
2 a crazy plan. absurd, cock-eyed
(*informal*), crackpot (*informal*), daft
(*informal*), foolish, hare-brained, idiotic,
impractical, lunatic, mad, outrageous,
preposterous, ridiculous, senseless,

silly, stupid, unwise, unworkable, zany.
OPPOSITE sensible.
3 *crazy about tennis.* enthusiastic,
fanatical, keen, mad, nuts (*informal*),
obsessed, passionate, wild.

creak *verb*
The door creaked. screech, squeak.

cream *noun*
She applied sunburn cream. lotion,
ointment.

crease *noun*
He smoothed out the creases. crinkle,
crumple, fold, furrow, groove, line,
pucker, ridge, wrinkle.
crease *verb*
He creased the paper. crimp, crinkle,
crumple, fold, pleat, pucker, rumple,
wrinkle.
OPPOSITE smooth.

create *verb*
1 *He created a masterpiece.* bring into
being, compose, conceive, construct,
design, devise, form, invent, make,
originate, produce, think up.
2 *She created a fund to help the victims.*
establish, found, initiate, institute,
pioneer, set up.
3 *The solution created more problems.*
beget, generate, give rise to, lead to,
make, produce.

creation *noun*
*The creation of the world is described in
Genesis.* beginning, birth, formation,
foundation, genesis, invention, origin.

creative *adjective*
a creative mind. fertile, imaginative,
ingenious, inventive, original,
productive, resourceful.
OPPOSITE unimaginative.

creator *noun*
the creator of the universe. author,
designer, inventor, maker, originator.

creature *noun*
They care for all creatures. animal, beast,
being, living thing, organism.

crèche *noun*
child care centre, nursery, preschool.

credible *adjective*
Her story was credible. believable,
conceivable, plausible, reasonable.
OPPOSITE incredible.

credit *noun*
She brought credit to her family. acclaim,
esteem, glory, honour, merit, praise,
recognition, reputation.
OPPOSITE disgrace, reproach.
on credit *buy on credit.* by instalments,
on hire purchase, on the never-never
(*informal*), on the slate (*informal*), on tick
(*informal*).

creditable *adjective*
a creditable performance. admirable,
commendable, honourable,
meritorious, praiseworthy, respectable,
worthy.
OPPOSITE discreditable, shameful.

creed *noun*
regardless of colour or creed. belief(s),
conviction(s), doctrine, dogma, faith,
principles, religion.

creek *noun* (*Australian*)
The creek dries up in summer. brook,
river, rivulet, stream, tributary,
watercourse.

creep *verb*
1 *She crept under the sofa.* crawl, move
on all fours, slither, squirm, worm your
way, wriggle, writhe.
2 *He crept quietly out of the room.* edge,
inch, slink, slip, sneak, steal, tiptoe.

creepy *adjective*
a creepy film. disturbing, eerie,
frightening, hair-raising, scary, spooky
(*informal*), uncanny, weird.

crest *noun*
1 *The cockatoo has a yellow crest.* comb,
topknot, tuft.
2 *The walkers reached the crest of the hill.*
apex, brow, crown, peak, pinnacle,
summit, top.
OPPOSITE base.
3 *He designed the school crest.* badge,
emblem, insignia, symbol.

crevice *noun*
a rock crevice. cleft, crack, cranny,
fissure, gap, rift, split.

a
b
c
d
e
f
g
h
i
j
k
l
m
n
o
p
q
r
s
t
u
v
w
x
y
z

crew *noun*
1 *the ship's crew.* company, personnel, squad, staff, team, workforce.
2 *Come and join our happy crew.* band, bunch, crowd, gang, group, mob, troop.

crib *noun*
a baby's crib. cot, cradle.

crime *noun*
He was guilty of the crime. felony (*old use*), misdeed, misdemeanour, offence, wrong, wrongdoing; see also SIN.

criminal *noun*
The police caught the criminal. baddy (*informal*), convict, crim (*Australian informal*), crook (*informal*), culprit, delinquent, desperado, felon, jailbird, lawbreaker, malefactor, miscreant, offender, outlaw, transgressor, villain, wrongdoer.
criminal *adjective*
criminal behaviour. corrupt, crooked, dishonest, illegal, illicit, unlawful, wrong.
OPPOSITE legal.

cringe *verb*
The sight of the cane made him cringe. cower, crouch, draw back, flinch, quail, recoil, shrink back, wince.

crinkle *verb & noun*
see CREASE.

cripple *verb*
1 *The disease is gradually crippling him.* disable, incapacitate, lame, maim, paralyse, weaken.
2 *The strike crippled industry.* bring to a standstill, damage, hurt, immobilise, paralyse.

crippled *adjective*
a crippled person. disabled, handicapped, incapacitated, lame, maimed, paralysed.

crisis *noun*
1 *the crisis in an illness.* climax, crunch (*informal*), crux, danger period, turning point.
2 *He can handle any crisis.* calamity, catastrophe, difficulty, disaster, emergency, predicament.

crisp *adjective*
1 *crisp pastry.* brittle, crispy, crunchy, crusty.
OPPOSITE soft, soggy.
2 *a crisp winter morning.* bracing, chilly, cold, cool, fresh, nippy (*informal*).
OPPOSITE balmy, warm.

critic *noun*
1 *The scheme has its critics.* attacker, detractor, fault-finder, knocker (*informal*), objector, opponent.
OPPOSITE supporter.
2 *a film critic.* evaluator, judge, reviewer.

critical *adjective*
1 *critical comments.* disapproving, disparaging, judgemental, nit-picking (*informal*), uncomplimentary.
OPPOSITE complimentary.
2 *of critical importance.* acute, crucial, decisive, key, main, major, momentous, pivotal, serious, vital.
3 *The patient is in a critical condition.* dangerous, grave, perilous, precarious, risky, serious.

criticise *verb*
He criticised their work. She's always criticising people. bag (*Australian informal*), belittle, censure, condemn, find fault with, knock (*informal*), object to, pan (*informal*), pick holes in, rebuke, reprimand, rubbish, slam (*informal*), slate (*informal*), tell off (*informal*), tick off (*informal*).
OPPOSITE praise.

criticism *noun*
1 *He faced hostile criticism of his decision.* censure, condemnation, disapproval, fault-finding, flak (*informal*), nit-picking (*informal*), reproach.
OPPOSITE approval, praise.
2 *literary criticism.* analysis, appraisal, critique, evaluation, review.

croaky *adjective*
a croaky voice. hoarse, husky, rasping, rough, throaty.
OPPOSITE mellow.

crockery *noun*
They washed the crockery. china, dishes, earthenware, plates, tableware.

crook *noun*
1 *a shepherd's crook.* staff, stick.
2 (*informal*) *Don't trust him. He's a crook.*
baddy (*informal*), cheat, criminal, knave
(*old use*), lawbreaker, malefactor, rogue,
scoundrel, swindler, thief, villain,
wrongdoer.
crook *adjective* (*Australian informal*)
1 *She did a crook job.* bad, inferior, poor,
shoddy, unsatisfactory.
OPPOSITE good.
2 *He feels crook.* ailing, ill, lousy
(*informal*), poorly, rotten (*informal*), sick,
unwell.
OPPOSITE well.

go crook at *or* **on** (*Australian informal*)
*His parents went crook on him for
smashing the window.* get mad with,
rebuke, reprimand, reproach, rouse on
(*Australian informal*), scold, tick off
(*informal*), upbraid.
OPPOSITE praise.

crooked *adjective*
1 *a crooked path.* bent, curved,
serpentine, twisted, winding, zigzag.
OPPOSITE straight.
2 *a crooked painting.* askew, awry, cock-
eyed (*informal*), lopsided, off-centre,
slanting, uneven.
OPPOSITE level, straight.
3 *a crooked body.* bent, bowed, contorted,
crippled, deformed, lopsided.
OPPOSITE straight.
4 *a crooked accountant.* bent (*slang*),
corrupt, criminal, dishonest, fraudulent,
shady, shonky (*Australian informal*),
underhand, unscrupulous,
untrustworthy.
OPPOSITE honest, straight.

crop *noun*
1 *The farmer's crop was affected by the hail.*
harvest, produce, vintage, yield.
2 *a new crop of weeds.* batch, outcrop.
crop *verb*
1 *The sheep crop the grass closely.* browse,
eat, graze, nibble.
2 *She had her hair cropped.* bob, clip, cut,
shear, snip, trim.
crop up *A problem has cropped up.*
appear, arise, come up, emerge,
happen, occur, turn up.

cross *noun*
1 *In the church there is a wooden cross.*
crucifix, rood.
2 *The dog is a cross.* bitser (*Australian
informal*), blend, combination, cross-
breed, hybrid, mixture, mongrel.
cross *verb*
1 *The lines cross.* criss-cross, intersect.
2 *He crossed the road.* cut across, go
across, traverse.
3 *The bridge crosses the river.* extend
across, pass over, span, straddle.
4 *He crossed a Great Dane with an
Alsatian.* cross-breed, interbreed, mate.
cross *adjective*
a cross old lady. angry, annoyed, bad-
tempered, crabby, cranky, crotchety,
disagreeable, grouchy (*informal*),
grumpy, ill-tempered, impatient, irate,
irritable, peevish, petulant, shirty
(*informal*), snaky (*Australian informal*),
surly.
OPPOSITE agreeable.
cross out *They crossed out her name.*
cancel, delete, scratch out, strike out.

crossing *noun*
1 *The travellers had a rough crossing.*
journey, passage, voyage.
2 *the crossing of two paths.* crossroads,
intersection, junction.
3 *a shallow river crossing.* causeway,
ford.

cross-section *noun*
a cross-section of the community. sample,
section.

crouch *verb*
She crouched under the bed. bend, cower,
duck, huddle, hunch, squat, stoop.
OPPOSITE stand up.

crow *verb*
nothing to crow about. blow your own
trumpet, boast, brag, gloat, show off,
skite (*Australian informal*), swank
(*informal*).

crowd *noun*
1 *He spoke to the crowd.* assembly,
company, congregation, crush, flock,
gathering, herd, horde, host, mass,
mob, multitude, rabble, swarm, throng.
2 *The game drew a big crowd.* attendance,
audience, onlookers, spectators,
turnout.

a b c d e f g h i j k l m n o p q r s t u v w x y z

3 *He's not one of their crowd.* bunch (*informal*), circle, crew, gang, group, lot, mob, set, troop.

crowd *verb*
1 *The people crowded along the streets to watch the parade.* assemble, cluster, collect, congregate, flock, gather, herd, mill, swarm, throng.
OPPOSITE disperse.
2 *We were crowded into a ferry.* cram, huddle, jam, pack, pile, press, shove, squash, squeeze.

crowded *adjective*
1 *a crowded train.* congested, full, jam-packed, overflowing, packed.
OPPOSITE empty.
2 *a crowded city.* over-populated, populous.
OPPOSITE uninhabited.

crown *noun*
1 *the Queen's crown.* coronet, diadem, tiara.
2 *the crown of the hill.* apex, crest, peak, pinnacle, summit, top.

crown *verb*
1 *He was crowned the new king.* enthrone, install.
2 *The publication of the book crowned an illustrious career.* cap, complete, top off.

crowning *noun*
coronation, enthronement.

crucial *adjective*
a crucial matter. critical, decisive, important, key, momentous, pivotal, serious, significant, vital.
OPPOSITE unimportant.

crude *adjective*
1 *crude oil.* natural, raw, unprocessed, unrefined.
OPPOSITE refined.
2 *crude tools.* improvised, makeshift, primitive, rough, simple, unsophisticated.
OPPOSITE sophisticated.
3 *a crude joke.* coarse, improper, indecent, obscene, rude, vulgar.
OPPOSITE polite.

cruel *adjective*
a cruel person. a cruel act. atrocious, barbaric, beastly, bloodthirsty, brutal, callous, cold-blooded, ferocious, fiendish, hard-hearted, harsh, heartless, inhuman, inhumane, mean, merciless, monstrous, pitiless, ruthless, sadistic, savage, severe, tyrannical, unkind, vicious, violent.
OPPOSITE humane, kind.

cruelty *noun*
atrocity, barbarity, bestiality, brutality, callousness, ferocity, fiendishness, hard-heartedness, harshness, heartlessness, inhumanity, meanness, mercilessness, monstrousness, pitilessness, ruthlessness, sadism, savagery, severity, tyranny, unkindness, viciousness, violence.
OPPOSITE humanity, kindness.

cruise *verb*
They cruised the Pacific. sail, voyage.
cruise *noun*
a harbour cruise. journey, sail, trip, voyage.

crumb *noun*
bread crumbs. bit, fragment, morsel, particle, piece, scrap, speck.

crumble *verb*
1 *She crumbled the stock cube.* crush, grind, pulverise.
2 *The rock crumbled.* break up, disintegrate, fall apart, go to pieces.

crumple *verb*
1 *He crumpled his shirt.* crease, crinkle, crush, rumple, screw up, wrinkle.
OPPOSITE smooth.
2 *She crumpled into a heap.* collapse, fall down, flop.

crunch *verb*
1 *She crunched an apple.* chew, chomp, gnaw, masticate, munch.
2 *He crunched the leaves as he walked.* crush, scrunch, squash.
crunch *noun*
when it comes to the crunch. acid test, moment of truth, showdown, test.

crusade *noun*
She led the crusade against tobacco advertising. campaign, drive, movement, push, struggle, war.

crush *verb*
1 *The machine crushed the metal.* buckle, compress, mangle, press, smash, squash, squeeze.
2 *She crushed the clothes in packing them.* crease, crinkle, crumple, rumple, wrinkle.
3 *He crushed the fruit.* liquidise, mash, pound, pulp, squash.
4 *She crushed the biscuits.* crumble, crunch, grind, pound, pulverise, shatter.
5 *They crushed the enemy.* conquer, defeat, overcome, overpower, overthrow, overwhelm, rout, subdue, suppress, thrash, trounce, vanquish.

crust *noun*
a crust on a kettle, sore, cheese, etc. coating, incrustation, outside, rind, scab, skin.

crutch *noun*
He used crutches when he walked. prop, support.

cry *noun*
1 *She let out a cry.* bellow, call, exclamation, howl, scream, screech, shout, shriek, squawk, squeak, squeal, wail, whimper, whine, yell, yelp, yowl.
2 *a cry for help.* appeal, call, demand, entreaty, plea, request.
cry *verb*
1 *He cries over little things.* bawl, blubber, break down, grizzle, howl, shed tears, sob, wail, weep, whimper.
2 *She cried out from across the road.* bellow, call out, exclaim, roar, scream, shout, yell.

cry-baby *noun*
sissy, sook (*Australian informal*), wimp (*informal*), wuss (*slang*).

cubby hole *noun*
carrel, compartment, cubicle, niche, nook, pigeon-hole.

cube *noun*
a baby's building cubes. block, brick.
cube *verb*
She cubed the carrots. chop, cut, dice.

cubicle *noun*
Each cubicle is fitted with a tape recorder. booth, carrel, compartment, cubby hole, stall.

cuddle *verb*
1 *The mother cuddled her child.* caress, clasp, embrace, fondle, hug, nurse, squeeze.
2 *She cuddled up to him in bed.* huddle, nestle, snuggle.

cue *noun*
She missed her cue to speak. hint, prompt, reminder, sign, signal.

cuff *noun*
off the cuff *He spoke off the cuff.* ad lib, extempore, impromptu, spontaneously, unprepared, unrehearsed.

cul-de-sac *noun*
blind alley, close, dead end.

culminate *verb*
The argument culminated in a fight. climax, conclude, end up, finish, terminate, wind up.

culprit *noun*
They caught the culprit. lawbreaker, miscreant, offender, troublemaker, wrongdoer.

cult *noun*
members of a new cult. religion, sect.

cultivate *verb*
1 *He cultivated the land.* farm, till, work.
2 *They cultivated wheat.* grow, produce, raise, tend.
3 *She cultivated the skill.* develop, foster, nurture, refine, work on.

culture *noun*
1 *They studied French language and culture.* art, arts, civilisation, customs, literature, music, society, traditions.
2 *classes in physical culture.* development, education, training.

cultured *adjective*
a cultured person. civilised, cultivated, educated, highbrow, intellectual, refined, sophisticated, well-bred. OPPOSITE uncouth.

cunning *adjective*
a cunning ploy. a cunning person. artful, astute, calculating, clever, crafty, deceitful, devious, dodgy (*informal*), foxy, ingenious, knowing, scheming, sharp, shifty, shrewd, sly, sneaky,

a
b
c
d
e
f
g
h
i
j
k
l
m
n
o
p
q
r
s
t
u
v
w
x
y
z

subtle, tricky, underhand, wily.
OPPOSITE guileless.

cunning *noun*
The fox is noted for his cunning.
cleverness, craftiness, deceitfulness,
deviousness, guile, ingenuity,
shrewdness, slyness, subtlety, trickery,
wiliness.

cup *noun*
1 *He drank from the cup.* beaker, chalice,
goblet, mug, tankard, teacup.
2 *Their team won the cup.* award, prize,
trophy.

cupboard *noun*
[*kinds of cupboard*] buffet, built-in,
cabinet, chest, closet, dresser, larder,
linen press, locker, pantry, safe,
sideboard, wardrobe.

curator *noun*
the museum curator. conservator,
custodian, keeper, manager.

curb *verb*
They tried to curb their spending. check,
contain, control, hold back, limit,
moderate, rein in, restrain, restrict, slow
down.

cure *verb*
1 *She could not cure the patient's problem.*
heal, make better, remedy.
2 *The technician cured the fault.* correct,
fix, mend, put right, rectify, remedy,
repair.
cure *noun*
a cure for the disease. antidote, medicine,
remedy, therapy, treatment.

curiosity *noun*
Curiosity killed the cat. inquisitiveness,
interest, nosiness (*informal*), prying,
snooping (*informal*).
OPPOSITE indifference.

curious *adjective*
1 *a curious neighbour.* inquiring,
inquisitive, interested, nosy (*informal*),
prying, snoopy (*informal*).
OPPOSITE uninterested.
2 *frightened by curious noises.* abnormal,
bizarre, extraordinary, funny,
mysterious, odd, peculiar, queer,
strange, unusual, weird.
OPPOSITE normal.

curl *verb*
1 *The snake curled round the branch.* bend,
coil, curve, loop, spiral, turn, twist,
wind.
2 *She curled her hair.* crimp, frizz, perm,
wave.
OPPOSITE straighten.
curl *noun*
She has curls in her hair. dreadlock, kink,
ringlet, wave.

curly *adjective*
curly hair. crimped, frizzed, frizzy,
permed, wavy.

currency *noun*
*She exchanged a traveller's cheque for
French currency.* cash, coinage, legal
tender, money.

current *adjective*
current practices. actual, contemporary,
existing, latest, modern, present,
present-day, prevailing, prevalent,
up-to-date.
OPPOSITE past.
current *noun*
The river has a strong current. flow,
stream, tide.

curse *noun*
1 *The bad fairy's curse came to pass.* evil
spell, hex, jinx (*informal*), malediction.
OPPOSITE blessing.
2 *The injured man uttered a curse.*
expletive, oath, obscenity, profanity,
swear-word.
curse *verb*
He cursed the other driver. damn, revile,
swear at.
OPPOSITE bless.
be cursed with *He was cursed with poor
eyesight.* be afflicted with, be troubled
with, suffer from.

curtain *noun*
drape, hanging, screen.

curtsy *noun*
She made a curtsy to the Queen. bob, bow.
curtsy *verb*
see BOW[1].

curve *noun*
arc, arch, bend, bow, crescent, crook,
curl, kink, loop, spiral, turn, twist.

curve *verb*
arc, arch, bend, bow, circle, coil, kink, loop, spiral, turn, twist, wind.

curved *adjective*
1 *a curved path.* crescent-shaped, crooked, looped, serpentine, spiral, twisting, winding.
OPPOSITE straight.
2 *a curved surface.* arched, bent, bowed, concave, convex, humped, rounded.
OPPOSITE flat.

cushion *noun*
bolster, hassock, kneeler, pad, pillow.
cushion *verb*
A rubber pad cushioned the impact.
absorb, buffer, damp, dampen, deaden, lessen, reduce, soften.

custodian *noun*
the gallery's custodian. curator, guardian, keeper, steward, warden.

custody *noun*
1 *She has custody of the children.* care, charge, guardianship.
2 *The papers are in safe custody.* care, hands, keeping.
3 *He was being held in custody.* detention, imprisonment, jail, prison.
take into custody see ARREST.

custom *noun*
1 *It is their custom to shake hands.*
convention, habit, practice, routine, tradition, way, wont.
2 *The owner appreciated their custom.*
business, patronage, support, trade.

customary *adjective*
with her customary politeness.
accustomed, habitual, normal, ordinary, regular, standard, traditional, typical, usual.
OPPOSITE unusual.

customer *noun*
buyer, client, consumer, patron, purchaser, shopper.
OPPOSITE vendor.

customs *noun*
The government collects customs on imports. duty, import tax, levy, tariff.

cut *verb*
1 amputate, bisect, carve, chip, chisel, chop, cleave, clip, crop, cube, detach,
dice, dissect, divide, dock, engrave, fell, gash, gouge, guillotine, hack, hew, knife, lacerate, lance, lop, mangle, mince, mow, mutilate, nick, notch, pare, pierce, pink, prune, reap, remove, saw, score, scythe, sever, shave, shear, shred, slash, slice, slit, snick, snip, split, stab, trim, wound.
2 *The lines cut at right angles.* cross, go across, intersect.
3 *He cut his paper by 1000 words.*
abbreviate, abridge, condense, reduce, shorten.
OPPOSITE lengthen.

cut *noun*
1 *She had a cut on her leg.* gash, incision, laceration, slash, wound.
2 *He made a cut in the timber.* channel, furrow, groove, indentation, nick, notch, slit.
3 *a cut in interest rates.* decline, decrease, fall, lowering, reduction.
OPPOSITE increase.
4 *a power cut.* disruption, failure, stoppage.
5 *(informal) a cut of the profits.*
commission, percentage, portion, rake-off *(informal)*, share, slice.
cut back *The company was forced to cut back staff.* downsize *(informal)*, rationalise, reduce, retrench; see also ECONOMISE.
cut down on *He has to cut down on fat intake.* decrease, lessen, lower, reduce.
OPPOSITE increase.
cut in *He cut in on our conversation.*
break in, butt in, interrupt, intervene.
cut off
1 *The gas supply has been cut off.*
disconnect, discontinue, halt, stop, suspend.
2 *The farm was cut off from the town by the floods.* isolate, maroon, separate.
cut out *She cut out the offending part.*
censor, delete, eliminate, exclude, leave out, omit, remove.
OPPOSITE include.

cute *adjective (informal)*
a cute baby. adorable, attractive, pretty, sweet *(informal)*.

cutting *adjective*
cutting remarks. harsh, hurtful, sarcastic, scathing, sharp, stinging, wounding.

a
b
c
d
e
f
g
h
i
j
k
l
m
n
o
p
q
r
s
t
u
v
w
x
y
z

cutting *noun*
1 *a newspaper cutting.* clipping, extract, piece, section.
2 *a plant cutting.* slip.

cycle *noun*
1 *the cycle of the seasons.* repetition, rotation, round, sequence, series.
2 *He rides a cycle.* bicycle, moped, motor cycle, motor scooter, penny farthing, scooter, tandem, tricycle.

cycle *verb*
He cycles to work. bicycle, bike (*informal*), pedal, ride.

cyclone *noun*
hurricane, tropical cyclone, typhoon.

cynical *adjective*
a cynical view of politicians. jaundiced, sardonic, sceptical, scoffing, suspicious.
OPPOSITE optimistic.

Dd

dab *noun*
a dab of polish. bit, pat, touch.
dab *verb*
She dabbed paint on the wall. apply, daub, pat.

dabble *verb*
They dabbled at the water's edge. dip, paddle, splash.

daily *adjective*
a daily occurrence. day-to-day, everyday.

dainty *adjective*
dainty coffee cups. delicate, dinky (*informal*), exquisite, fine, pretty, small.

dally *verb*
They dallied on the way home. dawdle, delay, dilly-dally (*informal*), hang about, linger, loiter, take your time, tarry.
OPPOSITE hurry.

dam *noun*
1 A dam was built across the river. bank, barrage, barrier, embankment, wall, weir.
2 (*Australian*) The farmer's dam is full after rain. pond, reservoir, tank (*Australian*).

damage *noun*
The accident caused a lot of damage. destruction, devastation, harm, havoc, hurt, injury, loss, mutilation, ruin.
damage *verb*
1 damage a thing. break, bruise, bust (*informal*), chip, cripple, dent, destroy, devastate, harm, hurt, impair, injure, mangle, mar, mutilate, ravage, ruin, sabotage, scratch, spoil, vandalise, wound, wreck.
OPPOSITE mend.
2 damage a reputation. blemish, stain, sully, tarnish.
OPPOSITE enhance.
damages *plural noun*
The court ordered the guilty party to pay damages. compensation, costs, reparations, restitution.

damp *adjective*
damp weather. clammy, dank, humid, moist, muggy, steamy, sticky, wet.
OPPOSITE dry.
damp *verb*
1 He damped the clothes before ironing them. dampen, moisten, sprinkle, wet.
2 She damped their enthusiasm. cool, dampen, dash, discourage, dull, restrain.
OPPOSITE kindle.

dance *verb*
The children danced around. bob, caper, frolic, jig, jump, leap, pirouette, prance, romp, skip, trip, twirl.
dance *noun*
1 [*kinds of dance or dancing*] ballet, ballroom dancing, belly dance, cancan, corroboree, flamenco, folk dancing, foxtrot, hornpipe, jazz ballet, jig, jive, limbo, line dancing, minuet, polka, quickstep, reel, square dance, tango, tap dance, waltz.
2 They went to a dance. ball, disco (*informal*), formal, prom (*American*), social.

danger *noun*
1 There is no danger of losing. chance, possibility, risk, threat.
2 the dangers of diving in shallow water. hazard, jeopardy, peril, pitfall, risk, snare, trouble.
OPPOSITE safety.

dangerous *adjective*
1 a dangerous undertaking. chancy, dicey (*slang*), dodgy (*informal*), hairy (*slang*), hazardous, perilous, precarious, risky, tricky, uncertain, unsafe.
OPPOSITE safe.
2 a dangerous animal. destructive, ferocious, savage, treacherous, vicious, wild.
OPPOSITE harmless.
3 a dangerous criminal. desperate, threatening, violent.

dangle *verb*
The apples dangled from strings. hang, sway, swing.

dare *verb*
1 She wouldn't dare to interrupt. be bold enough, be game, have the nerve, presume, venture.
2 They dared him to jump. challenge, defy, taunt.

daring *noun*
He was rewarded for his daring. boldness, bravery, courage, pluck, prowess, valour.
OPPOSITE cowardice.
daring *adjective*
a daring rescuer. adventurous, bold, brave, courageous, fearless, game, heroic, intrepid, plucky, reckless, valiant.
OPPOSITE cowardly.

dark *adjective*
1 a dark night. black, dim, dingy, dull, gloomy, moonless, murky, overcast, pitch-dark, shadowy, shady, starless, unlit.
OPPOSITE bright.
2 dark skin. black, brown, dusky, olive, swarthy, tanned.
OPPOSITE fair.
3 dark hair. black, brown, brunette.
OPPOSITE blond.
dark *noun*
out after dark. darkness, dusk, evening, night, nightfall, night-time, sunset, twilight.

darken *verb*
The sky darkened. blacken, cloud over.
OPPOSITE brighten.

darling *noun*
beloved, dear, love, pet, sweet, sweetheart.
darling *adjective*
her darling husband. beloved, dear, lovable, loved, precious.

darn *verb*
He darned his socks. mend, repair, sew.

dart *noun*
a poisoned dart. arrow, missile, projectile.

dart *verb*
She darted out in front of a car. bolt, dash, jump, leap, race, run, scoot, shoot, spring, streak, tear, zip.

dash *verb*
1 The runners dashed past him. bolt, dart, fly, gallop, hasten, hurry, hurtle, hustle, race, run, rush, scoot, shoot, speed, sprint, stampede, streak, sweep, tear, whiz, zip, zoom.
2 She dashed the glass against the wall. fling, hurl, knock, shatter, smash, strike, throw.
3 Their hopes were dashed. destroy, disappoint, frustrate, ruin, shatter, spoil.
OPPOSITE fulfil, raise.
dash *noun*
1 a last-minute dash. bolt, run, rush, sprint, spurt.
2 a dash of vanilla. drop, hint, splash, sprinkling, suggestion, touch.

data *plural noun*
He analysed the data. evidence, facts, figures, information, material.

date *noun*
1 objects of prehistoric date. age, epoch, era, period, time, vintage.
2 (informal) They had a date for lunch together. appointment, arrangement, booking, engagement, meeting.
3 (informal) Lots of people go to the formal without a date. boyfriend, companion, escort, girlfriend, partner.
date *verb*
The custom dates from ancient times. see ORIGINATE.

daunting *adjective*
a daunting task. awesome, fearsome, forbidding, frightening.

dawdle *verb*
They were late home because they dawdled. dally, delay, dilly-dally (informal), hang about, lag behind, linger, loiter, straggle, take your time.
OPPOSITE hurry.

dawn *noun*
1 He woke up at dawn. break of day, cock-crow, daybreak, first light, sunrise.
OPPOSITE dusk.

2 *the dawn of an era.* beginning, birth, start, threshold.
OPPOSITE end.

day *noun*
1 *She works during the day.* daylight, daytime.
OPPOSITE night.
2 *He died on this day last year.* date.
3 *the olden days. the present day.* age, epoch, era, period, time.

daydream *noun*
The whole idea was only a daydream. dream, fantasy, illusion, reverie.
daydream *verb*
She was daydreaming instead of concentrating. dream, fantasise, muse.

daylight *noun*
1 *eight hours of daylight.* daytime, light, sunlight, sunshine.
2 *He was up before daylight.* break of day, dawn, morning, sunrise.

daze *verb*
The knock on the head dazed him. bewilder, confuse, stun, stupefy.
daze *noun*
She walked around in a daze. bewilderment, confusion, muddle, shock, stupor, trance.

dazzle *verb*
1 *The headlights dazzled the pedestrian.* blind, daze.
2 *He dazzled them with his knowledge.* amaze, awe, blind, confuse, impress, overawe, stun.

dazzling *adjective*
a dazzling light. blinding, brilliant, radiant, sparkling.

dead *adjective*
1 *a dead person.* deceased, departed, late.
OPPOSITE alive, living.
2 *Her foot felt dead.* numb, paralysed.
3 *a dead language.* defunct, disused, extinct, obsolete.
OPPOSITE living.
4 *Business is dead.* dormant, inactive, inert, quiet, slow, sluggish, stagnant.
OPPOSITE active, booming.
5 *dead silence.* absolute, complete, thorough, total, utter.

dead end blind alley, close, cul-de-sac.
dead heat draw, tie.

deaden *verb*
1 *The medicine deadened the pain.* anaesthetise, dull, kill, numb, subdue.
OPPOSITE intensify.
2 *The muffler deadens the noise.* damp, muffle, mute, quieten, soften, stifle, suppress.
OPPOSITE amplify.

deadline *noun*
time limit.

deadlock *noun*
The talks reached a deadlock. halt, stalemate, stand-off, standstill.

deadly *adjective*
a deadly disease. fatal, lethal, mortal, terminal.

deaf *adjective*
hard of hearing, hearing-impaired.

deafening *adjective*
a deafening sound. booming, ear-piercing, loud, noisy, thunderous.

deal *verb*
1 *She dealt the cards.* allocate, allot, apportion, distribute, divide, dole out, give out, hand out, share out.
2 *They deal in antiques.* do business, handle, market, sell, trade, traffic.
deal *noun*
1 *a deal of cards.* distribution, hand, round.
2 *The two parties made a deal.* agreement, arrangement, bargain, contract, pact, settlement, transaction.
3 (*informal*) *a great deal of money.* amount, lot, quantity, volume.
deal with
1 *He dealt with the problem.* attend to, cope with, grapple with, handle, look after, manage, see to, sort out, tackle, take care of, treat.
OPPOSITE ignore.
2 *The book deals with various subjects.* be about, be concerned with, consider, cover, touch on, treat.

dealer *noun*
distributor, merchant, peddler (*of drugs*), retailer, salesperson, seller, shopkeeper, supplier, trader, trafficker.

a
b
c
d
e
f
g
h
i
j
k
l
m
n
o
p
q
r
s
t
u
v
w
x
y
z

dear *adjective*
1 *a dear friend.* beloved, cherished, close, darling, loved, precious, treasured, valued.
2 *Everything they sell is dear.* costly, exorbitant, expensive, pricey (*informal*).
OPPOSITE cheap.

death *noun*
decease (*formal*), demise (*formal*), dying, end, passing.
OPPOSITE birth, life.
put to death execute, kill, slay.

debate *noun*
a political debate. argument, conference, controversy, discussion, dispute, wrangle.
debate *verb*
They debated the issue. argue, contest, discuss, dispute, wrangle over.

debris *noun*
They cleaned up the debris. flotsam, fragments, remains, rubbish, rubble, wreckage.

debt *noun*
He paid off his debts. due, liability, obligation.

decapitate *verb*
behead, guillotine.

decay *verb*
The food decayed in the heat. break down, decompose, deteriorate, disintegrate, go bad, go off, go rotten, perish, putrefy, rot, spoil.
decay *noun*
tooth decay. caries, cavity, rot.

deceased *adjective*
the deceased man. dead, departed, late.
OPPOSITE alive, living.

deceit *noun*
full of lies and deceit. cheating, cunning, deceitfulness, deception, dishonesty, double-dealing, fraud, humbug, hypocrisy, lies, misrepresentation, pretence, skulduggery (*informal*), treachery, trickery, untruthfulness.
OPPOSITE honesty, openness.

deceitful *adjective*
a deceitful person. crooked, cunning, devious, dishonest, false, hypocritical, lying, phoney (*informal*), shifty, sneaky, treacherous, tricky, two-faced, underhand, unfaithful, untrustworthy.
OPPOSITE honest.

deceive *verb*
He cannot easily be deceived. bluff, cheat, con (*informal*), defraud, delude, diddle (*informal*), double-cross, dupe, fool, have (*slang*), have on (*informal*), hoax, hoodwink, kid (*informal*), mislead, rip off (*informal*), string along (*informal*), suck in (*informal*), swindle, take for a ride (*informal*), take in, trick.

decent *adjective*
1 *decent behaviour.* acceptable, appropriate, becoming, correct, decorous, honourable, law-abiding, proper, respectable, seemly, upright.
OPPOSITE immodest.
2 *a decent joke.* clean, inoffensive, polite.
OPPOSITE indecent, obscene.
3 (*informal*) *That's very decent of you.* civil, considerate, fair, generous, good, kind, obliging, sporting.
4 *a decent meal.* adequate, satisfactory, square.
OPPOSITE unsatisfactory.

deception *noun*
We could see through this little deception. bluff, con (*informal*), fraud, hoax, lie, pretence, ruse, sham, swindle, swizz (*informal*), trick; see also DECEIT.

deceptive *adjective*
Appearances can be deceptive. deceiving, false, misleading, unreliable.
OPPOSITE trustworthy.

decide *verb*
1 *She decided on the red dress.* choose, elect, opt for, pick, select.
2 *The jury decided that he was guilty.* adjudicate, conclude, determine, judge, resolve, rule, settle.
3 *The goal decided the match.* clinch, determine, seal, settle.

decipher *verb*
She deciphered the message. crack, decode, figure out, interpret, make out, read, translate.
OPPOSITE code, encode.

decision *noun*
　The judge's decision is final. adjudication,
　conclusion, determination, finding,
　judgement, ruling, sentence, verdict;
　see also CHOICE.

decisive *adjective*
　1 a decisive battle. conclusive, critical,
　crucial, deciding, significant.
　2 a decisive person. decided, determined,
　firm, resolute, unhesitating.
　OPPOSITE indecisive, non-committal.

deck[1] *noun*
　the top deck. floor, level, platform,
　storey.

deck[2] *verb*
　The hall was decked with streamers. adorn,
　decorate, festoon, trim.

declaration *noun*
　a declaration of innocence. affirmation,
　announcement, assertion, confession,
　proclamation, profession,
　pronouncement, protestation,
　statement, testimony.

declare *verb*
　She declared her intentions. He declared
　that he was leaving. affirm, announce,
　assert, confess, contend, make known,
　proclaim, profess, pronounce, reveal,
　state, testify, voice.
　OPPOSITE hide.

decline *verb*
　1 He declined the invitation. pass up,
　refuse, reject, turn down.
　OPPOSITE accept.
　2 Business declined. His health declined.
　decrease, deteriorate, diminish, ebb, fall
　off, flag, go downhill, go to the pack
　(Australian informal), sink, slip, slump,
　wane, weaken, worsen.
　OPPOSITE improve, increase.
　decline *noun*
　a decline in interest. a decline in business.
　decrease, deterioration, downturn,
　drop, falling off, recession, slump,
　wane.
　OPPOSITE improvement.

decode *verb*
　see DECIPHER.

decompose *verb*
　The food decomposed in the heat. decay,
　disintegrate, go bad, go off, go rotten,
　perish, putrefy, rot, spoil.

decorate *verb*
　1 They decorated the Christmas tree.
　adorn, deck, festoon, ornament, tizzy
　(Australian informal), trim.
　2 The house has been newly decorated. do
　up (informal), paint, paper, refurbish,
　renovate.

decoration *noun*
　1 Christmas decorations. adornment,
　ornament, trimming.
　2 a decoration for bravery. award, badge,
　medal, medallion.

decorative *adjective*
　The roof was both decorative and
　functional. fancy, ornamental, pretty.

decorum *noun*
　He behaved with decorum. correctness,
　decency, dignity, propriety, seemliness.

decoy *noun*
　The police used a decoy to catch the
　criminal. bait, enticement, lure, stool-
　pigeon, trap.

decrease *verb*
　1 They decreased the number of holidays.
　cut, lower, reduce, shorten.
　OPPOSITE increase.
　2 Interest has decreased. abate, drop off,
　ebb, lessen, subside, wane.
　OPPOSITE intensify.
　3 The numbers have decreased. contract,
　decline, diminish, drop, dwindle, fall,
　reduce, shrink, taper off.
　OPPOSITE increase.
　decrease *noun*
　contraction, cut, cutback, decline, drop,
　ebb, fall, reduction.
　OPPOSITE increase.

decree *noun*
　1 They obeyed the royal decree. command,
　commandment, dictate, direction,
　directive, edict, instruction, law, order,
　proclamation, statute.
　2 the judge's decree. decision, judgement,
　ruling, verdict.
　decree *verb*
　The government decreed that the day would
　be a holiday. command, declare, dictate,

a
b
c
d
e
f
g
h
i
j
k
l
m
n
o
p
q
r
s
t
u
v
w
x
y
z

direct, enact, ordain, order, proclaim, rule.

decrepit *adjective*
a decrepit old house. battered, derelict, dilapidated, ramshackle, rickety, run-down, tumbledown.

dedicate *verb*
1 *She dedicated her life to God's service.* commit, consecrate, devote, give, pledge.
2 *The book is dedicated to her father.* address, inscribe.

deduct *verb*
She deducted $5 from the total. knock off (*informal*), subtract, take away, take off. OPPOSITE add.

deduction *noun*
1 *a deduction of $5 from the bill.* discount, rebate, subtraction.
2 *a logical deduction.* conclusion, inference, reasoning.

deed *noun*
1 *praised for his good deeds.* accomplishment, achievement, act, action, exploit, feat, work.
2 *the deeds to the house.* contract, document, paper.

deep *adjective*
1 *a deep crater.* bottomless, cavernous, profound, unfathomed. OPPOSITE shallow.
2 *a deep sleep.* heavy, profound, sound. OPPOSITE light.
3 *a deep colour.* dark, intense, rich, strong, vivid. OPPOSITE pale.
4 *a deep voice.* bass, booming, low, resonant, sonorous. OPPOSITE high-pitched.
5 *deep in thought.* absorbed, engrossed, immersed, lost, occupied, preoccupied.
6 *a deep interest.* burning, earnest, extreme, fervent, heartfelt, intense, keen, profound, serious. OPPOSITE superficial.
7 *a deep discussion.* intellectual, learned, thoughtful. OPPOSITE superficial.

deer *noun*
[*male deer*] buck, hart, stag; [*female deer*] doe, hind; [*young deer*] fawn.

deface *verb*
Vandals defaced the front of the building. damage, disfigure, mar, spoil.

defame *verb*
His opponents tried to defame him. blacken, denigrate, discredit, disparage, libel, malign, slander, smear, vilify.

defeat *verb*
1 *Their team defeated the others.* beat, clobber (*slang*), conquer, crush, euchre, get the better of, lick (*informal*), outclass, outdo, outwit, overcome, overpower, overthrow, overwhelm, paste (*slang*), prevail over, pulverise (*informal*), rout, slaughter (*informal*), stonker (*Australian slang*), surpass, thrash, triumph over, trounce, vanquish. OPPOSITE lose to.
2 *The problem defeats me.* baffle, beat, confound, frustrate, perplex, puzzle.
defeat *noun*
suffer defeat. beating, conquest, failure, licking (*informal*), loss, overthrow, pasting (*informal*), thrashing. OPPOSITE victory.

defect *noun*
1 *a defect in the paintwork. a mechanical defect.* blemish, bug (*informal*), fault, flaw, imperfection, mark, spot, stain.
2 *a personality defect.* deficiency, failing, fault, flaw, shortcoming, weakness.
defect *verb*
The traitor defected to the other country. change sides, desert, go over.

defective *adjective*
a defective machine. crook (*Australian informal*), dud (*informal*), faulty, imperfect, malfunctioning, out of order. OPPOSITE perfect.

defence *noun*
1 *The soldiers ensured the country's defence.* preservation, protection, security.
2 *The wall acts as a defence against attack.* buffer, cover, guard, protection, safeguard, shield.
3 *What was his defence when you challenged him?* excuse, explanation, justification, plea.

defenceless *adjective*
defenceless children. helpless, powerless, vulnerable, weak.

defend *verb*
1 *They defended the city against attack.* fortify, guard, preserve, protect, safeguard, secure, shelter, shield.
OPPOSITE attack.
2 *He defended their right to speak.* champion, justify, stand up for, support, uphold, vindicate.

defer *verb*
The programme was deferred to next month. adjourn, delay, hold over, postpone, put off, shelve.

defiant *adjective*
The child was strong-willed and defiant. contrary, disobedient, insubordinate, mutinous, obstinate, rebellious, recalcitrant, truculent.
OPPOSITE compliant, obedient.

deficiency *noun*
1 *a calcium deficiency.* absence, dearth, deficit, insufficiency, lack, shortage, want.
OPPOSITE abundance.
2 *aware of his own deficiencies.* failing, fault, flaw, imperfection, shortcoming, weakness.
OPPOSITE strength.

deficient *adjective*
1 *deficient in vitamins.* lacking, light on (*Australian informal*), short, wanting.
OPPOSITE abundant, rich.
2 *a deficient memory.* defective, faulty, imperfect, inadequate, unsatisfactory.

deficit *noun*
deficiency, shortfall.
OPPOSITE surplus.

define *verb*
1 *The dictionary defines words.* clarify, explain.
2 *The document defines the conditions.* delineate, describe, detail, set out, specify, spell out, state.

definite *adjective*
1 *a definite time and place.* defined, exact, fixed, particular, precise, specific.
OPPOSITE indefinite.

2 *a definite coolness in his manner.* clear, distinct, marked, noticeable, obvious, pronounced, unmistakable.
OPPOSITE vague.
3 *Is it definite that we are to move?* certain, decided, fixed, positive, settled, sure.
OPPOSITE uncertain.

definition *noun*
a dictionary definition. description, explanation, interpretation.

deformed *adjective*
a deformed body. contorted, crooked, disfigured, distorted, grotesque, lopsided, malformed, misshapen, twisted, warped.

defraud *verb*
They were defrauded by a con man. cheat, con (*informal*), deceive, diddle (*informal*), dupe, fleece, have (*slang*), hoodwink, rip off (*informal*), rook, swindle, take for a ride (*informal*), trick.

defrost *verb*
defrost a freezer. de-ice, melt, thaw, unfreeze.

deft *adjective*
deft movements. adroit, agile, dexterous, expert, neat, nimble, proficient, skilful.
OPPOSITE clumsy.

defy *verb*
1 *He defied his teachers.* confront, disobey, flout, oppose, resist, stand up to.
OPPOSITE obey.
2 *He defied them to try it.* challenge, dare.

degenerate *verb*
The debate degenerated into a brawl. decline, deteriorate, sink, worsen.
OPPOSITE improve.

degrade *verb*
She degrades herself by the way she speaks. cheapen, debase, demean, disgrace, humiliate.
OPPOSITE dignify, upgrade.

degrading *adjective*
degrading work. demeaning, humiliating, menial, undignified.

a
b
c
d
e
f
g
h
i
j
k
l
m
n
o
p
q
r
s
t
u
v
w
x
y
z

degree *noun*
1 *the degree of difficulty.* grade, level, order, rank.
2 *move up by degrees.* stage, step.

deity *noun*
They worshipped several deities. divinity, god, goddess.

delay *verb*
1 *We were delayed by an accident.* detain, hamper, hinder, hold up, impede, inhibit, obstruct, retard, slow.
OPPOSITE advance.
2 *He delayed leaving until the weather became cooler.* defer, postpone, put off, shelve.
OPPOSITE hasten.
3 *Act now. Do not delay.* dilly-dally (*informal*), hang back, hesitate, pause, procrastinate, stall, wait.
OPPOSITE hurry.
delay *noun*
Bad weather caused delays. hold-up, interruption, pause, postponement, setback, wait.

delegate *noun*
We dealt with her delegate. agent, ambassador, deputy, emissary, envoy, proxy, representative, spokesperson.
delegate *verb*
He delegated responsibility to his staff. assign, entrust, hand over, transfer.

delete *verb*
She deleted the offending words. cancel, cross out, cut out, edit out, efface, erase, obliterate, remove, rub out, strike out, take out, wipe out.
OPPOSITE insert.

deliberate *adjective*
1 *a deliberate insult.* calculated, conscious, intended, intentional, planned, premeditated, wilful.
OPPOSITE accidental.
2 *Her footsteps were deliberate.* careful, cautious, measured, painstaking, slow, unhurried.
OPPOSITE hasty.

delicate *adjective*
1 *a delicate fabric.* filmy, fine, flimsy, lacy, light, sheer, thin.
OPPOSITE coarse.

2 *a delicate ornament.* breakable, dainty, flimsy, fragile, frail.
OPPOSITE sturdy.
3 *a delicate flavour.* faint, gentle, mild, subtle.
OPPOSITE intense, strong.
4 *a delicate child.* feeble, frail, sickly, unhealthy, weak.
OPPOSITE healthy, strong.
5 *delicate plants.* frail, tender.
OPPOSITE hardy.
6 *a delicate situation.* awkward, hazardous, precarious, sensitive, ticklish, touchy, tricky.
7 *The situation requires delicate handling.* careful, diplomatic, discreet, sensitive, skilful, tactful.
OPPOSITE insensitive.

delicious *adjective*
a delicious meal. appetising, delectable, luscious, mouth-watering, scrumptious (*informal*), tasty, yummy (*informal*).
OPPOSITE revolting.

delight *verb*
1 *The performers delighted the audience.* amuse, captivate, charm, enchant, enrapture, entertain, entrance, fascinate, please, thrill.
OPPOSITE disappoint.
2 *She delights in teasing people.* revel, take pleasure; see also ENJOY.
delight *noun*
a source of great delight. bliss, ecstasy, enjoyment, happiness, joy, pleasure, satisfaction.
OPPOSITE displeasure.

delightful *adjective*
adorable, agreeable, attractive, beautiful, charming, enchanting, enjoyable, heavenly, lovable, lovely, nice, pleasant, pleasurable, wonderful.
OPPOSITE obnoxious.

delinquent *noun*
a home for delinquents. criminal, hooligan, lawbreaker, miscreant, offender, troublemaker, wrongdoer.

delirious *adjective*
1 *The fever made him delirious.* demented, frantic, frenzied, hysterical, incoherent, light-headed, mad, raving.
2 *delirious with joy.* ecstatic, excited, wild.

deliver *verb*
  1 *He delivered the letters.* bring, carry, convey, distribute, give out, hand over, take, transport.
  OPPOSITE receive.
  2 *The head girl delivered the speech.* give, make, present, utter.
  3 *The bowler delivered a fast ball.* bowl, throw, toss.
  4 *Deliver us from evil.* free, liberate, release, rescue, save, set free.

delivery *noun*
  1 *The price includes free delivery.* conveyance, dispatch, distribution, transport.
  2 *He received a new delivery of goods.* batch, consignment, load, shipment.
  3 *the delivery of a baby.* birth, childbirth.

delude *verb*
  He was deluded into thinking he needed a new car. bluff, con (*informal*), deceive, dupe, fool, have on (*informal*), hoax, hoodwink, kid (*informal*), mislead, trick.

deluge *noun*
  1 *The shed was washed away in the deluge.* flood, inundation.
  2 *Sunshine followed the deluge.* cloudburst, downpour, rain, torrent.
  3 *a deluge of fan mail.* flood, rush, shower, spate, stream, torrent.
  deluge *verb*
  She was deluged with letters. flood, inundate, overrun, overwhelm, swamp.

delusion *noun*
  delusions of grandeur. illusion, misbelief, misconception.

de luxe *adjective*
  a de luxe hotel. elegant, first-class, grand, luxurious, posh (*informal*), superior, upmarket.
  OPPOSITE basic, ordinary.

demand *noun*
  1 *comply with his demands.* command, order, request, summons.
  2 *a demand for their goods.* call, need, requirement, want.
  demand *verb*
  1 *He demanded his money.* ask for, claim, insist on, order, press for, request, require.
  2 *This work demands great skill.* call for, need, require.

demanding *adjective*
  a demanding job. arduous, difficult, exacting, hard, onerous, strenuous, taxing, tough.
  OPPOSITE easy.

demean *verb*
  She won't demean herself to ask for help. degrade, humble, humiliate, lower.

democratic *adjective*
  democratic government. elected, popular, representative.

demolish *verb*
  The workmen demolished the old house. destroy, dismantle, knock down, level, pull down, raze, tear down; see also WRECK.
  OPPOSITE construct, erect.

demon *noun*
  bogy, devil, evil spirit, fiend, goblin, hobgoblin, imp.

demonstrate *verb*
  1 *He demonstrated that sugar dissolves in water.* confirm, establish, prove, show.
  2 *He demonstrated his invention.* display, exhibit, present, show.
  3 *She demonstrated how it worked.* describe, explain, illustrate, show, teach.
  4 *The students demonstrated against increased fees.* march, parade, protest, rally.

demonstration *noun*
  1 *a ballet demonstration.* display, exhibition, presentation, show.
  2 *Conservationists staged a demonstration.* demo (*informal*), march, parade, protest, rally, sit-in.

demoralise *verb*
  She was demoralised by her poor results. depress, discourage, dishearten.
  OPPOSITE encourage.

den *noun*
  1 *an animal's den.* burrow, hole, lair, nest.
  2 *He sought the privacy of his den.* hideaway, hide-out (*informal*), retreat, study.

denial *noun*
  1 *a denial of the statement.* contradiction, disclaimer, negation, rejection,

a
b
c
d
e
f
g
h
i
j
k
l
m
n
o
p
q
r
s
t
u
v
w
x
y
z

repudiation.
OPPOSITE affirmation.
2 *a denial of rights.* deprivation, refusal, withholding.

denomination *noun*
various Christian denominations. church, persuasion, sect.

denote *verb*
A red symbol denotes danger. express, indicate, mean, represent, signal, signify, symbolise.

denounce *verb*
1 *He denounced their harsh policies.* attack, condemn, criticise, object to.
OPPOSITE praise.
2 *She denounced him as a spy.* accuse, betray, dob in (*Australian informal*), incriminate, inform against, report.

dense *adjective*
1 *dense fog.* heavy, impenetrable, thick.
OPPOSITE light.
2 *a dense weave.* close, compact, heavy.
OPPOSITE loose, open.
3 *a dense crowd.* packed, solid, thick.
OPPOSITE sparse.
4 *She was too dense to understand.* dim (*informal*), dull, dumb (*informal*), feeble-minded, foolish, obtuse, slow, stupid, thick, unintelligent.
OPPOSITE bright.

dent *noun*
a dent in the bodywork. depression, dimple, dint, hollow, indentation.

deny *verb*
1 *She denied the statement.* contradict, disclaim, reject, repudiate.
OPPOSITE affirm.
2 *He was denied his rights.* deprive of, disallow, refuse, withhold.
OPPOSITE grant.

depart *verb*
They packed their bags and departed. clear off (*informal*), embark, emigrate, escape, exit, go away, leave, make off, make tracks (*informal*), nick off (*Australian slang*), push off (*informal*), retire, run away, run off, scarper (*informal*), scram (*informal*), set off, set out, shoot through (*Australian informal*), skedaddle (*informal*), take your leave, withdraw.
OPPOSITE arrive, stay.

department *noun*
the departments of a hospital. a government department. branch, bureau, division, office, part, section, unit.

departure *noun*
exit, exodus, going away, leaving, retreat, withdrawal.
OPPOSITE arrival, return.

depend *verb*
depend on
1 *Whether we can swim depends on the weather.* hang on, hinge on, rest on, turn on.
2 *She depends on my help.* bank on, count on, need, reckon on, rely on.

dependable *adjective*
a dependable person. consistent, constant, faithful, loyal, reliable, stalwart, steadfast, steady, true, trustworthy.
OPPOSITE unreliable.

dependent *adjective*
dependent on *He is dependent on drugs.* addicted to, hooked on (*slang*), reliant on.

depict *verb*
1 *The artist depicted the scene in bright colours.* draw, illustrate, paint, picture, portray, represent, show, sketch.
2 *The writer depicted the events.* describe, narrate, outline, record, relate.

deplorable *adjective*
1 *deplorable behaviour.* abominable, disgraceful, lamentable, regrettable, reprehensible, shameful.
OPPOSITE praiseworthy.
2 *deplorable conditions.* appalling, awful, dreadful, pathetic, shocking, wretched; see also BAD.
OPPOSITE good.

deplore *verb*
1 *We deplore his death.* grieve over, lament, mourn.
2 *She deplores waste.* condemn, disapprove of, regret.

deport *verb*
The illegal immigrants were deported. banish, exile, expatriate, expel, send away, transport.

deportment *noun*
The girls were assessed on dress and deportment. bearing, behaviour, carriage, conduct, demeanour, manner.

deposit *noun*
1 *He paid a deposit on the car.* down payment, first instalment.
2 *a deposit of mud.* crust, dregs, lees, sediment, silt.
deposit *verb*
1 *They deposited their bags inside the door.* drop, dump, lay, leave, park (*informal*), place, put down, set down.
2 *She deposits her wages in the account.* bank, pay in, save.
OPPOSITE withdraw.

depot *noun*
1 *Extra supplies are kept at the depot.* base, cache, headquarters, store, storehouse, warehouse.
2 *a bus depot.* garage, station, terminal, terminus.

depress *verb*
His circumstances depressed him. dishearten, oppress, sadden, weigh down.
OPPOSITE cheer.

depressed *adjective*
feeling depressed. blue, dejected, desolate, despondent, disconsolate, disheartened, dismal, dispirited, down, downcast, down in the dumps, gloomy, glum, heavy-hearted, hopeless, low, melancholy, miserable, out of sorts, pessimistic, sad, unhappy, wretched.
OPPOSITE elated, exhilarated.

depression *noun*
1 *He was overcome by depression.* the blues, dejection, despair, despondency, gloom, hopelessness, low spirits, melancholy, pessimism, sadness, unhappiness, wretchedness.
OPPOSITE light-heartedness.
2 *Economists forecast a depression.* decline, downturn, recession, slump.
OPPOSITE boom.
3 *The weather map shows a depression.* cyclone, low, trough.
OPPOSITE anticyclone, high.
4 *a depression in the ground.* basin, cavity, crabhole (*Australian*), crater, dent, dip, gilgai (*Australian*), hole,

hollow, indentation, pit, trough.
OPPOSITE elevation.

deprive *verb*
deprive of *The cat deprived her of her chair.* deny, dispossess of, refuse, rob of, take away.

depth *noun*
depth of feeling. deepness, intensity, profundity, strength.
in depth *study a subject in depth.* comprehensively, extensively, in detail, intensively, thoroughly.

deputy *noun*
Her deputy has to stand in for her quite often. assistant, lieutenant, locum, offsider (*Australian*), proxy, relief, replacement, representative, reserve, stand-in, substitute, surrogate, understudy.

derelict *adjective*
a derelict building. abandoned, decrepit, deserted, dilapidated, forsaken, neglected, run-down, tumbledown.
derelict *noun*
The derelict slept on a park bench. down-and-out, outcast, tramp, vagrant.

derivation *noun*
the derivation of a word. etymology, origin, root, source.

derive *verb*
1 *She derives pleasure from cooking.* draw, gain, get, glean, obtain, receive.
2 *The word derives from Latin.* come, originate, stem.

descend *verb*
1 *We descended the mountain.* climb down, come down, go down.
OPPOSITE climb.
2 *The plane suddenly descended.* come down, drop, fall, nosedive, plummet, plunge, sink, swoop down.
OPPOSITE ascend.

descendants *plural noun*
children, heirs, issue, offspring, progeny.
OPPOSITE ancestors.

descent *noun*
1 *the parachuter's descent.* coming down, dive, drop, fall, plunge.

a
b
c
d
e
f
g
h
i
j
k
l
m
n
o
p
q
r
s
t
u
v
w
x
y
z

2 *a steep descent in the road.* decline, downward slope.
OPPOSITE ascent, rise.
3 *They are of noble descent.* ancestry, birth, blood, extraction, genealogy, lineage, origin, parentage, stock, strain.

describe *verb*
He described the events and the people. depict, detail, elaborate, explain, express, narrate, outline, portray, recount, relate, represent, tell (about).

description *noun*
a description of a person or an event. account, commentary, depiction, explanation, outline, picture, portrait, portrayal, profile, record, report, representation, sketch, story.

desert[1] *noun*
wasteland, wilderness.
desert *adjective*
1 *The interior is desert country.* arid, barren, dry, infertile, uncultivated, waste, wild.
2 *a desert island.* desolate, uninhabited.
OPPOSITE inhabited.

desert[2] *verb*
1 *He deserted his wife.* abandon, ditch (*informal*), dump (*informal*), forsake, jilt, leave, leave in the lurch, walk out on.
OPPOSITE stand by.
2 *He was disillusioned with the party and deserted.* defect, run away.
OPPOSITE stay.

deserter *noun*
an army deserter. absconder, defector, escapee, fugitive, runaway.

deserve *verb*
The work deserves praise. be entitled to, be worthy of, command, earn, justify, merit, warrant.

design *noun*
1 *She drew a design of the finished structure.* blueprint, diagram, draft, drawing, outline, pattern, plan, sketch.
2 *fashion design.* couture.
3 *an efficient kitchen design.* arrangement, form, layout.
4 *the newest design of blender.* model, style, type, version.
5 *fabric with a floral design.* motif, pattern.

design *verb*
1 *He designed the building.* conceive, draft, draw, lay out, plan, sketch.
2 *The speech was designed to make an impact.* calculate, intend, mean, plan.

designer *noun*
architect, couturier, creator, inventor, planner.

desirable *adjective*
1 *a desirable person. a desirable quality.* alluring, appealing, attractive, popular, sought-after, worthwhile.
2 *It is desirable that you wear a tie.* advisable, preferable, recommended.

desire *noun*
satisfy a desire for adventure. ambition, appetite, aspiration, craving, fancy, hunger, itch, longing, lust, passion, thirst, urge, wish, yen.
desire *verb*
She desires fame. covet, crave, fancy, hanker after, hope for, hunger for, long for, set your heart on, thirst for, want, wish for, yearn for.

desolate *adjective*
1 *a desolate landscape.* barren, bleak, deserted, dismal, dreary, empty, isolated, lonely, remote, stark, uninhabited, wild, windswept.
2 *Her father's death left her feeling desolate.* depressed, despondent, disconsolate, forlorn, forsaken, glum, heavy-hearted, lonely, melancholy, miserable, unhappy, wretched.
OPPOSITE cheerful.

despair *noun*
She wrung her hands in despair. depression, desperation, despondency, hopelessness.

desperate *adjective*
1 *The situation is desperate.* acute, bad, critical, dire, grave, hopeless, serious, urgent.
2 *a desperate criminal.* dangerous, daring, rash, reckless, violent, wild.

despicable *adjective*
abominable, bad, base, contemptible, detestable, evil, hateful, loathsome, low, mean, odious, outrageous, reprehensible, rotten, shameful, vile,

wicked.
OPPOSITE admirable.

despise *verb*
She despised them because they told on her.
detest, disdain, dislike, feel contempt
for, hate, loathe, look down on, scorn.
OPPOSITE revere.

dessert *noun*
afters (*informal*), pudding, sweet.

destination *noun*
They reached their destination. end, goal,
target.

destined *adjective*
destined to happen. doomed, fated,
intended, meant, ordained.

destiny *noun*
1 *She left it to destiny.* chance, fate,
fortune, luck, providence.
2 *Her destiny was to be a martyr.* doom,
fate, fortune, lot, portion.

destroy *verb*
1 *destroy a building, car, city, etc.*
annihilate, blow up, break, bust
(*informal*), demolish, devastate,
dismantle, eliminate, exterminate,
knock down, lay waste, level, mutilate,
obliterate, pull down, pull to pieces, put
an end to, ravage, raze, ruin, sabotage,
smash, spoil, tear down, vandalise,
wipe out, wreck, zap (*slang*).
OPPOSITE construct.
2 *The vet destroyed the sick cow.* finish off,
kill, put down, put to sleep, slaughter,
slay.
OPPOSITE save.
3 *destroy confidence.* crush, dash, erode,
extinguish, put an end to, shatter,
undermine.
OPPOSITE build.

destruction *noun*
weapons of mass destruction. annihilation,
damage, demolition, devastation,
elimination, extermination, extinction,
havoc, killing, massacre, ruin, sabotage,
slaughter, vandalism, wreckage.

destructive *adjective*
a destructive influence. adverse,
damaging, dangerous, detrimental,
devastating, disastrous, harmful,
injurious, negative, ruinous.
OPPOSITE constructive.

detach *verb*
He detached the wheels from the suitcase.
disconnect, part, pull off, release,
remove, separate, slip off, take off,
undo, unfasten.
OPPOSITE attach.

detached *adjective*
1 *a detached house.* free-standing,
separate.
OPPOSITE attached.
2 *a detached view of the matter.*
disinterested, impartial, neutral,
objective, unbiased, uninvolved.
OPPOSITE involved.

detail *noun*
a minor detail. aspect, circumstance, fact,
factor, feature, item, particular, point,
respect.

detailed *adjective*
a detailed account. blow-by-blow,
comprehensive, elaborate, exact,
exhaustive, full, graphic, in-depth,
itemised, minute, rigorous, thorough.
OPPOSITE sketchy.

detain *verb*
1 *The police detained the suspect.* arrest,
capture, confine, hold in custody,
imprison, jail.
OPPOSITE release.
2 *Her friend detained her at the shops.* bail
up (*Australian*), buttonhole, delay, hold
up, keep, waylay.

detect *verb*
*She detected the leak. He detected that
something was wrong.* discern, discover,
find, identify, locate, notice, observe,
perceive, see, sense, spot, track down,
uncover.
OPPOSITE overlook.

detective *noun*
cop (*slang*), investigator, policeman,
police officer, policewoman, private eye
(*informal*), sleuth.

detention *noun*
kept in police detention. captivity,
confinement, custody, imprisonment.

a
b
c
d
e
f
g
h
i
j
k
l
m
n
o
p
q
r
s
t
u
v
w
x
y
z

deter *verb*
The fear of punishment deterred them.
daunt, discourage, dissuade, hinder,
impede, obstruct, prevent, put off, scare
off.
OPPOSITE encourage.

deteriorate *verb*
Her health has deteriorated. decline,
diminish, go backwards, go downhill,
go to the pack (*Australian informal*),
sink, slip, wane, weaken, worsen.
OPPOSITE improve.

determination *noun*
*He will succeed because he has
determination.* backbone, courage,
fortitude, grit, guts (*informal*),
perseverance, persistence, resolve,
spirit, tenacity, will-power.

determine *verb*
1 *He determined how much he would get.*
calculate, discover, establish, find out,
work out.
2 *The committee determined what had to be
done.* agree on, decide, resolve, settle.
3 *Many factors determine the result.* affect,
control, decide, dictate, influence,
shape.

determined *adjective*
a determined person. adamant, dogged,
firm, headstrong, persistent, resolute,
single-minded, strong-willed, stubborn,
tenacious.
OPPOSITE irresolute.

detest *verb*
He detests work. abhor, abominate,
despise, dislike, hate, loathe.
OPPOSITE love.

detestable *adjective*
see HATEFUL.

detonate *verb*
They detonated a bomb. discharge,
explode, let off, set off.

detour *noun*
a detour to avoid the roadworks. bypass,
deviation, diversion.

devastated *adjective*
devastated by the news. appalled,
dismayed, overcome, overwhelmed,
shattered, shocked, traumatised.

devastating *adjective*
a devastating earthquake. catastrophic,
destructive, disastrous.

develop *verb*
1 *The child developed.* advance, blossom,
grow, mature.
2 *He developed the business.* build up,
diversify, enlarge, expand, improve,
increase.
3 *The company developed rapidly.* expand,
flourish, grow, progress.
OPPOSITE stagnate.
4 *She developed a sore throat.* acquire,
contract, get, pick up.

development *noun*
1 *the development of the business.*
building, evolution, expansion, growth,
progress, spread.
2 *the latest developments.* circumstance,
event, happening, incident.

deviate *verb*
She deviated from the rules. depart,
digress, diverge, stray, turn aside.
OPPOSITE adhere to.

device *noun*
a kitchen full of modern devices.
apparatus, appliance, contraption
(*informal*), gadget, implement,
instrument, invention, machine, tool,
utensil.

devil *noun*
1 *He was plagued by devils.* bogy, demon,
evil spirit, fiend.
2 *He was a devil to take things which
weren't his.* monster, rascal, rogue,
scamp, scoundrel.
the Devil Old Nick, Satan.

devilish *adjective*
demonic, diabolical, evil, fiendish,
hellish, satanic, ungodly, villainous,
wicked.
OPPOSITE angelic.

devious *adjective*
1 *a devious route.* circuitous, indirect,
roundabout, winding.
OPPOSITE direct.
2 *a devious person.* crafty, cunning,
deceitful, dishonest, sly, sneaky,
underhand, wily.
OPPOSITE straightforward.

devise *verb*
He devised a scheme. conceive, concoct, contrive, create, design, dream up, hatch, invent, make up, plan, produce, think up, work out.

devote *verb*
She devotes her time to helping others. commit, consecrate, dedicate, give, set aside.

devoted *adjective*
a devoted friend. close, committed, constant, dedicated, enthusiastic, faithful, loving, loyal, reliable, staunch.
OPPOSITE disloyal.

devotee *noun*
a devotee of tennis. buff (*informal*), enthusiast, fan, fanatic, follower, lover, supporter.

devotion *noun*
devotion to the party. affection, allegiance, attachment, commitment, dedication, love, loyalty.
devotions *plural noun*
He joined in morning devotions. prayers, worship.

devour *verb*
They devoured the food in five minutes. bolt, consume, demolish (*informal*), eat, gobble, gorge, gulp down, guzzle, knock back, scoff (*informal*), swallow, wolf.

devout *adjective*
a devout Jew. ardent, committed, dedicated, devoted, earnest, fervent, genuine, godly, holy, pious, religious, sincere, staunch.
OPPOSITE impious.

diabolical *adjective*
a diabolical deed. devilish, evil, fiendish, hellish, satanic, ungodly, villainous, wicked.

diagnose *verb*
diagnose the problem. detect, identify, name, recognise.

diagonal *adjective*
a diagonal line. oblique, slanting, sloping.

diagram *noun*
chart, drawing, figure, graph, illustration, outline, plan, sketch.

dial *verb*
She dialled her friend's house. call, phone, ring, telephone.

dialect *noun*
They speak different dialects of English. accent, brogue, lingo (*informal*), variety; see also LANGUAGE.

dialogue *noun*
A dialogue between the parties resolved the matter. communication, conference, conversation, discussion, talk.

diameter *noun*
thickness, width.

diary *noun*
He kept a diary of daily happenings. chronicle, journal, log, record.

dictate *verb*
He tried to dictate what she should wear. command, decree, lay down the law on, ordain, order, prescribe.

dictator *noun*
The country is ruled by a dictator. autocrat, despot, tyrant.

dictatorial *adjective*
His dictatorial approach made people resentful. authoritarian, autocratic, bossy, despotic, domineering, totalitarian, tyrannical.
OPPOSITE democratic.

die *verb*
1 He died at eighty. breathe your last, depart this world, expire, kick the bucket (*slang*), lose your life, pass away, pass on, perish.
OPPOSITE live, survive.
2 The engine died. break down, conk out (*informal*), fail.
3 She is dying for an ice cream. hanker, hunger, long, thirst, yearn.
die down Interest died down. decline, decrease, diminish, fade, lessen, peter out, subside, taper off, wane.
OPPOSITE grow.
die out The custom has died out. cease, disappear, end, pass, vanish.
OPPOSITE endure, survive.

a
b
c
d
e
f
g
h
i
j
k
l
m
n
o
p
q
r
s
t
u
v
w
x
y
z

diet *noun*
She eats a healthy diet. food intake, nourishment, nutrition.

differ *verb*
1 The twins differ in temperament. be different, be dissimilar, be distinguishable, be poles apart, be unlike, contrast.
OPPOSITE be alike.
2 They differed on the matter. be at odds, clash, disagree, quarrel.
OPPOSITE agree.

difference *noun*
1 a difference in meaning. contrast, deviation, distinction, divergence, nuance.
OPPOSITE likeness, similarity.
2 make up the difference. balance, deficit, gap.
3 a difference in her mood. alteration, change, modification, transformation, variation.
4 They settled their differences. argument, conflict, disagreement, dispute, quarrel.
OPPOSITE agreement.

different *adjective*
1 They have completely different ideas. conflicting, contradictory, contrary, contrasting, dissimilar, distinct, unlike.
OPPOSITE identical.
2 a collection of different stamps. assorted, diverse, miscellaneous, mixed, sundry, various.
OPPOSITE identical.
3 a different way of looking at things. alternative, new, novel, other.
OPPOSITE same.
4 He's different now. altered, changed, modified, transformed.
5 There is a different peg for each person's coat. distinct, individual, particular, separate, special, unique.

difficult *adjective*
1 a difficult maths problem. baffling, challenging, complex, complicated, confusing, hard, knotty, perplexing, problematical, puzzling, thorny, ticklish, tough, tricky.
OPPOSITE easy.
2 Moving the piano is a difficult task. arduous, demanding, exhausting, gruelling, hard, laborious, strenuous,

taxing, tiring, tough, uphill.
OPPOSITE easy.
3 difficult times. bad, hard, harsh, oppressive, rough, severe, tough, troubled.
4 a difficult person to deal with. awkward, demanding, fussy, obstreperous, recalcitrant, stroppy (*informal*), stubborn, troublesome, trying, uncooperative.

difficulty *noun*
He overcame many difficulties. adversity, complication, hang-up (*informal*), hardship, hassle (*informal*), hindrance, hitch, hurdle, impediment, obstacle, ordeal, pitfall, pressure, problem, snag, stumbling block, trouble.
in difficulties in a bind (*informal*), in a fix, in a jam (*informal*), in a mess, in a pickle (*informal*), in a plight, in a predicament, in a quandary, in a spot (*informal*), in dire straits, in hot water (*informal*), in strife (*Australian informal*), in the soup (*informal*), in trouble, up the creek (*informal*).

dig *verb*
1 The wombat dug under the fence. burrow, delve (*old use*), excavate, tunnel.
2 He dug a hole. gouge out, hollow out, scoop out.
3 He dug his fork into the meat. jab, plunge, poke, prod, thrust.
dig *noun*
1 an archaeological dig. excavation.
2 a dig in the ribs. nudge, poke, prod, thrust.
dig up She dug up some useful facts. discover, dredge up, ferret out, find, fossick out (*Australian informal*), root out, seek, uncover, unearth.

digest *verb*
1 digest food. absorb, assimilate, break down.
2 digest information. absorb, assimilate, comprehend, grasp, take in, understand.

dignified *adjective*
a dignified air. a dignified person. calm, decorous, elegant, formal, grand, honourable, imposing, majestic, noble, proper, sedate, serious, sober, solemn,

staid, stately.
OPPOSITE undignified.

dignity *noun*
1 *He behaved with dignity.* decorum, formality, gravity, majesty, nobility, poise, propriety, self-respect, solemnity, stateliness.
2 *a job beneath his dignity.* position, rank, standing, station, status.

dike *noun*
see DYKE.

dilemma *noun (informal)*
in a dilemma. bind (*informal*), catch-22 (*informal*), difficulty, fix, hole (*informal*), jam (*informal*), mess, plight, predicament, problem, quandary, spot (*informal*).

diligent *adjective*
a diligent student. attentive, careful, conscientious, earnest, hard-working, industrious, meticulous, painstaking, persevering, scrupulous, studious, thorough.
OPPOSITE slack.

dilute *verb*
She diluted the soup. thin, water down, weaken.
OPPOSITE concentrate.

dim *adjective*
1 *dim light.* cloudy, dark, dingy, dull, dusky, faint, gloomy, low, murky, pale, shadowy, weak.
OPPOSITE bright.
2 *a dim memory.* blurred, faint, fuzzy, hazy, indistinct, obscure, vague.
OPPOSITE clear.
3 *He's too dim to understand that.* see STUPID.

dimension *noun*
A solid has three dimensions. breadth, depth, height, length, measurement, thickness, width.
dimensions *plural noun*
1 *the room's dimensions.* area, capacity, measurements, proportions, size, volume.
2 *the dimensions of a problem.* extent, magnitude, scale, scope, size.

diminish *verb*
Interest has diminished. abate, decline, decrease, dwindle, fade, lessen, reduce, shrink, subside, wane.
OPPOSITE increase.

din *noun*
She could not hear her friend above the din. bedlam, clamour, clatter, commotion, hubbub, hullabaloo, noise, pandemonium, racket, row (*informal*), rumpus, shindy (*informal*), tumult, uproar.
OPPOSITE silence.

dine *verb*
eat, feast, have dinner, sup.

dingy *adjective*
He felt depressed in his dingy office. dark, dirty, dismal, drab, dreary, dull, gloomy, shabby.
OPPOSITE bright.

dinner *noun*
a farewell dinner. banquet, feast, meal, repast (*formal*), supper, tea.

dinosaur *noun*
[*various dinosaurs*] allosaurus, ankylosaurus, apatosaurus, brachiosaurus, diplodocus, iguanodon, stegosaurus, triceratops, tyrannosaurus.

dip *verb*
1 *She dips her biscuit in her tea.* dunk, immerse, plunge, sink, steep, submerge, wet.
2 *The road dips.* descend, drop, slope downwards.
OPPOSITE rise.
dip *noun*
1 *a dip in the pool.* bathe, bogey (*Australian*), plunge, swim.
2 *a dip in the road.* depression, hollow.
OPPOSITE hump.
dip into *He dipped into the book.* browse, glance at, sample.

diplomat *noun*
ambassador, attaché, consul, envoy, representative.

diplomatic *adjective*
He was diplomatic in his reply. courteous, discreet, polite, sensitive, tactful.
OPPOSITE tactless.

a
b
c
d
e
f
g
h
i
j
k
l
m
n
o
p
q
r
s
t
u
v
w
x
y
z

dire *adjective*
1 *dire consequences.* appalling, calamitous, catastrophic, disastrous, dreadful, horrible, serious, terrible.
2 *dire warnings.* gloomy, grave, grim, ominous.
3 *in dire need.* critical, desperate, drastic, extreme, pressing, urgent.

direct *adjective*
1 *a direct route.* straight, unswerving.
OPPOSITE indirect, roundabout.
2 *a direct way of speaking.* blunt, candid, forthright, frank, honest, open, outspoken, plain, straight, straightforward.
OPPOSITE evasive.

direct *verb*
1 *She directed me to the office.* conduct, guide, lead, navigate, point, show, steer, usher.
2 *They directed their guns at the crowd.* aim, level, point, train, turn.
3 *She directed the meeting.* administer, command, control, govern, head, lead, manage, oversee, preside over, run, superintend, supervise.
4 *He directed them to leave.* command, instruct, order, tell.

direction *noun*
1 *under her direction.* administration, charge, command, control, guidance, leadership, management, supervision.
2 *travelling in a northerly direction.* course, line, route, tack, way.
directions *plural noun*
He followed the directions. guidelines, instructions, recipe, rules.

director *noun*
the director of a company, orchestra, etc. administrator, boss, captain, chairperson, chief, commander, conductor, coordinator, executive, governor, head, leader, manager, superintendent, supervisor.

directory *noun*
Her name is in the directory. index, list, register.

dirt *noun*
1 *Clean the dirt off your shoes.* dust, filth, grime, muck, mud, soot.
2 *planted in the dirt.* earth, soil.

dirty *adjective*
1 *dirty clothes. a dirty place.* blackened, dingy, dusty, filthy, foul, grimy, grotty (*slang*), grubby, insanitary, messy, muddy, soiled, sooty, sordid, squalid, stained, unclean.
OPPOSITE clean.
2 *a dirty trick.* contemptible, despicable, dishonest, dishonourable, low, mean, nasty, shabby, underhand, unfair, unsporting.
OPPOSITE above board.
3 *a dirty joke.* coarse, crude, filthy, improper, indecent, obscene, offensive, pornographic, rude, smutty, tasteless, vulgar.
OPPOSITE clean.

dirty *verb*
Mud dirtied the water. blacken, foul, muddy, pollute, soil, stain, sully, tarnish.
OPPOSITE clean.

disability *noun*
mental or physical disability. handicap, impairment, incapacity.

disabled *adjective*
a disabled person. crippled, handicapped, incapacitated, lame, maimed.
OPPOSITE able-bodied.

disadvantage *noun*
Her shortness was a disadvantage in netball. drawback, handicap, hindrance, impediment, inconvenience, liability, minus.
OPPOSITE advantage, benefit.

disadvantaged *adjective*
a disadvantaged group in society. deprived, underprivileged.
OPPOSITE favoured.

disagree *verb*
1 *the right to disagree.* differ, dissent, diverge.
OPPOSITE agree.
2 *His statement disagrees with theirs.* be at odds, be incompatible, clash, conflict, contrast, differ (from).
OPPOSITE coincide.
3 *The sisters disagree over everything.* argue, be at loggerheads, differ, quarrel.
OPPOSITE agree.

disagreeable *adjective*

1 *a disagreeable smell.* disgusting, distasteful, nasty, objectionable, obnoxious, offensive, repulsive, revolting, unpleasant.
OPPOSITE pleasant.
2 *He is disagreeable when he first gets up.* bad-tempered, crabby, cross, crotchety, grouchy (*informal*), grumpy, irritable, shirty (*informal*), snaky (*Australian informal*), stroppy (*informal*), surly, unfriendly.
OPPOSITE affable.

disagreement *noun*

There was a disagreement over boundaries. argument, clash, conflict, controversy, dispute, quarrel, row, tiff, wrangle.
OPPOSITE consensus.

disappear *verb*

1 *The man disappeared before we could find out his name.* clear off (*informal*), flee, go away, nick off (*Australian slang*), retire, retreat, run away, run off, scarper (*informal*), scram (*informal*), shoot through (*Australian informal*), vanish, withdraw.
OPPOSITE appear, arrive.
2 *The fog disappeared.* clear, evaporate, fade, melt away, pass, vanish.

disappoint *verb*

1 *The attendance disappointed the organisers.* discourage, dishearten, disillusion, let down, sadden.
OPPOSITE gratify.
2 *He disappointed their hopes.* dash, destroy, frustrate, shatter, thwart.
OPPOSITE satisfy.

disappointment *noun*

1 *feel disappointment.* disenchantment, disillusionment, dissatisfaction, frustration, regret, sadness, unhappiness.
OPPOSITE fulfilment.
2 *The actual event was a bit of a disappointment.* anticlimax, comedown, failure, fiasco, fizzer (*Australian informal*), flop (*slang*), let-down, non-event, wash-out (*slang*).
OPPOSITE success.

disapproval *noun*

She viewed the deal with disapproval. censure, condemnation, criticism, disfavour, dissatisfaction; see also OPPOSITION.

disapprove *verb*

disapprove of *He disapproved of what they did.* censure, condemn, criticise, deplore, frown on, object to, take a dim view of (*informal*).
OPPOSITE approve.

disaster *noun*

1 *natural disasters.* accident, adversity, calamity, catastrophe, misfortune, mishap, tragedy.
2 *The dinner was a disaster.* failure, fiasco, fizzer (*Australian informal*), flop (*slang*), wash-out (*slang*).
OPPOSITE success.

disastrous *adjective*

disastrous consequences. appalling, calamitous, catastrophic, devastating, dire, dreadful, ruinous, terrible, tragic.

disbelieve *verb*

She disbelieved their explanation. distrust, doubt, mistrust, question.
OPPOSITE believe.

disc *noun*

1 *The game is played with coloured discs.* circle, counter, token.
2 *music discs.* album, compact disc, record, recording, single.

discard *verb*

They discarded their old clothes. cast off, chuck out (*informal*), dice (*Australian informal*), dispose of, ditch (*informal*), dump, get rid of, reject, scrap, shed, throw away.
OPPOSITE keep.

discharge *verb*

1 *discharge fluid.* belch, eject, emit, empty out, expel, give out, leak, ooze, pour out, release, secrete, send out, spurt.
2 *discharge a missile.* detonate, explode, fire, let off, set off, shoot, trigger.
3 *discharge an employee.* dismiss, fire, kick out (*informal*), sack (*informal*).
OPPOSITE hire.
4 *discharge from hospital.* free, liberate, release.
OPPOSITE admit.

a
b
c
d
e
f
g
h
i
j
k
l
m
n
o
p
q
r
s
t
u
v
w
x
y
z

disciple *noun*
a disciple of the famous teacher. follower, pupil, supporter.

discipline *noun*
The teacher maintains good discipline. control, order, routine, system.
discipline *verb*
1 She disciplined them to say 'Please'. coach, drill, educate, indoctrinate, instruct, train.
2 He disciplined them harshly. chastise, correct, punish, rebuke, reprimand.

disclose *verb*
disclose a secret. air, betray, blab, blow (slang), bring to light, divulge, expose, give away, impart, leak, let out, let slip, make known, make public, publish, reveal, tell, uncover.
OPPOSITE cover up.

disco *noun* (informal)
club, discothèque, nightclub; see also DANCE.

discolour *verb*
The material has discoloured. bleach, fade, scorch, stain, tarnish, tinge.

discomfort *noun*
physical or mental discomfort. ache, affliction, distress, hardship, irritation, misery, pain, soreness, suffering, uneasiness.
OPPOSITE comfort.

disconnect *verb*
disconnect the power supply. cut off, detach, switch off, turn off, undo, unplug.
OPPOSITE connect.

discontented *adjective*
He was discontented with his job. browned off (slang), disenchanted, disgruntled, displeased, dissatisfied, fed up (informal), miserable, unhappy.
OPPOSITE contented.

discontinue *verb*
They discontinued the class. abandon, break off, cancel, cease, cut, end, finish, interrupt, stop, suspend, terminate.
OPPOSITE continue.

discount *noun*
a 5% discount on the full price. concession, deduction, rebate, reduction.

discourage *verb*
1 She was discouraged by her failure. daunt, demoralise, depress, dishearten, dismay, intimidate.
OPPOSITE encourage.
2 They discouraged him from applying. deter, dissuade, put off, talk out of.
OPPOSITE persuade.

discourteous *adjective*
bad-mannered, cheeky, disrespectful, impertinent, impolite, impudent, insolent, insulting, rude, uncivil, uncouth.
OPPOSITE polite.

discover *verb*
She discovered the solution. come across, come upon, detect, dig up, ferret out, find, hear of, hit on, identify, learn, light on, locate, perceive, read of, realise, spot, stumble on, track down, uncover, unearth, work out.

discoverer *noun*
creator, explorer, inventor, pioneer.

discreet *adjective*
She was discreet in her comments. careful, cautious, circumspect, diplomatic, guarded, prudent, tactful, wary.
OPPOSITE indiscreet.

discretion *noun*
He acted with discretion. care, discernment, judgement, prudence, sense, sensitivity, tact, wisdom.
OPPOSITE indiscretion.

discriminate *verb*
He can't discriminate between the two brands. differentiate, distinguish, tell apart.

discrimination *noun*
sexual discrimination. bias, favouritism, prejudice, unfairness.
OPPOSITE impartiality.

discuss *verb*
They discussed the matter. argue, consider, debate, examine, have out, speak about, talk about, thrash out.

discussion *noun*
a discussion between management and the union. argument, conference, consultation, conversation, debate, dialogue, talk.

disdain *noun*
treat with disdain. contempt, derision, scorn.
OPPOSITE respect.
disdain *verb*
He disdained their attempts at reconciliation. despise, look down on, reject, scorn, sneer at, spurn.

disdainful *adjective*
a disdainful attitude. arrogant, contemptuous, haughty, proud, scornful, sneering, snobbish, snooty (*informal*), supercilious, superior.

disease *noun*
affliction, ailment, bug (*informal*), complaint, condition, disorder, illness, infection, malady, plague, sickness.

disembark *verb*
alight, get off, get out, go ashore, land.
OPPOSITE board.

disfigured *adjective*
The accident left him disfigured. defaced, deformed, mutilated, scarred.

disgrace *noun*
He brought disgrace upon himself. discredit, dishonour, disrepute, humiliation, reproach, shame.
OPPOSITE honour.
disgrace *verb*
He disgraced his family. bring dishonour to, bring shame on, embarrass, humiliate, let down.

disgraceful *adjective*
disgraceful conduct. discreditable, dishonourable, outrageous, scandalous, shameful, unbecoming, unseemly.
OPPOSITE creditable.

disguise *verb*
1 He disguised himself as a priest. dress up, masquerade; see also IMPERSONATE.
2 He could not disguise his true feelings. camouflage, conceal, cover up, hide, mask, veil.

disguise *noun*
We were taken in by the disguise. camouflage, costume, mask, masquerade.

disgust *noun*
overcome feelings of disgust. abhorrence, aversion, contempt, dislike, distaste, hatred, loathing, nausea, repugnance, repulsion, revulsion.
disgust *verb*
The battle scene disgusted them. appal, horrify, nauseate, offend, repel, revolt, shock, sicken, turn someone's stomach.

disgusting *adjective*
a disgusting habit. appalling, detestable, distasteful, dreadful, filthy, foul, gross (*informal*), loathsome, nauseating, objectionable, offensive, off-putting, repulsive, revolting, shocking, sickening, unpleasant, vile, yucky (*informal*).
OPPOSITE delightful.

dish *noun*
basin, bowl, container, plate, platter, ramekin, receptacle; [*dishes*] crockery.
dish out see DISTRIBUTE.

dishevelled *adjective*
The runners were dishevelled. bedraggled, messy, ruffled, scruffy, tangled, tousled, unkempt, untidy.
OPPOSITE neat.

dishonest *adjective*
a dishonest person. a dishonest act. bent (*slang*), corrupt, criminal, crooked, deceitful, deceptive, dodgy (*informal*), false, fraudulent, hypocritical, insincere, lying, misleading, shady, shonky (*Australian informal*), two-faced, underhand, unscrupulous, untrustworthy, untruthful.
OPPOSITE honest.

disinfect *verb*
clean, cleanse, fumigate, purify, sanitise, sterilise.

disinfectant *noun*
antiseptic, bactericide, germicide, sanitiser, steriliser.

disintegrate *verb*
The structure disintegrated after many years. break up, collapse, crumble,

a
b
c
d
e
f
g
h
i
j
k
l
m
n
o
p
q
r
s
t
u
v
w
x
y
z

decay, decompose, deteriorate, fall apart, perish, rot, shatter.

disinterested *adjective*
The adjudicator must be a disinterested party. dispassionate, impartial, neutral, objective, unbiased, uninvolved, unprejudiced.
OPPOSITE biased, interested.

disjointed *adjective*
a disjointed speech. disconnected, disorganised, fragmented, incoherent, jumbled, mixed up, rambling.
OPPOSITE coherent.

dislike *noun*
a dislike of something or someone. abhorrence, antipathy, aversion, contempt, detestation, disgust, distaste, hatred, horror, loathing, repugnance, resentment, revulsion.
OPPOSITE liking.
dislike *verb*
She dislikes liars. abominate, despise, detest, hate, loathe, object to, resent, take exception to.
OPPOSITE like.

disloyal *adjective*
He was disloyal to his friends. faithless, false, treacherous, two-faced, unfaithful, untrue.
OPPOSITE loyal.

dismal *adjective*
dismal songs. black, bleak, cheerless, depressing, dreary, gloomy, grim, melancholy, miserable, mournful, sad, sombre.
OPPOSITE cheerful.

dismantle *verb*
They dismantled the trampoline for storage. demolish, knock down, pull to pieces, take apart, take down, undo.
OPPOSITE assemble, erect.

dismay *noun*
The thought of war filled them with dismay. agitation, alarm, anxiety, apprehension, consternation, dread, fear, horror, shock, terror, trepidation.
OPPOSITE delight.
dismay *verb*
The amount of work dismayed her. alarm, appal, daunt, depress, disconcert, discourage, dishearten, distress,

frighten, horrify, scare, shock, terrify, unnerve.
OPPOSITE cheer.

dismiss *verb*
1 *The teacher dismissed the class.* disband, let go, release, send away.
2 *The boss dismissed him.* discharge, fire, get rid of, give notice to, give the boot to (*slang*), give the sack to (*informal*), kick out (*informal*), lay off, make redundant, pension off, remove, sack (*informal*).
OPPOSITE hire, reinstate.
3 *He was quick to dismiss the idea.* discard, give up, pooh-pooh, reject, set aside.
OPPOSITE accept.

disobedient *adjective*
a disobedient person. contrary, defiant, insubordinate, mutinous, naughty, obstreperous, perverse, rebellious, recalcitrant, unmanageable, unruly, wayward.
OPPOSITE compliant, obedient.

disobey *verb*
She disobeyed the rules. break, defy, disregard, flout, ignore, infringe, transgress, violate.
OPPOSITE obey, observe.

disorder *noun*
1 *The room was in disorder.* chaos, confusion, disarray, mess, muddle, shambles, untidiness.
OPPOSITE order.
2 *public disorder.* anarchy, bedlam, chaos, commotion, confusion, havoc, lawlessness, mayhem, pandemonium, rioting, trouble, turmoil, unrest, uproar.
OPPOSITE order, peace.
3 *a nervous disorder.* ailment, complaint, condition, disease, illness, malady, sickness.

disorderly *adjective*
1 *a disorderly crowd.* badly-behaved, boisterous, lawless, obstreperous, riotous, rowdy, turbulent, undisciplined, unruly, wild.
OPPOSITE well-behaved.
2 *a disorderly office.* chaotic, confused, disorganised, higgledy-piggledy, jumbled, messy, muddled, topsy-turvy,

unsystematic, untidy.
OPPOSITE tidy.

disorganised *adjective*
disorganised work. careless, confused,
disorderly, haphazard, messy, slipshod,
sloppy, unmethodical, unsystematic.
OPPOSITE methodical.

dispatch *verb*
1 *They dispatched the parcel.* consign,
convey, deliver, forward, mail, post,
send, transmit.
OPPOSITE receive.
2 *The farmer dispatched the sick cow.* see
KILL.
dispatch *noun*
a government dispatch. bulletin,
communication, communiqué, letter,
message, report.

dispense *verb*
1 *She dispensed their pocket money.*
allocate, allot, apportion, deal out, dish
out (*informal*), distribute, dole out, give
out, hand out, issue.
2 *The chemist dispenses medicines.* give
out, make up, prepare, provide, supply.
dispense with *We can dispense with the
car.* dispose of, do without, forgo, get
rid of, relinquish.
OPPOSITE retain.

disperse *verb*
The crowd dispersed. break up, disband,
scatter, spread out.
OPPOSITE congregate, gather.

displace *verb*
She was displaced in his affections. oust,
replace, supersede, supplant.

display *verb*
He displayed confidence. demonstrate,
exhibit, flaunt, parade, present, reveal,
show.
OPPOSITE conceal.
display *noun*
a doll display. a ballet display. array,
demonstration, exhibition, exposition,
presentation, show, spectacle.

displease *verb*
His behaviour displeased them. anger,
annoy, irritate, offend, trouble, upset,
vex, worry.
OPPOSITE please.

disposable *adjective*
1 *disposable income.* available, net,
usable.
2 *disposable cups.* discardable, throw-
away.
OPPOSITE reusable.

dispose *verb*
dispose of *She disposed of her old car.*
discard, dispatch, ditch (*informal*),
dump, get rid of, give away, scrap, sell,
throw away, throw out.
OPPOSITE keep.

disposition *noun*
a kindly disposition. attitude, character,
make-up, nature, personality, spirit,
temperament.

disprove *verb*
He disproved the theory. discredit,
explode, negate, rebut, refute.
OPPOSITE confirm, prove.

dispute *verb*
1 *The brothers disputed about the money.*
argue, bicker, clash, debate, disagree,
haggle, quarrel, squabble, wrangle.
2 *He disputed their right to be there.*
challenge, contest, query, question.
OPPOSITE accept.
dispute *noun*
a dispute about ownership. argument,
battle, conflict, controversy, debate,
disagreement, quarrel, row, squabble,
wrangle.

disqualify *verb*
He was disqualified from driving. ban, bar,
debar, outlaw, prohibit.

disregard *verb*
He disregarded my wishes. brush aside,
forget, ignore, neglect, overlook, pay no
attention to; see also DISOBEY.
OPPOSITE heed.

disrespect *noun*
He meant no disrespect. contempt,
impiety, impoliteness, insolence,
irreverence, rudeness.
OPPOSITE respect.

disrespectful *adjective*
She was disrespectful to her mother.
cheeky, contemptuous, discourteous,
impertinent, impolite, impudent,

a
b
c
d
e
f
g
h
i
j
k
l
m
n
o
p
q
r
s
t
u
v
w
x
y
z

insolent, offensive, rude.
OPPOSITE respectful.

disrupt *verb*
The strike disrupted progress on the site.
break up, cut into, disturb, interfere
with, interrupt, upset.

dissatisfied *adjective*
dissatisfied patrons. browned off (*slang*),
disappointed, discontented,
disenchanted, disgruntled, displeased,
fed up (*informal*), frustrated, unhappy.
OPPOSITE contented, satisfied.

dissect *verb*
The students dissected a rat. cut up,
dismember.

dissent *verb*
Only one member dissented. differ,
disagree, object, protest.
OPPOSITE assent.

dissolve *verb*
1 *The crystals dissolve in hot water.*
liquefy, melt.
2 *He dissolved into thin air.* disappear,
fade, melt, vanish.
3 *She dissolved into tears.* break, collapse,
melt.

dissuade *verb*
dissuade from *He dissuaded them from
running.* advise against, deter from,
discourage from, put off.
OPPOSITE persuade to.

distance *noun*
the distance between A and B. gap,
interval, length, range, space, span,
stretch.

distant *adjective*
1 *a distant place.* far, far-away, far-flung,
far-off, outlying, remote.
OPPOSITE close.
2 *The friends had become distant with one
another.* aloof, cold, cool, offhand,
remote, reserved, stand-offish,
unfriendly, withdrawn.
OPPOSITE close.

distasteful *adjective*
He found cleaning distasteful. detestable,
disagreeable, disgusting, loathsome,
nauseating, objectionable, off-putting,
repugnant, repulsive, revolting,

sickening, unpleasant, vile.
OPPOSITE pleasant.

distinct *adjective*
1 *a distinct improvement.* clear, clear-cut,
definite, marked, noticeable, obvious,
plain, pronounced, sharp, strong,
unmistakable.
OPPOSITE vague.
2 *two distinct problems.* different,
individual, separate, unconnected.

distinction *noun*
1 *a distinction between the two groups.*
contrast, difference.
OPPOSITE similarity.
2 *wines of distinction.* class, eminence,
excellence, fame, merit, note, prestige,
prominence, quality, renown, worth.
OPPOSITE mediocrity.

distinctive *adjective*
a distinctive footstep. characteristic,
different, distinguishing, idiosyncratic,
individual, peculiar, personal, special,
specific, unique.
OPPOSITE nondescript.

distinguish *verb*
1 *He cannot distinguish between blue and
black.* differentiate, discriminate,
separate, tell apart.
2 *His voice distinguished him from the
others.* differentiate, identify, mark, set
apart.
3 *She distinguished his footstep.* discern,
identify, make out, perceive, pick out,
recognise, single out.

distinguished *adjective*
1 *a distinguished pianist.* celebrated,
eminent, famed, famous, great,
illustrious, important, legendary,
notable, noted, outstanding, pre-
eminent, prominent, renowned,
respected, well-known.
OPPOSITE unknown.
2 *He had a distinguished air.* aristocratic,
dignified, grand, noble, refined, regal.

distort *verb*
1 *The heat distorted the metal.* bend,
buckle, contort, deform, skew, twist,
warp.
2 *He distorted the account.* colour, garble,
misrepresent, slant, twist.

distract *verb*
She was distracted by another customer.
divert, draw away, sidetrack.

distraction *noun*
Television is a useful distraction.
amusement, diversion, entertainment, escape, pastime, recreation.

distraught *adjective*
The police spoke to the distraught parents.
agitated, distressed, frantic, hysterical, overwrought, upset.

distress *noun*
1 *The man was in distress.* affliction, agony, anguish, discomfort, misery, pain, sorrow, suffering, torment, torture, woe.
OPPOSITE comfort.
2 *a ship in distress.* adversity, danger, difficulty, trouble.
OPPOSITE safety.

distress *verb*
The news distressed them. afflict, bother, dismay, disturb, grieve, hurt, pain, perturb, sadden, shake, shock, torment, torture, trouble, upset, worry.
OPPOSITE cheer.

distressing *adjective*
a distressing sight of suffering animals.
appalling, disturbing, grievous, heartbreaking, heart-rending, horrific, painful, pathetic, poignant, sad, terrible, tragic, traumatic, upsetting.
OPPOSITE heartening.

distribute *verb*
He distributed the lollies. allocate, allot, apportion, assign, circulate, deal out, deliver, dish out (*informal*), dispense, divide up, dole out, give out, hand out, issue, pass round, serve, share out.

district *noun*
area, community, electorate (*Australian*), locality, municipality, neighbourhood, precinct, province, region, shire, suburb, territory, vicinity, zone.

distrust *noun*
doubt, mistrust, suspicion.
OPPOSITE trust.

distrust *verb*
He distrusted their motives. doubt, mistrust, question, suspect.
OPPOSITE trust.

distrustful *adjective*
She was distrustful of strangers.
mistrustful, paranoid, suspicious, wary.
OPPOSITE trusting.

disturb *verb*
1 *The news disturbed him.* alarm, disconcert, distress, fluster, perturb, rattle (*informal*), startle, trouble, upset, worry.
2 *They try not to disturb her during the day.* annoy, bother, hassle (*informal*), interrupt, pester.
3 *The surface of the water was disturbed by a boat.* agitate, churn up, ripple, rock, ruffle, shake.

disturbance *noun*
The youths created a disturbance at the shops. commotion, fracas, hullabaloo, kerfuffle (*informal*), racket, riot, row, rumpus, stir, to-do, trouble, tumult, turmoil, unrest, uproar.

disturbed *adjective*
mentally disturbed. deranged, unbalanced, unstable.

disused *adjective*
a disused building. abandoned, idle, neglected, obsolete.

ditch *noun*
He dug a ditch. channel, drain, dyke, gutter, moat, trench.
ditch *verb* (*informal*)
She ditched her boyfriend. abandon, dice (*Australian informal*), discard, drop, dump (*informal*), get rid of, reject.
OPPOSITE keep.

dither *verb*
He dithered about signing the contract.
hesitate, hum and haw, shilly-shally, waver.

dive *verb*
1 *She dived under water.* dip, plunge, submerge.
2 *The aircraft suddenly dived.* descend, drop, nosedive, plummet, plunge, swoop.
OPPOSITE rise.

a
b
c
d
e
f
g
h
i
j
k
l
m
n
o
p
q
r
s
t
u
v
w
x
y
z

dive *noun*
a dive into the water. header, plunge.

diverge *verb*
The paths diverged. branch, divide, fork,
separate, split.
OPPOSITE converge.

diverse *adjective*
1 *a diverse group.* miscellaneous, mixed,
motley, varied.
OPPOSITE uniform.
2 *people of diverse backgrounds.* assorted,
different, various.
OPPOSITE similar.

diversion *noun*
1 *Reading is her favourite diversion.*
amusement, distraction, entertainment,
escape, game, hobby, pastime,
recreation, sport.
2 *a traffic diversion.* bypass, detour,
deviation.

divert *verb*
1 *The police diverted traffic.* deflect,
redirect, shunt, sidetrack, turn aside.
2 *The clown diverted the audience.* amuse,
cheer up, distract, entertain.

divide *verb*
1 *She divided the chicken into even
portions.* break up, carve up, cut up,
joint, part, partition, separate, split,
subdivide.
2 *The road divides here.* branch, diverge,
fork, split.
3 *He divided the food amongst them.* allot,
apportion, deal out, dish out (*informal*),
distribute, dole out, share.
4 *He divided the plants into varieties.*
arrange, categorise, class, classify,
group, sort.

divine *adjective*
divine intervention. celestial, godlike,
heavenly, holy, sacred, spiritual,
superhuman, supernatural.
OPPOSITE human.

division *noun*
1 *the division of the profits.* allocation,
distribution, sharing, splitting.
2 *arranged in separate divisions.* bay,
compartment, part, section, segment.
3 *the divisions of an organisation.* branch,
department, section, sector,
subdivision.
4 *The issue caused division in the party.*
disagreement, discord, dissension,
disunity.
OPPOSITE unity.

divorce *verb*
The couple divorced. break up, part,
separate, split up.
OPPOSITE marry.

dizziness *noun*
faintness, giddiness, light-headedness,
vertigo.

dizzy *adjective*
He felt dizzy on the roof. faint, giddy,
light-headed, reeling, unsteady, woozy
(*informal*).
OPPOSITE steady.

do *verb*
1 *She did her duty.* accomplish, carry out,
complete, execute, fulfil, perform,
undertake.
2 *What wrong has he done?* commit,
perpetrate.
3 *He did five copies.* make, prepare,
produce, turn out.
4 *He does the cleaning.* attend to, deal
with, handle, look after, manage.
5 *She couldn't do this problem.* answer,
solve, work out.
6 *Do as I say.* act, behave, conduct
yourself, practise.
7 *How is the patient doing?* fare, get on,
make out.
8 *That will never do.* be acceptable, be
adequate, be enough, be satisfactory, be
sufficient, be suitable, suffice.
do *noun* (*informal*)
a farewell do. event, function, occasion,
party, reception.
do away with *They did away with that
law.* abolish, axe, get rid of, scrap, stop.
OPPOSITE retain.
do up
1 *He did up his boots.* buckle, fasten, lace
up, zip.
2 *They did up the house.* redecorate,
renovate, repair, restore.
do without *They did without sugar.*
abstain from, dispense with, forgo, go
without.

dob *verb* (*Australian informal*)
dob in
1 He dobs in cheats. blow the whistle on, denounce, grass (on) (slang), inform on, report, shop (slang), split on (slang), tell on.
2 We all dobbed in $5 for his present. chip in (*informal*), contribute, donate, give, pitch in (*informal*), put in.

docile *adjective*
a docile creature. biddable, compliant, gentle, meek, mild, obedient, passive, submissive, tame.
OPPOSITE intractable.

dock *noun*
The ship is in the dock. berth, jetty, landing stage, pier, quay, slipway, wharf.
dock *verb*
The ship docked at Sydney. berth, moor, put in.
docks *plural noun*
dockyard, harbour, marina, port, shipyard.

doctor *noun*
consultant, general practitioner, GP, intern, locum, medical practitioner, medico (*informal*), physician, quack (*slang*), specialist, surgeon; [*various specialist doctors*] anaesthetist, cardiologist, dermatologist, gastroenterologist, gynaecologist, haematologist, neurologist, obstetrician, ophthalmologist, orthopaedic surgeon, paediatrician, plastic surgeon, psychiatrist, radiologist.

doctrine *noun*
a religious doctrine. belief, conviction, creed, dogma, philosophy, principle, teaching.

document *noun*
official documents. certificate, charter, contract, deed, form, licence, paper, policy, record, report.
document *verb*
1 They documented their claims with receipts. back up, prove, substantiate, support.
2 He documented the interview. chronicle, record, report, write up.

doddery *adjective*
a doddery old man. decrepit, frail, infirm, shaky, tottering, trembling, unsteady.

dodge *verb*
1 She dodged out of the way of the ball. duck, escape, sidestep, swerve, veer.
2 He dodged their questions. avoid, evade, fend off, sidestep, skirt round.
3 She dodged work. avoid, evade, get out of, shirk, shun, shy away from.
dodge *noun* (*informal*)
a tax dodge. lurk (*Australian informal*), racket, rort (*Australian slang*), ruse, scam (*slang*), scheme, trick.

dog *noun*
a dog as a pet. bitch (*female*), cur, hound, mongrel, mutt (*informal*), pooch (*slang*), pup, puppy, whelp; [*various breeds of dog*] Afghan hound, Alsatian, basset-hound, beagle, bloodhound, blue heeler, borzoi, boxer, bulldog, bull terrier, cattle dog, chihuahua, chow, cocker spaniel, collie, corgi, dachshund, Dalmatian, dingo, Dobermann pinscher, foxhound, fox terrier, Great Dane, greyhound, husky, kelpie, Labrador, mastiff, Newfoundland, Old English sheepdog, Pekingese, pit bull terrier, pointer, Pomeranian, poodle, pug, retriever, Rottweiler, St Bernard, Samoyed, setter, sheepdog, shih-tzu, spaniel, Sydney silky, terrier, whippet, wolfhound.

dogged *adjective*
She finished by dogged determination. determined, firm, obstinate, patient, persistent, resolute, single-minded, stubborn, tenacious, unwavering.

dogmatic *adjective*
a dogmatic manner. assertive, authoritative, categorical, cocksure, dictatorial, opinionated.

dogsbody *noun* (*informal*)
He was treated as the office dogsbody. drudge, slave.

dole *verb*
dole out He doles out the money. allocate, apportion, deal out, deliver, dish out

a
b
c
d
e
f
g
h
i
j
k
l
m
n
o
p
q
r
s
t
u
v
w
x
y
z

(*informal*), dispense, distribute, give out, hand out, share out.
dole *noun* (*informal*)
She finds it hard to live on the dole. benefit, social security, unemployment benefit.

dollop *noun*
a dollop of cream. blob, lump.

domain *noun*
1 *the king's domain.* dominion, empire, kingdom, land, province, realm, territory.
2 *the domain of science.* area, field, sphere.

dome *noun*
a church with a dome. cupola.

domestic *adjective*
1 *domestic duties.* family, home, household.
2 *a domestic flight.* internal, national.
OPPOSITE international.
3 *domestic animals.* domesticated, house-trained, pet, tame.
OPPOSITE wild.

dominant *adjective*
the dominant person in a group. the dominant features. chief, influential, leading, main, outstanding, paramount, predominant, prevailing, principal, ruling.

dominate *verb*
The television dominates their lives. control, govern, monopolise, rule.

dominion *noun*
1 *He has dominion over the country.* authority, control, power, rule, sway.
2 *ruler of several dominions.* domain, empire, kingdom, realm, state, territory.

donate *verb*
She donated $2000 to their cause. chip in (*informal*), contribute, fork out (*slang*), give, grant, present, provide, subscribe.
OPPOSITE receive.

donation *noun*
All donations will be gratefully received. contribution, gift, handout, offering, present.

donkey *noun*
ass, jackass (*male*), jenny (*female*).

donor *noun*
The money came from an anonymous donor. benefactor, contributor, giver, provider, sponsor.
OPPOSITE recipient.

doom *noun*
face your doom. death, destiny, destruction, end, fate, ruin.
doom *verb*
He was doomed to failure. destine, fate, ordain, predestine.

door *noun*
doorway, entrance, entry, exit, gate, hatch, portal, trapdoor.

doorstep *noun*
step, threshold.

dope *noun*
1 (*informal*) *They found dope in his possession.* drug, narcotic.
2 (*informal*) *She knew she'd been a dope.* ass (*informal*), clot (*informal*), fool, idiot (*informal*), imbecile, mug (*informal*), nincompoop, twit (*slang*).
dope *verb*
The man was doped. anaesthetise, drug, sedate.

dopey *adjective* (*informal*)
1 *He is dopey when he first gets up.* groggy, sleepy.
2 *a dopey thing to do.* dumb (*informal*), foolish, idiotic, reckless, senseless, silly, stupid, unwise.
OPPOSITE sensible.

dormant *adjective*
a dormant animal. asleep, hibernating, inactive, resting, sleeping.
OPPOSITE active, awake.

dose *noun*
a dose of medicine. dosage, measure, portion, quantity.

dot *noun*
fleck, mark, point, speck, speckle, spot.

dote *verb*
dote on *She dotes on her grandchildren.* adore, cherish, idolise, love, treasure, worship.

dotted *adjective*
dotted material. flecked, freckled, speckled, spotted.

double *adjective*
1 *double lines.* duplicate, paired, twin.
OPPOSITE single.
2 *a double purpose.* dual, twin, twofold.
OPPOSITE single.
double *noun*
She was shocked to see her double. clone,
copy, dead spit, duplicate, look-alike,
ringer (*informal*), spitting image, twin.
double *verb* (*Australian*)
He doubled his friend on his bike. dink
(*Australian*), dinky (*Australian*), donkey
(*Australian*), double-bank (*Australian*),
double-dink (*Australian*).

double-cross *verb*
The scoundrel double-crossed him. betray,
cheat, deceive, trick.

doubt *noun*
They have some doubts about the situation.
anxiety, concern, hesitation, misgiving,
qualm, reservation, uncertainty, worry.
OPPOSITE certainty.
doubt *verb*
He doubted their honesty. distrust,
mistrust, question, suspect.

doubtful *adjective*
He felt doubtful about the job. distrustful,
dubious, hesitant, mistrustful, sceptical,
suspicious, uncertain, undecided,
unsure.
OPPOSITE certain.

dowdy *adjective*
dowdy clothes. daggy (*Australian
informal*), drab, dull, old-fashioned,
shabby, sloppy, unattractive,
unfashionable.
OPPOSITE smart.

down¹ *verb* (*informal*)
He downed a glass of beer. drain, drink,
gulp down, swallow.
down *noun* (*informal*)
The man had a down on him. derry
(*Australian informal*), grudge, set
(*Australian informal*); see also DISLIKE.
down and out *The rich man helps those
who are down and out.* broke (*informal*),
destitute, hard up (*informal*), needy,
penniless, poor.
OPPOSITE rich.

down² *noun*
goose down. feathers, fluff, plumage.

downcast *adjective*
He was downcast and needed cheering up.
crestfallen, dejected, depressed,
despondent, discouraged, disheartened,
dispirited, down, down-hearted, down
in the dumps, heavy-hearted, low,
melancholy, miserable, sad, unhappy,
wretched.
OPPOSITE elated, happy.

downfall *noun*
Greed caused his downfall. collapse,
destruction, fall, ruin, undoing.

downpour *noun*
caught in a downpour. cloudburst,
deluge, rainstorm, shower, storm.

downright *adjective*
downright nonsense. absolute, complete,
out-and-out, outright, pure, sheer,
thorough, utter.

down-to-earth *adjective*
matter-of-fact, no-nonsense, practical,
realistic, sensible.
OPPOSITE airy-fairy.

doze *verb*
She dozed in a chair. drop off, nap, nod
off, sleep, slumber, snooze.

drab *adjective*
The place looks drab. cheerless,
colourless, dingy, dismal, dreary, dull,
sombre, unattractive.
OPPOSITE bright.

draft *noun*
a draft of the thesis. outline, plan, sketch.
draft *verb*
1 *She drafted a proposal.* draw up,
outline, plan.
2 (*American*) *He was drafted into the army.*
call up, conscript.

drag *verb*
He dragged a heavy load. draw, haul, lug,
pull, tow, tug.
drag *noun*
He found the work a drag. bind (*informal*),
bore, nuisance, strain.
drag out *He dragged out the discussions.*
draw out, extend, prolong, protract,
spin out.
OPPOSITE shorten.

a
b
c
d
e
f
g
h
i
j
k
l
m
n
o
p
q
r
s
t
u
v
w
x
y
z

drain *verb*

1 *He drained the water from the can.* draw off, empty, pour off.
2 *The bath water drained out.* discharge, empty, flow out.
3 *The mowing drained his energy.* consume, exhaust, sap, spend, use up.

drain *noun*

The drain is blocked. channel, ditch, gutter, outlet, pipe, sewer, trench.

drama *noun*

1 *a three-act drama.* play.
2 *They study drama at school.* acting, dramatics, stagecraft, theatre.
3 *Her life is full of drama.* action, excitement, suspense.

dramatic *adjective*

1 *dramatic works.* stage, theatrical.
2 *a dramatic change.* impressive, marked, noticeable, radical, spectacular, startling, striking.

dramatist *noun*

playwright.

drastic *adjective*

drastic measures. desperate, dire, extreme, radical, severe.

draught *noun*

He felt a cold draught. breeze, wind.

draw *verb*

1 *She likes to draw. He drew the scene.* depict, doodle, illustrate, outline, picture, portray, represent, scribble, sketch, trace.
2 *The car drew a heavy load.* drag, haul, lug, pull, tow, tug.
3 *The show drew a large crowd.* attract, bring in, entice, lure.
4 *The waiter drew the cork.* extract, remove, pull out, take out.
5 *Our team drew with theirs.* be equal, tie.

draw *noun*

1 *The band proved quite a draw.* attraction, drawcard, enticement, lure.
2 *The contest ended in a draw.* dead heat, deadlock, stalemate, tie.

draw back *He drew back in fear.* cringe, recoil, retreat, shrink back, withdraw.
draw out *He drew out the meeting with unnecessary questions.* drag out, extend, lengthen, prolong, protract, spin out. OPPOSITE shorten.

draw up

1 *The taxi drew up.* come to a stop, halt, pull up, stop.
2 *He drew up a contract.* compose, draft, prepare, write out.

drawback *noun*

The plan has no drawbacks. disadvantage, handicap, hindrance, inconvenience, liability, minus, shortcoming. OPPOSITE advantage.

drawers *plural noun*

see CHEST OF DRAWERS (at CHEST).

drawing *noun*

cartoon, chart, design, diagram, illustration, pattern, picture, plan, portrait, sketch.

dread *noun*

He faced the exams with dread. anxiety, apprehension, dismay, fear, foreboding, horror, panic, terror, trepidation. OPPOSITE confidence.

dread *verb*

She dreaded the punishment. be afraid of, be scared of, fear.

dreadful *adjective*

1 *a dreadful accident.* appalling, awful, bad, calamitous, catastrophic, disastrous, fearful, frightful, ghastly, grisly, hideous, horrendous, horrible, horrific, terrible, tragic.
2 *(informal) dreadful weather.* abominable *(informal)*, appalling *(informal)*, atrocious *(informal)*, bad, foul, lousy *(informal)*, miserable, nasty, rotten *(informal)*, shocking *(informal)*, terrible *(informal)*. OPPOSITE good, pleasant.

dream *noun*

1 *lost in a dream.* daydream, fantasy, hallucination, illusion, nightmare, reverie, trance, vision.
2 *His dream is to own a sports car.* ambition, aspiration, desire, goal, hope, wish.

dream *verb*

He dreamt he was flying. daydream, fancy, fantasise, hallucinate, imagine.
dream up *He dreamt up a silly scheme.* conceive, concoct, create, devise, imagine, invent, think up.

dreary *adjective*
1 *a dreary performance.* boring, deadly (*informal*), dull, humdrum, lacklustre, lifeless, monotonous, mundane, tedious, tiresome, uninteresting.
2 *a dreary place.* bleak, cheerless, colourless, depressing, dingy, dismal, drab, dull, gloomy, miserable, sombre. OPPOSITE bright.

drench *verb*
The sprinkler drenched them. douse, saturate, soak, wet.

dress *noun*
1 *appropriate dress for the occasion.* apparel (*formal*), attire (*formal*), clobber (*slang*), clothes, clothing, costume, garb, garments, gear (*informal*), outfit, raiment, wear.
2 *a woman's dress.* frock, gown, kimono, robe, sari.
dress *verb*
1 *They were dressed in their best clothes.* attire, clothe, deck out, doll up (*informal*), robe.
2 *The nurse dressed his wounds.* bandage, bind.

dresser *noun*
We put the dishes in the dresser. buffet, cupboard, sideboard.

dressing *noun*
1 *salad dressing.* mayonnaise, sauce, vinaigrette.
2 *the dressing on a wound.* bandage, plaster, poultice.

dressing gown *noun*
bath robe, brunch coat, housecoat, negligée, robe, wrapper.

dressmaker *noun*
couturier, couturière, seamstress, tailor.

dressy *adjective*
dressy clothes. chic, elegant, formal, smart, snazzy (*informal*), stylish. OPPOSITE casual.

dribble *verb*
1 *He dribbled as he looked at the food.* drool, salivate, slobber.
2 *The juice dribbled down his chin.* drip, flow, ooze, run, trickle.

dried *adjective*
1 *dried milk.* dehydrated, powdered.
2 *dried coconut.* desiccated, preserved.

drift *verb*
1 *The raft drifted downstream.* coast, float.
2 *He drifted idly through the streets.* meander, ramble, saunter, stray, wander.
drift *noun*
1 *They tried to stop the drift of people away from the town.* movement, shift, tide.
2 *Did you catch the drift of his speech?* gist, meaning, point.

drill *noun*
army drill. exercises, practice, training.
drill *verb*
1 *He drilled through the timber.* bore, penetrate, pierce.
2 *The students were drilled in vocabulary.* coach, instruct, teach, train.

drink *verb*
He drank his juice. down, drain, gulp, guzzle, lap, quaff, sip, swallow, swig (*informal*), swill.
drink *noun*
1 *hot or cold drinks.* beverage, liquid, refreshment.
2 *His work was affected by drink.* alcohol, booze (*informal*), grog (*Australian*), liquor.
3 *She took a drink from her glass.* gulp, mouthful, sip, swallow, swig (*informal*).

drip *verb*
Water dripped through the ceiling. dribble, drizzle, leak, sprinkle, trickle.
drip *noun*
1 *She cleaned up the drips.* drop, droplet, splash.
2 (*informal*) *She thinks he's a drip.* dope (*informal*), dork (*slang*), geek (*slang*), jerk (*slang*), nerd (*slang*), twit (*slang*), wally (*slang*), wimp (*informal*), wuss (*slang*).

drive *verb*
1 *He drove the animals into the yard.* herd, push, send, urge.
2 *He drove the ball a great distance.* hit, propel, push, strike.
3 *He drove the stake into the ground.* hammer, push, ram, send, sink, thrust.
4 *He can't drive the vehicle.* control, guide, handle, operate, pilot, steer.
5 *She drives to work.* motor, travel by car.

a
b
c
d
e
f
g
h
i
j
k
l
m
n
o
p
q
r
s
t
u
v
w
x
y
z

6 *He drives the boss to the office.* chauffeur, convey, run.
7 *What drove him to steal?* compel, force, motivate, oblige, pressure, push, spur.
drive *noun*
1 *Let's go for a drive.* excursion, jaunt, journey, outing, run, trip.
2 *We need a leader with drive.* ambition, determination, energy, enthusiasm, go, initiative, motivation, push, vigour, zeal.
3 *a sales drive.* campaign, crusade, push.
drive out *He was driven out of his own home.* banish, evict, expel, kick out (*informal*), remove, turn out.

driver *noun*
chauffeur, motorist.

drizzly *adjective*
drizzly weather. damp, misty, rainy, showery, wet.

drone *verb*
The machines droned continuously. buzz, hum, purr, whirr.

drool *verb*
The smell of fish makes the cat drool. dribble, salivate, slobber.

droop *verb*
The plant drooped in the heat. dangle, flop, hang down, sag, wilt, wither.

drop *noun*
1 *a drop of water.* bead, drip, droplet, spot.
2 *a drop of chilli sauce.* dash, hint, splash, sprinkling, touch, trace.
3 *a drop in prices.* cut, decline, decrease, fall, reduction, slump.
OPPOSITE rise.
4 *a steep drop to the sea.* descent.
OPPOSITE climb.
drop *verb*
1 *He dropped the parcel on the floor.* let fall, let go of, plonk.
2 *The engines failed and the plane dropped to the ground.* collapse, crash, descend, dive, fall, plummet, plunge, sink, tumble.
OPPOSITE soar.
3 *Prices dropped.* crash, decline, decrease, fall, nosedive, plummet, plunge, slump.
OPPOSITE rise.

4 *They dropped the price.* lower, reduce.
OPPOSITE increase.
5 *She dropped behind the others.* fall, lag, straggle, trail.
6 *He dropped his middle name.* eliminate, exclude, leave out, omit.
OPPOSITE include.
7 *He dropped his girlfriend.* abandon, desert, ditch (*informal*), dump, forsake, jilt, leave, reject.
8 *They dropped the idea.* abandon, discard, give up, scrap.
drop in on *They dropped in on grandmother.* call in on, look in on, pop in on, visit.
drop off *She dropped off in front of the TV.* doze, drowse, fall asleep, nap, nod off, sleep, snooze.

drown *verb*
1 *The fields were drowned by the floodwaters.* drench, engulf, flood, inundate, submerge, swamp.
2 *Their noise drowned ours.* overpower, overwhelm.

drowsy *adjective*
She stopped work when she felt drowsy. dopey (*informal*), dozy, sleepy, somnolent, tired, weary.
OPPOSITE wide awake.

drug *noun*
The doctor prescribed the drugs. medication, medicine, pill.
drug *verb*
The patient was drugged. anaesthetise, dope, knock out (*informal*), sedate.
drug user addict, druggie (*informal*), junkie (*slang*).

drum *noun*
1 *He plays the drums.* bongo, kettledrum, side drum, snare drum, tambour, timpano, tom-tom.
2 *He used the drum for storage.* barrel, cask, container, cylinder, keg, tub.
drum *verb*
She drummed on the table. beat, pound, rap, tap, thump.
drum up *drum up support.* canvass, gather, obtain, round up, summon, whip up.

drummer *noun*
timpanist.

drunk *adjective*
drunken, full (*slang*), inebriated, intoxicated, jolly (*informal*), merry (*informal*), paralytic (*informal*), plastered (*slang*), sloshed (*slang*), sozzled (*slang*), tiddly (*informal*), tipsy, under the influence (*informal*), under the weather.
OPPOSITE sober.

drunkard *noun*
alcoholic, boozer (*informal*), drunk, sot, tippler, wino (*informal*).
OPPOSITE teetotaller.

dry *adjective*
1 *dry land.* arid, bone-dry, dehydrated, parched, scorched, thirsty, waterless.
OPPOSITE wet.
2 *a dry book.* boring, dull, tedious, uninteresting.
OPPOSITE interesting.
dry *verb*
1 *The swimmer dried himself.* towel, wipe.
2 *She dried the food to preserve it.* cure, dehydrate, desiccate.
3 *The plant dried.* shrivel, wilt, wither.

dual *adjective*
a dual purpose. double, twin, twofold.
OPPOSITE single.

dub *verb*
Robert was dubbed 'Professor'. christen, name, nickname, rename.

dubious *adjective*
1 *She was dubious about his motives.* disbelieving, distrustful, doubtful, mistrustful, sceptical, suspicious, uncertain, unsure.
OPPOSITE certain.
2 *a dubious character.* dodgy (*informal*), fishy (*informal*), questionable, shady, suspect, suspicious, unreliable, untrustworthy.
OPPOSITE reliable.

duchess *noun*
see NOBLEWOMAN.

duck *noun*
drake (*male*), duckling (*young*).
duck *verb*
1 *She ducked under water.* bob, dip, dive, plunge, submerge.
2 *He ducked to avoid hitting his head.* bend down, bob down, crouch, stoop.

duct *noun*
The liquid flows through ducts. canal, channel, pipe, tube.

dud *adjective* (*informal*)
1 *a dud $10 note.* counterfeit, fake, forged, phoney (*informal*).
OPPOSITE genuine.
2 *a dud machine.* bung (*Australian informal*), defective, unusable, useless, worthless.
OPPOSITE working.

due *adjective*
1 *pay the amount due.* outstanding, owed, owing, payable, unpaid.
2 *with due respect.* adequate, appropriate, deserved, fitting, proper, rightful, suitable.
3 *When is the bus due?* expected, scheduled.
dues *plural noun*
pay your membership dues. fee, levy, sub (*informal*), subscription.

duel *noun*
combat, contest, fight.

duke *noun*
see NOBLEMAN.

dull *adjective*
1 *a dull day.* bleak, cloudy, dismal, grey, overcast, sunless.
OPPOSITE sunny.
2 *a dull student.* dense, dim, dumb (*informal*), obtuse, slow, stupid, thick.
OPPOSITE bright, intelligent.
3 *a dull edge.* blunt, blunted.
OPPOSITE keen, sharp.
4 *a dull colour.* dark, dingy, drab, dreary, faded, gloomy, sombre, subdued.
OPPOSITE bright.
5 *a dull sound.* deadened, indistinct, muffled, muted.
OPPOSITE sharp.
6 *a dull finish.* flat, matt, tarnished.
OPPOSITE glossy.
7 *a dull book.* bland, boring, dreary, dry, humdrum, lacklustre, lifeless, monotonous, mundane, ordinary, routine, stodgy, tedious, tiresome, unimaginative, uninteresting.
OPPOSITE exciting.

a
b
c
d
e
f
g
h
i
j
k
l
m
n
o
p
q
r
s
t
u
v
w
x
y
z

dull *verb*
The drugs dulled the pain. deaden, numb, relieve, soothe, subdue.
OPPOSITE accentuate.

dumb *adjective*
1 The child is deaf and dumb. mute, silent, speechless, tongue-tied.
2 (informal) Don't be so dumb. dense, dim (informal), foolish, obtuse, slow, stupid, thick, unintelligent.
OPPOSITE clever.

dumbfounded *adjective*
They were dumbfounded by the news. amazed, astonished, astounded, flabbergasted, nonplussed, speechless, staggered, stunned, thunderstruck.

dummy *noun*
1 The clothes were put on the dummy. lay figure, mannequin, model.
2 a baby's dummy. pacifier.

dump *verb*
1 He dumped the old car. chuck out (informal), discard, dispose of, ditch (informal), get rid of, scrap, throw out.
OPPOSITE keep.
2 She dumped the things on the counter. deposit, drop, place, plonk, put down, set down, throw down, unload.
3 She dumped him. abandon, desert, ditch (informal), jilt, leave.
dump *noun*
She took the rubbish to the dump. garbage dump, garbage tip, rubbish tip, scrap heap, tip.

dunce *noun*
see IDIOT.

dung *noun*
droppings, excrement, faeces, manure, muck.

dungeon *noun*
The prisoner is in the dungeon. cell, lock-up, prison.

duo *noun*
a comedy duo. couple, pair.

duplicate *noun*
a duplicate of the original. copy, facsimile, photocopy, replica, reproduction.

duplicate *verb*
1 He duplicated the letter. copy, photocopy, reproduce.
2 They duplicated our work. redo, repeat, replicate.

durable *adjective*
durable shoes. hard-wearing, indestructible, long-lasting, serviceable, solid, stout, strong, sturdy, tough.
OPPOSITE fragile.

duration *noun*
She slept for the duration of the concert. length, period, span, term, time.

dusk *noun*
They worked from dawn to dusk. evening, nightfall, sundown, sunset, twilight.
OPPOSITE dawn.

dust *noun*
bulldust (Australian), dirt, grime, grit, powder, sawdust, soot.
dust *verb*
1 Dust with icing sugar. dredge, sprinkle.
2 Dust the table. brush, clean, wipe.
dust storm Darling shower (Australian), dust devil, sandstorm, willy willy (Australian).

dutiful *adjective*
a dutiful daughter. conscientious, devoted, diligent, faithful, loyal, obedient, reliable, responsible.
OPPOSITE remiss.

duty *noun*
1 He acted out of a sense of duty. allegiance, loyalty, obligation, responsibility.
2 We each have a list of duties to perform. assignment, charge, chore, function, job, role, task.
3 You must pay a duty on these goods. customs, excise, levy, tariff, tax, toll.

dwarf *noun*
a fairy tale about a dwarf. elf, gnome, leprechaun, midget, pygmy, troll.
OPPOSITE giant.
dwarf *adjective*
a dwarf tree. bonsai, little, miniature, small, stunted.
OPPOSITE giant.

dwarf *verb*
The new tower dwarfs the older buildings.
dominate, overshadow, tower over.

dwell *verb*
She dwells in an old house. abide (*old use*),
live, reside; see also INHABIT.
dwell on She dwelt on their faults.
concentrate on, focus on, harp on.
OPPOSITE pass over.

dwelling *noun*
abode (*old use*), domicile, home, house,
lodging, residence; see also FLAT, HOUSE.

dwindle *verb*
The number of members has dwindled.
contract, decline, decrease, diminish,
lessen, reduce, shrink, wane.
OPPOSITE increase.

dye *verb*
He dyed his shoes black. colour, paint,
stain, tint.

dye *noun*
fabric dye. colour, colouring, pigment,
stain, tint.

dying *adjective*
a dying industry. obsolescent, vanishing,
waning.
OPPOSITE thriving.

dyke *noun*
1 They built a dyke to hold back the flood
waters. embankment, levee, stopbank.
2 The water runs away in a dyke. canal,
channel, ditch, furrow, gutter.

dynamic *adjective*
a dynamic person. active, energetic,
forceful, go-ahead, high-powered,
lively, powerful, progressive, vigorous.

dynasty *noun*
a royal dynasty. family, house, line,
lineage.

a
b
c
d
e
f
g
h
i
j
k
l
m
n
o
p
q
r
s
t
u
v
w
x
y
z

Ee

eager *adjective*
1 *an eager student.* ardent, avid, earnest, enthusiastic, fervent, interested, keen, motivated, passionate, willing, zealous.
OPPOSITE apathetic.
2 *He was eager to find out more.* anxious, bursting, desirous, dying (*informal*), impatient, itching, keen, longing, raring (*informal*), yearning.
OPPOSITE reluctant.

earl *noun*
see NOBLEMAN.

earlier *adverb*
He left earlier. before, beforehand, previously.
OPPOSITE later.
earlier *adjective*
an earlier conversation. previous, prior.
OPPOSITE later.

earliest *adjective*
the earliest inhabitants. aboriginal, first, initial, original.
OPPOSITE latest.

early *adverb*
She arrived early. ahead of time, prematurely, too soon.
OPPOSITE late, punctually.
early *adjective*
1 *an early arrival.* premature.
OPPOSITE late, punctual.
2 *in the early days.* ancient, old, olden, prehistoric, primitive.
OPPOSITE modern.
3 *the early part of summer.* beginning, first, initial, preliminary.
OPPOSITE later.

earn *verb*
1 *She earned their respect.* be entitled to, be worthy of, deserve, gain, merit, win.
2 *He earns $400 a week.* clear, collect, draw, get, make, obtain, receive, take home, work for.

earnest *adjective*
1 *an earnest desire.* ardent, fervent, heartfelt, impassioned, intense,

passionate, serious, sincere, strong, wholehearted.
OPPOSITE half-hearted.
2 *an earnest person.* conscientious, determined, diligent, grave, serious, sober, solemn, thoughtful, zealous.
OPPOSITE frivolous.

earnings *plural noun*
income, pay, salary, wages.

earth *noun*
1 *life on earth.* globe, planet, world.
2 *The earth is hard to dig.* clay, dirt, ground, land, loam, soil.

earthly *adjective*
our earthly existence. mortal, mundane, physical, secular, terrestrial, worldly.
OPPOSITE heavenly, spiritual.

earthquake *noun*
quake (*informal*), shock, tremor.

ease *noun*
a life of ease. comfort, leisure, luxury, prosperity, relaxation, repose, rest.
OPPOSITE hardship.
ease *verb*
1 *The medicine eased the pain.* alleviate, lessen, lighten, reduce, relieve, soothe, subdue.
OPPOSITE exacerbate.
2 *She eased their fears.* allay, calm, pacify, quieten, relieve, soothe, still, subdue.
OPPOSITE intensify.
3 *They eased the pressure.* reduce, relax, slacken.
OPPOSITE tighten.
4 *The pain eased.* abate, diminish, let up, moderate, slacken.
OPPOSITE intensify.

easy *adjective*
1 *an easy job.* cushy (*informal*), effortless, elementary, light, painless, soft (*informal*), undemanding.
OPPOSITE hard.
2 *The gadget is easy to use.* foolproof, simple, straightforward,

uncomplicated, user-friendly.
OPPOSITE difficult.
3 *an easy conscience.* carefree, clear, untroubled, unworried.
OPPOSITE troubled.
4 *She has an easy existence.* carefree, comfortable, cosy, leisurely, peaceful, relaxed, restful, soft (*informal*), tranquil, untroubled.
OPPOSITE hard.

easygoing *adjective*
an easygoing person. calm, carefree, casual, even-tempered, happy-go-lucky, indulgent, laid-back (*informal*), lenient, liberal, nonchalant, open-minded, permissive, placid, relaxed, soft, tolerant, unflappable (*informal*).
OPPOSITE strict, tense.

eat *verb*
1 *He ate his food.* bite, bolt, chew, chomp, consume, devour, feast on, feed on, gnaw, gobble, gorge, gulp, guzzle, knock back (*informal*), munch, nibble, peck, pick at, polish off, scoff, stuff, swallow, tuck in (*informal*), wolf.
2 *She eats at a set time.* breakfast, dine, lunch, snack, sup.
eat into
1 *Acids eat into metals.* attack, corrode, destroy, rot, wear away.
2 *The expenses gradually ate into their savings.* consume, erode, make a hole in, use up.

eatable *adjective*
digestible, edible.

eavesdrop *verb*
eavesdrop on *He eavesdropped on their conversation.* bug (*informal*), listen in on, monitor, overhear, tap.

ebb *verb*
1 *The tide ebbed.* flow back, go out, recede, retreat.
OPPOSITE flow, rise.
2 *His strength ebbed.* decline, decrease, diminish, dwindle, fade, wane, weaken.
OPPOSITE grow.

eccentric *adjective*
an eccentric person. eccentric habits. abnormal, bizarre, cranky, dotty (*informal*), freakish, odd, offbeat, outlandish, peculiar, queer, singular, strange, unconventional, unusual,

way-out, weird, zany.
OPPOSITE normal, ordinary.
eccentric *noun*
He was regarded as an eccentric. character, crackpot (*informal*), crank, dag (*Australian informal*), dingbat (*informal*), freak, hard case (*Australian informal*), nonconformist, nut (*informal*), oddball (*informal*), oddity, screwball (*informal*), weirdo (*informal*).

echo *noun*
The circular wall created an echo. resonance, reverberation.
echo *verb*
1 *The music echoed in the valley.* reflect, resound, reverberate.
2 *The clown echoed everything she said.* ape, copy, imitate, mimic, parrot, repeat, reproduce.

eclipse *noun*
an eclipse of the sun. blocking out, covering, darkening, obscuring, shadowing.

economic *adjective*
1 *economic policy.* budgetary, financial, fiscal, monetary, trade.
2 *It is not economic to stay open late.* cost-effective, profitable.
OPPOSITE uneconomic.

economical *adjective*
1 *an economical housekeeper.* careful, frugal, sparing, thrifty.
OPPOSITE extravagant, wasteful.
2 *an economical way to buy shampoo.* cheap, inexpensive, reasonable.
OPPOSITE expensive.

economise *verb*
They had to economise on heating. be economical, conserve, cut back, cut costs, save, scrimp, skimp, stint, tighten your belt.
OPPOSITE splash out.

ecstasy *noun*
She was in ecstasy at the news. bliss, delight, elation, euphoria, happiness, joy, rapture.
OPPOSITE misery.

ecstatic *adjective*
He was ecstatic at the results. blissful, delighted, elated, euphoric, exultant,

a
b
c
d
e
f
g
h
i
j
k
l
m
n
o
p
q
r
s
t
u
v
w
x
y
z

happy, joyful, overjoyed, rapturous.
OPPOSITE miserable.

edge *noun*
1 *the edge of the cup.* brim, brink, lip, rim.
2 *the edge of the town.* border, boundary,
circumference, end, extremity, fringe,
limit, margin, outskirts, perimeter,
periphery.
OPPOSITE centre, interior.
3 *the edge of the road.* kerb, roadside,
shoulder, side, verge.
4 *a fabric edge.* selvedge.
edge *verb*
1 *The blanket is edged with satin.* bind,
border, fringe, hem, trim.
2 *She edged her way out of the room.*
crawl, creep, inch, sidle, slink, steal,
worm.

edgy *adjective*
She was edgy, waiting for some news.
anxious, irritable, jittery (*informal*),
jumpy, nervous, nervy, on edge, on
tenterhooks, tense, uptight (*informal*).
OPPOSITE calm.

edible *adjective*
Witchetty grubs are edible. digestible,
eatable.
OPPOSITE inedible.

edit *verb*
1 *The text was edited before publication.*
adapt, adjust, alter, check, correct,
modify, polish, revise, rewrite.
2 *He edited a set of essays on language.*
assemble, collate, compile, put together.

edition *noun*
1 *the paperback edition.* copy, form,
version.
2 *this month's edition of the magazine.*
issue, number, publication.

educate *verb*
*The child was educated by both parents and
school.* bring up, coach, edify, enlighten,
indoctrinate, inform, instruct, nurture,
rear, school, teach, train, tutor.

educated *adjective*
He was addressing an educated audience.
cultivated, cultured, enlightened,
informed, knowledgeable, learned,
literate, scholarly.
OPPOSITE ignorant, uneducated.

education *noun*
cultivation, development, edification,
enlightenment, instruction, schooling,
teaching, training, tuition, upbringing.

educational *adjective*
1 *an educational institution.* academic,
scholastic.
2 *The programme was both educational and
entertaining.* edifying, educative,
enlightening, informative, instructive.

eerie *adjective*
an eerie atmosphere. creepy, frightening,
ghostly, mysterious, scary, spooky
(*informal*), uncanny, weird.

effect *noun*
1 *the effect of his decision.* consequence,
impact, outcome, repercussion, result,
upshot.
OPPOSITE cause.
2 *Special lighting gave the effect of
moonlight.* impression.
3 *The law came into effect last week.* force,
operation, play.

effective *adjective*
an effective advertisement. convincing,
forceful, impressive, persuasive, potent,
powerful, striking, successful.
OPPOSITE ineffective.

effeminate *adjective*
He had an effeminate voice and walk.
camp, unmanly, womanish.
OPPOSITE macho, manly.

efficient *adjective*
an efficient worker. businesslike, capable,
competent, effective, effectual,
organised, productive, proficient,
skilful.
OPPOSITE inefficient.

effort *noun*
1 *The job required a lot of effort.* elbow
grease, energy, exertion, labour, pains,
strain, struggle, toil, trouble, work.
2 *He made no effort to help us.* attempt,
endeavour, try.

effortless *adjective*
an effortless task. cushy (*informal*), easy,
painless, simple, undemanding.
OPPOSITE difficult.

egg *verb*
egg on *They egged him on to do it.*
encourage, goad, incite, prompt, push,
sool on (*Australian informal*), spur on,
urge.
OPPOSITE discourage.

egotistic *adjective*
conceited, egotistical, proud, self-
centred, self-important, vain.

eject *verb*
The police ejected them from the disco.
banish, chuck out (*informal*), evict,
expel, get rid of, kick out (*informal*),
remove, throw out, turf out (*informal*),
turn out.

elaborate *adjective*
1 *an elaborate design.* busy, detailed,
fancy, fussy, intricate, ornate, showy.
OPPOSITE plain, simple.
2 *an elaborate technique.* complex,
complicated, intricate, involved,
sophisticated.
OPPOSITE simple.
elaborate *verb*
elaborate on *He elaborated on his idea.*
enlarge on, expand on, flesh out, work
out.

elastic *adjective*
an elastic material. expandable, resilient,
rubbery, springy, stretchy.
OPPOSITE rigid.

elated *adjective*
She was elated at the news. delighted,
ecstatic, euphoric, exhilarated, exultant,
happy, joyful, jubilant, overjoyed,
thrilled.
OPPOSITE depressed.

elbow *verb*
He elbowed his way past the others. jostle,
nudge, push, shove, thrust.

elder *adjective*
an elder brother. big, older.
OPPOSITE younger.
elder *noun*
He is my elder by one year. senior.
OPPOSITE junior.

elderly *adjective*
elderly people. aged, ageing, old, oldish,
retired, senior.
OPPOSITE young.

eldest *adjective*
the eldest child. first-born, oldest.
OPPOSITE youngest.

elect *verb*
They elected a new Prime Minister.
appoint, choose, opt for, pick, select,
vote for.

election *noun*
a federal election. ballot, poll, vote.

elegant *adjective*
1 *an elegant person.* chic, dignified,
fashionable, graceful, gracious,
handsome, refined, smart, stylish.
OPPOSITE unrefined.
2 *elegant surroundings.* grand, luxurious,
opulent, plush, posh (*informal*), stately,
stylish, sumptuous, tasteful.

element *noun*
broken down into its elements.
component, constituent, factor,
ingredient, member, part, unit.
elements *plural noun*
1 *Man against the elements.* weather.
2 *He has mastered the elements of the
subject.* basics, essentials, fundamentals,
principles, rudiments.

elementary *adjective*
elementary mathematics. basic,
fundamental, introductory, primary,
rudimentary, simple.
OPPOSITE advanced.

elevator *noun*
The elevator holds twelve people. lift.

elf *noun*
The elf played a trick on the man. fairy,
gnome, goblin, gremlin (*informal*),
hobgoblin, imp, leprechaun, pixie,
spirit, sprite.

eligible *adjective*
*She is eligible to compete in the
tournament.* acceptable, allowed,
authorised, entitled, qualified, suitable.
OPPOSITE ineligible.

eliminate *verb*
1 *eliminate errors. eliminate weeds.*
abolish, cut out, delete, destroy, do
away with, eradicate, exterminate, get
rid of, omit, remove, root out, stamp

a
b
c
d
e
f
g
h
i
j
k
l
m
n
o
p
q
r
s
t
u
v
w
x
y
z

out, weed out.
OPPOSITE include, retain.
2 *He was eliminated in the second round.*
defeat, exclude, knock out.

elite *noun*
the elite of society. best, choice, cream,
pick.

eloquent *adjective*
an eloquent speech. an eloquent speaker.
articulate, expressive, fluent, forceful,
persuasive, powerful.
OPPOSITE inarticulate.

elude *verb*
He eluded his pursuers. avoid, dodge,
escape from, evade, give the slip to,
shake off.

emancipate *verb*
They emancipated the slave. deliver, free,
liberate, release, set free.
OPPOSITE enslave.

embankment *noun*
*The flood waters rushed over the
embankment.* bank, levee, stopbank.

embark *verb*
The travellers embarked in Sydney. board
ship, get on, go aboard.
OPPOSITE disembark.
embark on *He embarked on further study.*
begin, commence, enter on, start,
undertake.

embarrass *verb*
*She embarrassed them by mentioning the
matter.* abash, distress, humiliate,
mortify, shame.

embarrassed *adjective*
abashed, ashamed, awkward,
distressed, flustered, humiliated,
mortified, self-conscious, shamefaced,
sheepish, uncomfortable, upset.

emblem *noun*
a school emblem. badge, coat of arms,
crest, hallmark, insignia, logo, seal,
sign, symbol.

embrace *verb*
He embraced his wife affectionately. clasp,
cuddle, hold, hug.

embroidery *noun*
needlework, sewing.

emerge *verb*
1 *The child emerged from behind the
curtain.* appear, come out, peep out,
show up, surface.
OPPOSITE disappear.
2 *It emerged that several people were
involved in the crime.* become known, be
revealed, come out, come to light,
transpire, turn out.

emergency *noun*
She stays calm in an emergency. crisis,
danger, difficulty, predicament.
emergency *adjective*
an emergency supply. backup, reserve,
spare.

emigrate *verb*
He emigrated from England. depart, leave,
migrate, move, quit, relocate.
OPPOSITE immigrate.

eminent *adjective*
an eminent scholar. celebrated,
distinguished, famous, great,
illustrious, important, notable, noted,
outstanding, pre-eminent, prominent,
renowned, respected, well-known.
OPPOSITE undistinguished.

emit *verb*
emit light, heat, fumes, etc. beam,
discharge, expel, give off, give out,
issue, leak, ooze, pour forth, radiate,
send out, shed, transmit.

emotion *noun*
He showed no emotion when the cat died.
feeling, passion, sentiment.

emotional *adjective*
1 *an emotional speech.* emotive,
impassioned, moving, passionate,
poignant, sentimental, stirring,
touching.
2 *an emotional person.* ardent,
demonstrative, excitable, fervent,
passionate, sensitive, sentimental,
temperamental.
OPPOSITE unemotional.

emperor *noun*
Caesar, czar, head of state, kaiser,
mikado, monarch, ruler, sovereign, tsar.

emphasis *noun*
The emphasis is on quality. accent, attention, importance, prominence, stress.

emphasise *verb*
She emphasised the importance of exercise. accent, accentuate, draw attention to, highlight, impress, insist on, point up, stress, underline.
OPPOSITE play down.

emphatic *adjective*
His answer was an emphatic 'No'. categorical, decisive, definite, forceful, strong, vigorous.
OPPOSITE tentative.

empire *noun*
These countries were once part of his empire. domain, dominion, kingdom, realm, territory.

employ *verb*
1 The company employed extra workers. appoint, engage, give work to, hire, take on.
2 He employed a new technique. apply, make use of, use, utilise.

employed *adjective*
an employed person. working.
OPPOSITE jobless, unemployed.

employee *noun*
The firm has 100 employees. hand, wage-earner, worker; [employees] human resources, labour, personnel, staff, workforce.
OPPOSITE employer.

employer *noun*
1 He was a kind employer. boss, chief, manager, master, proprietor.
OPPOSITE employee.
2 Her new employer was one of the big banks. business, company, firm, organisation.

employment *noun*
She was looking for new employment. business, calling, career, job, occupation, profession, pursuit, trade, vocation, work.
OPPOSITE leisure, unemployment.

empty *adjective*
1 an empty box. hollow, unfilled, void.
OPPOSITE full.
2 an empty house. bare, deserted, unfurnished, uninhabited, unoccupied, vacant.
OPPOSITE occupied.
3 an empty page. blank, clean, clear, unused.
OPPOSITE used.

empty *verb*
1 She emptied the contents of her purse. pour out, remove, tip out.
2 She emptied the bath water. drain, let out, pour out.
3 The police emptied the building. clear, evacuate.

enable *verb*
1 The gift enabled her to visit Italy. allow, let, permit.
2 The certificate enables him to work in Australia. allow, authorise, entitle, license, permit, qualify.
OPPOSITE prevent (from).

enchant *verb*
She enchanted the audience with her singing. bewitch, captivate, charm, delight, enthral, entrance, fascinate, hold spellbound, hypnotise, mesmerise, thrill.

enchanter *noun*
magician, sorcerer, warlock, wizard.

enchantress *noun*
magician, siren, sorceress, witch.

encircle *verb*
Troops encircled the city. besiege, circle, enclose, encompass, hem in, ring, surround.

enclose *verb*
1 He enclosed the area with a fence, rope, etc. circle, cordon off, encircle, encompass, ring, surround, wall in.
2 The animals are enclosed in cages. box in, close in, confine, fence in, pen, restrict, shut in.
3 She enclosed a card with the parcel. include, insert, send with.

enclosure *noun*
The animals are kept in enclosures. cage, compound, coop, corral, fold, hutch,

a
b
c
d
e
f
g
h
i
j
k
l
m
n
o
p
q
r
s
t
u
v
w
x
y
z

paddock, pen, pound, run, stall, sty, yard.

encounter *verb*
1 *They encountered a stranger on the path.* bump into (*informal*), chance upon, meet, run into.
2 *He encountered many problems.* be faced with, come up against, confront, contend with, experience, face, grapple with, meet with, run into.

encounter *noun*
1 *a brief encounter.* meeting.
2 *an encounter with the authorities.* battle, brush, clash, conflict, confrontation, fight, run-in.

encourage *verb*
1 *She encourages her students.* buck up (*informal*), build up, buoy up, cheer up, comfort, hearten, inspire, reassure.
OPPOSITE discourage.
2 *They encouraged him to keep trying.* egg on, exhort, persuade, spur, urge.
OPPOSITE deter, dissuade.
3 *Cutting back encourages new growth.* aid, assist, boost, foster, help, promote, stimulate.
OPPOSITE hinder.

encouragement *noun*
His praise was all the encouragement she needed. boost, incentive, inspiration, reassurance, shot in the arm, stimulus, support.

end *noun*
1 *the end of the bus route.* limit, terminus.
OPPOSITE start.
2 *the end of the queue.* back, rear, tail.
OPPOSITE beginning, head.
3 *The pencil has a sharp end.* point, tip.
4 *cigarette ends.* butt, remains, remnant, stub.
5 *the end of the session.* close, completion, conclusion, culmination, ending, finale, finish, termination.
OPPOSITE beginning, opening.
6 *the end of the lending period.* expiration, expiry, termination.
7 *He came to an unfortunate end.* death, demise (*formal*), destruction, downfall, extinction, fall, passing, ruin.
8 *The end does not justify the means.* aim, design, goal, intention, object, objective, purpose.

end *verb*
1 *He ended the concert with an old favourite.* bring to an end, close, complete, conclude, finish, round off, terminate, wind up.
OPPOSITE begin.
2 *They ended the cruel practice.* abolish, eliminate, eradicate, get rid of, put an end to, put a stop to, stamp out, stop, wipe out.
3 *They ended their relationship.* break off, cut, discontinue, sever, terminate.
OPPOSITE commence.
4 *Work has ended for the day.* cease, come to an end, finish, halt, peter out, run out, stop.
OPPOSITE start.
5 *The contract ended.* cease, expire, run out.

end up *He ended up in jail.* finish up, land, wind up.
in the end eventually, finally, in the long run, ultimately.

endanger *verb*
Their lives were endangered by his driving. imperil, jeopardise, put at risk, threaten.
OPPOSITE safeguard.

endeavour *verb*
They endeavour to please customers. aim, attempt, make an effort, strive, try.
endeavour *noun*
Her endeavour to please them succeeded. attempt, effort, try.

ending *noun*
a surprise ending. conclusion, end, finale, finish, resolution, termination.
OPPOSITE beginning.

endless *adjective*
1 *endless love.* abiding, boundless, ceaseless, constant, eternal, everlasting, infinite, limitless, never-ending, permanent, perpetual, unending.
OPPOSITE finite.
2 *an endless din.* constant, continual, continuous, incessant, interminable, non-stop, ongoing, perpetual, persistent.
OPPOSITE passing.

endurance *noun*
The race was a test of endurance. fortitude, hardiness, patience, perseverance,

persistence, stamina, staying power,
strength, tenacity.

endure *verb*
1 *He endured great hardship.* bear, brave,
cope with, experience, stand up to,
suffer, undergo, weather, withstand.
OPPOSITE escape.
2 *She cannot endure their insolence.* abide,
bear, put up with, stand, tolerate.
3 *The tradition has endured.* carry on,
continue, last, live on, persist, prevail,
remain, stay, survive.
OPPOSITE die.

enemy *noun*
adversary, antagonist, foe, opponent,
opposition, rival.
OPPOSITE ally, friend.

energetic *adjective*
1 *an energetic person.* active, animated,
dynamic, forceful, full of beans
(*informal*), go-ahead, hard-working,
high-powered, indefatigable,
industrious, lively, perky, spirited,
sprightly, spry, tireless, vibrant,
vigorous, zippy.
OPPOSITE listless.
2 *an energetic game of tennis.* brisk,
strenuous, vigorous.

energy *noun*
He never runs out of energy. drive,
enthusiasm, force, go, gusto, liveliness,
oomph (*informal*), pep, power, stamina,
verve, vigour, vitality, vivacity, zeal,
zest, zing (*informal*), zip.
OPPOSITE lethargy.

enforce *verb*
He enforces the rules. administer, apply,
carry out, implement, impose, insist on.
OPPOSITE waive.

engage *verb*
1 *He engaged a secretary.* appoint,
employ, hire, recruit, take on.
OPPOSITE dismiss.
2 *They engaged her in conversation.*
absorb, engross, involve, occupy.

engaged *adjective*
1 *an engaged couple.* betrothed (*formal*).
2 *The line is engaged.* busy, in use,
occupied.
OPPOSITE free.

engagement *noun*
1 *the couple's engagement.* betrothal.
2 *He could not attend because of a previous
engagement.* appointment, arrangement,
booking, commitment, date (*informal*),
meeting.

engine *noun*
1 *a car engine.* motor.
2 *a railway engine.* locomotive.

engrave *verb*
Her name was engraved on the medal.
carve, cut, etch, inscribe.

engrossed *adjective*
engrossed in a book. absorbed, immersed,
involved, lost, occupied, preoccupied.

engulf *verb*
The waters engulfed the town. flood,
inundate, overrun, submerge, swallow
up, swamp.

enhance *verb*
Salt enhances the flavour. boost, enrich,
heighten, improve, increase, intensify,
strengthen.
OPPOSITE detract from, diminish.

enjoy *verb*
She enjoys the attention. appreciate, be
fond of, be keen on, delight in, fancy,
lap up, like, love, relish, revel in,
savour.
OPPOSITE dislike.
enjoy yourself be happy, have a ball
(*informal*), have a good time, have fun.

enjoyable *adjective*
an enjoyable evening. agreeable, cool
(*informal*), delightful, good, lovely
(*informal*), nice, pleasant, pleasurable,
satisfying.
OPPOSITE unpleasant.

enjoyment *noun*
She gets enjoyment out of life. amusement,
delight, entertainment, fun, happiness,
joy, kick (*informal*), pleasure, recreation,
satisfaction, thrill, zest.

enlarge *verb*
1 *They enlarged the shop.* add to,
broaden, expand, extend, lengthen,
widen.
2 *Her stomach has enlarged over the years.*
bulge, distend, expand, fill out, grow

a
b
c
d
e
f
g
h
i
j
k
l
m
n
o
p
q
r
s
t
u
v
w
x
y
z

bigger, stretch, swell.
OPPOSITE diminish.
3 *She enlarged the photo.* blow up
(*informal*), magnify.
OPPOSITE reduce.

enlist *verb*
1 *He enlisted as a soldier.* enrol, join up,
register, sign on, volunteer.
2 *The government enlisted troops.* call up,
conscript, draft (*American*), enrol,
recruit.
3 *Try to enlist their support.* drum up,
gather, get, muster, obtain, secure.

enmity *noun*
enmity between neighbours. animosity,
antagonism, bitterness, hatred,
hostility, ill will, malevolence,
opposition.
OPPOSITE friendship.

enormous *adjective*
an enormous house. an enormous amount.
astronomical, big, colossal, giant,
gigantic, ginormous (*slang*), great, huge,
humungous (*slang*), immeasurable,
immense, incalculable, jumbo, king-
sized, large, mammoth, massive,
mighty, monstrous, monumental,
outsize, spacious, staggering,
stupendous, sweeping, tremendous,
vast.
OPPOSITE tiny.

enough *adjective*
They have enough money. adequate,
ample, sufficient.
OPPOSITE insufficient.

enquire *verb*
He enquired about the patient's condition.
ask, inquire, query, question.

enquiry *noun*
The counter officer handles enquiries.
inquiry, query, question.

enrage *verb*
His lateness enraged his team mates.
anger, annoy, exasperate, incense,
infuriate, irritate, madden, outrage,
provoke, rile (*informal*).

enrol *verb*
1 *He enrolled in the swimming club.* enlist,
join up, register, sign on.
OPPOSITE withdraw (from).

2 *The college enrolled her as a student.*
accept, admit, enlist, recruit, take on.
OPPOSITE expel.

ensemble *noun*
a string ensemble. band, group,
orchestra.

ensure *verb*
Good food will ensure good health.
guarantee, make certain, make sure,
secure.

entangle *verb*
1 *She entangled the strands of cotton.*
entwine, interlace, intertwine, mat,
snarl, tangle, twist.
OPPOSITE unravel.
2 *The animal was entangled in the net.*
catch, ensnare, snare, trap.
3 *He became entangled in a dangerous
situation.* catch up, embroil, involve,
mix up.

enter *verb*
1 *They entered the country.* come in, go
in, intrude in, invade, penetrate.
OPPOSITE leave.
2 *He entered the army.* enlist in, enrol in,
join, register for, sign up for.
OPPOSITE leave.
3 *She entered his name in her book.*
inscribe, jot, list, note, record, register,
write.
4 *They will enter the race.* compete in, go
in, participate in, register for, take part
in.
OPPOSITE withdraw (from).

enterprise *noun*
1 *a difficult enterprise.* endeavour,
mission, operation, project,
undertaking, venture.
2 *The new person shows enterprise.* drive,
get-up-and-go, initiative,
resourcefulness.
3 *a large family enterprise.* business,
company, concern, establishment, firm,
organisation.

enterprising *adjective*
an enterprising person. adventurous,
bold, daring, energetic, go-ahead,
imaginative, intrepid, resourceful.

entertain *verb*
1 *She entertained her audience.* amuse,
delight, divert, please.

2 *They enjoy entertaining visitors.* play host to, receive, welcome.

entertainer *noun*
artist, artiste, performer, player; [*various entertainers*] actor, actress, busker, clown, comedian, comic, conjuror, dancer, instrumentalist, jester, juggler, magician, minstrel, musician, singer, vocalist.

entertainment *noun*
He dances for entertainment. amusement, diversion, enjoyment, fun, pastime, pleasure, recreation, sport.

enthusiasm *noun*
She does everything with enthusiasm. ardour, eagerness, excitement, exuberance, fervour, gusto, keenness, passion, relish, verve, zeal, zest.

enthusiast *noun*
a tennis enthusiast. addict, buff (*informal*), devotee, fan, fanatic, follower, freak (*informal*), lover, nut (*informal*), supporter, zealot.

enthusiastic *adjective*
1 *an enthusiastic member.* ardent, avid, committed, eager, excited, exuberant, fervent, keen, passionate, zealous.
OPPOSITE apathetic.
2 *an enthusiastic welcome.* hearty, warm, wholehearted.
OPPOSITE half-hearted.

entice *verb*
He enticed the cat inside with a fish. attract, bribe, cajole, coax, decoy, lure, persuade, seduce, tempt.

entire *adjective*
an entire tea set. complete, full, intact, total, unbroken, whole.
OPPOSITE incomplete, partial.

entirely *adverb*
entirely correct. absolutely, altogether, completely, fully, one hundred per cent, perfectly, quite, totally, utterly, wholly.
OPPOSITE partially.

entitle *verb*
1 *The chapter is entitled 'Peace'.* call, name, title.

2 *The ticket entitles you to a seat.* allow, authorise, permit, qualify.

entrance[1] *noun*
1 *the entrance to a house.* access, door, doorway, entry, foyer, gate, gateway, opening, passage, porch, portal, threshold, way in.
OPPOSITE exit.
2 *She made a grand entrance.* appearance, arrival, entry.
OPPOSITE departure, exit.
3 *Entrance is refused to people in thongs.* access, admission, admittance, entry.

entrance[2] *verb*
She entranced them with her song. bewitch, captivate, charm, delight, enchant, enrapture, enthral, fascinate, hold spellbound, hypnotise, mesmerise, transport.

entrant *noun*
ten entrants in the competition. applicant, candidate, competitor, contestant, participant.

entreat *verb*
He entreated the giant to have mercy on him. appeal to, beg, beseech, implore, plead with, pray, request.

entrust *verb*
1 *He entrusted them with the job.* assign, charge, delegate, trust.
2 *She entrusted the children to the nanny's care.* commit, consign, hand over.

entry *noun*
1 *She was refused entry.* admission, admittance, entrance.
2 *He made his entry.* appearance, arrival, entrance.
3 *the entry to a building.* access, approach, door, doorway, entrance, gate, gateway, opening, way in.
4 *an entry in a diary.* item, jotting, note, record.

envelop *verb*
1 *The baby was enveloped in a warm rug.* swaddle, swathe, wrap.
2 *The hill was enveloped in mist.* blanket, cloak, conceal, cover, shroud, surround, veil.

a
b
c
d
e
f
g
h
i
j
k
l
m
n
o
p
q
r
s
t
u
v
w
x
y
z

envelope *noun*
The passbook fits in a plastic envelope.
case, cover, covering, jacket, pocket,
wrapper.

envious *adjective*
envious of their good fortune. covetous,
green, grudging, jealous, resentful.

environment *noun*
a change of environment. atmosphere,
circumstances, conditions, context,
habitat, setting, situation, surroundings.

environmentalist *noun*
conservationist, ecologist, green,
greenie (*Australian informal*).

envisage *verb*
They did not envisage any problems.
conceive of, contemplate, foresee,
imagine, picture, predict, visualise.

envy *noun*
covetousness, jealousy, resentment.
envy *verb*
She envies them their independence.
begrudge, be jealous of, covet, grudge,
resent.

epidemic *noun*
a flu epidemic. outbreak, pestilence,
plague.

episode *noun*
1 a memorable episode in history. affair
(*informal*), event, happening, incident,
occasion, occurrence.
2 an episode of a serial. chapter,
instalment, part, scene, section.

epistle *noun*
He wrote them a long epistle.
communication, letter, note.

epoch *noun*
the dawn of a new epoch. age, era, period,
time.

equal *adjective*
equal amounts. equivalent, even,
identical, level, like, matching, parallel,
same, uniform.
OPPOSITE unequal.
equal *noun*
At chess he has no equal. match, parallel,
peer, rival.

equal *verb*
1 Two plus two equals four. add up to, be
equivalent to, come to, make, total.
2 He equalled his opponent's score. draw
with, match, reach, tie with.

equality *noun*
equality in pay and conditions.
egalitarianism, equivalence, evenness,
parity, sameness, uniformity.
OPPOSITE inequality.

equip *verb*
We were equipped for our journey. arm, fit
out, furnish, kit out, provide, rig out,
supply.

equipment *noun*
the equipment for a job. apparatus,
appliances, gear, hardware,
implements, instruments, kit,
machinery, materials, outfit, plant, rig,
supplies, tackle, tools.

equivalent *adjective*
two items of equivalent value.
corresponding, equal, identical,
matching, same.
OPPOSITE different.

era *noun*
They belonged to a different era. age, day,
epoch, period, time.

eradicate *verb*
He cannot eradicate the weeds. annihilate,
destroy, eliminate, exterminate, get rid
of, obliterate, remove, root out, uproot,
weed out, wipe out.

erase *verb*
She erased her mistake. blot out, cancel,
delete, efface, obliterate, remove, rub
out, wipe out.

erect *adjective*
an erect stance. bolt upright, standing,
upright, vertical.
erect *verb*
1 erect a tent. pitch, put up, set up.
OPPOSITE dismantle.
2 erect a building. build, construct, raise.
OPPOSITE demolish.

erode *verb*
The surface is being eroded by water, wind,
acid, etc. corrode, destroy, eat away,
grind down, rub away, wear away,
weather.

errand *noun*
> She sent the child on an errand. chore, job, mission, task.

erratic *adjective*
> erratic behaviour. capricious, changeable, fickle, inconsistent, irregular, spasmodic, uneven, unpredictable, variable.
> OPPOSITE consistent.

error *noun*
> He corrected the errors. blue (*Australian informal*), blunder, booboo (*slang*), clanger (*informal*), fault, flaw, howler (*informal*), inaccuracy, lapse, miscalculation, misprint, mistake, oversight, slip, slip-up (*informal*), typo (*informal*).

erupt *verb*
> Lava erupted from the volcano. be discharged, belch, burst out, gush out, issue, pour out, shoot forth, spew, spurt out.

escalate *verb*
> 1 Prices have escalated. increase, jump, multiply, rise, skyrocket, soar.
> OPPOSITE drop.
> 2 The tension escalated. blow up, heighten, intensify, mount, rise, step up, worsen.
> OPPOSITE lessen.

escape *verb*
> 1 The prisoner escaped. abscond, bolt, break free, break out, flee, get away, run away, scarper, slip away, take flight.
> 2 He escaped punishment. avoid, dodge, elude, evade, get out of, wriggle out of.

escape *noun*
> 1 They planned their escape from prison. breakout, flight, getaway.
> OPPOSITE capture.
> 2 a fire escape. exit, way out.
> 3 Reading is a pleasant escape from the chores. distraction, diversion, outlet, relief.

escort *noun*
> 1 a police escort. bodyguard, chaperone, convoy, guard, minder, protector.
> 2 The girl has a charming escort. companion, date (*informal*), partner.

escort *verb*
> He escorted them to the police station. accompany, chaperone, conduct, guide, lead, take, usher.

especially *adverb*
> 1 He made it especially for them. chiefly, expressly, particularly, primarily, specially, specifically.
> 2 It was not especially good. exceptionally, extraordinarily, outstandingly, particularly.

essay *noun*
> She wrote an essay. article, composition, critique, paper, thesis.

essence *noun*
> 1 the essence of her argument. core, crux, gist, heart, substance.
> 2 vanilla essence. concentrate, extract.

essential *adjective*
> 1 A toothbrush is essential. imperative, indispensable, necessary, vital.
> OPPOSITE dispensable.
> 2 its essential qualities. basic, central, chief, fundamental, inherent, intrinsic, key, main, primary, principal.
> OPPOSITE incidental.

essential *noun*
> Tact is an essential for this job. must, necessity, prerequisite, requirement.

establish *verb*
> 1 She established a new company. begin, build, construct, create, found, initiate, institute, introduce, originate, pioneer, set up, start.
> 2 You must establish your innocence. confirm, demonstrate, prove, show, substantiate, verify.
> OPPOSITE disprove.

establishment *noun*
> They run a large establishment. business, company, concern, corporation, enterprise, firm, institution, organisation, plant.

estate *noun*
> 1 a housing estate. area, development.
> 2 His estate was left to the children. assets, fortune, money, property, wealth.

esteem *noun*
> His father was held in high esteem. admiration, appreciation, estimation,

a
b
c
d
e
f
g
h
i
j
k
l
m
n
o
p
q
r
s
t
u
v
w
x
y
z

regard, respect, reverence, veneration.
OPPOSITE disdain.

estimate *noun*
1 *an estimate of a thing's worth.* appraisal, assessment, calculation, evaluation, guesstimate (*informal*), judgement, opinion, valuation.
2 *a builder's estimate.* quotation, quote (*informal*), tender.

estimate *verb*
She estimated the watch's value at $500. appraise, assess, calculate, evaluate, guess, judge, put, rate, reckon, size up, value.

etch *verb*
The scene is etched on my mind. carve, engrave, impress, imprint, inscribe, stamp.

eternal *adjective*
see EVERLASTING.

ethics *plural noun*
medical ethics. moral code, morality, morals, principles, scruples.

ethnic *adjective*
ethnic differences. cultural, national, racial.

evacuate *verb*
1 *The townspeople were evacuated.* move out, relocate, remove, send away.
2 *The police evacuated the nursing home.* clear, empty.
3 *The residents evacuated the building.* abandon, desert, flee, leave, quit, vacate.

evade *verb*
evade a person. evade a responsibility. avoid, dodge, duck, elude, escape from, shirk, shun, sidestep, steer clear of.
OPPOSITE face.

evaluate *verb*
1 *Evaluate 'x' in these equations.* calculate, compute, work out.
2 *She evaluated the scheme.* appraise, assess, judge, review, value.

evaporate *verb*
The water evaporated in the sun. dry up, vaporise.
OPPOSITE condense.

even *adjective*
1 *an even surface.* flat, level, plane, smooth.
OPPOSITE rough, uneven.
2 *Her hair is even.* straight.
OPPOSITE crooked.
3 *an even climate.* consistent, constant, regular, steady, unchanging, uniform, unvarying.
OPPOSITE variable.
4 *The scores were even.* balanced, drawn, equal, identical, level, neck and neck, square, the same, tied.
OPPOSITE different.

even *verb*
1 *The hairdresser evened the ends.* level, straighten.
2 *The last point evened the scores.* balance, equalise, level, tie.

evening *noun*
dusk, eventide (*old use*), night, nightfall, sundown, sunset, twilight.
OPPOSITE dawn, morning.

event *noun*
1 *an unlikely event.* affair, circumstance, episode, experience, happening, incident, occasion, occurrence.
2 *a grand social event.* ceremony, function, occasion, proceedings.
3 *a sporting event.* championship, competition, contest, fixture, meet, meeting, tournament.
4 *The next event in the carnival is the 100m freestyle.* competition, contest, item, race.

even-tempered *adjective*
calm, easygoing, placid, serene, steady, tranquil, unfazed (*informal*), unflappable (*informal*).
OPPOSITE volatile.

eventful *adjective*
an eventful holiday. action-packed, busy, exciting, full, memorable, momentous, unforgettable.
OPPOSITE uneventful.

eventually *adverb*
She arrived at the party eventually. at last, finally, in the end, ultimately.

everlasting *adjective*
1 *everlasting life.* endless, eternal, immortal, infinite, limitless, never-

ending, timeless, unending, unlimited.
OPPOSITE finite, transitory.
2 *an everlasting problem.* abiding,
ceaseless, chronic, constant, continual,
continuous, endless, eternal, incessant,
interminable, non-stop, perennial,
permanent, perpetual, persistent,
recurrent, repeated.
OPPOSITE occasional, temporary.

everybody *pronoun*
all, all and sundry, everyone, one and
all, the world.
OPPOSITE nobody.

everyday *adjective*
everyday clothes. an everyday event.
common, commonplace, customary,
daily, day-to-day, familiar, mundane,
normal, ordinary, regular, routine,
usual.
OPPOSITE unusual.

everywhere *adverb*
extensively, far and wide, globally, high
and low, near and far, universally.

evict *verb*
The landlord evicted his tenant. drive out,
eject, expel, get rid of, kick out
(*informal*), remove, throw out, turf out
(*informal*), turn out.

evidence *noun*
1 *They had enough evidence to convict him.*
data, documentation, facts, grounds,
information.
2 *Her tears were evidence of her true
feelings.* indication, manifestation,
proof, sign, symptom, testimony, token.

evident *adjective*
It was evident that she enjoyed reading.
apparent, clear, noticeable, obvious,
plain, unmistakable.
OPPOSITE dubious.

evil *adjective*
an evil person. an evil act. abominable,
atrocious, bad, base, beastly, corrupt,
demonic, depraved, despicable,
detestable, diabolical, foul, hateful,
immoral, infamous, iniquitous,
loathsome, malevolent, malicious,
satanic, sinful, sinister, ungodly,
unrighteous, vicious, vile, villainous,
wicked.
OPPOSITE good.

evil *noun*
He wanted to root out evil. corruption,
depravity, immorality, iniquity, sin,
vice, wickedness, wrong, wrongdoing.
OPPOSITE goodness.

evolve *verb*
The scheme evolved gradually. develop,
grow, unfold.

exact *adjective*
1 *an exact answer.* accurate, correct,
literal, perfect, precise, right, spot-on
(*informal*), true.
OPPOSITE approximate.
2 *exact instructions.* detailed, explicit,
minute, particular, precise, rigorous,
specific, strict.
3 *an exact worker.* careful, fastidious,
meticulous, painstaking, scrupulous.
OPPOSITE careless.

exaggerate *verb*
1 *He exaggerated the size of the problem.*
blow up, magnify, overestimate,
overstate.
OPPOSITE understate.
2 *She likes to exaggerate.* ham it up
(*informal*), lay it on thick (*informal*),
make a mountain out of a molehill, pile
it on (*informal*).

exalt *verb*
1 *They exalted him to a senior position.*
advance, elevate, promote, raise,
upgrade.
OPPOSITE demote.
2 *Christians exalt Jesus.* adore, glorify,
hallow, honour, laud (*formal*), praise,
revere, venerate, worship.

examination *noun*
1 *an examination of the college records.*
analysis, audit, check, inspection,
investigation, observation, probe,
review, scrutiny, study, survey.
2 *school examinations.* exam (*informal*),
oral (*informal*), quiz, test.
3 *examination of the witness.* cross-
examination, interrogation,
questioning.

examine *verb*
1 *He examined the documents, evidence,
etc.* analyse, audit, check, consider, go
over, inquire into, inspect, investigate,
look at, look over, probe, research,

a
b
c
d
e
f
g
h
i
j
k
l
m
n
o
p
q
r
s
t
u
v
w
x
y
z

example 164 exchange

review, scrutinise, sift, study, survey, vet.
2 *The students are examined on their knowledge.* question, quiz, sound out, test.
3 *He examined the witness.* cross-examine, cross-question, grill, interrogate, question.

example *noun*
1 *The lawyer cited examples of the same situation.* case, illustration, instance, model, precedent.
2 *She sent in an example of her work.* prototype, sample, specimen.
3 *Set a good example.* model, pattern, standard.

exasperate *verb*
He was exasperated by their slowness. anger, annoy, bug (*informal*), enrage, get on someone's nerves, infuriate, irk, irritate, madden, needle (*informal*), peeve (*informal*), provoke, rile (*informal*), vex.
OPPOSITE appease, please.

excavate *verb*
1 *He excavated a cellar.* burrow, dig, hollow out, mine, scoop out, shovel out, tunnel.
OPPOSITE fill in.
2 *He excavated some old bones.* dig up, uncover, unearth.
OPPOSITE bury.

exceed *verb*
The attendance exceeded last year's record. beat, better, excel, go beyond, go over, outdo, outnumber, overtake, pass, surpass, top.

excel *verb*
She excels at music. be outstanding, shine, stand out.

excellent *adjective*
an excellent performance, dinner, job, etc. ace (*informal*), admirable, awesome (*informal*), beaut (*Australian informal*), brilliant (*informal*), capital, choice, classic, cool (*informal*), exceptional, fabulous, fantastic, far-out (*informal*), fine, first-class, first-rate, great, impressive, magnificent, marvellous, meritorious, model, outstanding, peerless, perfect, prize, remarkable,

sensational, splendid, super (*informal*), superb, superior, superlative, supreme, swell (*informal*), terrific (*informal*), top-notch (*informal*), tremendous, wicked (*slang*), wizard (*informal*), wonderful.
OPPOSITE bad, inferior.

except *preposition*
No one was left except me. apart from, besides, but, excluding, other than, save.
OPPOSITE including.

exception *noun*
a rule without exceptions. departure, deviation, exclusion, inconsistency, irregularity.

exceptional *adjective*
1 *an exceptional case.* abnormal, atypical, extraordinary, odd, phenomenal, rare, remarkable, singular, special, uncommon, unusual.
OPPOSITE normal, typical.
2 *an exceptional pianist.* see EXCELLENT.

excerpt *noun*
excerpts from a film, book, etc. clip, extract, quotation, selection, trailer.

excess *noun*
1 *an excess of grapes.* glut, over-abundance, overflow, oversupply, superfluity, surfeit.
OPPOSITE shortage.
2 *Take what you need and dispose of the excess.* balance, leftovers, remainder, residue, surplus.
OPPOSITE deficit.

excessive *adjective*
1 *excessive prices.* exorbitant, extortionate, extreme, inordinate, outrageous, steep, unreasonable.
OPPOSITE reasonable.
2 *excessive drinking.* heavy, immoderate, intemperate.
OPPOSITE moderate.
3 *excessive flattery.* exaggerated, extravagant, fulsome, overdone, profuse, superfluous.

exchange *verb*
The children exchanged stamps. barter, change, interchange, substitute, swap, trade.

excitable *adjective*
   an excitable person. emotional, highly-
   strung, hotheaded, nervous,
   temperamental, volatile.
   OPPOSITE placid.

excite *verb*
   1 *Do not excite the patient.* agitate,
   animate, arouse, disturb, fluster, rouse,
   stir up, thrill, upset, wind up (*informal*),
   work up.
   OPPOSITE lull.
   2 *It excited curiosity.* arouse, awaken,
   incite, inspire, kindle, provoke,
   stimulate.
   OPPOSITE dampen.

excitement *noun*
   action, activity, ado, adventure,
   agitation, frenzy, furore, fuss, kerfuffle,
   sensation, stir, thrill, to-do, unrest.

exciting *adjective*
   an exciting story. breathtaking,
   electrifying, exhilarating, gripping,
   heady, moving, riveting, rousing,
   sensational, spectacular, stimulating,
   stirring, suspenseful, thrilling.
   OPPOSITE boring.

exclaim *verb*
   bawl, bellow, call out, cry out, shout,
   yell.

exclude *verb*
   1 *He was excluded from the group.* ban,
   bar, debar, expel, forbid, keep out,
   leave out, ostracise, prohibit, shut out.
   OPPOSITE admit, include.
   2 *She excluded that possibility.* eliminate,
   omit, preclude, reject, rule out.
   OPPOSITE admit.

exclusive *adjective*
   1 *He belongs to an exclusive club.* closed,
   private, restricted, select.
   OPPOSITE open.
   2 *an exclusive boutique.* expensive, high-
   class, upmarket.
   3 *They have the exclusive rights.* full, sole,
   undivided, unique.
   OPPOSITE shared.

excursion *noun*
   an excursion into the hills. drive,
   expedition, hike, holiday, jaunt,

journey, outing, pleasure-trip, ramble,
   ride, run, tour, trek, trip, walk.

excusable *adjective*
   an excusable mistake. forgivable,
   pardonable.
   OPPOSITE inexcusable.

excuse *verb*
   1 *The teacher excused her for being late.*
   forgive, let off, pardon.
   OPPOSITE punish.
   2 *Nothing can excuse such rudeness.*
   explain, justify, warrant.
   3 *He was excused from attending the
   lesson.* exempt, free, let off, release.
   OPPOSITE compel.

   excuse *noun*
   an excuse for her absence. defence,
   explanation, justification, plod
   (*Australian informal*), pretext, reason.

execute *verb*
   1 *He executes the boss's orders.*
   accomplish, carry out, complete, do,
   effect, fulfil, implement, perform.
   2 *The murderer was executed.* kill, put to
   death, slay; [*various ways to execute*]
   behead, crucify, electrocute, gas,
   guillotine, hang, lynch, shoot, stone.

executive *noun*
   a business executive. administrator, chief,
   director, manager.

exempt *adjective*
   He is exempt from paying tax. excused,
   freed, immune, released, relieved,
   spared.
   OPPOSITE liable.

   exempt *verb*
   They exempted him from playing football.
   excuse, free, let off, release, relieve,
   spare.

exercise *noun*
   1 *She keeps fit through exercise.* activity,
   aerobics, callisthenics, games,
   gymnastics, PE, physical education,
   physical training, PT, sport.
   2 *military exercises.* drill, manoeuvres,
   movements, practice, training.

   exercise *verb*
   1 *He exercised his power of veto.* apply,
   employ, exert, use, utilise, wield.
   2 *She exercises daily at the gym.* limber
   up, loosen up, practise, train, work out.

a
b
c
d
e
f
g
h
i
j
k
l
m
n
o
p
q
r
s
t
u
v
w
x
y
z

exert *verb*
He exerted all his strength. apply, employ, exercise, use, utilise, wield.

exertion *noun*
physical and mental exertion. effort, exercise, labour, strain, toil, work.
OPPOSITE inertia.

exhale *verb*
blow, breathe out, expire, pant, puff.
OPPOSITE inhale.

exhaust *verb*
1 Playing in the heat exhausted them. drain, fatigue, tire out, weaken, wear out, weary.
OPPOSITE refresh.
2 He exhausted their funds. blow (slang), consume, deplete, spend, use up.
OPPOSITE replenish.

exhaust *noun*
car exhaust. emissions, fumes, gases, smoke.

exhausted *adjective*
The players were exhausted. burnt out, bushed (informal), dog-tired, done in (informal), drained, fagged out (informal), fatigued, pooped (informal), run down, sapped, tired out, washed out, weak, weary, whacked (informal), worn out, zapped (slang), zonked (slang).
OPPOSITE invigorated.

exhausting *adjective*
an exhausting job. arduous, difficult, gruelling, hard, heavy, laborious, strenuous, tiring.
OPPOSITE easy.

exhibit *verb*
They exhibited their paintings. display, present, show.

exhibition *noun*
an art exhibition. demonstration, display, expo, exposition, presentation, show.

exile *noun*
1 She lived in exile. banishment, expulsion.
2 a political exile. deportee, expatriate, outcast.

exile *verb*
He was exiled for political reasons. banish, deport, expatriate, expel, send away.

exist *verb*
1 Do fairies exist? be, be real, live, occur.
2 They cannot exist on that income. keep going, live, subsist, survive.
OPPOSITE die.

existence *noun*
1 He does not believe in the existence of fairies. presence, reality.
OPPOSITE non-existence.
2 the struggle for existence. being, life, subsistence, survival.
OPPOSITE death.

exit *noun*
1 She made her exit. departure, escape, retreat.
OPPOSITE entrance.
2 The room has an emergency exit. door, outlet, way out.
OPPOSITE entrance.

exit *verb*
We exited by the rear door. see LEAVE.

exotic *adjective*
exotic plants. alien, foreign, imported; see also UNUSUAL.
OPPOSITE native.

expand *verb*
1 The business expanded. build up, develop, enlarge, grow, increase.
OPPOSITE contract.
2 His stomach expanded. bloat, broaden, distend, fatten, grow, stretch, swell, widen.
OPPOSITE shrink.
3 The pelican expanded its wings. extend, open out, spread out, stretch out.
OPPOSITE close up.
4 He expanded his story. amplify, elaborate upon, enlarge upon, flesh out, pad out.
OPPOSITE abridge.

expanse *noun*
She painted an expanse of blue. area, extent, sea, stretch, sweep.

expect *verb*
1 She didn't expect these problems. anticipate, bargain for, forecast, foresee, predict.

2 *He expects obedience.* count on, demand, insist on, rely on, require.
3 *He expected that she would ring up.* assume, believe, guess, imagine, presume, suppose, think.

expectant *adjective*
1 *an expectant mother.* expecting, pregnant.
2 *expectant fans.* eager, hopeful, ready, waiting, watchful.

expectation *noun*
little expectation of success. anticipation, hope, likelihood, probability, prospect.

expedition *noun*
a polar expedition. excursion, exploration, journey, mission, outing, safari, tour, trek, trip, voyage.

expel *verb*
He was expelled from his school, the country, etc. banish, chuck out (*informal*), deport, discharge, dismiss, drive out, eject, evict, exile, get rid of, kick out (*informal*), remove, send away, throw out, turf out (*informal*).
OPPOSITE admit.

expenditure *noun*
They cut their expenditure. expenses, outgoings, outlay, overheads, spending.
OPPOSITE income.

expense *noun*
Expenses were high and income was low. charge, cost, fee, payment, price; see EXPENDITURE.

expensive *adjective*
an expensive watch. costly, dear, exorbitant, extravagant, luxurious, precious, priceless, pricey (*informal*), valuable.
OPPOSITE cheap.

experience *noun*
1 *Has he any experience in child-minding?* background, familiarity, involvement, practice.
2 *a frightening experience.* adventure, episode, event, happening, incident, occurrence, ordeal.
experience *verb*
She experienced pain, hardship, etc. bear, encounter, endure, face, feel, go

through, know, meet with, suffer, undergo.

experienced *adjective*
an experienced teacher. accomplished, competent, expert, fully-fledged, practised, proficient, seasoned, skilled, veteran, well-versed.
OPPOSITE inexperienced, raw.

experiment *noun*
a scientific experiment. investigation, test, trial.

experimental *adjective*
an experimental programme. pilot, test, trial.

expert *noun*
an expert in economics, wine, cooking, etc. authority, buff (*informal*), connoisseur, consultant, genius, know-all (*informal*), maestro, old hand, past master, professional, pundit, scholar, specialist, virtuoso, whiz (*informal*).
OPPOSITE novice.
expert *adjective*
an expert jeweller. accomplished, capable, competent, experienced, knowledgeable, practised, professional, proficient, qualified, skilful, skilled, talented.
OPPOSITE incompetent.

expertise *noun*
She has the expertise for the job. know-how, knowledge, mastery, proficiency, skill.

expire *verb*
1 *The sick man finally expired.* breathe your last, die, pass away, perish.
2 *His permit has expired.* cease, end, finish, lapse, run out, stop, terminate.
OPPOSITE continue, start.

explain *verb*
1 *He explained what the writer meant.* clarify, clear up, decipher, define, demonstrate, describe, detail, elaborate, expound, illustrate, interpret, show, spell out, teach.
2 *That explains his strange behaviour.* account for, justify.

a
b
c
d
e
f
g
h
i
j
k
l
m
n
o
p
q
r
s
t
u
v
w
x
y
z

explanation *noun*
1 *an explanation of a word, theory, etc.*
account, clarification, commentary,
definition, description, interpretation,
key.
2 *She gave no explanation for her
behaviour.* account, excuse, justification,
reason.

explode *verb*
1 *The army bomb squad exploded the bomb.*
detonate, discharge, let off, set off.
2 *The bomb exploded.* blast, blow up,
burst, detonate, erupt, go off.
3 *Her father exploded with anger.* see
BECOME ANGRY (at ANGRY).

exploit *noun*
his noble exploits. act, adventure, deed,
escapade, feat.
exploit *verb*
1 *He exploited the opportunity.* capitalise
on, cash in on, make the most of, profit
from, take advantage of, use, utilise.
2 *The company exploits their workers.*
abuse, misuse, take advantage of, use.

explore *verb*
1 *He explored the country.* check out,
inspect, look around, prospect, scout,
survey, tour, travel about.
2 *She explored the problem.* analyse,
examine, inquire into, investigate, look
into, probe, research, study, survey.

explorer *noun*
discoverer, pioneer, prospector,
surveyor, trailblazer, traveller.

explosion *noun*
1 *We heard an explosion.* bang, blast,
boom, detonation, discharge, eruption,
outburst, pop, report, shot.
2 *an explosion of laughter.* burst,
eruption, fit, outburst.

explosive *adjective*
an explosive situation. charged,
dangerous, dicey (*slang*), precarious,
tense, unstable, volatile.
explosive *noun*
He used explosives to open the safe.
dynamite, gelignite, gunpowder, jelly
(*slang*), nitroglycerine, TNT.

expose *verb*
1 *He exposed himself to danger.* lay open,
put at risk, subject.

2 *She did not expose her legs.* bare,
display, reveal, show, uncover.
OPPOSITE cover.
3 *He exposed the plot.* betray, disclose,
divulge, leak, let out, make known,
reveal, uncover.
OPPOSITE conceal.

express[1] *adjective*
1 *an express train.* fast, high-speed,
non-stop, rapid-transit, through.
OPPOSITE slow.
2 *an express postal service.* fast, hasty,
prompt, quick, rapid, speedy, swift.

express[2] *verb*
1 *They expressed their feelings.* air,
communicate, convey, disclose, put into
words, reveal, speak, state, utter, vent,
voice.
2 *An 'X' expresses a kiss.* denote,
indicate, mean, represent, signify, stand
for, symbolise.

expression *noun*
1 *a slang expression.* idiom, phrase,
saying, term, word.
2 *a sad expression on her face.* air, aspect,
countenance, face, look.
3 *He read it with expression.* eloquence,
emotion, feeling, intonation, meaning,
sensitivity.

expressionless *adjective*
an expressionless stare. blank, deadpan,
empty, poker-faced, vacant, wooden.
OPPOSITE expressive.

expressive *adjective*
an expressive look. meaningful, revealing,
significant, telling.
OPPOSITE vacant.

expulsion *noun*
expulsion from school. banishment,
eviction, exclusion, removal.

exquisite *adjective*
an exquisite ring. beautiful, dainty,
delicate, elegant, fine, lovely, perfect.
OPPOSITE ugly.

extend *verb*
1 *He extended the line.* continue,
elongate, enlarge, lengthen, stretch.
OPPOSITE shorten.

2 *They extended their stay.* drag out, lengthen, prolong, protract, spin out.
OPPOSITE curtail.
3 *He extended his arm.* hold out, reach out, straighten out, stretch out.
4 *Their land extends to the river.* carry on, continue, reach, stretch.
5 *The load extended beyond the end of the truck.* jut out, project, protrude, stick out.
6 *He extended a welcome.* give, grant, offer.

extension *noun*
They built an extension to their house. addition, annexe, wing.

extensive *adjective*
1 *extensive gardens.* ample, big, huge, immense, large, spacious, vast.
OPPOSITE small.
2 *extensive knowledge.* broad, comprehensive, encyclopedic, thorough, vast, wide.
OPPOSITE restricted.
3 *extensive damage.* sweeping, vast, wholesale, widespread.
OPPOSITE slight.

extent *noun*
1 *the extent of the property.* area, breadth, expanse, length, size, spread, width.
2 *the extent of the problem.* amount, degree, limit, range, scale, scope.

exterior *adjective*
the exterior wall. external, outer, outside, outward, superficial.
OPPOSITE interior.
exterior *noun*
the house exterior. façade, face, outside, shell, surface.
OPPOSITE interior.

exterminate *verb*
He exterminated the blowflies. annihilate, destroy, eliminate, eradicate, get rid of, kill, murder, root out, slaughter, wipe out.

external *adjective*
an external appearance. exterior, outer, outside, outward, superficial.
OPPOSITE internal.

extinct *adjective*
1 *an extinct fire, volcano, etc.* burnt out, extinguished, inactive.
OPPOSITE active.

2 *extinct animals.* dead, died out.
OPPOSITE extant.

extinguish *verb*
extinguish a light, fire, etc. put out, quench, snuff out.
OPPOSITE kindle.

extra *adjective*
extra supplies. additional, excess, further, more, other, reserve, spare, superfluous, supplementary, surplus.
extra *adverb*
It is extra cold today. especially, exceptionally, particularly, unusually.
extra *noun*
1 *You have to pay for the extras.* accessory, addition, add-on, attachment, bonus, luxury, supplement.
2 *He kept what he needed and gave away the extra.* excess, remainder, rest, surplus.

extract *verb*
The dentist extracted the tooth. draw out, pull out, remove, take out.
OPPOSITE insert.
extract *noun*
1 *a vegetable extract.* concentrate, essence.
2 *an extract from the book, film, etc.* clip, cutting, excerpt, passage, quotation, snippet, trailer.

extraordinary *adjective*
an extraordinary person. extraordinary events. abnormal, amazing, astonishing, bizarre, curious, exceptional, incredible, miraculous, odd, outstanding, peculiar, phenomenal, rare, remarkable, singular, special, strange, striking, uncommon, unusual, weird.
OPPOSITE everyday, ordinary.

extravagant *adjective*
1 *He is extravagant when buying presents.* lavish, over-generous, prodigal, spendthrift, wasteful.
OPPOSITE economical, mean.
2 *an extravagant present.* costly, expensive, sumptuous.
OPPOSITE cheap.

extreme *adjective*
1 *extreme pain.* acute, excessive, great, intense, severe.
OPPOSITE mild.

a
b
c
d
e
f
g
h
i
j
k
l
m
n
o
p
q
r
s
t
u
v
w
x
y
z

2 *the extreme end of the hall.* farthest, furthermost, furthest, utmost, uttermost.
OPPOSITE closest.
3 *extreme measures.* drastic, harsh, radical, severe, stiff, stringent.
OPPOSITE moderate.
4 *an extreme view.* fanatical, hard-line, immoderate, radical, unreasonable, way-out (*informal*).
OPPOSITE moderate.

extreme *noun*
midway between the two extremes. boundary, end, extremity, limit, maximum, minimum, pole.

extremely *adverb*
extremely lucky. awfully (*informal*), especially, exceedingly, exceptionally, extraordinarily, remarkably, terribly (*informal*), very.

exuberant *adjective*
exuberant children. animated, boisterous, energetic, excited, full of beans (*informal*), high-spirited, irrepressible, lively, spirited, vivacious.
OPPOSITE listless, subdued.

exultant *adjective*
an exultant winner. delighted, ecstatic, elated, gleeful, jubilant, overjoyed, triumphant.

eye *verb*
The boy eyed the girl. behold (*old use*), contemplate, gaze at, look at, observe, ogle, peer at, stare at, study, view, watch.

eye-doctor *noun*
oculist, ophthalmologist.

eyesight *noun*
good eyesight. sight, vision.

eyesore *noun*
The building is an eyesore. blight, blot, monstrosity.

eyewitness *noun*
an eyewitness to the crash. bystander, observer, onlooker, spectator, witness.

Ff

fable *noun*
Aesop's fables. allegory, legend, myth, parable, story, tale.

fabric *noun*
The fabric was draped over the dummy. cloth, material, stuff, textile; [*kinds of fabric*] brocade, calico, corduroy, cotton, crepe, denim, drill, felt, flannel, flannelette, gabardine, gauze, georgette, gingham, hessian, jersey, lace, linen, Lycra (*trade mark*), muslin, plaid, polyester, poplin, rayon, satin, silk, taffeta, tartan, tweed, twill, velvet, velveteen, viscose, voile, wool.

fabulous *adjective*
1 *stories of fabulous creatures.* fabled, fictional, imaginary, legendary, mythical.
OPPOSITE real.
2 *fabulous wealth.* extraordinary, great, incredible, mind-boggling (*informal*), stupendous, tremendous, unbelievable.
3 (*informal*) *We had a fabulous time.* see EXCELLENT.

face *noun*
1 *a cheerful face.* air, countenance, expression, look.
2 *the northern face of the building.* façade, front, side, surface.
face *verb*
1 *The house faces a park.* front on, lie opposite, look out on, overlook.
2 *She faced many trials.* brave, confront, encounter, experience, meet.
face up to *He couldn't face up to his problems.* accept, come to terms with, cope with, deal with.
OPPOSITE evade.

facecloth *noun*
face washer, flannel, washer (*Australian*).

facetious *adjective*
a facetious comment. amusing, comical, flippant, funny, humorous, joking,
witty.
OPPOSITE serious.

facility *noun*
laundry facilities. amenity, convenience, resource.

fact *noun*
1 *Sort out fact from fiction.* actuality, certainty, reality, truth.
OPPOSITE fiction.
2 *He gave me the facts.* circumstance, detail, particular; [*facts*] data, evidence, information, low-down (*slang*).

factor *noun*
The human factor must be taken into account. aspect, circumstance, component, element, influence, part.

factory *noun*
forge, foundry, mill, plant, refinery, works, workshop.

factual *adjective*
a factual account. accurate, faithful, objective, strict, true, truthful.
OPPOSITE false, fanciful.

fad *noun*
a yo-yo fad. craze, cult, fashion, mania, passion, rage, vogue.

fade *verb*
1 *Her jeans have faded.* bleach, dull, lighten, pale, wash out, whiten.
OPPOSITE brighten.
2 *The image faded.* dim, disappear, grow faint, vanish, weaken.
3 *Interest faded. The sound faded.* decline, decrease, die away, diminish, dwindle, ebb, peter out, trail away, wane.
OPPOSITE increase.
fade away *You'll fade away if you don't eat.* die, pass away, shrivel, waste away, wither.

fail *verb*
1 *She failed her exam.* be unsuccessful in, bomb out in (*informal*), flunk (*informal*).
OPPOSITE pass.

171

2 *Their plan failed.* backfire, be unsuccessful, come unstuck (*informal*), fall through, flop (*slang*), founder, misfire.
OPPOSITE succeed, work.
3 *The supply failed.* be exhausted, be insufficient, be used up, run out.
OPPOSITE hold out.
4 *Her eyesight is failing.* decline, deteriorate, dim, diminish, dwindle, fade, wane, weaken.
OPPOSITE improve.
5 *The engine failed.* break down, conk out (*informal*), malfunction.
OPPOSITE work.
6 *He failed to write.* forget, neglect, omit.

failing *noun*
Pride was one of his failings. fault, flaw, foible, imperfection, shortcoming, vice, weakness.
OPPOSITE strength.

failure *noun*
The programme was a failure. disaster, fiasco, fizzer (*Australian informal*), flop (*slang*), non-event, wash-out (*slang*).
OPPOSITE success.

faint *adjective*
1 *The picture is faint.* blurred, dim, hazy, indistinct, misty, unclear.
OPPOSITE clear, distinct.
2 *a faint colour.* delicate, faded, light, pale, pastel, soft, subdued, subtle.
OPPOSITE intense.
3 *a faint sound.* low, muffled, muted, soft, subdued.
OPPOSITE loud.
4 *a faint hope.* feeble, remote, slender, slight, slim, small, vague, weak.
OPPOSITE strong.
5 *He felt faint.* dizzy, giddy, light-headed, unsteady, weak, woozy (*informal*).
faint *verb*
He fainted at the sight of blood. black out, collapse, flake out (*informal*), keel over, lose consciousness, pass out (*informal*), swoon.
OPPOSITE come round.

faint-hearted *adjective*
chicken-hearted, cowardly, diffident, fearful, lily-livered, timid, timorous.
OPPOSITE bold.

fair¹ *noun*
1 *a craft stall at the school fair.* bazaar, fête, gala, market.
2 *a book fair.* exhibition, expo, exposition, sale, show.
3 *a merry-go-round at the fair.* carnival, funfair, show.

fair² *adjective*
1 *fair hair.* blond, golden, light.
OPPOSITE dark.
2 *fair weather.* bright, clear, cloudless, fine, sunny, unclouded.
OPPOSITE cloudy.
3 *a fair decision.* even-handed, honest, impartial, just, legitimate, objective, open-minded, proper, reasonable, right, sporting, sportsmanlike, unbiased, unprejudiced.
OPPOSITE unfair.
4 *The meal was fair.* all right, average, indifferent, mediocre, middling, OK (*informal*), passable, reasonable, satisfactory, so-so (*informal*), tolerable.

fairly *adverb*
1 *They acted fairly.* honestly, impartially, justly, objectively, properly, reasonably.
2 *fairly fast.* moderately, pretty, quite, rather, reasonably, somewhat.

fairness *noun*
equity, even-handedness, impartiality, justice, neutrality, objectivity.

fairy *noun*
elf, imp, pixie, sprite.

faith *noun*
1 *He has faith in you.* belief, confidence, reliance, trust.
2 *people of many faiths.* belief, church, conviction, creed, persuasion, religion.

faithful *adjective*
1 *a faithful supporter.* committed, constant, dedicated, dependable, devoted, dutiful, loyal, reliable, staunch, steadfast, true, trustworthy, trusty.
OPPOSITE disloyal, unfaithful.
2 *a faithful account.* accurate, correct, factual, honest, strict, true, truthful.
OPPOSITE inaccurate.

fake *noun*
1 *The note was a fake.* copy, counterfeit, duplicate, forgery, fraud, hoax,

imitation, phoney (*informal*), replica, reproduction.
2 *The doctor was a fake.* charlatan, cheat, con man (*informal*), fraud, humbug, impostor, phoney (*informal*), quack.
fake *adjective*
fake diamonds. artificial, bogus, counterfeit, false, forged, imitation, phoney (*informal*), pretend (*informal*), pseudo, sham, synthetic.
OPPOSITE authentic, genuine.
fake *verb*
1 *They faked the document.* copy, counterfeit, fabricate, forge, reproduce.
2 *He faked illness.* feign, pretend, simulate.

fall *verb*
1 *He fell down the hill.* collapse, come a buster (*Australian informal*), come a cropper (*informal*), come a gutser (*Australian slang*), crash, overbalance, plummet, plunge, slide, slip, spill, stumble, topple, trip, tumble.
2 *Night fell.* descend.
3 *The material falls gracefully.* cascade, dangle, hang.
4 *Prices fell. The numbers fell.* crash, decline, decrease, diminish, drop, dwindle, nosedive, plummet, plunge, reduce, slump.
OPPOSITE rise.
5 *Many men fell in the battle.* be killed, die, perish.
6 *Easter fell early.* happen, occur, take place.
fall *noun*
1 *the fall of the government.* collapse, defeat, downfall, overthrow.
2 *a fall in interest rates.* decline, decrease, dip, dive, drop, reduction, slump.
fall out *The couple fell out over the incident.* argue, disagree, fight, quarrel, squabble.
fall through see FAIL.

fallacy *noun*
1 *That people can't change their nature is a fallacy.* delusion, misconception, mistake, myth.
2 *a fallacy in the reasoning.* error, flaw, inaccuracy, inconsistency, mistake.

falls *plural noun*
cascade, cataract, waterfall.

false *adjective*
1 *a false argument.* erroneous, faulty, inaccurate, incorrect, invalid, misleading, unsound, untrue, wrong.
OPPOSITE correct, true.
2 *a false friend.* deceitful, dishonest, disloyal, faithless, hypocritical, insincere, lying, treacherous, two-faced, unfaithful, untruthful.
OPPOSITE faithful, true.
3 *false pearls.* artificial, bogus, counterfeit, fake, imitation, phoney (*informal*), pretend (*informal*), pseudo, sham, synthetic.
OPPOSITE genuine.
4 *a false name.* assumed, fictitious, made-up.
OPPOSITE real.

falter *verb*
1 *The old man faltered and fell.* stagger, stumble, totter.
2 *She faltered in front of the microphone.* hesitate, pause, stammer, stutter.

fame *noun*
celebrity, distinction, eminence, glory, honour, prestige, prominence, recognition, renown, reputation, repute.
OPPOSITE obscurity.

familiar *adjective*
1 *a familiar experience.* common, commonplace, customary, everyday, habitual, normal, regular, routine, usual, well-known.
OPPOSITE strange, unfamiliar.
2 *They are on familiar terms.* chummy (*informal*), close, friendly, informal, intimate, matey, pally (*informal*).
OPPOSITE distant, formal.
be familiar with *He is familiar with computers.* be acquainted with, be at home with, be used to, be versed in, know about.

family *noun*
1 *a single-income family.* household.
2 *The couple want to raise a family.* brood, children, kids (*informal*), offspring.
3 *a reunion of the whole family.* clan, flesh and blood, folk, kin, kindred, kinsmen, kinswomen, kith and kin, people, relations, relatives, tribe.

a
b
c
d
e
f
g
h
i
j
k
l
m
n
o
p
q
r
s
t
u
v
w
x
y
z

4 *He comes from a noble family.* ancestry, dynasty, forebears, genealogy, line, lineage, parentage, pedigree, roots, stock.

famished *adjective*
The children were famished after school. hungry, peckish (*informal*), ravenous, starving.

famous *adjective*
a famous person. celebrated, distinguished, eminent, famed, great, illustrious, important, legendary, notable, noted, outstanding, pre-eminent, prominent, renowned, well-known.
OPPOSITE unknown.

fan *noun*
jazz fans. tennis fans. addict, admirer, buff (*informal*), devotee, enthusiast, fanatic, follower, lover, nut (*informal*), supporter.

fanatic *noun*
a religious fanatic. enthusiast, extremist, maniac, zealot.

fancy *noun*
1 *flights of fancy.* delusion, fantasy, imagination, make-believe.
OPPOSITE reality.
2 *He had a fancy for a hamburger.* craving, desire, hunger, liking, longing.
OPPOSITE dislike.
fancy *adjective*
a fancy design. complicated, decorative, detailed, elaborate, intricate, ornamental, ornate, showy.
OPPOSITE plain, simple.
fancy *verb*
1 *He fancied that he was in another place.* dream, fantasise, imagine, picture, think.
2 *She fancies the red dress.* desire, hanker after, like, long for, prefer, want, wish for, yearn for.
3 (*informal*) *He fancies her.* be attracted to, like, take a fancy to, take a liking to, take a shine to (*informal*).
OPPOSITE dislike.

fantastic *adjective*
1 *a fantastic story.* absurd, amazing, bizarre, extraordinary, fanciful, far-fetched, implausible, incredible,

outlandish, preposterous, strange, unbelievable, unreal, unrealistic, weird, whimsical, wild.
OPPOSITE credible.
2 *a fantastic sum of money.* enormous, extravagant, great, huge, immense, terrific (*informal*), tremendous, vast.
3 (*informal*) *a fantastic show.* exceptional, fabulous (*informal*), first-rate, great, magnificent, marvellous, remarkable, sensational, splendid, wonderful; see also EXCELLENT.

fantasy *noun*
1 *in the realms of fantasy.* fancy, imagination, invention, make-believe.
OPPOSITE reality.
2 *a fantasy about his past.* daydream, dream, illusion, reverie.

far *adjective*
in a far country. distant, far-away, far-off, remote.
OPPOSITE near.

farce *noun*
He described the proceedings as a farce. charade, joke, mockery, sham.

farcical *adjective*
a farcical situation. absurd, comical, laughable, ludicrous, preposterous, ridiculous.

fare *noun*
1 *bus fares.* charge, cost, fee, payment, price, rate.
2 *The café provides stodgy fare.* food, meals, tucker (*Australian informal*).
fare *verb*
How did he fare? do, get on, make out, manage.

farewell *interjection*
adieu, au revoir, bye (*informal*), bye-bye (*informal*), cheerio (*informal*), cheers (*informal*), goodbye, hooray (*Australian informal*), see you (*informal*), see you later (*informal*), so long (*informal*).
farewell *adjective*
a farewell speech. parting, valedictory.

far-fetched *adjective*
a far-fetched explanation. dubious, fanciful, implausible, improbable, incredible, unconvincing, unlikely.
OPPOSITE plausible.

farm *noun*
plantation, property, ranch, run (*Australian*), station (*Australian*).
farm *verb*
They farm the land. cultivate, till, work.

farmer *noun*
agriculturalist, cocky (*Australian informal*), grazier (*Australian*), pastoralist (*Australian*), peasant, sharefarmer (*Australian*).

far-reaching *adjective*
far-reaching policy changes. broad, extensive, sweeping, wide-ranging.

far-sighted *adjective*
A far-sighted person wears glasses for close work. hypermetropic, long-sighted.
OPPOSITE myopic, short-sighted.

fascinate *verb*
The dancer fascinated the audience. attract, bewitch, captivate, charm, enchant, enthral, entrance, hold spellbound, hypnotise, mesmerise, rivet.

fashion *noun*
1 *Continue in this fashion.* manner, method, mode, way.
2 *the fashion of short skirts.* craze, fad, rage, style, trend, vogue.
fashion *verb*
She fashions new things out of scrap. carve, construct, create, form, make, manufacture, model, mould, produce, shape.

fashionable *adjective*
fashionable clothes. chic, classy (*informal*), contemporary, elegant, in, in fashion, latest, modern, smart, stylish, swish (*informal*), trendy (*informal*), up-to-date, with it (*informal*).
OPPOSITE old-fashioned.

fast^1 *adjective*
1 *a fast pace.* breakneck, brisk, express, fleet, hasty, high-speed, nippy (*informal*), quick, rapid, speedy, swift, zippy.
OPPOSITE slow.
2 *fast colours.* fixed, indelible, permanent.
fast *adverb*
1 *Run as fast as you can.* at full pelt, at full speed, at the double, briskly, hastily, hurriedly, like lightning (*informal*), like mad (*informal*), quickly, rapidly, speedily, swiftly.
OPPOSITE slowly.
2 *The car was stuck fast.* firmly, securely, solidly, tightly.

fast^2 *verb*
They binged after fasting. go without food, starve.
OPPOSITE eat.

fasten *verb*
adhere, affix, anchor, attach, bind, bolt, bond, buckle, button, chain, clamp, clasp, clip, close, connect, couple, do up, fix, hitch, hook, join, knot, lace, lash, latch, link, lock, moor, nail, peg, pin, rivet, screw, seal, secure, sew, shut, staple, stick, strap, tack, tape, tether, tie, truss, zip up.
OPPOSITE unfasten.

fat *noun*
1 *body fat.* blubber, flab (*informal*).
2 *He cooks with fat.* butter, dripping, grease, lard, margarine, suet.
fat *adjective*
1 *a fat person.* chubby, dumpy, flabby, gross, heavy, large, obese, overweight, plump, podgy, portly, roly-poly, rotund, squat, stout, tubby.
OPPOSITE slim, thin.
2 *a fat book.* bulky, thick, weighty.
OPPOSITE thin.

fatal *adjective*
a fatal disease. deadly, lethal, mortal, terminal.

fatality *noun*
road fatalities. casualty, death.

fate *noun*
1 *Fate had brought them together.* chance, destiny, fortune, luck, predestination, providence.
2 *a person's fate.* destiny, doom, fortune, lot.

father *noun*
1 [*informal terms of address*] dad, daddy, pa, papa, pop.
2 *land of our fathers.* ancestor, forebear, forefather, patriarch.
3 *the father of modern medicine.* creator, founder, inventor, originator.

a
b
c
d
e
f
g
h
i
j
k
l
m
n
o
p
q
r
s
t
u
v
w
x
y
z

fatherly *adjective*
He showed fatherly concern. fatherlike, kind, paternal, protective.

fatigue *noun*
After working for twenty hours he was overcome with fatigue. exhaustion, tiredness, weariness.
OPPOSITE energy.

fatty *adjective*
greasy, oily.

fault *noun*
1 faults in the paintwork. blemish, defect, flaw, imperfection.
OPPOSITE perfection.
2 a mechanical fault. bug (informal), defect, glitch (informal), malfunction, trouble.
3 He forgave their faults. error, failing, foible, imperfection, misdeed, mistake, offence, shortcoming, sin, slip-up (informal), trespass (old use), vice, weakness, wrongdoing.
OPPOSITE strength.
4 The other driver admitted fault. blame, responsibility.

fault *verb*
You can't fault his work. criticise, find fault with, knock (informal), pick holes in.
OPPOSITE commend.
at fault culpable, guilty, in the wrong, responsible, to blame.

faultless *adjective*
a faultless performance. correct, flawless, ideal, immaculate, perfect, unblemished.
OPPOSITE imperfect.

faulty *adjective*
The toaster is faulty. defective, imperfect, kaput (informal), malfunctioning, on the blink (informal), out of order.
OPPOSITE sound, working.

favour *noun*
1 He was looked upon with favour. approval, goodwill, support, sympathy.
OPPOSITE disfavour.
2 Can you do me a favour? courtesy, good deed, good turn, kindness, service.
OPPOSITE disservice.

3 He showed favour to one team. bias, favouritism, partiality, preference.
OPPOSITE even-handedness.

favour *verb*
1 Which method do you favour? advocate, approve, back, choose, endorse, opt for, prefer, recommend, select, support.
OPPOSITE oppose.
2 The wet track favoured our horse. assist, benefit, give an advantage to, help.
OPPOSITE hinder.

favourable *adjective*
1 a favourable response. approving, encouraging, good, positive, reassuring, supportive, sympathetic.
OPPOSITE hostile, unfavourable.
2 favourable conditions. advantageous, auspicious, beneficial, helpful, promising, propitious.
OPPOSITE adverse.

favourite *adjective*
her favourite doll. best, chosen, pet, preferred.

favourite *noun*
1 the teacher's favourite. darling, pet.
2 the favourite in the race. front runner.
OPPOSITE outsider.

favouritism *noun*
bias, partiality, positive discrimination, preference, prejudice.
OPPOSITE even-handedness.

fawn *adjective*
a fawn colour. beige, buff, camel, khaki, light brown, neutral.

fear *noun*
1 trembling with fear. alarm, anxiety, apprehension, awe, consternation, dismay, dread, fright, horror, panic, terror, trepidation, worry.
OPPOSITE courage.
2 a fear of flying. aversion, dread, phobia.

fear *verb*
He feared the punishment. be afraid of, be frightened of, be scared of, dread, worry about.

fearful *adjective*
1 a fearful explosion. alarming, appalling, awful, dreadful, fearsome, frightening, frightful, ghastly, horrendous, horrific,

scary, shocking, terrible, terrific,
terrifying.
2 *He is fearful in new situations.* afraid,
alarmed, anxious, apprehensive,
cowardly, faint-hearted, frightened,
nervous, panicky, scared, terrified,
timid, timorous, worried.
OPPOSITE fearless.

fearless *adjective*
a fearless policeman. bold, brave,
courageous, daring, dauntless, gallant,
game, heroic, intrepid, lion-hearted,
plucky, unafraid, undaunted, valiant.
OPPOSITE cowardly.

feast *noun*
a ten-course feast. banquet, dinner, meal,
repast (*formal*), spread.
feast *verb*
They feasted on smoked salmon. dine, eat,
gorge, tuck in (*informal*).

feat *noun*
the amazing feats of the riders.
achievement, act, action, deed, exploit,
performance, stunt.

feather *noun*
a bird's feather. hackle, plume, quill;
[*feathers*] down, plumage.

feature *noun*
The plan has good and bad features. aspect,
attribute, characteristic, detail, point,
property, quality, respect, trait.

federation *noun*
a federation of driving instructors.
alliance, association, confederation,
league, syndicate, union.

fee *noun*
pay a fee. charge a fee. brokerage, charge,
commission, cost, dues, levy, payment,
price, rate, subscription, tariff, toll.

feeble *adjective*
1 *He was too feeble to carry the suitcase.*
decrepit, delicate, frail, helpless, infirm,
listless, poorly, puny, sickly, weak,
weedy.
OPPOSITE strong.
2 *a feeble excuse.* flimsy, lame, paltry,
poor, tame, unconvincing, weak.
OPPOSITE convincing.
3 *He's too feeble to stand up to them.*
ineffectual, powerless, soft, spineless,

weak, wimpish (*informal*).
OPPOSITE powerful, strong.

feed *verb*
1 *She fed the baby.* nourish, nurse, suckle.
OPPOSITE starve.
2 *The animals are feeding.* browse, eat,
graze.
3 *They feed on insects.* dine, live, prey;
see also EAT.

feedback *noun*
reaction, response.

feel *verb*
1 *She felt the parcel and guessed its
contents.* finger, handle, manipulate,
maul, stroke, touch.
2 *He felt his way.* fumble, grope.
3 *He felt a severe pain.* be aware of, be
conscious of, experience, notice,
perceive, sense, suffer.
4 *I feel that you're right.* believe,
consider, think.

feeler *noun*
the insect's feelers. antenna.

feeling *noun*
1 *a tingling feeling in his fingers.*
awareness, sensation.
2 *the feeling of the place.* air, atmosphere,
climate, feel, mood, spirit, tone, vibes
(*informal*).
3 *He showed no feeling.* compassion,
concern, emotion, empathy, passion,
sensitivity, sympathy, tenderness,
understanding.
OPPOSITE apathy.
4 *He had a feeling that they would not turn
up.* hunch, idea, impression, inkling,
instinct, intuition, notion, premonition,
suspicion, thought.
5 *The feeling of the meeting was against it.*
attitude, opinion, sentiment, view.

fell *verb*
He felled the tree. chop down, cut down,
knock down.

fellow *noun*
1 *She gets on well with her fellows.*
associate, colleague, companion,
comrade, mate, peer.
2 (*informal*) *He was a strange fellow.* bloke
(*informal*), boy, chap (*informal*),
gentleman, guy (*informal*), lad, man; see
also PERSON.

a
b
c
d
e
f
g
h
i
j
k
l
m
n
o
p
q
r
s
t
u
v
w
x
y
z

fellowship *noun*
1 *She enjoys the fellowship of others.* companionship, company, friendship, society.
2 *He belongs to a student fellowship.* association, club, league, society.

female *adjective*
see FEMININE.
OPPOSITE male.
female *noun*
see GIRL, WOMAN.

feminine *adjective*
female, girlish, ladylike, womanly.
OPPOSITE masculine.

fence *noun*
barricade, barrier, hoarding, palings, railing, stockade, wall.
fence *verb*
fence in box in, close in, confine, coop up, enclose, hedge in, hem in, surround, wall in.

fend *verb*
fend for *They were left to fend for themselves.* look after, shift for, support, take care of.
fend off *They fended off their attackers.* hold at bay, keep off, parry, repel, repulse, ward off.

ferocious *adjective*
1 *Lions are ferocious.* fierce, savage, vicious, wild.
OPPOSITE gentle, tame.
2 *a ferocious assault.* barbarous, bestial, bloodthirsty, brutal, cruel, fierce, ruthless, sadistic, savage, vicious, violent.

ferret *verb*
1 *She ferreted about in the drawer.* forage, fossick (*Australian informal*), hunt, rummage, search.
2 *He ferreted out the information.* dig out, discover, find, root out, unearth.

ferry *verb*
They ferried the cars across the river. carry, convey, ship, take, transfer, transport.

fertile *adjective*
1 *fertile soil.* fruitful, productive, rich.
OPPOSITE barren.
2 *a fertile animal.* fruitful, productive.
OPPOSITE infertile, sterile.

3 *a fertile imagination.* creative, imaginative, inventive, productive, prolific, rich.
OPPOSITE unimaginative.

fertilise *verb*
1 *fertilise the garden.* compost, feed, top-dress.
2 *fertilise a cow.* impregnate, inseminate.
3 *fertilise a plant.* pollinate.

fervent *adjective*
a fervent supporter. ardent, devout, eager, earnest, emotional, enthusiastic, impassioned, keen, passionate, vehement, warm, zealous.
OPPOSITE apathetic.

festival *noun*
anniversary, carnival, celebration, eisteddfod, fair, fête, fiesta, gala, holiday, jamboree, jubilee, pageant, party, show.

festive *adjective*
a festive spirit. cheerful, gay, happy, jovial, joyous, light-hearted, merry.
OPPOSITE gloomy.

festivity *noun*
They joined in the festivities. celebration, gaiety, merrymaking, party, revelry.

fetch *verb*
1 *He fetched the luggage.* bring, carry, collect, get, pick up, retrieve.
2 *The car won't fetch much.* bring in, go for, raise, sell for, yield.

fête *noun*
the school fête. bazaar, fair, gala, jumble sale; see also FESTIVAL.

fetters *plural noun*
The prisoners are in fetters. bonds, chains, irons, manacles, shackles.

feud *noun*
a feud between the two families. conflict, dispute, quarrel, row, vendetta.

few *adjective*
few visitors. infrequent, rare, scarce, sparse.
OPPOSITE many.
few *noun*
We have only a few left. handful, remnant, sprinkling.
OPPOSITE lot.

fiasco *noun*
The party was a fiasco. catastrophe, disaster, failure, fizzer (*Australian informal*), flop (*slang*), non-event, wash-out (*slang*).
OPPOSITE success.

fib *noun*
telling fibs. fabrication, falsehood, lie, porky (*slang*), story, untruth, white lie (*informal*).
OPPOSITE truth.

fibre *noun*
The fibre is spun. filament, strand, thread.

fickle *adjective*
a fickle person. fickle weather. capricious, changeable, erratic, inconsistent, inconstant, temperamental, unfaithful, unpredictable, unreliable, variable.
OPPOSITE constant.

fiction *noun*
1 *His explanation was pure fiction.* fabrication, fib, invention, lie, make-believe.
OPPOSITE fact.
2 *She prefers to read fiction.* fable, fairy story, fantasy, legend, myth, novel, romance, story, tale.
OPPOSITE non-fiction.

fictitious *adjective*
a fictitious character, account, etc. bogus, fabled, false, fanciful, fictional, imaginary, invented, legendary, made-up, mythical, phoney (*informal*), untrue.
OPPOSITE factual, true.

fiddle *noun*
1 (*informal*) *He plays the fiddle.* violin.
2 (*slang*) *The accountant was involved in a big fiddle.* fraud, racket, rort (*Australian slang*), scam (*slang*), swindle, swizz (*informal*).
fiddle *verb*
1 *She fiddled with the beads.* fidget, finger, jiggle, juggle, play, toy, twiddle.
2 *He fiddled with the radio to make it work.* mess about, muck around, tamper, tinker, twiddle.

fiddly *adjective* (*informal*)
a fiddly job. awkward, messy, ticklish, tricky.

fidelity *noun*
1 *marital fidelity. fidelity to the king.* allegiance, devotion, faithfulness, loyalty.
OPPOSITE disloyalty, infidelity.
2 *fidelity in newspaper reporting.* accuracy, faithfulness, honesty, integrity, truthfulness.
OPPOSITE inaccuracy.

fidget *verb*
They fidgeted nervously. fiddle, jiggle around, shuffle, squirm, twitch, wriggle.

fidgety *adjective*
a fidgety audience. jittery (*informal*), nervous, restless, twitchy.

field *noun*
1 *sheep in the field.* lea (*poetical*), meadow, paddock, paddy (*for rice*), pasture.
2 *a sports field.* arena, ground, oval, pitch, stadium.
3 *her field of vision.* range, scope.
4 *an expert in his field.* area, domain, province, sphere, subject.

fiend *noun*
The hero saved them from the fiend. brute, demon, devil, monster, ogre.

fierce *adjective*
1 *a fierce battle.* bloodthirsty, bloody, brutal, cutthroat, ferocious, merciless, relentless, savage, vicious, violent, wild.
OPPOSITE gentle.
2 *the fierce heat.* extreme, great, intense, severe, strong.
OPPOSITE mild.

fiery *adjective*
1 *a fiery incinerator.* blazing, burning, flaming, hot, red-hot.
2 *a fiery temper.* hot, impetuous, irascible, passionate, violent.
OPPOSITE calm.

fight *verb*
1 *The enemies fought.* argue, battle, be at loggerheads, bicker, box, brawl, clash, combat, duel, feud, grapple, joust, quarrel, scrap (*informal*), scuffle, skirmish, spar, squabble, stoush (*Australian slang*), strive, struggle, tussle, war, wrestle.

a b c d e f g h i j k l m n o p q r s t u v w x y z

2 *They fought a war.* carry on, conduct, wage.

3 *He is fighting for justice.* campaign, crusade, lobby, strive, struggle.

4 *You can't fight progress.* defy, oppose, resist.

fight *noun*

1 *He was injured in a fight.* action, affray, aggression, altercation, argument, barney (*informal*), battle, blue (*Australian informal*), brawl, campaign, clash, combat, conflict, confrontation, contest, dispute, duel, dust-up (*informal*), encounter, feud, fisticuffs, fracas, free-for-all, hostilities, joust, punch-up (*informal*), quarrel, row, scrap (*informal*), scrimmage, scuffle, set-to, skirmish, squabble, stoush (*Australian slang*), strife, struggle, tussle, war, wrestle.

2 *The boxers began their fight.* bout, boxing match.

fight back counter, counter-attack, hit back, retaliate.

fighter *noun*

boxer, campaigner, combatant, duellist, gladiator, guerrilla, marine, mercenary, partisan, pugilist, soldier, warrior, wrestler.

figure *noun*

1 *She wrote down the figures.* digit, integer, number, numeral.

2 *The figure was carved out of wood.* effigy, figurine, image, sculpture, statue.

3 *an important figure in politics.* character, identity (*Australian*), person, personality.

4 *She has a good figure.* body, build, form, outline, physique, shape.

figure *verb*

Where does he figure in the story. appear, feature, play a part.

figure out

1 *She figured out what was owing.* add up, calculate, compute, work out.

2 *He can't figure out what's going on.* comprehend, grasp, interpret, suss out (*informal*), understand, work out.

file^1 *verb*

He filed the metal. rub, shape, smooth.

file^2 *noun*

1 *She keeps her papers in a file.* binder, folder, holder, portfolio.

2 *They keep a file on each person.* dossier, papers, records.

3 *a long file of cars.* column, line, queue, row, string, train.

file *verb*

1 *The clerk filed the papers.* arrange, catalogue, pigeon-hole, put away, store.

2 *The competitors filed past the flag.* march, parade, troop.

fill *verb*

1 *He filled his case with clothes.* cram, jam, load up, pack, stuff.
OPPOSITE empty.

2 *The builders filled the hole.* block up, bung up, close, plug, seal, stop up.
OPPOSITE excavate, hollow out.

3 *He was appointed to fill the position.* hold, occupy, take up.
OPPOSITE vacate.

4 *The new deli fills a need.* answer, fulfil, meet, satisfy.

5 *He filled the time wisely.* pass, spend, use.

fill in

1 *She filled in the form.* answer, complete, fill out.

2 (*informal*) *He filled me in on what had happened.* acquaint, brief, inform, tell.

3 *Another player filled in for her.* cover, deputise, relieve, stand in, substitute.

filling *noun*

cushion filling. contents, padding, stuffing, wadding.

film *noun*

1 *plastic film.* coating, covering, layer, sheet.

2 *They watched a film about the war.* feature, flick (*informal*), motion picture, movie, picture, video.

film *verb*

They filmed the scene four times. photograph, record, shoot, video.

filter *noun*

Pass the liquid through a filter. screen, sieve, strainer.

filter *verb*

They filter the water. clarify, purify, refine, sieve, strain.

filth *noun*
dirt, grime, gunk (*informal*), muck (*informal*), mud, slime, sludge.

filthy *adjective*
1 *filthy buildings.* blackened, dirty, dusty, grimy, grubby, muddy, soiled, squalid.
OPPOSITE clean.
2 *filthy language.* coarse, crude, dirty, foul, improper, indecent, obscene, offensive, rude, smutty, vulgar.

final *adjective*
1 *the final chapter.* closing, concluding, end, finishing, last, ultimate.
OPPOSITE opening.
2 *The judge's decision is final.* conclusive, definitive, indisputable, irrevocable, unalterable.

finale *noun*
see ENDING.

finally *adverb*
at last, eventually, in the end, lastly, once and for all, ultimately.

finance *verb*
The bank financed the scheme. back, fund, pay for, sponsor, subsidise, underwrite.
finances *plural noun*
His finances are limited. assets, capital, cash, funds, means, money, resources.

find *verb*
1 *He found his missing keys.* come across, come upon, dig up, discover, locate, recover, regain, retrieve, spot, stumble on, uncover, unearth.
OPPOSITE lose.
2 *She found the cause of the problem.* detect, determine, diagnose, discover, identify, trace, track down, work out.
3 *They can't find work.* acquire, gain, get, obtain, procure.
4 *The court found her innocent.* declare, judge, pronounce, rule.
find out *She found out the results.* ascertain, discover, hear, learn.

findings *plural noun*
the findings of a court. conclusion, decision, judgement, verdict.

fine[1] *noun*
a parking fine. charge, penalty, ticket.

fine *verb*
He was fined for speeding. book, charge, penalise.

fine[2] *adjective*
1 *a fine performance.* accomplished, brilliant, excellent, exceptional, fantastic, first-class, first-rate, great, high-quality, impressive, magnificent, marvellous, masterly, meritorious, meticulous, outstanding, peerless, praiseworthy, prize, sensational, skilful, splendid, super (*informal*), superb, superior, superlative, top-notch (*informal*), wonderful.
OPPOSITE inferior, poor.
2 *fine weather.* bright, clear, fair, sunny.
OPPOSITE overcast, wet.
3 *fine material.* delicate, flimsy, gauzy, lacy, light, sheer, thin, transparent.
OPPOSITE coarse, heavy.
4 *a fine line.* narrow, slender, slim, thin.
OPPOSITE thick.
5 *fine workmanship.* beautiful, dainty, delicate, excellent, exquisite, flawless.
6 *I'm fine, thank you.* all right, OK (*informal*), well.

finicky *adjective*
a finicky eater. choosy (*informal*), fastidious, fussy, pernickety (*informal*), picky (*informal*).

finish *verb*
1 *He finished the lecture with a question.* close, complete, conclude, discontinue, end, halt, round off, terminate, wind up, wrap up (*informal*).
OPPOSITE begin.
2 *The lesson finished early.* cease, close, come to an end, conclude, end, stop, terminate.
OPPOSITE start.
3 *The work was finished on time.* accomplish, achieve, carry out, complete, finalise.
OPPOSITE start.
4 *Who finished the biscuits?* consume, eat up, get through, knock off (*informal*), polish off.
finish *noun*
1 *the finish of a race, job, etc.* cessation, close, completion, conclusion, end, ending, finale, termination.
OPPOSITE beginning.

a
b
c
d
e
f
g
h
i
j
k
l
m
n
o
p
q
r
s
t
u
v
w
x
y
z

2 *The shelves have a glossy finish.* coating, exterior, surface, veneer.

fire *noun*
1 *Where there's smoke there's fire.* burning, combustion, flames.
2 *The firemen fought the fire.* blaze, bonfire, bushfire (*Australian*), inferno.
3 *The leader was full of fire.* ardour, energy, enthusiasm, fervour, inspiration, passion, spirit, vigour.

fire *verb*
1 *The soldier fired at the crowd.* open fire, shoot, snipe.
2 *They fired their missiles.* detonate, discharge, explode, launch, let off, set off.
3 *The boss fired her.* dismiss, give someone notice, give someone the boot (*informal*), remove, sack (*informal*).
OPPOSITE hire.
4 *He fired the pile of sticks.* ignite, kindle, light, set ablaze, set fire to, set on fire.
5 *He fired the students with enthusiasm.* animate, excite, inspire, motivate, stimulate.
on fire ablaze, aflame, alight, blazing, burning, in flames.

firearm *noun*
see GUN.

fireplace *noun*
fire, grate, hearth, range.

fireproof *adjective*
flameproof, incombustible, non-flammable, non-inflammable.
OPPOSITE flammable, inflammable.

fireworks *plural noun*
crackers, pyrotechnics.

firm¹ *noun*
They are partners in a firm. business, company, corporation, enterprise, establishment, organisation, partnership.

firm² *adjective*
1 *a firm mixture.* compact, hard, rigid, set, solid, stable, stiff, unyielding.
OPPOSITE soft.
2 *a firm grip.* secure, steady, strong, sure, tenacious, tight.
OPPOSITE loose.
3 *He remained firm in his opinion.* adamant, definite, dogged, inflexible,

obstinate, persistent, resolute, rigid, steadfast, stubborn, unshakeable, unwavering, unyielding.
OPPOSITE irresolute.
4 *a firm arrangement.* agreed, definite, fixed, settled, unalterable, unchangeable.
OPPOSITE tentative.
5 *firm friends.* constant, dependable, faithful, loyal, reliable, solid, staunch, steadfast.

firm *verb*
The mixture firmed up. compact, harden, jell, set, solidify, stiffen.

first *adjective*
1 *the first child in the family.* eldest, first-born, oldest.
OPPOSITE last, youngest.
2 *a ship's first voyage.* initial, maiden, original.
OPPOSITE last.
3 *the first stage.* earliest, initial, introductory, opening, preliminary.
OPPOSITE final.
4 *of first importance.* basic, chief, foremost, fundamental, greatest, highest, leading, main, major, primary, prime, principal, supreme.
OPPOSITE least.

first-class *adjective*
see EXCELLENT.

fish *noun*
[*various fishes*] anchovy, barracouta, barramundi, bass, bream, butterfish, callop, carp, cod, eel, flathead, flounder, garfish, gemfish, goby, golden perch, goldfish, groper, haddock, hake, herring, hoki, jewfish, John Dory, kingfish, leatherjacket, ling, luderick, lungfish, mackerel, marlin, minnow, morwong, mullet, mulloway, Murray cod, nannygai, perch, pike, pilchard, piranha, plaice, ray, redfin, redfish, roughy, salmon, sardine, sea horse, shark, skate, skipjack, snapper, snook, sole, sprat, stingray, stonefish, swordfish, tommy ruff, trevally, trout, tuna, whitebait, whiting, wrasse, yellowbelly.

fish *verb*
1 *He fished from the side of the boat.* angle, go fishing, trawl.

2 *He's fishing for clues.* fossick
(*Australian informal*), hunt, look, probe,
search, seek.

fishy *adjective* (*informal*)
There's something fishy about him.
doubtful, dubious, shady, strange,
suspect, suspicious, suss (*informal*).

fit[1] *noun*
a fit of sneezing. attack, bout, burst,
convulsion, outbreak, seizure, spasm,
spell.

fit[2] *adjective*
1 *a dinner fit for a king.* appropriate,
fitting, proper, right, suitable, worthy.
OPPOSITE unfit, unsuitable.
2 *She does not feel fit to take on the job.*
able, capable, competent, prepared,
qualified, ready.
3 *He keeps fit by running daily.* hardy,
healthy, in condition, in fine fettle, in
training, robust, well.
OPPOSITE unfit, unhealthy.
fit *verb*
1 *The tailor fitted the jacket on him.* adapt,
adjust, alter, modify, shape.
2 *He fitted a lock on the door.* install.
3 *The pieces fitted together.* connect,
dovetail, go, interlock, join.
4 *This fits our requirements.* correspond
to, match, meet, satisfy, suit.
fit in
1 *The doctor fitted us in.* accommodate,
make room for, make time for, slot in,
squeeze in.
2 *He feels he doesn't fit in.* belong,
conform, feel at home.
fit out *They fitted out the team.* equip, kit
out, rig out, supply.

fitting *adjective*
a fitting comment. appropriate, apt, fit,
proper, right, suitable, timely.
OPPOSITE unsuitable.

fix *verb*
1 *He fixed the mirror to the wall.* anchor,
attach, cement, fasten, fit, glue, mount,
nail, peg, pin, rivet, screw, secure, stick,
tape.
2 *The number is fixed in her mind.*
implant, plant, root.
3 *They fixed a time for their next meeting.*
agree on, arrange, decide on, establish,
organise, set, settle on, specify.

4 *He fixed the car's problem.* correct, cure,
mend, put right, rectify, remedy, repair,
sort out.
fix *noun* (*informal*)
He was in a real fix. bind (*informal*),
catch-22 (*informal*), difficulty, dilemma,
jam (*informal*), mess, pickle (*informal*),
plight, predicament, quandary, spot
(*informal*).

fixed *adjective*
1 *fixed cupboards.* built-in, permanent.
OPPOSITE movable.
2 *fixed prices.* constant, level, pegged,
stable, static.
OPPOSITE fluctuating.
3 *a fixed look.* intent, steady, stony.
OPPOSITE wavering.

fixture *noun*
1 *The insurance covers fixtures.* fitment,
fitting.
OPPOSITE movable.
2 *a sporting fixture.* engagement, event,
match, meet, meeting.

fizz *verb*
bubble, fizzle, froth, hiss, sparkle,
sputter.

fizzer *noun* (*Australian informal*)
*The party was a fizzer because of poor
publicity.* disappointment, failure,
fiasco, flop (*slang*).

fizzy *adjective*
a fizzy drink. aerated, bubbly,
carbonated, effervescent, sparkling.
OPPOSITE still.

flabbergasted *adjective*
We were flabbergasted at the results.
astonished, astounded, dumbfounded,
overwhelmed, speechless, staggered,
stunned, surprised, thunderstruck.

flabby *adjective*
a flabby stomach. flaccid, limp, soft,
weak.
OPPOSITE firm, taut.

flag[1] *noun*
a team's flag. banner, colours, ensign,
jack, pennant, standard, streamer.
flag *verb*
We flagged down their car. hail, signal,
wave.

a
b
c
d
e
f
g
h
i
j
k
l
m
n
o
p
q
r
s
t
u
v
w
x
y
z

flag² *verb*
1 *He started to flag after the third lap.* droop, tire, weary, wilt.
2 *Their interest never flagged.* decline, fail, wane, weaken.

flake *noun*
soap flakes. bit, leaf, piece, scale, shaving, sliver.

flame *verb*
The fire began to flame more brightly. blaze, burn, flare.
in flames ablaze, aflame, alight, blazing, burning, on fire.

flammable *adjective*
flammable material. combustible, inflammable.
OPPOSITE non-flammable, non-inflammable.

flap *verb*
The clothes flapped on the line. flutter, swing, wave.
flap *noun* (*informal*)
She got herself in a flap about the arrangements. bother, flat spin (*informal*), fluster, panic, state, tizzy (*informal*).

flare *verb*
1 *The bushfire flared.* blaze, burn, flame.
2 *Her jeans flared.* broaden, widen.
OPPOSITE taper.

flash *verb*
The lights flashed. blink, flicker, gleam, glimmer, glint, sparkle, twinkle, wink.
flash *noun*
1 *a flash of light.* blaze, flare, gleam, ray, shaft.
2 *a flash of inspiration.* burst, spark, spurt.
3 *He was back in a flash.* instant, jiffy (*informal*), moment, second, split second, tick (*informal*), trice.

flashy *adjective*
a flashy outfit. flamboyant, flash (*informal*), garish, gaudy, jazzy, lairy (*Australian informal*), loud, ostentatious, showy, tacky (*informal*), tasteless.

flat *adjective*
1 *a flat surface.* even, horizontal, level, plane, smooth.
OPPOSITE uneven.

2 *a flat dish.* low-sided, shallow.
OPPOSITE deep.
3 *a flat refusal.* absolute, categorical, definite, firm.
4 *flat seas.* calm, smooth, unruffled.
OPPOSITE choppy.
5 *She answered in a flat voice.* boring, dull, lifeless, monotonous, unemotional, uninteresting.
OPPOSITE excited.
6 *The drink has gone flat.* stale, still.
OPPOSITE fizzy.
flat *noun*
She lives in a flat. apartment, bedsit (*British*), condominium (*American*), home unit (*Australian*), penthouse, unit (*Australian*).

flatten *verb*
1 *The machine flattens the ground.* compress, iron out, level, pat down, press, roll, smooth.
2 *They flattened her flowers.* crush, run over, squash, trample.
3 *The storm flattened the building.* demolish, destroy, knock down, level, raze.

flatter *verb*
1 *She flattered him to get his help.* butter up (*informal*), compliment, crawl to, play up to, praise, suck up to (*informal*), sweet-talk (*informal*).
2 *The dress flatters her.* become, do something for, suit.

flattery *noun*
compliments, praise, smooth talk, soft soap (*informal*), sweet talk (*informal*).

flavour *noun*
1 *the flavour of the food.* savour, taste.
2 *the flavour of a book.* character, essence, quality, tone.
flavour *verb*
The cook flavoured the food. season, spice.

flaw *noun*
1 *a flaw in the work.* blemish, bug, defect, error, fault, imperfection, mistake.
2 *a flaw in his character.* failing, fault, foible, shortcoming, weakness.

fleck *noun*
flecks of a different colour. dot, freckle, patch, speck, speckle, spot.

flee *verb*

He took his bags and fled. abscond, beat it (*slang*), bolt, disappear, do a bunk (*slang*), escape, leave, retreat, run away, scarper (*slang*), scram (*slang*), shoot through (*Australian informal*), skedaddle (*informal*), take flight, vanish.

fleet[1] *noun*

a fleet of ships. armada, convoy, flotilla, line, navy, squadron.

fleet[2] *adjective*

fast, nimble, quick, rapid, speedy, swift. OPPOSITE slow.

fleeting *adjective*

fleeting sadness. brief, ephemeral, momentary, passing, short-lived, temporary, transient, transitory. OPPOSITE lasting.

flesh *noun*

1 *the flesh of animals.* meat.
2 *the flesh of the apricot.* pulp, substance.

flex *noun*

electrical flex. cable, cord, lead, wire.

flexible *adjective*

1 *a flexible body, wire, etc.* bendable, elastic, lithe, pliable, resilient, springy, supple. OPPOSITE rigid, stiff.
2 *a flexible arrangement.* adaptable, adjustable, versatile. OPPOSITE inflexible.

flick *verb*

1 *He flicked the dust off the table.* brush, flip, sweep, whisk.
2 *She flicked through the cards.* flip, leaf, skim, thumb.

flicker *verb*

The candle flickered. blink, glimmer, quiver, shimmer, tremble, twinkle, waver, wink.

flight[1] *noun*

1 *the science of flight.* see FLYING.
2 *a one-hour flight between cities.* hop, journey, trip.
flight attendant air hostess, hostess, hostie (*Australian informal*), steward, stewardess.

flight[2] *noun*

a hasty flight from danger. departure, escape, exit, exodus, fleeing, getaway, retreat.

flimsy *adjective*

1 *a flimsy structure.* breakable, fragile, frail, ramshackle, rickety, shaky, weak. OPPOSITE solid, strong.
2 *flimsy curtains.* delicate, filmy, fine, gossamer, lacy, see-through, sheer, thin. OPPOSITE thick.
3 *a flimsy excuse.* feeble, implausible, inadequate, lame, paltry, poor, weak. OPPOSITE sound.

flinch *verb*

He flinched when he saw the whip. cower, cringe, draw back, duck, quail, recoil, shrink, wince.

fling *verb*

1 *Don't fling stones.* cast, catapult, chuck (*informal*), heave, hurl, launch, pitch, shy, sling, throw, toss. OPPOSITE catch.
2 *She flung her bags down.* bung (*informal*), chuck (*informal*), plonk, shove, throw, toss (*informal*).

flip *verb*

1 *flip a coin.* flick, spin, throw, toss.
2 *He flipped through the pages of his magazine.* flick, leaf, skim, thumb.
flip over *The boat flipped over.* capsize, overturn, roll over, topple over, turn over, turn turtle.

flit *verb*

Moths flitted round the light. dart, flitter, flutter, fly.

float *verb*

float on water. float on air. bob, drift, glide, hover, sail, waft. OPPOSITE sink.

flock *noun*

a flock of birds, sheep, visitors, etc. assembly, band, bevy, brood, bunch, cluster, collection, colony, community, company, congregation, contingent, crowd, drove, flight, gaggle, gathering, herd, horde, mob, multitude, pack, swarm, throng, troop.

flock *verb*

People flocked to see the Prince. assemble, cluster, collect, congregate, converge,

a
b
c
d
e
f
g
h
i
j
k
l
m
n
o
p
q
r
s
t
u
v
w
x
y
z

crowd, gather, herd, huddle, mass, mob, swarm, throng.

flog *verb*
The thief was flogged. beat, belt (*slang*), cane, chastise, lash, scourge, thrash, whip.

flood *noun*
1 They were drowned in the flood. deluge, inundation, spate, torrent.
2 a flood of questions. deluge, outpouring, rush, shower, spate, stream, torrent, wave.
flood *verb*
1 The water flooded the town. deluge, drown, engulf, inundate, submerge, swamp.
2 The river flooded. overflow, run a banker (*Australian*).
3 Letters flooded in. flow, pour.

floor *noun*
a building with five floors. deck, level, storey.
floor *verb*
1 The boxer floored his opponent. bowl over, knock down.
2 The problem completely floored him. baffle, bamboozle (*informal*), confuse, flummox (*informal*), perplex, stump (*informal*), throw.

flop *verb*
1 The doll's arms flop. dangle, droop, hang down, sag.
2 She flopped into a chair. collapse, drop, fall, loll, slump, tumble.
flop *noun* (*slang*)
The show was a flop. disaster, failure, fiasco, fizzer (*Australian informal*), non-event, wash-out (*slang*).
OPPOSITE hit, success.

floppy *adjective*
baggy, drooping, limp, loose, wilting.
OPPOSITE firm, rigid.

flounder *verb*
The walkers floundered in the mud. bumble, fumble, stagger, struggle, stumble, wallow.

flourish *verb*
1 The plants flourished. bloom, blossom, flower, grow, thrive.

2 Business flourished. be successful, boom, grow, prosper, succeed, thrive.
OPPOSITE decline.
3 He flourished the trophy. brandish, display, flaunt, wave.

flow *verb*
1 Water flows through the pipes. circulate, course, run.
2 The river flows into the lake. discharge, empty.
3 The water flowed from the hose. dribble, drip, gush, leak, ooze, pour, run, rush, seep, spill, spout, spurt, squirt, stream, trickle.
flow *noun*
1 carried by the river's flow. course, current, drift, stream.
2 a flow of tears. a flow of words. flood, gush, outpouring, stream, torrent.
3 a steady flow of visitors. influx, spate, stream, succession, tide, train.

flower *noun*
1 The plant is covered in flowers. bloom, blossom, bud; [*various flowers*] alyssum, aster, banksia, begonia, bluebell, buttercup, camellia, carnation, chrysanthemum, cornflower, crocus, daffodil, dahlia, daisy, dandelion, flannel flower, forget-me-not, freesia, gardenia, geranium, gladiolus, hollyhock, hyacinth, hydrangea, iris, jonquil, kangaroo paw, lily, marigold, nasturtium, orchid, pansy, peony, petunia, phlox, pigface, poppy, primrose, protea, rhododendron, rose, snapdragon, snowdrop, stock, Sturt's desert pea, Sturt's desert rose, sunflower, sweet pea, tulip, viola, violet, waratah, zinnia.
2 She was presented with flowers. bouquet, corsage, garland, posy, spray, wreath.
flower *verb*
The plant flowers in spring. bloom, blossom.

fluctuate *verb*
His mood fluctuates. change, see-saw, shift, swing, vary, waver.

fluent *adjective*
a fluent speaker. articulate, eloquent, smooth-spoken.
OPPOSITE hesitant.

fluff *noun*
The clothes had fluff on them. down, fuzz, lint.

fluffy *adjective*
downy, fleecy, furry, fuzzy, woolly.

fluid *noun*
gas, liquid, solution.
OPPOSITE solid.
fluid *adjective*
a fluid substance. flowing, gaseous, liquid, molten, runny, sloppy, watery.
OPPOSITE solid, stiff.

fluke *noun*
It was a fluke that he passed. accident, chance, stroke of luck.

flush *verb*
1 Her cheeks flushed with embarrassment. blush, colour, glow, redden.
OPPOSITE pale.
2 The plumber flushed the drains. clean out, rinse out, wash out.
flush *adjective*
1 flush with the wall. flat, level.
2 (informal) He has just been paid and is feeling flush. rich, wealthy, well in (Australian informal), well off.
OPPOSITE hard up (informal).

flustered *adjective*
He gets flustered easily. agitated, bothered, confused, fazed (informal), in a dither, in a flap (informal), in a state, in a tizzy (informal), nervous, panicky, rattled (informal).

flutter *verb*
1 The butterfly fluttered away. flit, flitter, fly.
2 The insect fluttered its wings. bat, flap, vibrate, wave.
3 Her heart fluttered. palpitate, quiver, shake, tremble.
flutter *noun*
1 He was in a flutter before his exam. dither, flap (informal), fluster, tizzy (informal).
2 The news caused a flutter in the classroom. commotion, ripple, stir.
3 (informal) We had a flutter at the races. bet, gamble, punt, wager.

fly *verb*
1 The bird flew from tree to tree. flit, flitter, flutter, glide, hover, soar, swoop, wing.

2 She flew to London. jet.
3 The flag is flying at half-mast. flap, flutter, wave.
4 She flew out of the room. burst, dart, dash, hurry, hurtle, race, run, rush, scoot, shoot, speed, sweep, tear, whiz, zoom.

flying *noun*
aeronautics, aviation, flight.

foal *noun*
a horse and foal. colt (male), filly (female).

foam *noun*
1 The water was covered in foam. bubbles, froth, lather, suds.
2 a cushion made of foam. rubber, sponge.
foam *verb*
The drink foamed. bubble, effervesce, fizz, froth.

focus *noun*
the focus of their attention. centre, core, hub.
focus *verb*
He focused his attention on this issue. centre, concentrate, fix, home in, zero in.

fodder *noun*
animal fodder. feed, food, forage, provender, silage.

foe *noun*
They beat their foes. adversary, antagonist, enemy, opponent, rival.
OPPOSITE ally, friend.

fog *noun*
We couldn't see through the fog. cloud, haze, mist, murkiness, smog.
fog *verb*
Her glasses fogged up. cloud, mist, steam.

foggy *adjective*
1 foggy weather. hazy, misty, murky.
OPPOSITE clear.
2 only a foggy idea. fuzzy, hazy, imprecise, inexact, obscure, vague.
OPPOSITE clear.

foil *verb*
He foiled their plans. frustrate, hamper, hinder, obstruct, stonker (Australian slang), thwart.

a b c d e f g h i j k l m n o p q r s t u v w x y z

fold[1] *verb*
1 *He folded the material.* bend, crease, double over, pleat, wrinkle.
OPPOSITE unfold.
2 *The bed folds for storage.* collapse.
fold *noun*
folds in the material. crease, crinkle, gather, pleat, pucker, tuck, wrinkle.

fold[2] *noun*
the sheep fold. compound, enclosure, pen, yard.

folder *noun*
The papers are in a folder. binder, cover, file, portfolio, ringbinder.

folk *noun*
1 *ordinary folk.* human beings, people.
2 *Her folk are in New Zealand.* family, kin, kinsfolk, parents, people, relations, relatives.

folklore *noun*
beliefs, legends, lore, myths, traditions.

follow *verb*
1 *The police followed the suspect.* chase, go after, hound, hunt, pursue, run after, shadow, stalk, tail (*informal*), track, trail.
OPPOSITE lead.
2 *She followed the path.* go along, keep to, proceed along, take.
OPPOSITE stray from.
3 *Which king followed Henry VII?* come after, replace, succeed.
OPPOSITE precede.
4 *Follow her example.* copy, emulate, imitate.
5 *Follow the rules.* abide by, comply with, heed, keep, obey, observe.
OPPOSITE disobey.
6 *She didn't follow what you said.* comprehend, cotton on to (*informal*), get (*informal*), grasp, latch on to (*informal*), take in, understand.
OPPOSITE misunderstand.
7 *He follows cricket.* be interested in, support.
8 *What followed is history.* come next, ensue, result.

follower *noun*
The great man had many followers. admirer, devotee, disciple, fan, hanger-on, supporter.
OPPOSITE leader.

following *adjective*
in the following days. ensuing, next, subsequent, succeeding, successive.
OPPOSITE preceding, previous.

fond *adjective*
1 *fond parents.* adoring, affectionate, caring, devoted, doting, indulgent, loving, tender, warm.
OPPOSITE unloving.
2 *fond hopes.* absurd, foolish, naive, silly, vain.
fond of *fond of jazz.* crazy about, keen on, nuts about (*informal*), partial to.

fondness *noun*
1 *a fondness for chocolates.* liking, partiality, taste, weakness.
OPPOSITE dislike.
2 *fondness for a person.* affection, attachment, love, tenderness.
OPPOSITE hostility.

food *noun*
chow (*slang*), delicacies, diet, eats (*informal*), fare, feed, fodder, foodstuff, forage, grub (*slang*), nosh (*slang*), nourishment, produce, provisions, rations, refreshments, sustenance, tucker (*Australian informal*).

fool *noun*
1 *He realised what a fool he'd been.* ass (*informal*), blockhead, bonehead, boofhead (*Australian informal*), chump (*informal*), clot (*informal*), cretin, dill (*Australian informal*), dimwit (*informal*), dingbat (*informal*), dodo (*informal*), dolt, dope (*informal*), drongo (*Australian informal*), duffer, dummy (*informal*), dunce, fat-head (*informal*), galah (*Australian slang*), gig (*Australian informal*), git (*informal*), goof (*slang*), goon (*slang*), goose (*informal*), half-wit, idiot (*informal*), ignoramus, imbecile, jerk (*slang*), lunatic, moron (*informal*), mug (*informal*), nincompoop, ninny, nitwit (*informal*), nong (*Australian informal*), numskull, nut (*informal*), sap (*informal*), silly (*informal*), silly billy (*informal*), simpleton, sucker (*informal*), thickhead (*informal*), twerp (*slang*), twit (*slang*), wally (*slang*).
2 *the court fool.* buffoon, clown, comic, entertainer, jester, zany.

fool *verb*
1 *They didn't mean it seriously: they were just fooling.* jest, joke, kid (*informal*), make believe, pretend.
2 *You can't fool her.* bluff, con (*informal*), deceive, delude, dupe, hoax, hoodwink, mislead, take in, trick.
fool around clown around, mess around, monkey about, play around, play the fool.

foolhardy *adjective*
a foolhardy action. bold, daredevil, daring, impetuous, imprudent, irresponsible, rash, reckless, unwise.
OPPOSITE cautious.

foolish *adjective*
a foolish person, scheme, etc. absurd, barmy (*slang*), crazy, daft (*informal*), dopey (*informal*), goofy (*slang*), hare-brained, idiotic, illogical, imprudent, inane, insane, irrational, ludicrous, lunatic, mad, madcap, misguided, nonsensical, nutty (*informal*), potty (*informal*), ridiculous, senseless, silly, stupid, unintelligent, unwise.
OPPOSITE wise.

foolishness *noun*
folly, idiocy, insanity, lunacy, madness, silliness, stupidity.
OPPOSITE wisdom.

foot *noun*
1 *an animal's foot.* hoof, pad, paw, trotter.
2 *the foot of the hill.* base, bottom.
OPPOSITE top.

footing *noun*
on an equal footing. basis, standing, status, terms.

footpath *noun*
footway, path, pavement, sidewalk (*American*).

footprint *noun*
footmark, footstep, track.

forbid *verb*
She forbids talking in class. ban, bar, outlaw, prohibit, proscribe, veto.
OPPOSITE allow.

forbidding *adjective*
a forbidding appearance. grim, harsh, hostile, inhospitable, menacing, off-putting, ominous, severe, stern, threatening, unfriendly, uninviting.

force *noun*
1 *Force was needed to shift it.* effort, energy, exertion, might, power, pressure, strength, vigour.
2 *a police force. a force of workers.* body, corps, squad, team, unit.
3 *The new rules come into force next week.* effect, operation, play, use.

force *verb*
1 *They forced him to sign the paper.* bully, coerce, compel, constrain, drive, make, oblige, order, pressure.
2 *He forced a confession from her.* drag, extract, wrest, wring.
3 *He forced the lock.* break open, burst open, prise open, push open, wrench open.

forceful *adjective*
1 *a forceful personality.* aggressive, assertive, dynamic, energetic, masterful, pushy, strong, vigorous.
OPPOSITE weak.
2 *a forceful argument.* cogent, compelling, convincing, effective, persuasive, potent, powerful, strong, telling, weighty.
OPPOSITE feeble.

forecast *verb*
They forecast that it would rain. foretell, forewarn, predict, prophesy.
forecast *noun*
an economic forecast. outlook, prediction, prognosis, projection, prophecy.

forefather *noun*
ancestor, forebear, predecessor.

forehead *noun*
brow.

foreign *adjective*
1 *foreign goods.* alien, exotic, imported, overseas, strange, unfamiliar.
OPPOSITE native.
2 *foreign affairs.* external, international, overseas.
OPPOSITE domestic.
3 *Jealousy is foreign to her nature.* alien, outside, uncharacteristic, unnatural.
OPPOSITE intrinsic.

a b c d e f g h i j k l m n o p q r s t u v w x y z

foreigner *noun*
alien, immigrant, new chum (*Australian informal*), newcomer, outsider, stranger, visitor.
OPPOSITE native.

foreman *noun*
1 *a factory foreman.* boss, overseer, superintendent, supervisor.
2 *a jury foreman.* spokesman, spokesperson, spokeswoman.

foremost *adjective*
their foremost scientists. best, chief, greatest, leading, main, major, pre-eminent, principal, supreme, top.

foresee *verb*
She foresaw the dangers. anticipate, envisage, expect, forecast, foretell, predict, prophesy.

foresight *noun*
They showed foresight in their town planning. far-sightedness, forethought, providence, vision.
OPPOSITE hindsight, short-sightedness.

forest *noun*
brush, jungle, plantation, thicket, wood, woodland, woods.

foretell *verb*
The prophets foretold future events. forecast, foresee, predict, prophesy.

forever *adverb*
always, constantly, continually, eternally, everlastingly, evermore, incessantly, permanently, perpetually.

forfeit *noun*
They had to pay a forfeit. fine, penalty.
forfeit *verb*
She forfeited her rights. forgo, give up, relinquish, renounce, sacrifice, surrender, waive.

forge *noun*
a blacksmith's forge. furnace, smithy.
forge *verb*
1 *The blacksmith forged the horse's shoes.* fashion, form, hammer out, mould, shape.
2 *The crooks forged $20 notes.* copy, counterfeit, fake.

forged *adjective*
a forged $20 bill. bogus, counterfeit, dud (*informal*), fake, false, imitation, phoney (*informal*).
OPPOSITE genuine.

forgery *noun*
The passport was a forgery. copy, counterfeit, fake, fraud, imitation, phoney (*informal*), replica, reproduction.

forget *verb*
1 *He forgot a few people.* leave out, miss, neglect, omit, overlook, pass over, skip.
OPPOSITE remember.
2 *He forgot his umbrella.* leave behind.
OPPOSITE remember, take.

forgetful *adjective*
absent-minded, careless, inattentive, neglectful, negligent, remiss, scatterbrained, vague.

forgive *verb*
forgive a sin. forgive a sinner. absolve, excuse, exonerate, let off, overlook, pardon, remit.
OPPOSITE condemn.

forgiveness *noun*
absolution, amnesty, exoneration, pardon, remission.

forgo *verb*
You will have to forgo rich food. abandon, abstain from, give up, go without, renounce.

fork *noun*
a fork in the road. Y-junction.
fork *verb*
The road forks. branch, divide, split.

forlorn *adjective*
She was forlorn after he left. dejected, depressed, desolate, forsaken, heavy-hearted, lonely, melancholy, miserable, sad, unhappy, woebegone, wretched.
OPPOSITE happy.

form *noun*
1 *He is more interested in the form of things than their substance.* appearance, arrangement, composition, configuration, construction, contour, design, figure, format, formation, layout, mould, organisation, outline,

pattern, profile, shape, silhouette, structure.
2 *different forms of the same thing.* brand, breed, class, edition, genus, kind, model, sort, species, style, type, variety, version.
3 *Sixth form at school.* class, grade, year.
4 *They filled in a form.* application, coupon, document, paper, questionnaire.
5 *The runners were in fine form.* condition, fettle, fitness, health, shape, trim.
6 *We sat on wooden forms.* bench, seat.

form *verb*
1 *The sculptor formed a horse out of clay, stone, etc.* build, carve, cast, construct, create, fashion, forge, make, model, mould, produce, sculpt, shape, work.
2 *We formed a fundraising committee.* establish, found, set up.
3 *Twelve members form a team.* compose, constitute, make up.
4 *He formed a habit.* acquire, develop, pick up.

formal *adjective*
1 *She wears a hat on formal occasions.* ceremonial, official, solemn, stately.
OPPOSITE informal.
2 *a formal manner.* ceremonious, conventional, dignified, pompous, prim, proper, reserved, starchy, stiff, stilted.
OPPOSITE casual.

format *noun*
the format of a book. arrangement, design, form, layout, organisation, shape, size, structure.

former *adjective*
in former times. ancient, bygone, earlier, old, olden, past, previous.

formerly *adverb*
in the past, once, previously.

formidable *adjective*
a formidable task. arduous, challenging, daunting, difficult, mammoth, onerous, overwhelming, tough.
OPPOSITE easy.

formula *noun*
1 *a formula for success.* blueprint, method, prescription, recipe.

2 *a mathematical formula.* algorithm, rule, statement, theorem.

formulate *verb*
She formulated her response carefully. articulate, compose, express, form, frame, phrase, work out.

forsake *verb*
He promised never to forsake her. abandon, desert, leave, reject.

fort *noun*
see FORTRESS.

forte *noun*
Debating is her forte. speciality, specialty, strength, strong point.

fortify *verb*
1 *They fortified the town against the invaders.* defend, protect, reinforce, secure, strengthen.
2 *The hot food fortified the walkers.* boost, invigorate, strengthen, sustain.

fortress *noun*
acropolis, castle, citadel, fort, garrison, stronghold.

fortunate *adjective*
1 *a fortunate person.* blessed, favoured, happy, lucky, prosperous.
2 *a fortunate choice.* auspicious, favourable, lucky, propitious, providential, timely.
OPPOSITE disastrous.

fortune *noun*
1 *Fortune smiled on their venture.* chance, destiny, fate, luck, providence.
2 *He inherited the family fortune.* assets, estate, inheritance, property, riches, wealth.
3 *It cost a fortune. He made a fortune.* big bickies (*Australian informal*), bundle (*informal*), heaps (*informal*), megabucks (*informal*), mint, packet (*informal*), pots (*informal*).

fortune-teller *noun*
astrologer, clairvoyant, crystal-gazer, diviner, palmist, prophet, seer, soothsayer.

forward *adjective*
She was too forward for her own good. assertive, audacious, bold, brazen, cheeky, fresh (*informal*), impertinent,

a
b
c
d
e
f
g
h
i
j
k
l
m
n
o
p
q
r
s
t
u
v
w
x
y
z

impudent, presumptuous, pushy; see also PRECOCIOUS.
OPPOSITE retiring.

forward *verb*
1 *The neighbours forwarded the mail.* readdress, redirect, send on.
2 *The company forwards parcels to Europe.* deliver, dispatch, freight, send, ship, transport.

forwards *adverb*
ahead, forward, frontwards, onwards.
OPPOSITE backwards.

fossil *noun*
plant and animal fossils. relic, remains.

foster *verb*
foster an interest. advance, cultivate, encourage, further, nurture, promote.

foul *adjective*
1 *a foul smell.* bad, disgusting, horrible, nauseating, objectionable, obnoxious, off (*informal*), offensive, putrid, rank, revolting, rotten, smelly, stinking, vile.
OPPOSITE fragrant, sweet.
2 *a foul crime.* abhorrent, appalling, atrocious, beastly, contemptible, despicable, detestable, evil, loathsome, monstrous, shocking, terrible, vicious, vile, villainous, violent, wicked.
3 *foul language.* abusive, bad, blasphemous, coarse, crude, dirty, disgusting, filthy, impolite, indecent, obscene, offensive, rude, smutty, vulgar.
OPPOSITE polite.
4 *foul weather.* atrocious (*informal*), crook (*Australian informal*), dreadful (*informal*), lousy (*informal*), rough, shocking (*informal*), stormy, terrible (*informal*), wild.
OPPOSITE fair, fine.

foul *verb*
1 *The sewage fouled the water.* contaminate, pollute, taint.
OPPOSITE cleanse.
2 *His line fouled theirs.* entangle, snarl, tangle.

found *verb*
1 *He founded the scheme.* begin, create, establish, initiate, institute, originate, pioneer, set up, start.
2 *The story is founded on fact.* base, build, ground, root.

foundation *noun*
1 *a foundation for medical research.* establishment, institution, organisation.
2 *The building has a strong foundation.* base, footing, substructure.
3 *Her claims are without foundation.* base, basis, grounds, justification, support.

fountain *noun*
1 *a fountain of water.* jet, shower, spout, spray, spring.
2 *the fountain of wisdom.* beginning, fount, origin, source.

fowl *noun*
bantam, bird, chicken, chook (*Australian informal*), cock, duck, goose, guinea fowl, hen, rooster, turkey; [*fowls*] poultry.

fox *noun*
cub (*young*), kit (*young*), vixen (*female*).

foyer *noun*
the hotel foyer. entrance hall, lobby, vestibule.

fraction *noun*
Only a fraction was left. bit, fragment, part, piece, portion, section.

fracture *noun*
a fracture in the rock. break, cleft, crack, fissure, rift, split.
fracture *verb*
She fractured her arm. break, crack.

fragile *noun*
a fragile vase. breakable, brittle, delicate, flimsy, frail, weak.
OPPOSITE strong.

fragment *noun*
1 *fragments of glass, food, etc.* bit, chip, crumb, morsel, part, particle, piece, remnant, scrap, shred, sliver, speck, splinter; [*fragments*] smithereens.
2 *a fragment of the conversation.* bit, snatch, snippet.

fragrance *noun*
the fragrance of roses. aroma, balm, bouquet, odour, perfume, scent, smell.
OPPOSITE stink.

frail *adjective*
1 *a frail structure.* delicate, flimsy, fragile, rickety, unsound, weak.
OPPOSITE strong.

2 *a frail old lady.* ailing, decrepit, feeble, infirm, sickly, weak.
OPPOSITE robust.

frame *noun*
1 *a house with a timber frame. a car frame.* chassis, framework, shell, skeleton, structure, substructure.
2 *a picture frame. a window frame.* border, case, edge, margin, mount, surround.
3 *a woman with a large frame.* body, build, figure, physique, skeleton.
frame *verb*
She framed the photo. enclose, mount, surround.
frame of mind attitude, disposition, humour, mood, outlook, state, temper.

framework *noun*
1 *the timber framework of a house.* chassis, frame, shell, skeleton, structure, substructure.
2 *the framework of a book.* outline, plan, skeleton.

franchise *noun*
When were women given the franchise? suffrage, right to vote, vote.

frank *adjective*
He was frank in his criticism. blunt, candid, direct, forthright, honest, open, outspoken, straightforward, truthful, upfront (*informal*).
OPPOSITE evasive.

frantic *adjective*
Their mother was frantic when they didn't arrive. agitated, anxious, berserk, beside yourself, crazy, desperate, distraught, frenzied, hysterical, overwrought, panic-stricken, worried.
OPPOSITE calm.

fraud *noun*
1 *She was found guilty of fraud.* cheating, deceit, deception, dishonesty, fraudulence, rorting (*Australian slang*), swindling, trickery.
2 *The doctor was a fraud.* charlatan, cheat, con man (*informal*), fake, humbug, impostor, phoney (*informal*), quack, sham, swindler, trickster.

fraudulent *adjective*
a fraudulent social security claim. crooked, deceitful, dishonest, false, phoney (*informal*), shady, shonky (*Australian*

informal), unscrupulous.
OPPOSITE honest.

frayed *adjective*
frayed material. ragged, shabby, tattered, tatty (*informal*), threadbare, unravelled, worn.

freak *noun*
1 *He was considered a freak because he had an extra toe.* monster, monstrosity, mutant, oddity, weirdo (*informal*).
2 (*informal*) *a health freak.* crank, eccentric, fanatic, maniac, nut (*informal*).
freak *verb* (*informal*)
1 *He freaked when he saw the damage to his car.* see BECOME ANGRY (at ANGRY).
2 *Exams freak me out.* see FRIGHTEN.

freakish *adjective*
freakish behaviour. abnormal, atypical, bizarre, eccentric, exceptional, extraordinary, freak, odd, peculiar, queer, strange, unusual, weird.
OPPOSITE normal.

free *adjective*
1 *a free person.* emancipated, liberated, released.
OPPOSITE enslaved.
2 *a free country.* autonomous, democratic, independent, self-governing.
3 *the free end.* loose, unattached, untied.
4 *free of responsibility.* absolved, exempt (from), immune (from), rid, without.
5 *a free sample.* complimentary, gratis, on the house (*informal*), unpaid.
6 *free time.* leisure, spare, uncommitted.
7 *The toilet is free.* available, unoccupied, vacant.
OPPOSITE engaged.
8 *He was free to leave.* able, allowed, at liberty, permitted.
OPPOSITE forbidden.
9 *She is very free with her money.* bountiful, generous, lavish, liberal, unstinting.
OPPOSITE stingy.
free *verb*
1 *He freed the slaves.* deliver, emancipate, liberate, release, rescue, save, set free.
OPPOSITE capture.
2 *He freed the animals.* let loose, let out, uncage, unchain, unleash.
OPPOSITE confine.

a
b
c
d
e
f
g
h
i
j
k
l
m
n
o
p
q
r
s
t
u
v
w
x
y
z

3 *He was freed from his obligations.*
excuse, exempt, let off, release, relieve,
save, spare.
4 *He freed his line from the tangled mess.*
clear, detach, disentangle, extricate,
loosen, remove, untangle.

freedom *noun*
1 *political freedom.* autonomy,
independence, liberty, self-
determination, self-government.
OPPOSITE dependence.
2 *freedom of speech.* candour, directness,
frankness, openness, outspokenness.
OPPOSITE censorship.
3 *freedom after captivity.* deliverance,
emancipation, liberation, liberty,
release.
OPPOSITE captivity.
4 *freedom to do as you wish.* discretion,
free hand, free rein, latitude, licence,
scope.

freeway *noun*
expressway, highway, motorway.

freeze *verb*
1 *The lake froze.* ice over, turn to ice.
OPPOSITE thaw.
2 *She froze the drinks.* chill, cool,
refrigerate.
OPPOSITE thaw.
3 *He froze on the spot.* halt, petrify, stop.
4 *Prices have been frozen.* fix, hold, peg.

freezing *adjective*
freezing weather. arctic, bitter, chilly,
cold, frigid, frosty, ice-cold, icy, nippy
(*informal*), perishing (*informal*), subzero.
OPPOSITE sweltering.

freight *noun*
1 *The price includes freight.* carriage,
cartage, conveyance, haulage,
shipment, shipping, transport.
2 *The train carries freight and passengers.*
cargo, consignment, goods, lading,
load.
freight *verb*
The company freights goods overseas.
carry, cart, dispatch, forward, move,
send, ship, transport.

frenzied *adjective*
frenzied activity. a frenzied crowd.
agitated, berserk, crazy, delirious,
demented, distraught, excited, feverish,
frantic, frenetic, hectic, hysterical, mad,

wild.
OPPOSITE calm.

frenzy *noun*
He worked himself into a frenzy. agitation,
excitement, fever, hysteria, insanity,
madness, mania.

frequent *adjective*
1 *a frequent problem.* common, continual,
eternal, perpetual, persistent, recurrent,
repeated.
OPPOSITE rare.
2 *They had frequent phone calls.* constant,
continual, countless, incessant, many,
numerous.
OPPOSITE few.
3 *a frequent visitor.* familiar, habitual,
regular.
OPPOSITE infrequent, occasional.
frequent *verb*
He frequents that shop. haunt, patronise,
visit.

fresh *adjective*
1 *fresh news.* hot, latest, new, recent,
up-to-date, up-to-the-minute.
OPPOSITE old, stale.
2 *a fresh approach.* alternative, different,
innovative, new, newfangled
(*derogatory*), novel, original, untried.
OPPOSITE old.
3 *a fresh sheet of paper.* clean, pristine,
untouched, unused.
OPPOSITE used.
4 *fresh air.* clean, cool, crisp, pure,
refreshing, unpolluted.
OPPOSITE stale.
5 *He was fresh after his rest.* alert,
energetic, invigorated, lively, perky,
refreshed, revived.
OPPOSITE weary.

freshen *verb*
She freshened the room. air, clean,
ventilate.

fret *verb*
She fretted when her friend went away.
brood, distress yourself, grieve, mope,
pine, worry.

friar *noun*
brother, monk, religious.

friction *noun*
1 *The sore was caused by friction.*
abrasion, chafing, fretting, rubbing.

2 *There was friction between the sisters.*
antagonism, conflict, disagreement,
discord, quarrelling, strife.

friend *noun*
1 *confide in a friend.* acquaintance, ally,
boyfriend, buddy (*informal*), chum
(*informal*), cobber (*Australian informal*),
companion, comrade, confidant,
confidante, crony, girlfriend, mate, pal
(*informal*), partner, penfriend, playmate,
steady.
OPPOSITE enemy.
2 *the friends of the library.* backer,
benefactor, helper, patron, supporter,
sympathiser.

friendly *adjective*
1 *a friendly person.* affable, affectionate,
amiable, amicable, approachable,
brotherly, chummy (*informal*), genial,
good-natured, gracious, hospitable,
kind, kind-hearted, kindly, loving,
matey, neighbourly, outgoing, pally
(*informal*), sisterly, sociable,
sympathetic, tender, warm-hearted,
welcoming.
OPPOSITE hostile.
2 *on friendly terms.* amicable, close,
cordial, familiar, good, harmonious,
intimate.
OPPOSITE unfriendly.

friendship *noun*
1 *The club aims to promote friendship.*
amity, camaraderie, companionship,
comradeship, cordiality, friendliness,
harmony, mateship.
OPPOSITE hostility.
2 *a long-standing friendship.* alliance,
association, partnership, relationship.

fright *noun*
1 *The noise made her jump in fright.*
alarm, anxiety, apprehension,
consternation, dismay, dread, fear,
horror, panic, terror, trepidation.
2 *He gave me a fright.* scare, shock, start,
turn.

frighten *verb*
Dogs frighten him. alarm, cow, daunt,
dismay, freak out (*informal*), horrify,
intimidate, menace, perturb, petrify,
put the wind up (*informal*), rattle
(*informal*), scare, startle, terrify,
terrorise, unnerve.
OPPOSITE reassure.

frightened *adjective*
afraid, alarmed, anxious, apprehensive,
chicken (*informal*), faint-hearted, fearful,
nervous, panic-stricken, petrified,
scared, terrified, terror-stricken.
OPPOSITE unafraid.

frightening *adjective*
a frightening experience. alarming,
chilling, creepy, eerie, fearful, fearsome,
frightful, hair-raising, horrifying,
nightmarish, scary, sinister, spine-
chilling, spooky, terrifying.
OPPOSITE reassuring.

frightful *adjective*
Something frightful has happened.
appalling, awful, bad, dreadful, fearful,
fearsome, ghastly, grisly, gruesome,
hideous, horrendous, horrible, horrid,
horrific, shocking, terrible.

frill *noun*
1 *a frill on a dress.* flounce, ruff, ruffle.
2 *simple accommodation with no frills.*
addition, extra, supplement, trimming.

fringe *noun*
1 *the fringe of a scarf.* border, edge,
edging, tassels.
2 *the fringe of a town.* borders, edge,
limits, margin, outskirts, perimeter,
periphery.
fringe benefit *A company car is one of his
fringe benefits.* bonus, extra, perk
(*informal*), side benefit.

frisk *verb*
1 *The lambs frisked about in the field.*
caper, cavort, dance, frolic, gambol,
jump, leap, play, prance, romp, skip.
2 *The police frisked everyone.* check,
inspect, search.

frisky *adjective*
a frisky kitten. active, lively, perky,
playful, spirited.

fritter *verb*
fritter away *She frittered away all her
money.* misspend, squander, waste.

frivolous *adjective*
1 *frivolous conversation.* facetious,
flippant, inane, petty, ridiculous, silly,
superficial, trivial, unimportant.
OPPOSITE serious.
2 *a frivolous person.* flighty, giddy,
irresponsible, light-hearted, shallow,

a
b
c
d
e
f
g
h
i
j
k
l
m
n
o
p
q
r
s
t
u
v
w
x
y
z

silly, superficial.
OPPOSITE earnest.

frizzy *adjective*
frizzy hair. Afro, bushy, curly, fuzzy.

frock *noun*
dress, gown, robe.

frolic *verb*
The children frolicked in the yard. caper, cavort, frisk, gambol, let off steam, play, romp, skip.

front *noun*
1 *the front of an object.* face, head, nose.
OPPOSITE back.
2 *a ship's front.* bow, fore.
OPPOSITE stern.
3 *a house front.* façade, face, frontage.
4 *the front of the line.* beginning, head, start, top.
OPPOSITE back.
5 *a military front.* forefront, front line, spearhead, van, vanguard.
OPPOSITE rearguard.
6 *She put on a brave front.* air, appearance, exterior, façade, face, look, show.
front *adjective*
1 *front legs.* fore.
OPPOSITE hind, rear.
2 *the front page.* first, initial, leading.
OPPOSITE back.

frontier *noun*
a country's frontiers. border, boundary.

frost *noun*
The ground was covered in frost. hoarfrost, rime.

frosty *adjective*
see COLD.

froth *noun*
bubbles, foam, lather, scum, suds.

frown *verb*
He looked ugly when he frowned. glare, glower, grimace, knit your brow, lour, scowl.
OPPOSITE smile.

frozen *adjective*
see COLD.

fruit *noun*
[*various fruits*] apple, apricot, avocado, banana, blackberry, blackcurrant, blueberry, boysenberry, breadfruit, cherry, cranberry, date, fig, gooseberry, grape, grapefruit, guava, honeydew melon, kiwi fruit, lemon, lime, loganberry, loquat, lychee, mandarin, mango, mulberry, nectarine, olive, orange, passion fruit, pawpaw, peach, peacharine, pear, pineapple, plum, pomegranate, quince, raspberry, redcurrant, rockmelon, starfruit, strawberry, tamarillo, tangelo, tangerine, tomato, watermelon.

fruitful *adjective*
1 *fruitful soil.* fertile, productive, rich.
OPPOSITE barren.
2 *a fruitful discussion.* productive, profitable, rewarding, successful, useful, valuable, worthwhile.
OPPOSITE fruitless.

fruitless *adjective*
a fruitless attempt. futile, ineffective, pointless, unproductive, unsuccessful, useless, vain.
OPPOSITE fruitful.

frustrate *verb*
The weather frustrated their efforts. block, check, foil, hamper, hinder, impede, prevent, stonker (*Australian slang*), stop, stymie, thwart.
OPPOSITE facilitate.

fry *verb*
She fried the meat. brown, sauté.

fugitive *noun*
The police finally caught the fugitive. deserter, escapee, renegade, runaway.

fulfil *verb*
1 *She fulfilled her task.* accomplish, achieve, carry out, complete, discharge, execute, perform.
2 *He fulfilled all the requirements.* answer, comply with, fill, meet, satisfy.
3 *She fulfilled her promise.* abide by, keep, live up to.
OPPOSITE break.

full *adjective*
1 *a full glass of water.* brimming, filled, overflowing.
OPPOSITE empty.
2 *The place was full.* bursting, chock-a-block, chockers (*Australian informal*), chock-full, congested, crammed, crowded, filled, jam-packed,

overcrowded, packed, stuffed.
OPPOSITE empty.
3 *full of ideas.* abounding (in), rich (in), teeming (with).
OPPOSITE devoid (of).
4 *He felt full after his meal.* gorged, replete, sated, satiated, stuffed.
OPPOSITE hungry.
5 *a full account.* complete, comprehensive, detailed, entire, exhaustive, thorough, total, unabridged, whole.
OPPOSITE partial.

fumbling *adjective*
a fumbling attempt at fielding. awkward, bumbling, bungling, clumsy, inept.

fume *verb*
1 *The chimney fumed.* smoke, smoulder.
2 *He fumed when they were late again.* blow up (*informal*), blow your stack (*informal*), blow your top (*informal*), explode, flare up, lose your temper, rage, seethe, smoulder.
fumes *plural noun*
exhaust, gas, smoke, vapour.

fun *noun*
They had fun and games. She does it for fun. amusement, diversion, enjoyment, entertainment, frivolity, gaiety, hilarity, jollity, kicks (*informal*), laughter, merriment, mirth, play, pleasure, recreation, relaxation, sport.
OPPOSITE misery.
make fun of deride, jeer at, joke about, laugh at, mimic, mock, parody, poke fun at, ridicule, satirise, send up (*informal*), sling off at (*Australian informal*), take off, take the mickey out of (*informal*), taunt, tease.

function *noun*
1 *a person's function. a thing's function.* activity, duty, job, purpose, role, task, use.
2 *attend a social function.* affair (*informal*), ceremony, do (*informal*), event, gathering, occasion, party, reception.
function *verb*
1 *The machine is not functioning correctly.* behave, go, operate, perform, run, work.
2 *It functions as an office and play room.* act, serve.

fund *noun*
1 *his retirement fund.* kitty, nest egg, pool, reserve.
2 *a fund of jokes.* hoard, mine, reserve, stock, store, supply.
fund *verb*
The company funded the project. back, finance, pay for, sponsor, subsidise.
funds *plural noun*
He manages the company's funds. capital, cash, finances, means, money, resources, savings, wealth.

fundamental *adjective*
a fundamental rule. basic, cardinal, crucial, elementary, essential, important, key, primary, principal, underlying, vital.
OPPOSITE secondary.
fundamentals *plural noun*
The course deals with the fundamentals of programming. basics, elements, essentials, principles, rudiments.

funeral *noun*
burial, cremation, interment.

fungus *noun*
[*kinds of fungus*] mildew, mould, mushroom, toadstool, truffle.

funnel *noun*
a ship's funnel. chimney, smokestack.

funny *adjective*
1 *She told a funny joke.* amusing, comical, crazy, droll, entertaining, facetious, hilarious, humorous, laughable, ludicrous, priceless (*informal*), ridiculous, witty, zany.
OPPOSITE sad.
2 *A funny thing happened.* abnormal, bizarre, curious, extraordinary, odd, peculiar, queer, strange, unusual, weird.

fur *noun*
an animal's fur. coat, down, fleece, hair, hide, pelt, skin.

furious *adjective*
1 *He was furious when he found out.* angry, cross, enraged, hopping mad (*informal*), incensed, indignant, infuriated, irate, livid, mad, rabid, ropeable (*Australian informal*).
OPPOSITE calm.
2 *a furious storm.* fierce, intense, raging, savage, tempestuous, violent, wild.

a
b
c
d
e
f
g
h
i
j
k
l
m
n
o
p
q
r
s
t
u
v
w
x
y
z

furnace *noun*
boiler, forge, incinerator, kiln, oven.

furnish *verb*
1 *She furnished the house luxuriously.* equip, fit out.
2 *Each person was furnished with stationery.* arm, equip, provide, supply.

furniture *noun*
effects, furnishings, movables.

furrow *noun*
1 *Plant in the furrows.* channel, ditch, drill, groove, rut, trench.
2 *skin furrows.* crease, line, wrinkle.

furry *adjective*
downy, fleecy, fluffy, fuzzy, hairy, woolly.

further *adjective*
further details. additional, extra, fresh, more, new, other, supplementary.
further *verb*
They furthered the cause. advance, aid, assist, boost, champion, forward, help, promote.
OPPOSITE hinder.

furthermore *adverb*
also, besides, in addition, moreover, too.

furthest *adjective*
the furthest point. extreme, farthest, furthermost, outermost, ultimate, uttermost.
OPPOSITE closest.

furtive *adjective*
a furtive glance. covert, secretive, shifty, sly, sneaky, stealthy, surreptitious, wily.
OPPOSITE open.

fury *noun*
1 *Her eyes were wild with fury.* anger, exasperation, frenzy, ire, paddy (*informal*), rage, temper, wrath.
2 *the fury of the storm.* ferocity, violence.

fuse *verb*
The parts fused together. amalgamate, blend, bond, combine, consolidate, incorporate, merge, stick, synthesise, unite, weld.
OPPOSITE separate.

fuss *noun*
a lot of fuss over nothing. ado, bother, bustle, commotion, excitement, flurry, fluster, furore, hue and cry, hullabaloo, kerfuffle (*informal*), palaver (*informal*), rumpus, stir, to-do, uproar.
fuss *verb*
She fussed over every little thing. carry on, complain, create (*slang*), flap (*informal*), fret, niggle, quibble, worry.

fussy *adjective*
1 *a fussy person.* choosy (*informal*), faddy, fastidious, finicky, hard to please, particular, pernickety (*informal*), picky (*informal*), selective.
OPPOSITE easygoing.
2 *a fussy design.* busy, cluttered, detailed, elaborate, fancy, intricate, ornate.
OPPOSITE simple.

futile *adjective*
a futile attempt. fruitless, ineffective, pointless, senseless, unsuccessful, useless, vain, worthless.
OPPOSITE effective.

future *adjective*
future programmes. approaching, coming, forthcoming, prospective, subsequent.
CONTRASTS WITH past, present.
future *noun*
1 *no worries about the future.* hereafter, tomorrow.
2 *The future is promising.* outlook, prospect.

fuzzy *adjective*
1 *fuzzy material.* downy, fleecy, fluffy, frizzy, furry, woolly.
2 *fuzzy images.* blurred, dim, hazy, imprecise, indistinct, unclear, vague, woolly.
OPPOSITE clear.

Gg

gabble *verb*
She gabbled unintelligibly. babble, chatter, jabber, prattle, yabber (*Australian informal*).

gadget *noun*
a useful kitchen gadget. apparatus, appliance, contraption (*informal*), device, gizmo (*informal*), implement, instrument, machine, tool, utensil.

gag *noun*
They laughed at his gags. jest, joke, wisecrack.
gag *verb*
The burglar gagged the shop owner. muzzle, silence.

gaiety *noun*
Christmas is a time of gaiety. celebration, cheer, festivity, fun, glee, happiness, hilarity, jollity, joy, merriment, merrymaking, mirth.
OPPOSITE melancholy.

gain *verb*
1 He gained the prize. She gained recognition. achieve, acquire, attain, earn, get, obtain, procure, receive, score, secure, win.
OPPOSITE forfeit, lose.
2 They gained out of the sale. make a profit, profit.
OPPOSITE lose.
3 He gained two kilos. add on, increase, put on.
OPPOSITE lose.
gain *noun*
1 a financial gain. advantage, benefit, dividend, income, profit, return, reward.
OPPOSITE loss.
2 a gain in weight. increase, jump, rise.
OPPOSITE loss.
gains *plural noun*
ill-gotten gains. booty, loot, proceeds, profits, takings, winnings.

gala *noun*
carnival, fair, festival, fête, pageant.

gale *noun*
The tree was blown over in the gale. blast, cyclone, gust, hurricane, storm, tempest, tornado, typhoon, wind.

gallant *adjective*
1 a gallant officer. brave, courageous, daring, fearless, heroic, intrepid, manly, noble, valiant.
OPPOSITE cowardly.
2 a gallant man. chivalrous, considerate, courteous, gentlemanly, kind, polite, suave.
OPPOSITE discourteous.

gallop *verb*
The horse galloped home. bolt, bound, dash, fly, hurry, hurtle, race, run, rush, shoot, speed, sprint, tear, whiz.

gallows *noun*
hanged on the gallows. gibbet, scaffold.

gamble *verb*
1 She gambles on the horses. bet, have a flutter (*informal*), punt.
2 He gambled his week's wages. bet, chance, risk, stake, venture, wager.
gamble *noun*
The enterprise is a bit of a gamble. chance, lottery, punt, risk, uncertainty.

gambler *noun*
better, punter, speculator.

game *noun*
1 They enjoy games. amusement, diversion, entertainment, pastime, playing, recreation, sport.
2 They won all their games in the tournament. bout, competition, contest, event, match, round.
game *adjective*
He wasn't game to tell them. bold, brave, courageous, daring, fearless, intrepid, plucky; see also WILLING.
OPPOSITE afraid.

gang *noun*
1 a gang of road workers. crew, squad, team, troop.

2 *a gang of ruffians.* band, bunch, group, mob (*informal*), pack, push (*Australian old use*).

gangster *noun*
bandit, brigand, criminal, crook (*informal*), desperado, robber, ruffian, thug, tough.

gangway *noun*
A gangway was left between the seats. aisle, gap, passage.

gaol *noun & verb*
see JAIL.

gaoler *noun*
see JAILER.

gap *noun*
1 *a narrow gap.* aisle, aperture, break, chasm, crack, cranny, crevice, gangway, hole, opening, space.
2 *a gap between items in the concert.* break, intermission, interval, lull, pause, recess.

gape *verb*
1 *He gaped at the magician.* gawp (*informal*), gaze, goggle, stare.
2 *The seam gaped.* come apart, open up, split open.

garage *noun*
1 *He parked the car in the garage.* shed.
2 *The garage serves petrol.* filling station, petrol station, service station.

garbage *noun*
debris, junk, litter, refuse, rubbish, scraps, trash, waste.
garbage bin see BIN.

garbled *adjective*
a garbled account. confused, incoherent, jumbled, mixed-up, unclear.

garden *noun*
allotment, grounds, lawn, patch, plot, yard.

garish *adjective*
He drives a garish green car. bright, flashy, gaudy, lairy (*Australian informal*), loud, showy.
OPPOSITE unobtrusive.

garland *noun*
a garland of flowers. festoon, lei, wreath.

garments *plural noun*
apparel (*formal*), attire (*formal*), clothes, clothing, costume, dress, garb, gear (*informal*), outfit, raiment (*old use*), vestments, wear.

garnish *verb*
The soup was garnished with coriander. decorate, embellish.

garrison *noun*
an army garrison. citadel, fort, fortress, stronghold.
garrison *verb*
Troops garrisoned the town. defend, guard, occupy, protect.

gas *noun*
He breathed in the gas. exhaust, fumes, vapour.

gash *noun*
a deep gash in the leg. cut, laceration, slash, slit, tear, wound.
gash *verb*
cut, lacerate, slash, slit, tear, wound.

gasp *verb*
He gasped for air. choke, pant, puff, wheeze.

gate *noun*
barrier, door, entrance, entry, exit, gateway, portal, portcullis, turnstile.

gather *verb*
1 *The people gathered outside the church.* assemble, concentrate, congregate, convene, crowd, flock, herd, mass, meet, rally, rendezvous, swarm, throng.
OPPOSITE disperse.
2 *He gathered his forces.* marshal, mobilise, muster, rally, round up, summon.
3 *He gathered supplies for the winter.* accumulate, collect, hoard, pile up, stack up, stockpile, store.
4 *They gathered mushrooms.* collect, garner, glean, harvest, pick, pluck, reap.
5 *The car gathered speed.* gain, increase, pick up.
6 *I gather your proposal was accepted.* conclude, infer, learn, take it, understand.
7 *She gathered the material.* ruffle, shirr.

gathering *noun*
a gathering of all her relatives. assembly, collection, congregation, congress, convention, crowd, flock, get-together (*informal*), group, meeting, mob, muster, party, rally, reunion, social, swarm, throng.

gaudy *adjective*
He wore a gaudy orange shirt. bright, colourful, flamboyant, flashy, garish, jazzy, lairy (*Australian informal*), loud, lurid, showy, tawdry.
OPPOSITE drab.

gauge *noun*
1 *heavy-gauge wire.* diameter, thickness.
2 *a gauge of their support.* guide, indicator, measure, yardstick.
3 *The amount registered on the gauge.* meter, scale.
gauge *verb*
It is easy to gauge their interest. assess, estimate, judge, measure.

gaunt *adjective*
He lost too much weight and looked gaunt. bony, emaciated, haggard, lanky, lean, scraggy, scrawny, skinny, thin.
OPPOSITE fat.

gay *adjective*
1 *The mood was gay.* blithe, bright, cheerful, happy, jolly, jovial, light-hearted, lively, merry.
OPPOSITE glum, unhappy.
2 *gay colours.* bright, colourful, gaudy, showy, vivid.
OPPOSITE dull.
3 (*informal*) *gay rights.* homosexual, lesbian (*female*).
OPPOSITE heterosexual.

gaze *verb*
gaze at *They gazed at the scene.* behold (*old use*), contemplate, eye, gape at, gawp at (*informal*), look at, observe, peer at, stare at, study, survey, view, watch.
gaze *noun*
She shifted her gaze. look, stare.

gear *noun*
1 *fishing gear.* apparatus, appliances, equipment, implements, instruments, kit, materials, paraphernalia, rig, stuff, tackle, things, tools.

2 (*informal*) *Dress in casual gear.* apparel (*formal*), attire (*formal*), clothes, clothing, dress, garments, get-up (*informal*), outfit, wear.

gem *noun*
a bangle studded with gems. gemstone, jewel, precious stone; [*various gems*] amethyst, aquamarine, diamond, emerald, garnet, jade, opal, ruby, sapphire, topaz, turquoise.

genealogy *noun*
She traced her genealogy back 200 years. ancestry, family history, lineage, pedigree.

general *adjective*
1 *general support.* broad, common, extensive, global, overall, popular, public, sweeping, universal, wholesale, widespread, worldwide.
OPPOSITE local.
2 *good general knowledge.* all-round, broad, comprehensive, encyclopedic.
OPPOSITE specialised.
3 *a general occurrence.* customary, everyday, familiar, habitual, normal, ordinary, regular, standard, typical, usual.
OPPOSITE exceptional.
4 *She spoke only in general terms.* broad, imprecise, indefinite, vague.
OPPOSITE specific.

generally *adverb*
1 *He is generally happy.* by and large, for the most part, in general, largely, mainly, mostly, normally, on the whole, usually.
OPPOSITE rarely.
2 *The rules apply generally.* across the board, always, everywhere, globally, universally.
OPPOSITE locally.

generate *verb*
She could not generate any enthusiasm. bring about, create, drum up, give rise to, produce, whip up.

generous *adjective*
1 *a generous giver.* benevolent, big-hearted, bountiful, charitable, kind-hearted, lavish, magnanimous, open-handed, philanthropic, selfless,

a
b
c
d
e
f
g
h
i
j
k
l
m
n
o
p
q
r
s
t
u
v
w
x
y
z

unselfish, unstinting.
OPPOSITE mean.
2 *a generous amount.* abundant, ample, copious, lavish, liberal, plentiful, sizeable.
OPPOSITE meagre.

genesis *noun*
beginning, birth, commencement, creation, origin, start.
OPPOSITE end.

genial *adjective*
genial people. affable, amiable, easygoing, friendly, hospitable, kind, outgoing, pleasant, sociable, warm-hearted.
OPPOSITE unfriendly.

genius *noun*
She was a true genius. brain (*informal*), expert, know-all, mastermind, prodigy, virtuoso, whiz-kid (*informal*).
OPPOSITE moron.

gentle *adjective*
1 *a gentle breeze.* balmy, faint, light, mild, moderate, soft.
OPPOSITE strong.
2 *a gentle voice.* calm, mild, pleasant, quiet, soft, soothing, sweet, tender.
OPPOSITE raucous.
3 *a gentle person.* compassionate, humane, kind, kind-hearted, kindly, lenient, meek, merciful, mild, peaceful, placid, serene, soft-hearted, sympathetic, tender-hearted.
OPPOSITE harsh, rough.
4 *a gentle animal.* docile, harmless, manageable, meek, placid, tame.
OPPOSITE wild.
5 *a gentle slope.* easy, gradual, moderate, slight.
OPPOSITE steep.
6 *a gentle hint.* faint, indirect, mild, slight, subtle.
OPPOSITE strong.

genuine *adjective*
1 *the genuine article.* actual, authentic, dinkum (*Australian informal*), dinky-di (*Australian informal*), honest-to-goodness (*informal*), real, ridgy-didge (*Australian informal*), true.
OPPOSITE fake.

2 *He showed genuine concern.* heartfelt, honest, real, sincere, true.
OPPOSITE insincere.

germ *noun*
Cleanliness prevents the spread of these germs. bacterium, bug (*informal*), microbe, micro-organism, virus.

germinate *verb*
The seeds germinated after a week. come up, grow, shoot, spring up, sprout.

gesture *noun*
Her gestures indicated her true feelings. action, motion, movement, sign, signal.
gesture *verb*
He gestured to them to approach. beckon, motion, nod, point, signal, wave.

get *verb*
1 *She got a new book.* acquire, be given, buy, come by, get hold of, obtain, procure, purchase, receive.
2 *He got all the prizes.* earn, gain, land, receive, scoop, score, take, win.
OPPOSITE lose.
3 *Go and get your umbrella.* bring, collect, fetch, pick up, retrieve.
4 *She got a cold.* catch, come down with, contract, develop, pick up, suffer from.
5 *The police will get the culprit.* arrest, capture, catch, grab, nab (*informal*), seize.
6 *Try to get his attention.* attract, capture, catch, draw.
7 (*informal*) *He didn't get what I meant.* comprehend, cotton on to (*informal*), fathom, follow, grasp, understand.
OPPOSITE misunderstand.
8 *I'll get lunch now.* fix, make ready, prepare.
9 *Try to get him to eat.* cause, convince, induce, influence, make, persuade.
OPPOSITE dissuade.
10 *The days are getting longer.* become, grow.
11 *How do you get to work?* go, journey, travel.
12 *He got home late.* arrive at, reach.
get at (*informal*)
What are you getting at? drive at, hint at, imply, insinuate, mean, suggest.
get away *The thieves got away in a stolen car.* abscond, bolt, break free, do a bunk (*slang*), escape, flee, leave, nick off

(*Australian slang*), push off (*informal*), scarper, shoot through (*Australian informal*), slip away.
OPPOSITE stay.

get back
1 *She got back her purse.* recover, regain, retrieve.
2 *Things got back to normal.* go back, return.

get down *The rider got down.* dismount, get off.

get off *The passengers got off.* alight, descend, disembark, get out.

get on
1 *get on a bus.* board, climb on.
2 *get on a horse.* mount.
3 *How's she getting on?* cope, fare, get along, make out (*informal*), manage.

get out of *She got out of doing the cleaning again.* avoid, dodge, escape, evade, shirk, wriggle out of.

get over
1 *He got over the problem.* master, overcome, surmount.
2 *He has got over his illness.* pull through, recover from, survive.

get through *He got through his exam.* pass, succeed in.
OPPOSITE fail.

get up *She gets up at 7 o'clock.* arise (*old use*), rise, surface.
OPPOSITE retire.

get your own back (*informal*) get even, have your revenge, pay back, retaliate.

getaway *noun*
He made a quick getaway. escape, flight, retreat.

get-together *noun* (*informal*)
The friends arranged a get-together. function, gathering, meeting, party, reunion, social.

ghastly *adjective*
1 *a ghastly accident.* appalling, awful, dreadful, frightful, gruesome, hideous, horrendous, horrible, repulsive, shocking, terrible.
2 *He looked ghastly.* ashen, deathly, ghostly, pale, pallid, pasty, sickly, wan, washed out.
OPPOSITE blooming, healthy.

ghost *noun*
He doesn't believe in ghosts. apparition, phantom, poltergeist, spectre, spirit, spook (*informal*), vision.

ghostly *adjective*
ghostly noises. creepy, eerie, sinister, spooky (*informal*), uncanny, unearthly, weird.

giant *noun*
a fairy-tale giant. monster, ogre.
OPPOSITE dwarf.
giant *adjective*
see GIGANTIC.

giddiness *noun*
dizziness, light-headedness, unsteadiness, vertigo.

giddy *adjective*
He felt giddy standing on the roof. dizzy, faint, light-headed, unsteady.
OPPOSITE steady.

gift *noun*
1 *a generous gift.* alms, bequest, contribution, donation, freebie (*informal*), give-away (*informal*), handout, legacy, offering, offertory, present, tip.
2 *He has a gift for mathematics.* ability, aptitude, flair, genius, head, knack, talent.

gifted *adjective*
a gifted pupil. able, accomplished, bright, brilliant, capable, clever, intelligent, skilful, skilled, talented.
OPPOSITE inept.

gigantic *adjective*
a gigantic building, amount, etc. big, boomer (*Australian informal*), colossal, enormous, extensive, gargantuan, giant, ginormous (*slang*), huge, humungous (*slang*), immeasurable, immense, jumbo-sized, king-sized, large, mammoth, massive, mighty, monstrous, monumental, stupendous, tremendous, vast, whopping (*slang*).
OPPOSITE small, tiny.

giggle *verb*
She giggled nervously. chuckle, laugh, snicker, snigger, titter.

a
b
c
d
e
f
g
h
i
j
k
l
m
n
o
p
q
r
s
t
u
v
w
x
y
z

giggle *noun*
He let out a giggle. chuckle, laugh, snicker, snigger, titter.

gimmick *noun*
an advertising gimmick. device, ploy, stratagem, trick.

gingerly *adverb*
She touched the controls gingerly. carefully, cautiously, warily.
OPPOSITE confidently.

girdle *noun*
1 *He tied the robe with a girdle.* belt, cord.
2 *She wears a girdle to pull her stomach in.* corset, stays (*old use*), truss.

girl *noun*
babe (*informal*), bird (*informal*), chick (*slang*), damsel (*old use*), female, gal (*informal*), lass, lassie (*informal*), maid (*old use*), maiden (*old use*), miss, schoolgirl, sheila (*Australian slang*); see also CHILD, WOMAN.

girlfriend *noun*
date (*informal*), steady, sweetheart.

give *verb*
1 *He gave them money.* allot, allow, award, bestow, deal out, dish out (*informal*), distribute, dole out, entrust with, equip with, grant, hand out, hand over, offer, pay, present, provide with, ration out, supply with.
OPPOSITE receive, take.
2 *They give to various charities.* contribute, donate, subscribe.
3 *He gave me the message.* communicate, convey, deliver, impart, pass on, report, tell, transmit.
4 *She gave a scream.* emit, let out, utter.
5 *The children give an annual show.* perform, play, present, put on, stage.
6 *They gave a party.* hold, host, organise, provide, put on, throw (*informal*).
7 *The chair will give under her weight.* break, buckle, collapse, crack, fold up, give way, yield.
give away
1 *She gave away the old clothes.* cast off, discard, part with, throw out, toss out.
2 *She gave away their secret.* betray, blab, divulge, leak, let out, make known, reveal.
give back *They gave back the deposit.* pay back, refund, reimburse, repay,

return.
OPPOSITE retain.
give in *He will fight and not give in.* capitulate, concede, give up, submit, surrender, yield.
give off *It gave off a strong smell.* emit, exude, give out, release.
give out
1 *The candle gives out light.* emit, produce, put out, radiate, shed.
2 *The supply gave out.* dry up (*informal*), fail, peter out, run out, stop.
give up
1 *He gave up smoking.* cease, discontinue, give away (*Australian*), quit, stop.
OPPOSITE continue.
2 *She gave up her job.* abandon, chuck in (*informal*), leave, quit, resign, retire from.
OPPOSITE keep.
3 *Her opponent gave up.* capitulate, concede, give in, retire, surrender, throw in the towel, throw up the sponge, yield.
OPPOSITE persevere.
give way *The bridge gave way under the car's weight.* break, buckle, cave in, collapse, crumble, give, snap.

giver *noun*
benefactor, contributor, donor, sponsor.

glad *adjective*
They were glad to hear he was well. delighted, happy, joyful, pleased, thrilled.
OPPOSITE sad, sorry.

gladden *verb*
The news gladdened their hearts. brighten, cheer, delight, please.
OPPOSITE sadden.

glamorous *adjective*
a glamorous woman. attractive, beautiful, bewitching, charming, elegant, exciting, fascinating.
OPPOSITE unattractive.

glance *verb*
He glanced through the advertisements. look, peek, peep, scan, skim.
glance *noun*
He took a glance at the paper. glimpse, look, peek, peep, squiz (*Australian slang*).

glare *verb*
She glared at them. frown, glower, lour, scowl, stare.
glare *noun*
1 *sun glare.* brightness, dazzle, radiance.
2 *He gave them a hard glare.* frown, glower, lour, scowl, stare.

glaring *adjective*
1 *glaring headlights.* blinding, bright, dazzling, harsh, strong.
OPPOSITE dim.
2 *glaring inconsistencies.* blatant, conspicuous, flagrant, obvious, patent, plain, unmistakable.
OPPOSITE subtle.

glass *noun*
1 *She polished the glass.* crystal, pane, plate glass.
2 *She admired herself in the glass.* looking-glass, mirror.
3 *She drinks from a glass.* beaker, goblet, tumbler, wineglass.
glasses *plural noun*
optical glasses. binoculars, goggles, opera glasses, specs (*informal*), spectacles, sunglasses.

glasshouse *noun*
conservatory, greenhouse, hothouse.

glassy *adjective*
1 *a glassy surface.* reflective, shiny, smooth.
2 *a glassy look.* blank, deadpan, expressionless, glazed, vacant.

glaze *noun*
the glaze on the pots. enamel, finish, lustre.

gleam *noun*
a gleam of light. beam, flash, glimmer, glint, ray, shimmer, spark.
gleam *verb*
The sink gleamed. flash, glimmer, glisten, shimmer, shine, sparkle.

glee *noun*
She jumped with glee. cheerfulness, delight, ecstasy, excitement, exhilaration, happiness, joy, jubilation, mirth.
OPPOSITE misery.

glide *verb*
1 *glide on ice.* aquaplane, coast, skate, skid, skim, slide, slip.
2 *glide through the air.* drift, float, fly, sail, soar.

glimmer *noun*
1 *a glimmer of light.* flash, flicker, gleam, glint, glow, ray, shimmer, sparkle.
2 *a glimmer of hope.* flicker, gleam, ray, spark, speck.
glimmer *verb*
The city lights glimmered. flicker, gleam, glint, glow, shimmer, shine, twinkle.

glimpse *noun*
He caught a brief glimpse. glance, look, peek, peep, squiz (*Australian slang*), view.
glimpse *verb*
She glimpsed a bird in the tree. catch sight of, discern, espy, notice, peep at, see, sight, spot.

glint *noun*
the glint in his eye. flash, gleam, sparkle.
glint *verb*
The metal glinted in the sun. flash, gleam, glimmer, glisten, glitter, shine, sparkle, twinkle.

glisten *verb*
The bath glistened after being cleaned. gleam, shimmer, shine, sparkle.

glitter *verb*
All that glitters is not gold. glimmer, shimmer, shine, sparkle, twinkle.
glitter *noun*
the glitter of crystal. gleam, sparkle, twinkle.
OPPOSITE dullness.

glittering *adjective*
a glittering display. brilliant, dazzling, glitzy (*slang*), splendid.

gloat *verb*
She gloated over her success. crow, delight, exult, glory, rejoice, revel; see also BOAST.

global *adjective*
a global problem. general, international, universal, widespread, worldwide.
OPPOSITE local.

globe *noun*
1 *a light globe.* ball, bulb, sphere.
2 *He has travelled the globe.* earth, world.

a
b
c
d
e
f
g
h
i
j
k
l
m
n
o
p
q
r
s
t
u
v
w
x
y
z

gloom *noun*
1 *He could not see in the gloom.* darkness, dimness, dusk, semi-darkness, shadows, twilight.
OPPOSITE brightness.
2 *a feeling of gloom.* depression, despair, glumness, melancholy, misery, pessimism, sadness, unhappiness.
OPPOSITE cheerfulness.

gloomy *adjective*
1 *a gloomy day.* black, bleak, cheerless, cloudy, dark, depressing, dismal, dreary, dull, murky, overcast.
OPPOSITE sunny.
2 *a gloomy man. a gloomy expression.* depressed, desolate, dismal, glum, heavy-hearted, melancholy, moody, morbid, morose, mournful, pessimistic, sad, sombre, sullen, unhappy.
OPPOSITE cheerful.

glorify *verb*
The people glorified God. adore, exalt, extol, hallow, honour, laud (*formal*), praise, revere, venerate, worship.
OPPOSITE denigrate.

glorious *adjective*
1 *a glorious achievement.* famous, grand, heroic, illustrious, impressive, noble.
OPPOSITE inglorious.
2 *a glorious day.* beautiful, brilliant, excellent, fine, grand, magnificent, majestic, marvellous, spectacular, splendid, stunning, superb, terrific (*informal*), wonderful.
OPPOSITE dull.

glory *noun*
1 *She brought glory to her school.* credit, distinction, esteem, fame, honour, kudos (*informal*), prestige, renown.
OPPOSITE shame.
2 *glory to God.* adoration, exaltation, honour, praise, reverence, veneration, worship.
OPPOSITE blasphemy.
3 *the glory of a sunset.* beauty, grandeur, greatness, magnificence, majesty, splendour.
glory *verb*
They gloried in their success. delight, exult, pride yourself, rejoice, revel, take pride.

gloss *noun*
The woodwork has a high gloss. brightness, lustre, polish, sheen, shine, sparkle.
gloss over *He glossed over the faults.* conceal, cover up, hide, make light of, whitewash.
OPPOSITE emphasise, highlight.

glossy *adjective*
glossy paint. gleaming, glistening, lustrous, shining, shiny.
OPPOSITE matt.

glove *noun*
gauntlet, mitt, mitten.

glow *verb*
1 *The fire glowed.* gleam, radiate, shine.
2 *Her cheeks glowed.* blush, colour, flush, redden, shine.
OPPOSITE pale.
glow *noun*
1 *the glow from the fire.* brightness, gleam, heat, light, radiance, warmth.
2 *a healthy glow.* blush, colour, flush, radiance, redness, rosiness, ruddiness.
OPPOSITE pallor.

glue *noun*
stuck with glue. adhesive, cement, gum, paste.
glue *verb*
She glued the parts together. affix, attach, cement, fasten, gum, paste, stick.

gluey *adjective*
a gluey mixture. adhesive, sticky, tacky.

glum *adjective*
He was all alone, feeling glum. cheerless, crestfallen, depressed, despondent, doleful, down-hearted, down in the mouth, forlorn, gloomy, melancholy, miserable, moody, morose, mournful, sad, unhappy, woebegone.
OPPOSITE cheerful.

glut *noun*
a glut of potatoes. excess, overabundance, oversupply, surfeit, surplus.
OPPOSITE shortage.

glutton *noun*
gormandiser, greedy-guts (*informal*), guts (*informal*), guzzler, pig (*informal*).

gluttonous *adjective*
greedy, gutsy (*slang*), insatiable,
voracious.

gnarled *adjective*
a gnarled tree trunk. distorted, knobbly,
knotty, lumpy, misshapen, rough,
twisted.
OPPOSITE smooth.

gnash *verb*
He gnashed his teeth in fury. grate, grind.

gnaw *verb*
She gnawed a carrot. bite, chew, chomp,
munch, nibble.

gnome *noun*
dwarf, elf, goblin, troll.

go *verb*
1 *He is going home.* head for, journey,
make for, nip (*informal*), pop, proceed,
set out for, start for, travel, visit, zip off;
see also ADVANCE.
2 *It's time to go.* beat it (*slang*), be off,
buzz off (*slang*), clear off (*informal*),
depart, disappear, exit, get away, go
away, hop it (*slang*), leave, make tracks
(*informal*), make yourself scarce, nick off
(*Australian slang*), push off (*informal*),
retire, retreat, run off, scarper (*informal*),
scoot, scram (*informal*), set off, shoot
through (*Australian informal*), shove off
(*informal*), skedaddle (*informal*), take
your leave, take yourself off, vanish,
withdraw.
OPPOSITE arrive.
3 *The road goes to Dungog.* extend, lead,
reach, run, stretch.
4 *The car won't go.* function, move,
operate, perform, run, work.
5 *The time went quickly.* elapse, pass, slip
by.
6 *The glasses go in this case.* belong, fit.
7 *The milk went sour.* become, turn.
8 *Things went well.* fare, proceed,
progress, turn out, work out.
9 *The money has all gone.* be spent, be
used, dry up, run out.
10 *The elastic has gone.* disintegrate, fail,
give way, perish.

go *noun*
1 *a man with plenty of go.* dash, drive,
dynamism, energy, vigour, vim
(*informal*), vivacity.
2 *It's your go.* shot, turn.
3 (*informal*) *Have a go at it.* attempt, bash
(*informal*), crack (*informal*), shot, stab
(*informal*), try.

go about *He went about the task the
wrong way.* approach, attack, deal with,
handle, set about, tackle, undertake.

go across *He went across their field.*
cross, cut across, traverse.

go after chase, follow, pursue, tail
(*informal*), track, trail.
OPPOSITE precede.

go along with *We don't go along with
their ideas.* agree with, be in sympathy
with.

go back on *She went back on her word.*
break, recant, renege on, repudiate.
OPPOSITE keep.

go back to *He went back to his former
habits.* resume, return to, revert to.

go before lead, precede.
OPPOSITE follow.

go beyond *go beyond your expectations.*
exceed, pass, surpass.

go for *She always goes for the dearest
item.* choose, opt for, prefer.

go off
1 *The bomb went off.* blow up, detonate,
explode.
2 *The meat went off.* decay, deteriorate,
go bad, go rotten, perish, rot, spoil.
OPPOSITE keep.

go on
1 *They went on with their work.* carry on,
continue, keep on, persevere, persist,
proceed.
2 (*informal*) *He kept going on about the
olden days.* carry on (*informal*), rabbit on
(*informal*), ramble on, waffle (*informal*).

go over
1 *Let's go over the evidence.* examine,
recap (*informal*), recapitulate, review.
2 *The actor goes over his lines.* practise,
rehearse, run through.

go round circle, gyrate, orbit, revolve,
rotate, spin, swirl, swivel, turn, twirl,
whirl.

go through
1 *The arrow went through his heart.* enter,
penetrate, pierce, puncture.
2 *He has gone through an ordeal.* bear,
endure, experience, suffer, undergo.

a
b
c
d
e
f
g
h
i
j
k
l
m
n
o
p
q
r
s
t
u
v
w
x
y
z

3 *They went through his papers.* check, inspect, look through, search, sift through.

go up

1 *We'll go up the stairs.* ascend, climb, mount.
OPPOSITE descend.

2 *Prices are going up.* escalate, increase, rise, rocket, soar.
OPPOSITE fall.

go with

1 *She went with them.* accompany, escort.

2 *The shoes go with the dress.* match, suit.
OPPOSITE clash with.

go without *go without sleep.* be deprived of, deny yourself, do without, forgo, give up, sacrifice.

go-ahead *adjective*
a go-ahead employee. ambitious, enterprising, forward-looking, progressive.

goal *noun*
They worked towards a common goal. aim, ambition, end, object, objective, purpose, target.

goat *noun*
billy goat, he-goat, kid, nanny goat.

gobble *verb*
He gobbled his food and left. bolt, devour, gulp, guzzle, scoff (*informal*), wolf.

go-between *noun*
agent, broker, intermediary, mediator, messenger, middleman, negotiator.

goblin *noun*
Goblins exist in fairy tales. bogy, elf, gnome, hobgoblin, imp, leprechaun, sprite.

go-cart *noun*
billycart, hill trolley.

god *noun*
The Greeks worshipped many gods. deity, divinity.
God *They worship God as creator and ruler of the universe.* Allah, the Almighty, the Creator, the Father, Jehovah, the Lord, Yahweh.

goddess *noun*
deity, divinity.

godless *adjective*
a godless society. atheistic, evil, heathen, impious, irreligious, pagan, sacrilegious, ungodly, wicked.
OPPOSITE God-fearing.

godly *adjective*
a godly man. devout, God-fearing, holy, pious, religious, saintly.
OPPOSITE ungodly.

godsend *noun*
The lottery prize was a godsend. blessing, bonanza, boon, windfall.

goggles *plural noun*
glasses, spectacles.

gold *adjective*
a gold frame. gilded, gilt, golden, gold-plated.

golden *adjective*
1 *golden curls.* blond, flaxen, gold, yellow.
2 *a golden opportunity.* excellent, favourable, precious, priceless, valuable.

good *adjective*
1 *good food.* beneficial, delicious, healthy, nutritious, scrumptious (*informal*), tasty, wholesome.
OPPOSITE harmful.
2 *a good reason.* cogent, genuine, legitimate, powerful, satisfactory, solid, sound, strong, valid.
OPPOSITE weak.
3 *He made a good decision.* appropriate, fitting, proper, prudent, right, sensible, wise.
OPPOSITE bad.
4 *in a good position. at a good time.* advantageous, auspicious, convenient, desirable, favourable, fortunate, lucky, opportune, propitious, suitable.
OPPOSITE adverse, bad.
5 *a good person.* benevolent, blameless, considerate, decent, ethical, godly, holy, honest, honourable, innocent, just, kind, law-abiding, moral, noble, righteous, upright, virtuous, well-intentioned, well-meaning, worthy.
OPPOSITE wicked.
6 *good conduct.* admirable, commendable, correct, exemplary, honourable, meritorious, praiseworthy,

worthy.
OPPOSITE unseemly.
7 *a good child.* biddable, courteous, dutiful, helpful, obedient, polite, well-behaved, well-mannered.
OPPOSITE ill-mannered, naughty.
8 *We had a good time.* agreeable, cool (*informal*), delightful, enjoyable, excellent, fabulous (*informal*), fantastic (*informal*), fine, great (*informal*), happy, lovely, marvellous, nice, outstanding, pleasant, satisfying, superb, terrific (*informal*), tremendous (*informal*), wonderful.
OPPOSITE rotten.
9 *a good player. a good worker.* able, accomplished, capable, competent, conscientious, dependable, diligent, effective, efficient, expert, first-rate, proficient, reliable, skilful, skilled, sound, thorough.
OPPOSITE poor.

good *noun*
1 *Look for the good in people.* goodness, merit, virtue.
OPPOSITE bad, evil.
2 *It is for his own good.* advantage, benefit, interest, profit, welfare, well-being.
OPPOSITE harm.
good point *The plan has its good points.* advantage, merit, strength, strong point, virtue.
OPPOSITE drawback, weakness.

goodbye *interjection & noun*
adieu, au revoir, bon voyage, bye-bye (*informal*), cheerio (*informal*), cheers (*informal*), ciao (*informal*), farewell, hooray (*Australian informal*), see you (*informal*), see you later (*informal*), so long (*informal*), ta-ta (*informal*).

good-looking *adjective*
attractive, beautiful, bonny (*Scottish*), fair (*old use*), handsome, lovely, pretty.
OPPOSITE plain.

good-natured *adjective*
benevolent, compassionate, easygoing, forgiving, friendly, generous, genial, gracious, helpful, kind, kind-hearted, kindly, obliging, sympathetic, tender-hearted, thoughtful, tolerant, unselfish.
OPPOSITE unkind.

goodness *noun*
benevolence, generosity, honour, integrity, kindness, merit, morality, righteousness, virtue.
OPPOSITE evil.

goods *plural noun*
1 *one's worldly goods.* belongings, possessions, property, things.
2 *a tax on goods and services.* articles, commodities, merchandise, products, wares.
3 *a goods train.* cargo, freight.

good-tempered *adjective*
affable, amiable, amicable, cheerful, easygoing, even-tempered, gentle, good-humoured, happy, happy-go-lucky, jovial, mild, pleasant.
OPPOSITE peevish, testy.

goodwill *noun*
an act of goodwill towards a stranger. benevolence, charity, friendliness, grace, kindness.
OPPOSITE hostility.

gooey *adjective* (*informal*)
a gooey mixture. gluey, mushy, slimy, sloppy, sludgy, slushy, squidgy, sticky, tacky.

goose *noun*
gander (*male*), gosling (*young*).

gorge *noun*
They drove through the gorge. canyon, chasm, gully, pass, ravine, valley.
gorge *verb*
She gorged herself on cakes. feast, fill, overeat, stuff.
OPPOSITE starve.

gorgeous *adjective*
1 *a gorgeous tapestry.* colourful, exquisite, magnificent, rich, splendid, sumptuous.
OPPOSITE drab.
2 *a gorgeous woman.* attractive, beautiful, good-looking, smashing (*informal*), stunning (*informal*).
OPPOSITE ugly.

gory *adjective*
a gory film. bloody, grisly, gruesome, macabre, violent.

a
b
c
d
e
f
g
h
i
j
k
l
m
n
o
p
q
r
s
t
u
v
w
x
y
z

gossip *noun*
1 *a piece of idle gossip.* backbiting, hearsay, rumour, scandal, tittle-tattle.
2 *Don't tell her your secrets. She's a gossip.* busybody, gossip-monger, rumour-monger, scandalmonger, tattler.
gossip *verb*
They gossiped for hours. blab, chat, natter (*informal*), prattle, tattle, tell tales, tittle-tattle.

got
see GET.

gouge *verb*
She gouged out a hole in the log. bore, cut, dig, groove, hollow, scoop.

govern *verb*
Who governs the country? administer, be in charge of, command, control, direct, guide, head, lead, manage, rule, run, superintend, supervise.

government *noun*
the government of the country. administration, command, control, leadership, management, regime, rule.

governor *noun*
the governor of a province, state, etc. chief, head, ruler, viceroy.

gown *noun*
wearing a long gown. dress, frock, habit, robe, vestment.

grab *verb*
He grabbed her handbag. clasp, clutch, grasp, hold, nab (*informal*), pluck, seize, snatch, swipe (*informal*).
OPPOSITE release.

grace *noun*
1 *She dances with grace.* elegance, gracefulness, smoothness.
OPPOSITE clumsiness.
2 *The teacher gave him a week's grace.* extension, postponement, reprieve.
3 *the grace of God.* favour, forbearance, forgiveness, goodness, goodwill, lenience, mercy.
4 *They said grace before eating.* benediction, blessing, prayer, thanksgiving.

graceful *adjective*
a graceful dancer. agile, elegant, lithe, nimble, supple.
OPPOSITE clumsy, ungainly.

gracious *adjective*
1 *a gracious person.* amiable, courteous, friendly, good-natured, hospitable, kind, kindly, polite, tactful.
2 *gracious living.* elegant, luxurious, refined.

grade *noun*
1 *several grades of potatoes.* category, class, quality, standard.
2 *a student's grade for an essay.* assessment, mark, rank, rating, result, score.
3 *What grade are you in at school?* class, form, year.
grade *verb*
1 *The wool has been graded.* class, classify, rank, sort.
2 *The teacher graded the assignments.* assess, mark, rate, score.

gradient *noun*
The road has a steep gradient. grade, hill, incline, slope.

gradual *adjective*
a gradual increase. gentle, piecemeal, progressive, slow, steady.
OPPOSITE sharp, sudden.

gradually *adverb*
bit by bit, by degrees, progressively, slowly, steadily, step by step.

grain *noun*
1 *Birds eat grain.* cereal, corn, granule, grist, kernel, seed.
2 *a grain of sand.* bit, particle, speck.
3 *a grain of truth.* bit, hint, jot, ounce, shred, skerrick (*Australian informal*), trace.

grand *adjective*
1 *a grand house.* elegant, imposing, impressive, large, luxurious, magnificent, majestic, opulent, palatial, posh (*informal*), splendid, stately, sumptuous, superb.
OPPOSITE humble.
2 (*informal*) *We had a grand time.* see GREAT.
3 *the grand total.* all-inclusive, complete, comprehensive, full.

grandeur *noun*
the grandeur of the occasion. dignity, magnificence, majesty, pomp, splendour.

grant *verb*
1 She granted them permission to leave. allow, give.
OPPOSITE refuse.
2 The government granted subsidies. allocate, award, bestow, donate, give, pay, provide.
grant *noun*
She receives a study grant. allowance, award, bursary, endowment, scholarship, subsidy.

grapevine *noun*
I heard it on the grapevine. bush telegraph, mulga wire.

graphic *adjective*
1 a graphic presentation. diagrammatic, drawn, illustrated, pictorial, visual.
2 a graphic account. colourful, descriptive, detailed, explicit, vivid.

grapple *verb*
grapple with
1 He grappled with the man. fight, struggle with, tackle, wrestle with.
2 She grappled with the problem. address, come to grips with, contend with, deal with, struggle with, tackle, wrestle with.

grasp *verb*
1 She grasped his hand. clasp, clench, cling to, clutch, grab, grip, hang on to, hold, seize, snatch, take, take hold of.
OPPOSITE release.
2 He couldn't grasp what we meant. comprehend, cotton on to (*informal*), fathom, follow, get (*informal*), latch on to (*informal*), see, understand.
grasp *noun*
1 a powerful grasp. clasp, clutch, grip, hold.
2 a grasp of the subject. command, mastery, understanding.

grasping *adjective*
He's mean and grasping. avaricious, covetous, greedy, mercenary.
OPPOSITE generous.

grass *noun*
a picnic on the grass. green, lawn, pasture, sward, turf.
grass *verb* (*slang*)
He grassed his mates. betray, blow the whistle on (*informal*), dob in (*Australian informal*), inform on, rat on (*informal*), shelf (*Australian slang*), shop (*slang*), sneak on (*informal*), split on (*slang*).

grassland *noun*
field, meadow, pampas, pasture, plain, prairie, range, savannah, steppe.

grate[1] *noun*
fireplace, hearth.

grate[2] *verb*
1 She grated the ginger. grind, mince, shred.
2 His finger grated on the blackboard. grind, rub, scrape, scratch.
grate on Her laugh grates on people. annoy, get on someone's nerves, irritate, jar on, rub someone up the wrong way.

grateful *adjective*
She was grateful for their concern. appreciative, thankful.
OPPOSITE resentful.

grating[1] *noun*
A grating covers the hole. grate, grid, grille.

grating[2] *adjective*
a grating voice. discordant, harsh, jarring, rasping, raucous, shrill, strident.

gratitude *noun*
He showed his gratitude. appreciation, thankfulness, thanks.
OPPOSITE ingratitude.

grave[1] *noun*
buried in a grave. burial place, crypt, mausoleum, sepulchre, tomb, vault.

grave[2] *adjective*
1 a grave matter. critical, crucial, important, momentous, serious, weighty.
OPPOSITE petty.
2 grave faces. earnest, gloomy, grim, pensive, serious, sober, solemn, sombre,

a
b
c
d
e
f
g
h
i
j
k
l
m
n
o
p
q
r
s
t
u
v
w
x
y
z

staid, thoughtful.
OPPOSITE merry.

gravel *noun*
a path of gravel. pebbles, road metal,
shingle, stones.

gravestone *noun*
headstone, monument, tombstone.

graveyard *noun*
burial ground, cemetery, churchyard.

graze[1] *verb*
The sheep are grazing in the paddock.
browse, feed.

graze[2] *verb*
He grazed his knee. bark, scrape, scratch,
skin.
graze *noun*
a graze on the knee. abrasion, scrape,
scratch.

grazier *noun* (*Australian*)
cattle farmer, pastoralist (*Australian*),
sheep farmer.

grease *noun*
dripping, fat, lard, lubricant, oil, suet,
tallow.
grease *verb*
He greased the engine. lubricate, oil.

greasy *adjective*
fatty, oily, slick.

great *adjective*
1 a great amount. big, colossal,
enormous, gigantic, huge, humungous
(*slang*), immense, large, massive,
phenomenal, stupendous, vast.
OPPOSITE slight.
2 The storm caused great damage.
considerable, extensive, immeasurable,
sweeping, vast, widespread.
OPPOSITE minor.
3 a great success. notable, outstanding,
profound, remarkable, resounding,
splendid, tremendous.
4 great joy. deep, indescribable, intense,
profound, unspeakable.
5 great pain. acute, extreme, intense,
severe, strong.
OPPOSITE mild.
6 a great mathematician. brilliant,
celebrated, distinguished, eminent,
first-class, gifted, illustrious, important,
leading, noted, outstanding, prominent,

renowned, superior, talented, well-
known.
7 one of the great events of history. grand,
historic, important, momentous,
significant.
OPPOSITE unimportant.
8 She's a great reader. avid, eager, keen,
passionate.
9 (*informal*) It was a great party. brilliant
(*informal*), cool (*informal*), delightful,
enjoyable, excellent, fabulous (*informal*),
fantastic (*informal*), fine, first-rate, good,
grand (*informal*), lovely, magnificent,
marvellous, outstanding, pleasant,
splendid, super (*informal*), superb,
terrific (*informal*), tremendous
(*informal*), wonderful.
OPPOSITE bad, lousy (*informal*).

greatest *adjective*
best, chief, highest, main, maximum,
paramount, supreme, top, utmost.
OPPOSITE least.

greatness *noun*
Some people achieve greatness. distinction,
eminence, grandeur, importance,
stature.

greed *noun*
greed for food. greed for money. avarice,
covetousness, gluttony.
OPPOSITE unselfishness.

greedy *adjective*
1 The greedy child ate all the biscuits.
gluttonous, ravenous, voracious.
2 greedy moneylenders. avaricious,
covetous, grasping, miserly, money-
hungry, on the make (*informal*).
OPPOSITE generous.

greedy-guts *noun*
see GLUTTON.

green *adjective*
1 a green colour. apple green,
aquamarine, beryl, bottle green,
chartreuse, emerald, jade, lime, olive,
pea green, sea green.
2 green pastures. green trees. leafy, lush,
verdant.
3 The fruit is still green. raw, unripe.
OPPOSITE ripe.
green *noun*
a political green. conservationist,
environmentalist, greenie (*Australian
informal*).

greenhouse *noun*
conservatory, glasshouse, hothouse.

greet *verb*
She greeted her friend. address, receive, welcome.

greeting *noun*
They were given a warm greeting. reception, salutation, welcome.
greetings *plural noun*
birthday greetings. compliments, congratulations, regards, wishes.

grey *adjective*
1 *a grey colour. grey hair.* charcoal grey, grizzled, grizzly, gunmetal, hoary, mousy, silver, slate, smoky, steely.
2 *grey skies.* cloudy, dark, dull, gloomy, heavy, leaden, overcast.
OPPOSITE sunny.
3 *a grey area.* doubtful, hazy, intermediate, uncertain, unclear.

grid *noun*
1 *The drain was covered with a grid.* grating, grille.
2 *The cables are laid in a grid.* lattice, network.

grief *noun*
overcome with grief. anguish, desolation, distress, heartache, heartbreak, misery, regret, remorse, sadness, sorrow, suffering, unhappiness, woe.
OPPOSITE joy.

grievance *noun*
He aired his grievances. beef (*slang*), complaint, gripe (*informal*), objection.

grieve *verb*
1 *She grieved them with her thoughtlessness.* distress, hurt, pain, sadden, upset.
OPPOSITE hearten.
2 *He grieved for his dead friend.* fret, lament, mope, mourn, pine, weep.
OPPOSITE rejoice.

grill *verb*
1 *He grilled the meat.* barbecue, broil, brown, toast.
2 *The police grilled them over the incident.* cross-examine, interrogate, question.

grim *adjective*
1 *grim faces.* dour, forbidding, gloomy, glum, harsh, severe, stern.
OPPOSITE smiling.

2 *The future looks grim.* bleak, desolate, dire, dismal, dreadful, forbidding, frightful, ghastly, gloomy, horrible, unpleasant.

grimace *verb*
She grimaced with pain. frown, pull a face, scowl, wince.

grimy *adjective*
grimy hands. blackened, dirty, filthy, grubby, soiled, sooty.
OPPOSITE clean.

grin *verb*
beam, smile, smirk.

grind *verb*
1 *She ground the pepper.* crush, granulate, mill, pound, pulverise.
2 *a tool for grinding metal.* file, polish, sharpen, smooth, whet.
3 *He grinds his teeth.* gnash, grate.

grip *verb*
1 *She gripped his arm.* clasp, clutch, grab, grasp, hang on to, hold, seize, snatch, take hold of.
OPPOSITE let go.
2 *The story gripped him.* captivate, enthral, hold spellbound, rivet.
grip *noun*
1 *He had a powerful grip.* clasp, clutch, grasp, hold.
2 *She has a good grip of her subject.* command, comprehension, grasp, hold, mastery, understanding.

grisly *adjective*
a grisly murder. appalling, dreadful, frightful, ghastly, gory, grim, gruesome, hideous, horrendous, horrible, horrid, macabre, repulsive, shocking, vile.
OPPOSITE pleasant.

gristly *adjective*
gristly meat. leathery, tough.

grit *noun*
1 *She had grit in her eyes.* dirt, dust, sand.
2 *a man of true grit.* backbone, courage, determination, endurance, guts (*informal*), mettle, pluck, spirit, spunk (*informal*).
OPPOSITE cowardice.
grit *verb*
He gritted his teeth. clench, set.

a
b
c
d
e
f
g
h
i
j
k
l
m
n
o
p
q
r
s
t
u
v
w
x
y
z

grizzle verb (informal)
The child grizzled continuously. cry, moan, whimper, whine, whinge (informal); see also COMPLAIN.

groan verb
He groaned in pain. cry, howl, moan, wail.

grog noun (Australian informal)
alcohol, liquor.

groggy adjective
The patient was groggy from the anaesthetic. dazed, dopey (informal), shaky, unsteady, wonky (informal), woozy (informal).

groom noun
the bride and groom. bridegroom, husband.
groom verb
1 He groomed the horse. brush, comb, curry.
2 The cat groomed herself. clean up, preen, spruce up, tidy, wash.
3 He was groomed for the job. prepare, prime, train.

groove noun
a groove in wood. channel, cut, furrow, rut, score, slot.
OPPOSITE ridge.

grope verb
He groped for a match in the dark. feel about, fish, fossick (Australian informal), fumble, rummage, search.

gross adjective
1 He became gross through overeating. enormous, fat, flabby, huge, obese, overweight, rotund.
OPPOSITE emaciated.
2 gross manners. boorish, coarse, crass, crude, rude, unrefined, vulgar.
OPPOSITE refined.
3 gross negligence. blatant, clear, flagrant, obvious, outrageous.
4 gross income. entire, pre-tax, total, whole.
OPPOSITE net.
5 (informal) The food was gross. see DISGUSTING.

grotesque adjective
a grotesque face. absurd, bizarre, deformed, distorted, fantastic, freakish, hideous, misshapen, monstrous, odd, ugly, weird.

grouch noun (informal)
Who invited that old grouch? crosspatch, grumbler, grump (informal), killjoy, malcontent, misery (informal), sourpuss (informal), wet blanket, whinger (informal).

grouchy adjective
a grouchy person. bad-tempered, cantankerous, crabby, cranky, cross, crotchety, crusty, discontented, disgruntled, grumpy, irritable, sullen, surly, testy, tetchy.

ground noun
1 She kept her feet on the ground. earth, land.
2 Plant the rose in the ground. dirt, earth, loam, soil.
3 a sports ground. arena, field, oval, pitch, stadium.
ground verb
1 The ship was grounded in the storm. beach, run aground, shipwreck, strand.
OPPOSITE launch.
2 The children were grounded in the three Rs. drill, educate, instruct, teach, train.
3 The story is grounded on fact. base, establish, found, root.
grounds plural noun
1 the house and grounds. campus, estate, garden(s), lawn(s), surroundings.
2 He has no grounds for complaint. basis, cause, evidence, justification, reason.

groundwork noun
Others had done the groundwork. preparation, spadework.

group noun
1 The specimens were classified into four groups. category, class, classification, division, family, genus, kind, order, phylum, race, sort, species, type, variety.
2 a group of people, animals, things, etc. alliance, assembly, association, assortment, band, batch, battery, bevy, body, bracket, brigade, brood, bunch, circle, clan, clique, club, cluster, collection, colony, combination, community, company, congregation, consortium, constellation (of stars), contingent, convoy, corps, crew, crop, crowd, drove, ensemble, faction,

federation, fleet, flock, flotilla, force, gaggle (*of geese*), galaxy (*of stars*), gang, gathering, herd, horde, host, league, legion, litter, lot, mass, mob, movement, multitude, organisation, pack, panel, party, pod (*of seals, dolphins, or whales*), pride (*of lions*), rabble, ring, school (*of fish, dolphins, or whales*), series, set, shoal (*of fish*), society, squad, subset, swarm (*of bees*), syndicate, team, throng, tribe, troop, troupe (*of actors*), union.

group *verb*
1 *They were grouped by age.* arrange, class, classify, organise, sort.
2 *The new children grouped together.* associate, band, cluster, collect, congregate, gather.
OPPOSITE disperse.

grove *noun*
an olive grove. orchard, plantation.

grovel *verb*
He was not prepared to grovel to the boss. crawl (*informal*), kowtow, suck up (*informal*), toady.

grow *verb*
1 *The child grew quickly.* become bigger, become taller, develop, fill out, grow up, mature, shoot up.
OPPOSITE shrink.
2 *The line of people grew.* become longer, extend, lengthen.
OPPOSITE shorten.
3 *The business has grown.* boom, build up, develop, enlarge, evolve, expand, flourish, increase, mushroom, progress, prosper, snowball, spread, thrive.
OPPOSITE decline.
4 *The plants won't grow without water.* flourish, germinate, live, shoot, spring up, sprout, survive, thrive.
OPPOSITE die.
5 *He grew resentful.* become, get, turn.
6 *She grows vegetables.* cultivate, produce, raise.

growl *verb*
The dog growled. snarl.

grown-up *adjective*
grown-up behaviour. adult, mature.
OPPOSITE immature.
grown-up *noun*
adult, oldie (*informal*).
OPPOSITE child.

growth *noun*
1 *growth in numbers.* enlargement, expansion, increase, proliferation.
OPPOSITE decrease.
2 *strong economic growth.* advancement, development, improvement, progress.
OPPOSITE decline.
3 *The doctor removed the growth.* cancer, cyst, lump, polyp, tumour.

grub *noun*
caterpillar, larva, maggot.

grubby *adjective*
grubby feet. blackened, dirty, dusty, filthy, grimy, soiled.
OPPOSITE clean.

grudge *noun*
She bore no grudges. grievance, hard feelings, ill will, resentment.
hold a grudge against have a derry on (*Australian informal*), have a down on (*informal*), have a set on (*Australian informal*).

grudging *adjective*
grudging in his praise. envious, jealous, reluctant, resentful, sparing.
OPPOSITE generous.

gruelling *adjective*
a gruelling task. arduous, demanding, exhausting, hard, laborious, strenuous, tiring, tough.
OPPOSITE easy.

gruesome *adjective*
the gruesome details of the murder. ghastly, gory, grisly, hideous, horrible, macabre, repulsive, revolting, shocking, sickening.
OPPOSITE pleasant.

gruff *adjective*
1 *a gruff voice.* gravelly, harsh, hoarse, husky, rough, throaty.
2 *a gruff reply. a gruff manner.* abrupt, bad-tempered, crabby, crusty, curt, grouchy (*informal*), grumpy, sullen, surly, unfriendly.
OPPOSITE friendly.

grumble *verb*
She grumbled about everything. beef (*slang*), bitch (*informal*), complain, find fault with, gripe (*informal*), grizzle (*informal*), groan, moan, object, protest, whine, whinge (*informal*).

a
b
c
d
e
f
g
h
i
j
k
l
m
n
o
p
q
r
s
t
u
v
w
x
y
z

grumpy *adjective*
He was feeling tired and grumpy. bad-tempered, cantankerous, crabby, cranky, cross, crotchety, grouchy, irritable, peevish, petulant, sullen, surly, testy, tetchy.

grunt *verb*
The pig grunted. snort.

guarantee *noun*
1 *She gave her guarantee that it would be finished.* assurance, pledge, promise, word.
2 *a 12-month guarantee on all parts.* warranty.

guarantee *verb*
1 *Your privacy is guaranteed.* ensure, protect, secure.
2 *He guaranteed that they were genuine.* certify, pledge, promise, swear, vow.

guard *verb*
1 *The cat guarded her kittens.* defend, look after, mind, preserve, protect, safeguard, shelter, shield, watch over.
2 *He guarded the prisoner.* keep an eye on, supervise, watch over.

guard *noun*
1 *an armed guard.* bodyguard, chaperone, escort, garrison, guardian, guardsman, lookout, minder, patrol, security officer, sentinel, sentry, warder, watchman.
2 *a mouth guard.* protector, screen, shield.
off (one's) guard napping, unprepared, unready.
on (one's) guard alert, careful, on the watch, ready, vigilant, wary, watchful.
stand guard guard, keep a lookout, keep watch, patrol.

guardian *noun*
the guardian of their faith. custodian, defender, keeper, preserver, protector, trustee, warden, watchdog.

guardianship *noun*
care, charge, custody, keeping, protection.

guess *verb*
1 *She guessed the answer.* estimate, have a stab at (*informal*).
OPPOSITE know.

2 *I guess he'll be back.* assume, expect, imagine, predict, reckon, speculate, suppose, surmise, suspect, think.

guess *noun*
Her guess turned out to be correct. assumption, conjecture, estimate, guesstimate (*informal*), hunch, hypothesis, prediction, shot in the dark, supposition, surmise, suspicion, theory.

guest *noun*
1 *a house guest.* billet, caller, company, visitor.
OPPOSITE host, hostess.
2 *a hotel guest.* patron, resident, visitor.
guest house hostel, hotel, pension.

guidance *noun*
guidance on careers. advice, counselling, direction, help, information, instruction.

guide *noun*
1 *a tour guide.* conductor, director, escort, leader, pilot, usher.
2 *a friend and guide.* adviser, counsellor, guru, mentor, teacher.

guide *verb*
She guided them through the town. conduct, direct, escort, lead, manoeuvre, navigate, pilot, show the way, steer, usher.

guidebook *noun*
a restaurant guidebook. directory, guide, handbook, manual.

guideline *noun*
instruction, principle, regulation, requirement, rule, standard.

guild *noun*
the pharmacists' guild. association, federation, league, organisation, society, union.

guilt *noun*
1 *They could not establish his guilt.* blame, fault, responsibility.
OPPOSITE innocence.
2 *She was overcome by feelings of guilt.* disgrace, remorse, shame.

guilty *adjective*
1 *He was proven guilty.* culpable, responsible.
OPPOSITE innocent.

2 *a guilty look.* ashamed, hangdog, remorseful, shamefaced, sheepish.
OPPOSITE innocent.

gulf *noun*
1 *ships in the gulf.* bay, cove, inlet.
2 *a gulf between people.* chasm, gap, rift.

gullet *noun*
The food was stuck in his gullet.
oesophagus, throat.

gullible *adjective*
With experience she became less gullible.
believing, green, naive, trusting,
unsuspecting.
OPPOSITE suspicious.

gully *noun*
1 *a stormwater gully.* channel, ditch,
drain, gutter.
2 *(Australian) The car rolled down the
gully.* gorge, ravine, valley.

gulp *verb*
He gulped his food greedily. bolt, devour,
gobble, guzzle, wolf.
gulp *noun*
She took a big gulp. mouthful, swallow,
swig (*informal*).

gum *noun*
The pictures are stuck with gum. adhesive,
glue, paste.
gum *verb*
He gummed the pieces together. glue,
paste, stick.

gun *noun*
arm, firearm; [*various guns*] airgun,
automatic, blunderbuss, cannon,
carbine, handgun, machine-gun,
mortar, musket, pistol, revolver, rifle,
semi-automatic, shotgun, sub-machine-
gun.

gunman *noun*
assassin, marksman, sniper.

gurgle *noun*
a gurgle of water in the pipe. babble,
burble.

guru *noun*
They respected him as their guru. leader,
master, mentor, sage, teacher.

gush *verb*
1 *Water gushed from the hose.* flow, pour,
run, rush, spout, spurt, stream, surge.
OPPOSITE trickle.
2 *She gushed about her new friend.* babble
on, get carried away (*informal*), go
overboard (*informal*), rave (*informal*).
gush *noun*
a gush of water. cascade, flood, jet,
outpouring, rush, spurt, stream, torrent.

gust *noun*
a gust of wind. blast, rush, squall.

gusty *adjective*
a gusty day. blowy, blustery, squally,
stormy, windy.
OPPOSITE calm.

gut *noun*
a pain in the gut. abdomen, bowel, colon,
insides (*informal*), intestine.
gut *adjective*
a gut reaction. instinctive, intuitive,
spontaneous, subconscious.
gut *verb*
The building was gutted by fire. destroy,
devastate, ravage.
guts *plural noun* (*informal*)
It took guts to say that. courage,
determination, grit (*informal*), nerve,
pluck, spunk (*informal*).

gutter *noun*
Water runs off in the gutters. channel,
ditch, drain, sewer, trough.

guy *noun* (*informal*)
The party was only for guys. bloke
(*informal*), boy, chap (*informal*), fellow
(*informal*), gentleman, lad, male, man.

guzzle *verb*
They guzzled their dinner. bolt, devour,
gobble, gulp, scoff (*informal*), wolf.

gymnastics *plural noun*
acrobatics, callisthenics.

gypsy *noun*
He sold all his possessions and joined the
gypsies. nomad, traveller, vagabond,
wanderer.

a
b
c
d
e
f
g
h
i
j
k
l
m
n
o
p
q
r
s
t
u
v
w
x
y
z

Hh

habit *noun*
1 *good study habits.* custom, practice, routine, way.
2 *a drug habit.* addiction, dependence.

habitat *noun*
the koala's native habitat. domain, environment, home, setting, surroundings, territory.

habitual *adjective*
1 *habitual lying.* constant, continual, frequent, persistent, regular, repeated, routine, standard, usual.
OPPOSITE occasional.
2 *waiting in his habitual place.* accustomed, customary, established, familiar, fixed, normal, regular, set, traditional, usual.
3 *a habitual smoker.* addicted, chronic, confirmed, hardened, inveterate.
OPPOSITE occasional.

hack *verb*
He hacked the shrub to pieces. chop, cut, hew, mutilate, slash.

hag *noun*
She was an old hag. bag (*slang*), battleaxe (*informal*), crone, witch.

haggard *adjective*
She looked haggard after her illness. careworn, drawn, exhausted, gaunt, worn.
OPPOSITE radiant.

haggle *verb*
They haggled over the price. argue, bargain, dispute, negotiate, quarrel, wrangle.

hail *verb*
She hailed a taxi. call to, flag down, signal to, wave to.

hair *noun*
1 *Each hair is extremely fine.* bristle, filament, strand.
2 *He admired her hair.* curls, locks, ringlets, tresses.

3 *facial hair.* beard, bristles, fuzz, moustache, sideburns, whiskers.
4 *an animal's hair.* coat, down, fleece, fur, mane, pelt, wool.

hairdresser *noun*
barber, haircutter, hair stylist.

hair-raising *adjective*
frightening, hairy (*slang*), nerve-racking, scary, spine-chilling, terrifying.

hairy *adjective*
1 *hairy skin.* bristly, bushy, downy, fleecy, furry, fuzzy, hirsute, shaggy, stubbly, unshaven, whiskery, woolly.
OPPOSITE bald, hairless.
2 (*slang*) *The drive was rather hairy.* dangerous, dicey (*slang*), frightening, hair-raising, nerve-racking, scary, terrifying.

half-hearted *adjective*
a half-hearted attempt. half-hearted support. apathetic, feeble, indifferent, lackadaisical, lukewarm, unenthusiastic.
OPPOSITE hearty, wholehearted.

halfway *adjective*
They have reached the halfway point. intermediate, mid, middle, midway.

hall *noun*
1 *The hall was packed for the concert.* assembly hall, auditorium, concert hall, theatre.
2 *They left their coats in the hall.* corridor, entrance hall, foyer, lobby, passage, vestibule.

hallucination *noun*
This drug produces hallucinations. apparition, dream, fantasy, illusion, mirage, nightmare, vision.

halt *noun*
a halt in proceedings. break, close, delay, intermission, interruption, pause, recess, shut-down, standstill, stop, stoppage, suspension, termination.

halt *verb*
1 *The cars must halt at a red light.* come to a stop, pull up, stop, wait.
OPPOSITE proceed, start.
2 *They have halted the spread of the disease.* arrest, block, check, stop.

halve *verb*
1 *Draw a line which halves the square.* bisect.
2 *The price was halved.* cut by half, reduce to half.
OPPOSITE double.

hammer *verb*
1 *He hammered the nails back in.* bang, drive, hit, knock, nail, tack.
2 *She hammered the table.* bash, batter, beat, hit, knock, pound, strike, thump.
hammer out *They hammered out a plan.* devise, thrash out, work out.

hamper *verb*
The splint hampered his movements. curb, hinder, impede, inhibit, limit, obstruct, restrict.
OPPOSITE assist.

hand *noun*
1 *a clean pair of hands.* fist, mitt (*slang*), palm.
2 *He was employed as a factory hand.* assistant, employee, labourer, worker.
3 (*informal*) *They gave her a big hand.* applause, clap, ovation.
hand *verb*
She handed him his hat. give, pass.
by hand *She whipped the cream by hand.* manually.
hand in *She handed in her essay.* deliver, give, present, submit.
hand out *He handed out the lollies.* dish out (*informal*), dispense, distribute, dole out, give out, share out.
hand over
1 *He handed over the money.* donate, give, pass, pay, surrender.
2 *He was handed over to the authorities.* deliver, present, turn over.
on hand *a helper on hand.* available, handy, present.

handbag *noun*
ladies' handbags. bag, purse (*American*).

handbook *noun*
a motorist's handbook. guidebook, manual.

handcuffs *plural noun*
manacles, shackles.

handful *noun*
A handful of students remained. few, remnant, sprinkling.
OPPOSITE crowd.

handicap *noun*
1 *a physical handicap.* disability, disadvantage, impairment.
2 *Lack of experience was a handicap.* barrier, disadvantage, drawback, hindrance, impediment, limitation, obstacle, stumbling block.
OPPOSITE advantage.
handicap *verb*
Lack of light handicapped the search party. disadvantage, hamper, hinder, impede, limit, restrict.
OPPOSITE help.

handle *noun*
held by the handle. grip, haft, hilt, knob, shaft.
handle *verb*
1 *Please do not handle the fruit.* feel, finger, pick up, poke, touch.
2 *He can handle the car well.* control, drive, manoeuvre, operate, steer.
3 *She can handle any problem.* cope with, deal with, look after, manage, tackle, take care of.

handout *noun*
1 *He survives on handouts.* donation, freebie (*informal*), gift.
2 *She never reads the handouts.* brochure, bulletin, circular, leaflet, pamphlet.

handsome *adjective*
1 *a handsome man.* attractive, fine-looking, good-looking.
OPPOSITE ugly.
2 *a handsome woman.* attractive, beautiful, elegant, good-looking, smart.
3 *a handsome amount of money.* ample, considerable, generous, large, lavish, liberal, sizeable.
OPPOSITE stingy.

handwriting *noun*
calligraphy, hand, scrawl, scribble, script, writing.

a
b
c
d
e
f
g
h
i
j
k
l
m
n
o
p
q
r
s
t
u
v
w
x
y
z

handy *adjective*
1 *a handy gadget.* convenient, helpful, practical, useful.
OPPOSITE useless.
2 *The pens are handy by the telephone.* accessible, at hand, available, convenient, on hand.
OPPOSITE inaccessible.
3 *He is handy with cars.* adept, capable, competent, deft, expert, good, proficient, skilful.
OPPOSITE inept.

hang *verb*
1 *She hung the lights in the tree.* dangle, drape, string, suspend.
2 *The material hangs well.* drape, fall.
3 *She hung her head in shame.* bend, bow, droop, drop, lower.
4 *The smoke is hanging over the city.* hover, linger, remain, rest, stay.
OPPOSITE disperse.
get the hang of *(informal)*
He has finally got the hang of it. come to grips with, comprehend, figure out, get the knack of, grasp, master, understand.
hang around *They were still hanging around when we left.* hang about, linger, loiter, lurk, remain, stay, wait.
OPPOSITE leave.
hang on *(informal) He asked me to hang on.* hold on, hold the line, wait.
hang on to
1 *The child hung on to my hand.* cling to, clutch, grip, hold on to.
2 *He hung on to his job.* hold on to, keep, remain in, retain.
OPPOSITE lose.
hang out *(informal) He found somewhere else to hang out.* dwell, live, reside.

hang-up *noun (informal)*
He has a hang-up about eating in public. difficulty, inhibition, mental block, phobia, problem, thing *(informal)*.

haphazard *adjective*
She works in a haphazard fashion. arbitrary, chaotic, disorganised, hit-or-miss, random, slapdash, unplanned, unsystematic.
OPPOSITE methodical, systematic.

happen *verb*
An accident is bound to happen. arise, come about, come to pass, crop up, eventuate, occur, result, take place.

happen to *Whatever will happen to her?* become of, befall *(formal)*.

happening *noun*
strange happenings. episode, event, incident, occasion, occurrence, proceeding.

happiness *noun*
bliss, cheerfulness, contentment, delight, ecstasy, elation, enjoyment, euphoria, exhilaration, exuberance, gladness, glee, joy, jubilation, light-heartedness, merriment, mirth, pleasure, rapture, satisfaction.
OPPOSITE sadness.

happy *adjective*
1 *She was happy when the exams were over.* blissful, blithe, cheerful, contented, delighted, ecstatic, elated, enraptured, euphoric, exhilarated, glad, gleeful, gratified, joyful, joyous, jubilant, light-hearted, merry, overjoyed, pleased, rapturous, satisfied, thrilled.
OPPOSITE sad.
2 *a happy coincidence.* favourable, fortunate, lucky, opportune, timely.
OPPOSITE unfortunate.
3 *I am happy to help.* delighted, eager, glad, keen, pleased, willing.
OPPOSITE reluctant.

happy-go-lucky *adjective*
see CAREFREE.

harass *verb*
He'll work better if you stop harassing him. annoy, badger, bother, bug *(informal)*, disturb, hassle *(informal)*, hound, pester, plague, stand over *(Australian)*, trouble, worry.

harbour *noun*
The harbour was filled with ships. anchorage, dock, haven, marina, port, shelter.
harbour *verb*
He harboured the escapee. conceal, hide, house, protect, shelter, shield.

hard *adjective*
1 *hard cardboard.* dense, firm, inflexible, rigid, solid, stiff, tough.
OPPOSITE soft.
2 *hard facts.* definite, indisputable, irrefutable, solid, true.
OPPOSITE disputable.

3 *a hard job.* arduous, back-breaking, demanding, difficult, exacting, gruelling, heavy, laborious, onerous, strenuous, taxing, tiring, tough.
OPPOSITE easy.

4 *a hard question.* awkward, baffling, complex, complicated, confusing, cryptic, difficult, puzzling, tricky.
OPPOSITE easy, simple.

5 *She has gone through hard times.* bad, difficult, grim, harsh, oppressive, painful, rough, severe, tough, unbearable, unpleasant.
OPPOSITE pleasant.

6 *take a hard line.* severe, stern, strict, unbending, uncompromising.
OPPOSITE lenient.

7 *a hard worker.* conscientious, diligent, earnest, energetic, industrious, painstaking, unflagging, untiring.
OPPOSITE lazy.

8 *a hard voice.* grating, harsh, sharp, shrill, unpleasant.
OPPOSITE gentle, pleasant.

hard *adverb*
1 *He worked hard.* conscientiously, diligently, doggedly, energetically, industriously, strenuously, untiringly.
OPPOSITE lazily.

2 *She pressed the lid down hard.* firmly, forcefully, forcibly, powerfully, strongly, violently.
OPPOSITE gently, lightly.

3 *It's raining hard.* heavily, intensely.
OPPOSITE lightly.

hard up (*informal*)
too hard up to give a donation. broke (*informal*), penniless, poor, poverty-stricken, skint (*informal*).
OPPOSITE well off.

harden *verb*
The mixture hardened in the sun. firm, set, solidify, stiffen, strengthen, toughen.
OPPOSITE soften.

hard-hearted *adjective*
callous, cold, cruel, hard, harsh, heartless, indifferent, inhuman, insensitive, mean, merciless, pitiless, remorseless, ruthless, stony-hearted, uncaring, unfeeling, unforgiving, unkind, unrepentant, unsympathetic.
OPPOSITE compassionate.

hardly *adverb*
There is hardly any petrol left. barely, scarcely.

hardship *noun*
The family suffered severe financial hardship. adversity, affliction, difficulty, distress, misery, misfortune, need, poverty, strain, suffering, tribulation, woe.
OPPOSITE ease.

hardware *noun*
equipment, implements, instruments, ironmongery, machinery, tools.

hard-wearing *adjective*
hard-wearing shoes. durable, heavy-duty, long-lasting, strong, tough.
OPPOSITE flimsy.

hardy *adjective*
a hardy plant. drought-resistant, frost-resistant, robust, strong, sturdy, tough, vigorous.
OPPOSITE tender.

hare *noun*
buck (*male*), doe (*female*), leveret (*young*).

hark *verb*
Hark! the dogs are barking. listen.
hark back *He keeps harking back to his favourite subject.* go back, return, revert.

harm *noun*
1 *grievous bodily harm.* hurt, injury, pain, suffering.
2 *Clearing has caused a great deal of harm to the land.* damage, destruction, detriment, havoc.
OPPOSITE benefit, good.

harm *verb*
1 *Do not harm the cat.* abuse, hurt, ill-treat, injure, maltreat, mistreat, molest, wound.
2 *Smoking can harm your health.* damage, destroy, impair, injure, ruin, spoil, undermine.
OPPOSITE benefit, improve.

harmful *adjective*
harmful practices. harmful chemicals. adverse, bad, damaging, dangerous, destructive, detrimental, injurious, ruinous, unhealthy.
OPPOSITE beneficial, harmless.

a
b
c
d
e
f
g
h
i
j
k
l
m
n
o
p
q
r
s
t
u
v
w
x
y
z

harmless *adjective*
1 *a harmless drug.* non-toxic, safe.
OPPOSITE dangerous, harmful.
2 *a bit of harmless fun.* gentle, innocent,
innocuous, inoffensive, mild.

harmonious *adjective*
1 *harmonious sounds.* euphonious,
melodious, musical, sweet, tuneful.
OPPOSITE cacophonous, discordant.
2 *a harmonious relationship.* amicable,
compatible, congenial, friendly,
pleasant.
OPPOSITE incompatible.

harmony *noun*
a state of harmony among the people.
accord, agreement, compatibility,
concord, friendliness, peace, unanimity,
unity.
OPPOSITE conflict.

harness *verb*
1 *He harnessed the horse.* bridle, yoke.
2 *They are able to harness the energy of the
waterfall.* capture, control, exploit, use.

harsh *adjective*
1 *a harsh voice.* cacophonous,
discordant, grating, gruff, jarring,
rasping, raucous, rough, shrill, stern,
strident.
OPPOSITE gentle.
2 *a harsh light.* bright, brilliant, dazzling,
glaring.
OPPOSITE soft.
3 *a harsh environment.* austere, hard,
inhospitable, rough, severe, stark,
tough, unpleasant.
OPPOSITE mild, pleasant.
4 *harsh words. harsh treatment.*
aggressive, bitter, brutal, cruel, cutting,
hard, hostile, hurtful, malicious, mean,
merciless, nasty, severe, spiteful, stern,
unfeeling, unfriendly, unkind,
unsympathetic, vicious, vindictive.
OPPOSITE gentle, lenient.

harvest *noun*
We expect a good tomato harvest this year.
crop, produce, yield.
harvest *verb*
The crops have all been harvested. collect,
garner, gather, glean, pick, reap.
OPPOSITE plant, sow.

hash *noun*
make a hash of (*informal*)
botch, bungle, make a mess of, mess up,
ruin, spoil.

hassle *noun* (*informal*)
1 *She had no hassles exchanging the
present.* bother, difficulty, problem,
trouble, worry.
2 *They're always having hassles about the
rent money.* argument, disagreement,
fight, quarrel, squabble, wrangle.
hassle *verb* (*informal*)
*He keeps on hassling her when she is trying
to work.* annoy, badger, bother, bug
(*informal*), harass, hound, nag, pester,
worry.

hasty *adjective*
1 *a hasty retreat.* fast, hurried, prompt,
quick, rapid, speedy, sudden, swift.
OPPOSITE slow.
2 *a hasty decision.* careless, headlong,
hurried, impetuous, impulsive, quick,
rash, rushed, snap.
OPPOSITE considered.

hat *noun*
[*kinds of hat*] Akubra (*trade mark*),
beanie, bearskin, beret, boater, bonnet,
bowler hat, busby, cabbage-tree hat
(*Australian*), cap, deerstalker, fez,
panama, slouch hat, sombrero,
sou'wester, stetson, sunhat, tam
o'shanter, top hat; see also HEADGEAR.

hatch[1] *noun*
He passed the boxes through the hatch.
manhole, opening.

hatch[2] *verb*
1 *hatch eggs.* brood, incubate.
2 *They have hatched a money-making
scheme.* concoct, cook up (*informal*),
design, devise, dream up, invent, think
up.

hatchet *noun*
axe, mogo (*Australian*), tomahawk.

hate *noun*
1 *He was filled with hate.* see HATRED.
2 (*informal*) *a pet hate.* aversion, dislike.
OPPOSITE love.
hate *verb*
1 *hate a person or a thing.* abhor, despise,
detest, dislike, loathe.
OPPOSITE love.

2 (*informal*) *She hated to wake the baby.* be reluctant, be unwilling, dislike.
OPPOSITE like.

hateful *adjective*
a hateful person. a hateful job. abhorrent, abominable, atrocious, contemptible, despicable, detestable, disgusting, horrid, loathsome, nasty, obnoxious, odious, repugnant, repulsive, revolting, vile.
OPPOSITE lovable, pleasant.

hatred *noun*
abhorrence, animosity, antagonism, antipathy, aversion, bitterness, contempt, detestation, disgust, dislike, enmity, hate, hostility, loathing, malevolence, repugnance, resentment, revulsion.
OPPOSITE affection, love.

haughty *adjective*
He has a haughty manner. arrogant, conceited, condescending, contemptuous, disdainful, high and mighty, hoity-toity, patronising, proud, scornful, self-important, snobbish, snooty (*informal*), stuck-up (*informal*), supercilious, superior.
OPPOSITE humble.

haul *verb*
1 *He was hauled out of the wreckage.* drag, draw, heave, hoick (*slang*), pull, tug, wrench, yank (*informal*).
2 *The truck was hauling a heavy load.* carry, cart, convey, lug, tow, transport.

haunt *verb*
1 *She haunts the shop.* frequent, hang around, loiter around, patronise.
2 *The memory haunts me.* linger with, obsess, plague, prey on, stay with.
haunt *noun*
one of their favourite haunts. hang-out (*informal*), meeting-place, resort, retreat, stamping ground (*informal*).

have *verb*
1 *They have two cars.* keep, own, possess.
2 *The library has many rare books.* contain, hold, include.
3 *She's had a shock.* endure, experience, go through, suffer, undergo.
4 *They had a conversation.* carry on, conduct, engage in.

5 *I won't have it any longer.* accept, allow, permit, put up with, stand for (*informal*), take, tolerate.
6 *She asked me to have a biscuit.* eat, take.
have on (*informal*)
You're having me on! fool, hoax, kid (*informal*), pull someone's leg, tease.
have to *We have to go.* be forced to, be obliged to, must, need to.

haven *noun*
His home was a haven from his fans. asylum, hide-out, refuge, retreat, sanctuary, shelter; see also HARBOUR.

haversack *noun*
backpack, knapsack, pack, rucksack, satchel.

havoc *noun*
The floods caused widespread havoc. chaos, confusion, destruction, devastation, disorder, ruin, upheaval.

hazard *noun*
Beware of unseen hazards. danger, peril, pitfall, risk, threat.

hazardous *adjective*
a hazardous undertaking. chancy, dangerous, dicey (*slang*), hairy (*slang*), perilous, precarious, risky, tricky, uncertain.
OPPOSITE safe.

haze *noun*
We couldn't see the view through the haze. cloud, fog, mist, smog.

hazy *adjective*
1 *a hazy day.* foggy, misty, smoggy.
OPPOSITE clear.
2 *a hazy idea.* blurred, confused, faint, fuzzy, imprecise, indefinite, indistinct, sketchy, unclear, vague.
OPPOSITE precise.

head *noun*
1 *He fell and hit his head.* cranium, skull.
2 *Use your head!* brain, intellect, intelligence, loaf (*slang*), mind, nut (*informal*).
3 *It costs $50 per head.* capita, person.
4 *the head of the line.* front, top.
OPPOSITE end.
5 *the head of the river.* beginning, origin, source.
OPPOSITE mouth.

a
b
c
d
e
f
g
h
i
j
k
l
m
n
o
p
q
r
s
t
u
v
w
x
y
z

6 *the head of the organisation.* boss, captain, chairman, chief, commander, director, leader, manager, superintendent, supervisor.
OPPOSITE subordinate.
7 *The school has a new head.* headmaster, headmistress, head teacher, principal.
8 *heads of countries. heads of governments.* emperor, governor, king, leader, monarch, premier, president, prime minister, queen, ruler, sovereign.
9 *Matters have come to a head.* climax, crisis.

head *verb*
1 *He heads the organisation.* be in charge of, command, control, direct, govern, lead, manage, rule, superintend, supervise.
2 *She headed the procession.* be at the front of, begin, lead, start.
3 *They headed home.* aim for, go, make for, proceed, set off for, start for, turn for.

head off
1 *Let's head them off.* block, cut off, divert, intercept, turn aside.
2 *They headed off a disaster.* avert, fend off, forestall, prevent, ward off.

headgear *noun*
[*kinds of headgear*] balaclava, cap, crown, hat, headdress, helmet, hood, kerchief, scarf, skullcap, snood, tiara, turban, veil, wimple; see also HAT.

heading *noun*
caption, headline, title.

headland *noun*
cape, head, promontory.

headline *noun*
caption, heading, title.

headlong *adverb*
1 *They ran headlong into one another.* head first, head-on.
2 *He rushed headlong into the decision.* hastily, impetuously, impulsively, rashly, recklessly.

headmaster, headmistress *noun*
head, head teacher, principal.

headquarters *plural noun*
base, central office, depot, head office.

headstrong *adjective*
a headstrong child. determined, intractable, obstinate, pigheaded, self-willed, strong-willed, stubborn, uncontrollable, wilful.
OPPOSITE docile, tractable.

heal *verb*
1 *The wound has healed.* knit, mend.
2 *The doctor healed the sick people.* cure, restore, treat.

health *noun*
1 *in sickness and in health.* fitness, healthiness, robustness, vitality, well-being.
OPPOSITE sickness.
2 *in good health. in bad health.* condition, fettle, form, shape, state.

healthy *adjective*
1 *a healthy person.* fit, hale, hearty, robust, strapping, well.
OPPOSITE sick, sickly.
2 *a healthy climate.* beneficial, health-giving, invigorating, salubrious, wholesome.
OPPOSITE unhealthy.
3 *a healthy economy.* flourishing, sound, strong, thriving.
OPPOSITE unsound.

heap *noun*
A heap of rubbish lay on the ground. bundle, mass, mound, mountain, pile, stack.

heap *verb*
1 *We heaped the leaves under the trees.* accumulate, collect, gather, pile, stack.
OPPOSITE scatter.
2 *She heaped his plate with food.* fill, load, pile.
3 *They heaped praise upon him.* lavish, pour, shower.

heaps *plural noun* (*informal*)
There's heaps of food. loads (*informal*), lots (*informal*), masses, mountains, oodles (*informal*), piles (*informal*), plenty, stacks (*informal*), tons (*informal*), whips (*Australian informal*).
OPPOSITE little.

hear *verb*
1 *We heard their conversation.* catch, listen to, overhear, pick up.
2 *I heard about it in the paper.* discover, find out, gather, learn, read.

hearing *noun*
1 *in her hearing.* earshot, presence.
2 *an official hearing in the court.* inquiry, investigation, trial.

hearsay *noun*
The evidence is only hearsay. gossip, rumour, tittle-tattle.
OPPOSITE fact.

heart *noun*
1 *a healthy heart.* ticker (*informal*).
2 *That was cruel: have you no heart?* compassion, consideration, emotions, feelings, humanity, love, sympathy, tenderness.
3 *He was losing heart.* courage, determination, enthusiasm, guts (*informal*), nerve, pluck, spirit, spunk (*informal*).
4 *the heart of the problem.* core, crux, essence, nitty-gritty (*informal*), nub.
5 *the heart of the city.* centre, hub, middle, nucleus.
OPPOSITE outskirts.
by heart *learn by heart.* by memory, by rote, parrot-fashion.

heartbroken *adjective*
see BROKEN-HEARTED.

hearten *verb*
She was heartened by the news. cheer, comfort, encourage, please.
OPPOSITE dishearten.

hearth *noun*
fireplace, fireside.

heartless *adjective*
a heartless person. callous, cold, cruel, hard-hearted, harsh, merciless, pitiless, ruthless, unfeeling, unkind, unsympathetic.
OPPOSITE kind.

heart-warming *adjective*
a heart-warming story. cheering, encouraging, heartening, inspiring, pleasing, touching.
OPPOSITE disheartening.

hearty *adjective*
1 *hearty applause. a hearty welcome.* enthusiastic, exuberant, heartfelt, lively, sincere, vigorous, warm, wholehearted.
OPPOSITE half-hearted.

2 *a hale and hearty eighty-year-old.* energetic, hardy, healthy, robust, sprightly, spry, strong, vigorous.
OPPOSITE frail.
3 *a hearty meal.* big, large, solid.
OPPOSITE skimpy.

heat *noun*
1 *A thermometer measures heat.* hotness, temperature, warmth.
2 *He won his heat.* preliminary, round.
heat *verb*
She heated the pie. reheat, warm up.
OPPOSITE cool down.

heated *adjective*
a heated argument. angry, emotional, excited, fervent, fierce, passionate, stormy, tense, vehement, violent.
OPPOSITE calm.

heathen *noun*
infidel, non-believer, pagan, unbeliever.

heave *verb*
1 *He heaved the case on to the platform.* drag, draw, haul, hoick (*slang*), hoist, lift, pull, raise, yank (*informal*).
2 *She heaved a sigh.* emit, let out, utter.
3 *He heaved a rock at it.* cast, chuck (*informal*), fling, hurl, pitch, sling, throw, toss.

heaven *noun*
1 *Heaven is the abode of God.* Elysium, paradise.
OPPOSITE hell.
2 *A dip in the pool is heaven on a hot day.* bliss, delight, ecstasy, happiness, joy, paradise.
OPPOSITE hell.
the heavens sky.

heavenly *adjective*
1 *heavenly creatures.* angelic, celestial, divine.
OPPOSITE earthly.
2 (*informal*) *The music was heavenly.* beautiful, blissful, delightful, divine (*informal*), exquisite, glorious, sublime, wonderful.

heavy *adjective*
1 *a heavy parcel.* bulky, cumbersome, hefty, massive, ponderous, unwieldy, weighty.
OPPOSITE light.

a
b
c
d
e
f
g
h
i
j
k
l
m
n
o
p
q
r
s
t
u
v
w
x
y
z

2 *a heavy man.* big, burly, fat, hefty, hulking, large, solid, stocky, stout, sturdy, thickset.
OPPOSITE lean.
3 *heavy rain.* copious, hard, pouring, profuse, torrential.
OPPOSITE light.
4 *a heavy drinker.* excessive, immoderate, intemperate, unrestrained.
OPPOSITE moderate.
5 *heavy work.* arduous, exhausting, hard, laborious, onerous, strenuous, tiring.
OPPOSITE light.
6 *Their army suffered heavy losses.* considerable, extensive, severe, substantial.
OPPOSITE small.
7 *heavy fighting.* concentrated, intense, relentless, severe, unrelenting.
OPPOSITE sporadic.
8 *heavy mist.* dense, thick.
OPPOSITE fine.
9 *a heavy heart.* depressed, downcast, forlorn, gloomy, melancholy, miserable, sad, sorrowful, unhappy.
OPPOSITE happy, light.

heckle *verb*
The demonstrators heckled the speaker. harass, interrupt, jeer at, taunt.

hectic *adjective*
a hectic holiday. active, busy, exciting, frantic, frenzied, lively, wild.
OPPOSITE leisurely.

hedge *noun*
They planted a hedge. hedgerow, screen, windbreak.
hedge *verb*
He keeps hedging on the issue. beat about the bush, dodge, equivocate, play for time, stall.
OPPOSITE commit yourself.

heed *verb*
Heed his advice. bear in mind, listen to, mark, mind, pay attention to, take notice of.
OPPOSITE disregard, ignore.
heed *noun*
He paid no heed. attention, notice, regard, thought.

hefty *adjective*
1 *a hefty footballer.* beefy, big, brawny, burly, muscular, solid, strong, sturdy, tough.
OPPOSITE weedy.
2 *a hefty blow.* forceful, heavy, mighty, powerful, strong, vigorous.
OPPOSITE light.
3 *a hefty amount.* big, huge, large, massive, sizeable, substantial.
OPPOSITE little.

height *noun*
1 *a person's height.* stature, tallness.
2 *The mountain's height is 1500 metres.* altitude, elevation.
3 *the view from the heights.* cliff, highland, hilltop, peak, pinnacle, rise, summit, top.
4 *at the height of her career.* apex, climax, heyday, peak, pinnacle, zenith.
OPPOSITE nadir.

heighten *verb*
Her fears heightened. grow, increase, intensify.
OPPOSITE diminish.

heir, heiress *noun*
beneficiary, inheritor, legatee, successor.

hell *noun*
1 Hades, inferno, underworld.
OPPOSITE heaven.
2 *He made their life hell.* agony, misery, torment, torture.
OPPOSITE bliss.

help *verb*
1 *He helped the criminal to escape. He helped to write the book.* abet, aid, assist, collaborate, cooperate, lend a hand.
2 *They helped the cause.* advance, back, boost, champion, further, promote, serve, stand up for, support.
OPPOSITE hinder.
3 *These pills should help the headache.* alleviate, cure, ease, improve, relieve, remedy, soothe.
OPPOSITE aggravate.
help *noun*
1 *She could not have managed without their help.* advice, aid, assistance, backing, backup, collaboration, contribution, cooperation,

encouragement, succour, support.
OPPOSITE opposition.
2 *Knowledge of another language is a help.*
advantage, asset, benefit, boon.
OPPOSITE handicap.

helper *noun*
abetter, accessory, accomplice, aid, aide,
assistant, collaborator, offsider
(*Australian*), partner, sidekick (*informal*),
supporter.

helpful *adjective*
1 *a helpful person.* accommodating,
considerate, cooperative, kind,
neighbourly, obliging, supportive,
willing.
OPPOSITE unhelpful.
2 *a helpful gadget.* convenient, handy,
practical, useful.
OPPOSITE useless.
3 *helpful criticism.* constructive,
instructive, useful, valuable,
worthwhile.
OPPOSITE useless.

helping *noun*
a second helping of dessert. portion,
serving.

helpless *adjective*
helpless as a baby. dependent, feeble,
incapable, powerless, vulnerable.
OPPOSITE capable.

hem *verb*
hem in *He was hemmed in by reporters.*
beset, box in, encircle, enclose, fence in,
hedge in, restrict, surround.

herald *noun*
The herald proclaimed the king's message.
announcer, messenger, town crier.
herald *verb*
*John the Baptist heralded the coming of
Jesus.* announce, foretell, proclaim,
signal, usher in.

herb *noun*
She uses herbs in cooking. flavouring,
seasoning, spice; [*various herbs*] basil,
chive, coriander, dill, mint, oregano,
parsley, rosemary, sage, tarragon,
thyme.

herd *noun*
1 *a herd of animals.* drove, flock, mob
(*Australian*), pack.

2 *a herd of shoppers.* army, company,
crowd, drove, flock, group, horde, host,
mass, mob, multitude, swarm, throng.
herd *verb*
1 *The people herded together under the
shelter.* assemble, congregate, crowd,
flock, gather, group, huddle, mob,
muster, throng.
2 *He herded the sheep into the yard.* drive,
guide, lead, round up, shepherd.

hereditary *adjective*
a hereditary disease. genetic, inbred,
inherited.
OPPOSITE acquired.

heritage *noun*
proud of his country's heritage.
background, history, inheritance,
legacy, past, tradition.

hermit *noun*
a religious hermit. loner, recluse, solitary.

hero, heroine *noun*
1 *The firefighters were honoured as heroes.*
celebrity, champion, idol, legend
(*informal*), star, superstar.
OPPOSITE coward.
2 *the hero in the film.* goody (*informal*),
protagonist.
OPPOSITE villain.

heroic *adjective*
a heroic act. a heroic person. bold, brave,
chivalrous, courageous, daring,
dauntless, fearless, gallant, intrepid,
lion-hearted, plucky, valiant.
OPPOSITE cowardly.

hero-worship *noun*
idolatry, idolisation.

hesitant *adjective*
1 *Her speech was hesitant.* faltering,
halting, slow, stammering, stuttering.
OPPOSITE fluent.
2 *He was hesitant about interfering.*
diffident, dubious, indecisive, in two
minds, reluctant, uncertain, unsure.
OPPOSITE confident.

hesitate *verb*
He who hesitates is lost. delay, dilly-dally
(*informal*), dither, hang back, hum and
haw, pause, shilly-shally, waver.

a b c d e f g h i j k l m n o p q r s t u v w x y z

hibernate *verb*
The animal hibernates for six months. be dormant, be inactive, sleep.

hidden *adjective*
a hidden meaning. concealed, cryptic, disguised, obscure, secret.
OPPOSITE obvious.

hide *verb*
1 She hid her money. bury, conceal, put away, stash (*informal*).
OPPOSITE display.
2 He hid his true feelings. bottle up, conceal, cover up, disguise, mask, repress, suppress.
OPPOSITE reveal.
3 She hid until they'd gone. conceal yourself, go into hiding, lie low, take cover.

hideous *adjective*
a hideous crime. a hideous picture. abominable, appalling, atrocious, dreadful, frightful, ghastly, grim, grisly, grotesque, gruesome, horrendous, horrible, monstrous, objectionable, odious, repulsive, revolting, shocking, sickening, ugly, unsightly, vile.
OPPOSITE beautiful, pleasant.

hideout *noun* (*informal*)
den, hidey-hole (*informal*), hiding place, lair, refuge.

hiding *noun* (*informal*)
beating, caning, flogging, spanking, thrashing, whipping.

higgledy-piggledy *adjective*
chaotic, confused, disorderly, jumbled, mixed-up, muddled.
OPPOSITE orderly.

high *adjective*
1 a high building. high-rise, lofty, soaring, tall, towering.
OPPOSITE low.
2 a high platform. elevated, raised.
OPPOSITE low.
3 She has a high position in the company. exalted, important, powerful, prominent, senior, top.
OPPOSITE lowly.
4 high quality. best, first, superior, supreme, top.
OPPOSITE inferior, low.

5 high temperatures. above average, extreme, great, intense.
OPPOSITE low.
6 high prices. dear, excessive, exorbitant, expensive, steep (*informal*), stiff (*informal*).
OPPOSITE cheap.
7 a high voice. high-pitched, piercing, sharp, shrill, soprano, treble.
OPPOSITE deep, low.

highlands *plural noun*
heights, hills, mountains, plateau, ranges, tableland.
OPPOSITE lowlands.

highlight *noun*
It was the highlight of the trip. climax, feature, high point, high spot.
highlight *verb*
This case highlighted the problem. accent, accentuate, emphasise, point up, spotlight, stress, underline.
OPPOSITE play down.

highly-strung *adjective*
edgy, excitable, jumpy, nervous, nervy, stressed, tense, touchy, uneasy, uptight (*informal*), volatile.
OPPOSITE calm, placid.

high-spirited *adjective*
boisterous, excited, exhilarated, exuberant, full of beans (*informal*), jolly, lively, merry, vivacious.
OPPOSITE depressed.

highway *noun*
a national highway. expressway, freeway, main road, motorway, tollway.

highwayman *noun*
Travellers feared being held up by a highwayman. bandit, brigand, bushranger, robber, thief.

hike *noun*
an afternoon hike through the bush. bushwalk, ramble, tramp, trek, walk.
hike *verb*
They hiked for seven hours through the scrub. backpack, ramble, roam, rove, tramp, trek, walk.

hiker *noun*
backpacker, bushwalker, rambler, trekker, walker.

hilarious *adjective*
a hilarious story. amusing, comical,
funny, humorous, witty.
OPPOSITE sad, serious.

hill *noun*
They climbed the hill to admire the view.
bluff, dune, foothill, headland, hillock,
mesa, mountain, peak, promontory,
rise, summit.
OPPOSITE valley.

hillside *noun*
bank, slope.

hind *adjective*
hind legs. back, rear.
OPPOSITE fore, front.

hinder *verb*
The accident hindered progress. block,
curb, delay, frustrate, hamper,
handicap, hold back, hold up, impede,
inhibit, obstruct, prevent, restrict, slow,
stop, thwart.
OPPOSITE advance, help.

hindrance *noun*
The roadworks were a hindrance to traffic.
barrier, handicap, impediment,
obstacle, obstruction, restriction, snag,
stumbling block.
OPPOSITE help.

hinge *noun*
The door swings on a hinge. joint, pivot.
hinge *verb*
It all hinges on the examination. depend,
hang, pivot, rest, revolve (around),
turn.

hint *noun*
1 He gave no hint of his plans. clue,
indication, inkling, lead, suggestion.
2 cleaning hints. pointer, suggestion, tip.
hint *verb*
She hinted that he was unwelcome. imply,
indicate, insinuate, intimate, suggest.

hire *verb*
1 She hires the workers. appoint, employ,
engage, take on.
OPPOSITE dismiss.
2 They hired a car for their holiday.
charter, lease, rent.

hiss *verb*
The audience hissed. boo, deride, heckle,
hoot, jeer.
OPPOSITE applaud.

historic *adjective*
a historic event. celebrated, famous,
important, memorable, momentous,
significant.
OPPOSITE unimportant.

historical *adjective*
a study based on historical evidence. actual,
authentic, documented, factual, real,
recorded, true.
OPPOSITE fictional, fictitious.

history *noun*
1 He has written a history of Australia.
account, annals, chronicle, record, saga.
2 She told them a little of her history.
background, biography, life story,
memoirs, past, story.

hit *verb*
1 He hit his opponent. bash, batter, beat,
belt (*slang*), box, buffet, butt, clip
(*informal*), clobber (*slang*), clout
(*informal*), club, dong (*Australian
informal*), flog, hammer, job (*informal*),
knock, lash, lay into (*informal*), pound,
pummel, punch, quilt (*Australian slang*),
rap, slap, slog, slug, smack, smite, sock
(*slang*), spank, stoush (*Australian slang*),
strike, swat, swipe (*informal*), tap,
thrash, thump, trounce, wallop (*slang*),
whack, whip.
2 They hit the city with several bombs.
assail, attack, strike.
3 The truck hit the car. bang into, bump
into, collide with, crash into, ram into,
run into, slam into, smash into.
OPPOSITE miss.
4 He hit the ball. bat, cut, drive, kick,
knock, putt, strike.
5 The loss hit her deeply. affect, move,
touch, upset, wound.
hit *noun*
1 He received such a hit that he couldn't get
up. bash, blow, buffet, bump, clip
(*informal*), clout (*informal*), dong
(*Australian informal*), king-hit
(*Australian informal*), knock, knock-out,
punch, slap, slog, slug, smack, stroke,
swipe (*informal*), thump, wallop (*slang*),
whack.

a
b
c
d
e
f
g
h
i
j
k
l
m
n
o
p
q
r
s
t
u
v
w
x
y
z

2 *The play was a hit.* sell-out, sensation, smash hit (*informal*), success, triumph, winner.
OPPOSITE failure.
hit back see RETALIATE.
hit on *He hit on a method which worked.* chance on, come up with, discover, stumble on.
hit out at *He hit out at the authorities.* attack, condemn, criticise, denounce, lash out at.

hitch *verb*
1 *He hitched the animal to the cart.* attach, connect, couple, fasten, harness, join, tie, yoke.
OPPOSITE unfasten.
2 see HITCHHIKE.
3 *He hitched up his trousers.* jerk, pull, tug, yank (*informal*).
hitch *noun*
a slight hitch in the proceedings. catch, difficulty, hiccup, hold-up, interruption, obstacle, problem, snag, stumbling block.

hitchhike *verb*
He hitchhiked from Adelaide to Darwin. hitch, thumb a lift.

hit-or-miss *adjective*
His methods were rather hit-or-miss. careless, casual, haphazard, random.
OPPOSITE precise.

hive *noun*
a hive of bees. apiary, beehive.

hoard *noun*
He kept a hoard of nuts for the winter. cache, fund, reserve, stash (*informal*), stock, stockpile, store, supply, treasure trove.
hoard *verb*
He hoards tiny jars. accumulate, amass, collect, gather, hang on to, hold on to, keep, lay up, save, stash away (*informal*), stockpile, store.

hoarse *adjective*
a hoarse voice. croaky, gruff, harsh, husky, rasping, rough, scratchy.
OPPOSITE smooth.

hoax *verb*
Don't let him hoax you. bluff, con (*informal*), deceive, delude, dupe, fool, have on (*informal*), hoodwink, pull someone's leg, swindle, take in (*informal*), trick.
hoax *noun*
We soon realised that it was a hoax. con (*informal*), confidence trick, deception, fraud, prank, scam (*slang*), spoof (*informal*), swindle, trick.

hobble *verb*
He hobbled about in plaster for six weeks. limp, shuffle, stumble.

hobby *noun*
Building boats is his hobby, not his job. diversion, interest, leisure activity, pastime, recreation, relaxation.
OPPOSITE job.

hoist *verb*
He hoisted the box on to his shoulder. haul, heave, hoick (*slang*), lift, pull up, raise, winch.
OPPOSITE lower.

hold *verb*
1 *He held the bag.* bring, carry, clasp, clutch, grasp, grip, hang on to, keep, retain, seize, take.
OPPOSITE let go.
2 *The police held the suspected person.* arrest, confine, detain, keep, lock up.
OPPOSITE release.
3 *The hall holds 1000 people.* accommodate, have a capacity of, house, seat, take.
4 *This beam won't hold the roof.* bear, carry, support, take.
5 *The fine weather is expected to hold until the weekend.* carry on, continue, endure, last, persist, stay.
6 *The play held their interest.* captivate, capture, keep, maintain, sustain.
OPPOSITE lose.
7 *He held an important job.* have, hold down, occupy, possess.
8 *They held a meeting.* call, conduct, convene, run.
9 *Hold your tongue.* check, control, curb, restrain.
10 *She holds me responsible.* consider, deem, judge, reckon, think.
hold *noun*
1 *He kept a firm hold on the railing.* clasp, clutch, grasp, grip.
2 *The blackmailer has a hold over them.* control, influence, power, sway.

hold back *She held back her tears. They held back information.* block, check, control, curb, halt, keep back, repress, restrain, stop, suppress, withhold.

hold off *They held off making a decision.* defer, delay, postpone, put off, stall.

hold out *She held out her hand.* extend, put out, reach out, stretch out.

hold up

1 *This held up the decision.* delay, hinder, obstruct, slow down.

2 *The bushrangers held them up.* bail up (*Australian*), mug, rob, stick up (*informal*), waylay.

hold-up *noun*

1 *a traffic hold-up.* delay, jam, snarl, stoppage.

2 *an armed hold-up.* burglary, robbery, stick-up (*informal*).

hole *noun*

1 *a hole in the wall.* aperture, breach, break, cavity, chink, crack, gap, opening, slit, slot, space.

2 *The ground was uneven with holes.* cavity, crabhole (*Australian*), depression, gilgai (*Australian*), gnamma hole (*Australian*), hollow, melon hole (*Australian*), pit, pocket, pothole, tunnel. OPPOSITE mound.

3 *a hole in the tyre.* gash, leak, puncture, split, tear.

4 *The animals returned to their holes.* burrow, den, hideout (*informal*), lair, warren.

holiday *noun*

1 *Christmas and Easter are holidays.* feast day, festival.

2 *a holiday from school and work.* break, leave, rest, time off, vacation.

3 *an overseas holiday.* cruise, excursion, honeymoon, safari, tour, trip.

hollow *adjective*

1 *a hollow Easter egg.* empty, unfilled, void. OPPOSITE solid.

2 *hollow cheeks.* concave, sunken. OPPOSITE rounded.

3 *hollow promises.* empty, false, hypocritical, insincere. OPPOSITE genuine.

hollow *noun*

1 *a hollow in the ground.* basin, bunker (*Golf*), cave, cavern, cavity, crabhole (*Australian*), crater, depression, ditch, gilgai (*Australian*), gnamma (*Australian*), hole, pit, pothole, trough. OPPOSITE mound.

2 *It is cool in the hollows.* dell, glen, gully (*Australian*), valley. OPPOSITE hill.

hollow *verb*

He hollowed out a spot for the plant. dig, excavate, gouge, scoop. OPPOSITE fill.

holy *adjective*

1 *Holy Bible. holy ground.* blessed, consecrated, divine, hallowed, heavenly, sacred. OPPOSITE Satanic.

2 *He led a holy life.* blameless, devout, godly, pious, religious, righteous, saintly, virtuous. OPPOSITE sinful.

homage *noun*

The people paid homage to the king. honour, respect, tribute. OPPOSITE disrespect.

home *noun*

1 *The family moved into a new home.* abode (*old use*), dwelling, habitation, house, place, residence; see also FLAT, HOUSE.

2 *He left his home to come to Australia.* see HOMELAND.

3 *a home for sick or elderly people.* hospice, hostel, institution, nursing home, rest home, retirement home.

4 *the home of the quokka.* habitat, territory; [*various homes built by animals*] burrow, den, hole, lair, nest, warren; [*various man-made homes for animals*] apiary, aviary, cage, coop, fold, hive, hutch, kennel, pen, shed, stable, stall, sty.

homeland *noun*

She longed to return to her homeland. birthplace, fatherland, home, motherland, native land.

homeless *adjective*

1 *a homeless kitten.* abandoned, lost, stray.

a
b
c
d
e
f
g
h
i
j
k
l
m
n
o
p
q
r
s
t
u
v
w
x
y
z

2 *a homeless person.* displaced, evicted, exiled, itinerant, nomadic, vagabond, vagrant, wandering.

homely *adjective*
1 *a homely guest house.* comfortable, cosy, friendly, informal, liveable, simple, unpretentious, welcoming.
OPPOSITE formal.
2 (*American*) *a homely girl.* ordinary, plain, unattractive.
OPPOSITE attractive.

homestead *noun*
the homestead on a sheep station. farmhouse, home, house, residence.

homework *noun*
two hours' homework per night. assignment, prep, preparation, study, work.

homicide *noun*
assassination, killing, manslaughter, murder, slaying.

homosexual *adjective*
gay (*informal*), lesbian (*female*).
CONTRASTS WITH bisexual, heterosexual.

honest *adjective*
1 *an honest businessman.* honourable, law-abiding, principled, scrupulous, straight, trustworthy, truthful, upright.
OPPOSITE corrupt, dishonest.
2 *an honest opinion.* blunt, candid, direct, forthright, frank, genuine, open, sincere, straightforward, truthful.
OPPOSITE dishonest, insincere.
3 *honest dealings.* above board, ethical, fair, honourable, lawful, legal, legitimate, proper.
OPPOSITE fraudulent, unethical.

honesty *noun*
She was admired for her honesty. frankness, genuineness, integrity, openness, sincerity, trustworthiness, truthfulness, uprightness.
OPPOSITE dishonesty.

honour *noun*
1 *She treated him with great honour.* admiration, esteem, homage, respect, reverence, veneration, worship.
OPPOSITE contempt.
2 *He brought great honour to his school.* acclaim, credit, distinction, fame, glory,

prestige, recognition, renown.
OPPOSITE discredit, dishonour.
3 *He deemed it an honour to have been chosen.* compliment, privilege.
OPPOSITE insult.
4 *a man of honour.* decency, fairness, honesty, integrity, morality, principle, virtue.
OPPOSITE dishonour.

honour *verb*
1 *They honoured the dead with two minutes' silence.* pay homage to, pay tribute to, pay your respects to, praise, salute.
OPPOSITE insult.
2 *She honours God before people.* admire, esteem, glorify, hallow, praise, respect, revere, venerate, worship.
OPPOSITE disrespect.
3 *Honour a promise.* abide by, keep, stand by, stick to.
OPPOSITE break.

honourable *adjective*
an honourable businessman. above board, decent, ethical, high-minded, honest, principled, respectable, scrupulous, upright.
OPPOSITE dishonourable.

hook *noun*
Hang your hat on the hook. peg, nail.
hook *verb*
1 *He hooked a large fish.* capture, catch, take.
2 *He hooked the gate behind him.* fasten, hitch, latch, secure.
OPPOSITE unhook.

be hooked on (*slang*)
He is hooked on dope. be addicted to, be dependent on.

hooligan *noun*
The police arrested the young hooligans. delinquent, hoodlum, hoon (*Australian informal*), larrikin (*Australian*), lout, ruffian, tearaway, thug, tough, troublemaker, vandal, yob (*informal*).

hoop *noun*
He jumped through a series of hoops. band, circle, ring.

hoot *noun*
1 *The owl's hoots woke the other animals.* cry, scream, screech, shriek, whoop.

2 *The audience sent him off the stage with hoots.* boo, catcall, hiss, jeer.
OPPOSITE cheer.

hoot *verb*
1 *The train hooted as it neared the station.* screech, whistle.
2 *The audience hooted the speaker off the stage.* boo, hiss, jeer, mock.
OPPOSITE cheer.
3 *The driver hooted his horn.* blast, blow, honk, sound, toot.

hooter *noun*
horn, siren, whistle.

hop *verb*
The rabbit hopped out of the way. bob, bound, jump, leap, skip, spring.
hop *noun*
1 *With one hop he reached the chair.* bob, bounce, bound, jump, leap, spring.
2 *a short hop between towns.* distance, flight, stage, trip.

hope *noun*
1 *They live in hope that one day he'll return.* confidence, expectation, faith, optimism, trust.
OPPOSITE despair.
2 *no hope of winning.* chance, likelihood, probability, prospect.
3 *filled with hopes of happiness.* ambition, aspiration, desire, dream, longing, wish.
hope *verb*
He is hoping for a promotion. He hopes to be famous. aspire, desire, dream, expect, long, trust, wish.
OPPOSITE despair of.

hopeful *adjective*
1 *They were hopeful of a cure.* confident, expectant, optimistic, trusting.
OPPOSITE pessimistic.
2 *a hopeful sign.* encouraging, favourable, heartening, positive, promising, reassuring.
OPPOSITE discouraging.

hopeless *adjective*
1 *He felt hopeless in the face of all these problems.* dejected, demoralised, depressed, despairing, despondent, downcast, forlorn, pessimistic, wretched.
OPPOSITE hopeful, optimistic.

2 *Her condition is hopeless.* bad, desperate, incurable.
3 *a hopeless cook.* feeble, inadequate, incompetent, poor, useless.
OPPOSITE competent, good.

horde *noun*
She avoided the hordes of shoppers. crowd, drove, mass, mob, multitude, swarm, throng.

horizontal *adjective*
a horizontal surface. flat, level.
OPPOSITE vertical.

horn *noun*
1 *a deer's horns.* antler.
2 *a car horn.* hooter.

horrible *adjective*
1 *a horrible crime.* abhorrent, abominable, appalling, atrocious, awful, despicable, detestable, dreadful, foul, frightful, ghastly, grisly, gruesome, hideous, horrendous, horrid, horrific, loathsome, monstrous, odious, repugnant, repulsive, revolting, shocking, sickening, terrible, vile.
OPPOSITE pleasant.
2 *(informal) a horrible person.* awful, disagreeable, horrid, mean, nasty, objectionable, obnoxious, offensive, unbearable, unkind, unpleasant.
OPPOSITE charming, kind.

horrify *verb*
The news horrified her. alarm, appal, disgust, frighten, revolt, scare, shock, terrify.
OPPOSITE delight, please.

horror *noun*
1 *He felt horror at the sight of the bushfire.* alarm, dismay, dread, fear, panic, terror, trepidation.
2 *He has a horror of spiders.* aversion, dislike, dread, fear, hatred, loathing, revulsion.
OPPOSITE liking.
3 *The little horror had locked them out.* devil, rascal, scallywag, scamp, scoundrel, terror *(informal)*, wretch.
OPPOSITE angel.

horse *noun*
bronco, brumby *(Australian)*, carthorse, charger, draughthorse, gee-gee *(informal)*, hack, moke *(Australian)*,

a
b
c
d
e
f
g
h
i
j
k
l
m
n
o
p
q
r
s
t
u
v
w
x
y
z

mount, mustang, nag (*informal*), nanto (*Australian old use*), neddy (*informal*), pacer, pony, racehorse, steed (*poetical*), trotter, yarraman (*Australian*); [*male horses*] colt, gelding, sire, stallion; [*female horses*] filly, mare; [*young horses*] colt, filly, foal.

horse-rider *noun*
equestrian, horseman, horsewoman, jockey, rider.

hospitable *adjective*
hospitable hosts. amiable, cordial, friendly, generous, genial, gracious, kind, sociable, warm, welcoming.
OPPOSITE inhospitable.

hospital *noun*
The city is served by several hospitals. clinic, hospice, infirmary, medical centre, nursing home, sanatorium.

host[1] *noun*
A host of people attended. army, crowd, horde, lot, mass, mob, multitude, myriad, swarm, throng; see also GROUP.
OPPOSITE handful.

host[2] *noun*
the host of the show. anchorperson, announcer, compère, disc jockey, DJ, Master of Ceremonies, MC, presenter.

hostage *noun*
captive, prisoner.

hostel *noun*
They stayed at a students' hostel. boarding house, guest house, home.

hostess *noun*
She works as a hostess with the airline. air hostess, flight attendant, hostie (*Australian informal*), steward, stewardess.

hostile *adjective*
1 *hostile aircraft.* attacking, enemy, warring.
OPPOSITE friendly.
2 *We were given a hostile reception.* chilly, cold, cool, frosty, icy, unfriendly.
OPPOSITE friendly, warm.
3 *They exchanged hostile words.* aggressive, angry, belligerent, spiteful, unfriendly, unkind, vicious.
OPPOSITE kind.

hostility *noun*
There was open hostility between the former friends. aggression, animosity, antagonism, antipathy, enmity, friction, opposition, resentment, unfriendliness.
OPPOSITE friendship.
hostilities *plural noun*
see WAR.

hot *adjective*
1 *hot weather.* scorching, sultry, summery, sweltering, warm.
OPPOSITE cold.
2 *a hot fire. a hot pan.* baking, blazing, boiling, burning, fiery, flaming, glowing, piping hot, red-hot, roasting, scalding, scorching, searing, sizzling, steaming.
OPPOSITE cold.
3 *a hot flavour.* burning, peppery, piquant, pungent, sharp, spicy.
OPPOSITE mild.
4 *a hot debate.* angry, animated, ardent, emotional, fervent, fiery, heated, intense, lively, passionate, stormy.
OPPOSITE calm.
5 *The news is hot.* fresh, latest, new, recent.
OPPOSITE stale.
6 *He's not too hot at chess any more.* capable, competent, good, skilful.
hot *verb* (*informal*)
She hotted up the bath. heat up, reheat, warm up.
OPPOSITE cool.

hotel *noun*
guest house, inn, local (*informal*), motel, pub (*informal*), public house, tavern.

hothouse *noun*
Tomatoes may be cultivated in a hothouse. conservatory, glasshouse, greenhouse.

hot-tempered *adjective*
angry, bad-tempered, fiery, irritable, quick-tempered, short-tempered, tempestuous.
OPPOSITE placid.

hound *noun*
a pack of hounds. beagle, bloodhound, dog, foxhound, greyhound, hunting dog, wolfhound.

hound *verb*
He hounded them for the money. badger, chase, dog, harass, hunt, keep at, nag, pester, pursue.

house *noun*
1 *They have moved into a new house.* abode (*old use*), accommodation, dwelling, home, place, residence; [*kinds of house*] bungalow, chalet, cottage, farmhouse, homestead, hut, igloo, maisonette, manor, manse, mansion, presbytery, rectory, shack, shanty, terrace house, town house, vicarage, villa.
2 *two houses of parliament.* assembly, chamber, council, legislative body.
3 *They played to a packed house.* auditorium, hall, theatre.
house *verb*
Several families housed the students. accommodate, billet, put up, shelter.

housebreaker *noun*
burglar, intruder, robber, thief.

household *noun*
The work is shared in their household. family, home, house.
household *adjective*
a household name. familiar, well-known.

householder *noun*
a letter addressed to the householder. occupant, owner, resident, tenant.

housework *noun*
cleaning, cooking, home duties, housekeeping.

housing *noun*
1 *The government provides housing.* accommodation, dwellings, homes, houses, lodging(s), quarters, residences, shelter.
2 *The machine's housing is cracked.* case, casing, cover.

hovel *noun*
The poor man lived in a dreadful hovel. dump (*informal*), hole (*informal*), hut, shack, shanty, shed.
OPPOSITE palace.

hover *verb*
1 *The butterfly hovered over the flower.* float, flutter.

2 *The sales assistant hovered over the customer.* hang about, linger, wait near.

howl *noun*
1 *the howl of a dog.* bay, cry, wail, whine, yelp, yowl.
2 *a howl of pain.* bellow, cry, groan, scream, shout, shriek, wail, yell, yowl.
howl *verb*
1 *He howled in pain.* bawl, bellow, cry, roar, scream, shout, shriek, wail, whine, yell, yelp, yowl; see also WEEP.
2 *They howled with laughter.* cry, hoot, roar, scream, shriek.
howl down *The speaker was howled down.* boo, heckle, hiss, hoot, jeer, shout down.

hub *noun*
the hub of the universe. centre, core, focus, heart, middle.

huddle *verb*
1 *Fifteen people huddled into a lift.* cluster, cram, crowd, flock, herd, jam, pile, press, squash, squeeze, throng.
2 *He huddled up in a chair by the fire.* curl up, nestle, snuggle.

hue *noun*
colour, shade, tinge, tint, tone.

hug *verb*
He hugged her and kissed her. clasp, cuddle, embrace, hold, squeeze.

huge *adjective*
a huge amount, object, task, etc. astronomical, big, colossal, enormous, exorbitant, giant, gigantic, great, humungous (*slang*), immense, large, mammoth, massive, mighty, monstrous, staggering, stupendous, sweeping, vast.
OPPOSITE tiny.

hull *noun*
a ship's hull. body, frame, framework, skeleton.

hullabaloo *noun*
They made such a hullabaloo when she left. clamour, commotion, din, fracas, fuss, hubbub, racket, rumpus, uproar.

hum *verb*
The motor hummed. buzz, drone, purr, vibrate, whirr.

a
b
c
d
e
f
g
h
i
j
k
l
m
n
o
p
q
r
s
t
u
v
w
x
y
z

hum *noun*
There was an unpleasant hum in the amplifier. buzz, drone, purr, vibration, whirr.

human *adjective*
human being child, human, individual, man, mortal, person, woman.

humane *adjective*
a humane judge. compassionate, humanitarian, kind, kind-hearted, merciful, sympathetic, understanding.
OPPOSITE cruel, inhumane.

humanity *noun*
1 crimes against humanity. humankind, human race, man, mankind, people, society.
2 The politician was admired for his humanity. compassion, goodness, kindness, mercy, sympathy, understanding.
OPPOSITE cruelty, inhumanity.

humble *adjective*
1 He is humble about his talents. meek, modest, unassertive, unassuming.
OPPOSITE proud.
2 a humble house. modest, ordinary, plain, simple, unpretentious.
OPPOSITE grand.
humble *verb*
The experience humbled him. disgrace, humiliate, mortify, shame, take down a peg (informal).
OPPOSITE exalt.

humid *adjective*
The humid atmosphere was oppressive. clammy, close, damp, dank, moist, muggy, steamy, sticky, sultry.
OPPOSITE dry.

humiliate *verb*
He humiliated his son by correcting him in public. disgrace, embarrass, humble, mortify, put down, shame, take down a peg (informal).
OPPOSITE exalt.

humiliation *noun*
He suffered humiliation at the announcement. disgrace, embarrassment, indignity, mortification, shame.
OPPOSITE pride.

humility *noun*
a great man with true humility. humbleness, lowliness, meekness, modesty.
OPPOSITE pride.

humorous *adjective*
a humorous story. a humorous person. amusing, comic, comical, facetious, funny, hilarious, laughable, ridiculous, witty.
OPPOSITE serious.

humour *noun*
1 She appreciated the humour of the situation. absurdity, comedy, funniness, ludicrousness, ridiculousness.
OPPOSITE gravity.
2 His stories are full of humour. comedy, jokes, wit, wittiness.
OPPOSITE seriousness.
3 Is he in a good humour? mood, spirits, temper.
humour *verb*
They only agreed to attend in order to humour him. go along with, indulge, pamper, pander to, play up to.

hump *noun*
a camel's hump. bulge, bump, hunch, lump, swelling.

hunch *verb*
She was hunched over her work. arch, bend, crouch, hump.
hunch *noun*
I have a hunch about that. feeling, idea, intuition, premonition, suspicion.

hunger *noun*
1 He nearly died of hunger. malnutrition, starvation.
OPPOSITE overeating.
2 a hunger for knowledge. appetite, craving, desire, longing, thirst.

hungry *adjective*
After their long walk they were hungry. famished, peckish (informal), ravenous, starved, starving.
OPPOSITE full.

hunk *noun*
a big hunk of cake. block, chunk, lump, piece, slab, wedge.

hunt *verb*
1 *He is hunting wild pigs.* chase, pursue, stalk, track, trail.
2 *She was hunting for her stapler.* ferret out, forage for, fossick for (*Australian informal*), look for, rummage for, search for, seek.
hunt *noun*
the hunt for clues. chase, pursuit, quest, search.

hunter *noun*
huntsman, predator, tracker.

hurdle *noun*
1 *He jumped all the hurdles.* barricade, barrier, fence.
2 *The language was another hurdle to overcome.* barrier, difficulty, impediment, obstacle, problem, snag, stumbling block.

hurl *verb*
He hurled a ball through the window. cast, chuck (*informal*), fling, heave, pitch, propel, sling (*informal*), throw, toss.

hurricane *noun*
cyclone, tropical cyclone, typhoon; see also STORM, WIND[1].

hurry *noun*
No need for all the hurry. bustle, haste, hustle, rush, scurry, urgency.
OPPOSITE delay.
hurry *verb*
1 *He hurried home.* bolt, dash, fly, hasten, hurtle, hustle, race, rush, scoot, scurry, scuttle, speed, whiz, zip, zoom.
OPPOSITE dawdle.
2 *He told me to hurry.* be quick, get a move on (*informal*), get cracking (*informal*), get your skates on (*informal*), make haste, make it snappy (*informal*), step on it (*informal*).
OPPOSITE slow down.
3 *They hurried the work along.* accelerate, expedite, fast-track (*informal*), hasten, push, quicken, speed up.
OPPOSITE delay.

hurt *verb*
1 *He hurt his leg. He was severely hurt.* cripple, damage, disable, injure, maim, mutilate, wound.

2 *Oil won't hurt the machine.* damage, harm, impair, spoil.
OPPOSITE improve.
3 *She was hurt by his tactless remark.* distress, grieve, offend, pain, trouble, upset, wound.
OPPOSITE cheer.
4 *My head hurts.* ache, be painful, be sore, smart, sting, throb.
hurt *noun*
mental hurt. physical hurt. ache, affliction, agony, anguish, damage, discomfort, distress, grief, harm, injury, misery, pain, sadness, soreness, sorrow, suffering, torment, torture.

hurtful *adjective*
a hurtful comment. brutal, cruel, cutting, distressing, malicious, mean, nasty, unkind, upsetting.
OPPOSITE helpful, kind.

hurtle *verb*
The car hurtled along. fly, race, shoot, speed, tear, whiz, zip, zoom.
OPPOSITE crawl.

husband *noun*
bridegroom, groom, mate, partner, spouse.

hush *verb*
She hushed the baby. calm, lull, quieten, shush (*informal*), silence, soothe.
hush *noun*
There was a hush in the room. quietness, silence, stillness.
OPPOSITE noise.

hushed *adjective*
They spoke in hushed voices. low, quiet, soft, subdued.
OPPOSITE loud.

husk *noun*
He removed the seeds from the husks. hull, pod, shell.

husky *adjective*
1 *a husky voice.* croaking, dry, gruff, harsh, hoarse, rasping, rough, throaty.
2 *a husky young man.* beefy, brawny, burly, hefty, muscular, nuggety (*Australian*), solid, stocky, strapping, strong, sturdy, tough.
OPPOSITE puny.

a
b
c
d
e
f
g
h
i
j
k
l
m
n
o
p
q
r
s
t
u
v
w
x
y
z

hustle *verb*
1 *They hustled the man out of the building.*
bundle, bustle, jostle, push, shove,
thrust.
2 *He hustled her into buying the computer.*
force, pressure, push, rush.

hustle *noun*
the hustle of the big city. activity, bustle,
haste, hurly-burly, hurry, rush, tumult.

hut *noun*
cabin, chalet, gunyah (*Australian*),
house, hovel, humpy (*Australian*), lean-
to, mia mia (*Australian*), shack, shanty,
shed, shelter, skillion (*Australian*),
wurley (*Australian*).

hutch *noun*
a rabbit hutch. box, cage, coop,
enclosure, pen.

hybrid *noun*
The gardener has produced a hybrid. blend,
cross, cross-breed, half-breed, mixture.
OPPOSITE thoroughbred.

hygienic *adjective*
a hygienic hospital ward. clean,
disinfected, germ-free, healthy,
sanitary, sterile, sterilised.
OPPOSITE dirty.

hymn *noun*
Hymns are sung in church. anthem, carol,
chorus, introit, psalm, song.

hypnotise *verb*
He was hypnotised by her looks. bewitch,
enthral, entrance, fascinate, mesmerise.

hypocrisy *noun*
His speech was full of hypocrisy. deceit,
dishonesty, falseness, insincerity.
OPPOSITE sincerity.

hypocritical *adjective*
*It is hypocritical not to practise what you
preach.* false, inconsistent, insincere,
two-faced.
OPPOSITE sincere.

hysterical *adjective*
*The woman was hysterical after the
accident.* berserk, distraught, frantic,
frenzied, overwrought, raving,
uncontrollable.
OPPOSITE composed.

Ii

ice *noun*
Ice is frozen water. black ice, floe, frost, glacier, iceberg, icicle, pack ice, rime.

icing *noun*
lemon icing on the cake. frosting, glaze.

icon *noun*
a religious icon. idol, image, statue.

icy *adjective*
1 *icy winds. icy temperatures.* biting, bitter, chilly, cold, freezing, frosty, glacial, nippy (*informal*), subzero.
OPPOSITE blazing, hot.
2 *icy roads.* frosty, frozen, slippery.

idea *noun*
1 *She has lots of good ideas.* brainwave (*informal*), concept, notion, plan, proposal, scheme, suggestion, thought.
2 *Can you give him some idea of what is needed?* clue, hint, impression, indication, inkling.
3 *He tested his idea.* hunch, hypothesis, suspicion, theory.
4 *They have different ideas about discipline.* attitude, belief, conviction, opinion, thought, view.

ideal *adjective*
ideal conditions. excellent, faultless, model, optimal, optimum, perfect.

identical *adjective*
identical stories, faces, etc. alike, duplicate, indistinguishable, matching, same, twin.
OPPOSITE different.

identify *verb*
1 *The victim was able to identify her attacker in the line-up.* distinguish, name, pick out, recognise, single out, spot.
2 *The mechanic identified the problem.* detect, diagnose, discover, pinpoint, work out.
identify with *She could not identify with the characters.* empathise with, relate to, respond to, sympathise with.

identity *noun*
1 *proof of identity.* ID, name.
2 *She worried about losing her identity.* individuality, personality, uniqueness.
3 (*Australian informal*) *a television identity.* celebrity, personality, star.
OPPOSITE nonentity.

idiom *noun*
Some idioms are hard to translate. expression, phrase.

idiot *noun* (*informal*)
Don't be such an idiot! ass (*informal*), blockhead, bonehead, chump (*informal*), clot (*informal*), cretin, dill (*Australian informal*), dimwit (*informal*), dodo (*informal*), dolt, dope (*informal*), drongo (*Australian informal*), dummy (*informal*), dunce, fat-head (*informal*), fool, galah (*Australian slang*), half-wit, ignoramus, imbecile, jerk (*slang*), lunatic, moron (*informal*), nincompoop, ninny, nitwit (*informal*), nong (*Australian informal*), numskull, nut (*informal*), simpleton, thickhead (*informal*), twerp (*slang*), twit (*slang*).
OPPOSITE genius.

idiotic *adjective*
It was an idiotic thing to do. absurd, crazy, dumb (*informal*), foolhardy, foolish, irrational, lunatic, mad, nutty (*informal*), reckless, ridiculous, senseless, silly, stupid, unintelligent, unwise.
OPPOSITE sensible.

idle *adjective*
1 *The tractor lay idle.* inactive, out of action, unused.
2 *an idle fellow.* lazy, shiftless, slothful, sluggish.
OPPOSITE busy.
3 *idle time.* free, unfilled, unoccupied, unproductive.
4 *idle chatter.* empty, frivolous, pointless, trivial, useless, worthless.

idol *noun*
1 *They worshipped idols.* graven image, icon, image, statue.
2 *a sporting idol.* celebrity, heart-throb (*slang*), hero, heroine, star, superstar.

idolise *verb*
She idolised her brother. adore, dote on, look up to, love, revere, worship.
OPPOSITE despise.

ignite *verb*
1 *She ignited the pile of wood.* fire, kindle, light, set fire to.
2 *The wood ignited.* burn, catch fire, kindle.

ignorant *adjective*
1 *ignorant of the road rules.* unaware, unfamiliar (with), uninformed (about).
OPPOSITE aware.
2 *She was ignorant because she didn't want to learn.* illiterate, uneducated.
OPPOSITE educated.

ignore *verb*
1 *She ignored his rudeness.* close your eyes to, disregard, neglect, overlook, pass over.
2 *He ignored the new boy.* cold-shoulder, send to Coventry, slight, take no notice of.

ill *adjective*
1 *She felt ill.* crook (*Australian informal*), diseased, indisposed, infirm, nauseous, off colour, out of sorts, poorly, queasy, rotten, seedy (*informal*), sick, sickly, under the weather, unhealthy, unwell.
OPPOSITE well.
2 *no ill effects.* adverse, bad, damaging, destructive, detrimental, evil, harmful, unfavourable.
OPPOSITE good.

illegal *adjective*
an illegal activity. an illegal drug. banned, criminal, forbidden, illegitimate, illicit, outlawed, prohibited, unauthorised, unlawful.
OPPOSITE legal.

illegible *adjective*
Her writing is illegible. indecipherable, unreadable.
OPPOSITE clear, legible.

illegitimate *adjective*
1 *an illegitimate child.* bastard, love.
2 *an illegitimate move in chess.* illegal, improper, inadmissible, wrong.
OPPOSITE legal, legitimate.

illiterate *adjective*
computer illiterate. ignorant, uneducated, uninformed, unknowledgeable.
OPPOSITE literate.

illness *noun*
affliction, ailment, bug (*informal*), complaint, condition, disease, disorder, indisposition, infection, infirmity, malady, sickness, trouble, wog (*Australian informal*).
OPPOSITE health.

illogical *adjective*
Their findings were illogical. absurd, irrational, unreasonable, unsound.
OPPOSITE logical.

ill-treat *verb*
abuse, harm, injure, maltreat, mistreat, molest, persecute, wrong.

illuminate *verb*
1 *They illuminated the streets.* brighten up, floodlight, light up.
OPPOSITE darken.
2 *He illuminated the subject.* clarify, explain, shed light on, throw light on.

illusion *noun*
an optical illusion. deception, hallucination, mirage, trick.

illustrate *verb*
1 *The artist illustrated the courtroom scene.* depict, draw, picture, portray, represent.
2 *The sentence illustrates the word's usage.* demonstrate, exemplify, explain, show.

illustration *noun*
1 *The book has coloured illustrations.* diagram, drawing, figure, picture, plate.
2 *an illustration of usage.* example, instance, sample, specimen.

image *noun*
1 *a graven image.* carving, figure, icon, idol, representation, statue.
2 *She studied her image in the mirror.* appearance, likeness, reflection.

3 *She is the image of her mother.* copy, dead ringer (*informal*), duplicate, replica, spit, spitting image.
4 *a mental image.* concept, conception, idea, impression, perception, picture, vision.

imaginary *adjective*
an imaginary friend. fancied, fanciful, fictitious, hypothetical, illusory, invented, legendary, made-up, mythical, non-existent, pretend (*informal*), unreal.
OPPOSITE real.

imagination *noun*
1 *The story shows imagination.* creativity, ingenuity, innovation, inspiration, inventiveness, vision.
2 *in your imagination.* fancy, fantasy, mind's eye.

imaginative *adjective*
an imaginative architect, cook, etc. creative, ingenious, innovative, inspired, inventive, visionary.
OPPOSITE unimaginative.

imagine *verb*
1 *He imagined what it would be like.* conceive, dream up, envisage, fantasise, picture, speculate, think up, visualise.
2 *What do you imagine has happened?* assume, believe, expect, guess, presume, suppose, think.

imitate *verb*
1 *He imitated the professor.* ape, copy, echo, impersonate, mimic, send up (*informal*), take off.
2 *They imitated the sound of the sea.* copy, counterfeit, duplicate, replicate, reproduce, simulate.

imitation *noun*
1 *She distinguished the imitation from the real article.* copy, counterfeit, duplicate, fake, forgery, replica, reproduction.
2 *He does imitations of celebrities.* impersonation, impression, parody, send-up (*informal*), spoof (*informal*), take-off.
imitation *adjective*
imitation cream. artificial, fake, mock, phoney (*informal*), synthetic.
OPPOSITE real.

immature *adjective*
an immature attitude. babyish, childish, inexperienced, infantile, juvenile, naive, puerile, youthful.
OPPOSITE mature.

immediate *adjective*
1 *an immediate reply.* direct, instant, instantaneous, prompt, speedy, swift, unhesitating.
OPPOSITE delayed.
2 *in the immediate neighbourhood.* adjacent, closest, nearest, next.

immediately *adverb*
She paid up immediately. at once, directly, instantly, on the knocker (*Australian informal*), on the spot, promptly, right away, straight away, then and there.

immense *adjective*
an immense amount. astronomical, big, colossal, considerable, enormous, excessive, exorbitant, extensive, gigantic, great, hefty, huge, immeasurable, large, mammoth, massive, monstrous, staggering, stupendous, terrific, tremendous, vast.
OPPOSITE small.

immerse *verb*
1 *She immersed the clothes in soapy water.* dip, drench, dunk, plunge, soak, submerge, wet.
2 *He immersed himself in history.* absorb, bury, engross, occupy, preoccupy.

immigrant *noun*
She helps immigrants settle in. migrant, newcomer, settler.
CONTRASTS WITH emigrant.

immobile *adjective*
1 *With its wheels clamped, the car was immobile.* fast, fixed, immobilised, immovable, stationary, stuck.
2 *The patient was immobile.* motionless, paralysed, still.
OPPOSITE mobile.

immodest *adjective*
People were shocked by her immodest behaviour. brazen, forward, improper, indecent, shameless, wanton.
OPPOSITE modest.

a
b
c
d
e
f
g
h
i
j
k
l
m
n
o
p
q
r
s
t
u
v
w
x
y
z

immoral *adjective*
immoral behaviour. bad, base, corrupt, depraved, evil, iniquitous, shameless, sinful, unethical, unprincipled, unscrupulous, wicked.
OPPOSITE moral, virtuous.

immortal *adjective*
God is immortal. abiding, enduring, eternal, everlasting, undying.
OPPOSITE mortal.

immune *adjective*
immune to criticism. immune to mumps. exempt (from), free (from), protected (from), resistant (to), safe (from).
OPPOSITE liable, susceptible.

immunisation *noun*
rubella immunisation. inoculation, vaccination; see also INJECTION.

immunity *noun*
an immunity to mumps. protection, resistance.
OPPOSITE susceptibility.

imp *noun*
1 *fairy-tale imps.* demon, devil, elf, fairy, goblin, hobgoblin, pixie, spirit, sprite.
2 *The little imp had tied his shoelaces together.* devil, monkey, rascal, scallywag, scamp.

impact *noun*
1 *The impact caused severe injuries.* bump, collision, crash, knock, smash.
2 *The war had a big impact on their lives.* consequence, effect, influence.

impair *verb*
Smoking impairs your health. damage, harm, hurt, injure, ruin, spoil, weaken.
OPPOSITE improve.

impart *verb*
He was eager to impart the information. communicate, convey, disclose, make known, pass on, report, reveal, tell, transmit.
OPPOSITE withhold.

impartial *adjective*
an impartial observer. disinterested, even-handed, fair, just, neutral, non-partisan, objective, unbiased.
OPPOSITE biased.

impatient *adjective*
1 *They were impatient to leave.* anxious, eager, itching, keen, raring.
2 *The audience was getting impatient.* edgy, fidgety, nervous, nervy, restive, restless, toey (*Australian informal*).
OPPOSITE patient.

impediment *noun*
a speech impediment. defect, handicap, lisp, stammer, stutter.

imperfect *adjective*
imperfect work. defective, faulty, flawed, incomplete, shoddy, substandard.
OPPOSITE perfect.

imperfection *noun*
The polish showed up the imperfections. blemish, defect, fault, flaw, shortcoming, weakness.

impersonate *verb*
He impersonates well-known figures. ape, imitate, masquerade as, mimic, portray, pose as, pretend to be, take off.

impertinence *noun*
He was offended by her impertinence. cheek, effrontery, gall, hide, impudence, insolence, nerve, rudeness.

impertinent *adjective*
an impertinent person. an impertinent question. cheeky, disrespectful, impolite, impudent, insolent, presumptuous, rude.
OPPOSITE polite.

impetuous *adjective*
1 *an impetuous dash.* hasty, headlong, impulsive, quick, spontaneous, spur-of-the-moment, sudden, wild.
2 *an impetuous person.* foolhardy, headstrong, hotheaded, impulsive, rash, reckless, spontaneous.
OPPOSITE cautious.

implement *noun*
cooking implements. device, gadget, instrument, tool, utensil.
implement *verb*
They implemented the proposed changes. carry out, enforce, put into effect.

implicit *adjective*
implicit agreement. implied, understood, unsaid, unspoken.
OPPOSITE explicit.

implore *verb*
> *She implored them to stay.* appeal to, ask, beg, beseech, entreat, plead with, request.

imply *verb*
> *He implied that he thought they were wrong.* hint, indicate, insinuate, intimate, suggest.

impolite *adjective*
> bad-mannered, cheeky, coarse, discourteous, disrespectful, impudent, insolent, insulting, loutish, rude, tactless, uncivil, vulgar.
> OPPOSITE polite.

importance *noun*
> **1** *a person of importance.* distinction, eminence, influence, note, prominence, renown, status.
> **2** *place importance on manners.* emphasis, stress, value, weight.
> **3** *matters of little importance.* account, consequence, import, significance.

important *adjective*
> **1** *an important decision.* big, consequential, critical, crucial, fateful, grave, historic, key, life and death, major, momentous, newsworthy, noteworthy, pressing, primary, serious, significant, urgent, vital, weighty.
> OPPOSITE trivial.
> **2** *an important person.* celebrated, distinguished, eminent, famed, famous, great, influential, leading, notable, outstanding, powerful, pre-eminent, prominent, renowned, well-known.
> OPPOSITE unimportant.

impose *verb*
> **1** *They imposed a tax on clothing.* enforce, inflict, levy, put.
> **2** *He imposed his ideas on the class.* force, inflict.
> **impose on** *We don't want to impose on your hospitality.* abuse, exploit, presume on, take advantage of.

imposing *adjective*
> *an imposing building.* big, grand, impressive, magnificent, majestic, ostentatious, splendid, stately, striking.
> OPPOSITE unimposing.

impossible *adjective*
> *an impossible task.* hopeless, impracticable, inconceivable, insoluble, unachievable, unthinkable.
> OPPOSITE feasible, possible.

impostor *noun*
> *They got rid of the impostor.* charlatan, con man (*informal*), fraud, impersonator, phoney (*informal*), pretender.

impotent *adjective*
> *She was impotent to help.* helpless, powerless, unable; see also WEAK.

impractical *adjective*
> **1** *an impractical person.* airy-fairy, idealistic, starry-eyed, unrealistic, visionary.
> OPPOSITE practical, realistic.
> **2** *an impractical scheme.* half-baked, hare-brained, impossible, impracticable, unworkable.
> OPPOSITE feasible, workable.

imprecise *adjective*
> *an imprecise idea.* approximate, fuzzy, general, hazy, indefinite, inexact, nebulous, rough, sketchy, vague.
> OPPOSITE precise.

impress *verb*
> *They were impressed by her singing.* affect, move, stir, strike, touch.

impression *noun*
> **1** *He wanted to make a good impression.* effect, impact, mark.
> **2** *He had an impression that they knew the way.* belief, feeling, hunch, idea, notion, opinion, sense, suspicion.
> **3** *She does impressions of famous people.* imitation, impersonation, parody, send-up (*informal*), take-off.

impressive *adjective*
> *an impressive display. an impressive occasion.* awe-inspiring, grand, great, imposing, magnificent, majestic, memorable, moving, outstanding, remarkable, sensational, spectacular, splendid, stately, striking, superb.
> OPPOSITE ordinary.

imprint *noun*
> *the imprint of a paw.* impression, mark, print, seal, stamp.

a b c d e f g h i j k l m n o p q r s t u v w x y z

imprint *verb*
The scene is imprinted on his mind.
engrave, etch, implant, impress, stamp.

imprison *verb*
The murderer was imprisoned for life.
confine, detain, incarcerate, intern, jail,
lock up, place in custody, shut up.
OPPOSITE free.

imprisonment *noun*
The murderer was sentenced to life
imprisonment. confinement, custody,
detention, incarceration, jail.

improbable *adjective*
an improbable explanation. far-fetched,
implausible, incredible, unbelievable,
unlikely.
OPPOSITE likely.

impromptu *adjective*
an impromptu speech. ad lib, extempore,
off the cuff, spontaneous, unprepared,
unrehearsed, unscripted.
OPPOSITE prepared.

improper *adjective*
improper conduct. improper language.
coarse, crude, inappropriate, indecent,
irreverent, obscene, offensive, rude,
unbecoming, unseemly, unsuitable,
vulgar.
OPPOSITE decent.

improve *verb*
1 Business is improving. advance,
develop, pick up, progress.
OPPOSITE decline.
2 The patient is improving. be on the
mend, get better, perk up, rally,
recover, recuperate, take a turn for the
better.
OPPOSITE deteriorate.
3 He improved his work. enhance, fix up,
polish, refine, revise, touch up,
upgrade.
OPPOSITE spoil, worsen.
4 They promised to improve standards.
boost, lift, raise.
OPPOSITE lower.

improvement *noun*
advance, development, enhancement,
progress, rally, recovery, refinement,
reform, revamp, revision, touch-up,
upgrade, upturn.

improvise *verb*
They had no music, but they improvised an
accompaniment. ad lib (informal),
extemporise, invent, make up, play by
ear.

impudent *adjective*
Don't be impudent! brazen, cheeky,
discourteous, disrespectful, fresh
(informal), impertinent, impolite,
insolent, pert, rude, saucy.
OPPOSITE polite.

impulsive *adjective*
1 an impulsive person. capricious,
hotheaded, impetuous, rash, reckless.
OPPOSITE cautious.
2 an impulsive action. automatic, hasty,
headlong, impetuous, instinctive, rash,
reckless, spontaneous, spur-of-the-
moment, unplanned.
OPPOSITE premeditated.

impure *adjective*
The water was impure. adulterated,
contaminated, dirty, filthy, foul,
polluted, tainted, unclean.
OPPOSITE clean, pure.

in *adjective*
Hats are in again. fashionable, in fashion,
in vogue, trendy (informal).
OPPOSITE out of fashion.

inability *noun*
an inability to speak. helplessness,
incapacity, powerlessness.
OPPOSITE ability.

inaccessible *adjective*
The area was inaccessible except by boat.
cut off, isolated, out of reach, remote,
unreachable.
OPPOSITE accessible.

inaccuracy *noun*
inaccuracies in the text. error, fault,
misprint, mistake, slip-up (informal),
typo (informal).

inaccurate *adjective*
inaccurate reporting. careless, false,
imprecise, incorrect, inexact, sloppy,
untruthful, wrong.
OPPOSITE accurate.

inactive *adjective*
an inactive animal. asleep, dormant, hibernating, idle, inert, lazy, passive, resting, sedentary, sleepy, slothful, sluggish.
OPPOSITE active.

inadequate *adjective*
inadequate information. deficient, insufficient, scanty, sketchy, skimpy, sparse, wanting.
OPPOSITE adequate.

inanimate *adjective*
an inanimate object. lifeless.
OPPOSITE animate.

inappropriate *adjective*
an inappropriate choice, remark, etc. improper, incongruous, irrelevant, unbecoming, unsatisfactory, unsuitable, wrong.
OPPOSITE appropriate.

inattentive *adjective*
Inattentive driving causes accidents. absent-minded, careless, distracted, heedless, negligent.
OPPOSITE attentive, cautious.

inborn *adjective*
an inborn ability. congenital, hereditary, inbred, inherent, innate, native, natural.
OPPOSITE acquired.

incapable *adjective*
an incapable worker. incompetent, ineffective, ineffectual, inept, useless.
OPPOSITE capable, competent.

incense *verb*
He was incensed by their selfish attitude. anger, enrage, exasperate, infuriate, madden, outrage, provoke, rile (*informal*), vex.

incentive *noun*
The workers are offered incentives to work harder. encouragement, inducement, lure, spur, stimulus.
OPPOSITE deterrent.

incessant *adjective*
their incessant chatter. ceaseless, chronic, constant, continual, continuous, endless, eternal, everlasting, interminable, non-stop, permanent, perpetual, persistent, relentless.
OPPOSITE occasional.

incident *noun*
an amusing incident. affair, episode, event, experience, happening, occasion, occurrence.

incidental *adjective*
incidental costs. minor, secondary.
OPPOSITE major.

incite *verb*
He incited the crowd to revolt. arouse, egg on, encourage, excite, goad, provoke, rouse, spur, stir up, urge.

inclination *noun*
He has an inclination to overeat. habit, predisposition, propensity, tendency.

incline *verb*
1 *The roof inclines steeply.* pitch, slant, slope.
2 *He inclined his head to see.* bend, bow, lean, tilt, tip.
incline *noun*
a steep incline. grade, gradient, hill, inclination, pinch (*Australian*), pitch, rise, slant, slope.
be inclined *She was inclined to give up easily.* be apt, be liable, be prone, be wont (*old use*), tend.

include *verb*
1 *The course includes practical and theoretical subjects.* comprise, consist of, contain, cover, incorporate, take in.
OPPOSITE exclude.
2 *He included her on his birthday list.* add, count, list, number.
OPPOSITE omit.

incoherent *adjective*
When he was tired his speech became incoherent. confused, illogical, jumbled, muddled, rambling, unclear, unintelligible.
OPPOSITE coherent.

income *noun*
Income exceeds expenditure. earnings, livelihood, pay, receipts, revenue, salary, takings, wages.
OPPOSITE expenditure.

a
b
c
d
e
f
g
h
i
j
k
l
m
n
o
p
q
r
s
t
u
v
w
x
y
z

incompatible *adjective*
incompatible statements. conflicting, contradictory, incongruous, inconsistent, irreconcilable.
OPPOSITE consistent.

incompetent *adjective*
an incompetent cook. clueless (*informal*), hopeless, inadequate, incapable, ineffectual, inefficient, inept, inexpert, unskilful, useless.
OPPOSITE competent, skilful.

incomplete *adjective*
an incomplete manuscript. abridged, fragmentary, imperfect, partial, sketchy, unfinished.
OPPOSITE complete.

incongruous *adjective*
The log cabin looked incongruous in suburbia. inappropriate, odd, out of keeping, out of place.
OPPOSITE congruous.

inconsiderate *adjective*
an inconsiderate person, action, etc. careless, insensitive, rude, selfish, tactless, thoughtless, uncaring, unthinking.
OPPOSITE considerate.

inconsistent *adjective*
1 *inconsistent behaviour.* capricious, changeable, erratic, fickle, patchy, temperamental, unpredictable, unreliable, variable.
2 *These actions are inconsistent with his philosophy.* at odds, conflicting, contradictory, incompatible.
OPPOSITE consistent.

inconspicuous *adjective*
The shy man tried to be inconspicuous. unnoticeable, unobtrusive.
OPPOSITE prominent.

inconvenience *noun*
They put up with many inconveniences. bother, disruption, disturbance, hassle (*informal*), irritation, nuisance, trouble.
inconvenience *verb*
He didn't mean to inconvenience us. bother, disrupt, disturb, hassle (*informal*), impose on, put out (*informal*), trouble.

inconvenient *adjective*
an inconvenient time. awkward, bothersome, ill-timed, inopportune, troublesome, unsuitable, untimely.
OPPOSITE convenient.

incorporate *verb*
The three councils were incorporated into one. amalgamate, blend, combine, consolidate, integrate, merge, mix, unite; see also INCLUDE.

incorrect *adjective*
an incorrect answer. erroneous, false, inaccurate, mistaken, untrue, wrong.
OPPOSITE correct.

increase *verb*
1 *They increased the size of the club.* add to, augment, boost, build up, enlarge, expand, lift, raise, supplement, swell.
OPPOSITE decrease, reduce.
2 *The shares increased in value.* appreciate, escalate, gain, go up, grow, improve, jump, multiply, rise, skyrocket, soar.
OPPOSITE decrease, drop.
3 *The treatment increased the pain.* aggravate, compound, exacerbate, heighten, intensify, step up, strengthen.
OPPOSITE ease.
4 *He increased the time allowed for the project.* extend, lengthen, prolong, protract.
OPPOSITE decrease, shorten.
increase *noun*
1 *an increase in size, numbers, etc.* boost, build-up, enlargement, escalation, expansion, explosion, extension, growth, inflation, rise, upsurge.
2 *an increase of $20.* addition, gain, increment, jump, rise.
OPPOSITE decrease.

incredible *adjective*
an incredible story. amazing, extraordinary, far-fetched, implausible, improbable, inconceivable, miraculous, unbelievable, unlikely.
OPPOSITE credible.

incredulous *adjective*
He was incredulous when they told him. disbelieving, doubtful, dubious, sceptical, unbelieving.
OPPOSITE credulous.

incriminate *verb*
He said nothing which would incriminate his friends. accuse, blame, implicate.

incubate *verb*
The hen incubated the eggs. brood, hatch.

incurable *adjective*
1 *an incurable squint.* inoperable, uncorrectable, untreatable.
OPPOSITE curable.
2 *an incurable flirt.* hopeless, incorrigible, inveterate.

indebted *adjective*
She was indebted to her friend for her help. grateful, obliged, thankful.

indecent *adjective*
an indecent joke. indecent language. coarse, crude, dirty, filthy, foul, improper, obscene, offensive, pornographic, rude, suggestive, tasteless, unprintable, unseemly, vulgar.
OPPOSITE decent.

indecisive *adjective*
She was indecisive about whether to go. hesitant, in two minds, irresolute, tentative, uncertain, undecided, unsure.
OPPOSITE decisive.

indefinite *adjective*
1 *an indefinite period.* open-ended, unlimited, unspecified.
OPPOSITE fixed.
2 *He was indefinite about his return date.* non-committal, tentative, uncertain, undecided, unsure, vague.
OPPOSITE specific.
3 *an indefinite idea.* confused, fuzzy, general, hazy, imprecise, inexact, obscure, vague.
OPPOSITE precise.

indelible *adjective*
indelible ink. fast, fixed, lasting, permanent.

independent *adjective*
1 *an independent state.* autonomous, free, self-determining, self-governing, self-ruling, self-sufficient, sovereign.
OPPOSITE dependent.
2 *an independent commentator.* impartial, non-partisan.

indestructible *adjective*
1 *indestructible plastic.* durable, strong, sturdy, tough, unbreakable.
OPPOSITE breakable, fragile.
2 *an indestructible friendship.* enduring, eternal, everlasting, lasting, permanent, undying.

index *noun*
an index of names. catalogue, directory, list, register.

indicate *verb*
1 *The signs indicate the way.* make known, point out, reveal, show, signal, specify, tell.
2 *A nod indicates agreement.* be a sign of, denote, imply, mean, show, signify, spell.

indication *noun*
The tears were an indication of tiredness. clue, evidence, hint, mark, sign, signal, symptom, token, warning.

indifferent *adjective*
1 *an indifferent attitude.* apathetic, cold, cool, dispassionate, half-hearted, lukewarm, neutral, uncaring, unconcerned, uninterested.
OPPOSITE interested.
2 *indifferent playing.* fair, mediocre, middling, ordinary, passable, so-so, unexciting, uninspired.
OPPOSITE exceptional.

indigenous *adjective*
indigenous plants. indigenous people. aboriginal, native, original.
OPPOSITE foreign, imported.

indignant *adjective*
an indignant customer. angry, cross, infuriated, irate, irritated, livid (*informal*), riled (*informal*), ropeable (*Australian informal*), up in arms (*informal*).
OPPOSITE delighted.

indignation *noun*
righteous indignation. anger, fury, ire, irritation, outrage, wrath.

indirect *adjective*
an indirect route. circuitous, devious, meandering, rambling, roundabout.
OPPOSITE straight.

a
b
c
d
e
f
g
h
i
j
k
l
m
n
o
p
q
r
s
t
u
v
w
x
y
z

indispensable *adjective*
an indispensable gadget. essential, key,
necessary, required, vital.
OPPOSITE redundant.

indisposed *adjective*
A relief teacher replaced our teacher who
was indisposed. crook (*Australian
informal*), ill, poorly, sick, unwell.
OPPOSITE well.

indistinct *adjective*
indistinct shapes. blurred, confused,
faint, fuzzy, hazy, indefinite, obscure,
unclear, vague.
OPPOSITE clear, distinct.

individual *adjective*
1 individual serves. separate, single.
OPPOSITE shared.
2 The artist has his individual style.
characteristic, distinct, distinctive,
exclusive, own, particular, peculiar,
personal, special, specific, unique.
OPPOSITE universal.
individual *noun* (*informal*)
an unpleasant individual. character,
fellow, human being, man, person,
woman.

indoctrinate *verb*
brainwash; see also TEACH.

induce *verb*
I don't know what induced him to buy a
car. cause, coax, influence, inspire, lead,
motivate, move, persuade, prompt,
provoke, sway, tempt.
OPPOSITE deter.

inducement *noun*
They offered him inducements to stay.
attraction, carrot, enticement, goad,
incentive, spur, stimulus.
OPPOSITE deterrent.

indulge *verb*
1 He indulges his children. mollycoddle,
pamper, pander to, spoil.
2 She indulged her craving for chocolate.
cater to, give in to, gratify, satisfy.

indulgent *adjective*
an indulgent father. easygoing,
forbearing, forgiving, kind, lenient,
merciful, permissive, soft, tolerant.
OPPOSITE strict.

industrious *adjective*
an industrious worker. conscientious,
diligent, energetic, hard-working,
indefatigable, tireless, unflagging,
zealous.
OPPOSITE lazy.

industry *noun*
the car industry. business, commerce,
manufacturing, trade.

inedible *adjective*
The food was inedible. uneatable.
OPPOSITE edible.

ineffective *adjective*
The treatment was ineffective. futile,
unsuccessful, useless.
OPPOSITE effective.

inefficient *adjective*
1 an inefficient system. ineffective,
uneconomic, unproductive, wasteful.
2 an inefficient worker. disorganised,
incapable, incompetent, ineffective,
ineffectual.
OPPOSITE efficient.

inequality *noun*
bias, difference, discrimination,
imbalance, prejudice.
OPPOSITE equality.

inertia *noun*
a feeling of inertia. inactivity, laziness,
lethargy, listlessness, sluggishness.
OPPOSITE action, vitality.

inevitable *adjective*
an inevitable accident. certain,
inescapable, sure, unavoidable.
OPPOSITE avoidable.

inexact *adjective*
an inexact translation. approximate,
imprecise, inaccurate, loose, rough.
OPPOSITE exact.

inexcusable *adjective*
Her bad behaviour was inexcusable.
unforgivable, unjustifiable,
unpardonable.
OPPOSITE excusable.

inexpensive *adjective*
budget-priced, cheap, economical,
low-priced, reasonable.
OPPOSITE expensive.

inexperienced *adjective*
an inexperienced youth. green, immature, naive, unsophisticated, unworldly.
OPPOSITE experienced.

inexplicable *adjective*
The disappearance was inexplicable. baffling, incomprehensible, mysterious, puzzling, unaccountable, unexplainable.

infallible *adjective*
an infallible cure. certain, dependable, foolproof, guaranteed, perfect, reliable, sure, unfailing.
OPPOSITE fallible, uncertain.

infamous *adjective*
an infamous villain. his infamous deeds. disgraceful, dishonourable, evil, notorious, outrageous, scandalous, wicked.
OPPOSITE honourable.

infant *noun*
babe, baby, child, piccaninny, toddler, tot.

infantile *adjective*
His behaviour is infantile. babyish, childish, immature, juvenile, puerile.
OPPOSITE mature.

infatuated *adjective*
infatuated with She was infatuated with him. besotted with, crazy about, in love with, mad about.

infatuation *noun*
crush (*informal*), obsession, passion.

infect *verb*
The water was infected by the chemicals. contaminate, poison, pollute, taint.

infection *noun*
She caught a respiratory infection. ailment, bug (*informal*), disease, illness, virus, wog (*Australian informal*).

infectious *adjective*
infectious diseases. catching, communicable, contagious.

infer *verb*
From the state of his clothes we inferred that it was raining. conclude, deduce, gather, reason, surmise.

inferior *adjective*
1 inferior rank. junior, lower, subordinate.
OPPOSITE superior.
2 inferior work. inferior quality. cheap, crook (*Australian informal*), faulty, imperfect, inadequate, indifferent, mediocre, poor, second-rate, shoddy, substandard, third-rate.
OPPOSITE superior.

infertile *adjective*
infertile soil. barren, poor, sterile, unproductive.
OPPOSITE fertile.

infest *verb*
Rats infested the shed. invade, overrun, swarm, take over.

infidelity *noun*
his wife's infidelity. adultery, disloyalty, unfaithfulness.
OPPOSITE faithfulness, fidelity.

infinite *adjective*
1 an infinite number of possibilities. endless, immeasurable, immense, incalculable, inexhaustible, innumerable, limitless, myriad, unlimited.
2 He believes that space is infinite. boundless, endless, interminable, never-ending, unbounded, unending.
OPPOSITE finite.

infirm *adjective*
A nurse looks after the infirm people. ailing, decrepit, feeble, frail, ill, poorly, senile, unwell, weak.
OPPOSITE healthy.

inflame *verb*
His speech inflamed the crowd. anger, arouse, enrage, fire up, incense, incite, infuriate, provoke, rouse, stir up.
OPPOSITE calm.

inflamed *adjective*
an inflamed tonsil. festering, infected, red, sore, swollen.

inflammable *adjective*
Petrol is highly inflammable. combustible, flammable.
OPPOSITE non-flammable, non-inflammable.

a
b
c
d
e
f
g
h
i
j
k
l
m
n
o
p
q
r
s
t
u
v
w
x
y
z

inflate *verb*
1 *inflate a tyre.* blow up, fill, pump up.
OPPOSITE deflate.
2 *inflate the price.* increase, raise.

inflexible *adjective*
1 *The ruler is made of inflexible plastic.*
firm, hard, rigid, solid, stiff.
2 *an inflexible person, attitude, etc.*
adamant, firm, obstinate, rigid,
stubborn, unbending, uncompromising.
OPPOSITE flexible.

inflict *verb*
inflict a penalty. administer, impose.

influence *noun*
1 *Television had an influence on her.*
effect, hold, impact.
2 *political influence.* authority, clout
(*informal*), control, leverage, muscle,
power, pressure, sway, weight.
influence *verb*
Don't try to influence her. affect, bias,
change, control, lead, manipulate,
motivate, move, persuade, predispose,
prejudice, sway.

influential *adjective*
an influential person. authoritative,
important, persuasive, powerful,
strong.
OPPOSITE weak.

inform *verb*
She informed them of their rights. advise,
brief, enlighten, fill in (*informal*),
instruct, keep posted, notify, tell, warn.
inform on *They informed on the con man.*
betray, blow the whistle on (*informal*),
denounce, dob in (*Australian informal*),
grass (on) (*slang*), rat on (*informal*),
report, shop (*slang*), sneak on (*informal*),
split on (*slang*), tell on.

informal *adjective*
1 *an informal atmosphere.* casual,
easygoing, homely, natural, relaxed.
2 *informal language.* colloquial,
everyday, slangy.
OPPOSITE formal.

information *noun*
*The police received new information. She
read the information she was given.* advice,
communication, data, evidence, facts,
info (*informal*), intelligence, knowledge,
low-down (*informal*), material, message,
news, notice, notification, particulars,
report, tidings.

informer *noun*
a police informer. dobber (*Australian
informal*), dog (*slang*), grass (*slang*),
informant, source, stool-pigeon,
tell-tale, whistle-blower (*informal*).

infrequent *adjective*
infrequent visits. irregular, occasional,
rare, sporadic, uncommon.
OPPOSITE frequent.

infuriate *verb*
Her selfishness infuriated the others. anger,
enrage, exasperate, incense, irritate,
madden, needle (*informal*), outrage, rile
(*informal*), vex.

ingenious *adjective*
an ingenious idea. artful, brilliant, clever,
crafty, cunning, imaginative, inventive,
neat, nifty (*informal*), resourceful,
shrewd, skilful, smart.
OPPOSITE unimaginative.

ingrained *adjective*
an ingrained scepticism. confirmed, deep-
rooted, deep-seated.

ingredient *noun*
Mix all the ingredients. component,
constituent, element, part.

inhabit *verb*
They inhabited the place. dwell in, live in,
occupy, people, populate, reside in,
settle in.

inhabitant *noun*
citizen, dweller, inmate, native,
occupant, resident, tenant; see also
POPULATION.

inhale *verb*
She inhaled the fumes. breathe in, draw
in, suck in.
OPPOSITE exhale.

inherent *adjective*
inherent goodness. essential, inborn,
inbred, innate, intrinsic, native, natural.

inheritance *noun*
He received an inheritance. bequest,
birthright, estate, heritage, legacy.

inheritor *noun*
beneficiary, heir, heiress.

inhibit *verb*
inhibit progress. inhibit growth. block, check, curb, hamper, hinder, hold back, impede, limit, obstruct, prevent, restrain, restrict, retard, stunt.
OPPOSITE promote.

inhospitable *adjective*
1 *inhospitable people.* cool, unfriendly, unsociable, unwelcoming.
OPPOSITE hospitable.
2 *an inhospitable place.* bleak, desolate, forbidding, uninviting.

inhuman *adjective*
inhuman treatment of prisoners. barbarous, brutal, cold-hearted, cruel, heartless, inhumane, merciless, ruthless, savage, unfeeling, vicious.
OPPOSITE human, humane.

initial *adjective*
the initial stage. beginning, early, first, introductory, opening, original, preliminary, starting.
OPPOSITE final.

initiate *verb*
He initiated the discussions. begin, commence, embark on, instigate, institute, launch, open, originate, set in motion, start.
OPPOSITE conclude.

initiative *noun*
He lacks initiative. drive, dynamism, enterprise, resourcefulness.
take the initiative begin, commence, make the first move, start, take the lead.

injection *noun*
a tetanus injection. booster, immunisation, inoculation, jab (*informal*), shot, vaccination.

injure *verb*
He injured his leg. bruise, cripple, cut, damage, disable, fracture, harm, hurt, impair, lacerate, maim, mangle, mutilate, scar, sprain, strain, wound.

injury *noun*
minor injuries. abrasion, bruise, cut, damage, fracture, harm, hurt, laceration, lesion, scrape, scratch, wound.

injustice *noun*
1 *the injustice of the system.* bias, discrimination, inequity, prejudice, unfairness, unjustness.
OPPOSITE justice.
2 *They committed many injustices.* abuse, injury, offence, wrong.

inkling *noun*
She had no inkling of what was happening. clue, hint, idea, suspicion.

inland *noun*
He lives in the inland. backblocks (*Australian*), back of beyond, bush, interior, never-never (*Australian*), outback (*Australian*), sticks (*informal*).

inlet *noun*
They rowed up the inlet. bay, cove, creek (*British*), estuary, fiord, harbour, sound.

inn *noun*
hotel, pub (*informal*), public house, tavern.

innate *adjective*
innate ability. congenital, hereditary, inborn, inbred, inherent, inherited, native, natural.
OPPOSITE acquired.

inner *adjective*
an inner wall. central, inside, interior, internal.
OPPOSITE outer.

innocent *adjective*
1 *innocent until proven guilty.* blameless, guiltless.
OPPOSITE guilty.
2 *as innocent as a baby.* angelic, moral, pure, righteous, sinless, virtuous.
OPPOSITE sinful.
3 *an innocent remark.* harmless, innocuous, inoffensive.
OPPOSITE harmful.
4 *young and innocent.* green, gullible, inexperienced, naive, trusting, unworldly.
OPPOSITE experienced.

innovative *adjective*
an innovative design. creative, imaginative, new, novel, original.
OPPOSITE unoriginal.

a
b
c
d
e
f
g
h
i
j
k
l
m
n
o
p
q
r
s
t
u
v
w
x
y
z

innumerable *adjective*
innumerable grains of sand. countless, myriad, numberless, numerous.

inoculate *verb*
inoculate against disease. immunise, vaccinate.

inoffensive *adjective*
an inoffensive remark. harmless, innocuous, safe, unoffending.
OPPOSITE objectionable.

inquest *noun*
see INQUIRY.

inquire *verb*
The man inquired about her health. ask, check, enquire, query, question, quiz.
inquire into *He inquired into their financial dealings.* examine, explore, inspect, investigate, look into, probe, research, study.

inquiry *noun*
1 *an official inquiry.* enquiry, hearing, inquest, inquisition, investigation, post-mortem, probe, review, study.
2 *a telephone number for inquiries.* enquiry, query, question.

inquisitive *adjective*
The stranger was too inquisitive. curious, nosy (*informal*), prying, snoopy (*informal*).
OPPOSITE uninterested.

insane *adjective*
The murderer was insane. berserk, crazy, demented, deranged, irrational, lunatic, mad, mental (*informal*), nutty (*informal*), unbalanced, unhinged.
OPPOSITE sane.

inscribe *verb*
He inscribed his name in the wood. carve, engrave, etch, write.

inscription *noun*
an inscription on a tombstone. engraving, epitaph, words, writing.

insect *noun*
bug (*informal*), creepy-crawly (*informal*); [*various insects*] ant, aphid, bee, beetle, blowfly, borer, bug, butterfly, cicada, cockroach, crane-fly, cricket, dragonfly, earwig, firefly, flea, fly, glow-worm, gnat, grasshopper, hornet, ladybird, locust, louse, midge, mosquito, moth, praying mantis, silverfish, termite, wasp, weevil.

insecure *adjective*
1 *The ladder is insecure.* dangerous, precarious, rickety, rocky, shaky, unsafe, unsteady, wobbly.
OPPOSITE secure.
2 *She feels insecure.* anxious, diffident, fearful, timid, vulnerable.
OPPOSITE confident.

insensitive *adjective*
an insensitive person. callous, cold-hearted, hard-hearted, heartless, indifferent, tactless, thick-skinned, thoughtless, uncaring, unfeeling, unsympathetic.
OPPOSITE sensitive.

inseparable *adjective*
The friends were inseparable. attached, close, thick as thieves (*informal*).

insert *verb*
She inserted old coins in the pudding. implant, put in, slip in, stick in, tuck in.
OPPOSITE remove.

inside *noun*
the inside of an object. centre, core, heart, interior, middle.
OPPOSITE outside.
inside *adjective*
the inside surface. inmost, inner, innermost, interior, internal.
OPPOSITE outside.
insides *plural noun* (*informal*)
the insides of an animal. bowels, entrails, guts, innards (*informal*), intestines.

insight *noun*
He showed great insight into human behaviour. discernment, intuition, judgement, perception, understanding.

insignificant *adjective*
1 *an insignificant increase.* little, minor, minute, negligible, paltry, petty, slight, tiny, trifling, trivial.
OPPOSITE substantial.
2 *an insignificant person.* unimportant, useless, worthless.
OPPOSITE important.

insincere *adjective*
insincere words. an insincere person. deceitful, dishonest, false, hypocritical,

phoney (*informal*), two-faced.
OPPOSITE sincere.

insist *verb*
1 *She insisted that she was right.* assert, claim, declare, emphasise, maintain, stress.
2 *He insisted that we attend the ceremony.* command, demand, put your foot down, require, stipulate.

insolence *noun*
She won't put up with his insolence. arrogance, audacity, backchat (*informal*), cheek, impertinence, impudence, rudeness.

insolent *adjective*
The insolent boy had to apologise. arrogant, brazen, cheeky, contemptuous, disrespectful, impertinent, impolite, impudent, presumptuous, rude.
OPPOSITE polite.

insoluble *adjective*
an insoluble problem. baffling, inexplicable, mysterious, perplexing, puzzling, unanswerable, unsolvable.
OPPOSITE soluble.

inspect *verb*
They inspected the site. check, examine, investigate, look over, scrutinise, survey, suss out (*informal*), view.

inspection *noun*
The car passed the inspection. check, check-up, examination, going-over (*informal*), investigation, once-over (*informal*), scrutiny.

inspire *verb*
His action was inspired by jealousy. animate, drive, encourage, motivate, move, prompt, provoke, spur, stimulate, stir.

install *verb*
1 *The machine was installed in its correct position.* establish, fit, fix, mount, place, put, set up.
OPPOSITE remove.
2 *He was installed as chairman.* induct, invest, ordain.

instalment *noun*
We read the first instalment of the novel. chapter, episode, part, section.

instance *noun*
She gave an instance of their carelessness. case, example, illustration, sample.

instant *adjective*
instant answers. immediate, instantaneous, prompt, quick, ready, speedy, unhesitating.
OPPOSITE slow.
instant *noun*
It happened in an instant. flash, jiffy (*informal*), moment, split second, trice, twinkling of an eye.
OPPOSITE age.

instantaneous *adjective*
Death was instantaneous. immediate, instant, quick, swift.
OPPOSITE gradual, slow.

instead *adverb*
instead of in place of, in lieu of.

instinct *noun*
1 *She knows what to do by instinct.* intuition, nature.
2 *He has an instinct for finding a good place.* aptitude, gift, knack, skill, talent.

instinctive *adjective*
an instinctive reaction. automatic, inborn, innate, intuitive, natural, reflex, spontaneous, subconscious, unlearned.
OPPOSITE learned.

institute *noun*
an institute for learning. academy, college, establishment, institution, organisation, school, society.
institute *verb*
They instituted a new practice. begin, create, establish, found, initiate, originate, start.
OPPOSITE abolish.

institution *noun*
1 *a charitable institution.* establishment, organisation, society.
2 *Bedtime stories were a family institution.* custom, habit, practice, routine, tradition.

instruct *verb*
1 *He instructed the class in life-saving.* coach, drill, educate, lecture, teach, train, tutor.
2 *He instructed them to start.* bid, command, direct, order, tell.

a
b
c
d
e
f
g
h
i
j
k
l
m
n
o
p
q
r
s
t
u
v
w
x
y
z

instruction *noun*
1 *religious instruction.* education, guidance, lessons, schooling, teaching, training, tuition.
2 *He followed the instructions.* command, direction, guideline, order, prescription, recipe, rule.

instructive *adjective*
an instructive film. educational, enlightening, helpful, informative.

instructor *noun*
coach, educator, lecturer, mentor, teacher, trainer, tutor.

instrument *noun*
The technician uses many instruments. apparatus, appliance, device, gadget, implement, machine, tool, utensil; see also EQUIPMENT.

insufficient *adjective*
insufficient money. deficient, inadequate, meagre, scant, scanty, scarce, wanting.
OPPOSITE enough.

insulate *verb*
1 *insulate a pipe.* clad, cover, lag, protect, wrap.
2 *insulate a person from the outside world.* isolate, protect, separate, shelter, shield.

insult *verb*
He was reprimanded for insulting his sister. abuse, be rude to, disparage, offend, put down, slight, snub.
OPPOSITE compliment.

insult *noun*
She tried to ignore his insults. abuse, affront, insolence, put-down (*informal*), rudeness, slight, snub.

insulting *adjective*
an insulting remark. abusive, derogatory, disparaging, offensive, rude, uncomplimentary.
OPPOSITE complimentary.

insurance *noun*
life insurance. car insurance. assurance, cover, indemnity, protection.

intact *adjective*
The ornament was no longer intact after being dropped. complete, entire, perfect, unbroken, undamaged, whole.
OPPOSITE broken, damaged.

integral *adjective*
an integral part of the organisation. basic, essential, indispensable, necessary, vital.
OPPOSITE dispensable.

integrate *verb*
The two plans were integrated into one. amalgamate, blend, combine, incorporate, join, merge, mix, unite.
OPPOSITE separate.

integrity *noun*
Friends vouched for his integrity. honesty, honour, morality, scrupulousness, trustworthiness, truthfulness, uprightness, virtue.
OPPOSITE dishonesty.

intellect *noun*
Use your intellect. brains, intelligence, mental ability, mind, reason, sense, understanding.

intellectual *adjective*
1 *an intellectual challenge.* academic, mental.
2 *an intellectual person.* academic, bookish, brainy, erudite, intelligent, learned, scholarly, studious, thinking.

intellectual *noun*
a discussion among intellectuals. academic, brain (*informal*), highbrow, scholar, thinker.

intelligence *noun*
1 *The test measures intelligence.* brains, cleverness, intellect, mental ability, reason, sense, understanding, wisdom.
2 *He received secret intelligence.* advice, information, knowledge, news, notification, report, tidings, word.
3 *He works in intelligence.* espionage, spying.

intelligent *adjective*
an intelligent person. astute, brainy, bright, clever, intellectual, perceptive, quick, reasoning, sensible, sharp, shrewd, smart, thinking, wise.
OPPOSITE stupid.

intend *verb*
1 *She intends to become a dentist.* aim, mean, plan, propose.
2 *The comment was intended to shock.* calculate, design, mean.

intense *adjective*
1 *intense pain.* acute, concentrated, excruciating, extreme, great, piercing, raging, severe, sharp, strong, violent.
OPPOSITE mild.
2 *an intense love.* ardent, burning, deep, earnest, fervent, keen, passionate, powerful, profound, strong, vehement.
OPPOSITE cool, indifferent.

intensify *verb*
1 *The troubles intensified.* escalate, mount, multiply, worsen.
OPPOSITE ease.
2 *The humidity intensified the problem.* aggravate, boost, compound, exacerbate, heighten, increase, reinforce, strengthen.
OPPOSITE reduce.

intensive *adjective*
intensive care. comprehensive, concentrated, in-depth, thorough.

intent *noun*
with intent to kill. intention, object, objective, plan, purpose.
intent *adjective*
1 *intent on destruction.* bent, determined, resolved, set.
2 *an intent gaze.* absorbed, concentrated, engrossed, fixed, intense, keen, steadfast, steady.

intention *noun*
The intention was to please. aim, ambition, goal, intent, object, objective, plan, purpose.

intentional *adjective*
an intentional insult. conscious, deliberate, intended, planned, premeditated, purposeful, wilful.
OPPOSITE accidental.

intercept *verb*
The bus was intercepted before it reached its destination. ambush, cut off, head off, obstruct, stop, waylay.

interchange *noun*
a traffic interchange. crossroads, intersection, junction.

interest *noun*
1 *He has no interest in the subject.* concern, curiosity, enthusiasm,

fascination.
OPPOSITE indifference.
2 *His interests are philately and reading.* hobby, pastime, pursuit.
interest *verb*
The subject interests him. absorb, appeal to, attract, concern, engross, excite, fascinate, intrigue.
OPPOSITE bore.

interested *adjective*
1 *an interested student.* absorbed, attentive, concerned, curious, engrossed, enthusiastic, inquisitive, keen.
OPPOSITE uninterested.
2 *an interested party.* concerned, involved, partisan.
OPPOSITE disinterested, neutral.

interesting *adjective*
an interesting book. absorbing, engrossing, exciting, fascinating, gripping, intriguing, readable, riveting, stimulating.
OPPOSITE uninteresting.

interfere *verb*
1 *Do not interfere in their business. You must not interfere.* butt in, intervene, intrude, meddle, poke your nose in, pry.
2 *Someone has interfered with the radio.* fiddle, tamper, tinker.
3 *It doesn't interfere with his work.* conflict, get in the way of, hamper.

interior *adjective*
the interior surface. inner, inside, internal.
OPPOSITE exterior.
interior *noun*
They explored the interior. backblocks (*Australian*), centre, inland, outback (*Australian*).
OPPOSITE coast.

interlude *noun*
a refreshing interlude. break, gap, intermission, interval, pause, recess, rest.

intermediate *adjective*
an intermediate position. halfway, middle, neutral.

intermission *noun*
see INTERVAL.

a
b
c
d
e
f
g
h
i
j
k
l
m
n
o
p
q
r
s
t
u
v
w
x
y
z

intermittent *adjective*
intermittent rain. fitful, occasional, on and off, spasmodic, sporadic.
OPPOSITE continuous.

intern *verb*
They interned aliens. confine, detain, imprison, jail, lock up.
OPPOSITE free.

internal *adjective*
an internal wall. inner, inside, interior.
OPPOSITE external.

international *adjective*
1 *an international phone call.* long-distance, overseas.
OPPOSITE domestic.
2 *an international problem.* global, universal, worldwide.
OPPOSITE local, national.

interpret *verb*
He interpreted the words incorrectly. construe, decipher, decode, explain, read, take, translate, understand.

interrogate *verb*
The police interrogated the suspect. cross-examine, examine, grill, question, quiz.

interrogation *noun*
cross-examination, examination, inquisition, questioning, third degree.

interrupt *verb*
1 *A phone call interrupted the game.* break up, disrupt, disturb, halt, hold up, interfere with, stop.
2 *The speaker asked her to stop interrupting.* break in, butt in, chip in, cut in, interject.

interruption *noun*
a short interruption to her work. break, disruption, gap, halt, pause, stop, stoppage.

intersect *verb*
The two roads intersect. converge, cross, cut.

intersection *noun*
corner, crossroads, interchange, junction.

interval *noun*
1 *an interval of half an hour.* break, gap, interlude, intermission, interruption,

lapse, lull, pause, recess, respite, rest, space, spell.
2 *the interval measured two centimetres.* gap, opening, space.

intervene *verb*
She does not intervene in their disputes. butt in, interfere, intrude, meddle, mediate, step in.

interview *noun*
conversation, dialogue, discussion, meeting.

intestines *plural noun*
bowels, colon, entrails, guts, innards (*informal*), insides (*informal*).

intimate[1] *adjective*
1 *intimate friends.* affectionate, bosom, close, familiar.
OPPOSITE distant.
2 *an intimate conversation.* confidential, heart-to-heart, personal, private.
OPPOSITE public.
3 *an intimate knowledge of computers.* deep, detailed, firsthand, in-depth, thorough.
OPPOSITE superficial.

intimate[2] *verb*
She intimated that she was going to resign. hint, imply, indicate, insinuate, make known, suggest.

intimidate *verb*
They were intimidated into signing the consent form. bully, coerce, cow, frighten, scare, stand over (*Australian*), terrorise, threaten.

intolerable *adjective*
intolerable pain. agonising, excruciating, insufferable, unbearable.
OPPOSITE tolerable.

intolerant *adjective*
He was intolerant of people with different views. bigoted, narrow-minded, prejudiced.
OPPOSITE tolerant.

intoxicated *adjective*
drunk, drunken, fuddled, high (*informal*), high as a kite (*informal*), inebriated, merry (*informal*), plastered (*slang*), smashed (*slang*), sozzled (*slang*), stoned (*slang*), tiddly (*informal*), tipsy,

under the influence.
OPPOSITE sober.

intoxicating *adjective*
intoxicating drinks. alcoholic, heady,
spirituous, strong.
OPPOSITE soft.

intrepid *adjective*
an intrepid knight. bold, brave,
courageous, daring, fearless, gallant,
game, heroic, plucky, valiant.
OPPOSITE cowardly.

intricate *adjective*
an intricate design. complex,
complicated, detailed, elaborate, fancy,
involved, ornate.
OPPOSITE simple.

intrigue *verb*
The story intrigued her. appeal to,
fascinate, interest.
intrigue *noun*
a political intrigue. conspiracy, plot,
scheme.

introduce *verb*
1 *She introduced him to her mother.*
acquaint (with), make known, present.
2 *He introduced the next item.* announce,
present.
3 *They introduced a new system.* begin,
bring in, establish, initiate, institute,
launch, phase in, set up, start.

introduction *noun*
the introduction of a book. beginning,
foreword, opening, preamble, preface,
prelude, prologue.
OPPOSITE epilogue.

introductory *adjective*
introductory remarks. opening,
preliminary, preparatory.
OPPOSITE concluding.

intrude *verb*
They intruded on a private meeting. barge
in, break in, butt in, gatecrash, interfere,
intervene, muscle in (*slang*), trespass.

intruder *noun*
The owner surprised the intruder. burglar,
gatecrasher, housebreaker, invader,
robber, thief, trespasser.

intuition *noun*
He acted on his intuition. feeling, hunch,
instinct, sixth sense.

intuitive *adjective*
see INSTINCTIVE.

inundate *verb*
1 *The river inundated the town.* drown,
engulf, flood, overflow, submerge,
swamp.
2 *She was inundated with letters.* deluge,
overwhelm, swamp.

invade *verb*
1 *Enemy forces invaded the country.*
attack, enter, occupy, overrun, raid.
2 *Do not invade their privacy.* encroach
on, infringe upon, intrude on, trespass
on.

invalid[1] *noun*
The invalid is bedridden. patient, sufferer.

invalid[2] *adjective*
His licence is invalid. expired, illegal, out
of date, unusable, useless, void.
OPPOSITE valid.

invaluable *adjective*
His support was invaluable. precious,
useful, valuable.
OPPOSITE useless, worthless.

invariable *adjective*
her invariable response. consistent,
constant, regular, set, unchangeable,
unchanging, uniform.

invasion *noun*
1 *an invasion into a neighbouring country.*
attack, foray, incursion, onslaught, raid.
2 *invasion of privacy.* infringement,
intrusion, violation.

invent *verb*
1 *invent a tool, word, etc.* coin, conceive,
create, design, devise, make,
manufacture, mint, originate.
2 *invent an excuse.* concoct, cook up
(*informal*), dream up, fabricate, make
up, think up.

invention *noun*
a useful invention. coinage, contraption,
creation, device, innovation.

inventive *adjective*
an inventive person. clever, creative,
enterprising, imaginative, ingenious,
innovative, resourceful.
OPPOSITE unimaginative.

a
b
c
d
e
f
g
h
i
j
k
l
m
n
o
p
q
r
s
t
u
v
w
x
y
z

inventor *noun*
creator, designer, discoverer, innovator, maker, originator.

invest *verb*
1 *He invested his money in the business.* place, put.
2 *He invested much time in study.* devote, give, put in, spend.

investigate *verb*
They investigated his disappearance. check on, examine, explore, go into, inquire into, look into, probe, research, study, suss out (*informal*).

investigation *noun*
a police investigation. a scientific investigation. examination, exploration, inquest, inquiry, inspection, research, scrutiny, study, survey.

investment *noun*
a good return on an investment. capital, outlay, principal, stake.

invigorate *verb*
The walk invigorated her. enliven, pep up (*informal*), perk up, refresh, rejuvenate.
OPPOSITE tire.

invigorating *adjective*
an invigorating walk. bracing, healthy, refreshing, stimulating.
OPPOSITE exhausting.

invincible *adjective*
an invincible team. unbeatable, unconquerable, undefeatable, unstoppable.
OPPOSITE conquerable.

invisible *adjective*
invisible stitching. concealed, hidden, imperceptible, inconspicuous, undetectable, unnoticeable, unseen.
OPPOSITE visible.

invite *verb*
They invited him to speak. ask, bid, call on, request, urge.

inviting *adjective*
an inviting place. appealing, attractive, enticing, tempting.
OPPOSITE uninviting.

invoice *noun*
The goods came with an invoice. account, bill, statement.

involuntary *adjective*
an involuntary movement. automatic, impulsive, instinctive, mechanical, reflex, spontaneous, unconscious, unintentional.
OPPOSITE deliberate, voluntary.

involve *verb*
1 *The plan involves much expense.* entail, mean, necessitate, require.
2 *The scheme involves ordinary people.* affect, concern, include, touch.
3 *He was not involved in the robbery.* embroil, entangle, implicate, incriminate, mix up.

involved *adjective*
1 *a long and involved story.* complex, complicated, elaborate, intricate.
OPPOSITE straightforward.
2 *deeply involved in her work.* absorbed, busy, caught up, engaged, engrossed, occupied, preoccupied, wrapped up.

irate *adjective*
an irate customer. angry, annoyed, cross, enraged, furious, indignant, infuriated, livid (*informal*), mad, ropeable (*Australian informal*).

iron *verb*
He ironed the clothes. press, smooth.
irons *plural noun*
The prisoner was in irons. bonds, chains, fetters, shackles.

irrational *adjective*
irrational behaviour. crazy, illogical, mad, nonsensical, senseless, unreasonable.
OPPOSITE rational.

irregular *adjective*
1 *an irregular surface.* bumpy, pitted, rough, rugged, uneven.
OPPOSITE even, level.
2 *an irregular shape.* asymmetric, lopsided.
OPPOSITE regular.
3 *She made irregular visits.* erratic, infrequent, occasional, random, spasmodic, sporadic.
OPPOSITE regular.
4 *irregular behaviour.* abnormal, eccentric, extraordinary, odd, peculiar,

strange, unconventional, unusual.
OPPOSITE normal.

irrelevant *adjective*
This information is irrelevant. beside the point, inapplicable, neither here nor there, unconnected.
OPPOSITE pertinent.

irreligious *adjective*
an irreligious person. agnostic, atheistic, godless, heathen, impious, irreverent, pagan, unbelieving, ungodly.
OPPOSITE religious.

irresistible *adjective*
an irresistible desire. compelling, overpowering, overwhelming, powerful; see also TEMPTING.

irresponsible *adjective*
an irresponsible babysitter. careless, negligent, reckless, thoughtless, unthinking, untrustworthy.
OPPOSITE responsible.

irreverent *adjective*
an irreverent joke. blasphemous, disrespectful, impious, irreligious, profane, sacrilegious, ungodly.
OPPOSITE reverent.

irritable *adjective*
He is irritable when tired. bad-tempered, cantankerous, crabby, cranky, cross, crotchety, fractious, grouchy (*informal*), grumpy, irascible, peevish, petulant, prickly, ratty (*informal*), short-tempered, snaky (*Australian informal*), snappy, testy.
OPPOSITE cheerful.

irritate *verb*
anger, annoy, bother, bug (*informal*), drive someone mad (*informal*), drive someone up the wall (*informal*), exasperate, get on someone's nerves, give someone the pip (*informal*), harass, infuriate, irk, nark (*informal*), needle (*informal*), pester, plague, provoke, rankle, rile (*informal*), rub someone up the wrong way (*informal*), trouble, upset, vex.

irritating *adjective*
annoying, bothersome, exasperating, tiresome, trying, upsetting.

irritation *noun*
He could not hide his irritation. anger, annoyance, displeasure, exasperation, impatience, vexation.

island *noun*
isle, islet.

isolate *verb*
He isolated himself from the community. cut off, detach, insulate, separate, set apart.

isolated *adjective*
an isolated homestead. cut-off, desolate, lone, lonely, outlying, remote, secluded, solitary.

issue *noun*
1 *the latest issue of the magazine.* edition, number, publication.
2 *They discussed serious issues.* matter, point, question, subject, topic.
issue *verb*
1 *They issued safety helmets to visitors.* distribute, give out, provide, supply.
2 *The principal issues a weekly bulletin.* circulate, distribute, publish, put out, release, send out.

itch *noun*
1 *The bite left an itch.* irritation, prickling, tickle, tingling.
2 *She has an itch to fly.* desire, longing, urge, yearning.
itch *verb*
1 *Scratch where it itches.* prickle, tickle, tingle.
2 *He is itching to find out.* be desperate, be eager, hanker, long, thirst, yearn.

item *noun*
1 *The items were listed individually.* article, detail, entry, object, piece, point, product, thing.
2 *a news item.* article, feature, piece, report, story.

itemise *verb*
Phone calls are itemised on the bill. detail, list, specify, spell out.

a
b
c
d
e
f
g
h
i
j
k
l
m
n
o
p
q
r
s
t
u
v
w
x
y
z

Jj

jab *verb*
He jabbed the needle into her arm. poke, prod, stab, thrust.
jab *noun*
1 He received a jab in his side. dig, nudge, poke, prod, stab, thrust.
2 (*informal*) a tetanus jab. immunisation, injection, shot, vaccination.

jack *verb*
jack up You need to jack up the car to change the tyre. hoist, lift, raise.

jacket *noun*
1 They wore jackets. anorak, blazer, bolero, cagoule, coat, parka, tuxedo, windcheater.
2 a book jacket. cover, dust cover, dust jacket, wrapper.

jaded *adjective*
He was feeling jaded. done in (*informal*), fatigued, tired, weary, worn out.
OPPOSITE energetic.

jagged *adjective*
a jagged edge. chipped, notched, ragged, rough, serrated, uneven.
OPPOSITE smooth.

jail or **gaol** *noun*
1 The jail was built by convicts. detention centre, lock-up, nick (*slang*), penitentiary (*American*), prison, remand centre, watch-house.
2 He was sentenced to two years' jail. confinement, custody, imprisonment, porridge (*slang*), prison.
jail *verb*
He was jailed for ten years. imprison, intern, lock up, put away, put behind bars.
OPPOSITE release.

jailer or **gaoler** *noun*
keeper, prison officer, warder.

jam¹ *verb*
1 I jammed the books in tightly. pack, push, ram, squash, squeeze, stuff, wedge.

2 The tape has jammed. catch, snarl, stick.
3 The shoppers jammed the entrance to the store. block, clog, cram, crowd, fill, jam-pack, obstruct, pack.
jam *noun*
1 a traffic jam. build-up, congestion, hold-up, snarl.
2 (*informal*) I'm in a jam. bind (*informal*), difficulty, fix (*informal*), mess, plight, predicament, spot (*informal*).

jam² *noun*
toast and jam. conserve, jelly, marmalade, preserve.

jamboree *noun*
They attended the Scout jamboree. carnival, celebration, convention, gathering, rally.

jam-packed *adjective* (*informal*)
The hall was jam-packed. chock-a-block, chockers (*informal*), crammed, crowded, filled, full, packed.
OPPOSITE empty, half-empty.

jangle *verb*
The keys jangled. clang, clank, clink, jingle, rattle.

jar¹ *noun*
a glass jar. bottle, container, crock, jug, pot, receptacle, vase, vessel.

jar² *verb*
She jarred her neck in the accident. jerk, jolt, shake.

jargon *noun*
He didn't understand the scientist's jargon. cant, gobbledegook (*informal*), idiom, lingo (*informal*), slang.

jarring *adjective*
a jarring noise. discordant, grating, harsh, irritating, raucous.

jaunt *noun*
a Sunday afternoon jaunt in the car. drive, excursion, expedition, outing, trip.

jazz *verb*
jazz up *She jazzes up her clothes with ribbons.* adorn, brighten up, liven up.

jazzy *adjective*
a jazzy sports car. flash (*informal*), flashy, gaudy, showy, smart, snazzy (*informal*).

jealous *adjective*
He was jealous of his brother's popularity. covetous, envious, grudging, resentful.

jeer *verb*
The crowd jeered him rudely. boo, chiack (*Australian informal*), gibe, heckle, hiss, laugh at, make fun of, mock, ridicule, scoff at, sneer at, taunt.
OPPOSITE cheer.
jeer *noun*
He was driven off the stage with jeers. boo, catcall, gibe, hiss, scoff, sneer, taunt.
OPPOSITE cheer.

jelly *noun*
quince jelly. conserve, jam, preserve.

jeopardise *verb*
His reckless driving jeopardised their lives. endanger, imperil, put on the line, risk, threaten.

jeopardy *noun*
Their lives were in jeopardy. danger, peril, risk, threat.
OPPOSITE safety.

jerk *noun*
1 *It opened with a jerk.* jig, jiggle, jog, jolt, pull, rock, shake, thrust, tug, twist, twitch.
2 (*slang*) *He's such a jerk.* see FOOL.
jerk *verb*
1 *She jerked the camera as she took the photo.* jiggle, move, shake.
2 *The car jerked down the road.* bounce, jolt, kangaroo, kangaroo-hop, lurch.
3 *The door had to be jerked open.* jiggle, pull, tug, twist, wrench, yank.

jerky *adjective*
jerky movements. disconnected, rough, spasmodic, uncoordinated, uneven.
OPPOSITE smooth.

jersey *noun*
jumper, pullover, sweater, top.

jest *noun*
He told a jest. gag, joke, wisecrack (*informal*), witticism.
jest *verb*
He didn't mean it: he was only jesting. joke, kid (*informal*), pull someone's leg (*informal*), tease.

jester *noun*
the court jester. buffoon, clown, comedian, comic, fool, joker, wag, zany.

jet *noun*
1 *a jet of water.* fountain, gush, spray, spurt, stream.
2 *a blocked jet.* nozzle, spout, sprinkler.
3 *They travelled on a jet.* jumbo, jumbo jet, plane; see also AIRCRAFT.

jetty *noun*
They boarded the ferry at the jetty. landing stage, pier, quay, wharf.

jewel *noun*
a gold ring set with jewels. gem, gemstone, precious stone.

jewellery *noun*
adornments, jewels, ornaments, trinkets; [*kinds of jewellery*] anklet, bangle, beads, bracelet, brooch, chain, charm, cuff link, earring, locket, necklace, pendant, ring, stud, tiepin.

jib *verb*
The horse jibbed at the fence. baulk, prop (*Australian*), pull up, stop.

jiffy *noun* (*informal*)
in a jiffy. flash, instant, minute, moment, second (*informal*), tick (*informal*).

jig *verb*
The toddler jigged up and down. bob, bounce, dance, hop, jump.

jiggle *verb*
He jiggled the key in the lock. jerk, shake, wiggle.

jilt *verb*
After a long courtship he jilted her. abandon, drop (*informal*), dump (*informal*), forsake, reject.

jingle *verb*
The coins jingled in his pocket. clink, jangle, rattle, ring, tinkle.

a
b
c
d
e
f
g
h
i
j
k
l
m
n
o
p
q
r
s
t
u
v
w
x
y
z

jingle *noun*
1 *the jingle of coins. the jingle of sleigh bells.* clink, jangle, rattle, ring, tinkle.
2 *a catchy advertising jingle.* chorus, poem, rhyme, song, tune, verse.

jinx *noun*
There seems to be a jinx on them. curse, hex, spell.

jinxed *adjective*
see UNLUCKY.

jitters *plural noun* (*informal*)
He had the jitters before his driving test. butterflies (*informal*), collywobbles (*informal*), heebie-jeebies (*informal*), jim-jams (*informal*), nerves, shakes, willies (*informal*).

jittery *adjective* (*informal*)
The dentist calmed the jittery patient. anxious, frightened, jumpy, nervous, nervy, quivering, shaky, uneasy.
OPPOSITE calm.

job *noun*
1 *He is paid at the end of each job.* assignment, chore, errand, piece of work, project, task.
2 *He changed his job.* appointment, career, employment, occupation, position, post, profession, situation, trade, vocation, work.
3 *It's his job to lock up.* duty, function, responsibility, role.

jobless *adjective*
out of work, unemployed.
OPPOSITE employed.

jockey *noun*
a horse and jockey. hoop (*Australian informal*), horseman, horse-rider, horsewoman, rider.

jog *verb*
1 *She needed to jog him a little to wake him up.* jerk, jolt, knock, nudge, push, shake.
2 *Let me jog your memory.* prompt, refresh, stimulate, stir.
3 *He jogs for exercise.* run, trot.

join *verb*
1 *He joined the two bits together.* add, attach, bind, bracket, cement, combine, connect, couple, fasten, fit, fuse, glue, link, put together, solder, splice, stick, tack, tie, unite, weld.
OPPOSITE separate.
2 *The two roads join at Hay.* come together, converge, meet, merge.
3 *She joined in the fun.* participate, share, take part.
4 *She joined the army.* enlist in, enrol in, enter, register for, sign up for, volunteer for.
OPPOSITE leave.

join *noun*
You can't see the join. connection, joint, knot, link, seam.

joint *adjective*
a joint decision. a joint effort. collective, combined, common, cooperative, shared.
OPPOSITE individual.

jointly *adverb*
They do everything jointly. as a team, cooperatively, in partnership, together.
OPPOSITE individually.

joke *noun*
1 *He tells jokes.* gag, jest, pun, wisecrack (*informal*), witticism.
2 *She played a joke on them.* hoax, practical joke, prank, trick.

joke *verb*
Don't joke: this is serious. crack jokes, jest, kid (*informal*), pun, tease.

joker *noun*
The joker cheered them up. buffoon, clown, comedian, comic, jester, prankster, wag, zany.

jolly *adjective*
a jolly person. bright, cheerful, cheery, exuberant, good-humoured, happy, high-spirited, jovial, joyful, merry.
OPPOSITE miserable.

jolt *verb*
1 *They were jolted out of their seats by the impact.* bump, dislodge, jerk, shake.
2 *The car jolted along the road.* bounce, bump, jerk, kangaroo, kangaroo-hop, lurch.

jolt *noun*
1 *The jolts of the train kept the passengers awake.* bounce, bump, jerk, lurch.

2 *The news of the accident gave her a jolt.* shock, start, surprise.

jostle *verb*
They had to jostle their way through the crowd. bump, elbow, knock, push, shove.

jot *verb*
jot down *He jotted down the address.* note, scribble, take down, write down.

jotter *noun*
notebook, notepad, pad, writing pad.

journal *noun*
1 *The explorer kept a journal of his expedition.* diary, logbook, record.
2 *an article in a scientific journal.* magazine, newspaper, paper, periodical.

journalist *noun*
columnist, correspondent, editor, journo (*Australian informal*), reporter.

journey *noun*
cruise, drive, excursion, expedition, flight, jaunt, mission, outing, pilgrimage, ride, safari, tour, trek, trip, voyage, walk.
journey *verb*
see TRAVEL.

jovial *adjective*
a jovial person. breezy, bright, cheerful, good-humoured, happy, jolly, joyful, lively, merry.
OPPOSITE melancholy.

joy *noun*
The news of the birth filled them with joy. bliss, contentment, delight, ecstasy, elation, euphoria, exultation, gladness, happiness, jubilation, pleasure, rapture.

joyful *adjective*
She was joyful at the news. blithe, cheerful, content, delighted, ecstatic, elated, euphoric, exultant, glad, happy, jolly, jovial, joyous, jubilant, merry, overjoyed.
OPPOSITE miserable.

jubilant *adjective*
the jubilant prizewinner. delighted, exultant, gleeful, happy, joyful, overjoyed, rejoicing, triumphant.

jubilation *noun*
We shared in the team's jubilation after they won the match. delight, exultation, glee, happiness, joy, rejoicing, triumph.

jubilee *noun*
the State's jubilee. anniversary, celebration, commemoration, festival.

judge *noun*
1 *a judge of a court.* justice, magistrate.
2 *a judge of a competition.* adjudicator, arbiter, arbitrator, referee, umpire.
judge *verb*
1 *Who is judging the case?* decide, hear, try.
2 *She judged the pet show.* adjudicate, arbitrate, referee, umpire.
3 *You can't judge a book by its cover.* assess, evaluate, rate, size up (*informal*).
4 *He judged the distance accurately.* assess, estimate, gauge, guess.

judgement *noun*
1 *The judgement was in his favour.* adjudication, decision, ruling, sentence, verdict.
2 *He lacks judgement.* discernment, discretion, discrimination, good sense, insight, shrewdness, wisdom.
3 *in the judgement of most people.* assessment, belief, mind, opinion, view.

judicial *adjective*
the judicial system. legal.

judicious *adjective*
a judicious decision. discerning, politic, prudent, sensible, shrewd, wise.
OPPOSITE unwise.

jug *noun*
a jug of water. carafe, ewer, pitcher.

juice *noun*
fruit or vegetable juice. drink, liquid, nectar.

juicy *adjective*
a juicy pear. moist, ripe, succulent.
OPPOSITE dry.

jumble *verb*
All their clothes were jumbled up. confuse, disorganise, mix, mix up, muddle.

a b c d e f g h i j k l m n o p q r s t u v w x y z

jumble *noun*
a jumble of papers. confusion, hotchpotch, mess, mixture, muddle.
jumble sale bazaar, boot sale, bring-and-buy-sale, garage sale, rummage sale.

jump *verb*
1 *The cat jumped on to the bed.* bounce, bound, hop, leap, pounce, spring.
2 *She can jump the fence.* clear, go over, hurdle, pass over, vault.
3 *The reader jumped a line.* leave out, miss, omit, overlook, pass over, skip.
4 *The horse jumped when he heard the shot.* buck, flinch, rear, recoil, shy, start.
5 *Prices have jumped recently.* escalate, increase, rise, shoot up.
jump *noun*
1 *a running jump.* bounce, bound, hop, leap, pounce, spring, vault.
2 *a jump in house prices.* escalation, increase, rise.
3 *The horse baulked at the last jump.* fence, gate, hurdle, obstacle.
jump at *She jumped at the opportunity.* grab, leap at, seize, snatch.

jumper *noun*
guernsey, jersey, pullover, skivvy, sweater, top.

jumpy *adjective*
anxious, edgy, jittery (*informal*), nervous, nervy, tense, uneasy, uptight (*informal*).
OPPOSITE calm.

junction *noun*
a road junction. corner, crossroads, interchange, intersection, meeting point, T-junction, Y-junction.

jungle *noun*
a tropical jungle. forest, rainforest.

junior *adjective*
1 *John Smith junior.* younger.
OPPOSITE older, senior.
2 *a junior officer.* inferior, lower-ranking, subordinate.
OPPOSITE senior, superior.
3 *junior primary school.* lower.

junk *noun*
They threw out their junk. cast-offs, clutter, garbage, odds and ends, rubbish, scrap, trash.

junkie *noun* (*slang*)
addict, drug addict, druggie (*informal*), drug user.

just *adjective*
1 *a just decision.* even-handed, fair, impartial, neutral, reasonable, unbiased, unprejudiced.
OPPOSITE unjust.
2 *a just reward.* appropriate, deserved, fair, fitting, right.
just *adverb*
1 *It happened just at that spot.* exactly, precisely, right.
2 (*informal*) *We are just good friends.* merely, no more than, only, simply.
just about (*informal*)
just about ready. almost, close to, more or less, nearly, practically.

justice *noun*
1 *She appealed to his sense of justice.* equity, even-handedness, fairness, fair play, impartiality, right.
OPPOSITE injustice.
2 *the Chief Justice.* judge, magistrate.

justifiable *adjective*
He has a justifiable complaint. fair, legitimate, reasonable, valid.
OPPOSITE unjustifiable.

justification *noun*
no justification for his actions. defence, excuse, explanation, grounds, reason.

justify *verb*
His actions could never be justified. defend, excuse, explain.

jut *verb*
The bags jutted into the aisle. poke out, project, protrude, stick out.

juvenile *adjective*
1 *juvenile behaviour.* childish, immature, infantile, puerile, youthful.
OPPOSITE mature.
2 *juvenile offenders.* adolescent, teenage, young.
OPPOSITE adult.
juvenile *noun*
The crime was committed by juveniles. adolescent, child, kid (*informal*), minor, teenager, youngster, youth.
OPPOSITE adult.

Kk

kangaroo *noun*
a mob of kangaroos. boomer (*male*), doe (*female*), joey (*young*), old man (*male*), roo (*informal*); [*various kangaroos*] eastern grey kangaroo, euro, forester, red kangaroo, tree-kangaroo, wallaroo, western grey kangaroo.

keel *noun*
the ship's keel. base, bottom, underside.
keel *verb*
keel over *The ship keeled over.* capsize, collapse, fall over, heel over, overturn, tilt, turn over, upset.

keen *adjective*
1 *The knife had a keen edge.* sharp.
OPPOSITE blunt.
2 *A keen wind was blowing.* biting, bitter, cold, piercing, severe.
OPPOSITE gentle.
3 *He showed a keen interest.* ardent, avid, deep, eager, enthusiastic, fervent, intense, lively, strong, zealous.
OPPOSITE apathetic.
4 *She is keen to start work.* anxious, eager, impatient, itching, raring.
5 *The blind man has a keen sense of smell.* acute, penetrating, sensitive, sharp.
OPPOSITE poor.
keen on (*informal*)
He is keen on her. attracted to, fond of, infatuated by, interested in, mad about, nuts on (*informal*), rapt in, taken with.
OPPOSITE uninterested in.

keep *verb*
1 *You must keep some for later.* conserve, hang on to, hold on to, preserve, put aside, put away, reserve, retain, save, store, withhold.
OPPOSITE get rid of.
2 *They had to keep still.* hold, remain, stay.
3 *What kept you?* delay, detain, hinder, hold up, obstruct, prevent.
4 *He keeps his promises. Keep to the rules.* abide by, comply with, conform to, fulfil, honour, obey, stick to.
OPPOSITE break.

5 *They keep the Passover.* celebrate, commemorate, honour, observe.
OPPOSITE ignore.
6 *She keeps goal for the team.* defend, guard, protect.
7 *He can't keep a family on his income.* feed, maintain, provide for, support.
8 *He keeps bees.* care for, look after, own, tend.
9 *They keep trying.* carry on, continue, persevere in, persist in.
OPPOSITE give up.
10 *Margarine will keep for a long time.* be usable, last, stay fresh.
OPPOSITE deteriorate, go off.
keep *noun*
1 *She earns her keep.* board, food, maintenance, subsistence.
2 *the castle's keep.* donjon, stronghold, tower.
for keeps (*informal*)
The trophy was hers for keeps. forever, for good, permanently.
OPPOSITE temporarily.
keep away from *He tried to keep away from her.* avoid, dodge, evade, shun, stay away from, steer clear of.
keep down *We have to keep the numbers down.* limit, restrict.
OPPOSITE increase.
keep on *He just keeps on doing it.* carry on, continue, go on, keep, persist in.
OPPOSITE stop.
keep on at *He keeps on at me.* badger, harass, hassle (*informal*), nag, pester.
keep up *Keep up the good work.* carry on with, continue, maintain.

keeper *noun*
1 *a zoo keeper. a museum keeper.* caretaker, curator, custodian, guardian, ranger.
2 *a jail keeper.* guard, jailer, warder, watchman.

keeping *noun*
in safe keeping. care, charge, custody, guardianship, hands.

in keeping with *a house in keeping with its surroundings.* fitting, in harmony with, in line with, in step with, in tune with, suiting.

keepsake *noun*
a keepsake from her grandmother. memento, reminder, souvenir.

keg *noun*
a keg of beer. barrel, cask, hogshead.

kernel *noun*
almond kernels. nut, seed.

key *noun*
1 *the key to the door.* latchkey, master key, passkey, skeleton key.
2 *the key to the mystery.* answer, clue, secret, solution.
3 *a key to the symbols used in the book.* code, explanation, guide, interpretation, legend.
4 *Press the keys on the pad.* button.
key *verb*
key in *She keyed in the data.* enter, input, type.
key *adjective*
a key industry. critical, crucial, essential, important, major, vital.

kick *verb*
1 *He kicked the ball.* boot, punt.
2 *The gun kicked.* recoil, spring back.
3 *(slang) He has kicked the habit.* give up, quit, stop.
kick *noun*
1 *She gave the ball a hard kick.* boot, punt.
2 *(informal) She gets a kick out of giving presents.* buzz *(informal)*, enjoyment, excitement, fun, pleasure, satisfaction, thrill.
kick off see BEGIN.
kick out *(informal) She broke the rules and was kicked out.* dismiss, drive out, evict, expel, fire, oust, sack, throw out.

kid *noun*
1 see GOAT.
2 *(informal) a film for kids.* child, youngster.
OPPOSITE adult.
kid *verb (informal)*
1 *He tried to kid them that he was really sick.* bluff, deceive, fool, have on *(informal)*, hoax, hoodwink, lie to, trick.
2 *He was just kidding.* jest, joke, pull someone's leg *(informal)*, tease.

kidnap *verb*
They kidnapped his child. abduct, carry off, seize, snatch.

kill *verb*
1 *kill an animal or a person.* annihilate, assassinate, bump off *(slang)*, butcher, cull, destroy, do away with, do in *(slang)*, eliminate, execute, exterminate, finish off, knock off *(informal)*, martyr, massacre, mow down, murder, put down, put to death, put to sleep, slaughter, slay, take someone's life, wipe out, zap *(slang)*; *[various ways to kill]* behead, choke, crucify, decapitate, drown, electrocute, gas, guillotine, gun down, hang, knife, poison, shoot, stab, starve, stifle, stone, strangle, suffocate, throttle.
2 *The medicine killed the pain.* deaden, dull, numb, put an end to, stop.

killer *noun*
The police hunted for the killer. assassin, executioner, hit man *(slang)*, murderer, slayer.

killing *noun*
annihilation, assassination, bloodshed, butchery, carnage, destruction, euthanasia, execution, extermination, genocide, homicide, manslaughter, massacre, murder, slaughter, slaying, suicide.

killjoy *noun*
Who invited that killjoy to the party? party-pooper *(informal)*, spoilsport, wet blanket, wowser *(Australian)*.

kin *noun*
next of kin. family, kindred, kinsfolk, kith and kin, relations, relatives.

kind[1] *noun*
of the same kind. brand, breed, category, class, classification, form, ilk *(informal)*, make, nature, set, sort, species, style, type, variety.

kind[2] *adjective*
a kind person. a kind deed. affectionate, amiable, attentive, benevolent, big-hearted, caring, charitable, compassionate, considerate, fatherly, friendly, generous, genial, gentle, good, good-natured, gracious, helpful, hospitable, humane, kind-hearted, kindly, lenient, loving, merciful,

motherly, neighbourly, nice, obliging, philanthropic, soft-hearted, sympathetic, tender-hearted, thoughtful, understanding, unselfish, warm-hearted, well-meaning.
OPPOSITE unkind.

kindergarten *noun*
nursery school, preschool.

kindle *verb*
1 *He kindled the fire.* fire, ignite, light, set fire to.
OPPOSITE extinguish.
2 *The teacher kindled his interest in history.* arouse, awaken, excite, inspire, spark off, stimulate, stir.
OPPOSITE extinguish.

kindred *noun*
see KIN.

king *noun*
monarch, ruler, sovereign; see also RULER.

kingdom *noun*
1 *The King was respected throughout his kingdom.* country, domain, dominion, empire, land, monarchy, nation, realm, state, territory.
2 *a member of the animal kingdom.* classification, division, world.

kingly *adjective*
regal, royal.

kink *noun*
1 *a kink in a piece of wire.* bend, coil, crinkle, curve, loop, tangle, twist.
2 *a kink in his personality.* eccentricity, foible, peculiarity, quirk.

kiosk *noun*
1 *a newspaper kiosk.* booth, stall, stand.
2 (*Australian*) *They had Devonshire tea at the kiosk.* café, snack bar, tea room.

kiss *noun*
a kiss on the cheek. caress, peck, smack, smooch (*informal*).

kit *noun*
Each recruit is supplied with his kit. equipment, gear, outfit, rig, tackle, things.

kitchen *noun*
galley, kitchenette, scullery.

kitty *noun*
Each person contributes $5 to the kitty. fund, pool, reserve.

knack *noun*
She has a knack for making people laugh. ability, aptitude, art, expertise, gift, skill, talent, trick.

knapsack *noun*
backpack, haversack, pack, rucksack; see also BAG.

knave *noun*
The knave in the story got his just deserts. baddy (*informal*), blackguard, rascal, rogue, scoundrel, villain.

kneel *verb*
She knelt to say her prayers. bend, bow, crouch, genuflect, stoop.

knickers *plural noun*
ladies' knickers. briefs, drawers, panties (*informal*), pants (*informal*), underpants, underwear, undies (*informal*).

knick-knack *noun*
She bought some knick-knacks as souvenirs. curio, ornament, trifle, trinket.

knife *noun*
blade, cutter; [*kinds of knife*] carving knife, chopper, clasp-knife, cleaver, flick knife, jackknife, lancet, machete, paperknife, penknife, pocket knife, scalpel, sheath knife.
knife *verb*
The victim was knifed. cut, slash, slit, stab.

knit *verb*
The broken bones will knit in six weeks. grow together, heal, join, mend.

knob *noun*
1 *the door knob.* handle.
2 *He turned the knobs on the radio.* button, control, switch.
3 *a smooth surface without any knobs.* bulge, bump, knot, lump, node, nodule, projection, swelling.
4 *a knob of butter.* lump, nub, pat.

knobbly *adjective*
The tree has a knobbly trunk. gnarled, knotty, lumpy, rough, uneven.
OPPOSITE smooth.

a
b
c
d
e
f
g
h
i
j
k
l
m
n
o
p
q
r
s
t
u
v
w
x
y
z

knock *verb*
1 *He knocked the man unconscious.* bash, batter, beat, belt, clip (*informal*), clout (*informal*), dong (*Australian informal*), hit, kick, pummel, punch, smite, sock (*slang*), strike, thrash, wallop (*slang*), whack.
2 *She knocked at the door.* bang, hammer, hit, pound, rap, strike, tap, thud, thump.
3 *He knocked a nail in the wall.* drive, hammer, hit.
4 (*informal*) *He knocks everything they do.* bag (*Australian informal*), belittle, bucket (*Australian informal*), criticise, disparage, find fault with, insult, pan (*informal*), pick holes in, rubbish (*Australian informal*), run down, slam (*informal*), tear to pieces.

knock *noun*
He received a knock on the head. He heard a loud knock. bang, blow, bump, clip (*informal*), clout (*informal*), dong (*Australian informal*), hit, kick, punch, rap, slap, smack, tap, thud, thump, wallop (*slang*), whack, wham (*informal*).

knock back (*informal*)
She knocked back his offer. see REFUSE[1].

knock down
1 *They knocked down the old building.* demolish, destroy, pull down, raze.
OPPOSITE erect.
2 *He knocked down the price to $20.* bring down, decrease, lower, reduce.
OPPOSITE raise.

knock into *He knocked into another car.* bang into, bump into, collide with, crash into, run into, slam into, smash into.

knock off
1 (*informal*) *He has knocked off work for today.* cease, finish, stop.
OPPOSITE start.
2 (*informal*) *She knocked $10 off the bill.* deduct, subtract, take off.
OPPOSITE add on.
3 (*slang*) *He knocked off the jewels.* nick (*slang*), pinch (*informal*), steal, thieve.

knock out
1 *The top player was knocked out in the second round.* beat, defeat, eliminate.
2 *He knocked himself out running the marathon.* exhaust, tire out, wear out.

knock-back *noun* (*informal*)
He was depressed by the knock-backs he received. refusal, rejection, turn-down.

knot *noun*
1 *She tied a knot in the rope.* loop, twist; [*kinds of knot*] bow, bowline, clove hitch, granny knot, hitch, reef knot, slip knot.
2 *She has knots in her hair.* snarl, tangle.
3 *knots on a tree trunk.* knob, lump, node, nodule.

knot *verb*
He knotted one string to the other. bind, fasten, hitch, join, lash, loop, tie.

knotty *adjective*
1 *knotty timber.* gnarled, knobbly, uneven.
OPPOSITE smooth.
2 *a knotty problem.* baffling, complex, complicated, difficult, intricate, perplexing, puzzling, thorny, tricky.
OPPOSITE straightforward.

know *verb*
1 *They know their tables.* have learnt, have memorised, remember.
2 *He did not know what was going on.* be aware of, comprehend, realise, understand.
OPPOSITE be ignorant of.
3 *He knows which twin is which.* discern, discriminate, distinguish, identify, recognise, remember.
4 *I know I left it here.* be certain, be confident, be positive, be sure.
OPPOSITE be unsure.
5 *She did not know any of the other people.* be acquainted with, be a friend of, be familiar with.
6 *Does he know French?* comprehend, speak, understand.

know-all *noun*
expert, genius, smart alec (*informal*), wise guy (*informal*).

know-how *noun*
They need someone with the technical know-how. ability, competence, expertise, knack, knowledge, skill.

knowing *adjective*
a knowing look. artful, astute, aware, crafty, cunning, meaningful, perceptive, shrewd, sly, wily.
OPPOSITE innocent.

knowledge *noun*
1 *She has the knowledge but lacks experience.* education, facts, information, learning, scholarship, science.
OPPOSITE ignorance.
2 *He had a working knowledge of computers.* experience, expertise, familiarity, grasp, know-how, understanding.
3 *He had no knowledge of what had happened.* awareness, consciousness, inkling, memory, perception, realisation.

knowledgeable *adjective*
a knowledgeable speaker. educated, enlightened, erudite, intelligent, learned, well-informed.
OPPOSITE ignorant.

known *adjective*
a known author. acknowledged, famous, noted, recognised, renowned, well-known.
OPPOSITE anonymous, unknown.

kowtow *verb*
He refused to kowtow to the boss. bow and scrape, crawl (*informal*), grovel, lick someone's boots, suck up (*informal*), toady.

kudos *noun* (*informal*)
She liked the kudos that went with the job. acclaim, fame, glory, honour, prestige, renown, respect.

a
b
c
d
e
f
g
h
i
j
k
l
m
n
o
p
q
r
s
t
u
v
w
x
y
z

Ll

label *noun*
1 *The clothes have labels on them.* sticker, tag, ticket.
2 *the company's label.* brand, logo, trade mark.
label *verb*
1 *All the goods are labelled.* identify, mark, name, stamp, tag.
2 *He was labelled a bully.* brand, call, describe, identify.

laborious *adjective*
a laborious task. arduous, difficult, exhausting, hard, onerous, strenuous, taxing, tiring.
OPPOSITE easy.

labour *noun*
1 *One cannot put a price on his labour.* effort, exertion, toil, work.
2 *She went to hospital when labour started.* childbirth, contractions, travail (*old use*).
3 *Relations between labour and management are good.* employees, workers, workforce.

labourer *noun*
He prefers to work as a labourer. hand, manual worker, unskilled worker, worker, workman.

labyrinth *noun*
maze, network, warren.

lace *verb*
1 *She can now lace her own shoes.* do up, fasten, tie.
2 *The plant's shoots are laced through the wire.* entwine, intertwine, weave.

lack *noun*
a lack of knowledge on the subject. absence, deficiency, insufficiency, need, scarcity, shortage, want.
OPPOSITE abundance.
lack *verb*
She lacks some of the ingredients. be short of, be without, miss, need.
OPPOSITE have.

lacquer *noun*
gloss, varnish.

lacy *adjective*
lacy curtains. delicate, fine, flimsy, net.

lad *noun*
1 *a lad of school age.* boy, child, kid (*informal*), youngster, youth.
2 (*informal*) *They like the lad she's marrying.* bloke (*informal*), boy, chap (*informal*), fellow (*informal*), guy (*informal*), young man.

laden *adjective*
laden with parcels. burdened, encumbered, loaded, weighed down.

lady *noun*
see WOMAN.

ladylike *adjective*
A tomboy doesn't like to be ladylike. dignified, genteel, polite, posh (*informal*), refined.

lag¹ *verb*
Some of the younger children lagged behind. dawdle, drag the chain (*Australian*), drop back, drop behind, fall behind, go slow, straggle, trail.
OPPOSITE keep up.

lag² *verb*
They lag the pipes to prevent heat loss. encase, insulate, wrap.

lagoon *noun*
billabong, lake, pond, pool.

laid-back *adjective* (*informal*)
He is very laid-back about his studies. calm, casual, easygoing, relaxed, unfazed (*informal*).
OPPOSITE uptight (*informal*).

lair *noun*
an animal's lair. burrow, den, hideout (*informal*), hidey-hole (*informal*), hiding place, hole, home, shelter.

lairy *adjective* (*Australian informal*)
a lairy shirt. bright, flash (*informal*),
flashy, garish, gaudy, loud, showy.
OPPOSITE subdued.

lake *noun*
lagoon, loch (*Scottish*), pond, reservoir,
sea, tarn.

lame *adjective*
1 *He has been lame since an accident.*
crippled, disabled, maimed, paralysed,
paraplegic.
OPPOSITE able-bodied.
2 *Don't give me that lame excuse.* feeble,
flimsy, unconvincing, unsatisfactory,
weak.
OPPOSITE persuasive.

lament *noun*
The choir sang a lament at the funeral.
dirge, elegy, keen, lamentation,
requiem.
lament *verb*
We lament the death of our friend. bewail,
grieve over, mourn, regret, wail over,
weep over.

lamp *noun*
see LIGHT[1].

lance *noun*
They spear fish with lances. harpoon,
javelin, pike, shaft, spear.
lance *verb*
The doctor will have to lance that boil. cut
open, jab, pierce, prick.

land *noun*
1 *good farming land.* earth, ground, soil.
2 *forest land.* area, country, region,
terrain, tract.
3 *people from different lands.* country,
empire, nation, state, territory.
4 *They own land in the south-east.*
property, real estate.
land *verb*
1 *The ship landed.* arrive, berth, dock,
moor, put into port.
2 *The aircraft landed.* arrive, come down,
touch down.
3 *We landed in Hobart.* alight, arrive,
disembark, go ashore.
4 *He was lucky to land the job.* get, obtain,
secure, win.

5 *He landed in jail.* end up, fetch up
(*informal*), find yourself, finish up, wind
up.

landing *noun*
1 *The trainee pilot was pleased with his
landing.* arrival, touchdown.
OPPOSITE take-off.
2 *The boat stopped at several landings.*
jetty, landing stage, pier, quay, wharf.

landlady, landlord *noun*
The tenant paid his rent to his landlady.
owner, proprietor.

landmark *noun*
1 *From the lookout we could see all the
important landmarks.* feature.
2 *a landmark in world history.* milestone,
turning point, watershed.

landowner *noun*
grazier (*Australian*), landholder,
pastoralist (*Australian*), squire.

landscape *noun*
panorama, scene, scenery, view, vista.
landscape *verb*
*The garden has been landscaped
professionally.* design, lay out, plan.

landslide *noun*
avalanche, landslip.

lane *noun*
Their house is on a quiet lane. alley, path,
road, track.

language *noun*
1 *an unfamiliar language.* dialect, speech,
tongue.
2 *scientific language.* idiom, jargon, lingo
(*informal*), slang, terminology,
vocabulary, words.

lanky *adjective*
a lanky young man. gangling, gawky,
lank, lean, skinny, thin.

lantern *noun*
a gas lantern. lamp.

lap[1] *noun*
a lap of the oval. circuit.

lap[2] *verb*
1 *The cat lapped up all the milk.* drink,
lick, sip.

a
b
c
d
e
f
g
h
i
j
k
l
m
n
o
p
q
r
s
t
u
v
w
x
y
z

2 *The waves lapped against the shore.*
splash, wash.

lapse *noun*
1 *He can be forgiven for this lapse.* error,
fault, mistake, omission, oversight, slip,
slip-up.
2 *after a lapse of five years.* break, gap,
interlude, interruption, interval,
passage.
lapse *verb*
1 *He lapsed into baby talk.* degenerate,
fall, regress, slip.
2 *She let her membership lapse.* expire,
run out, stop, terminate.
OPPOSITE continue.

larder *noun*
Food is kept in the larder. food cupboard,
pantry.

large *adjective*
1 *a large meal, amount, etc.* ample, big,
colossal, considerable, copious,
enormous, extensive, generous, giant,
gigantic, ginormous (*slang*), great,
handsome, huge, humungous (*slang*),
immeasurable, immense, infinite,
jumbo-sized, king-sized, mammoth,
massive, monstrous, outsize, oversized,
stupendous, substantial, tremendous,
unlimited, vast, whopping (*slang*).
OPPOSITE small.
2 *a large person.* big, broad, bulky, fat,
hefty, huge, hulking (*informal*), obese,
overweight, portly, stout.
OPPOSITE small.
3 *a large house.* big, grand, imposing,
roomy, sizeable, spacious.
OPPOSITE compact, small.
at large
1 *At night the dogs are at large.* free,
loose, unconfined, unrestrained.
2 *the population at large.* as a whole, in
general.

largely *adverb*
He did it largely for his own family.
chiefly, in the main, mainly, mostly,
primarily, principally.

large-scale *adjective*
a large-scale review. big, comprehensive,
extensive, major, wholesale, wide-
ranging.
OPPOSITE small-scale.

lark *noun*
They only did it for a bit of a lark. joke,
prank, tease, trick.

larrikin *noun* (*Australian*)
hooligan, hoon (*Australian informal*), lair
(*Australian informal*), rowdy, ruffian,
tearaway.

larva *noun*
caterpillar, grub, maggot.

lash *verb*
1 *He lashed the boy for his rudeness.* beat,
belt, cane, flog, hit, lay into (*informal*),
strike, thrash, whip.
2 *The blind was lashed down.* fasten,
secure, tie.
lash *noun*
He received forty lashes as punishment.
blow, cut, stroke.

lass *noun*
damsel (*old use*), girl, lassie (*informal*),
maid (*old use*), maiden (*old use*), young
woman.

lasso *noun*
lariat, rope.

last[1] *adjective*
1 *the last item on the programme.* closing,
concluding, final, ultimate.
OPPOSITE first.
2 *replying to your last letter.* latest, most
recent.
3 *our last hope.* only remaining.
at last eventually, finally, in the end,
ultimately.

last[2] *verb*
How long can this pain last? carry on,
continue, endure, go on, keep on,
persist.

lasting *adjective*
a lasting relationship. enduring,
everlasting, long-lasting, long-lived,
long-term, permanent.
OPPOSITE short-lived, temporary.

latch *noun*
a latch on a gate. bolt, catch, lock.
latch *verb*
latch the doors. bolt, fasten, lock, secure.

latch on to (*informal*)
Has he latched on to the idea yet? catch on to, cotton on to (*informal*), get (*informal*), grasp, understand.

late *adjective*
1 *late birthday wishes.* belated, delayed, held up, overdue, tardy.
OPPOSITE early.
2 *her late husband.* dead, deceased.
OPPOSITE living.

lately *adverb*
latterly, nowadays, of late, recently.
OPPOSITE formerly.

latent *adjective*
latent talent. concealed, dormant, hidden, invisible, potential, undeveloped.
OPPOSITE manifest.

later *adverb*
Their friends arrived later. after, afterwards, presently, subsequently.
OPPOSITE earlier.

latest *adjective*
the latest news. current, freshest, newest, up-to-date, up-to-the-minute.

lather *noun*
shampoo lather. bubbles, foam, froth, suds.

lattice *noun*
The plant grows on a lattice. framework, trellis.

laugh *verb*
be in stitches (*informal*), cackle, chortle, chuckle, crack up (*informal*), giggle, guffaw, snicker, snigger, split your sides, titter.
laugh *noun*
1 *The joke raised a few laughs.* cackle, chortle, chuckle, giggle, guffaw, snicker, snigger, titter.
2 (*informal*) *What a laugh that was!* hoot (*informal*), joke, scream (*informal*).
laugh at *They were laughing at him.*
deride, jeer at, joke about, make fun of, mock, poke fun at, ridicule, satirise, sling off at (*Australian informal*), take the mickey out of (*informal*), taunt, tease.

laughable *adjective*
The amount being offered is laughable. absurd, farcical, ludicrous, nonsensical, outrageous, preposterous, ridiculous.

laughter *noun*
cackling, chuckling, giggling, glee, hilarity, hysterics, laughing, merriment, mirth, sniggering.

launch[1] *verb*
1 *launch a rocket.* fire, project, propel, send forth, send off.
2 *launch a ship.* float, set afloat.
OPPOSITE ground.
3 *They launched their campaign.* begin, embark upon, introduce, open, set going, start.
OPPOSITE stop.
launch *noun*
The launch of the spacecraft was set for noon. blast-off, lift-off, take-off.

launch[2] *noun*
motor boat; see also BOAT.

lavatory *noun*
see TOILET.

lavish *adjective*
1 *He was always lavish with his money.* extravagant, generous, liberal, unstinting.
OPPOSITE stingy.
2 *There were lavish supplies of food in the cupboards.* abundant, bountiful, copious, plentiful, profuse.

law *noun*
1 *the laws of a country.* act, by-law, commandment, decree, edict, regulation, rule, statute.
2 *the laws of physics.* axiom, formula, principle, rule, theorem.

law-abiding *adjective*
honest, obedient, orderly, upstanding.
OPPOSITE lawless.

lawbreaker *noun*
criminal, delinquent, felon, miscreant, offender, wrongdoer.

lawful *adjective*
allowable, authorised, legal, legitimate, permissible, permitted, valid.
OPPOSITE illegal, unlawful.

a
b
c
d
e
f
g
h
i
j
k
l
m
n
o
p
q
r
s
t
u
v
w
x
y
z

lawless *adjective*
1 *a lawless country.* anarchic, chaotic, ungoverned.
2 *lawless brigands.* insubordinate, rebellious, riotous, uncontrolled, unruly, wild.
OPPOSITE law-abiding.

lawn *noun*
grass, sward, turf.

lawsuit *noun*
action, case, legal proceedings, suit, trial.

lawyer *noun*
advocate, attorney, barrister, counsel, legal adviser, Queen's Counsel (QC), solicitor.

lax *adjective*
They had been far too lax about discipline. careless, casual, easygoing, indulgent, lenient, permissive, relaxed, slack.
OPPOSITE strict.

lay *verb*
1 *Lay your bags on the bed.* deposit, leave, place, put, rest, set down.
2 *Lay the table.* arrange, set, spread.
lay down
1 *He laid down his life.* give up, sacrifice, surrender, yield.
2 *She laid down the rules.* dictate, establish, prescribe, set.
lay off *Workers were laid off when business went quiet.* stand down, suspend; see also DISMISS.
lay on *Meals were laid on.* provide, supply.
lay out *The editor laid out the page.* arrange, design, plan, set out.

layer *noun*
peel off the top layer. coating, film, level, ply, sheet, stratum, thickness, tier.

layout *noun*
arrangement, composition, design, organisation, plan, structure.

laze *verb*
They lazed in the sun for the afternoon. loaf, lounge, put your feet up, relax, rest, take it easy.

lazy *adjective*
The less he has to do, the more lazy he becomes. idle, inactive, indolent, languid, lethargic, listless, shiftless, slack, slothful, sluggish.
OPPOSITE energetic, industrious.

lazybones *noun*
couch potato (*informal*), good-for-nothing, idler, layabout, loafer, slacker, sluggard.

lead *verb*
1 *The usher leads people to their seats.* conduct, escort, guide, pilot, steer, usher.
2 *What led you to take this on?* cause, induce, influence, persuade, prompt.
3 *He led the attack.* be in charge of, command, control, direct, head, spearhead, supervise.
lead *noun*
1 *Follow his lead.* direction, example, guidance, leadership.
2 *He gave us a lead.* clue, hint, indication, tip-off.
3 *a dog's lead.* leash.

leader *noun*
They look up to their leader. boss, captain, chief, chieftain, commander, conductor, director, governor, head, manager, premier, president, prime minister, principal, ringleader, ruler.
OPPOSITE follower.

leaf *noun*
1 *a leaf of a plant.* blade, frond, needle; [*leaves*] foliage, greenery.
2 *a leaf of a book.* folio, page, sheet.

leaflet *noun*
an information leaflet. booklet, brochure, flyer, handout, pamphlet.

league *noun*
the league of old scholars. alliance, association, group, organisation, society, union.

leak *noun*
1 *a leak in a tyre.* crack, gash, hole, puncture, split.
2 *a government leak.* disclosure, revelation.
leak *verb*
1 *Water leaked from the tap.* discharge, drip, escape, ooze, seep, trickle.
2 *The employee leaked the news to a journalist.* disclose, divulge, let out, reveal.

lean[1] *adjective*
a lean beast. a lean person. bony, gaunt, lanky, scraggy, scrawny, skinny, slender, slim, thin, weedy, wiry.
OPPOSITE fat, hefty.

lean[2] *verb*
1 *The ship leaned to one side.* incline, list, slant, slope, tilt, tip.
2 *He leans on his stick.* prop yourself, rest, support yourself.
3 *He leans heavily on his wife for her support.* depend, rely.

leap *verb*
He leaps in the air. bounce, bound, jump, pounce, spring, vault.
leap *noun*
The cat took a huge leap. bounce, bound, jump, pounce, spring, vault.

learn *verb*
1 *She learned the road rules.* grasp, master, memorise, pick up, study.
2 *He learned that his friend had died.* become aware, discover, find out, gather, hear.

learned *adjective*
learned people. clever, educated, erudite, informed, intellectual, knowledgeable, scholarly, well-informed, well-read.
OPPOSITE uneducated.

learner *noun*
apprentice, beginner, cadet, novice, pupil, rookie (*informal*), student, trainee.

lease *verb*
lease a property. lease a car. hire, let, rent.

leash *noun*
a dog's leash. lead.

least *adjective*
the least amount. barest, faintest, littlest, lowest, minimum, scantiest, slightest, smallest, tiniest.
OPPOSITE greatest.

leather *noun*
hide, skin, suede.

leave *verb*
1 *He left without saying goodbye.* beat it (*slang*), buzz off (*slang*), clear off (*informal*), depart, disappear, do a bunk (*slang*), escape, exit, flee, get away, go away, head off, make off, make yourself scarce, nick off (*Australian slang*), push off (*informal*), rack off (*Australian slang*), retire, retreat, run away, run off, scarper (*informal*), scram (*informal*), set off, shoot through (*Australian informal*), shove off (*informal*), skedaddle (*informal*), take off, take your leave, vanish, withdraw.
OPPOSITE arrive, enter.
2 *He left his job.* abandon, chuck in (*informal*), give up, quit, resign, retire from, walk out of.
OPPOSITE retain.
3 *She left the house to a nephew.* bequeath, give, hand down, will.
4 *He left his wife and children.* abandon, desert, forsake, leave in the lurch, part from, separate from.

leave *noun*
1 *He begged leave to speak.* consent, permission.
2 *He has not returned from his leave.* break, exeat, furlough, holiday, sabbatical, vacation.
leave out *leave out a word in the sentence.* drop, exclude, miss out, omit, skip.
OPPOSITE include.

lecture *noun*
1 *a physics lecture.* address, speech, talk.
2 *He knew he was in for a lecture over the incident.* earbashing (*Australian informal*), reprimand, scolding, sermon, serve (*Australian informal*), talking-to (*informal*), telling-off (*informal*).

ledge *noun*
mantelpiece, shelf, sill.

left *adjective*
the ship's left side. larboard (*old use*), port.
OPPOSITE right, starboard.

leftovers *plural noun*
dregs, excess, remainder(s), residue, scraps, surplus.

leg *noun*
1 *quick on his legs.* limb, pin (*informal*), shank.
2 *The first leg of the trip was the most strenuous.* lap, part, section, stage.

legacy *noun*
Her aunt left her a legacy of $5000 in her will. bequest, inheritance.

a
b
c
d
e
f
g
h
i
j
k
l
m
n
o
p
q
r
s
t
u
v
w
x
y
z

legal *adjective*
1 *Is it legal to drive without wearing a seat belt?* allowed, authorised, lawful, permissible, permitted.
OPPOSITE illegal.
2 *the legal heir.* legitimate, proper, rightful.

legalise *verb*
The use of the drug has not been legalised. allow, authorise, decriminalise, permit.
OPPOSITE prohibit.

legend *noun*
1 *an old Russian legend.* folk tale, myth, saga, story, tale.
2 *the legend on a map.* code, key.

legendary *adjective*
1 *a legendary figure.* fabled, fictional, fictitious, mythical, traditional.
OPPOSITE historical.
2 *(informal) His soufflés were legendary.* famous, renowned, well-known.

legible *adjective*
His writing is legible. clear, neat, plain, readable, tidy.
OPPOSITE illegible.

legislation *noun*
the Native Title legislation. act, bill, law, statute.

legitimate *adjective*
1 *legitimate business activities.* lawful, legal, permissible.
OPPOSITE illegal.
2 *a legitimate excuse.* acceptable, fair, reasonable, valid.
OPPOSITE unacceptable.

leisure *noun*
free time, recreation, relaxation, spare time, time off.
OPPOSITE work.

leisurely *adjective*
at a leisurely pace. calm, easy, gentle, relaxed, restful, slow, unhurried.
OPPOSITE brisk.

lend *verb*
The bank will lend you the money. advance, loan.
OPPOSITE borrow.

length *noun*
1 *The bridge is a kilometre in length.* distance, extent, measurement, size, span.
CONTRASTS WITH breadth, depth.
2 *the length of his life.* duration, period, span, term, time.
at length
1 *At length the jury came to a decision.* at last, eventually, finally, in the end.
2 *He spoke at length about his problems.* fully, in depth, in detail.

lengthen *verb*
1 *The teacher lengthened the music lesson.* draw out, prolong, protract, spin out, stretch out.
2 *Lengthen the sides.* elongate, extend, increase.
OPPOSITE shorten.

lengthy *adjective*
a lengthy explanation. drawn-out, extended, long, long-winded, prolonged, protracted.
OPPOSITE brief.

lenient *adjective*
The judge was lenient. compassionate, easygoing, forbearing, indulgent, merciful, mild, soft, sparing.
OPPOSITE harsh, severe.

lesbian *adjective*
gay *(informal)*, homosexual.

less *adjective*
of less importance. slighter, smaller.
OPPOSITE more.
less *preposition*
She is paid $500, less tax. deducting, minus, subtracting, taking away.

lessen *verb*
1 *The cushions lessen the impact.* cut down, deaden, decrease, diminish, minimise, reduce.
OPPOSITE intensify.
2 *The wind has lessened.* abate, die down, ease, let up, moderate, subside.
OPPOSITE strengthen.

lesser *adjective*
a lesser problem. minor, secondary, slighter, smaller.
OPPOSITE greater.

lesson *noun*
  1 *The school day is divided into eight lessons.* class, period, session.
  2 *There was a lesson to be learnt from the accident.* message, moral, principle, rule, warning.
  3 *the New Testament lesson.* passage, reading.

let *verb*
  1 *They let her see the baby.* agree to, allow, consent to, enable, permit.
  OPPOSITE forbid.
  2 *room to let.* lease, rent.
  let down
  1 *He let down the tyres.* deflate.
  OPPOSITE inflate, pump up.
  2 *I don't want to let him down.* disappoint, fail, leave high and dry, leave in the lurch.
  3 *She let down her dress.* lengthen.
  OPPOSITE shorten, take up.
  let go *She let all the animals go.* free, let loose, liberate, release, set free.
  let off
  1 *They let off a bomb.* detonate, discharge, explode, set off.
  2 *They knew he was guilty, but they let him off.* excuse, exempt, pardon, release, reprieve, spare.
  let on *(informal)* *She never let on what had happened.* admit, confess, disclose, divulge, give away, let slip, reveal.
  let out
  1 *She opened the cage and let the bird out.* free, let go, liberate, release, set free.
  2 *The dress needs letting out.* enlarge, loosen.
  let up *(informal)* *The rain let up after lunch.* abate, ease, lessen, subside.
  OPPOSITE increase.

let-down *noun*
  see DISAPPOINTMENT.

lethal *adjective*
  a lethal injection. deadly, fatal, mortal, poisonous, toxic.
  OPPOSITE harmless.

letter *noun*
  1 *How many letters fit on one line?* character, symbol.
  2 *What did the letter say?* communication, epistle, message, note; [*letters*] correspondence, mail, post.

letterbox *noun*
  mailbox, pillar box (*old use*), postbox.

level *noun*
  1 *We climbed to a higher level.* altitude, elevation, height.
  2 *the level of alcohol in the blood.* amount, degree, measure, value.
  3 *He reached a high level in his job.* grade, position, rank, stage, standard.
  4 *He works on the third level of the building.* floor, storey.
  level *adjective*
  1 *a level surface.* even, flat, horizontal, plane, smooth.
  OPPOSITE bumpy, undulating.
  2 *They are level in first place.* equal, even, neck and neck, tied.
  level *verb*
  1 *The last shot levelled the scores.* even out, tie.
  2 *The workers levelled the building.* demolish, flatten, knock down, raze, tear down, topple.
  3 *He levelled the gun at him.* aim, direct, point, train.

lever *noun*
  It opens with a lever. control, handle.
  lever *verb*
  He levered the lid off the tea chest. prise, wrench.

levy *verb*
  The library levied a small fine. charge, collect, impose.
  levy *noun*
  The government funded the scheme by imposing a levy. charge, duty, excise, tariff, tax, toll.

liable *adjective*
  1 *She was liable for the debts.* accountable, answerable, responsible.
  2 *She is liable to cry.* apt, inclined, likely, prone.

liar *noun*
  You can't trust him: he's a liar. fibber, storyteller (*informal*).

liberal *adjective*
  1 *liberal quantities of food.* abundant, ample, copious, extravagant, generous, lavish, plentiful.
  OPPOSITE skimpy.

a
b
c
d
e
f
g
h
i
j
k
l
m
n
o
p
q
r
s
t
u
v
w
x
y
z

2 *liberal in his attitude.* broad-minded, enlightened, open-minded, permissive, tolerant, unprejudiced.
OPPOSITE narrow-minded.

liberate *verb*
The prisoners were liberated by the new president. emancipate, free, let go, release, set free.
OPPOSITE enslave, imprison.

liberty *noun*
They fought to preserve their country's liberty. autonomy, freedom, independence.

licence *noun*
You need a licence to sell those goods. authorisation, franchise, permit.

license *verb*
He is licensed to sell liquor. allow, authorise, permit.
OPPOSITE forbid.

lick *verb*
The cat licked up her milk. lap, tongue.

licking *noun* (*informal*)
1 *Their team came in for a licking.* beating, clobbering (*slang*), defeat, thrashing, trouncing.
2 *He got a licking for being cheeky.* beating, belting, flogging, hiding (*informal*), spanking, thrashing.

lid *noun*
All the jars had lids. cap, cover, top.

lie[1] *noun*
She was punished for telling lies. falsehood, fib, porky (*slang*), story (*informal*), untruth, whopper (*slang*).
OPPOSITE fact, truth.
lie *verb*
You never know when she's lying. bluff, deceive, fib, perjure yourself.

lie[2] *verb*
1 *She is lying on the bed.* recline, rest, sprawl.
2 *The machinery lay idle.* be, remain, stay.
3 *The land lies to the east.* be, be found, be located, be situated.
lie low go into hiding, hide, keep a low profile (*informal*), take cover.

lieutenant *noun*
assistant, deputy.

life *noun*
1 *the right to life.* being, existence, survival.
OPPOSITE death.
2 *Is there life on Mars?* flora and fauna, living things.
3 *full of life.* animation, energy, exuberance, liveliness, vigour, vitality, vivacity.
4 *The life of Luther makes interesting reading.* autobiography, biography.

lifeless *adjective*
1 *a lifeless body.* dead, deceased, inanimate, inert, non-living.
OPPOSITE living.
2 *a lifeless performance.* boring, dull, lacklustre, soulless, unexciting.
OPPOSITE lively.

lifelike *adjective*
The wax models are lifelike. accurate, authentic, realistic, true to life.

lifelong *adjective*
a lifelong friendship. enduring, lasting, permanent.
OPPOSITE short-lived.

lifetime *noun*
existence, life, life span.

lift *verb*
1 *He can lift heavy objects.* elevate, hoist, jack up, pick up, raise.
OPPOSITE lower.
2 *This lifted her spirits.* boost, cheer up, improve, raise.
OPPOSITE depress.
3 (*informal*) *He was caught lifting jewellery.* see STEAL.
4 *The fog lifted.* disperse, dissipate, rise.
OPPOSITE descend.
5 *The ban has been lifted.* cancel, remove, revoke, withdraw.
OPPOSITE enforce.
lift *noun*
1 *He gave her a lift to the station.* ride.
2 *Tall buildings need lifts.* elevator.
3 *The compliment gave her a lift.* boost, encouragement, reassurance, shot in the arm.

lift-off *noun*
blast-off, launch, take-off.

light¹ *noun*

1 *The light from the fire, torch, sun, etc.* blaze, brightness, brilliance, flash, glare, glow, illumination, radiance, reflection.
OPPOSITE darkness.

2 *a light to read by.* beacon, candle, floodlight, headlight, lamp, lantern, spotlight, torch.

light *adjective*

1 *The room was very light.* bright, illuminated, well-lit.
OPPOSITE dark.

2 *light blue.* delicate, pale, pastel, soft.
OPPOSITE dark.

light *verb*

Light the fire. ignite, kindle, set alight, start.
OPPOSITE extinguish.

bring to light *New evidence was brought to light.* disclose, expose, reveal, uncover.

come to light *It came to light that he had been at the scene of the crime.* appear, become apparent, come out, emerge, transpire.

light up *light up the room.* brighten, illuminate, lighten.
OPPOSITE darken.

light² *adjective*

1 *a light parcel.* lightweight, portable.
OPPOSITE heavy.

2 *a light blanket.* flimsy, lightweight, thin.
OPPOSITE heavy.

3 *light rainfall.* low, moderate, slight.
OPPOSITE heavy.

4 *light duties.* easy, effortless, simple, undemanding.
OPPOSITE arduous.

5 *light mist.* faint, fine, thin.
OPPOSITE dense.

6 *She is light on her feet.* agile, graceful, lithe, nimble, supple.
OPPOSITE clumsy.

7 *light music.* entertaining, frivolous, superficial.
OPPOSITE serious.

light on

1 *We're light on bread.* low on, short on.

2 *(Australian informal) The drinks were a bit light on.* in short supply, scarce.
OPPOSITE plentiful.

lighten¹ *verb*

The new paint lightened the room. brighten, light up, liven up.
OPPOSITE darken.

lighten² *verb*

1 *They tossed the cargo overboard to lighten the load.* cut down, diminish, ease, reduce.
OPPOSITE increase.

2 *The tablets lightened the pain.* alleviate, ease, lessen, reduce, relieve.
OPPOSITE increase.

3 *Her spirits were lightened by the news.* lift, raise, uplift.
OPPOSITE depress.

light-headed *adjective*

dizzy, faint, giddy, woozy (*informal*).

light-hearted *adjective*

blithe, bright, carefree, cheerful, gay, happy, jolly, merry.
OPPOSITE gloomy, heavy-hearted.

lighthouse *noun*

beacon.

like¹ *adjective*

The twins are of like temperament. corresponding, identical, matching, similar, the same.
OPPOSITE unlike.

like² *verb*

1 *He likes her.* admire, appreciate, approve of, be fond of, be keen on, fancy; see also LOVE.

2 *She doesn't like housework.* be keen on, enjoy, fancy, relish.
OPPOSITE dislike, hate.

3 *Would you like to try abseiling?* care, desire, have a mind, want, wish.

likeable *adjective*

agreeable, amiable, attractive, charming, congenial, friendly, genial, pleasant, pleasing.
OPPOSITE disagreeable.

likelihood *noun*

The likelihood of his winning is strong. chance, possibility, probability, prospect.

likely *adjective*

1 *I knew that was likely to happen.* bound, destined, liable, to be expected.

a b c d e f g h i j k l m n o p q r s t u v w x y z

2 *That doesn't sound very likely.*
believable, credible, plausible, probable.
OPPOSITE dubious.
3 *She was the most likely person for the job.*
appropriate, fitting, promising,
qualified, suitable.

liken *verb*
compare, draw an analogy between,
equate.

likeness *noun*
1 *There is a strong family likeness.*
resemblance, sameness, similarity.
OPPOSITE difference.
2 *She drew a good likeness of him.* copy,
picture, portrait, replica, representation.

liking *noun*
She has developed a liking for poetry.
appetite, appreciation, fondness,
partiality, penchant, preference, taste.
OPPOSITE aversion, dislike.

limb *noun*
1 *an animal with long limbs.* appendage,
arm, leg, wing.
2 *the limb of a tree.* bough, branch.

limbo *noun*
in limbo *The project has been left in limbo.*
half-finished, suspended, unfinished,
up in the air.

limit *noun*
1 *the school limits.* border, boundary,
bounds, confines, edge, frontier,
perimeter.
2 *the limit of your patience.* breaking-
point, end, extent.
3 *a limit on the number of books you can
borrow.* ceiling, cut-off, limitation,
quota, restriction.
limit *verb*
We need to limit our spending. check,
confine, contain, control, curb, restrain,
restrict.

limitation *noun*
He is aware of his own limitations.
deficiency, shortcoming, weakness.

limited *adjective*
limited resources. restricted, scanty,
small.
OPPOSITE unlimited.

limp[1] *verb*
He limped after injuring his knee. falter,
hobble, shuffle.

limp[2] *adjective*
The flowers are looking limp. droopy,
floppy, lifeless, wilted.

line *noun*
1 *draw a line through a word.* dash, mark,
score, slash, stroke.
2 *paint a line of red.* band, streak, strip,
stripe.
3 *lines on his face.* crease, crow's-foot,
furrow, wrinkle.
4 *a dividing line.* border, borderline,
boundary, limit.
5 *a line of people.* chain, column,
crocodile, file, procession, queue, row,
series.
6 *She dropped me a line at Christmas.*
card, letter, note, postcard.
7 *a railway line.* branch, route, track.
8 *a shipping line.* company, fleet.
9 *a line of kings.* dynasty, family,
lineage.
10 *a line of thought.* course, direction,
tack, tendency, trend.
11 *tied to the end of a line.* cable, cord,
hawser, lead, rope, string, wire.
line *verb*
1 *Someone has already lined the paper.*
rule.
2 *The street is lined with trees.* border,
edge, fringe.
in line with conforming with, in
accordance with, in agreement with, in
keeping with, in step with.
line up
1 *The passengers lined up.* form a line,
queue up.
2 *She lined the chairs up.* align,
straighten.
3 *He lined up a surprise for her birthday.*
arrange, organise, prepare, set up.

linen *noun*
bed and table linen. manchester, napery.

liner *noun*
see SHIP.

linger *verb*
1 *She knew she must not linger as she was
due home shortly.* dally, dawdle, delay,
dilly-dally, hang about, loiter, remain,
stay, take your time.

2 *He lingered on until he was 99.* hang on, last, survive.
3 *The smell lingered.* continue, hang around, persist, remain, stay.

lingerie *noun*
corsetry, underclothes, undergarments, underwear, undies (*informal*).

lining *noun*
backing, facing, interfacing.

link *noun*
1 *a link in a chain.* loop, ring.
2 *She was his only link with the outside world.* bond, connection, tie.
3 *a link between diet and the disease.* association, connection, relationship, tie-up.
link *verb*
1 *The two rooms are linked by telephone.* connect, join, unite.
OPPOSITE separate.
2 *The disease is linked with poor diet.* associate, connect, identify, relate, tie up.

lion *noun*
cub (*young*), king of beasts, lioness (*female*).

lip *noun*
the lip of a jug. brim, edge, rim, spout.

liquid *noun*
The patient can only have liquids. beverage, drink, fluid.
OPPOSITE solid.
liquid *adjective*
a liquid substance. flowing, fluid, molten, runny, watery.
OPPOSITE solid.

liquor *noun*
under the influence of liquor. alcohol, drink, grog (*Australian*).

list *noun*
a list of names. catalogue, directory, index, register, roll, schedule, series, table.
list *verb*
He listed the students' names in his book. catalogue, enter, index, itemise, note, record, register, write down.

listen *verb*
If you listen you'll find out. lend an ear, pay attention, pay heed, take notice, tune in.
listen in *She listened in on their conversation.* bug (*informal*), eavesdrop, intercept, overhear, tap.

listless *adjective*
He was listless following his illness. apathetic, languid, lethargic, lifeless, sluggish, tired, unenthusiastic.
OPPOSITE energetic, lively.

literal *adjective*
1 *the literal meaning.* basic, main, original, primary.
OPPOSITE figurative, metaphorical.
2 *a literal translation.* exact, precise, strict, true, verbatim, word for word.
OPPOSITE free.

literature *noun*
1 *He studies literature as well as language.* writings, written works.
2 (*informal*) *The tourist office provides literature on the city's attractions.* booklets, brochures, handouts, information, leaflets, material, pamphlets.

litter *noun*
1 *The streets were strewn with litter.* debris, garbage, mess, refuse, rubbish, trash, waste.
2 *the prettiest kitten in the litter.* brood, family, group.
litter *verb*
The room was littered with toys. clutter, mess up, scatter, strew.

little *adjective*
1 *a little person, object, etc.* compact, concise, diminutive, dwarf, microscopic, midget, miniature, minute, pocket-sized, puny, short, slight, small, stunted, tiny, undersized, wee.
OPPOSITE big.
2 *It only took a little time.* brief, short.
OPPOSITE long.
3 *It made only a little difference.* insignificant, marginal, minimal, negligible, slight.
OPPOSITE considerable.
4 *It was only a little point.* minor, petty, trivial, unimportant.
OPPOSITE major.

a
b
c
d
e
f
g
h
i
j
k
l
m
n
o
p
q
r
s
t
u
v
w
x
y
z

5 *The restaurant gives little portions.* inadequate, meagre, measly (*informal*), scanty, small, stingy.
OPPOSITE ample.
6 *her little brother.* baby, young, younger.
OPPOSITE big, older.
little by little bit by bit, gradually, progressively, slowly.

live[1] *adjective*
1 *live specimens.* alive, animate, breathing, living, surviving.
OPPOSITE dead.
2 *live embers.* burning, glowing, hot.
3 *very much a live issue.* active, burning, current, topical.
4 *a live broadcast.* direct.
OPPOSITE pre-recorded.

live[2] *verb*
1 *Do you eat to live or live to eat?* be, be alive, breathe, exist, survive.
OPPOSITE die.
2 *The memory will live with me.* continue, endure, last, persist, remain, stay.
3 *She lives on fruit.* feed, keep going, survive.
4 *Where does he live?* abide (*old use*), dwell, reside; see also INHABIT.

livelihood *noun*
earn a livelihood. crust (*Australian informal*), income, living.

lively *adjective*
a lively person. active, animated, boisterous, cheerful, chirpy, energetic, enthusiastic, full of beans (*informal*), irrepressible, perky, spirited, sprightly, spry, vigorous, vivacious.
OPPOSITE listless.

liven *verb*
She livened up when her visitors came. brighten up, buck up (*informal*), cheer up, perk up.

livestock *noun*
animals, stock.

living *adjective*
living creatures. alive, animate, breathing, live.
OPPOSITE dead.
living *noun*
1 *the joy of living.* being alive, existence, life.
OPPOSITE dying.

2 *What do you do for a living?* crust (*Australian informal*), income, livelihood, means of support; see also JOB.
living room drawing room, family room, lounge, lounge room, parlour (*old use*), sitting room.

lizard *noun*
[*various lizards*] bearded dragon, bluetongue, bobtail, boggi, chameleon, frilled lizard, gecko, goanna, iguana, jacky lizard, moloch, monitor lizard, mountain devil, perentie, skink, sleepy lizard, stumpy tail.

load *noun*
1 *a load of timber.* cargo, consignment, freight, shipment.
2 *That will be a load off her mind.* burden, weight.
load *verb*
They loaded the car with the luggage. fill, pack, pile up.
loads *plural noun* (*informal*)
loads of room. heaps (*informal*), lots (*informal*), masses, piles (*informal*), plenty.

loaf *verb*
He spends the weekend loafing around. idle, laze, lounge, take it easy, veg out (*slang*).

loafer *noun*
bludger (*Australian informal*), bum (*slang*), couch potato (*informal*), good-for-nothing, idler, layabout, lazybones (*informal*), shirker, skiver (*informal*), slacker.

loan *noun*
They took out a loan with the bank. advance, mortgage.
loan *verb*
see LEND.

loathe *verb*
She loathes cigarette smoke. abhor, abominate, despise, detest, dislike, hate.
OPPOSITE love.

loathsome *adjective*
a loathsome habit of spitting. abominable, despicable, detestable, disgusting, hateful, odious, offensive, repulsive.
OPPOSITE delightful, lovable.

lob *verb*
He lobbed the ball. see THROW.

lob in (*Australian slang*)
He lobbed in an hour late. appear, arrive, rock up (*slang*), show up (*informal*), turn up.

lobby *noun*
1 *We waited in the lobby.* corridor, entrance hall, foyer, hall, porch, vestibule.
2 *the anti-nuclear lobby.* body, force, pressure group.
lobby *verb*
They lobbied for free bus travel. campaign, petition, push.

local *adjective*
1 *the local newspaper.* area, community, district, neighbourhood, provincial, regional.
OPPOSITE national.
2 *local pain. local anaesthetic.* confined, localised, restricted.
OPPOSITE general.
local *noun*
If you need directions ask one of the locals. inhabitant, native, resident.

locality *noun*
They live in the same locality. area, community, district, neighbourhood, region, suburb, vicinity.

locate *verb*
The mechanic located the problem. detect, discover, find, identify, pinpoint.
be located *The church is located on a hill.* be, be found, be situated.

location *noun*
1 *The house is in a beautiful location.* area, locality, place, position, setting, site, spot.
2 *Can you give your location to help us find you?* bearings, position, whereabouts.

lock¹ *noun*
a lock of hair. tress, tuft.

lock² *noun*
The locks were broken. bar, bolt, catch, latch, padlock.
lock *verb*
He locked the door. bar, bolt, fasten, secure.
OPPOSITE unlock.
lock up *He will be locked up for life.* imprison, intern, jail, put away.

locker *noun*
cabinet, compartment, cupboard.

locomotive *noun*
a diesel locomotive. engine.

lodge *noun*
1 *the gatekeeper's lodge.* cottage, gatehouse, home, house, residence.
2 *a new lodge for skiers.* cabin, chalet, hostel, hotel, motel, resort.
lodge *verb*
1 *He lodges with a family.* board, live, reside, stay.
2 *The bone has lodged in her throat.* become embedded, get stuck, stick.
3 *You must lodge a complaint.* file, lay, make, register, submit.

lodging *noun*
His allowance covers board and lodging. accommodation, housing, shelter.
lodgings *plural noun*
He returned to his lodgings for the night. accommodation, billet, digs (*informal*), quarters, residence, room(s).

loft *noun*
The house has a loft. attic.

lofty *adjective*
1 *a lofty building.* high, soaring, tall, towering.
2 *a lofty manner.* arrogant, disdainful, haughty, high and mighty, proud, scornful, snooty (*informal*), supercilious.
OPPOSITE humble, lowly.

log *noun*
1 *He cut the branch into logs.* block, piece, stump.
2 *They kept a log of their trip.* diary, journal, logbook, record.

logger *noun*
The loggers were at work in the forest. lumberjack (*American*), timber-getter, tree-feller.

logical *adjective*
1 *a logical argument.* coherent, rational, reasoned, sound, valid.
OPPOSITE illogical.
2 *a logical person.* intelligent, rational, reasonable, sensible, thinking.

logo *noun*
They designed a new logo for their company. emblem, symbol, trade mark.

a
b
c
d
e
f
g
h
i
j
k
l
m
n
o
p
q
r
s
t
u
v
w
x
y
z

loiter *verb*
The people were asked not to loiter, but to return home quickly. dally, dawdle, hang around, linger, lurk, skulk.

loll *verb*
She lolled on the sofa. lie, lounge, recline, relax, slump, sprawl.

lolly *noun*
candy (*American*), sweet, toffee.

lone *adjective*
a lone passenger on the bus. alone, lonely, single, sole, solitary, unaccompanied.

lonely *adjective*
1 She often felt lonely after her husband died. forlorn, forsaken, friendless, lonesome.
OPPOSITE befriended.
2 a lonely place. deserted, isolated, remote, secluded, unfrequented, uninhabited.
OPPOSITE busy, crowded.

long[1] *adjective*
1 a long silence. big, drawn-out, endless, interminable, lengthy, prolonged, protracted, sustained, unending.
OPPOSITE short.
2 a long table. elongated, extended.
OPPOSITE short.
3 a long friendship. enduring, lasting, long-lasting, long-lived, long-standing, long-term.
OPPOSITE brief.

long[2] *verb*
long for I long for the sunshine. crave, desire, hanker after, hunger for, pine for, thirst for, want, wish for, yearn for.

longing *noun*
satisfy a deep longing. appetite, craving, desire, hunger, thirst, urge, wish, yearning, yen.

long-sighted *adjective*
far-sighted, hypermetropic.
OPPOSITE myopic, short-sighted.

long-suffering *adjective*
a long-suffering partner. forbearing, patient, tolerant.
OPPOSITE impatient.

long-term *adjective*
a long-term illness. chronic, long, long-lasting, persistent.
OPPOSITE short-term, temporary.

long-winded *adjective*
a long-winded description. lengthy, rambling, tedious, verbose, wordy.
OPPOSITE succinct.

look *verb*
1 He looked at their faces. gape, gaze, glance, glare, goggle, peek, peep, peer, squint, stare; see also LOOK AT.
2 Look to the front. face.
3 The work looked easy. appear, seem.
look *noun*
1 Take a look at this. gaze, glance, glare, glimpse, peek, peep, squint (*informal*), squiz (*Australian slang*), stare, stickybeak (*Australian informal*).
2 Have a look for it. check, rummage, search.
3 She had a strange look. appearance, countenance, expression, face.
look after She looks after her elderly parents. attend to, care for, guard, mind, protect, take care of.
OPPOSITE neglect.
look at
1 They looked at the painting. behold (*old use*), contemplate, examine, eye, glimpse, inspect, observe, see, study, survey, view, watch.
2 The department will look at your case. see CONSIDER.
look down on He looks down on other people. despise, disdain, look down your nose at, patronise, scorn.
OPPOSITE look up to.
look for She looked for her purse. check for, fossick for (*Australian informal*), hunt for, rummage for, search for, seek.
look forward to I look forward to your letter. anticipate, await, long for.
look in The doctor looked in every day. call in, drop in, visit.
look into The police are looking into the matter. check on, examine, explore, go into, inquire into, investigate, probe, research.
look on The crowd looked on helplessly. observe, stand by, view, watch, witness.
OPPOSITE participate.
look out Look out when you cross the

road. beware, keep your eyes open, pay attention, take care, watch out.

look up
1 *You'll need to look up the address in my book.* check, find, search for.
2 *Look up the book.* check, consult, refer to.
3 *Things are looking up.* get better, improve, pick up.
4 *When he was in town he looked us up.* call on, drop in on, look in on, visit.

look up to *He looks up to his brother.* admire, respect, revere, worship.
OPPOSITE look down on.

look-alike *noun*
dead spit, double, ringer (*informal*), spitting image, twin.

look-in *noun*
He didn't give anyone else a look-in. chance, go (*informal*), show (*informal*).

lookout *noun*
He was appointed lookout. guard, picket, sentinel, sentry, watchman.

loom *verb*
Giant trees loomed before him. appear, rise, soar, stand out, tower.

loop *noun*
circle, circuit, coil, curl, knot, noose, ring, twirl, twist.
loop *verb*
The wire had looped around the chair. coil, curl, entwine, kink, twist, wind.

loophole *noun*
1 *a loophole in the wall of the castle.* aperture, gap, opening, slit.
2 *loopholes in a contract.* escape, get-out, let-out, way out.

loose *adjective*
1 *The animals were loose.* at large, free, uncaged, unconfined, unleashed, unrestrained, untethered, untied.
OPPOSITE enclosed, tethered.
2 *a loose button.* detached, unattached, unfastened, unstuck.
OPPOSITE fixed.
3 *a loose board.* rickety, shaky, unsteady, wobbly.
OPPOSITE secure.

4 *loose clothes.* baggy, floppy.
OPPOSITE tight.
5 *The shop sells loose biscuits.* bulk, unpackaged.
OPPOSITE packaged.
6 *The rope is too loose.* slack.
OPPOSITE taut, tight.
7 *a loose definition.* broad, imprecise, inexact, rough, sloppy, vague.
OPPOSITE precise.

loose *verb*
1 *They loosed the dogs.* free, let go, let loose, liberate, release, set free.
OPPOSITE shut in, tie up.
2 *The ropes were loosed.* loosen, undo, unfasten, untie.
OPPOSITE tie, tighten.

loosen *verb*
1 *He loosened his grip.* ease, relax, slacken.
OPPOSITE tighten.
2 *He managed to loosen the screw.* free, loose, release, undo, unfasten.
OPPOSITE tighten.

loot *noun*
The thief ran off with the loot. booty, goods, pillage, plunder, spoils, swag (*informal*), takings.
loot *verb*
After the earthquake many people looted the damaged buildings. pillage, plunder, raid, ransack, rob, sack.

lop *verb*
The trees were lopped to clear the power lines. chop, cut, prune.

lopsided *adjective*
The painting is lopsided. askew, asymmetrical, crooked, unbalanced, uneven.
OPPOSITE even, symmetrical.

lord *noun*
1 *The lion is considered lord of the jungle.* king, master, monarch, ruler, sovereign.
2 *He was made a lord.* aristocrat, noble, nobleman, peer.
the Lord God, Jehovah, Jesus Christ, Yahweh.

lore *noun*
He had studied the lore of these people. folklore, legends, myths, traditions.

a b c d e f g h i j k l m n o p q r s t u v w x y z

lorry *noun*
pick-up, road train (*Australian*), semi (*Australian informal*), semitrailer, transport, truck, van.

lose *verb*
1 *He has lost his pen.* mislay, misplace.
OPPOSITE find.
2 *So much was lost in the accident.* destroy, obliterate, wipe out.
OPPOSITE save.
3 *They lost their way.* miss, stray from, wander from.
4 *She has lost weight.* get rid of, shed.
OPPOSITE gain.
5 *It doesn't matter whether you win or lose.* be defeated, get beaten.
OPPOSITE win.

loss *noun*
1 *loss of sight.* deprivation, impairment, reduction.
OPPOSITE gain.
2 *a widow's loss.* bereavement.
3 *Both armies suffered heavy losses.* casualty, death, fatality.
at a loss *I am at a loss as to how it could have happened.* baffled, mystified, perplexed, puzzled.

lost *adjective*
1 *a lost child. a lost purse.* mislaid, misplaced, missing, strayed, vanished.
OPPOSITE found.
2 *lost in wonder.* absorbed, engrossed, preoccupied, rapt.

lot[1] *noun*
1 *We were each given our lot.* allocation, allotment, part, portion, ration, share.
2 *her lot in life.* destiny, fate, fortune.
3 *a building lot.* allotment, block, plot.
4 *We took delivery of a new lot of chairs.* batch, collection, group, set.

lot[2] *noun (informal)*
1 *a lot of letters. lots of lollies.* dozens (*informal*), heaps (*informal*), loads (*informal*), many, masses, piles (*informal*), plenty, scores, stacks (*informal*), swag (*Australian informal*), tons (*informal*).
2 *She's a lot happier now.* a good deal, a great deal, much.

lotion *noun*
hand lotion. balm, cream, moisturiser, ointment.

loud *adjective*
1 *loud music. loud voices.* amplified, blaring, booming, deafening, noisy, penetrating, piercing, raucous, resounding, rowdy, thundering.
OPPOSITE soft.
2 *loud colours.* bold, bright, flashy, garish, gaudy, showy.
OPPOSITE pastel, subdued.

loudness *noun*
volume.

lounge *verb*
On the weekend she just lounges around. laze, lie, loaf, loll, recline, relax, sprawl, veg out (*slang*).
lounge *noun*
1 *They waited in the airport lounge.* waiting room.
2 *The lounge is a room for all the family.* drawing room, living room, lounge room, parlour (*old use*), sitting room.

lousy *adjective (informal)*
He had a lousy time. awful (*informal*), bad, dreadful (*informal*), miserable, nasty, rotten (*informal*), terrible (*informal*); see also BAD.
OPPOSITE wonderful.

loutish *adjective*
loutish behaviour. discourteous, ill-mannered, impolite, rough, rude, uncouth.
OPPOSITE polite.

lovable *adjective*
a lovable child. adorable, appealing, charming, darling, dear, delightful, endearing, lovely, sweet.
OPPOSITE detestable.

love *noun*
1 *She feels love towards him.* adoration, affection, devotion, fondness, tenderness, warmth; see also PASSION.
OPPOSITE hate, hatred.
2 *She is his one true love.* beloved, darling, lover, sweetheart.
love *verb*
1 *She loves him.* adore, be devoted to, be fond of, cherish, dote on, hold dear,

idolise, revere, treasure.
OPPOSITE hate.
2 *He loves good books.* appreciate, be
fond of, delight in, enjoy, like, relish,
treasure.
OPPOSITE hate.

lovely *adjective*
1 *She looked lovely.* adorable, attractive,
beautiful, charming, good-looking,
gorgeous, pretty.
OPPOSITE unattractive.
2 *(informal) I had a lovely time.* cool
(informal), delightful, enjoyable,
excellent, fantastic *(informal)*, good,
great *(informal)*, nice, pleasant, terrific
(informal), wonderful.
OPPOSITE terrible.

lover *noun*
1 *send a valentine to your lover.* admirer,
beloved, boyfriend, girlfriend, suitor,
sweetheart.
2 *art lovers.* admirer, buff *(informal)*,
devotee, enthusiast, fan.

loving *adjective*
adoring, affectionate, amorous, caring,
close, devoted, doting, fond, friendly,
kind, kind-hearted, passionate,
sympathetic, tender, warm, warm-
hearted.
OPPOSITE indifferent, unloving.

low[1] *verb*
The cattle are lowing. moo.

low[2] *adjective*
1 *low trees.* dwarf, little, miniature,
short, small, squat, stunted.
OPPOSITE high, tall.
2 *His position in the firm is quite low.*
humble, inferior, junior, lowly,
unimportant.
OPPOSITE high, superior.
3 *low prices.* budget, cheap, cut-price,
inexpensive, modest, reduced.
OPPOSITE high.
4 *a low opinion of somebody.* bad,
negative, poor, unfavourable.
OPPOSITE high.
5 *The singer has a low voice.* bass, deep.
OPPOSITE high-pitched.
6 *He spoke in a low voice so as not to be
overheard.* faint, hushed, muffled, quiet,

soft, subdued.
OPPOSITE loud.
7 *She's feeling rather low.* blue, dejected,
depressed, despondent, down,
downcast, forlorn, gloomy, glum,
listless, melancholy, miserable, sad.
OPPOSITE happy.

lower *verb*
1 *He lowered the flag.* bring down, drop,
let down, pull down, take down.
OPPOSITE hoist, raise.
2 *She lowered her voice.* quieten, soften,
subdue, tone down.
OPPOSITE raise.
3 *The lights may be lowered.* dim, dip,
fade, subdue, turn down.
OPPOSITE turn up.
4 *They lowered their prices.* cut, decrease,
discount, drop, mark down, reduce.
OPPOSITE increase.

lowly *adjective*
She came from a lowly background.
humble, modest, unassuming,
unpretentious.

loyal *adjective*
He remained a loyal friend. constant,
dedicated, dependable, devoted,
faithful, patriotic, staunch, steadfast,
true, true-blue, trustworthy.
OPPOSITE disloyal.

loyalty *noun*
allegiance, constancy, devotion,
faithfulness, fidelity, steadfastness,
trustworthiness.
OPPOSITE disloyalty.

lubricate *verb*
All the moving parts need to be lubricated.
grease, oil.

luck *noun*
1 *We found it by sheer luck.* accident,
chance, coincidence, destiny, fate, fluke,
good fortune, serendipity.
2 *We wish you luck.* good fortune,
prosperity, success.

lucky *adjective*
1 *a lucky person.* blessed, fortunate.
OPPOSITE unfortunate.
2 *a lucky find.* accidental, chance, fluky,
serendipitous.

a
b
c
d
e
f
g
h
i
j
k
l
m
n
o
p
q
r
s
t
u
v
w
x
y
z

ludicrous *adjective*
a ludicrous proposal. absurd, crazy, farcical, laughable, nonsensical, preposterous, ridiculous.
OPPOSITE sensible, serious.

lug *verb*
She lugged the parcel up the stairs. carry, drag, haul, heave, pull.

luggage *noun*
They search through all your luggage. baggage, bags, cases, gear, ports (*Australian*), suitcases, trunks; see also BELONGINGS.

lukewarm *adjective*
1 *She likes her tea lukewarm.* tepid, warm.
2 *He got a lukewarm reception.* cool, half-hearted, indifferent, unenthusiastic.
OPPOSITE enthusiastic.

lull *verb*
The music lulled her to sleep. calm, hush, pacify, quieten, relax, soothe.
OPPOSITE excite.
lull *noun*
a lull in the conversation. break, gap, interval, let-up (*informal*), pause, silence.

lumber *verb*
1 *They lumbered him with the job.* burden, encumber, saddle.
2 *The man lumbered up the stairs.* clump, plod, shuffle, trudge, waddle.

luminous *adjective*
The hands of the clock are luminous. bright, glowing, luminescent, phosphorescent, radiant, shining.

lump *noun*
1 *a lump of cheese.* ball, bit, chunk, cube, hunk, piece, wedge.
2 *The doctor examined the lump on her arm.* bulge, bump, growth, swelling.
lump *verb*
They lumped them together. combine, group, mix.

lumpy *adjective*
bumpy, chunky, uneven.
OPPOSITE smooth.

lunatic *noun*
loony (*informal*), madman, madwoman, maniac, nut (*informal*), nutter (*informal*).

lunch *noun*
He likes a hot lunch at about one o'clock. dinner, luncheon (*formal*), midday meal.

lunge *noun*
1 *He made a lunge to catch the ball.* dive, plunge, stretch.
2 *a lunge with the sword.* charge, jab, stab, thrust.
lunge *verb*
He lunged towards the man with his knife. charge, dive, plunge, pounce, rush.

lurch[1] *noun*
leave in the lurch abandon, desert, forsake, leave high and dry, leave stranded.

lurch[2] *verb*
The drunken man lurched and fell. flounder, reel, stagger, stumble, sway, totter.

lure *noun*
the lure of a big salary. attraction, bait, decoy, draw, drawcard.
lure *verb*
People are often lured by money. attract, draw, entice, seduce, tempt.

lurk *verb*
There was someone lurking in the bushes. hide, lie in wait, linger, skulk.

luscious *adjective*
luscious grapes. delicious, juicy, rich, succulent, sweet.

lush *adjective*
The grass is lush after the winter rains. green, luxuriant, profuse, strong, thick.

lust *noun*
a lust for money. appetite, craving, desire, greed, hunger, longing, passion.

lustre *noun*
The table had a lustre after polishing. brightness, brilliance, gleam, gloss, sheen, shine, sparkle.

luxurious *adjective*
luxurious hotels. de luxe, elegant, expensive, first-class, grand, opulent,

plush, posh (*informal*), sumptuous, swish (*informal*), upmarket.
OPPOSITE cheap.

luxury *noun*
1 *They live a life of luxury.* affluence, comfort, ease, opulence, self-indulgence.
2 *An overseas holiday is a luxury.* extra, extravagance, indulgence, treat.
OPPOSITE necessity.

lying *noun*
punished for lying. deception, dishonesty, fibbing, perjury, prevarication.
lying *adjective*
the lying scoundrel. deceitful, dishonest, mendacious, untruthful.
OPPOSITE truthful.

lyrics *plural noun*
the lyrics of a song. text, words.

a
b
c
d
e
f
g
h
i
j
k
l
m
n
o
p
q
r
s
t
u
v
w
x
y
z

Mm

machine *noun*
The tedious work is now done by a machine. apparatus, appliance, computer, contraption, device, engine, gadget, instrument, mechanism, robot, tool.

machinery *noun*
farm machinery. equipment, gear, machines, plant.

macho *adjective*
Macho men don't cry. manly, masculine, tough, virile.
OPPOSITE effeminate.

mad *adjective*
1 She has gone mad. bananas (*slang*), barmy (*slang*), batty (*slang*), berserk, bonkers (*slang*), crackers (*slang*), crazy, demented, deranged, dotty (*informal*), flaky (*slang*), frenzied, insane, irrational, loony (*informal*), lunatic, manic, mental (*informal*), nuts (*informal*), nutty (*informal*), off your head, out of your mind, potty (*informal*), psychotic, round the bend (*informal*), screwy (*informal*), troppo (*Australian slang*), unbalanced, unhinged.
OPPOSITE sane.
2 a mad plan. absurd, crazy, daft (*informal*), foolhardy, foolish, hare-brained, idiotic, illogical, insane, lunatic, nonsensical, preposterous, rash, reckless, silly, stupid, unwise, wild.
OPPOSITE sensible.
3 She is mad about horses and riding. crazy, enthusiastic, fanatical, infatuated, keen, nuts (*informal*), obsessed, passionate, wild.
OPPOSITE indifferent.
4 (*informal*) He'll be really mad when he finds out. angry, annoyed, cross, enraged, furious, infuriated, irate, livid, riled (*informal*), ropeable (*Australian informal*), wild.
OPPOSITE calm.

madden *verb*
His hesitation maddens me. anger, annoy, bug (*informal*), drive someone mad, enrage, exasperate, incense, infuriate, irritate, needle (*informal*), rile (*informal*), vex, wind up (*informal*).
OPPOSITE soothe.

madman, madwoman *noun*
crackpot (*informal*), loony (*slang*), lunatic, maniac, nut (*informal*), nutcase (*informal*), nutter (*informal*), psychopath.

madness *noun*
1 The hospital cured his madness. dementia, insanity, lunacy, mania, mental illness, psychosis.
OPPOSITE sanity.
2 (*informal*) It was sheer madness to buy it. folly, foolishness, idiocy, lunacy, stupidity.

magazine *noun*
She likes to read magazines. bulletin, journal, newsletter, pamphlet, periodical.

maggot *noun*
grub, larva.

magic *noun*
black magic, conjuring, divination, illusion, sleight of hand, sorcery, spells, trickery, voodoo, witchcraft, wizardry.

magician *noun*
We were captivated by the magician's tricks. conjuror, enchanter, enchantress, illusionist, medicine man, sorcerer, sorceress, warlock (*old use*), witch, witchdoctor, wizard.

magnificent *adjective*
a magnificent house. a magnificent performance. beautiful, brilliant, excellent, exquisite, extraordinary, fine, glorious, gorgeous, grand, great, imposing, impressive, majestic, marvellous, opulent, spectacular, splendid, stately, striking, stunning, sumptuous, superb, terrific (*informal*), wonderful.
OPPOSITE ordinary.

magnify *verb*
1 *The lens magnifies objects.* blow up (*informal*), enlarge.
OPPOSITE reduce.
2 *The newspaper magnified the seriousness of the incident.* amplify, blow up (*informal*), exaggerate, overstate.
OPPOSITE understate.

magnitude *noun*
the magnitude of the problem. extent, importance, scale, significance, size.

maid *noun*
The lady employs a maid. chambermaid, domestic, help, housemaid, lady's maid, maidservant, parlourmaid, servant.

maiden *noun* (*old use*)
young maidens and lads. damsel (*old use*), girl, lass, lassie (*informal*), maid (*old use*).
maiden *adjective*
1 *a maiden aunt.* spinster, unmarried, unwed.
2 *a maiden voyage.* first, initial.

mail *noun*
The mail is delivered daily. correspondence, letters, packages, parcels, post.
mail *verb*
She mailed it immediately. dispatch, post, send.

maim *verb*
The accident maimed him for life. cripple, disable, incapacitate, injure, lame, mutilate, wound.

main *adjective*
the main problem. the main office. biggest, central, chief, critical, crucial, essential, first, foremost, greatest, head, largest, leading, major, most important, outstanding, predominant, primary, prime, principal, vital.
OPPOSITE minor, secondary.

mainly *adverb*
The concert was attended mainly by teenagers. chiefly, especially, generally, in the main, largely, mostly, predominantly, primarily, principally.

mainstream *noun*
the mainstream of political opinion. current, direction, tide, trend.

maintain *verb*
1 *They maintained the custom.* carry on, continue, keep, keep up, preserve, prolong, uphold.
OPPOSITE break.
2 *He maintains his car.* care for, keep in good repair, look after, preserve, service, take care of.
OPPOSITE neglect.
3 *They maintain three children at university.* finance, keep, provide for, support.
4 *He still maintains that he is right.* assert, claim, contend, declare, hold, insist.
OPPOSITE deny.

maintenance *noun*
1 *He looks after the maintenance of the car.* care, preservation, repairs, running, servicing, upkeep.
2 *She is paid maintenance for the children.* alimony, allowance.

majestic *adjective*
a majestic house. a majestic air. august, dignified, glorious, grand, imperial, imposing, impressive, lordly, magnificent, noble, regal, royal, splendid, stately.
OPPOSITE humble.

majesty *noun*
the majesty of the occasion. dignity, grandeur, magnificence, splendour, stateliness.

major *adjective*
1 *The major part of the work is finished.* bigger, greater, larger, main.
2 *a major consideration.* central, chief, crucial, important, key, main, primary, prime, principal, significant.
OPPOSITE minor.

majority *noun*
1 *He ate the majority of the chocolates.* bulk, greater part, lion's share, most.
OPPOSITE minority.
2 *They won by a handsome majority.* excess, margin.

make *verb*
1 *She makes dresses, pots, boats, etc.* assemble, build, carve, construct, create, erect, fabricate, form, invent, manufacture, model, mould, produce, put together, sculpture, sew, shape.

a
b
c
d
e
f
g
h
i
j
k
l
m
n
o
p
q
r
s
t
u
v
w
x
y
z

2 *She made the dessert.* bake, concoct, cook, prepare, produce.
3 *Who made the rules? Make a list.* compile, compose, devise, draw up, establish, formulate, frame, invent, think up, write.
4 *They made a time for their next meeting.* agree on, arrange, decide on, fix, organise, settle on.
5 *They made him their spokesman.* appoint, elect, nominate.
6 *Please make your bed.* arrange, prepare, straighten, tidy.
7 *He likes to make difficulties.* bring about, cause, create, provoke.
8 *Five and five make ten.* add up to, amount to, come to, equal, total.
9 *Can she make her goal?* accomplish, achieve, arrive at, attain, reach.
10 *He made a good teacher.* become, end up, turn into, turn out.
11 *He made a lot of money.* acquire, earn, gain, get, obtain.
12 *She made him sign it.* cause, compel, force, oblige, order, pressure.
13 *He made a speech.* deliver, give, present, utter.

make *noun*
The car is a French make. brand, kind, sort, type.

make do *They had to make do with what they had.* get by, improvise, manage.

make for *They made for home.* aim for, go towards, head for, proceed towards.

make out
1 *I can't make out his writing.* decipher, figure out, read, understand, work out.
2 *She made out a shadowy figure.* discern, distinguish, espy, perceive, see.

make over *He made the car over to his daughter.* sign over, transfer.

make up
1 *The seven of us made up a team.* compose, constitute, form.
2 *He made up the whole story.* concoct, fabricate, invent, manufacture, think up.

make up for *Nothing will make up for the loss.* atone for, compensate for, offset, recompense.

make up your mind choose, come to a decision, decide, resolve, settle.

make-believe *noun*
daydreaming, dreaming, fantasy, imagination, play-acting, pretence.

make-over *noun*
a bathroom make-over. redecoration, remodelling, renovation, transformation, upgrade.

maker *noun*
builder, constructor, creator, inventor, manufacturer, producer.

makeshift *adjective*
a makeshift shelter. improvised, provisional, stopgap, temporary.
OPPOSITE permanent.

make-up *noun*
1 *Actors wear make-up.* cosmetics, face paint, greasepaint; [*various items of make-up*] blusher, eye liner, eye shadow, foundation, lipstick, mascara, powder.
2 *Depression is in his make-up.* character, nature, personality, temperament.

male *adjective*
masculine.
OPPOSITE female.
male *noun*
see BOY, MAN.

malevolent *adjective*
a malevolent character. a malevolent look. hostile, malicious, malignant, nasty, sinister, spiteful, vicious, vindictive.
OPPOSITE benevolent, kind.

malice *noun*
done with malice aforethought. animosity, bitterness, enmity, hostility, ill will, malevolence, maliciousness, spite, spitefulness, vindictiveness.
OPPOSITE benevolence, kindness.

malicious *adjective*
malicious gossip. bitchy (*informal*), hostile, malevolent, malignant, mean, mischievous, nasty, spiteful, unkind, vicious, vindictive.
OPPOSITE benevolent, friendly.

malignant *adjective*
1 *a malignant tumour.* cancerous, deadly, fatal.
OPPOSITE benign, non-malignant.
2 *a malignant look.* destructive, evil, harmful, hostile, malevolent, malicious,

spiteful, vicious, vindictive.
OPPOSITE benign, kindly.

mall *noun*
a shopping mall. arcade, centre, complex, plaza, precinct.

malnutrition *noun*
She was suffering from malnutrition. emaciation, hunger, starvation, undernourishment.

mammoth *adjective*
a mammoth task. colossal, enormous, giant, gigantic, huge, immense, large, massive, mighty, stupendous, tremendous.
OPPOSITE tiny.

man *noun*
1 *All men are equal. Every man for himself.* human, human being, individual, mortal, person.
2 *Man is responsible for the welfare of animals.* human beings, humanity, humankind, human race, humans, mankind, people.
3 *The club is for men only: women are not allowed.* bloke (*informal*), chap (*informal*), fellow (*informal*), gentleman, guy (*informal*), lad (*informal*), male.
man *verb*
The students manned the counter. attend, operate, staff.

manage *verb*
1 *He manages the business.* administer, be in charge of, conduct, control, direct, head, oversee, run, superintend, supervise.
2 *Can she manage scissors yet?* control, handle, manipulate, operate, use, wield.
3 *He is good at managing people.* cope with, deal with, handle.
4 *She managed the task.* accomplish, carry out, do, perform, succeed in, undertake.
OPPOSITE fail.

manageable *adjective*
1 *a manageable size.* convenient, handy.
OPPOSITE unwieldy.
2 *a manageable task.* feasible, possible, practicable.
OPPOSITE impossible.
3 *a manageable child.* biddable, compliant, controllable, docile,

tractable.
OPPOSITE rebellious.

management *noun*
1 *experts in project management.* administration, control, direction, handling, organisation, running, supervision.
2 *a disagreement between management and the workers.* administrators, bosses, directors, employers, executives, managers.

manager *noun*
1 *the manager of the repair division.* administrator, boss, chief, director, foreman, head, overseer, proprietor, superintendent, supervisor.
2 *A singer needs a manager.* agent, organiser.

mandate *noun*
The Government was given a mandate to reform the tax system. approval, authorisation, authority, permission.

manger *noun*
The horse's hay was in the manger. feeding trough.

mangle *verb*
His body was mangled in the accident. crush, cut, damage, disfigure, injure, lacerate, maim, mutilate.

manhole *noun*
Access to the pipe is through a manhole. hatch, opening, trapdoor.

mania *noun*
tennis mania. craze, enthusiasm, fad, obsession, passion; see also MADNESS.

maniac *noun*
The fire was started by a maniac. crackpot (*informal*), loony (*slang*), lunatic, madman, madwoman, nut (*informal*), nutcase (*informal*), nutter (*informal*), psychopath.

manipulate *verb*
1 *She is good at manipulating the gadget.* control, handle, manage, operate, use, wield, work.
2 *He manipulated the figures.* adjust, cook (*informal*), falsify, fiddle (*slang*), juggle, massage, rig.

a
b
c
d
e
f
g
h
i
j
k
l
m
n
o
p
q
r
s
t
u
v
w
x
y
z

mankind *noun*
the history of mankind. human beings, humanity, humankind, human race, man, people, society.

manly *adjective*
1 *a manly appearance.* male, masculine.
OPPOSITE effeminate, feminine.
2 *He was expected to behave in a manly fashion.* brave, chivalrous, courageous, fearless, gallant, heroic, macho, valiant.
OPPOSITE cowardly.

man-made *adjective*
a man-made product. artificial, made, manufactured, synthetic.
OPPOSITE natural.

manner *noun*
1 *He described the manner in which he makes the dough.* fashion, method, procedure, style, technique, way.
2 *She has a friendly manner.* air, attitude, bearing, demeanour, disposition.
manners *plural noun*
1 *bad manners. good manners.* behaviour, conduct, form.
2 *He hasn't learned any manners.* courtesy, decorum, etiquette, politeness, social graces, tact.

mannerism *noun*
He had a mannerism of pulling his ear as he spoke. habit, idiosyncrasy, peculiarity, quirk, trait.

manoeuvre *noun*
1 *army manoeuvres.* exercise, movement, operation.
2 *He used a clever manoeuvre to achieve his ends.* device, dodge (*informal*), move, ploy, ruse, scheme, stratagem, tactic, trick.
manoeuvre *verb*
1 *He manoeuvred the car into the front position.* edge, guide, jockey, move, position, steer.
2 *She manoeuvred the conversation towards money.* direct, guide, manipulate, steer.

mansion *noun*
The original homestead was a grand two-storeyed mansion. castle, manor, manor house, palace.
OPPOSITE hovel.

manslaughter *noun*
He was tried for manslaughter. homicide, killing.
CONTRASTS WITH murder.

manual *adjective*
1 *a manual gear-change.* hand-operated.
OPPOSITE automatic.
2 *manual labour.* blue-collar, physical.
OPPOSITE mental.
manual *noun*
a manual for the car. handbook, primer, reference book, textbook.

manufacture *verb*
1 *They manufacture cars.* assemble, build, construct, make, process, produce.
2 *He manufactured an excuse.* concoct, cook up (*informal*), dream up, fabricate, invent, make up, think up.
manufacture *noun*
the manufacture of bags. construction, making, production.

manure *noun*
He spread the manure over the garden. compost, dung, fertiliser, muck.

manuscript *noun*
He studies ancient manuscripts. document, script.

many *adjective*
He received many letters. a lot of (*informal*), copious, countless, dozens of (*informal*), heaps of (*informal*), innumerable, lots of (*informal*), myriad, numbers of, numerous, oodles of (*informal*), piles of (*informal*), plenty of, scores of, umpteen (*informal*).
OPPOSITE few.

map *noun*
a map of the world. chart, diagram, plan, projection.
map *verb*
Cook mapped the east coast of Australia. chart, survey.
map out *He had to map out a programme.* arrange, devise, organise, plan, plot, prepare.

mar *verb*
1 *A scratch marred the surface.* blemish, damage, deface, disfigure, flaw, scar, spoil, stain.
2 *A poor accompaniment marred the performance.* detract from, ruin, spoil,

tarnish.
OPPOSITE enhance.

marauder *noun*
The town was raided by marauders. bandit, buccaneer, looter, pillager, pirate, plunderer, robber.

march *verb*
The soldiers marched past. file, parade, stride, tramp, troop, walk.
march *noun*
a protest march. demo (informal), demonstration, parade, procession.

margin *noun*
1 The writing filled the page leaving a narrow margin. border, boundary, edge, frame, fringe.
2 She won by a narrow margin. difference, gap.

marginal *adjective*
of marginal importance. little, minimal, minor, slight.
OPPOSITE central, major.

marina *noun*
see HARBOUR.

marine *adjective*
1 marine creatures. oceanic, salt-water, sea.
CONTRASTS WITH freshwater, terrestrial.
2 marine vessels. maritime, nautical, naval, ocean-going, seafaring, seagoing.

mariner *noun*
sailor, seafarer, seaman.

maritime *adjective*
a maritime nation. a maritime museum. marine, nautical, naval, seafaring, seagoing, shipping.

mark *noun*
1 The vase left a mark on the table. There were paint marks on his clothes. blemish, blotch, dot, impression, line, patch, scar, scratch, smear, smudge, spatter, speck, speckle, splash, splotch, spot, stain, streak, trace.
2 a mark of respect. indication, proof, sign, signal, token.
3 The clock bears the mark of the maker. badge, brand, emblem, hallmark, imprint, label, logo, seal, stamp, symbol, trade mark.

4 The student was pleased with his mark for English. assessment, grade, rating, result, score.
mark *verb*
1 Something has marked the surface. blemish, deface, disfigure, mar, scar, score, scratch, scuff, smudge, spot, stain.
2 A tree marks the spot. designate, identify, indicate, show, signify.
3 She marked all her belongings. brand, identify, label, name.
4 The teacher marked the students' work. assess, correct, evaluate, grade, judge, rate, score.
5 Mark my words! heed, mind, note, pay attention to.
OPPOSITE ignore.

marked *adjective*
a marked accent. definite, distinct, noticeable, obvious, pronounced, strong, unmistakable.
OPPOSITE imperceptible.

market *noun*
a craft market. bazaar, fair, mart, sale.
market *verb*
see SELL.

maroon *verb*
He was marooned on an island. abandon, desert, forsake, isolate, leave, strand.

marriage *noun*
1 the state of marriage. matrimony, wedlock.
2 a long and happy marriage. match, partnership, union.
3 We attended their marriage. marriage ceremony, wedding.

married *adjective*
marital, matrimonial, nuptial, wedded.

marry *verb*
Let's get married. become husband and wife, become man and wife, get hitched (informal), tie the knot (informal), wed.

marsh *noun*
bog, fen, mire, quagmire, slough, swamp.

marsupial *noun*
[various marsupials] bandicoot, bettong, bilby, cuscus, dunnart, glider, kangaroo, koala, marsupial mole,

a
b
c
d
e
f
g
h
i
j
k
l
m
n
o
p
q
r
s
t
u
v
w
x
y
z

numbat, opossum, pademelon, phalanger, possum, potoroo, quokka, quoll, rat-kangaroo, Tasmanian devil, Tasmanian tiger (= thylacine), wallaby, wallaroo, wombat.

martial *adjective*
martial music. military, warlike.

martyr *noun*
a martyr to arthritis. sufferer, victim.
martyr *verb*
Stephen was martyred for his faith. kill, put to death, torment, torture.

marvel *noun*
the marvels of modern medicine. miracle, wonder.
marvel *verb*
marvel at *They marvelled at his achievements.* admire, be amazed by, be astonished by, be staggered by, be surprised by, wonder at.

marvellous *adjective*
a marvellous view, result, meal, etc. amazing, astonishing, astounding, breathtaking, brilliant (*informal*), cool (*informal*), excellent, extraordinary, fabulous (*informal*), fantastic (*informal*), fine, first-rate, glorious, grand, great, magnificent, miraculous, outstanding, phenomenal, remarkable, sensational, spectacular, splendid, stunning (*informal*), stupendous, superb, terrific (*informal*), tremendous (*informal*), wonderful.
OPPOSITE ordinary, terrible.

mascot *noun*
The team's mascot was a teddy bear. charm, emblem, symbol, talisman.

masculine *adjective*
1 *a masculine hero.* macho, male, manly, virile.
OPPOSITE effeminate, feminine.
2 *She is masculine-looking.* butch (*slang*), mannish.
OPPOSITE feminine.

mash *verb*
He mashed the pumpkin. crush, pound, pulp, purée, squash.

mask *noun*
1 *a dentist's protective mask.* covering, goggles, shield, visor.

2 *I could not tell who it was behind the mask.* cover-up, disguise.
mask *verb*
The robber's face was masked. She masked her feelings. camouflage, conceal, cover up, disguise, hide, obscure, screen.
OPPOSITE reveal.

mass^1 *noun*
1 *a mass of soap.* blob, block, cake, chunk, hunk, lump.
OPPOSITE fragments.
2 *a mass of papers.* bundle, collection, heap, mound, mountain, pile, quantity, stack.
3 *a mass of people.* body, congregation, crowd, flock, gathering, herd, horde, host, mob, multitude, sea, swarm, throng.
mass *verb*
People massed outside Parliament House. assemble, collect, congregate, flock, gather, herd, muster, rally.
OPPOSITE disperse.
mass *adjective*
weapons of mass destruction. extensive, general, large-scale, universal, wholesale, widespread.

mass^2 *noun*
They go to mass every Sunday. Communion, Eucharist, Holy Communion, Lord's Supper.

massacre *noun*
the senseless massacre of thousands of people. bloodbath, carnage, extermination, killing, murder, slaughter, slaying.
massacre *verb*
Thousands were massacred. butcher, execute, exterminate, kill, murder, slaughter, slay.

massage *noun*
The massage relieved his aching back. kneading, manipulation, rubbing.

massive *adjective*
1 *a massive statue.* colossal, enormous, giant, gigantic, heavy, hefty, hulking, immense, large, mammoth, monumental, solid.
OPPOSITE tiny.
2 *a massive telephone bill.* astronomical, enormous, exorbitant, hefty, high, huge, large.
OPPOSITE tiny.

3 *massive changes.* considerable, extensive, far-reaching, substantial, sweeping, vast, wide-ranging.
OPPOSITE slight.

mast *noun*
a ship's mast. pole, post, spar.

master *noun*
1 *He is the master of the house.* head, leader, lord, owner, ruler.
2 *masters and servants.* boss (*informal*), chief, employer, governor (*slang*), overseer.
3 *a ship's master.* captain, skipper.
4 *the senior science master.* schoolmaster, teacher.
5 *a master at the piano.* ace, expert, genius, maestro, past master, professional, virtuoso, wizard.
6 *Many copies may be made from the one master.* original.
master *verb*
1 *She has mastered her fear of the dark.* conquer, control, overcome, subdue, vanquish.
OPPOSITE surrender to.
2 *He has mastered the secrets of Asian cookery.* get the hang of (*informal*), get the knack of, grasp, learn, understand.

masterly *adjective*
a masterly performance. accomplished, brilliant, deft, excellent, expert, skilful, virtuoso.
OPPOSITE inept.

mastermind *noun*
a mastermind at bridge. ace, brain (*informal*), expert, genius, master, wizard.
mastermind *verb*
He masterminded the attack. conceive, devise, direct, engineer, lead, orchestrate, organise, plan.

mat *noun*
carpet, doormat, matting, rug.

matador *noun*
bullfighter, toreador.

match *noun*
1 *His team won the match.* bout, competition, contest, game, rubber, tournament.
2 *He met his match.* equal, equivalent, peer, rival.
CONTRASTS WITH inferior, superior.

match *verb*
1 *Her qualifications matched the requirements of the job.* agree with, coincide with, correspond with, equal, fit, meet, suit.
OPPOSITE differ from.
2 *The jacket matches the dress.* coordinate with, go with, harmonise with, team with, tone with.
OPPOSITE clash with.
3 *He matched the names with the faces.* connect, couple, fit, join, link, pair, put together, unite.
OPPOSITE mismatch.

mate *noun*
1 *A man always looks after his mates.* buddy (*informal*), chum (*informal*), cobber (*Australian informal*), companion, comrade, crony, friend, pal (*informal*).
2 (*informal*) *a single person in search of a mate.* husband, partner, spouse, wife.
mate *verb*
The animals mate once a year. breed, copulate, couple, pair up.

material *noun*
1 *one of the essential raw materials.* constituent, element, ingredient, matter, stuff, substance.
2 *The dress is made from a fine material.* cloth, fabric, textile.
3 *She is gathering material for her project.* data, facts, ideas, information, observations.
materials *plural noun*
cleaning materials. equipment, gear, supplies, tools, utensils.

materialise *verb*
The ghost did not materialise. appear, emerge, show up (*informal*), turn up.
OPPOSITE vanish.

maternal *adjective*
see MOTHERLY.

maternity *noun*
1 motherhood, motherliness.
2 *a maternity hospital.* see BIRTH.

mateship *noun* (*Australian*)
A spirit of mateship existed between the workers. camaraderie, comradeship, friendship.

matey *adjective*
He found the new neighbour very matey. chummy (*informal*), familiar, friendly,

a b c d e f g h i j k l m n o p q r s t u v w x y z

pally (*informal*), sociable.
OPPOSITE unsociable.

matrimony *noun*
united in holy matrimony. marriage, wedlock.

matt *adjective*
The walls are covered with a matt paint. dull, flat.
OPPOSITE gloss, glossy.

matted *adjective*
matted hair. knotted, knotty, tangled, unkempt.

matter *noun*
1 *foreign matter. vegetable matter.* material, stuff, substance, thing.
2 *It's a serious matter.* affair, business, concern, issue, question, situation, subject, topic.
3 *What is the matter?* difficulty, problem, trouble, worry.
matter *verb*
It doesn't matter. be important.

matter-of-fact *adjective*
He was matter-of-fact about the accident. down-to-earth, factual, unemotional.
OPPOSITE emotional.

mature *adjective*
1 *a mature animal.* adult, developed, fully-fledged, grown, grown-up.
OPPOSITE immature.
2 *a mature cheddar.* ripe, ripened.
OPPOSITE unripe.
mature *verb*
1 *The child matured.* develop, grow up.
2 *The cheese matured.* age, mellow, ripen.

maturity *noun*
The child has reached maturity. adulthood, coming of age, majority, manhood, womanhood.

maul *verb*
The lion mauled the boy. claw, lacerate, mutilate, savage, tear to pieces.

maximum *noun*
1 *The temperature reached a maximum of 35°.* peak, top.
OPPOSITE minimum.
2 *They allow a maximum of three visitors at a time.* ceiling, upper limit.

maximum *adjective*
maximum speed. maximum security. extreme, full, greatest, highest, most, top, utmost.
OPPOSITE least, minimal.

maybe *adverb*
perchance (*old use*), perhaps, possibly.
OPPOSITE definitely.

maze *noun*
The children were lost in the maze. labyrinth, network, warren.

meadow *noun*
field, grassland, paddock, pasture.

meagre *adjective*
a meagre serving of peas. mean, measly (*informal*), mingy (*informal*), scanty, skimpy, small, stingy.
OPPOSITE ample, generous.

meal *noun*
The meal was served in the dining room. banquet, breakfast, brunch, dinner, feast, lunch, luncheon, repast (*formal*), spread, supper, tea.

mean[1] *verb*
1 *I didn't mean to hurt you.* aim, intend, plan.
2 *Helmets are meant to protect cyclists.* design, intend.
3 *What does that word mean to you?* communicate, convey, denote, express, imply, indicate, say, signify, stand for, symbolise.

mean[2] *adjective*
1 *She's too mean to make a donation.* miserly, niggardly, penny-pinching, stingy, tight-fisted.
OPPOSITE generous.
2 *a mean trick. a mean person.* base, beastly (*informal*), contemptible, cruel, despicable, hard-hearted, lousy (*informal*), malicious, nasty, spiteful, unkind.
OPPOSITE kind.

mean[3] *adjective*
The mean mark was 65%. average.

meander *verb*
1 *The stream meanders.* loop, snake, twist, wind, zigzag.
2 *They meandered through the bush.* ramble, roam, rove, wander.

meaning *noun*
1 *the meaning of a word.* sense, significance.
2 *a life full of meaning.* importance, point, purpose, significance, value.
OPPOSITE absurdity.

meaningful *adjective*
1 *a meaningful look.* deep, expressive, pointed, significant, telling.
OPPOSITE meaningless.
2 *He was seeking more meaningful work.* rewarding, satisfying, useful, worthwhile.

meaningless *adjective*
1 *meaningless words.* empty, hollow, superficial, trite.
OPPOSITE meaningful.
2 *The abbreviations were meaningless to outsiders.* baffling, incomprehensible, nonsensical, puzzling, unintelligible.
OPPOSITE comprehensible.
3 *His existence was no longer meaningless.* absurd, aimless, pointless, senseless, useless, worthless.
OPPOSITE meaningful.

means *noun*
a means of achieving change. manner, medium, method, mode, process, way.
means *plural noun*
a man of some means. assets, funds, income, money, property, resources, riches, wealth.

measly *adjective* (*informal*)
a measly amount. meagre, mean, mingy (*informal*), miserable, paltry, stingy.
OPPOSITE generous, lavish.

measure *noun*
1 *the measure of an object.* amount, capacity, dimensions, extent, magnitude, mass, measurement, proportions, quantity, size.
2 *The metre is a measure of length.* standard, unit.
3 *We used the measure to find out the object's size.* callipers, gauge, rule, ruler, scale, tape-measure, yardstick.
4 *measures to prevent accidents.* action, course, law, means, method, procedure, process, step, way.

measure *verb*
1 *He measured its size.* assess, calculate, compute, determine, estimate, gauge, quantify, weigh.
2 *He measured the depth.* fathom, plumb, sound.
measure out *She measured out their drinks.* apportion, deal out, dispense, distribute, dole out, mete out, ration out.
measure up to *He doesn't measure up to their standards.* come up to, fulfil, meet, pass, reach, satisfy.

measurement *noun*
1 *the measurement of performance.* assessment, evaluation.
2 *He recorded the measurements of each of the items.* area, breadth, capacity, depth, dimension, extent, height, length, magnitude, mass, size, volume, weight, width.

meat *noun*
flesh; [*kinds of meat*] beef, kangaroo, lamb, mutton, pork, rabbit, veal, venison.

meat-eating *adjective*
carnivorous, flesh-eating.
CONTRASTS WITH herbivorous, vegetarian.

mechanic *noun*
The mechanic fixed the washing machine. repairman, technician, workman.

mechanical *adjective*
1 *The production is mechanical.* automated, mechanised.
OPPOSITE manual.
2 *a mechanical response.* automatic, instinctive, involuntary, reflex, unconscious, unthinking.
OPPOSITE conscious.

mechanism *noun*
the clock mechanism. action, machinery, movement, workings, works.

medal *noun*
a medal for bravery. award, decoration, gong (*slang*), medallion, prize.

meddle *verb*
She likes to meddle in people's affairs. butt in, interfere, intervene, intrude, poke your nose in, pry.

a
b
c
d
e
f
g
h
i
j
k
l
m
n
o
p
q
r
s
t
u
v
w
x
y
z

meddler *noun*
busybody, intruder, Nosy Parker, stickybeak (*Australian informal*).

mediator *noun*
He acted as mediator between the two sides. arbitrator, broker, go-between, intermediary, middleman, negotiator, referee, umpire.

medical *adjective*
medical insurance. health.
medical *noun* (*informal*)
The applicants had to undergo a medical. check-up, health check, medical examination, physical (*informal*).
medical centre clinic, health centre, hospital, infirmary, surgery.

medicinal *adjective*
The herb has medicinal properties. curative, healing, restorative, therapeutic.

medicine *noun*
The doctor prescribed a new medicine. capsule, cure, drug, linctus, medication, pill, remedy, tablet, treatment.

mediocre *adjective*
of mediocre quality. average, fair, indifferent, middling, ordinary, passable, run-of-the-mill, second-rate, so-so (*informal*).
OPPOSITE outstanding.

meditate *verb*
1 *She meditated on his words.* deliberate, muse, ponder, reflect, think.
2 *He was meditating what action he would take.* consider, contemplate, plan, think over.

medium *noun*
1 *the happy medium.* average, compromise, mean, middle ground.
OPPOSITE extreme.
2 *the use of television as a medium for advertising.* agency, channel, instrument, means, vehicle.
medium *adjective*
of medium size. average, intermediate, middling, moderate.

meek *adjective*
a meek and mild person. compliant, docile, gentle, humble, mild, obedient,
submissive, tame, unassuming.
OPPOSITE assertive.

meet *verb*
1 *The friends meet every Friday in the mall.* assemble, come together, congregate, gather, get together, muster, rally, rendezvous.
2 *She met an old acquaintance today.* bump into (*informal*), come across, encounter, run into, see.
3 *There is a line where the two pieces meet.* butt, converge, join, touch.
4 *Have you met the new teacher?* be introduced to, make the acquaintance of.
5 *Australia meets England at the MCG.* compete against, oppose, play, take on.
6 *He did not know what dangers he would meet.* come up against, confront, encounter, experience, face, run into.
7 *This does not meet our standards.* come up to, comply with, measure up to, reach, satisfy.
OPPOSITE fall short of.
8 *She agreed to meet the costs.* cover, deal with, pay, take care of.

meeting *noun*
1 *It was our first meeting.* appointment, date (*informal*), encounter, engagement, get-together (*informal*), rendezvous.
2 *a meeting of heads of churches.* assembly, conference, congregation, congress, convention, council, forum, gathering, rally, summit, synod.
3 *an athletics meeting.* competition, contest, event, fixture, meet.

melancholy *adjective*
She remained melancholy after her husband's death. dejected, depressed, despondent, dismal, doleful, down, down in the dumps (*informal*), forlorn, gloomy, glum, heavy-hearted, miserable, sad.
OPPOSITE happy.

mellow *adjective*
1 *mellow fruit.* juicy, luscious, mature, ripe, sweet.
OPPOSITE unripe.
2 *mellow sounds.* rich, smooth, velvety.
OPPOSITE harsh.

3 *He has become more mellow with age.* affable, amiable, easygoing, gentle, kindly, pleasant, sympathetic.
mellow *verb*
The wine has mellowed. develop, mature, soften.

melodious *adjective*
melodious music. dulcet, euphonious, harmonious, musical, sweet, tuneful.
OPPOSITE cacophonous.

melodramatic *adjective*
a melodramatic account of a minor incident. exaggerated, histrionic, overdone, sensational, theatrical.
OPPOSITE matter-of-fact.

melody *noun*
We sang familiar melodies. air, strain, theme, tune.

melt *verb*
1 *The ice melted.* liquefy, thaw.
OPPOSITE freeze, solidify.
2 *The lolly melts in the mouth.* dissolve, soften.
OPPOSITE harden.
3 *Her compassion melted his hard heart.* disarm, soften, touch.
OPPOSITE harden.
melt away *Gradually the crowd melted away.* disappear, disperse, evaporate, fade away, vanish.
OPPOSITE gather.

member *noun*
1 *a member of an association.* associate, fellow, subscriber.
2 *members of the same subset.* component, constituent, element.

memoirs *plural noun*
You don't have to be famous to write your memoirs. autobiography, diary, life story, memories, recollections, reminiscences.

memorable *adjective*
a memorable speech. a memorable holiday. historic, impressive, momentous, noteworthy, outstanding, remarkable, significant, striking, unforgettable.
OPPOSITE unimpressive.

memorial *noun*
see MONUMENT.

memorise *verb*
She memorised the address. commit to memory, learn by heart, learn by rote, remember.

memory *noun*
1 *He is losing his memory.* recall, retention.
2 *memories of childhood.* recollection, remembrance, reminder, reminiscence, souvenir.

menace *noun*
1 *a menace to civilisation.* danger, hazard, risk, threat.
2 *It is unkind to call someone a menace.* nuisance, pest.
menace *verb*
The dog menaced the visitor. bully, frighten, intimidate, terrify, terrorise, threaten.

menacing *adjective*
a menacing look. black, forbidding, hostile, intimidating, malignant, ominous, sinister, threatening.
OPPOSITE friendly.

mend *verb*
1 *He mends cars.* fix, patch up, put right, repair, restore.
OPPOSITE break, damage.
2 *You must mend your manners.* correct, improve, rectify, reform.
on the mend *The patient is on the mend.* convalescing, getting better, improving, recovering, recuperating.

mental *adjective*
1 *a mental challenge.* intellectual.
2 *mental illness.* psychiatric.
OPPOSITE physical.
3 *(informal) The work is driving him mental.* see MAD.

mentality *noun*
1 *a child of above-average mentality.* ability, brains, intellect, intelligence, IQ.
2 *He has a strange mentality.* attitude, mindset, outlook.

mention *verb*
He didn't mention the incident. allude to, bring up, comment on, hint at, refer to, speak of, touch on.
mention *noun*
She made no mention of her discovery. hint, indication, reference, remark.

a
b
c
d
e
f
g
h
i
j
k
l
m
n
o
p
q
r
s
t
u
v
w
x
y
z

merchant *noun*
a *wine merchant.* dealer, distributor, exporter, importer, salesman, supplier, trader, wholesaler.

merciful *adjective*
a *merciful judge.* compassionate, forbearing, forgiving, gentle, humane, kind, lenient, mild, sympathetic, tender-hearted, tolerant.
OPPOSITE merciless.

merciless *adjective*
a *merciless judge.* callous, cruel, hard-hearted, harsh, heartless, inhuman, inhumane, pitiless, relentless, remorseless, ruthless, severe, strict, unforgiving, unsympathetic.
OPPOSITE merciful.

mercy *noun*
He *showed great mercy towards the offender.* clemency, compassion, forbearance, forgiveness, grace, kindness, lenience, pity, sympathy, tolerance.
OPPOSITE harshness.

merge *verb*
1 *The two companies merged.* amalgamate, combine, consolidate, join forces, unite.
OPPOSITE separate.
2 *The two lanes merge.* converge, join, meet.

merit *noun*
1 *This book shows merit.* excellence, goodness, quality, value, worth.
2 *Each of the proposals had its merits.* advantage, good point, strength, virtue.
OPPOSITE fault.

merit *verb*
This *article merits your attention.* be entitled to, be worthy of, deserve, justify, warrant.

merriment *noun*
see MIRTH.

merry *adjective*
All *the party guests felt merry.* cheerful, gleeful, happy, high-spirited, jolly, jovial, joyous, light-hearted, lively.
OPPOSITE sad.

merry-go-round *noun*
carousel, roundabout, whirligig.

merrymaking *noun*
The *merrymaking went on until two in the morning.* celebrations, festivities, fun, partying, revelry.

mesh *noun*
The *bag was made of mesh.* lacework, net, netting, network.

mess *noun*
1 *The bedroom was in a mess.* chaos, confusion, disarray, muddle, shambles, shemozzle (*informal*), untidiness.
2 *Mess lay everywhere.* clutter, jumble, litter.
3 *He was in a mess.* difficulty, fix (*informal*), hot water (*informal*), pickle (*informal*), predicament, spot (*informal*), trouble.
4 *the officers' mess.* canteen, dining room, refectory.

mess *verb*
1 *They messed up their desks.* clutter up, jumble, litter, muck up, untidy.
OPPOSITE tidy.
2 *He messed up our plans.* botch, bungle, muck up (*informal*), ruin, spoil.
3 *The clock doesn't work since he messed around with it.* fiddle, meddle, play, tamper, tinker.

make a mess of botch, bungle, make a hash of (*informal*), mess up, muddle, ruin, spoil.

message *noun*
1 *He sent a message to the minister.* announcement, bulletin, communication, communiqué, dispatch, letter, memo (*informal*), news, note, notice, report, statement, tidings, word.
2 *a book's message.* meaning, moral, point, teaching, theme.

get the message (*informal*)
I *had to tell him many times before he got the message.* catch on, comprehend, cotton on (*informal*), get it (*informal*), grasp it, latch on (*informal*), twig (*informal*), understand.

messenger *noun*
He *acted as a messenger between the two parties.* ambassador, courier, envoy, go-between, herald.

messy *adjective*
1 *a messy room.* chaotic, cluttered, dirty, disorderly, jumbled, littered, mucked-up, muddled, topsy-turvy, untidy.
OPPOSITE clean, neat, tidy.
2 *The customer had a messy appearance.* bedraggled, dirty, dishevelled, sloppy, slovenly, unkempt.
OPPOSITE neat.
3 *a messy situation.* awkward, complicated, difficult, embarrassing, problematical, sticky (*informal*), ticklish, tricky.

metal *noun*
[*various metals*] aluminium, brass, bronze, chromium, cobalt, copper, gold, iron, lead, lithium, magnesium, mercury, nickel, pewter, platinum, potassium, silver, sodium, solder, steel, tin, uranium, zinc.

metallic *adjective*
1 *metallic paint.* gleaming, glistening, lustrous, shiny.
2 *a metallic sound.* brassy, clanging, clanking, clinking, jangling, ringing, tinny.

metaphorical *adjective*
a metaphorical use of a word. figurative.
OPPOSITE literal.

meter *noun*
The man read the electricity meter. clock, dial, gauge, indicator.

method *noun*
1 *research method.* approach, knack, manner, means, procedure, process, routine, system, technique, way.
2 *There's method in her madness.* design, order, orderliness, pattern, plan, structure, system.

methodical *adjective*
a methodical approach to his work. careful, disciplined, logical, meticulous, orderly, organised, structured, systematic, tidy.
OPPOSITE careless, haphazard.

microbe *noun*
The microbe was examined under a microscope. bacterium, bug (*informal*), germ, micro-organism, virus.

microphone *noun*
He installed a hidden microphone. bug (*informal*), mike (*informal*).

microscopic *adjective*
microscopic writing. little, minuscule, minute, small, tiny.
OPPOSITE large.

middle *adjective*
1 *in middle position.* central, halfway, median, mid, midway.
2 *of middle height.* average, intermediate, medium, moderate.
middle *noun*
1 *in the middle of Melbourne.* centre, core, heart, hub, nucleus.
OPPOSITE outskirts.
2 *It goes round your middle.* midriff, stomach, waist.

midget *noun*
The film starred a midget. dwarf, lilliputian, pygmy.
OPPOSITE giant.
midget *adjective*
a midget television set. little, miniature, minuscule, minute, small, tiny.
OPPOSITE gigantic.

midst *noun*
in the midst of
1 *in the midst of her friends.* amidst, among, surrounded by.
2 *In the midst of their discussion the telephone rang.* during, halfway through, in the middle of.

might *noun*
He tugged with all his might. energy, force, power, strength.

mighty *adjective*
1 *a mighty army.* invincible, powerful, robust, strong, sturdy.
OPPOSITE feeble.
2 *a mighty aircraft.* big, bulky, colossal, enormous, huge, immense, large, mammoth, massive, monstrous.
OPPOSITE small.

migrant *noun*
emigrant, immigrant, newcomer.

migrate *verb*
The birds migrate each winter. emigrate, go overseas, immigrate, move, relocate, travel.

a
b
c
d
e
f
g
h
i
j
k
l
m
n
o
p
q
r
s
t
u
v
w
x
y
z

mild *adjective*
1 *In spring the weather is mild.* balmy, moderate, temperate, warm.
OPPOSITE severe.
2 *She has a mild nature.* calm, docile, easygoing, gentle, kind, placid, serene.
OPPOSITE harsh.
3 *mild flavours.* bland, delicate, faint, subtle.
OPPOSITE sharp, strong.

militant *adjective*
militant unionists. aggressive, assertive, belligerent, defiant, pugnacious, pushy (*informal*), uncompromising.
OPPOSITE passive.

military *adjective*
military personnel. armed, army, defence, service.
military *noun*
The country is being ruled by the military. armed forces, army, defence forces, soldiers.

milky *adjective*
a milky liquid. cloudy, opaque, white, whitish.
OPPOSITE clear.

mill *noun*
a pepper mill. grinder.
mill *verb*
1 *They are milling the corn.* crush, granulate, grind.
2 *People milled around the entrance.* congregate, crowd, hover, mass, swarm, throng.

mimic *verb*
He mimics the politicians brilliantly. ape, copy, imitate, impersonate, parody, send up (*informal*), take off.

mince *verb*
The butcher minced the beef finely. chop, cut, grind, hash.

mind *noun*
1 *He doesn't use his mind sometimes.* brain, common sense, head, imagination, intellect, intelligence, reasoning, sense, understanding, wits.
2 *He changed his mind.* attitude, intention, judgement, opinion, outlook, point of view, position, view.
3 *She has a suspicious mind.* attitude, mentality, mindset.

mind *verb*
1 *He is minding the baby.* babysit, keep an eye on, look after, take care of, tend.
OPPOSITE neglect.
2 *He doesn't mind the music.* be bothered by, dislike, object to, resent, take exception to.
OPPOSITE like.
3 *Mind the low ceilings.* be careful of, beware of, look out for, take care with, watch out for.
4 *Mind what she says.* heed, mark, note, pay attention to, remember, take notice of.
OPPOSITE ignore.
bring to mind *He can't bring the name to mind.* recall, recollect, remember.

mind-boggling *adjective*
amazing, astonishing, astounding, incredible, staggering, startling, unbelievable.

minder *noun*
babysitter, bodyguard, carer, child-minder.

mindless *adjective*
1 *the mindless dumping of waste into rivers.* careless, heedless, senseless, thoughtless, unintelligent, unthinking.
2 *Packing bags is a mindless job.* boring, mechanical, routine, tedious.
OPPOSITE stimulating.

mine *noun*
1 *a coal mine.* colliery, excavation, pit, quarry, workings.
2 *a mine of information.* fund, source, storehouse, supply, treasury.
mine *verb*
He made his fortune mining gold. dig for, excavate, extract.

mingle *verb*
1 *The flavours mingled.* blend, combine, merge, mix.
OPPOSITE separate.
2 *The host found it hard to mingle.* circulate, mix, socialise.

mingy *adjective* (*informal*)
a mingy increase of $2. meagre, mean, measly (*informal*), paltry, stingy.

miniature *adjective*
a doll's house with miniature furniture. dwarf, little, microscopic, minuscule, minute, pocket-size, small, small-scale,

tiny.
OPPOSITE full-scale, large.

minimal *adjective*
minimal change. imperceptible,
marginal, minuscule, minute,
negligible, slight, small, subtle, token.
OPPOSITE maximum.

minimise *verb*
The firm tried to minimise costs. cut,
decrease, diminish, keep down, lessen,
reduce.
OPPOSITE maximise.

minimum *noun*
1 *The minimum required to be present is
fifteen.* least, lowest.
2 *an overnight minimum of 5°.* low.
OPPOSITE maximum.
minimum *adjective*
a minimum wage. basic, least, lowest,
smallest.
OPPOSITE maximum.

minister *noun*
a church minister. archbishop,
archdeacon, bishop, chaplain,
clergyman, clergywoman, cleric, curate,
deacon, dean, evangelist, father, padre,
parson, pastor, preacher, priest, rector,
vicar.
OPPOSITE layperson.

minor *adjective*
a minor issue. insignificant, lesser, petty,
slight, small, trivial, unimportant.
OPPOSITE major.
minor *noun*
Minors are not allowed in the club.
adolescent, child, juvenile, teenager,
youngster, youth.
OPPOSITE adult.

minstrel *noun*
a medieval minstrel. bard, entertainer,
musician, performer, singer.

mint *verb*
1 *They minted a new dollar coin.* cast,
coin, make, produce, strike.
2 *The word has been recently minted.* coin,
invent, make up.

minute¹ *noun*
It was all over in a minute. flash, instant,
jiffy (*informal*), moment, tick (*informal*),
trice.

minutes *plural noun*
We read the minutes of the last meeting.
account, notes, proceedings, record,
summary.

minute² *adjective*
1 *She took minute sips.* little, microscopic,
minuscule, small, tiny.
OPPOSITE huge.
2 *a minute examination.* close, detailed,
exhaustive, meticulous, thorough.
OPPOSITE superficial.

miracle *noun*
Jesus performed many miracles. marvel,
wonder.

miraculous *adjective*
a miraculous recovery. amazing,
astonishing, astounding, extraordinary,
incredible, marvellous, mysterious,
phenomenal, remarkable, supernatural,
unbelievable, wonderful.

mirage *noun*
a mirage in the desert. hallucination,
illusion, vision.

mirror *noun*
He admired himself in the mirror. glass,
looking-glass.
mirror *verb*
The trees were mirrored in the lake. reflect.

mirth *noun*
The mood at the party was one of mirth.
amusement, cheerfulness, fun, gaiety,
glee, happiness, hilarity, jollity,
laughter, merriment, merrymaking,
rejoicing, revelry.
OPPOSITE sadness.

misbehaviour *noun*
*Unhappiness was the cause of her
misbehaviour.* bad manners,
delinquency, disobedience, misconduct,
naughtiness, playing up (*informal*),
rebelliousness, unruliness.

miscellaneous *adjective*
a miscellaneous collection of games.
assorted, different, diverse, mixed,
motley, varied, various.

mischief *noun*
1 *Left alone, they got up to mischief.* high
jinks, misbehaviour, misconduct,
naughtiness, playfulness, playing up

a b c d e f g h i j k l m n o p q r s t u v w x y z

(*informal*), pranks, shenanigans
(*informal*).
2 *He caused a lot of mischief with this
rumour.* damage, harm, hurt, injury,
trouble.

mischievous *adjective*
1 *a mischievous child.* devilish, impish,
naughty, playful, roguish.
OPPOSITE goody-goody.
2 *mischievous gossip.* destructive,
harmful, hurtful, injurious, malicious,
spiteful.
OPPOSITE harmless.

miser *noun*
That miser won't give you anything.
hoarder, Scrooge, skinflint, tightwad
(*informal*).
OPPOSITE spendthrift.

miserable *adjective*
1 *He was miserable while his friend was
away.* dejected, depressed, desolate,
despondent, doleful, downcast, down-
hearted, forlorn, gloomy, glum, heavy-
hearted, melancholy, sad, sorrowful,
unhappy, wretched.
OPPOSITE happy.
2 *miserable weather.* abysmal (*informal*),
appalling (*informal*), atrocious
(*informal*), depressing, dismal, dreadful
(*informal*), dreary, terrible (*informal*),
unpleasant.
OPPOSITE fine.

miserly *adjective*
a miserly person. close-fisted, mean,
mingy (*informal*), niggardly, penny-
pinching, stingy, tight-fisted.
OPPOSITE generous.

misery *noun*
1 *Nothing will lift her out of her misery.*
blues, depression, despair, distress,
gloom, grief, melancholy, sadness,
sorrow, unhappiness, woe,
wretchedness.
OPPOSITE happiness.
2 *the misery associated with poverty.*
affliction, discomfort, hardship,
misfortune, suffering, trouble.
OPPOSITE comfort.

misfortune *noun*
1 *a series of misfortunes.* accident,
affliction, blow, calamity, catastrophe,
disaster, misadventure, mishap,
setback, trial, tribulation, trouble.
2 *a victim of misfortune.* adversity, bad
luck, mischance.
OPPOSITE good luck.

misguided *adjective*
*The officer was well-intentioned but
misguided.* foolish, misinformed, misled,
mistaken, unwise.

mislay *verb*
He has mislaid his keys. lose, misplace.

mislead *verb*
*The advertiser misled people about the
product's usefulness.* bluff, con (*informal*),
deceive, delude, dupe, fool, hoax,
hoodwink, kid (*informal*), lead astray,
lie, misguide, misinform, take for a ride
(*informal*), take in, trick.

misprint *noun*
see MISTAKE.

misrepresent *verb*
*The papers misrepresented the committee's
findings.* distort, falsify, misquote,
misreport, twist.

miss *verb*
1 *He missed football to play chess.* absent
yourself from, forgo, give up, skip.
OPPOSITE attend.
2 *She missed her opportunity.* let go, let
pass, let slip, lose, pass up.
OPPOSITE seize.
3 *Miss a line.* leave, omit, skip.
4 *He never misses a mistake.* disregard,
gloss over, ignore, overlook, pass over.
5 *Would you miss television if you didn't
have a set?* crave for, long for, pine for,
want, yearn for.
6 *If we go this way we can miss the centre
of the city.* avoid, bypass, dodge, steer
clear of.
OPPOSITE hit, reach.
miss out *He missed out a word.* forget,
leave out, omit, overlook, pass over,
skip.
OPPOSITE include.

missile *noun*
They attacked the target with missiles.
projectile; [*kinds of missile*] arrow,
ballistic missile, bomb, boomerang,
bullet, dart, grenade, guided missile,

harpoon, javelin, rocket, shell, spear, torpedo.

missing *adjective*
1 *One volume was missing.* gone, lost, mislaid, misplaced, removed.
2 *The cat is missing.* absent, disappeared, gone, lost.
OPPOSITE present.

mission *noun*
1 *The group was sent on a fact-finding mission.* assignment, campaign, exercise, expedition, operation, quest.
2 *She knows her mission in life.* calling, purpose, vocation.

missionary *noun*
apostle, evangelist, preacher.

mist *noun*
It was hard to see through the mist. cloud, fog, haze, smog, steam, vapour.

mistake *noun*
He made a mistake. blooper (*informal*), blue (*Australian informal*), blunder, booboo (*slang*), clanger (*informal*), error, howler (*informal*), miscalculation, misjudgement, misprint, mix-up, oversight, slip, slip-up (*informal*), typo (*informal*).
mistake *verb*
1 *He mistook my meaning.* confuse, get wrong, misconstrue, misinterpret, misunderstand.
2 *I mistook her for her sister.* confuse with, mix up with, take for.

mistreat *verb*
He was fined for mistreating the dog. abuse, harm, hurt, ill-treat, maltreat, manhandle, molest, torment.

mistress *noun*
1 *the cat's mistress.* keeper, owner.
2 *the senior science mistress.* schoolmistress, teacher.
3 *His wife discovered he had a mistress.* girlfriend, lover.

mistrust *verb*
She mistrusted their methods. distrust, doubt, have misgivings about, question, suspect.
OPPOSITE trust.

mistrust *noun*
a mistrust of science. distrust, scepticism, suspicion, wariness.
OPPOSITE trust.

misty *adjective*
a misty day. foggy, hazy.
OPPOSITE clear.

misunderstand *verb*
The student misunderstood the teacher's comments. get wrong, misconstrue, misinterpret, misjudge, misread, mistake.
OPPOSITE understand.

misunderstanding *noun*
a misunderstanding of the rules. confusion, misconception, misinterpretation, misjudgement, misreading, mistake, mix-up.

misuse *noun*
a misuse of funds. a misuse of power. abuse, misappropriation, squandering, waste.

mix *verb*
1 *Mix the eggs into the butter and sugar mixture.* add, beat, blend, combine, fold, incorporate, integrate, stir, whip, whisk.
2 *She mixes business with pleasure.* combine, join, merge, mingle, unite.
OPPOSITE separate.
3 *He mixes well at parties.* be sociable, fraternise, mingle, socialise.
mix *noun*
The correct mix of oil and vinegar. proportions, ratio; see also MIXTURE.
mix up
1 *They mixed up the cards.* jumble up, muddle up, rearrange, shuffle.
2 *He mixed up their names.* confuse, muddle.
3 *She was mixed up in the robbery.* implicate, involve, tie up.

mixed *adjective*
1 *a mixed group of people.* assorted, diverse, miscellaneous, motley, varied.
OPPOSITE uniform.
2 *a mixed breed.* cross-bred, hybrid, mongrel.

mixed-up *adjective* (*informal*)
The doctor helps mixed-up people. confused, muddled, screwed-up (*informal*).

a
b
c
d
e
f
g
h
i
j
k
l
m
n
o
p
q
r
s
t
u
v
w
x
y
z

mixture *noun*
alloy, assortment, blend, collection, combination, compound, concoction, cross, hash, hotchpotch, hybrid, jumble, medley, mix, patchwork, rag-bag, variety.

moan *noun*
1 *The patient's moans were pitiful.* groan, wail, whimper.
2 *She had a moan about the amount of homework.* beef (*slang*), complaint, grievance, gripe (*informal*), grizzle (*informal*), grumble, whine, whinge (*informal*).

moan *verb*
1 *The dog moaned with pain.* groan, howl, wail, whimper, whine.
2 *He's always moaning about something.* beef (*slang*), complain, gripe (*informal*), grizzle (*informal*), grumble, whine, whinge (*informal*).

mob *noun*
1 *an angry mob of protesters.* bunch, crowd, crush, gathering, herd, horde, lot, mass, pack, rabble, throng.
2 (*Australian*) *a mob of animals.* flock, group, herd.

mob *verb*
The princess's admirers mobbed her. besiege, crowd round, gather round, surround, swarm round.

mobile *adjective*
a mobile toy library. movable, portable, transportable, travelling.
OPPOSITE stationary.

mobilise *verb*
They mobilised their troops. assemble, gather, marshal, muster, organise, rally.
OPPOSITE demobilise.

mock *verb*
The spectators mocked him when he dropped the ball. jeer at, make fun of, pay out (*informal*), poke fun at, ridicule, scoff at, scorn, sling off at (*Australian informal*), sneer at, take the mickey out of (*informal*), taunt.
OPPOSITE praise.

mock *adjective*
a mock battle. fake, imitation, pretend (*informal*), pretended, simulated.
OPPOSITE real.

mockery *noun*
1 *He was subjected to public mockery.* derision, jeering, ridicule, scorn.
2 *They made a mockery of justice.* farce, joke, pretence, travesty.

mode *noun*
a mode of instruction. approach, fashion, form, manner, means, method, practice, procedure, system, technique, way.

model *noun*
1 *a model of the finished house.* archetype, copy, dummy, miniature, mock-up, prototype, replica, representation.
2 *the latest model of car.* design, style, type, version.
3 *The clothes are displayed by the models.* mannequin.

model *adjective*
a model pupil. excellent, exemplary, ideal, perfect.

model *verb*
1 *He modelled a pig out of clay.* cast, form, make, mould, sculpt (*informal*), shape.
2 *The programme is modelled on a British one.* base, copy.

moderate *adjective*
1 *moderate prices.* average, fair, intermediate, medium, middling, modest, reasonable.
OPPOSITE excessive.
2 *a moderate climate.* mild, temperate.
OPPOSITE extreme.

moderate *verb*
1 *He moderated his behaviour. She moderated her voice.* check, curb, quieten down, restrain, soften, subdue, tame, temper, tone down.
2 *The wind moderated.* abate, calm down, die down, ease, subside.

modern *adjective*
modern ideas. contemporary, current, fashionable, innovative, new, newfangled (*derogatory*), present, progressive, recent, trendy (*informal*), up-to-date, with it (*informal*).
OPPOSITE old, old-fashioned.

modernise *verb*
They modernised the bathroom. rejuvenate, renovate, update.

modest *adjective*
1 *He was modest about his achievements.* humble, quiet, unassertive, unassuming.
OPPOSITE conceited.
2 *a modest increase.* moderate, slight, small.
OPPOSITE substantial.
3 *a modest house.* humble, lowly, ordinary, simple, unpretentious.
OPPOSITE ostentatious.
4 *The modest ones undressed in the cubicles.* bashful, coy, self-conscious, shy.
OPPOSITE brazen, immodest.

modify *verb*
1 *They modified their original design.* adapt, adjust, alter, change, refine, revise, transform, vary.
2 *The adjective modifies the noun.* limit, qualify, restrict.

module *noun*
The furniture comes in modules. component, part, piece, unit.

moist *adjective*
a moist atmosphere. clammy, damp, dank, dewy, humid, muggy, steamy, wet.
OPPOSITE dry.

moisten *verb*
Moisten the soil. damp, dampen, irrigate, soak, spray, water, wet.
OPPOSITE dry.

moisture *noun*
The timber was damaged by moisture. condensation, damp, dampness, dew, humidity, liquid, steam, vapour, water, wetness.
OPPOSITE dryness.

molest *verb*
The child molested the cat. abuse, annoy, bother, harass, ill-treat, mistreat, pester, tease, torment.

moment *noun*
1 *I'll be with you in a moment.* flash, instant, jiffy (*informal*), minute, second, tick (*informal*), trice, two shakes (*informal*).
OPPOSITE eternity (*informal*).
2 *At this moment he walked in.* instant, juncture, point, stage.

momentary *adjective*
a momentary feeling of happiness. brief, ephemeral, fleeting, passing, short, short-lived, temporary, transient.
OPPOSITE lasting.

momentous *adjective*
a momentous decision. crucial, fateful, grave, historic, important, significant, weighty.
OPPOSITE unimportant.

momentum *noun*
The campaign is gathering momentum. force, impetus, strength.

monarch *noun*
emperor, empress, head, king, queen, ruler, sovereign.

monarchist *noun*
royalist.

monarchy *noun*
empire, kingdom, realm.

monastery *noun*
Monks live in a monastery. abbey, cloister, friary, lamasery (*Buddhism*), priory, religious house.
CONTRASTS WITH convent.

money *noun*
1 *He never carries any money.* banknotes, cash, coins, currency, dosh (*slang*), dough (*slang*), notes, paper money, ready money.
2 *You need money to start a business.* assets, capital, finance, funds, means, resources, riches, wealth.

mongrel *noun*
Our dog is a mongrel. bitser (*Australian informal*), cross-breed, hybrid.
OPPOSITE pedigree dog.

monitor *noun*
1 *a school monitor.* prefect.
2 *a computer monitor.* display terminal, screen, VDU, visual display unit.
monitor *verb*
The doctor monitored the baby's progress. check, keep an eye on, keep track of, observe, record, watch.

monk *noun*
abbot, brother, friar, lama (*Buddhism*), prior, religious.

a
b
c
d
e
f
g
h
i
j
k
l
m
n
o
p
q
r
s
t
u
v
w
x
y
z

monkey *noun*
1 [*kinds of monkey*] baboon, Barbary ape, capuchin, langur, macaque, mandrill, marmoset, rhesus monkey, tamarin, vervet.
2 *The child's a little monkey.* devil, imp, rascal, rogue, scallywag, scamp.

monologue *noun*
They listened patiently to his monologue. address, lecture, oration, sermon, soliloquy, speech.

monopolise *verb*
The project monopolised his time. dominate, preoccupy, take over.
OPPOSITE share.

monotonous *adjective*
1 *a monotonous voice.* boring, droning, dull, expressionless, flat, singsong, soporific, unexpressive.
OPPOSITE expressive.
2 *monotonous work.* boring, dreary, dull, humdrum, mechanical, repetitive, routine, tedious, unvarying.
OPPOSITE interesting, varied.

monster *noun*
He was frightened by the monster in the story. beast, bogyman, brute, bunyip (*Australian*), demon, devil, dragon, fiend, giant, ogre.

monstrosity *noun*
The new skyscraper is a monstrosity. eyesore, horror, monster.

monstrous *adjective*
1 *a monstrous plant.* abnormal, freakish, grotesque, misshapen, odd, ugly, unnatural, weird.
2 *a monstrous building.* colossal, enormous, gigantic, huge, immense, massive.
3 *a monstrous crime.* abhorrent, appalling, atrocious, brutal, cruel, despicable, detestable, fiendish, ghastly, heinous, hideous, horrible, horrid, outrageous, repulsive, savage, shocking, vile, wicked.

monument *noun*
a monument to our forefathers. cairn, cenotaph, gravestone, headstone, mausoleum, memorial, obelisk, plaque, shrine, statue, tombstone.

monumental *adjective*
1 *a monumental novel.* classic, enduring, great, impressive, lasting, major.
2 *a monumental waste of money.* colossal, enormous, great, huge, immense, large, massive, monstrous, terrific (*informal*).

mood *noun*
1 *Her mood changed.* disposition, frame of mind, humour, spirits, state of mind, temper.
2 *the mood of the meeting.* atmosphere, attitude, feeling.

moody *adjective*
1 *His financial problems made him moody.* blue, depressed, dismal, gloomy, glum, irritable, melancholy, morose, peevish, sulky, sullen, testy, tetchy, unhappy.
OPPOSITE cheerful.
2 *You don't know what to expect with such a moody person.* changeable, erratic, inconsistent, temperamental, unpredictable, volatile.
OPPOSITE stable.

moon *noun*
Triton is a moon of Neptune. satellite.

moor[1] *noun* (*British*)
They walked on the moor. fell, heath.

moor[2] *verb*
He moored the boat. anchor, berth, dock, secure, tie up.

mop *verb*
She mopped the floor. clean, wash, wipe.
mop up
1 *He mopped up the spill.* clean up, soak up, sponge, wipe.
2 *He was left to mop up the job.* clean up, clear up, finish off.

mope *verb*
She spent days moping after her friend went away. brood, fret, mooch (*informal*), moon, pine.

moral *adjective*
1 *a moral code.* ethical.
2 *His behaviour was entirely moral.* above board, blameless, decent, ethical, good, honourable, principled, proper, right, righteous, upright, virtuous.
OPPOSITE immoral, unethical.
moral *noun*
The story has a moral. lesson, message, principle, teaching.

morale *noun*
The team's morale is high. confidence, self-confidence, spirit.

morality *noun*
a person of the highest morality. decency, ethics, fairness, goodness, honour, integrity, morals, principles, scruples, standards, virtue.

more *adjective*
more lollies. more income. additional, extra, further, other, reserve, spare.
OPPOSITE fewer, less.

moreover *adverb*
It was an unkind remark; moreover, it was untrue. also, besides, further, furthermore, in addition.

morgue *noun*
mortuary.

moron *noun*
see IDIOT.

morsel *noun*
a morsel of cheese. bit, bite, fragment, mouthful, nibble, piece, scrap, sliver, taste, titbit.

mortal *adjective*
1 our mortal existence. earthly, ephemeral, human, transient, worldly.
OPPOSITE immortal.
2 a mortal wound. deadly, fatal, lethal.
3 in mortal fear. deep, extreme, grave, intense, severe.
mortal *noun*
a mere mortal. human being, man, person, woman.

mortuary *noun*
morgue.

most *noun*
He received the most. bulk, lion's share, majority.
OPPOSITE least.
most *adverb*
That's most amusing. exceedingly, extremely, highly, very.
make the most of He makes the most of every opportunity. capitalise on, exploit, profit by, take advantage of.

mostly *adverb*
She works mostly at home. chiefly, for the most part, generally, in general, largely, mainly, on the whole, primarily, usually.

motel *noun*
They spent the night at a motel. hotel, inn, motor inn.

mother *noun*
[informal terms of address] ma, mama, mamma, mammy, mom (American), mum, mummy.
mother *verb*
She was good at mothering her children. care for, fuss over, look after, nurse, nurture, protect, raise, rear, tend.

motherly *adjective*
The child had a motherly way with the kittens. caring, gentle, kind, loving, maternal, protective, tender.

motion *noun*
1 All motion is restricted. locomotion, mobility, movement.
2 The motion was read to the meeting. proposal, recommendation, suggestion.
motion *verb*
He motioned to her to come forward. beckon, gesture, nod, signal, wave.

motionless *adjective*
He remained motionless. at rest, immobile, inert, paralysed, stationary, still, stock-still, transfixed.
OPPOSITE moving.

motivate *verb*
1 His action was motivated by self-interest. drive, influence, inspire, prompt, provoke.
2 The teacher wasn't able to motivate her pupils. inspire, stimulate.

motivation *noun*
She was lacking in motivation. ambition, drive, impetus, inspiration, stimulus.

motive *noun*
a motive for the crime. grounds, motivation, purpose, reason.

motor *noun*
engine.
motor car see CAR.

motorcycle *noun*
bike (informal), motor bike (informal).

a
b
c
d
e
f
g
h
i
j
k
l
m
n
o
p
q
r
s
t
u
v
w
x
y
z

motorcyclist *noun*
biker, bikie (*Australian informal*).

mottled *adjective*
mottled eggs. blotchy, dappled, flecked, marbled, motley, speckled, spotty, variegated.
OPPOSITE plain.

motto *noun*
The school motto is 'Semper fidelis'. adage, maxim, proverb, saying, slogan.

mould[1] *verb*
1 *She moulded a cup out of clay.* cast, form, model, sculpt, shape.
2 *The school helped to mould his character.* develop, form, influence, make, shape.

mould[2] *noun*
fungus, mildew.

mouldy *adjective*
1 *The food went mouldy.* bad, mildewed, off, rotten, stale.
2 *The cupboard smelt mouldy.* damp, musty, stale.

mound *noun*
a mound of stones. heap, hill, pile, pyramid, stack.

mount *verb*
1 *She mounted the stairs.* ascend, clamber up, climb, go up.
OPPOSITE descend.
2 *He mounted the horse.* climb on, get astride, get on, straddle.
OPPOSITE dismount.
3 *Fears mounted for their safety.* escalate, grow, heighten, increase, rise.
OPPOSITE diminish.
4 *They mounted the photographs in the album.* fix, install, place, position, put.
5 *They mounted an attack.* arrange, carry out, launch, organise, set up, stage.

mountain *noun*
1 *He climbed the mountain.* alp, bluff, hill, mount, peak, pinnacle, range.
2 *a mountain of letters. mountains of work.* heap (*informal*), load (*informal*), lot (*informal*), pile (*informal*), stack (*informal*).

mourn *verb*
He mourned for his dead wife. grieve, lament, sorrow, weep.
OPPOSITE rejoice.

mournful *adjective*
a mournful expression. dismal, doleful, funereal, gloomy, melancholy, sad, sombre, sorrowful.
OPPOSITE joyful.

mouth *noun*
1 *She closed her mouth.* gob (*slang*), jaws, lips, trap (*slang*).
2 *the mouth of a cave.* entrance, opening, outlet, portal.
3 *the mouth of the river.* estuary.
OPPOSITE head, source.

mouthful *noun*
1 *only one mouthful of pie left.* bit, bite, morsel, nibble, spoonful.
2 *He took a mouthful of tea.* gulp, sip, sup, swallow, swig (*informal*).

movable *adjective*
movable furniture. mobile, portable, transportable.
OPPOSITE built-in, fixed.

move *verb*
1 *They've moved things around.* change, remove, shift, swap, switch, transfer, transport.
2 *I moved out of the way of the ball.* bolt, dart, jump, leap, shift, step; see also RUN.
3 *Don't move!* budge, fidget, flinch, jerk, quiver, shift, stir, sway, tremble, turn, twitch, wince, wriggle.
4 *The snake moved through the grass.* slink, slip, slither, wiggle, wriggle, writhe.
5 *The skater moves gracefully on the ice.* dance, flow, glide, skate, slide.
6 *They sold their house and moved to a new suburb.* relocate, shift, transfer, transplant; see also MIGRATE.
7 *The work moves slowly.* advance, develop, go on, proceed, progress.
OPPOSITE stagnate.
8 *The sad news moved them deeply.* affect, impress, stir, touch.

move *noun*
1 *You mustn't make a move.* gesture, motion, movement.

2 *Each player has had his move.* chance, go, opportunity, shot (*informal*), turn.
3 *a wise move.* act, action, initiative, measure, step, tactic.

movement *noun*
1 *Every movement is painful to him.* action, activity, gesture, motion, move, step, stroke.
2 *army movements.* exercise, manoeuvre, operation.
3 *the anti-nuclear movement.* group, lobby, organisation, party; see also CAMPAIGN.
4 *a movement towards shorter working hours.* evolution, progress, shift, swing, tendency, trend.
5 *the movements of a symphony.* division, part, section.

movie *noun* (*informal*)
They watched a movie. film, flick (*informal*), motion picture, moving picture, picture, video.

moving *adjective*
a very moving performance. emotional, inspiring, poignant, rousing, stirring, touching.
OPPOSITE unemotional.

mow *verb*
clip, cut, trim.

much *adjective*
They don't have much money. abundant, a lot of (*informal*), ample, copious, plentiful.
OPPOSITE little.
much *noun*
He has much to say. a great deal, heaps (*informal*), loads (*informal*), lots (*informal*), plenty, stacks (*informal*), volumes.
OPPOSITE little.
much *adverb*
1 *He feels much better.* a great deal, a lot, considerably, decidedly, far.
OPPOSITE slightly.
2 *much the same.* about, almost, approximately, nearly, virtually.

muck *noun*
1 *The farmer's boots were covered in muck.* droppings, dung, manure.

2 (*informal*) *The children traipsed muck into the house.* dirt, filth, mud.
3 (*informal*) *What's that muck you're watching?* garbage, rubbish, trash.
muck *verb*
muck up
1 *She mucked up the room in five minutes.* disorganise, jumble, mess up, muddle, turn upside down.
OPPOSITE tidy up.
2 *We mucked up the dinner.* botch, bungle, mess up, ruin, spoil.

mud *noun*
Her boots were covered in mud. dirt, filth, mire, muck (*informal*), silt, slime, sludge.

muddle *verb*
1 *Her papers were muddled.* disorganise, jumble, mess up, mix up, muck up.
2 *He gets muddled when you interrupt him.* bewilder, confuse, fluster, mix up.
muddle *noun*
The place is in a muddle. chaos, clutter, confusion, disarray, jumble, mess, shambles.

muddy *adjective*
1 *muddy ground.* boggy, slimy, waterlogged, wet.
OPPOSITE dry.
2 *muddy shoes.* dirty, filthy, mucky (*informal*).
3 *muddy liquid.* cloudy, impure, murky.
OPPOSITE clear.

muffle *verb*
1 *He muffled himself up before going out in the cold.* cover, wrap.
2 *The blanket muffled the sounds.* dampen, deaden, dull, quieten, soften, stifle, suppress.
OPPOSITE amplify.

mug *noun*
1 *She drank from a mug.* beaker, cup.
2 (*informal*) *There's always some mug who'll buy it.* bunny (*Australian informal*), duffer, dupe, fool, muggins (*informal*), simpleton, soft touch, sucker (*informal*).
mug *verb*
The lady was mugged outside the bank. assault, attack, rob.

a
b
c
d
e
f
g
h
i
j
k
l
m
n
o
p
q
r
s
t
u
v
w
x
y
z

muggy *adjective*
The muggy weather made people irritable.
close, humid, oppressive, steamy,
sticky, stuffy, sultry.

mulga *noun* (*Australian*)
They live out in the mulga. backblocks
(*Australian*), bush, country, donga
(*Australian*), mallee (*Australian*), never-
never (*Australian*), outback (*Australian*),
scrub, sticks (*informal*).

multicoloured *adjective*
a multicoloured shirt. harlequin, motley,
pied, variegated.
OPPOSITE plain.

multicultural *adjective*
a multicultural society. cosmopolitan,
multiracial, pluralist.

multinational *adjective*
a multinational company. international,
worldwide.

multiple *adjective*
This gadget has multiple uses. many,
numerous, several, sundry, various.

multiply *verb*
Rabbits multiply rapidly. breed, increase,
proliferate, reproduce.

multitude *noun*
1 *He was greeted by an angry multitude.*
crowd, horde, mob, rabble, throng.
2 *a multitude of problems.* host, mass,
myriad, swag (*Australian informal*).

mumble *verb*
He mumbled something unintelligible.
babble, grunt, murmur, mutter.
mumble *noun*
All he heard was a mumble. babble,
murmur, mutter.

munch *verb*
He munched a carrot. bite, chew, chomp,
crunch, eat, gnaw.

mundane *adjective*
*mundane tasks such as cleaning and
shopping.* commonplace, dreary, dull,
everyday, ordinary, routine, unexciting,
uninspiring, uninteresting.

municipal *adjective*
a municipal library. civic, community,
council, district, local.

mural *noun*
They painted a mural on the old building.
fresco, wall-painting.

murder *noun*
found guilty of murder. assassination,
extermination, genocide, homicide,
killing, massacre, slaughter, slaying.
CONTRASTS WITH manslaughter.
murder *verb*
He murdered many people. assassinate,
bump off (*slang*), do in (*slang*),
exterminate, kill, massacre, slaughter,
slay.

murderer *noun*
assassin, cutthroat, hit man (*slang*),
killer, murderess.

murderous *adjective*
murderous tendencies. bloodthirsty,
brutal, deadly, homicidal, savage,
vicious.

murky *adjective*
1 *It was too murky to see clearly.* dark,
dim, dull, dusky, foggy, gloomy,
shadowy.
OPPOSITE bright.
2 *murky waters.* cloudy, impure, muddy.
OPPOSITE clear.

murmur *noun*
1 *the murmur of the stream.* babble,
burble, drone, hum.
2 *There wasn't a murmur from them.*
peep, sigh, sound.
murmur *verb*
He murmured to the person next to him.
mumble, mutter, whisper.

muscle *noun*
1 *It takes a bit of muscle to lift an engine.*
brawn, might, muscularity, strength.
2 *Trade unions with plenty of muscle.*
clout (*informal*), influence, power,
strength.
muscle *verb*
muscle in on (*informal*)
He muscled in on our game. butt in on,
force your way into, intrude on, push
your way into.

muscular *adjective*
He became more muscular through rowing.
athletic, beefy, brawny, burly, hefty,
nuggety (*Australian*), robust, strapping,

strong, sturdy, thickset.
OPPOSITE weedy.

muse *verb*
He mused upon the meaning of life.
contemplate, meditate, ponder, reflect,
speculate, think.

mushy *adjective*
mushy vegetables. mashed, puréed,
sloppy, soft, squidgy (*informal*), squishy
(*informal*).

music *noun*
1 *music-making.* harmony, melody;
[*kinds of music*] blues, classical music,
country music, folk, jazz, opera, pop,
rock, sacred music, soul.
2 *the music for the film.* score,
soundtrack.

musical *adjective*
musical sounds. dulcet, euphonious,
harmonious, lyrical, melodic,
melodious, sweet, tuneful.
OPPOSITE cacophonous.

musical instrument [*various musical
instruments*] accordion, bagpipes, banjo,
bassoon, bells, bugle, castanets, cello,
clarinet, clavichord, cor anglais, cornet,
cymbals, didgeridoo, double bass,
drum, euphonium, fife, flute, French
horn, glockenspiel, guitar, harmonica,
harmonium, harp, harpsichord,
keyboard, lute, lyre, mandolin,
marimba, mouth organ, oboe, organ,
pan pipes, piano, piccolo, recorder,
saxophone, sitar, synthesiser,
tambourine, timpani, triangle,
trombone, trumpet, tuba, ukulele, viola,
violin, xylophone, zither.

musician *noun*
artist, composer, instrumentalist, muso
(*slang*), performer, player, soloist,
virtuoso, vocalist.

must *noun* (*informal*)
An umbrella is a must. essential,
necessity, requirement.

muster *verb*
1 *He mustered his troops.* assemble,
collect, gather, marshal, mobilise, rally.
2 *She finally mustered the courage to tell
him.* find, gather, screw up, summon.

3 (*Australian*) *They mustered the cattle.*
herd, round up.

musty *adjective*
The house had a musty smell. damp,
mildewed, mouldy, stale, stuffy.
OPPOSITE fresh.

mutation *noun*
a gene mutation. alteration, change,
transformation.

mute *adjective*
1 *He has been mute from birth.* dumb,
speechless.
2 *She remained mute during the discussion.*
quiet, silent, tight-lipped, tongue-tied,
uncommunicative.
OPPOSITE vocal.

muted *adjective*
muted colours. pale, pastel, soft,
subdued, toned down.
OPPOSITE intense.

mutilate *verb*
The body was badly mutilated. damage,
destroy, disfigure, dismember, injure,
maim, mangle.

mutinous *adjective*
The crew became mutinous. defiant,
disobedient, insubordinate, rebellious.
OPPOSITE compliant.

mutiny *noun*
The sailors planned a mutiny.
insurrection, rebellion, revolt, riot,
rising, uprising.
mutiny *verb*
They mutinied soon after leaving port.
rebel, revolt, riot, rise up.

mutter *verb*
He muttered his disapproval. grumble,
mumble, murmur.
mutter *noun*
We heard a mutter from behind us.
complaint, grumble, mumble, murmur.

mutual *adjective*
1 *The feeling is mutual.* reciprocal,
reciprocated, requited.
2 (*informal*) *our mutual friend.* common,
joint, shared.

muzzle *noun*
an animal's muzzle. jaws, mouth, nose,
snout.

a
b
c
d
e
f
g
h
i
j
k
l
m
n
o
p
q
r
s
t
u
v
w
x
y
z

muzzle *verb*
He has to muzzle his greyhound. bridle, control, gag, restrain.

mysterious *adjective*
1 *mysterious events.* baffling, bizarre, curious, incomprehensible, inexplicable, mystifying, puzzling, strange, supernatural, uncanny, weird. OPPOSITE straightforward.
2 *He was mysterious about his past.* cagey (*informal*), cryptic, enigmatic, evasive, secretive.
OPPOSITE open.

mystery *noun*
1 *the mystery of their disappearance.* conundrum, enigma, problem, puzzle, riddle, secret.
2 *divine mysteries.* miracle, wonder.

mystify *verb*
The police were mystified by the disappearance. baffle, bamboozle (*informal*), bewilder, confound, confuse, puzzle.

myth *noun*
1 *He is reading the Greek myths.* fable, legend, narrative, story, tale.
2 *It is a myth that all natural foods are good for you.* delusion, fallacy, falsehood, fantasy, fiction, lie, untruth.

mythical *adjective*
1 *Theseus was a mythical hero.* fabled, legendary, mythological.
2 *a mythical friend.* fictitious, imaginary, invented, made-up, non-existent.
OPPOSITE real.

Nn

nab *verb* (*informal*)
The police nabbed the culprit. apprehend, arrest, capture, catch, nail, nick (*slang*), seize.

nag *verb*
He nagged them to clean their rooms. badger, harass, harp on at, hassle (*informal*), henpeck, keep on at, pester, scold.

nagging *adjective*
a nagging suspicion. a nagging toothache. continuous, niggling, persistent.

nail *verb*
She nailed the top to the uprights. hammer, pin, tack; see also FASTEN.
nail down It was hard to nail him down to a time. bind, commit, pin down.

naive *adjective*
1 naive children. artless, ingenuous, innocent, simple, unaffected, unsophisticated.
OPPOSITE sophisticated.
2 He must be naive to believe that. credulous, green, gullible, inexperienced, unsuspecting, unworldly.
OPPOSITE wary.

naked *adjective*
The swimmers were naked. bare, in the altogether (*informal*), in your birthday suit (*informal*), nude, starkers (*slang*), unclothed, uncovered, undressed.
OPPOSITE clothed.

name *noun*
1 What name does she go by? alias, assumed name, Christian name, false name, family name, first name, given name, last name, maiden name, nickname, pen-name, pet name, pseudonym, surname, title.
2 Another name for a 'Nosy Parker' is a 'stickybeak'. label, term, word.
name *verb*
1 They named him 'Peter'. baptise, call, christen, dub, nickname.

2 She named the book 'Life'. call, entitle, title.
3 He was named as the next leader. appoint, choose, designate, nominate, pick, select.
4 The report named the culprits. identify, mention, specify.

nameless *adjective*
The donor wished to remain nameless. anonymous, unidentified, unnamed.

nanny *noun*
A nanny looks after their children. nurse, nursemaid.

nap *noun*
He has a nap after lunch. catnap, doze, forty winks, kip (*slang*), lie-down, rest, shut-eye (*informal*), siesta, sleep, slumber, snooze.
nap *verb*
no time to nap. catnap, doze, drop off, kip (*slang*), nod off, sleep, slumber, snooze.

napkin *noun*
table napkins. serviette.

nappy *noun*
a baby's nappy. diaper (*American*), napkin.

narcotic *adjective*
The drug has a narcotic effect. anaesthetic, hypnotic, numbing, sedative, soporific.

narrate *verb*
She narrated the episode to me. describe, recount, relate, tell.

narrative *noun*
a narrative of her misfortunes. account, chronicle, report, saga, story, tale, yarn.

narrow *adjective*
1 a narrow passage. confined, constricted, cramped, strait (*old use*), tight.
OPPOSITE broad, wide.
2 a narrow tube. fine, slender, slim, thin.
OPPOSITE thick.

3 *a narrow escape.* close, near.
narrow *verb*
They have narrowed the gap. close up,
diminish, lessen, reduce.
OPPOSITE widen.

narrow-minded *adjective*
biased, bigoted, inflexible, intolerant,
petty, prejudiced, rigid, small-minded.
OPPOSITE broad-minded.

nasty *adjective*
1 *a nasty taste.* awful, disagreeable,
disgusting, foul, nauseating,
objectionable, offensive, repulsive,
revolting, sickening, unpalatable,
unpleasant, vile, yucky (*informal*).
OPPOSITE pleasant.
2 *nasty weather.* appalling (*informal*),
atrocious (*informal*), bad, dreadful
(*informal*), foul, lousy (*informal*), rotten
(*informal*), shocking (*informal*), stormy,
terrible (*informal*).
OPPOSITE fair, fine.
3 *a nasty person.* beastly, contemptible,
ill-tempered, malevolent, malicious,
mean, obnoxious, sinister, spiteful,
unkind, vicious, vindictive.
OPPOSITE kind.
4 *a nasty thing to do.* abominable,
beastly, cowardly, dastardly,
detestable, horrible, horrid, loathsome,
lousy (*informal*), low-down, mean,
rotten.
OPPOSITE kind.
5 *a nasty problem.* annoying, bad,
difficult, serious, tricky, troublesome.

nation *noun*
people of all nations. community,
country, land, people, race, society,
state.

national *adjective*
1 *national costume.* ethnic.
2 *a national strike.* countrywide, general,
nationwide.

nationalism *noun*
patriotism.

native *adjective*
1 *She developed her native talent.* inborn,
innate, natural.
OPPOSITE acquired.
2 *a native inhabitant.* aboriginal,
indigenous, original.

native *noun*
If you want to know the way, ask a native.
inhabitant, local, resident.

natural *adjective*
1 *natural resources.* crude, raw,
unprocessed, unrefined.
OPPOSITE man-made, refined.
2 *Her reaction was quite natural.* normal,
ordinary, reasonable, understandable.
OPPOSITE surprising, unnatural.
3 *natural leadership skills.* inborn, innate,
instinctive, intuitive, native.
OPPOSITE acquired.
4 *He's a very natural person.* artless,
authentic, down-to-earth, genuine,
spontaneous, unaffected,
unpretentious, unsophisticated.
OPPOSITE artificial.

nature *noun*
1 *She has a kind nature.* character,
disposition, heart, make-up,
personality, spirit, temperament.
2 *the nature of the disease.* character,
characteristics, features, peculiarities,
properties, qualities.
3 *subjects of this nature.* kind, sort, type,
variety.

naughty *adjective*
a naughty child. bad, contrary,
disobedient, impish, incorrigible,
mischievous, perverse, undisciplined,
unruly, wayward, wilful.
OPPOSITE well-behaved.

nausea *noun*
*Her nausea was caused by the rocking of the
ship.* biliousness, motion-sickness,
queasiness, seasickness, sickness,
travel-sickness.

nautical *adjective*
marine, maritime, naval, seafaring,
seagoing.

navigate *verb*
He navigated the boat through the channel.
direct, guide, pilot, sail, steer.

navy *noun*
armada, fleet, flotilla.

near *adverb*
She came near. alongside, close, nigh,
within close range, within cooee
(*Australian informal*).

near *preposition*
near the school. adjacent to, around, close to.

near *adjective*
1 *The end is near.* approaching, at hand, close, imminent, in sight, looming.
2 *a near escape.* close, narrow.

near *verb*
We neared the shore. approach, draw near to.

nearby *adjective*
a nearby field. adjacent, adjoining, close, neighbouring.

nearly *adverb*
1 *nearly a thousand people.* about, almost, approximately, around, close to, in the vicinity of, roughly.
2 *He is nearly forty.* almost, approaching, nigh on, pushing (*informal*).
3 *He is nearly ready.* almost, practically, virtually.

near-sighted *adjective*
myopic, short-sighted.
OPPOSITE hypermetropic, long-sighted.

neat *adjective*
1 *a neat appearance.* clean, dapper, natty (*informal*), smart, spruce, tidy, trim.
OPPOSITE scruffy, untidy.
2 *a neat office.* orderly, organised, shipshape, straight, tidy.
OPPOSITE disorderly.
3 *neat writing.* careful, legible, readable.
OPPOSITE messy.

necessary *adjective*
1 *the necessary items for a trip.* compulsory, essential, indispensable, needed, obligatory, required.
OPPOSITE non-essential, unnecessary.
2 *the necessary consequence.* inevitable, unavoidable.

necessitate *verb*
The new job will necessitate moving house. call for, entail, involve, mean, require.

necessity *noun*
1 *A degree in computing is not a necessity.* essential, must (*informal*), prerequisite, requirement.
2 *The family is in dire necessity.* hardship, need, poverty, want.

necklace *noun*
beads, chain, choker.

need *noun*
1 *Her needs are few.* demand, desire, necessity, requirement, want.
2 *There is no need to worry.* call, cause, necessity, reason.
3 *The family is in need.* hardship, poverty, want.

need *verb*
1 *He needs a torch.* be short of, lack, require, want.
2 *They need your help.* depend on, rely on.
3 *Do you need to ask permission?* be obliged to, be required to, have to, must.

needless *adjective*
needless worry. inessential, pointless, uncalled-for, unjustifiable, unnecessary, useless.
OPPOSITE necessary.

needlework *noun*
embroidery, sewing.

needy *adjective*
The family is very needy. deprived, destitute, disadvantaged, down and out, hard up (*informal*), impoverished, penniless, poor, poverty-stricken, skint (*informal*).
OPPOSITE affluent.

negative *adjective*
1 *a negative reply.* contradictory, dissenting, objecting, opposing, refusing, rejecting.
OPPOSITE affirmative, positive.
2 *a negative attitude.* antagonistic, defeatist, gloomy, pessimistic, reluctant, uncooperative, unenthusiastic, unwilling.
OPPOSITE optimistic, positive.

neglect *verb*
1 *Don't neglect your duty.* disregard, forget, ignore, let go, let slide, let slip, overlook, shirk.
OPPOSITE attend to.
2 *I neglected to tell you.* fail, forget, omit.

negligence *noun*
The accident was caused by negligence. carelessness, forgetfulness, inattention,

a
b
c
d
e
f
g
h
i
j
k
l
m
n
o
p
q
r
s
t
u
v
w
x
y
z

laxity, slackness, thoughtlessness.
OPPOSITE attention, care.

negligent *adjective*
negligent in his duty. careless, heedless,
inattentive, neglectful, remiss, slack,
thoughtless, unthinking.
OPPOSITE careful.

negligible *adjective*
He drank a negligible amount.
imperceptible, insignificant, minuscule,
minute, small, tiny, trifling,
unimportant.
OPPOSITE substantial.

negotiate *verb*
1 *The two sides are negotiating.* bargain,
discuss, haggle, talk.
2 *They negotiated a contract.* agree on,
arrange, settle, work out.
3 *She negotiated the fence.* clear, cross, get
over.

negotiator *noun*
broker, go-between, intermediary,
mediator, peacemaker.

neighbourhood *noun*
a quiet neighbourhood. area, community,
district, locality, spot, suburb.

neighbouring *adjective*
a neighbouring block. adjacent, adjoining,
close, nearby.

neighbourly *adjective*
a neighbourly person. affable,
considerate, friendly, helpful,
hospitable, kind, obliging, sociable,
thoughtful.
OPPOSITE unfriendly.

nerve *noun*
1 *You need nerve to be a stuntman.*
bravery, coolness, courage, daring,
fearlessness, guts (*informal*), pluck,
spunk (*informal*).
2 (*informal*) *She had the nerve to ask for
more.* audacity, boldness, cheek, gall
(*slang*), hide (*informal*), impertinence,
impudence, insolence.
get on someone's nerves annoy, drive
someone up the wall (*informal*),
exasperate, irritate, worry.
nerves *plural noun* see NERVOUSNESS.

nerve-racking *adjective*
a nerve-racking experience. stressful,
tense, testing, trying, unnerving,
worrying.

nervous *adjective*
*a nervous person. The strange noises made
him feel nervous.* afraid, agitated,
alarmed, anxious, apprehensive, edgy,
fidgety, flustered, frightened, highly-
strung, jittery (*informal*), jumpy, nervy,
neurotic, shaky, tense, timid, twitchy,
uneasy, uptight (*informal*), worried.
OPPOSITE calm.

nervousness *noun*
*Her nervousness disappeared after a minute
on stage.* agitation, anxiety,
apprehension, butterflies (*informal*),
heebie-jeebies (*informal*), jitters
(*informal*), nerves, stage fright, tension,
trembling, uneasiness.
OPPOSITE composure.

nestle *verb*
She nestled in my arms. cuddle, curl up,
huddle, snuggle.

net[1] *noun*
Little creatures were caught in the net.
mesh, netting, network, web.
net *verb*
He netted a big fish. capture, catch, snare,
trap.

net[2] *adjective*
net income. clear, disposable.
OPPOSITE gross.

network *noun*
a network of highways. complex, grid,
system.

neurotic *adjective*
He has become neurotic about security.
anxious, obsessive, unbalanced.

neuter *verb*
The animals have been neutered. castrate,
de-sex, doctor, geld, spay, sterilise.

neutral *adjective*
1 *a neutral umpire.* detached,
disinterested, impartial, independent,
non-aligned, non-partisan, unbiased,
uninvolved.
OPPOSITE interested.

2 *a neutral colour.* beige, colourless, indefinite, wishy-washy.
OPPOSITE strong.

neutralise *verb*
The acid neutralises the alkali. cancel (out), counteract, counterbalance, offset.

never-ending *adjective*
a never-ending supply of jokes. constant, continuous, endless, everlasting, inexhaustible, infinite, limitless, unlimited.
OPPOSITE limited.

never-never *noun* (*Australian informal*)
They live in the never-never. backblocks (*Australian*), back of beyond, outback (*Australian*), the sticks (*Australian informal*).

nevertheless *adverb*
It was strange, nevertheless true. but, however, none the less, still, yet.

new *adjective*
1 *He bought a new car.* brand-new, unused.
OPPOSITE second-hand, used.
2 *new ideas.* fresh, hot, innovative, latest, modern, newfangled (*derogatory*), novel, original, recent, red-hot, trendy (*informal*), up-to-date.
OPPOSITE old.
3 *Everything was new to me.* strange, unfamiliar, unheard-of.
OPPOSITE familiar.
4 *We have a new member.* additional, another, extra.
OPPOSITE long-standing.
5 *the new president.* incoming, succeeding.
OPPOSITE past, retiring.
6 *The house was given a new appearance.* altered, changed, different, rejuvenated, renovated, restored, transformed.
OPPOSITE same.

newcomer *noun*
1 *The town welcomes newcomers.* immigrant, migrant, new chum (*Australian informal*), stranger.
2 *a newcomer to the job.* beginner, novice, probationer, trainee.
OPPOSITE old hand.

newly *adverb*
The house was newly painted. freshly, just, lately, recently.

news *noun*
1 *She was anxious for news from home.* information, intelligence, tidings, word.
2 *He read the news.* announcement, bulletin, communication, communiqué, dispatch, message, press release, report, statement, story.

newsletter *noun*
Members are sent a monthly newsletter. bulletin, magazine, report.

newspaper *noun*
broadsheet, daily, journal, paper, rag (*derogatory*), tabloid, weekly.

newsworthy *adjective*
a newsworthy story. important, interesting, noteworthy, significant.

newsy *adjective* (*informal*)
a newsy letter. gossipy, informative, interesting.

next *adjective*
1 *She was in the next room.* adjacent, adjoining, closest, nearest, neighbouring, next-door.
2 *the next day.* following, subsequent, succeeding.
OPPOSITE preceding.
next *adverb*
What happened next? afterwards, subsequently, then.
next to
1 *He placed his chair next to mine.* alongside, beside, by, closest to, nearest to.
2 *next to impossible.* almost, close to, nearly, pretty well, virtually, well nigh.

nibble *verb*
He nibbled his food. bite, gnaw, munch, peck at, pick at; see also EAT.

nice *adjective*
1 *a nice day.* agreeable, delightful, enjoyable, fabulous (*informal*), fantastic (*informal*), fine, good, great (*informal*), lovely, marvellous, pleasant, satisfactory, splendid, wonderful; see also EXCELLENT, GOOD.
OPPOSITE awful, dreadful.
2 *a nice person.* agreeable, amiable, amicable, attractive, benevolent,

a
b
c
d
e
f
g
h
i
j
k
l
m
n
o
p
q
r
s
t
u
v
w
x
y
z

benign, caring, charming, compassionate, congenial, considerate, delightful, friendly, good, good-natured, gracious, kind, kindly, likeable, pleasant, polite, sweet, sympathetic, thoughtful, understanding.
OPPOSITE disagreeable, unpleasant.
3 *a nice distinction.* careful, delicate, fine, minute, precise, subtle.
OPPOSITE approximate, rough.

niche *noun*
1 *a niche in the wall.* alcove, bay, nook, recess.
2 *She found her niche in life.* calling, place, slot, vocation.

nick *noun*
He made nicks in the timber with a knife. cut, notch, score, scratch, snick.
nick *verb*
1 *He nicked himself while shaving.* cut, gash, scratch, snick.
2 (*slang*) *He was caught nicking books.* knock off (*slang*), lift, pilfer, pinch (*informal*), snatch, snitch (*slang*), steal, swipe (*informal*), take.
3 (*slang*) *The burglar expected to be nicked one day.* arrest, catch, nab (*informal*), pick up.
in good nick (*informal*)
in good condition, in good health, in good trim.

nickname *noun*
alias, pet name.
nickname *verb*
He was nicknamed 'Professor'. call, christen, dub, rename.

niggle *verb*
He kept niggling over trifles. fuss, nag, nit-pick (*informal*), quibble.

niggling *adjective*
a niggling doubt. annoying, lurking, nagging, persistent, worrying.

night *noun*
dark, darkness, dusk, evening, nightfall, night-time.

nightly *adjective*
nightly wanderings. after-dark, evening, night-time, nocturnal.

nightmarish *adjective*
a nightmarish experience. dreadful, frightening, horrible, horrifying, scary, terrible, terrifying.

nil *noun*
The score was two games to nil. love, none, nothing, nought, zero.

nimble *adjective*
a nimble ninety-year old. active, agile, lithe, lively, nippy (*informal*), quick, sprightly, spry, swift.
OPPOSITE clumsy, slow.

nip *verb*
1 *He nipped himself with the tweezers.* pinch, squeeze, tweak.
2 *The cat nipped her ankle.* bite.
3 *She nipped off the sideshoots.* break, clip, cut, snip.

nipple *noun*
teat.

nippy *adjective* (*informal*)
nippy weather. biting, bitter, chilly, cold, freezing, icy.

nit-picking *noun* (*informal*)
His constant nit-picking hindered progress. fault-finding, niggling, quibbling.

nobility *noun*
a member of the nobility. aristocracy, peerage, upper class, upper crust (*informal*).
OPPOSITE commoners.

noble *adjective*
1 *of noble birth.* aristocratic, blue-blooded, titled.
OPPOSITE lowly.
2 *a noble character. noble sentiments.* exalted, generous, high-minded, honourable, lofty, selfless, virtuous, worthy.
OPPOSITE base, ignoble.
3 *a noble building.* fine, grand, imposing, impressive, magnificent, majestic, splendid, stately.
OPPOSITE modest.

nobleman *noun*
aristocrat, grandee, lord, noble, peer; [*kinds of nobleman*] baron, count, duke, earl, marquess, marquis, viscount.

noblewoman *noun*
aristocrat, lady, noble, peeress; [*kinds of noblewoman*] baroness, countess, duchess, marchioness, marquise, viscountess.

nobody *pronoun*
none, no one.
nobody *noun*
He's a nobody. lightweight, nonentity, nothing, pipsqueak (*informal*), unknown.
OPPOSITE somebody.

nocturnal *adjective*
nocturnal activities. after-dark, evening, nightly, night-time.
OPPOSITE diurnal.

nod *verb*
1 He nodded to the next customer. gesture, motion, signal.
2 She nodded her head. bob, bow, incline.
nod *noun*
They were given a nod to begin. gesture, sign, signal.
nod off doze off, drop off, drowse, fall asleep.

node *noun*
a node on a tree trunk. bump, knob, knot, lump, nodule, swelling.

noise *noun*
She could not sleep because of the dreadful noise. bedlam, clamour, clatter, commotion, din, hubbub, hullabaloo, outcry, pandemonium, racket, row, rumpus, sound, tumult, uproar.

noisy *adjective*
1 a noisy crowd. boisterous, lively, rowdy, tumultuous, turbulent, uproarious, vociferous.
OPPOSITE quiet.
2 noisy music. blaring, booming, deafening, loud, piercing, raucous, shrill, strident, thundering.
OPPOSITE soft.

nomad *noun*
He sold his house and became a nomad. gypsy, itinerant, rover, traveller, vagabond, wanderer.

nomadic *adjective*
a nomadic life. itinerant, migratory, roving, travelling, vagabond, vagrant, wandering.

nominal *adjective*
1 a nominal Christian. in name only, ostensible, professed, so-called, theoretical.
OPPOSITE real, true.
2 They paid only a nominal rent. minimal, small, token.

nominate *verb*
1 Five films were nominated for the award. name, propose, put forward, recommend, submit, suggest.
2 He was nominated as their spokesman. appoint, choose, elect, name, pick, select.

non-believer *noun*
agnostic, atheist, heathen, pagan, sceptic, unbeliever.

nondescript *adjective*
a nondescript room. bland, characterless, ordinary, plain, unexceptional, uninteresting, unremarkable.
OPPOSITE distinctive.

non-event *noun*
The fair turned out to be a non-event. anticlimax, disappointment, fizzer (*Australian informal*).

non-existent *adjective*
a non-existent monster. fictitious, imaginary, make-believe, mythical, pretend (*informal*), pretended, unreal.
OPPOSITE real.

non-flammable *adjective*
see NON-INFLAMMABLE.

non-inflammable *adjective*
Pyjamas should be made of non-inflammable material. fireproof, flameproof, incombustible, non-flammable.
OPPOSITE flammable, inflammable.

nonplussed *adjective*
The strange events left us nonplussed. amazed, baffled, bamboozled (*informal*), bewildered, confused, dumbfounded,

a
b
c
d
e
f
g
h
i
j
k
l
m
n
o
p
q
r
s
t
u
v
w
x
y
z

flabbergasted, perplexed, puzzled, speechless, stunned, surprised.

nonsense *noun*
He talked a lot of nonsense. balderdash, boloney (*informal*), bunkum, claptrap, drivel, foolishness, garbage, gibberish, gobbledegook (*informal*), guff (*slang*), hogwash (*informal*), hooey (*informal*), humbug, inanity, kidstakes (*Australian informal*), mumbo-jumbo, piffle (*informal*), poppycock (*slang*), rot (*slang*), rubbish, silliness, stupidity, tommyrot (*slang*), trash, tripe (*informal*), twaddle. OPPOSITE reason, sense.

nonsensical *adjective*
a nonsensical idea. absurd, crazy, foolish, idiotic, inane, laughable, ludicrous, meaningless, preposterous, ridiculous, senseless, silly, stupid. OPPOSITE sensible.

non-stop *adjective*
1 *a non-stop train.* direct, express, fast, through.
2 *non-stop laughter.* ceaseless, constant, continuous, endless, incessant, persistent, steady.

nook *noun*
She sat in her nook and sewed. alcove, corner, cubby hole, niche, recess.

noon *noun*
midday, noonday, twelve o'clock.

norm *noun*
compared to the norm. average, benchmark, mean, rule, standard, usual, yardstick.

normal *adjective*
1 *under normal conditions.* average, conventional, customary, habitual, ordinary, regular, routine, standard, typical, usual. OPPOSITE abnormal.
2 *He wasn't normal after the accident.* balanced, rational, reasonable, sane. OPPOSITE odd, unbalanced.

nose *noun*
a bump on the nose. beak (*informal*), conk (*slang*), muzzle, proboscis, snout.
nose *verb*
1 *The dog nosed her leg.* nudge, nuzzle, smell, sniff.

2 *Someone's been nosing around.* poke, prowl, pry, search, snoop (*informal*), stickybeak (*Australian informal*).
3 *The car nosed past them.* ease, edge, inch.

nostalgia *noun*
nostalgia for the early days. longing, pining, yearning.

nostalgic *adjective*
The photos of home made him nostalgic. homesick, sentimental, wistful.

nosy *adjective* (*informal*)
a nosy visitor. curious, inquisitive, prying, snoopy (*informal*).

notable *adjective*
1 *a notable success. a notable omission.* conspicuous, important, noticeable, obvious, outstanding, remarkable, significant, striking. OPPOSITE insignificant.
2 *a notable historian.* celebrated, distinguished, eminent, famous, noted, prominent, renowned, well-known. OPPOSITE obscure, unknown.

notch *noun*
The walker made notches in the trunks of the trees. cut, nick, score, snick.
notch *verb*
He notched every tree which he passed. cut, nick, score, snick.
notch up *They notched up another victory.* achieve, gain, score.

note *noun*
1 *He made notes of their conversation.* minute, record.
2 *She wrote a note to the principal.* communication, epistle, letter, memo (*informal*), memorandum, message.
3 *Buy an edition of the play with notes.* annotation, comment, endnote, explanation, footnote.
4 *a $100 note.* banknote, bill. OPPOSITE coin.
5 *He detected a note of optimism.* air, feeling, sound, tone.
6 *Take note of what she says.* attention, heed, notice.
note *verb*
1 *We noted that he was smiling.* be aware, notice, observe, perceive, see.

2 *Note what he is telling you.* heed, mind,
pay attention to.
OPPOSITE ignore.
3 *He noted it in his diary.* enter, jot down,
mark, record, write down.

notebook *noun*
exercise book, jotter, journal, logbook,
memo book, pocketbook.

noted *adjective*
see NOTABLE.

nothing *noun*
We were left with nothing. nil, nought,
zero, zilch (*informal*).

notice *noun*
1 *He read the notice about coming events.*
advertisement, announcement, circular,
flyer, leaflet, letter, memo (*informal*),
message, note, pamphlet, placard,
poster, sign.
2 *She brought the matter to his notice.*
attention, consideration.
3 *He gave two days' notice of the test.*
advice, notification, warning.
notice *verb*
He noticed nothing unusual. be aware of,
catch sight of, detect, discern, note,
observe, perceive, see, spot.
OPPOSITE disregard, overlook.

noticeable *adjective*
a noticeable change. conspicuous,
definite, discernible, distinct, marked,
obvious, perceptible, pronounced,
striking, visible.
OPPOSITE imperceptible.

notification *noun*
You will receive official notification.
advice, announcement, communication,
information, notice.

notify *verb*
1 *They haven't notified the relatives yet.*
advise, alert, inform, tell, warn.
2 *He notified his intentions.* announce,
declare, disclose, make known, publish,
report, reveal.

notion *noun*
a weird notion. belief, concept, idea,
opinion, thought.

notoriety *noun*
disrepute, infamy, scandal.

notorious *adjective*
a notorious criminal. disreputable,
infamous, scandalous, well-known.

nought *noun*
nil, nothing, zero, zilch (*informal*).

nourish *verb*
She nourishes her children well. feed,
nurture, provide for.

nourishing *adjective*
Eat nourishing food. healthy, nutritious,
wholesome.

novel *noun*
He reads historical novels. fiction, saga,
story, tale.
novel *adjective*
a novel idea. different, innovative, new,
original, strange, unfamiliar, unusual.
OPPOSITE familiar, old.

novelty *noun*
1 *The novelty has worn off.* newness,
originality.
2 *The show bags contain a few novelties.*
knick-knack, trifle, trinket.

novice *noun*
a novice in the trade. apprentice,
beginner, learner, new chum (*Australian
informal*), rookie (*informal*), trainee.
OPPOSITE master, old hand.

now *adverb*
at present, at the moment, at this
moment, at this point, at this stage, at
this time, currently, nowadays.

nuclear *adjective*
nuclear energy. atomic.

nucleus *noun*
the nucleus of a new congregation. basis,
centre, core, heart, kernel.

nude *adjective*
nude bodies on the beach. bare, exposed,
naked, stripped, unclothed, undressed.
OPPOSITE clothed.
in the nude in the altogether (*informal*),
in the raw, in your birthday suit
(*informal*), starkers (*slang*).

nudge *verb*
He nudged the boy sitting next to him.
bump, dig in the ribs, elbow, jog, poke,
prod, push, touch.

a
b
c
d
e
f
g
h
i
j
k
l
m
n
o
p
q
r
s
t
u
v
w
x
y
z

nuisance *noun*
Her broken leg was a nuisance.
annoyance, bother, drag, hassle
(*informal*), inconvenience, irritation,
menace, pain (*informal*), pest, problem,
trouble.

null *adjective*
The agreement was declared null and void.
invalid, nullified, worthless.
OPPOSITE valid.

numb *adjective*
Her fingers were numb with cold.
deadened, paralysed.
numb *verb*
The ice pack numbed his foot. anaesthetise,
deaden, dull.

number *noun*
1 *the numbers from 1 to 5.* digit, figure,
integer, numeral.
2 *The December number of the magazine is
the biggest.* copy, edition, issue,
publication.
3 *She sang two numbers at the concert.*
item, piece, song.
4 *the number of those present.* amount,
quantity, sum, total.
number *verb*
1 *They can be numbered on the fingers of
one hand.* calculate, count, reckon, tally,
tot up.
2 *The crowd numbered five thousand.* add
up to, amount to, come to, total.
a number of *a number of friends.* a few,
several, some.
numbers of *numbers of fans.* see MANY.

numeral *noun*
*The children can write all their numerals
legibly now.* digit, figure, integer,
number.

numerous *adjective*
numerous examples. abundant, copious,
countless, innumerable, many, myriad,
numberless, numbers of, untold.
OPPOSITE few.

nun *noun*
abbess, prioress, religious, sister.

nunnery *noun*
abbey, cloister, convent, priory,
religious house.
CONTRASTS WITH monastery.

nurse *noun*
1 *a nurse in a hospital.* sister.
2 *The children had a nurse at home.* nanny,
nursemaid.
nurse *verb*
1 *She was employed to nurse the invalid.*
care for, look after, tend.
2 *She nursed the baby for nine months.*
breastfeed, feed, suckle.

nursing home *noun*
convalescent home, hospice, hospital,
hostel, institution, rest home,
sanatorium.

nurture *verb*
1 *They nurtured their children lovingly.*
bring up, care for, feed, look after,
nourish, raise, rear.
2 *The school nurtures the pupils.* develop,
discipline, educate, instruct, school,
train.

nut *noun*
1 kernel; [*various nuts*] almond, Brazil
nut, cashew, chestnut, coconut,
hazelnut, macadamia, peanut, pecan,
pine nut, pistachio, walnut.
2 (*informal*) *The person who did this was a
nut.* crackpot (*informal*), crank, fruitcake
(*informal*), loony (*informal*), lunatic,
madman, madwoman, maniac, nutcase
(*informal*), nutter (*informal*), psychopath,
weirdo (*informal*).

nutritious *adjective*
He only eats nutritious food. healthy,
nourishing, wholesome.
OPPOSITE unhealthy.

nutty *adjective*
see CRAZY.

oath *noun*
1 *They swore an oath of allegiance.* pledge, promise, vow.
CONTRASTS WITH affirmation.
2 *In his rage he uttered several unrepeatable oaths.* blasphemy, curse, obscenity, profanity, swear-word.

obedient *adjective*
an obedient child. biddable, compliant, disciplined, docile, dutiful, meek, submissive.
OPPOSITE defiant, disobedient.

obese *adjective*
see FAT.

obey *verb*
She obeys all the rules. abide by, adhere to, comply with, follow, heed, keep to, observe, stick to.
OPPOSITE break, disobey.

object *noun*
1 *an unidentified flying object.* article, body, contraption (*informal*), device, item, thing.
2 *The object of the exercise is to win support.* aim, goal, intention, objective, point, purpose.
object *verb*
object to *He objects to all their ideas.* complain about, criticise, disapprove of, dislike, find fault with, grumble at, knock (*informal*), mind, oppose, protest at.
OPPOSITE accept, approve.

objection *noun*
1 *He voiced his objection.* disagreement, disapproval, opposition, protest.
OPPOSITE approval.
2 *Please state your objections in writing.* complaint, criticism, grievance, quibble, reservation.

objectionable *adjective*
objectionable behaviour. an objectionable smell. disgusting, foul, intolerable, nasty, nauseating, obnoxious, offensive, repugnant, repulsive, revolting, unacceptable, unbearable, unpleasant, vile.
OPPOSITE acceptable, pleasant.

objective *adjective*
1 *objective evidence.* actual, concrete, observable, real.
2 *an objective assessment.* detached, dispassionate, fair, impartial, just, unbiased, unprejudiced.
OPPOSITE subjective.
objective *noun*
The group formulated its objectives. aim, design, goal, intention, mission, object, purpose, target.

obligation *noun*
He has an obligation to attend practices. commitment, duty, onus, requirement, responsibility.

oblige *verb*
He was obliged to go. bind, compel, constrain, force, require.

obliging *adjective*
An obliging man pushed the car to the side of the road. accommodating, considerate, cooperative, courteous, helpful, kind, neighbourly.
OPPOSITE unhelpful.

oblique *adjective*
an oblique line. angled, diagonal, slanting, sloping.

oblivious *adjective*
oblivious of her surroundings. forgetful, heedless, insensible, unaware, unconscious, unmindful.
OPPOSITE aware.

oblong *noun*
rectangle.

obnoxious *adjective*
an obnoxious character. despicable, detestable, disagreeable, disgusting, hateful, horrible, insufferable, loathsome, nasty, objectionable, odious, offensive, repulsive, unpleasant, vile.
OPPOSITE delightful, likeable.

obscene *adjective*
obscene language. crude, dirty, filthy, foul, improper, indecent, offensive, pornographic, rude, smutty, unprintable, vulgar.
OPPOSITE decent.

obscure *adjective*
1 *an obscure shape at the window.* dim, faint, fuzzy, hazy, indistinct, misty, murky, shadowy.
OPPOSITE distinct.
2 *an obscure writer.* forgotten, little-known, unheard-of, unimportant, unknown.
OPPOSITE famous.
3 *The meaning is obscure.* cryptic, enigmatic, hidden, mysterious, uncertain, unclear, vague.
OPPOSITE plain.

obscure *verb*
The peak was obscured by mist. blot out, cloud, conceal, cover, envelop, hide, mask, shroud.

observant *adjective*
The postman is observant. alert, attentive, aware, perceptive, sharp-eyed, shrewd, vigilant, watchful, wide awake (*informal*).
OPPOSITE unobservant.

observation *noun*
1 *The tower is for the observation of wild animals.* surveillance, viewing, watching.
2 *She made an observation about the lateness of the hour.* comment, remark, statement.

observe *verb*
1 *He observed the children playing. He observed changes.* contemplate, detect, discover, look at, monitor, note, notice, perceive, see, spot, study, survey, view, watch, witness.
2 *Observe the law.* abide by, adhere to, comply with, follow, heed, keep, obey.
OPPOSITE disobey.
3 *Do they observe Remembrance Day?* celebrate, commemorate, honour, keep.
4 *He quietly observed that they were all wrong.* comment, remark, say, state.

observer *noun*
He attended as an observer. bystander, eyewitness, onlooker, spectator, viewer, witness.
OPPOSITE participant.

obsession *noun*
Cleanliness became an obsession. fixation, hobby horse, infatuation, mania, passion, preoccupation.

obsolescent *adjective*
Typewriters are obsolescent. declining, disappearing, dying out, moribund, on the way out (*informal*).

obsolete *adjective*
The word 'apothecary' is now obsolete. antiquated, archaic, dead, disused, old-fashioned, outdated, out of date.
OPPOSITE current.

obstacle *noun*
an obstacle to progress. bar, barrier, blockage, difficulty, hindrance, hurdle, obstruction, snag, stumbling block.

obstinate *adjective*
The obstinate man continued to refuse help. defiant, dogged, headstrong, inflexible, mulish, perverse, pigheaded, recalcitrant, resolute, stiff-necked, strong-willed, stubborn, uncompromising, unyielding, wilful.
OPPOSITE compliant.

obstreperous *adjective*
The teacher could not control the obstreperous children. boisterous, disorderly, irrepressible, noisy, rowdy, stroppy (*informal*), uncontrollable, unmanageable, unruly, wild.
OPPOSITE docile, well-behaved.

obstruct *verb*
1 *Leaves obstructed the drain.* block, choke, clog, jam, plug up, stop up.
OPPOSITE clear.
2 *The workmen tried to obstruct progress.* block, delay, deter, frustrate, halt, hamper, hinder, hold up, impede, prevent, slow down, stall, stop, thwart.
OPPOSITE help.

obstruction *noun*
The obstruction has been removed. barricade, barrier, blockage, obstacle.

obtain *verb*
1 *She obtained the book from a new shop.* acquire, buy, come by, get, get hold of, pick up, procure, purchase.
2 *He obtained the information.* gain, gather, get, glean, receive.
3 *He obtained 65%.* achieve, attain, earn.

obtuse *adjective*
It was impossible to explain it to the obtuse clerk. dense, dopey (*informal*), dumb (*informal*), slow, stupid, thick.
OPPOSITE bright.

obvious *adjective*
an obvious error. blatant, clear, conspicuous, evident, glaring, noticeable, patent, plain, prominent, pronounced, unconcealed, unmistakable, visible.
OPPOSITE hidden, obscure.

occasion *noun*
1 *a joyous occasion.* ceremony, episode, event, function, happening, incident, occurrence.
2 *It was an occasion to use her new camera.* chance, moment, opportunity, time.

occasional *adjective*
occasional showers. fitful, infrequent, intermittent, irregular, odd, random, rare, scattered, spasmodic, sporadic.
OPPOSITE constant, frequent.

occasionally *adverb*
The car breaks down occasionally. at times, every so often, from time to time, now and then, once in a while, on occasion, sometimes.
OPPOSITE constantly, often.

occult *adjective*
occult powers. magic, mysterious, mystic, mystical, supernatural.

occupant *noun*
the occupant of a house. householder, inhabitant, occupier, resident, tenant.

occupation *noun*
the occupation of gardener. business, calling, career, employment, job, profession, trade, vocation, work.

occupied *adjective*
The sign on the toilet door read 'occupied'. engaged, in use.
OPPOSITE vacant.

occupy *verb*
1 *They occupy the third flat.* dwell in, inhabit, live in, reside in.
2 *The enemy occupied the country.* capture, conquer, invade, seize, take over, take possession of.
3 *The man occupied two seats.* fill, take up, use.
4 *He occupies the position of treasurer.* fill, hold, hold down.
5 *She is fully occupied with study.* absorb, employ, engross, involve, keep busy, preoccupy.

occur *verb*
1 *They expected an accident to occur.* befall, come about, come off, come to pass, eventuate, happen, take place.
2 *The problem occurs wherever water is scarce.* appear, arise, be found, crop up, emerge, exist, show up, surface.
occur to *It did not occur to him to tell anybody.* dawn on, enter your head, suggest itself to.

occurrence *noun*
a rare occurrence of snow. the latest occurrence. bout, episode, event, happening, incident, instance, occasion, phenomenon.

ocean *noun*
the blue, the deep, sea.

odd *adjective*
1 *odd behaviour.* abnormal, bizarre, curious, eccentric, extraordinary, freakish, funny, incongruous, irregular, offbeat, peculiar, queer, quirky, singular, strange, uncommon, unconventional, unnatural, unusual, weird.
OPPOSITE normal.
2 *He does odd jobs.* casual, miscellaneous, occasional, random, sundry, various.
OPPOSITE regular.
3 *an odd number.* uneven.
OPPOSITE even.
4 *an odd knitting needle.* leftover, lone, single, spare, surplus, unpaired.
OPPOSITE paired.

a b c d e f g h i j k l m n o p q r s t u v w x y z

oddity *noun*
1 *the oddity of her appearance.*
eccentricity, incongruity, peculiarity,
strangeness.
2 *He was considered rather an oddity.*
character, curiosity, eccentric, freak,
misfit, nut (*informal*), weirdo (*informal*).

oddments *plural noun*
a sale of oddments. leftovers, odds and
ends, odds and sods (*informal*),
remainders, remnants.

odious *adjective*
an odious crime. abhorrent, abominable,
contemptible, despicable, detestable,
hateful, horrible, loathsome, monstrous,
obnoxious, repugnant, repulsive, vile.

odour *noun*
1 *a pleasant odour.* aroma, bouquet,
fragrance, perfume, scent, smell.
2 *an unpleasant odour.* pong (*informal*),
reek, smell, stench, stink.

offbeat *adjective*
an offbeat sense of humour. bizarre,
eccentric, odd, strange, unconventional,
unusual, way-out, weird.

offcuts *plural noun*
The timber offcuts are sold cheaply.
leftovers, remnants, scraps.

offence *noun*
1 *a punishable offence.* crime, felony (*old
use*), misdeed, misdemeanour, sin,
transgression, trespass (*old use*),
wickedness, wrongdoing.
2 *She meant no offence.* disrespect, harm,
hurt, insult, wrong.
take offence *He took offence at the
remark.* be affronted, be offended, take
umbrage.

offend *verb*
1 *Try not to offend anyone.* affront, anger,
disgust, displease, hurt someone's
feelings, insult, outrage, upset.
OPPOSITE please.
2 *He offended against the law.* do wrong,
sin, transgress, trespass (*old use*).

offender *noun*
criminal, culprit, felon, lawbreaker,
malefactor, sinner, transgressor,
trespasser (*old use*), wrongdoer.

offensive *adjective*
1 *offensive remarks.* abusive,
disrespectful, improper, indecent,
insolent, insulting, nasty, objectionable,
obscene, odious, off-putting (*informal*),
rude.
OPPOSITE polite.
2 *an offensive smell.* bad, disgusting,
foul, nasty, nauseating, obnoxious,
repulsive, revolting, sickening, yucky
(*informal*).
OPPOSITE pleasant.
3 *offensive weapons.* aggressive,
attacking.
OPPOSITE defensive.

offensive *noun*
a military offensive. assault, attack, blitz,
onslaught, raid.

offer *verb*
1 *She offered her a biscuit.* give, hand,
present.
OPPOSITE deny, withhold.
2 *He offered a suggestion.* propose, put
forward, submit, suggest, tender,
volunteer.
OPPOSITE refuse.

offer *noun*
He made an offer too good to refuse. bid,
proposal, proposition, suggestion,
tender.

offering *noun*
a generous offering. contribution,
donation, gift, offertory, present,
sacrifice.

offhand *adjective*
They were hurt by his offhand manner.
casual, curt, perfunctory, rude,
unceremonious, unconcerned.
OPPOSITE concerned.

office *noun*
1 *One room of the house is an office.* den,
study, workroom.
2 *She took up the office of treasurer.*
appointment, duty, function, job,
position, post, role.

officer *noun*
1 *a customs officer.* functionary, official.
2 *a police officer.* see POLICE.

official *adjective*
an official announcement. approved, authorised, certified, endorsed, formal, proper.
OPPOSITE unauthorised, unofficial.
official *noun*
The decision rests with the official. bureaucrat, functionary, office-bearer, officer.

officious *adjective*
The clerk was too officious. bossy, bumptious, cocky, interfering, intrusive, meddlesome, self-important.

off-putting *adjective* (*informal*)
He had an off-putting manner. disconcerting, disgusting, offensive, repellent, repulsive, unpleasant.
OPPOSITE attractive.

offset *verb*
The salary increase was offset by a rise in prices. balance, cancel out, compensate for, counteract, counterbalance.

offshoot *noun*
1 *The plant developed offshoots.* branch, side shoot.
2 *an offshoot of the main research.* by-product, development, spin-off.

offsider *noun* (*Australian informal*)
He works as an electrician's offsider. assistant, associate, helper, partner, sidekick (*informal*).

offspring *noun*
1 *The couple have no offspring.* child(ren), descendant(s), family, heir(s), kid(s) (*informal*), progeny.
2 *an animal's offspring.* brood, litter, young.

often *adverb*
They see each other often. constantly, continually, frequently, regularly, repeatedly.
OPPOSITE never, seldom.

ogre, ogress *noun*
1 *a fairy-tale ogre.* bogyman, giant, monster.
2 *He wasn't really such an ogre.* beast, brute, bully, fiend, monster, tyrant.

oil *verb*
She oiled the machine. grease, lubricate.

oily *adjective*
The food was oily. fatty, greasy.

ointment *noun*
He applied ointment to the sores. balm, cream, liniment, lotion, oil, salve.

OK or **okay** *adjective* (*informal*)
The meal was OK. adequate, all right, fine, passable, reasonable, satisfactory, so-so (*informal*), tolerable.

old *adjective*
1 *an old person.* aged, elderly, geriatric, senior.
OPPOSITE young.
2 *The museum houses old cars.* antiquated, antique, archaic, obsolescent, obsolete, outdated, primitive, veteran, vintage.
OPPOSITE modern.
3 *They keep the old customs.* age-old, ancient, early, long-standing, time-honoured, traditional.
OPPOSITE modern, recent.
4 *Wear old clothes.* decrepit, dilapidated, ragged, tatty (*informal*), worn, worn-out.
OPPOSITE new.
5 *He always tells old jokes.* familiar, hackneyed, stale, unoriginal.
OPPOSITE fresh, original.
6 *the old days.* bygone, early, former, olden (*old use*), prehistoric.
OPPOSITE present.
7 *He went back to his old job.* earlier, former, previous, prior.
OPPOSITE new.

older *adjective*
1 *my older brother.* big, elder.
2 *older citizens.* senior.
OPPOSITE younger.

old-fashioned *adjective*
old-fashioned clothes. old-fashioned ideas. antiquated, archaic, behind the times, conservative, conventional, fuddy-duddy (*informal*), obsolete, old hat (*informal*), outdated, out-of-date, traditional, unfashionable.
OPPOSITE fashionable, up-to-date.

a
b
c
d
e
f
g
h
i
j
k
l
m
n
o
p
q
r
s
t
u
v
w
x
y
z

omen *noun*
The grey clouds were a bad omen.
indication, sign, warning.

ominous *adjective*
ominous clouds. inauspicious, menacing,
sinister, threatening.
OPPOSITE auspicious.

omission *noun*
1 her omission from the party list.
exclusion, non-inclusion.
OPPOSITE inclusion.
2 errors of omission. neglect, negligence,
oversight.
OPPOSITE commission.

omit *verb*
1 The author omitted an important name.
drop, exclude, ignore, leave out, miss,
overlook, pass over, skip.
OPPOSITE include.
2 He omitted to sign the cheque. fail,
forget, neglect.
OPPOSITE remember.

omnipotent *adjective*
omnipotent God. all-powerful, almighty,
sovereign, supreme.
OPPOSITE powerless.

once *adverb*
People once lived there. formerly, in days
gone by, in the past, previously.

oncoming *adjective*
oncoming traffic. advancing,
approaching.
OPPOSITE receding.

onerous *adjective*
an onerous task. arduous, burdensome,
difficult, hard, heavy, oppressive,
taxing, tiring.
OPPOSITE easy.

one-sided *adjective*
1 They gave a one-sided version of events.
biased, unfair, prejudiced.
OPPOSITE unbiased.
2 a one-sided contest. unbalanced,
unequal, uneven, unfair.
OPPOSITE balanced.

ongoing *adjective*
an ongoing debate. continuing, current,
running.

onlooker *noun*
a crowd of onlookers at the scene of the
accident. bystander, eyewitness,
observer, spectator, viewer, witness.
OPPOSITE participant.

only *adjective*
our only hope. lone, one, single, sole,
solitary.
only *adverb*
He only says it to annoy people. just,
merely, purely, simply.

onset *noun*
the onset of war. beginning,
commencement, outbreak, outset, start.

onslaught *noun*
They could not survive the fierce onslaught.
aggression, assault, attack, blitz,
bombardment, charge, offensive, raid.

onus *noun*
The onus of proof rests with you. burden,
duty, obligation, responsibility.

ooze *verb*
Blood oozed from the wound. discharge,
dribble, drip, leak, seep, trickle.

opaque *adjective*
an opaque liquid. cloudy, milky, muddy,
murky, unclear.
CONTRASTS WITH translucent,
transparent.

open *adjective*
1 The door is open. ajar, unbolted,
undone, unfastened, unlatched,
unlocked.
OPPOSITE shut.
2 She likes the wide open spaces. broad,
clear, empty, extensive, unbounded,
uncluttered, uncrowded, unfenced,
unobstructed.
OPPOSITE confined.
3 an open meeting. general, public,
unrestricted.
OPPOSITE closed, exclusive.
4 an open newspaper. spread-out,
unfolded.
5 welcomed with open arms. outspread,
outstretched.
6 He was open about his motives. candid,
communicative, direct, forthright,
frank, honest, outspoken,
straightforward.
OPPOSITE secretive.

7 *open contempt.* blatant, flagrant, obvious, patent, unconcealed, undisguised.
OPPOSITE covert, secret.
8 *keeping their options open.* undecided, unresolved, unsettled.

open *verb*
1 *open a door, parcel, bottle, etc.* unbolt, unclasp, uncork, undo, unfasten, unhook, unlatch, unlock, unroll, unseal, untie, unwrap, unzip.
OPPOSITE close, fasten.
2 *The chairman opened the proceedings.* begin, commence, initiate, kick off (*informal*), launch, start.
OPPOSITE close.

open-air *adjective*
an open-air cinema. alfresco, outdoor, outside.
OPPOSITE indoor.

opening *noun*
1 *They blocked up the opening.* aperture, breach, break, chink, cleft, crack, cut, fissure, gap, hatch, hole, leak, manhole, mouth, orifice, outlet, passage, rift, slit, slot, space, vent.
2 *the opening of business.* beginning, commencement, launch, outset, start.
OPPOSITE close.
3 *the opening of a book, opera, etc.* introduction, overture, preface, prelude.
OPPOSITE conclusion, finale.
4 *He sought an opening in the housing industry.* break (*informal*), opportunity, position, vacancy.

open-minded *adjective*
He remained open-minded as he listened to both sides. fair, impartial, just, objective, tolerant, unbiased, unprejudiced.
OPPOSITE narrow-minded.

operate *verb*
1 *The torch operates with a battery.* function, go, perform, run, work.
2 *He operates the machine.* control, handle, manage, manipulate, use, wield, work.

operation *noun*
1 *a delicate operation. a military operation.* action, business, campaign, exercise, manoeuvre, procedure, process, task, undertaking.

2 *The doctor performed a knee operation.* op (*informal*), surgery.

opinion *noun*
She keeps her opinions to herself. belief, conclusion, conviction, creed, feeling, idea, impression, judgement, point of view, sentiment, thought, view, viewpoint.
opinion poll see POLL.

opponent *noun*
She thought she could beat all her opponents. adversary, competitor, contender, enemy, foe, opposition, rival.

opportunity *noun*
He never got an opportunity to speak. break (*informal*), chance, moment, occasion, opening, time.

oppose *verb*
1 *She opposed the changes.* argue against, buck (*informal*), contest, defy, fight, object to, resist, withstand.
OPPOSITE support.
2 *Team A opposes Team B in the final.* compete against, meet, play, rival.
opposed to *opposed to capital punishment.* against, anti, averse to.
OPPOSITE in favour of, pro.

opposite *adjective*
1 *the opposite wall.* facing.
OPPOSITE same.
2 *opposite points of view.* conflicting, contradictory, contrary, contrasting, incompatible, opposing.
OPPOSITE like, same.
opposite *noun*
The two words are opposites. antonym.
OPPOSITE synonym.

opposition *noun*
1 *They voiced their opposition to the proposal.* antagonism, disagreement, disapproval, hostility, objection, resistance.
OPPOSITE backing.
2 *He left the company and joined the opposition.* competitor, enemy, opponent, rival.

oppress *verb*
1 *The new government oppressed the people.* abuse, bully, crush, exploit, maltreat, persecute, tyrannise.

a
b
c
d
e
f
g
h
i
j
k
l
m
n
o
p
q
r
s
t
u
v
w
x
y
z

2 *Her worries oppressed her.* afflict, burden, depress, overwhelm, torment, trouble, weigh down, worry.
OPPOSITE cheer up.

oppressive *adjective*
1 *an oppressive master.* cruel, hard, harsh, repressive, severe, tyrannical, unjust.
OPPOSITE humane, lenient.
2 *The weather was oppressive.* close, humid, muggy, stifling, stuffy, sultry, uncomfortable.

opt *verb*
opt for *We each opted for a different chocolate.* choose, decide on, go for, pick, select, settle on, vote for.

optical *adjective*
see VISUAL.

optimistic *adjective*
She was optimistic about the outcome. cheerful, confident, expectant, hopeful, positive.
OPPOSITE pessimistic.

option *noun*
He disliked both the options. alternative, choice, possibility.

optional *adjective*
optional subjects. elective, non-essential, voluntary.
OPPOSITE compulsory.

opulent *adjective*
1 *an opulent family.* affluent, prosperous, rich, wealthy, well off.
OPPOSITE impoverished.
2 *an opulent hotel suite.* luxurious, plush (*informal*), splendid, sumptuous.
OPPOSITE squalid.

oral *adjective*
an oral examination. spoken.
OPPOSITE written.

orange *adjective*
an orange colour. amber, apricot, carroty, coral, ginger, saffron, salmon, tangerine.

oration *noun*
a funeral oration. address, eulogy, homily, speech.

orbit *noun*
the orbit of the planet. circuit, course, path, revolution, track, trajectory.
orbit *verb*
The spaceship orbited the earth. circle, circumnavigate, revolve around.

orchestra *noun*
band, ensemble.

orchestrate *verb*
1 *She orchestrated the music.* arrange, score.
2 *He orchestrated the protest campaign.* coordinate, mastermind, organise, stage-manage.

ordain *verb*
1 *He was ordained as a minister.* appoint, consecrate, induct, install, invest.
2 *The king ordained that all prisoners would be pardoned.* command, decree, dictate, order, rule.

ordeal *noun*
She survived the ordeal. affliction, distress, hardship, nightmare, suffering, test, trial, tribulation, trouble.

order *noun*
1 *The books are in alphabetical order.* arrangement, classification, grouping, layout, organisation, sequence, series, system.
2 *She had the room back in order quickly.* neatness, orderliness, shape, tidiness.
OPPOSITE disarray, disorder.
3 *The car is in good running order.* condition, nick (*informal*), repair, state.
4 *law and order.* calm, control, discipline, harmony, peace.
OPPOSITE anarchy, chaos.
5 *He follows the boss's orders.* command, decree, direction, edict, injunction, instruction.
OPPOSITE request.
6 *He showed courage of the highest order.* degree, kind, level, quality, sort, type.
7 *a religious order.* association, brotherhood, community, fraternity, sisterhood, society.
order *verb*
1 *The medical records are ordered alphabetically.* arrange, classify, group, lay out, organise, sort.

2 *He ordered them to leave.* bid, charge, command, direct, instruct, tell.
OPPOSITE entreat.
3 *He ordered tickets for the play.* apply for, book, request, reserve.
order about boss around, bully, control, push around, tell someone what to do.
out of order *The machine is out of order.* broken, bung (*Australian informal*), damaged, kaput (*informal*), on the blink (*informal*).
OPPOSITE working.

orderly *adjective*
1 *He keeps his things in an orderly fashion.* methodical, neat, ordered, organised, shipshape, spick and span, straight, systematic, tidy.
OPPOSITE chaotic.
2 *orderly behaviour.* controlled, disciplined, law-abiding, quiet, well-behaved.
OPPOSITE disorderly, unruly.

ordinary *adjective*
an ordinary man, performance, house, etc. average, common, commonplace, conventional, customary, everyday, familiar, humble, humdrum, mediocre, middling, mundane, nondescript, normal, orthodox, plain, regular, routine, simple, so-so (*informal*), standard, typical, undistinguished, unexciting, unimpressive, uninspired, uninteresting, unremarkable, usual.
OPPOSITE exceptional, extraordinary.

organisation *noun*
1 *They belong to a peacemaking organisation.* alliance, association, body, club, company, corps, federation, fellowship, fraternity, group, league, movement, order, party, society, union.
2 *He works for a large banking organisation.* business, company, corporation, enterprise, establishment, firm, house, institution.
3 *The organisation of the essay was clear.* arrangement, design, form, format, layout, ordering, presentation, structure.
4 *The organisation of the event was a nightmare.* administration, coordination, management, planning, running.

organise *verb*
1 *She organised her papers.* arrange, catalogue, classify, group, order, put in order, sort, tidy.
OPPOSITE disorganise.
2 *The event was organised with military precision.* arrange, control, coordinate, manage, orchestrate, plan, run, stage-manage.
3 *The police organised a search party.* assemble, establish, form, mobilise, put together, set up.

organised *adjective*
an organised approach. businesslike, careful, efficient, methodical, neat, orderly, planned, structured, systematic.
OPPOSITE disorganised.

organism *noun*
microscopic organisms. being, creature, living thing.

orgy *noun*
a drunken orgy. party, revelry, spree (*informal*).

orientate *verb*
The course is orientated towards teachers. aim, direct, gear, orient, slant.
orientate yourself
1 *He used the tower to orientate himself.* find your position, get your bearings, orient yourself.
2 *It can take a few weeks for you to orientate yourself.* acclimatise, adapt, adjust, familiarise yourself, orient yourself, settle in.

origin *noun*
1 *the origin of life.* basis, beginning, birth, cause, commencement, creation, derivation, emergence, foundation, genesis, root, source, start, starting point.
OPPOSITE end.
2 *a man of humble origin.* ancestry, birth, descent, extraction, lineage, parentage.

original *adjective*
1 *the original vegetation.* aboriginal, earliest, first, initial, native, primeval.
OPPOSITE imported.
2 *an original story.* creative, firsthand, fresh, imaginative, innovative, inventive, new, novel, unconventional,

a b c d e f g h i j k l m n o p q r s t u v w x y z

unique.
OPPOSITE hackneyed, unoriginal.

original *noun*
The original is housed in the museum: this is a copy. archetype, master, prototype.
OPPOSITE copy, replica.

originate *verb*
The tradition originated centuries ago. arise, begin, commence, date from, emerge, spring up, start.

ornament *noun*
1 She displays her ornaments in a cabinet. bric-à-brac, knick-knack, trinket.
2 The dress needs some ornament to make it less plain. adornment, decoration, jewellery, trimming.

ornate *adjective*
ornate furnishings. decorated, elaborate, fancy, flamboyant, ornamented, showy.
OPPOSITE plain.

orthodox *adjective*
orthodox beliefs. accepted, conventional, established, mainstream, official, ordinary, standard, traditional.
OPPOSITE heretical.

oscillate *verb*
1 The pendulum oscillates. sway, swing.
2 Her mood oscillates between depression and ecstasy. fluctuate, see-saw, swing, vary, waver.

ostentatious *adjective*
an ostentatious house. conspicuous, extravagant, flamboyant, flash (informal), flashy, grandiose, imposing, pretentious, showy.
OPPOSITE modest.

other *adjective*
1 He has no other income. additional, extra, further, more, supplementary.
2 There can be no other explanation. alternative, different.
OPPOSITE same.
other than She has no friends other than her family. apart from, aside from, besides, except.

oust *verb*
He was ousted from his job. banish, dismiss, drive out, eject, expel, fire, give the boot (slang), give the sack (informal),

kick out (informal), sack (informal), throw out.

outback *noun* (Australian)
He grew up in the city but now lives in the outback. backblocks (Australian), back of beyond, bush, interior, never-never (Australian), sticks (informal).

outbreak *noun*
an outbreak of fighting. a new outbreak of cholera. epidemic, eruption, outburst.

outburst *noun*
an outburst of anger. an outburst of laughter. blaze, eruption, explosion, fit, flood, outbreak, spasm.

outcast *noun*
He was treated as an outcast. deportee, exile, outlaw, refugee.

outcome *noun*
The outcome of the talks was a peaceful settlement. consequence, effect, result, sequel, upshot.

outcrop *noun*
a fresh outcrop of spots. burst, crop, eruption, outbreak.

outcry *noun*
The umpire's decision brought an angry outcry. clamour, hue and cry, objection, protest, uproar.

outdated *adjective*
outdated customs. antiquated, archaic, obsolete, old, old-fashioned, out-of-date, unfashionable.
OPPOSITE current, modern.

outdo *verb*
She can outdo all her competitors. beat, defeat, exceed, excel, outclass, outshine, outstrip, surpass, top.

outdoors *adverb*
They eat outdoors in summer. al fresco, in the open air, out of doors, outside.
OPPOSITE indoors.

outer *adjective*
1 an outer layer. exterior, external, outside, superficial, surface.
OPPOSITE inner, internal.
2 an outer suburb. outlying, remote.
OPPOSITE inner.

outfit *noun*
1 *She wore her new outfit to the party.* clothes, clothing, costume, gear (*informal*), get-up (*informal*).
2 *an emergency survival outfit.* equipment, gear, kit.

outgoing *adjective*
1 *an outgoing personality.* extroverted, friendly, gregarious, sociable, warm.
OPPOSITE retiring, shy.
2 *the outgoing president.* departing, ex-, past, retiring.
OPPOSITE incoming.

outhouse *noun*
barn, outbuilding, shed.

outing *noun*
an outing to the zoo. drive, excursion, expedition, hike, jaunt, tour, trip.

outlandish *adjective*
a contest for the most outlandish outfit. bizarre, exotic, freakish, odd, outrageous, peculiar, strange, unusual, way-out, weird.
OPPOSITE ordinary.

outlaw *noun*
The carriage was attacked by a band of outlaws. bandit, brigand, criminal, desperado, fugitive, marauder, outcast.
outlaw *verb*
Smoking is outlawed on public transport. ban, forbid, prohibit.
OPPOSITE allow.

outlay *noun*
a small outlay of ten dollars. charge, cost, expenditure, expense.
OPPOSITE return.

outlet *noun*
1 *a safety outlet.* duct, escape, exit, hole, opening, overflow, vent, way out.
2 *an outlet for her imagination.* channel, release.
3 *a fast-food outlet.* shop, store.

outline *noun*
1 *the outline of a person.* contour, profile, shadow, shape, silhouette, tracing.
2 *an outline of the story.* abstract, draft, framework, plan, précis, résumé, sketch, summary, synopsis.

outlook *noun*
1 *a pleasant outlook over the lake.* aspect, panorama, prospect, scene, sight, view, vista.
2 *He has an optimistic outlook.* attitude, perspective, view, viewpoint.
3 *a grim economic outlook.* forecast, prediction, prospect.

outlying *adjective*
outlying areas. distant, far-flung, outer, remote.
OPPOSITE inner.

outnumber *verb*
Boys outnumbered girls. exceed.

output *noun*
Their output was diminished because of the power failure. production, yield.
OPPOSITE input.

outrage *noun*
1 *an outrage against society.* atrocity, crime, evil, insult, offence, scandal.
2 *He felt outrage at the incident.* anger, disgust, indignation, rage, shock.
outrage *verb*
He was outraged at the suggestion. affront, anger, incense, infuriate, insult, offend, scandalise, shock.

outrageous *adjective*
1 *outrageous prices.* absurd, excessive, exorbitant, preposterous, shocking, unreasonable.
OPPOSITE reasonable.
2 *an outrageous crime.* atrocious, barbarous, despicable, disgraceful, infamous, monstrous, notorious, offensive, scandalous, shocking, vile, wicked.

outright *adverb*
1 *She was killed outright.* at once, immediately, instantly.
2 *Smoking is banned outright.* absolutely, altogether, completely, entirely, utterly.
outright *adjective*
outright stupidity. absolute, complete, downright, out-and-out, sheer, utter.

outset *noun*
from the outset. beginning, commencement, start.
OPPOSITE finish.

a
b
c
d
e
f
g
h
i
j
k
l
m
n
o
p
q
r
s
t
u
v
w
x
y
z

outside *noun*
It looked perfect on the outside. coating, cover, covering, crust, exterior, face, shell, skin, surface.
OPPOSITE inside.
outside *adjective*
an outside wall. exterior, external, outer.
OPPOSITE interior, internal.
outside *adverb*
They like eating outside. al fresco, in the open air, outdoors, out of doors.
OPPOSITE inside.
outside *preposition*
no interests outside his work. apart from, aside from, beyond, except, other than.

outsider *noun*
He felt like an outsider. alien, foreigner, immigrant, newcomer, odd man out, ring-in (*Australian informal*), stranger, visitor.
OPPOSITE member.

outskirts *plural noun*
on the outskirts of town. edge, fringe, limits.
OPPOSITE centre.

outspoken *adjective*
an outspoken critic of the government. blunt, candid, forthright, frank, open, straightforward, unreserved.
OPPOSITE reticent.

outstanding *adjective*
1 *outstanding work. an outstanding student.* distinguished, eminent, excellent, exceptional, exemplary, extraordinary, great, impressive, memorable, notable, pre-eminent, remarkable, sensational, special, splendid, superior.
OPPOSITE mediocre.
2 *an outstanding amount.* due, overdue, owing, unpaid.
OPPOSITE paid.

outward *adjective*
an outward sign of an inward change. exterior, external, observable, outer, outside, superficial, visible.
OPPOSITE inward.

outweigh *verb*
The advantages outweigh the disadvantages. exceed, override, predominate over, surpass.

outwit *verb*
She outwitted her opponent. dupe, hoodwink, outfox (*informal*), outsmart, trick.

oval *noun*
1 ellipse.
2 (*Australian*) Games are played on the oval. playing field, sports field, sportsground.
oval *adjective*
an oval garden. egg-shaped, elliptical.

ovation *noun*
The audience gave the pianist a big ovation. applause, clap, hand (*informal*).

oven *noun*
cooker, furnace, kiln, microwave, range, stove.

overall *adjective*
the overall effect. all-inclusive, broad, complete, general, total.

overalls *plural noun*
Overalls keep his clothes clean. boiler suit, dungarees.

overbearing *adjective*
an overbearing woman with a timid husband. arrogant, bossy, domineering, imperious, officious.
OPPOSITE unassuming.

overcast *adjective*
overcast skies. cloudy, dull, foggy, gloomy, grey, heavy, leaden, misty.
OPPOSITE clear, sunny.

overcoat *noun*
greatcoat, topcoat; see also COAT.

overcome *verb*
1 *They overcame the enemy.* beat, conquer, crush, defeat, master, overpower, overthrow, quell, subdue, thrash, triumph over, vanquish.
OPPOSITE surrender to.
2 *She overcame the problem.* conquer, lick (*informal*), resolve, rise above, surmount.
OPPOSITE give in to.

overdo *verb*
He overdid the praise. exaggerate, lay (it) on a bit thick (*informal*), overstate, pile (it) on (*informal*).
OPPOSITE understate.

overdue *adjective*
The payment was overdue. in arrears, late, outstanding, owing.
OPPOSITE early, premature.

overeat *verb*
If you overeat, you might feel sick. binge (*informal*), gorge yourself, overindulge, pig out (*informal*), stuff yourself.
OPPOSITE starve yourself.

overestimate *verb*
He overestimated the size of the problem. exaggerate, overrate, overstate.
OPPOSITE underestimate.

overflow *verb*
The water overflowed. brim over, flood, flow over, pour over, run over, slop over, spill over.
overflow *noun*
We needed a bucket to catch the overflow. excess, spillage, surplus.

overgrown *adjective*
1 *an overgrown zucchini.* enormous, gigantic, large, outsize, oversized.
OPPOSITE undersized.
2 *The cats liked the overgrown garden.* tangled, uncut, unkempt, untidy, wild.

overhang *verb*
The tree overhangs the fence. jut out over, project over, protrude over, stick out over.

overhaul *verb*
He overhauled the engine. recondition, repair, restore, service.

overhear *verb*
He overheard a private conversation. eavesdrop on, hear, listen in on.

overjoyed *adjective*
He was overjoyed at the news. delighted, ecstatic, elated, euphoric, exuberant, exultant, happy, joyful, joyous, jubilant, over the moon (*informal*), rapt, thrilled.
OPPOSITE downcast.

overload *verb*
He is overloaded with work. overburden, overtax, weigh down.

overlook *verb*
1 *The castle overlooks the lake.* face, front on to, look out on, look over.

2 *He overlooked an important point.* forget, ignore, leave out, miss, neglect, omit, skip.
3 *She overlooks his faults.* disregard, excuse, forgive, ignore, pardon, pass over, turn a blind eye to.
OPPOSITE notice.

overpower *verb*
He overpowered the madman. beat, defeat, get the better of, overcome, overwhelm, subdue.

overpowering *adjective*
an overpowering feeling of tiredness. irresistible, overwhelming, powerful, uncontrollable.

overrate *verb*
He overrated his abilities. exaggerate, overestimate.
OPPOSITE underrate.

overrule *verb*
The court overruled his decision. disallow, override, overturn, reject, reverse, set aside, veto.
OPPOSITE uphold.

overrun *verb*
The rabbits soon overran the country. cover, infest, invade, occupy, spread over, swarm over, take over.

overseas *adverb*
He travels overseas. abroad.
overseas *adjective*
an overseas investment. foreign, offshore.

oversee *verb*
He oversees the work. be in charge of, direct, manage, run, superintend, supervise.

overseer *noun*
He was appointed overseer of the men. boss, foreman, forewoman, manager, superintendent, supervisor.

overshadow *verb*
This achievement overshadowed all the others. dwarf, eclipse, outshine, put in the shade, surpass, tower over.

oversight *noun*
The letter wasn't sent because of an oversight. blunder, carelessness, error, lapse, mistake, omission, slip-up (*informal*).

a
b
c
d
e
f
g
h
i
j
k
l
m
n
o
p
q
r
s
t
u
v
w
x
y
z

overstate *verb*
He has overstated the problem. blow up, exaggerate, inflate, magnify.
OPPOSITE understate.

overstatement *noun*
exaggeration, hyperbole.
OPPOSITE understatement.

overt *adjective*
overt hostility. blatant, evident, obvious, open, patent, plain, unconcealed, visible.
OPPOSITE covert, secret.

overtake *verb*
The leader could see the others gradually overtaking her. catch up with, go past, outpace, outstrip, overhaul, pass.

overthrow *verb*
They overthrew the government, the president, etc. bring down, defeat, depose, oust, overturn, topple, unseat.

overtone *noun*
The sermon had political overtones. connotation, hint, implication, innuendo, suggestion, undercurrent.

overture *noun*
the overture of an opera. beginning, introduction, opening, prelude.

overturn *verb*
1 The boat overturned. capsize, keel over, topple over, turn over, turn turtle.
2 He overturned the flowerpot. invert, knock over, spill, tip over, up-end, upset, upturn.

overused *adjective*
an overused phrase. clichéd, common, hackneyed, overworked, stale.
OPPOSITE original.

overview *noun*
an overview of the subject. outline, sketch, survey.

overweight *adjective*
chubby, dumpy, fat, gross, heavy, obese, plump, podgy, portly, rotund, stout, tubby.
OPPOSITE thin.

overwhelm *verb*
1 The floodwaters overwhelmed the town. bury, cover, drown, engulf, flood, inundate, submerge, swamp.
2 Their army was overwhelmed by the enemy. beat, conquer, crush, defeat, overcome, overpower, rout, vanquish.

overwhelming *adjective*
an overwhelming urge to speak. irresistible, overpowering, uncontrollable.

overwrought *adjective*
The parents of the missing child were overwrought. agitated, beside yourself, distressed, frantic, hysterical, nervous, nervy, on edge, overexcited, uptight (*informal*), worked up.
OPPOSITE calm.

owe *verb*
He doesn't owe you anything. be beholden to, be indebted to, be in debt to, be under an obligation to.

owing *adjective*
the amount owing. due, outstanding, overdue, unpaid.
owing to She was late, owing to a derailment. because of, caused by, on account of, thanks to.

own[1] *adjective*
Bring your own chair. individual, personal, private.
on your own She did it on her own. alone, by yourself, independently, single-handed, solo, unaccompanied, unaided, unassisted.

own[2] *verb*
He owns shares. be the owner of, have, hold, keep, possess.
own up (*informal*)
The culprit would not own up. admit, come clean (*informal*), confess.

owner *noun*
the owner of the property. holder, landlady, landlord, master, mistress, possessor, proprietor, proprietress.

ox *noun*
bull, bullock, cow, steer.

Pp

pace *noun*
  1 *The room measured five paces.* step, stride.
  2 *He works at a fast pace.* rate, speed, velocity.
pace *verb*
  He paced up and down. see WALK.

pacify *verb*
  She pacified the baby by feeding him. appease, calm, quieten, settle, soothe.
  OPPOSITE agitate, provoke.

pack *noun*
  1 *There are six candles in a pack.* bag, box, bundle, carton, package, packet, parcel.
  2 *He carried the food in his pack.* backpack, haversack, kitbag, knapsack, rucksack, satchel; see also SWAG.
  3 *a pack of thieves.* band, gang, group, mob, push (*Australian*).
  4 *a pack of lies.* heap, load, lot, set.
pack *verb*
  1 *She packed the glasses in padded boxes.* load, package, parcel, place, put, store, stow, stuff, wrap up.
  2 *He packed his bags.* fill, load.
  OPPOSITE unpack.
  3 *We were packed into the room like sardines.* cram, crowd, jam, squash, squeeze, stuff.
  4 *She packed the soil down tightly.* compact, compress, press, ram.
pack off *They packed him off to the country.* bundle off, send away, send off.

package *noun*
  a heavy package. bag, bale, box, bundle, carton, container, pack, packet, parcel.
package *verb*
  She packaged the present neatly. pack (up), parcel (up), wrap (up).

packet *noun*
  Yeast comes in little packets. bag, envelope, pack, package, parcel, sachet.

pact *noun*
  The two sides signed a pact. accord, agreement, bargain, contract, covenant, deal, treaty, understanding.

pad *noun*
  1 *a protective pad.* buffer, cushion, padding, pillow, wad.
  2 *a writing pad.* jotter, notepad.
pad *verb*
  1 *They padded the seat with foam.* cushion, fill, line, protect, stuff, upholster.
  2 *He padded out his speech with jokes.* bulk out, lengthen, spin out, stretch out.

padding *noun*
  The boxes were lined with kapok for padding. cushioning, filling, stuffing, wadding.

paddle[1] *noun*
  a paddle for a boat. oar, scull.
paddle *verb*
  She paddled the canoe. row, scull.

paddle[2] *verb*
  The toddlers paddled in the little pool. dabble, splash about, wade.

paddock *noun* (*Australian*)
  The sheep are in the paddock. field, meadow, pasture.

pagan *noun*
  heathen, non-believer, unbeliever.

page *noun*
  a page of a book. folio, leaf, sheet.

pageant *noun*
  We went to see the Christmas pageant. display, parade, procession, show, spectacle.

pain *noun*
  1 *She has no physical pain.* ache, discomfort, hurt, pang, soreness, sting, throb, twinge.
  2 *The news caused him pain.* affliction, agony, anguish, distress, grief, heartache, hurt, sadness, sorrow,

suffering, torment, torture, woe.
OPPOSITE joy.
pains *plural noun*
He takes pains with his work. care, effort,
trouble.

painful *adjective*
1 *painful fingers.* aching, hurting, raw,
sensitive, smarting, sore, stinging,
tender, throbbing.
2 *a painful headache.* agonising,
excruciating, shooting, splitting,
stabbing.
3 *a painful subject. a painful situation.*
awkward, delicate, distressing,
embarrassing, traumatic,
uncomfortable, unpleasant, upsetting.
OPPOSITE pleasant.

painless *adjective*
1 *a painless operation.* comfortable,
pain-free.
OPPOSITE painful.
2 *a painless way to lose weight.* easy,
effortless, simple.
OPPOSITE difficult.

painstaking *adjective*
a painstaking craftsman. careful,
conscientious, diligent, hard-working,
meticulous, precise, scrupulous,
thorough.
OPPOSITE careless.

paint *noun*
colour, colouring, dye, pigment, stain,
tint.
paint *verb*
1 *She painted the room blue.* coat, colour,
daub, decorate.
2 *She painted the scene.* depict, portray,
represent.

painter *noun*
artist, decorator.

painting *noun*
His paintings are in the art gallery.
picture, work of art; [*kinds of painting*]
abstract, fresco, landscape, mural, oil
painting, portrait, seascape, still life,
water colour.

pair *noun*
They make a good pair. couple, duo,
partnership, twosome.

pal *noun* (*informal*)
A good pal won't let you down. buddy
(*informal*), chum (*informal*), cobber
(*Australian informal*), comrade, crony,
friend, mate.
OPPOSITE enemy.

palace *noun*
The duke lives in a palace. castle, château,
mansion.
OPPOSITE hovel.

pale *adjective*
1 *The patient looks pale.* anaemic, ashen,
colourless, deathly, ghostly, pallid,
pasty, wan, washed out, white.
OPPOSITE ruddy.
2 *a pale colour.* bleached, dim, faint,
light, misty, muted, pastel, soft,
subdued.
OPPOSITE deep, vivid.

pamper *verb*
They pamper their children. humour,
indulge, mollycoddle, spoil.

pamphlet *noun*
He read the pamphlet about immunisation.
booklet, brochure, flyer, handout,
leaflet, notice, tract.

pan *noun*
cooking pans. billy (*Australian*),
casserole, cauldron, Dutch oven, frying
pan, frypan, griddle, pot, pressure
cooker, saucepan, skillet, wok.

pancake *noun*
crêpe, flapjack, pikelet.

pandemonium *noun*
*There was pandemonium after the
earthquake.* bedlam, chaos, commotion,
confusion, disorder, hubbub,
hullabaloo, racket, rumpus, tumult,
turmoil, uproar.
OPPOSITE order, peace.

pander *verb*
pander to *The newspaper panders to the
public interest in scandal.* cater for,
gratify, indulge.

panel *noun*
1 *a wall panel. tapestry panel.* insert,
piece, section, strip.
2 *a panel of adjudicators.* body,
committee, group, jury, team.

pang *noun*
1 *hunger pangs.* ache, pain, spasm, stab, sting, twinge.
2 *pangs of remorse.* see QUALM.

panic *noun*
Panic seized him. alarm, anxiety, consternation, dismay, dread, fear, fright, horror, hysteria, terror, trepidation.
OPPOSITE calmness.
panic *verb*
She panics when it is better to stay calm. drop your bundle (*Australian informal*), freak out (*informal*), get into a state, get into a tizzy (*informal*), get the jitters (*informal*), go to pieces, lose your cool (*informal*).

panicky *adjective*
She was panicky before the exam. agitated, flustered, frantic, frightened, jittery (*informal*), nervous, nervy, panic-stricken, petrified, scared, terrified, terror-stricken.
OPPOSITE calm.

panorama *noun*
They admired the panorama from the lookout. landscape, prospect, scene, view, vista.

pant *verb*
The dog was panting in the sun. gasp, huff, puff, wheeze.

pantry *noun*
Flour is kept in the pantry. cupboard, larder, storeroom.

pants *plural noun* (*informal*)
1 *She prefers skirts to pants.* slacks, trousers.
2 *Pants are their only underwear.* boxer shorts, briefs, drawers, jocks (*slang*), knickers, panties (*informal*), trunks, underpants, undies (*informal*).

paper *noun*
1 *written on paper.* card, letterhead, notepaper, papyrus, parchment, stationery, writing paper.
2 *He reads the paper every day.* see NEWSPAPER.
3 *Keep important papers in a safe place.* certificate, deed, document, form, record.

parable *noun*
allegory, fable, story, tale.

parade *noun*
1 *a parade of floats and bands through the city.* cavalcade, march, march-past, motorcade, pageant, procession.
2 *The street is called 'Anzac Parade'.* avenue, boulevard, road, street.
parade *verb*
The children paraded in the main street. file past, march.

paradise *noun*
1 *The dying woman looked forward to being in paradise.* heaven.
OPPOSITE hell.
2 *Adam and Eve lived in an earthly paradise.* Eden, Garden of Eden.
3 *a shopper's paradise.* delight, heaven, joy, wonderland.

paralysed *adjective*
1 *The accident left him paralysed.* crippled, immobile, lame, numb, paraplegic, quadriplegic.
2 *paralysed with fear.* frozen, petrified, rigid.

paramount *adjective*
of paramount importance. chief, foremost, greatest, highest, main, major, primary, prime, supreme, utmost.
OPPOSITE secondary.

parapet *noun*
The soldiers were protected by the parapet. battlements, rampart.

paraphernalia *noun*
He brought a lot of paraphernalia for just a weekend. accessories, belongings, effects, equipment, gear, materials, odds and ends, possessions, stuff, tackle, things.

paraphrase *verb*
She paraphrased the hymn. rephrase, reword, rewrite.

parasol *noun*
sunshade, umbrella.

parcel *noun*
bale, bundle, pack, package, packet.

parch *verb*
The hot sun parches the land. bake, burn, dry out, scorch, sear.
OPPOSITE wet.

a
b
c
d
e
f
g
h
i
j
k
l
m
n
o
p
q
r
s
t
u
v
w
x
y
z

parched *adjective*
1 *parched ground.* arid, dry, waterless.
OPPOSITE wet.
2 *The walkers were parched.* dehydrated, dry, thirsty.

pardon *noun*
The repentant sinner received God's pardon. absolution, amnesty, forgiveness, mercy, remission, reprieve.
OPPOSITE punishment.

pardon *verb*
1 *She pardoned the offence.* excuse, forgive, overlook.
2 *The judge pardoned the prisoner.* absolve, acquit, exonerate, forgive, let off, reprieve.
OPPOSITE punish.

parent *noun*
the child's parents. father, mother.

park *noun*
a picnic in the park. gardens, parklands, playground, recreation ground, reserve.

parka *noun*
anorak; see also JACKET.

parlour *noun* (*old use*)
The front room is the parlour. drawing room, living room, lounge, salon, sitting room.

parson *noun*
The parson married them. chaplain, clergyman, clergywoman, minister, padre, pastor, preacher, priest, rector, vicar.

part *noun*
1 *part of the profits. part of a pie.* bit, chunk, division, fraction, fragment, percentage, piece, portion, proportion, section, sector, segment, share, slice, subdivision.
OPPOSITE total.
2 *The story is issued in five parts.* chapter, episode, instalment, issue, section, volume.
3 *He comes from another part of the state.* area, district, region.
4 *He assembled the parts.* component, constituent, element, ingredient, module, unit.
5 *the early part of your life.* period, point, stage.

6 *The actor enjoyed his part.* character, role.

part *verb*
They parted amicably. break up, divorce, separate, split up.
OPPOSITE marry.

part with *She won't part with her teddy.* give away, give up, hand over, relinquish, spare, surrender.
OPPOSITE keep.

take part see PARTICIPATE.

partial *adjective*
a partial eclipse. imperfect, incomplete, limited.
OPPOSITE total.

be partial to *She is partial to chocolate.* be fond of, be keen on, enjoy, like, love.
OPPOSITE dislike.

participant *noun*
a participant in the discussions. contributor, party, player.

participate *verb*
She participated in the game. be active, be involved, join, partake, play a part, share, take part.

particle *noun*
1 *food particles.* bit, crumb, fragment, grain, morsel.
2 *He hasn't a particle of sense.* atom, iota, jot, scrap, shred, skerrick (*Australian informal*), speck, trace.

particular *adjective*
1 *made for a particular purpose.* distinct, individual, special, specific.
OPPOSITE general.
2 *He took particular care.* especial, exceptional, special.
OPPOSITE ordinary.
3 *He is particular about what he eats.* choosy (*informal*), fastidious, finicky, fussy, pernickety (*informal*), selective.
OPPOSITE indifferent.

particulars *plural noun*
She was familiar with the particulars of the case. circumstances, details, facts, information.

partition *noun*
He hid behind the partition. barrier, divider, panel, room divider, screen, wall.

partition *verb*
The space was partitioned into poky offices. break up, divide, separate, split up, subdivide.

partly *adverb*
That's partly true. half, in part, partially, semi-.
OPPOSITE completely.

partner *noun*
1 *a business partner. a partner in crime.* accessory, accomplice, ally, associate, collaborator, colleague, helper, offsider (*Australian informal*), sidekick (*informal*).
2 *None of the guests had partners.* companion, consort, husband, mate, spouse, wife.

partnership *noun*
Both members benefit from the partnership. alliance, association, collaboration, marriage, relationship, union.

party *noun*
1 *The guests enjoyed the party.* at-home, ball, banquet, bash (*informal*), celebration, do (*informal*), feast, festivity, formal, function, gathering, get-together (*informal*), orgy, rave (*informal*), reception, shindig (*informal*), shivoo (*Australian informal*), social.
2 *a search party.* band, body, crew, force, group, squad, team.
3 *a political party.* camp, faction, league, side.

pass *verb*
1 *We watched the procession pass.* file past, go by, go past, move on, proceed, progress.
2 *The car passed theirs on the bridge.* get ahead of, outstrip, overhaul, overtake.
3 *He passed the ball from one hand to the other.* juggle, shuffle, slide, slip, toss, transfer.
4 *It helps to pass the time.* fill, occupy, take up, use up, while away.
5 *Time passed quickly.* elapse, fly, go by, roll by, slip away.
6 *The storm passed.* blow over, die away, disappear, evaporate, fade, peter out, vanish.
7 *The parliament passed the new law.* adopt, approve, authorise, decree, enact, ratify.

8 *Not all the candidates pass.* get through, qualify, succeed.
OPPOSITE fail.

pass *noun*
1 *The students have a travel pass.* permit, ticket.
2 *a mountain pass.* canyon, defile, gap, gorge, ravine.

pass away *Father passed away after a long illness.* see DIE.

pass out (*informal*) *He passes out at the sight of blood.* black out, collapse, faint, keel over, swoon.
OPPOSITE come round.

pass over
1 *They passed over the next item on the agenda.* disregard, ignore, miss, omit, skip.
2 *He was passed over for the job.* ignore, overlook, reject.

pass round *She passed the biscuits round.* circulate, deal out, distribute, dole out, hand round, offer, share.

pass up (*informal*) *She passed up an opportunity.* decline, forgo, let go, let slip, neglect, turn down.

passable *adjective*
1 *The road was not passable in snow.* clear, open.
OPPOSITE impassable.
2 *His work was passable.* acceptable, adequate, all right, fair, mediocre, OK (*informal*), reasonable, satisfactory, so-so (*informal*), tolerable.
OPPOSITE unsatisfactory.

passage *noun*
1 *We wished the travellers a safe passage.* crossing, journey, trip, voyage.
2 *We walked along the narrow passage.* aisle, alley, arcade, corridor, gangway, hall, opening, passageway, shaft, tunnel.
3 *She copied the passage from a book.* episode, excerpt, extract, paragraph, piece, portion, quotation, section.

passenger *noun*
a bus passenger. commuter, traveller.

passing *adjective*
a passing glance. brief, cursory, fleeting, hasty, momentary, quick, short, superficial.

passion *noun*
1 *He expressed his hatred with passion.* ardour, earnestness, emotion, feeling, fervour, intensity, zeal.
OPPOSITE apathy.
2 *sexual passion.* amorousness, ardour, desire, love, lust.
OPPOSITE frigidity.
3 *She has a passion for cricket.* craze, enthusiasm, infatuation, mania, obsession.

passionate *adjective*
a passionate plea. ardent, burning, eager, earnest, emotional, enthusiastic, fervent, heartfelt, heated, impassioned, intense, vehement, zealous.
OPPOSITE apathetic.

passive *adjective*
a passive creature. apathetic, docile, inactive, inert, resigned, submissive, unassertive, unresisting, unresponsive.
OPPOSITE active.

password *noun*
She gave the password to enter. countersign, sign, signal, watchword.

past *adjective*
1 *in past times.* bygone, earlier, former, previous, prior.
CONTRASTS WITH future, present.
2 *the past president.* ex-, former, previous.
past *noun*
1 *She dwelt in the past.* old days, olden days.
2 *He talked about his past.* background, history.
past *preposition*
He drove past our house. beyond, by, in front of.

paste *noun*
1 *wallpaper paste.* adhesive, glue, gum.
2 *tuna paste.* pâté, purée, spread.
paste *verb*
She pasted the pieces together. glue, gum, stick.

pastel *adjective*
painted in pastel shades. delicate, faint, light, muted, pale, soft, subdued.
OPPOSITE bright, dark.

pastime *noun*
Reading and cricket are his pastimes. activity, amusement, diversion, entertainment, game, hobby, interest, leisure pursuit, recreation, sport.

pastor *noun*
The congregation has two pastors. chaplain, clergyman, clergywoman, minister, padre, parson, preacher, priest, rector, vicar.

pastoral *adjective*
pastoral lands. agricultural, farming, grazing, rural, stock-raising.

pastoralist *noun* (*Australian*)
cattle farmer, grazier (*Australian*), sheep farmer, squatter (*Australian*).

pasture *noun*
The sheep are in the pasture. field, meadow, paddock, run (*Australian*).

pat *verb*
1 *She patted his back gently.* caress, massage, rub, stroke.
2 *He patted down the pastry.* dab, flatten, slap, tap.
pat *noun*
He gave him a little pat on the wrist. hit, rap, slap, smack, tap.

patch *noun*
1 *She sewed a patch on her jeans.* mend, reinforcement, repair.
2 *He had a patch over the wound.* bandage, cover, dressing, pad, plaster.
3 *black patches on a white background.* area, blob, blotch, mark, speck, speckle, splash, splotch, spot.
4 *a vegetable patch.* area, garden, lot, plot.
patch *verb*
He patched his trousers. mend, reinforce, repair.
patch up *After their quarrel they tried to patch things up.* make up, resolve, set right, settle.

patchy *adjective*
1 *The colour is rather patchy.* blotchy, dappled, inconsistent, mottled, speckled, uneven, variable.
OPPOSITE uniform.
2 *We only have patchy information.* incomplete, rough, sketchy.
OPPOSITE complete.

paternal *adjective*
a paternal interest. fatherlike, fatherly, kindly, protective.

paternity *noun*
fatherhood, fathership.

path *noun*
1 *They walked up the path.* aisle, alley, footpath, footway, lane, passage, pathway, pavement, sidewalk (*American*), track, trail, walkway, way.
2 *the path of a moving vehicle.* course, line, orbit, route, trajectory, way.

pathetic *adjective*
1 *pathetic sights of starving children.* distressing, heartbreaking, moving, piteous, pitiable, pitiful, poignant, sad, touching, tragic, wretched.
OPPOSITE heart-warming.
2 *a pathetic amount.* meagre, measly (*informal*), miserable, paltry, stingy, woeful.

patience *noun*
1 *He showed patience as he waited in the line.* calmness, endurance, forbearance, restraint, self-control, tolerance.
OPPOSITE impatience.
2 *With patience he can learn to walk again.* determination, doggedness, perseverance, persistence, staying power, tenacity.
OPPOSITE impatience.

patient *adjective*
1 *a patient sufferer.* calm, forbearing, long-suffering, resigned, tolerant.
2 *a patient worker.* determined, dogged, persistent, tenacious, tireless, unflagging.
OPPOSITE impatient.

patient *noun*
The doctor has many patients. case, client, invalid, sufferer.

patio *noun*
The patio is used for outdoor parties. courtyard, terrace.

patriotic *adjective*
patriotic soldiers. loyal, nationalistic.

patrol *verb*
The police patrol the area. guard, police, watch.

patrol *noun*
The patrol must stay awake all night. guard, lookout, sentinel, sentry, watch, watchman.

patron *noun*
1 *a patron of the arts.* backer, benefactor, champion, promoter, sponsor, supporter.
2 *a restaurant patron.* client, customer, regular.

patronage *noun*
1 *government patronage of the arts.* aid, backing, help, promotion, sponsorship, support.
2 *The store appreciated our patronage.* business, custom.

patronising *adjective*
He spoke to us in a patronising way. condescending, disdainful, haughty, supercilious, superior.

patter[1] *verb*
The rain pattered on the windows. beat, rap, tap.
patter *noun*
the patter of the rain. beating, pit-a-pat, pitter-patter, tapping.

patter[2] *noun*
the salesman's patter. pitch, spiel (*slang*).

pattern *noun*
1 *The curtains have a floral pattern.* decoration, design, marking, motif.
2 *a sewing pattern.* design, guide, model, template.
3 *There was a pattern to the crimes.* consistency, formula, order, regularity, system.
pattern *verb*
The play was patterned on an older one. model, mould, shape, style.

patterned *adjective*
patterned material. decorated, figured, ornamented.
OPPOSITE plain.

patty *noun*
a fish patty. cake, croquette, rissole.

pause *noun*
a pause in the conversation. break, breather, gap, halt, hesitation, interlude, interruption, let-up, lull, rest, spell,

a
b
c
d
e
f
g
h
i
j
k
l
m
n
o
p
q
r
s
t
u
v
w
x
y
z

stop.
OPPOSITE continuity.

pause *verb*
She paused for the others to catch up. break off, delay, halt, hesitate, rest, stop, wait.
OPPOSITE continue.

pavement *noun*
footpath, path, pathway, sidewalk (*American*).

paw *noun*
a dog's paw. foot, pad.

pawn *verb*
She pawned her watch to get the money. hock (*slang*), pledge.

pay *verb*
1 He paid $200. advance, chip in (*informal*), contribute, cough up (*informal*), fork out (*slang*), give, hand over, outlay, part with, refund, shell out (*informal*), spend.
2 He had to pay the owner for the damage. compensate, recompense, reimburse, repay.
3 Crime doesn't pay. be advantageous, be profitable, be worthwhile, pay off.
4 He paid her a compliment. bestow, extend, give, grant, present.
OPPOSITE withhold.

pay *noun*
He saves some of his pay. earnings, fee, income, remuneration, salary, stipend, wages.

pay back see REPAY, RETALIATE.

pay for You'll pay for your foolishness. be punished for, pay a penalty for, pay the price for, suffer for.

payment *noun*
She received a handsome payment. They make regular payments. advance, allowance, award, benefit, bonus, commission, compensation, contribution, donation, fee, instalment, outlay, pay, pay-off (*informal*), payout, premium, recompense, refund, reimbursement, remittance, remuneration, repayment, reward, royalty, salary, subscription, surcharge, tip, toll, wage(s).

peace *noun*
1 a time of peace between the wars. accord, concord, harmony, order.
OPPOSITE war.

2 the peace of the bush. calm, calmness, quiet, quietness, serenity, stillness, tranquillity.
OPPOSITE noise.

peaceful *adjective*
1 a peaceful holiday. balmy, calm, quiet, restful, serene, still, tranquil, undisturbed, untroubled.
OPPOSITE hectic.
2 a peaceful discussion. amicable, friendly, harmonious, non-violent, peaceable.
OPPOSITE hostile, violent.

peacemaker *noun*
She acted as a peacemaker between the two parties. conciliator, mediator, negotiator.

peak *noun*
1 mountain peaks. apex, crest, pinnacle, summit, tip, top, zenith.
OPPOSITE base, foot.
2 the peak of his career. climax, culmination, height, heyday, pinnacle, summit, top, zenith.
OPPOSITE nadir.

peal *noun*
1 the peal of bells. carillon, chime, ringing, toll.
2 a peal of thunder. blast, burst, clap, crash, roar, rumble.

peal *verb*
The bells pealed each Sunday. chime, ring, toll.

pebbles *plural noun*
a path made of pebbles. cobbles, gravel, shingle, stones.

peck *verb*
1 The bird pecked me. bite, nip.
2 She pecks at her food. nibble, pick.

peculiar *adjective*
1 a peculiar person. abnormal, bizarre, crazy, curious, eccentric, extraordinary, freakish, funny, odd, offbeat, outlandish, quaint, queer, strange, unconventional, unusual, weird.
OPPOSITE normal, ordinary.
2 his own peculiar style. characteristic, different, distinctive, exclusive, individual, particular, personal, special, specific, unique.
OPPOSITE common.

peculiarity *noun*
She knows all his peculiarities.
characteristic, eccentricity, foible,
idiosyncrasy, mannerism, quirk, trait.

pedantic *adjective*
*The teacher was pedantic about his use of
words.* exact, hair-splitting, meticulous,
nit-picking, particular, precise.

pedestrian *noun*
The track was only for pedestrians. hiker,
rambler, walker.

pedigree *noun*
They studied the dog's pedigree. ancestry,
background, family, genealogy, line,
lineage, stock.
pedigree *adjective*
a pedigree poodle. pure-bred,
thoroughbred.

peel *noun*
grated lemon peel. rind, skin, zest.
peel *verb*
1 *She peeled off the dead skin.* flake,
remove, scale, strip.
2 *He peeled the vegetables.* pare, skin.

peep[1] *verb*
1 *She peeped from behind the curtain.*
glance, look, peek, peer.
2 *The sun peeped out from behind the
cloud.* appear, come into view, emerge,
show.
peep *noun*
He took a peep at the presents. glance,
glimpse, look, peek.

peep[2] *noun*
1 *the peep of sparrows.* cheep, chirp,
squeak, tweet, twitter.
2 *not a peep from the children.* cry,
murmur, sound, squeak, whimper,
whisper.
peep *verb*
The sparrows peeped. cheep, chirp,
squeak, tweet, twitter.

peer[1] *verb*
He peered at them over his glasses. gaze,
look, peek, peep, stare.

peer[2] *noun*
1 *peers of the realm.* aristocrat, lord,
noble, nobleman; [*kinds of peer*] baron,
duke, earl, marquess, viscount.

2 *She gets on well with her peers.*
contemporary, equal, fellow.

peeress *noun*
aristocrat, lady, noblewoman; [*kinds of
peeress*] baroness, countess, duchess,
marchioness, viscountess.

peeve *verb* (*informal*)
His remark really peeved her. annoy, bug
(*informal*), irritate, miff (*informal*),
needle, provoke, rile, upset, vex.

peevish *adjective*
*She's peevish when she does not get what
she wants.* bad-tempered, crabby,
cranky, cross, grouchy, grumpy,
irritable, petulant, snaky (*Australian
informal*), sulky, surly, testy.
OPPOSITE good-tempered.

peg *noun*
1 *He hung his coat on the peg.* hook, nail.
2 *a tent peg.* pin, skewer, spike.
peg *verb*
1 *She pegged the washing on the line.*
attach, fasten, pin, secure.
2 *Prices have been pegged.* control, fix,
freeze, limit, set.

pellet *noun*
1 *pellets of pet food.* ball, bead, pill.
2 *He fired a pellet into the tree.* shot, slug.

pelt[1] *noun*
The animals are killed for their pelts. coat,
fleece, hide, skin.

pelt[2] *verb*
1 *She pelted the thieves with stones.* assail,
batter, bombard, pepper, shower.
2 *The rain was pelting down.* bucket,
pour, teem.

pen[1] *noun*
The animals are in the pen. cage,
compound, coop, corral, enclosure,
fold, hutch, pound, run, stall, sty.
pen *verb*
The animals were penned. close in,
confine, coop up, enclose, fence in,
impound, restrict, shut in.

pen[2] *noun*
He writes with a pen. ballpoint, Biro
(*trade mark*), felt-tipped pen, fountain
pen, marker, quill, Texta (*trade mark*).

a
b
c
d
e
f
g
h
i
j
k
l
m
n
o
p
q
r
s
t
u
v
w
x
y
z

penalise *verb*
He was penalised for using bad language.
fine, handicap, punish.

penalty *noun*
1 He paid the penalty for his misdeeds.
fine, forfeit, price, punishment.
OPPOSITE reward.
2 The team is playing with a penalty.
disadvantage, handicap.

penetrate *verb*
1 The prongs penetrated the rubber boot.
break through, drill through, enter,
perforate, pierce, prick, probe,
puncture, spike.
2 The rain penetrated their clothes.
permeate, saturate, seep through, soak
through.

penetrating *adjective*
a penetrating cry. carrying, harsh, loud,
piercing, sharp, shrill.
OPPOSITE soft.

penitent *adjective*
The driver was penitent after the accident.
apologetic, contrite, regretful,
remorseful, repentant, sorry.
OPPOSITE impenitent.

pen-name *noun*
She writes under a pen-name. alias,
assumed name, nom de plume,
pseudonym.

pennant *noun*
The team carried the school pennant.
banner, flag, standard.

penniless *adjective*
He cannot pay his bills: he is penniless.
broke, destitute, hard up (*informal*),
impoverished, needy, poor, poverty-
stricken, skint (*informal*).
OPPOSITE affluent, rich.

pension *noun*
annuity, benefit, super (*informal*),
superannuation.

pensive *adjective*
photographed in pensive mood. daydreaming, dreamy, introspective,
meditative, reflective, serious,
thoughtful.
OPPOSITE carefree.

people *plural noun*
1 He prefers animals to people. human
beings, humanity, humans, mankind,
men and women, persons.
2 the Australian people. citizens,
community, electorate, inhabitants,
nation, populace, population, public,
residents, society.

pepper *noun*
green or red peppers. capsicum.
pepper *verb*
The body was peppered with bullets.
bombard, pelt, riddle, shower, spray.

perceive *verb*
He perceived a change in their attitude.
become aware of, detect, discern,
notice, observe, recognise, see, sense.

perceptive *adjective*
a perceptive judge of character. astute,
clever, discerning, keen, observant,
quick, sensitive, sharp, shrewd,
understanding.
OPPOSITE obtuse.

perch *noun*
a bird's perch. roost.
perch *verb*
The bird perched on the branch. alight,
land, rest, roost, settle, sit.

perennial *adjective*
a perennial problem. chronic, constant,
continuous, eternal, everlasting, lasting,
never-ending, permanent, perpetual,
persistent.
OPPOSITE occasional, temporary.

perfect *adjective*
1 a perfect answer. accurate, complete,
correct, exact, precise, right.
OPPOSITE wrong.
2 a perfect specimen. excellent, faultless,
flawless, immaculate, in mint condition,
spotless, unblemished, undamaged.
OPPOSITE faulty, imperfect.
3 perfect conditions for sailing. ideal,
model, optimum.
OPPOSITE poor.
4 perfect nonsense. absolute, complete,
out-and-out, pure, sheer, thorough,
total, utter.

perforate *verb*
The spikes perforated the skin. penetrate,
pierce, prick, puncture.

perform *verb*
1 *He performs his job well.* accomplish, achieve, carry out, complete, do, execute, fulfil.
2 *The car performs well.* behave, function, go, operate, run, work.
3 *He is performing in a new play.* act, appear, play, star.
4 *They performed a play.* enact, present, put on, stage.

performance *noun*
a performance of the play. enactment, presentation, production, showing, staging; see also SHOW.

performer *noun*
actor, actress, artist, artiste, busker, dancer, entertainer, instrumentalist, musician, player, singer, star, vocalist.

perfume *noun*
the sweet perfume of the flowers. aroma, bouquet, fragrance, odour, scent, smell.
OPPOSITE stink.

perhaps *adverb*
maybe, perchance (*old use*), possibly.

peril *noun*
The walkers were in grave peril. danger, hazard, jeopardy, risk, threat.
OPPOSITE safety.

perilous *adjective*
a perilous journey. chancy, dangerous, hazardous, precarious, risky, unsafe.
OPPOSITE safe.

perimeter *noun*
the perimeter of the school. border, boundary, circumference, edge, fringe, limits, margin.
OPPOSITE centre.

period *noun*
1 *a period of ill health. He went away for a long period.* bout, interval, patch, phase, season, space, span, spell, stage, stint, stretch, term, time, while.
2 *relics of an earlier period.* aeon, age, epoch, era, time.
3 *They have two art periods a week.* class, lesson, session.

periodic *adjective*
a periodic change. cyclical, periodical, recurrent, regular, seasonal.

periodical *noun*
The library does not lend periodicals. journal, magazine, newspaper, paper.

perish *verb*
1 *He perished in the desert.* die, expire, lose your life, pass away.
2 *The elastic has perished.* disintegrate, give way, go, rot.

perk¹ *verb*
perk up *He perked up after the shower.* brighten up, buck up, liven up, pep up, revive.

perk² *noun* (*informal*)
the perks of the job. bonus, extra, fringe benefit, perquisite.

perky *adjective*
He felt perky again after his illness. animated, bright, cheerful, energetic, lively, sprightly, spry, vivacious.
OPPOSITE lethargic.

permanent *adjective*
1 *a permanent problem.* chronic, constant, continual, continuous, enduring, everlasting, lasting, lifelong, long-lasting, never-ending, ongoing, perennial, perpetual, persistent.
OPPOSITE temporary.
2 *a permanent structure.* durable, fixed, indestructible, stable.
OPPOSITE impermanent, temporary.
3 *a permanent stain.* indelible, ingrained, persistent.
OPPOSITE removable.

permanently *adverb*
always, constantly, continuously, eternally, forever, for good, for keeps (*informal*), perpetually, persistently.

permissible *adjective*
a permissible amount. acceptable, admissible, allowable, authorised, lawful, legal, legitimate, permitted, proper, right, valid.
OPPOSITE forbidden, illegal.

permission *noun*
He granted them permission to publish his story. approval, authorisation, authority, clearance, consent, go-ahead, leave.
OPPOSITE prohibition.

a
b
c
d
e
f
g
h
i
j
k
l
m
n
o
p
q
r
s
t
u
v
w
x
y
z

permissive *adjective*
a permissive society. broad-minded,
easygoing, indulgent, lenient, tolerant.
OPPOSITE strict.

permit *verb*
He does not permit smoking. agree to,
allow, approve of, authorise, consent to,
legalise, license, put up with, sanction,
tolerate.
OPPOSITE ban, prohibit.
permit *noun*
a parking permit. authorisation, licence,
pass, warrant.

perpendicular *adjective*
The walls should be perpendicular.
upright, vertical.
OPPOSITE horizontal.

perpetual *adjective*
1 *a state of perpetual bliss.* endless,
enduring, eternal, everlasting, lasting,
never-ending, permanent, unending.
OPPOSITE temporary.
2 *(informal) Her perpetual whinging was
tiring.* ceaseless, constant, continual,
endless, incessant, interminable, non-
stop, persistent, recurrent, repeated,
unceasing.
OPPOSITE occasional.

perplex *verb*
Her behaviour perplexed people. baffle,
bamboozle *(informal)*, bewilder,
confuse, mystify, nonplus, puzzle,
stump *(informal)*, throw *(informal)*.

persecute *verb*
He was persecuted for his religious beliefs.
bully, harass, hassle, intimidate,
maltreat, mistreat, oppress, terrorise,
torment, torture, victimise.

perseverance *noun*
*In the end he was rewarded for his
perseverance.* determination, diligence,
doggedness, endurance, patience,
persistence, stamina, staying power,
sticking power, tenacity.

persevere *verb*
*She persevered at the task until it was
mastered.* battle on, carry on, continue,
endure, keep on, persist, plug away,
stick at *(informal)*.
OPPOSITE give up.

persist *verb*
1 *He persisted in cheating.* carry on,
continue, go on, keep on, persevere,
stick at *(informal)*.
OPPOSITE give up, stop.
2 *The rain persisted for a week.* continue,
hold, last.

persistent *adjective*
1 *He was persistent in his fight for truth.*
determined, diligent, dogged, firm,
obstinate, patient, relentless, resolute,
steadfast, stubborn, tenacious, tireless,
unwavering.
OPPOSITE irresolute.
2 *The pain is persistent.* chronic, constant,
continuous, endless, eternal,
everlasting, incessant, interminable,
nagging, obstinate, permanent,
perpetual, recurrent, unceasing,
unrelenting.
OPPOSITE intermittent.

person *noun*
a lucky person. a funny person. chap
(informal), character, creature, fellow
(informal), human, human being,
individual, mortal, sort *(informal)*, soul,
type *(informal)*; see also CHILD, MAN,
WOMAN.

personal *adjective*
1 *his personal touch.* characteristic,
distinctive, individual, special, unique.
2 *a personal opinion.* individual, private,
subjective.
3 *her personal diary.* confidential,
intimate, own, private, secret.
OPPOSITE public.
4 *personal hygiene.* bodily, physical.

personality *noun*
1 *He has a charming personality.*
character, disposition, make-up, nature,
temperament.
2 *a television personality.* celebrity,
identity *(Australian informal)*, star.

personnel *noun*
The firm looks after its personnel.
employees, human resources, staff,
workers, workforce.

perspective *noun*
She could see things from his perspective.
angle, outlook, point of view,
standpoint, viewpoint.

perspiration *noun*
sweat.

perspire *verb*
sweat.

persuade *verb*
She finally persuaded them to go. cajole,
coax, convert, convince, entice, induce,
influence, lead, move, sway, talk into,
tempt, win over.
OPPOSITE dissuade.

persuasion *noun*
*It did not take much persuasion to make
them come.* argument, cajolery, coaxing,
convincing, influence.

persuasive *adjective*
a persuasive argument. compelling,
convincing, forceful, plausible,
powerful, telling, weighty.
OPPOSITE weak.

perturb *verb*
He was not perturbed by their absence.
agitate, alarm, bother, disconcert,
distress, disturb, frighten, scare,
trouble, upset, worry.
OPPOSITE reassure.

perverse *adjective*
a perverse child, delighting in disobedience.
contrary, disobedient, headstrong,
intractable, obstinate, pigheaded
(*informal*), rebellious, recalcitrant,
stroppy (*informal*), stubborn,
unreasonable, wayward, wilful.
OPPOSITE cooperative, reasonable.

pervert *verb*
He tried to pervert the witness. bribe,
corrupt, lead astray.
pervert *noun*
a sexual pervert. deviant, weirdo
(*informal*).

perverted *adjective*
a perverted mind. corrupt, depraved,
deviant, kinky (*informal*), sick, twisted,
warped.
OPPOSITE normal.

pessimistic *adjective*
He was pessimistic about his results.
cynical, defeatist, despairing,
despondent, fatalistic, gloomy,
hopeless, negative, resigned, unhappy.
OPPOSITE optimistic.

pest *noun*
The telephone is sometimes a pest.
annoyance, bother, curse,
inconvenience, menace, nuisance, pain
(*informal*).

pester *verb*
*He pestered his mother for his pocket
money.* annoy, badger, bother, harass,
hassle (*informal*), hound, irritate, keep
on at, nag, plague, torment, trouble,
worry.

pet *noun*
the teacher's pet. apple of someone's eye,
darling, favourite.
pet *adjective*
1 *a pet wallaby.* domestic, domesticated,
tame.
2 *a pet subject.* favourite, special.
pet *verb*
She petted the cat. caress, cuddle, fondle,
pat, stroke.

peter *verb*
peter out *The supply petered out.*
diminish, end, fail, give out, run out,
stop.
OPPOSITE continue.

petition *noun*
*The residents signed a petition to keep the
shop open.* appeal, entreaty, plea,
request, supplication.

petrify *verb*
The noises petrified her. appal, frighten,
numb, paralyse, scare stiff (*informal*),
terrify.

petrol *noun*
fuel, gas (*American informal*), gasoline
(*American*).
petrol station filling station, garage,
roadhouse, service station, servo
(*Australian informal*).

petticoat *noun*
slip, underskirt.

petty *adjective*
petty details. insignificant, minor,
piffling (*informal*), small, trifling, trivial,
unimportant.
OPPOSITE important.

a
b
c
d
e
f
g
h
i
j
k
l
m
n
o
p
q
r
s
t
u
v
w
x
y
z

petulant *adjective*
They ignored him when he became petulant.
bad-tempered, crabby, cross, grouchy,
grumpy, huffy, irritable, peevish,
snappy, sulky, sullen, testy, tetchy.

phantom *noun*
She thought she saw a phantom.
apparition, ghost, poltergeist, spectre,
spirit, spook (*informal*).

pharmacist *noun*
The pharmacist made up the prescription.
apothecary (*old use*), chemist, dispenser,
druggist, pharmaceutical chemist.

pharmacy *noun*
Medicines are sold at the pharmacy.
dispensary, drugstore (*American*).

phase *noun*
the introductory phase. period, point,
stage, step, time.

phenomenal *adjective*
a phenomenal achievement. amazing,
exceptional, extraordinary, fabulous
(*informal*), fantastic (*informal*), great,
incredible (*informal*), marvellous,
miraculous, noteworthy, outstanding,
rare, remarkable, sensational, singular,
stupendous, uncommon, wonderful.
OPPOSITE ordinary.

phenomenon *noun*
*Snow is a rare phenomenon in most parts of
Australia.* event, experience, happening,
occurrence.

philosophical *adjective*
He was philosophical about the loss. calm,
fatalistic, logical, rational, reasonable,
resigned, serene, stoical, unemotional.
OPPOSITE upset.

philosophy *noun*
a philosophy of life. belief system,
convictions, doctrine, ideology, view.

phobia *noun*
He was cured of his phobia about cats.
aversion, dislike, dread, fear, hang-up
(*informal*), horror; [*various phobias*]
acrophobia (*of heights*), agoraphobia (*of
open spaces*), arachnophobia (*of spiders*),
claustrophobia (*of confined places*),
hydrophobia (*of water*), nyctophobia (*of
night or of darkness*), xenophobia (*of

foreigners*).
OPPOSITE liking.

phone *noun*
blower (*informal*), telephone.
phone *verb*
He phoned his parents. call, dial, ring
(up), telephone.

phoney *adjective* (*informal*)
a phoney diamond. artificial, bogus,
counterfeit, fake, false, forged,
imitation, pseudo, sham, synthetic.
OPPOSITE genuine.

photocopy *noun*
a photocopy of the document. copy,
duplicate.
photocopy *verb*
*He photocopied the letter for his own
records.* copy, duplicate, reproduce.

photograph *noun*
photo (*informal*), picture, print, shot,
snap, snapshot.
photograph *verb*
shoot, snap.

phrase *noun*
1 *a French phrase book.* expression,
idiom, term.
2 *It became a famous phrase.* catchphrase,
cliché, dictum, maxim, motto, proverb,
saying, slogan.
phrase *verb*
He phrased the statement carefully.
express, formulate, frame, put, word.

physical *adjective*
1 *physical punishment.* bodily, corporal.
CONTRASTS WITH mental, spiritual.
2 *the physical world.* actual, concrete,
material, real, solid, tangible.
OPPOSITE intangible.

physician *noun*
doctor, medical practitioner.

physique *noun*
a healthy physique. body, build, figure,
shape.

pick *verb*
1 *He only picks at his food.* nibble, peck.
2 *She picked some grapes.* collect, cut,
gather, harvest, pluck, pull off.
3 *She was picked to be captain.* choose,
decide on, elect, name, nominate, opt

for, select, settle on, single out, vote for.
OPPOSITE reject.

pick *noun*
1 *He had first pick.* choice, option, preference, selection.
2 *the pick of the crop.* best, choice, cream, elite.
OPPOSITE worst.

pick on *Stop picking on her.* bully, criticise, find fault with, get at (*informal*), harass, nag.

pick out *He picked her out easily in the crowd.* distinguish, make out, notice, recognise, spot.

pick up
1 *Friends picked him up at the airport.* call for, collect, fetch, get.
2 *The police picked him up for shoplifting.* apprehend, arrest, catch, detain, nab (*informal*), nick (*slang*), take into custody.
3 *She picked up a bargain.* acquire, come by, find, get, obtain, snaffle (*informal*).
4 *He picked up a bad cold.* catch, come down with, contract.
5 *Business is picking up.* get better, improve, recover.

pickle *noun*
He got himself into a pickle. fix (*informal*), jam (*informal*), mess, predicament, spot (*informal*).
pickle *verb*
He pickled the olives in brine. preserve.

picture *noun*
1 *a picture in a book. pictures on the walls.* cartoon, collage, design, diagram, drawing, engraving, etching, illustration, image, landscape, likeness, mosaic, mural, painting, photo, photograph, plate, portrait, print, representation, reproduction, sketch, snapshot; [*pictures*] graphics.
2 *They watched a picture in black and white.* film, flick (*informal*), motion picture, movie (*informal*), moving picture, video.
picture *verb*
1 *The artist pictured the scene on her canvas.* depict, draw, illustrate, paint, portray, represent, reproduce, sketch.
2 *Picture yourself by a mountain stream.* conceive, dream up, envisage, fancy, imagine, see, visualise.

picturesque *adjective*
1 *a picturesque landscape.* attractive, beautiful, charming, pretty, quaint, scenic.
OPPOSITE ugly.
2 *picturesque language.* colourful, descriptive, expressive, graphic, imaginative, striking, vivid.
OPPOSITE dull.

pie *noun*
flan, quiche, tart.

piece *noun*
1 *a piece of chocolate, material, timber, etc.* amount, bar, bit, bite, block, chip, chunk, division, fraction, fragment, hunk, length, lump, morsel, part, portion, quantity, remnant, scrap, section, segment, share, shred, slab, slice, sliver, snippet, stick, titbit, wedge.
2 *There are fifty pieces in the set.* component, element, module, part, unit.
3 *a piece of embroidery. a museum piece.* article, example, instance, item, object, sample, specimen, thing.
4 *She played her new piece on the piano.* composition, creation, item, number, work.
piece *verb*
piece together *He pieced the saucer together again.* assemble, join together, mend, patch up, put together, reassemble.

pier *noun*
fishing from the pier. breakwater, jetty, landing stage, quay, wharf.

pierce *verb*
The nail pierced his foot. bore through, enter, gore, impale, jab, lance, penetrate, perforate, prick, puncture, skewer, spear, spike, stab, wound.

piercing *adjective*
1 *a piercing wind.* biting, bitter, cutting.
OPPOSITE gentle.
2 *a piercing voice.* deafening, loud, noisy, penetrating, screeching, sharp, shrill, strident.
OPPOSITE soft.

pig *noun*
1 *a herd of pigs.* boar, hog, piglet, porker, sow (*female*), swine.

a
b
c
d
e
f
g
h
i
j
k
l
m
n
o
p
q
r
s
t
u
v
w
x
y
z

2 (*informal*) *Some pig has eaten all of the pie.* see GLUTTON.

pigeon-hole *noun*
The letter is in your pigeon-hole. compartment, cubby hole, niche.

pigheaded *adjective*
She is too pigheaded to listen to your advice. headstrong, mulish, obstinate, refractory, self-willed, stiff-necked, stubborn, wilful.
OPPOSITE tractable.

pigment *noun*
painted in natural pigments. colour, colouring, dye, tint.

pikelet *noun*
drop scone, flapjack, pancake.

pile¹ *noun*
The house is built on piles. column, pillar, post, stilt, support, upright.

pile² *noun*
1 *a pile of clothes, leaves, etc.* batch, collection, heap, hoard, mass, mound, mountain, pyramid, stack, stockpile.
2 (*informal*) *She has a pile of work. piles of work to do.* heap (*informal*), load (*informal*), lot (*informal*), mountain, oodles (*informal*), plenty, stack (*informal*), ton (*informal*).
pile *verb*
1 *She piled the toys in the corner.* accumulate, assemble, collect, gather, heap (up), load, mass, stack (up), stockpile.
OPPOSITE scatter.
2 *They piled into the car.* crowd, huddle, pack, squeeze.

pile³ *noun*
The carpet has a thick pile. nap, surface.

pilfer *verb*
She pilfered lollies from the shop. help yourself to, lift (*informal*), nick (*slang*), pinch (*informal*), snitch (*slang*), souvenir (*slang*), steal, take.

pill *noun*
The pills are available on prescription. capsule, lozenge, pellet, tablet.

pillage *verb & noun*
see PLUNDER.

pillar *noun*
a tall supporting pillar. column, obelisk, pile, post, prop, shaft, support, upright.

pillow *noun*
bolster, cushion.

pilot *noun*
1 *an aeroplane pilot.* airman, airwoman, aviator, captain.
2 *The pilot steered the boat.* coxswain, guide, helmsman, navigator, steersman.
pilot *verb*
His job is to pilot the boats through the harbour. conduct, escort, guide, lead, navigate, steer.
pilot *adjective*
a pilot programme. experimental, preliminary, test, trial.

pimple *noun*
blackhead, spot, whitehead, zit (*slang*); [*pimples*] acne.

pin *noun*
brooch, drawing pin, hairpin, hatpin, nappy pin, safety pin, skewer, spike, split pin, staple, tack, tiepin.
pin *verb*
1 *The picture was pinned on the board.* affix, attach, fasten, fix, nail, secure, spike, staple, stick, tack.
2 *He was pinned under the car.* hold down, hold fast, immobilise.
pin down *He pinned him down to a time.* bind, commit, nail down.

pinafore *noun*
apron.

pinch *verb*
1 *She pinched my arm.* nip, squeeze, tweak.
2 (*informal*) *She pinched a watch from behind the counter.* lift (*informal*), nick (*slang*), pilfer, snatch, snavel (*Australian informal*), snitch (*slang*), steal, swipe (*informal*), take.
pinch *noun*
1 *The baby gave her a pinch.* nip, squeeze, tweak.
2 *a pinch of salt.* bit, smidgen, speck, touch, trace.

pine *verb*
1 *He pined when his wife died.* grieve, languish, mope, mourn, waste away.

2 *She is pining for home.* crave for, hanker after, hunger for, long for, thirst for, yearn for.

pink *adjective*
a pink colour. coral, flesh-coloured, peach, rose, rosy, salmon-pink, shell-pink, skin-coloured.

pinnacle *noun*
1 *The pinnacle was covered with snow.* apex, cap, crest, peak, summit, tip, top.
2 *the pinnacle of her career.* climax, culmination, height, heyday, peak, summit, top, zenith.
OPPOSITE nadir.

pinpoint *verb*
He pinpointed their position. discover, find, identify, locate, spot.

pioneer *noun*
1 *Her ancestors were Australian pioneers.* colonist, discoverer, explorer, settler.
2 *pioneers in the fast-food industry.* founder, innovator, trailblazer.
pioneer *verb*
He pioneered the procedure. create, develop, discover, establish, found, introduce, start.

pious *adjective*
a pious man, inspired by his love for God. devout, faithful, God-fearing, godly, holy, religious, reverent, saintly.
OPPOSITE impious.

pip *noun*
lemon pips. seed.

pipe *noun*
The pipe is blocked. channel, conduit, drainpipe, duct, hose, main, pipeline, tube.

pirate *noun*
buccaneer, corsair, marauder, privateer.

pit *noun*
1 *The ball fell into a pit.* abyss, bunker, cavity, crater, depression, ditch, gully, hole, hollow, trench.
2 *The miners went into the pit.* coalmine, colliery, mine, quarry, shaft, working.
pit *verb*
The surface was pitted. dent, gouge, nick, pock-mark, scar.

pitch *verb*
1 *He pitched the ball.* bowl, cast, chuck (*informal*), fling, heave, hurl, lob, sling, throw, toss.
2 *He pitched the tent.* erect, put up, raise, set up.
3 *The ship pitched in heavy seas.* lurch, plunge, rock, roll, toss about.
pitch *noun*
1 *The roof has a gentle pitch.* angle, grade, gradient, incline, slope.
2 *Their excitement had reached fever pitch.* degree, height, intensity, level, point.
3 *He has no ear for recognising differences in pitch.* highness, lowness, tone.
4 *sales pitch.* line (*informal*), patter, spiel (*slang*), talk.

pitcher *noun*
a pitcher of water. ewer, jug.

pitfall *noun*
warned of the pitfalls. danger, difficulty, hazard, peril, snag, snare, trap.

pitiful *adjective*
1 *the pitiful sight of an injured animal.* forlorn, heartbreaking, moving, pathetic, poignant, sad, touching, wretched.
2 *a pitiful attempt.* contemptible, hopeless, miserable, pathetic, poor, sorry, useless, woeful.

pitiless *adjective*
a pitiless tyrant. brutal, callous, cruel, hard-hearted, heartless, inhuman, merciless, relentless, remorseless, ruthless.
OPPOSITE compassionate, merciful.

pity *noun*
1 *He felt pity for the victims.* commiseration, compassion, condolence, regret, sorrow, sympathy.
OPPOSITE indifference.
2 *The judge showed no pity.* charity, clemency, compassion, forbearance, lenience, mercy, tenderness.
OPPOSITE severity.
3 *What a pity!* shame.
pity *verb*
He pitied those who were not chosen. commiserate with, feel for, feel sorry for, sympathise with.

a
b
c
d
e
f
g
h
i
j
k
l
m
n
o
p
q
r
s
t
u
v
w
x
y
z

pivot *noun*
The arms turn on a pivot. axis, fulcrum, shaft, spindle.
pivot *verb*
The spinning top pivots on this point. revolve, rotate, spin, swivel, turn.

placard *noun*
The wall was covered with placards. advertisement, bill, notice, poster, sign.

place *noun*
1 *This is the place where it happened.* address, location, scene, setting, site, situation, spot, venue.
2 *We visited many interesting places.* area, city, country, district, locality, neighbourhood, region, town, township, village.
3 *The meeting is at his place.* dwelling, home, house, premises, residence.
4 *Someone is sitting in that place.* chair, position, seat, space, spot.
place *verb*
1 *She placed the parcels on the table.* arrange, deposit, dump, lay, leave, locate, plant, plonk, position, put, rest, set, situate, stand, station, stick (*informal*).
OPPOSITE remove.
2 *I can't place him.* identify, recognise, remember.
in place of in lieu of, instead of.

placid *adjective*
a placid nature. calm, even-tempered, level-headed, mild, peaceable, quiet, sedate, serene, tranquil, unexcitable, unruffled.
OPPOSITE excitable.

plague *noun*
1 *bubonic plague.* epidemic, pestilence.
2 *a plague of mice.* infestation, invasion, scourge.
plague *verb*
We were plagued by mosquitoes. annoy, bother, bug (*informal*), disturb, harass, hassle (*informal*), irritate, pester, torment, trouble, vex, worry.

plain *adjective*
1 *The meaning was plain.* apparent, certain, clear, evident, explicit, obvious, patent, transparent, unambiguous, understandable, unmistakable.
OPPOSITE obscure.

2 *a plain dress.* austere, basic, homely, ordinary, simple.
OPPOSITE elaborate, fancy.
3 *The food tastes plain.* bland, insipid, tasteless, uninteresting, wishy-washy.
OPPOSITE tasty.
4 *plain paper.* blank, unlined, unmarked, unpatterned.
OPPOSITE patterned.
5 *some plain speaking.* blunt, candid, direct, forthright, frank, honest, open, outspoken, straightforward, unambiguous.
OPPOSITE evasive.
6 *She thought she looked plain.* homely (*American*), ordinary, unattractive.
OPPOSITE attractive.
plain *noun*
The hills overlook sweeping plains. flat, grassland, pampas, prairie, savannah, steppe, tundra, veld.

plait *verb*
She plaited the three strands. braid, intertwine, interweave.

plan *noun*
1 *They looked at the plan of the building.* blueprint, chart, design, diagram, drawing, layout, map, sketch.
2 *They worked according to a plan.* aim, formula, intention, method, outline, plot, policy, procedure, programme, project, proposal, schedule, scheme, strategy.
plan *verb*
1 *The city developed as it had been planned.* design, draw, lay out, map out.
2 *They planned their action.* arrange, design, devise, organise, plot, premeditate, prepare, scheme, think up.
3 *Do you plan to come?* aim, intend, mean, propose.

plane *noun*
1 *points on the same plane.* level, surface.
2 *They travelled to England by plane.* aeroplane, aircraft, jet, jumbo.

plank *noun*
The floor is made of planks. board, slab, timber.

planned *adjective*
a planned attack. calculated, deliberate, intentional, organised, premeditated.
OPPOSITE unplanned.

plant *noun*

1 *A botanist studies plants.* flora, greenery, vegetation; [*kinds of plant*] alga, annual, bulb, bush, cactus, fern, flower, fungus, grass, herb, lichen, moss, perennial, seedling, shrub, succulent, tree, vegetable, vine, weed.
2 *an engineering plant.* factory, foundry, mill, works, workshop.
3 *The firm is insured for damage to plant.* equipment, gear, machinery.

plant *verb*

1 *He planted seeds and seedlings.* set out, sow, transplant.
2 *She planted the idea in his head.* fix, implant, put.
3 *He planted the tapes in her house.* conceal, hide, secrete.

plaster *noun*

She had a plaster on her cut finger. bandage, dressing.

plaster *verb*

He plastered the table with finger paint. coat, cover, daub, smear, spread.

plate *noun*

1 *a plate for food.* dish, platter.
2 *a plate of glass.* layer, pane, panel, sheet.
3 *His name was on a brass plate on the wall.* plaque, shingle, sign, tablet.

plateau *noun*

After an uphill climb we reached a plateau. highland, tableland.

platform *noun*

1 *She addressed us from the platform.* dais, podium, pulpit, rostrum, stage, stand.
2 *a political party's platform.* manifesto, policy, programme.

platter *noun*

platters of food. dish, plate, tray.

platypus *noun*

duckbill, water mole (*old use*).

plausible *adjective*

a plausible explanation. believable, credible, likely, reasonable.
OPPOSITE implausible, unlikely.

play *verb*

1 *She is playing with her sister.* amuse yourself, enjoy yourself, entertain yourself, fool about, frisk, frolic, have fun, mess about, romp, skylark.
2 *He plays cricket.* join in, participate in, take part in.
3 *Our team plays your school next week.* challenge, compete against, meet, oppose, take on, vie with.
4 *She played the fairy in the play.* act as, impersonate, perform as, portray, pretend to be, represent, star as.
5 *She plays the flute.* perform on.

play *noun*

1 *a mixture of work and play.* amusement, diversion, entertainment, fun, leisure, pleasure, recreation, sport.
2 *a stage play.* drama, entertainment, production, show.
play down *He played down the incident.* downplay, gloss over, make light of, minimise.
play for time delay, hedge, procrastinate, stall.
play up (*informal*) *The children played up for the babysitter.* be disobedient, be mischievous, be naughty, misbehave, muck up (*informal*).

player *noun*

1 *a tennis player.* competitor, contestant, participant, sportsperson.
2 *the piano player.* artist, artiste, entertainer, musician, performer.
3 *The players bowed before the curtain fell.* actor, actress, performer.

playful *adjective*

1 *playful kittens.* active, frisky, high-spirited, lively, mischievous, skittish, spirited, sprightly, vivacious.
OPPOSITE sedate.
2 *a playful remark.* facetious, humorous, jesting, jocular, light-hearted, teasing, tongue-in-cheek.
OPPOSITE serious.

playground *noun*

park, recreation ground.

playwright *noun*

dramatist.

plaza *noun*

market place, square.

plea *noun*

a plea for mercy. appeal, entreaty, petition, request, supplication.

a b c d e f g h i j k l m n o p q r s t u v w x y z

plead *verb*
plead with *He pleaded with them to let him go.* appeal to, ask, beg, beseech, entreat, implore, petition, request.

pleasant *noun*
1 *a pleasant day, place, etc.* agreeable, attractive, beautiful, delightful, enjoyable, fine, good, inviting, lovely, mild, nice, peaceful, pleasing, pleasurable, relaxing, satisfying, serene.
OPPOSITE nasty, unpleasant.
2 *pleasant sounds.* euphonious, gentle, harmonious, mellow, melodious, musical, pretty, soothing, sweet, tuneful.
OPPOSITE harsh.
3 *a pleasant companion.* affable, amiable, amicable, charming, cheerful, congenial, cordial, friendly, genial, good-humoured, hospitable, jolly, jovial, kindly, likeable, nice, sweet, sympathetic.
OPPOSITE obnoxious.

please *verb*
1 *The shopkeeper likes to please his customers.* content, delight, gratify, satisfy, suit.
OPPOSITE annoy, displease.
2 *You may do as you please.* choose, decide, like, prefer, want, wish.

pleased *adjective*
She was pleased when it was all over. content, contented, delighted, glad, grateful, happy, joyful, satisfied, thankful.
OPPOSITE displeased, unhappy.

pleasure *noun*
He gets pleasure out of helping people. He walks for pleasure. amusement, bliss, delight, diversion, enjoyment, entertainment, fulfilment, fun, gratification, happiness, joy, kick(s) (*informal*), recreation, satisfaction, thrill.
OPPOSITE displeasure, pain.

pleat *noun*
a skirt with pleats. crease, fold, tuck.

pledge *noun*
a pledge of loyalty. assurance, commitment, guarantee, oath, promise, vow, word.

pledge *verb*
He pledged his support. guarantee, promise, swear, vow.

plentiful *adjective*
a plentiful supply of tomatoes. abundant, ample, bountiful, copious, generous, large, lavish, liberal, profuse, prolific.
OPPOSITE meagre.

plenty *noun*
plenty of cream. heaps (*informal*), lashings (*informal*), loads (*informal*), lots (*informal*), masses, much, oodles (*informal*), piles (*informal*), stacks (*informal*), tons (*informal*).
OPPOSITE shortage.

pliable *adjective*
1 *a pliable material.* bendable, flexible, malleable, plastic, pliant, springy, supple.
OPPOSITE rigid.
2 *a pliable person.* adaptable, amenable, compliant, flexible, tractable.
OPPOSITE intractable.

plight *noun*
a sad and sorry plight. difficulty, jam (*informal*), mess, pickle (*informal*), predicament, situation, state.

plod *verb*
1 *She plodded slowly through the mud.* lumber, plough, slog, traipse (*informal*), tramp, trudge.
2 *She plodded on with the work.* beaver on, grind away, peg away, persevere, plug away, soldier on.

plot *noun*
1 *a plot for vegetables.* allotment, block (*Australian*), field, garden, lot, patch.
2 *the film's plot.* outline, scenario, story, storyline, synopsis.
3 *a plot to bring down the government.* conspiracy, intrigue, plan, scheme.
plot *verb*
1 *He plotted the course for the rally.* chart, draw, map out, outline, sketch.
2 *They plotted to overthrow the government.* conspire, plan, scheme.

pluck *verb*
1 *She plucked some flowers.* gather, harvest, pick, pull off, yank (*informal*).
2 *He plucks his eyebrows.* pull out, remove.

3 *He plucked the letter from her hand.*
grab, grasp, seize, snatch, tug.
pluck *noun*
The rescuer showed great pluck. bravery,
courage, daring, grit, guts (*informal*),
nerve, spunk (*informal*), valour.

plucky *adjective*
the plucky hero. bold, brave, courageous,
daring, fearless, game, hardy, heroic,
intrepid, spirited, valiant.
OPPOSITE faint-hearted.

plug *noun*
1 *The plug came out of the hole.* bung,
cork, stopper.
2 (*informal*) *The broadcaster gave their
product a free plug.* advertisement, boost,
commercial, promotion, publicity.
plug *verb*
He plugged the gaps. block up, close up,
fill, seal, stop up.

plummet *verb*
*The bird plummeted to the ground. Prices
plummeted.* crash, drop, fall, nosedive,
plunge, take a dive, tumble.
OPPOSITE soar.

plump *adjective*
*She needs to lose weight before she becomes
too plump.* chubby, dumpy, fat, obese,
overweight, podgy, portly, roly-poly,
rotund, squat, stout, tubby.
OPPOSITE skinny.

plunder *verb*
The soldiers plundered the town. loot,
pillage, raid, ransack, rob.
plunder *noun*
He loaded the plunder in his truck. booty,
loot, pillage, spoils, swag (*informal*),
takings.

plunge *verb*
1 *He plunged the sword into his side.* force,
jab, push, stick, thrust.
2 *The lift plunged when the cable broke.*
drop, fall, nosedive, plummet.
OPPOSITE soar.
3 *The boy plunged into the icy water.* dive,
duck, fall, jump, leap, sink, throw
yourself, tumble.
4 *She plunged the clothes in the water.* dip,
douse, immerse, lower, steep,
submerge.

plunge *noun*
a plunge from the ten-metre tower. dive,
drop, fall, header, jump, leap, nosedive,
tumble.

plus *noun*
The scheme has several pluses. advantage,
asset, benefit, bonus.
OPPOSITE drawback, minus.

poach[1] *verb*
He poached the fish in wine. simmer.

poach[2] *verb*
He poached the owner's pheasants. hunt,
steal.

pocket *noun*
The passbook fits in a plastic pocket. bag,
compartment, envelope, pouch.
pocket *verb*
He pocketed the money. pilfer, steal, take.
pocket knife clasp-knife, jackknife,
penknife.
pocket money allowance.

pod *noun*
She removed the peas from the pod. case,
hull, husk, shell.

podgy *adjective*
*He was teased at school because he was
podgy.* chubby, dumpy, fat, overweight,
plump, portly, roly-poly, rotund, squat,
stout, tubby.
OPPOSITE skinny.

poem *noun*
ballad, doggerel, elegy, epic, haiku,
idyll, jingle, lay, limerick, lyric, ode,
rhyme, sonnet, verse.

poet *noun*
bard.

poetic *adjective*
poetic writing. lyrical, metrical, poetical,
rhythmic.

poetry *noun*
poems, verse.
CONTRASTS WITH prose.

point *noun*
1 *It narrows to a sharp point.* apex,
extremity, nib, prong, spike, tip, vertex.
2 *The house is on the point.* cape,
headland, promontory.
3 *a decimal point.* dot, spot.

a
b
c
d
e
f
g
h
i
j
k
l
m
n
o
p
q
r
s
t
u
v
w
x
y
z

4 *They agreed to meet at a certain point.* location, place, position, site, situation, spot.
5 *At that point she wanted to give up.* instant, juncture, moment, stage, time.
6 *The judges award points.* mark, score.
7 *The house has its good points.* aspect, attribute, characteristic, feature, property, quality, trait.
8 *They differed on several points.* detail, issue, item, matter, particular.
9 *the point of the story.* argument, drift, essence, gist, meaning, message, thrust.
10 *The exercise has no point.* aim, goal, intention, object, purpose, reason, sense, use, value.
point *verb*
1 *He pointed the gun at the fox.* aim, direct, level, train.
2 *He pointed the car towards home.* aim, direct, guide, lead, steer.
on the point of *She was on the point of leaving.* about to, close to, near to, on the brink of, on the verge of.
point of view *They have different points of view.* opinion, outlook, stance, standpoint, viewpoint.
point out *She pointed out the sights.* draw attention to, indicate, show.
to the point *The comments were to the point.* apposite, apt, pertinent, relevant. OPPOSITE beside the point, irrelevant.

pointed *adjective*
1 *a pointed object.* pointy, sharp, tapering.
2 *a pointed comment.* barbed, cutting, penetrating, sharp.

pointer *noun* (*informal*)
1 *helpful pointers on removing stains.* hint, recommendation, suggestion, tip, wrinkle (*informal*).
2 *pointers to underlying problems.* clue, indication, indicator, lead, sign.

pointless *adjective*
a pointless discussion. a pointless task. aimless, futile, irrelevant, meaningless, needless, senseless, unnecessary, unproductive, useless, worthless. OPPOSITE useful.

poise *verb*
She poised the book on her head. balance, steady.

poise *noun*
1 *The gymnasts were awarded marks for poise.* balance, carriage, deportment, equilibrium, steadiness.
2 *She handled the situation with poise.* calmness, composure, confidence, self-assurance, self-confidence, self-control.

poison *noun*
toxin, venom.
poison *verb*
1 *We poisoned the grass.* kill.
2 *The chemicals poisoned the water supply.* contaminate, infect, pollute, taint.

poisonous *adjective*
1 *Poisonous substances are locked away.* deadly, harmful, lethal, toxic. OPPOSITE non-toxic.
2 *a poisonous spider-bite.* deadly, fatal, lethal, venomous. OPPOSITE non-venomous.

poke *verb*
1 *He poked him in the back.* butt, dig, elbow, jab, nudge, prod, push.
2 *Poke your fork in your meat.* jab, stab, stick, thrust.
3 *She is poking about in the drawer.* forage, fossick (*Australian informal*), rummage, search, snoop (*informal*).
poke fun at jeer at, make fun of, mock, rib (*informal*), ridicule, sling off at (*Australian informal*), take the mickey out of (*informal*), tease.
poke out *The label is poking out.* jut out, protrude, stick out.
poke your nose in *He always pokes his nose in other people's affairs.* interfere in, intrude in, meddle in, pry in.

pole *noun*
a wooden pole. bar, boom, column, mast, post, rod, shaft, spar, staff, stick, stilt, upright.

police *noun*
The police were called to the accident scene. constabulary, cops (*slang*), fuzz (*slang*), law (*informal*).
police *verb*
The streets are policed. control, patrol, supervise.
police officer constable, cop (*slang*), copper (*slang*), detective, inspector, officer, policeman, policewoman, sergeant, superintendent.

policy[1] *noun*

defence policy. a policy on discipline. code, guidelines, line, manifesto, plan, platform, principles, procedure, rules, strategy, system, tactics.

policy[2] *noun*

an insurance policy. contract.

polish *verb*

1 *He polished the lamp.* buff, burnish, rub (up), shine, smooth.
2 *She polished her performance.* brush up, improve, perfect, refine, smarten up, touch up.

polish *noun*

The furniture has a fine polish. brilliance, gloss, lustre, sheen, shine, smoothness, sparkle.
OPPOSITE dullness.

polite *adjective*

a polite person. attentive, chivalrous, civil, civilised, considerate, courteous, diplomatic, gallant, genteel, gentlemanly, ladylike, refined, respectful, suave, tactful, thoughtful, urbane, well-behaved, well-bred, well-mannered.
OPPOSITE impolite, rude.

politician *noun*

Member of Parliament, MP, parliamentarian, polly (*slang*), senator, statesman.

poll *noun*

1 *The people go to the polls this Saturday.* ballot, election, vote.
2 *a public opinion poll.* Gallup poll, straw poll, survey.

poll *verb*

She polled sixty per cent of the votes. gain, get, receive, win.

pollute *verb*

We must stop polluting our rivers with chemical waste. contaminate, defile, dirty, foul, infect, poison, soil, taint.

pomp *noun*

great pomp and ceremony. ceremony, display, glory, grandeur, magnificence, ostentation, pageantry, show, solemnity, spectacle, splendour, style.

pompous *adjective*

His pompous manner upsets some people. arrogant, bombastic, grandiose, haughty, high and mighty, hoity-toity, imperious, overbearing, pretentious, self-important, snobbish, stuck-up (*informal*), supercilious, superior.
OPPOSITE modest.

pond *noun*

ducks on the pond. dam (*Australian*), lake, pool, waterhole.

ponder *verb*

She likes to sit and ponder. brood, contemplate, meditate, muse, reflect, think.
ponder over *He pondered over the problem.* consider, dwell on, mull over, muse over, puzzle over, reflect on, study, think about.

pong *noun* (*informal*)

The pong from the rotten meat was unbearable. reek, stench, stink.

pong *verb* (*informal*)

Bad fish pongs. reek, smell, stink.

pool[1] *noun*

1 *a swim in a mountain pool.* bogey hole (*Australian informal*), lagoon, lake, pond, swimming hole, waterhole.
2 *The rain left pools of water.* puddle.
3 *a swim at the municipal pool.* aquatic centre, baths, swimming pool.

pool[2] *noun*

They each put $2 a week into a pool for joint spending. bank, fund, kitty, reserve.

pool *verb*

They pooled their resources. combine, merge, share.

poor *adjective*

1 *too poor to afford new shoes.* bankrupt, broke (*informal*), destitute, hard up (*informal*), impoverished, needy, penniless, poverty-stricken.
OPPOSITE affluent, rich.
2 *poor soil.* barren, infertile, sterile, unproductive, useless.
OPPOSITE fertile, productive.
3 *poor workmanship. poor quality.* bad, crummy (*informal*), defective, faulty, imperfect, inadequate, inferior, rotten, rubbishy, second-rate, shoddy,

a b c d e f g h i j k l m n o p q r s t u v w x y z

slipshod, substandard, unsatisfactory.
OPPOSITE good.
4 *The poor kitten lost her mother.*
miserable, pathetic, sorry, unfortunate,
unlucky, wretched.
OPPOSITE lucky.

pop *noun*
the pop of a balloon bursting. bang, burst,
crack, explosion, snap.
pop *verb*
The popcorn started to pop. bang, burst,
crackle, explode.
pop in *The doctor popped in each day.* call
in, drop in, nip in (*informal*), stop by,
visit.
pop up *The problem will pop up again.*
appear, come up, crop up, emerge,
surface.

pope *noun*
Holy Father, pontiff.

popular *adjective*
1 *a popular person.* admired, celebrated,
famous, favourite, renowned, sought-
after, well-known, well-liked.
OPPOSITE unpopular.
2 *a popular opinion.* common, general,
mainstream, universal, widely-held,
widespread.

populate *verb*
*The area was populated by post-war
immigrants.* colonise, inhabit, occupy,
people, settle.

population *noun*
The city's population is three million.
citizens, inhabitants, occupants, people,
populace, public, residents.

porch *noun*
The visitors waited in the porch. entrance
hall, lobby, portico, vestibule.

pore¹ *noun*
skin pores. hole, opening.

pore² *verb*
pore over *The student pored over his
notes.* examine, go over, peruse, read,
study.

pornographic *adjective*
pornographic films. blue, dirty, erotic,
indecent, lewd, obscene, smutty.

porous *adjective*
a porous material. absorbent, spongy.

port *noun*
The ship was in the port. anchorage, dock,
dockyard, harbour, marina, seaport.

portable *adjective*
a portable cot. compact, light, movable,
transportable.

porter¹ *noun*
a hotel porter. commissionaire,
concierge, doorkeeper, doorman,
gatekeeper, janitor.

porter² *noun*
A railway porter carried our bags.
attendant, carrier.

portion *noun*
*They each received a portion of the profits,
cake, etc.* allocation, allotment, bit, cut
(*informal*), division, fraction, helping,
part, piece, quantity, quota, ration,
section, segment, serving, share, slice.

portly *noun*
a portly bear. bulky, fat, obese,
overweight, rotund, stocky, stout,
tubby.
OPPOSITE thin.

portrait *noun*
a portrait of her parents. drawing, image,
likeness, painting, photograph, picture,
sketch.

portray *verb*
1 *The writer portrays the evil side of the
characters.* depict, describe, represent,
show.
2 *She portrayed the duchess in the play.* act
as, impersonate, perform as, play, pose
as, represent.

pose *verb*
1 *They posed for the photo.* model, sit.
2 *She posed a difficult question.* ask,
present, put forward, raise.
pose *noun*
photographed in a reclining pose. attitude,
position, posture, stance.
pose as *He posed as an expert.* act as,
impersonate, masquerade as, pass
yourself off as, pretend to be.

posh *adjective* (*informal*)
a posh hotel. elegant, grand, luxurious, opulent, smart, stylish, sumptuous, swanky (*informal*), swish (*informal*), upmarket.
OPPOSITE downmarket.

position *noun*
1 *We found their position on the map.* locality, location, place, point, site, situation, spot, whereabouts.
2 *out of its correct position.* niche, place, possie (*Australian informal*), setting, slot, spot.
3 *a difficult yoga position.* pose, posture, stance.
4 *a person's financial position.* circumstances, condition, situation, state.
5 *What is his position on uranium mining?* attitude, line, opinion, stance, stand, standpoint, view, viewpoint.
6 *She has taken up a position in a legal firm.* appointment, job, occupation, office, post, situation.
position *verb*
She positioned the photographs in the album. arrange, lay out, line up, mount, place, put, set.

positive *adjective*
1 *He was positive that he was right.* assured, certain, cocksure, confident, convinced, definite, sure.
OPPOSITE unsure.
2 *They had positive proof.* absolute, conclusive, definite, firm, indisputable, irrefutable, sure, undeniable.
OPPOSITE inconclusive.
3 (*informal*) *He's a positive genius.* absolute, complete, downright, real, true, utter.
4 *She made some positive suggestions.* beneficial, constructive, helpful, practical, useful.
OPPOSITE negative, useless.
5 *a positive answer.* affirmative.
OPPOSITE negative.
6 *Maintain a positive attitude.* hopeful, optimistic.
OPPOSITE negative, pessimistic.

possess *verb*
1 *He possesses a large fortune.* have, hold, own.

2 *He was possessed by a demon.* control, dominate, govern, influence, rule.

possessions *plural noun*
He looks after his possessions. assets, belongings, effects, gear, goods, property, stuff, things.

possessive *adjective*
He was possessive about his friends. clinging, domineering, jealous, proprietorial.

possibility *noun*
1 *the possibility of rain.* chance, likelihood, probability, risk.
2 *The plan has possibilities.* potential, potentiality, promise, prospects.

possible *adjective*
1 *It is not possible to do that.* achievable, attainable, feasible, manageable, practicable, viable, workable.
OPPOSITE impossible, impracticable.
2 *a possible solution.* admissible, conceivable, credible, reasonable.
OPPOSITE impossible, unthinkable.
3 *a possible winner.* likely, potential.
OPPOSITE unlikely.

possibly *adverb*
Possibly, he might come. maybe, perchance, perhaps.

post¹ *noun*
The post is leaning over. column, paling, picket, pier, pile, pillar, pole, prop, shaft, stake, stilt, support, upright.
post *verb*
He posted the notice on the board. display, paste up, pin up, put up, stick up.

post² *noun*
1 *The sentries are at their posts.* place, point, position, station.
2 *She resigned her post in the company.* appointment, employment, job, occupation, office, position, situation, work.
post *verb*
1 *They posted lookouts at the entrances.* install, place, position, put, set, station.
2 *The journalist was posted to New York.* appoint, assign, send.

post³ *noun*
We received some interesting post today. correspondence, letters, mail, packets.

a
b
c
d
e
f
g
h
i
j
k
l
m
n
o
p
q
r
s
t
u
v
w
x
y
z

post *verb*
He posted two letters. dispatch, mail, send.
keep posted *Keep me posted on what's happening.* advise, brief, inform, notify.

postbox *noun*
letterbox, mailbox, pillar box (*old use*).

poster *noun*
Posters were stuck up on the walls. advertisement, bill, notice, placard, sign.

posterity *noun*
1 *Posterity will judge the merits of his plan.* future generations.
2 *The benefits will go to his posterity.* children, descendants, heirs, offspring, progeny.

post-mortem *noun*
A post-mortem was carried out on the victim. autopsy.

postpone *verb*
They postponed their holiday. defer, delay, hold over, put off, shelve.
OPPOSITE bring forward.

postscript *noun*
a postscript to the report. addendum, addition, afterthought, epilogue, PS.

posture *noun*
Fitness classes improved his posture. bearing, carriage, deportment, stance.

posy *noun*
a posy of carnations. bouquet, bunch, corsage, nosegay, spray.

pot *noun*
1 *a cooking pot.* billy, casserole, cauldron, crockpot, dixie, pan, quartpot, saucepan, urn, vessel.
2 *He put the plant in a pot.* flowerpot, planter.

potent *adjective*
a potent drug. effective, heady, intoxicating, overpowering, powerful, strong.
OPPOSITE weak.

potential *adjective*
a potential genius. budding, likely, possible, promising.

potential *noun*
This candidate shows a lot of potential. ability, aptitude, capability, possibility, promise.

potion *noun*
He drank the magic potion. brew, concoction, drink, liquid, mixture.

pottery *noun*
ceramics, china, crockery, earthenware, porcelain, stoneware, terracotta.

potty *adjective*
see CRAZY.

pouch *noun*
a money pouch. bag, dillybag (*Australian*), holder, pocket, purse, sack, wallet.

poultry *noun*
[*kinds of poultry*] bantam, chicken, chook (*Australian informal*), cock, cockerel, duck, fowl, goose, guinea fowl, hen, pullet, rooster, turkey.

pounce *verb*
pounce on *The cat pounced on the sparrow.* ambush, attack, fall upon, jump on, leap on, seize, spring on, swoop down on.
pounce *noun*
With a single pounce the cat had stunned the mouse. jump, leap, spring, swoop.

pound[1] *noun*
Stray dogs are taken to the pound. compound, enclosure, pen, yard.

pound[2] *verb*
1 *He pounded the seeds into a powder.* crush, grind, pulverise.
2 *She pounded the vegetables into a purée.* mash, pulp, squash.
3 *She pounded on the door. He pounded the man's back.* bang, batter, beat, clobber (*slang*), hammer, hit, knock, pummel, thump.
4 *Her heart was pounding.* beat, palpitate, pulsate, throb, thump.

pour *verb*
1 *Water was pouring out of the burst pipe.* cascade, discharge, flow, gush, issue, run, spill, spout, spurt, stream.

2 *We stayed indoors because it was pouring.* bucket, deluge, pelt, rain cats and dogs (*informal*), teem.
3 *The shoppers poured into the store.* flood, rush, stream, swarm, throng.

poverty *noun*
Many people live in poverty. beggary, deprivation, destitution, hardship, impoverishment, need, want.
OPPOSITE wealth.

poverty-stricken *adjective*
see POOR.

power *noun*
1 *It taxed his mental powers.* ability, capability, capacity, competence, faculty, skill, talent.
2 *a man of great physical power.* energy, force, might, muscle, strength, vigour.
OPPOSITE weakness.
3 *political power.* authority, clout (*informal*), control, dominance, dominion, influence, leverage, muscle, sway.
OPPOSITE impotence.
4 *They have no legal power to do that.* authority, jurisdiction, licence, right.

powerful *adjective*
1 *a powerful footballer.* dynamic, energetic, hefty, invincible, mighty, robust, strong, sturdy.
OPPOSITE weak, weedy.
2 *a powerful argument.* authoritative, convincing, effective, forceful, influential, persuasive, potent, sound, strong, weighty.
OPPOSITE weak.
3 *a powerful voice.* loud, penetrating, resonant, sonorous, strong.
OPPOSITE gentle, soft.

powerless *adjective*
1 *He takes advantage of powerless people.* defenceless, feeble, helpless, impotent, weak.
OPPOSITE powerful.
2 *powerless to help.* incapable (of), unable.
OPPOSITE able.

practicable *adjective*
The proposal to interview everyone is not practicable. feasible, manageable, possible, practical, realistic, viable, workable.
OPPOSITE impracticable.

practical *adjective*
1 *no practical experience.* applied, hands-on.
OPPOSITE theoretical.
2 *a practical gadget.* functional, handy, usable, useful.
OPPOSITE impractical, useless.
3 *a practical handyman.* capable, competent, handy, proficient, skilled.
4 *It's nice to dream, but let's be practical.* businesslike, down-to-earth, pragmatic, realistic, sensible.
OPPOSITE impractical, unrealistic.
practical joke hoax, prank, trick.

practically *adverb*
There was practically no hope. almost, close to, essentially, nearly, virtually.

practice *noun*
1 *It works well in practice.* action, effect, operation, use.
OPPOSITE theory.
2 *It is his practice to shake each person's hand.* convention, custom, habit, procedure, ritual, routine, tradition.
3 *Practice makes perfect.* drill, preparation, rehearsal, training.

practise *verb*
1 *She is practising for the exam.* brush up, drill, exercise, rehearse, train.
2 *He did not practise what he preached.* apply, carry out, do, perform.
3 *She no longer practises medicine.* engage in, pursue, work at.

praise *verb*
1 *The paper praised the rescuer for his actions.* acclaim, applaud, commend, compliment, congratulate, honour, pay homage to, pay tribute to.
OPPOSITE criticise.
2 *The people praise God.* adore, exalt, glorify, hallow, honour, laud (*formal*), magnify (*old use*), revere, venerate, worship.

praise *noun*
The praise was deserved. acclaim, accolade, applause, commendation, compliment, congratulations, eulogy, homage, honour, ovation, tribute.
OPPOSITE criticism.

a
b
c
d
e
f
g
h
i
j
k
l
m
n
o
p
q
r
s
t
u
v
w
x
y
z

praiseworthy *adjective*
a praiseworthy result. admirable, commendable, creditable, deserving, honourable, laudable, meritorious, worthy.
OPPOSITE dishonourable.

pram *noun*
baby buggy, baby carriage, perambulator, pushchair, pusher (*Australian*), stroller.

prance *verb*
They pranced happily around the stage. caper, cavort, dance, frisk, frolic, jump, leap, romp, skip.

prank *noun*
The first day of April is a day of pranks. antic, caper, escapade, hoax, lark, practical joke, trick.

pray *verb*
I pray you not to touch anything. appeal to, ask, beg, beseech, entreat, implore, plead with, urge.

prayer *noun*
The service included prayers and hymns. benediction, blessing, collect, devotion, entreaty, intercession, litany, petition, request, supplication, thanksgiving.

preach *verb*
1 *He preached a provocative sermon.* deliver.
2 *He preached the gospel.* expound, proclaim, teach.
3 *She's always preaching at them.* lecture, moralise, sermonise.

preacher *noun*
The preacher had an attentive audience. chaplain, clergyman, clergywoman, curate, evangelist, minister, missionary, padre, parson, pastor, priest, rector, vicar.

prearrange *verb*
They prearranged the meeting place. fix, plan, predetermine.

precarious *adjective*
1 *a precarious position on the edge of the cliff.* dangerous, hazardous, insecure, perilous, rocky, shaky, unsafe, unstable, unsteady, vulnerable.
OPPOSITE secure.
2 *a precarious operation.* chancy, delicate, dicey (*slang*), dodgy (*informal*), risky, ticklish, touch-and-go.
OPPOSITE safe.

precaution *noun*
a precaution against sunburn. defence, preventive measure, protection, safeguard, safety measure.

precede *verb*
Summer precedes autumn. come before, go before, lead into, usher in.
OPPOSITE follow, succeed.

precedent *noun*
The ruling in the case set a precedent. example, model, pattern, standard.

precious *adjective*
1 *precious jewels.* costly, dear, expensive, invaluable, priceless, valuable.
OPPOSITE worthless.
2 *precious memories.* beloved, cherished, dear, prized, treasured, valuable.

precipice *noun*
He injured his back when he fell down the precipice. bluff, cliff, crag, escarpment, rockface, scarp.

precipitation *noun*
Annual precipitation is 100 centimetres. dew, hail, rain, rainfall, sleet, snow, snowfall.

précis *noun*
He read a précis of the document. abstract, outline, résumé, summary, synopsis.

precise *adjective*
1 *at that precise moment.* exact, particular, specific, very.
2 *precise details.* clear, definite, exact, explicit, minute, specific.
OPPOSITE hazy, imprecise.
3 *He is very precise in his work.* accurate, careful, correct, fastidious, finicky, meticulous, painstaking, particular, pernickety (*informal*), scrupulous.
OPPOSITE careless, hit-or-miss.

precisely *adverb*
1 *precisely in the middle.* bang (*informal*), exactly, right, smack (*informal*).

2 *at six o'clock precisely.* on the dot, on the knocker (*Australian informal*), punctually, sharp.

precocious *adjective*
a precocious child. advanced, bright, forward, gifted, mature, quick.
OPPOSITE backward.

predator *noun*
the animal is a predator. hunter, marauder.
OPPOSITE prey.

predecessor *noun*
a history of the man's predecessors. ancestor, forebear, forefather.
OPPOSITE descendant.

predestine *verb*
She believed that she was predestined to work there. destine, fate, intend, mean, preordain.

predicament *noun*
He found himself in a terrible predicament. difficulty, dilemma, emergency, fix (*informal*), jam (*informal*), mess, pickle (*informal*), plight, quandary, spot (*informal*), trouble.

predict *verb*
He predicted that it would be fine. forecast, foretell, prophesy.

predictable *adjective*
The result was predictable. expected, foreseeable, on the cards, unsurprising.
OPPOSITE unpredictable.

prediction *noun*
His prediction turned out to be spot on. forecast, prognosis, prophecy.

predominant *adjective*
The predominant feeling was anger. chief, dominant, main, major, paramount, prevailing, primary.
OPPOSITE subordinate.

preen *verb*
The bird was preening itself. clean, groom, neaten, plume, smarten, tidy.

preface *noun*
He read the preface to the book. foreword, introduction, preamble, prologue.
OPPOSITE epilogue.

prefer *verb*
She prefers those chocolates. choose, fancy, favour, like better, opt for, pick out, select.

preference *noun*
1 *a preference for classical music.* fondness, inclination, leaning, liking, partiality, predilection.
OPPOSITE dislike.
2 *They were given their first preference.* choice, option, pick, selection.

pregnant *adjective*
The woman is pregnant. expectant, expecting, with child (*literary*).

prehistoric *adjective*
prehistoric times. ancient, earliest, olden (*old use*), primeval, primitive.
OPPOSITE future.

prejudice *noun*
a victim of racial prejudice. bias, bigotry, discrimination, intolerance, unfairness.

prejudiced *adjective*
The adjudicator was prejudiced. biased, bigoted, discriminatory, intolerant, narrow-minded, one-sided, partisan, unfair.
OPPOSITE unbiased.

preliminary *adjective*
preliminary lessons. preliminary remarks. early, first, initial, introductory, opening, preparatory.
OPPOSITE concluding.
preliminary *noun*
He played better in the preliminaries. elimination round, heat, qualifying round.
OPPOSITE final.

prelude *noun*
The parade was a colourful prelude to the festival. beginning, curtain-raiser, introduction, opening, overture, precursor, preface, prologue, start.
OPPOSITE conclusion.

premature *adjective*
a premature decision. hasty, precipitate, too early, too soon, untimely.

a
b
c
d
e
f
g
h
i
j
k
l
m
n
o
p
q
r
s
t
u
v
w
x
y
z

premises *plural noun*
They moved to new premises.
accommodation, building, campus,
house, property, site.

premonition *noun*
He had a premonition that an accident
would happen. feeling, foreboding,
hunch, intuition, suspicion.

preoccupied *adjective*
1 He was preoccupied with work.
absorbed, engrossed, immersed,
wrapped up.
2 He wasn't listening properly because he
was preoccupied. absent-minded, lost in
thought, pensive.

preparation *noun*
1 All the preparations for the event were
completed. arrangement, groundwork,
organisation, plan, planning,
spadework.
2 She did her preparation for her music
lesson. homework, practice, prep.
3 The doctor prescribed a skin preparation.
concoction, mixture, product,
substance.

preparatory *adjective*
a preparatory lesson. introductory,
preliminary.

prepare *verb*
1 She prepared the table for dinner.
arrange, get ready, lay, organise, set.
2 He was well prepared for the job. brief,
equip, groom, prime, train.
3 She prepared her item for the concert.
practise, rehearse, work on.
4 She prepared an interesting programme.
arrange, design, develop, devise, map
out, organise, plan.
5 She prepared a delicious dessert. concoct,
cook, make, mix, produce, put together,
whip up.
be prepared to He was not prepared to
resign. be minded to, be ready to, be
willing to.

preposterous *adjective*
What a preposterous idea! absurd, crazy,
farcical, laughable, ludicrous,
monstrous, nonsensical, outrageous,
ridiculous, unthinkable, weird.

prerequisite *noun*
Ability to drive a car is a prerequisite for
the job. condition, essential, must
(*informal*), necessity, pre-condition,
requirement.

preschool *noun*
kindergarten, nursery school.

prescribe *verb*
1 The doctor prescribed an antibiotic.
advise, order, recommend, suggest.
2 He likes to prescribe what others should
do. dictate, lay down, ordain, order,
specify, stipulate.

presence *noun*
His presence is required. attendance,
company.
OPPOSITE absence.

present[1] *adjective*
1 Is there a doctor present? about, at
hand, here, in attendance, on the scene,
on the spot.
OPPOSITE absent.
2 the present situation. contemporary,
current, existing, immediate.
3 the present champion. current, existing,
reigning.
present *noun*
He lives for the present. here and now,
now, today.
CONTRASTS WITH future, past.

present[2] *noun*
They gave a costly present. contribution,
donation, gift, offering, tip.
present *verb*
1 She presented the prizes. award, bestow,
confer, distribute, donate, give, hand
out, hand over.
2 He presented his views clearly.
communicate, declare, give, impart,
make known, put forward, recount,
relate, state.
3 He presented her to his parents.
introduce, make known.
4 They presented their latest products at the
show. demonstrate, display, exhibit,
reveal, show.
5 The students presented a French comedy.
act, mount, perform, put on, stage.
present itself No suitable occasion
presented itself. arise, eventuate, happen,
occur.

present yourself *They presented themselves in court.* appear, arrive, attend, front up (*informal*), turn up.

presentable *adjective*
He looked presentable in a borrowed suit. acceptable, all right, decent, neat, OK (*informal*), passable, respectable, satisfactory, suitable, tidy.

presentation *noun*
1 *The project was marked on both content and presentation.* appearance, arrangement, form, layout, structure, style.
2 *We enjoyed the children's end-of-year presentation.* demonstration, display, exhibition, performance, production, show.

presently *adverb*
1 *We shall see you again presently.* before long, directly, in a moment, shortly, soon.
2 *He is in a meeting presently.* at present, currently, now.

preserve *verb*
1 *We want to preserve our heritage.* conserve, defend, guard, keep, keep safe, look after, maintain, protect, retain, safeguard, save, secure.
OPPOSITE destroy.
2 *She learned ways to preserve fruit, meat, fish, etc.* bottle, can, corn, cure, dry, freeze, pickle, salt, smoke, tin.
preserve *noun*
She eats quince preserve on her toast. conserve, jam, jelly.

preside *verb*
preside over *She is presiding over the meeting.* be in charge of, chair, conduct, control, direct, run.

president *noun*
the society's president. chairman, chairperson, chairwoman, director, head, leader.

press *verb*
1 *Press the button.* depress, push.
2 *The recipe says to press the fruit.* compress, crush, mash, squash, squeeze.
3 *She presses her own clothes.* flatten, iron, smooth.

4 *They pressed him to make a speech.* coerce, compel, constrain, force, implore, order, persuade, pressure, require, urge.
5 *He pressed for a higher salary.* campaign, demand, hold out, insist on, push, stick out (*informal*).
press *noun*
good coverage in the press. journals, magazines, newspapers, papers, periodicals, print media.

pressing *adjective*
a pressing need. critical, crucial, essential, important, urgent, vital.
OPPOSITE unimportant.

pressure *noun*
1 *He applied pressure to the wound to stop the bleeding.* compression, force.
2 *financial pressures.* burden, constraint, demand, difficulty, hardship, hassle (*informal*), load, oppression, strain, stress, tension.
3 *They put pressure on him to resign.* coercion, compulsion, force.
pressure *verb*
They pressured him into signing. bully, coerce, compel, constrain, drive, force, lean on (*informal*), persuade, press, put pressure on, railroad.

prestige *noun*
Her job gave her prestige. celebrity, fame, glamour, glory, honour, kudos, renown, reputation, status.

presume *verb*
1 *He presumed that she was telling the truth.* assume, believe, guess, imagine, presuppose, suppose, surmise, take for granted, take it.
2 *He presumed to advise a stranger.* be so bold as, dare, have the audacity, take the liberty, venture.

presumption *noun*
1 *Their action was based on a wrong presumption.* assumption, belief, premise, presupposition, supposition, surmise.
2 *He had the presumption to put himself at the head of the table.* arrogance, audacity, boldness, cheek, impertinence, impudence, nerve (*informal*), presumptuousness.

a
b
c
d
e
f
g
h
i
j
k
l
m
n
o
p
q
r
s
t
u
v
w
x
y
z

presumptuous *adjective*
It was presumptuous to come without an invitation. arrogant, audacious, bold, cheeky, cocky, forward, impertinent, impudent, overconfident.

pretence *noun*
Her sympathy was all a pretence. act, charade, cover, deception, front, hoax, hypocrisy, lie, make-believe, masquerade, put-on (*informal*), ruse, sham, show, trick.

pretend *verb*
1 She isn't sick: she's just pretending. act, bluff, deceive, fake, kid (*informal*), make believe, put it on (*informal*), sham.
2 He pretended to be a policeman. act as, impersonate, masquerade as, pass yourself off as, pose as.
3 He pretended that he knew. claim, make believe, make out, profess.

pretentious *adjective*
He felt uncomfortable with such pretentious people. affected, arty (*informal*), la-di-da (*informal*), ostentatious, pompous, self-important, snobbish, stuck-up (*informal*), toffee-nosed (*informal*).
OPPOSITE unpretentious.

pretty *adjective*
1 a pretty girl. appealing, attractive, beautiful, bonny (*Scottish*), captivating, charming, dainty, fair (*old use*), fetching, good-looking, handsome, lovely, nice, pleasing, sweet (*informal*).
OPPOSITE plain, ugly.
2 pretty scenery. attractive, beautiful, breathtaking, picturesque, scenic, spectacular.
OPPOSITE drab.
pretty *adverb*
pretty good. fairly, moderately, quite, rather, reasonably, somewhat.

prevailing *adjective*
the prevailing wind. chief, common, dominant, main, predominant, usual.

prevalent *adjective*
the prevalent view. common, current, dominant, general, popular, predominant, prevailing, usual, widespread.
OPPOSITE rare.

prevent *verb*
The vaccine will prevent the spread of the disease. avert, avoid, block, curb, deter, fend off, halt, hamper, hinder, impede, inhibit, obstruct, stave off, stop, thwart, ward off.
OPPOSITE cause, enable.

previous *adjective*
1 his previous boss. ex-, former, past.
2 The article was in a previous issue. back, earlier, past, preceding, prior.
OPPOSITE subsequent.

previously *adverb*
the article mentioned previously. above, before, earlier.
OPPOSITE subsequently.

prey *noun*
The cat killed its prey. quarry, victim.
OPPOSITE predator.
prey *verb*
prey on
1 The cat preys on mice. devour, eat, feed on, hunt, kill.
2 It preyed on his conscience. haunt, trouble, weigh on, worry.

price *noun*
1 the price of goods or services. amount, charge, cost, fare, fee, payment, rate, sum, terms, toll, value, worth.
2 That's the price you pay for foolishness. consequence, cost, penalty, punishment, sacrifice.

priceless *adjective*
1 priceless antiques. costly, dear, expensive, invaluable, irreplaceable, precious, pricey (*informal*), valuable.
OPPOSITE cheap, worthless.
2 (*informal*) The story she told us was priceless. absurd, amusing, funny, hilarious.

prick *verb*
The needle pricked his skin. jab, lance, perforate, pierce, puncture, stab.
prick *noun*
He felt a sharp prick. jab, pinprick, prickle, stab, sting.

prickle *noun*
The plant had sharp prickles. barb, needle, spike, spine, thorn.
prickle *verb*
His skin prickled after he touched the plant. itch, smart, sting, tingle.

pride *noun*
1 *She takes pride in her work.* delight, enjoyment, gratification, happiness, joy, pleasure, satisfaction.
2 *His new baby is his pride and joy.* delight, joy, pleasure.
3 *He wouldn't do that. He has his pride.* dignity, honour, self-esteem, self-respect.
4 *Pride goeth before a fall.* arrogance, conceit, egotism, self-importance, self-love, self-satisfaction, smugness, vanity.
OPPOSITE humility.

pride *verb*
pride yourself on *He prided himself on his ironing.* be proud of, boast about, congratulate yourself on, flatter yourself on.

priest *noun*
a priest in the Christian church. archdeacon, chaplain, chief priest, clergyman, clergywoman, cleric, father, high priest, minister, padre, parson, pastor, rector, vicar.

prim *adjective*
The children's behaviour offended the prim old lady. demure, formal, old-fashioned, precise, prissy, proper, prudish, starchy, strait-laced, stuffy.
OPPOSITE broad-minded.

primarily *adverb*
His tasks are primarily administrative. basically, chiefly, essentially, firstly, fundamentally, generally, largely, mainly, mostly, predominantly, principally.
OPPOSITE secondarily.

primary *adjective*
1 *primary education.* basic, elementary, first.
OPPOSITE secondary.
2 *our primary purpose.* chief, essential, fundamental, key, main, major, paramount, prime, principal.
OPPOSITE secondary.

prime *adjective*
1 *the prime motive.* chief, key, leading, main, major, primary, principal.
OPPOSITE secondary.
2 *prime beef.* best, excellent, first-class, superior, top-quality.
OPPOSITE inferior.

prime *noun*
past their prime. best, heyday, peak, zenith.

primitive *adjective*
1 *a primitive tribe.* ancient, old, prehistoric, primeval, uncivilised.
OPPOSITE civilised.
2 *primitive methods.* archaic, basic, crude, elementary, obsolete, old-fashioned, rough, rudimentary, simple, unsophisticated.
OPPOSITE advanced.

principal *adjective*
1 *the principal features.* basic, chief, dominant, essential, foremost, fundamental, leading, main, major, outstanding, predominant, primary, prime, supreme.
OPPOSITE minor, secondary.
2 *the principal city.* capital, chief, main, major.

principal *noun*
1 *the school principal.* head, headmaster, headmistress, head teacher.
2 *She was paid interest on the principal.* capital.

principle *noun*
1 *a scientific principle.* assumption, axiom, law, rule, truth.
2 *She follows certain principles of behaviour.* belief, guideline, precept, rule, standard, tenet.
3 *a man of principle.* conscience, ethics, honesty, honour, integrity, morality, morals, scruples, standards, virtue.

print *verb*
They print 100 copies of the newsletter. produce, reproduce, run off; see also PUBLISH.

print *noun*
1 *His feet left prints in the cement.* impression, imprint, indentation, mark, stamp, track.
2 *The book has large print.* font, letters, type, typeface.
3 *a print of the original drawing.* copy, duplicate, facsimile, replica, reproduction.

printout *noun*
He read the computer printout. hard copy, output.

a
b
c
d
e
f
g
h
i
j
k
l
m
n
o
p
q
r
s
t
u
v
w
x
y
z

prior *adjective*
a prior engagement. a prior claim. earlier, pre-existing, previous.
OPPOSITE subsequent.
prior *adverb*
prior to see BEFORE.

priority *noun*
His request was given priority. precedence, preference.

priory *noun*
abbey, cloister, convent, friary, monastery, nunnery, religious house.

prise *verb*
She prised the lid off. force, lever, wrench.

prison *noun*
The prison was built last century. detention centre, dungeon, jail, lock-up, nick (*slang*), penitentiary (*American*), remand centre.

prisoner *noun*
captive, convict, detainee, hostage, inmate, internee, jailbird, lag (*slang*).

private *adjective*
1 *a private club.* closed, exclusive, restricted, special.
OPPOSITE public.
2 *private property.* individual, own, personal.
OPPOSITE public.
3 *private thoughts.* innermost, intimate, personal, secret.
4 *The information was to be kept private.* classified, confidential, hush-hush (*informal*), quiet, secret.
OPPOSITE open, public.
5 *a private retreat.* hidden, isolated, off-limits, quiet, remote, secluded.
6 *private school.* independent, non-government.
OPPOSITE state.

privilege *noun*
a staff privilege. advantage, benefit, concession, entitlement, exemption, perk (*informal*), prerogative, right.

prize *noun*
He won the prize. award, crown, cup, jackpot, medal, reward, trophy.

prize *adjective*
a prize pumpkin. award-winning, champion, excellent, first-rate, prize-winning, top, winning.
prize *verb*
She prized the necklace. appreciate, cherish, esteem, treasure, value.

probability *noun*
There is no probability of rain. chance, likelihood, possibility, prospect.

probable *adjective*
It's probable the match will end in a draw. expected, likely, on the cards, predictable.
OPPOSITE improbable.

probe *noun*
They conducted a probe into his business dealings. examination, exploration, inquiry, inspection, investigation, study.
probe *verb*
1 *He probed the wound for bits of glass.* examine, explore, feel around, poke, prod.
2 *She probed his motives.* examine, inquire into, investigate, look into, question, scrutinise, sound out.

problem *noun*
1 *mathematical problems.* conundrum, mystery, poser, puzzle, question, riddle, sum, teaser.
2 *technical problems. financial problems.* bug (*informal*), burden, complication, concern, difficulty, dilemma, hassle (*informal*), headache, hitch, predicament, setback, snag, strife (*Australian informal*), trouble, worry.

procedure *noun*
He followed the procedure for handling enquiries. method, operation, practice, process, routine, system, technique, way.

proceed *verb*
1 *They proceeded to the hotel.* advance, go on, head, make your way, move on, progress, push on.
OPPOSITE retreat.
2 *Business proceeded, uninterrupted.* carry on, continue, go on, keep going.
OPPOSITE halt.

proceedings *plural noun*
1 *She instituted divorce proceedings.*
action, lawsuit, legal action.
2 *He was present during the entire proceedings.* actions, activities, business, events, goings-on, happenings.

proceeds *plural noun*
He gave away the proceeds from the sale.
earnings, gain, income, profit(s), revenue, takings.

process *noun*
1 *a process for making paper.* means, method, operation, procedure, system, technique, way.
2 *It was in the process of being built.*
course, progress.
process *verb*
1 *They process the raw materials.* change, convert, refine, transform, treat.
2 *They processed her application.* deal with, handle, take care of.

procession *noun*
Shoppers stopped to watch the procession along the street. cavalcade, cortège, line, march, motorcade, pageant, parade.

proclaim *verb*
The officer proclaimed the good news.
advertise, announce, broadcast, circulate, declare, make known, pronounce, publicise, publish, tell, trumpet.

procrastinate *verb*
He procrastinated too long over the decision. dally, delay, dilly-dally *(informal)*, dither, drag your feet, hesitate, hold off, play for time, stall.

procure *verb*
The book is difficult to procure. acquire, buy, come by, find, get, get hold of, obtain, pick up.

prod *verb*
1 *She prodded him to wake him up.* butt, elbow, jab, nudge, poke.
2 *They need to be prodded into action.*
goad, prompt, push, rouse, spur, stimulate, stir, urge.
prod *noun*
1 *She gave the bundle a prod.* butt, elbow, jab, nudge, poke.

2 *He needs a prod to get started on the cleaning.* prompt, reminder, spur, stimulus.

prodigal *adjective*
the prodigal son. extravagant, improvident, profligate, spendthrift, wasteful.
OPPOSITE thrifty.

prodigy *noun*
a musical prodigy. genius, marvel, sensation, virtuoso, whiz-kid *(informal)*, wizard.

produce *verb*
1 *She produced new evidence.* bring forward, come up with, disclose, display, exhibit, present, provide, reveal, show, supply.
OPPOSITE withhold.
2 *The tree will produce a lot of fruit.* bear, bring forth, generate, yield.
3 *They produced offspring.* bear, beget, breed, bring forth, give birth to, raise, rear, reproduce.
4 *This produced a sensation.* bring about, cause, create, give rise to, provoke, raise.
5 *The firm produces electrical appliances.* assemble, build, construct, create, fabricate, form, invent, make, manufacture, turn out.
6 *He produced a piece of music.* compose, create, devise, think up, write.
produce *noun*
They cook with fresh garden produce. crops, foodstuffs, harvest, products, yield.

product *noun*
manufactured products. artefact, article, commodity, creation, item, object, production, thing; [*products*] goods, merchandise, output, produce, wares.

productive *adjective*
1 *The soil is productive.* fertile, fruitful, prolific, rich.
OPPOSITE barren, sterile.
2 *productive workers.* active, busy, dynamic, effective, efficient, energetic, prolific.
OPPOSITE unproductive.
3 *a productive meeting.* beneficial, constructive, profitable, useful,

a
b
c
d
e
f
g
h
i
j
k
l
m
n
o
p
q
r
s
t
u
v
w
x
y
z

valuable, worthwhile.
OPPOSITE unproductive, useless.

profess *verb*
1 *She professed a liking for classical music.* assert, claim, confess, declare, pronounce, state.
2 *He professed to be an expert.* allege, claim, make out, pretend, purport.

profession *noun*
a profession in journalism. calling, career, employment, job, occupation, vocation.

professional *adjective*
1 *a professional opinion.* expert, knowledgeable, qualified, skilled, trained.
OPPOSITE amateur.
2 *He did a professional job.* competent, expert, proficient, skilful.
OPPOSITE amateurish, unprofessional.
3 *a professional tennis-player.* paid.
OPPOSITE amateur.

professional *noun*
The job was done by a professional. authority, expert, master, pro (*informal*), specialist.
OPPOSITE amateur.

proficient *adjective*
a proficient carpenter. able, accomplished, adept, capable, competent, deft, dexterous, expert, skilful, skilled, trained.
OPPOSITE inept.

profile *noun*
1 *They traced each other's profile.* contour, outline, shape, silhouette.
2 *The book contains profiles of our prime ministers.* account, biography, character sketch, description.

profit *noun*
1 *She could see no profit in reading those magazines.* advantage, benefit, gain, good, use, value.
OPPOSITE disadvantage.
2 *The company made a big profit.* gain, proceeds, return.
OPPOSITE loss.

profit *verb*
profit from *He profited from the time spent in the library.* be helped by, benefit from, gain from, make the most of.

profitable *adjective*
1 *a profitable meeting.* advantageous, beneficial, helpful, productive, rewarding, useful, valuable, worthwhile.
2 *a profitable enterprise.* lucrative, moneymaking, paying, remunerative.
OPPOSITE unprofitable.

profound *adjective*
1 *He expressed profound sympathy.* deep, great, heartfelt, sincere.
OPPOSITE insincere.
2 *a profound discussion.* deep, intellectual, learned, serious, thoughtful, wise.
OPPOSITE shallow, superficial.

profuse *adjective*
1 *profuse apologies.* abundant, ample, copious, plentiful.
OPPOSITE sparing.
2 *a profuse sweat.* copious, excessive, heavy.
OPPOSITE light.

prognosis *noun*
The patient's prognosis was good. forecast, prediction.

programme *noun*
1 *the programme of events.* agenda, calendar, plan, schedule, timetable.
2 *a TV or radio programme.* broadcast, performance, presentation, production, show, telecast.

programme *verb*
She programmed her appointments for Monday. arrange, line up, organise, plan, schedule.

progress *noun*
1 *The hikers were making good progress each day.* advance, headway, strides.
2 *He surveyed the progress of scientific knowledge.* advance, advancement, development, evolution, expansion, growth, improvement, march.
OPPOSITE regression.

progress *verb*
The work progressed quickly. advance, come along, come on, continue, develop, go ahead, improve, make headway, move ahead, move forward, move on, proceed.
OPPOSITE regress.

in progress *The demolition is in progress.*
going on, happening, proceeding,
taking place, under way.

progression *noun*
The children had a progression of nannies.
sequence, series, string, succession.

progressive *adjective*
1 *a progressive improvement.* continuous,
gradual, ongoing, steady.
OPPOSITE sudden, uneven.
2 *a progressive company.* avant-garde,
enlightened, enterprising, forward-
thinking, go-ahead, innovative,
modern, up-and-coming (*informal*).
OPPOSITE conservative.

prohibit *verb*
1 *Smoking is prohibited in the lifts.* ban,
bar, forbid, outlaw, proscribe, veto.
OPPOSITE permit.
2 *His blindness prohibits his becoming a
pilot.* preclude, prevent, rule out, stop.

project *verb*
1 *The shelf projects over the fireplace.*
extend, jut out, overhang, protrude,
stand out, stick out.
2 *He projected the missile at the target.*
cast, fling, hurl, launch, propel, shoot,
throw.
project *noun*
1 *a redevelopment project.* plan, proposal,
scheme, undertaking, venture.
2 *Students did projects on various subjects.*
assignment, exercise, task.

projection *noun*
1 *They stood on a narrow projection.*
ledge, overhang, ridge, shelf.
2 *projections of unemployment figures.*
estimate, estimation, forecast,
prediction.

prolific *adjective*
a prolific peach tree. fertile, fruitful,
productive.
OPPOSITE unproductive.

prologue *noun*
The play begins with a prologue. foreword,
introduction, preamble, preface,
prelude.
OPPOSITE epilogue.

prolong *verb*
He tried not to prolong the pain. drag out,
draw out, extend, lengthen, protract,
spin out, stretch out, string out.
OPPOSITE shorten.

promenade *noun*
1 *He went for a promenade along the beach.*
amble, saunter, stroll, walk.
2 *People enjoy walking along the
promenade.* boulevard, esplanade, mall,
parade.

prominent *adjective*
1 *She had her prominent nose reshaped.*
jutting out, projecting, protruding,
sticking out.
2 *the prominent features.* conspicuous,
noticeable, obtrusive, obvious,
pronounced, striking.
OPPOSITE inconspicuous.
3 *a prominent academic.* celebrated,
distinguished, eminent, famous,
illustrious, important, notable,
outstanding, pre-eminent, renowned,
well-known.
OPPOSITE unknown.

promise *noun*
1 *He broke his promise.* assurance,
commitment, contract, covenant,
guarantee, oath, pledge, vow, word,
word of honour.
2 *His work shows promise.* aptitude,
capability, potential, talent.
promise *verb*
*He promised us that he would be there. He
promised to come.* agree, assure, commit
yourself, give your word, guarantee,
pledge, swear, undertake, vow.

promising *adjective*
1 *a promising start to the day.* auspicious,
encouraging, favourable, propitious,
reassuring.
OPPOSITE discouraging.
2 *a promising actor.* able, gifted, talented,
up-and-coming (*informal*).

promontory *noun*
*The view from the promontory out to sea
was superb.* cape, head, headland, point.

promote *verb*
1 *He was promoted to a supervisory
position.* elevate, move up, raise,

a b c d e f g h i j k l m n o p q r s t u v w x y z

upgrade.
OPPOSITE demote.
2 *The society promotes understanding.* advance, boost, encourage, foster, further, help, sponsor, support.
OPPOSITE obstruct.
3 *They need to promote their product.* advertise, make known, market, plug (*informal*), publicise, push.

prompt *adjective*
1 *He received a prompt answer.* early, immediate, instant, instantaneous, quick, speedy, swift.
OPPOSITE belated.
2 *Please be prompt.* on time, punctual.
OPPOSITE late.
prompt *verb*
1 *His comments prompted her to apologise.* egg on, encourage, induce, influence, inspire, motivate, move, spur, stimulate.
2 *She prompted the actors when they forgot their lines.* cue, jog the memory of, remind.

promptly *adverb*
1 *He dealt promptly with the problem.* at once, immediately, quickly, readily, right away, speedily, straight away, swiftly, without delay.
2 *The guests left promptly at eight o'clock.* on the dot, on the knocker (*Australian informal*), on time, punctually.
OPPOSITE late.

prone *adjective*
1 *He was lying prone on the bed.* face down, flat, horizontal, prostrate.
CONTRASTS WITH supine, upright.
2 *prone to headaches.* inclined, liable, predisposed, subject, susceptible.
OPPOSITE immune.

prong *noun*
The fork has four prongs. point, spike, tine.

pronounce *verb*
1 *The b is not pronounced in 'lamb'.* articulate, enunciate, say, sound, speak, utter, voice.
2 *The play was pronounced a success.* announce, declare, proclaim.

pronounced *adjective*
The differences were becoming more pronounced. apparent, clear, conspicuous, definite, distinct, evident, marked, noticeable, obvious, prominent, striking, strong, unmistakable.
OPPOSITE faint.

proof *noun*
He has no proof of their guilt. confirmation, demonstration, documentation, evidence, facts, grounds, substantiation, testimony, verification.

prop *noun*
The fence was held up with props. brace, buttress, post, reinforcement, stake, stay, strut, support.
prop *verb*
He propped his bicycle against the tree. lean, rest, stand.
prop up *Two posts propped up the wall.* brace, buttress, hold up, reinforce, shore up, stake, strengthen, support.

propel *verb*
She was propelled from her chair when the spring snapped. catapult, drive, eject, fling, push, send, throw, thrust.

proper *adjective*
1 *This isn't the proper time to tell her.* appropriate, apt, fitting, right, suitable.
OPPOSITE inappropriate.
2 *She learnt to do it the proper way.* accepted, conventional, correct, established, orthodox, right, standard.
OPPOSITE wrong.
3 *Her language and manners were very proper.* conventional, courteous, decent, decorous, dignified, formal, polite, prim, respectable, seemly.
OPPOSITE improper.
4 (*informal*) *We were in a proper mess.* absolute, complete, real, thorough, utter.

property *noun*
1 *Look after your personal property.* belongings, effects, gear, goods, possessions, things.
2 *His property passes to his children on his death.* assets, fortune, riches, wealth.

3 *He invested in property.* buildings, land, real estate.
4 *It has the property of removing stains.* characteristic, feature, quality, trait.

prophecy *noun*
We saw the fulfilment of his prophecy. forecast, prediction.

prophesy *verb*
He prophesied a period of war. forecast, foresee, foretell, predict.

prophet *noun*
The words of the prophet came true. forecaster, fortune-teller, oracle, prophetess (*female*), seer, soothsayer.

proportion *noun*
1 *He is paid a proportion of the profits.* division, fraction, part, percentage, piece, portion, quota, section, share.
2 *The proportion of red to blue varies in each of these purple paints.* balance, ratio, relationship.
proportions *plural noun*
a house of large proportions. dimensions, extent, magnitude, measurements, size.

proposal *noun*
The proposal to build the hall needs council approval. bid, offer, plan, project, proposition, recommendation, scheme, submission, suggestion.

propose *verb*
1 *She proposed a simple solution.* advance, offer, present, put forward, recommend, submit, suggest, tender.
2 *He proposed to ring them back.* aim, intend, mean, plan.

proprietor *noun*
a hotel proprietor. hotel-keeper, landlady, landlord, licensee, manager, owner, proprietress, publican.

propriety *noun*
act with propriety. correctness, courtesy, decency, decorum, politeness, respectability, seemliness.
OPPOSITE impropriety.

prosecute *verb*
They were prosecuted for trespassing. accuse, bring to trial, charge, sue, take to court, try.

prospect *noun*
1 *The prospects of winning were slim.* chance, hope, likelihood, odds, outlook, possibility, probability.
2 *a splendid prospect from the lookout.* outlook, panorama, scene, sight, view, vista.
prospect *verb*
They prospected for gold. explore, fossick (*Australian informal*), look, search.

prosper *verb*
The business prospered. boom, do well, flourish, grow, make money, succeed, thrive.
OPPOSITE fail.

prosperity *noun*
a life of prosperity. affluence, fortune, plenty, riches, success, wealth.

prosperous *adjective*
a prosperous businessman. affluent, flourishing, rich, successful, thriving, wealthy, well off, well-to-do.
OPPOSITE poor, unsuccessful.

protect *verb*
1 *The shepherd protects his flock.* care for, cherish, defend, guard, keep safe, look after, mind, take care of, tend, watch over.
2 *The house is protected from the wind by a row of trees.* screen, shelter, shield.
OPPOSITE expose.
3 *Take insurance to protect yourself against loss.* cover, insure, safeguard, secure.
4 *The wax protects the surface.* coat, insulate, preserve, seal.
OPPOSITE expose.

protection *noun*
protection against disease, loss, etc. armour, barrier, buffer, cover, defence, immunity, insurance, refuge, safeguard, screen, security, shelter, shield.

protective *adjective*
1 *protective towards their children.* possessive, solicitous, vigilant, watchful.
2 *a protective cloth.* covering, insulating, protecting, waterproof.

a
b
c
d
e
f
g
h
i
j
k
l
m
n
o
p
q
r
s
t
u
v
w
x
y
z

protest *noun*
1 *The changes were accepted without any protest.* beef (*slang*), complaint, grumble, hue and cry, objection, outcry.
2 *The workers staged a protest.* boycott, demo (*informal*), demonstration, rally, sit-in, strike.

protest *verb*
They protested at the decision. beef (*slang*), be up in arms, complain, demonstrate, grumble, moan, object, strike.
OPPOSITE approve, support.

protester *noun*
agitator, complainer, demonstrator, objector, striker.
OPPOSITE supporter.

prototype *noun*
the prototype of the car. original, sample, trial model.

protract *verb*
He tried to protract the conversation. drag out, draw out, extend, lengthen, prolong, spin out, stretch out.
OPPOSITE shorten.

protrude *verb*
His stomach protrudes. bulge, jut out, poke out, project, stand out, stick out.

proud *adjective*
1 *proud parents of a new baby.* delighted, happy, pleased, satisfied.
OPPOSITE ashamed, displeased.
2 *They were too proud to ask for help.* dignified, independent, self-respecting.
OPPOSITE humble.
3 *She was so proud that we found her insufferable.* arrogant, boastful, cocky, conceited, disdainful, egotistic(al), haughty, hoity-toity, self-satisfied, smug, snobbish, snooty (*informal*), stuck-up (*informal*), supercilious, superior, vain.
OPPOSITE humble, modest.

prove *verb*
1 *This evidence proves his guilt.* bear out, confirm, corroborate, demonstrate, document, establish, show, substantiate, verify.
OPPOSITE disprove.
2 *It proved to be a mistake.* be found, turn out.

proverb *noun*
His favourite proverb is 'Too many cooks spoil the broth'. adage, axiom, catchphrase, dictum, maxim, motto, saying, slogan.

provide *verb*
1 *He provided them with everything they needed.* arm, equip, furnish, supply.
OPPOSITE deprive of.
2 *He provided the money.* allot, contribute, donate, give, grant, offer, present, supply.

provide for
1 *He can no longer provide for his family.* keep, maintain, support, take care of.
2 *They tried to provide for every possibility.* allow for, anticipate, cater for, make provision for, plan for, prepare for.

province *noun*
1 *The country is divided into provinces.* area, district, region, state, territory.
2 *Teaching history is within her province.* area, domain, field, responsibility, sphere.

provincial *adjective*
a provincial newspaper. country, district, local, regional, rural.
OPPOSITE national.

provision *noun*
1 *He made provision for their future.* arrangement, plan, preparation.
2 *under the provisions of the will.* condition, proviso, requirement, specification, stipulation, term.

provisions *plural noun*
They laid up their provisions for the winter. food, groceries, rations, stores, supplies.

provisional *adjective*
a provisional appointment. interim, stopgap, temporary.
OPPOSITE permanent.

proviso *noun*
She gave her approval with one proviso. condition, provision, qualification, requirement, rider, stipulation.

provocative *adjective*
1 *a provocative dress.* alluring, inviting, seductive, sexy, tantalising, tempting.
2 *The interviewer was deliberately provocative.* annoying, exasperating, infuriating, irritating, maddening.

provoke *verb*
1 *He provoked people with his snide remarks.* anger, annoy, enrage, exasperate, incense, infuriate, irritate, madden, needle (*informal*), outrage, rile (*informal*), upset, vex, wind up (*informal*).
OPPOSITE pacify.
2 *The sharp comment provoked an angry response.* arouse, cause, draw, elicit, evoke, generate, inspire, produce, prompt, spark, stimulate, trigger.

prowess *noun*
1 *mathematical prowess.* ability, aptitude, competence, expertise, genius, proficiency, skill, talent.
OPPOSITE incompetence.
2 *a warrior's prowess.* boldness, bravery, courage, daring, heroism, valour.
OPPOSITE cowardice.

prowl *verb*
Wild animals prowled around the tents. lurk, roam, skulk, slink, sneak, steal.

prudent *adjective*
It seemed prudent to make further enquiries. careful, cautious, far-sighted, judicious, politic, sensible, shrewd, smart, wise.
OPPOSITE imprudent, unwise.

prudish *adjective*
The film upset some prudish viewers. demure, narrow-minded, old-fashioned, prim, prissy, puritanical, strait-laced.
OPPOSITE open-minded.

prune *verb*
He pruned the dead branches of the fruit trees. chop, cut back, lop, remove, snip off, trim.

pry *verb*
He's always prying into other people's affairs. delve, inquire, interfere, meddle, poke about, probe, snoop (*informal*), stickybeak (*Australian informal*).

psych *verb*
psych up *He psyched himself up for the interview.* gear up, prepare, steel.

psychic *adjective*
inexplicable psychic powers, outside the natural laws. clairvoyant, extrasensory, occult, paranormal, supernatural, telepathic.

psychological *adjective*
a psychological problem. emotional, mental.
OPPOSITE physical.

pub *noun* (*informal*)
They had a drink at the pub. bar, hotel (*Australian*), inn, local (*informal*), public house, saloon (*American*), tavern.

puberty *noun*
The child had reached puberty. adolescence, pubescence, teens.

public *adjective*
1 *a public library.* civic, community, council, government, municipal, national, state.
OPPOSITE private.
2 *the public interest.* common, community, general, national, popular.
OPPOSITE private.
3 *The information was now public.* disclosed, familiar, known, official, open, published, unconcealed.
OPPOSITE secret.
public *noun*
members of the Australian public. citizens, community, country, electorate, nation, people, populace, population, society, voters.
in public *She said these things in public.* openly, publicly.
OPPOSITE in private.
public servant bureaucrat, civil servant (*British & American*), government employee, official.

publicise *verb*
The event was well publicised. advertise, announce, make known, plug (*informal*), promote, publish, push.

publicity *noun*
1 *The rescuer tried to avoid publicity.* attention, fame, limelight, notice.
2 *After all the publicity, the show was disappointing.* advertising, build-up, hype (*slang*), marketing, plug (*informal*), promotion, propaganda.

publish *verb*
1 *The book was published in 1839.* bring out, issue, release; see also PRINT.

a
b
c
d
e
f
g
h
i
j
k
l
m
n
o
p
q
r
s
t
u
v
w
x
y
z

2 *The results were published in the newspaper.* advertise, announce, broadcast, disclose, make known, make public, proclaim, publicise, report, reveal.
OPPOSITE suppress.

pucker *verb*
She puckered her brow. The material puckered. contract, crinkle, furrow, gather, screw up, wrinkle.
pucker *noun*
She sewed the seam without any puckers. crease, crinkle, fold, gather, pleat, tuck, wrinkle.

puddle *noun*
He stepped in a puddle. pool.

puff *noun*
a puff of wind. blast, breath, draught, gust.
puff *verb*
The wolf huffed and puffed. blow, exhale, gasp, heave, huff, pant, wheeze.
puff up *Her stomach puffed up.* bloat, blow up, distend, expand, inflate, swell.

puffy *adjective*
His eyes were puffy from crying. puffed up, swollen.

pull *verb*
1 *The engine could not pull the heavy load.* drag, draw, haul, heave, lug, tow, trail, tug.
OPPOSITE push.
2 *He pulled my hair.* grab, jerk, tug, wrench, yank (*informal*).
3 *He pulled a muscle.* sprain, strain, stretch, tear, wrench.
pull down
1 *He pulled down the sign.* lower, remove, take down.
OPPOSITE raise.
2 *They pulled down the building.* demolish, destroy, dismantle, level, raze, tear down.
OPPOSITE erect.
pull in *The train pulled in to the station.* arrive (at), draw in, enter, stop (at).
pull off *He pulled off the stunt without much trouble.* accomplish, achieve, carry off, do, manage.
pull out
1 *The train pulled out of the station.* draw out, leave, move out.
OPPOSITE enter.

2 *She pulled out her tooth.* draw, extract, remove, take out.
OPPOSITE insert.
pull someone's leg *Don't believe him: he's just pulling your leg.* have on (*informal*), kid (*informal*), tease, trick.
pull through *The doctor didn't expect him to pull through.* get better, rally, recover, survive.
pull up *The car pulled up at the lights.* draw up, halt, stop.

pullover *noun*
He wore a pullover for warmth. jersey, jumper, sweater.

pulp *noun*
fruit pulp. flesh, mash, mush, purée.
pulp *verb*
She pulped the fruit in the blender. crush, liquidise, mash, pound, purée, smash, squash.

pulse *noun*
She could not feel any pulse. beat, pulsation, rhythm, throb, vibration.

pulverise *verb*
1 *He pulverised the seeds.* crush, grind, mill, pound.
2 *They pulverised the opposition.* beat, clobber (*slang*), defeat, thrash, trounce.

pump *verb*
1 *The doctor pumped her stomach to remove the poison.* drain, empty.
2 *He pumped the man for information.* grill, interrogate, probe, question, quiz.
pump up *He pumped up the tyres.* blow up, fill, inflate.
OPPOSITE let down.

pun *noun*
play on words.

punch *verb*
He punched the other man. bash, box, clout (*informal*), cuff, dong (*Australian informal*), hit, pummel, slog, slug, sock (*slang*), stoush (*Australian slang*), strike, thump.
punch *noun*
1 *He gave the man a punch in the stomach.* blow, box, clout (*informal*), hit, slog, slug, sock (*slang*), thump.
2 (*informal*) *His sermon lacked punch.* force, forcefulness, power, vigour.

punctual *adjective*
The doctor was punctual. on schedule, on the dot, on the knocker (*Australian informal*), on time, prompt.
CONTRASTS WITH early, late.

puncture *noun*
The tyre has a puncture. hole, leak, slit, tear.
puncture *verb*
A thorn punctured the tyre. penetrate, perforate, pierce, prick.

pungent *adjective*
a pungent smell or taste. acid, acrid, aromatic, hot, piquant, sharp, spicy, strong, tangy, tart.
OPPOSITE bland, delicate.

punish *verb*
He was punished for his misdeeds. chastise, discipline, make to suffer, penalise, sentence.
OPPOSITE pardon, reward.

punishment *noun*
Make the punishment fit the crime. chastisement, discipline, fine, imposition, penalty, sentence.
OPPOSITE reward.

punt *verb* (*informal*)
He punted $10 on one horse. bet, gamble, risk, stake, wager.
punt *noun*
He had a punt on the outcome. bet, gamble, wager.

puny *adjective*
1 *He is too puny to do such heavy work.* feeble, frail, sickly, skinny, small, undersized, weak, weedy.
OPPOSITE strapping.
2 *a puny amount.* feeble, paltry, pathetic, petty, small, tiny, trifling, trivial.
OPPOSITE large.

pup *noun*
The dog had a litter of three pups. puppy, whelp.

pupil *noun*
1 *Each teacher has twenty pupils.* learner, scholar, schoolboy, schoolchild, schoolgirl, student.
2 *a pupil of the great painter.* apprentice, disciple.

puppet *noun*
The story was told using puppets. doll, finger puppet, glove puppet, marionette, string puppet.

purchase *verb*
They purchased a television. acquire, buy, get, obtain, pay for.
OPPOSITE sell.
purchase *noun*
She took her purchases home. acquisition, buy.

purchaser *noun*
buyer, customer.
OPPOSITE vendor.

pure *adjective*
1 *pure gold.* solid, unadulterated, unalloyed, unmixed.
OPPOSITE adulterated.
2 *pure water.* clean, clear, fresh, straight, uncontaminated, undiluted, unpolluted, untainted.
OPPOSITE impure, polluted.
3 *a pure person.* blameless, chaste, decent, good, innocent, modest, moral, sinless, upright, virtuous.
OPPOSITE immoral.
4 *pure nonsense.* absolute, complete, downright, perfect, sheer, thorough, total, utter.

purée *noun*
The baby eats apple purée. mash, mush, pulp.
purée *verb*
Purée the pumpkin. liquidise, mash, pulp.

purify *verb*
The water has to be purified. clean, disinfect, distil, filter, refine, sterilise.
OPPOSITE contaminate.

puritanical *adjective*
a serious and puritanical old man. austere, moralistic, prim, prudish, strait-laced, strict, wowserish (*Australian*).
OPPOSITE permissive.

purple *adjective*
a purple colour. amethyst, hyacinth, jacaranda, lavender, lilac, mauve, mulberry, plum, violet.

purpose *noun*
The task has an educational purpose. aim, function, goal, intent, intention,

a
b
c
d
e
f
g
h
i
j
k
l
m
n
o
p
q
r
s
t
u
v
w
x
y
z

justification, motive, object, objective, point, use, value.

on purpose *He tripped her up on purpose.* consciously, deliberately, intentionally, knowingly.
OPPOSITE accidentally.

purposeless *adjective*
a purposeless activity. aimless, meaningless, pointless, senseless, useless.
OPPOSITE purposeful.

purse *noun*
1 *The money is in the purse.* pouch, wallet.
2 (*American*) *She carries her glasses in her purse.* bag, handbag.
purse *verb*
He pursed his lips. press together, pucker, squeeze.

pursue *verb*
1 *The police pursued the villains.* chase, follow, go after, hound, hunt, run after, shadow, stalk, tail (*informal*), track down, trail.
2 *She pursued her studies at university.* carry on, conduct, continue, engage in, follow, work at.

pursuit *noun*
1 *The cat gave up her pursuit of the mouse.* chase, hunt, stalking, tracking.
2 *intellectual and recreational pursuits.* activity, hobby, interest, occupation, pastime, recreation.

push *verb*
1 *He pushed the trolley out of the way.* drive, move, propel, shove, thrust.
2 *She pushed her way through the crowd.* advance, butt, elbow, force, jostle, nudge, press, ram, shoulder, shove, thrust.
3 *She pushed the filling into the hole.* compress, cram, force, pack, press, ram, squash, squeeze, stick (*informal*), stuff.
4 *They pushed him into entering the contest.* bully, coerce, compel, drive, egg on, encourage, force, goad, hound, press, pressure, spur, urge.
OPPOSITE discourage.
5 *They like to push new products.* advertise, plug (*informal*), promote, publicise.

pusher *noun*
1 *a drug pusher.* dealer, peddler, seller.
2 (*Australian*) *a baby's pusher.* pushchair, stroller.

pushover *noun* (*informal*)
1 *She found the test a pushover.* bludge (*Australian informal*), breeze (*informal*), cinch (*informal*), piece of cake (*informal*), snack (*Australian informal*), walkover.
OPPOSITE struggle.
2 *He'll be a pushover for that trickster.* dupe, easy prey, mug (*informal*), sitter (*informal*), sitting duck (*informal*), soft touch, sucker (*informal*).

pushy *adjective*
a pushy salesman. aggressive, assertive, bumptious, forceful, forward, self-assertive.
OPPOSITE retiring.

put *verb*
1 *He put the ornaments on the shelf.* arrange, bung (*informal*), deposit, dump, lay, leave, locate, place, plant, plonk, pop, position, rest, set down, settle, situate, slap, stand, station, stick.
2 *He put the pictures on the wall.* arrange, hang, mount, place, position.
3 *She put the battery in the camera.* fit, insert, install, load, place.
OPPOSITE remove.
4 *Who put that idea in his head?* implant, insert, instil, plant.
5 *They put the death toll at 350.* calculate, estimate, reckon.
6 *He put his theory very simply.* express, formulate, phrase, say, state, word.
7 *He put the idea to us for comment.* offer, present, put forward, submit, suggest.
8 *The government put a tax on wine.* apply, impose, levy, place.
9 *She put the blame on others.* cast, lay, pin.
put by *They put some money by each week for their holiday.* put aside, reserve, save, set aside, stash (*informal*).
OPPOSITE spend.
put down
1 *The army put down the rebellion.* crush, quell, stop, subdue, suppress.
2 *She felt he was putting her down.* belittle, denigrate, disparage, humiliate, slight, snub.

3 *The dog had to be put down.* destroy, kill, put to sleep.
4 *She put it down to tiredness.* ascribe, attribute, blame on.

put forward
1 *They put forward their ideas.* advance, offer, present, propose, put up, submit, suggest.
2 *His name was put forward.* nominate, propose, recommend, submit, suggest.

put in
1 *He put in many extra hours.* devote, give, spend.
2 *She put in for the job.* apply, go, try.

put off
1 *She had to put off the party.* defer, delay, hold off, postpone, reschedule, shelve.
2 *The fish looked good to eat, but the smell put him off.* disgust, repel, revolt, sicken. OPPOSITE attract.
3 *His father tried to put him off becoming an actor.* deter from, discourage from, dissuade from, talk out of. OPPOSITE encourage.

put on
1 *She put on her new outfit.* change into, don, dress in, slip into, wear. OPPOSITE take off.
2 *They put on a play.* mount, perform, present, produce, stage.
3 *She put on a funny voice.* adopt, affect, assume.
4 *They put cream on their skin.* apply, slap, spread. OPPOSITE remove.
5 *She put on weight.* gain, increase. OPPOSITE lose.
6 *He put on the heater.* plug in, switch on, turn on. OPPOSITE turn off.

put out
1 *He put out his hand to save them.* extend, hold out, reach out, stick out, stretch out. OPPOSITE withdraw.
2 *They tried not to put her out by their visit.* annoy, bother, inconvenience, irritate, trouble.
3 *They put out the fire.* douse, extinguish, quench, snuff out. OPPOSITE light.

put together *He put the model together.* assemble, build, construct, join, make. OPPOSITE dismantle.

put up
1 *They put up the house in six weeks.* build, construct, erect. OPPOSITE demolish.
2 *He put up the tent.* erect, pitch, set up.
3 *They are putting up their prices.* boost, bump up (*informal*), increase, jack up (*informal*), raise. OPPOSITE lower.
4 *The company put up the money for the venture.* contribute, donate, pay, provide, supply.
5 *They put us up for the night.* accommodate, billet, house, lodge, take in.

put up with *She won't put up with any rudeness.* abide, accept, bear, brook, endure, stand for, suffer, take, tolerate.

putrid *adjective*
The meat had to be thrown out because it was putrid. bad, decayed, decomposed, foul, rotten, smelly, stinking. OPPOSITE fresh.

puzzle *noun*
They all tried to solve the puzzle. brainteaser, conundrum, dilemma, enigma, mystery, paradox, problem, question, riddle.

puzzle *verb*
1 *She was puzzled by the message.* baffle, bamboozle (*informal*), bewilder, confuse, mystify, nonplus, perplex, stump (*informal*), throw (*informal*).
2 *She puzzled over the strange events.* brood, muse, ponder, rack your brains, wonder.

puzzling *adjective*
puzzling behaviour. a puzzling problem. baffling, difficult, enigmatic, inexplicable, insoluble, mysterious, perplexing, strange, unfathomable. OPPOSITE straightforward.

pygmy *noun*
a fairy tale of pygmies and giants. dwarf, lilliputian, midget. OPPOSITE giant.

pygmy *adjective*
a pygmy kangaroo. dwarf, miniature, small, tiny, undersized. OPPOSITE giant.

a
b
c
d
e
f
g
h
i
j
k
l
m
n
o
p
q
r
s
t
u
v
w
x
y
z

Qq

quack *noun*
1 *He isn't qualified. He's a quack.*
charlatan, fake, impostor, phoney
(*informal*).
2 (*slang*) *He went to the quack for a check-up.* see DOCTOR.

quadrangle *noun*
The offices are arranged around a quadrangle. courtyard, quad.

quail *verb*
He quailed at the sight of the cane. cower, cringe, flinch, recoil, shrink, wince.

quaint *adjective*
a quaint old cottage. attractive, charming, curious, odd, old-fashioned, picturesque, unusual.

quake *verb*
She quaked with fear at the thunder.
quaver, quiver, shake, shudder, tremble.
quake *noun* (*informal*)
The quake caused buildings to collapse.
earthquake, tremor.

qualification *noun*
1 *Do you have the right qualifications for the job?* ability, aptitude, attribute, competence, credentials, experience, knowledge, prerequisite, quality, skill, training.
2 *After four years of study he gained his teaching qualification.* certificate, degree, diploma.
3 *This statement needs some qualification.* condition, modification, proviso, reservation, restriction, stipulation.

qualified *adjective*
a qualified mechanic. certificated, certified, competent, licensed, skilled, trained.

qualify *verb*
1 *His studies qualified him to practise as a therapist.* allow, authorise, entitle, equip, fit, licence, make eligible, permit, prepare, train.

2 *She qualified the phrase 'all students' to 'nearly all students'.* limit, modify, restrict.

quality *noun*
1 *His work is of the highest quality.* calibre, class, grade, level, standard.
2 *It's quality that matters, not quantity.* excellence, merit, value, worth.
3 *He has many good qualities.* attribute, characteristic, feature, trait.

qualm *noun*
He has no qualms about stealing.
compunction, misgiving, pang of conscience, scruple.

quantity *noun*
a small quantity. amount, dose, extent, load, lot, measure, number, portion, sum, volume.

quarantine *noun*
The animals were kept in quarantine after the journey. isolation, segregation.

quarrel *noun*
They had a quarrel over money.
altercation, argument, barney (*informal*), clash, conflict, controversy, disagreement, dispute, feud, fight, row, squabble, tiff, wrangle.
quarrel *verb*
The children quarrel constantly. argue, bicker, brawl, differ, fall out, fight, row (*informal*), scrap, squabble, wrangle.

quarrelsome *adjective*
argumentative, belligerent, cantankerous, contentious, contrary, cross, irritable, petulant, pugnacious, truculent.
OPPOSITE peaceable.

quarry[1] *noun*
a wild animal's quarry. prey, victim.

quarry[2] *noun*
They filled in the old stone quarry.
excavation, mine, pit, working.

quarters *plural noun*
the soldiers' quarters. accommodation,
barracks, billet, digs (*informal*), housing,
lodgings.

quaver *verb*
Her voice quavered. quiver, shake,
tremble, waver.
quaver *noun*
a quaver in her voice. quiver, trembling,
tremor, wavering.

quay *noun*
The ferry drew close to the quay. berth,
dock, jetty, landing stage, pier, wharf.

queasy *adjective*
He felt queasy after the rich food. bilious,
ill, nauseous, off colour, sick.

queen *noun*
monarch, ruler, sovereign.

queer *adjective*
1 Her behaviour was a bit queer.
abnormal, bizarre, curious, eccentric,
funny, odd, peculiar, strange,
unconventional, unusual, weird.
OPPOSITE normal.
2 She felt a bit queer. dizzy, faint, giddy,
ill, off colour, out of sorts, poorly,
queasy, unwell.

quench *verb*
1 The rain quenched the fire. douse,
extinguish, put out, smother.
2 The drink quenched his thirst. satisfy,
slake.

query *noun*
The officer answered our query. enquiry,
inquiry, question.
query *verb*
He queried our explanation. challenge,
dispute, doubt, question.

quest *noun*
a quest for knowledge. hunt, pursuit,
search.

question *noun*
1 Did you answer her question?
conundrum, enquiry, inquiry, poser,
puzzle, query, riddle.
OPPOSITE answer, statement.
2 unresolved questions. issue, matter,
point, problem.

3 There is no question that he is guilty.
dispute, doubt, uncertainty.
question *verb*
1 The police questioned him about the
incident. ask, cross-examine, enquire of,
examine, grill, inquire of, interrogate,
interview, probe, quiz.
2 She questioned the spokesperson's
authority. call into question, cast doubt
on, challenge, dispute, doubt, query.

questionable *adjective*
His motives are rather questionable.
doubtful, dubious, suspect, suss
(*informal*), uncertain.

questionnaire *noun*
set of questions, survey.

queue *noun*
a queue of people. chain, column, file,
line, row.
queue *verb*
They queued for the bus. line up.

quibble *noun*
a quibble about the price. complaint,
objection, protest.
quibble *verb*
It's not worth quibbling about. argue, find
fault, niggle, nit-pick (*informal*), object,
protest, quarrel, split hairs.

quiche *noun*
a leek quiche. flan, pie, tart.

quick *adjective*
1 a quick pace. breakneck, brisk, express,
fast, fleet, rapid, speedy, swift, zippy.
OPPOSITE slow.
2 The old man was quick on his feet. agile,
lively, nimble, nippy (*informal*),
sprightly, spry.
OPPOSITE slow.
3 a quick visit. brief, fleeting, hasty,
hurried, short.
OPPOSITE long.
4 a quick response. immediate, instant,
instantaneous, prompt, speedy, swift.
OPPOSITE slow.
5 She is quick at mathematics. able, astute,
bright, clever, intelligent, perceptive,
sharp, shrewd, smart.
OPPOSITE slow.
6 He has a quick temper. fiery, hot, sharp,
short.

a
b
c
d
e
f
g
h
i
j
k
l
m
n
o
p
q
r
s
t
u
v
w
x
y
z

quicken *verb*
They quickened their pace. accelerate, hasten, hurry, speed up.
OPPOSITE slacken, slow down.

quickly *adverb*
briskly, fast, hastily, hurriedly, in a flash, in a jiffy (*informal*), in no time, instantly, promptly, rapidly, speedily, swiftly.
OPPOSITE slowly.

quiet *adjective*
1 *The examination room was quiet.* silent, soundless, still.
OPPOSITE noisy.
2 *The wombat was so quiet that we thought he was dead.* inactive, inert, motionless, still.
OPPOSITE active.
3 *The streets were quiet after the riot.* calm, peaceful, tranquil, undisturbed.
OPPOSITE busy, rowdy.
4 *a quiet voice.* gentle, hushed, inaudible, low, soft.
OPPOSITE loud.
5 *She is a quiet person.* gentle, introverted, mild, placid, reserved, reticent, retiring, sedate, serene, shy, silent, taciturn, uncommunicative.
OPPOSITE noisy, talkative.
6 *quiet colours.* muted, restful, soft, subdued, unobtrusive.
OPPOSITE loud, showy.

quieten *verb*
He quietened the children. calm, hush, pacify, quiet, restrain, shush (*informal*), silence, soothe, subdue.

quietness *noun*
calm, hush, peace, quiet, serenity, silence, stillness, tranquillity.
OPPOSITE noise.

quill *noun*
1 *a bird's quills.* feather, plume.
2 *a porcupine's quills.* spine.

quilt *noun*
continental quilt, coverlet, Doona (*trade mark*), duvet, eiderdown.

quit *verb*
1 *They quit the campsite at dawn.* depart from, desert, go away from, leave, vacate.
OPPOSITE arrive at.
2 *He quit his job.* abandon, chuck in (*informal*), forsake, give up, leave, resign from.
OPPOSITE continue, start.
3 (*informal*) *Quit moaning.* cease, desist from, stop.
OPPOSITE keep on.

quite *adverb*
1 *Are you quite certain?* absolutely, altogether, completely, entirely, fully, perfectly, positively, totally, utterly.
2 *He is quite fat.* comparatively, fairly, moderately, pretty, rather, reasonably, relatively, somewhat.

quiver *verb*
The boy quivered with fear. quake, quaver, shake, shiver, shudder, tremble, vibrate.

quiz *noun*
competition, examination, questionnaire, test.
quiz *verb*
She quizzed the witnesses about what they had seen. ask, examine, grill, interrogate, question, test.

quota *noun*
They received their quota of the money. allocation, allowance, cut (*informal*), lot, part, portion, proportion, ration, share.

quotation *noun*
1 *The essay contained quotations from the Bible.* citation, excerpt, extract, passage, quote (*informal*), reference.
2 *The painter gave us a quotation for the job.* estimate, quote (*informal*), tender.

quote *verb*
1 *He is fond of quoting Shakespeare.* recite, repeat.
2 *Can you quote a recent example?* call up, cite, mention, name, refer to.
3 *The painter quoted $1000 for the job.* estimate, tender.

Rr

rabbit *noun*
buck (*male*), bunny (*informal*), doe
(*female*), kitten (*young*).

rabble *noun*
He tried to quieten the noisy rabble. crowd,
horde, mob, swarm, throng.

race¹ *noun*
She won the race. chase, competition,
contest, heat, marathon, rally, relay.
race *verb*
1 *She raced against her brother.* compete.
2 *He raced past me.* dart, dash, fly, hurry,
hurtle, run, rush, shoot, speed, sprint,
sweep, tear, whiz, zip, zoom.

race² *noun*
the different races of the world. ethnic
group, nation, people, tribe.

racetrack *noun*
circuit, course, racecourse, speedway,
track.

racial *adjective*
racial background. ethnic, national, tribal.

racism *noun*
racial discrimination, racial intolerance,
racialism, racial prejudice.

rack *noun*
a rack for mugs. framework, shelf, stand,
support.

racket *noun*
1 *The racket made it impossible to
concentrate.* clamour, commotion, din,
hubbub, hullabaloo, noise,
pandemonium, row, ruckus, rumpus,
uproar.
OPPOSITE quietness.
2 *a tax racket.* dodge (*informal*), lurk
(*Australian informal*), rort (*Australian
slang*), scam (*slang*), scheme, swindle.

radiant *adjective*
1 *a radiant light.* bright, brilliant,
dazzling, gleaming, glowing,
incandescent, luminous, shining.
OPPOSITE dark, dull.

2 *the radiant mother-to-be.* beaming,
beautiful, blissful, ecstatic, glowing,
happy, joyful, overjoyed.
OPPOSITE unhappy.

radiate *verb*
1 *Five roads radiate from this point.*
branch out, diverge, spread out.
OPPOSITE converge.
2 *The heater radiates warmth.* emit, give
out, send out, shed, transmit.

radical *adjective*
1 *radical changes.* complete, drastic,
far-reaching, fundamental, major,
profound, sweeping, thorough.
OPPOSITE minimal, superficial.
2 *radical policies.* extreme, extremist,
immoderate, revolutionary.
OPPOSITE conservative, moderate.

radio *noun*
He listened to the programme on the radio.
receiver, set, transistor, tuner, wireless.

raffle *noun*
art union (*Australian*), draw, lottery,
sweep, sweepstake.

rag *noun*
He wiped his hands on a rag. cloth,
fragment, remnant, scrap.
rags *plural noun*
dressed in rags. shreds, tatters.

rage *noun*
1 *a fit of rage.* anger, exasperation,
frenzy, fury, paddy (*informal*), tantrum,
temper, wrath.
2 *Big hats were all the rage.* craze,
fashion, trend, vogue.
rage *verb*
He raged at the unfairness of the system. be
angry, be furious, blow your stack
(*informal*), blow your top (*informal*), do
your block (*Australian informal*), fly off
the handle (*informal*), fume, go off the
deep end (*informal*), let off steam, lose
your cool (*informal*), lose your temper,
rail, rant, rave, seethe.

ragged *adjective*
1 *ragged clothes.* dilapidated, frayed, holey, scruffy, shabby, tattered, tatty (*informal*), threadbare, torn, worn-out.
2 *a ragged edge.* jagged, rough, uneven.
OPPOSITE even, smooth.

raging *adjective*
1 *raging seas.* heavy, roaring, stormy, turbulent, wild.
OPPOSITE calm.
2 *a raging headache.* excruciating, intense, severe.
OPPOSITE mild.

raid *noun*
1 *a midnight raid on the town.* assault, attack, blitz, foray, incursion, invasion, offensive, onslaught, swoop.
2 *a police raid.* bust (*informal*), search.
raid *verb*
1 *The soldiers raided the town.* attack, invade, storm, swoop on.
2 *The thieves raided the store.* loot, pillage, plunder, ransack, rob.

rail *noun*
1 *He held on to the rail.* banisters, bar, handrail, railing.
2 *They travelled by rail.* railway, train.

railing *noun*
He stood on the other side of the railing. balustrade, barrier, fence, rails.

railway *noun*
travel by railway. rail, railroad (*American*), train.

rain *noun*
After the rain we can go outside. cloudburst, deluge, downpour, drizzle, shower, storm, thunderstorm; see also RAINFALL.
rain *verb*
It is raining. bucket down, drizzle, pelt, pour, rain cats and dogs (*informal*), spit, sprinkle, teem.

raincoat *noun*
anorak, mac (*informal*), mackintosh, oilskin, trench coat, waterproof.

rainfall *noun*
annual rainfall. precipitation.

rainy *adjective*
rainy weather. damp, drizzly, showery, wet.
OPPOSITE dry.

raise *verb*
1 *He raised the weight off the ground.* elevate, heave, hoist, jack, lift, pick up.
OPPOSITE lower.
2 *He raised a monument on the site.* build, construct, erect, put up.
OPPOSITE pull down.
3 *They raised their prices.* bump up (*informal*), increase, inflate, mark up, put up.
OPPOSITE reduce.
4 *She raised our hopes.* arouse, boost, build up, heighten, increase, kindle, stimulate.
OPPOSITE dash.
5 *He raises roses.* breed, cultivate, grow, produce, propagate.
6 *They raised four children.* bring up, nurture, rear.
7 *They raised the amount needed.* amass, collect, gather, get, obtain.
8 *She raised the question.* bring up, introduce, pose, put forward.
raise *noun*
He asked for a raise. increase, rise.
raise from the dead restore to life, resurrect, resuscitate, revive.

rake *verb*
1 *She raked the leaves.* collect, gather, sweep up.
2 *They raked through the old papers.* comb, forage, fossick (*Australian informal*), rummage, scour, search.

rally *verb*
1 *The people rallied in support.* assemble, come together, gather, unite.
2 *The leader rallied his troops.* assemble, marshal, mobilise, muster.
3 *The old man rallied after weeks of being ill.* get better, improve, pull through, recover, revive.
OPPOSITE deteriorate.
rally *noun*
1 *The students held a rally.* convention, demo (*informal*), demonstration, jamboree, gathering, meeting.
2 *Fifty cars competed in the rally.* competition, race.

ram *verb*
   1 *He rammed the filling into the cushion.* force, jam, pack, push, stuff.
   2 *He rammed the nail into the wood.* drive, force, hammer, push.
   3 *Her car rammed the one in front.* bump into, collide with, crash into, hit, run into, slam into, smash into.

ramble *verb*
   1 *They rambled through the bush.* amble, hike, roam, rove, stroll, traipse, tramp, trek, walk, wander.
   2 *The audience lost interest as the speaker rambled.* digress, waffle (*informal*), witter on (*informal*).
   ramble *noun*
   a ramble in the bush. hike, roam, stroll, trek, walk.

ramp *noun*
   a steep ramp. incline, slope.

rampage *verb*
   The gang rampaged through the city streets. go berserk, go wild, run amok, run riot.

ramshackle *adjective*
   a ramshackle old cottage. decrepit, dilapidated, rickety, run-down, shaky, tumbledown.

ranch *noun*
   farm, stud.

random *adjective*
   a random choice. accidental, arbitrary, chance, haphazard, hit-or-miss, indiscriminate, unplanned.
   OPPOSITE deliberate, systematic.

range *noun*
   1 *a range of mountains.* chain, line, row, series.
   2 *a specific age range.* bracket, group, span.
   3 *The shop stocks a wide range of shoes.* assortment, selection, set, variety.
   4 *outside the range of her duties.* area, bounds, domain, extent, field, limits, scope, sphere.
   5 *She warmed herself by the range.* cooker, fireplace, oven, stove.
   range *verb*
   1 *The prices ranged from $100 to $500.* differ, extend, go, vary.

2 *The sheep ranged over the hills.* ramble, roam, rove, stray, travel, wander.
   ranges *plural noun*
   The ranges were covered with stringybarks. highlands, hills, mountains.

ranger *noun*
   a park ranger. curator, keeper, warden.

rank *noun*
   1 *They stood in two ranks.* column, file, line, queue, row.
   2 *a person of lower rank.* class, grade, level, position, station, status.
   rank *verb*
   He ranked them in order of merit. arrange, class, grade, order, place, rate.

ransack *verb*
   1 *She ransacked her drawer for a safety pin.* comb, fossick in (*Australian informal*), rummage in, scour, search.
   2 *Thieves ransacked the house.* loot, pillage, plunder, raid, rob, sack.

rap *noun*
   1 *He gave him a rap on the back of the hand.* hit, knock, tap.
   2 (*informal*) *He took the rap for what happened.* blame, punishment.
   rap *verb*
   He rapped on the window. hit, knock, strike, tap.

rape *verb*
   assault sexually, ravish, violate.

rapid *adjective*
   a rapid decision. rapid progress. brisk, fast, hasty, high-speed, meteoric, prompt, quick, speedy, sudden, swift, whirlwind.
   OPPOSITE slow.

rapidly *adverb*
   see QUICKLY.

rapt *adjective*
   The audience was rapt. absorbed, captivated, engrossed, enraptured, enthralled, entranced, spellbound.
   OPPOSITE uninterested.

rapture *noun*
   The music filled her with rapture. bliss, delight, ecstasy, elation, happiness, joy.
   OPPOSITE sorrow.

a
b
c
d
e
f
g
h
i
j
k
l
m
n
o
p
q
r
s
t
u
v
w
x
y
z

rare[1] *adjective*
1 *These animals have become rare.* scarce, uncommon.
OPPOSITE common, plentiful.
2 *a rare sight.* abnormal, infrequent, occasional, odd, strange, uncommon, unfamiliar, unusual.
OPPOSITE common.

rare[2] *adjective*
rare steak. pink, undercooked, underdone.

rarely *adverb*
only seen rarely. infrequently, occasionally, once in a blue moon, seldom.
OPPOSITE often.

rascal *noun*
1 *The police caught the rascal.* blackguard, knave (*old use*), miscreant, rogue, scoundrel, villain, wretch.
2 *She was a rascal to scare her mother like that.* imp, monkey, scallywag, scamp.

rash[1] *noun*
an itchy rash on the body. dermatitis, eczema, spots.

rash[2] *adjective*
a rash decision. foolhardy, hasty, headlong, heedless, hotheaded, impetuous, impulsive, madcap, reckless.
OPPOSITE cautious.

rate *noun*
1 *a rate of six kilometres per hour.* pace, speed, velocity.
2 *Cheaper rates apply at weekends.* charge, cost, fare, fee, price, tariff.
3 *council rates.* levy, tax, taxation.
rate *verb*
1 *She rated her chances as good.* assess, class, consider, deem, estimate, reckon, regard.
2 *His essay was rated highly.* judge, rank, regard, value.

rather *adverb*
It is rather dark. comparatively, fairly, moderately, pretty, quite, relatively, somewhat.

ratio *noun*
The ratio of blue to red is 2:1. proportion, relationship.

ration *noun*
She gave away her ration of butter. allocation, allowance, portion, quota, share.
ration out *The food was rationed out among the starving people.* allocate, apportion, distribute, dole out, share out.

rational *adjective*
1 *a rational person.* intelligent, lucid, normal, sane, sensible.
OPPOSITE irrational, mad.
2 *a rational explanation.* logical, reasonable, sensible, sound.
OPPOSITE illogical, irrational.

rationalise *verb*
1 *She tried to rationalise her fears.* account for, excuse, explain away, justify.
2 *The industry has been rationalised.* make efficient, streamline.

rattle *verb*
1 *The glasses rattled in the box.* clank, clatter, clink, jangle, shake.
2 (*informal*) *Nothing seems to rattle him.* agitate, alarm, disconcert, faze (*informal*), fluster, frighten, perturb, shake, throw, unnerve, upset, worry.
rattle off *He rattled off his story.* recite, recount, reel off, relate.

rave *verb*
1 *He ranted and raved like a madman.* carry on (*informal*), go on (*informal*), rant, sound off (*informal*).
2 *She raved about my new dress.* be enthusiastic, go overboard (*informal*), gush.

ravenous *adjective*
They were ravenous after their long hike. famished, hungry, starving.

ravine *noun*
canyon, defile, gorge, gully, valley.

raw *adjective*
1 *raw meat.* uncooked.
OPPOSITE cooked.
2 *raw sugar.* crude, natural, unprocessed, unrefined, untreated.
OPPOSITE processed.
3 *The firm took on a raw graduate and trained him.* fresh, inexperienced, new,

untrained.
OPPOSITE experienced.
4 *His knee was raw.* grazed, skinned.

ray *noun*
1 *a ray of sunlight.* beam, shaft.
2 *a ray of hope.* flicker, glimmer, spark, trace.

raze *verb*
Workmen razed the building. demolish, destroy, flatten, knock down, level, tear down, wreck.
OPPOSITE erect.

reach *verb*
1 *He reached out his hand to save the man.* extend, hold out, put out, stretch out.
2 *They reached Sydney in daylight.* arrive at, get to, hit, make.
3 *They reached him by telephone.* catch up with, communicate with, contact, get hold of, get in touch with.
4 *They reached their goal.* accomplish, achieve, attain.
5 *The temperature reached 40°.* climb to, go to, hit, rise to.
6 *Prices reached rock-bottom.* descend to, fall to, hit, strike.
reach *noun*
1 *The glasses are beyond the child's reach.* grasp.
2 *The shops are within easy reach.* distance, range.

react *verb*
She reacted unexpectedly. act, behave, respond.

reaction *noun*
a reaction to a request. answer, feedback, reply, response.

read *verb*
1 *She could not read his handwriting.* decipher, interpret, make out, understand.
2 *He read the book.* browse through, dip into, glance at, peruse, pore through, scan, skim, study, wade through.
3 *She read the poem to the class.* present, quote, recite, reel off.
4 *He read about it in the newspaper.* discover, find out, hear, learn.
5 *The thermometer reads 20°.* indicate, register, show.

readable *adjective*
1 *readable writing.* clear, legible, neat, plain, understandable.
OPPOSITE illegible.
2 *a readable book.* absorbing, enjoyable, entertaining, interesting.
OPPOSITE boring, unreadable.

ready *adjective*
1 *The officers were ready for action.* equipped, organised, prepared, set.
OPPOSITE unprepared.
2 *She is always ready to help a friend.* disposed, eager, game, glad, happy, inclined, keen, willing.
OPPOSITE reluctant.
3 *He always has a ready answer.* immediate, instant, pat, prompt, quick, speedy.
4 *She has a ready supply of tissues.* accessible, available, handy.

real *adjective*
1 *The film is based on real events and real people.* actual, factual, historical, true.
OPPOSITE imaginary.
2 *real butter.* authentic, dinkum (*Australian informal*), dinky-di (*Australian informal*), genuine, honest-to-goodness (*informal*), natural, proper.
OPPOSITE artificial.
3 *Her faith was real.* genuine, heartfelt, honest, sincere, solid, true.
OPPOSITE nominal.

realise *verb*
She didn't realise what was going on. appreciate, become aware of, comprehend, cotton on to (*informal*), grasp, know, perceive, sense, suss out (*informal*), twig (*informal*), understand, wake up to.

realistic *adjective*
1 *a realistic painting.* accurate, authentic, faithful, lifelike, natural, true-to-life.
OPPOSITE unrealistic.
2 *a realistic proposal.* feasible, practicable, practical, viable, workable.
OPPOSITE impractical.

really *adverb*
He really meant it. actually, certainly, definitely, genuinely, honestly, indeed, in fact, positively, sincerely, truly.

a
b
c
d
e
f
g
h
i
j
k
l
m
n
o
p
q
r
s
t
u
v
w
x
y
z

realm *noun*
1 *the queen's realm.* country, domain, dominion, empire, kingdom, monarchy, territory.
2 *the realm of science.* area, domain, field, sphere, world.

reap *verb*
1 *The wheat is ready to be reaped.* cut, gather in, harvest.
2 *She reaped the benefits of their experience.* gain, obtain, receive.

rear[1] *noun*
She stood towards the rear. back, end, stern, tail.
OPPOSITE front.
rear *adjective*
rear legs. back, hind.
OPPOSITE fore, front.

rear[2] *verb*
1 *She reared the family on her own.* bring up, care for, look after, nurture, raise.
2 *The farmer rears pigs.* breed, keep, produce, raise.

rearrange *verb*
She rearranged their places at the table. change, interchange, reorganise, reshuffle, shift, shuffle, swap, switch.

reason *noun*
1 *the reason for her odd behaviour.* cause, excuse, explanation, grounds, justification, motive, pretext, rationale.
2 *He has lost his reason.* faculties, intellect, intelligence, judgement, mind, sanity, wits.
OPPOSITE insanity.
3 *He won't listen to reason.* common sense, good sense, logic, sense, wisdom.
reason *verb*
1 *She reasoned that they must have known.* conclude, deduce, infer, work out.
2 *He tried to reason with her.* argue, debate, discuss.
reason out *He reasoned the problem out.* figure out, solve, think through, work out, work through.

reasonable *adjective*
1 *any reasonable person.* intelligent, logical, rational, sane, sensible, thinking.
OPPOSITE unreasonable.

2 *a reasonable explanation.* logical, plausible, rational, sensible, sound, tenable.
OPPOSITE absurd.
3 *The fine was reasonable.* equitable, fair, just, justifiable, moderate.
OPPOSITE excessive.

reassure *verb*
She reassured the others that all would be well. assure, comfort, encourage, set someone's mind at rest.
OPPOSITE perturb.

reassuring *adjective*
a reassuring sign. comforting, encouraging, favourable, hopeful, promising.
OPPOSITE discouraging.

rebel *noun*
The army fought against the rebels. dissenter, insurgent, malcontent, mutineer, nonconformist, revolutionary.
rebel *verb*
They rebelled against the authorities. mutiny, revolt, rise up.
OPPOSITE obey.

rebellion *noun*
insurrection, mutiny, revolt, revolution, rising, uprising.

rebellious *adjective*
The rebellious youth became an ardent reformer. defiant, disobedient, insubordinate, mutinous, recalcitrant, unmanageable, unruly, wild.
OPPOSITE obedient.

rebound *verb*
1 *The ball rebounded off the wall.* bounce back, ricochet, spring back.
2 *The nasty trick rebounded on them.* backfire, boomerang, recoil.

rebuild *verb*
They rebuilt the bridge after the collapse. reconstruct, remake, renew, restore.

rebuke *verb*
Her parents rebuked her for her insolence. admonish, castigate, censure, chide (*old use*), reprimand, reproach, reprove, scold, tell off (*informal*), tick off (*informal*), upbraid.
OPPOSITE praise.

rebuke *noun*
He was given a stern rebuke. admonition, censure, dressing down (*informal*), rap over the knuckles, reprimand, reproof, scolding.
OPPOSITE commendation.

recall *verb*
She recalled the incident. call to mind, recollect, remember.

recap *verb* (*informal*)
The chairman recapped what the other speakers had said. go over, recapitulate, repeat, restate, summarise, sum up.
recap *noun* (*informal*)
a recap of the previous lesson. recapitulation, résumé, summary, summing up.

recede *verb*
The floodwaters receded. ebb, go back, retreat, subside.
OPPOSITE advance.

receipt *noun*
She returned the goods with the receipt. docket, proof of purchase.

receive *verb*
1 She received the award. accept, acquire, collect, gain, get, land, obtain, take, win.
OPPOSITE give.
2 He received unfair treatment. be subjected to, experience, meet with, suffer, undergo.
OPPOSITE inflict.
3 She received her guests at the door. greet, meet, welcome.

recent *adjective*
recent news. contemporary, current, fresh, latest, new, up-to-date.
OPPOSITE old.

receptacle *noun*
carrier, container, holder, vessel.

reception *noun*
1 a cool reception. greeting, welcome.
2 a wedding reception. do (*informal*), function, gathering, party.

recess *noun*
1 The cave had many recesses. alcove, bay, niche, nook.

2 She eats an apple at recess. break, little lunch, morning tea, playlunch, playtime.

recession *noun*
The country is facing a recession. decline, depression, downturn, slump.

recipe *noun*
He made the cake without a recipe. directions, formula, instructions.

reciprocal *adjective*
She loved him, but the feeling was not reciprocal. mutual, reciprocated, returned.
OPPOSITE one-sided.

recital *noun*
an organ recital. concert, performance.

recite *verb*
She recited the poem. deliver, narrate, perform, rattle off, reel off, repeat, say, tell.

reckless *adjective*
a reckless driver. careless, daredevil, foolhardy, hotheaded, impetuous, impulsive, irresponsible, mad, negligent, rash, unthinking, wild.
OPPOSITE careful, cautious.

reckon *verb*
1 He reckoned how much it had all cost. add up, assess, calculate, compute, count, figure out, tally, tot up (*informal*), work out.
2 She reckoned they would win. believe, consider, fancy, think.

recline *verb*
He reclined on the sofa. lean back, lie, loll, lounge, rest, sprawl.

recognise *verb*
1 She didn't recognise their faces. identify, know, place, recall, recollect, remember.
2 He recognised the hopelessness of the situation. accept, acknowledge, admit, be aware of, perceive, realise, see, understand.

recognition *noun*
She received public recognition for her work. acknowledgement, appreciation, notice.

a
b
c
d
e
f
g
h
i
j
k
l
m
n
o
p
q
r
s
t
u
v
w
x
y
z

recoil *verb*
1 *He was injured when his gun recoiled.* kick, kick back, spring back.
2 *She recoiled at the sight of the dead body.* draw back, flinch, jump back, shrink, shy away, start, wince.

recollect *verb*
see REMEMBER.

recommend *verb*
1 *He recommended a different treatment.* advise, advocate, prescribe, propose, suggest.
2 *She recommended the book.* approve of, commend, endorse, laud (*formal*), praise, speak well of.
OPPOSITE condemn.

reconcile *verb*
1 *The counsellor reconciled the man and woman.* bring together, reunite.
2 *They reconciled their differences.* fix up, mend, patch up, resolve, settle.

recondition *verb*
He reconditioned the engine. overhaul, rebuild, renovate, repair, restore.

reconstruct *verb*
1 *They reconstructed the model.* reassemble, rebuild, remake, repair, restore.
2 *Police reconstructed the crime.* re-create, re-enact.

record *noun*
1 *He kept a record of events.* account, chronicle, diary, document, dossier, history, journal, log, memorandum, narrative, note, register, report, transcription.
2 *He likes listening to records.* see RECORDING.
3 *She has a good employment record.* background, curriculum vitae, CV, experience, history.
record *verb*
1 *She records what is said at meetings.* document, enter, jot down, list, minute, note, register, take down, transcribe, write down.
2 *They recorded the show.* film, tape, video.

recording *noun*
album, CD, compact disc, disc, record, release, tape, video.

recount *verb*
She recounted the whole sad tale. describe, narrate, recite, relate, report, tell.

recover *verb*
1 *He recovered his car which had been stolen.* find, get back, reclaim, recoup, redeem, retrieve, salvage, track down.
2 *She recovered from her illness.* convalesce, get better, heal, improve, mend, pick up, pull through, rally, recuperate.
OPPOSITE deteriorate.

recreation *noun*
He fixes cars for recreation. amusement, diversion, enjoyment, entertainment, fun, hobby, leisure, pastime, play, pleasure, sport.

recruit *verb*
He recruited extra staff. engage, enlist, take on.
recruit *noun*
The new recruits attended a training course. apprentice, newcomer, novice, rookie (*informal*), trainee.

rectangle *noun*
oblong, square.

rectify *verb*
He rectified the problem. correct, cure, fix, mend, put right, remedy, repair.

rector *noun*
see CLERGY.

recuperate *verb*
The patient recuperated at home. convalesce, get better, improve, mend, recover, regain health.

recur *verb*
The problem recurs each summer. be repeated, happen again, reappear, resurface, return.

recurrent *adjective*
a recurrent problem. chronic, continual, frequent, perennial, periodic, perpetual, recurring, repeated.
OPPOSITE isolated.

recycle *verb*
Cans may be recycled. reprocess, reuse, use again.

red *adjective*
1 *a red colour.* blood-red, brick-red, burgundy, carmine, cerise, cherry, claret, cochineal, crimson, flame, garnet, maroon, ruby, russet, scarlet, vermilion.
2 *red hair.* auburn, carroty, ginger.
3 *a red face.* florid, flushed, ruddy.
OPPOSITE pale.
4 *red eyes.* bloodshot.

redden *verb*
His cheeks reddened. blush, colour, flush, glow.
OPPOSITE whiten.

redeem *verb*
1 *He redeemed his watch at the pawnshop.* buy back, reclaim, recover, repurchase.
2 *Christians believe that Jesus died to redeem sinners.* atone for, ransom, rescue, save, set free.

reduce *verb*
1 *They reduced their spending.* cut, cut back, cut down, decrease, diminish, lessen, slash, trim.
OPPOSITE increase.
2 *He reduced the price.* cut, decrease, discount, drop, lower, mark down, slash.
OPPOSITE increase.
3 *He reduced the message to a few lines.* abbreviate, abridge, condense, prune, shorten.
OPPOSITE lengthen.
4 *The treatment reduced the pain.* alleviate, ease, lessen, lighten, minimise.
OPPOSITE increase, intensify.
5 *He reduced the page to A4.* scale down, shrink.
OPPOSITE enlarge.

reduction *noun*
1 *reductions in staff.* cut, cutback, decrease, downsizing, retrenchment.
OPPOSITE increase.
2 *Pensioners are entitled to a 5% reduction on rates.* concession, discount, rebate.
OPPOSITE surcharge.

redundant *adjective*
The essay included redundant information. excess, superfluous, unnecessary, unwanted.

reek *noun*
the reek of tobacco. odour, pong (*informal*), smell, stench, stink.
reek *verb*
The house reeked after the dinner party. pong (*informal*), smell, stink.

reel *noun*
a reel of yarn. bobbin, spindle, spool.
reel *verb*
1 *The wounded man reeled, and finally collapsed.* lurch, rock, stagger, stumble, sway, teeter, totter, wobble.
2 *Her head reeled when she tried to get up.* spin, swim, whirl.
reel off *He reeled off the dates.* rattle off, recite.

refer *verb*
refer to
1 *He didn't refer to the incident again.* allude to, bring up, comment on, mention, speak of.
2 *He referred the matter to his solicitor.* direct, pass, send.
3 *She referred to her handbook.* consult, look up in, turn to.

referee *noun*
The players respected the referee's decision. adjudicator, ref (*informal*), umpire.

reference *noun*
1 *He made no reference to recent events.* allusion, hint, mention.
2 *a biblical reference.* citation, example, quotation.
3 *The principal wrote a reference for each student.* testimonial.

referendum *noun*
ballot, plebiscite, poll, vote.

refill *verb*
replenish, restock, top up.

refine *verb*
The liquid has been refined. clarify, distil, filter, process, purify.

refined *adjective*
a refined person. civilised, cultivated, dignified, elegant, genteel, gentlemanly, ladylike, polished, polite, sophisticated, well-bred.
OPPOSITE uncouth.

reflect *verb*
1 *The tree was reflected in the lake.* mirror.

a
b
c
d
e
f
g
h
i
j
k
l
m
n
o
p
q
r
s
t
u
v
w
x
y
z

2 *His exam mark did not reflect his real ability.* demonstrate, display, indicate, reveal, show.

reflect on *He reflected on what had been said.* brood on, consider, contemplate, deliberate on, meditate on, mull over, ponder, think about.

reflection *noun*
a reflection in the mirror. image, likeness.

reform *verb*
1 *He reformed the tax system.* amend, change, correct, improve, mend, rectify, revolutionise, transform.
2 *She used to be an alcoholic, but she has reformed.* mend your ways, turn over a new leaf.

refrain[1] *noun*
They all sang the refrain. chorus.

refrain[2] *verb*
refrain from *Please refrain from coughing.* abstain from, avoid, desist from, stop.
OPPOSITE persist in.

refresh *verb*
1 *The drink refreshed him.* freshen, invigorate, perk up (*informal*), revive.
2 *Let me refresh your memory.* jog, prod, prompt, stimulate.

refreshments *plural noun*
drinks, eats (*informal*), food, nibbles (*informal*), snacks.

refrigerate *verb*
chill, cool, freeze.

refuge *noun*
1 *The cave was a refuge from the bushfire.* haven, hideout (*informal*), hidey-hole (*informal*), hiding place, retreat, sanctuary, shelter.
2 *He took refuge in the hut.* asylum, cover, protection, safety, sanctuary, shelter.

refugee *noun*
displaced person, exile, fugitive, runaway.

refund *verb*
He refunded them the money. give back, pay back, reimburse, repay, return.
refund *noun*
a tax refund. reimbursement, repayment.

refusal *noun*
knock-back (*informal*), rejection, veto.
OPPOSITE acceptance.

refuse[1] *verb*
1 *He refused their offers of help.* decline, knock back (*informal*), pass up (*informal*), reject, scorn, spurn, turn down.
OPPOSITE accept.
2 *They were refused entry.* deny, forbid, prohibit, withhold.
OPPOSITE grant.

refuse[2] *noun*
He put the refuse in the bin. debris, garbage, junk, litter, rubbish, scrap, trash, waste.

refute *verb*
He refuted the other man's statement. disprove, negate, rebut.
OPPOSITE prove.

regain *verb*
He regained the trophy. get back, recoup, recover, retrieve, win back.

regal *adjective*
regal splendour. kingly, lordly, majestic, princely, queenly, royal, stately.

regard *verb*
1 *She regarded him studiously.* behold (*old use*), contemplate, eye, gaze at, look at, observe, stare at, view, watch.
OPPOSITE ignore.
2 *We regard the matter as serious.* consider, judge, look upon, reckon, view.
3 *His work is highly regarded.* esteem, respect, value.
regard *noun*
1 *He pays no regard to the rules.* attention, care, concern, consideration, heed, notice, thought.
OPPOSITE disregard.
2 *He is held in high regard.* admiration, esteem, honour, respect.
OPPOSITE contempt.

regarding *preposition*
He spoke to them regarding the matter. about, concerning, with reference to, with respect to.

regardless *adverb*
Carry on regardless. anyway, heedlessly, nevertheless.
regardless of *Regardless of what you say, I still want to go.* despite, in spite of, irrespective of, notwithstanding.

region *noun*
They live in an arid region. area, district, land, locality, neighbourhood, place, spot, territory, zone.

regional *adjective*
regional cookery. local, provincial.

register *noun*
His name is in the register. catalogue, directory, index, list, record, roll.
register *verb*
1 *He registered for swimming lessons.* enlist, enrol, join up, sign up.
2 *She registered a complaint.* file, place on record, record, write down.
3 *The thermometer registered 100°.* indicate, record, show.
4 *His face registered his true feelings.* betray, express, indicate, reflect, reveal, show.

regret *noun*
He had no regrets about the incident. disappointment, penitence, remorse, repentance, sorrow.
regret *verb*
She regretted what had happened. be sad about, be sorry about, deplore, lament, repent, rue.

regretful *adjective*
She was regretful about the accident. apologetic, contrite, penitent, remorseful, repentant, rueful, sorry.
OPPOSITE unrepentant.

regular *adjective*
1 *She makes regular visits to her aunt.* frequent, periodic, repeated, routine.
OPPOSITE occasional.
2 *a regular bedtime.* consistent, fixed, normal, predictable, set, standard, unchanging.
OPPOSITE variable.
3 *This is not the regular way of doing it.* conventional, correct, customary, established, habitual, normal, ordinary, orthodox, proper, routine, standard,

traditional, typical, usual.
OPPOSITE unorthodox.
4 *regular footsteps.* even, measured, rhythmic, steady, uniform.
OPPOSITE uneven.
5 *a regular shape.* even, symmetrical.
OPPOSITE irregular.

regulate *verb*
1 *The traffic is regulated by police.* control, direct, govern, manage, supervise.
2 *The sound is regulated with this knob.* adjust, alter, change, modulate, vary.

regulation *noun*
local government regulations. by-law, law, rule, statute.

rehearse *verb*
They rehearsed the play many times. go over, practise, prepare, run through.

reign *noun*
under the reign of Henry VII. kingship, rule, sovereignty.
reign *verb*
The Queen reigned for three years. be on the throne, govern, rule.

rein *verb*
rein in *He reined in their spending.* check, control, curb, keep a tight rein on, limit, restrain.

reinforce *verb*
1 *He reinforced the wall.* brace, buttress, fortify, prop up, strengthen, toughen.
OPPOSITE weaken.
2 *This reinforced their argument.* add weight to, assist, bolster, enhance, strengthen, support.
OPPOSITE weaken.

reject *verb*
1 *She rejected the offer.* decline, dismiss, knock back (*informal*), pass up (*informal*), refuse, spurn, turn down, turn your nose up at.
OPPOSITE accept.
2 *He rejected all their gifts.* discard, get rid of, send back, throw out.
OPPOSITE accept.
3 *His friends rejected him.* brush off, disown, ditch (*informal*), drop, dump, forsake, renounce, snub.
reject *noun*
The shop sells rejects. cast-off, discard, second.

a
b
c
d
e
f
g
h
i
j
k
l
m
n
o
p
q
r
s
t
u
v
w
x
y
z

rejection *noun*
Her application met with another rejection. brush-off, knock-back (*informal*), refusal, snub, thumbs down, veto.
OPPOSITE acceptance.

rejoice *verb*
They rejoiced at the good news. be happy, be joyful, be overjoyed, celebrate, crow, delight, revel.
OPPOSITE be sad.

relate *verb*
She related their exciting tale. describe, narrate, recite, recount, report, spin, tell.
relate to
1 *These facts relate to the case.* apply to, be connected with, belong to, be relevant to, concern, pertain to, refer to.
2 *She does not relate well to children.* get on with, interact with, understand.

related *adjective*
They are related problems. allied, associated, connected, interconnected, interrelated.
OPPOSITE separate.

relation *noun*
1 *the relation between fact and fiction.* association, connection, correlation, correspondence, link, relationship, tie-in.
2 *friends and relations.* see RELATIVE.

relationship *noun*
The relationship between the two is very close. association, attachment, bond, connection, link, rapport, tie.

relative *adjective*
She did it with relative ease. comparative.
relative *noun*
She visited her relative. kinsman, kinswoman, relation; [*relatives*] clan, family, flesh and blood, folk, kin, kindred, kith and kin.

relax *verb*
1 *He relaxed in front of television.* calm down, laze, lounge, rest, take it easy, unwind, veg out (*slang*).
OPPOSITE tense.
2 *She relaxed her grip.* ease off, loosen, slacken, weaken.
OPPOSITE tighten.

3 *They relaxed the rules.* bend, ease, stretch.
OPPOSITE tighten.

relaxation *noun*
He plays cards for relaxation. diversion, enjoyment, fun, hobby, leisure, pastime, pleasure, recreation.
OPPOSITE work.

relaxed *adjective*
a relaxed attitude. calm, casual, easygoing, informal, laid-back (*informal*), nonchalant, slack.
OPPOSITE tense.

relay *verb*
He relayed the information. communicate, pass on, send on, transmit.

release *verb*
1 *They released the captives.* deliver, discharge, emancipate, free, let go, let loose, let out, liberate, set free.
OPPOSITE detain.
2 *They released their seat belts.* unbuckle, undo, unfasten, untie.
OPPOSITE fasten.
3 *They released the new book.* circulate, distribute, issue, launch, publish.
OPPOSITE suppress.

relent *verb*
He finally relented and allowed them to go. be merciful, capitulate, give in, have pity, yield.

relentless *adjective*
1 *a relentless tyrant.* harsh, merciless, remorseless, ruthless, severe, unyielding.
OPPOSITE lenient.
2 *The crying was relentless.* constant, continuous, endless, incessant, persistent.

relevant *adjective*
The comment was not relevant to the subject. applicable, appropriate, connected, pertinent, related, to the point.
OPPOSITE irrelevant.

reliable *adjective*
a reliable friend. constant, dependable, faithful, loyal, staunch, steadfast, steady, sure, true, trusted, trustworthy.
OPPOSITE unreliable.

relic *noun*
relics of the past. antique, heirloom, keepsake, memento, reminder, souvenir.

relief *noun*
1 He sought relief from the pain. comfort, ease, let-up, remission, respite, rest, solace.
2 A fund offered relief to flood victims. aid, assistance, help, support.

relieve *verb*
1 Nothing will relieve the pain. alleviate, ease, help, lessen, lighten, reduce, soothe, subdue.
OPPOSITE aggravate.
2 The money will relieve the bushfire victims. aid, assist, help.
3 She relieves the teacher when he is ill. cover for, fill in for, stand in for, substitute for, take the place of.

religion *noun*
a comparative study of the world's religions. belief, creed, cult, denomination, faith, sect; [various religions] Buddhism, Christianity, Hinduism, Islam, Judaism.

religious *adjective*
1 a religious service. devotional, divine, holy, sacred, spiritual.
OPPOSITE secular.
2 religious instruction. doctrinal, scriptural, spiritual, theological.
OPPOSITE secular.
3 a religious person. devout, God-fearing, godly, pious, spiritual.
OPPOSITE impious, irreligious.

relish *verb*
She relished the thought. delight in, enjoy, fancy, like, love, savour.
OPPOSITE dislike.

reluctant *adjective*
They were reluctant to commit themselves. disinclined, hesitant, loath, unwilling.
OPPOSITE eager.

rely *verb*
rely on Can you rely on him? bank on, count on, depend on, reckon on, trust.

remain *verb*
1 Two pieces of cake remain. be left.

2 The old customs remain. continue, endure, go on, live on, persist, prevail, survive.
OPPOSITE die.
3 She remained in Bendigo. hang around, keep on, linger, stay, stick around (informal), tarry, wait.
OPPOSITE leave.

remainder *noun*
He threw out the remainder. balance, excess, leftovers, remnant, residue, rest, surplus.

remains *plural noun*
1 the remains of the meal. dregs, leftovers, remnants, scraps.
2 the castle remains. ruins, wreckage.
3 They buried his remains. body, carcass, corpse.

remark *noun*
He addressed his remarks to me. comment, observation, opinion, statement, word.
remark *verb*
'You've had your hair cut,' he remarked. comment, mention, note, observe, say.

remarkable *adjective*
a remarkable achievement. amazing, astounding, exceptional, extraordinary, impressive, marvellous, memorable, notable, noteworthy, outstanding, phenomenal, sensational, significant, singular, special, startling, striking, surprising, uncommon, unusual, wonderful.
OPPOSITE ordinary.

remedy *noun*
1 a remedy for many illnesses. antidote, cure, medicine, therapy, treatment.
2 The problem has an easy remedy. answer, cure, solution.
remedy *verb*
The technician remedied the problem. correct, cure, fix, put right, rectify, repair, solve.

remember *verb*
1 He remembered what we told him. keep in mind, memorise, recall, recollect.
OPPOSITE forget.
2 They were remembering old times. look back on, recall, recollect, reflect on, reminisce about, think back on.

a
b
c
d
e
f
g
h
i
j
k
l
m
n
o
p
q
r
s
t
u
v
w
x
y
z

remembrance *noun*
They were silent in remembrance of the dead. commemoration, memory, recollection.

remind *verb*
Remind her to withdraw the money. jog someone's memory, prompt, refresh someone's memory.

reminder *noun*
The photo was a reminder of happier times. keepsake, memento, remembrance, souvenir.

reminiscences *plural noun*
He wrote his reminiscences. memoirs, memories, recollections.

remnant *noun*
She made a quilt out of the remnants. fragment, leftover, offcut, piece, remainder, remains, residue, scrap.

remorse *noun*
He felt no remorse for his crime. contrition, guilt, penitence, regret, repentance, shame, sorrow.

remote *adjective*
1 *a remote place.* distant, far-away, inaccessible, isolated, outlying, out of the way, secluded.
OPPOSITE near.
2 *a remote chance.* faint, outside, slender, slight, slim, unlikely.
OPPOSITE likely.

remove *verb*
1 *They were removed from the building.* drive out, eject, evacuate, evict, expel, kick out (*informal*), throw out, turn out.
2 *He removed a branch of the tree.* chop off, cut off, lop off, prune.
3 *He was removed to a different hospital.* cart off, convey, move, relocate, shift, take away, transfer, transport.
4 *She removed her savings from the bank.* take out, withdraw.
OPPOSITE deposit.
5 *He removed the splinter.* extract, pull out, take out.
6 *He removed his clothes.* peel off, pull off, shed, strip off, take off.
OPPOSITE don, put on.
7 *He was removed from the job.* dismiss, expel, fire, get rid of, kick out (*informal*),

oust, sack (*informal*), transfer.
OPPOSITE install.
8 *He removed the graffiti.* delete, erase, get rid of, rub out, wash off, wipe out.

render *verb*
1 *a reward for services rendered.* do, give, perform, provide, supply.
2 *The accident rendered him helpless.* make.

rendezvous *noun*
They arranged a rendezvous at four o'clock. appointment, date (*informal*), engagement, meeting.

renew *verb*
1 *Her energy was renewed by the holiday.* refresh, rejuvenate, restore, revive.
2 *The tyres need renewing.* change, replace.
3 *He renewed his subscription.* continue, extend, prolong.
OPPOSITE cancel.

renovate *verb*
The new owners renovated the house. do up (*informal*), modernise, redecorate, refurbish, rejuvenate, remodel, restore, update.

renown *noun*
She won renown as a ballerina. distinction, fame, importance, note, prestige, reputation, repute.
OPPOSITE obscurity.

renowned *adjective*
the renowned pianist. celebrated, distinguished, eminent, famous, illustrious, noted, prominent, well-known.
OPPOSITE obscure.

rent *verb*
He bought a houseboat and rents it out. charter, hire, lease, let.

reorganise *verb*
He reorganised the office. change, rationalise, rearrange, restructure, transform.

repair *verb*
1 *They repaired the car.* fix, overhaul, recondition, restore, service.
2 *She repaired the hole in her stockings.* darn, mend, patch, sew up.

repair *noun*
in good repair. condition, nick (*informal*), order, shape, state.

repay *verb*
He repaid me the money he had borrowed. pay back, recompense, refund, reimburse.

repeat *verb*
1 *He repeated what he had been told to say.* echo, quote, recite, reiterate, retell, say again, tell again.
2 *They repeated their mistake.* duplicate, reproduce.
repeat *noun*
The programme was a repeat. rebroadcast, replay, rerun.
OPPOSITE première.

repeated *adjective*
repeated interruptions. continual, frequent, recurrent.
OPPOSITE one-off.

repeatedly *adverb*
again and again, continually, frequently, often, over and over, time and time again.

repel *verb*
1 *They repelled the attacker.* drive away, fend off, force back, keep at bay, parry, repulse, stave off, ward off.
2 *The foul smell repelled her.* disgust, nauseate, offend, put off, revolt, sicken.
OPPOSITE attract.

repent *verb*
He repented of his sins. be sorry, feel remorse, lament, regret.

repentant *adjective*
a repentant sinner. contrite, penitent, regretful, remorseful, sorry.
OPPOSITE unrepentant.

repetitive *adjective*
a repetitive job. boring, humdrum, monotonous, repetitious, tedious, unchanging, unvaried.

replace *verb*
1 *He replaced the vase on the shelf.* put back, restore, return.
2 *She replaced the unpopular secretary.* come after, follow, oust, substitute for, succeed, supersede, supplant, take the place of.
3 *She replaces the water daily.* change, renew, replenish.

replacement *noun*
deputy, locum, proxy, stand-in, substitute, successor, surrogate.

replica *noun*
a replica of a painting. copy, duplicate, facsimile, imitation, likeness, model, reproduction.
OPPOSITE original.

reply *verb*
'That's not what I've heard,' he replied. answer, rejoin, respond, retort.
OPPOSITE ask.
reply *noun*
a reply to a letter or question. acknowledgement, answer, comeback (*informal*), rejoinder, response, retort.
OPPOSITE question.

report *verb*
1 *They reported their results.* announce, communicate, declare, disclose, document, notify, publish, record, say, state, tell, write up.
OPPOSITE withhold.
2 *He reported them to the Tax Office.* denounce, dob in (*Australian informal*), grass (on) (*slang*), inform on, shop (*slang*), tell on.
3 *Report to the office.* front up (*informal*), introduce yourself, present yourself.
report *noun*
1 *He read the report.* account, announcement, article, bulletin, communiqué, description, narrative, news, paper, proceedings, record, statement, story, write-up.
2 *The gun went off with a loud report.* bang, blast, explosion, noise.

reporter *noun*
a newspaper reporter. correspondent, journalist, writer.

represent *verb*
1 *She represented the Queen in the play.* act as, appear as, perform as, play, portray.
2 *The hotel was not as it had been represented in the brochure.* depict,

a
b
c
d
e
f
g
h
i
j
k
l
m
n
o
p
q
r
s
t
u
v
w
x
y
z

describe, illustrate, picture, portray, present.
3 *Each dot on the map represents a town.* correspond to, denote, express, indicate, mean, signify, stand for, symbolise.
4 *He represents the tourism industry.* act for, act on behalf of, speak for.

representative *noun*
1 *an official representative.* ambassador, delegate, deputy, emissary, envoy, mouthpiece, proxy, spokesperson, stand-in, substitute.
2 *the company's sales representatives.* agent, rep (*informal*), salesman, salesperson, saleswoman.

repress *verb*
1 *The government repressed the people severely.* control, crush, keep down, oppress, subjugate.
2 *They repressed the revolt.* quash, quell, subdue, suppress.
3 *She repressed her emotions.* bottle up, check, control, curb, hold back, restrain, stifle, suppress.
OPPOSITE release.

reprieve *noun*
The judge granted him a reprieve. pardon, postponement, remission, stay of execution.
reprieve *verb*
The prisoner was reprieved. let off, pardon, spare.

reprimand *noun*
He was given a stern reprimand. admonition, dressing down (*informal*), lecture, rebuke, reproof, scolding, talking-to (*informal*).
OPPOSITE commendation.
reprimand *verb*
She reprimanded them for speaking rudely. admonish, castigate, censure, chastise, chide (*old use*), go crook at (*Australian informal*), lecture, rap over the knuckles, rebuke, reproach, reprove, rouse on (*Australian informal*), scold, take to task, tell off (*informal*), tick off (*informal*), upbraid.
OPPOSITE praise.

reprisal *noun*
They did nothing for fear of reprisal. retaliation, retribution, revenge, vengeance.

reproach *verb*
She reproached herself for not doing enough. admonish, castigate, censure, chide (*old use*), criticise, rebuke, reprimand, reprove, scold, upbraid.
OPPOSITE commend.
reproach *noun*
His action brought reproach upon the family. discredit, disgrace, disrepute, humiliation, shame.
OPPOSITE honour.

reproduce *verb*
1 *They reproduced the document.* copy, duplicate, fax, photocopy, print.
2 *The rabbits are constantly reproducing.* breed, multiply, procreate, proliferate, propagate.

reproduction *noun*
a reproduction of a painting. copy, duplicate, facsimile, imitation, print, replica.
OPPOSITE original.

reptile *noun*
[*various reptiles*] alligator, crocodile, lizard, snake, tortoise, turtle; see also LIZARD, SNAKE.

repulsive *adjective*
a repulsive sight. abominable, disgusting, distasteful, foul, gross (*informal*), hideous, horrible, loathsome, nasty, nauseating, objectionable, obnoxious, odious, offensive, off-putting, repellent, repugnant, revolting, sickening, ugly, vile, yucky (*informal*).
OPPOSITE attractive.

reputable *adjective*
a reputable dealer. above board, honest, honourable, reliable, respectable, respected, trustworthy.
OPPOSITE disreputable.

reputation *noun*
The carpenter had a good reputation. fame, name, prestige, renown, repute, standing.

request *noun*
He granted her request for funds. appeal, application, entreaty, petition, plea.
request *verb*
1 *She requested a job.* apply for, ask for, beg for, petition for, plead for, solicit.

2 *He requested them not to smoke.* appeal to, ask, beseech, entreat, implore.

require *verb*
1 *The patient requires help to get dressed.* depend on, need, rely on.
2 *She bought the things she required.* be missing, be short of, lack, need, want.
3 *The job requires skill.* call for, demand, necessitate.
4 *You are required to be there.* command, compel, direct, oblige, order.

required *adjective*
required reading for the course. compulsory, essential, mandatory, necessary, obligatory, prescribed, requisite.

requirement *noun*
A degree is a requirement for the job. essential, must, necessity, prerequisite, requisite, specification, stipulation.

rescue *verb*
1 *They rescued the hostages.* deliver, free, liberate, release, save.
2 *They rescued a few things from the burning house.* recover, retrieve, salvage.
rescue *noun*
deliverance, liberation, recovery, release, retrieval.

research *noun*
He conducts cancer research. experimentation, exploration, inquiry, investigation, study.
research *verb*
He researched his family's history. delve into, explore, inquire into, investigate, study.

resemblance *noun*
There is a resemblance between him and his father. correspondence, likeness, similarity.
OPPOSITE difference.

resemble *verb*
She resembles her sister. be like, be similar to, look like, take after.

resent *verb*
He resents having to pay. begrudge, dislike, mind, object to, take exception to, take umbrage at.
OPPOSITE like.

resentful *adjective*
a resentful attitude. angry, bitter, discontented, disgruntled, envious, grudging, indignant, jealous, sullen.

resentment *noun*
She felt resentment at their good fortune. anger, animosity, bitterness, discontent, envy, hatred, hostility, ill will, indignation, jealousy, rancour.

reservation *noun*
1 *a hotel reservation.* booking.
2 *They had no reservations about the proposal.* doubt, hesitation, misgiving, objection, qualm, scruple.

reserve *verb*
1 *He reserved some chocolates for later.* hold back, keep, keep back, preserve, put aside, retain, save, spare, withhold.
2 *She reserved a room for the night.* book, order, prearrange, secure.
reserve *noun*
1 *a reserve of lollies.* cache, fund, hoard, kitty, pool, stock, stockpile, store, supply.
2 *The team has two reserves.* backup, deputy, stand-by, stand-in, substitute, understudy.
3 *a nature reserve.* conservation park, game park, safari park, sanctuary, wildlife park.

reserved *adjective*
a reserved person. aloof, bashful, distant, restrained, reticent, shy, stand-offish, uncommunicative, undemonstrative, unemotional, withdrawn.
OPPOSITE open, outgoing.

reservoir *noun*
The water is low in the reservoir. dam, lake, pond.

reshuffle *noun*
a Cabinet reshuffle. rearrangement, reorganisation, shake-up, spill (*Australian informal*).

reside *verb*
reside in *She resides in a converted barn.*

a
b
c
d
e
f
g
h
i
j
k
l
m
n
o
p
q
r
s
t
u
v
w
x
y
z

dwell in, hang out in (*informal*), inhabit, live in, lodge in, occupy, stay in.

residence *noun*
the governor's official residence. abode (*old use*), domicile, dwelling, home, house, place.

resident *noun*
1 *a resident of Hobart.* citizen, householder, inhabitant, local, native.
2 *a hotel resident.* guest, inmate, lodger, occupant, visitor.

resign *verb*
She resigned her position. abdicate, give up, leave, quit, relinquish, stand down from, step down from.
resign yourself to *She resigned herself to defeat.* accept, reconcile yourself to.

resist *verb*
1 *They resisted their attackers.* defy, fight, oppose, stand up to, withstand.
OPPOSITE surrender to.
2 *He resisted the proposed changes.* buck (*informal*), fight against, jack up at (*Australian slang*), oppose, rebel against.
OPPOSITE accept.

resistant *adjective*
resistant to disease. water-resistant. immune, impervious, proof, unaffected.
OPPOSITE susceptible.

resolute *adjective*
He was resolute in his support of the new law. adamant, determined, dogged, firm, persistent, resolved, staunch, steadfast, tenacious, unwavering.
OPPOSITE irresolute, vacillating.

resolution *noun*
1 *She has the resolution to complete the job.* determination, doggedness, persistence, purpose, resolve, tenacity, will-power.
2 *a New Year's resolution.* commitment, decision, intention, pledge, promise, resolve.

resolve *verb*
1 *She resolved to tell him.* decide, determine.
OPPOSITE hesitate.
2 *The problem has been resolved.* clear up, fix, remedy, settle, solve, sort out.

resolve *noun*
1 *She kept her resolve.* intention, pledge, promise, resolution.
2 *They fought with resolve.* determination, doggedness, purpose, resolution, steadfastness, will-power.

resort *verb*
resort to *He resorted to violence.* adopt, fall back on, have recourse to, turn to, use, utilise.

resort *noun*
1 *She will only do it as a last resort.* choice, option, recourse.
2 *a tourist resort.* centre, haunt, retreat, spot.

resound *verb*
The organ resounded in the church. echo, resonate, reverberate, ring.

resounding *adjective*
a resounding success. enormous, great, marked, notable, outstanding, remarkable, striking, tremendous (*informal*).

resource *noun*
The library is full of study resources. aid, help, material.
resources *plural noun*
They pooled their resources. assets, funds, means, money, reserves, riches, wealth.

resourceful *adjective*
a resourceful student. clever, creative, enterprising, ingenious, innovative, inventive, shrewd.
OPPOSITE unimaginative.

respect *noun*
1 *She treated her parents with respect.* admiration, awe, consideration, courtesy, deference, honour, politeness, regard, reverence, veneration.
OPPOSITE disrespect.
2 *with respect to.* reference, regard, relation.
3 *They differ in several respects.* aspect, detail, feature, particular, point, regard, way.

respect *verb*
1 *They respected their grandparents.* admire, esteem, honour, look up to, revere, venerate.
OPPOSITE scorn.

2 *He respected her wishes.* comply with, consider, follow, heed, honour, obey, observe.
OPPOSITE ignore.

respectable *adjective*
1 *a respectable family.* decent, honest, honourable, reputable, upright, worthy.
2 *He did not look respectable in his gardening clothes.* decent, presentable, proper, tidy.
OPPOSITE disreputable.
3 *a respectable score.* acceptable, adequate, fair, passable, reasonable, satisfactory.
OPPOSITE disgraceful.

respected *adjective*
a respected academic. celebrated, distinguished, esteemed, highly-regarded.

respectful *adjective*
civil, considerate, courteous, deferential, polite, well-mannered.
OPPOSITE disrespectful.

respond *verb*
She responded rudely to the question. answer, react, rejoin, reply, retort.
OPPOSITE ask.

response *noun*
1 *an immediate response to the question.* answer, rejoinder, reply, retort.
OPPOSITE question.
2 *The report met with little response.* acknowledgement, feedback, reaction.

responsibility *noun*
1 *They accepted responsibility for the accident.* blame, fault, guilt, liability.
2 *He had the responsibility of telling the family.* burden, duty, job, obligation, onus, task.

responsible *adjective*
1 *She was responsible for the accident.* at fault, guilty, to blame.
2 *a responsible person.* conscientious, dependable, dutiful, honest, law-abiding, mature, reliable, sensible, trustworthy.
OPPOSITE irresponsible.
3 *a responsible job.* executive, important, managerial, senior, supervisory.

rest[1] *verb*
1 *He worked hard and then rested.* lie down, pause, relax, sleep, take it easy.
2 *He rested the rake against the tree.* lean, perch, place, prop, stand, support.
3 *The case rests on scanty evidence.* be based, depend, hang, hinge, rely.
rest *noun*
1 *He had a rest on the sofa.* lie-down, nap, siesta, sleep, snooze.
2 *The body needs periods of rest.* ease, idleness, inactivity, leisure, relaxation, repose.
OPPOSITE activity.
3 *She stopped work for a short rest.* break, breather, holiday, interlude, intermission, interval, pause, recess, respite, spell (*Australian*), time off, vacation.
4 *a rest for a telescope.* base, holder, prop, stand, support, tripod.
at rest inactive, inert, motionless, still.
OPPOSITE moving.

rest[2] *noun*
They sold some and gave away the rest. balance, excess, leftovers, remainder, remnant, residue, surplus.

restaurant *noun*
bistro, brasserie, buffet, café, cafeteria, canteen, diner (*American*), eatery (*informal*).

restless *adjective*
1 *a restless horse.* agitated, edgy, excitable, fidgety, frisky, impatient, lively, nervous, skittish.
OPPOSITE calm.
2 *a restless night.* disturbed, sleepless, wakeful.

restore *verb*
1 *They restored the old car.* do up (*informal*), fix, mend, rebuild, recondition, remodel, renovate, repair.
2 *He was restored to good health.* bring back, rehabilitate, return.
3 *The stolen painting was restored to its owners.* give back, hand back, return.

restrain *verb*
1 *He restrained the prisoner.* bind, chain, fetter, shackle, tie up.
2 *He restrained his temper.* bottle up, bridle, contain, control, keep in check, repress, suppress.

a
b
c
d
e
f
g
h
i
j
k
l
m
n
o
p
q
r
s
t
u
v
w
x
y
z

3 *They restrained their spending.* check, curb, curtail, keep a tight rein on, limit, moderate, rein in, restrict.

restraint *noun*
1 *The car is fitted with child restraints.* harness, seat belt.
2 *She showed great restraint in not saying anything.* control, self-control, self-discipline, self-restraint.

restrict *verb*
1 *Her movements were restricted.* check, cramp, curb, hamper, impede, limit.
2 *The animals were restricted in small cages.* box in, confine, coop up, enclose, hem in, pen, shut in.

restriction *noun*
no restrictions on how the money is to be spent. condition, constraint, control, limitation, proviso, qualification, stipulation.

result *noun*
1 *the result of his research.* consequence, effect, fruit, outcome, output, repercussion, upshot.
2 *exam results.* grade, mark, score.
3 *She came up with the correct result.* answer, finding, solution.
result *verb*
1 *The headache resulted from too much reading.* arise, come about, follow, happen, occur, originate, spring, stem.
2 *Disobedience resulted in tragedy.* culminate, end, finish.

resume *verb*
1 *They resumed their seats.* reoccupy, return to, take again.
2 *They resumed lessons after lunch.* begin again, carry on, continue, recommence, restart.

retain *verb*
1 *She retained the lid.* hang on to, hold on to, keep, save.
OPPOSITE discard.
2 *He retains information easily.* learn, memorise, recall, recollect, remember.
OPPOSITE forget.

retaliate *verb*
It was hard not to retaliate after having been punched. counter-attack, get even, get your own back (*informal*), hit back,

pay back, reciprocate, seek retribution, take reprisals, take revenge.

retard *verb*
Poor diet can retard growth. delay, hamper, handicap, hinder, impede, inhibit, obstruct, slow down, stunt.
OPPOSITE speed up.

retire *verb*
1 *He retired at 55.* give up work, leave work, quit work, stop working.
2 *They retired to the sitting room.* go, retreat, withdraw.
3 *She retires at 9 o'clock.* go to bed, hit the sack (*informal*), turn in (*informal*).
OPPOSITE get up.

retiring *adjective*
a retiring disposition. bashful, diffident, meek, modest, reserved, shy, timid, uncommunicative, withdrawn.
OPPOSITE outgoing.

retort *verb*
He retorted angrily. answer, counter, react, rejoin, reply, respond.
retort *noun*
His sharp retort took her by surprise. answer, comeback, rejoinder, reply, response.

retrace *verb*
retrace your steps backtrack, go back, return.

retreat *verb*
They retreated in terror from the scene. back away, depart, escape, flee, go away, leave, retire, run away, shrink back, withdraw.
OPPOSITE advance.
retreat *noun*
1 *He made a hasty retreat.* departure, escape, exit, flight, getaway.
2 *They ran to their cosy retreat in the hills.* asylum, haven, hideout (*informal*), hiding-place, refuge, resort, sanctuary, shelter.

retrench *verb*
1 *In hard times the company was forced to retrench.* cut back, downsize, economise, rationalise, tighten your belt.
2 (*Australian*) *They retrenched fifty workers.* dismiss, get rid of, lay off, make redundant, sack (*informal*), shed.

retrieve *verb*
1 *The dog retrieved the ball.* bring back, fetch, find, get back, recapture, recover, regain.
2 *He retrieved the information.* access, find, recover, track down.

return *verb*
1 *He returns on Monday.* come back, go back, reappear.
OPPOSITE leave.
2 *She returned the books.* bring back, give back, hand back, put back, replace, restore, send back, take back.
OPPOSITE keep.
3 *She returned the favour.* pay back, reciprocate, repay.
4 *The rash returned.* come back, reappear, recur, resurface.
return *noun*
1 *She was greeted on her return.* arrival, homecoming, reappearance.
OPPOSITE departure.
2 *a poor return on an investment.* earnings, income, profit, revenue, yield.
OPPOSITE outlay.

reunion *noun*
gathering, get-together.

reuse *verb*
recycle, use again.

reveal *verb*
1 *The paper revealed the true story.* bring to light, disclose, divulge, expose, leak, let out, let slip, proclaim, publish, tell.
OPPOSITE cover up.
2 *He revealed his real feelings.* admit, air, betray, confess, declare, show, voice.
OPPOSITE hide.
3 *She lifted her veil to reveal her face.* bare, display, expose, show, uncover.
OPPOSITE cover.

revel *verb*
revel in *She revels in all the attention.* bask in, delight in, enjoy, glory in, rejoice in, relish, savour, wallow in.

revelation *noun*
astonishing revelations about their past. disclosure, discovery, eye-opener, leak.

revenge *noun*
He sought revenge for the murder. reprisal, retaliation, retribution, vengeance.

take revenge avenge yourself, get even, get your own back, pay back, retaliate, take reprisals.

revenue *noun*
income, proceeds, receipts, return, takings.
OPPOSITE expenditure.

revere *verb*
She reveres God. They revered their mother. admire, adore, glorify, hold in awe, honour, idolise, look up to, respect, reverence, venerate, worship.
OPPOSITE despise.

reverence *noun*
They treated his name with reverence. admiration, adoration, awe, devotion, esteem, honour, respect, veneration.
OPPOSITE irreverence.

reversal *noun*
a complete reversal of policy. about-face, about-turn, backflip, change, turn-about, turn-around, U-turn.

reverse *noun*
1 *Sign on the reverse.* back, flip side (*informal*), other side, underside.
2 *It was the reverse of what she expected.* antithesis, contrary, converse, opposite.
reverse *verb*
1 *They reversed the order.* invert, transpose, turn round, turn upside down.
2 *He reversed his decision.* do a backflip on (*informal*), override, overrule, overturn, revoke, undo.
OPPOSITE uphold.
3 *She reversed the car.* back, drive backwards.
OPPOSITE advance.

review *noun*
1 *a review of the firm's performance.* analysis, examination, reappraisal, reassessment, re-examination, stocktaking, study, survey.
2 *The play received good reviews.* criticism, critique, notice, write-up.
review *verb*
1 *He reviewed the situation.* analyse, assess, examine, go over, investigate, reappraise, reassess, reconsider, re-examine, study, survey, take stock of, think over.

a
b
c
d
e
f
g
h
i
j
k
l
m
n
o
p
q
r
s
t
u
v
w
x
y
z

2 *She enjoyed reviewing the book.*
appraise, assess, comment on, criticise,
evaluate, judge.

revise *verb*
1 *He revised the article for publication.*
alter, amend, change, edit, modify,
rework, rewrite, update.
2 *They revised their physics for the test.*
brush up on, cram, go over, learn,
study, swot (*informal*).

revival *noun*
a revival of interest. reawakening,
renewal, resurgence.

revive *verb*
1 *The doctor revived the patient.* bring
round, resuscitate.
2 *The patient did not revive.* come round,
rally, recover, regain consciousness.
3 *He revived the custom.* bring back,
reintroduce, restore.

revolt *verb*
1 *The people revolted against the
government.* disobey, mutiny, rebel, rise
up.
2 *They were revolted by what they saw.*
appal, disgust, horrify, nauseate, repel,
shock, sicken.
revolt *noun*
The people's revolt was quashed. mutiny,
rebellion, revolution, rising, uprising.

revolting *adjective*
a revolting smell, sight, etc. abominable,
detestable, disgusting, distasteful, foul,
gross (*informal*), gruesome, hateful,
hideous, horrible, loathsome, nasty,
nauseating, objectionable, obnoxious,
odious, offensive, off-putting, repellent,
repugnant, repulsive, vile.
OPPOSITE attractive, pleasant.

revolution *noun*
1 *the French Revolution.* coup, coup
d'état, mutiny, rebellion, revolt, rising,
uprising.
2 *a medical revolution.* change,
reformation, shift, transformation.
3 *a revolution of the wheel.* rotation, spin,
turn.

revolve *verb*
The planet revolves around the sun. circle,
go round, orbit.

reward *noun*
a reward for a job well done. award,
bounty, compensation, payment, prize,
recompense, remuneration.
OPPOSITE punishment.
reward *verb*
He was rewarded for his efforts.
compensate, pay, recompense,
remunerate.
OPPOSITE penalise.

rewarding *adjective*
a rewarding job. fulfilling, gratifying,
profitable, satisfying, worthwhile.

rewrite *verb*
He rewrote the book. adapt, edit,
paraphrase, revise, rework.

rhyme *noun*
a nursery rhyme. jingle, poem, verse.

rhythm *noun*
the rhythm of music, poetry, etc. beat,
cadence, lilt, metre, pattern, pulse.

rhythmic *adjective*
rhythmic music. metrical, regular,
rhythmical, steady.

ribbon *noun*
band, braid, strip, tape.

rich *adjective*
1 *a rich businessman.* affluent, moneyed,
prosperous, wealthy, well-heeled
(*informal*), well off, well-to-do.
OPPOSITE poor.
2 *rich in natural resources.* abounding,
abundant, well endowed, well
supplied.
OPPOSITE deficient.
3 *rich furnishings.* costly, expensive,
grand, lavish, luxurious, magnificent,
opulent, splendid, sumptuous.
OPPOSITE cheap.
4 *a rich soil.* fertile, fruitful, lush,
productive.
OPPOSITE unproductive.
riches *plural noun*
assets, fortune, means, money,
property, resources, wealth.

rickety *adjective*
a rickety table. decrepit, dilapidated,
flimsy, ramshackle, shaky,
tumbledown, unstable, unsteady, weak,

wobbly.
OPPOSITE steady.

ricochet *verb*
The ball rebounded off the wall. bounce, rebound.

rid *verb*
He rid the dog of fleas. clear, free.
get rid of They got rid of the things they didn't want. chuck out (*informal*), discard, dispense with, dispose of, ditch (*informal*), drive out, dump, eject, eliminate, eradicate, evict, expel, exterminate, remove, scrap, throw away, throw out, weed out.
OPPOSITE acquire.

riddle *noun*
He enjoys solving riddles. brainteaser, conundrum, enigma, mystery, problem, puzzle, teaser.

ride *verb*
1 She cannot ride a horse. control, handle, manage.
2 He likes riding on buses. go, journey, travel.
3 He bought a bike, and now he rides to work. bicycle, cycle, pedal.
ride *noun*
She had a ride in his car. drive, journey, lift, outing, spin (*informal*), trip.

rider *noun*
1 horses and riders. equestrian, hoop (*Australian slang*), horseman, horse-rider, horsewoman, jockey.
2 bicycle riders. bicyclist, biker, bikie (*Australian informal*), cyclist, motorcyclist.

ridge *noun*
The views from the ridge were spectacular. crest, hilltop, saddle.

ridicule *noun*
an object of ridicule. banter, derision, mockery, sarcasm, satire, scorn.
ridicule *verb*
They love to ridicule important people. caricature, deride, jeer at, laugh at, make fun of, mock, parody, poke fun at, satirise, scoff at, send up (*informal*), sling off at (*Australian informal*), sneer at, take off, take the mickey out of (*informal*), taunt, tease.

ridiculous *adjective*
a ridiculous idea. absurd, comical, crazy, droll, farcical, foolish, funny, hare-brained, hilarious, idiotic, laughable, ludicrous, mad, nonsensical, outrageous, preposterous, silly, stupid, zany.
OPPOSITE sensible.

rife *adjective*
Disease was rife in the city. common, prevalent, rampant, widespread.

rift *noun*
1 a rift in the rock. break, chink, cleft, crack, crevasse, crevice, fissure, fracture, split.
2 a rift between friends. breach, disagreement, split.

right *adjective*
1 right conduct. decent, ethical, fair, good, honest, honourable, just, lawful, legal, moral, proper, virtuous.
OPPOSITE wrong.
2 the right word for the occasion. appropriate, apt, fitting, proper, suitable.
OPPOSITE inappropriate.
3 the right answer. accurate, correct, exact, perfect, precise, proper, true, valid.
OPPOSITE incorrect.
right *noun*
1 You don't have the right to do that. authority, entitlement, licence, permission, power, prerogative, privilege.
2 a ship's right. starboard.
OPPOSITE port.
right *verb*
1 They managed to right the boat. set upright, stand upright, straighten up.
2 She tried to right the wrong. correct, put right, rectify, redress, repair, set right.

righteous *adjective*
a righteous person. blameless, ethical, good, holy, honest, honourable, just, law-abiding, moral, upright, virtuous.
OPPOSITE wicked.

rightful *adjective*
the rightful owner. lawful, legal, legitimate, proper, true.
OPPOSITE unlawful.

a
b
c
d
e
f
g
h
i
j
k
l
m
n
o
p
q
r
s
t
u
v
w
x
y
z

rigid *adjective*
1 *rigid materials.* firm, hard, inflexible, stiff, unbending.
OPPOSITE flexible.
2 *The rules are rigid.* cut and dried, firm, hard and fast, inflexible, rigorous, strict, stringent.
OPPOSITE flexible.

rim *noun*
the rim of a cup, lake, etc. border, brim, brink, circumference, edge, lip, perimeter, verge.

rind *noun*
He peeled off the rind. crust, husk, peel, skin.

ring[1] *noun*
1 *a gold ring. a ring of light.* band, circle, disc, halo, hoop, loop.
2 *a wrestling ring.* arena, enclosure.
ring *verb*
Police ringed the house. circle, encircle, enclose, encompass, hem in, surround.

ring[2] *verb*
1 *The bell rang.* chime, clang, ding, dong, jingle, peal, tinkle, toll.
2 *The hall rang with cheers.* echo, resonate, resound, reverberate.
3 *He rang the police.* call, phone, ring up, telephone.
ring *noun*
1 *They heard a ring of bells.* chime, clang, jingle, knell, peal, tinkle, toll.
2 *(informal) Give me a ring next week.* bell *(informal)*, buzz *(informal)*, call, phone call.

rinse *verb*
Rinse the plates in clean water. clean, swill, wash.

riot *noun*
People were hurt in the riot which broke out. brawl, commotion, disorder, disturbance, fracas, mutiny, pandemonium, revolt, rising, tumult, turmoil, uprising, uproar.
riot *verb*
The people rioted in the city. mutiny, rampage, rebel, revolt, run amok, run riot.

riotous *adjective*
a riotous crowd. anarchic, boisterous, disorderly, lawless, mutinous,

rebellious, rowdy, unruly, wild.
OPPOSITE orderly.

rip *verb*
The barbed wire ripped his skin. gash, lacerate, rupture, sever, slash, slit, split, tear.
rip *noun*
gash, laceration, rupture, slash, slit, split, tear.
rip off *(informal)*
The company makes money by ripping people off. cheat, con *(informal)*, defraud, diddle *(informal)*, fleece, rob, rook, swindle, take for a ride *(informal)*.

ripe *adjective*
1 *The fruit is ripe.* in season, mature, mellow.
OPPOSITE green, unripe.
2 *He lived to a ripe age.* advanced, mature, old.
OPPOSITE tender.

ripen *verb*
The cheese needs to ripen. age, develop, mature, mellow.

rip-off *noun (informal)*
con *(informal)*, swindle, swizz *(informal)*.

ripple *noun*
wave, wavelet.
ripple *verb*
The breeze rippled the surface. agitate, disturb, ruffle, stir.

rise *verb*
1 *The plane is rising.* ascend, climb, go up, soar.
OPPOSITE descend.
2 *The building rose above them.* loom, tower.
3 *She rose to greet us.* arise *(old use)*, get up, stand up.
OPPOSITE lie down, sit down.
4 *The people rose against the government.* mutiny, rebel, revolt, take up arms.
5 *The waves rose.* billow, heave, surge, swell.
OPPOSITE subside.
6 *The shares rose in value.* appreciate, escalate, go up, grow, increase, jump, rocket, shoot up, skyrocket.
OPPOSITE decrease.
7 *Her spirits rose.* improve, lift, soar.
OPPOSITE fall.

8 *The dough rises.* expand, prove, puff up, swell.

9 *The river rises in these mountains.* begin, commence, flow (from), originate, spring (from), start.

rise *noun*

1 *The car overheated after the steep rise.* ascent, climb.
OPPOSITE descent.

2 *The house is visible from the rise.* hill, incline, slope.

3 *Employees receive an annual rise.* increase, increment, raise.

4 *her rise to fame.* advance, advancement, climb, march, progress.

risk *noun*

There was a risk of being caught. chance, danger, possibility.

risk *verb*

1 *He risked his life.* endanger, imperil, jeopardise.

2 *He risked his wages on a horse.* bet, chance, gamble, stake, venture, wager.

risky *adjective*

chancy, dangerous, dicey (*slang*), dodgy (*informal*), hairy (*slang*), hazardous, perilous, precarious, uncertain, unsafe.
OPPOSITE safe.

ritual *noun*

1 *a marriage ritual.* ceremony, rite, service.

2 *a bedtime ritual.* practice, procedure, routine, tradition.

rival *noun*

He beat his rival. adversary, challenger, enemy, foe, opponent.
OPPOSITE ally.

rival *verb*

1 *They rivalled one another for first place.* compete with, contend with, contest, oppose, vie with.

2 *His cooking rivals that of the best restaurant chefs.* compare with, equal, match.

river *noun*

brook, creek, rivulet, stream, tributary, watercourse, waterway.

road *noun*

1 [*kinds of road*] alley, avenue, boulevard, bypass, byway, causeway, clearway, close, crescent, cul-de-sac, dead end, drive, expressway, freeway, highway, lane, motorway, parade, ring road, route, street, thoroughfare, tollway, track, turnpike (*historical* & *American*), way.

2 *the road to success.* path, route, way.

road train (*Australian*)

juggernaut (*informal*), lorry, semi (*Australian informal*), semitrailer, truck.

roadside *noun*

edge, kerb, verge, wayside.

roadway *noun*

carriageway, road.

roam *verb*

He roamed through the town. meander, ramble, range, rove, saunter, stroll, tootle around (*informal*), travel, wander.

roar *noun*

1 *the lion's roar.* bellow, howl, shout, yell.

2 *the roar of the engines.* blare, clamour, din, noise, racket, thunder.

3 *roars of laughter.* guffaw, hoot (*informal*), howl, scream, shout, shriek.

roar *verb*

1 *He roared with pain.* bawl, bellow, howl, scream, shout, yell.

2 *They roared at his jokes.* guffaw, laugh.

roast *verb*

He roasted the turkey. bake.

rob *verb*

1 *He robbed the man. They robbed a bank.* burgle, hold up, loot, mug, pilfer from, plunder, ransack, steal from, stick up (*informal*).

2 *He robs his customers.* cheat, diddle (*informal*), fleece, overcharge, rip off (*informal*), short-change, swindle.

robber *noun*

bandit, brigand, buccaneer, burglar, bushranger, crook (*informal*), highwayman, housebreaker, looter, marauder, mugger, pickpocket, pilferer, pirate, plunderer, shoplifter, thief.

robbery *noun*

1 *The robbery was committed at 9 o'clock.* burglary, hold-up, mugging, raid, stick-up (*informal*).

2 *He was in jail for robbery.* larceny, stealing, theft.

a
b
c
d
e
f
g
h
i
j
k
l
m
n
o
p
q
r
s
t
u
v
w
x
y
z

robe *noun*
dress, dressing gown, gown, habit, kimono, vestment.

robot *noun*
android, automaton, machine.

robust *adjective*
a robust youth. brawny, hardy, healthy, muscular, powerful, strapping, strong, sturdy, tough, vigorous.
OPPOSITE weak.

rock[1] *noun*
The ground was covered with rocks. boulder, crag, outcrop, pebble, stone; [*various rocks*] basalt, chalk, coal, granite, lava, limestone, marble, pumice, quartzite, sandstone, shale, slate.

rock[2] *verb*
1 *The boat rocked when he stood up.* lurch, pitch, reel, roll, shake, sway, toss, totter, wobble.
2 *The country was rocked by the news of his death.* disturb, shake, shock, stagger, stun, upset.

rocky[1] *adjective*
a rocky path. gravelly, pebbly, rugged, stony.

rocky[2] *adjective*
a rocky start. precarious, shaky, unstable, unsteady.

rod *noun*
bar, baton, cane, cue, dowel, mace, poker, pole, sceptre, staff, stick, wand.

rogue *noun*
1 *The police caught the rogues.* blackguard, con man (*informal*), crook (*informal*), good-for-nothing, knave (*old use*), miscreant, rascal, scoundrel, villain, wretch.
2 *The little rogue hid their shoes.* devil, imp, monkey, rascal, scallywag, scamp, wag.

role *noun*
1 *She played the title role.* character, part.
2 *the role of computers in schools.* function, job, part, place.

roll *verb*
1 *He rolled the wheelchair down the path.* trundle, wheel.

2 *The child rolled over.* flip, somersault, tumble, turn.
3 *The wheels rolled.* go round, revolve, rotate, spin, turn, twirl, whirl.
4 *She rolled up the flag.* furl, wind.
OPPOSITE unfurl.
5 *The cat rolled herself up in a ball.* coil, curl, twist, wind, wrap.
6 *He rolled out the pastry.* flatten, level, smooth.
7 *The ship rolled on heavy seas.* lurch, pitch, reel, rock, sway, toss, totter.

roll *noun*
1 *a roll of paper.* cylinder, reel, spool.
2 *bread rolls.* bagel, bap, bun.
3 *The teacher read the roll.* list, register.
4 *a roll of drums.* boom, reverberation, rumble, thunder.

roller coaster *noun*
big dipper, switchback.

romance *noun*
She reads romances. love story.

romantic *adjective*
a romantic film. emotional, mushy, nostalgic, sentimental, soppy (*informal*).

romp *verb*
The children romped around. caper, dance, frisk, frolic, gambol, jump, play, prance, run, skip.

room *noun*
1 *There was no room to move.* area, elbow room, space.
2 *Each person has his own room.* cell, chamber (*old use*), office.

roomy *adjective*
a roomy bag, house, etc. ample, big, commodious, huge, large, spacious, vast.
OPPOSITE small.

roost *verb*
The birds roosted under the eaves. nest, perch, settle, sleep.

rooster *noun*
cock, cockerel.

root *noun*
1 *plant roots.* radicle, rhizome, rootlet, tuber.
2 *the root of all evil.* basis, bottom, cause, foundation, origin, source.

root *verb*
He was rooted to the spot. anchor, fix, stick.
root out They rooted out crime. eliminate, eradicate, get rid of, remove, weed out.
take root The idea took root. become established, catch on, take hold.

rope *noun*
cable, cord, guy, hawser, lariat, lasso, line, noose, painter, stay, tether.
rope *verb*
The car was roped to the one in front for towing. attach, bind, fasten, hitch, secure, tie.

rort *noun (Australian slang)*
a tax rort. dodge (*informal*), lurk (*Australian informal*), racket, scam (*slang*), scheme, swindle.

roster *noun*
the canteen roster. list, rota.

rosy *adjective*
1 rosy cheeks. blushing, florid, flushed, glowing, pink, red, rose, ruddy.
OPPOSITE pale.
2 a rosy future. auspicious, bright, encouraging, hopeful, optimistic, promising.
OPPOSITE bleak.

rot *verb*
The food rotted. decay, decompose, disintegrate, go bad, go off, perish, putrefy, spoil.
rot *noun (slang)*
He talks a lot of rot. see NONSENSE.

rotate *verb*
1 The table-top rotates. revolve, spin, swivel, turn, twirl, whirl.
2 They rotate jobs in the office. alternate, swap, take turns at.

rotten *adjective*
1 rotten food. bad, decayed, decomposed, mouldy, off, perished, putrid, rancid, stinking.
OPPOSITE fresh.
2 Replace the rotten elastic. crumbling, disintegrated, perished, worn-out.
3 That was a rotten thing to do. beastly, contemptible, despicable, lousy (*informal*), mean, nasty, unkind.

4 (*informal*) She felt rotten with her cold. ill, miserable, poorly, seedy (*informal*), sick, unwell, wretched.
5 (*informal*) rotten weather. abysmal (*informal*), appalling (*informal*), atrocious (*informal*), bad, dreadful (*informal*), foul, shocking (*informal*), terrible (*informal*).

rotund *adjective*
The man grew rotund. chubby, fat, obese, overweight, plump, podgy, portly, stout, tubby.
OPPOSITE skinny.

rough *adjective*
1 a rough surface, edge, etc. bumpy, irregular, jagged, pitted, ragged, rugged, uneven.
OPPOSITE smooth.
2 rough skin. calloused, chapped, hard, scaly, unshaven.
OPPOSITE smooth.
3 a rough person. rough manners. coarse, crude, impolite, loutish, rude, uncouth, unrefined, vulgar.
OPPOSITE refined.
4 a rough voice. grating, gruff, harsh, hoarse, husky, raucous.
OPPOSITE gentle.
5 hurt in rough play. boisterous, lively, rowdy, unrestrained, wild.
OPPOSITE gentle.
6 rough weather. blustery, inclement, squally, stormy, tempestuous, turbulent, violent, wild.
OPPOSITE calm.
7 They had a rough time. difficult, hard, rugged, tough, unpleasant.
OPPOSITE easy.
8 The painter did a rough job. careless, clumsy, hasty, imperfect, patchy, unfinished.
OPPOSITE perfect.
9 Their dwellings were rough and temporary. crude, makeshift, primitive, rough-and-ready, rudimentary.
OPPOSITE elaborate.
10 a rough idea. approximate, general, hazy, imprecise, inexact, sketchy, vague.
OPPOSITE exact.

roughly *adverb*
about, approximately, around, close to, in the vicinity of, nearly, round about.

a b c d e f g h i j k l m n o p q **r** s t u v w x y z

round *adjective*

1 *a round object.* bulbous, circular, curved, globular, rotund, spherical.
2 *a round dozen.* complete, entire, full, whole.

round *noun*

1 *another round of talks.* course, cycle, series, succession.
2 *She won the first round in the contest.* bout, division, game, heat, section, stage.

round *verb*

The car rounded the corner. go round, turn.

round off *She rounded off the conversation.* bring to a close, close, complete, conclude, end, finish, terminate.

round up *They rounded up the cattle.* assemble, collect, gather, herd, muster.

roundabout *noun*

carousel, merry-go-round, whirligig.

roundabout *adjective*

1 *a roundabout way to the shops.* circuitous, devious, indirect, meandering.
OPPOSITE straight.
2 *He asked in a roundabout way.* devious, indirect, oblique.
OPPOSITE direct.

rouse *verb*

1 *She could not rouse him from his sleep.* arouse, awaken, stir, waken, wake up.
2 *He was easily roused to anger.* excite, incite, move, provoke, stimulate, stir.

rousing *adjective*

1 *three rousing cheers.* hearty, loud, strong, vigorous.
2 *a rousing speech.* inspiring, moving, powerful, provoking, stirring.

rout *verb*

They routed their opponents, enemies, etc. beat, conquer, crush, defeat, overpower, put to flight, scatter, thrash, trounce, vanquish.

route *noun*

They drove the scenic route. course, itinerary, path, road, way.

routine *noun*

a daily routine. custom, habit, method, pattern, practice, procedure, ritual, system, way.

routine *adjective*

1 *a routine check of bags.* customary, habitual, normal, regular, standard, usual.
OPPOSITE one-off.
2 *The work had become routine.* boring, dull, familiar, humdrum, mechanical, monotonous, ordinary, predictable, tedious.
OPPOSITE exciting.

rove *verb*

The cat likes to rove. prowl, ramble, roam, stray, wander.

rover *noun*

gypsy, itinerant, nomad, traveller, vagabond, wanderer, wayfarer.

row[1] *noun*

They were arranged in rows. chain, column, file, line, queue, rank, sequence, series, tier.

row[2] *verb*

She rowed the boat. paddle, propel, scull.

row[3] *noun (informal)*

1 *What's all the row about?* clamour, commotion, din, disturbance, fuss, hullabaloo, noise, racket, rumpus, tumult, uproar.
2 *They had a row over money.* altercation, argument, barney (*informal*), blue (*Australian informal*), bust-up (*informal*), dispute, fight, quarrel, run-in, scrap (*informal*), squabble, tiff, wrangle.

rowdy *adjective*

a rowdy crowd. boisterous, disorderly, lawless, noisy, obstreperous, riotous, rough, unruly, wild.
OPPOSITE quiet.

royal *adjective*

the royal seal. kingly, monarchic, queenly, regal, sovereign.

rub *verb*

1 *He rubbed her back.* caress, massage, pat, stroke.
2 *She has a blister where the shoe rubs.* chafe, gall.
3 *He rubbed cream on the sunburn.* apply, smear, spread, wipe, work in.
4 *She rubbed the silver.* buff, burnish, polish, shine, wipe.

rub out *She rubbed out the mistake.* blot out, cancel, delete, erase, obliterate, remove, wipe out.

rubbish *noun*
1 *They removed the rubbish.* debris, garbage, junk, litter, muck (*informal*), mullock (*Australian*), refuse, rubble, scrap, trash, waste.
2 *He talks a lot of rubbish.* balderdash, boloney (*informal*), bunkum, claptrap, cobblers (*slang*), codswallop (*slang*), drivel, garbage, gibberish, gobbledegook (*informal*), guff (*slang*), hogwash (*informal*), humbug, nonsense, piffle (*informal*), poppycock (*slang*), rot (*slang*), stuff and nonsense (*informal*), tommyrot (*slang*), tripe (*informal*), twaddle.
OPPOSITE sense.
rubbish *verb* (*Australian informal*)
He rubbished their proposal. bag (*Australian informal*), belittle, disparage, knock (*informal*), pan (*informal*), pick holes in, pooh-pooh, run down, scoff at, tear to pieces.

rubble *noun*
building rubble. debris.

rucksack *noun*
backpack, haversack, knapsack, pack.

ruddy *adjective*
a ruddy face. florid, flushed, red, rosy.
OPPOSITE pale.

rude *adjective*
1 *a rude person.* abusive, bad-mannered, brazen, cheeky, discourteous, disrespectful, foul-mouthed, impertinent, impolite, impudent, inconsiderate, insolent, insulting, loutish, offensive, offhand, rough, saucy, surly, uncivil, uncouth, vulgar.
OPPOSITE polite.
2 *rude jokes.* coarse, crude, dirty, filthy, foul, improper, indecent, lewd, obscene, offensive, pornographic, tasteless, unprintable, vulgar.
OPPOSITE clean.

ruffian *noun*
attacked by ruffians. bully, gangster, hood (*informal*), hoodlum, hooligan, hoon (*Australian informal*), larrikin

(*Australian*), lout, mugger, rogue, rough, scoundrel, thug, tough, villain.

ruffle *verb*
1 *The pebble ruffled the surface of the lake.* disturb, ripple, stir.
2 *He was not ruffled by the news.* agitate, disconcert, disturb, faze (*informal*), fluster, perturb, rattle (*informal*), unsettle, upset.
OPPOSITE calm.
ruffle *noun*
The dress had ruffles. flounce, frill, ruff.

ruffled *adjective*
Her hair was ruffled. dishevelled, messed up, tangled, tousled, untidy.

rug *noun*
1 *a floor rug.* mat.
2 *a rug for the bed.* blanket, coverlet.

rugged *adjective*
1 *rugged country.* bumpy, craggy, jagged, rocky, rough, stony, uneven, wild.
2 *a rugged face.* craggy, furrowed, leathery, lined, weather-beaten, wrinkled.
OPPOSITE smooth.

ruin *noun*
1 *The house was in a state of ruin.* decay, destruction, dilapidation, disrepair, rack and ruin.
2 *He suffered financial ruin.* collapse, defeat, downfall, failure, fall, loss, undoing.
ruin *verb*
She ruined their plans. The crop was ruined. damage, demolish, destroy, devastate, mess up, muck up, sabotage, spoil, undermine, vandalise, wreck.
ruins *plural noun*
They sifted through the ruins of their house. remains, rubble, shell, wreck, wreckage.

rule *noun*
1 *They followed the rules.* by-law, code, commandment, convention, formula, guideline, instruction, law, order, policy, principle, protocol, regulation, statute.
2 *Getting up at 6 o'clock is the rule.* convention, custom, norm, routine, standard.
OPPOSITE exception.

a
b
c
d
e
f
g
h
i
j
k
l
m
n
o
p
q
r
s
t
u
v
w
x
y
z

3 *under the rule of Elizabeth I.* authority, control, government, jurisdiction, leadership, regime, reign, sovereignty.
rule *verb*
1 *He rules the country.* administer, command, control, direct, govern, lead, manage, reign over, run.
2 *The judge ruled that they were innocent.* adjudicate, decide, decree, find, judge, pronounce.
as a rule for the most part, generally, normally, ordinarily, usually.
rule out *The possibility has been ruled out.* dismiss, eliminate, exclude.

ruler *noun*
1 *the ruler of the people.* chief, commander, emir, emperor, empress, governor, head, head of state, king, leader, lord, monarch, president, prince, princess, queen, sovereign, sultan.
2 *He measured the distance with a ruler.* measure, rule, yardstick.

rumble *noun*
the rumble of aeroplanes. boom, roar, thunder.

rummage *verb*
He rummaged through the drawer to find the key. comb, ferret, fossick (*Australian informal*), hunt, ransack, rifle, scour, search.

rumour *noun*
He didn't believe the rumours he heard. bush telegraph, furphy (*Australian informal*), gossip, hearsay, mulga wire (*Australian informal*), tale.
rumour *verb*
It was rumoured that he had been poisoned. bandy about, gossip, report, spread about, whisper.

rumpus *noun*
They kicked up a rumpus. commotion, din, disturbance, fuss, hullabaloo, pandemonium, protest, racket, row, storm, to-do, uproar.

run *verb*
1 *The boys ran past quickly.* bound, dart, dash, fly, gallop, hurry, hurtle, jog, race, rush, scamper, scoot, scurry, scuttle, shoot, speed, sprint, spurt, stampede, streak, sweep, tear, trot, zip.

2 *The car ran down the hill.* plunge, roll, slide.
3 *The colour ran in the wash.* bleed, come out, spread.
4 *The water ran from the tap.* drip, flow, gush, leak, pour, stream, trickle.
5 *The car runs well.* behave, function, go, perform, work.
6 *The bus runs every hour.* go, operate, travel.
7 *A friend ran her home.* drive, take, transport.
8 *The lease runs for six months.* be current, be valid, continue, last.
OPPOSITE expire.
9 *He runs the business.* administer, conduct, control, direct, govern, look after, maintain, manage, organise, oversee, supervise.

run *noun*
1 *They went for a run in the car.* drive, excursion, outing, ride, trip.
2 *a run of disasters.* sequence, series, spate, succession.
3 *a chicken run.* compound, coop, enclosure, pen.
4 (*Australian*) *He owns a cattle run.* farm, property, station (*Australian*).
run after chase, follow, pursue.
run away abscond, beat it (*slang*), bolt, clear off (*informal*), depart, disappear, do a runner (*slang*), escape, flee, go away, leave, make off, nick off (*Australian slang*), retreat, run off, scarper (*informal*), scoot, scram (*informal*), shoot through (*Australian informal*), skedaddle (*informal*), take flight, take off, take to your heels, withdraw.
OPPOSITE arrive.
run down *The writer is always running politicians down.* bag (*Australian informal*), belittle, criticise, disparage, knock (*informal*), malign, pan (*informal*), rubbish, slate (*informal*).
OPPOSITE praise.
run into
1 *They ran into another car.* bump into, collide with, crash into, hit, knock into, smash into, strike.
2 *She ran into an old school friend in town.* bump into, come across, meet, run across.

run over
1 *The driver ran over a cat.* hit, knock down, run down.
2 *He ran over his lines.* go over, practise, rehearse, run through.

runaway *noun*
bolter, deserter, escapee, fugitive.

run-down *noun*
a run-down of the day's events. outline, recap (*informal*), report, review, round-up, summary, survey.

runny *adjective*
a runny mixture. fluid, liquid, sloppy, thin, watery.
OPPOSITE solid.

runway *noun*
airstrip, landing strip.

rural *adjective*
rural scenery. country, pastoral, rustic.
OPPOSITE urban.

rush *verb*
1 *They rushed to the hospital.* charge, dash, fly, gallop, hasten, hurry, hustle, race, run, scoot, scurry, shoot off, speed, sprint, storm, tear, whiz, zip, zoom.
OPPOSITE dawdle.
2 *They rushed the building.* attack, capture, charge, seize, storm.

rush *noun*
They are always in a rush to be on time. haste, hurry, hustle, race.

rust *verb*
The iron roof rusted. corrode, oxidise, rot.

rustic *adjective*
a rustic atmosphere. country, pastoral, rural.
OPPOSITE urban.

rustle *noun*
a rustle of leaves. swish, whisper.

rut *noun*
1 *The wheels were caught in the rut.* furrow, groove.
2 *He was in a rut.* grind, habit, routine.

ruthless *adjective*
a ruthless killer. brutal, callous, cruel, ferocious, harsh, heartless, merciless, pitiless, relentless, remorseless, savage, vicious.
OPPOSITE compassionate.

a
b
c
d
e
f
g
h
i
j
k
l
m
n
o
p
q
r
s
t
u
v
w
x
y
z

Ss

sabotage *noun*
an act of sabotage. damage, destruction, disruption, vandalism.
sabotage *verb*
He sabotaged my plans. destroy, disrupt, ruin, spoil, undermine, wreck.

sachet *noun*
a sachet of sherbet. bag, pack, packet.

sack *noun*
a sack of potatoes. bag, pack, package.
sack *verb* (*informal*)
The boss sacked half his workers. discharge, dismiss, fire, give notice to, lay off, make redundant.
OPPOSITE hire.

sacred *adjective*
a sacred place. sacred music. blessed, consecrated, divine, hallowed, holy, religious, revered, sanctified, spiritual.
OPPOSITE profane, secular.

sacrifice *noun*
animal sacrifices to their god. offering.
sacrifice *verb*
He sacrifices his free time to help others. forfeit, forgo, give up, offer, renounce, surrender.

sad *adjective*
1 *He felt sad.* blue, dejected, depressed, desolate, despondent, discontented, dismal, distressed, doleful, downcast, gloomy, glum, heartbroken, heavy-hearted, melancholy, miserable, mournful, rueful, sorrowful, unhappy, woebegone, wretched.
OPPOSITE happy.
2 *a sad film.* dismal, distressing, gloomy, heartbreaking, pessimistic, touching, tragic, upsetting.
OPPOSITE comic.

sadden *verb*
He was saddened by their selfishness. depress, dishearten, distress, grieve, upset.
OPPOSITE cheer.

sadistic *adjective*
brutal, cruel, inhuman, monstrous, vicious.

sadness *noun*
dejection, depression, desolation, despondency, discontent, distress, gloom, glumness, melancholy, misery, sorrow, unhappiness, woe, wretchedness.
OPPOSITE happiness.

safari *noun*
an African safari. expedition, tour, trip.

safe *adjective*
1 *safe medicines.* harmless, innocuous, non-toxic.
OPPOSITE dangerous, harmful.
2 *a safe car.* dependable, reliable, roadworthy, sound.
OPPOSITE dangerous.
3 *They remained safe because they stayed inside.* all right, OK (*informal*), safe and sound, unharmed, uninjured, unscathed.
OPPOSITE endangered.
4 *a safe place.* defended, protected, secure, sheltered.
OPPOSITE unprotected.
safe *noun*
She keeps her jewels in a safe. strongbox, vault.

safeguard *noun*
environmental safeguards. defence, precaution, protection.
safeguard *verb*
The lawyer will safeguard their interests. defend, guard, look after, preserve, protect.
OPPOSITE jeopardise.

safely *adverb*
Drive safely. carefully, cautiously, prudently.
OPPOSITE dangerously.

safety *noun*
The helmet is for your safety. protection, security.
OPPOSITE danger.

sag *verb*
The bed sagged in the middle. bow, droop, flop, sink, slump, subside.

saga *noun*
Icelandic sagas. epic, history, legend, story, tale.

sail *noun*
Devonport is an overnight sail from Melbourne. cruise, journey, trip, voyage.
sail *verb*
1 We sail next week. cruise, embark, put to sea, set out, set sail.
2 Who was sailing the boat? navigate, pilot, skipper, steer.

sailor *noun*
mariner, navigator, seafarer, seaman, yachtsman, yachtswoman.

saintly *adjective*
a saintly person. blameless, God-fearing, godly, holy, innocent, pious, righteous, upright, virtuous.
OPPOSITE ungodly.

salary *noun*
The company's executives receive a monthly salary. earnings, income, pay, stipend.
CONTRASTS WITH wage.

sale *noun*
1 the sale of goods. selling, vending.
OPPOSITE buying, purchase.
2 make a sale. deal, transaction.
3 He bought the cupboard at a sale. auction, clearance, sell-out.

salesperson *noun*
You pay the salesperson at the counter. sales assistant, salesman, saleswoman, shop assistant.

salon *noun*
She runs a beauty salon. establishment, parlour, shop.

salty *adjective*
salty water. brackish, briny, saline, salt.

salute *noun*
greeting, salutation, welcome.
salute *verb*
He saluted each person as they entered. acknowledge, greet, nod to.

salvage *verb*
He salvages old bicycles. recover, recycle, rescue, retrieve, save.

salvation *noun*
the salvation of souls. deliverance, redemption, saving.
OPPOSITE damnation.

same *adjective*
1 We see the same man every day. identical, selfsame.
OPPOSITE different.
2 The two girls have the same features. alike, identical, indistinguishable.
OPPOSITE dissimilar.
3 He continued at the same speed. constant, unchanged, uniform, unvarying.
OPPOSITE variable.

sameness *noun*
There's a sameness about his writing. evenness, monotony, similarity, uniformity.
OPPOSITE variety.

sample *noun*
He sent them a sample of his work. example, foretaste, specimen, taste.
sample *verb*
He sampled the soup. taste, test, try.

sanction *noun*
1 The practice will never be given official sanction. approval, authorisation, consent, go-ahead, OK (*informal*), permission, support.
2 Other countries imposed political sanctions against the offending country. ban, boycott, embargo, penalty.
sanction *verb*
The government will not sanction euthanasia. allow, approve, authorise, consent to, legalise, permit, support.
OPPOSITE prohibit.

sanctuary *noun*
1 The priest is in the sanctuary. chapel, church, sanctum, shrine, temple.

a b c d e f g h i j k l m n o p q r s t u v w x y z

2 *a koala sanctuary.* conservation park, reservation, reserve, wildlife park.
3 *The refugees were seeking sanctuary.* asylum, haven, protection, refuge, safety, shelter.

sand *verb*
He sanded the timber. polish, sandpaper, smooth.

sandbank *noun*
reef, sandbar, shoal.

sandwich *noun*
sambo (*Australian slang*), sanger (*Australian slang*).
sandwich *verb*
The car was sandwiched between two trucks. jam, squash, squeeze, wedge.

sane *adjective*
1 *The doctors declared the man to be sane.* all there (*informal*), lucid, normal, of sound mind, rational.
OPPOSITE insane, mad.
2 *a sane approach.* logical, rational, reasonable, sensible, sound.
OPPOSITE foolish.

sanitary *adjective*
a sanitary cooking environment. clean, germ-free, healthy, hygienic, sanitised, sterile, sterilised.
OPPOSITE unhygienic.

sanity *noun*
normality, rationality, reason, saneness, sense, soundness.
OPPOSITE insanity, madness.

sap *noun*
tree sap. juice, lifeblood.
sap *verb*
The disease had sapped his strength. deplete, drain, exhaust, rob, weaken.

sarcastic *adjective*
a sarcastic comment. derisive, ironic, mocking, satirical, scornful, sneering, taunting.

sash *noun*
The dress has a sash at the waist. cummerbund, girdle, tie.

satanic *adjective*
demonic, devilish, diabolic, evil, fiendish, hellish, infernal, wicked.

satchel *noun*
a school satchel. backpack, bag, pack, schoolbag.

satellite *noun*
a satellite orbiting the planet. moon, space station, sputnik.

satin *adjective*
a satin finish. glossy, shiny, smooth.
OPPOSITE matt.

satire *noun*
1 *He uses satire in his essays.* irony, mockery, ridicule, sarcasm.
2 *The play was a satire on school life.* burlesque, parody, send-up (*informal*), skit, spoof (*informal*), take-off.

satirical *adjective*
a satirical play. derisive, ironic, mocking, sarcastic.

satisfaction *noun*
Her success was a source of great satisfaction to them. contentment, fulfilment, gratification, happiness, pleasure, pride.
OPPOSITE dissatisfaction.

satisfactory *adjective*
His marks are satisfactory. acceptable, adequate, all right, enough, fine, OK (*informal*), passable, sufficient, up to scratch.
OPPOSITE unsatisfactory.

satisfy *verb*
1 *Nothing seems to satisfy him.* content, fulfil, gratify, please.
2 *This should satisfy their needs.* answer, comply with, fulfil, meet.
3 *Water will satisfy his thirst.* appease, assuage, quench, slake.
4 *She satisfied the examiners that she knew her subject.* convince, persuade, prove to.

satisfying *adjective*
a satisfying job. enjoyable, fulfilling, gratifying, pleasing, rewarding.

saturate *verb*
The clothes were saturated in the rain. drench, soak, wet through.

sauce *noun*
a meat pie with sauce. dressing, gravy, relish.

saunter *verb*
The tourists sauntered through the grounds. amble, ramble, roam, stroll, wander.

sausage *noun*
barbecued sausages. banger (*slang*), snag (*Australian slang*).

savage *adjective*
1 *savage tribes.* barbaric, primitive, uncivilised.
OPPOSITE civilised.
2 *savage animals.* ferocious, fierce, untamed, wild.
OPPOSITE domesticated, tame.
3 *a savage attack.* brutal, callous, cruel, ferocious, inhuman, merciless, ruthless, vicious, violent.
OPPOSITE mild.
savage *verb*
The sheep were savaged by a pack of dogs. attack, maul.

save *verb*
1 *He saved the boy from drowning.* preserve, protect, rescue, spare.
2 *They have been saved from their sins.* deliver, ransom, redeem, set free.
3 *Save water.* conserve, economise on, use sparingly.
OPPOSITE waste.
4 *She saves plastic bags.* collect, hoard, hold on to, keep, preserve, reserve, retain, store.
5 *They are saving money for a holiday.* accumulate, bank, deposit, invest, lay by, put aside, put by, set aside.

savings *plural noun*
capital, funds, investments, nest egg.

saviour *noun*
1 deliverer, liberator, protector, redeemer, rescuer.
2 *the Saviour.* Christ, Jesus, Messiah.

savoury *adjective*
savoury biscuits with cheese. appetising, piquant, salty, tasty.
OPPOSITE sweet.

saw *noun*
[*kinds of saw*] chainsaw, circular saw, fretsaw, hacksaw, jigsaw.
saw *verb*
see CUT.

say *verb*
1 '*Good,' she said.* announce, answer, bellow, blurt out, call out, comment, cry, declare, exclaim, moan, mumble, murmur, mutter, recite, remark, repeat, reply, scream, shout, shriek, snap, snarl, speak, splutter, squawk, squeal, stammer, state, stutter, tell, utter, whisper, yell.
2 *Does she say much in her letter?* communicate, convey, disclose, express, impart, mention, refer to, report, reveal, speak of, tell.

saying *noun*
a famous saying. adage, byword, catchphrase, maxim, motto, proverb, quotation, slogan.

scab *noun*
a scab on a sore. crust.

scabbard *noun*
He returned his sword to its scabbard. sheath.

scaffold *noun*
The prisoner was sent to the scaffold. gallows, gibbet.

scaffolding *noun*
The painters erected scaffolding around the building. frame, framework, platform.

scald *verb*
see BURN.

scale[1] *noun*
1 *The fish has scales.* flake, lamina, plate.
2 *She removed the scale from the inside of the kettle.* coating, crust, deposit, encrustation.

scale[2] *noun*
1 *a scale of fees.* hierarchy, ladder, progression, range, sequence, series, spectrum.
2 *a map with a scale of 1 cm to 1 km.* proportion, ratio.
3 *the scale of the problem.* dimensions, extent, level, scope, size.
scale *verb*
He scaled the cliff. ascend, clamber up, climb, mount.

scales *plural noun*
balance, weighing machine.

a
b
c
d
e
f
g
h
i
j
k
l
m
n
o
p
q
r
s
t
u
v
w
x
y
z

scallywag *noun*
devil, imp, knave, miscreant, rascal,
rogue, scamp, wretch.

scamper *verb*
She scampered off before I could talk to her.
dash, hurry, race, run, rush, scoot,
scurry, scuttle, skip.

scan *verb*
1 *He scanned their faces for clues.*
examine, look at, scrutinise, study,
survey.
2 *He quickly scanned the book.* flick
through, flip through, glance at, skim.

scandal *noun*
1 *His abuse of his position is a scandal!*
crime, disgrace, outrage, shame, sin.
2 *Have you heard the latest scandal?*
gossip, rumour, tattle, tittle-tattle.

scandalous *adjective*
scandalous behaviour. disgraceful,
improper, outrageous, shameful,
shocking, unseemly, wicked.

scant *adjective*
scant consideration for others. inadequate,
insufficient, limited, little, minimal,
scanty.

scapegoat *noun*
bunny (*Australian informal*), fall guy
(*slang*), victim, whipping boy.

scar *noun*
The cut left a scar. mark, scratch, wound.
scar *verb*
His arm was scarred by the cat. damage,
disfigure, mark, scratch, wound.

scarce *adjective*
Copies of the book were scarce. in short
supply, insufficient, rare, scanty.
OPPOSITE plentiful.

scarcely *adverb*
I scarcely know her. barely, hardly, only
just.

scare *verb*
The man scares people. alarm, dismay,
frighten, intimidate, shock, startle,
terrify, terrorise, unnerve.
OPPOSITE reassure.

scared *adjective*
afraid, alarmed, fearful, frightened,
intimidated, nervous, panic-stricken,
petrified, terrified.

scarf *noun*
headscarf, kerchief, muffler,
neckerchief.

scary *adjective*
a scary story. alarming, creepy, eerie,
frightening, hair-raising, spine-chilling,
spooky (*informal*), terrifying.

scatter *verb*
1 *The gardener scattered the seeds.*
broadcast, sow, spread, sprinkle, strew,
throw about.
2 *The crowd scattered.* disband, disperse,
dissipate.

scatterbrained *adjective*
absent-minded, disorganised, forgetful,
muddle-headed, scatty (*informal*), silly,
vague.

scene *noun*
1 *the scene of the crime.* locality, location,
place, setting, site.
2 *Please don't create a scene.* exhibition,
fuss, incident, outburst, spectacle.
3 *We admired the scene from the lookout.*
landscape, panorama, scenery, sight,
view, vista.

scenery *noun*
1 *mountain scenery.* landscape,
panorama, view, vista.
2 *stage scenery.* backdrop, set.

scenic *adjective*
a scenic drive. beautiful, panoramic,
picturesque, pretty.

scent *noun*
1 *the scent of roses.* aroma, fragrance,
odour, perfume, smell.
2 *The dogs lost the scent.* spoor, track,
trail.

sceptical *adjective*
He was sceptical about the man's claims.
disbelieving, distrustful, doubting,
dubious, incredulous, mistrustful,
questioning, suspicious.
OPPOSITE convinced.

schedule *noun*
The surgeon has a busy schedule. agenda, plan, programme, timetable.
schedule *verb*
The interview is scheduled for Friday. book, list, plan, programme, timetable.

scheme *noun*
1 *a job creation scheme.* plan, programme, project, strategy.
2 *a tax-avoidance scheme.* conspiracy, dodge (*informal*), plot, racket, rort (*Australian slang*), scam (*slang*).
3 *a colour scheme.* arrangement, design, system.
scheme *verb*
They were scheming to oust the President. conspire, intrigue, plan, plot.

scholar *noun*
1 *a classics scholar.* academic, intellectual.
2 *Many schools have an association of old scholars.* collegian, pupil, student.

scholarly *adjective*
a scholarly person. academic, bookish, erudite, intellectual, learned, studious.
OPPOSITE ignorant.

scholarship *noun*
The scholarship pays the university fees. award, bursary, fellowship, grant.

scholastic *adjective*
scholastic achievements. academic, educational.

school¹ *noun*
a school of fish. shoal.

school² *noun*
educational institution; [*kinds of school*] academy, area school (*Australian*), boarding school, central school (*Australian*), coeducational school, college, comprehensive school (*British*), consolidated school (*Australian*), convent school, day school, district school (*Australian*), government school, grammar school, high school, independent school, infant school, junior school, kindergarten, middle school, non-government school, nursery school, preparatory school, prep school, preschool, primary school, private school, public school, secondary school, senior school, state school, Sunday school, technical school.

schoolchild *noun*
collegian, pupil, scholar, schoolboy, schoolgirl, student.

schooling *noun*
education, instruction, learning, tuition.

schoolteacher *noun*
chalkie (*Australian slang*), master, mistress, schoolmaster, schoolmistress, teacher.

science *noun*
[*various sciences*] astronomy, biology, botany, chemistry, geology, physics, zoology.

scientific *adjective*
a scientific approach. analytical, methodical, precise, rigorous, systematic.

scissors *plural noun*
clippers, cutters, secateurs, shears, snips.

scoff *verb*
scoff at He scoffed at her efforts. deride, disparage, jeer at, knock (*informal*), make fun of, mock, ridicule, rubbish (*Australian informal*), scorn, sling off at (*Australian informal*), sneer at.

scold *verb*
He scolded them for being late. admonish, censure, chastise, chide (*old use*), go crook at (*Australian informal*), rap over the knuckles, rebuke, reprimand, reproach, rouse on (*Australian informal*), tell off (*informal*), tick off (*informal*), upbraid.
OPPOSITE praise.

scolding *noun*
dressing down (*informal*), lecture, rap over the knuckles, rebuke, reprimand, reproof, talking-to (*informal*).

scoop *noun*
a scoop of flour. ladle, shovel, spoon.
scoop *verb*
He scooped out a hole in the soil. dig, excavate, gouge, hollow.

a
b
c
d
e
f
g
h
i
j
k
l
m
n
o
p
q
r
s
t
u
v
w
x
y
z

scope *noun*
1 *It does not fall within the scope of this inquiry.* area, bounds, extent, limits, range.
2 *In this job there is scope for initiative.* opportunity, outlet, room.

scorch *verb*
The iron was too hot and scorched the shirt. brown, burn, discolour, sear, singe.

scorching *adjective*
see HOT.

score *noun*
He improved his score in maths. grade, mark, points, result, tally.
score *verb*
1 *She scored ten points.* gain, get, make, notch up.
2 *The timber had been heavily scored.* cut, gash, gouge, groove, notch, scratch.
3 *The music was scored for string ensemble.* arrange, orchestrate, write.

scorn *noun*
He treated the suggestion with scorn. contempt, derision, disdain, ridicule.
scorn *verb*
He scorned their attempts to include him. despise, disdain, rebuff, reject, shun, snub, spurn.

scornful *adjective*
a scornful look. contemptuous, disdainful, jeering, mocking, sarcastic, scathing, scoffing, sneering, snide (*informal*).

scoundrel *noun*
blackguard, crook (*informal*), knave (*old use*), miscreant, rascal, rogue, villain.

scour[1] *verb*
She scoured the pans until they shone. clean, cleanse, polish, rub, scrub.

scour[2] *verb*
They scoured the area for clues. comb, rake through, ransack, search.

scout *noun*
lookout, spy, vanguard.
scout *verb*
He scouted around for evidence. ferret, fossick (*Australian informal*), hunt, look, search, snoop (*informal*).

scowl *verb*
frown, glare, glower, lour.

scramble *verb*
1 *We scrambled over the rocks.* clamber, climb, crawl, struggle.
2 *They scrambled to the exits.* dash, hurry, race, run, rush, scurry.
scramble *noun*
There was a mad scramble for the ball. race, run, rush, struggle, tussle.

scrap[1] *noun*
1 *scraps of material.* fragment, piece, rag, remnant, shred, tatter.
2 *not a scrap of evidence.* bit, fragment, jot, shred, skerrick (*Australian informal*), trace.
3 *He makes money out of scrap.* junk, refuse, rubbish, salvage, trash.
scrap *verb*
They scrapped that idea and started again. abandon, discard, ditch (*informal*), do away with, drop, get rid of, give up.
OPPOSITE retain.

scrap[2] *noun* (*informal*)
The boys had a scrap over the toy. altercation, argument, dispute, fight, quarrel, row, squabble.

scrape *verb*
1 *He scraped the mud off his shoes.* clean, remove, rub, scrub.
2 *The teacher scraped the blackboard with her fingernail.* grate, scratch.
3 *He scraped his knee.* graze, scratch, skin.
scrape *noun*
1 *It's hard to avoid scrapes especially on knees.* abrasion, cut, graze, injury, scratch.
2 *He's always getting into scrapes.* difficulty, plight, predicament, trouble.

scrappy *adjective*
a scrappy piece of work. bitty, disjointed, fragmentary.

scratch *verb*
1 *The timber had been badly scratched.* gouge, mark, score, scuff.
2 *She scratched her leg on the fence.* cut, graze, scrape, skin.
3 *The horse was scratched.* withdraw.

scratch *noun*
scratches on his legs. abrasion, graze, laceration, scrape, wound.

scrawl *verb*
He scrawls illegibly. scribble; see also WRITE.

scream *verb*
She screamed in pain. bawl, cry out, howl, screech, shriek, squeal, wail, yell, yowl.
scream *noun*
1 *The screams could be heard for some distance.* cry, howl, screech, shriek, squeal, yell, yowl.
2 (*informal*) *We thought the play was a scream.* hoot (*informal*), laugh, riot (*informal*).

screech *noun & verb*
see SCREAM.

screen *noun*
1 *They were separated by a screen.* divider, partition.
2 *a window screen.* blind, curtain, flyscreen.
3 *He planted trees as a screen from the wind.* barrier, protection, shelter, shield.
4 *a computer screen.* monitor, VDU, visual display unit.
screen *verb*
1 *The house was screened from public view.* camouflage, conceal, hide, protect, shelter, shield.
2 *The television channel screened a series of French films.* broadcast, present, show.
3 *Volunteers are screened before being appointed.* check, examine, investigate, test, vet.

scribble *verb*
She scribbled on a sheet of paper. doodle, jot, scrawl.

script *noun*
1 *in legible script.* handwriting, writing.
2 *a film script.* lines, screenplay, text, words.

scripture *noun*
Each religion has its scripture. sacred writings.
Scripture the Bible, the Word of God.

scrounge *verb*
He's always without money and scrounging off friends. beg, bludge (*Australian informal*), borrow, cadge, scab (*Australian slang*), sponge.

scrub¹ *noun*
The land was covered with scrub. bush, mallee, mulga.

scrub² *verb*
1 *They helped to scrub the pans.* clean, scour, wash.
2 (*informal*) *We had to scrub our plans.* abandon, cancel, drop, forget, scrap.

scruffy *adjective*
a scruffy appearance. bedraggled, dishevelled, messy, shabby, slovenly, tatty (*informal*), unkempt, untidy.
OPPOSITE neat.

scrupulous *adjective*
1 *scrupulous attention to detail.* careful, conscientious, fastidious, meticulous, painstaking, rigorous, thorough.
OPPOSITE careless.
2 *A treasurer must be scrupulous.* ethical, honest, honourable, principled.
OPPOSITE unscrupulous.

scrutinise *verb*
He scrutinised the document. examine, inspect, look over, peruse, study, survey.

scrutiny *noun*
The work was subjected to close scrutiny. examination, inspection, investigation, study.

scuffle *noun*
The policeman was injured in the scuffle. brawl, fight, fisticuffs, scrap (*informal*), skirmish, stoush (*Australian slang*), struggle, tussle.

sculpture *noun*
bust, carving, cast, figure, figurine, statue, statuette.
sculpture *verb*
The man sculptured a dolphin out of wood. carve, form, make, model, sculpt (*informal*), shape.

scum *noun*
the scum on the top of the liquid. film, foam, froth.

a
b
c
d
e
f
g
h
i
j
k
l
m
n
o
p
q
r
s
t
u
v
w
x
y
z

scurry *verb*
The mice scurried away at the sound of the cat. flit, hurry, run, rush, scamper, scoot, scuttle.

scuttle¹ *verb*
They scuttled the ship. scupper, sink.

scuttle² *verb*
see SCURRY.

sea *noun*
1 *a ship on the open sea.* the blue, the deep, the main (*old use*), ocean. OPPOSITE land.
2 *a sea of faces.* expanse, mass.
at sea baffled, bewildered, confused, perplexed, puzzled, uncertain.

seafarer *noun*
mariner, sailor, seaman. OPPOSITE landsman.

seafaring *adjective*
a seafaring nation. maritime, nautical, naval, sailing, seagoing.

seal *noun*
This seal guarantees its authenticity. crest, emblem, imprint, insignia, stamp, sticker, symbol.
seal *verb*
1 *The envelope was sealed.* close, fasten, secure, stick down.
2 *The timber has been sealed.* coat, protect, surface.
3 *His fate was sealed.* decide, determine, secure, settle.
4 (*Australian*) *Most of the roads are sealed.* bituminise, macadamise, tar, tarmac, tar-seal (*Australian*).
seal off *The police sealed off the area.* block off, close off, cordon off. OPPOSITE open up.

seam *noun*
1 *a dress seam.* join, stitching.
2 *the seam of coal.* layer, lode, stratum, vein.

seaman *noun*
mariner, sailor, seafarer.

search *verb*
1 *They searched the area for clues.* comb, examine, explore, hunt, look over, ransack, scour, survey.

2 *She searched through her handbag to find a pen.* check, ferret, forage, fossick (*Australian informal*), look, rummage.
3 *The authorities searched all the new arrivals.* check, examine, frisk, inspect.
search *noun*
a search for survivors. hunt, inspection, investigation, look, quest.

searching *adjective*
a searching examination. careful, in-depth, probing, testing, thorough.

seasick *adjective*
nauseous, queasy, sick.

season *noun*
Christmas is a festive season. period, time.
season *verb*
1 *The food has already been seasoned.* flavour, pepper, salt, spice.
2 *The wood has been seasoned.* age, condition, dry, harden, mature.

seasoning *noun*
What seasoning did you put in the sauce? condiment, flavour, herb, relish, spice.

seat *noun*
1 *a seat to sit on.* armchair, bench, chair, couch, form, lounge, pew, settee, sofa, stall, stool, throne.
2 *We reserved seats.* place.
3 *a safe Labor seat.* constituency, electorate.
seat *verb*
1 *The usher seated them in the front row.* place, position, put, situate.
2 *The hall seats two hundred.* accommodate, hold, take.
seat belt restraint, safety belt.

secluded *adjective*
a secluded place. hidden, isolated, lonely, private, remote, sheltered.

second *adjective*
1 *There won't be a second time.* following, next, subsequent.
2 *The team has a second driver.* additional, alternative, backup, extra, other, substitute, supplementary.
second *noun* (*informal*)
I'll be with you in a second. flash, instant, jiffy (*informal*), minute, moment, tick (*informal*).

second *verb*
He seconded the motion. back, endorse, support.

secondary *adjective*
1 *a secondary consideration.* lesser, minor, subordinate, subsidiary.
OPPOSITE primary.
2 *secondary colours.* derivative, derived.
OPPOSITE primary.

second-hand *adjective*
second-hand clothes. hand-me-down, pre-loved, pre-owned, recycled, used, worn.
OPPOSITE new.

secret *adjective*
1 *The details of the project were kept secret.* classified, concealed, confidential, hidden, hush-hush (*informal*), private, undisclosed.
OPPOSITE public.
2 *a secret meeting.* clandestine, private, undercover.
OPPOSITE public.
secret *noun*
1 *She can be trusted with a secret.* confidence.
2 *the secrets of nature.* enigma, mystery, puzzle.
secret agent see SPY.

secrete *verb*
1 *He secreted the key in a flowerpot.* conceal, hide, stash.
OPPOSITE display.
2 *Resin is secreted by pine trees.* discharge, exude, give off, produce.
OPPOSITE absorb.

secretive *adjective*
There is no need to be so secretive. cagey (*informal*), evasive, furtive, mysterious, reticent, tight-lipped, uncommunicative.
OPPOSITE candid, open.

sect *noun*
a religious sect. cult, denomination, faction, party.

section *noun*
1 *The whole is divided into sections.* bit, compartment, division, fraction, part, piece, portion, sector, segment, slice, subdivision.

2 *The novel was published in six sections.* chapter, instalment, part.
3 *sections of an organisation.* branch, department, division.
4 *a section of a journey.* leg, stage.

sector *noun*
The city was divided into sectors. area, district, division, part, quarter, region, section, zone.

secure *adjective*
1 *The people thought their walled town was secure.* defended, impregnable, protected, safe, unassailable.
OPPOSITE vulnerable.
2 *He felt his position was secure.* assured, certain, guaranteed, reliable, safe, solid, sound, steady, sure.
OPPOSITE shaky.
3 *She felt secure in her mother's arms.* confident, protected, safe, snug.
OPPOSITE insecure.
secure *verb*
1 *They secured the city from attack.* defend, fortify, guard, make safe, protect, safeguard.
2 *Secure the doors and windows before the winds start.* batten down, bolt, fasten, lock.
3 *He secured the necessary items.* acquire, come by, get, obtain, procure.

security *noun*
1 *lulled into a false sense of security.* assurance, confidence, protection, safety.
OPPOSITE anxiety.
2 *The house is the security for the loan.* guarantee, pledge, surety.

sedate *adjective*
a sedate person. sedate music. calm, collected, composed, decorous, dignified, peaceful, placid, serious, sober, tranquil.
OPPOSITE lively.
sedate *verb*
The medicine sedated him. calm, pacify, quieten, relax, soothe, subdue, tranquillise.
OPPOSITE agitate, stimulate.

sedative *adjective*
The medicine had a sedative effect. calming, relaxing, soothing, soporific, tranquillising.

a
b
c
d
e
f
g
h
i
j
k
l
m
n
o
p
q
r
s
t
u
v
w
x
y
z

sedative *noun*
The doctor prescribed a sedative. narcotic, opiate, sleeping pill, tranquilliser. OPPOSITE stimulant.

sediment *noun*
the sediment in a bottle of wine. deposit, dregs, lees, residue.

seductive *adjective*
a seductive outfit. alluring, attractive, enticing, inviting, provocative, sexy, tempting.

see *verb*
1 She could see the fine detail with her new glasses. behold (old use), discern, distinguish, glimpse, make out, notice, observe, perceive, recognise, spot.
2 I don't see what you mean. appreciate, comprehend, get (informal), grasp, perceive, realise, understand.
3 I just can't see it happening. conceive, envisage, foresee, imagine, picture, visualise.
4 I see things differently now. consider, look at, regard, view.
5 He saw the programme. look at, view, watch.
6 He went to see what happened. ascertain, discover, find out, investigate, learn.
7 She went to see the principal. call on, consult, meet with, speak to, talk to, visit.
8 Please see her out. accompany, conduct, escort, lead, show, take, usher.
9 See that he gets this. ensure, make sure, mind, take care.
see to Please see to this matter. attend to, deal with, look after, sort out, take care of.

seed *noun*
The plant grew from a seed. grain, pip, stone.

seek *verb*
1 She sought help. ask for, go for, look for, request, solicit.
2 Whom are you seeking? look for, search for.
3 What are you seeking to achieve? aim, aspire, attempt, endeavour, try.

seem *verb*
It seems likely. appear, feel, look, sound.

seep *verb*
Oil seeped through the hole. dribble, filter, flow, leak, ooze, trickle.

seethe *verb*
1 The waters are seething. boil, bubble, churn, foam, surge.
2 She seethed with rage. be furious, be livid, boil, fume.

see-through *adjective*
a see-through blouse. sheer, transparent. OPPOSITE opaque.

segment *noun*
a segment of the pie. division, part, piece, portion, section, slice, wedge.

segregate *verb*
Schools used to segregate the girls from the boys. isolate, keep apart, separate.

seize *verb*
1 She seized her bag and ran outside. clutch, grab, grasp, pluck, snatch, take hold of.
2 He was seized by the police. apprehend, arrest, capture, catch, collar (informal), nab (informal), nick (slang).
3 Customs officers seized the goods. confiscate, impound, take away, take possession of.

seldom *adverb*
hardly ever, infrequently, once in a blue moon, rarely. OPPOSITE often.

select *verb*
She was selected as captain. appoint, choose, elect, nominate, pick.
select *adjective*
one of a select group. choice, elite, exclusive.

selection *noun*
1 She took time to make her selection. choice, decision, pick.
2 a selection of chocolates. assortment, collection, mixture, variety.

selective *adjective*
He is selective in what he reads. careful, choosy (informal), discriminating, fussy, particular, picky (informal).

self-centred *adjective*
People avoid him because he is so self-centred. egocentric, egotistic, selfish,

self-seeking, wrapped up in yourself.
OPPOSITE selfless.

self-confident *adjective*
He got the job because he was self-confident. assured, bold, confident, self-assured.
OPPOSITE insecure.

self-conscious *adjective*
She felt self-conscious as she walked across the stage. awkward, bashful, embarrassed, insecure, shy, uncomfortable.

self-control *noun*
She lacked the self-control to resist chocolates. restraint, self-discipline, self-restraint, will-power.

self-esteem *noun*
pride, self-respect, self-worth.

selfish *adjective*
egocentric, greedy, inconsiderate, mean, miserly, self-centred, stingy, thoughtless, wrapped up in yourself.
OPPOSITE generous, unselfish.

selfless *adjective*
a selfless volunteer. altruistic, generous, kind, self-denying, self-sacrificing, unselfish.
OPPOSITE selfish.

self-respect *noun*
dignity, pride, self-esteem.

self-righteous *adjective*
He rejected the criticism with self-righteous indignation. holier-than-thou, pompous, priggish, sanctimonious, self-satisfied, smug.

self-sufficient *adjective*
With his farm he was able to be self-sufficient. independent, self-contained, self-reliant, self-supporting.

sell *verb*
1 *He sells stamps.* auction, barter, deal in, handle, market, peddle, retail, stock, trade in, traffic in.
OPPOSITE buy.
2 *The book sells for $20.* be priced at, cost.

seller *noun*
dealer, hawker, merchant, peddler, pedlar, retailer, salesman, salesperson,

saleswoman, shopkeeper, supplier, trader, trafficker, vendor, wholesaler.
OPPOSITE buyer.

sell-out *noun*
The concert was a sell-out. hit, success, winner.

semitrailer *noun*
lorry, road train (*Australian*), semi (*Australian informal*), transport, truck.

send *verb*
1 *He sent them a message. She sent the parcel.* consign, convey, dispatch, email, fax, forward, pass on, post, relay, ship, transmit, write.
2 *He sent the arrow into the air.* direct, fire, launch, propel, shoot.
send away see DISMISS.
send for *We sent for the doctor.* ask for, call, order, summon.
send up (*informal*) *The show sends up politicians.* caricature, make fun of, mimic, parody, satirise, take off.

send-up *noun* (*informal*)
a send-up of parliament. burlesque, caricature, parody, satire, spoof (*informal*), take-off.

senile *adjective*
She dreaded becoming senile. decrepit, doddery, feeble-minded, infirm.

senior *adjective*
1 *Tom Brown senior.* elder, older.
OPPOSITE junior.
2 *a senior officer.* higher-ranking, superior.
OPPOSITE junior.
senior *noun*
concessions for seniors. pensioner, retiree, senior citizen.

sensation *noun*
1 *the sensation of pain.* awareness, consciousness, feeling, perception, sense.
2 *The news caused a sensation.* commotion, excitement, stir.

sensational *adjective*
1 *It was a sensational finish to the tennis match.* dramatic, electrifying, exciting, spectacular, striking, stunning, terrific (*informal*), thrilling.

a
b
c
d
e
f
g
h
i
j
k
l
m
n
o
p
q
r
s
t
u
v
w
x
y
z

2 *That newspaper goes for the sensational news.* lurid, scandalous, shocking, startling.

sense *noun*
1 *a sense of smell.* faculty, perception, power, sensation.
2 *a sense of decency.* awareness, consciousness, perception, recognition.
3 *She has no sense.* brains (*informal*), common sense, gumption, intelligence, judgement, nous (*informal*), reason, wisdom, wit.
4 *What is the sense of the word?* meaning, signification.
5 *What is the sense of doing that?* point, purpose, use, value.
sense *verb*
She sensed that something was wrong. be aware, detect, discern, feel, perceive, realise, suspect.

senseless *adjective*
1 *a senseless act.* absurd, foolish, inane, mad, meaningless, nonsensical, pointless, silly, stupid.
OPPOSITE sensible.
2 *He was knocked senseless.* insensible, out, unconscious.
OPPOSITE conscious.

sensible *adjective*
1 *a sensible person.* intelligent, level-headed, logical, prudent, rational, reasonable, thoughtful, wise.
OPPOSITE foolish.
2 *sensible clothes.* functional, practical, serviceable.

sensitive *adjective*
1 *a sensitive listener.* considerate, perceptive, sympathetic, understanding.
OPPOSITE insensitive.
2 *Be careful what you say as she's very sensitive.* hypersensitive, thin-skinned, touchy.
OPPOSITE thick-skinned.
3 *The skin was sensitive at the site of the scar.* delicate, painful, sore, tender.

sentence *noun*
The judge passed the sentence. decision, judgement, penalty, punishment.

sentence *verb*
The judge sentenced him to two years' jail. condemn, penalise, punish.

sentiment *noun*
1 *I do not share his political sentiments.* attitude, belief, feeling, opinion, thought, view.
2 *She acted out of sentiment rather than reason.* emotion, feeling, sentimentality.

sentimental *adjective*
a sentimental film. corny (*informal*), emotional, mushy, nostalgic, romantic, soppy (*informal*).

sentry *noun*
guard, lookout, sentinel, watchman.

separate *adjective*
1 *a separate matter.* unconnected, unrelated.
OPPOSITE connected, same.
2 *They live in separate houses.* detached, free-standing, individual, single.
3 *They lead separate lives.* independent.
separate *verb*
1 *The glued parts could not be separated.* break apart, detach, disconnect, divide, split, take apart.
2 *The teacher separated the class into three groups.* break, divide, segregate, sort, split.
OPPOSITE merge.
3 *The couple separated.* break up, divorce, part, split up.

separation *noun*
1 *separation into groups.* break, division, partition, segregation, split.
OPPOSITE union.
2 *separation after twenty years of marriage.* break-up, divorce, parting, split-up.

sequel *noun*
Have you read the sequel? continuation, development, follow-up.

sequence *noun*
the logical sequence of events. chain, course, order, progression, series, succession, train.

serene *adjective*
She remained serene throughout her ordeal. calm, composed, peaceful, placid, quiet, tranquil, unperturbed, unruffled.
OPPOSITE agitated.

series *noun*
a series of disasters. chain, cycle, group, line, order, progression, row, sequence, set, string, succession, train.

serious *adjective*
1 a serious person. earnest, grave, long-faced, pensive, sedate, sober, solemn, staid, steady, thoughtful.
OPPOSITE frivolous.
2 He is serious about doing it. determined, earnest, genuine, keen, resolute, sincere.
OPPOSITE joking.
3 a serious decision. crucial, important, momentous, vital, weighty.
OPPOSITE unimportant.
4 a serious illness. bad, critical, dangerous, grave, life-threatening, major, severe.
OPPOSITE minor.

sermon *noun*
a sermon in church. address, homily, talk.

servant *noun*
The master treats his servants well. attendant, butler, domestic, footman, housekeeper, maid, maidservant, manservant, page, slave, valet.

serve *verb*
1 He served his country. help, work for.
2 That box will serve as a table. act, be suitable, do, function.
3 He has served his sentence. complete, undergo.
4 One person served the food to everybody. dish up, distribute, dole out, give, hand, present.
5 She serves the customers. assist, attend to, look after, wait on.
serve *noun*
a small serve of potatoes. helping, portion, serving.

service *noun*
1 He left the firm after 30 years of service. employment, labour, work.
2 Can I be of service? aid, assistance, benefit, help, use.
3 a church service. ceremony, rite, ritual, sacrament.
4 a warranty on service and parts. maintenance, overhaul, repair.
service *verb*
The mechanic services our car. fix, maintain, overhaul, repair.
service station filling station, garage, petrol station, roadhouse, servo (*Australian informal*).

serviette *noun*
napkin, table napkin.

serving *noun*
helping, portion, serve.

session *noun*
1 a parliamentary session. meeting, sitting.
2 a long session on the telephone. period, spell, time.

set *verb*
1 She set the vase on the shelf. bung (*informal*), deposit, dump, install, leave, place, plonk, position, put, rest, stand.
2 He set the clock. adjust, regulate.
3 She set the table. arrange, lay, prepare.
4 The jelly has set. firm, gel, jell, solidify, stiffen.
5 They set a date for their next meeting. appoint, choose, decide on, determine, establish, fix, name, settle on, specify.
6 The post is set in concrete. embed, fix, lodge, mount, stick.
7 He set a new record for the 100 metres. create, establish.
8 The teacher set them homework. allot, assign, give, prescribe.
set *noun*
a set of stamps, people, etc. assortment, batch, bunch, class, collection, group, series.
set about He set about building a bookcase. begin, commence, start.
set back The work was set back by rain. delay, hamper, hinder, hold back, impede, slow.
OPPOSITE advance.
set off
1 They set off for Melbourne. depart, leave, set forth, set out, start.
2 This set off a chain reaction. cause, spark, start, stimulate, trigger.
3 They set off their fireworks. detonate, explode, ignite, let off.

a
b
c
d
e
f
g
h
i
j
k
l
m
n
o
p
q
r
s
t
u
v
w
x
y
z

set out

1 *The report sets out the terms of reference.* declare, detail, make known, present, state.

2 *They set out on a long journey.* begin, depart, embark, leave, set forth, set off, start.

set sail depart, leave, put to sea, sail.

set up

1 *He set up the hall before the party.* arrange, organise, prepare.

2 *They set up a business.* begin, create, develop, establish, found, start.

setback *noun*

He succeeded despite many setbacks. complication, hiccup, hitch, obstacle, problem, snag.

settee *noun*

They sat together on the settee. couch, lounge, sofa.

setting *noun*

a house's setting. a historical setting. background, context, environment, locale, locality, place, scene, site, surroundings.

settle *verb*

1 *They settled in Perth.* establish yourself, immigrate, move, put down roots. OPPOSITE emigrate, uproot.

2 *Englishmen settled the east coast.* colonise, occupy, populate.

3 *The dove settled on an olive branch.* alight, come to rest, land, perch.

4 *They left the dust to settle.* fall, sink, subside.

5 *They settled on a meeting point.* agree, choose, decide, fix.

6 *The dispute has been settled.* clear up, deal with, resolve, straighten out, work out.

7 *She couldn't settle the baby.* calm, pacify, quieten, soothe. OPPOSITE agitate.

8 *The debt has been settled.* clear, discharge, liquidate, pay. OPPOSITE incur.

settlement *noun*

1 *The two parties have reached a settlement.* agreement, arrangement, reconciliation, resolution.

2 *Life was hard in the new settlement.* colony, community, outpost, township.

settler *noun*

colonist, immigrant, pioneer.

set-up *noun*

arrangement, format, organisation, structure, system.

sever *verb*

see CUT.

several *adjective*

She sent out several invitations. a few, a good many, a number of, some.

severe *adjective*

1 *a severe person.* austere, cruel, forbidding, hard, harsh, merciless, ruthless, stern, strict, unsympathetic. OPPOSITE gentle.

2 *They took severe measures.* Draconian, drastic, extreme, harsh, stringent, strong, tough. OPPOSITE lenient.

3 *severe storms.* fierce, intense, strong, violent. OPPOSITE mild.

4 *a severe illness.* acute, bad, critical, dangerous, grave, serious. OPPOSITE mild.

sew *verb*

baste, darn, embroider, mend, smock, stitch, tack.

sewage *noun*

effluent, waste.

sex *noun*

1 *the sex of the baby.* gender.

2 *have sex.* see SEXUAL INTERCOURSE (at SEXUAL).

sexism *noun*

male chauvinism, sexual discrimination; see also PREJUDICE.

sexual *adjective*

1 *sexual organs.* genital, reproductive, sex.

2 *sexual attraction.* erotic, physical, sensual.

sexual intercourse coitus, copulation, intercourse, love-making, mating, sex.

shabby *adjective*
1 *shabby clothes.* frayed, ragged, scruffy, tattered, tatty (*informal*), threadbare, worn.
2 *shabby old buildings.* dilapidated, dingy, drab, neglected, ramshackle, run-down, tumbledown.
OPPOSITE neat.
3 *a shabby trick.* contemptible, despicable, dirty, dishonourable, low-down, mean, unfair.

shack *noun*
cabin, hovel, hut, shanty, weekender (*Australian*).

shade *noun*
1 *At midday there is little shade.* semi-darkness, shadow.
2 *different shades of pink.* colour, degree, hue, intensity, tinge, tint, tone.
3 *a shade better.* bit, degree, fraction, tad (*informal*), touch, trace.
4 *shades of meaning.* difference, nuance, variation.
5 *a shade for the light.* blind, cover, screen, shield.
shade *verb*
1 *The tree shades the house.* cast shadow on, screen, shelter.
2 *He had shaded the area on the map.* darken, hatch.

shadow *noun*
1 *The photo was taken in shadow.* darkness, gloom, semi-darkness, shade.
2 *The man cast a longer shadow.* outline, shape, silhouette.
shadow *verb*
The detective shadowed the suspect. follow, pursue, stalk, tail (*informal*), track, trail.

shady *adjective*
1 *a shady corner.* cool, dark, dim, shaded, shadowy.
OPPOSITE sunny.
2 *shady dealings.* dubious, fishy (*informal*), questionable, shonky (*Australian informal*), suspect, suspicious.
OPPOSITE above board.

shaft *noun*
1 *He sent a shaft through the air.* arrow, lance, spear.
2 *a shaft of light.* beam, ray, streak.

3 *a shaft of lightning.* bolt, streak.
4 *the shaft of a tool.* handle, pole, shank, stem, stick.
5 *a mine shaft.* entrance, opening, passage, tunnel.
6 *a lift shaft.* well.

shaggy *adjective*
shaggy hair. bushy, messy, rough, thick, tousled, unkempt, untidy, woolly.

shake *verb*
1 *He shook his stick.* brandish, jiggle, swing, wag, waggle, wave, wiggle.
2 *The explosion made the house shake.* rock, sway, vibrate, wobble.
3 *She shook with fear.* quake, quaver, quiver, shiver, shudder, totter, tremble.
4 *The news had shaken them.* agitate, distress, disturb, jolt, perturb, rattle (*informal*), shock, stun, unnerve, upset.
5 *Her voice shook.* falter, quaver, tremble, wobble.

shaky *adjective*
1 *He is a bit shaky on his legs.* doddery, trembling, unsteady, wobbly.
OPPOSITE steady.
2 *a shaky start.* doubtful, hesitant, rocky (*informal*), uncertain.

shallow *adjective*
1 *a shallow wound.* skin-deep, superficial, surface.
OPPOSITE deep.
2 *shallow talk.* empty, frivolous, superficial, trivial.
OPPOSITE profound.

sham *noun*
1 *His penitence was a sham.* act, charade, pretence, put-on (*informal*).
2 *They soon realised the financial adviser was a sham.* charlatan, cheat, con man (*informal*), fake, fraud, impostor, phoney (*informal*).

shambles *noun*
Their bedroom was a shambles. disaster area (*informal*), mess, muddle, pigsty, shemozzle (*informal*).

shame *noun*
1 *He felt shame over the incident.* embarrassment, guilt, humiliation, mortification, regret, remorse.
OPPOSITE pride.

a
b
c
d
e
f
g
h
i
j
k
l
m
n
o
p
q
r
s
t
u
v
w
x
y
z

2 *He brought shame on himself.* discredit,
disgrace, dishonour, humiliation,
scandal, stigma.
OPPOSITE honour.
3 *It's a shame that you won't be there.*
disappointment, pity.
shame *verb*
*He would not shame him in front of his
friends.* disgrace, embarrass, humble,
humiliate, mortify.

shameful *adjective*
shameful behaviour. contemptible,
deplorable, disgraceful, dishonourable,
reprehensible, scandalous, shocking,
unbecoming.
OPPOSITE honourable.

shameless *adjective*
shameless conduct. bold, brazen, cheeky,
immodest, impudent, unashamed,
unseemly.

shanty *noun*
hovel, hut, shack.

shape *noun*
1 *He recognised the object by its shape.*
contour, form, outline, profile,
silhouette; [*various two-dimensional
shapes*] circle, decagon, diamond,
ellipse, heptagon, hexagon, nonagon,
oblong, octagon, oval, parallelogram,
pentagon, polygon, quadrilateral,
rectangle, rhombus, semicircle, square,
trapezium, triangle.
2 *He wasn't in good shape.* condition,
form, health, state.
shape *verb*
The sculptor shaped the head. construct,
fashion, form, frame, make, model,
mould, sculpt, sculpture.

share *noun*
They each got their fair share. allocation,
allotment, allowance, bit, cut (*informal*),
fraction, helping, part, portion, quota,
ration.
share *verb*
She shared the pencils among the children.
allocate, allot, apportion, deal out,
distribute, divide.

shark *noun*
[*various sharks*] blue pointer, carpet
shark, dogfish, grey nurse shark,

gummy shark, hammerhead, Port
Jackson shark, school shark, whale
shark, white pointer, wobbegong.

sharp *adjective*
1 *a sharp knife.* keen, pointed.
OPPOSITE blunt.
2 *a sharp slope.* abrupt, precipitous,
sheer, steep, vertical.
OPPOSITE gentle, gradual.
3 *a sharp turn.* acute, hairpin, sudden.
OPPOSITE gradual.
4 *in sharp focus.* clear, distinct,
well-defined.
OPPOSITE indistinct.
5 *sharp pain.* acute, intense, severe,
shooting, stabbing.
OPPOSITE mild.
6 *a sharp voice.* high-pitched,
penetrating, piercing, shrill, strident.
OPPOSITE soft.
7 *sharp words.* angry, bitter, caustic,
cutting, harsh, stinging, unkind.
OPPOSITE gentle.
8 *a sharp taste or smell.* acid, acrid, bitter,
pungent, sour, strong, tangy, tart,
vinegary.
OPPOSITE bland, mild.
9 *He is very sharp: you won't fool him.*
alert, astute, bright, clever, intelligent,
knowing, perceptive, quick, shrewd,
smart.
OPPOSITE dull, slow.
sharp *adverb*
1 *He arrived at six o'clock sharp.* exactly,
on the dot, on the knocker (*Australian
informal*), precisely, promptly,
punctually.
OPPOSITE approximately.
2 *She pulled up sharp.* abruptly,
suddenly.
OPPOSITE gradually.

sharpen *verb*
sharpen a knife. grind, hone, whet.
OPPOSITE blunt.

shatter *verb*
1 *The glass shattered.* break, burst, crack,
explode, smash, splinter.
2 *All our hopes were shattered.* dash,
destroy.
3 *We were shattered by the news.* crush,
devastate, disturb, upset.

shave *verb*
1 *He shaved his whiskers.* cut off, snip off, trim.
2 *He shaved a millimetre off the door.* pare, plane, slice, trim.
shave *noun*
close shave (*informal*)
close call (*informal*), narrow escape.

shawl *noun*
a *woollen shawl.* scarf, stole.

shear *verb*
He shears sheep. clip, crop, strip; see also CUT.

shears *plural noun*
clippers, cutters, scissors.

sheath *noun*
He replaced the knife in its sheath. case, cover, scabbard, sleeve.

shed[1] *noun*
barn, garage, hut, lean-to, outbuilding, outhouse, shelter, workshop.

shed[2] *verb*
1 *Deciduous trees shed their leaves.* drop, lose.
2 *The snake shed its skin.* cast, lose, slough.
3 *The birds shed their feathers.* lose, moult.
4 *He shed his clothes before stepping into his bath.* cast off, discard, remove, take off, throw off.
OPPOSITE don, put on.

sheen *noun*
The woodwork has a sheen after polishing. brightness, gleam, gloss, lustre, polish, shine.

sheep *noun*
ewe (*female*), jumbuck (*Australian*), lamb, ram (*male*), wether (*male*).

sheepish *adjective*
a *sheepish look.* ashamed, bashful, coy, embarrassed, self-conscious, shamefaced, shy, timid.
OPPOSITE brazen.

sheer *adjective*
1 *sheer happiness.* absolute, complete, pure, total, utter.
2 *sheer cliffs.* abrupt, perpendicular, precipitous, sharp, steep, vertical.

3 *sheer stockings.* fine, flimsy, gauzy, see-through, thin, transparent.
OPPOSITE opaque, thick.

sheet *noun*
1 *a sheet of paper.* folio, leaf, page.
2 *a sheet of glass.* pane, panel, plate.
3 *She put a sheet of plastic over the food.* cover, film, layer.

shelf *noun*
ledge, mantelpiece, sill.

shell *noun*
1 *The hard shell protects the soft contents.* case, cover, covering, exterior, outside.
2 *a turtle's shell.* carapace.
3 *the shell of seeds, nuts, etc.* case, hull, husk, pod.
4 *the shell of a ship.* body, chassis, frame, framework, hull.
shell *verb*
The town was shelled. bomb, bombard, fire on.

shellfish *noun*
crustacean, mollusc; [*various shellfish*] abalone, Balmain bug, barnacle, clam, cockle, crab, crayfish, limpet, lobster, marron, Moreton Bay bug, mussel, oyster, prawn, scallop, shrimp, whelk, yabby.

shelter *noun*
1 *The people sought shelter from the bombs.* asylum, cover, haven, protection, refuge, safety, sanctuary.
2 *The walkers crowded into the tiny shelter.* bunker, hut, shed.
shelter *verb*
1 *The wall shelters the garden.* protect, screen, shield.
2 *They sheltered the escapee.* conceal, give refuge to, harbour, hide.
3 *They sheltered under the eaves until the rain had eased.* take cover, take refuge.

shelve *verb*
The plans have been shelved. defer, postpone, put aside, put on the back burner (*informal*), put on hold, suspend.

shield *noun*
a *shield against attack.* barrier, defence, guard, protection, refuge, safeguard, screen, shelter.

a
b
c
d
e
f
g
h
i
j
k
l
m
n
o
p
q
r
s
t
u
v
w
x
y
z

shield *verb*
We were shielded from danger. defend,
guard, preserve, protect, safeguard,
screen, shelter.
OPPOSITE expose.

shift *verb*
They are always shifting things around.
change, move, rearrange, relocate,
switch, transfer.
shift *noun*
a shift in position. alteration, change,
move, relocation, switch, transfer,
variation.

shifty *adjective*
a shifty character. deceitful, dodgy
(*informal*), shonky (*Australian informal*),
slippery, sly, sneaky, underhand,
untrustworthy, wily.
OPPOSITE trustworthy.

shimmer *verb*
The lights shimmered in the water. flicker,
gleam, glimmer, glisten, sparkle,
twinkle.
shimmer *noun*
the shimmer of the lights reflecting in the
water. flicker, gleam, glimmer, glitter,
sparkle, twinkle.

shine *verb*
1 The lights are shining. beam, blaze,
dazzle, flash, flicker, gleam, glimmer,
glint, glisten, glitter, glow, radiate,
reflect, shimmer, sparkle, twinkle.
2 The sun shone today. be visible, come
out.
3 What does she shine at? do well, excel,
stand out.
4 I had to shine all the brass. buff,
burnish, clean, polish.
shine *noun*
The silver cup has lost its shine.
brightness, gleam, glint, gloss, glow,
lustre, polish, radiance, sheen,
shimmer, sparkle.

shiny *adjective*
a shiny surface. bright, gleaming,
glistening, glossy, lustrous, polished,
satin, shimmering.
OPPOSITE dull.

ship *noun*
vessel; [*various ships*] aircraft carrier,
battleship, brig, clipper, container ship,

corvette, cruiser, destroyer, flagship,
freighter, frigate, galleon, galley,
gunboat, ice-breaker, liner, merchant
ship, minesweeper, sailing ship,
steamship, submarine, tanker, warship;
see also BOAT.
ship *verb*
They had their furniture shipped
beforehand. consign, convey, dispatch,
export, freight, send, transport.

shipment *noun*
cargo, consignment, load.

shirk *verb*
He shirks the jobs which he doesn't like.
avoid, dodge, evade, get out of, shun,
shy away from.

shiver *verb*
The thought made her shiver. quake,
quaver, quiver, shake, shudder,
tremble.

shoal *noun*
a shoal of fish. school.

shock *noun*
1 Several minor shocks were detected after
the initial earthquake. impact, jolt, quake,
shake, tremor.
2 The news came as a terrible shock. bolt
from the blue, bombshell, surprise.
shock *verb*
1 News of the murder shocked everyone.
appal, disgust, dismay, horrify, offend,
outrage, scandalise, upset.
2 He was shocked by the findings. amaze,
astonish, astound, stagger, stun,
surprise, take aback.

shocking *adjective*
1 a shocking crime. appalling, atrocious,
disgusting, disturbing, horrific,
horrifying, monstrous, outrageous,
scandalous, terrible.
2 (*informal*) shocking weather.
abominable (*informal*), appalling
(*informal*), atrocious (*informal*), bad,
dreadful (*informal*), foul, terrible
(*informal*), unpleasant.

shoddy *adjective*
shoddy work. bad, careless, inferior,
poor, slipshod, sloppy, substandard.
OPPOSITE careful.

shoe *noun*
[*kinds of shoe*] boot, clog, court shoe, sandal, sandshoe, slipper, sneaker, thong, trainer.

shoemaker *noun*
bootmaker, cobbler, shoe repairer.

shoot *verb*
1 *He shot the last round of ammunition.* discharge, fire.
2 *He shot the man.* gun down, hit, kill, snipe at, wound.
3 *The others shot past me.* charge, dash, fly, race, rush, speed, tear.
4 *The film was shot on location.* film, photograph.
shoot *noun*
The plant has new shoots. branch, bud, offshoot, sprig, sprout, sucker, tendril.
shoot up *The child has shot up.* grow, sprout.

shop *noun*
boutique, department store, mart, retailer, salon, store, supermarket.

shore *noun*
1 *They walked along the shore, picking up shells.* beach, coast, foreshore, seashore, seaside.
2 *They had their picnic on the shore of the lake.* bank, edge, side.

short *adjective*
1 *a short person. a short tree.* dwarf, little, miniature, petite, pygmy, small, squat, stubby, stunted, tiny.
OPPOSITE tall.
2 *a short visit.* brief, fleeting, momentary, passing, quick, short-lived.
OPPOSITE long.
3 *Money was short.* deficient, insufficient, lacking, light on (*Australian informal*), limited, low, scanty, scarce, wanting.
OPPOSITE abundant.
4 *The speech was short.* brief, concise, succinct, terse, to the point.
OPPOSITE long-winded.
5 *He was very short with people.* abrupt, blunt, brusque, curt, gruff, impatient, sharp, snappy.
OPPOSITE patient.
short *adverb*
She stopped short. abruptly, suddenly, unexpectedly.

shortage *noun*
a shortage of information. food shortages. dearth, deficiency, deficit, famine, insufficiency, lack, scarcity, shortfall, want.
OPPOSITE abundance.

shortcoming *noun*
She knows her shortcomings. deficiency, failing, fault, imperfection, limitation, weakness.
OPPOSITE strength.

shorten *verb*
He shortened the book. abbreviate, abridge, condense, cut down, diminish, prune, reduce.
OPPOSITE lengthen.

short-lived *adjective*
His joy was short-lived. ephemeral, fleeting, passing, temporary, transient.
OPPOSITE lasting.

shortly *adverb*
1 *I'll be leaving shortly.* before long, directly, presently, soon.
2 *He answered her shortly.* abruptly, brusquely, curtly, gruffly, impatiently, sharply, tersely.
OPPOSITE patiently.

short-sighted *adjective*
She wears glasses because she is short-sighted. myopic, near-sighted.
OPPOSITE hypermetropic, long-sighted.

short-tempered *adjective*
cross, grumpy, hot-tempered, impatient, irascible, irritable, quick-tempered, snappy, testy, tetchy.

shot *noun*
1 *He heard five shots.* bang, blast, discharge, explosion, report.
2 *He's a good shot.* archer, marksman, sharpshooter, shooter, sniper.
3 *The gunman fired his last shot.* bullet, pellet, slug.
4 *You get three shots at the bull's-eye.* attempt, chance, go, try.
5 *They don't need any shots before this trip.* immunisation, injection, jab (*informal*), vaccination.
6 *holiday shots of scenery.* photo (*informal*), photograph, picture, snapshot.

a
b
c
d
e
f
g
h
i
j
k
l
m
n
o
p
q
r
s
t
u
v
w
x
y
z

shoulder *verb*

1 *He shouldered his way through to the front.* elbow, jostle, push, shove.
2 *She shouldered the responsibility.* assume, bear, carry, take on, take upon yourself.
OPPOSITE shirk.

shout *noun*

1 *We heard a shout.* bellow, cry, outcry, roar, scream, screech, shriek, yell.
2 *(informal) He said that it was his shout.* round, treat, turn.

shout *verb*

1 *He shouted to the people behind him.* bawl, bellow, call, cry out, roar, scream, screech, shriek, thunder, yell.
2 *(Australian informal) He shouted everyone a drink.* pay for, stand, treat.

shove *noun*

He gave the boy a shove. push, thrust.

shove *verb*

1 *He shoved his way through the crowd.* elbow, jostle, push, shoulder, thrust.
2 *(informal) Shove it in the drawer.* place, put, stash *(informal)*, stick *(informal)*, stuff.

shovel *verb*

He shovelled soil. dig, excavate, scoop, shift.

show *verb*

1 *He doesn't usually show his feelings.* disclose, express, indicate, reveal.
OPPOSITE conceal.
2 *He showed us how it works.* demonstrate, describe, explain, illustrate, instruct, point out, teach.
3 *This shows that it can be done.* demonstrate, prove.
4 *Show the man out.* conduct, direct, escort, guide, lead, usher.
5 *The gallery is showing all her work.* display, exhibit, present.
6 *The label shows.* be visible, stick out.

show *noun*

1 *a craft show.* display, exhibition, expo *(informal)*, exposition, fair, pageant.
2 *(informal) In the evening they went to see a show.* entertainment, gig *(informal)*, performance, play, production.

show off

1 *He showed off his new car.* display, flaunt, parade.
2 *He loves to show off.* boast, brag, skite *(Australian informal)*, swagger, swank *(informal)*.

show up

1 *This latest incident has shown up his nasty streak.* expose, highlight, reveal.
2 *(informal) He always shows up in the end.* appear, be present, come, front up *(informal)*, materialise, turn up.

shower *noun*

A light shower is forecast. drizzle, rain, sprinkle.

shower *verb*

1 *He showered them with the hose.* spatter, spray, sprinkle.
2 *He was showered with presents.* deluge, flood, inundate, overwhelm.

show-off *noun*

boaster, braggart, exhibitionist, lair *(Australian informal)*, skite *(Australian informal)*.

showy *adjective*

a showy outfit. bright, brilliant, flamboyant, flashy, garish, gaudy, lairy *(Australian informal)*, ostentatious, striking.

shred *noun*

1 *shreds of material.* bit, fragment, piece, scrap, strip; [*shreds*] rags, tatters.
2 *not a shred of evidence.* bit, jot, particle, scrap, skerrick *(Australian informal)*, trace.

shred *verb*

The documents had to be shredded. cut up, destroy, rip up, tear up.

shrew *noun*

The woman had become a bitter old shrew. battleaxe *(informal)*, nag, scold *(old use)*.

shrewd *adjective*

a shrewd businesswoman. astute, canny, clever, crafty, cunning, far-sighted, ingenious, intelligent, knowing, perceptive, savvy *(informal)*, sharp, sly, smart, wise.
OPPOSITE stupid.

shriek *noun & verb*

cry, howl, scream, screech, squeal, yell.

shrill *adjective*
a shrill voice. high-pitched, penetrating, piercing, screeching, sharp.
OPPOSITE low.

shrine *noun*
1 *They worshipped at the shrine.* chapel, church, mosque, sanctuary, temple.
2 *a shrine of remembrance.* cenotaph, memorial, monument.

shrink *verb*
1 *The membership was shrinking as people drifted away.* contract, decline, diminish, dwindle, reduce.
OPPOSITE expand.
2 *He shrank from the accident scene in horror.* back away, draw back, recoil, retire, retreat, withdraw.

shrivel *verb*
The plant has shrivelled. dehydrate, dry up, shrink, wilt, wither, wrinkle.

shroud *noun*
The corpse was wrapped in a shroud. winding-sheet.
shroud *verb*
1 *The body was shrouded.* cover, swathe, wrap.
2 *His past life is shrouded in mystery.* cloak, clothe, conceal, cover, envelop, hide, veil.

shrub *noun*
bush, plant; [*various shrubs*] acacia, azalea, banksia, boronia, bottlebrush, camellia, cassia, daphne, erica, fuchsia, gardenia, geranium, grevillea, hakea, heather, hibiscus, honeysuckle, hydrangea, jasmine, lavender, lilac, melaleuca, myrtle, oleander, poinsettia, protea, rhododendron, rosemary, tea-tree, waratah, wax plant.

shudder *verb*
He shuddered at the thought. quake, quaver, quiver, shake, shiver, tremble.
shudder *noun*
She gave a shudder as she thought of the accident. quake, quiver, shake, shiver, spasm, tremble, tremor, vibration.

shuffle *verb*
1 *He is able to shuffle about now.* hobble, shamble.

2 *Please don't shuffle your feet.* drag, scrape, scuff.
3 *He has shuffled the cards.* jumble, mix, rearrange.

shunt *verb*
The train was shunted on to a siding. divert, sidetrack.

shut *verb*
I shut the door. bolt, close, fasten, latch, lock, secure.
OPPOSITE open.
shut out *They were shut out of the meeting.* bar, exclude, keep out, leave out, lock out.
shut up
1 *He will soon be shut up for five years.* confine, imprison, intern, jail, lock up, put away (*informal*).
OPPOSITE release.
2 (*informal*) *It is impolite to tell someone to shut up.* be quiet, be silent, stop talking.

shy *adjective*
She was shy in the company of strangers. bashful, coy, diffident, hesitant, nervous, reserved, retiring, self-conscious, timid.
OPPOSITE confident.
shy *verb*
The horse shied at the noise. buck, jump, recoil, start.

sick *adjective*
1 *He is too sick to go to work.* ailing, bedridden, crook (*Australian informal*), diseased, ill, indisposed, infirm, poorly, sickly, unwell.
OPPOSITE well.
2 *She had eaten too much and felt a bit sick.* bilious, nauseous, queasy.
3 *What he has done makes me sick.* angry, annoyed, disgusted, distressed, mad, sickened, upset.
be sick *The cat was sick on the carpet.* barf (*slang*), chuck (*informal*), chunder (*Australian slang*), puke (*informal*), sick up (*informal*), spew, throw up, vomit.
sick of *He is sick of reading.* bored with, fed up with (*informal*), jack of (*Australian slang*), tired of.

a
b
c
d
e
f
g
h
i
j
k
l
m
n
o
p
q
r
s
t
u
v
w
x
y
z

sicken *verb*
She was sickened by what she saw. disgust, distress, horrify, nauseate, offend, repel, revolt, upset.

sickly *adjective*
1 *a sickly child.* delicate, frail, ill, sick, unhealthy, unwell, weak.
OPPOSITE healthy.
2 *She looks sickly.* ashen, green, grey, pale, wan, yellow.
3 *a sickly taste.* cloying, nauseating, over-sweet, saccharine, sugary, syrupy.

sickness *noun*
1 *They promised to love one another in sickness and in health.* ill health, illness, infirmity.
OPPOSITE health.
2 *What are the symptoms of this sickness?* affliction, ailment, bug (*informal*), complaint, disease, disorder, illness, malady.
3 *Many people suffer from motion sickness.* biliousness, nausea, queasiness, vomiting.

side *noun*
1 *Write on the ruled side of the paper.* face, surface.
2 *He stood at the side of the pool.* boundary, brink, edge, limit, margin, perimeter, verge.
OPPOSITE centre.
3 *the side of a hill.* face, flank, slope.
4 *They studied the problem from every side.* aspect, facet, position, slant, standpoint, viewpoint.
5 *the opposing side.* camp, faction, party, team.
side *adjective*
1 *a side shoot.* lateral.
2 *a side matter.* incidental, marginal, secondary.
OPPOSITE main.
side *verb*
side with *She sided with them.* ally with, back, defend, go along with, stand up for, stick up for (*informal*), support.

sideboard *noun*
The china goes in the sideboard. buffet, cabinet, cupboard, dresser.

sidestep *verb*
He neatly sidestepped the issue. avoid, bypass, dodge, duck, evade, skirt round.

sidewalk *noun* (*American*)
footpath, pavement.

sideways *adjective*
a sideways glance. indirect, oblique, sidelong.
OPPOSITE direct.

siege *noun*
blockade.

sieve *noun*
Pass the mixture through a sieve. colander, filter, riddle, screen, sifter, strainer.
sieve *verb*
Sieve the flour. filter, riddle, sift, strain.

sift *verb*
Sift the flour. see SIEVE.

sight *noun*
1 *His sight is poor.* eyesight, vision.
2 *at first sight.* appearance, glance, glimpse, look, view.
3 *He disappeared from my sight.* range of vision, view.
4 *The tourists were told of the sights to visit.* display, scene, spectacle.
sight *verb*
We sighted land. behold (*old use*), catch sight of, espy, glimpse, make out, observe, see, spot, spy.

sightseer *noun*
holidaymaker, tourist, traveller, visitor.

sign *noun*
1 *a sign of love. no sign of trouble.* clue, evidence, hint, indication, symptom, token, trace, warning.
2 *We saw the sign of the red cross and felt safe.* badge, emblem, insignia, logo, mark, symbol.
3 *He read the sign.* notice, placard, plaque, poster, signboard.
4 *The policeman will give you the sign to go.* cue, gesture, nod, signal.
sign *verb*
She signed the document. autograph, countersign, endorse, undersign.
sign up *He signed up at the beginning of the war.* enlist, join up, register, sign on, volunteer.

signal *noun*
1 *We waited for the signal to proceed.* gesture, indication, nod, semaphore, sign, wave.

2 *This was her signal to leave.* cue, sign, warning.
signal *verb*
He signalled to them to come through. beckon, direct, gesture, indicate, motion, nod, sign, wave.

significance *noun*
1 *What is the significance of this symbol?* import, meaning, point, sense.
2 *an event of historical significance.* consequence, importance, moment.

significant *adjective*
a significant achievement. considerable, great, important, momentous, noteworthy, outstanding, remarkable.
OPPOSITE insignificant.

signify *verb*
1 *Red signifies danger. What does this word signify?* be a sign of, denote, imply, indicate, mean, represent, stand for, symbolise.
2 *They signified their appreciation by applauding.* convey, demonstrate, express, indicate, make known, show.

silence *noun*
the silence of the night. calm, hush, peace, quietness, stillness, tranquillity.
OPPOSITE noise.
silence *verb*
They managed to silence the protesters. gag, hush, quieten.

silent *adjective*
1 *a silent person, unable to speak.* dumb, mute, speechless, tongue-tied.
2 *a silent night.* calm, peaceful, quiet, soundless, still, tranquil.
OPPOSITE noisy.
3 *She was silent about the incident.* quiet, reserved, reticent, secretive, taciturn, tight-lipped, uncommunicative.
OPPOSITE talkative.
4 *a silent telephone number.* ex-directory, unlisted.
OPPOSITE listed.

silhouette *noun*
I could see his silhouette through the curtain. contour, form, outline, profile, shadow, shape.

silky *adjective*
silky material. fine, satiny, sleek, smooth, soft.

sill *noun*
ledge.

silly *adjective*
1 *a silly thing to do.* absurd, crazy, foolish, idiotic, illogical, inane, ludicrous, mad, pointless, reckless, ridiculous, senseless, stupid, unwise.
OPPOSITE sensible.
2 *a silly person.* barmy (*slang*), batty (*slang*), crazy, daft (*informal*), dopey (*informal*), dotty (*informal*), feeble-minded, foolish, goofy (*slang*), half-witted, insane, mad, potty (*informal*), scatty (*informal*), stupid.
OPPOSITE sensible.

similar *adjective*
similar problems. alike, analogous, comparable, parallel.
OPPOSITE dissimilar.

similarity *noun*
The similarity of the paintings is striking. correspondence, likeness, resemblance.
OPPOSITE difference, dissimilarity.

simmer *verb*
The casserole simmered for an hour. boil, bubble, stew.

simple *adjective*
1 *simple arithmetic.* basic, easy, elementary, rudimentary, straightforward, uncomplicated.
OPPOSITE complex, difficult.
2 *simple clothes.* austere, modest, plain, unsophisticated.
OPPOSITE fancy.
3 *a simple person who doesn't put on airs.* artless, genuine, honest, natural, sincere, straightforward, unaffected, unpretentious, unsophisticated.
OPPOSITE sophisticated.
4 *He was a bit simple and people took advantage of him.* backward, childish, dumb (*informal*), feeble-minded, naive, obtuse, simple-minded, slow, stupid.

simulate *verb*
He simulated a heart attack. act, fake, feign, imitate, pretend, sham.

simultaneous *adjective*
simultaneous events. coexistent, coincident, concurrent, parallel.

a b c d e f g h i j k l m n o p q r s t u v w x y z

sin *noun*
1 *a world of sin.* corruption, crime, evil, immorality, iniquity, sinfulness, ungodliness, unrighteousness, vice, wickedness, wrongdoing.
OPPOSITE righteousness.
2 *Forgive us our sins.* crime, fault, iniquity, misdeed, misdemeanour, offence, transgression, trespass (*old use*), vice, wrong, wrongdoing.
OPPOSITE virtue.
sin *verb*
do wrong, err, go astray, offend, transgress, trespass (*old use*).

sincere *adjective*
a sincere apology. a sincere person. authentic, dinkum (*Australian informal*), dinky-di (*Australian informal*), earnest, frank, genuine, heartfelt, honest, natural, open, real, true.
OPPOSITE false, insincere.

sinful *adjective*
They were punished for their sinful conduct. bad, blasphemous, corrupt, evil, immoral, iniquitous, sacrilegious, ungodly, unrighteous, wicked, wrong.
OPPOSITE righteous, sinless.

sing *verb*
1 *The man was singing.* carol, chant, croon, hum, serenade, trill, yodel.
2 *The birds were singing.* chirp, chirrup, tweet, twitter, warble.

singe *verb*
She singed the sheet she was ironing. burn, scorch, sear.

singer *noun*
chorister, crooner, minstrel, songster, vocalist.

single *adjective*
1 *They had a single copy of the book.* isolated, lone, odd, one, sole, solitary, unique.
2 *single beds.* individual, separate.
3 *a club for single people.* unattached, unmarried.
OPPOSITE married.
single *verb*
single out *He was singled out for special treatment.* choose, earmark, pick out, select.

singular *adjective*
1 *singular behaviour.* abnormal, bizarre, curious, eccentric, extraordinary, odd, outlandish, peculiar, strange, unconventional, unusual.
OPPOSITE common.
2 *a singular talent for music.* exceptional, extraordinary, outstanding, rare, remarkable, unique.
OPPOSITE ordinary.

sinister *adjective*
1 *a sinister look.* alarming, disturbing, frightening, menacing, ominous, threatening.
OPPOSITE benign.
2 *sinister intentions.* bad, criminal, diabolical, evil, malevolent, vile, villainous, wicked.
OPPOSITE good.

sink *verb*
1 *She sank to the ground.* descend, dip, droop, drop, fall, slump, subside.
2 *The sun sank below the horizon.* go down, set.
OPPOSITE rise.
3 *The ship sank.* founder, go down, submerge.
4 *They sank the ship.* scupper, scuttle.
5 *He was sinking in strength.* decline, deteriorate, diminish, fade, fail, go downhill, languish, slip.
OPPOSITE rally.
6 *sink a shaft. sink a well.* bore, dig, drill, excavate.
sink *noun*
Wash your hands in the sink. basin, washbasin.
sink in *The news hasn't sunk in yet.* be absorbed, go in, penetrate, register.

sinner *noun*
a repentant sinner. evildoer, malefactor, miscreant, offender, transgressor, trespasser (*old use*), wrongdoer.

sip *noun*
He had one sip and left the rest. drink, drop, mouthful, swallow, swig (*informal*), taste.

siren *noun*
an ambulance siren. alarm, signal.

sit *verb*
1 *He sat on the window sill.* be seated, perch yourself, rest, settle, squat.
2 *The car sits in the garage unused.* lie, remain, stand, stay.
3 *The committee will sit again in a month's time.* assemble, convene, meet.

site *noun*
the site for the event. location, place, position, setting, spot, venue.

sitting room *noun*
drawing room, living room, lounge, parlour (*old use*).

situation *noun*
1 *Their house is in a beautiful situation.* locality, location, place, position, setting, site, spot.
2 *He was in a difficult situation.* circumstances, plight, position, predicament.
3 *He looked every day in the 'Situations Vacant' column.* employment, job, position, post.

size *noun*
the size of a thing, a problem, etc. amount, area, bulk, capacity, dimensions, extent, magnitude, measurements, proportions, scale, scope.
size *verb*
size up (*informal*)
He sized up the situation very quickly. assess, gauge, judge, weigh up (*informal*).

sizeable *adjective*
a sizeable sum. ample, big, considerable, handsome, hefty, large, substantial.
OPPOSITE small.

sizzle *verb*
The sausages sizzled in the pan. hiss, sputter.

skate *verb*
She skated across the ice. glide, skid, skim, slide.

skeleton *noun*
1 *an animal's skeleton.* bones, frame.
2 *the skeleton of a building.* framework, shell, structure.

skerrick *noun* (*Australian informal*)
She didn't leave a skerrick. bit, crumb, fragment, jot, particle, scrap, shred, trace.

sketch *noun*
1 *a sketch of the finished house.* design, diagram, drawing, picture.
2 *a sketch of the finished book.* abstract, draft, outline, plan, synopsis.

skid *verb*
The car skidded on the wet road. aquaplane, slide, slip.

skilful *adjective*
a skilful performer. skilful work. able, accomplished, adept, brilliant, capable, clever, competent, deft, dexterous, expert, gifted, ingenious, masterly, professional, proficient, skilled, talented.
OPPOSITE incompetent.

skill *noun*
a job requiring skill. ability, aptitude, art, capability, cleverness, competence, dexterity, expertise, ingenuity, knack, know-how, mastery, proficiency, prowess, talent.
OPPOSITE incompetence.

skim *verb*
1 *He skimmed the fat off the stock.* remove, scrape.
2 *He skimmed over the water in his boat.* fly, glide, sail, sweep.
3 *She skimmed through several books.* flick, flip, glance, scan, thumb.
OPPOSITE pore over.

skin *noun*
1 *His skin was damaged by chemicals.* dermis, epidermis.
2 *animal skins.* coat, fur, hide, pelt.
3 *a plastic skin.* casing, coating, covering, exterior, film, membrane.
4 *the skin of fruit and vegetables.* husk, jacket (*of a potato*), peel, rind, shell.
skin *verb*
He skinned his knee on his first day at school. graze, scrape, scratch.

skinny *adjective*
Since dieting he has become too skinny. bony, emaciated, gaunt, lanky, lean, scraggy, scrawny, slender, thin.
OPPOSITE fat.

a
b
c
d
e
f
g
h
i
j
k
l
m
n
o
p
q
r
s
t
u
v
w
x
y
z

skip *verb*
1 *They skipped off happily.* bob, bound, caper, dance, frisk, gambol, hop, leap, prance, romp, run, trip.
2 *They skipped from one subject to another.* flit, jump, pass.
3 *He skipped that page.* leave out, miss, neglect, omit, overlook, pass over.
4 *She skipped the lecture that day.* absent yourself from, cut (*informal*), miss, play truant from, wag (*informal*).
OPPOSITE attend.

skipper *noun*
see CAPTAIN.

skirt *verb*
1 *Skirting the property is a low hedge.* border, bound, encircle, fringe, surround.
2 *He skirted the issue.* avoid, bypass, dodge, evade, sidestep.

skit *noun*
The revue consisted of several very funny skits. burlesque, parody, send-up (*informal*), sketch, spoof (*informal*), take-off.

skite *verb* (*Australian informal*)
He was skiting about his achievement. blow your own trumpet, boast, brag, congratulate yourself, crow, show off, vaunt.
skite *noun* (*Australian informal*)
boaster, braggart, show-off.

sky *noun*
air, atmosphere, heavens.

slab *noun*
a slab of cake. block, chunk, hunk, piece, slice, wedge.

slack *adjective*
1 *a slack rope.* floppy, limp, loose, relaxed.
OPPOSITE taut, tight.
2 *She's been slack in her work.* careless, casual, lackadaisical, lax, lazy, negligent, offhand, remiss, slapdash, slipshod, sloppy.
OPPOSITE diligent.
3 *Business is slack.* inactive, quiet, slow, sluggish.
OPPOSITE booming, busy.

slack *verb*
Don't let him catch you slacking. be lazy, ease off, idle, take it easy.

slacken *verb*
1 *You can slacken the rope now.* let go, loosen, relax, release, slack.
OPPOSITE tighten.
2 *They slackened their pace too early.* decrease, ease, reduce, relax, slow down.
OPPOSITE increase.

slam *verb*
1 *He slammed the door.* bang, close, shut.
2 *The red car slammed into the white one.* bump, crash, knock, ram, run, smash.

slant *verb*
1 *The floor slants downwards near the drain hole.* incline, lean, list, slope, tilt.
2 *The story has been slanted in his favour.* angle, bias, distort.
slant *noun*
1 *The floor is on a slant.* angle, incline, list, slope, tilt.
2 *a different slant on the news.* angle, attitude, bias, perspective, prejudice, view.

slap *verb*
She slapped his face. cuff, hit, smack, spank, strike, whack.
slap *noun*
She received a slap on the bottom. blow, cuff, hit, smack, whack.
slap *adverb*
He ran slap into the teacher. bang, directly, headlong, smack (*informal*), straight.

slash *verb*
1 *The box has been slashed open.* cut, gash, hack, rip, slice, slit, tear.
2 *Prices were slashed.* cut, drop, lower, reduce.
slash *noun*
1 *a slash made by a knife.* cut, gash, incision, laceration, rip, slit.
2 *Put a slash through the mistake.* line, oblique, stroke.

slaughter *noun*
the slaughter of innocent people. carnage, killing, massacre, murder, slaying.

slaughter *verb*
1 *The animals were slaughtered.* butcher, destroy, kill.
2 *The soldiers slaughtered civilians.* execute, exterminate, kill, massacre, murder, slay.
3 (*informal*) *We were slaughtered by the other team.* beat, defeat, thrash, trounce.

slave *noun*
The boy was sold as a slave. serf, servant, vassal.
slave *verb*
She slaves all day in the kitchen. grind away, labour, slog, sweat, toil, work hard.

slave-driver *noun*
oppressor, taskmaster, tyrant.

slavery *noun*
He was sold into slavery. bondage, captivity, enslavement, serfdom, servitude.
OPPOSITE freedom.

slay *verb*
assassinate, execute, kill, massacre, murder, put to death, slaughter.

sledge *noun*
bob-sled, bob-sleigh, luge, sled, sleigh, toboggan.

sleek *adjective*
She has beautiful sleek hair. glossy, shiny, silky, smooth.
OPPOSITE dull.

sleep *noun*
1 *an afternoon sleep.* catnap, doze, forty winks, kip (*slang*), nap, repose, rest, shut-eye (*informal*), siesta, slumber, snooze.
2 *the animal's winter sleep.* dormancy, hibernation.
sleep *verb*
He can sleep anywhere. catnap, doze, drop off, kip (*slang*), nap, nod off, rest, slumber, snooze.

sleepless *adjective*
a sleepless night. disturbed, restless, wakeful.

sleeplessness *noun*
insomnia, wakefulness.

sleepwalker *noun*
somnambulist.

sleepy *adjective*
1 *The hot weather makes him feel sleepy.* dopey (*informal*), drowsy, lethargic, somnolent, tired, weary.
OPPOSITE wide awake.
2 *a sleepy little outback town.* dormant, inactive, peaceful, quiet.
OPPOSITE busy.

sleeve *noun*
a protective sleeve. case, cover, sheath.

sleigh *noun*
see SLEDGE.

slender *adjective*
1 *a slender figure.* lean, slight, slim, thin.
OPPOSITE stout.
2 *a slender hope.* faint, feeble, slight, slim, small, weak.
OPPOSITE strong.

slice *noun*
1 *a slice of cake.* chunk, piece, portion, segment, sliver, wedge.
2 *a slice of the profits.* cut, part, portion, proportion, share.
slice *verb*
1 *He sliced the chicken.* carve, cut, divide.
2 *He sliced off the top layer.* pare, peel, shave, trim.

slick *adjective*
a slick salesman. clever, cunning, glib, sly, smarmy (*informal*), smooth.

slide *verb*
The smooth downhill slope made it easy to slide. coast, glide, skate, skid, slip, slither.
slide *noun*
1 *The books passed down the slide.* chute, ramp, slope.
2 *The child plays on the slide.* slippery dip (*Australian*).

slight *adjective*
1 *a slight difference.* imperceptible, insignificant, little, minute, negligible, small, subtle, superficial, tiny, trivial.
OPPOSITE considerable, great.
2 *a person of slight build.* delicate, frail, lean, slender, slim, thin.
OPPOSITE heavy, large.

a
b
c
d
e
f
g
h
i
j
k
l
m
n
o
p
q
r
s
t
u
v
w
x
y
z

slim *adjective*
1 *a slim person.* lean, slender, slight, thin.
OPPOSITE fat.
2 *Her chances are slim.* faint, remote, slender, slight, small.
OPPOSITE strong.

slime *noun*
The pipes were full of slime. goo (*informal*), gunge (*informal*), gunk (*informal*), muck, mud, ooze, sludge.

slimy *adjective*
a slimy substance. gooey (*informal*), gungy (*informal*), mucky, muddy, oozy, slippery, sludgy.

sling *noun*
1 *His injured arm was in a sling.* bandage, belt, strap, support.
2 *He shot stones using his sling.* catapult, shanghai (*Australian*), slingshot.
sling *verb*
1 *He slung the hammock between two trees.* dangle, hang, suspend, swing.
2 (*informal*) *He slung his bag on the floor.* cast, chuck (*informal*), fling, hurl, throw, toss.

slink *verb*
He slunk out of the room. creep, skulk, slip, sneak, steal.

slip *verb*
1 *She slipped on the wet floor.* fall, glide, skid, slide, slither.
2 *She slipped out of the room.* creep, skulk, slink, sneak, steal.
3 *Slip these stitches off the needle.* detach, release.
slip *noun*
1 *Avoid slips by moving slowly.* fall, glide, skid, slide.
2 *He can be forgiven for a minor slip.* blue (*Australian informal*), blunder, booboo (*slang*), error, lapse, mistake, slip-up (*informal*).
3 *The dress needs a slip underneath.* petticoat.
4 *The pillows need clean slips.* case, cover, pillowcase, pillowslip.
5 *He handed me a slip of paper.* piece, scrap, sheet, strip.
give the slip *He gave me the slip.* avoid, dodge, elude, escape, evade, lose.

slip up (*informal*) *We rely on you not to slip up.* blunder, err, goof (*slang*), make a mistake.

slippery *adjective*
a slippery surface. greasy, oily, slick, slithery, smooth, wet.

slit *noun*
a slit in the wall. a slit in her skirt. crack, cut, gash, hole, incision, opening, rip, slash, slot, split, tear.
slit *verb*
She slit the seam. cut, gash, rip, slash, split, tear.

slither *verb*
The snake slithered across the path. slide, slink, slip.

slog *verb*
1 *He slogged the ball.* hit, strike, thump, whack.
2 *He slogged away at his work for hours.* labour, plod, plough, toil, work.
3 *They slogged on through the scrub for another ten kilometres.* plod, plough, tramp, trudge.

slogan *noun*
an advertising slogan. catchphrase, jingle, motto.

slop *verb*
She slopped her tea over her books. slosh (*informal*), spill, splash, splatter.

slope *verb*
The road slopes steeply. ascend, bank, descend, drop, incline, rise, slant, tilt, tip.
slope *noun*
a steep slope. angle, ascent, bank, descent, escarpment, grade, gradient, hill, hillside, inclination, incline, pitch, rake, rise, scarp, slant, tilt.

sloppy *adjective*
1 *sloppy food.* gooey (*informal*), liquid, runny, watery.
OPPOSITE solid.
2 *sloppy work.* careless, lax, messy, shoddy, slapdash, slipshod, slovenly, unmethodical, untidy.
OPPOSITE careful, meticulous.
3 *sloppy love letters.* mushy, romantic, sentimental, soppy (*informal*).

slot *noun*
1 *He put the coin in the slot.* groove, hole, opening, slit.
2 *Each patient has a ten-minute slot.* place, position, space, spot, time.
slot *verb*
The doctor slotted two extra patients in. fit, schedule.

slouch *verb*
When he's tired he tends to slouch. droop, hunch, loll, sag, slump, stoop.

slovenly *adjective*
1 *a slovenly appearance.* careless, dirty, disreputable, messy, scruffy, slatternly, unkempt, untidy.
OPPOSITE neat.
2 *slovenly work.* see SLOPPY.

slow *adjective*
1 *a slow pace.* dawdling, leisurely, measured, plodding, sluggish, steady, unhurried.
OPPOSITE fast.
2 *a slow process.* drawn-out, endless, gradual, interminable, long, prolonged, protracted, time-consuming.
OPPOSITE quick.
3 *a slow response.* delayed, late, tardy.
OPPOSITE hasty, quick.
4 *You may need to explain it again, as he is a bit slow.* dense, dim, dull, dumb (*informal*), obtuse, stupid, thick (*informal*).
OPPOSITE clever, quick.
5 *Business is slow today.* dull, quiet, slack, sluggish.
OPPOSITE brisk, lively.
slow *verb*
1 *Cars must slow down for this corner.* brake, decelerate, reduce speed.
OPPOSITE accelerate.
2 *Illness has slowed her progress on the work.* hinder, hold back, impede, retard.
OPPOSITE speed up.

slowly *adverb*
at a snail's pace, gradually, leisurely, sluggishly, steadily, unhurriedly.
OPPOSITE quickly.

sludge *noun*
The drain was blocked with sludge. goo (*informal*), mire, muck, mud, silt, slime, slush.

slug *verb*
1 *He slugged his opponent.* see HIT.
2 (*Australian informal*) *He was slugged with a huge fine.* charge, hit, tax.

slumber *noun*
The princess fell into a deep slumber. repose, rest, sleep.
slumber *verb*
He found the princess slumbering. doze, nap, rest, sleep, snooze.

slump *noun*
1 *The country was facing a slump.* decline, depression, downturn, recession, setback.
OPPOSITE upturn.
2 *a slump in prices.* collapse, crash, decline, drop, fall, tumble.
OPPOSITE improvement, increase.
slump *verb*
1 *The value of his shares slumped.* collapse, crash, decline, drop, fall, plummet, plunge, tumble.
OPPOSITE improve.
2 *She slumped into the chair.* collapse, drop, fall, flop, sink, tumble.

sly *adjective*
1 *He is a sly character.* artful, crafty, cunning, devious, furtive, secretive, shrewd, sneaky, underhand, wily.
OPPOSITE straightforward.
2 *She did it with a sly smile.* arch, knowing, mischievous, playful, roguish.

smack *noun*
a smack on the bottom. blow, hit, rap, slap, spanking, whack.
smack *verb*
He smacked the child. belt (*slang*), hit, rap, slap, spank, strike, wallop (*slang*), whack.
smack *adverb* (*informal*)
He ran smack into the car in front. bang, directly, slap, straight.

small *adjective*
1 *a small person, plant, house, etc.* compact, diminutive, dwarf, little, microscopic, miniature, minuscule, minute, petite, pocket-sized, poky, puny, short, slender, slight, stunted, tiny, undersized, wee (*informal*).
OPPOSITE big, large.

a
b
c
d
e
f
g
h
i
j
k
l
m
n
o
p
q
r
s
t
u
v
w
x
y
z

2 *a small amount.* imperceptible, infinitesimal, insignificant, little, meagre, measly (*informal*), minimal, negligible, paltry, petty, scant, scanty, trifling, trivial.
OPPOSITE big.
3 *He said it in a small voice.* faint, feeble, little, quiet, soft, subdued, weak.
OPPOSITE loud, strong.

smart *adjective*
1 *a smart pace.* brisk, energetic, fast, quick, swift, vigorous.
OPPOSITE slow.
2 *a smart student.* able, astute, brainy, bright, capable, clever, ingenious, intelligent, keen, sharp.
OPPOSITE dull.
3 *That wasn't a very smart thing to do.* clever, prudent, sensible, shrewd, wise.
OPPOSITE silly, stupid.
4 *a smart appearance.* chic, dapper, elegant, fashionable, neat, posh (*informal*), snazzy (*informal*), spruce, stylish, swanky (*informal*), swish (*informal*), trim.
OPPOSITE dowdy, untidy.
smart *verb*
Her finger smarted. hurt, sting, throb.

smash *verb*
1 *The glass smashed.* break, shatter, splinter.
2 *He smashed the door down.* bash, batter, break, hammer, hit, knock, pound, strike.
3 *The car smashed into the bus.* bang, bump, collide (with), crash, hit, knock, ram, run, slam.
smash *noun*
a smash on the freeway. accident, collision, crash, pile-up (*informal*), prang (*slang*).
smash hit (*informal*)
The song was a smash hit. hit, success, triumph, winner.
OPPOSITE flop (*slang*).

smear *verb*
1 *The baby smeared her high chair with jam.* coat, cover, plaster, rub, spread.
2 *The newspaper smeared the doctor's reputation.* blacken, defame, denigrate, malign, slur, sully.

smear *noun*
paint smears on his face. blotch, mark, smudge, splotch, stain, streak.

smell *noun*
1 *What sort of smell was it?* aroma, bouquet, fragrance, odour, perfume, scent, whiff.
2 *The smell of rotten meat filled the shop.* pong (*informal*), reek, stench, stink.
smell *verb*
1 *She smelt the wine before sipping it.* nose, scent, sniff.
2 *The refrigerator smells.* pong (*informal*), reek, stink.

smelly *adjective*
a smelly rubbish dump. foul-smelling, on the nose (*Australian informal*), pongy (*informal*), putrid, rancid, rank, stinking.
OPPOSITE fragrant, odourless.

smile *noun & verb*
beam, grin, simper, smirk.
OPPOSITE frown.

smoke *noun*
1 *The smoke was choking them.* exhaust, fumes, smog.
2 (*informal*) *a packet of smokes.* cigar, cigarette, fag (*slang*).
smoke *verb*
The fire is only smoking now. fume, smoulder.

smooth *adjective*
1 *a smooth surface.* even, flat, level.
OPPOSITE rough.
2 *smooth hair.* shiny, silky, sleek, soft, velvety.
3 *a smooth batter.* creamy, flowing, runny.
OPPOSITE lumpy.
4 *a smooth voice.* mellow, pleasant, soothing, sweet.
OPPOSITE harsh.
5 *smooth seas.* calm, even, flat, peaceful, still, unruffled.
OPPOSITE rough.
smooth *verb*
1 *She smoothed the sheets.* even, flatten, iron, level, press.
2 *He went ahead to smooth the way.* ease, open, pave, prepare.

smoothly *adverb*
All went smoothly. easily, straightforwardly, well, without a hitch.

smother *verb*
1 *He smothered his victim with a pillow.* asphyxiate, choke, stifle, suffocate.
2 *They smothered the fire with a blanket.* extinguish, put out, quench, snuff.
3 *The pie was smothered with cream.* cover.

smoulder *verb*
The fire was still smouldering. burn, smoke.

smudge *noun*
There were smudges of ink on her book. blot, blotch, mark, smear, splash, splotch, spot, stain, streak.
smudge *verb*
He smudged his work. blot, smear, stain, streak.

smug *adjective*
He was so smug about his win. complacent, conceited, self-righteous, self-satisfied, supercilious, superior.
OPPOSITE humble.

smuggling *noun*
bootlegging, contraband, drug running, gunrunning.

snack *noun*
1 *We have a snack at about 11 o'clock.* playlunch, recess, refreshments.
2 *(Australian informal) The exam was a snack.* bludge (*Australian informal*), breeze (*informal*), cinch (*informal*), doddle (*informal*), piece of cake (*informal*), pushover (*informal*).
snack bar canteen, deli (*informal*), kiosk (*Australian*), milk bar, sandwich shop, takeaway.

snag *noun*
There's just one snag. catch, difficulty, hitch, impediment, obstacle, obstruction, problem, stumbling block.
snag *verb*
She snagged her stockings. catch, rip, tear.

snake *noun*
serpent; [*various snakes*] adder, anaconda, asp, black snake, boa constrictor, brown snake, carpet snake, cobra, copperhead, death adder, diamond snake, dugite, python, rattlesnake, red-bellied black snake, taipan, tiger snake, viper, whip snake, womma.

snaky *adjective* (*Australian informal*)
He got quite snaky when asked for money. angry, annoyed, bad-tempered, crabby, irritable, shirty (*informal*).

snap *verb*
1 *The teacher snapped his fingers.* click, crack.
2 *The branch snapped.* break, crack, fracture, give way, split.
3 *The dog snapped at his heels.* bite, gnash, nip.
snap *noun*
1 *They heard a snap.* click, crack, fracture, pop.
2 *a cold snap.* period, spell.
3 *holiday snaps.* photo (*informal*), photograph, picture, snapshot.
snap *adjective*
a snap decision. hasty, quick, sudden.
snap up *If an opportunity comes, snap it up.* accept, grab, seize, snatch, take.

snappy *adjective* (*informal*)
1 *a snappy performance.* brisk, energetic, lively, vigorous, zippy.
OPPOSITE slow.
2 *a snappy dresser.* chic, dapper, elegant, fashionable, neat, smart, trendy (*informal*).
OPPOSITE dowdy.
3 *a snappy mood.* crabby, cross, grumpy, irritable, testy, tetchy.

snare *noun*
1 *snares for animals.* net, noose, trap.
2 *I warned him of the many snares.* danger, peril, pitfall, trap.
snare *verb*
He snared a fox. capture, catch, trap.

snarl[1] *verb*
The dog snarled at the postman. bare your teeth, growl.

snarl[2] *verb*
The thread has snarled. entangle, entwine, knot, tangle, twist.
snarl *noun*
a traffic snarl. blockage, hold-up, jam, obstruction, tangle.

a
b
c
d
e
f
g
h
i
j
k
l
m
n
o
p
q
r
s
t
u
v
w
x
y
z

snatch *verb*
He snatched her handbag. grab, nab (*informal*), pluck, seize, snitch (*slang*), steal, swipe (*informal*), take.

sneak *verb*
1 He is sneaking out. creep, slink, slip, steal, tiptoe.
2 (*informal*) He sneaked a book from the library. smuggle, snitch (*informal*), steal.
3 (*informal*) We couldn't trust him not to sneak on us. betray, dob (*Australian informal*), grass (*slang*), inform, rat (*informal*), report, shop (*slang*), split (*slang*), tell, tell tales.
sneak *noun* (*informal*)
He was the sneak who told on them. dobber (*Australian informal*), grass (*slang*), informer, pimp (*Australian slang*), tale-bearer, tell-tale.

sneaky *adjective*
a sneaky person. crafty, cunning, devious, furtive, secretive, shifty, slippery, sly, stealthy, treacherous, underhand, wily.
OPPOSITE open.

sneer *verb*
sneer at He sneered at their efforts. disdain, jeer at, laugh at, mock, ridicule, scoff at, scorn, snigger at.

sniff *verb*
1 Blow your nose instead of sniffing. sniffle, snivel, snuffle.
2 She sniffed the wine. nose, smell.

sniffle *verb & noun*
sniff, snivel, snuffle.

snigger *noun & verb*
chuckle, giggle, simper, snicker, titter; see also SNEER.

snip *verb*
She snipped her hair. clip, crop, cut, lop, prune, trim.

snipe *verb*
The gunman sniped at the president from a tall building. fire, shoot.

snippet *noun*
He only caught snippets of the news. bit, extract, fragment, part, snatch.

snivel *verb*
What was she snivelling about? blubber, cry, sob, weep, whimper, whine; see also SNIFFLE.

snobbish *adjective*
A snobbish person has few friends. condescending, disdainful, haughty, patronising, pompous, pretentious, snooty (*informal*), stuck-up (*informal*), superior, toffee-nosed (*informal*).
OPPOSITE humble.

snoop *verb* (*informal*)
The police have been snooping around. nose, poke your nose, pry, spy, stickybeak (*Australian informal*).

snooze *noun*
She had a snooze in the armchair. catnap, doze, forty winks, kip (*slang*), nap, rest, siesta, sleep.
snooze *verb*
She snoozed in the chair in the evening. catnap, doze, kip (*slang*), nap, rest, sleep.

snub *verb*
She snubbed him publicly. cold-shoulder, give someone the brush-off, humiliate, ignore, insult, rebuff, reject, scorn.

snuffle *verb & noun*
sniff, sniffle, snivel.

snug *adjective*
1 snug in bed. comfortable, comfy (*informal*), cosy, secure, warm.
2 a snug fit. close, tight.

snuggle *verb*
The cat snuggled up on her lap. cuddle, curl up, huddle, nestle.

soak *verb*
1 Soak the stained clothes in bleach. immerse, steep, submerge, wet.
2 The dye soaked through. penetrate, permeate, seep.
3 The rain soaked the washing. drench, saturate, wet.
soak up They soaked up the spill with an old nappy. absorb, sop up, take up.

soar *verb*
1 The bird soared higher and higher. ascend, fly, rise.
OPPOSITE descend.

2 *The price of new cars has soared.* climb, escalate, increase, mount, rise, rocket.
OPPOSITE drop.

sob *verb*
He sobbed uncontrollably. bawl, blubber, cry, snivel, wail, weep.

sober *adjective*
1 *Her friends got drunk but she stayed sober.* abstemious, abstinent, clear-headed, on the wagon (*informal*), teetotal, temperate.
OPPOSITE drunk.
2 *She is a sober person, not given to frivolity.* earnest, grave, level-headed, restrained, sedate, self-controlled, sensible, serious, solemn, staid.
OPPOSITE frivolous.
3 *sober colours.* drab, dreary, dull, inconspicuous, sombre, subdued.
OPPOSITE bright, gaudy.

sociable *adjective*
She has become more sociable as she has grown older. affable, communicative, extroverted, friendly, gregarious, outgoing, social.
OPPOSITE unsociable.

social *adjective*
1 *Ants are social creatures.* cooperative, interdependent.
OPPOSITE independent, solitary.
2 *social problems.* community, public.
3 *She is not a social person.* see SOCIABLE.
social *noun*
They went to the social on Saturday night. dance, disco (*informal*), do (*informal*), gathering, get-together (*informal*), party.

society *noun*
1 *an outrage against society.* community, humanity, mankind.
2 *members of different societies.* community, culture, nation, people.
3 *They are happy in each other's society.* company, fellowship, presence.
4 *They joined a historical society.* association, body, club, group, guild, organisation, union.

socket *noun*
a tooth socket. hole, hollow.

sofa *noun*
couch, settee.

soft *adjective*
1 *soft plastics.* flexible, malleable, pliable, supple.
OPPOSITE hard.
2 *a soft pillow.* floppy, limp, spongy, springy.
OPPOSITE firm.
3 *soft fabrics.* fleecy, satiny, silky, sleek, smooth, velvety.
OPPOSITE rough.
4 *soft voices.* faint, gentle, hushed, inaudible, low, muted, quiet, subdued.
OPPOSITE loud.
5 *His muscles have gone soft through lack of exercise.* feeble, flabby, weak.
OPPOSITE firm.
6 *He's too soft with the children: they need a firmer hand.* easygoing, indulgent, lax, lenient, permissive; see also SOFT-HEARTED.
OPPOSITE firm, tough.
7 (*informal*) *a soft job.* comfortable, cosy, cushy (*informal*), easy, undemanding.
OPPOSITE demanding, difficult.
8 *soft drink.* non-alcoholic.
OPPOSITE alcoholic.
9 *soft colours.* delicate, light, pale, pastel, subdued.
OPPOSITE bright.

soften *verb*
1 *He softened his voice to speak to the child.* lower, moderate, quieten, subdue, tone down.
OPPOSITE raise.
2 *This will soften the impact.* buffer, cushion, dampen, deaden, lessen, reduce.
OPPOSITE intensify.

soft-hearted *adjective*
caring, compassionate, generous, gentle, kind, merciful, mild, soft, sympathetic, tender-hearted, understanding, warm-hearted.

soggy *adjective*
1 *The washing was still soggy.* drenched, saturated, soaked, sodden, sopping, waterlogged, wet.
OPPOSITE dry.
2 *soggy damper.* doughy, heavy, stodgy.
OPPOSITE light.

a
b
c
d
e
f
g
h
i
j
k
l
m
n
o
p
q
r
s
t
u
v
w
x
y
z

soil[1] noun
1 *He tills the soil.* dirt, earth, ground, loam.
2 *on her home soil.* country, ground, land, territory.

soil[2] verb
He soiled his new jumper. blacken, dirty, stain.
OPPOSITE clean.

soldier noun
commando, conscript, fighter, GI (*American*), marine, mercenary, NCO, private, regular, serviceman, servicewoman, trooper, warrior.

sole adjective
1 *the sole survivor.* lone, only, single, solitary.
2 *The channel has the sole right to show the tennis.* exclusive.
OPPOSITE joint.

solemn adjective
1 *We don't want any solemn faces in this room.* earnest, glum, grave, sad, sedate, serious, sober, sombre, staid, unsmiling.
OPPOSITE cheerful.
2 *a solemn occasion.* awesome, ceremonial, ceremonious, dignified, formal, grand, important, impressive, stately.
OPPOSITE frivolous.

solicitor noun
see LAWYER.

solid adjective
1 *a solid substance.* dense, firm, hard, rigid, stable.
OPPOSITE fluid, hollow.
2 *solid silver.* pure, unadulterated, unalloyed.
3 *a solid table.* durable, robust, sound, strong, sturdy, substantial.
OPPOSITE flimsy.
4 *solid evidence.* concrete, reliable, sound, strong, tangible, weighty.
OPPOSITE flimsy.

solidify verb
The mixture solidified. congeal, gel, harden, jell, set.
OPPOSITE liquefy.

solitary adjective
1 *a solitary walker.* alone, lone, single, sole, solo, unaccompanied.
2 *a solitary example.* isolated, one and only, single, sole.
3 *He found a solitary spot to meditate and pray.* deserted, desolate, empty, isolated, lonely, remote, secluded, unfrequented.
OPPOSITE busy.

solo adjective & adverb
alone, independent, single-handed, unaccompanied.

solution noun
1 *a solution of salt and water.* blend, mixture.
2 *a solution to the problem.* answer, explanation, key, remedy, resolution, result.

solve verb
He has solved the puzzle. answer, crack, figure out, resolve, work out.

sombre adjective
1 *sombre colours.* dark, drab, dreary, dull, gloomy, sober.
OPPOSITE bright.
2 *sombre mood.* dismal, gloomy, grave, melancholy, sad, serious, sober, solemn.
OPPOSITE cheerful.

sometimes adverb
They call in sometimes. every so often, from time to time, now and then, occasionally, on and off.
OPPOSITE never.

song noun
air, anthem, aria, ballad, carol, chorus, ditty, hymn, jingle, lullaby, madrigal, number, psalm, serenade, shanty.

sook noun (*Australian informal*)
coward, cry-baby, sissy, softie (*informal*), wimp (*informal*), wuss (*slang*).

soon adverb
1 *They'll be here soon.* before long, by and by, presently, shortly.
2 *The rain came too soon.* early, quickly.
OPPOSITE late.

soothe verb
1 *It was hard to soothe the dissatisfied customer.* appease, calm, pacify.
OPPOSITE upset.

2 *The ointment soothed the pain.* alleviate, ease, reduce, relieve.
OPPOSITE aggravate.

sooty *adjective*
1 *a sooty chimney.* dirty, grimy.
2 *The cat was a sooty colour.* black, blackish, charcoal.

sophisticated *adjective*
1 *a sophisticated audience.* cosmopolitan, cultivated, cultured, experienced, knowledgeable, refined, worldly-wise.
OPPOSITE naive, unsophisticated.
2 *a sophisticated gadget.* advanced, complex, complicated, elaborate, intricate.
OPPOSITE crude.

sopping *adjective*
She came home sopping. drenched, dripping, saturated, soaked, sodden, wet.
OPPOSITE dry.

sorcerer *noun*
enchanter, magician, warlock, wizard.

sorceress *noun*
enchantress, magician, witch.

sorcery *noun*
black magic, enchantment, magic, witchcraft, wizardry.

sordid *adjective*
1 *sordid living conditions.* dirty, filthy, foul, putrid, sleazy, squalid.
OPPOSITE clean.
2 *a sordid business.* base, dishonourable, mean, mercenary, shabby, vile.
OPPOSITE honourable.

sore *adjective*
1 *a sore ankle.* aching, bruised, chafed, grazed, hurting, inflamed, injured, painful, sensitive, smarting, stinging, tender, uncomfortable.
2 *He was feeling sore about his failure.* angry, annoyed, distressed, irritated, peeved (*informal*), touchy, upset, vexed.
sore *noun*
The sores took a long time to heal. abrasion, abscess, blister, boil, burn, graze, inflammation, laceration, scratch, ulcer, wound.

sorrow *noun*
His death caused her great sorrow. anguish, distress, grief, heartache, misery, regret, sadness, suffering, unhappiness, woe.
OPPOSITE joy.

sorry *adjective*
1 *She was sorry about what she had done.* apologetic, contrite, penitent, regretful, remorseful, repentant, sad, sorrowful.
OPPOSITE unrepentant.
2 *She felt sorry for the victims.* compassionate, pitying, sympathetic, understanding.
OPPOSITE unsympathetic.
3 *Things were in a sorry state.* bad, deplorable, dreadful, miserable, pitiful, terrible, woeful, wretched.

sort *noun*
different sorts of things. brand, breed, category, class, form, genus, group, kind, species, style, type, variety.
sort *verb*
1 *The specimens have been sorted into groups.* arrange, class, classify, divide, group, organise.
2 *Sort the grain from the chaff.* pick out, separate, sift.
OPPOSITE mix.
sort out
1 *They sorted out the pile of ribbons.* disentangle, organise, straighten out, tidy.
2 *He will sort out the problem.* attend to, clear up, deal with, handle, resolve, solve.

soul *noun*
1 *a person's soul.* spirit.
2 *not a soul in sight.* creature, individual, person.

sound¹ *noun*
He didn't hear a sound. noise.
sound *verb*
1 *The g in 'gnat' is not sounded.* enunciate, pronounce, speak, utter, voice.
2 *It sounds all right.* appear, seem.
3 *The bells sounded the start of business.* announce, signal.

sound² *adjective*
1 *sound in mind and body.* fit, healthy, robust, well.
OPPOSITE unhealthy.

a
b
c
d
e
f
g
h
i
j
k
l
m
n
o
p
q
r
s
t
u
v
w
x
y
z

2 *The house was structurally sound.* intact, solid, strong, sturdy, well-built.
OPPOSITE damaged.
3 *a sound argument.* cogent, coherent, logical, rational, reasonable, solid.
OPPOSITE illogical.
4 *a sound investment.* reliable, safe, secure, solid.
OPPOSITE risky.
5 *a sound sleep.* continuous, deep, unbroken, uninterrupted.
OPPOSITE disturbed, light.

sound³ *verb*
He sounded the depth of the river. fathom, measure, plumb, test.
sound out see QUESTION.

soup *noun*
broth, chowder, consommé.

sour *adjective*
1 *a sour taste.* acid, astringent, mouth-puckering, sharp, tangy, tart, vinegary.
OPPOSITE sweet.
2 *The milk has gone sour.* bad, curdled, fermented, off, rancid, stale.
OPPOSITE fresh.
3 *Nobody liked the new teacher who always looked so sour.* bad-tempered, bitter, crabby, embittered, grouchy (*informal*), irritable, nasty, peevish, sullen, surly, testy, tetchy, unpleasant.
OPPOSITE amiable.

source *noun*
1 *Smoking was the source of her ill health.* cause, origin, root.
OPPOSITE consequence.
2 *Some dictionaries give the source of words.* derivation, origin.
3 *the source of the river.* beginning, head, spring, start.
OPPOSITE mouth.
4 *The evidence comes from a reliable source.* informant.

souvenir *noun*
He was given a tie as a souvenir of his visit. keepsake, memento, reminder.

sovereign *noun*
emperor, empress, king, monarch, queen, ruler, sultan.

sow *verb*
1 *The farmer sowed the seeds in the field.* broadcast, plant, scatter, strew.

2 *He sowed discontent in the group.* implant, introduce, spread.

space *noun*
1 *There's plenty of space in the hall.* area, capacity, room, volume.
2 *a parking space.* bay, place, position, spot.
3 *Fill in the spaces.* blank.
4 *There was a big space between them.* break, distance, gap, hole, interval, opening.
5 *She wanted to be an astronaut and explore space.* the heavens, outer space, the universe.
6 *in a short space of time.* duration, interval, period, span, stretch.

space *verb*
The teacher spaced the children an arm's length apart. arrange, place, position, separate, spread.

spacious *adjective*
a spacious house. big, enormous, extensive, large, roomy, sizeable, vast.
OPPOSITE compact, small.

span *noun*
1 *the wing span.* breadth, distance, extent, length, measure, reach, spread, stretch.
2 *over a span of five years.* duration, interval, length, period, space, spell, stretch, term.

span *verb*
The viaduct spans the valley. bridge, cross, extend across, straddle, stretch across.

spank *verb*
hit, slap, smack.

spare *verb*
1 *He wanted to spare me the pain.* protect from, relieve of, save, shield from.
OPPOSITE expose to.
2 *He could not spare me his time.* afford, give, grant, part with.

spare *adjective*
spare space. additional, available, extra, free, leftover, surplus, unoccupied.

sparing *adjective*
He was sparing with the club's money. careful, economical, frugal, miserly, penny-pinching, stingy, thrifty.
OPPOSITE extravagant.

spark *noun*
a spark of light. flash, flicker, glimmer, glint, sparkle.
spark *verb*
spark off *The article sparked off a heated debate.* provoke, set off, start, touch off, trigger off.

sparkle *verb*
The jewels sparkled in the light. flash, gleam, glint, glitter, scintillate, shimmer, shine, twinkle.

sparkling *adjective*
1 *a sparkling light.* bright, brilliant, dazzling, gleaming, glittering, glowing, scintillating, shining, twinkling.
OPPOSITE dull.
2 *a sparkling personality.* animated, bright, exuberant, lively, vibrant, vivacious, witty.
OPPOSITE dull.
3 *sparkling wine.* bubbly, carbonated, effervescent, fizzy.
OPPOSITE still.

sparse *adjective*
The population of these animals is sparse. meagre, scanty, scarce, scattered, sporadic, thin.
OPPOSITE dense.

spasm *noun*
1 *The tablets control the spasm.* convulsion, cramp, fit, jerk, seizure, shudder, twitch.
2 *a spasm of coughing.* attack, bout, burst, fit, outburst, spell, spurt.

spatter *verb*
Her clothes were spattered with fat. shower, splash, splatter, spot, spray, sprinkle, stain.

speak *verb*
1 *He does not speak clearly.* articulate, enunciate, pronounce, talk.
2 *The two leaders spoke about many matters.* chat, converse, talk; see also DISCUSS.
3 *The minister spoke to the congregation.* address, lecture, preach, talk.
4 *She spoke the thoughts of everyone present.* communicate, convey, declare, express, relate, say, state, utter, voice.

speak of *He never spoke of it again.* discuss, mention, refer to, talk about.
speak out *She always speaks out on issues which concern her.* be outspoken, sound off (*informal*), speak up, speak your mind.

speaker *noun*
lecturer, orator, preacher, spokesman, spokesperson, spokeswoman, talker.
OPPOSITE listener.

spear *noun*
harpoon, javelin, lance, pike, trident.
spear *verb*
spear a fish. harpoon, impale, lance, pierce, stab.

special *adjective*
1 *She has a special way of doing her hair.* certain, characteristic, distinctive, individual, particular, specific, unique.
OPPOSITE general.
2 *She has a special gift for music.* exceptional, extraordinary, outstanding, rare, remarkable, singular, uncommon, unusual.
OPPOSITE ordinary.

specialist *noun*
a specialist on frogs. authority, connoisseur, consultant, expert, professional.

speciality *noun*
Wedding cakes are her speciality. forte, line, specialty, strong point, talent, thing (*informal*).

species *noun*
a species of animal. breed, class, classification, strain.

specific *adjective*
1 *The client described his specific problem.* individual, particular, special, unique.
OPPOSITE general.
2 *He was quite specific in what he said.* definite, exact, explicit, precise, unambiguous.
OPPOSITE vague.

specify *verb*
The ingredients are specified on the label. detail, identify, itemise, list, mention, name, spell out, state.

a
b
c
d
e
f
g
h
i
j
k
l
m
n
o
p
q
r
s
t
u
v
w
x
y
z

specimen *noun*
They collected plant specimens from the garden. example, model, representative, sample.

speck *noun*
There was not a speck of dust to be seen. bit, fleck, grain, particle, skerrick (*Australian informal*), speckle, spot, trace.

speckled *adjective*
a speckled egg. flecked, freckled, mottled, spotted.

spectacle *noun*
1 the spectacle of snow-capped mountains. scene, sight.
2 A large crowd attended the spectacle. display, exhibition, exposition, extravaganza, pageant, show, spectacular.
spectacles *plural noun*
see GLASSES (at GLASS).

spectacular *adjective*
spectacular feats. amazing, breathtaking, dramatic, electrifying, exciting, impressive, magnificent, marvellous, sensational, splendid, thrilling.
OPPOSITE ordinary.

spectator *noun*
bystander, eyewitness, observer, onlooker, viewer, witness; [*spectators*] audience, crowd.
OPPOSITE participant.

spectre *noun*
apparition, ghost, phantom, poltergeist, spirit, spook (*informal*), vision.

spectrum *noun*
a broad spectrum of abilities. compass, gamut, range, span, spread.

speech *noun*
1 She has lost the power of speech. communication, speaking, talking, utterance.
2 He won an award for clear speech. articulation, diction, elocution, enunciation, pronunciation.
3 They sat quietly throughout his speech. address, lecture, monologue, sermon, soliloquy, spiel (*slang*), talk.
4 in colloquial speech. dialect, idiom, language, lingo (*informal*), parlance.

speechless *adjective*
dumb, dumbfounded, mute, silent, tongue-tied.

speed *noun*
1 a speed of 60 kilometres per hour. pace, rate, velocity.
2 We were bewildered by the speed with which he did it all. briskness, haste, promptness, quickness, rapidity, swiftness.
OPPOSITE slowness.

speed *verb*
She sped home to tell the news. bolt, dash, fly, gallop, hasten, hurry, race, run, rush, shoot, streak, tear, zip.
speed up
1 He sped up to get home on time. accelerate, get a move on (*informal*), hurry up, quicken, step on it (*informal*).
OPPOSITE slow down.
2 They tried to speed up her application. accelerate, expedite, fast-track (*informal*), hasten, hurry along.
OPPOSITE delay.

speedy *adjective*
1 a speedy ride. fast, quick, rapid, swift.
OPPOSITE slow.
2 a speedy reply. early, immediate, prompt, quick, ready.
OPPOSITE tardy.

spell[1] *noun*
a magic spell. charm, curse, hex, incantation.

spell[2] *verb*
This decision spelt disaster. mean, signal, signify.
spell out All the conditions of employment were clearly spelt out. detail, explain, set out, specify.

spell[3] *noun*
1 They had not seen each other for a long spell. interval, period, time, while.
2 They were having a cold spell. period, snap, wave.
3 a spell of work. bout, period, session, shift, stint, stretch, term, turn.
4 (*Australian*) After working for two hours they needed a spell. break, breather, pause, rest, smoko (*Australian informal*).

spellbound *adjective*
spellbound by the dancing. bewitched, captivated, charmed, enchanted, enraptured, enthralled, entranced, fascinated, hypnotised, mesmerised, rapt.

spend *verb*
1 *She spent all her money.* blow (*slang*), fork out (*slang*), outlay, pay out, shell out (*informal*), splurge, squander, use up.
OPPOSITE save.
2 *She spends an hour a day reading.* devote, fill, occupy, pass, use, while away.

spendthrift *noun*
prodigal, profligate, squanderer, wastrel.
OPPOSITE miser.

sphere *noun*
1 *a sphere the size of an orange.* ball, globe, orb.
2 *His sphere of influence is small.* area, circle, domain, field, range, scope.

spice *noun*
He uses spices in his cooking. condiment, flavouring, herb, seasoning; [*various spices*] allspice, aniseed, cardamom, cayenne, chilli, cinnamon, cloves, coriander, cumin, ginger, mace, nutmeg, paprika, pepper, saffron, turmeric.

spicy *adjective*
a spicy curry. aromatic, fragrant, hot, piquant, pungent, sharp, strong.
OPPOSITE bland.

spider *noun*
[*various spiders*] black widow, daddy-long-legs, funnel-web, huntsman, jockey spider, money spider, red-back, St Andrew's Cross spider, tarantula, trapdoor spider, white-tailed spider.

spike *noun*
He caught his clothes on the spike. barb, point, prong, spine, stake, thorn.
spike *verb*
The pitchfork spiked his foot. impale, pierce, skewer, spear, stab.

spill *verb*
1 *She spilt her cup of milk.* knock over, overturn, tip over, upset.
2 *The tea spilt on the saucer.* brim over, overflow, pour, run over, slop.

spin *verb*
1 *He spun round to face us.* gyrate, pirouette, revolve, rotate, swirl, turn, twirl, twist, wheel, whirl.
2 *He can spin a good yarn.* concoct, invent, make up, relate, tell.
spin *noun*
He took us for a spin in his new car. drive, ride, run, trip.
spin out *He spun the story out over two episodes.* drag out, draw out, extend, prolong, protract.

spindle *noun*
The disc revolves on a spindle. axle, pin, rod, shaft.

spindly *adjective*
spindly legs. lanky, long, skinny, thin.

spine *noun*
1 *an injured spine.* backbone, spinal column, vertebral column.
2 *a plant with spines.* barb, needle, prickle, spike, thorn.
3 *The porcupine has sharp spines.* bristle, prickle, quill, spike.

spine-chilling *adjective*
a spine-chilling murder story. chilling, frightening, hair-raising, horrifying, scary, terrifying.

spin-off *noun*
by-product, offshoot, side benefit.

spiral *noun*
coil, corkscrew, helix.

spirit *noun*
1 *I shall be with you in spirit.* soul.
OPPOSITE body.
2 *The castle was said to be haunted by spirits.* apparition, genie, ghost, gremlin (*informal*), phantom, poltergeist, spectre, spook (*informal*), sprite.
3 *He has a generous spirit.* character, disposition, heart, nature, temperament.
4 *They will never break his spirit.* courage, determination, drive, endurance,

a
b
c
d
e
f
g
h
i
j
k
l
m
n
o
p
q
r
s
t
u
v
w
x
y
z

fearlessness, grit, guts (*informal*), pluck, spunk (*informal*), will, zeal.

spirits *plural noun*
The patient is in good spirits. feelings, frame of mind, humour, mood, morale, temper.

spirited *adjective*
1 *a spirited discussion.* animated, ardent, energetic, fervent, lively, passionate, vigorous.
OPPOSITE lifeless, spiritless.
2 *the spirited hero of the story.* bold, brave, courageous, daring, determined, fearless, feisty (*informal*), intrepid, plucky, valiant.
OPPOSITE timid.

spiritual *adjective*
1 *Spiritual well-being is more important than physical health.* emotional, inner, mental, psychic, psychological.
OPPOSITE material, physical.
2 *spiritual music.* divine, religious, sacred.
OPPOSITE secular.

spit[1] *verb*
1 *He spat out the pips.* eject, spew.
2 *The fat was spitting in the pan.* hiss, pop, splutter, sputter.
spit *noun*
1 *a ball of spit.* saliva, slag (*Australian slang*), spittle, sputum.
2 *She is the dead spit of her sister.* double, image, likeness, look-alike, ringer (*informal*), spitting image.

spit[2] *noun*
They keep their boat at the spit. peninsula, point, promontory.

spite *noun*
She did it out of spite. animosity, bitterness, hatred, hostility, ill will, malevolence, malice, rancour, resentment, revenge, vengeance, vindictiveness.
OPPOSITE benevolence.
spite *verb*
She did it to spite me. annoy, get at (*informal*), hurt, irritate, provoke, put out, thwart, upset, wound.
OPPOSITE please.
in spite of *She loved him in spite of his faults.* despite, notwithstanding, regardless of.

spiteful *adjective*
a spiteful person. bitchy (*informal*), bitter, catty, malevolent, malicious, nasty, resentful, revengeful, unkind, vindictive.
OPPOSITE benevolent.

splash *verb*
1 *The passing car splashed mud on the pedestrians.* fling, shower, spatter, splatter, spray, throw up.
2 *She splashed about in the pool.* paddle, slosh, wade.
3 *His picture was splashed across the front page.* display, plaster, spread.
splash *noun*
1 *He loves to hear the splash of the waves on the rocks.* breaking, crash, smashing, splatter.
2 *splashes of ink on the page.* blob, blotch, mark, smear, smudge, splotch, stain, streak.
3 *tea with a splash of milk.* dash, drop, touch.

splendid *adjective*
1 *a splendid display.* beautiful, brilliant, dazzling, fine, glittering, glorious, gorgeous, grand, imposing, impressive, lavish, magnificent, showy, spectacular, sumptuous, superb.
OPPOSITE poor.
2 *splendid results.* brilliant, excellent, exceptional, fabulous (*informal*), fantastic (*informal*), first-rate, great, marvellous, outstanding, remarkable, stupendous, super (*informal*), superb, terrific (*informal*), wonderful.
OPPOSITE poor.

splendour *noun*
beauty, brilliance, glory, grandeur, greatness, magnificence, majesty, richness, show.

splinter *noun*
She had a splinter of glass in her foot. fragment, sliver.
splinter *verb*
The timber splinters easily. fracture, shatter, split.

split *verb*
1 *The axeman split the log.* break, chop, crack, fracture, hew, splinter.

2 *They split the profits between them.* apportion, carve up, distribute, divide, dole out, share.
3 *His trousers have split.* burst, come apart, rip, tear.
4 *They were split into two groups.* break, divide, segregate, separate.
OPPOSITE unite.

split *noun*
1 *a split in the rock.* breach, break, cleft, crack, fissure, fracture, slit.
2 *There was a split in the party over the issue.* breach, division, rift.
OPPOSITE unity.
split up *His parents have split up.* break up, divorce, part, separate.

splutter *verb*
1 *The sausages spluttered in the pan.* hiss, sizzle, spit, sputter.
2 *She spluttered unintelligibly.* mumble, stammer, stutter.

spoil *verb*
1 *The work was spoilt by carelessness.* blight, botch, bungle, damage, destroy, mar, mess up, ruin, undo, wreck.
OPPOSITE improve.
2 *Food spoils if it is left out of the refrigerator.* decay, deteriorate, go bad, go off, perish, rot.
OPPOSITE keep.
3 *The parents are spoiling their child with too many toys.* indulge, lavish, mollycoddle, overindulge, pamper.
OPPOSITE deprive.

spoilsport *noun*
We don't want that spoilsport at our party. killjoy, nark (*Australian informal*), party-pooper (*informal*), wet blanket (*informal*), wowser (*Australian informal*).

spoken *adjective*
a spoken message. oral, unwritten, verbal.

spokesperson *noun*
delegate, mouthpiece, representative, speaker, spokesman, spokeswoman.

sponge *verb*
She sponged the floors. clean, mop, wash, wipe.
sponge off, sponge on *He doesn't work and likes to sponge on people.* bludge on

(*Australian informal*), cadge from, impose on, live off, scrounge from.

sponger *noun*
bludger (*Australian informal*), cadger, freeloader (*informal*), hanger-on, parasite, scrounger.

spongy *adjective*
spongy ground. absorbent, boggy, marshy, porous, soft, springy, swampy.
OPPOSITE firm.

sponsor *noun*
The football club has a new sponsor. backer, benefactor, financier, patron, promoter, supporter.
sponsor *verb*
The match was sponsored by their company. back, finance, fund, promote, subsidise, support.

spontaneous *adjective*
1 *a spontaneous response.* automatic, impetuous, impulsive, instinctive, involuntary, natural, reflex, unconscious, unforced.
OPPOSITE considered.
2 *A spontaneous speech is often better than a prepared one.* ad lib, extempore, impromptu, off-the-cuff, unprepared, unrehearsed.
OPPOSITE prepared.

spooky *adjective* (*informal*)
It was spooky in the old house. creepy, eerie, frightening, ghostly, scary, uncanny, weird.

spool *noun*
The cotton is wound on a spool. bobbin, reel.

sport *noun*
1 *His favourite sport is badminton.* diversion, game, pastime, physical activity, recreation; [*various sports*] aerobics, archery, athletics, Australian Rules, badminton, baseball, basketball, bowls, boxing, canoeing, cricket, croquet, cycling, discus, diving, fencing, fishing, football, golf, gymnastics, hockey, horse racing, hunting, ice skating, javelin, judo, karate, kung fu, lacrosse, motorcycle racing, motor racing, mountaineering, netball, orienteering, pole-vaulting, polo, rock-climbing, rowing, Rugby League,

a
b
c
d
e
f
g
h
i
j
k
l
m
n
o
p
q
r
s
t
u
v
w
x
y
z

Rugby Union, running, sailing, shooting, shot-put, skiing, soccer, softball, squash, surfing, swimming, table tennis, tae kwon do, tennis, tenpin bowling, tobogganing, trampolining, triathlon, volleyball, water polo, water-skiing, weightlifting, windsurfing, wrestling, yachting.
2 (*informal*) *He's a good sport.* sportsman, sportswoman.

sporting *adjective*
It was very sporting of him to let you go first. considerate, decent, fair, generous, sportsmanlike.

sportsground *noun*
arena, field, ground, oval, pitch, playing field, stadium.

sportsman, sportswoman *noun*
contestant, participant, player, sportsperson.

sportsmanlike *adjective*
see SPORTING.

spot *noun*
1 *a white dog with black spots.* blot, blotch, dot, fleck, mark, patch, smudge, speck, speckle, splash, splotch, stain.
2 *skin without a spot.* birthmark, blackhead, blemish, freckle, mole, pimple, whitehead, zit (*informal*); [*spots*] rash.
3 *a beautiful spot for a house.* area, district, locality, location, neighbourhood, place, position, region, setting, site, situation.
4 *a five-minute spot before the news.* segment, slot, time.
5 *a few spots of rain.* bead, blob, drop.
spot *verb*
1 *The material is spotted with grease.* dot, mark, smudge, soil, spatter, speckle, splash, splotch, spray, stain.
2 (*informal*) *I could not spot her in the crowd.* catch sight of, detect, discover, distinguish, espy, find, identify, locate, notice, pick out, recognise, see.
in a spot (*informal*)
He was in a bit of a spot and needed help. in a bind (*informal*), in a fix (*informal*), in a jam (*informal*), in a mess, in a pickle (*informal*), in a plight, in a predicament, in a quandary.
on the spot *The policeman fined him on*

the spot. at the scene, immediately, right away, straight away, then and there.

spotless *adjective*
1 *She has a spotless record.* clean, faultless, flawless, immaculate, impeccable, perfect, unblemished, untarnished.
OPPOSITE blemished.
2 *The floor is spotless.* clean, immaculate, unstained.
OPPOSITE dirty.

spotty *adjective*
blotchy, brindled, dappled, dotted, flecked, freckled, mottled, pimply, speckled, splotchy, spotted.

spouse *noun*
husband, mate (*informal*), partner, wife.

spout *noun*
Water comes out the spout. jet, nozzle, outlet.
spout *verb*
1 *The water spouted from the hose.* flow, gush, jet, spray, spurt, squirt, stream.
2 (*informal*) *He's always spouting about what's wrong with the world.* carry on (*informal*), go on (*informal*), hold forth, rant, rave.

sprain *verb*
She has sprained her ankle. twist, wrench.

sprawl *verb*
He sprawled on the bed. flop, lie spread-eagled, loll, lounge, recline, slouch, slump, spread yourself out, stretch out.
sprawl *noun*
the urban sprawl. expansion, spread.

spray[1] *noun*
a spray of flowers. bouquet, bunch, corsage, posy, sprig.

spray[2] *noun*
1 *The liquid comes out in a fine spray.* drizzle, droplets, mist, shower, vapour.
2 *a perfume spray.* aerosol, atomiser, vaporiser.
spray *verb*
He sprayed the stove with sauce. shower, spatter, splash, sprinkle, wet.

spread *verb*
1 *He spread the newspaper on the floor.* lay out, open out, unfold, unroll.

2 *The stain spread as she treated it.* diffuse, disperse, enlarge, extend, grow, widen.
3 *She spread the glue thickly.* apply, coat, lay on, paste, plaster, smear.
4 *The gardener spread the seeds.* broadcast, distribute, scatter, sprinkle, strew.
5 *He helped to spread the news.* broadcast, circulate, disseminate, publicise, transmit.
6 *The rabbit population is spreading.* expand, grow, increase, multiply, proliferate.
OPPOSITE diminish.
7 *The store spread the payments over six months.* distribute, space.
spread *noun*
1 *They measured the spread of the wings.* breadth, coverage, expanse, extent, range, reach, scope, span, stretch, sweep, width.
2 *the spread of the disease.* advance, expansion, increase, proliferation.
3 *(informal) The caterers put on a fine spread for the visitors.* banquet, feast, meal.

sprightly *adjective*
a sprightly old gentleman. active, agile, dynamic, energetic, hale, lively, nimble, perky, spry, vivacious.
OPPOSITE doddery.

spring *verb*
1 *He sprang from behind the chair and startled her.* bounce, bound, dart, hop, jump, leap, pounce, shoot out.
2 *The enmity sprang from a misunderstanding.* arise, derive, grow, originate, stem.
spring *noun*
1 *With one spring he was by her side.* bound, hop, jump, leap, vault.
2 *There's plenty of spring left in the mattress.* bounce, elasticity, resilience, springiness.
3 *The water comes from a spring.* fountain, geyser, spa, well-spring.
spring back *The door sprang back in his face.* bounce back, fly back, rebound, recoil.

springy *adjective*
a springy cushion. bouncy, elastic, resilient, spongy.

sprinkle *verb*
1 *He sprinkled the plants with the hose.* shower, spatter, splash, spray.
2 *She sprinkled cocoa on her cappuccino.* dust, scatter, strew.

sprint *verb*
He sprinted to the corner when he heard the crash. dash, race, run, rush, speed, tear.

sprout *verb*
The plants are sprouting. bud, develop, germinate, grow, shoot.

spruce *adjective*
He looked spruce in his new suit. chic, neat, smart, tidy, trim, well-groomed.
OPPOSITE shabby.

spunk *noun (informal)*
This business needs people with spunk. courage, determination, grit, guts *(informal)*, pluck.

spur *verb*
The good reviews spurred him on to greater success. egg on, encourage, motivate, prompt, stimulate, urge.
OPPOSITE discourage.

spurt *verb*
1 *The water spurted out of the hose.* burst, flow, gush, jet, shoot, spout, spray, squirt, stream, surge.
OPPOSITE trickle.
2 *He spurted ahead after the final turn.* dash, race, shoot, speed, sprint, tear.
spurt *noun*
The water came out in a spurt. burst, gush, jet, rush, spray, squirt, stream, surge.
OPPOSITE trickle.

spy *noun*
double agent, informer, intelligence agent, mole, secret agent, undercover agent.
spy *verb*
He spied a new star with the telescope. discern, discover, espy, make out, notice, observe, perceive, see, spot.
spy on *He knew that someone was spying on him.* keep under surveillance, keep watch on, observe, peep on, shadow, snoop on *(informal)*, tail *(informal)*, watch.

a
b
c
d
e
f
g
h
i
j
k
l
m
n
o
p
q
r
s
t
u
v
w
x
y
z

spying *noun*
espionage, intelligence, surveillance.

squabble *verb*
The twins often squabbled over their toys.
argue, bicker, fight, quarrel, scrap
(*informal*), wrangle.
squabble *noun*
*They finished their squabble and were
friends again.* argument, barney
(*informal*), dispute, fight, quarrel, row,
scrap (*informal*), tiff, wrangle.

squad *noun*
a squad of workers. band, force, gang,
group, team, unit.

squalid *adjective*
squalid living conditions. dilapidated,
dirty, filthy, run-down, seedy, shabby,
sordid, wretched.
OPPOSITE clean.

squall *noun*
The weather bureau forecast squalls. gust,
storm, wind.

squander *verb*
He squanders all his money on cigarettes.
blow (*slang*), fritter away, throw away,
waste.
OPPOSITE save.

square *noun*
1 *Put a tick in the square.* box, space.
2 (*informal*) *The students considered her a
square.* conservative, fuddy-duddy
(*informal*), old fogy, stick-in-the-mud
(*informal*).
square *adjective*
1 *The corners are square.* right-angled.
2 *We need to get your room square.* in
order, neat, orderly, tidy.
3 *The teams are all square at this stage of
the competition.* equal, even, level, tied.
4 *three square meals a day.* decent,
satisfying, substantial.
OPPOSITE inadequate.
5 *a square deal.* above board, fair, honest,
just, straight.
OPPOSITE crooked.
6 (*informal*) *She thinks all old people are
square.* conservative, conventional, old-
fashioned, out of date, out of touch.
OPPOSITE trendy (*informal*).

square *verb*
His story squares with hers. agree, be
consistent, correspond, fit, match, tally.

squash *verb*
1 *Don't squash the tomatoes.* compress,
crush, flatten, mangle, mash, press,
pulp, squeeze.
2 *The children were squashed into a small
classroom.* cram, crowd, crush, jam,
pack, squeeze.

squat *verb*
She squatted under the table. crouch.
squat *adjective*
a squat figure. dumpy, nuggety
(*Australian*), short, stocky, thickset.
OPPOSITE lanky.

squatter *noun* (*Australian*)
a wealthy squatter. grazier, pastoralist,
sheep farmer.

squawk *verb*
The ducks are squawking. cry, scream,
screech.

squeak *noun* & *verb*
cheep, chirp, cry, peep, screech, shriek,
squeal, yelp.

squeal *noun*
1 *the squeal of brakes.* scream, screech.
2 *a squeal of pain.* cry, scream, screech,
shriek, wail, yell.
squeal *verb*
She squealed when she was pinched. cry,
scream, screech, shriek, wail, yell.

squeeze *verb*
1 *He squeezed the rubbish so that it took up
less space.* compact, compress, crush,
press, squash, wring.
2 *Squeeze the shampoo out of the bottle.*
extract, force, press, push.
3 *We all squeezed into the little car.* cram,
crowd, jam, pack, pile, squash.
squeeze *noun*
He gave her an affectionate squeeze. clasp,
cuddle, embrace, hug.

squelch *verb*
We squelched through the mud. slosh,
splash, wade.

squirm *verb*
1 *Worms squirm.* twist, wiggle, wriggle,
writhe.

2 *He squirmed with embarrassment.*
fidget, wince, writhe.

squirt *verb*
1 *The doctor squirted water in her ear.*
shoot, spray, syringe.
2 *He squirted me with lemon juice.*
shower, spatter, splash, splatter, spray,
sprinkle, spurt.

stab *verb*
The man was stabbed to death. jab, knife,
lance, pierce, spear, spike, wound.
stab *noun*
1 *She felt a stab of pain.* jab, pang, prick,
tweak, twinge.
2 *(informal) Have a stab at it.* attempt,
crack *(informal)*, go *(Australian informal)*,
shot *(informal)*, smack *(informal)*, try.

stable[1] *adjective*
1 *The base of the structure must be stable.*
anchored, firm, fixed, secure, solid,
sound, steady, sturdy.
OPPOSITE shaky.
2 *A stable partnership had built up over
many years.* enduring, lasting,
permanent, reliable, solid, steady,
strong.
OPPOSITE insecure.
3 *The patient remains in a stable condition.*
constant, steady, unchanged.
OPPOSITE fluctuating.
4 *a stable person.* balanced, sane,
sensible, steady, together *(informal)*.
OPPOSITE unstable.

stable[2] *noun*
The horse is in his stable. stall.

stack *noun*
1 *a stack of books.* bundle, heap, load,
mound, mountain, pile.
2 *stacks of hay.* cock, haycock, hayrick,
haystack, rick.
3 *(informal) a stack of work. stacks of time.*
heap, load, lot *(informal)*, mass,
mountain, pile *(informal)*, plenty, ton
(informal).
stack *verb*
Her job was to stack the plates. collect,
heap, pile.

stadium *noun*
an athletic stadium. amphitheatre, arena,
ground, sportsground.

staff *noun*
1 *He supported himself on his staff.* cane,
crook, crosier, crutch, pole, stick.
2 *The company has a staff of forty.* crew,
employees, manpower, personnel,
team, workers, workforce.
staff *verb*
The new office is staffed by three officers.
man, run, service, tend.

stage *noun*
1 *The speakers addressed us from the stage.*
dais, platform, podium, rostrum.
2 *Negotiations had reached a critical stage.*
period, phase, point.
3 *The first stage of their journey was the
longest.* hop, leg, part, section.
stage *verb*
1 *The school staged a play for the parents.*
mount, perform, present, produce, put
on.
2 *They staged a demonstration.* arrange,
carry out, hold, organise, plan.

stagger *verb*
1 *He staggered from his bed to the
telephone.* falter, lurch, reel, stumble,
teeter, totter.
2 *He was staggered by the news.* astonish,
astound, dumbfound, flabbergast,
overwhelm, shake, shock, startle, stun,
surprise, take aback.

stagnant *adjective*
1 *The water in the creek was stagnant.*
motionless, stale, standing, still.
OPPOSITE flowing.
2 *Business was stagnant.* dead, dormant,
slow, sluggish, static.
OPPOSITE booming.

stain *verb*
Her dress is stained with paint. discolour,
mark, smear, smudge, soil, spot.
stain *noun*
1 *stains on her dress.* blotch, mark,
smudge, speck, splotch, spot.
2 *a stain on his reputation.* blemish, blot,
flaw, stigma, taint, tarnish.
3 *They used a walnut stain on the timber.*
dye, tint.

stairs *plural noun*
I climbed up the stairs. staircase,
stairway, steps.

a
b
c
d
e
f
g
h
i
j
k
l
m
n
o
p
q
r
s
t
u
v
w
x
y
z

stake *noun*
1 *The tomato bushes are supported by stakes.* picket, pole, post, spike, stick.
2 *He could afford the stake of $5 on the game.* bet, wager.
3 *He has a stake in the business.* concern, interest, investment, share.
stake *verb*
1 *He has staked the plants.* brace, prop, support.
2 *I'll stake my life on it.* bet, chance, risk, wager.

stale *adjective*
1 *The bread has gone stale.* dry, mouldy.
OPPOSITE fresh.
2 *The room smelt stale because it had been closed up.* close, musty, stuffy.
OPPOSITE fresh.
3 *His jokes are stale.* familiar, hackneyed, old, out of date, unoriginal.
OPPOSITE new.
4 *After ten years in the same job he is feeling stale.* bored, jaded, stagnant.

stalk¹ *noun*
The flowers have long stalks. shoot, stem.

stalk² *verb*
1 *She stalked out with her nose in the air.* flounce, march, stride, strut.
2 *He stalked his victim.* follow, hound, prowl after, pursue, shadow, tail (*informal*), track, trail.

stall *noun*
1 *The animals are all in their stalls.* pen, shed, stable.
2 *The room was divided into stalls for privacy.* booth, cell, compartment, cubicle, enclosure.
3 *He helped on the lolly stall at the fair.* booth, counter, kiosk, stand, table.
stall *verb*
Quit stalling! delay, hedge, play for time, procrastinate.

stamina *noun*
He doesn't have the stamina to run five kilometres. endurance, energy, perseverance, staying power, strength, vigour.

stammer *verb*
falter, splutter, stumble, stutter.

stamp *verb*
1 *He stamped on the snails.* crush, flatten, squash, step, stomp, tramp, trample, tread.
OPPOSITE tiptoe.
2 *He had his initials stamped on his wallet.* brand, emboss, engrave, imprint, inscribe, print.
stamp *noun*
the maker's official stamp. brand, hallmark, imprint, logo, mark, seal, trade mark.
stamp out *They tried to stamp out sexism.* abolish, eliminate, eradicate, put an end to, stop.

stamp-collecting *noun*
philately.

stampede *noun*
There was a stampede for the exits. charge, dash, race, run, rush.
stampede *verb*
The crowd stampeded into the arena. bolt, charge, dash, race, rush.

stand *verb*
1 *The court stands when the judge enters.* get up, rise.
OPPOSITE sit.
2 *Their house stands on the edge of a park.* be, be located, be situated, lie.
3 *She stood the vase on the table.* deposit, place, position, put, set.
4 *It has stood the test of time.* bear, endure, survive, weather, withstand.
5 *The traffic stood still.* remain, stay, stop.
6 *She is standing for parliament.* run.
7 *She stood trial for the murder of the child.* face, undergo.
8 *He couldn't stand the noise.* abide, bear, endure, put up with, suffer, take, tolerate.
9 *He stood everyone a drink.* pay for, provide, shout (*Australian informal*), treat to.
stand *noun*
1 *He took his stand near the door.* place, position.
2 *What is his stand on this issue?* see STANDPOINT.
3 *a stand for a camera, ornaments, etc.* base, rack, support, tripod.
4 *He works on a newspaper stand.* booth, counter, kiosk, stall.
5 *a taxi stand.* rank.

6 *The witness took the stand.* witness box.
stand by
1 *She stood by helplessly.* look on, stay on
the sidelines, watch.
2 *She will always stand by her children.*
defend, side with, stick by, support.
3 *Stand by for lift-off.* be ready, wait.
4 *He always stands by his promises.* abide
by, adhere to, honour, keep, stick to.
stand down
1 *The chairman was asked to stand down.*
resign, step down, withdraw.
2 *The firm has begun standing down
workers.* lay off, stand off, suspend.
stand for
1 *What do the letters 'TLC' stand for?* be
short for, denote, indicate, mean,
represent, signify.
2 *(informal) He won't stand for any
nonsense.* put up with, suffer, take,
tolerate.
stand in for *He'll stand in for me if I can't
be there.* cover for, deputise for, fill in
for, relieve, replace, substitute for, take
the place of.
stand out *He stood out in his purple shirt.*
be conspicuous, be noticeable, be
prominent, stick out.
stand up for *He can be relied upon to
stand up for you.* defend, speak up for,
stand by, stick up for, support.
stand up to
1 *He was too weak to stand up to the boss.*
challenge, confront, defy, face up to,
oppose, resist.
2 *This carpet should stand up to heavy use.*
endure, last through, resist, survive,
withstand.

standard *noun*
1 *Does this meet the company's standards?*
benchmark, criterion, guideline,
requirement, specification, yardstick.
2 *Her work is of a high standard.* grade,
level, quality.
3 *the royal standard.* banner, ensign, flag,
pennant.
standard *adjective*
the standard treatment for burns.
accepted, conventional, customary,
normal, ordinary, orthodox, prescribed,
recognised, regular, routine, set, usual.
OPPOSITE unorthodox.

stand-by *noun*
The team has a second car as a stand-by.
backup, replacement, reserve,
substitute.

stand-in *noun*
He acts as a stand-in when someone's sick.
deputy, locum, relief, replacement,
reserve, stand-by, substitute, surrogate.

stand-offish *adjective*
aloof, cold, cool, detached, distant,
remote, reserved, unapproachable,
unsociable.
OPPOSITE friendly.

standpoint *noun*
*He looked at the situation from a different
standpoint.* angle, attitude, opinion,
point of view, position, stance, stand,
viewpoint.

standstill *noun*
The accident brought work to a standstill.
halt, stop.

stanza *noun*
The poem has four stanzas. verse.

staple *adjective*
Bread is their staple food. basic, chief,
essential, main, principal, standard.

star *noun*
1 *the stars in the sky.* celestial body,
heavenly body; [*group of stars*]
constellation, galaxy.
2 *a printed star.* asterisk.
3 *a film star.* celebrity, idol, megastar
(*informal*), superstar.
star *verb*
The Frenchman stars in the film. act,
appear, feature, perform, play.

stare *verb*
He stood and stared in amazement. gape,
gawk (*informal*), gawp (*informal*), gaze,
glare, goggle, look, peer, watch.
stare *noun*
He gave a hard stare. gape, gaze, glare,
look.

start *verb*
1 *He started his musical career at seven.*
begin, commence, embark on, enter
upon, take up.
OPPOSITE finish.

a
b
c
d
e
f
g
h
i
j
k
l
m
n
o
p
q
r
s
t
u
v
w
x
y
z

2 *He started the machine.* activate, switch on, turn on.
OPPOSITE stop.
3 *He started a fund for research into leukaemia.* create, establish, found, initiate, institute, launch, originate, pioneer, set up.
4 *They started for Sydney first thing in the morning.* depart, get going, leave, set off, set out.
OPPOSITE arrive.
5 *The sudden noise made him start.* blench, flinch, jump, recoil, twitch, wince.
6 *She started from her seat.* bound, jump, leap, shoot, spring.

start *noun*
1 *the start of an era, enterprise, etc.* beginning, birth, commencement, dawn, inception, kick-off (*informal*), launch, onset, opening, origin, outset.
OPPOSITE finish.
2 *She was given a fresh start.* break (*informal*), chance, opening, opportunity.
3 *He had a head start.* advantage, edge, lead.
4 *The knock at the door gave her a start.* jolt, jump, shock, surprise.

starting point *noun*
the starting point of a discussion. basis, beginning, foundation.

startle *verb*
The sound of footsteps startled him. alarm, disturb, frighten, scare, shake, surprise, unsettle, upset.

startling *adjective*
startling news. alarming, astonishing, disturbing, dramatic, remarkable, shocking, staggering, surprising, unexpected.

starvation *noun*
They will die of starvation. famine, hunger, malnutrition, undernourishment.

starve *verb*
starve yourself fast, go hungry, go without food.
OPPOSITE overeat.

starving *adjective* (*informal*)
After their long walk they were starving. famished, hungry, ravenous.

state *noun*
1 *the state of the economy.* circumstances, condition, health, shape, situation.
2 *She remained in a depressed state.* attitude, condition, frame of mind, mood.
3 *She got into a state.* dither, flap (*informal*), fluster, panic, stew (*informal*), tizzy (*informal*).
4 *The funeral was attended by many heads of state.* country, kingdom, land, nation, republic.
5 *Those services are run by the state.* government.

state *adjective*
1 *state schools.* government, public.
OPPOSITE independent, private.
2 *on state occasions.* ceremonial, formal, official.

state *verb*
He stated his opinion. announce, assert, declare, express, proclaim, report, say, voice.

stately *adjective*
a stately mansion. grand, imposing, impressive, magnificent, majestic.
OPPOSITE modest.

statement *noun*
1 *Each person made a brief statement.* account, affidavit, affirmation, announcement, assertion, comment, communication, communiqué, confession, declaration, proclamation, remark, report, utterance.
2 *The company sends me a monthly statement.* account, bill, invoice.

static *adjective*
Prices remained static. constant, fixed, frozen, pegged, stable, stationary, steady, unchanging.
OPPOSITE variable.

station *noun*
1 *All stations were manned.* location, place, position, post, site.
2 *a radio station.* broadcaster, channel.
3 *a bus station.* depot, stop, terminal, terminus.
4 (*Australian*) *a cattle station.* estate, property, ranch (*American*), run (*Australian*).

station *verb*
He is stationed at Richmond. assign, base, locate, place, position, post.

stationary *adjective*
a stationary vehicle. immobile, motionless, parked, standing, static, still, unmoving.
OPPOSITE moving.

stationery *noun*
office supplies, paper, writing materials.

statue *noun*
bust, carving, cast, figurine, sculpture, statuette.

status *noun*
1 *two employees of equal status.* level, position, rank, standing, station.
2 *He thought the new job would give him status.* distinction, importance, prestige, recognition.

stay *verb*
1 *Her friend stayed until the taxi arrived.* linger, remain, tarry, wait.
OPPOSITE leave.
2 *The child stayed awake until everyone had gone.* continue, keep, remain.
3 *She is staying at a friend's house.* dwell, live, lodge, reside, sleep, sleep over, visit.
stay *noun*
They had a brief stay in Hobart. holiday, sojourn, stop, stopover, time, visit.

staying power *noun*
To run a marathon you need staying power. endurance, grit, perseverance, persistence, stamina, sticking power.

steadfast *adjective*
Her faith remained steadfast throughout her illness. constant, determined, firm, persistent, resolute, steady, sure, unshakeable.
OPPOSITE wavering.

steady *adjective*
1 *The ladder is not steady on that surface.* balanced, firm, immovable, secure, stable.
OPPOSITE unsteady, wobbly.
2 *Maintain steady pressure.* consistent, constant, continuous, even, regular, unchanging, uniform.
OPPOSITE variable.
3 *a steady worker.* careful, conscientious, dependable, diligent, reliable.
OPPOSITE unreliable.

steady *verb*
1 *Nobody helped to steady the ladder.* balance, secure, stabilise, support.
2 *She steadied herself before walking into the examination room.* calm, compose, control.

steal *verb*
1 *He stole their property.* appropriate, embezzle, help yourself to, knock off (*slang*), lift (*informal*), make off with, misappropriate, nick (*slang*), pilfer, pinch (*informal*), poach, pocket, seize, snaffle (*informal*), snatch, snavel (*Australian informal*), snitch (*slang*), souvenir (*slang*), swipe (*informal*), take, thieve.
2 *He stole out of the room when nobody was looking.* creep, skulk, slink, slip, sneak, tiptoe.

stealing *noun*
see THEFT.

stealthy *adjective*
stealthy steps. covert, furtive, secret, secretive, sly, sneaky, surreptitious, unobtrusive.
OPPOSITE open.

steam *noun*
1 *The bathroom was full of steam after his shower.* mist, vapour.
2 *He's run out of steam.* energy, momentum, power, puff (*informal*), stamina.

steep *adjective*
1 *a steep slope.* abrupt, precipitous, sharp, sheer, vertical.
OPPOSITE gentle.
2 (*informal*) *Their prices are a bit steep.* dear, excessive, exorbitant, expensive, extortionate, high.
OPPOSITE reasonable.

steer *verb*
He steered the boat into port. conduct, direct, guide, lead, navigate, pilot.
steer clear of *They steered clear of one another.* avoid, bypass, dodge, give a wide berth to, keep away from.

stem *noun*
The plant has a strong stem. stalk, trunk.
stem *verb*
stem from *Her dissatisfaction stems from a misunderstanding.* arise from, derive

a
b
c
d
e
f
g
h
i
j
k
l
m
n
o
p
q
r
s
t
u
v
w
x
y
z

from, originate in, result from, spring from.

stench *noun*
The stench from the dump was intolerable. pong (*informal*), reek, stink.
OPPOSITE fragrance.

step *verb*
She tries not to step on ants. trample, tread, walk.

step *noun*
1 *Some people take longer steps than others.* pace, stride.
2 *She recognised his step.* footstep, gait, tread, walk.
3 *There are three steps in the solution of the problem.* part, phase, stage.
4 *What steps have you taken to find a job?* action, measure, move.
5 *She finds it difficult to climb steps.* rung, stair.
step in see INTERVENE.
step on it see HURRY.
step up *He stepped up the dose.* boost, build up, increase, raise.
OPPOSITE decrease.

sterile *adjective*
1 *a sterile couple.* barren, childless, infertile.
OPPOSITE fertile.
2 *sterile country.* arid, bare, barren, desert, unfruitful, unproductive, waste.
OPPOSITE fertile.
3 *a sterile sickroom.* antiseptic, aseptic, clean, disinfected, germ-free, hygienic, sanitary, sterilised.
OPPOSITE septic.

sterilise *verb*
1 *The equipment must be sterilised.* clean, disinfect, fumigate, sanitise.
2 *The food was sterilised.* pasteurise, purify.
3 *The animals were sterilised.* castrate, de-sex, doctor, geld, neuter, spay.

stern¹ *adjective*
a stern headmaster. austere, authoritarian, dour, forbidding, grim, harsh, inflexible, severe, strict, tyrannical.
OPPOSITE lenient.

stern² *noun*
the ship's stern. back, rear.
OPPOSITE bow.

stew *verb*
She stewed the hare for our dinner. braise, casserole.

stew *noun*
beef stew. casserole, fricassee, goulash, hotpot, ragout.

steward *noun*
an airline steward. flight attendant, stewardess (*female*).

stewardess *noun*
an airline stewardess. air hostess, flight attendant, hostie (*Australian informal*), steward.

stick¹ *noun*
1 *We collected sticks for the fire.* branch, twig.
2 *The gardener uses sticks to support his plants.* cane, pole, stake.
3 *He hit the animal with a stick.* bludgeon, cane, club, cudgel, rod, truncheon, waddy (*Australian*).
4 *He walks with a stick.* cane, crook, staff, walking stick.
5 *Some sports use a stick.* bat, club, cue.
6 *a magician's stick.* baton, rod, wand.
the sticks (*informal*)
They left the city and went to live in the sticks. the backblocks (*Australian*), the back of beyond, the backwoods, the bush, the country, the outback (*Australian*), Woop Woop (*Australian informal*).

stick² *verb*
1 *She stuck the needle in her finger.* insert, jab, poke, push, thrust.
2 *They stick their pictures on the pinboard.* attach, fasten, fix, nail, pin, tack.
OPPOSITE remove.
3 (*informal*) *He stuck a copy in each letterbox.* place, put, shove (*informal*), thrust.
4 *He stuck the label on the box.* affix, attach, glue, gum, paste, tape.
OPPOSITE remove.
5 *The two surfaces have stuck together.* adhere, bind, bond, cement, fuse, glue, join, seal, weld.
OPPOSITE separate.

6 *The coin stuck in her throat.* catch, jam, lodge, wedge.
OPPOSITE dislodge.
7 *They were stuck for hours in the traffic.* catch, detain, hold up, immobilise, trap.
8 (*informal*) *She likes to stick at home.* remain, stay, stop.
stick at (*informal*)
He stuck at the job. continue, keep at, last at, persevere with, persist at.
stick by *She stuck by her friend.* stand by, support.
OPPOSITE desert.
stick out
1 *The branch stuck out through the fence.* extend, jut out, poke out, project, protrude.
2 *The purple house sticks out.* be conspicuous, be noticeable, stand out.
stick to *He stuck to the rules.* abide by, adhere to, follow, keep to.
stick up for (*informal*) *She always sticks up for her friends.* back, back up, defend, side with, stand by, stand up for, support.
OPPOSITE abandon.

sticker *noun*
Her suitcase was covered in stickers. label, notice, seal, sign.

stick-up *noun* (*informal*)
a bank stick-up. hold-up, robbery.

sticky *adjective*
1 *a sticky mixture.* gluey, gooey (*informal*), tacky.
OPPOSITE runny.
2 *sticky tape.* adhesive, gummed.
3 *sticky weather.* clammy, humid, muggy, steamy, sultry.
OPPOSITE dry.

stickybeak *noun* (*Australian informal*)
She's such a stickybeak. busybody, Nosy Parker (*informal*), snooper (*informal*).

stiff *adjective*
1 *stiff cardboard.* firm, hard, inflexible, rigid.
OPPOSITE flexible.
2 *stiff muscles.* rigid, taut, tense, tight.
OPPOSITE relaxed, supple.
3 *a stiff mixture.* dense, firm, heavy, solid, thick.
OPPOSITE fluid.

4 *a stiff test.* arduous, challenging, difficult, exacting, hard, rigorous, tough.
OPPOSITE easy.
5 *She always is so stiff and difficult to talk to.* aloof, austere, cold, cool, formal, prim, reserved, starchy, stilted, strait-laced.
OPPOSITE relaxed.
6 *a stiff sentence.* drastic, hard, harsh, merciless, severe, tough.
OPPOSITE lenient.
7 *a stiff breeze.* brisk, keen, strong.
OPPOSITE gentle.
8 *a stiff drink.* potent, powerful, strong.
OPPOSITE weak.

stiffen *verb*
The mixture stiffened. coagulate, congeal, firm up, harden, jell (*informal*), set, solidify, thicken.

stifle *verb*
1 *He was stifled with a pillow.* asphyxiate, smother, suffocate.
2 *He stifled a giggle.* hold back, restrain, smother, suppress.

still *adjective*
1 *Try to keep still.* immobile, inert, motionless, stationary, stock-still.
OPPOSITE moving.
2 *a still night.* calm, noiseless, peaceful, quiet, silent, soundless, tranquil.
OPPOSITE noisy.
3 *still water.* calm, stagnant, undisturbed.
OPPOSITE flowing.
still *noun*
in the still of the night. calm, peace, quietness, silence, stillness, tranquillity.

stilt *noun*
The houses are built on stilts. block, pile, pillar, post.

stilted *adjective*
The language is stilted. artificial, awkward, forced, formal, laboured, pompous, stiff, unnatural.
OPPOSITE natural.

stimulate *verb*
The excursion stimulated an interest in zoology. arouse, awaken, encourage, inspire, prompt, provoke, rouse, spur,

a
b
c
d
e
f
g
h
i
j
k
l
m
n
o
p
q
r
s
t
u
v
w
x
y
z

stir up, whet.
OPPOSITE discourage.

stimulus *noun*
The reward acted as a stimulus.
encouragement, incentive, inducement,
shot in the arm, spur.
OPPOSITE deterrent.

sting *noun*
The ointment relieves stings. bite, prick,
tingle, wound.
sting *verb*
1 *The bee stung her on the foot.* bite, nip,
prick, wound.
2 *The onion made his eyes sting.* burn,
hurt, smart, tingle.

stingy *adjective*
1 *a stingy person.* close-fisted, mean,
miserly, niggardly, parsimonious,
penny-pinching, tight, tight-fisted.
OPPOSITE generous.
2 *a stingy amount.* inadequate,
insufficient, meagre, measly (*informal*),
paltry, scanty, skimpy, small.
OPPOSITE lavish.

stink *noun*
the stink of the rubbish dump. pong
(*informal*), reek, stench.
OPPOSITE fragrance.
stink *verb*
The place stinks. pong (*informal*), reek.

stinking *adjective*
see SMELLY.

stint *noun*
He did his stint of serving on the counter.
period, shift, spell, stretch, term.

stir *verb*
1 *Not even the leaves were stirring.* flutter,
move, quiver, rustle, twitch.
2 *She stirred the pudding mixture.* beat,
blend, mix, whip, whisk.
3 *The story stirred their interest.* arouse,
awaken, excite, inspire, provoke,
stimulate.
4 (*informal*) *He's only stirring you.* get
someone going (*informal*), provoke,
tease, wind up (*informal*).
stir *noun*
He caused a stir with the news.
commotion, disturbance, excitement,
fuss, to-do.

stirring *adjective*
a stirring speech. exciting, inspiring,
moving, provocative, rousing,
stimulating.

stitch *noun*
The wound needed five stitches. suture.
stitch *verb*
She stitched the dress. baste, darn,
embroider, mend, sew, tack.

stock *noun*
1 *She keeps a stock of soap.* accumulation,
hoard, reserve, stockpile, store, supply.
2 *The farmer sold half his stock.* animals,
beasts, livestock.
3 *He comes of German stock.* ancestry,
background, descent, extraction,
lineage.
4 *chicken stock.* bouillon, broth.
stock *adjective*
That is his stock reply. customary,
routine, set, standard, usual.
stock *verb*
They stock her favourite chocolates. carry,
handle, have, keep, sell.
stock up on *She stocked up on cat food.*
accumulate, buy up, hoard, lay in,
stockpile.

stockings *plural noun*
hosiery, pantihose, tights.

stockman *noun* (*Australian*)
drover (*Australian*), herdsman,
stockrider (*Australian*).

stocky *adjective*
a stocky man. burly, nuggety
(*Australian*), solid, stout, sturdy,
thickset.
OPPOSITE lanky.

stodgy *adjective*
1 *stodgy porridge.* heavy, indigestible,
starchy.
OPPOSITE light.
2 *a stodgy book.* boring, dreary, dull,
tedious, uninteresting.
OPPOSITE interesting.

stole *noun*
scarf, shawl, wrap.

stomach *noun*
a protruding stomach. abdomen, belly,
paunch, tummy (*informal*).

stone *noun*
1 *The surface was covered with stones.* boulder, cobble, gibber (*Australian*), pebble, rock; [*stones*] gravel, scree, shingle.
2 *a ring with a precious stone.* gem, jewel.
3 *cherry stones.* pip, pit, seed.

stoned *adjective*
see INTOXICATED.

stony *adjective*
1 *stony paths.* cobbled, gravelly, pebbly, rocky, rough, rugged.
OPPOSITE smooth.
2 *He was given a stony look.* blank, chilly, cold, fixed, hard, icy, indifferent, unfeeling, unresponsive.
OPPOSITE friendly.

stoop *verb*
1 *He stooped to go through the low doorway.* bend down, crouch, duck, kneel, lean over.
OPPOSITE straighten up.
2 *He hasn't stooped to lying, has he?* descend, fall, lower yourself, resort, sink.

stoop *noun*
She walks with a stoop. droop, hunch, slouch.

stop *verb*
1 *He stopped the car.* brake, halt, pull up, stall, switch off, turn off.
OPPOSITE start.
2 *She danced until the music stopped.* cease, come to an end, end, finish, terminate.
OPPOSITE start.
3 *He tried to stop them from going.* bar, hinder, keep, preclude, prevent.
OPPOSITE allow.
4 *The accident stopped traffic.* block, halt, hamper, immobilise, impede, obstruct.
5 *They have stopped these illegal practices.* abolish, discontinue, do away with, put an end to.
OPPOSITE introduce.
6 *She stopped reading and looked up.* abandon, break off, cease, conclude, desist, discontinue, finish, give up, halt, interrupt, knock off (*informal*), leave off, quit, refrain from.
OPPOSITE begin, continue.

7 *The supply has stopped.* expire, peter out, run out.
OPPOSITE continue.
8 (*informal*) *They stopped at a friend's place for the weekend.* rest, stay, stop off, stop over.
9 *They cannot stop the bleeding.* arrest, check, curb, stanch, stem.
10 *All the gaps have been stopped.* block, close, fill, plug, seal.

stop *noun*
1 *Everything has come to a stop.* close, end, finish, halt, rest, standstill, termination.
OPPOSITE start.
2 *a stop in proceedings.* break, interlude, intermission, pause, recess, suspension.
OPPOSITE resumption.

stopper *noun*
a stopper for a cask. bung, cork, plug.

store *noun*
1 *She has a store of toothpaste in her cupboard.* cache, hoard, pile, reserve, stock, stockpile, supply.
2 *She shops at the store.* department store, general store, megastore, retailer, shop, supermarket.
3 *The truck collected the furniture from the store.* depot, storehouse, warehouse.

store *verb*
She is storing empty jars for future use. accumulate, collect, hoard, keep, preserve, put aside, reserve, save, stockpile, stow.
OPPOSITE discard.

storey *noun*
a building of twenty storeys. floor, level.

storm *noun*
1 *Houses were damaged in the storm.* blizzard, cloudburst, cyclone, deluge, downpour, dust storm, gale, hailstorm, hurricane, rainstorm, sandstorm, snowstorm, squall, tempest, thunderstorm, tornado, typhoon, willy willy (*Australian*).
2 *a storm of protest.* commotion, furore, fuss, outcry, row, stir, to-do, uproar.

storm *verb*
1 *She stormed out of the room.* charge, rush, stamp, tear.
2 *The soldiers stormed the building.* attack, charge, invade, raid, rush, take over.

a
b
c
d
e
f
g
h
i
j
k
l
m
n
o
p
q
r
s
t
u
v
w
x
y
z

stormy *adjective*
Stormy weather has been forecast.
blustery, foul, gusty, inclement, squally,
tempestuous, turbulent, violent, wild,
windy.
OPPOSITE mild.

story *noun*
1 *She is absorbed in the story she's reading.*
anecdote, fable, legend, myth,
narrative, novel, parable, tale, yarn.
2 *He's sticking to his story of what
happened.* account, record, report,
statement, version.
3 *(informal) Stop telling stories and tell the
truth.* falsehood, fib, fiction, lie, untruth.

stout *adjective*
1 *a stout stick.* fat, solid, strong, sturdy,
thick.
OPPOSITE thin.
2 *a stout person.* fat, obese, overweight,
plump, portly, rotund, stocky, tubby.
OPPOSITE skinny.

stow *verb*
The luggage was stowed in the boot. load,
pack, put, stash *(informal)*, store, stuff.

straggle *verb*
*The young ones straggled behind the older
children.* dawdle, lag, loiter, stray, trail.

straggler *noun*
They had to wait for the stragglers.
dawdler, loiterer, slowcoach, stray.

straggly *adjective*
long straggly hair. lank, loose, unkempt,
untidy.
OPPOSITE neat.

straight *adjective*
1 *in a straight line.* direct, unbending,
unswerving.
OPPOSITE curved.
2 *The paintings are straight.* level, square.
OPPOSITE crooked.
3 *The room is now straight.* neat, orderly,
shipshape, tidy.
OPPOSITE untidy.
4 *He won in straight sets.* consecutive,
successive, unbroken.
5 *I want you to be straight with me.*
candid, direct, frank, honest,
straightforward, truthful, upfront
(informal).
OPPOSITE evasive.

straight *adverb*
1 *Go straight to bed.* directly,
immediately, instantly.
2 *I told him straight.* candidly, directly,
frankly, honestly, without beating
about the bush.
straight away at once, directly,
immediately, instantly, on the spot,
right away, without delay.

straightforward *adjective*
1 *a straightforward person.* candid, frank,
honest, open, straight, truthful.
OPPOSITE devious.
2 *a straightforward procedure.* easy,
simple, uncomplicated.
OPPOSITE complex.

strain[1] *verb*
1 *Our patience was strained to the limit.*
push, stretch, tax, test.
2 *He has strained a muscle.* injure, pull,
rick, sprain, wrench.
3 *He strained to lift the heavy box.* exert
yourself, heave, strive, struggle, try.
4 *He strained the mixture.* filter, sieve,
sift.

strain *noun*
1 *muscle strain.* injury, pull, rick, sprain,
wrench.
2 *Even the simplest things are a strain for
her.* burden, drag, effort, exertion,
struggle.
3 *She felt under too much strain in her job.*
pressure, stress, tension.

strain[2] *noun*
a new strain of roses. breed, kind, type,
variety.

strainer *noun*
a food strainer. colander, filter, sieve,
sifter.

strait *noun*
The ship crossed the strait. channel,
narrows, passage.

strand *noun*
She separated the cotton into six strands.
fibre, filament, thread.

stranded *adjective*
1 *a stranded ship.* beached, grounded,
shipwrecked.
2 *They left us stranded without our bags.*
abandoned, high and dry, in the lurch,
marooned.

strange *adjective*

1 *She likes to visit strange places.* alien, exotic, foreign, unfamiliar, unknown.
OPPOSITE familiar.
2 *a strange idea. a strange person.* abnormal, bizarre, curious, eccentric, extraordinary, funny, new, novel, odd, outlandish, peculiar, queer, surprising, unconventional, unusual, way-out (*informal*), weird, zany.
OPPOSITE ordinary.

stranger *noun*

They welcome strangers into their home. alien, foreigner, newcomer, outsider, visitor.
OPPOSITE friend.

strangle *verb*

He strangled his victim. asphyxiate, choke, suffocate, throttle.

strap *noun*

band, belt, cord, thong, tie; [*straps*] braces.
strap *verb*
The baggage is strapped on the roof. attach, bind, fasten, lash, secure, tie, truss.

strategic *adjective*

a strategic move. calculated, planned, politic, tactical.

strategy *noun*

the strategy for winning the game. approach, method, plan, policy, scheme, tactics.

stray *verb*

1 *One member of the party strayed from the group.* go astray, roam, rove, straggle, wander.
2 *Do not stray from the subject.* deviate, digress, drift, get away, wander.
stray *adjective*
a stray animal. abandoned, homeless, lost, roaming, wandering.

streak *noun*

She has streaks of pink in her hair. band, line, stripe.
streak *verb*
1 *Her clothes were streaked with paint.* mark, smear, stain, stripe.
2 *He streaked ahead.* dart, dash, run, rush, speed, tear, whiz, zoom.

stream *noun*

1 *The streams are marked in blue on the map.* brook, creek, river, tributary, watercourse.
2 *a steady stream of traffic.* flow, line.
3 *a stream of water.* flood, flow, gush, jet, rush, surge, torrent.
4 *She moves against the stream.* current, flow, tide.
stream *verb*
Water streamed from the end of the hose. flood, gush, pour, run, rush, shoot, spout, spurt, surge.

streamer *noun*

The streets were decorated with streamers. bunting, flag, pennant, ribbon.

streamlined *adjective*

1 *a streamlined car.* aerodynamic, sleek, smooth.
2 *a streamlined process.* efficient, rationalised, simplified, smooth.

street *noun*

They live in the same street. alley, avenue, boulevard, close, crescent, cul-de-sac, drive, highway, lane, place, road, terrace, thoroughfare.

strength *noun*

1 *a man of great strength.* endurance, might, muscle, power, robustness, stamina, toughness.
OPPOSITE weakness.
2 *the strength of the earthquake.* force, intensity, power.
3 *the strength of the mixture.* concentration, potency.
4 *Diplomacy is one of her strengths.* asset, forte, strong point.
OPPOSITE weakness.

strengthen *verb*

1 *The fence needs to be strengthened.* brace, buttress, prop up, reinforce, shore up, support.
2 *The wind strengthened.* heighten, increase, intensify.
OPPOSITE lessen.
3 *This has strengthened their relationship.* bolster, boost, build up, develop, enhance, fortify, improve.
OPPOSITE weaken.

a
b
c
d
e
f
g
h
i
j
k
l
m
n
o
p
q
r
s
t
u
v
w
x
y
z

strenuous *adjective*

1 *a strenuous worker.* dynamic, energetic, enthusiastic, hard-working, industrious, untiring.
OPPOSITE lazy.
2 *a strenuous task.* arduous, demanding, difficult, exhausting, hard, laborious, taxing, tough, uphill.
OPPOSITE effortless.

stress *noun*

1 *Her headaches are caused by stress.* anxiety, pressure, strain, tension, worry.
2 *He puts a lot of stress on correct spelling.* emphasis, importance, priority, value, weight.
3 *The stress is on the last syllable.* accent, beat, emphasis, force.
stress *verb*
He stressed the point. dwell on, emphasise, highlight, impress, labour, underline.
OPPOSITE play down.

stressful *adjective*

a stressful job. demanding, difficult, draining, exhausting, pressured, trying, worrying.
OPPOSITE easy.

stretch *verb*

1 *He stretched the material.* draw out, elongate, expand, extend, lengthen, pull out.
OPPOSITE shrink.
2 *Knitted fabrics stretch.* be elastic, expand.
3 *The land stretches from here to the river.* cover, extend, reach, spread.
4 *My patience was stretched to the limit.* challenge, strain, tax, test.
stretch *noun*
1 *The material has lost its stretch.* elasticity, give, stretchiness.
2 *a stretch of land.* area, distance, expanse, length, section, tract.
3 *a ten-minute stretch of skipping.* period, spell, stint, term.

stricken *adjective*

stricken with polio. affected, afflicted, smitten, struck down.

strict *adjective*

1 *a strict translation.* close, exact, literal, precise.
OPPOSITE loose.
2 *strict rules.* absolute, firm, hard and fast, inflexible, rigid, stringent.
OPPOSITE flexible.
3 *a strict teacher.* authoritarian, firm, inflexible, rigid, severe, stern, tough, uncompromising.
OPPOSITE indulgent, lenient.

stride *verb*

He strides around the yard. march, pace, stalk, walk.
stride *noun*
He takes long strides. pace, step.

strife *noun*

There is strife between the unions and the government. conflict, disagreement, friction, trouble, unrest.
OPPOSITE harmony.
in strife (*Australian informal*)
She's always in strife and needing help. in a mess, in difficulties, in hot water (*informal*), in the soup (*slang*), in trouble.

strike *verb*

1 *He struck the other man.* bash, batter, beat, belt (*slang*), box, clobber (*slang*), clout (*informal*), cuff, dong (*Australian informal*), flog, hit, job (*informal*), knock, lash, punch, quilt (*Australian slang*), rap, slap, smack, smite, sock (*slang*), spank, swipe (*informal*), tap, thrash, thump, trounce, wallop (*slang*), whack, whip.
2 *The car struck an oncoming car.* bump into, collide with, crash into, hit, knock into, run into, smash into.
3 *The virus strikes the nervous system.* affect, afflict, attack.
4 *The clock struck one.* chime, peal, sound, toll.
5 *The diggers struck gold.* discover, find, reach, stumble on.
6 *The idea struck me.* come to, dawn upon, hit, occur to.
7 *The workers are striking for improved rosters.* down tools (*informal*), go on strike, stop work, take industrial action, walk out.
strike *noun*
The strike was over working conditions. industrial action, stoppage, walk-out.

striking *adjective*
  a striking likeness. amazing, astounding, conspicuous, extraordinary, impressive, noticeable, obvious, remarkable.

string *noun*
  1 *He wrapped the parcel with string.* cord, rope, twine.
  2 *a string of beads.* chain, necklace, strand.
  3 *A string of people were already waiting.* column, file, line, queue, row.
  4 *a string of events.* chain, sequence, series, succession.
  string *verb*
  She likes stringing beads. lace, thread.

strip[1] *verb*
  1 *He stripped the paint.* peel off, remove, shave off, take off.
  2 *The doctor asked him to strip to the waist.* disrobe, expose yourself, undress.

strip[2] *noun*
  a strip of land. a strip of material. band, bar, belt, ribbon, stripe.

stripe *noun*
  The uniform has blue and white stripes. band, bar, line, strip.

strive *verb*
  His report praised him for striving to do his best. aim, attempt, endeavour, make an effort, struggle, try.

stroke[1] *noun*
  1 *As punishment he received six strokes of the cane.* blow, hit, lash, whack.
  2 *She suffered a stroke.* apoplexy, cerebral haemorrhage, seizure.

stroke[2] *verb*
  The cat likes having her back stroked. caress, massage, pat, rub, touch.

stroll *verb*
  They strolled beside the river. amble, promenade, ramble, saunter, walk, wander.

stroller *noun*
  a baby's stroller. pushchair, pusher (*Australian*).

strong *adjective*
  1 *strong furniture.* durable, heavy-duty, indestructible, sound, stout, sturdy, tough, unbreakable.
  OPPOSITE flimsy.
  2 *a man as strong as Hercules.* brawny, burly, hardy, hefty, mighty, muscular, robust, sturdy, tough.
  OPPOSITE weak.
  3 *a strong argument.* cogent, compelling, convincing, forceful, persuasive, powerful, solid, sound, weighty.
  OPPOSITE unconvincing.
  4 *a strong wind.* mighty, powerful, violent.
  OPPOSITE mild.
  5 *a strong team.* formidable, invincible, powerful, unbeatable, unconquerable.
  OPPOSITE weak.
  6 *a strong curry.* aromatic, hot, piquant, pungent, sharp, spicy.
  OPPOSITE mild.
  7 *strong colours.* bold, bright, dark, deep, intense, loud, solid, vivid.
  OPPOSITE pale.
  8 *a strong accent.* clear, definite, distinct, marked, noticeable, obvious, pronounced, unmistakable.
  OPPOSITE faint.
  9 *a strong drink.* alcoholic, concentrated, fortified, heady, intoxicating, potent, stiff.
  OPPOSITE low-alcohol, soft.
  10 *a strong faith.* ardent, earnest, fervent, firm, intense, keen, passionate, powerful, steadfast, unshakeable.
  OPPOSITE half-hearted, weak.
  strong point asset, attribute, forte, quality, speciality, strength.
  OPPOSITE weakness.

stronghold *noun*
  They bombed all the enemy's strongholds. bastion, castle, citadel, fort, fortification, fortress.

structure *noun*
  1 *the structure of a book.* arrangement, composition, design, form, framework, layout, organisation, shape.
  2 *The architect has designed a magnificent structure.* building, construction, edifice.
  structure *verb*
  The course is structured to meet the different needs of students. arrange, design, organise, put together.

a
b
c
d
e
f
g
h
i
j
k
l
m
n
o
p
q
r
s
t
u
v
w
x
y
z

struggle *verb*

1 *They struggled to make ends meet.* battle, endeavour, labour, strain, strive, toil, try, work hard.

2 *The man struggled with his opponent.* battle, contend, fight, grapple, scuffle, spar, tussle, vie, wrestle.

struggle *noun*

1 *After a brief struggle he surrendered.* battle, conflict, confrontation, contest, fight, scuffle, skirmish, tussle.

2 *She finds writing a struggle.* effort, grind, hassle (*informal*), strain, trial.
OPPOSITE cinch (*informal*).

strut *verb*

He strutted into the room wanting to be noticed. flounce, parade, prance, stride, swagger.
OPPOSITE sneak.

stub *noun*

1 *Cigarette stubs leave a stale smell in a room.* butt, end, stump.

2 *He wrote the details of the cheque on the stub.* butt, counterfoil.

stub *verb*

1 *He stubbed his toe.* bump, hit, knock, strike.

2 *He stubbed his cigarette out.* extinguish, put out, snuff.

stubborn *adjective*

a stubborn person. adamant, defiant, dogged, headstrong, inflexible, intransigent, obstinate, pigheaded, recalcitrant, strong-minded, uncompromising, unyielding.
OPPOSITE docile.

stuck *adjective*

1 *He was stuck in the traffic.* caught, held up, stranded, trapped.

2 *She was stuck on the hard questions.* at a loss, baffled, bushed (*Australian informal*), stumped (*informal*).

stuck-up *adjective* (*informal*)

a stuck-up prig. arrogant, conceited, condescending, haughty, patronising, pretentious, proud, snobbish, snooty (*informal*), toffee-nosed (*informal*), uppity (*informal*).
OPPOSITE modest.

student *noun*

apprentice, learner, postgraduate, pupil, scholar, schoolboy, schoolchild, schoolgirl, trainee, undergraduate.

studio *noun*

a craftsman's studio. workroom, workshop.

studious *adjective*

a studious child. academic, bookish, diligent, intellectual, scholarly.

study *noun*

1 *She went to university to pursue her studies.* education, instruction, learning, research, scholarship, training.

2 *The government commissioned a study of poverty.* analysis, examination, inquiry, investigation, review, survey.

3 *He works in the study.* den, office, studio.

study *verb*

1 *He is studying law at university.* learn, read, take.

2 *She needs to study for the test.* cram, learn, memorise, revise, swot (*informal*).

3 *The medical team studied the drug's side effects.* analyse, examine, inquire into, investigate, look at, research, survey.

stuff *noun*

1 *sticky stuff.* material, matter, substance.

2 *They leave their stuff wherever they want.* belongings, bits and pieces, gear, junk (*informal*), odds and ends, paraphernalia, possessions, things.

stuff *verb*

1 *She stuffed her clothes in the drawer.* cram, jam, pack, push, put, ram, shove (*informal*), squash, squeeze, stash (*informal*), stow.

2 *He stuffed the cushion with feathers.* fill, pack, pad, wad.

stuffing *noun*

1 *The cushions need new stuffing.* filling, padding, wadding.

2 *roast chicken with stuffing.* filling, seasoning.

stuffy *adjective*

1 *a stuffy atmosphere.* airless, close, humid, muggy, musty, oppressive, stale, stifling, suffocating, sultry,

unventilated.
OPPOSITE airy.
2 *Her nose is stuffy.* blocked up, clogged up, congested, stuffed up.
OPPOSITE clear.
3 *a stuffy lecturer.* dreary, dull, narrow-minded, old-fashioned, priggish, prim, staid, strait-laced.

stumble *verb*
1 *She stumbled on the rocky path.* fall, falter, sprawl, stagger, topple, totter, trip.
2 *She stumbled through the sonata.* blunder, falter, flounder.
stumble on *I stumbled on the solution by accident.* chance on, come across, discover, find, happen on, hit on.

stumbling block *noun*
difficulty, hindrance, hitch, hurdle, impediment, obstacle, snag.

stump *noun*
a tree stump. the stump of a tooth. base, butt, end, remnant, stub.
stump *verb* (*informal*)
The question stumped him. baffle, bewilder, perplex, puzzle, throw (*informal*).

stun *verb*
1 *She was stunned by a blow on the head.* daze, knock out, numb.
2 *The news stunned me.* amaze, astonish, astound, bewilder, bowl over, dumbfound, flabbergast, floor, overwhelm, shock, stagger, stupefy, surprise.

stunning *adjective* (*informal*)
What a stunning dress! attractive, beautiful, exquisite, fantastic (*informal*), gorgeous (*informal*), sensational (*informal*), spectacular, splendid, striking, stupendous, wonderful.
OPPOSITE plain.

stunt[1] *verb*
His growth was stunted by poor diet. check, curb, hamper, hinder, impede, inhibit, restrict, retard.
OPPOSITE promote.

stunt[2] *noun*
The crowd was impressed with his brave stunts. act, exploit, feat, performance, trick.

stupendous *adjective*
a stupendous achievement. amazing, astonishing, astounding, colossal, enormous, exciting, extraordinary, great, huge, immense, incredible, marvellous, phenomenal, sensational (*informal*), spectacular, stunning (*informal*), terrific (*informal*), tremendous (*informal*), unbelievable, unreal (*slang*), wonderful.
OPPOSITE ordinary.

stupid *adjective*
1 *a stupid person.* brainless, clueless (*informal*), dense, dim (*informal*), dopey (*informal*), dull, dumb (*informal*), feeble-minded, foolish, half-witted, idiotic, obtuse, simple-minded, slow, thick, unintelligent.
OPPOSITE intelligent.
2 *It was a stupid thing to do.* absurd, crazy, foolhardy, foolish, idiotic, inane, irrational, ludicrous, mad, nonsensical, reckless, senseless, silly, unwise.
OPPOSITE sensible.

sturdy *adjective*
1 *a sturdy person.* brawny, burly, hardy, hefty, mighty, muscular, nuggety (*Australian*), robust, stout, strapping, strong, tough.
OPPOSITE weak.
2 *a sturdy chair.* durable, indestructible, solid, sound, strong, tough, unbreakable.
OPPOSITE flimsy.

stutter *verb*
He stutters when he speaks. falter, stammer.

style *noun*
1 *The essay was marked for style and content.* expression, language, wording.
2 *a style of painting.* approach, manner, method, mode, technique, way.
3 *various styles of jacket.* design, fashion, kind, pattern, shape, sort, type, version.
4 *a woman with style.* chic, class, elegance, flair, polish, sophistication.
style *verb*
He styled the woman's hair. arrange, cut, design, shape.

stylish *adjective*
a stylish outfit. chic, classy (*informal*), elegant, fashionable, smart, trendy

a
b
c
d
e
f
g
h
i
j
k
l
m
n
o
p
q
r
s
t
u
v
w
x
y
z

(*informal*), up-to-date, with it (*informal*).
OPPOSITE dowdy.

subconscious *adjective*
a subconscious desire. instinctive,
intuitive, unconscious.

subdue *verb*
1 *The police subdued the demonstrators.*
control, defeat, overcome, overpower,
repress, restrain, suppress.
2 *They subdued their voices.* hush, lower,
moderate, quieten, soften, tone down.
OPPOSITE raise.

subject *noun*
1 *Her favourite subject is mathematics.*
course, discipline, field.
2 *The subject of her lecture is safety in the
home.* issue, matter, theme, topic.
subject *verb*
*The doctor subjected him to a battery of
tests.* expose, put through, submit, treat.
subject *adjective*
subject to
1 *He is subject to colds.* liable to, prone
to, susceptible to.
2 *She accepted the invitation, subject to her
parents' approval.* conditional upon,
contingent on, dependent upon.

subjective *adjective*
a subjective criticism. biased, personal,
prejudiced.
OPPOSITE objective.

sublime *adjective*
sublime music. awe-inspiring, exalted,
glorious, grand, magnificent, majestic,
noble, wonderful.
OPPOSITE ordinary.

submerge *verb*
1 *The olives must be submerged in brine.*
dunk, immerse, plunge, soak, steep.
2 *All the low-lying land was submerged.*
cover, engulf, flood, inundate, swamp.
3 *The submarine submerged.* dive, go
under.
OPPOSITE surface.

submissive *adjective*
She became bolder and less submissive.
compliant, docile, meek, obedient,
passive, unassertive, yielding.
OPPOSITE defiant.

submit *verb*
1 *They had to submit to the enemy in the
end.* capitulate, give in, surrender,
throw in the towel, yield.
OPPOSITE resist.
2 *She submitted her proposal.* give in,
hand in, offer, present, put forward,
tender.
OPPOSITE withdraw.

subordinate *adjective*
1 *a subordinate consideration.* lesser,
secondary.
OPPOSITE primary.
2 *subordinate officers.* inferior, junior,
lower.
OPPOSITE senior.

subscribe *verb*
subscribe to *She subscribes generously to
various charities.* contribute to, donate
to, give to, help, support.

subscription *noun*
She has paid her subscription to the club.
contribution, dues, fee, membership
fee, sub (*informal*).

subsequent *adjective*
subsequent discoveries. ensuing,
following, later, succeeding.
OPPOSITE previous.

subside *verb*
1 *The land has subsided.* cave in, collapse,
drop, settle, sink.
OPPOSITE rise.
2 *The storm subsided.* abate, decrease, die
down, diminish, let up, moderate,
recede, weaken.
OPPOSITE intensify.

subsidise *verb*
The government subsidised the scheme.
back, contribute to, sponsor, support,
underwrite.

subsidy *noun*
*The centre is paid a government subsidy for
each user.* assistance, contribution, grant.

substance *noun*
1 *They have identified the substance.*
material, matter, stuff.
2 *the substance of an argument.* essence,
gist, heart, nub, thrust.

substantial *adjective*
  1 *a substantial house.* solid, strong, well-built.
  OPPOSITE flimsy.
  2 *a substantial amount.* big, considerable, large, significant, sizeable.
  OPPOSITE insignificant.
  3 *in substantial agreement.* basic, essential, fundamental.

substitute *noun*
  a substitute for a teacher, doctor, actor, etc. deputy, fill-in, locum, proxy, relief, replacement, reserve, ring-in (*Australian informal*), stand-in, stopgap, sub (*informal*), surrogate, understudy.
substitute *verb*
  1 *The copy was substituted for the original painting.* exchange, interchange, replace, swap, switch.
  2 *He will substitute for you while you are away.* cover, deputise, fill in, relieve, stand in.

subtle *adjective*
  1 *a subtle difference.* fine, imperceptible, minor, slight, tiny.
  OPPOSITE obvious.
  2 *a subtle fragrance.* delicate, faint, gentle, mild.
  OPPOSITE strong.
  3 *subtle methods.* clever, devious, ingenious, sly, sneaky, wily.
  OPPOSITE crude.

subtract *verb*
  deduct, remove, take away, take off.
  OPPOSITE add.

suburb *noun*
  They live in a quiet suburb. area, community, district, neighbourhood.

subway *noun*
  tunnel, underpass.

succeed *verb*
  1 *His plan succeeded.* bear fruit, be effective, be successful, work.
  OPPOSITE fail.
  2 *She finally succeeded as an actress.* achieve success, make good, make it, prosper.
  3 *He succeeded his brother as captain.* come after, follow, replace, take over from.
  OPPOSITE precede.

success *noun*
  1 *We wished him success.* achievement, attainment, prosperity, triumph, victory.
  OPPOSITE failure.
  2 *The play was a success.* hit, sell-out (*informal*), smash hit (*informal*), triumph, winner.
  OPPOSITE failure, flop (*slang*).

successful *adjective*
  1 *a successful enterprise.* booming, flourishing, fruitful, productive, profitable, prosperous, thriving.
  OPPOSITE unsuccessful.
  2 *the successful team.* triumphant, victorious, winning.
  OPPOSITE losing.

succession *noun*
  a succession of mishaps. chain, cycle, line, round, run, sequence, series, string, train.
  in succession consecutively, in a row, one after the other, running.

successive *adjective*
  three successive wins. consecutive, straight.

suck *verb*
  suck up *The vacuum cleaner sucks up the dirt.* draw up, pick up, pull up.
  suck up to (*informal*) *He was despised because he sucked up to the teacher.* crawl to (*informal*), fawn on, flatter, grovel to, kowtow to, play up to, toady to.

sucker *noun* (*informal*)
  He was a sucker to fall for that. dupe, mug (*informal*), muggins (*informal*), pushover (*informal*), sap (*informal*).

suckle *verb*
  The animal suckles its young. breastfeed, feed, nurse.

sudden *adjective*
  a sudden decision. abrupt, hasty, impetuous, instant, quick, rapid, rash, snap, surprise, swift, unexpected.
  OPPOSITE gradual.
  all of a sudden abruptly, all at once, in an instant, in the twinkling of an eye, out of the blue, quickly, suddenly, unexpectedly, without warning.
  OPPOSITE gradually, slowly.

a
b
c
d
e
f
g
h
i
j
k
l
m
n
o
p
q
r
s
t
u
v
w
x
y
z

suds *plural noun*
bubbles, foam, froth, lather.

suffer *verb*
1 *She suffered a lot of pain.* bear, cope with, endure, experience, feel, go through, put up with, undergo.
2 *He wouldn't let the dog suffer.* be in pain, feel pain, hurt.

suffering *noun*
Nothing could ease the suffering. affliction, agony, anguish, discomfort, distress, grief, heartache, hurt, misery, pain, sorrow, torment, torture, tribulation, woe.

sufficient *adjective*
sufficient food to feed a family. adequate, ample, enough.
OPPOSITE insufficient.

suffocate *verb*
asphyxiate, choke, smother, stifle, strangle, throttle.

sugary *adjective*
a sugary taste. cloying, saccharine, sickly, sweet.
OPPOSITE sour.

suggest *verb*
1 *The rash suggests rubella.* be a sign of, indicate, signal.
2 *Was he suggesting that she was lying?* hint, imply, insinuate, intimate.
3 *He suggested that we take a rest.* advise, advocate, propose, recommend.

suggestion *noun*
He would not follow her suggestion. advice, proposal, recommendation, tip.

suicidal *adjective*
suicidal behaviour. self-destructive.

suit *noun*
1 *a bathing suit.* costume, outfit.
2 *a criminal suit.* case, lawsuit, proceedings.
suit *verb*
1 *That time suits me.* be acceptable to, be convenient for, be right for, be suitable for, fit in with, please.
OPPOSITE be inconvenient to.
2 *That dress suits her.* become, look good on.

suitable *adjective*
a suitable remark. acceptable, appropriate, apt, becoming, befitting, convenient, fitting, proper, relevant, right, satisfactory, seemly, timely.
OPPOSITE inappropriate, unsuitable.

suitcase *noun*
bag, case, port (*Australian*), portmanteau, trunk.

suitor *noun*
The lady has several suitors. admirer, boyfriend, lover, sweetheart.

sulky *adjective*
a sulky child. bad-tempered, disgruntled, moody, peevish, petulant, pouting, resentful, scowling, sullen.

sullen *adjective*
a sullen man. bad-tempered, dismal, gloomy, grouchy (*informal*), grumpy, melancholy, moody, morose, resentful, sour, sulky, surly, unsociable.
OPPOSITE cheerful.

sultry *adjective*
sultry weather. close, hot, humid, muggy, oppressive, sticky, stifling, stuffy, suffocating.

sum *noun*
1 *the sum of the first five numbers.* addition, subtotal, total.
2 *a tidy sum of money.* amount.
3 *The teacher set ten sums for homework.* calculation, problem.
sum *verb*
sum up *He summed up all that had been said.* recap (*informal*), recapitulate, review, summarise.

summarise *verb*
see SUM UP (at SUM).

summary *noun*
a summary of the report. abstract, outline, précis, recap (*informal*), recapitulation, résumé, synopsis.

summit *noun*
They reached the summit of the mountain. apex, crest, crown, peak, pinnacle, top, zenith.
OPPOSITE base.

summon *verb*
1 *She summoned the fire brigade.* call out, send for.
2 *He was summoned to appear in court.* call, command, order, subpoena, summons.

summons *noun*
I received a summons to appear in court. command, demand, order, subpoena, writ.

sunbathe *verb*
bask, sunbake, sun yourself.

sunny *adjective*
a sunny day. bright, clear, cloudless, fair, fine, sunlit.
OPPOSITE dull.

sunrise *noun*
cock-crow, dawn, daybreak, first light, sun-up.

sunset *noun*
dusk, evening, nightfall, sundown, twilight.

sunshade *noun*
protected by a sunshade. awning, canopy, parasol.

superb *adjective*
a superb meal. a superb performance. brilliant (*informal*), cool (*informal*), excellent, exceptional, fabulous (*informal*), fantastic (*informal*), fine, first-class, first-rate, grand, great, impressive, magnificent, marvellous, outstanding, remarkable, splendid, stupendous, super (*informal*), superlative, terrific (*informal*), wonderful.
OPPOSITE inferior, poor.

superficial *adjective*
1 *a superficial wound.* exterior, external, shallow, skin-deep, slight, surface.
OPPOSITE deep.
2 *superficial knowledge.* cursory, limited, partial, sketchy, slight.
OPPOSITE thorough.

superfluous *adjective*
He gave away the superfluous copies. excess, extra, redundant, spare, surplus, unnecessary.

superintendent *noun*
boss, chief, foreman, head, manager, overseer, supervisor, warden.

superior *adjective*
1 *a superior officer.* higher, senior.
OPPOSITE inferior.
2 *superior quality.* better, excellent, first-class, greater, outstanding, super (*informal*), top, unequalled.
OPPOSITE inferior, poor.
3 *a superior tone of voice.* arrogant, condescending, disdainful, haughty, lofty, patronising, self-important, smug, snobbish, stuck-up (*informal*), supercilious.

supernatural *adjective*
supernatural power. extraordinary, miraculous, mysterious, occult, paranormal, psychic, unearthly.

supersede *verb*
This model supersedes the original one. replace, take the place of.

supervise *verb*
He supervised the work. control, direct, head, manage, orchestrate, organise, oversee, preside over, run, stage-manage, superintend.

supervision *noun*
1 *He was praised for his supervision of the project.* administration, direction, management, organisation, oversight.
2 *The prisoners are under close supervision.* control, observation, scrutiny, surveillance, watch.

supervisor *noun*
administrator, boss, chief, director, foreman, head, manager, overseer, superintendent, superior.

supple *adjective*
a supple body. flexible, limber, lithe, pliable.
OPPOSITE stiff.

supplement *noun*
1 *a single-person supplement.* add-on, extra, surcharge.
2 *a supplement to the document.* addendum, addition, appendix, codicil, insert, postscript, rider.

a
b
c
d
e
f
g
h
i
j
k
l
m
n
o
p
q
r
s
t
u
v
w
x
y
z

supplement *verb*
The second job is to supplement his income. add to, augment, boost, increase, top up.

supplementary *adjective*
a supplementary income. additional, extra.

supply *verb*
They will supply you with a car. equip, furnish, give, provide.
supply *noun*
1 the supply of gas to homes. delivery, provision.
2 He has laid in a supply of matches. hoard, reserve, stock, stockpile, store.

support *verb*
1 He used a plank to support the fence. brace, buttress, hold up, prop up, reinforce, shore up.
2 That chair won't support two of you. bear, carry, hold, take.
3 He supports a family of five. keep, maintain, provide for.
4 She supports the club. back, barrack for (Australian), contribute to, patronise, subsidise.
5 She supported him in his campaign. assist, back, defend, endorse, help, side with, stand up for, stick by, stick up for.
6 Witnesses supported her story. back up, confirm, corroborate, verify.
support *noun*
1 He promised his support to the club. aid, assistance, backing, help, patronage, sponsorship.
2 One of the supports has collapsed. bolster, brace, bracket, buttress, calliper, foundation, joist, pillar, post, prop, stay, stilt, strut.

supporter *noun*
They thanked their supporters. ally, backer, benefactor, fan, follower, patron, well-wisher.
OPPOSITE opponent.

supportive *adjective*
a supportive wife. caring, encouraging, helpful, sympathetic, understanding.

suppose *verb*
I suppose that he will show up. assume, believe, expect, fancy, guess, imagine, presume, think.

be supposed to *You are supposed to attend.* be expected to, be meant to, be obliged to.

suppress *verb*
1 They suppressed the riot. crush, overcome, overpower, put an end to, quash, quell, stop.
2 They can't suppress the truth. censor, conceal, cover up, hide, keep secret, silence, withhold.
OPPOSITE expose.
3 He suppressed his anger. bottle up, control, keep in check, repress, restrain, stifle.
OPPOSITE express.

supreme *adjective*
He has supreme authority. chief, greatest, highest, leading, paramount, principal, sovereign.

sure *adjective*
1 I am sure you are right. assured, certain, confident, convinced, positive.
OPPOSITE unsure.
2 The play is sure to be a hit. bound, certain, guaranteed.
3 One thing is sure. certain, clear, definite, indisputable, true.
OPPOSITE uncertain.
4 a sure cure. certain, dependable, fail-safe, infallible, reliable, sure-fire (informal), trustworthy, unfailing.
OPPOSITE unreliable.
make sure *She made sure that there was a train.* ascertain, check, confirm, double-check, make certain, verify.

surface *noun*
a smooth surface. coating, covering, exterior, finish, outside, shell, skin, top.
OPPOSITE inside.
surface *adjective*
surface damage. exterior, external, superficial.
surface *verb*
The diver surfaced. come up, emerge, rise.
OPPOSITE submerge.

surge *verb*
1 The sea surged. billow, heave, roll, swell.
2 The crowd surged forward. push, rush, stream.

surge *noun*
1 *a surge of water.* flow, gush, rush, stream, wave.
2 *a surge of interest.* growth, increase, rise, upsurge.

surly *adjective*
His surly manner turned people away. bad-tempered, crabby, crusty, grouchy (*informal*), gruff, grumpy, rude, snaky (*Australian informal*), sullen, unfriendly.
OPPOSITE friendly.

surname *noun*
family name, last name.

surpass *verb*
1 *She surpasses the others at mathematics.* beat, do better than, outclass, outdo, outshine, outstrip, overshadow, top.
2 *This surpasses all expectation.* exceed, go beyond, transcend.

surplus *noun*
We gave away our surplus of grapes. excess, glut, surfeit.
OPPOSITE deficit.

surprise *noun*
1 *They were filled with surprise.* amazement, astonishment, shock, wonder.
2 *The news came as a complete surprise.* bolt from the blue, bombshell, shock.
surprise *verb*
1 *The news surprised them.* amaze, astonish, astound, dumbfound, flabbergast, shock, stagger, startle, stun, take aback.
2 *He surprised them eating in the library.* catch, catch red-handed, discover, spring (*Australian informal*), take unawares.

surprised *adjective*
amazed, astonished, astounded, dumbfounded, flabbergasted, shocked, speechless, staggered, startled, stunned, taken aback, thunderstruck.

surprising *adjective*
a surprising result. amazing, astonishing, astounding, incredible, mind-boggling (*informal*), staggering, startling, unexpected.
OPPOSITE predictable.

surrender *verb*
1 *He surrendered his licence to the policeman.* give, hand over, relinquish.
2 *Finally the gunman surrendered.* capitulate, give in, give yourself up, submit, throw in the towel, yield.
OPPOSITE resist.

surrogate *noun*
see SUBSTITUTE.

surround *verb*
1 *A fence surrounds the garden.* encircle, enclose, ring, skirt.
2 *She was surrounded by fans.* beset, besiege, encircle, hem in.

surroundings *plural noun*
He works in pleasant surroundings. environment, setting.

survey *verb*
1 *He surveyed the scene from the lookout.* contemplate, look at, observe, view.
2 *This chapter surveys other theories.* consider, examine, explore, inspect, investigate, look at, review.
3 *His job is to survey the land.* map out, measure, plot.
survey *noun*
a survey of voting trends in Australia. examination, inquiry, inspection, investigation, poll, review, study.

survival *noun*
the fight for survival. existence, life.
OPPOSITE extinction.

survive *verb*
1 *They cannot survive on one income.* exist, live, make ends meet, subsist.
2 *Some traditions have survived.* continue, endure, keep on, last, live on, persist.
OPPOSITE die.
3 *He won't survive the winter.* come through, endure, last, live through.
4 *She survived her husband by ten years.* outlast, outlive.
OPPOSITE predecease.

suspect *verb*
1 *I suspect that you're right.* believe, fancy, guess, have a feeling, have a hunch, imagine, suppose, think.
OPPOSITE know.
2 *They suspected his reliability.* distrust, doubt, have misgivings about, mistrust,

a
b
c
d
e
f
g
h
i
j
k
l
m
n
o
p
q
r
s
t
u
v
w
x
y
z

question.
OPPOSITE trust.

suspend *verb*
1 *Decorations were suspended from the ceiling.* dangle, hang, sling.
2 *He suspended the inquiry.* adjourn, defer, delay, postpone, put off, shelve.
3 *They suspended payments while she was sick.* discontinue, interrupt, stop.
OPPOSITE continue, resume.
4 *He was suspended from his job.* lay off, stand down.

suspense *noun*
The suspense was intolerable. anticipation, tension, uncertainty.
OPPOSITE certainty.

suspicion *noun*
1 *filled with suspicion.* distrust, doubt, misgiving, mistrust, scepticism.
2 *She had a suspicion that they would win.* feeling, hunch, idea, notion.
3 *a suspicion of garlic in the soup.* dash, hint, suggestion, touch, trace.

suspicious *adjective*
1 *a suspicious mind.* disbelieving, distrustful, doubting, incredulous, mistrustful, sceptical, wary.
OPPOSITE trusting.
2 *suspicious activities.* dubious, fishy (*informal*), questionable, shady, suspect, untrustworthy.
OPPOSITE above board.

sustain *verb*
1 *The walls were built to sustain the weight of the roof.* bear, carry, hold, support, take.
2 *The book sustained his interest.* hold, keep, maintain.

swag *noun*
1 (*informal*) *The thief dropped the swag.* booty, loot, plunder, spoils, takings.
2 (*Australian*) *The tramp carries his belongings in his swag.* bluey (*Australian*), drum (*Australian*), matilda (*Australian*), shiralee (*Australian*).
3 (*Australian informal*) *a swag of bills to pay.* heap (*informal*), lot, masses, mountain, pile (*informal*).

swagger *verb*
All eyes turned as he swaggered down the mall. parade, prance, strut.

swagman *noun* (*Australian*)
bagman (*Australian*), sundowner (*Australian*), swaggie (*Australian*), tramp.

swallow *verb*
1 *She swallowed her food.* devour, eat, gobble, gulp, guzzle, scoff (*informal*).
2 *He swallowed his drink.* down (*informal*), gulp, guzzle, quaff, swig (*informal*), swill.
swallow up *He was swallowed up in the crowd.* absorb, engulf, swamp.

swamp *noun*
bog, fen, marsh, quagmire, slough.
swamp *verb*
1 *The waves swamped the boat.* engulf, fill, flood, inundate, submerge.
2 *They were swamped with orders.* deluge, flood, inundate, overwhelm, snow under.

swan *noun*
cob (*male*), cygnet (*young*), pen (*female*).

swap *verb*
1 *They swapped stamps.* barter, exchange, trade.
2 *They swapped the paintings and no one noticed.* exchange, interchange, substitute, switch.
swap *noun*
They did a swap while nobody was looking. exchange, substitution.

swarm *noun*
a swarm of insects. a swarm of people. army, cluster, crowd, drove, flock, herd, host, mass, mob, multitude, myriad, throng.
swarm *verb*
1 *The children swarmed into the hall.* crowd, flock, pour, rush, stream, surge.
2 *The people swarmed outside the building.* cluster, congregate, crowd, flock, herd, mass, mob, throng.
swarm with *The place swarmed with journalists.* be alive with, be crowded with, be overflowing with, be overrun by, crawl with, teem with.

sway *verb*
1 *He swayed unsteadily and then fell.* reel, rock, stagger, swing, totter, wobble.
2 *We were swayed by his stirring speech.* influence, move, persuade, win over.

swear *verb*
1 *He swore to tell the truth.* pledge, promise, vow.
2 *He swears when he's angry.* blaspheme, curse.
swear word blasphemy, expletive, obscenity, profanity.

sweat *noun*
in a sweat after exercise. lather, perspiration.
sweat *verb*
He sweats heavily. perspire.

sweater *noun*
jersey, jumper, pullover, skivvy (*Australian*), sweatshirt, top, windcheater.

sweep *verb*
1 *He swept the floor.* brush, clean, clear.
2 *They all swept past him.* belt (*slang*), charge, dash, fly, race, rush, sail, speed, tear, zoom.
sweep *noun*
1 *a long sweep of coastline.* arc, curve, expanse, extent, stretch.
2 *She gave the rugs a sweep.* brush, clean.

sweeping *adjective*
1 *He has made sweeping changes.* broad, extensive, far-reaching, huge, massive, radical, wholesale, wide-ranging.
OPPOSITE minor.
2 *a sweeping statement.* broad, general, unqualified.
OPPOSITE specific.

sweet *adjective*
1 *a sweet taste.* cloying, luscious, saccharine, sickly, sugary, syrupy.
OPPOSITE bitter, savoury, sour.
2 *a sweet smell.* balmy, fragrant, perfumed, scented.
OPPOSITE foul.
3 *sweet sounds.* dulcet, euphonious, harmonious, melodious, pleasant, tuneful.
OPPOSITE harsh.
4 (*informal*) *She has such a sweet face.* appealing, attractive, cute, lovely, pretty.
5 (*informal*) *What a sweet person she is!* amiable, charming, considerate, dear, delightful, generous, gentle, good-natured, kind, likeable, lovable, nice,

pleasant, thoughtful.
OPPOSITE disagreeable.

sweet *noun*
1 *a bag of sweets for sixty cents.* candy (*American*), lolly (*Australian*), toffee.
2 *No room for sweet after the roast.* afters (*informal*), dessert, pudding (*British*).

sweetheart *noun*
1 *'Let's go, sweetheart.'* darling, dear, honey (*informal*), love, sweet, sweetie (*informal*).
2 *cards to send to your sweetheart.* beloved, boyfriend, fiancé, fiancée, girlfriend, love, lover.

swell *verb*
1 *Her stomach swelled after overeating.* bloat, blow up, bulge, distend, expand, inflate, puff up.
OPPOSITE shrink.
2 *The visitors swelled the numbers.* augment, boost, increase, inflate.
OPPOSITE diminish.
3 *The crowd swelled.* build up, grow, increase, multiply.
OPPOSITE decrease.
4 *The music swelled.* grow louder, heighten, intensify.
OPPOSITE die away.
5 *The sea swelled.* billow, heave, mount, rise, surge.
OPPOSITE fall.
swell *noun*
1 *The boat was caught in a heavy swell.* billows, surge, waves.
2 *a swell in numbers.* increase, rise, surge.

swelling *noun*
The swelling went down after a day. blister, boil, bulge, bump, inflammation, lump.

sweltering *adjective*
a sweltering day. boiling, hot, scorching, stifling, sultry.
OPPOSITE freezing.

swerve *verb*
We swerved to avoid hitting the other car. deviate, turn, veer.

swift *adjective*
1 *swift on his feet.* brisk, fast, fleet, nimble, nippy (*informal*), quick, speedy.
OPPOSITE slow.

a b c d e f g h i j k l m n o p q r s t u v w x y z

2 *a swift response.* hasty, immediate, prompt, quick, rapid.
OPPOSITE slow.

swiftly *adverb*
see QUICKLY.

swill *verb*
He swilled the glasses under the tap. clean, rinse, wash.
swill *noun*
kitchen swill. pigswill, slop.

swim *verb*
She likes to swim after school. bathe, bogey (*Australian*), have a dip.
swimming costume bathers (*Australian*), bathing suit, bikini, cossie (*Australian informal*), swimmers (*Australian*), swimsuit, togs (*Australian informal*), trunks.
swimming pool aquatic centre, baths, pool.

swindle *verb*
They swindled her out of her savings. cheat, con (*informal*), deceive, defraud, diddle (*informal*), dupe, fleece, hoax, hoodwink, rip off (*informal*), rook, trick.
swindle *noun*
victims of a swindle. con (*informal*), confidence trick, deception, fraud, hoax, racket, rip-off (*informal*), swizz (*informal*), trick.

swindler *noun*
charlatan, cheat, con man (*informal*), crook (*informal*), fraud, racketeer, rogue, sharper, shicer (*Australian slang*), shyster (*informal*), trickster.

swing *verb*
1 *The plank swings up and down.* flap, oscillate, rock, see-saw, sway.
2 *She swung a rope between the trees.* dangle, hang, sling, suspend.
3 *She swung round to face the other way.* rotate, spin, swivel, turn.
4 *Her mood swings from hope to despair.* alter, change, fluctuate, shift, switch, vary, waver.
swing *noun*
1 *He took a swing with the bat.* stroke, sweep, swipe (*informal*).
2 *the swing in the vote.* change, movement, shift, turnaround.

swipe *verb* (*informal*)
1 *He swiped the ball.* belt (*slang*), hit, strike, swing at, whack.
2 *The thief swiped my bag.* grab, nab (*informal*), pinch (*informal*), seize, snatch, snitch (*slang*), steal.
swipe *noun* (*informal*)
He took a swipe at the ball. hit, stroke, swing.

swirl *verb*
It was windy and the dust was swirling. eddy, revolve, spin, spiral, twirl, twist, whirl.

switch *noun*
a switch in methods. about-face, change, changeover, shift, U-turn, variation.
switch *verb*
1 *Switch on the light.* flick, turn.
2 *He switched their glasses.* change, exchange, substitute, swap.

swivel *verb*
She likes to swivel on her chair. pivot, revolve, rotate, spin, turn, twirl, whirl.

swollen *adjective*
a swollen abdomen. bloated, bulging, distended, puffed-up.
OPPOSITE shrunken.

swoop *verb*
The bird swooped on the mouse. descend, dive, plunge, pounce, spring.
swoop on *The soldiers swooped on the town.* attack, descend on, raid, rush, storm.

sword *noun*
blade, broadsword, claymore, cutlass, foil, rapier, sabre, scimitar, steel (*literary*).

swot *verb*
see STUDY.

symbol *noun*
1 *the company's symbol.* badge, emblem, insignia, logo, sign, token, trade mark.
2 *The table explains the meaning of the symbols.* character, figure, ideogram, letter, pictogram, sign.

symbolise *verb*
White symbolises purity. denote, express, indicate, mean, represent, signify, stand for.

symmetrical *adjective*
a symmetrical shape. balanced, even, regular.
OPPOSITE asymmetrical, lopsided.

sympathetic *adjective*
a sympathetic judge. caring, compassionate, concerned, humane, kind, kindly, merciful, supportive, tender-hearted, understanding, warm-hearted.
OPPOSITE cold-hearted, unsympathetic.

sympathise *verb*
sympathise with
1 *We sympathised with the unhappy family.* commiserate with, feel compassion for, feel for, feel sorry for, offer condolences to, pity.
2 *I can sympathise with those feelings.* empathise with, identify with, understand.

sympathy *noun*
He felt deep sympathy for the victims. commiseration, compassion, concern, condolences, empathy, feeling, pity,
tenderness, understanding.
OPPOSITE indifference.

symptom *noun*
the symptoms of the disease. feature, indication, mark, pointer (*informal*), sign, signal.

synthetic *adjective*
synthetic grass. artificial, fake, imitation, man-made, manufactured.
OPPOSITE natural.

syringe *noun*
hypodermic, needle.

system *noun*
1 *a system of highways.* arrangement, network, organisation, set-up, structure.
2 *a system for doing the job.* approach, method, order, plan, procedure, routine, scheme, structure, technique, way.

systematic *adjective*
a systematic approach. businesslike, efficient, logical, methodical, ordered, orderly, organised, planned, scientific.
OPPOSITE haphazard.

a
b
c
d
e
f
g
h
i
j
k
l
m
n
o
p
q
r
s
t
u
v
w
x
y
z

Tt

table *noun*
1 *He put the things down on the table.* altar, bar, bench, buffet, counter, desk, lectern, stand.
2 *information presented in a table.* chart, list.

tableland *noun*
highland, plateau.

tablet *noun*
1 *The doctor prescribed some tablets.* capsule, lozenge, pill.
2 *The words were written on a stone tablet.* panel, plaque, plate, slab.

taboo *adjective*
taboo words. banned, forbidden, prohibited, unacceptable, unmentionable.
OPPOSITE acceptable.

tack *noun*
1 *fastened with tacks.* drawing pin, nail, pin, staple.
2 *He changed tack.* approach, course, direction, method, policy, strategy, tactic.

tack *verb*
1 *She tacked the picture to the board.* fasten, fix, nail, pin, staple.
2 *The dressmaker tacks the seam first.* baste, sew, stitch.
3 *She tacked an extra paragraph on the letter.* add, append, attach, tag.
OPPOSITE delete.

tackle *noun*
fishing tackle. apparatus, equipment, gear, kit.

tackle *verb*
1 *He tackled the problem systematically.* address, approach, attack, deal with, grapple with, handle, manage, set about.
2 *He successfully tackled the other player.* attack, challenge, intercept, take on.

tacky *adjective*
1 *The paint is still tacky.* sticky, wet.
OPPOSITE dry.

2 *(informal) tacky ornaments.* cheap, kitsch, shabby, tasteless, tawdry.

tact *noun*
She handled the situation with tact. courtesy, delicacy, diplomacy, discretion, sensitivity.
OPPOSITE tactlessness.

tactful *adjective*
a tactful comment. considerate, courteous, diplomatic, discreet, polite, sensitive, thoughtful.
OPPOSITE tactless.

tactic *noun*
He tried a different tactic. approach, manoeuvre, plan, ploy (*informal*), policy, scheme, strategy, tack.

tactless *adjective*
a tactless remark. impolite, inconsiderate, indiscreet, insensitive, thoughtless, undiplomatic.
OPPOSITE tactful.

tag *noun*
a name tag. label, sticker, tab, ticket.

tag *verb*
1 *The clothes have been tagged.* identify, label, mark, ticket.
2 *He tagged on an extra paragraph.* add, append, attach, tack.
tag along *Do you mind if he tags along with us?* accompany, come, follow, go, trail.

tail *noun*
His car was at the tail. back, end, rear.
OPPOSITE head, front.

tail *verb* (*informal*)
The police tailed the suspect. follow, pursue, shadow, stalk, track, trail.

take *verb*
1 *He took my hand.* clasp, clutch, grab, grasp, hold, pluck, seize, snatch.
OPPOSITE let go.
2 *They took many prisoners.* abduct, capture, carry off, catch, detain, seize.
OPPOSITE release.

3 *She took all the prizes.* gain, get, obtain, receive, scoop up, secure, win.

4 *Someone has taken my watch.* appropriate, help yourself to, lift (*informal*), make off with, nick (*slang*), pilfer, pinch (*informal*), poach, pocket, remove, snaffle (*informal*), snatch, snavel (*Australian informal*), snitch (*slang*), souvenir (*slang*), steal, swipe (*informal*).
OPPOSITE give back.

5 *He takes the eight o'clock train.* catch, travel by, use.

6 *It takes courage to speak out.* call for, demand, need, require.

7 *He offered to take us home.* accompany, bring, carry, conduct, convey, deliver, escort, guide, lead, run, transport.

8 *He took it that they were satisfied.* assume, conclude, gather, infer, interpret, suppose, understand.

9 *He took the blame.* accept, assume, bear, shoulder.

10 *She took her mother's advice.* accept, adopt, follow, heed.
OPPOSITE ignore.

11 *He couldn't take the strain.* bear, endure, put up with, stand, suffer, tolerate, undergo, withstand.

take after *She takes after her mother.* be the (spitting) image of, look like, resemble.

take away

1 *The teacher took away the comics.* confiscate, deprive someone of, impound, remove, seize.
OPPOSITE return.

2 *Take 5 away from 7.* deduct, subtract.
OPPOSITE add to.

take back *He took back his statement.* recant, retract, revoke, withdraw.

take in

1 *He did not take in all the information.* absorb, assimilate, digest, grasp, realise, understand.

2 *The scoundrel took them in with his smooth talk.* cheat, con (*informal*), deceive, dupe, fool, have on (*informal*), hoodwink, mislead, trick.

take off

1 *He took off his clothes, hat, etc.* doff, peel off, remove, shed, strip off.
OPPOSITE don.

2 *The actor took off important people cleverly.* imitate, mimic, parody, send up (*informal*).

3 *He took off in a waiting car.* see LEAVE.

take on

1 *She took on the extra responsibility.* accept, assume, shoulder, undertake.

2 *The firm took on two new people.* appoint, employ, engage, hire, recruit.
OPPOSITE dismiss.

take out *He took the splinter out.* draw out, extract, pull out, remove.
OPPOSITE insert.

take part *Ten children took part in the contest.* be involved, compete, enter, join, participate.

take place *The accident took place at noon.* come about, come to pass, happen, occur.

take up

1 *He took up a new career.* begin, commence, embark on, start.

2 *Sewing takes up her time.* consume, eat up, fill, make inroads into, occupy, use up.

3 *He took up from where he left off.* carry on, continue, pick up, recommence, resume.

take-off *noun*

1 *a brilliant take-off of the politician.* imitation, parody, send-up (*informal*), spoof (*informal*).

2 *the spacecraft's take-off.* blast-off, launch, lift-off.
OPPOSITE landing.

takings *plural noun*
The thief stole the day's takings. earnings, income, proceeds, receipts, revenue.

tale *noun*
a tale of adventure. account, anecdote, fable, fairy tale, legend, myth, narrative, saga, story, yarn (*informal*).

talent *noun*
artistic talent. a talent for mathematics. ability, accomplishment, aptitude, flair, genius, gift, knack, know-how, skill.

talk *verb*

1 *They talked for hours.* chat, chatter, converse, gabble, gossip, jabber, natter (*informal*), rabbit on (*informal*), speak, yabber (*Australian informal*), yak (*informal*).

a
b
c
d
e
f
g
h
i
j
k
l
m
n
o
p
q
r
s
t
u
v
w
x
y
z

2 *The baby has just learnt to talk.* babble, communicate, speak.
3 *The minister talked to the children.* address, lecture, preach, speak.
OPPOSITE listen.

talk *noun*
1 *The friends had a long talk.* chat, chinwag (*informal*), conference, consultation, conversation, dialogue, discussion, gossip, natter (*informal*), yabber (*Australian informal*), yak (*informal*).
2 *baby talk.* language, speech.
3 *He gave a talk on Mozart.* address, lecture, presentation, sermon, speech.
4 *There's been talk of a strike.* gossip, hearsay, report, rumour.
talk down to *He talks down to his pupils.* condescend to, patronise.
talk into *They talked him into resigning.* cajole into, coax into, convince to, persuade to.
talk out of *They talked him out of resigning.* deter from, discourage from, dissuade from, stop.

talkative *adjective*
chatty, communicative, garrulous, loquacious, voluble.
OPPOSITE taciturn.

talker *noun*
chatterbox, conversationalist, gasbag (*informal*), orator, speaker.
OPPOSITE listener.

tall *adjective*
1 *a tall person.* gangling, gigantic, lanky, leggy.
OPPOSITE short.
2 *a tall building.* high, lofty, multi-storey, towering.
OPPOSITE low.

tally *noun*
They kept a tally of their points. account, count, reckoning, record, score, total.
tally *verb*
Her story does not tally with theirs. agree, coincide, conform, correspond, match, square.

talon *noun*
a bird's talon. claw.

tame *adjective*
1 *a tame animal.* docile, domestic, domesticated, gentle.
OPPOSITE wild.
2 *The show was quite tame.* boring, dull, flat, unexciting, uninteresting.
OPPOSITE exciting.
tame *verb*
He tamed the horse. break in, domesticate, subdue, train.

tamper *verb*
tamper with *Someone had tampered with the controls.* fiddle with, interfere with, meddle with, muck around with, play with, tinker with.

tan *verb*
His skin has tanned. bronze, brown, suntan.
tan *adjective*
a tan colour. bronze, brownish-yellow, khaki, tawny, yellowish-brown.

tangible *adjective*
tangible proof. concrete, palpable, real, solid, substantial.
OPPOSITE intangible.

tangle *verb*
He tangled the wires. confuse, entangle, entwine, knot, snarl, twist.
OPPOSITE untangle.
tangle *noun*
a tangle of threads. confusion, jumble, jungle, knot, maze, muddle, snarl, web.

tangled *adjective*
tangled hair. dishevelled, knotted, knotty, matted, ruffled, tousled, unkempt.
OPPOSITE neat.

tangy *adjective*
a tangy lemon jelly. acid, piquant, sharp, sour, tart.

tank *noun*
1 *a water tank.* cistern, reservoir, vat.
2 *a fish tank.* aquarium.

tantalise *verb*
He tantalised the dog with a piece of meat. entice, lead on, tease, tempt, torment.
OPPOSITE gratify.

tantrum *noun*
fit of temper, hysterics, outburst, paddy (*informal*), rage.

tap[1] *noun*

Turn off the tap. faucet, stopcock, valve.

tap *verb*

They tapped the wine from the cask. drain, draw off, extract, siphon off.

tap[2] *verb*

She tapped on the glass. hit, knock, patter, rap, strike.

tape *noun*

1 *The labels are made from cotton tape.* binding, ribbon, strip.

2 *She fastened the package with tape.* adhesive tape, insulating tape, masking tape, packing tape, Sellotape (*trade mark*), sticky tape.

3 *a tape of the show.* audiotape, cassette, tape recording, video, videotape.

tape *verb*

1 *She taped the ends down.* fasten, fix, seal, sellotape, stick.

2 *He taped the concert.* record, tape-record, video, videotape.

taper *verb*

The stick tapers to a point. narrow, thin.

taper off *Business tapers off in winter.* decline, decrease, die down, diminish, peter out, reduce, slacken off, tail off, wane.

OPPOSITE expand.

target *noun*

a fundraising target. aim, goal, object, objective.

tarnish *verb*

1 *The metal tarnishes in damp conditions.* blacken, discolour, dull, stain.

OPPOSITE shine.

2 *His reputation was tarnished by the affair.* blacken, smirch, stain, sully, taint.

OPPOSITE enhance.

tart[1] *adjective*

1 *a tart flavour.* acid, acidic, astringent, piquant, sharp, sour, tangy.

OPPOSITE sweet.

2 *a tart reply.* acid, caustic, cutting, sharp.

OPPOSITE gentle.

tart[2] *noun*

a baked tart. flan, pastry, pie, quiche, tartlet.

task *noun*

They all have tasks to perform. assignment, charge, chore, commission, duty, errand, function, job, mission, work.

take to task admonish, castigate, censure, chastise, chide (*old use*), criticise, rebuke, reprimand, reproach, scold, tell off (*informal*), tick off (*informal*), upbraid.

OPPOSITE commend.

taste *noun*

1 *a pleasant taste.* flavour, savour.

2 *He had a small taste of the cheese.* bit, bite, morsel, mouthful, nibble, piece, sample, titbit.

3 *She had a taste of the juice.* mouthful, sample, sip, swallow.

4 *He developed a taste for travel.* appetite, fondness, inclination, liking, love.

OPPOSITE distaste.

5 *He has good taste in clothes.* discernment, discrimination, judgement, refinement.

taste *verb*

He tasted the soup. sample, sip, test, try.

tasteful *adjective*

tasteful furnishings. attractive, elegant, graceful, handsome, refined, stylish.

OPPOSITE tasteless.

tasteless *adjective*

1 *a tasteless drink.* bland, flavourless, insipid, weak, wishy-washy.

OPPOSITE tasty.

2 *a tasteless joke.* coarse, crude, improper, indelicate, offensive, unseemly, vulgar.

3 *tasteless decorations.* cheap, garish, gaudy, kitsch, showy, tawdry, unattractive.

OPPOSITE tasteful.

tasty *adjective*

a tasty meal. appetising, delectable, delicious, flavoursome, mouth-watering, palatable, scrumptious (*informal*), yummy (*informal*).

OPPOSITE bland.

tattered *adjective*

tattered clothes. frayed, holey, ragged, ripped, tatty (*informal*), threadbare, torn, worn-out.

a b c d e f g h i j k l m n o p q r s t u v w x y z

tatters *plural noun*
clothes in tatters. rags, shreds.

tatty *adjective* (*informal*)
tatty clothes. frayed, holey, moth-eaten, old, patched, ragged, scruffy, shabby, tattered, untidy, worn.

taunt *verb*
They taunted him because he was short. gibe, jeer at, make fun of, mock, poke fun at, ridicule, scoff at, sling off at (*Australian informal*), sneer at, take the mickey out of (*informal*), tease, torment.

taut *adjective*
a taut muscle. taut elastic. stretched, tense, tight.
OPPOSITE slack.

tavern *noun*
see PUB.

tax *noun*
a tax on wages, goods, services, etc. charge, customs, duty, excise, impost, levy, rates, slug (*Australian informal*), tariff, taxation, toll.

taxi *noun*
cab, taxicab.

taxing *adjective*
a taxing job. challenging, demanding, difficult, draining, exhausting, hard, onerous, strenuous, stressful, tiring, tough.
OPPOSITE easy.

teach *verb*
He has taught many students. coach, drill, educate, enlighten, indoctrinate, inform, instruct, lecture, school, train, tutor.

teacher *noun*
chalkie (*Australian slang*), coach, educator, governess, guru, headmaster, headmistress, instructor, lecturer, master, mentor, mistress, pedagogue (*old use*), preacher, principal, professor, rabbi, schoolmaster, schoolmistress, schoolteacher, trainer, tutor.

teaching *noun*
language teaching. education, instruction, training, tuition.

team *noun*
1 a netball team. club, line-up, side, squad.
2 a team of workers. band, corps, crew, force, gang, group, staff, unit.
team *verb*
team up They teamed up to do the research. band together, collaborate, combine, cooperate, join forces, unite.

tear *verb*
1 She tore her stockings. ladder, rip, shred, slash, slit, snag, split.
2 He tore his leg on the barbed wire. cut, gash, lacerate, mangle, mutilate.
3 He tore the photo away from them. grab, pluck, pull, rip, seize, snatch.
4 They tore past us. bolt, dart, dash, fly, gallop, hurry, hurtle, race, rip, run, rush, shoot, speed, sprint, spurt, streak, sweep, whiz, zip.
OPPOSITE crawl.
tear *noun*
a tear in clothes, skin, etc. gash, hole, laceration, rip, rupture, slash, slit, split.
tear apart The issue is tearing the people apart. break up, divide, split.
OPPOSITE unite.
tear down The men tore down the old shed. demolish, level, pull down, rip down.
OPPOSITE erect.

tearful *adjective*
tearful mourners at a funeral. crying, emotional, sobbing, teary (*informal*), upset, weepy (*informal*).

tease *verb*
1 They teased him because he wore glasses. gibe, make fun of, pay out, poke fun at, rag, rib (*informal*), ridicule, sling off at (*Australian informal*), stir (*informal*), take the mickey out of (*informal*).
2 The cat will bite you if you tease her. annoy, bait, bother, molest, pester, provoke, tantalise, taunt, torment.

teat *noun*
an animal's teats. dug, nipple.

technical *adjective*
1 technical studies. applied, mechanical, practical.
2 technical language. scientific, specialised, specialist.

technique *noun*
1 *a technique for removing splinters.* approach, knack, manner, method, procedure, system, trick, way.
2 *artististic technique.* art, craft, skill.

tedious *adjective*
a tedious book. tedious work. boring, dreary, dull, humdrum, laborious, long-winded, monotonous, stodgy, tiresome, tiring, unexciting, uninteresting, wearisome.
OPPOSITE interesting.

teem[1] *verb*
The river teemed with fish. abound, be full (of), be overrun, brim, overflow, seethe, swarm.

teem[2] *verb*
It teemed all day. bucket down, pelt, pour, rain, rain cats and dogs (*informal*).

teenager *noun*
adolescent, juvenile, minor, youth.

teetotaller *noun*
abstainer, non-drinker, wowser (*Australian*).
OPPOSITE drinker.

telepathic *adjective*
telepathic communication. psychic.

telephone *noun*
blower (*informal*), phone.
telephone *verb*
call, dial, give someone a bell (*informal*), give someone a buzz (*informal*), give someone a call, phone, ring (up).

televise *verb*
The tennis match will be televised. broadcast, screen, telecast, transmit.

television *noun*
television receiver, television set, telly (*informal*), the box (*informal*), TV.

tell *verb*
1 *He told the story.* announce, broadcast, communicate, confess, describe, disclose, divulge, explain, impart, make known, mention, narrate, proclaim, recite, recount, relate, report, reveal, state.
2 *He told them of the dangers.* acquaint (with), advise, inform, notify, warn.
OPPOSITE conceal.

3 *She told a lie.* say, speak, utter.
4 *He promised he wouldn't tell.* blab, let the cat out of the bag, spill the beans (*slang*), squeal (*slang*), talk, tittle-tattle.
5 *People can't tell which is which.* determine, discern, discover, distinguish, identify, make out, recognise.
6 *She told them to put pens down.* command, direct, instruct, order.
tell off (*informal*)
He told them off for being late. admonish, blast (*informal*), castigate, censure, chastise, go crook at (*Australian informal*), lecture, rebuke, reprimand, reproach, rouse on (*Australian informal*), scold, tick off (*informal*).
OPPOSITE commend.
tell on *He'll tell on you.* betray, dob in (*Australian informal*), grass (on) (*slang*), inform on, rat on (*slang*), report, shop (*slang*), sneak on (*slang*), split on (*slang*).

tell-tale *noun*
He was accused of being a tell-tale. blabbermouth, dobber (*Australian informal*), grass (*slang*), informer, sneak (*informal*), tale-bearer.
tell-tale *adjective*
a tell-tale blush. give-away (*informal*), indicative, revealing, significant.

temper *noun*
1 *He is in a good temper.* disposition, frame of mind, humour, mood.
2 *She did it in a temper.* fury, paddy (*informal*), rage, tantrum.
3 *a fit of temper.* anger, fury, hotheadedness, irritation, peevishness, petulance, rage, wrath.
4 *He kept his temper.* calmness, composure, cool, self-control.

temperament *noun*
a lively temperament. character, disposition, make-up, nature, personality, spirit, temper.

temperamental *adjective*
a temperamental person. capricious, changeable, emotional, erratic, excitable, fickle, hotheaded, moody, touchy, unpredictable, volatile.
OPPOSITE steady.

a b c d e f g h i j k l m n o p q r s t u v w x y z

temperate *adjective*
a temperate climate. gentle, mild, moderate.
OPPOSITE harsh.

tempest *noun*
The tempest raged. cyclone, gale, hurricane, storm, tornado, typhoon.

tempestuous *adjective*
tempestuous weather. blustery, rough, squally, stormy, turbulent, violent, wild, windy.
OPPOSITE calm.

temple *noun*
church, gurdwara, mosque, pagoda, sanctuary, shrine, stupa, synagogue, tabernacle.

tempo *noun*
a fast tempo. pace, rate, speed.

temporary *adjective*
1 *a temporary feeling.* brief, ephemeral, fleeting, momentary, passing, short-lived, transient, transitory.
OPPOSITE lasting.
2 *the temporary principal.* acting, provisional, relieving.
OPPOSITE permanent.
3 *temporary measures.* interim, short-term, stopgap.
OPPOSITE permanent.

tempt *verb*
He tempted the dog with a bone. attract, bait, coax, entice, lure, seduce, tantalise.

temptation *noun*
The chocolates were a big temptation. attraction, bait, draw, enticement, incentive, inducement, lure.

tempting *adjective*
a tempting offer. alluring, appealing, attractive, enticing, inviting, irresistible, seductive.

tenant *noun*
The owner leaves the gardening to the tenant. inhabitant, lessee, occupant, resident.

tend[1] *verb*
He tends the sheep. She tended the patient. attend to, care for, cherish, keep an eye on, keep watch over, look after, mind, nurse, take care of, watch.
OPPOSITE neglect.

tend[2] *verb*
She tends to cry a lot. be apt, be disposed, be inclined, be liable, be prone.

tendency *noun*
He has a tendency to mope. disposition, inclination, predisposition, propensity, readiness.

tender[1] *adjective*
1 *tender meat.* edible, soft, succulent.
OPPOSITE tough.
2 *tender plants.* delicate, fragile, frail.
OPPOSITE hardy.
3 *of tender age.* immature, vulnerable, young, youthful.
OPPOSITE old.
4 *His knee was tender after the accident.* painful, raw, sensitive, sore.
5 *They need tender care.* affectionate, compassionate, fond, gentle, kind, loving.

tender[2] *verb*
He tendered his resignation. give, hand in, offer, present, submit.
tender *noun*
Each company submitted a tender for the work. bid, offer, proposal, quotation, quote (*informal*).

tender-hearted *adjective*
caring, compassionate, humane, kind, kind-hearted, merciful, soft-hearted, sympathetic, warm-hearted.
OPPOSITE hard-hearted.

tense *adjective*
1 *a tense muscle.* stiff, strained, stretched, taut, tight.
OPPOSITE relaxed.
2 *He was tense before the interview.* anxious, apprehensive, edgy, highly-strung, jumpy, keyed up, nervous, nervy, uneasy, uptight (*informal*).
OPPOSITE calm, relaxed.
3 *a tense situation.* explosive, fraught, nerve-racking, strained, stressful, uneasy, volatile.
OPPOSITE calm.

tension *noun*
1 *the tension of a rope.* stiffness, tautness, tightness.
OPPOSITE slackness.

2 *headaches caused by tension.* anxiety, strain, stress, suspense.
OPPOSITE calmness.

tent *noun*
big top, marquee, tepee, wigwam.

tentative *adjective*
a tentative suggestion. cautious, experimental, hesitant, provisional, trial, unconfirmed.
OPPOSITE firm.

term *noun*
1 *a term of office.* course, period, session, spell, stint, stretch.
2 *a university term.* semester, trimester.
3 *a scientific term.* expression, name, phrase, word.
term *verb*
What is this condition termed? call, designate, label, name.
come to terms with *He came to terms with his disability.* accept, face up to, learn to live with, reconcile yourself to.
terms *plural noun*
1 *the terms of the settlement.* conditions, provisions, specifications, stipulations.
2 *interest-free terms.* charges, fees, prices, rates.

terminal *adjective*
a terminal illness. deadly, fatal, incurable, mortal.
terminal *noun*
the bus terminal. depot, station, terminus.

terminate *verb*
1 *She terminated the conversation.* close, conclude, cut off, end, finish, round off, stop, wind up.
2 *The music terminated abruptly.* cease, come to an end, conclude, end, finish, stop.
OPPOSITE start.

terminus *noun*
the bus terminus. depot, last stop, station, terminal.

terrain *noun*
rocky terrain. country, ground, land, landscape, region, territory.

terrestrial *adjective*
1 *terrestrial life.* earthly.
OPPOSITE extraterrestrial.

2 *Cats are terrestrial animals.* land.
OPPOSITE aquatic.

terrible *adjective*
1 *a terrible plane crash.* appalling, catastrophic, disastrous, dreadful, ghastly, hideous, horrendous, horrible, horrific, shocking, terrifying.
2 *She suffered terrible pain.* awful, distressing, excruciating, extreme, fierce, frightful, intense, intolerable, severe, unbearable.
OPPOSITE mild.
3 (*informal*) *The weather has been terrible.* abominable (*informal*), abysmal (*informal*), appalling (*informal*), atrocious (*informal*), awful (*informal*), bad, dreadful (*informal*), foul, lousy (*informal*), miserable, rotten (*informal*), shocking (*informal*), unpleasant.
OPPOSITE pleasant.
4 (*informal*) *He's terrible at ball games.* bad, hopeless, incompetent, pathetic, useless (*informal*), woeful (*informal*).
OPPOSITE brilliant.

terrific *adjective* (*informal*)
1 *It cost a terrific amount.* astronomical, colossal, enormous, excessive, exorbitant, extravagant, huge, large, monumental, staggering, stupendous, tremendous.
OPPOSITE tiny.
2 *a terrific storm.* colossal, fierce, intense, mighty, severe, terrible, violent.
3 *She does a terrific job.* admirable, brilliant, excellent, extraordinary, fabulous (*informal*), fantastic (*informal*), fine, first-class, great, incredible, magnificent, marvellous, outstanding, phenomenal, remarkable, sensational, spectacular, splendid, super (*informal*), superb, unbelievable, wonderful.
OPPOSITE terrible.

terrify *verb*
The sounds terrified him. alarm, appal, dismay, freak out (*informal*), frighten, horrify, petrify, scare, terrorise.
OPPOSITE reassure.

terrifying *adjective*
a terrifying experience. alarming, frightening, hair-raising, horrifying, nightmarish, scary, spine-chilling.

a
b
c
d
e
f
g
h
i
j
k
l
m
n
o
p
q
r
s
t
u
v
w
x
y
z

territory *noun*
unfamiliar territory. area, country, district, land, region, terrain, zone.

terror *noun*
They were seized with terror. alarm, consternation, dismay, dread, fear, fright, horror, panic, trepidation.

terrorise *verb*
The child terrorised smaller children. bully, frighten, intimidate, menace, persecute, terrify, torment.

test *noun*
1 *a test of the car's performance.* analysis, assessment, check, evaluation, experiment, trial.
2 *a screen test.* audition, check, try-out.
3 *school tests.* exam (*informal*), examination, quiz.
test *verb*
1 *He tested the candidates.* assess, audition, evaluate, examine, question, quiz, screen.
2 *They tested the drug on volunteers.* check, experiment with, sample, trial, try out.

testify *verb*
The man testified that the accused had been with him. affirm, attest, bear witness, declare, give evidence, state under oath, swear.

testimony *noun*
1 *The witness presented his testimony.* affidavit, declaration, deposition, evidence, statement.
2 *The sacrifice was testimony of his love.* demonstration, evidence, indication, proof.

tether *noun*
The animal is on a tether. chain, halter, lead, leash, rope.
tether *verb*
He tethered the horses. secure, tie up.
OPPOSITE untether.
at the end of your tether at the end of your patience, at your wits' end, desperate.

text *noun*
1 *the text of the speech.* content, script, transcript, wording, words.
2 *The sermon was based on a biblical text.* passage, quotation, verse.

textbook *noun*
manual, primer, schoolbook, text.

textile *noun*
woven and knitted textiles. cloth, fabric, material, stuff.

texture *noun*
a fabric's texture. appearance, consistency, feel, grain, structure, weave.

thank *verb*
She thanked them for the gift. acknowledge, express appreciation to, express gratitude to.
thanks *plural noun*
He expressed his thanks. acknowledgement, appreciation, gratitude, thankfulness.
OPPOSITE ingratitude.

thankful *adjective*
appreciative, grateful, indebted, obliged, pleased.
OPPOSITE unappreciative.

thankless *adjective*
a thankless task. unappreciated, unrewarding, useless, vain.
OPPOSITE appreciated.

thaw *verb*
The ice thawed. defrost, liquefy, melt, soften, unfreeze.
OPPOSITE freeze.

theatre *noun*
a theatre for plays and concerts. auditorium, hall, playhouse.

theatrical *adjective*
a theatrical company. drama, show business, stage.

theft *noun*
burglary, larceny, pilfering, poaching, robbery, shoplifting, stealing, thieving.

theme *noun*
1 *The theme of her speech.* argument, keynote, matter, subject, topic.
2 *a musical theme.* air, melody, motif, tune.

theology *noun*
a course in theology. divinity, religion.

theoretical *adjective*
theoretical physics. abstract, pure.
OPPOSITE applied, practical.

theory *noun*
1 *He based his theory on observations of many cases.* argument, assumption, explanation, hypothesis, idea, notion, supposition, thesis, view.
OPPOSITE fact.
2 *the theory of music.* laws, principles, rules, science, system.
OPPOSITE practice.

therapy *noun*
occupational therapy. speech therapy. cure, healing, remedy, treatment.

therefore *adverb*
a=b and b=c. Therefore a=c. accordingly, consequently, hence, so, thus.

thick *adjective*
1 *a thick stick.* broad, chunky, fat, squat, stout, stubby, wide.
OPPOSITE thin.
2 *a thick layer.* deep, dense, heavy, solid.
OPPOSITE thin.
3 *a thick jumper.* bulky, heavy, woolly.
OPPOSITE light.
4 *thick grass.* abundant, bushy, dense, impenetrable, lush, luxuriant, profuse.
OPPOSITE sparse.
5 *a thick paste.* concentrated, condensed, heavy, solid, stiff, viscous.
OPPOSITE thin, watery.
6 *He's a bit thick.* dense, dim (*informal*), dull, dumb (*informal*), half-witted, obtuse, slow, stupid, unintelligent.
OPPOSITE quick-witted.

thicken *verb*
1 *The custard thickened.* clot, coagulate, congeal, set, solidify, stiffen.
OPPOSITE thin.
2 *He thickened the sauce by boiling it down.* concentrate, condense, reduce.
OPPOSITE dilute.

thickness *noun*
1 *a metre in thickness.* breadth, depth, diameter, width.
2 *several thicknesses of wood.* layer, ply.

thick-skinned *adjective*
After years of receiving criticism she became thick-skinned. hardened,
insensitive, tough.
OPPOSITE thin-skinned.

thief *noun*
bandit, brigand, burglar, bushranger, crook (*informal*), highwayman, housebreaker, kleptomaniac, looter, mugger, pickpocket, pilferer, robber, shoplifter.

thieve *verb*
see STEAL.

thin *adjective*
1 *a thin pipe.* fine, narrow.
OPPOSITE thick.
2 *thin material.* delicate, fine, flimsy, fragile, light, see-through, sheer, transparent.
OPPOSITE thick.
3 *a thin person.* bony, emaciated, gangling, gaunt, lanky, lean, puny, scraggy, scrawny, skinny, slender, slight, slim, spindly, weedy, wiry.
OPPOSITE fat.
4 *a thin covering of hair.* light, meagre, scant, scanty, sparse, wispy.
OPPOSITE profuse.
5 *The sauce is too thin.* dilute, runny, watery.
OPPOSITE thick.
thin *verb*
She thinned the soup. dilute, water down, weaken.
OPPOSITE thicken.

thing *noun*
1 *The shop sells all sorts of things.* article, item, object, product.
2 *They witnessed strange things.* act, deed, doing, event, feat, happening, incident, occurrence, phenomenon.
3 *We have things to discuss.* affair, business, concern, matter.
4 *There are one or two odd things about the case.* aspect, detail, feature, particular, point.
things *plural noun*
1 *Take all your things when you leave.* belongings, bits and pieces, clothes, effects, equipment, gear, goods, paraphernalia, possessions, property, stuff.
2 *Things began to improve.* circumstances, conditions, matters, the situation.

a
b
c
d
e
f
g
h
i
j
k
l
m
n
o
p
q
r
s
t
u
v
w
x
y
z

think *verb*
1 *He spent his time thinking.* brood, contemplate, meditate, muse, ponder, reason, reflect.
2 *He is thinking of resigning.* consider, contemplate, entertain the thought, give thought to, mull over.
3 *She can't think where she put it.* bring to mind, call to mind, recall, recollect, remember.
OPPOSITE forget.
4 *What do you think will happen?* believe, expect, imagine, reckon, suppose.
5 *It is thought to be a fake.* assume, believe, consider, deem, hold, judge, regard (as).
think up (*informal*)
He thought up a clever scheme. conceive, concoct, create, devise, dream up, invent, make up.

thin-skinned *adjective*
hypersensitive, over-sensitive, sensitive, touchy.
OPPOSITE thick-skinned.

thirst *noun*
a thirst for adventure. appetite, craving, desire, fancy, hankering, hunger, longing, passion, yearning.
thirst *verb*
thirst for *He thirsts for knowledge.* crave, desire, hanker after, hunger for, long for, yearn for.

thirsty *adjective*
dehydrated, dry, parched.

thorn *noun*
The rose thorns pricked her. needle, prickle, spike, spine.

thorny *adjective*
1 *a thorny plant.* prickly, spiky, spiny.
2 *a thorny problem.* complicated, difficult, hard, intricate, knotty, ticklish, troublesome.
OPPOSITE easy.

thorough *adjective*
1 *a thorough account.* blow-by-blow, close, complete, comprehensive, detailed, exhaustive, extensive, full, in-depth, minute.
OPPOSITE incomplete, superficial.
2 *a thorough worker.* careful, conscientious, diligent, methodical,

meticulous, painstaking, rigorous, scrupulous, systematic.
OPPOSITE careless, perfunctory.
3 *a thorough waste of time.* absolute, complete, out-and-out, outright, total, utter.

thoroughbred *adjective*
a thoroughbred animal. pedigree, pure-bred.

thought *noun*
1 *deep in thought.* contemplation, daydreaming, introspection, meditation, reflection, reverie.
2 *an interesting thought. her thoughts on the matter.* belief, concept, idea, notion, opinion, sentiment, view.
3 *He paid little thought to their feelings.* attention, concern, consideration, regard.

thoughtful *adjective*
1 *a thoughtful expression.* absorbed, broody, contemplative, pensive, reflective, serious, wistful.
2 *It was thoughtful of him to ring.* attentive, caring, considerate, helpful, kind, obliging.
OPPOSITE thoughtless.

thoughtless *adjective*
1 *It was thoughtless not to take an umbrella.* absent-minded, careless, forgetful, heedless, negligent, scatterbrained, unthinking.
2 *a thoughtless remark.* inconsiderate, indiscreet, insensitive, rude, selfish, tactless, unfeeling.
OPPOSITE considerate, thoughtful.

thrash *verb*
1 *He thrashed the pupil for lying.* beat, belt (*slang*), cane, flog, hit, lash, lay into (*informal*), wallop (*slang*), whack, whip.
2 *Our team thrashed their team.* beat, clobber (*slang*), defeat, lick (*informal*), overwhelm, paste (*slang*), pulverise, rout, slaughter, trounce.

thread *noun*
1 *a silken thread.* fibre, filament, strand, yarn.
2 *He lost the thread of the argument.* drift, plot, storyline, train of thought.

threadbare *adjective*
Her clothes were threadbare. frayed, holey, ragged, shabby, tattered, tatty (*informal*), thin, worn.

threat *noun*
There's a threat of rain. danger, risk, warning.

threaten *verb*
1 *The robber threatened them with a gun.* bully, intimidate, menace, terrorise.
2 *The bushfire threatened homes.* endanger, imperil, jeopardise, put at risk.

threatening *adjective*
threatening clouds. looming, menacing, ominous, sinister.

threshold *noun*
1 *He carried his wife over the threshold.* doorstep, entrance.
2 *the threshold of a new era.* beginning, brink, dawn, outset, start.
OPPOSITE end.

thrifty *adjective*
a thrifty housewife. economical, frugal, provident, sparing.
OPPOSITE extravagant.

thrill *noun*
1 *a thrill of excitement.* flutter, quiver, shiver, throb, tingle, tremor.
2 *She gets a thrill from diving.* buzz (*informal*), enjoyment, excitement, kick (*informal*), pleasure.
thrill *verb*
He thrilled the crowd with his antics. delight, electrify, excite, rouse, stir, wow (*slang*).

thrilling *adjective*
a thrilling experience. electrifying, exciting, exhilarating, heady, rousing, sensational, stirring.
OPPOSITE boring.

thrive *verb*
The plants thrive in wet conditions. do well, flourish, grow well.
OPPOSITE wither.

thriving *adjective*
a thriving industry. booming, flourishing, healthy, prosperous, successful.
OPPOSITE languishing.

throb *verb*
His heart was throbbing. beat, palpitate, pound, pulsate, thump.
throb *noun*
the throb of the drums. beat, beating, pulse, vibration.

throng *noun*
She was lost in the throng of shoppers. crowd, gathering, herd, horde, host, mass, mob, multitude, swarm.
throng *verb*
The people thronged round the singer. congregate, crowd, flock, gather, herd, mill, swarm.

throttle *verb*
choke, strangle, suffocate.

throw *verb*
1 *He threw the ball.* bowl, cast, chuck (*informal*), fling, heave, hurl, launch, lob, pelt, pitch, project, propel, shy, sling, toss.
OPPOSITE catch.
2 *She threw the book down on the table.* bung (*informal*), chuck (*informal*), dump, plonk, slam, toss.
3 *The question threw me.* bewilder, confuse, disconcert, fluster, perplex, rattle (*informal*), stump (*informal*).
throw *noun*
an accurate throw. delivery, fling, hurl, launch, lob, pitch, shot, shy, toss.
throw away *He threw away his unwanted books.* cast off, chuck out (*informal*), discard, dispose of, ditch (*slang*), dump, get rid of, reject, scrap, throw out.
OPPOSITE keep.
throw out
1 *He was thrown out of the building.* chuck out (*informal*), eject, evict, expel, kick out (*informal*), remove, turf out (*informal*).
2 *He threw out his old coat.* see THROW AWAY.
throw up *The boy threw up after the party.* barf (*slang*), be ill, be sick, chuck (*informal*), chunder (*Australian slang*), puke (*informal*), sick up (*informal*), spew, vomit.

a b c d e f g h i j k l m n o p q r s t u v w x y z

thrust *verb*
1 *He thrust his way forward.* elbow, force, jostle, push, shoulder, shove.
2 *He thrust the sword into his side.* drive, jab, lunge, plunge, poke, stab, stick.

thud *noun*
They heard a thud when he fell. bang, bump, clunk, crash, thump.

thug *noun*
He was assaulted by thugs. bully, delinquent, gangster, hoodlum, hooligan, mugger, rough, ruffian, tough.

thumb *verb*
She thumbed through the book. browse, flick, flip, leaf, skim.

thump *verb*
1 *He thumped the other boy.* bash, batter, beat, clobber (*slang*), clout (*informal*), hammer, hit, knock, pound, punch, quilt (*Australian slang*), slog, slug, sock (*slang*), stoush (*Australian slang*), strike, wallop (*slang*), whack.
2 *Her heart was thumping.* pound, pulsate, throb.
thump *noun*
She came down with a thump. bang, bump, clunk, crash, thud.

thunder *noun*
the thunder of drums. boom, roar, roll, rumble.

thus *adverb*
We were early and thus able to get a seat. accordingly, consequently, hence, so, therefore.

thwart *verb*
They thwarted his attempts to escape. block, foil, frustrate, hamper, hinder, obstruct, prevent, stonker (*Australian slang*), stymie (*informal*).
OPPOSITE assist.

tick *noun* (*informal*)
He'll be with you in a tick. flash, instant, jiffy, minute, moment, second, trice.
tick off
1 *She ticked off the things she had.* check off, mark off.
2 (*informal*) *He was ticked off for being late.* admonish, castigate, censure, chastise, chide (*old use*), rap over the knuckles, rebuke, reprimand, reproach,
scold, tell off (*informal*), upbraid.
OPPOSITE praise.

ticket *noun*
1 *You need a ticket to enter.* coupon, pass, permit, token, voucher.
2 *a price ticket.* label, tab, tag.
3 *a parking ticket.* fine, notice, notification.

tickle *verb*
She tickled her under the arm. stroke, touch.
tickle *noun*
He felt a tickle in his throat. itch, tingle.

ticklish *adjective*
a ticklish problem. awkward, delicate, difficult, knotty, thorny, tricky.
OPPOSITE simple.

tide *noun*
The fisherman watches the tide. current, ebb and flow.

tidy *adjective*
1 *The office is tidy.* methodical, neat, orderly, shipshape, spick and span, straight, systematic, uncluttered.
OPPOSITE messy, untidy.
2 *She has a tidy appearance.* neat, presentable, smart, spruce, trim, well-groomed.
OPPOSITE scruffy.
3 *tidy writing.* careful, legible, neat, readable.
OPPOSITE messy.
tidy *verb*
1 *He tidied his room.* arrange, clean up, neaten, organise, sort out, straighten.
OPPOSITE mess up.
2 *She tidied herself up.* clean up, groom, smarten up, spruce up.

tie *verb*
1 *He tied the two pieces together.* attach, bind, connect, fasten, hitch, join, knot, lace, lash, link, strap, truss, unite, yoke.
OPPOSITE separate, untie.
2 *They tied for second place.* be equal, be even, be level, be neck and neck, draw.
tie *noun*
1 *He wears a tie.* bow tie, cravat, necktie.
2 *The result was a tie.* dead heat, draw, stalemate.
tie in *His statement tied in with the others.* agree, be consistent, correspond, fit,

tally.

tie up *They tied up the boat.* moor, secure.
OPPOSITE untie.

tier *noun*
1 *tiers of seats.* bank, line, row.
2 *a wedding cake with three tiers.* layer, level.

tie-up *noun*
a tie-up between the two ideas. association, connection, link, relationship.

tight *adjective*
1 *a tight screw.* fast, firm, fixed, secure.
OPPOSITE loose.
2 *tight jeans.* close-fitting, skintight, snug.
OPPOSITE loose.
3 *a tight seal.* airtight, watertight.
4 *tight elastic.* stiff, stretched, taut, tense.
OPPOSITE loose.
5 *He's tight with money.* mean, miserly, niggardly, penny-pinching, stingy.
OPPOSITE generous.

tighten *verb*
1 *They tightened the rope.* stiffen, stretch, tauten, tense.
OPPOSITE slacken.
2 *The blood vessel tightened.* constrict, contract, narrow.
OPPOSITE dilate.

till[1] *verb*
He tilled the soil. cultivate, farm, plough, work.

till[2] *noun*
The money is in the till. cash drawer, cash register, peter (*Australian slang*).

tilt *verb*
The boat tilted. incline, lean, list, sway, tip.
tilt *noun*
a tilt in the floor. cant, rake, slant, slope.

timber *noun*
beams, boards, logs, lumber, planks, wood.

time *noun*
1 *in Roman times.* age, days, epoch, era, period.

2 *at this time.* date, day, hour, instant, juncture, moment, occasion, opportunity, point, stage.
3 *a long time.* duration, interval, period, phase, season, session, spell, stretch, term, while.
on time *The bus arrived on time.* on schedule, on the dot, on the knocker (*Australian informal*), punctually.

timetable *noun*
a bus timetable. programme, schedule.

timid *adjective*
as timid as a mouse. bashful, chicken (*informal*), cowardly, coy, diffident, faint-hearted, fearful, frightened, mousy, nervous, pusillanimous, sheepish, shy, sooky (*Australian informal*), timorous, underconfident, unheroic, wussy (*slang*).
OPPOSITE bold.

tin *noun*
1 *The sugar is stored in a tin.* can, canister.
2 *a cake tin.* pan.

tinge *verb*
The sky was tinged with pink. colour, dye, stain, tint.
tinge *noun*
1 *a tinge of pink.* colour, shade, tint.
2 *a tinge of sadness.* hint, suggestion, touch, trace.

tingle *verb*
Her toes tingled. prickle, sting, tickle.

tinker *verb*
He likes to tinker with cars. fiddle, mess about, play.

tinkle *noun*
the tinkle of a bell. chime, ding, jingle, peal, ring.

tint *noun*
a bluish tint. colour, dye, hue, pigment, shade, stain, tinge, tone.

tiny *adjective*
baby, compact, diminutive, imperceptible, infinitesimal, insignificant, little, microscopic, midget, miniature, minuscule, minute, negligible, pocket-sized, skimpy, small, teeny (*informal*), undersized, wee

a
b
c
d
e
f
g
h
i
j
k
l
m
n
o
p
q
r
s
t
u
v
w
x
y
z

(*informal*), weeny (*informal*).
OPPOSITE enormous.

tip¹ *noun*

1 *a pencil with a sharp tip.* end, extremity, point.
2 *The tip of the mountain was covered in snow.* apex, cap, crest, crown, peak, pinnacle, summit, top.
OPPOSITE base.

tip² *verb*

The boat tipped. incline, lean, list, tilt.
tip *noun*
1 *The waitress receives tips.* gift, gratuity, present.
2 *a tip on how to peel onions.* advice, clue, hint, pointer, suggestion, warning, wrinkle (*informal*).
3 *a rubbish tip.* dump.
tip over
1 *The boat tipped over.* capsize, keel over, overturn, topple over.
2 *She tipped over the rubbish basket.* knock over, overturn, spill, up-end, upset, upturn.

tire *verb*

The walk tired her. drain, exhaust, fatigue, wear out, weary.
OPPOSITE invigorate.

tired *adjective*

He was tired after his hard work. bushed (*informal*), dog-tired, done in (*informal*), drained, drowsy, exhausted, fagged (*informal*), fatigued, jaded, languid, listless, pooped (*informal*), sapped, sleepy, weary, whacked (*informal*), worn out, zapped (*slang*), zonked (*slang*).
OPPOSITE energetic.
tired of *She was tired of cleaning.* bored of, browned off with (*slang*), fed up with, jack of (*Australian slang*), sick of.

tiredness *noun*

drowsiness, exhaustion, fatigue, languor, lassitude, lethargy, listlessness, sleepiness, weariness.
OPPOSITE vitality.

tireless *adjective*

a tireless person. energetic, hard-working, indefatigable, industrious, unflagging, untiring.
OPPOSITE lazy.

tiresome *adjective*

1 *a tiresome person.* annoying, bothersome, exasperating, irksome, irritating, troublesome.
2 *a tiresome book.* boring, dreary, dull, tedious, uninteresting, wearisome.
OPPOSITE interesting.

tiring *adjective*

a tiring job. arduous, exhausting, hard, laborious, strenuous, taxing, tiresome, wearing, wearisome, wearying.
OPPOSITE easy.

titbit *noun*

delicious titbits. bit, delicacy, morsel, nibble, snack.

title *noun*

1 *the title of a picture.* caption, heading, inscription, name.
2 *a person's title.* designation, position, rank, status.
title *verb*
She titled the book 'Dogs'. call, designate, entitle, label, name.

titter *noun*

titters from the ladies. chuckle, giggle, snicker, snigger.

tittle-tattle *verb*

They tittle-tattled about classmates. blab, chatter, gossip, tattle, tell tales.
tittle-tattle *noun*
Don't believe all that tittle-tattle you hear. chatter, chit-chat, gossip, hearsay, tattle.

toast *verb*

1 *He toasted the cheese.* brown, cook, grill.
2 *The guests toasted the bride and groom.* drink to, raise your glass to, salute.

toboggan *noun*

luge, sled, sledge.

toddler *noun*

baby, child, infant, preschooler.

together *adverb*

1 *They were working together.* closely, cooperatively, in collaboration, jointly, side by side.
OPPOSITE independently.
2 *They answered together.* in chorus, in unison, simultaneously.
OPPOSITE separately.

toil *verb*
She toiled for hours in the kitchen. beaver away, labour, slave, slog, strive, sweat, work.
toil *noun*
the reward after years of toil. drudgery, effort, exertion, grind, industry, labour, slog, sweat (*informal*), work, yakka (*Australian informal*).

toilet *noun*
bathroom, convenience, dunny (*Australian slang*), Gents (*informal*), Ladies, lavatory, loo (*informal*), men's, powder room, privy, rest room, toot (*Australian informal*), urinal, washroom, water closet, WC, women's.

token *noun*
1 *a token of our gratitude.* evidence, expression, indication, keepsake, mark, memento, sign, symbol.
2 *a book token.* coupon, voucher.
3 *The machine takes tokens.* counter, disc.

tolerable *adjective*
1 *The pain was only just tolerable.* bearable, endurable.
OPPOSITE intolerable.
2 *a tolerable meal.* acceptable, adequate, fair, OK (*informal*), passable, reasonable, satisfactory.

tolerant *adjective*
She is tolerant of other people. broad-minded, easygoing, forbearing, forgiving, indulgent, lenient, liberal, long-suffering, open-minded, patient, permissive, understanding.
OPPOSITE intolerant, narrow-minded.

tolerate *verb*
1 *They will not tolerate rudeness.* accept, admit, allow, condone, permit.
2 *He cannot tolerate the pain.* abide, bear, cope with, endure, put up with, stand, take.

toll[1] *noun*
1 *They pay a toll to use the expressway.* charge, fee, levy, payment, tax.
2 *the death toll.* cost, damage, loss.

toll[2] *verb*
The bell tolled. chime, peal, ring, sound, strike.

tollway *noun*
expressway, motorway, turnpike (*American*).

tomb *noun*
crypt, grave, mausoleum, sepulchre, vault.

tombstone *noun*
gravestone, headstone, monument.

tone *noun*
1 *an apologetic tone.* expression, intonation, manner, note, sound.
2 *autumn tones.* colour, hue, shade, tinge, tint.
3 *the tone of the place.* atmosphere, character, feeling, mood, spirit.
tone *verb*
The cushions tone with the sofa. blend, harmonise, match.
OPPOSITE clash.
tone down He toned down his criticism. moderate, play down, soften, subdue, temper.

tongue *noun*
the mother tongue. language.

tongue-tied *adjective*
She was tongue-tied in front of an audience. dumb, mute, silent, speechless.

too *adverb*
1 *She is too protective.* excessively, extremely, overly.
2 *intelligent, and good-looking too.* also, as well, besides, furthermore, in addition.

tool *noun*
tools of work. apparatus, appliance, contraption, device, gadget, implement, instrument, machine, utensil; [*tools*] equipment, gear, hardware.

toot *verb*
He tooted the horn. beep, blast, honk, hoot, sound.

tooth *noun*
[*kinds of tooth*] bicuspid, canine, eye tooth, fang, incisor, milk tooth, molar, permanent tooth, premolar, wisdom tooth.

top *noun*
1 *the top of the hill.* apex, brow, crest, crown, peak, pinnacle, summit, tip,

a
b
c
d
e
f
g
h
i
j
k
l
m
n
o
p
q
r
s
t
u
v
w
x
y
z

vertex, zenith.
OPPOSITE bottom.
2 *the top of the queue.* front, head.
OPPOSITE end.
3 *a bottle top.* cap, cover, covering, lid, stopper.
top *adjective*
1 *the top position.* highest, maximum, supreme, uppermost.
OPPOSITE lowest.
2 *the country's top designers.* best, foremost, greatest, leading, outstanding, pre-eminent.
top *verb*
1 *He topped the list.* head, lead.
2 *Nobody could top that score.* beat, better, exceed, improve on, outdo, surpass.
3 *The trifle was topped with strawberries.* cap, cover, crown, finish, garnish.

topic *noun*
a conversation topic. issue, matter, point, subject, theme.

topical *adjective*
a topical issue. contemporary, current, live, up-to-date, up-to-the-minute.

topple *verb*
1 *He toppled down the stairs.* fall, stumble, totter, tumble.
2 *The ornament toppled off the shelf.* crash, fall, tip over, tumble.
3 *The crisis toppled the government.* bring down, oust, overthrow, overturn, unseat.

topsy-turvy *adjective*
a topsy-turvy house. chaotic, confused, disorderly, higgledy-piggledy, messy, mixed-up, muddled, upside-down.
OPPOSITE orderly.

torch *noun*
flashlight.

torment *noun*
He suffered mental and physical torment. agony, anguish, distress, misery, pain, suffering, torture.
torment *verb*
1 *She was tormented by doubts.* afflict, distress, haunt, plague, rack, torture, trouble, worry.
2 *The dog tormented the cat.* annoy, bait, harass, intimidate, molest, oppress,

persecute, pester, plague, provoke, tease, victimise.

torn *adjective*
torn material. holey, ragged, ripped, slit, split, tattered, tatty (*informal*).
OPPOSITE intact.

tornado *noun*
twister (*American*), whirlwind; see also STORM.

torrent *noun*
They were swept away in the torrent of water. cascade, deluge, downpour, flood, rush, spate, stream.

torture *noun*
He suffered the torture of losing a child. agony, anguish, pain, suffering, torment.
torture *verb*
1 *The prisoner was tortured to try to make him confess.* abuse, maltreat, mistreat, persecute, punish, torment.
2 *She was tortured by self-doubts.* afflict, distress, plague, rack, torment, trouble, worry.

toss *verb*
1 *He tossed the ball.* bowl, cast, chuck (*informal*), fling, heave, hurl, launch, lob, pitch, propel, sling, throw.
OPPOSITE catch.
2 *The boat tossed in heavy seas.* bob, heave, pitch, reel, rock, roll.
3 *He tossed and turned all night.* squirm, thrash, wriggle, writhe.
toss *noun*
a toss of the ball. delivery, fling, hurl, launch, lob, pitch, throw.

total *adjective*
1 *the total number.* combined, complete, cumulative, entire, full, overall, whole.
2 *total chaos.* absolute, complete, outright, perfect, pure, sheer, thorough, utter.
total *noun*
The total is 500. aggregate, amount, sum, sum total, whole.
total *verb*
1 *She totalled the bill.* add up, calculate, compute, tot up (*informal*), work out.

2 *The donations totalled $400.* add up to, amount to, come to, make, tot up to (*informal*).

totally *adverb*
absolutely, completely, entirely, fully, utterly, wholly.
OPPOSITE partially.

totter *verb*
The old man tottered. dodder, falter, reel, rock, shake, stagger, stumble, sway, teeter, wobble.

touch *verb*
1 *touch someone or something.* be in contact with, brush, caress, dab, feel, finger, fondle, graze, handle, manipulate, massage, maul, nudge, pat, paw, poke, press, prod, rub, strike, stroke, tap, tickle.
2 *Do not touch the switches.* fiddle with, interfere with, meddle with, play with, tamper with, tinker with.
3 *She was touched by their kindness.* affect, impress, move, stir.

touch *noun*
just a touch of coriander. dash, hint, pinch, suggestion, suspicion, tinge, trace.

in touch with
1 *She kept in touch with her friend.* in contact with, in communication with, in correspondence with.
2 *He keeps in touch with the latest developments.* familiar with, informed on, up to date with.

touch down *The aircraft touched down.* arrive, land.
OPPOSITE take off.

touch on *The article touches on many subjects.* cover, deal with, mention, refer to, speak of.

touch up *He touched up the painting.* fix up, improve, repair.

touch-and-go *adjective*
It's touch-and-go whether he'll live. chancy, dicey (*slang*), doubtful, iffy (*informal*), precarious, uncertain.
OPPOSITE certain.

touching *adjective*
a touching story. emotional, moving, poignant, rousing, stirring.

touchy *adjective*
1 *He's very touchy on the subject.* oversensitive, prickly, sensitive, thin-skinned.
OPPOSITE thick-skinned.
2 *a touchy subject.* delicate, sensitive, sore, thorny, ticklish, tricky.

tough *adjective*
1 *tough steak.* chewy, gristly, leathery.
OPPOSITE tender.
2 *made of tough material.* durable, hard-wearing, hardy, heavy-duty, indestructible, resistant, strong, sturdy, unbreakable.
OPPOSITE weak.
3 *a physically tough person.* beefy, brawny, burly, fit, hardy, robust, rugged, strapping, strong, sturdy.
OPPOSITE weak.
4 *a tough disciplinarian.* firm, inflexible, merciless, rigid, strict, uncompromising.
OPPOSITE soft.
5 *a tough job.* arduous, demanding, difficult, exacting, gruelling, hard, laborious, onerous, stiff, strenuous, taxing, uphill.
OPPOSITE easy.

toughen *verb*
toughen glass. harden, reinforce, strengthen.
OPPOSITE weaken.

tour *noun*
a tour of the city. excursion, expedition, jaunt, journey, outing, trip.
tour *verb*
They are touring Europe. explore, go round, holiday in, travel round, visit.

tourist *noun*
globe-trotter, holidaymaker, sightseer, traveller, tripper, visitor.

tournament *noun*
This match is the last in the tournament. championship, competition, contest, series.

tow *verb*
The truck towed the car. drag, draw, haul, pull.
OPPOSITE push.

a
b
c
d
e
f
g
h
i
j
k
l
m
n
o
p
q
r
s
t
u
v
w
x
y
z

tower *noun*
belfry, keep, minaret, pagoda, skyscraper, steeple, turret.
tower *verb*
The new building towers above the rest. loom, rise, soar, stand out, stick up.

towering *adjective*
a towering office block. high, lofty, multi-storey, tall.

town *noun*
1 *a small country town.* community, hamlet, settlement, township, village.
2 *They moved from the town to the country.* big smoke (*informal*), city, metropolis.
OPPOSITE bush, country.

toxic *adjective*
a toxic chemical. deadly, lethal, poisonous.
OPPOSITE non-toxic.

toy *noun*
plaything.

trace *noun*
1 *They left without a trace.* evidence, indication, mark, sign, track, trail.
2 *a trace of bitterness in her voice.* element, hint, overtone, shade, shadow, tinge.
3 *The sauce had just a trace of vinegar.* bit, dash, drop, hint, pinch, suggestion, suspicion, touch.
trace *verb*
1 *They traced their missing cat.* discover, find, locate, recover, retrieve, track down.
2 *The book traces the development of the language.* chart, delineate, map, outline, record.
3 *They traced the map using greaseproof paper.* copy, draw over.

track *noun*
1 *animal tracks.* footprint, mark, print, scent, spoor, trace, trail.
2 *The researchers seem to be on the right track.* course, line, path, tack.
3 *a narrow bush track.* lane, path, road, trail.
4 *The horses raced round the track.* circuit, course, racecourse, racetrack.
5 *a train track.* line, rails, railway line.

track *verb*
The police tracked the thief. follow, hunt, pursue, shadow, stalk, tail (*informal*), trail.
track down *They tracked down the missing purse.* discover, find, locate, recover, retrieve, trace.

tract *noun*
large tracts of land. area, expanse, region, stretch, zone.

trade *noun*
1 *overseas trade.* business, buying and selling, commerce, dealing, traffic.
2 *She works in the clothing trade.* business, field, industry.
3 *He's a plumber by trade.* calling, career, craft, employment, job, occupation, vocation, work.
trade *verb*
1 *The two countries trade with one another.* buy and sell, deal, do business, market, traffic.
2 *She traded her stamps.* barter, exchange, swap.
trade mark brand, crest, emblem, hallmark, logo, name, proprietary name, symbol.

trader *noun*
suburban traders. dealer, merchant, retailer, shopkeeper, supplier.

tradesman, tradeswoman *noun*
a skilled tradesman. artisan, craftsman, workman.

tradition *noun*
Celebrating birthdays is a tradition. convention, custom, habit, practice.

traditional *adjective*
the traditional methods. classical, conventional, customary, established, habitual, orthodox, set, standard, time-honoured.
OPPOSITE new.

traffic *verb*
They were jailed for trafficking in heroin. deal, peddle, push (*informal*), sell, trade.

tragedy *noun*
the bushfire tragedy. calamity, catastrophe, disaster, misfortune.

tragic *adjective*
1 *a tragic sight.* distressing,
heartbreaking, pathetic, pitiful, sad,
wretched.
OPPOSITE happy.
2 *a tragic accident.* appalling, calamitous,
catastrophic, dire, disastrous, ghastly,
terrible, unfortunate.
OPPOSITE fortunate.

trail *verb*
1 *She trailed the blanket behind her.* drag,
draw, haul, pull, tow.
2 *Her dress trailed in the mud.* dangle,
drag, hang, sweep.
3 *He was tired and trailed behind the
others.* dally, dawdle, drop behind, fall
behind, lag, straggle.
OPPOSITE lead.
4 *They trailed the suspect.* follow, hound,
pursue, shadow, stalk, tail (*informal*),
track.
trail *noun*
1 *The ship left a trail.* mark, trace, wake,
wash.
2 *an animal's trail.* footmarks, footprints,
scent, spoor, track.
3 *a walking trail.* lane, path, track.
trail away *Her voice trailed away.* die
away, fade, grow fainter.

trailer *noun*
the trailers for films. advertisement, clip,
extract, preview.

train *noun*
1 *an endless train of cars.* cavalcade,
column, convoy, cortège, file, line,
motorcade, procession.
2 *a train of events.* chain, sequence,
series, set, string, succession.
train *verb*
1 *He trained the dog to stop at the corner.*
coach, condition, discipline, drill,
educate, instruct, teach.
2 *He's training for the big race.* exercise,
practise, prepare.
3 *She trained the gun on the tree.* aim,
direct, focus, level, point.

trainee *noun*
a clerical trainee. a trainee chef.
apprentice, cadet, learner, student.

trainer *noun*
a fitness trainer. coach, instructor,
teacher, tutor.

trait *noun*
an endearing trait. attribute,
characteristic, feature, idiosyncrasy,
peculiarity, quality.

traitor *noun*
a traitor to your country or friends.
betrayer, collaborator, deserter,
informer, Judas, quisling, renegade,
snake in the grass, turncoat.

tramp *verb*
1 *We heard him tramping along the
corridor.* clomp, clump, stamp, stomp,
stride.
2 *They tramped for miles through the
forest.* hike, march, plod, ramble, traipse
(*informal*), trek, trudge, walk.
tramp *noun*
The tramp slept under the bridge. beggar,
down-and-out, hobo, sundowner
(*Australian*), swagman (*Australian*),
vagabond, vagrant.

trample *verb*
He trampled the flowers. crush, flatten,
squash, stamp on, step on, tramp on,
tread on, walk on.

tranquil *adjective*
1 *a tranquil person.* calm, collected,
composed, peaceful, placid, sedate,
serene, unflappable (*informal*),
untroubled.
OPPOSITE agitated.
2 *tranquil surroundings.* peaceful, quiet,
restful, still, undisturbed.
OPPOSITE busy.

tranquillise *verb*
The medicine tranquillised her. calm,
quieten, relax, sedate, soothe.
OPPOSITE agitate.

transaction *noun*
a business transaction. deal, dealing,
negotiation, undertaking.

transfer *verb*
*They transferred the goods from the
warehouse to the shop.* carry, convey,
deliver, move, relocate, remove, shift,

a
b
c
d
e
f
g
h
i
j
k
l
m
n
o
p
q
r
s
t
u
v
w
x
y
z

shunt, switch, take, transplant, transport.

transform *verb*
The house was transformed into a hotel. alter, change, convert, modify, turn.

transformation *noun*
The old house has undergone a transformation. alteration, change, conversion, facelift, makeover, metamorphosis, revolution.

transient *adjective*
a transient feeling. brief, ephemeral, fleeting, momentary, passing, short-lived, temporary, transitory.
OPPOSITE permanent.

transition *noun*
1 *the transition from kindergarten to school.* change, changeover, move, progression, shift, switch.
2 *the transition from caterpillar to butterfly.* change, conversion, development, evolution, metamorphosis, transformation.

translate *verb*
Translate this sentence into simple English. change, convert, decode, interpret, paraphrase, render.

transmit *verb*
1 *The operator transmitted the message.* convey, dispatch, forward, pass on, relay, send.
OPPOSITE receive.
2 *The disease is transmitted by touch.* carry, communicate, pass on, spread, transfer.

transparent *adjective*
1 *transparent material.* filmy, gauzy, see-through, sheer.
2 *a transparent liquid.* clear, colourless, crystal-clear, limpid.
OPPOSITE cloudy, opaque.
3 *a transparent lie.* obvious, patent, unconcealed, undisguised, unmistakable.
OPPOSITE obscure.

transplant *verb*
The gardener transplanted the seedlings. move, relocate, shift, transfer.

transport *verb*
The company transports goods, people, etc. carry, cart, convey, ferry, freight, haul, move, shift, ship, take, transfer.

transport *noun*
He has no transport. conveyance, transportation, vehicle, wheels (*slang*).

trap *noun*
The animal was caught in the trap. ambush, booby trap, gin, net, pitfall, snare.

trap *verb*
1 *The farmer trapped the fox.* capture, catch, corner, ensnare, snare.
OPPOSITE release.
2 *He felt he'd been trapped into saying it.* deceive, dupe, set up (*informal*), trick.
3 *His leg was trapped under the car.* catch, hold, lock, pin down, stick.
OPPOSITE free.

trash *noun*
1 *He reads a lot of trash.* drivel, garbage, junk, nonsense, rubbish.
2 *Throw the trash in the bin.* garbage, junk, litter, refuse, rubbish, scraps, waste.

traumatic *adjective* (*informal*)
a traumatic experience. distressing, disturbing, painful, shocking, upsetting.

travel *verb*
1 *He travels to work by bus.* commute, go, journey.
2 *They travelled through South America.* cross, journey, roam, rove, tour, trek, voyage, wander.
3 *Good news travels fast.* be carried, be transmitted, move, spread.
4 *The walkers travelled thirty kilometres a day.* cover, go, progress.

travels *plural noun*
back from her travels. expedition, exploration, globe-trotting, journey, pilgrimage, tour, trip, voyage, wandering.

traveller *noun*
interstate and overseas travellers. backpacker, commuter, explorer, globe-trotter, gypsy, holidaymaker, nomad, passenger, sightseer, tourist, tripper,

vagabond, visitor, voyager, wanderer, wayfarer.

travelling *adjective*
a travelling musician. itinerant, peripatetic, roving, touring, vagabond, wandering.

treacherous *adjective*
1 *a treacherous person.* deceitful, disloyal, false, sneaky, traitorous, two-faced, untrustworthy.
OPPOSITE loyal.
2 *The roads were icy and treacherous.* dangerous, hazardous, perilous, precarious, unsafe.
OPPOSITE safe.

treachery *noun*
betrayal, disloyalty, treason.
OPPOSITE loyalty.

tread *verb*
She disliked treading on ants. stamp, step, tramp, trample, walk.

treason *noun*
executed for treason. betrayal, disloyalty, treachery.

treasure *noun*
The robbers buried the treasure. cache, fortune, hoard, riches, valuables, wealth.
treasure *verb*
She treasures the photo. appreciate, cherish, esteem, love, prize, value.
OPPOSITE despise.

treat *verb*
1 *He treated his staff badly.* behave towards, deal with, handle, manage.
2 *He treated it as a joke.* consider, look upon, regard, view.
3 *The subject is treated sensitively.* deal with, discuss, handle, present, tackle.
4 *The doctor treated the patient.* attend to, care for, look after, nurse, tend.
5 *The fabric has been treated with chemicals.* coat, dress, impregnate, process.
6 *She treated them to an ice cream.* shout (*Australian informal*), stand.
treat *noun*
1 *Going to a concert was a treat.* delight, joy, luxury, pleasure.

2 *The meal was his treat.* gift, present, shout (*Australian informal*).

treatment *noun*
cancer treatment. care, cure, medication, remedy, therapy.

treaty *noun*
The treaty was signed by both countries. agreement, alliance, armistice, convention, covenant, deal, pact.

tree *noun*
[*various trees*] acacia, ash, bangalay, bangalow, baobab, beech, birch, blackboy, blackbutt, bottlebrush, box, brigalow, cabbage tree, casuarina, cedar, coolibah, cypress, elm, eucalypt, fig, fir, flame tree, gidgee, grass-tree, gum, ironbark, jacaranda, jarrah, karri, kurrajong, lilly-pilly, mahogany, mallee, mangrove, maple, messmate, Moreton Bay fig, mulga, myall, oak, palm, paperbark, pine, plane, poplar, quandong, sally, sassafras, she-oak, spruce, stringybark, sycamore, tea-tree, wattle, wilga, willow, yarran, yew.

trek *noun*
a three-day bush trek. excursion, expedition, hike, journey, tramp, walk.
trek *verb*
They trekked through mud and long grass. hike, journey, traipse (*informal*), tramp, trudge, walk.

trellis *noun*
The plant grows on a trellis. frame, grille, lattice.

tremble *verb*
She trembled with fear. quake, quaver, quiver, shake, shiver, shudder, vibrate, wobble.
tremble *noun*
see TREMOR.

trembling *adjective*
His trembling voice revealed his nervousness. quavering, quivering, shaky, tremulous.

tremendous *adjective*
1 *a tremendous waste of money.* big, colossal, enormous, gigantic, huge, immense, large, mammoth, massive,

a
b
c
d
e
f
g
h
i
j
k
l
m
n
o
p
q
r
s
t
u
v
w
x
y
z

terrific (*informal*), vast.
OPPOSITE slight.
2 (*informal*) *a tremendous performance.*
excellent, exceptional, fabulous
(*informal*), fantastic (*informal*), fine,
great, impressive, magnificent,
marvellous, remarkable, stupendous,
superb, terrific (*informal*), wonderful.
OPPOSITE poor.

tremor *noun*
1 *a tremor in her voice, hands, etc.* quaver,
quiver, shake, shiver, shudder, tremble,
vibration, wobble.
2 *an earth tremor.* earthquake, quake
(*informal*), shock.

trench *noun*
The soldiers dug a trench. ditch, furrow,
sap.

trend *noun*
1 *an upward trend in prices.* drift,
inclination, movement, shift, tendency.
2 *She follows the trend in clothes.* craze,
fad, fashion, mode, style, vogue.

trendy *adjective* (*informal*)
trendy clothes. contemporary, cool
(*informal*), fashionable, in, modern,
stylish, up-to-date, with it (*informal*).
OPPOSITE old-fashioned.

trespass *verb*
1 *They trespassed on the farmer's land.*
encroach, intrude, invade.
2 (*old use*) *Forgive those who trespass
against you.* sin, transgress.
trespass *noun* (*old use*)
Forgive us our trespasses. iniquity,
misdeed, offence, sin, transgression,
wrong, wrongdoing.

trial *noun*
1 *a legal trial.* case, examination,
hearing, inquiry.
2 *The new machine underwent a trial.*
check, evaluation, experiment, test,
try-out.
3 *one of life's trials.* adversity, affliction,
hardship, ordeal, suffering, tribulation,
trouble, woe.
trial *adjective*
a trial period. experimental, pilot,
probationary, testing.

tribe *noun*
Each tribe has its own language. clan,
community, family, people, race.

tribunal *noun*
*The matter was reviewed by an independent
tribunal.* board, committee, court,
forum.

tributary *noun*
a tributary of the Murray. branch, creek,
rivulet.

tribute *noun*
pay tribute to *They paid tribute to his
leadership.* commend, compliment,
honour, pay homage to, praise.

trick *noun*
1 *He fell for that old trick.* bluff, con
(*informal*), confidence trick, deception,
dodge (*informal*), hoax, lurk (*Australian
informal*), manoeuvre, ploy, ruse,
stratagem, wile.
2 *a trick of the light.* illusion, mirage.
3 *There's a trick to making beds neatly.* art,
knack, method, secret, skill, technique,
way.
4 *conjuring tricks.* illusion, legerdemain,
magic, sleight of hand.
5 *She played a trick on the others.* gag,
hoax, joke, practical joke, prank.
trick *verb*
She tricked them into thinking they'd won.
bluff, cheat, con (*informal*), deceive,
defraud, dupe, fool, have on (*informal*),
hoax, hoodwink, kid (*informal*),
mislead, outwit, pull someone's leg,
swindle, take in.

trickery *noun*
They were taken in by his trickery.
cheating, craftiness, cunning, deceit,
deceitfulness, deception, fraud, hocus-
pocus, pretence, skulduggery, sleight of
hand, wiliness.
OPPOSITE honesty.

trickle *verb*
The water trickled from the hose. dribble,
drip, leak, ooze, seep.
OPPOSITE spurt.

trickster *noun*
charlatan, cheat, con man (*informal*),
crook (*informal*), fraud, racketeer, rogue,

sharp (*informal*), shicer (*Australian slang*), swindler.

tricky *adjective*
1 *a tricky person.* artful, crafty, cunning, deceitful, shifty, sly, underhand, wily.
OPPOSITE honest.
2 *a tricky task.* awkward, complicated, dangerous, delicate, difficult, hard, knotty, problematical, risky, ticklish.
OPPOSITE simple.

trifle *noun*
She worries over trifles. inessential, little thing, nothing, triviality.

trigger *verb*
This triggered a series of events. initiate, provoke, set off, spark off, start, touch off.

trim *adjective*
1 *He keeps trim by diet and exercise.* fit, lean, slender, slim.
OPPOSITE fat.
2 *a trim garden.* neat, orderly, shipshape, spick and span, spruce, tidy.
OPPOSITE untidy.
trim *verb*
1 *She trimmed their hair.* bob, clip, crop, cut, shear, snip.
2 *They trimmed the Christmas tree.* adorn, deck, decorate.

trimming *noun*
the dress trimming. decoration, ornamentation, trim.
trimmings *plural noun*
1 *wood trimmings. garden trimmings.* clippings, cuttings, scraps, shavings.
2 *roast pork with all the trimmings.* accompaniments, extras, frills, garnish.

trip *verb*
1 *They tripped lightly to the music.* dance, frolic, prance, skip.
2 *She tripped on the footpath.* fall over, slip, sprawl, stumble.
trip *noun*
an overseas trip. a trip in the car. cruise, drive, excursion, expedition, flight, holiday, jaunt, journey, outing, run, tour, trek, visit, voyage.

triumph *noun*
1 *the triumph of right over wrong.* conquest, success, victory.
OPPOSITE defeat.
2 *The play was a triumph.* hit (*informal*), sensation, smash hit (*informal*), success, winner.
OPPOSITE failure.
3 *Climbing the mountain was a great triumph.* accomplishment, achievement, conquest, feat.
triumph *verb*
He triumphed in battle. be victorious, conquer, succeed, win.
OPPOSITE lose.
triumph over *She triumphed over her enemies.* beat, conquer, defeat, overcome, overpower, vanquish.

triumphant *adjective*
the triumphant team. successful, victorious, winning.
OPPOSITE defeated, losing.

trivial *adjective*
a trivial matter. insignificant, little, minor, negligible, paltry, petty, small, superficial, trifling, unimportant.
OPPOSITE important.

troop *noun*
a troop of people. band, company, crew, flock, gang, group, horde, mob, pack.
troop *verb*
The children trooped in to their classroom. file, march, parade.
troops *plural noun*
armed forces, army, military, servicemen, servicewomen, soldiers.

trophy *noun*
a diving trophy. award, cup, medal, prize, shield.

trot *noun*
1 *A trot is faster than a walk.* jog, jogtrot, run.
2 (*Australian informal*) *She had a good trot.* innings, period, run, spell, spin (*Australian informal*).

trouble *noun*
1 *He offers help in times of trouble.* adversity, difficulty, distress, hardship, misfortune, sorrow, trial, tribulation.
OPPOSITE joy.

a
b
c
d
e
f
g
h
i
j
k
l
m
n
o
p
q
r
s
t
u
v
w
x
y
z

2 *She was weighed down by her troubles.* anxiety, burden, care, concern, problem, woe, worry.
3 *It's no trouble to do that.* bother, difficulty, hassle (*informal*), inconvenience, nuisance, problem.
4 *The finished product was worth the trouble it took.* care, effort, exertion, pains, struggle, work.
5 *Don't stir up trouble.* commotion, conflict, discord, disturbance, fuss, mischief, strife, turmoil, unrest.
OPPOSITE calm.
6 *engine trouble.* breakdown, defect, fault, malfunction, problem.
7 *stomach trouble.* affliction, ailment, disease, disorder, illness, pain, problem.

trouble *verb*
1 *What's troubling him?* ail, annoy, bother, bug (*informal*), distress, disturb, hassle (*informal*), hurt, inconvenience, irritate, oppress, perturb, plague, prey on, put out, upset, vex, worry.
OPPOSITE please.
2 *He didn't even trouble to find out.* bother, make the effort, take the time, take the trouble.
in trouble in a fix, in a jam (*informal*), in a mess, in a pickle (*informal*), in a predicament, in a scrape, in a spot (*informal*), in difficulties, in dire straits, in hot water (*informal*), in strife (*Australian informal*), in the soup (*informal*), up the creek (*informal*).

troublemaker *noun*
agitator, culprit, delinquent, hooligan, mischief-maker, rabble-rouser, ratbag (*Australian informal*), ringleader, stirrer (*Australian*).

troublesome *adjective*
1 *The mosquitoes are troublesome.* annoying, bothersome, distressing, irritating, pesky (*informal*), tiresome, vexing, worrying.
2 *a troublesome person.* disobedient, naughty, recalcitrant, trying, uncooperative, unmanageable, unruly.
OPPOSITE helpful.

trough *noun*
Water collected in the trough. channel, ditch, furrow, gully, gutter, trench.

troupe *noun*
a troupe of actors. band, company, group.

trousers *plural noun*
[*kinds of trousers*] bell-bottoms, breeches, chinos, cords, flares, hipsters, jeans, jodhpurs, moleskins, pants (*informal*), slacks, strides (*informal*).

truant *noun*
The school chases up truants. absentee, skiver (*informal*), wag (*informal*).
play truant absent yourself, bludge (*Australian informal*), play hookey (*informal*), skive (*informal*), stay away, wag (*informal*).

truce *noun*
The parties called for a truce. armistice, ceasefire, peace.

truck *noun*
He drives a truck. lorry, pick-up, road train (*Australian*), semi (*Australian informal*), semitrailer, van.

trudge *verb*
He trudged up the hill. lumber, plod, slog, traipse (*informal*), tramp, trek.

true *adjective*
1 *a true account.* accurate, actual, authentic, correct, exact, factual, faithful, genuine, honest, precise, reliable, right, strict, truthful.
OPPOSITE fictitious, untrue.
2 *He was the true heir.* authorised, genuine, legal, legitimate, proper, rightful.
OPPOSITE phoney (*informal*).
3 *a true friend.* constant, dependable, dinkum (*Australian informal*), dinky-di (*Australian informal*), faithful, loyal, real, reliable, sincere, true-blue, trustworthy.
OPPOSITE false.

trunk *noun*
1 *the trunk of a tree.* stem, stock.
2 *The rash was on her trunk but not on her limbs.* body, torso.
3 *She stores clothes in the trunk.* box, case, chest.
4 *an elephant's trunk.* proboscis, snout.

trunks *plural noun*
swimming trunks. bathers (*Australian*), costume, shorts, togs (*Australian informal*).

trust *noun*
1 *They have trust in God.* belief, confidence, conviction, faith, reliance.
OPPOSITE mistrust.
2 *a position of trust.* responsibility.
trust *verb*
1 *She trusted her children. He trusts in God.* believe in, depend on, have confidence in, have faith in, rely on.
OPPOSITE mistrust.
2 *We trust you will come to the party.* assume, expect, hope, presume, take it.

trusting *adjective*
He is too trusting when it comes to strangers. credulous, gullible, naive, unsuspecting, unsuspicious.
OPPOSITE suspicious.

trustworthy *adjective*
a trustworthy friend. dependable, faithful, honest, loyal, reliable, responsible, steadfast, sure, true, trusty (*old use*).
OPPOSITE unreliable, untrustworthy.

truth *noun*
1 *His story has the ring of truth.* accuracy, authenticity, reliability, truthfulness, veracity.
OPPOSITE falsity.
2 *Tell me the truth.* facts, reality.
OPPOSITE lies.

truthful *adjective*
1 *a truthful person.* frank, honest, open, sincere, straight, trustworthy.
OPPOSITE dishonest.
2 *a truthful account.* accurate, correct, factual, faithful, honest, reliable, true.
OPPOSITE inaccurate.

try *verb*
1 *He tried to answer the questions.* aim, attempt, endeavour, strive, struggle.
2 *He tried the ice cream.* sample, taste, test.
3 *They tried her patience.* strain, tax, test.
4 *A new judge tried the case.* adjudicate, hear, judge.

try *noun*
Have a try at it. attempt, bash (*informal*), crack (*informal*), go, shot (*informal*), stab (*informal*), whack (*informal*).
try out
1 *They tried out the treatment on volunteers.* check out, experiment with, test.
2 *He tried out for the school play.* audition, test.

trying *adjective*
a trying situation. annoying, difficult, exasperating, frustrating, irritating, stressful, taxing, tiresome, troublesome, vexing.

tub *noun*
He grew the plants in an old tub. barrel, bath, butt, cask, drum, pot.

tube *noun*
conduit, duct, hose, pipe.

tuberculosis *noun*
consumption (*old use*), TB (*informal*).

tuck *noun*
The dress has ornamental tucks. fold, pin-tuck, pleat.
tuck *verb*
She tucked her singlet into her pants. insert, push, shove, stick, stuff.

tuft *noun*
tufts of grass. bunch, clump, tussock.

tug *verb*
1 *He tugged the button off the mattress.* jerk, pluck, pull, wrench, yank.
2 *The ship was tugged into port.* drag, draw, haul, pull, tow.
OPPOSITE push.

tuition *noun*
private tuition. coaching, education, instruction, lessons, teaching, training.

tumble *verb*
1 *She tumbled down the stairs.* collapse, fall, plunge, roll, stumble, topple.
2 *Prices tumbled.* collapse, crash, drop, fall, nosedive, plummet, plunge, slump.
OPPOSITE increase.

tummy *noun* (*informal*)
abdomen, belly, paunch, stomach.

a
b
c
d
e
f
g
h
i
j
k
l
m
n
o
p
q
r
s
t
u
v
w
x
y
z

tumour *noun*

The surgeon removed the tumour. cancer, carcinoma, growth, lump.

tumult *noun*

The speaker could not be heard above the tumult. bedlam, chaos, commotion, confusion, din, disturbance, fracas, hubbub, hullabaloo, kerfuffle (*informal*), mayhem, noise, pandemonium, racket, riot, row, ruckus, rumpus, turmoil, uproar.
OPPOSITE peace.

tumultuous *adjective*

a tumultuous reception. boisterous, excited, noisy, rowdy, uproarious, wild.

tune *noun*

They sang a pleasant tune. air, melody, strain, theme.

tune *verb*

The engine needs to be tuned. adjust, regulate, set.

tuneful *adjective*

a tuneful song. catchy, harmonious, melodious, musical, pleasant.
OPPOSITE tuneless.

tunnel *noun*

adit, burrow, hole, mine, passage, shaft, subway, underpass.

tunnel *verb*

The wombat tunnelled under the fence. burrow, dig, excavate.

turbulent *adjective*

1 a turbulent mob. boisterous, disorderly, obstreperous, restless, riotous, rough, rowdy, unruly, violent, wild.
OPPOSITE peaceful.
2 turbulent weather. blustery, gusty, rough, stormy, tempestuous, violent, wild, windy.
OPPOSITE calm.

turf *noun*

grass, lawn, sod, sward.

turmoil *noun*

The place was in turmoil after the earthquake. agitation, bedlam, chaos, commotion, confusion, disorder, disturbance, mess, pandemonium,

tumult, upheaval, uproar.
OPPOSITE order.

turn *verb*

1 The merry-go-round turns. revolve, rotate, spin, swivel, twirl, whirl.
2 She turned to face me. circle, roll over, spin round, swing round, twist round, wheel round.
3 He turned the pages. flick, flip, leaf, riffle.
4 The truck turned the corner. go round, round.
5 Turn right. bear, deviate, diverge, veer.
6 He turned his thoughts to serious matters. direct, divert, shift, switch.
7 The grub turned into a moth. become, be transformed, change.
8 She turned the essay into a book. adapt, change, convert, make, modify, transform.

turn *noun*

1 a turn of the handle. revolution, rotation, twist, wind.
2 a road with many turns. angle, bend, corner, curve, hairpin bend, loop, turning, twist, wind.
3 She did me a good turn. act, action, deed, service.
4 Everyone had a turn. chance, go, move, opportunity, shot, spell, stint.
5 (*informal*) He gave me quite a turn. fright, scare, shock, start, surprise.

turn down He turned down their offer. decline, knock back (*informal*), pass up (*informal*), refuse, reject, spurn.
OPPOSITE accept.

turn off

1 He turned off the power. cut off, disconnect, switch off.
2 (*informal*) His bad manners turned people off. alienate, disgust, offend, put off, repel, repulse.

turn on

1 She turned on the washing machine. put on, start, switch on.
2 (*informal*) The idea didn't turn them on. animate, excite, interest, thrill.

turn out

1 He was turned out of his own home. chuck out (*informal*), eject, evict, expel, kick out (*informal*), remove, throw out, turf out (*informal*).

2 *Things turned out all right.* end up, happen, pan out, work out.

turn up
1 *The gloves eventually turned up.* be found, be located, materialise.
2 *She finally turned up.* appear, arrive, come, roll up (*informal*), show up.

turning point *noun*
a turning point in the research. breakthrough, crisis, crossroads, watershed.

tussle *noun*
Both men were injured in the tussle. battle, brawl, clash, conflict, fight, fracas, scrap (*informal*), scuffle, set-to, skirmish, squabble, struggle.

tutor *noun*
a private tutor. coach, educator, instructor, mentor, teacher.
tutor *verb*
He tutors students before exams. coach, instruct, teach.

tutorial *noun*
a university tutorial. class, discussion group, seminar.

tweet *verb*
The birds tweeted. cheep, chirp, chirrup, peep, twitter.

tweezers *plural noun*
pincers.

twiddle *verb*
He twiddled his pen. fiddle with, fidget with, play with, twirl.

twig *noun*
He collected twigs for the fire. shoot, stalk, stem, stick.

twilight *noun*
Headlights are needed at twilight. dusk, evening, gloaming, gloom, nightfall, sundown, sunset.
twilight *adjective*
the twilight hour. crepuscular.

twin *noun*
a person's twin. clone, double, look-alike.
twin *verb*
The towns were twinned. couple, link, match, pair.

twine *noun*
The parcel is tied with twine. cord, string, thread.

twinge *noun*
He felt a twinge in his stomach. ache, cramp, pain, pang, spasm, stitch, throb.

twinkle *verb*
The lights twinkled. blink, flash, flicker, glimmer, glitter, shimmer, shine, sparkle.

twirl *verb*
1 *The dancer twirled around the room.* loop, pirouette, revolve, rotate, spin, twist, whirl.
2 *He twirled his spaghetti round his fork.* coil, curl, twine, twist, wind.

twist *verb*
1 *He twisted the threads together.* braid, entwine, intertwine, interweave, plait, weave.
OPPOSITE unravel.
2 *He twisted the wire round a reel.* coil, curl, twine, twirl, wind, wrap.
3 *The road twists.* bend, curve, kink, loop, meander, turn, wind, zigzag.
OPPOSITE straighten out.
4 *She twisted her way through the tunnel.* squirm, worm, wriggle, writhe.
5 *He twisted his ankle.* pull, rick, sprain, wrench.
6 *The collision twisted the bodywork.* buckle, contort, crumple, distort, screw up, warp.
twist *noun*
1 *a road with many twists.* bend, corkscrew, curve, loop, turn, wind, zigzag.
2 *a twist in the hose.* coil, kink, knot, snarl, tangle.
3 *an unexpected twist in the story.* change, development, turn.

twisted *adjective*
1 *a twisted body.* bent, contorted, crooked, deformed, misshapen, screwed up.
2 *a twisted sense of humour.* kinky (*informal*), perverted, sick, warped.

twisty *adjective*
a twisty road. crooked, curved, serpentine, tortuous, winding, zigzag.
OPPOSITE straight.

a
b
c
d
e
f
g
h
i
j
k
l
m
n
o
p
q
r
s
t
u
v
w
x
y
z

twitch *verb*
He twitched when the needle pricked him.
fidget, flinch, jerk, jump, quiver, start,
wince, wriggle.
twitch *noun*
a facial twitch. blink, spasm, tic.

twitter *verb*
The birds twittered. cheep, chirp, chirrup,
peep, tweet.

two-faced *adjective*
deceitful, dishonest, false, hypocritical,
insincere.
OPPOSITE sincere.

type *noun*
1 *a type of dog, car, etc.* breed, category,
class, form, group, kind, make, model,
sort, species, strain, style, variety,
version.
2 *printed in bold type.* characters, font,
print, typeface.

typhoon *noun*
hurricane, tropical cyclone; see also
STORM.

typical *adjective*
1 *a typical winter's day.* average, normal,
ordinary, regular, representative,
standard.
OPPOSITE atypical.
2 *He answered with his typical rudeness.*
characteristic, customary, distinctive,
usual.
OPPOSITE uncharacteristic.

tyrannical *adjective*
a tyrannical leader. autocratic, cruel,
dictatorial, domineering, harsh,
oppressive, severe, unjust.
OPPOSITE democratic.

tyrant *noun*
The new king was a tyrant. autocrat,
bully, despot, dictator, slave-driver.

Uu

ugly *adjective*
1 *an ugly face, building, etc.* frightful, ghastly, grotesque, hideous, horrible, monstrous, repulsive, shocking, unattractive, unsightly.
OPPOSITE beautiful, handsome.
2 *The crowd was getting ugly.* hostile, menacing, nasty, threatening, unpleasant.
OPPOSITE pleasant.

ulterior *adjective*
ulterior motives. covert, hidden, secret, undisclosed.
OPPOSITE obvious.

ultimate *adjective*
1 *the ultimate syllable.* concluding, end, final, last.
OPPOSITE first.
2 *the ultimate cause.* basic, fundamental, primary, root, underlying.

umbrella *noun*
brolly (*informal*), parasol, sunshade.

umpire *noun*
Respect the umpire's decision. adjudicator, arbiter, arbitrator, judge, moderator, ref (*informal*), referee.
umpire *verb*
He umpired the contest. adjudicate, arbitrate, judge, moderate, referee.

unacceptable *adjective*
unacceptable language, behaviour, etc. improper, intolerable, objectionable, offensive, taboo, unsatisfactory, unseemly, unsuitable.
OPPOSITE acceptable.

unaccompanied *adjective*
an unaccompanied person. alone, lone, single, sole, solitary, solo, unescorted.
OPPOSITE accompanied.

unafraid *adjective*
bold, brave, courageous, dauntless, fearless, game, intrepid, plucky, undaunted, valiant.
OPPOSITE afraid.

unanimity *noun*
There was unanimity on the issue. accord, agreement, consensus, solidarity, unity.
OPPOSITE disagreement.

unassuming *adjective*
an unassuming person. diffident, modest, quiet, retiring, unassertive.
OPPOSITE bold.

unattractive *adjective*
an unattractive dress. drab, hideous, inelegant, plain, repulsive, tasteless, ugly, unappealing, unbecoming, unsightly.
OPPOSITE attractive.

unauthorised *adjective*
an unauthorised copy. illegal, pirated, unofficial.
OPPOSITE authorised.

unavoidable *adjective*
an unavoidable outcome. certain, destined, fated, inescapable, inevitable, necessary.
OPPOSITE avoidable.

unaware *adjective*
unaware of the dangers. ignorant, oblivious, unconscious, uninformed.
OPPOSITE aware.

unawares *adverb*
caught unawares. by surprise, off guard, unexpectedly.

unbalanced *adjective*
1 *The truck's load was unbalanced.* asymmetrical, lopsided, uneven.
2 *unbalanced reporting.* biased, one-sided, unfair.
OPPOSITE fair.
3 *mentally unbalanced.* crazy, deranged, insane, mad, unhinged, unsound, unstable.
OPPOSITE stable.

unbearable *adjective*
unbearable pain. excruciating, insufferable, intolerable.
OPPOSITE bearable.

unbeatable *adjective*
an unbeatable team. invincible, unconquerable, undefeatable, unstoppable.

unbecoming *adjective*
an unbecoming dress. unattractive, unflattering, unsuitable.
OPPOSITE becoming.

unbelievable *adjective*
an unbelievable story. amazing, astounding, extraordinary, far-fetched, implausible, incredible, unconvincing.
OPPOSITE credible.

unbeliever *noun*
see NON-BELIEVER.

unbiased *adjective*
an unbiased adjudicator. disinterested, fair, impartial, just, neutral, objective, open-minded, unprejudiced.
OPPOSITE biased.

unblock *verb*
unblock a drain. clear, free, unclog, unstop.

unbreakable *adjective*
unbreakable crockery. indestructible, solid, strong, sturdy, tough.
OPPOSITE fragile.

unbroken *adjective*
an unbroken series. complete, continuous, entire, intact, uninterrupted, whole.
OPPOSITE broken.

uncalled-for *adjective*
Her comments were uncalled-for. gratuitous, needless, unjustified, unnecessary, unsolicited, unwarranted.
OPPOSITE warranted.

uncanny *adjective*
1 uncanny noises. creepy, eerie, frightening, mysterious, scary, spooky (informal), strange, unearthly, weird.
2 uncanny accuracy. astonishing, extraordinary, incredible, remarkable, striking, unbelievable.

uncaring *adjective*
an uncaring person. callous, cold, hard-hearted, heartless, indifferent, insensitive, unfeeling, unsympathetic.
OPPOSITE compassionate.

uncertain *adjective*
1 She is uncertain about whether to go. doubtful, hesitant, indecisive, in two minds, undecided, unsure.
OPPOSITE decided.
2 uncertain weather. changeable, erratic, unpredictable, unreliable, variable.
OPPOSITE predictable.

unchangeable *adjective*
unchangeable quality. consistent, constant, dependable, reliable, unvarying.
OPPOSITE variable.

uncivilised *adjective*
1 an uncivilised tribe. barbarian, barbaric, barbarous, primitive, savage, wild.
2 uncivilised behaviour. boorish, rude, uncouth, uncultured, vulgar.
OPPOSITE civilised.

uncomfortable *adjective*
1 an uncomfortable situation. awkward, difficult, distressing, embarrassing, painful.
2 an uncomfortable feeling. anxious, awkward, embarrassed, nervous, troubled, uneasy, worried.
OPPOSITE comfortable.

uncommon *adjective*
an uncommon sight. abnormal, curious, exceptional, extraordinary, infrequent, odd, peculiar, rare, remarkable, special, strange, striking, unfamiliar, unusual.
OPPOSITE common.

uncommunicative *adjective*
He is shy and uncommunicative. quiet, reserved, reticent, retiring, secretive, silent, taciturn, tight-lipped, unforthcoming, unsociable.
OPPOSITE communicative.

uncomplimentary *adjective*
an uncomplimentary remark. critical, derogatory, disparaging, insulting, pejorative, rude, unkind.
OPPOSITE complimentary.

uncompromising *adjective*
an uncompromising attitude. hard-line, inflexible, rigid, strict, stubborn, unbending, unyielding.
OPPOSITE flexible.

unconditional *adjective*
unconditional love. absolute, complete, unlimited, unqualified, unreserved.
OPPOSITE conditional.

unconnected *adjective*
The two matters are unconnected. independent, separate, unrelated.
OPPOSITE connected.

unconscious *adjective*
1 *The victim was unconscious.* blacked out, insensible, knocked out, senseless.
OPPOSITE conscious.
2 *unconscious of what was happening.* oblivious, unaware.
OPPOSITE aware.
3 *an unconscious act.* automatic, instinctive, involuntary, mechanical, reflex, unintentional, unthinking.
OPPOSITE conscious.

uncontrollable *adjective*
1 *uncontrollable children.* headstrong, irrepressible, obstreperous, rebellious, undisciplined, unmanageable, unruly, wayward, wilful.
OPPOSITE manageable.
2 *an uncontrollable urge.* compulsive, irresistible, overwhelming.
OPPOSITE resistible.

unconventional *adjective*
unconventional behaviour. abnormal, eccentric, odd, offbeat, original, peculiar, strange, unorthodox, unusual, way-out, weird.
OPPOSITE conventional.

unconvincing *adjective*
an unconvincing excuse. feeble, flimsy, implausible, lame, unbelievable, unsatisfactory, weak.
OPPOSITE convincing.

uncooperative *adjective*
The workers were being deliberately uncooperative. difficult, obstructive, perverse, rebellious, stroppy *(informal)*, unhelpful.
OPPOSITE cooperative.

uncoordinated *adjective*
see CLUMSY.

uncouth *adjective*
an uncouth fellow. bad-mannered, coarse, loutish, rough, rude, uncivil, vulgar.
OPPOSITE polite.

uncover *verb*
They uncovered the truth. bare, dig up, disclose, discover, expose, reveal, unearth.
OPPOSITE cover up.

uncultivated *adjective*
uncultivated land. fallow, unused, virgin, waste, wild.
OPPOSITE cultivated.

undecided *adjective*
She is undecided about whether to go. ambivalent, in two minds, irresolute, open-minded, uncertain, unsure.
OPPOSITE decided.

undeniable *adjective*
an undeniable fact. certain, indisputable, indubitable, irrefutable, positive, sure, unquestionable.
OPPOSITE refutable.

under *preposition*
1 *a cellar under the house.* below, beneath, underneath.
OPPOSITE above.
2 *selling for under $20.* below, less than, lower than.
OPPOSITE over.
3 *He has several staff under him.* below, junior to, subordinate to.
OPPOSITE above.

underclothes *plural noun*
see UNDERWEAR.

underdone *adjective*
The meat was underdone. rare, undercooked.
OPPOSITE overcooked.

undergo *verb*
He must undergo treatment. bear, be subjected to, brave, endure, experience, go through, put up with, submit to.

underground *adjective*
1 *an underground cave.* subterranean.
2 *an underground organisation.* secret, undercover.

undergrowth *noun*
The rabbit hid in the undergrowth. brush, bushes, ground cover, shrubs.

a
b
c
d
e
f
g
h
i
j
k
l
m
n
o
p
q
r
s
t
u
v
w
x
y
z

underhand *adjective*
He used underhand methods to get what he wanted. crafty, crooked (*informal*), cunning, deceitful, devious, dishonest, fraudulent, shonky (*Australian informal*), sly, sneaky, unscrupulous.
OPPOSITE above board.

underline *verb*
This accident underlines the need for traffic lights. emphasise, highlight, point up, stress.

undermine *verb*
They undermined his leadership. destroy, erode, ruin, subvert, weaken.
OPPOSITE strengthen.

underneath *preposition*
underneath the floorboards. below, beneath, under.
OPPOSITE above.

underpants *plural noun*
boxer shorts, briefs, drawers, jocks (*slang*), knickers, panties (*informal*), pants, undies (*informal*).

underpass *noun*
subway, tunnel.
OPPOSITE overpass.

underprivileged *adjective*
underprivileged families. deprived, disadvantaged, needy, poor.

underrate *verb*
underrate a person. underestimate, undervalue.
OPPOSITE overrate.

underside *noun*
back, bottom, reverse, underneath, wrong side.

undersized *adjective*
an undersized person, plant, etc. diminutive, dwarf, little, midget, puny, short, small, stunted, tiny, underdeveloped.
OPPOSITE oversized.

understand *verb*
1 He couldn't understand what was going on. comprehend, cotton on to (*informal*), fathom, follow, get (*informal*), grasp, interpret, know, realise, see, take in.
OPPOSITE misunderstand.

2 Can you understand what he has written? decipher, decode, make head or tail of, make out.
3 He understands how you feel. appreciate, empathise with, sympathise with.
4 I understand she is in Paris. believe, gather, hear, learn.

understanding *adjective*
an understanding friend. compassionate, considerate, perceptive, sensitive, sympathetic, tolerant.
OPPOSITE unsympathetic.

understanding *noun*
1 beyond human understanding. intellect, intelligence, knowledge, mentality, perception, wisdom.
2 She has no understanding of the problems. appreciation, awareness, comprehension, conception, insight, perception, realisation.
3 His friends were lacking in understanding. compassion, consideration, empathy, feeling, sensitivity, sympathy, tolerance.
4 The parties reached an understanding. accord, agreement, arrangement, compromise, deal, pact, settlement.

undertake *verb*
1 She undertook to be treasurer. agree, consent, promise, volunteer.
2 He undertook the job. accept, embark on, start, tackle, take on.

undertaker *noun*
funeral director, mortician (*American*).

undertaking *noun*
1 He has the energy for this undertaking. endeavour, enterprise, job, project, task, venture, work.
2 He gave a solemn undertaking. assurance, commitment, guarantee, pledge, promise.

underwater *adjective*
subaquatic, submarine, undersea.

underwear *noun*
lingerie, underclothes, undergarments, undies (*informal*).

underworld *noun*
Hades, hell.

undeserved *adjective*
undeserved praise. unearned, unjustified, unmerited, unwarranted.
OPPOSITE deserved.

undesirable *adjective*
an undesirable state of affairs. objectionable, offensive, repugnant, unacceptable, unsatisfactory.
OPPOSITE desirable.

undivided *adjective*
his undivided attention. complete, exclusive, full, wholehearted.
OPPOSITE divided.

undo *verb*
1 *undo clothes, knots, etc.* detach, disconnect, loosen, open, release, unbuckle, unbutton, unclasp, unfasten, unhook, unpick, unravel, unscrew, untie, unzip.
OPPOSITE do up, fasten.
2 *Her carelessness undid all their good work.* destroy, ruin, spoil, wreck.

undoubted *adjective*
the undoubted winner. certain, clear, clear-cut, indisputable, sure, undisputed.

undress *verb*
She undressed in the bedroom. disrobe, strip, uncover yourself.
OPPOSITE dress.

undressed *adjective*
bare, naked, nude, unclothed.
OPPOSITE dressed.

unearth *verb*
The archaeologist unearthed several bones. dig up, discover, excavate, exhume, uncover.
OPPOSITE bury.

unearthly *adjective*
an unearthly sound. creepy, eerie, ghostly, spooky (*informal*), supernatural, uncanny, weird.

uneasy *adjective*
She feels uneasy about talking to strangers. anxious, apprehensive, edgy, ill at ease, nervous, nervy, tense, uncomfortable, worried.
OPPOSITE comfortable.

unemotional *adjective*
see COLD.

unemployed *adjective*
jobless, laid off, on the dole (*informal*), out of work, redundant.
OPPOSITE employed.

unequal *adjective*
1 *unequal amounts.* different, uneven.
OPPOSITE identical.
2 *unequal treatment.* biased, discriminatory, unbalanced, uneven, unfair, unjust.
OPPOSITE even-handed.

unethical *adjective*
unethical business practices. dishonest, dishonourable, immoral, shady, shonky (*Australian informal*), underhand, unprincipled, unscrupulous, wrong.
OPPOSITE ethical.

uneven *adjective*
1 *an uneven surface.* bumpy, irregular, lumpy, rough, rugged, undulating.
OPPOSITE level, smooth.
2 *an uneven edge.* crooked, jagged, ragged, wavy.
OPPOSITE straight.
3 *an uneven contest.* one-sided, unbalanced, unequal, unfair.
4 *uneven work.* erratic, inconsistent, patchy, variable.
OPPOSITE uniform.

unexciting *adjective*
an unexciting day, job, etc. boring, dreary, dull, humdrum, mundane, ordinary, run-of-the-mill, tame, tedious, uneventful, uninteresting.
OPPOSITE exciting.

unexpected *adjective*
an unexpected result. accidental, chance, surprising, undreamed-of, unforeseen.
OPPOSITE expected.

unfair *adjective*
unfair treatment. biased, inequitable, one-sided, partial, prejudiced, unjust, unreasonable.
OPPOSITE fair.

unfaithful *adjective*
1 *unfaithful to the party.* disloyal, false, traitorous, treacherous.

a
b
c
d
e
f
g
h
i
j
k
l
m
n
o
p
q
r
s
t
u
v
w
x
y
z

2 *an unfaithful husband.* adulterous, false, fickle, inconstant, two-timing (*informal*), untrue.
OPPOSITE faithful.

unfaithfulness *noun*
adultery, disloyalty, inconstancy, infidelity, treachery, treason.
OPPOSITE faithfulness.

unfamiliar *adjective*
an unfamiliar place, concept, etc. alien, exotic, foreign, new, novel, strange, unheard-of, unknown.
OPPOSITE familiar.

unfashionable *adjective*
unfashionable clothes, beliefs, etc. dated, obsolete, old-fashioned, outdated, out-of-date.
OPPOSITE fashionable.

unfasten *verb*
see UNDO, UNLOCK.

unfavourable *adjective*
1 *unfavourable conditions.* adverse, contrary, disadvantageous, inauspicious.
2 *an unfavourable response.* critical, hostile, negative.
OPPOSITE favourable.

unfeeling *adjective*
an unfeeling person. callous, clinical, cold, cold-hearted, cruel, hard, hard-hearted, harsh, heartless, insensitive, merciless, pitiless, ruthless, uncaring, unsympathetic.
OPPOSITE sensitive, sympathetic.

unfinished *adjective*
see INCOMPLETE.

unfit *adjective*
1 *The house is unfit for people to live in.* inappropriate, unsuitable, unusable, useless.
OPPOSITE suitable.
2 *He is unfit to be their leader.* inadequate, incapable, incompetent, unqualified, unsuited.
OPPOSITE qualified.
3 *The exercise showed how unfit she was.* out of condition, out of form, out of training, unhealthy.
OPPOSITE fit.

unflappable *adjective* (*informal*)
He remains unflappable even under extreme pressure. calm, collected, composed, cool, easygoing, nonchalant, placid, unexcitable.
OPPOSITE panicky.

unfold *verb*
1 *She unfolded the cloth.* open out, spread out, unfurl.
OPPOSITE fold up.
2 *The story gradually unfolded.* develop, emerge, evolve.

unforeseen *adjective*
see UNEXPECTED.

unforgettable *adjective*
an unforgettable evening. impressive, memorable, noteworthy, remarkable, striking.
OPPOSITE forgettable.

unforgiving *adjective*
an unforgiving person. hard-hearted, merciless, pitiless, remorseless, vengeful, vindictive.
OPPOSITE merciful.

unfortunate *adjective*
1 *an unfortunate error.* calamitous, disastrous, lamentable, regrettable, terrible, tragic.
2 *an unfortunate person.* hapless, ill-fated, jinxed (*informal*), luckless, unlucky, wretched.
OPPOSITE fortunate, lucky.

unfounded *adjective*
an unfounded fear. baseless, groundless, needless, unjustified, unwarranted.
OPPOSITE justified.

unfriendly *adjective*
an unfriendly person. aloof, antisocial, clinical, cool, distant, hostile, stand-offish, surly, uncaring, unfeeling, unkind, unneighbourly, unsociable.
OPPOSITE friendly.

ungainly *adjective*
an ungainly animal. awkward, clumsy, gangling, gawky, inelegant, ungraceful.
OPPOSITE graceful.

ungodly *adjective*
ungodly living. evil, godless, immoral, impious, iniquitous, irreligious, sinful,

wicked.
OPPOSITE godly.

ungrateful *adjective*
an ungrateful person. unappreciative,
unthankful.
OPPOSITE grateful.

unhappiness *noun*
see SADNESS.

unhappy *adjective*
1 *He was feeling unhappy.* dejected,
depressed, despondent, disconsolate,
discontented, dismal, distressed,
doleful, downcast, down-hearted, fed
up (*informal*), gloomy, glum,
heartbroken, heavy-hearted,
melancholy, miserable, mournful,
pessimistic, sad, sorrowful, woebegone,
wretched.
OPPOSITE happy.
2 *an unhappy choice.* bad, inappropriate,
poor, regrettable, unfortunate, unlucky,
unsatisfactory, unsuitable.
OPPOSITE satisfactory.

unharmed *adjective*
They escaped unharmed. safe, safe and
sound, undamaged, unhurt, uninjured,
unscathed.
OPPOSITE harmed.

unhealthy *adjective*
1 *an unhealthy person.* ailing, diseased,
poorly, sick, sickly, unwell.
OPPOSITE healthy.
2 *unhealthy living conditions.* harmful,
insanitary, unhygienic, unwholesome.
OPPOSITE healthy.

unhelpful *adjective*
an unhelpful person. obstructive, stroppy
(*informal*), uncooperative.
OPPOSITE helpful.

unidentified *adjective*
an unidentified victim. anonymous,
nameless, unknown, unnamed.
OPPOSITE identified.

uniform *adjective*
of uniform quality. consistent, constant,
even, identical, invariable, regular,
steady, unchanging.
OPPOSITE varying.

unify *verb*
see UNITE.

unimaginative *adjective*
an unimaginative composition. colourless,
dull, ordinary, pedestrian, unexciting,
uninspired, unoriginal.
OPPOSITE imaginative.

unimportant *adjective*
unimportant details. insignificant,
irrelevant, minor, obscure, petty, trivial.
OPPOSITE important.

uninhabited *adjective*
The house was uninhabited. deserted,
empty, unoccupied, vacant.
OPPOSITE inhabited.

uninhibited *adjective*
uninhibited behaviour. free, reckless,
spontaneous, unrepressed,
unrestrained.
OPPOSITE inhibited.

unintentional *adjective*
an unintentional meeting. accidental,
chance, inadvertent, unforeseen,
unplanned, unpremeditated.
OPPOSITE planned.

uninterested *adjective*
He was uninterested in what was going on.
apathetic, blasé, bored, detached,
indifferent, unconcerned.
OPPOSITE curious, interested.

uninteresting *adjective*
an uninteresting book, person, etc. boring,
commonplace, dreary, dull, humdrum,
monotonous, mundane, ordinary,
tedious, tiresome, uneventful,
unexciting, unimaginative, uninspiring.
OPPOSITE interesting.

uninterrupted *adjective*
uninterrupted sleep. continuous,
non-stop, solid, sound, unbroken,
undisturbed.
OPPOSITE interrupted.

uninvited *adjective*
an uninvited guest. unasked, unwanted,
unwelcome.
OPPOSITE invited.

uninviting *adjective*
an uninviting place. inhospitable,
unappealing, unattractive, unenticing,

a
b
c
d
e
f
g
h
i
j
k
l
m
n
o
p
q
r
s
t
u
v
w
x
y
z

unwelcoming.
OPPOSITE inviting.

union *noun*
1 *a union of several smaller firms.* alliance, amalgamation, association, coalition, combination, consortium, federation, league, merger, syndicate.
2 *the students' union.* club, group, society.
3 *a workers' union.* guild, trade union.

unique *adjective*
a unique voice. distinctive, inimitable, matchless, one-off, peculiar, singular.
OPPOSITE common.

unit *noun*
1 *The whole is composed of many units.* component, constituent, element, module, part, piece, section.
OPPOSITE whole.
2 *a unit of weight.* measure, measurement, quantity.
3 *The company has a research unit.* group, squad, team.
4 *She lives in a unit.* apartment, condominium (*American*), flat, home unit.

unite *verb*
1 *A common goal united them.* bind, bring together, join, link, tie, unify.
OPPOSITE divide.
2 *They united the two councils.* amalgamate, combine, consolidate, incorporate, integrate, join.
OPPOSITE split.
3 *The people united to block the development.* band together, collaborate, cooperate, join forces, team up.
OPPOSITE split.

unity *noun*
party unity. accord, agreement, consensus, harmony, oneness, solidarity, unanimity.
OPPOSITE disunity, division.

universal *adjective*
a universal problem. general, global, international, widespread, worldwide.
OPPOSITE localised.

universe *noun*
cosmos, Creation, world.

unjust *adjective*
an unjust decision. biased, inequitable, one-sided, prejudiced, unfair, unreasonable.
OPPOSITE just, reasonable.

unkempt *adjective*
He looked unkempt when he first got up. bedraggled, dishevelled, messy, scruffy, tousled, untidy.
OPPOSITE tidy.

unkind *adjective*
an unkind person. an unkind act. beastly (*informal*), callous, cold-hearted, cruel, hard-hearted, harsh, heartless, hurtful, inconsiderate, inhuman, inhumane, malicious, mean, merciless, nasty, pitiless, ruthless, sadistic, spiteful, thoughtless, uncaring, uncharitable, unfeeling, unfriendly, unneighbourly, unsympathetic, vicious.
OPPOSITE kind.

unknown *adjective*
1 *an unknown pianist.* obscure, unheard-of.
OPPOSITE well-known.
2 *an unknown benefactor.* anonymous, nameless, unidentified, unnamed.
OPPOSITE identified.

unlikely *adjective*
an unlikely tale. far-fetched, implausible, improbable, incredible, unbelievable.
OPPOSITE likely.

unlimited *adjective*
1 *a leader with unlimited power.* absolute, unqualified, unrestricted.
OPPOSITE restricted.
2 *unlimited patience.* boundless, endless, everlasting, inexhaustible, infinite, limitless, never-ending.
OPPOSITE limited.

unload *verb*
1 *He unloaded the cargo.* discharge, drop off, dump, offload, remove.
2 *He unloaded the car.* empty, unpack.
OPPOSITE load.

unlock *verb*
She unlocked the door. open, unbolt, undo, unfasten, unlatch.
OPPOSITE lock.

unlucky *adjective*
an unlucky person. accident-prone, hapless, ill-fated, jinxed (*informal*), luckless, unfortunate, wretched.
OPPOSITE lucky.

unmanageable *adjective*
1 *an unmanageable load.* awkward, cumbersome, unwieldy, weighty.
OPPOSITE manageable.
2 *an unmanageable person.* see UNCONTROLLABLE.

unmarried *adjective*
an unmarried aunt. maiden, single, unattached, unwed.

unmentionable *adjective*
an unmentionable word. forbidden, obscene, rude, shocking, taboo, unprintable.

unmistakable *adjective*
an unmistakable family likeness. apparent, blatant, clear, conspicuous, distinct, evident, glaring, noticeable, obvious, plain, pronounced.

unnatural *adjective*
1 *unnatural events.* abnormal, bizarre, freakish, odd, peculiar, strange, supernatural, unusual, weird.
2 *Her behaviour is very unnatural.* affected, artificial, contrived, forced, phoney (*informal*), stilted, theatrical.
OPPOSITE natural.

unnecessary *adjective*
unnecessary details. dispensable, excessive, inessential, needless, non-essential, redundant, superfluous, uncalled-for, unwanted.
OPPOSITE necessary.

unoccupied *adjective*
The house is unoccupied. deserted, empty, uninhabited, unlived-in, vacant.
OPPOSITE occupied.

unpaid *adjective*
1 *an unpaid account.* outstanding, overdue, owing.
2 *an unpaid worker.* honorary, unsalaried, unwaged, voluntary.
OPPOSITE paid.

unplanned *adjective*
an unplanned meeting. accidental, chance, unintended, unintentional, unpremeditated, unscheduled.
OPPOSITE planned.

unpleasant *adjective*
an unpleasant person, thing, etc. abominable, annoying, appalling, atrocious, awful, bad-tempered, beastly (*informal*), diabolical, disagreeable, disgusting, distasteful, dreadful, foul, frightful, ghastly, harsh, hateful, hideous, horrible, horrid, irksome, loathsome, nasty, nauseating, objectionable, obnoxious, offensive, off-putting, repugnant, repulsive, revolting, sickening, sordid, squalid, terrible, troublesome, unattractive, unfriendly, unlikeable, unsightly, upsetting, vile.
OPPOSITE pleasant.

unpopular *adjective*
He was unpopular at school. disliked, friendless, on the outer (*Australian informal*), unloved.
OPPOSITE popular.

unpredictable *adjective*
an unpredictable person. capricious, changeable, erratic, fickle, inconstant, moody, temperamental, unreliable.
OPPOSITE predictable.

unprejudiced *adjective*
an unprejudiced jury. disinterested, fair, impartial, objective, open-minded, unbiased.
OPPOSITE prejudiced.

unprepared *adjective*
She made an unprepared speech. ad lib, extempore, impromptu, off the cuff, spontaneous, unrehearsed.
OPPOSITE prepared.

unproductive *adjective*
1 *unproductive land.* barren, infertile, sterile, waste.
OPPOSITE fertile.
2 *an unproductive discussion.* fruitless, futile, unprofitable, useless.
OPPOSITE productive.

a
b
c
d
e
f
g
h
i
j
k
l
m
n
o
p
q
r
s
t
u
v
w
x
y
z

unprofessional *adjective*
1 *an unprofessional job.* amateurish, incompetent, inexpert, shoddy.
OPPOSITE professional.
2 *unprofessional conduct.* improper, negligent, unethical, unprincipled.
OPPOSITE ethical.

unprofitable *adjective*
1 *an unprofitable business.* uneconomic.
OPPOSITE profitable.
2 *unprofitable research.* fruitless, unproductive, useless, worthless.
OPPOSITE fruitful.

unravel *verb*
She unravelled the wool. disentangle, untangle, untwist.
OPPOSITE entangle.

unreadable *adjective*
unreadable writing. illegible, indecipherable.
OPPOSITE legible.

unreal *adjective*
an unreal world. artificial, fabulous, false, fantastic, fictitious, illusory, imaginary, make-believe, mythical, non-existent.
OPPOSITE real.

unrealistic *adjective*
unrealistic goals. idealistic, impracticable, impractical, unreasonable, unworkable.
OPPOSITE realistic.

unreasonable *adjective*
1 *an unreasonable person.* headstrong, illogical, irrational, obstinate, perverse, pigheaded, stiff-necked, stroppy (*informal*), stubborn, wilful.
OPPOSITE reasonable.
2 *an unreasonable price.* excessive, exorbitant, extortionate, steep (*informal*).
OPPOSITE moderate.
3 *an unreasonable request.* absurd, ludicrous, outrageous, preposterous.
OPPOSITE reasonable.

unreliable *adjective*
1 *The method is unreliable.* dicey (*slang*), dodgy (*informal*), risky, uncertain, unsound, unsure.

2 *an unreliable worker.* erratic, fickle, undependable, untrustworthy.
OPPOSITE reliable.

unrest *noun*
student unrest. agitation, disquiet, dissatisfaction, rebellion, rioting, strife, trouble, turmoil, unease, uprising.

unroll *verb*
unroll a flag. open out, spread out, unfurl.
OPPOSITE roll up.

unruly *adjective*
an unruly class. boisterous, disobedient, disorderly, lawless, obstreperous, riotous, rowdy, uncontrollable, undisciplined, unmanageable, wayward, wild.
OPPOSITE well-behaved.

unsafe *adjective*
The road is unsafe. dangerous, hazardous, perilous, precarious, risky, treacherous.
OPPOSITE safe.

unsatisfactory *adjective*
an unsatisfactory performance. defective, deficient, disappointing, faulty, inadequate, insufficient, substandard, unacceptable.
OPPOSITE satisfactory.

unscathed *adjective*
see UNHARMED.

unscrupulous *adjective*
an unscrupulous businessman. corrupt, crooked, deceitful, dishonest, dishonourable, immoral, shady, shonky (*Australian informal*), unethical, unprincipled.
OPPOSITE ethical, honest.

unseemly *adjective*
unseemly behaviour. improper, inappropriate, indecorous, offensive, tasteless, unbecoming, unfitting.
OPPOSITE seemly.

unseen *adjective*
concealed, hidden, invisible, out of sight, unnoticed.
OPPOSITE seen.

unselfish *adjective*
an unselfish person, action, etc. altruistic, considerate, generous, kind, magnanimous, selfless, thoughtful.
OPPOSITE selfish.

unsettled *adjective*
unsettled weather. changeable, erratic, patchy, unpredictable, unstable, variable.
OPPOSITE settled.

unsociable *adjective*
He lived alone and was unsociable. aloof, antisocial, reclusive, retiring, stand-offish, unfriendly, withdrawn.
OPPOSITE sociable.

unsophisticated *adjective*
1 *an unsophisticated person.* artless, ingenuous, naive, natural, unaffected, unpretentious, unworldly.
2 *Their methods were unsophisticated.* crude, primitive, simple, unrefined.
OPPOSITE sophisticated.

unstable *adjective*
an unstable situation. changeable, explosive, fluctuating, fluid, unpredictable, volatile.
OPPOSITE stable.

unsteady *adjective*
The ladder was unsteady. precarious, rickety, rocky, shaky, unstable, wobbly, wonky (*informal*).
OPPOSITE steady.

unsuccessful *adjective*
an unsuccessful try. failed, fruitless, futile, ineffective, ineffectual, vain.
OPPOSITE successful.

unsuitable *adjective*
inappropriate, out of place, unbecoming, unfitting, unseemly, wrong.
OPPOSITE suitable.

unsure *adjective*
see UNCERTAIN.

unsympathetic *adjective*
an unsympathetic official. callous, cold, hard-hearted, heartless, indifferent, insensitive, uncaring, uncompassionate, unfeeling.
OPPOSITE sympathetic.

untamed *adjective*
an untamed animal. feral, savage, unbroken, undomesticated, warrigal (*Australian*), wild.
OPPOSITE tame.

untangle *verb*
untangle a ball of wool. disentangle, unravel, unsnarl, untwist.
OPPOSITE tangle.

untidy *adjective*
1 *an untidy room.* chaotic, cluttered, disorderly, disorganised, higgledy-piggledy, jumbled, littered, messy, muddled, topsy-turvy.
OPPOSITE tidy.
2 *He has an untidy appearance.* bedraggled, dishevelled, ruffled, rumpled, scruffy, shaggy, sloppy, slovenly, straggly, tousled, unkempt.
OPPOSITE neat.

untie *verb*
see UNDO.

untold *adjective*
1 *There were untold problems.* countless, innumerable, numberless, numerous.
2 *untold misery.* great, immeasurable, incalculable, indescribable.

untrue *adjective*
1 *an untrue story.* false, fictitious, invented, made-up, untruthful, wrong.
OPPOSITE true.
2 *She was untrue to him.* disloyal, fickle, treacherous, unfaithful.
OPPOSITE loyal, true.

untruthful *adjective*
an untruthful witness. deceitful, dishonest, false, lying, mendacious.
OPPOSITE honest.

unused *adjective*
1 *an unused page.* blank, clean, empty, fresh, new, untouched.
OPPOSITE used.
2 *He was unused to country driving.* inexperienced (at), unaccustomed, unfamiliar (with).
OPPOSITE used.

unusual *adjective*
an unusual occurrence, person, etc. abnormal, atypical, bizarre, curious, different, eccentric, exceptional, exotic,

a
b
c
d
e
f
g
h
i
j
k
l
m
n
o
p
q
r
s
t
u
v
w
x
y
z

extraordinary, freakish, irregular, odd,
offbeat, outlandish, peculiar,
phenomenal, queer, rare, remarkable,
singular, special, strange, surprising,
uncommon, unfamiliar, unorthodox,
way-out (*informal*), weird.
OPPOSITE ordinary, usual.

unwanted *adjective*
1 *He gave away the unwanted items.* see
UNNECESSARY.
2 *She felt unwanted.* excluded, on the
outer (*Australian*), rejected, unpopular,
unwelcome.
OPPOSITE wanted.

unwell *adjective*
He felt unwell. bilious, crook (*Australian
informal*), funny (*informal*), ill,
indisposed, infirm, nauseous, off
colour, out of sorts, poorly, queasy,
rotten, seedy (*informal*), sick, sickly,
under the weather.
OPPOSITE well.

unwieldy *adjective*
an unwieldy tool. awkward, bulky,
clumsy, cumbersome, heavy, hefty.
OPPOSITE handy.

unwilling *adjective*
She was unwilling to help. disinclined,
hesitant, loath, reluctant.
OPPOSITE keen.

unwind *verb*
see RELAX.

unwise *adjective*
It is unwise to go there. crazy, foolish,
impolitic, imprudent, inadvisable, silly,
stupid, unintelligent.
OPPOSITE wise.

unworthy *adjective*
1 *He is unworthy of this honour.*
undeserving.
2 *Such conduct is unworthy of a king.*
beneath, inappropriate, unbecoming,
unbefitting, unfitting, unsuitable.
OPPOSITE worthy.

unwritten *adjective*
an unwritten law. implicit, oral, spoken,
tacit, unstated.
OPPOSITE written.

upbringing *noun*
the children's upbringing. education,
nurture, raising, rearing, training.

update *verb*
They updated their bathroom. modernise,
refurbish, remodel, renovate.

upgrade *verb*
He upgraded the computer. enhance,
improve.

upheaval *noun*
Their lives were full of upheaval. change,
chaos, disruption, disturbance, havoc,
turbulence, turmoil.

uphill *adjective*
an uphill battle. arduous, demanding,
difficult, exacting, gruelling, hard,
laborious, strenuous, tough.
OPPOSITE easy.

uphold *verb*
The court upheld the earlier decision.
confirm, endorse, maintain, stand by,
support, sustain.
OPPOSITE overrule.

upkeep *noun*
He paid for the car's upkeep. maintenance,
repairs, running.

uplift *verb*
Our spirits were uplifted by their singing.
buoy up, encourage, inspire, lift, raise.
OPPOSITE depress.

upmarket *adjective*
an upmarket hotel. classy (*informal*),
expensive, luxurious, superior.
OPPOSITE downmarket.

upper *adjective*
an upper level. higher, raised, superior.
OPPOSITE lower.

upright *adjective*
1 *an upright position.* erect,
perpendicular, standing, vertical.
OPPOSITE horizontal.
2 *an upright person.* ethical, good,
honest, honourable, just, moral,
principled, righteous, trustworthy,
upstanding, virtuous.
OPPOSITE dishonourable.

uprising *noun*
a students' uprising. insurrection, mutiny, rebellion, revolt, revolution.

uproar *noun*
1 *The party ended in uproar.* bedlam, chaos, commotion, confusion, disorder, mayhem, pandemonium, turmoil.
2 *The decision caused an uproar.* clamour, fracas, furore, hullabaloo, kerfuffle (*informal*), outcry, protest, riot, row, rumpus, stir, storm, to-do.

uproot *verb*
He uprooted the weeds. dig up, eradicate, get rid of, pull up, remove, root out.

upset *verb*
1 *He upset the trolley.* knock over, overturn, spill, tip up, topple, upturn.
OPPOSITE right.
2 *Fog upset the timetable.* affect, disrupt, interfere with, mess up.
3 *She upset her mother.* agitate, alarm, anger, annoy, bother, distress, disturb, fluster, frighten, grieve, hurt, offend, perturb, provoke, rattle (*informal*), trouble, vex, worry.
OPPOSITE pacify.
upset *noun*
a stomach upset. ailment, bug (*informal*), complaint, disorder.

upsetting *adjective*
an upsetting experience. distressing, disturbing, frightening, painful, traumatic, unnerving, worrying.

upshot *noun*
The upshot of the talks was that an inquiry was set up. consequence, effect, outcome, result.

upside-down *adjective*
an upside-down cake. inverted, topsy-turvy, upturned.

uptight *adjective* (*informal*)
He was uptight before the speech. anxious, apprehensive, edgy, jittery (*informal*), keyed up, nervous, tense, uneasy, worried.
OPPOSITE calm.

up-to-date *adjective*
an up-to-date kitchen. contemporary, current, fashionable, latest, modern, modernised, new, trendy (*informal*),

up-to-the-minute, with it (*informal*).
OPPOSITE antiquated.

upturn *noun*
an economic upturn. improvement, recovery, upswing.
OPPOSITE downturn.

urban *adjective*
an urban dweller. city, metropolitan, town.
OPPOSITE rural.

urge *verb*
1 *He urged them on.* drive, egg on, force, goad, prod, spur.
2 *She urged her to enter the contest.* coax, encourage, entreat, exhort, implore, plead with, press, prompt, push, recommend.
OPPOSITE discourage.
urge *noun*
an irresistible urge. compulsion, desire, drive, fancy, impulse, itch, longing, wish, yearning, yen.

urgent *adjective*
an urgent need. compelling, desperate, dire, immediate, important, necessary, pressing, vital.
OPPOSITE unimportant.

usable *adjective*
The car is not usable. available, functional, operational, working.
OPPOSITE unusable.

usage *noun*
1 *damaged by rough usage.* handling, treatment, use.
2 *established usage.* convention, custom, habit, practice, use.

use *verb*
1 *She learned how to use the gadget.* employ, handle, manage, manipulate, operate, utilise, wield, work.
2 *She used her brain.* apply, exercise, exert.
3 *The car uses a lot of petrol.* burn, consume, go through.
4 *He uses people for his own ends.* exploit, make use of, manipulate, take advantage of.
use *noun*
1 *The car has received a lot of use.* handling, usage.
OPPOSITE disuse.

a
b
c
d
e
f
g
h
i
j
k
l
m
n
o
p
q
r
s
t
u
v
w
x
y
z

2 *The product has various uses.*
application, function.
3 *What is the use of discussing it?*
advantage, benefit, good, point,
purpose, value.
use up *They used up all their cash.* blow
(*slang*), consume, deplete, exhaust,
fritter away, spend.

used[1] *adjective*
used clothes. hand-me-down, old,
recycled, second-hand, worn.
OPPOSITE new.

used[2] *adjective*
used to *He is used to the climate.*
acclimatised to, accustomed to, familiar
with.

useful *adjective*
1 *a useful device.* convenient, effective,
efficient, functional, handy, practical,
productive, serviceable, usable,
utilitarian.
OPPOSITE useless.
2 *a useful comment.* advantageous,
beneficial, constructive, helpful,
invaluable, positive, practical,
profitable, valuable, worthwhile.
OPPOSITE useless.

useless *adjective*
1 *The gadget is useless.* bung (*Australian
informal*), dud (*informal*), impractical,
ineffective, unusable, worthless.
OPPOSITE useful.
2 *It was useless trying to talk to him.*
fruitless, futile, hopeless, ineffectual,
pointless, unproductive, vain.
OPPOSITE productive.

user *noun*
consumer, operator.

usher *noun*
attendant, escort, guide, sidesman.
usher *verb*
He ushered them to their seats. conduct,
escort, guide, lead, show.

usual *adjective*
the usual method. accustomed, common,
conventional, customary, established,
everyday, familiar, general, habitual,
normal, ordinary, orthodox, regular,
routine, standard, traditional, typical.

utensil *noun*
kitchen utensils. appliance, device,
gadget, implement, instrument,
machine, tool.

uterus *noun*
womb.

utilise *verb*
see USE.

utmost *adjective*
of the utmost importance. extreme,
greatest, highest, maximum,
paramount, supreme.

utter[1] *adjective*
utter nonsense. absolute, complete,
downright, perfect, positive, pure,
sheer, thorough, total.

utter[2] *verb*
He did not utter a sound. come out with,
emit, express, let out, pronounce, say,
speak, voice.

U-turn *noun*
The politician did a U-turn. about-face,
about-turn, backflip, reversal.

Vv

vacancy *noun*
a vacancy for a clerk. job, opening, position, post, situation.

vacant *adjective*
1 *The house is vacant.* deserted, empty, uninhabited, unoccupied.
OPPOSITE occupied.
2 *a vacant space.* available, clear, empty, free, spare, unfilled, unoccupied, unused.
OPPOSITE filled.
3 *a vacant stare.* absent-minded, blank, deadpan, empty, expressionless.
OPPOSITE expressive.

vacation *noun*
He spent his vacation in Tasmania. break, holiday, leave, time off.

vaccination *noun*
a smallpox vaccination. booster, immunisation, injection, inoculation, jab (*informal*), shot.

vacuum *noun*
There was a vacuum inside the container. emptiness, nothingness, void.

vagrant *noun*
He was arrested as a vagrant. beggar, hobo, homeless person, itinerant, rover, tramp, vagabond.

vague *adjective*
a vague idea. a vague answer. ambiguous, fuzzy, general, hazy, imprecise, indefinite, loose, sketchy, uncertain, unclear, woolly.
OPPOSITE precise.

vain *adjective*
1 *She was so vain about her good looks.* arrogant, boastful, cocky, conceited, egotistical, proud, stuck-up (*informal*).
OPPOSITE modest.
2 *a vain attempt.* fruitless, futile, hopeless, unsuccessful, useless.
OPPOSITE successful.

valiant *adjective*
a valiant warrior. bold, brave, courageous, daring, dauntless, fearless, gallant, heroic, intrepid, lion-hearted, plucky, spirited, undaunted, valorous.
OPPOSITE cowardly.

valid *adjective*
1 *a valid driver's licence.* lawful, legal, legitimate, official.
OPPOSITE invalid.
2 *a valid excuse.* acceptable, allowable, permissible, proper, reasonable, sound.
OPPOSITE unacceptable.

valley *noun*
basin, canyon, dale, dell, glen, gorge, gully (*Australian*), hollow, pass, ravine, vale.

valour *noun*
an award for valour. bravery, courage, daring, gallantry, heroism, pluck.
OPPOSITE cowardice.

valuable *adjective*
1 *a valuable lesson.* beneficial, constructive, helpful, important, invaluable, profitable, useful, worthwhile.
OPPOSITE useless.
2 *valuable jewellery.* costly, expensive, precious, priceless, prized, treasured.
OPPOSITE cheap.

value *noun*
1 *The stamps increased in value.* price, worth.
2 *She can see the value of piano practice.* advantage, benefit, importance, merit, profit, use, usefulness, worth.
OPPOSITE uselessness.
value *verb*
1 *The dealer valued her coin collection.* appraise, assess, estimate, evaluate, price.
2 *She valued the friendship.* appreciate, cherish, esteem, prize, treasure.

values *plural noun*
moral values. ethics, morals, principles, standards.

van *noun*
All the luggage fitted in the van. campervan, lorry, panel van (*Australian*), truck, wagon.

vandal *noun*
Vandals had damaged the fence. delinquent, hoodlum, hooligan, ruffian, thug.

vanish *verb*
The stain has vanished. become invisible, disappear, evaporate, fade away, go away.
OPPOSITE appear.

vanity *noun*
Her vanity prevents her from seeing others' beauty. conceit, egotism, pride, self-admiration, self-love.
OPPOSITE modesty.

vanquish *verb*
He vanquished his enemies. beat, conquer, defeat, overcome, overpower, overthrow, rout, subdue, thrash, triumph over.
OPPOSITE surrender to.

vapour *noun*
The air was filled with the poisonous vapour. fog, fumes, gas, haze, mist, smoke, steam.

variable *adjective*
variable quality. variable winds. changeable, erratic, fickle, fluctuating, inconsistent, patchy, shifting, temperamental, unpredictable, unreliable.
OPPOSITE consistent.

variation *noun*
a variation in the order. alteration, change, deviation, difference, fluctuation, modification, permutation, shift.

variety *noun*
1 *The job has a lot of variety.* change, contrast, difference, diversity, variation.
OPPOSITE monotony.
2 *a wide variety of talents.* assortment, collection, combination, miscellany, mixture, range.

3 *a variety of tomato.* breed, class, form, kind, sort, strain, type.

various *adjective*
people from various backgrounds. assorted, different, diverse, many, miscellaneous, several, sundry, varied.

varnish *noun*
The shelves are finished with a varnish. coating, glaze, gloss, lacquer.

vary *verb*
1 *He varied the tone of his voice.* adjust, alter, change, modify.
2 *Her mood varies from hour to hour.* change, fluctuate, swing.
3 *Opinions vary on this point.* be at odds, conflict, differ, diverge.
OPPOSITE agree.

vast *adjective*
1 *a vast area.* big, broad, enormous, expansive, extensive, great, huge, immense, large, spacious, wide.
2 *a vast amount.* astronomical, colossal, exorbitant, gigantic, massive, sizeable, tremendous.
OPPOSITE tiny.

vat *noun*
a vat of beer. barrel, tank.

vault[1] *noun*
1 *The valuables are stored in a vault.* strongroom.
2 *a cathedral vault.* basement, cellar, crypt.

vault[2] *verb*
She vaulted the rail. bound over, clear, hurdle, jump over, leap over, spring over.
vault *noun*
a vault over the fence. bound, jump, leap, spring.

veer *verb*
The car suddenly veered to the right. bear, diverge, swerve, swing, turn, wheel.

vegetable *noun*
[*various vegetables*] artichoke, asparagus, bean, beetroot, bok choy, broccoli, Brussels sprout, cabbage, capsicum, carrot, cauliflower, celery, choko, cucumber, eggplant, endive, fennel, leek, lettuce, marrow, onion, parsnip, pea, pepper, potato, pumpkin, radish, shallot, silver beet, spinach, squash,

swede, sweet corn, sweet potato, tomato, turnip, zucchini.

vegetation *noun*
They cleared the natural vegetation. flora, greenery, growth, plants.

vehicle *noun*
People are transported in vehicles. conveyance; [*various vehicles*] bus, car, caravan, carriage, coach, cycle, tractor, trailer, train, tram, truck, van, wagon.

veil *noun*
She wore a veil. mantilla, yashmak.
veil *verb*
Her face was veiled. conceal, cover, disguise, hide, mask, obscure, shroud.
OPPOSITE reveal.

velocity *noun*
The car was travelling at a high velocity. pace, rate, speed.

vengeance *noun*
He sought vengeance for his brother's murder. reprisal, retaliation, retribution, revenge.

venom *noun*
snake venom. poison, toxin.

venomous *adjective*
That snake's bite is venomous. deadly, fatal, lethal, poisonous, toxic.
OPPOSITE harmless.

vent *noun*
The steam escapes through a vent in the lid. aperture, duct, hole, opening, outlet, slit.
vent *verb*
He vented his anger. air, express, give vent to, release.
OPPOSITE bottle up.

ventilate *verb*
The bathroom needs to be ventilated. air, freshen.

venture *noun*
a new business venture. endeavour, enterprise, project, undertaking.
venture *verb*
1 *She did not venture to stop them.* be so bold as, dare, presume.
2 *She ventured a suggestion.* advance, offer, put forward, volunteer.

3 *He ventured $20 on the horse.* chance, gamble, hazard, risk, stake, wager.

venue *noun*
The club meets at a new venue. location, meeting place, place, site.

verdict *noun*
a jury's verdict. adjudication, conclusion, decision, finding, judgement, opinion.

verge *noun*
the verge of the lake. border, brink, edge, margin, perimeter, rim, side, threshold.
on the verge of *on the verge of collapse.* close to, near to, on the brink of, on the point of.

verify *verb*
His statement can easily be verified. check, confirm, corroborate, prove, substantiate, support, uphold, validate.

vermin *noun*
parasites, pests.

versatile *adjective*
a versatile player. adaptable, all-round, flexible, handy, multi-skilled.
OPPOSITE specialised.

verse *noun*
1 *He writes verse.* poems, poetry; see also POEM.
2 *The poem has four verses.* stanza.

version *noun*
1 *She believed his version of the incident.* account, description, narrative, report, side, story.
2 *a modern version of the Bible.* edition, interpretation, reading, translation.
3 *a new version of an old song.* rendering, rendition, variation.
4 *the cheaper version of the sofa.* design, model, style, type.

vertex *noun*
the vertex of a hill. acme, apex, pinnacle, summit, top, zenith.

vertical *adjective*
1 *a vertical position.* erect, perpendicular, standing, upright.
OPPOSITE horizontal.
2 *a vertical rock face.* bluff, precipitous, sheer.

a
b
c
d
e
f
g
h
i
j
k
l
m
n
o
p
q
r
s
t
u
v
w
x
y
z

very *adverb*
very embarrassing. awfully, dreadfully (*informal*), especially, exceedingly, exceptionally, extraordinarily, extremely, frightfully, highly, immensely, jolly (*informal*), most, particularly, really, terribly, thoroughly, tremendously (*informal*), truly.
OPPOSITE slightly.
very *adjective*
the very thing we want. actual, exact, precise, selfsame.

vessel *noun*
1 *The vessel was not seaworthy.* boat, craft, ship; see BOAT, SHIP.
2 *He filled the vessel with water from the well.* container, holder, receptacle; [*various vessels*] crock, ewer, flask, jar, jug, pitcher, pot, urn, vase.

vet *noun*
veterinarian, veterinary surgeon.
vet *verb*
He vetted the applicants. check out, examine, investigate, screen.

veteran *noun*
Vietnam veterans. ex-serviceman, ex-servicewoman, returned serviceman, returned servicewoman, vet (*informal*).
veteran *adjective*
a veteran politician. experienced, long-serving, old, seasoned.
OPPOSITE inexperienced.

veto *noun*
the right of veto. prohibition, refusal, rejection.
OPPOSITE approval.
veto *verb*
She vetoed the plan. ban, bar, block, disallow, forbid, give the thumbs down to, prohibit, reject, rule out.
OPPOSITE approve.

vex *verb*
She was vexed by his behaviour. anger, annoy, bother, bug (*informal*), displease, disturb, exasperate, harass, hassle (*informal*), infuriate, irritate, nark (*informal*), needle, peeve (*informal*), perturb, plague, provoke, rile (*informal*), trouble, try, upset, worry.
OPPOSITE please.

viable *adjective*
a viable project. feasible, possible, practicable, practical, realistic, workable.
OPPOSITE unviable.

vibes *plural noun* (*informal*)
The house has good vibes. feelings, sensations, vibrations; see also ATMOSPHERE.

vibrant *adjective*
1 *vibrant colours.* bold, bright, brilliant, intense, radiant, striking, strong, vivid.
OPPOSITE dull.
2 *a vibrant personality.* animated, dynamic, energetic, enthusiastic, lively, sparkling, spirited, vivacious.
OPPOSITE lifeless.

vibrate *verb*
The glasses vibrated as the plane flew over the house. oscillate, quake, quiver, rattle, shake, shudder, throb, tremble, wobble.

vibration *noun*
a vibration in the pipes. oscillation, quaver, quiver, rattle, shaking, shudder, tremor.

vice[1] *noun*
1 *She was tempted into a life of vice.* corruption, evil, immorality, iniquity, sin, wickedness, wrongdoing.
2 *Smoking was not one of her vices.* defect, failing, fault, flaw, imperfection, shortcoming, weakness.
OPPOSITE virtue.

vice[2] *noun*
held in a vice. clamp.

vicinity *noun*
They live in the vicinity of the school. area, district, environs, locality, neighbourhood, precincts, region, zone.

vicious *adjective*
1 *a vicious crime.* atrocious, barbaric, beastly, brutal, callous, cruel, fiendish, heinous, inhuman, monstrous, ruthless, sadistic, savage, vile, violent.
2 *a vicious criminal.* depraved, evil, immoral, malevolent, malicious, spiteful, villainous, vindictive, wicked.
OPPOSITE kind.
3 *The dog looked vicious.* bad-tempered, dangerous, ferocious, fierce, mean,

nasty, savage, wild.
OPPOSITE tame.

victim *noun*
1 *accident victims.* casualty, fatality.
2 *the victim of a confidence trick.* bunny
(*Australian informal*), dupe, fall guy
(*slang*), mug (*informal*), scapegoat,
sucker (*informal*).
OPPOSITE perpetrator.
3 *The snake devours its victim.* prey,
quarry, target.

victimise *verb*
She felt victimised by everyone. bully,
cheat, exploit, oppress, persecute, pick
on, torment.

victor *noun*
champion, conqueror, vanquisher,
winner.
OPPOSITE loser.

victorious *adjective*
victorious in battle. conquering,
successful, triumphant, winning.
OPPOSITE defeated.

victory *noun*
a sporting victory. conquest, success,
triumph, walk-over, win.
OPPOSITE defeat.

vie *verb*
The two vied for first place. compete,
contend, contest, rival.

view *noun*
1 *the view from the summit.* landscape,
outlook, panorama, prospect, scene,
spectacle, vista.
2 *The procession came into view.* sight,
vision.
3 *He had strong views on the subject.*
attitude, belief, conviction, idea,
opinion, sentiment, thought; see also
VIEWPOINT.
view *verb*
1 *They viewed the scene.* behold (*old use*),
contemplate, eye, gaze at, look at,
observe, stare at, survey, take in, watch,
witness.
2 *He viewed the crime as serious.* consider,
judge, look upon, regard, see.

viewer *noun*
observer, onlooker, spectator, watcher;
[*viewers*] audience.

viewpoint *noun*
two conflicting viewpoints. angle,
attitude, opinion, outlook, perspective,
point of view, position, side, stance,
stand, standpoint, view.

vigilant *adjective*
The supervisor must be vigilant. alert,
attentive, awake, careful, observant, on
the lookout, on your guard, wary,
watchful.
OPPOSITE inattentive.

vigorous *adjective*
1 *a vigorous young man.* active, dynamic,
energetic, fit, hardy, lively, robust,
spirited, strapping, strenuous, strong.
OPPOSITE weak.
2 *vigorous efforts.* determined, forceful,
hearty, intense, keen, strenuous,
zealous.
OPPOSITE feeble.

vigour *noun*
He attacked the task with great vigour.
animation, drive, energy, enthusiasm,
gusto, liveliness, pep, power, spirit,
stamina, strength, verve, vitality,
vivacity, zeal, zest, zip.
OPPOSITE languor.

vile *adjective*
1 *a vile smell.* disgusting, foul, ghastly,
horrible, nasty, nauseating, obnoxious,
offensive, repulsive, revolting,
unpleasant.
OPPOSITE pleasant.
2 *a vile deed.* abominable, base,
contemptible, depraved, despicable,
evil, foul, hateful, heinous, hideous,
horrible, ignoble, immoral, loathsome,
nasty, odious, outrageous, shameful,
shocking, sinful, sordid, wicked.
OPPOSITE honourable.

village *noun*
community, hamlet, settlement,
township.

villain *noun*
The police captured the villain. baddy
(*informal*), blackguard, criminal, crook
(*informal*), knave (*old use*), miscreant,
rascal, rogue, scoundrel, wrongdoer.

vindictive *adjective*
*She had been hurt and was feeling
vindictive.* revengeful, spiteful,

a
b
c
d
e
f
g
h
i
j
k
l
m
n
o
p
q
r
s
t
u
v
w
x
y
z

unforgiving, vengeful.
OPPOSITE forgiving.

vintage *noun*
1 grape gathering, grape harvest.
2 *The cars are of the same vintage.* date,
era, period, year.

violate *verb*
1 *He was punished for violating the law.*
break, contravene, defy, disobey,
disregard, ignore, infringe, transgress.
OPPOSITE keep.
2 *The traders had violated the sacred place.*
defile, desecrate, dishonour, profane.
OPPOSITE revere.

violation *noun*
violation of human rights. abuse, breach,
disregard, infringement, transgression.
OPPOSITE upholding.

violent *adjective*
1 *a violent argument.* fierce, furious,
heated, impassioned, intense,
passionate, stormy, tempestuous,
vehement.
OPPOSITE calm.
2 *a violent person.* berserk, desperate,
destructive, frenzied, hotheaded,
uncontrollable, wild.
OPPOSITE gentle.
3 *a violent assault.* bloodthirsty, bloody,
brutal, cruel, ferocious, fierce,
murderous, savage, vicious, wild.
4 *a violent cyclone.* destructive, fierce,
intense, mighty, powerful, raging,
severe, tempestuous, turbulent, wild.
OPPOSITE mild.

violet *noun*
see PURPLE.

violin *noun*
fiddle (*informal*).

VIP *abbreviation*
The VIPs sit at the top table. big shot
(*informal*), bigwig (*informal*), celebrity,
dignitary.
OPPOSITE nobody.

virtually *adverb*
It is virtually impossible to tell them apart.
almost, effectively, essentially, more or
less, nearly, practically.

virtue *noun*
1 *Uphold virtue and hate vice.* decency,
goodness, honesty, honour, integrity,
morality, principle, probity, rectitude,
righteousness.
OPPOSITE vice.
2 *The house has few virtues to recommend
it.* advantage, asset, good point, merit,
plus, strength, strong point.
OPPOSITE disadvantage.

virtuous *adjective*
virtuous behaviour. blameless, chaste,
decent, good, honest, honourable,
moral, pure, righteous, saintly, upright.
OPPOSITE immoral.

virus *noun*
a flu virus. bug (*informal*), germ,
microbe, micro-organism.

visible *adjective*
1 *visible signs of distress.* apparent, clear,
conspicuous, discernible, evident,
noticeable, observable, obvious,
outward, plain, unmistakable.
OPPOSITE hidden, invisible.
2 *The ship was visible on the horizon.* in
sight, in view.

vision *noun*
1 *Spectacles improved her vision.* eyesight,
sight.
2 *He is seeing visions.* apparition, ghost,
hallucination, illusion, phantom,
spectre, spirit.
3 *a vision for the future.* dream, idea,
plan.
4 *They elected a man of vision.* far-
sightedness, foresight, imagination.
OPPOSITE short-sightedness.

visit *verb*
They visited their relatives in Sydney. call
in on, drop in on, go to see, look in on,
look up, pop in on, stay with, stop by.

visitor *noun*
1 *Visitors are always welcome.* blow-in
(*Australian informal*), caller, company,
guest.
2 *The city attracts many overseas visitors.*
holidaymaker, non-resident, sightseer,
tourist, traveller.
OPPOSITE local.

visual *adjective*
visual problems. ocular, ophthalmic,
optic, optical, sight.

visualise *verb*
It's hard to visualise what it will be like. conceive, envisage, imagine, picture, see.

vital *adjective*
a vital component. basic, critical, crucial, essential, fundamental, important, indispensable, key, necessary, significant.
OPPOSITE optional, unnecessary.

vitality *noun*
His holiday gave him renewed vitality. animation, energy, exuberance, gusto, liveliness, pep, strength, verve, vigour, vivacity, zeal, zest, zing (*informal*), zip.
OPPOSITE lethargy.

vivacious *adjective*
a vivacious young woman. animated, bubbly, exuberant, high-spirited, lively, perky, sparkling, spirited, vital.
OPPOSITE listless.

vivid *adjective*
1 vivid colours. bold, bright, brilliant, colourful, deep, garish, gaudy, gay, intense, loud, rich, striking, strong, vibrant.
OPPOSITE dull.
2 a vivid description. clear, detailed, graphic, lifelike, lively, realistic.
OPPOSITE dull, lifeless.

vocabulary *noun*
The technical words are in the vocabulary at the back of the book. dictionary, glossary, lexicon, word list.

vocal *adjective*
1 a vocal communication. oral, spoken, sung.
OPPOSITE written.
2 She was very vocal about her rights. forthright, outspoken, vociferous, voluble.
OPPOSITE reticent.

vocalist *noun*
see SINGER.

vocation *noun*
The employment counsellor discussed various vocations. calling, career, job, line of work, occupation, profession, trade.

vogue *noun*
Short skirts are the vogue. craze, fashion, rage, style, trend.
in vogue Hats are in vogue again. fashionable, in, in fashion, popular, trendy (*informal*).
OPPOSITE unfashionable.

voice *noun*
1 We heard voices. shouting, singing, speaking, speech.
2 [*kinds of singing voice*] alto, baritone, bass, contralto, counter-tenor, mezzo-soprano, soprano, tenor, treble.
voice *verb*
He voiced his opinion. air, articulate, communicate, declare, express, speak, state, utter.

void *adjective*
1 The room was void. bare, empty, unoccupied, vacant.
OPPOSITE full.
2 The contract was declared void. invalid, null and void.
OPPOSITE valid.

volley *noun*
a volley of bullets. barrage, bombardment, hail, shower.

volume *noun*
1 The dictionary is in two volumes. book, part, tome.
2 the volume of a container. capacity, dimensions, measure, size.
3 the volume of mail. amount, bulk, mass, quantity.
4 He turned up the volume of the music. loudness, sound.

voluntarily *adverb*
by choice, freely, of your own accord, of your own free will, of your own volition, willingly.

voluntary *adjective*
1 voluntary unionism. non-compulsory, optional, unforced.
OPPOSITE compulsory.
2 He does voluntary work. honorary, unpaid, volunteer.
OPPOSITE paid.

volunteer *verb*
1 She volunteered to do the job. nominate yourself, offer.
2 He volunteered for the army. enlist, join up, register, sign on.

a
b
c
d
e
f
g
h
i
j
k
l
m
n
o
p
q
r
s
t
u
v
w
x
y
z

vomit *verb*

barf (*slang*), be sick, bring up, chuck (*informal*), chunder (*Australian slang*), puke (*informal*), ralph (*slang*), sick up (*informal*), spew, throw up.

vote *noun*

1 *They held a vote for class captain.* ballot, election, poll, referendum.
2 *Eighteen-year-olds have the vote.* franchise, right to vote, suffrage.

vote *verb*

vote for *They each voted for a different candidate.* choose, elect, opt for, pick, select.

voter *noun*

elector.

voucher *noun*

a gift voucher. coupon, token.

vow *noun*

They made their vows in front of the congregation. oath, pledge, promise.

vow *verb*

She vowed that she would never smoke again. declare, give your word, pledge, promise, swear, take an oath.

voyage *noun*

The voyage took three weeks. crossing, cruise, journey, passage, sail, trip.

voyage *verb*

He voyaged to South America. cruise, journey, sail, travel.

vulgar *adjective*

1 *Burping in public is considered vulgar.* bad-mannered, coarse, common, ill-mannered, impolite, rough, rude, uncouth.
OPPOSITE polite.
2 *a vulgar joke.* coarse, crude, dirty, filthy, impolite, indecent, obscene, offensive, rude, smutty, tasteless.
OPPOSITE tasteful.

vulnerable *adjective*

1 *in a vulnerable position.* defenceless, exposed, insecure, precarious, unguarded, unprotected, weak.
OPPOSITE invulnerable.
2 *vulnerable to sun damage.* open, sensitive, subject, susceptible.
OPPOSITE immune.

Ww

wad *noun*
a wad of cotton wool. bundle, hunk, lump, mass, pad.

wadding *noun*
The box is lined with wadding. filling, lining, padding, stuffing.

waddle *verb*
The toddler waddled out of the room. shuffle, toddle, wobble.

waddy *noun*
The man was armed with a waddy. club, war club.

wade *verb*
1 She waded through the mud. paddle, plod, splash, trek, trudge.
2 He waded through the book. plod, plough, work your way.

waffle *verb* (*informal*)
The speaker waffled on for over an hour. prattle, rabbit (*informal*), ramble, witter (*informal*).

wag *verb*
1 The dog wagged his tail. shake, waggle, wave, wiggle.
2 His parents discovered he had been wagging school. absent yourself from, bludge (*Australian informal*) play hookey from (*informal*), play truant from, skive off (*informal*), stay away from.

wage[1] *verb*
They waged a war. carry on, conduct, engage in, fight.

wage[2] *noun*
He is paid an hourly wage. earnings, income, pay, wages.
CONTRASTS WITH salary.

wager *noun*
He had a small wager on the outcome. bet, flutter (*informal*), gamble, punt, speculation, stake.

wager *verb*
She wagered two dollars on the race. bet, gamble, hazard, punt (*informal*), risk, stake.

wagon *noun*
a horse-drawn wagon. cart, dray, wain (*old use*).

wail *verb*
The child was wailing with pain. bawl, caterwaul, cry, groan, howl, moan, shriek, sob, weep, whine.

waist *noun*
The apron ties around the waist. middle, midriff, waistline.

wait *verb*
1 They waited patiently for their turn. hang on, hold on, mark time, pause, sit tight (*informal*), stand by.
2 They waited behind to help clean up. dally, hang around, linger, loiter, lurk, remain, rest, stay, stop (*informal*), tarry.
wait *noun*
There was a long wait for a decision. adjournment, delay, hold-up, interval, pause, postponement, stay.
wait for She was waiting for a phone call. await, expect, look out for.
wait on She waited on the guests. attend to, serve.

waive *verb*
1 He waived his rights. forgo, forsake, give up, relinquish, renounce, surrender.
OPPOSITE claim.
2 They waived the normal rules. dispense with, set aside.
OPPOSITE enforce.

wake[1] *verb*
1 He did not wake until midday. awake, get up, stir, surface (*informal*), wake up.
2 She woke the baby. awaken, disturb, rouse, waken, wake up.
OPPOSITE put to sleep.

541

wake² *noun*
a wake for the dead man. vigil, watch.

wake³ *noun*
the ship's wake. backwash, track, trail, wash.
in the wake of after, behind, following, subsequent to.

walk *verb*
amble, bushwalk (*Australian*), creep, foot it, go on foot, hike, hobble, limp, march, pace, parade, plod, promenade, prowl, ramble, saunter, shuffle, slink, slog, stagger, stamp, step, stride, stroll, strut, swagger, tiptoe, toddle, totter, traipse (*informal*), tramp, trample, tread, trek, troop, trudge, waddle, wade.
walk *noun*
1 *They went for a walk.* amble, bushwalk (*Australian*), constitutional, hike, promenade, ramble, saunter, stroll, tramp, trek, walkabout, wander.
2 *He has a brisk walk.* gait, pace, step, stride.
3 *The map shows various walks through the forest.* path, pathway, route, track, trail.
walk out
1 *He became angry and walked out.* depart, flounce out, leave, storm out.
2 *The workers walked out.* down tools, go on strike, stop work, strike, take industrial action, walk off the job.
walk out on *He walked out on the people who needed him.* abandon, desert, forsake, leave, leave in the lurch.

walker *noun*
paths for walkers and cyclists.
bushwalker, hiker, pedestrian, rambler.

wall *noun*
barricade, barrier, battlements, bulkhead, dyke, embankment, fence, parapet, partition, rampart, stockade.

wallet *noun*
She keeps her money in a wallet. notecase, purse.

wallop *verb & noun*
see HIT.

wallow *verb*
1 *The hippopotamus was wallowing in the mud.* flounder, roll about, splash about.
2 *He wallowed in self-pity.* bask, delight, indulge, luxuriate, revel.

wall-painting *noun*
fresco, mural.

wan *adjective*
He felt better but still looked wan. pale, pallid, pasty, sickly, washed out, waxen.
OPPOSITE ruddy.

wand *noun*
She waved her magic wand. baton, cane, rod, staff, stick.

wander *verb*
1 *They wandered around the town.* meander, mooch (*informal*), mosey (*slang*), prowl, ramble, range, roam, rove, saunter, stroll, tootle (*informal*), travel, walk.
2 *She wandered from the subject.* deviate, digress, drift, stray.

wanderer *noun*
He's a wanderer: he'll never settle down. drifter, gypsy, hobo, itinerant, nomad, rambler, rover, swagman (*Australian*), traveller, vagabond, vagrant, wayfarer.

wane *verb*
Her strength is waning. decline, decrease, diminish, dwindle, ebb, fade, lessen, weaken.
OPPOSITE increase.

wangle *verb* (*slang*)
He should be able to wangle you an interview. fix (*informal*), get, pull off, swing (*informal*).

want *verb*
1 *He wants a new car.* covet, crave, desire, fancy, hanker after, long for, pine for, wish for, yearn for.
2 *They don't want for anything.* be short of, lack, need, require.
want *noun*
1 *a person of few wants.* desire, need, requirement, wish.
2 *a want of common sense.* absence, dearth, deficiency, insufficiency, lack, scarcity, shortage.
OPPOSITE abundance.

war *noun*
1 *The two countries were engaged in war.* battle, combat, conflict, fighting, hostilities, strife, warfare.
OPPOSITE peace.

2 *a war against crime.* attack, battle, blitz, campaign, crusade, fight.
war cry *The teams chanted their war cries.* battle-cry, motto, slogan.

ward *noun*
1 *The child became a ward of the state.* charge, dependant.
2 *a council ward.* area, district, division, section.
ward *verb*
ward off *He warded off his attackers.* avert, beat off, fend off, keep at bay, parry, repel, repulse, stave off.

warden *noun*
1 *a traffic warden.* superintendent, supervisor.
2 *a church warden.* attendant, sidesman, steward, verger.

warder *noun*
a prison warder. guard, jailer, prison officer.

wardrobe *noun*
closet, cupboard.

warehouse *noun*
The goods are stored in a warehouse. depot, store, storehouse.

wares *plural noun*
Traders displayed their wares. goods, merchandise, products, stock.

warfare *noun*
see WAR.

warlike *adjective*
1 *a warlike people.* aggressive, bellicose, belligerent, hostile, militant, militaristic, pugnacious.
OPPOSITE peaceable.
2 *warlike music.* martial, military.

warm *adjective*
1 *warm food.* lukewarm, tepid.
OPPOSITE cool.
2 *warm weather.* balmy, mild, sunny.
3 *a warm welcome.* cordial, enthusiastic, friendly, hearty, hospitable, rousing, sincere.
OPPOSITE cool, hostile.
warm *verb*
She warmed the milk. heat, heat up, hot up (*informal*), reheat, scald, warm up.
OPPOSITE chill.

warm up *The runner warmed up with gentle exercises.* limber up, loosen up, prepare.

warm-hearted *adjective*
a warm-hearted person. affectionate, caring, compassionate, friendly, genial, kind, kind-hearted, kindly, loving, sympathetic, tender-hearted, warm.
OPPOSITE cold-hearted.

warn *verb*
He was warned of the dangers. advise, alert, caution, forewarn, inform, make aware, notify, remind, tell, tip off.

warning *noun*
1 *He was not punished, but was given a warning.* admonition, advice, caution.
2 *There was no warning of any trouble.* forewarning, hint, indication, notice, notification, omen, sign, signal, threat, tip-off.

warp *verb*
1 *The timber warped because it had been left in the sun.* bend, bow, buckle, curve, distort, twist.
OPPOSITE straighten out.
2 *His mind has been warped.* corrupt, pervert, twist.

warrant *noun*
The police have a search warrant. authorisation, authority, entitlement, licence, permit.
warrant *verb*
Nothing can warrant such insolence. excuse, justify, permit.

warranty *noun*
The clock has a one-year warranty. guarantee.

warren *noun*
a rabbits' warren. burrow, maze.

warrigal *adjective* (*Australian*)
warrigal cattle. feral, unbroken, untamed, wild.

warrior *noun*
Their warriors were victorious. brave, fighter, gladiator, soldier.

warship *noun*
aircraft carrier, battleship, corvette, cruiser, destroyer, frigate, gunboat,

a
b
c
d
e
f
g
h
i
j
k
l
m
n
o
p
q
r
s
t
u
v
w
x
y
z

man-of-war, submarine, torpedo boat, trireme (*historical*).

wary *adjective*

1 *She was wary of anything new.* careful, cautious, circumspect, distrustful, guarded, suspicious.
OPPOSITE unwary.
2 *A sentry needs to be wary.* alert, observant, on the lookout, on your guard, vigilant, watchful.
OPPOSITE careless.

wash *verb*

1 *She washed the clothes, floors, etc.* clean, cleanse, douse, drench, launder, mop, rinse, scour, scrub, shampoo, soak, soap, sponge, swill, wipe.
2 *He washed before dinner.* bath, bathe, clean yourself, perform your ablutions, shower, wash yourself.
3 *The waves washed over the rocks.* break, flow, splash, sweep.
4 *The bottle was washed out to sea.* carry, sweep.
5 (*informal*) *That argument won't wash.* be accepted, hold water, stand up.

wash *noun*

1 *He had a wash before dinner.* bath, scrub, shower.
2 *the wash of the boats.* backwash, wake.

washed out

1 *His clothes had a washed-out look.* bleached, dull, faded.
OPPOSITE new.
2 *He was washed out after his long day.* done in (*informal*), drained, exhausted, jaded, tired, weary, worn out.
OPPOSITE invigorated.

washing *noun*

She pegged out the washing. clothes, laundry, wash.

wash-out *noun* (*slang*)

The concert was a wash-out. disaster, failure, fiasco, fizzer (*Australian informal*), flop (*slang*).

waste *verb*

1 *He wasted his money.* blow (*slang*), fritter away, misspend, misuse, squander.
OPPOSITE save.

2 *She wasted her opportunity.* let slip, miss, throw away.
OPPOSITE use.

waste *adjective*

1 *waste paper.* discarded, leftover, superfluous, unwanted, useless.
2 *waste land.* arid, barren, desert, uncultivated, unusable, wild.

waste *noun*

1 *a waste of resources.* misuse, squandering.
2 *The waste is dumped in a pit.* debris, effluent, garbage, junk, litter, refuse, rubbish, scraps, sewage, trash.
waste away *If she doesn't eat soon, she'll waste away.* become emaciated, fade away, grow thin, pine, shrivel, wither.

wasteful *adjective*

a wasteful use of paper. extravagant, improvident, prodigal, uneconomical.
OPPOSITE frugal, thrifty.

watch *verb*

1 *He watched what was happening.* attend to, behold (*old use*), concentrate on, contemplate, eye, gaze at, keep your eyes on, look at, mark, monitor, note, notice, observe, pay attention to, peep at, peer at, regard, stare at, survey, take notice of, view.
OPPOSITE ignore.
2 *He knew the police were watching him.* keep an eye on, keep under observation, keep under surveillance, spy on.
3 *Watch what you say.* be careful, beware, be wary, mind.
4 *He watched the baby while she went out.* guard, keep an eye on, look after, mind, supervise, take care of, tend.
OPPOSITE neglect.

watch *noun*

She read the time on her watch. pocket watch, stopwatch, timepiece, wristwatch.
keep watch *He stayed outside to keep watch.* be on the lookout, keep guard, keep vigil.

watchful *adjective*

a watchful teacher. alert, attentive, careful, eagle-eyed, observant, vigilant, wary.
OPPOSITE careless.

watchman *noun*
The watchman checks each floor of the building. guard, nightwatchman, patrol, security guard.

water *noun*
She fell in the water. creek, dam, lake, ocean, pond, pool, reservoir, river, sea, stream.
OPPOSITE land.

water *verb*
1 He watered his vegetable plot. dampen, flood, hose, irrigate, moisten, soak, spray, sprinkle, wet.
OPPOSITE parch.
2 Onions make her eyes water. run, stream, weep.
OPPOSITE dry up.
water down She waters down the juice for the baby. dilute, thin, weaken.
OPPOSITE concentrate.

waterfall *noun*
cascade, cataract, falls.

waterhole *noun*
All the waterholes were full after the rain. claypan (*Australian*), gilgai (*Australian*), gnamma hole (*Australian*), mickery (*Australian*), soak, watering hole.

waterlogged *adjective*
The ground is waterlogged. boggy, marshy, saturated, soaked, sodden, swampy.

waterproof *adjective*
Raincoats are made of waterproof material. impermeable, showerproof, water-repellent, water-resistant, watertight.

watershed *noun*
The decision was considered a watershed in the nation's history. crossroads, turning point.

watertight *adjective*
1 a watertight container. sealed, waterproof.
OPPOSITE leaky.
2 a watertight argument. irrefutable, sound.

waterway *noun*
The barges travel along a system of waterways. canal, channel, river, stream, watercourse.

watery *adjective*
1 a watery substance. aqueous, fluid, liquid.
OPPOSITE solid.
2 watery soup. diluted, runny, thin, watered down, weak, wishy-washy.
OPPOSITE thick.
3 watery eyes. bleary, damp, moist, streaming, tearful, teary, weepy, wet.
OPPOSITE dry.

wave *noun*
1 He goes to the beach to watch the waves. billow, boomer, breaker, comber, dumper (*Australian*), ripple, roller, surf, swell.
2 a wave of bombings. outbreak, spate, surge, upsurge.
3 He gave a farewell wave. gesture, salutation, signal.

wave *verb*
1 She waved her handkerchief. flap, flutter, shake, wag, wiggle.
2 He waved his knife about as he spoke. brandish, flourish, swing.
3 They waved goodbye. gesture, signal.
4 She waves her hair. coil, curl, kink, twirl.

waver *verb*
1 His courage never wavered. change, falter, vary.
2 The light from the lantern is wavering. flicker, quiver, shake, tremble, wobble.
3 He wavered between two opinions. dither, hesitate, hover, shilly-shally, swing, vacillate.

wavy *adjective*
1 wavy hair. crimped, curly, kinky, permed.
OPPOSITE straight.
2 a wavy line. curving, squiggly, undulating.
OPPOSITE straight.

wax *verb*
The moon waxes and wanes. enlarge, grow, increase.
OPPOSITE wane.

way *noun*
1 Which way did he take? course, direction, path, road, route, track, trail.
2 His way of doing it is different. approach, fashion, manner, means,

a
b
c
d
e
f
g
h
i
j
k
l
m
n
o
p
q
r
s
t
u
v
w
x
y
z

method, mode, procedure, process, style, system, technique.
3 *You'll soon get into our ways.* custom, habit, practice, routine, tradition.
4 *The patient is in a bad way.* condition, shape, state.
way in see ENTRANCE[1].
way out see EXIT.

way-out *adjective*
way-out clothes. bizarre, eccentric, exotic, offbeat, outlandish, outrageous, strange, unconventional, unusual, weird.
OPPOSITE conventional.

weak *adjective*
1 *The patient is still weak.* debilitated, delicate, exhausted, feeble, frail, infirm, sickly, weedy.
OPPOSITE robust.
2 *a weak fence.* decrepit, flimsy, fragile, rickety, shaky, unsteady.
OPPOSITE sturdy.
3 *a weak leader.* cowardly, ineffective, ineffectual, namby-pamby, powerless, soft, spineless, unassertive.
OPPOSITE strong.
4 *a weak excuse.* flimsy, implausible, lame, pathetic, unconvincing, unsatisfactory.
OPPOSITE persuasive.
5 *weak coffee.* dilute, insipid, tasteless, thin, watery, wishy-washy.
OPPOSITE strong.

weaken *verb*
1 *The disease weakened him.* debilitate, enfeeble, exhaust, sap.
OPPOSITE strengthen.
2 *The government is trying to weaken the group's influence.* decrease, diminish, erode, lessen, reduce, undermine.

weakling *noun*
coward, runt, sissy, softie (*informal*), sook (*Australian informal*), weed, wimp (*informal*), wuss (*slang*).

weakness *noun*
1 *He suffered increasing weakness in his muscles.* debility, feebleness, frailty.
OPPOSITE strength.
2 *He knows his own weaknesses.* defect, deficiency, failing, fault, flaw, foible, imperfection, shortcoming, weak point.
OPPOSITE forte, strength.

3 *a weakness for chocolate.* fondness, liking, passion, penchant, predilection, soft spot.
OPPOSITE dislike.

wealth *noun*
1 *He accumulated considerable wealth.* assets, capital, fortune, means, money, property, riches.
2 *They lived in wealth.* affluence, opulence, prosperity.
OPPOSITE poverty.
3 *a wealth of information.* abundance, fund, mine, profusion, store.
OPPOSITE dearth.

wealthy *adjective*
a wealthy merchant. affluent, loaded (*informal*), prosperous, rich, well-heeled (*informal*), well in (*Australian informal*), well off, well-to-do.
OPPOSITE poor.

weapons *plural noun*
armaments, arms, munitions, weaponry; [*various weapons*] axe, bayonet, bomb, boomerang, bow and arrow, catapult, club, dagger, dart, foil, grenade, gun, harpoon, hatchet, knife, lance, machete, mine, missile, nulla-nulla, shanghai, slingshot, spear, stick, sword, tomahawk, truncheon, waddy; see also GUN, MISSILE, SWORD.

wear *verb*
1 *She wore a dress.* be attired in, clothe yourself in, don, dress in, have on, put on, sport.
2 *Constant rubbing has worn the surface.* eat away, erode, grind down, rub away, scuff, wear away, wear down.
3 *This fabric wears well.* endure, last, stand up, survive.

wear *noun*
1 *summer wear. formal wear.* apparel (*formal*), attire (*formal*), clobber (*slang*), clothes, clothing, dress, garb, garments, gear (*informal*), raiment (*old use*).
2 *The carpet is showing signs of wear.* damage, deterioration, disrepair, wear and tear.
3 *This coat has a lot of wear left in it.* service, use.

wear off *The effect wore off.* decrease, diminish, dwindle, fade, lessen.
OPPOSITE intensify.

wear out
1 *The baby wore her parents out.* exhaust, fatigue, tire out, weary.
2 *His clothes wear out quickly.* become shabby, become threadbare, fray.

weariness *noun*
His illness left him with constant weariness. exhaustion, fatigue, languor, lassitude, lethargy, listlessness, tiredness.
OPPOSITE vitality.

weary *adjective*
She felt weary after her long day. dog-tired, done in (*informal*), drained, drowsy, exhausted, fagged out (*informal*), fatigued, jaded, pooped (*informal*), sleepy, tired, whacked (*informal*), worn out, zonked (*slang*).
OPPOSITE energetic.

weather *noun*
climate, the elements.
weather *verb*
1 *They weathered the timber before using it.* dry, season.
2 *They weathered the storm together.* brave, come through, endure, stand up to, survive, withstand.
weather bureau meteorological bureau.

weather-beaten *adjective*
weather-beaten skin. brown, dry, leathery, sunburnt, tanned, wrinkled.

weave[1] *verb*
She wove the different strands together. braid, entwine, interlace, intertwine, interweave, plait.

weave[2] *verb*
The car weaved its way through the traffic. meander, wind, zigzag.

web *noun*
a spider's web. cobweb, mesh, net, network.

wed *verb*
They will wed in December. get hitched (*informal*), marry, tie the knot (*informal*).

wedding *noun*
marriage.

wedge *noun*
1 *A wedge held the door open.* chock.
2 *a wedge of cake.* chunk, hunk, piece, slab, slice.
wedge *verb*
It was wedged between two books. jam, pack, sandwich, squeeze, stick.

wee *adjective*
see TINY.

weed *verb*
weed out *He weeded out the rotten ones.* eliminate, eradicate, get rid of, remove, root out.

weedy *adjective*
1 *a weedy garden.* overgrown, rank, wild.
2 *a weedy youth.* delicate, frail, puny, scrawny, thin, undersized, weak.
OPPOSITE strapping.

weep *verb*
He wept when his dog died. bawl, blubber, break down, cry, howl, shed tears, snivel, sob, wail.

weigh *verb*
He weighs sixty kilograms. measure.
weigh down *He was weighed down with cares.* burden, depress, encumber, load, oppress, overload, saddle.
weigh up *Weigh up the pros and cons.* assess, balance, compare, consider, evaluate.

weight *noun*
the weight of the package. heaviness, mass.

weighty *adjective*
1 *a weighty object.* burdensome, cumbersome, heavy, hefty, massive, ponderous.
OPPOSITE light.
2 *a weighty problem.* grave, important, momentous, pressing, serious.
OPPOSITE trifling.

weir *noun*
barrage, dam.

weird *adjective*
1 *weird events.* creepy, eerie, extraordinary, mysterious, peculiar, queer, spooky (*informal*), strange, supernatural, uncanny, unnatural.
OPPOSITE everyday, normal.

a b c d e f g h i j k l m n o p q r s t u v **w** x y z

2 *a weird person.* abnormal, bizarre, curious, eccentric, freakish, funny, kinky (*informal*), odd, offbeat, outlandish, peculiar, queer, strange, unconventional, unusual, wacky (*slang*), way-out (*informal*), zany.
OPPOSITE conventional, normal.

weirdo *noun* (*informal*)
crackpot (*informal*), dingbat (*informal*), eccentric, freak, fruitcake (*informal*), nut (*informal*), nutcase (*informal*), oddball (*informal*).

welcome *adjective*
a welcome donation. appreciated, gratifying, pleasing.
OPPOSITE unwanted.

welcome *verb*
1 *She welcomed her guests.* greet, meet, receive.
OPPOSITE ignore.
2 *They welcome new members.* accept, admit, let in, receive, take in.
OPPOSITE reject.

welcome *noun*
a warm welcome. greeting, reception, salutation.

welcoming *adjective*
cordial, friendly, hospitable, kind, warm.

welfare *noun*
1 *The school is concerned for its students' welfare.* happiness, health, security, well-being.
2 *The family is on welfare.* assistance, benefit, income support, social security.

well[1] *noun*
They draw water from the well. bore, shaft.

well[2] *adverb*
1 *He handled the problem well.* ably, commendably, competently, correctly, effectively, fairly, justly, properly, satisfactorily, skilfully.
OPPOSITE unsatisfactorily.
2 *Things went well.* famously, like a house on fire, nicely, smoothly, splendidly, successfully.
OPPOSITE badly.
3 *She cleaned it well.* carefully, completely, conscientiously,

meticulously, thoroughly.
OPPOSITE perfunctorily.
4 *He knows the man well.* closely, intimately, personally.
OPPOSITE superficially.
5 *He is well over eighty.* considerably, decidedly, much.
OPPOSITE slightly.
6 *They think well of him.* admiringly, approvingly, favourably, glowingly, highly.
OPPOSITE unfavourably.

well *adjective*
1 *She isn't well.* fit, hale and hearty, healthy, robust, sound, strong.
OPPOSITE sick.
2 *All's well.* all right, fine, OK (*informal*), satisfactory.
OPPOSITE unsatisfactory.

well off affluent, comfortable, loaded (*informal*), prosperous, rich, wealthy, well-heeled (*informal*), well in (*Australian informal*), well-to-do.
OPPOSITE hard up (*informal*), needy.

well-behaved *adjective*
disciplined, good, law-abiding, obedient, orderly, polite, well-mannered.
OPPOSITE naughty.

well-being *noun*
She looks after their well-being. good, happiness, health, welfare.

well-groomed *adjective*
clean, neat, smart, spruce, tidy, well-dressed.
OPPOSITE untidy.

well-known *adjective*
1 *a well-known author.* eminent, famous, illustrious, notable, noted, notorious, prominent, renowned.
OPPOSITE obscure, unknown.
2 *a well-known saying.* everyday, familiar, household, popular, proverbial.

well-mannered *adjective*
civil, correct, courteous, genteel, polite, refined, respectful, suave, thoughtful, well-behaved, well-bred.
OPPOSITE impolite.

wet *adjective*
1 *The ground is wet.* boggy, damp, dewy, moist, muddy, saturated, soaked, sodden, soggy, waterlogged.
OPPOSITE parched.
2 *He got wet because he did not have a raincoat.* drenched, dripping, saturated, soaked, sopping.
OPPOSITE dry.
3 *wet weather.* drizzly, rainy, showery, stormy.
OPPOSITE dry, fine.
4 *His skin felt wet.* clammy, damp, dank, humid, moist, sticky.
OPPOSITE dry.
5 *wet paint.* sticky, tacky.
OPPOSITE dry.

wet *verb*
1 *She wets the clothes before rubbing them with soap.* dampen, immerse, moisten, soak.
OPPOSITE dry.
2 *He wetted them with the hose.* douse, drench, saturate, splash, spray, sprinkle, squirt, water.
wet blanket *He spoilt the party by being a wet blanket.* damper, killjoy, party-pooper (*informal*), pessimist, spoilsport, wowser (*Australian*).

wetness *noun*
clamminess, condensation, damp, dampness, humidity, liquid, moisture, perspiration, sweat.

whack *noun & verb*
see HIT.

whale *noun*
[*various whales*] beaked whale, blue whale, bottlenose whale, fin whale, humpback whale, killer whale, minke whale, pilot whale, right whale, rorqual, southern right whale, sperm whale.

wharf *noun*
The ship is in at the wharf. dock, jetty, landing stage, pier, quay.

wharfie *noun* (*Australian informal*)
docker, stevedore, watersider (*Australian*), waterside worker (*Australian*), wharf labourer.

wheel *noun*
1 *The bed is on wheels.* castor, roller.

2 *a wheel of fire.* circle, disc, ring.
wheel *verb*
1 *He wheeled the invalid's chair up the ramp.* push, trundle.
2 *He wheeled round in astonishment.* pivot, spin, swing, swivel, turn, veer, whirl.
3 *The birds wheeled above us.* circle.

wheeze *verb & noun*
gasp, pant, puff.

whereabouts *noun*
They don't know his whereabouts. location, position, situation.

whiff *noun*
She caught a whiff of the curry. aroma, fragrance, odour, smell, stink.

while *noun*
He stayed for a while. period, spell, time.
while *verb*
while away *She whiled away the time reading.* fill, occupy, pass, spend.

whim *noun*
She bought the dress on a whim. caprice, fancy, impulse.

whimper *verb*
The child whimpered after stubbing his toe. cry, grizzle (*informal*), moan, snivel, wail, whine.
whimper *noun*
There wasn't a whimper from the baby. cry, moan, peep, whine.

whine *verb*
The dog whines when its owners go out. cry, moan, whimper.
whine *noun*
The child's whines were irritating. cry, moan, wail, whimper, whinge (*informal*).

whinge *verb* (*informal*)
He's never happy, always whinging about something. complain, gripe (*informal*), grizzle (*informal*), grumble, moan, whine.
whinge *noun* (*informal*)
She had a whinge to her friend about her problems. complaint, gripe (*informal*), grizzle (*informal*), grumble, moan, whine.

a
b
c
d
e
f
g
h
i
j
k
l
m
n
o
p
q
r
s
t
u
v
w
x
y
z

whip *noun*
The culprit was flogged with a whip. birch, crop, lash, rawhide, scourge, strap.
whip *verb*
1 He whipped the horse. beat, birch, flog, lash, scourge, thrash.
2 She whipped the eggs and sugar. beat, mix, whisk.
3 He whipped the letter out of her hand. pull, seize, snatch, swipe, whisk.

whirl *verb*
1 The carousel whirled round and round. revolve, rotate, spin, swirl, swivel, turn, twirl.
2 His head was whirling. reel, spin.
whirl *noun*
Her mind was in a whirl. confusion, daze, muddle, spin, turmoil.

whirlpool *noun*
eddy.

whirlwind *noun*
tornado, twister (*American*), willy willy (*Australian*).

whirr *verb*
The machine whirred. buzz, drone, hum.

whisk *verb*
1 He was whisked away to hospital. snatch, sweep, whip.
2 She whisked the egg whites. beat, mix, whip.

whiskers *plural noun*
The man shaved his whiskers. beard, bristles, facial hair, moustache, sideburns, stubble.

whisper *verb*
He whispered the words so softly that nobody else heard. breathe, murmur, mutter, say under your breath.
OPPOSITE shout.
whisper *noun*
He spoke in a whisper. hushed tone, murmur, undertone.

whistle *noun*
1 We heard a loud whistle. catcall, hoot.
2 He blew the whistle. hooter, siren.
whistle *verb*
He whistled a tune. hoot, pipe.

white *adjective*
1 a white colour. chalky, cream, hoary, ivory, lily-white, milky, off-white, platinum, silvery, snow-white, snowy.
OPPOSITE black.
2 a white race of people. Caucasian, fair-skinned, light-skinned.
3 His illness had made him turn very white. anaemic, ashen, bloodless, colourless, pale, pallid, pasty, wan, waxen.
OPPOSITE ruddy.
white *noun*
Separate the white and yolk of an egg. albumen.

whiten *verb*
The bleach whitened the nappies. bleach, fade, lighten.

whiz *verb*
The cars whizzed past her. dash, fly, hurry, hurtle, race, shoot, speed, tear, zip, zoom.

whiz-kid *noun* (*informal*)
expert, genius, prodigy, virtuoso, wizard.

whole *adjective*
1 the whole story. complete, entire, full, total, unabridged, uncut.
OPPOSITE partial.
2 There's not a plate left whole. intact, unbroken, undamaged.
OPPOSITE broken.
on the whole On the whole she likes her new school. all in all, altogether, by and large, for the most part, generally, in general, in the main.

wholesale *adjective*
wholesale destruction. comprehensive, extensive, general, large-scale, mass, sweeping, universal, widespread.
OPPOSITE partial.

wholesome *adjective*
wholesome food. healthy, nourishing, nutritious.
OPPOSITE unhealthy.

wicked *adjective*
1 a wicked person. a wicked action. atrocious, bad, base, beastly, contemptible, corrupt, degenerate, depraved, despicable, devilish, diabolical, evil, fiendish, foul, heinous,

immoral, incorrigible, infamous, iniquitous, lawless, malicious, monstrous, satanic, shameful, sinful, sinister, spiteful, ungodly, unholy, vicious, vile, villainous.
OPPOSITE good, righteous.
2 *a wicked grin.* devilish, impish, mischievous, naughty, roguish.
OPPOSITE angelic.

wickedness *noun*
He repented of his wickedness. depravity, evil, immorality, iniquity, sin, sinfulness, ungodliness, unrighteousness, vice, villainy, wrongdoing.
OPPOSITE righteousness.

wide *adjective*
1 *a wide chasm.* big, broad, expansive, extensive, immense, large, open, spacious, vast, yawning.
OPPOSITE narrow.
2 *He recommended wide changes.* big, broad, comprehensive, extensive, far-reaching, global, sweeping, vast, wide-ranging.
OPPOSITE limited.

widen *verb*
The river widens here. broaden, enlarge, expand, open out, spread.
OPPOSITE narrow.

widespread *adjective*
in widespread use. common, extensive, general, universal, wholesale.
OPPOSITE limited.

width *noun*
breadth, diameter, thickness.
OPPOSITE length.

wield *verb*
1 *He wielded the axe clumsily.* handle, manage, use.
2 *She wields considerable power.* command, exercise, exert, have.

wife *noun*
bride, partner, spouse.

wig *noun*
hairpiece, switch, toupee.

wiggle *verb*
She wiggled her hips. shake, sway, twitch, wag, waggle, wobble, wriggle.

wigwam *noun*
hut, tent, tepee.

wild *adjective*
1 *a wild animal.* feral, ferocious, free, myall (*Australian*), savage, unbroken, undomesticated, untamed, warrigal (*Australian*).
OPPOSITE tame.
2 *wild plants.* indigenous, myall (*Australian*), native, natural, uncultivated, warrigal (*Australian*).
OPPOSITE cultivated, introduced.
3 *The island was inhabited by a wild tribe.* barbarian, barbaric, barbarous, primitive, uncivilised.
OPPOSITE civilised.
4 *wild country.* bleak, desolate, rough, rugged, uninhabited, waste.
5 *wild behaviour.* berserk, boisterous, crazy, disorderly, excited, frenzied, hysterical, lawless, obstreperous, rebellious, reckless, riotous, rowdy, uncontrolled, unruly, violent.
OPPOSITE calm, orderly.
6 *wild weather.* blustery, rough, squally, stormy, tempestuous, turbulent, violent, windy.
OPPOSITE calm.

wilderness *noun*
He is trying to conserve the wilderness. bush, desert, wasteland, wilds.

wilful *adjective*
1 *a wilful person.* determined, dogged, headstrong, obstinate, perverse, pigheaded, recalcitrant, self-willed, strong-willed, stubborn, wayward.
OPPOSITE submissive.
2 *wilful murder.* calculated, deliberate, intentional, premeditated.
OPPOSITE accidental.

will *noun*
1 *He has the will to live.* desire, determination, inclination, intention, resolution, resolve, wish.
2 *She wrote her will.* testament.
will *verb*
He willed the house to his son. bequeath, leave, pass on.

willing *adjective*
1 *She was willing to participate.* eager, game, happy, inclined, keen, prepared,

a
b
c
d
e
f
g
h
i
j
k
l
m
n
o
p
q
r
s
t
u
v
w
x
y
z

ready.
OPPOSITE reluctant.
2 *a willing helper.* amenable,
cooperative, enthusiastic, keen,
obliging.
OPPOSITE unwilling.

willingly *adverb*
He signed up willingly. eagerly, happily,
like a shot, of your own accord, of your
own free will, readily, voluntarily.
OPPOSITE reluctantly.

will-power *noun*
commitment, determination, resolution,
resolve, self-control, self-discipline,
will.

willy willy *noun (Australian)*
dust devil, dust storm, sandstorm,
whirlwind.

wilt *verb*
1 *The flowers wilted in the stuffy
atmosphere.* become limp, deteriorate,
droop, shrivel, wither.
OPPOSITE thrive.
2 *The runners wilted after ten kilometres.*
droop, flag, languish, tire.

wily *adjective*
as wily as a fox. artful, astute, clever,
crafty, cunning, devious, knowing,
scheming, shrewd, sly, tricky.
OPPOSITE straightforward.

wimp *noun (informal)*
*He's such a wimp when it comes to
injections.* baby, coward, sissy, sook
(*Australian informal*), wuss (*slang*).

win *verb*
1 *The best team won.* be victorious, come
first, come top, succeed, triumph.
2 *He won the prize.* earn, gain, get, pick
up, receive, walk away with (*informal*).
OPPOSITE lose.
win *noun*
They scored a win. success, triumph,
victory.
OPPOSITE loss.
win over *He won his audience over.*
convert, convince, persuade, sway, talk
round.

wince *verb*
She winced as the splinter was removed.
cringe, flinch, grimace, recoil, start.

wind¹ *noun*
1 *The wind blew.* blast, breeze, draught,
gale, gust, squall; [*various winds*]
cyclone, Fremantle doctor (*Australian*),
hurricane, mistral, monsoon, sirocco,
southerly buster (*Australian*), tornado,
typhoon, whirlwind, willy willy
(*Australian*).
2 *After eating cabbage he has a lot of wind.*
flatulence, gas.
3 *The piper has run out of wind to keep
playing.* air, breath, puff.

wind² *verb*
1 *The river winds through pretty country.*
bend, curve, meander, snake, twist,
wander, zigzag.
2 *She wound the wool over her hand.* coil,
curl, loop, roll, turn, twirl, twist, wrap.
OPPOSITE unwind.
wind *noun*
a wind in the road. bend, curve, loop,
turn, twist.
wind up
1 *He wound up the business.* close down,
dissolve, liquidate.
2 (*informal*) *He wound up in jail.* end up,
finish up, land.

windbreak *noun*
The trees act as a windbreak. barrier,
breakwind, screen.

windcheater *noun*
*Their windcheaters keep out wind and
spray.* anorak, cagoule, jacket, parka; see
also SWEATER.

windfall *noun*
He has spent his little windfall. bonanza,
godsend.

winding *adjective*
a winding road. corkscrew, crooked,
serpentine, tortuous, twisting, zigzag.
OPPOSITE straight.

window *noun*
[*kinds of window*] bay window, bow
window, casement, dormer window,
fanlight, French window, oriel window,
porthole, quarterlight, skylight,
windscreen.

windy *adjective*
a windy night. blowy, blustery, breezy,
gusty, squally, stormy, tempestuous.
OPPOSITE calm.

wing *noun*
1 *a bird's wing.* pinion.
2 *the south wing of the mansion.* addition, annexe, extension.
3 *He belongs to the right wing of the party.* branch, faction, section.

wink *verb*
1 *He winked at her.* bat an eyelid, blink.
2 *The stars were winking.* blink, flash, flicker, sparkle, twinkle.

winner *noun*
1 *the winner of the competition.* champion, conqueror, victor.
2 *The soufflé was a real winner.* hit, knockout (*informal*), smash hit (*informal*), success.

wipe *verb*
1 *Wipe the dishes, floor, etc.* clean, dry, dust, mop, polish, rub, sponge, towel.
2 *He wiped grease on the moving parts.* apply, rub, smear, spread.
3 *The tape was wiped.* erase, scrub (*informal*); see also DELETE.
wipe out
1 *He wiped out my debts.* cancel, erase, get rid of, remove.
2 *The whole army was wiped out.* annihilate, destroy, exterminate, kill, obliterate.
wipe up *She wiped up the spill.* blot, clean up, mop up, soak up, sponge.

wire *noun*
electrical wire. cable, flex, lead.

wisdom *noun*
He had knowledge without wisdom. astuteness, discernment, insight, intellect, intelligence, judgement, prudence, sagacity, sense, shrewdness, understanding.
OPPOSITE folly.

wise *adjective*
1 *a wise decision.* advisable, appropriate, judicious, politic, prudent, sensible, shrewd, smart, sound.
OPPOSITE stupid, unwise.
2 *a wise person.* astute, discerning, intelligent, knowing, perceptive, prudent, sage, savvy (*informal*), sensible, shrewd, understanding.
OPPOSITE foolish.

wish *noun*
They tried to satisfy his wishes. ambition, aspiration, craving, desire, hope, longing, objective, want, whim, yearning, yen.
wish *verb*
1 *They wished for peace.* desire, hanker, hope, long, want, yearn.
2 *She wished them good evening.* bid.
3 *Do as you wish.* desire, fancy, like, please, want.

wishy-washy *adjective*
wishy-washy soup. bland, flavourless, insipid, tasteless, watery, weak.
OPPOSITE flavoursome.

wisp *noun*
a wisp of hair. piece, strand.

wistful *adjective*
a sad and wistful look. doleful, forlorn, longing, melancholy, nostalgic, pensive, pining, sad, yearning.

wit *noun*
1 *We enjoyed the speaker's sparkling wit.* banter, humour, jokes, puns, repartee.
2 *She had a reputation as a wit.* comedian, comic, humorist, jester, joker, punster, wag.
3 *Use your wits.* brains, common sense, intellect, intelligence, judgement, nous (*informal*), sense, understanding, wisdom.
OPPOSITE stupidity.

witch *noun*
1 *The witch cast a spell on the princess.* enchantress, magician, sorceress.
2 *an ugly old witch.* bag (*slang*), battleaxe (*informal*), hag.

witchcraft *noun*
black magic, magic, the occult, sorcery, voodoo, witchery, wizardry.

witchdoctor *noun*
medicine man, shaman.

withdraw *verb*
1 *He withdrew his troops.* pull out, recall, remove, take away.
2 *She withdrew her money from the bank.* remove, take out.
OPPOSITE deposit.

a
b
c
d
e
f
g
h
i
j
k
l
m
n
o
p
q
r
s
t
u
v
w
x
y
z

3 *He withdrew his statement.* cancel, recant, retract, revoke, take back.
OPPOSITE stand by.
4 *The troops withdrew.* back off, depart, leave, pull out, retire, retreat.
OPPOSITE advance.

wither *verb*
The flowers withered in the heat. dry out, shrivel, wilt.
OPPOSITE thrive.

withhold *verb*
You must not withhold information. conceal, hide, hold back, keep back, suppress.

withstand *verb*
They can withstand any attack. bear, cope with, endure, oppose, resist, stand up to, survive, tolerate, weather.
OPPOSITE yield.

witness *noun*
a witness to the accident. bystander, eyewitness, observer, onlooker, spectator, viewer.
witness *verb*
1 *She witnessed the crime.* be present at, observe, see, view, watch.
2 *A JP witnessed his signature.* countersign, endorse, validate.
bear witness to *His friend bore witness to his bravery.* attest to, confirm, testify to, vouch for, witness to.

witty *adjective*
a witty writer. amusing, clever, droll, funny, humorous, quick-witted, sharp-witted.
OPPOSITE dull.

wizard *noun*
1 *The wizard made a magic potion.* magician, medicine man, sorcerer, warlock (*old use*), witchdoctor.
2 *He's a wizard at chess.* expert, genius, maestro, master, virtuoso, whiz (*informal*).

wobble *verb*
She wobbled as she tried to stand up. quake, quiver, reel, rock, shake, stagger, sway, teeter, totter, tremble, waver.
wobble *noun*
a wobble in her voice. quaver, quiver, shaking, tremble, tremor.

wobbly *adjective*
1 *a wobbly tooth.* loose, wiggly.
OPPOSITE secure.
2 *The patient was a bit wobbly when she first got up.* groggy, shaky, unsteady, wonky (*informal*).

woe *noun*
1 *Her life was full of woe.* anguish, distress, grief, hardship, heartache, misery, misfortune, pain, sorrow, suffering, unhappiness.
OPPOSITE joy.
2 *She told them all her woes.* adversity, affliction, burden, misfortune, problem, trial, tribulation, trouble.

woman *noun*
bird (*informal*), chick (*slang*), dame (*old use or American slang*), damsel (*old use*), female, girl, lady, lass, maid (*old use*), maiden (*old use*), matron, sheila (*Australian slang*).

womb *noun*
uterus.

wonder *noun*
1 *He stared at the stars in wonder.* admiration, amazement, astonishment, awe, bewilderment, fascination, surprise.
2 *the wonders of nature.* curiosity, marvel, miracle, phenomenon.
wonder *verb*
1 *He wondered at their ingenuity.* be amazed, be stunned, be surprised, marvel.
2 *He wondered why they came.* ask yourself, be curious, muse, ponder, puzzle, question, speculate, think.

wonderful *adjective*
a wonderful achievement. wonderful scenery. admirable, amazing, astonishing, astounding, awe-inspiring, awesome, breathtaking, brilliant (*informal*), excellent, extraordinary, fabulous (*informal*), fantastic (*informal*), fine, first-class, impressive, incredible, magnificent, marvellous, miraculous, outstanding, phenomenal, remarkable, sensational, spectacular, splendid, staggering, stunning, stupendous, superb, terrific (*informal*), tremendous (*informal*), unbelievable, unreal (*slang*),

wondrous (*old use*).
OPPOSITE ordinary, terrible.

woo *verb*
1 (*old use*) *He wooed the woman.* court,
pursue, seek the hand of.
2 *He did it to woo supporters.* attract,
seek, seek to win.
OPPOSITE deter.

wood *noun*
1 *The house is made of wood.* boards, logs,
lumber (*American*), planks, slabs,
timber, weatherboards; [*kinds of wood*]
balsa, blackwood, cedar, ebony, elm,
jarrah, karri, kauri, mahogany, oak,
pine, rosewood, sandalwood, teak,
walnut.
2 *He put the wood on the fire.* firewood,
kindling, logs.
3 *The heroine got lost in the wood.* bush,
copse, forest, grove, jungle, scrub,
spinney, thicket, woodland, woods.

wooded *adjective*
wooded country. forested, timbered,
tree-covered.
OPPOSITE treeless.

wooden *adjective*
1 *a wooden house.* timber, weatherboard.
2 *wooden movements.* clumsy, leaden,
rigid, stiff.
OPPOSITE supple.
3 *a wooden stare.* blank, deadpan
(*informal*), empty, expressionless,
glassy, poker-faced, vacant.
OPPOSITE animated, expressive.

woodwork *noun*
cabinetmaking, carpentry, joinery.

wool *noun*
1 *The sheep is kept for its wool.* fleece,
hair.
2 *knitting wool.* yarn.

woolly *adjective*
1 *a woolly animal.* fleecy, fluffy, furry,
fuzzy, hairy, shaggy.
2 *a woolly jumper.* woollen.
3 *woolly ideas.* fuzzy, hazy, imprecise,
indefinite, muddled, unclear, vague.
OPPOSITE clear.

word *noun*
1 *He knew the word for a corkscrew in
French.* expression, name, term.

2 *Bring me word of where they are.* advice,
information, intelligence, message,
news, report, tidings.
3 *He gave us his word that he would do it.*
assurance, guarantee, pledge, promise,
undertaking, vow, word of honour.
4 *Don't fire till I give you the word.*
command, direction, instruction, order.

word *verb*
She worded the request carefully. express,
formulate, phrase, put.

word for word *He recorded it word for
word.* accurately, faithfully, literally,
precisely, verbatim.

words *plural noun*
1 *scientific words.* jargon, language,
terminology, vocabulary.
2 *the words of the opera.* libretto, lyrics,
script, text.

wordy *adjective*
1 *a wordy speaker.* garrulous, long-
winded, loquacious, rambling,
talkative, verbose, voluble.
OPPOSITE brief, succinct.
2 *a wordy definition.* circumlocutory,
roundabout, tautological.
OPPOSITE concise.

work *noun*
1 *Getting things ready requires hard work.*
drudgery, effort, elbow grease,
exertion, grind, industry, labour, slog,
sweat (*informal*), toil, travail (*old use*),
yakka (*Australian informal*).
OPPOSITE play.
2 *Each person was given his work to do.*
assignment, chore, duty, homework,
job, project, task, undertaking.
3 *literary and musical works.* book,
composition, creation, opus, piece,
writing.
4 *She enjoys her work and does not want to
retire.* business, career, employment,
job, occupation, profession, trade,
vocation.
OPPOSITE hobby.

work *verb*
1 *He worked for two years on the project.*
apply yourself, beaver away, be busy,
exert yourself, grind away, labour, plug
away, slave, slog, strive, sweat, toil.
2 *He worked until he was 65.* be
employed, have a job.
OPPOSITE be unemployed.

a
b
c
d
e
f
g
h
i
j
k
l
m
n
o
p
q
r
s
t
u
v
w
x
y
z

3 *The dishwasher is not working properly.* act, function, go, operate, perform, run.
4 *She can work the electric knife.* control, handle, manage, manipulate, operate, use, wield.
5 *The trick worked.* be effective, succeed. OPPOSITE fail.
6 *He works miracles.* accomplish, achieve, bring about, perform.
worked up *He became worked up over the issue.* agitated, excited, het up (*informal*), hot under the collar, stirred up, upset. OPPOSITE calm.

work out
1 *He worked out what was going on.* analyse, deduce, discover, fathom, figure out, gather, infer, reason.
2 *She worked out the answer.* calculate, compute, solve.
3 *They worked out a plan.* concoct, devise, draw up, formulate, produce.
4 *Things worked out well.* develop, evolve, go, pan out, turn out.

works *plural noun*
1 *the works of the clock.* insides (*informal*), machinery, mechanism, movement, workings.
2 *One hundred people are employed at the works.* factory, foundry, mill, plant, workshop.

workable *adjective*
a workable scheme. feasible, practicable, practical, viable. OPPOSITE unworkable.

worker *noun*
artisan, craftsman, craftswoman, employee, hand, labourer, operative, operator, wage-earner, workman. OPPOSITE employer.

workforce *noun*
The company looks after its workforce. employees, human resources, labour force, manpower, personnel, staff, workers.

working *adjective*
1 *a working person.* employed. OPPOSITE unemployed.
2 *a working computer.* functioning, going, operational, running, usable. OPPOSITE broken.

workman *noun*
The council employs workmen to do repairs. handyman, labourer, navvy, tradesman, worker.

workmanship *noun*
He deplored shoddy workmanship. craftsmanship, handiwork, skill, technique.

workout *noun*
exercise, practice, training session.

workshop *noun*
Repairs are done at the workshop. factory, laboratory, plant, workroom, works.

world *noun*
1 *the whole created world.* cosmos, Creation, universe.
2 *He has travelled the world.* earth, globe, planet.
3 *the world of politics.* area, circle, domain, realm, sphere.

worldwide *adjective*
global, international, universal.

worm *noun*
[*various worms*] earthworm, flatworm, fluke, hookworm, leech, roundworm, tapeworm, threadworm.
worm *verb*
He wormed his way through the tunnel. crawl, slither, squirm, twist, wriggle, writhe.

worn *adjective*
1 *The clothes were too worn to pass on.* dilapidated, frayed, holey, ragged, shabby, tattered, tatty (*informal*), thin, threadbare. OPPOSITE new.
2 *worn tyres.* bald, smooth. OPPOSITE new.
3 *She looked worn.* drawn, exhausted, haggard, tired, weary, worn out.
worn out *She was worn out after a hard day's work.* bushed (*informal*), dog-tired, done in (*informal*), drained, exhausted, fagged out (*informal*), fatigued, jaded, spent, tired out, whacked (*informal*). OPPOSITE energetic.

worried *adjective*
They comforted the worried parents. afraid, agitated, anxious, apprehensive, concerned, distraught, distressed,

fearful, frightened, nervous, perturbed, troubled, uneasy.
OPPOSITE serene.

worry *verb*
1 *Don't worry him now: I'll ring back later. The loud music does not worry her.* annoy, bother, disturb, harass, hassle, irritate, perturb, pester, plague, trouble, upset, vex.
2 *She worries about their safety.* be agitated, be anxious, fret.

worry *noun*
1 *They were caused a lot of worry by the absence of news.* anguish, anxiety, bother, concern, distress, stress, trouble, uneasiness.
OPPOSITE reassurance.
2 *Finances are his major worry.* bugbear, burden, concern, hassle (*informal*), headache, menace, nightmare (*informal*), problem, trouble.

worrying *adjective*
a worrying situation. alarming, distressing, disturbing, nerve-racking, stressful, upsetting.

worsen *verb*
1 *Her condition worsened.* decline, degenerate, deteriorate, go backwards, go downhill (*informal*).
2 *Exercise worsened the painful condition.* aggravate, exacerbate.
OPPOSITE improve.

worship *noun*
1 *the worship of God.* adoration, exaltation, glorification, praise, reverence, veneration.
2 *He attends worship.* church, service.
3 *an object of worship.* admiration, adoration, deification, devotion, hero-worship, idolisation.

worship *verb*
They worship many gods. admire, adore, dote on, exalt, extol, glorify, hallow, honour, idolise, look up to, love, praise, respect, revere, venerate.
OPPOSITE despise.

worth *noun*
the worth of education. benefit, good, importance, merit, use, usefulness, value.
OPPOSITE worthlessness.

worth *adjective*
be worth
1 *The book is worth $20.* be priced at, be valued at, cost, sell at.
2 *The book is worth reading.* be worthy of, deserve, justify, merit.

worthless *adjective*
a worthless exercise. futile, insignificant, meaningless, pointless, unimportant, unproductive, unprofitable, useless, vain, valueless.
OPPOSITE valuable.

worthwhile *adjective*
a worthwhile experience. advantageous, beneficial, important, productive, profitable, rewarding, useful, valuable.
OPPOSITE pointless.

worthy *adjective*
1 *a worthy cause.* commendable, deserving, good, meritorious, worthwhile.
OPPOSITE undeserving.
2 *our worthy leader.* admirable, creditable, honourable, praiseworthy, respectable.
OPPOSITE unworthy.

wound *noun*
The nurse bandaged his wounds. cut, gash, graze, incision, injury, laceration, lesion, scratch, sore.

wound *verb*
1 *The madman wounded ten people.* cut, damage, gash, graze, harm, hurt, injure, lacerate, maim, mutilate, shoot, stab.
2 *The criticism wounded her.* hurt, mortify, offend, pain, sting.

wrangle *verb*
They wrangled endlessly about minor details. argue, bicker, debate, disagree, dispute, fight, haggle, quarrel, quibble, squabble.

wrangle *noun*
a public wrangle over their respective rights. altercation, argument, barney (*informal*), brawl, clash, disagreement, dispute, quarrel, row, squabble.

wrap *verb*
She wrapped the bottle in paper. He wrapped himself in the blanket. bind, cover, encase, enclose, insulate, muffle, pack, package, parcel up, shroud, surround, swaddle, swathe.

a
b
c
d
e
f
g
h
i
j
k
l
m
n
o
p
q
r
s
t
u
v
w
x
y
z

wrapper *noun*
A plastic wrapper protects the book. case, casing, cover, envelope, jacket, packet, sleeve.

wrath *noun*
Do not incur his wrath by deliberate disobedience. anger, displeasure, exasperation, fury, indignation, ire, rage, temper.

wreath *noun*
The flowers were woven into a wreath. garland, lei.

wreck *verb*
1 The ship was wrecked on the coral reef. break up, destroy, ruin, scupper, scuttle, shatter, shipwreck, smash.
2 The building was wrecked by the rioters. demolish, destroy, devastate, raze, ruin, trash (*informal*), vandalise.
3 He wrecked their plans. botch, bungle, dash, destroy, muck up, ruin, sabotage, spoil, upset.

wreckage *noun*
He scavenged amongst the wreckage. debris, flotsam, remains, rubble, ruins, wreck.

wrench *verb*
He wrenched the knob off the door. force, jerk, lever, prise, pull, tear, tug, twist, yank (*informal*).

wrestle *verb*
1 He wrestled with his attacker. battle, contend, fight, grapple, scuffle, struggle, tussle.
2 He wrestled with the problem. contend, grapple, struggle.

wretch *noun*
1 a starving wretch. beggar, down-and-out, unfortunate.
2 the wretch who stole his car. rascal, ratbag (*informal*), rogue, rotter (*slang*), scoundrel, swine (*informal*), villain.

wretched *adjective*
1 She was all alone and feeling wretched. dejected, depressed, despondent, dismal, forlorn, hopeless, miserable, sad, sorrowful, unhappy, woebegone.
OPPOSITE happy.
2 She felt sorry for the wretched creature. pathetic, pitiful, poor, sorry, unfortunate.
OPPOSITE fortunate.

wriggle *verb*
He wriggled through the narrow opening. crawl, slither, squirm, twist, wiggle, worm your way, writhe.
wriggle out of She is able to wriggle out of anything. avoid, back out of, escape, evade, extricate yourself from, get out of.

wring *verb*
He wrung the clothes to remove the excess water. mangle, press, squeeze, twist.

wrinkle *noun*
1 He ironed out the wrinkles in the trousers. crease, crinkle, crumple, fold, pleat, pucker.
2 facial wrinkles. crow's-foot, furrow, line.
wrinkle *verb*
1 He wrinkled his sleeves. crease, crinkle, crumple, rumple.
2 She wrinkled her face. pucker, screw up.

wrinkled *adjective*
a wrinkled face. craggy, lined, rugged, shrivelled, wizened, wrinkly.
OPPOSITE smooth.

write *verb*
1 He wrote his name. inscribe, pen, pencil, print, scrawl, scribble, sign.
2 He writes books. compose, create, produce.
3 He wrote a letter. compose, dash off, draft, pen, send.
4 They agreed to write to each other. correspond, drop a line, send a letter.
write down She wrote down what the man said. document, jot down, list, make a note of, note, record, register, take down, transcribe.
write off
1 They wrote off the debt. cancel, erase, forget about, wipe out.
2 He wrote off his car. destroy, ruin, wreck.

writer *noun*
1 a neat writer. calligrapher, scribe.
2 She earns her living as a writer. author, columnist, correspondent, dramatist, essayist, journalist, novelist,

playwright, poet, screenwriter, scriptwriter.

write-up *noun*
The play received a good write-up. critique, notice, review.

writhe *verb*
The snakes writhed. squirm, twist, wriggle.

writing *noun*
1 *legible writing.* calligraphy, copperplate, graffiti, hand, handwriting, hieroglyphics, inscription, longhand, printing, scrawl, scribble, script, shorthand.
2 *an author's writings.* article, book, composition, diary, document, essay, journal, letter, literature, novel, poem, prose, publication, story, text, work.
writing paper letterhead, notepaper, paper, stationery.

wrong *adjective*
1 *He knows it is wrong to lie.* bad, corrupt, criminal, crooked, dishonest, evil, illegal, illicit, immoral, improper, iniquitous, naughty, sinful, unethical, unfair, unjust, unlawful, wicked.
OPPOSITE right.
2 *a wrong answer, impression, etc.* erroneous, false, imprecise, inaccurate, incorrect, inexact, mistaken, untrue.
OPPOSITE correct, true.

3 *She chose the wrong colour.* inappropriate, incongruous, undesirable, unsuitable.
OPPOSITE perfect.
4 *There is something wrong with the car.* amiss, awry, defective, faulty, kaput (*informal*), out of order, wonky (*informal*).
OPPOSITE right.
5 *the wrong side of the material.* reverse, under.
OPPOSITE right.

wrong *noun*
Two wrongs don't make a right. He knows the difference between right and wrong. abuse, crime, evil, immorality, iniquity, injustice, misdeed, misdemeanour, offence, sin, sinfulness, transgression, trespass (*old use*), vice, wickedness, wrongdoing.
OPPOSITE right.

wrong *verb*
She felt that they had wronged her. abuse, harm, ill-treat, maltreat, misrepresent, mistreat.

wrongdoer *noun*
The wrongdoer was punished. baddy (*informal*), criminal, crook (*informal*), culprit, evildoer, lawbreaker, malefactor, miscreant, offender, sinner, transgressor, villain.

wry *adjective*
a wry face. contorted, crooked, twisted.
OPPOSITE straight.

a b c d e f g h i j k l m n o p q r s t u v w x y z

Yy

yakka *noun (Australian informal)*
Clearing the yard was hard yakka. graft
(*slang*), grind, labour, slog, sweat, toil,
work.

yank *verb (informal)*
She yanked out her loose tooth. jerk, pull,
tug, wrench.
yank *noun (informal)*
The button came off with one sharp yank.
jerk, pull, tug, wrench.

yap *verb*
The dog wouldn't stop yapping. bark,
yelp.

yard *noun*
The children play in the yard. backyard,
courtyard, garden, quadrangle.

yarn *noun*
1 *woollen yarn.* fibre, strand, thread.
2 (*informal*) *He tells good yarns.* anecdote,
narrative, story, tale.

year *noun*
They are in Year 12. class, form, grade,
level.

yearbook *noun*
almanac, calendar.

yearly *adjective*
a yearly festival. annual.

yearn *verb*
He yearns for recognition. crave, hanker,
have a yen, hunger, long, pine, thirst;
see also DESIRE.

yell *verb*
yell for help. yell with pain. bawl, bellow,
call, cry, howl, roar, scream, screech,
shout, shriek.
yell *noun*
yells of pain, protest, etc. bellow, cry,
howl, roar, scream, screech, shout,
shriek.

yellow *adjective*
a yellow colour. amber, buttercup, canary,
daffodil, gold, golden, jaundiced, lemon,
mustard, primrose, saffron.

yelp *verb*
*The dog yelped after being hit by the
bicycle.* bark, cry, howl, squeal.

yet *adverb*
1 *They haven't seen the play yet.* so far, up
till now, up to now.
2 *She hates plays, yet she went to see this
one.* however, nevertheless, still.

yield *verb*
1 *The land yields good crops.* bear, give,
produce.
2 *The investment yields 5%.* bring in,
earn, pay, return.
3 *He yielded to pressure.* bow, capitulate,
cave in, give in, submit, surrender.
OPPOSITE resist.
yield *noun*
a farmer's yield. crop, harvest, output,
return.

yobbo *noun (informal)*
He was attacked by a bunch of yobbos.
hooligan, hoon (*Australian informal*),
larrikin (*Australian*), lout, ruffian, thug,
yob (*informal*).

young *adjective*
1 *a young industry.* developing,
fledgeling, growing, new, undeveloped.
OPPOSITE established, old.
2 *her young brother.* baby, little,
newborn.
3 *too young to understand.* babyish,
childish, immature, inexperienced,
infantile, juvenile.
OPPOSITE adult, mature.
young *noun*
The animals look after their young. babies,
brood, family, litter, offspring.

youngster *noun*
still only a youngster. adolescent, boy,
child, girl, juvenile, kid (*informal*), lad,
lass, teenager, youth.

youth *noun*
1 *in his youth.* adolescence, teenage
years, teens.
OPPOSITE old age.

2 *a youth of 16.* adolescent, boy, fellow, juvenile, kid (*informal*), lad, teenager, young man, youngster.
3 *the youth of the country.* kids (*informal*), young people.

youthful *adjective*
a youthful grandmother. active, energetic, sprightly, spry, young, young-looking.
OPPOSITE old.

yucky *adjective* (*informal*)
The food tastes yucky. disgusting, gross (*informal*), repulsive, revolting, sickening.

yummy *adjective* (*informal*)
a yummy dinner. appetising, delicious, mouth-watering, scrumptious (*informal*), tasty.

a
b
c
d
e
f
g
h
i
j
k
l
m
n
o
p
q
r
s
t
u
v
w
x
y
z

Zz

zany *adjective*
a zany sense of humour. absurd, bizarre, comical, crazy, eccentric, funny, idiotic, mad, odd, offbeat, peculiar, unconventional, unusual, wacky (*slang*), weird.
OPPOSITE conventional.

zap *verb*
see DESTROY, KILL.

zeal *noun*
He attacked the work with zeal. ardour, dedication, devotion, diligence, eagerness, earnestness, energy, enthusiasm, fanaticism, fervour, gusto, keenness, passion, vigour, zest.
OPPOSITE apathy.

zealous *adjective*
a zealous employee. ardent, conscientious, devoted, diligent, eager, earnest, energetic, enthusiastic, fanatical, fervent, keen, passionate.
OPPOSITE indifferent.

zero *noun*
The score was zero. duck (*Cricket*), love (*Tennis*), nil, nothing, nought, zilch (*slang*).

zest *noun*
1 *a zest for life.* eagerness, energy, enjoyment, enthusiasm, gusto, interest, keenness, pleasure, relish, zeal.
OPPOSITE apathy.

2 *The performance lacked zest.* excitement, liveliness, oomph (*informal*), sparkle, spirit, vigour, zing (*informal*).

zigzag *adjective*
a zigzag road. crooked, serpentine, tortuous, twisting, winding.
OPPOSITE straight.
zigzag *verb*
The road zigzags up the mountain. curve, meander, snake, twist, wind.

zip *noun*
a skirt zip. zip fastener, zipper.
zip *verb*
1 *He zipped his jacket.* close, do up, fasten.
OPPOSITE open, unzip.
2 *She zipped through her work in no time.* race, rush, speed, tear, whiz.

zit *noun*
see PIMPLE.

zone *noun*
an arid zone. a commercial zone. area, belt, district, locality, place, region, sector, territory.

zoo *noun*
conservation park, safari park, sanctuary, wildlife park, zoological gardens.

zoom *verb*
She zoomed off before I could tell her the news. dash, fly, hurry, race, rush, speed, tear, whiz, zip.